11th Conference on Empirical Methods in Natural Language Processing 2006

(EMNLP 2006)

Held in conjunction with COLING/ACL 2006

Sydney, Australia
22-23 July 2006

ISBN: 978-1-61738-500-1

Printed from e-media with permission by:

Curran Associates, Inc.
57 Morehouse Lane
Red Hook, NY 12571

CURRAN ASSOCIATES INC. proceedings.com

Some format issues inherent in the e-media version may also appear in this print version.

Printed by Curran Associates, Inc. (2010)

Association for Computational Linguistics
209 N. Eighth Street
Stroudsburg, Pennsylvania 18360

Phone: 1-570-476-8006
Fax: 1-570-476-0860

acl@aclweb.org

Additional copies of this publication are available from:

Curran Associates, Inc.
57 Morehouse Lane
Red Hook, NY 12571 USA
Phone: 845-758-0400
Fax: 845-758-2634
Email: curran@proceedings.com
Web: www.proceedings.com

Table of Contents

Preface

We are delighted to introduce the proceedings of the 11th Conference on Empirical Methods in Natural Language Proceessing, organized under the auspices of SIGDAT, the ACL Special Interest Group for linguistic data and corpus-based approaches to NLP.

This was a wonderfully fruitful year for EMNLP; we received 234 submissions, drawn from every area of language processing. Of these we were able to accept 73 papers (an acceptance rate of 31%), making for an unusually broad and exciting program. 43 of the papers were presented as talks, and 30 as posters.

The papers were selected by a program committee of 13 area chairs from Asia, Australia, Europe, and North America, ably assisted by a superb panel of 258 reviewers, also from all over the world. We are deeply indebted to the area chairs and the reviewers for their tireless and generous work.

Additional thanks to to the Publications Chair, Eric Ringger, who put this volume together, to the Local Arrangements Chair, James Curran, to the COLING/ACL Organizing Committee, especially Claire Cardie and Suzanne Stevenson, for constant advice, and to David Yarowsky and Ken Church of SIGDAT for fielding many questions. Special thanks go to the student volunteers at Stanford (Dan Cer, Pi-Chuan Chang, Surabhi Gupta, William Morgan, Yun-Hsuan Sung, and Huihsin Tseng).

We wish you all an enjoyable and thought-provoking conference.

Dan Jurafsky and Eric Gaussier
EMNLP Co-Chairs
June 2006

Organizers

Program Chairs:

Dan Jurafsky (Stanford University)
Eric Gaussier (Xerox Research Centre Europe)

Area Chairs:

Regina Barzilay (MIT)
Grace Chung
Jason Eisner (Johns Hopkins University)
Sanda M Harabagiu (University of Texas at Dallas)
James Henderson (University of Edinburgh)
Philipp Koehn (University of Edinburgh)
Paola Merlo (University of Geneva)
Rada Mihalcea (University of North Texas)
Grace Ngai (Hong Kong Polytechnic University)
Yan Qu (Clairvoyance Corporation)
Owen Rambow (Columbia University)
Dekai Wu (The Hong Kong University of Science and Technology)
Francois Yvon (ENST)

Local Arrangements Chair:

James Curran (University of Sydney)

Publications Chair:

Eric Ringger (Brigham Young University)

Reviewers:

Eneko Agirre, Yaser Al-Onaizan, Yasemin Altun, Sophia Ananiadou, Hidir Aras, Jason Baldridge, Srinivas Bangalore, Roberto Basili, Frederic Bechet, Oliver Bender, Nicola Bertoldi, Dan Bikel, Johan Bos, Costas Boulis, Chris Brew, Bill Byrne, Chris Callison-Burch, Nicola Cancedda, Yunbo Cao, Giuseppe Carenini, Michael Carl, Marine Carpuat, Xavier Carreras, Mauro Cettolo, Joyce Chai, Hsin-Hsi Chen, John Chen, Stanley Chen, Colin Cherry, Timothy Chklovski, Kenneth Church, Massimiliano Ciaramita, Stephen Clark, Nigel Collier, Michael Collins, Michael Connor, Koby Crammer, Josep Maria Crego, Andras Csomai, Silviu Cucerzan, Walter Daelemans, Hal Daume III, Adria de Gispert, Rodolfo Delmonte, Matthias Denecke, Maarten de Rijke, Mona Diab, Gaël Dias, Phil Edmonds, Andreas Eisele, Noemie Elhadad, Katrin Erk, Afsaneh Fazly, Marcello Federico, Radu Florian, George Foster, Alex Fraser, Pascale Fung, Jianfeng Gao, Claire Gardent, Dan Gildea, Jesus Gimenez, Roxana Girju, Natalie Glance, Sharon Goldwater, Gregory Grefenstette, Trond Grenager, Iryna Gurevych, Joakim Gustafson, Jan Hajic, Keith Hall, Sanda Harabagiu, Sasa Hasan, Vasileios Hatzivassiloglou, James Henderson, Iris Hendrickx, Andrew Hickl, Graeme Hirst, Julia Hockenmaier, Thomas Hofmann, Veronique Hoste, David Hull, Matthew Hurst, Rebecca Hwa, Martin Jansche, Michèle Jardino, Zhang Jie, Kristiina Jokinen, Min-Yen Kan, Nikiforos Karamanis, Jussi Karlgren, Adam Kilgarriff, Katrin Kirchhoff, Dan Klein, Alex Klemntiev, Kevin Knight, Philipp Koehn, Moshe Koppel, Roland Kuhn, Shankar Kumar, Olivia Kwong, Patrik Lambert, Irene Langkilde-Geary, Philippe Langlaise, Guy Lapalme, Yoong Keok Lee, Oliver Lemon, Roger Levy, Maggie Li, Chin-Yew Lin, Dekang Lin, Bing Liu, Hugo Liu, Berenike Loos, Qin Lu, Klaus Macherey, Bernardo Magnini, Steven Maiorano, Igor Malioutov, Gideon Mann, Christopher Manning, Daniel Marcu, Lluis Marquez, Jim Martin, David Martinez, Yuji Matsumoto, Takuya Matsuzaki, Andrew McCallum, Diana McCarthy, Kathy McKeown, I. Dan Melamed, Arul Menezes, Helen Meng, Eleni Miltsakaki, Sebastian Moeller, Jacques Moeschler, Dan Moldovan, Christof Monz, Robert C. Moore, Rumen Moralyiski, Dragos Stefan Munteanu, Gabriel Murray, Mikio Nakano, Alexis Nasr, Vivi Nastase, Roberto Navigli, Mark-Jan Nederhof, Ani Nenkova, Andrew Ng, Hwee Tou Ng Vincent Ng, Grace Ngai, Nicolas Nicolov, Malvina Nissim, Cheng Niu, Joakim Nivre, Franz Josef Och, Kemal Oflazer, Miles Osborne, Sebastian Pado, Tim Paek, Becky Passonneau, Jon Patrick, Fuchun Peng, Gerald Penn, Fernando Pereira, Fabio Pianesi, Joe Polifroni, Jay Ponte, Andrei Popescu-Belis, Robert Porzel, Oana Postolache, Pascal Poupart, John Prager, John Prange, Rashmi Prasad, James Pustejovsky, Chris Quirk, Steve Renals, German Rigau, Ellen Riloff, Brian Roark, Dan Roth, Alex Rudnicky, Marta Ruiz Costa-jussá, Fatiha Sadat, Kenji Sagae, Horacio Saggion, Franco Salvetti, Mark Sammons, Manabu Sassano, Charles Schafer, Holger Schwenk, Libin Shen, Wade Shen, Yihai Shen, Lei Shi, Advaith Siddharthan, Candy Sidner, Michel Simard, Noam Slonim, Kevin Small, David Smith, Noah Smith, Rion Snow, Caroline Sporleder, Mark Steedman, Amanda Stent, Suzanne Stevenson, Veselin Stoyanov, Carlo Strapparava, Jian Su, Zhifang Sui, Mihai Surdeanu, Charles Sutton, Chew Lim Tan, Franck Thollard, Christoph Tillmann, Kristina Toutanova, Roy Tromble, Huishin Tseng, Jun'ichi Tsujii, Yoshimasa Tsuruoka, Dan Tufis, Peter Turney, Nicola Ueffing, Takehito Utsuro, Kees Van Deemter, Antal van den Bosch, Sebastian Varges, Ashish Venugopal, David Vilar, Jean-Yves Vion-Dury, Stephan Vogel, Chao Wang, Haifeng Wang, Taro Watanabe, Andy Way, Bonnie Webber, Michael White, Janyce Wiebe, Jason Williams, Theresa Wilson, Dekai Wu, Peng Xu, XiaoFeng Yang, Deniz Yuret, Richard Zens, Tong Zhang, Jun Zhao, GuoDong Zhou, Liang Zhou, Ming Zhou, Michael Zock, Andreas Zollmann, Hans-Peter Zorn, Ingrid Zukerman

Conference Program Outline

Saturday, 22 July 2006

7:45–9:00	Registration
8:15–8:25	Welcome from the Organizers
8:25–10:30	Sessions 1a and 1b
10:30–11:00	Morning Coffee Break
11:00–12:15	Sessions 2a and 2b
12:15–1:45	Lunch
1:45–2:35	Sessions 3a and 3b
2:35–3:30	Invited Talk
3:30–4:00	Afternoon Coffee Break
4:00–6:30	Long Poster Session 1 and Welcome Reception

Sunday, 23 July 2006

8:25–10:30	Sessions 4a and 4b
10:30–11:00	Morning Coffee Break
11:00–12:30	Short Poster Session 2
12:30–1:45	Lunch
1:45–3:25	Sessions 5a and 5b
3:30-4:00	Afternoon Coffee Break
4:00-5:15	Sessions 6a and 6b

Conference Program In Detail

Saturday, 22 July 2006

Session 1a: Computational Semantics

8:25–8:50 *Unsupervised Discovery of a Statistical Verb Lexicon*
Trond Grenager and Christopher D. Manning

8:50–9:15 *An Empirical Approach to the Interpretation of Superlatives*
Johan Bos and Malvina Nissim

9:15–9:40 *Paraphrase Recognition via Dissimilarity Significance Classification*
Long Qiu, Min-Yen Kan and Tat-Seng Chua

9:40–10:05 *Detecting Parser Errors Using Web-based Semantic Filters*
Alexander Yates, Stefan Schoenmackers and Oren Etzioni

10:05–10:30 *Distributional measures of concept-distance: A task-oriented evaluation*
Saif Mohammad and Graeme Hirst

Session 1b: MT

8:25–8:50 *SPMT: Statistical Machine Translation with Syntactified Target Language Phrases*
Daniel Marcu, Wei Wang, Abdessamad Echihabi and Kevin Knight

8:50–9:15 *Phrasetable Smoothing for Statistical Machine Translation*
George Foster, Roland Kuhn and Howard Johnson

9:15–9:40 *The impact of parse quality on syntactically-informed statistical machine translation*
Chris Quirk and Simon Corston-Oliver

9:40–10:05 *Statistical Machine Reordering*
Marta R. Costa-jussà and José A. R. Fonollosa

10:05–10:30 *Re-evaluating Machine Translation Results with Paraphrase Support*
Liang Zhou, Chin-Yew Lin and Eduard Hovy

Saturday, 22 July 2006 (continued)

Session 2a: Discourse

11:00–11:25 *Exploiting Discourse Structure for Spoken Dialogue Performance Analysis*
Mihai Rotaru and Diane J. Litman

11:25–11:50 *Learning Information Status of Discourse Entities*
Malvina Nissim

11:50–12:15 *Automatic classification of citation function*
Simone Teufel, Advaith Siddharthan and Dan Tidhar

Session 2b: Parsing

11:00–11:25 *Is it Really that Difficult to Parse German?*
Sandra Kübler, Erhard W. Hinrichs and Wolfgang Maier

11:25–11:50 *Domain Adaptation with Structural Correspondence Learning*
John Blitzer, Ryan McDonald and Fernando Pereira

11:50–12:15 *Incremental Integer Linear Programming for Non-projective Dependency Parsing*
Sebastian Riedel and James Clarke

Session 3a: Computational Semantics

1:45–2:10 *Semantic Role Labeling of NomBank: A Maximum Entropy Approach*
Zheng Ping Jiang and Hwee Tou Ng

2:10–2:35 *Identification of Event Mentions and their Semantic Class*
Steven Bethard and James H. Martin

Session 3b: Parsing

1:45–2:10 *Extremely Lexicalized Models for Accurate and Fast HPSG Parsing*
Takashi Ninomiya, Takuya Matsuzaki, Yoshimasa Tsuruoka, Yusuke Miyao and Jun'ichi Tsujii

2:10–2:35 *Multilingual Deep Lexical Acquisition for HPSGs via Supertagging*
Phil Blunsom and Timothy Baldwin

Saturday, 22 July 2006 (continued)

Long Poster Session 1: Discourse, Dialogue, MT, Computational Semantics, Parsing (4:00–6:30)

Long Poster Session 1: Discourse, Dialogue, MT, Computational Semantics, Parsing (4:00–6:30) (continued)

Unsupervised Named Entity Transliteration Using Temporal and Phonetic Correlation
Tao Tao, Su-Youn Yoon, Andrew Fister, Richard Sproat and ChengXiang Zhai

Capturing Out-of-Vocabulary Words in Arabic Text
Abdusalam F.A. Nwesri, S.M.M. Tahaghoghi and Falk Scholer

Using linguistically motivated features for paragraph boundary identification
Katja Filippova and Michael Strube

BESTCUT: A Graph Algorithm for Coreference Resolution
Cristina Nicolae and Gabriel Nicolae

Automatic Construction of Predicate-argument Structure Patterns for Biomedical Information Extraction
Akane Yakushiji, Yusuke Miyao, Tomoko Ohta, Yuka Tateisi and Jun'ichi Tsujii

Protein folding and chart parsing
Julia Hockenmaier, Aravind K. Joshi and Ken A. Dill

Learning Phrasal Categories
William P. Headden III, Eugene Charniak and Mark Johnson

Priming Effects in Combinatory Categorial Grammar
David Reitter, Julia Hockenmaier and Frank Keller

Better Informed Training of Latent Syntactic Features
Markus Dreyer and Jason Eisner

Sunday, 23 July 2006

Sunday, 23 July 2006 (continued)

Short Poster Session 2: Sentiment, WSD, Machine Learning Models and Methods, Term and Entity Extraction (11:00–12:30)

Sunday, 23 July 2006 (continued)

Session 5a: Generation, Summarization, and Lexical Semantics

1:45–2:10 *Statistical Ranking in Tactical Generation*
Erik Velldal and Stephan Oepen

2:10–2:35 *Sentence ordering with manifold-based classification in multi-document summarization*
Paul D Ji and Stephen Pulman

2:35–3:00 *Quality Assessment of Large Scale Knowledge Resources*
Montse Cuadros and German Rigau

3:00–3:25 *Graph-based Word Clustering using a Web Search Engine*
Yutaka Matsuo, Takeshi Sakaki, Kôki Uchiyama and Mitsuru Ishizuka

Session 5b: Machine Learning Models and Methods

1:45–2:10 *Context-Dependent Term Relations for Information Retrieval*
Jing Bai, Jian-Yun Nie and Guihong Cao

2:10–2:35 *Loss Minimization in Parse Reranking*
Ivan Titov and James Henderson

2:35–3:00 *Unsupervised Relation Disambiguation with Order Identification Capabilities*
Jinxiu Chen, Donghong Ji, ChewLim Tan and Zhengyu Niu

3:00–3:25 *Competitive generative models with structure learning for NLP classification tasks*
Kristina Toutanova

Sunday, 23 July 2006 (continued)

Session 6a: Word Senses

4:00–4:25 *Two graph-based algorithms for state-of-the-art WSD*
Eneko Agirre, David Martínez, Oier López de Lacalle and Aitor Soroa

4:25–4:50 *Broad-Coverage Sense Disambiguation and Information Extraction with a Supersense Sequence Tagger*
Massimiliano Ciaramita and Yasemin Altun

Session 6b: Machine Learning Models and Methods

4:00–4:25 *Learning Field Compatibilities to Extract Database Records from Unstructured Text*
Michael Wick, Aron Culotta and Andrew McCallum

4:25–4:50 *Discriminative Methods for Transliteration*
Dmitry Zelenko and Chinatsu Aone

4:50–5:15 *Solving the Problem of Cascading Errors: Approximate Bayesian Inference for Linguistic Annotation Pipelines*
Jenny Rose Finkel, Christopher D. Manning and Andrew Y. Ng

Unsupervised Discovery of a Statistical Verb Lexicon

Trond Grenager and Christopher D. Manning
Computer Science Department
Stanford University
Stanford, CA 94305
{grenager, manning}@cs.stanford.edu

Abstract

This paper demonstrates how unsupervised techniques can be used to learn models of deep linguistic structure. Determining the *semantic roles* of a verb's dependents is an important step in natural language understanding. We present a method for learning models of verb argument patterns directly from unannotated text. The learned models are similar to existing verb lexicons such as VerbNet and PropBank, but additionally include statistics about the *linkings* used by each verb. The method is based on a structured probabilistic model of the domain, and unsupervised learning is performed with the EM algorithm. The learned models can also be used discriminatively as semantic role labelers, and when evaluated relative to the PropBank annotation, the best learned model reduces 28% of the error between an informed baseline and an oracle upper bound.

1 Introduction

An important source of ambiguity that must be resolved by any natural language understanding system is the mapping between syntactic dependents of a predicate and the *semantic roles*[1] that they each express. The ambiguity stems from the fact that each predicate can allow several alternate mappings, or *linkings*,[2] between its semantic roles and their syntactic realization. For example, the verb *increase* can be used in two ways:

(1) The Fed increased interest rates.
(2) Interest rates increased yesterday.

The instances have apparently similar surface syntax: they both have a subject and a noun phrase directly following the verb. However, while the subject of *increase* expresses the agent role in the first, it instead expresses the patient role in the second. Pairs of linkings such as this allowed by a single predicate are often called *diathesis alternations* (Levin, 1993).

The current state-of-the-art approach to resolving this ambiguity is to use discriminative classifiers, trained on hand-tagged data, to classify the semantic role of each dependent (Gildea and Jurafsky, 2002; Pradhan et al., 2005; Punyakanok et al., 2005). A drawback of this approach is that even a relatively large training corpus exhibits considerable sparsity of evidence. The two main hand-tagged corpora are PropBank (Palmer et al., 2003) and FrameNet (Baker et al., 1998), the former of which currently has broader coverage. However, even PropBank, which is based on the 1M word WSJ section of the Penn Treebank, is insufficient in quantity and genre to exhibit many things. A perfectly common verb like *flap* occurs only twice, across all morphological forms. The first example is an adjectival use (*flapping wings*), and the second is a rare intransitive use with an agent argument and a path (*ducks flapping over Washington*). From this data, one cannot learn the basic alternation pattern for *flap*: *the bird flapped its wings* vs. *the wings flapped*.

We propose to address the challenge of data sparsity by learning models of verb behavior directly from raw unannotated text, of which there is plenty. This has the added advantage of being easily extendible to novel text genres and languages, and the possibility of shedding light on the question of human language acquisition. The models learned by our unsupervised approach provide a new broad-coverage lexical resource which gives statistics about verb behavior, information that may prove useful in other language processing tasks, such as parsing. Moreover, they may be used discriminatively to label novel verb instances for semantic role. Thus we evaluate them both in terms of the verb alternations that they learn and their accuracy as semantic role labelers.

This work bears some similarity to the substantial literature on automatic subcategorization frame acquisition (see, e.g., Manning (1993), Briscoe and Carroll (1997), and Korhonen (2002)). However, that research is focused on acquiring verbs' syntactic behavior, and we are focused on the acquisition of verbs' linking behavior. More relevant is the work of McCarthy and

[1] Also called *thematic roles*, *theta roles*, or *deep cases*.
[2] Sometimes called *frames*.

Proceedings of the 2006 Conference on Empirical Methods in Natural Language Processing (EMNLP 2006), pages 1–8,
Sydney, July 2006.

Relation	Description
subj	NP preceding verb
np#n	NP in the nth position following verb
np	NP that is not the subject and not immediately following verb
cl#n	Complement clause in the nth position following verb
cl	Complement clause not immediately following verb
xcl#n	Complement clause without subject in the nth position following verb
xcl	Complement clause without subject not immediately following verb
acomp#n	Adjectival complement in the nth position following verb
acomp	Adjectival complement not immediately following verb
prep_x	Prepositional modifier with preposition x
advmod	Adverbial modifier
advcl	Adverbial clause

Table 1: The set of syntactic relations we use, where $n \in \{1, 2, 3\}$ and x is a preposition.

Korhonen (1998), which used a statistical model to identify verb alternations, relying on an existing taxonomy of possible alternations, as well as Lapata (1999), which searched a large corpus to find evidence of two particular verb alternations. There has also been some work on both clustering and supervised classification of verbs based on their alternation behavior (Stevenson and Merlo, 1999; Schulte im Walde, 2000; Merlo and Stevenson, 2001). Finally, Swier and Stevenson (2004) perform unsupervised semantic role labeling by using hand-crafted verb lexicons to replace supervised semantic role training data. However, we believe this is the first system to simultaneously discover verb roles and verb linking patterns from unsupervised data using a unified probabilistic model.

2 Learning Setting

Our goal is to learn a model which relates a verb, its semantic roles, and their possible syntactic realizations. As is the case with most semantic role labeling research, we do not attempt to model the syntax itself, and instead assume the existence of a syntactic parse of the sentence. The parse may be from a human annotator, where available, or from an automatic parser. We can easily run our system on completely unannotated text by first running an automatic tokenizer, part-of-speech tagger, and parser to turn the text into tokenized, tagged sentences with associated parse trees.

In order to keep the model simple, and independent of any particular choice of syntactic representation, we use an abstract representation of syntax. We define a small set of *syntactic relations*, listed in Table 1, each of which describes a possible syntactic relationship between the verb and a dependent. Our goal was to choose a set that provides sufficient syntactic information for the semantic role decision, while remaining accurately computable from any reasonable parse tree using simple deterministic rules. Our set does not include the relations *direct object* or *indirect object*, since this distinction can not be made deterministically on the basis of syntactic structure alone; instead, we opted to number the noun phrase (*np*), complement clause (*cl, xcl*), and adjectival complements (*acomp*) appearing in an unbroken sequence directly after the verb, since this is sufficient to capture the necessary syntactic information. The syntactic relations used in our experiments are computed from the typed dependencies returned by the Stanford Parser (Klein and Manning, 2003).

Sentence: *A deeper market plunge today could give them their first test.*

Verb: give		
Syntactic Relation	**Semantic Role**	**Head Word**
subj	ARG0	plunge/NN
np	ARGM	today/NN
np#1	ARG2	they/PRP
np#2	ARG1	test/NN

$v = give$
$\ell = \{ARG0 \rightarrow subj, ARG1 \rightarrow np\#2$
$\quad ARG2 \rightarrow np\#1\}$
$o = [(ARG0, subj), (ARGM, ?),$
$\quad (ARG2, np\#1), (ARG1, np\#2)]$
$(g_1, r_1, w_1) = (subj, ARG0, plunge/NN)$
$(g_2, r_2, w_2) = (np, ARG0, today/NN)$
$(g_3, r_3, w_3) = (np\#1, ARG2, they/PRP)$
$(g_4, r_4, w_4) = (np\#2, ARG1, test/NN)$

Figure 1: An example sentence taken from the Penn Treebank (wsj_2417), the verb instance extracted from it, and the values of the model variables for this instance. The semantic roles listed are taken from the PropBank annotation, but are not observed in the unsupervised training method.

We also must choose a representation for semantic roles. We allow each verb a small fixed number of roles, in the manner similar to PropBank's $ARG0 \ldots ARG5$. We also designate a single adjunct role which is shared by all verbs, similar to PropBank's $ARGM$ role. We say "similar" because our system never observes the PropBank roles (or any human annotated semantic roles) and so cannot possibly use the same names. Our system assigns arbitrary integer names to the roles it discovers, just as clustering systems give

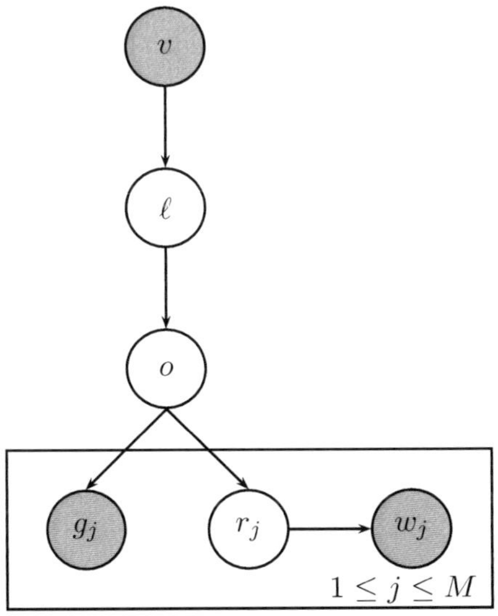

Figure 2: A graphical representation of the verb linking model, with example values for each variable. The rectangle is a *plate*, indicating that the model contains multiple copies of the variables shown within it: in this case, one for each dependent j. Variables observed during learning are shaded.

arbitrary names to the clusters they discover.[3]

Given these definitions, we convert our parsed corpora into a simple format: a set of *verb instances*, each of which represents an occurrence of a verb in a sentence. A verb instance consists of the base form (lemma) of the observed verb, and for each dependent of the verb, the dependent's syntactic relation and head word (represented as the base form with part of speech information). An example Penn Treebank sentence, and the verb instances extracted from it, are given in Figure 1.

3 Probabilistic Model

Our learning method is based on a structured probabilistic model of the domain. A graphical representation of the model is shown in Figure 2. The model encodes a joint probability distribution over the elements of a single verb instance, including the verb type, the particular linking, and for each dependent of the verb, its syntactic relation to the verb, semantic role, and head word.

We begin by describing the generative process to which our model corresponds, using as our running example the instance of the verb *give* shown in Figure 1. We begin by generating the verb lemma v, in this case *give*. Conditioned on the choice of verb *give*, we next generate a linking ℓ, which defines both the set of core semantic roles to be expressed, as well as the syntactic relations that express them. In our example, we sample the ditransitive linking $\ell = \{ARG0 \rightarrow subj, ARG1 \rightarrow np\#2, ARG2 \rightarrow np\#1\}$. Conditioned on this choice of linking, we next generate an *ordered* linking o, giving a final position in the dependent list for each role and relation in the linking ℓ, while also optionally inserting one or more adjunct roles. In our example, we generate the vector $o = [(ARG0, subj), (ARGM, ?), (ARG2, np\#1), (ARG1, np\#2)]$. In doing so we've specified positions for $ARG0$, $ARG1$, and $ARG2$ and added one adjunct role $ARGM$ in the second position. Note that the length of the ordered linking o is equal to the total number of dependents M of the verb instance. Now we iterate through each of the dependents $1 \leq j \leq M$, generating each in turn. For the core arguments, the semantic role r_j and syntactic relation g_j are completely determined by the ordered linking o, so it remains only to sample the syntactic relation for the adjunct role: here we sample $g_2 = np$. We finish by sampling the head word of each dependent, conditioned on the semantic role of that dependent. In this example, we generate the head words $w_1 = plunge/NN$, $w_2 = today/NN$, $w_3 = they/NN$, and $w_4 = test/NN$.

Before defining the model more formally, we pause to justify some of the choices made in designing the model. First, we chose to distinguish between a verb's *core arguments* and its *adjuncts*. While core arguments must be associated with a semantic role that is verb specific (such as the patient role of *increase*: the *rates* in our example), adjuncts are generated by a role that is verb independent (such as the time of a generic event: *last month* in our example). Linkings include mappings only for the core semantic roles, resulting in a small, focused set of possible linkings for each verb. A consequence of this choice is that we introduce uncertainty between the choice of linking and its realization in the dependent list, which we represent with ordered linking variable o.[4]

We now present the model formally as a factored joint probability distribution. We factor the joint probability distribution into a product of the

[3] In practice, while our system is not guaranteed to choose role names that are consistent with PropBank, it often does anyway, which is a consequence of the constrained form of the linking model.

[4] An alternative modeling choice would have been to add a state variable to each dependent, indicating which of the roles in the linking have been "used up" by previous dependents.

probabilities of each instance:

$$\mathrm{P}(\mathcal{D}) = \prod_{i=1}^{N} \mathrm{P}(v^i, \ell^i, o^i, \mathbf{g}^i, \mathbf{r}^i, \mathbf{w}^i)$$

where we assume there are N instances, and we have used the vector notation $\mathbf{g}$ to indicate the vector of variables g_j for all values of j (and similarly for $\mathbf{r}$ and $\mathbf{w}$). We then factor the probability of each instance using the independencies shown in Figure 2 as follows:

$$\mathrm{P}(v, \ell, o, \mathbf{g}, \mathbf{r}, \mathbf{w}) =$$
$$\mathrm{P}(v)\mathrm{P}(\ell|v)\mathrm{P}(o|\ell) \prod_{j=1}^{M} \mathrm{P}(g_j|o)\mathrm{P}(r_j|o)\mathrm{P}(w_j|r_j)$$

where we have assumed that there are M dependents of this instance. The verb v is always observed in our data, so we don't need to define $\mathrm{P}(v)$. The probability of generating the linking given the verb $\mathrm{P}(\ell|v)$ is a multinomial over possible linkings.[5] Next, the probability of a particular ordering of the linking $\mathrm{P}(o|\ell)$ is determined only by the number of adjunct dependents that are added to o. One pays a constant penalty for each adjunct that is added to the dependent list, but otherwise all orderings of the roles are equally likely. Formally, the ordering o is distributed according to the geometric distribution of the difference between its length and the length of ℓ, with constant parameter λ.[6] Next, $\mathrm{P}(g_j|o)$ and $\mathrm{P}(r_j|o)$ are completely deterministic for core roles: the syntactic relation and semantic role for position j are specified in the ordering o. For adjunct roles, we generate g_j from a multinomial over syntactic relations. Finally, the word given the role $\mathrm{P}(w_j|r_j)$ is distributed as a multinomial over words.

To allow for labeling elements of verb instances (verb types, syntactic relations, and head words) at test time that were unobserved in the training set, we must smooth our learned distributions. We use Bayesian smoothing: all of the learned distributions are multinomials, so we add *psuedocounts*, a generalization of the well-known *add-one smoothing* technique. Formally, this corresponds to a Bayesian model in which the parameters of these multinomial distributions are themselves random variables, distributed according to a Dirichlet distribution.[7]

[5]The way in which we estimate this multinomial from data is more complex, and is described in the next section.

[6]While this may seem simplistic, recall that all of the important ordering information is captured by the syntactic relations.

Role	Linking Operations
ARG0	Add $ARG0$ to subj
ARG1	No operation Add $ARG1$ to np#1 Add $ARG1$ to cl#1 Add $ARG1$ to xcl#1 Add $ARG1$ to acomp#1 Add $ARG1$ to subj, replacing $ARG0$
ARG2	No operation Add $ARG2$ to prep_x, $\forall x$ Add $ARG2$ to np#1, shifting $ARG1$ to np#2 Add $ARG2$ to np#1, shifting $ARG1$ to prep_with
ARG3	No operation Add $ARG3$ to prep_x, $\forall x$ Add $ARG3$ to cl#n, $1 < n < 3$
ARG4	No operation Add $ARG4$ to prep_x, $\forall x$

Table 2: The set of linking construction operations. To construct a linking, select one operation from each list.

3.1 Linking Model

The most straightforward choice of a distribution for $\mathrm{P}(\ell|v)$ would be a multinomial over all possible linkings. There are two problems with this simple implementation, both stemming from the fact that the space of possible linkings is large (there are $O(|\mathcal{G}+1|^{|\mathcal{R}|})$, where $\mathcal{G}$ is the set of syntactic relations and $\mathcal{R}$ is the set of semantic roles). First, most learning algorithms become intractable when they are required to represent uncertainty over such a large space. Second, the large space of linkings yields a large space of possible models, making learning more difficult.

As a consequence, we have two objectives when designing $\mathrm{P}(\ell|v)$: (1) constrain the set of linkings for each verb to a set of tractable size which are linguistically plausible, and (2) facilitate the construction of a structured prior distribution over this set, which gives higher weight to linkings that are known to be more common. Our solution is to model the *derivation* of each linking as a sequence of *construction operations*, an idea which is similar in spirit to that used by Eisner (2001). Each operation adds a new role to the linking, possibly replacing or displacing one of the existing roles. The complete list of linking operations is given in Table 2. To build a linking we select one operation from each list; the presence of a no-operation for each role means that a linking doesn't have to include all roles. Note that this linking derivation process is not shown in Figure 2, since it is possi-

[7]For a more detailed presentation of Bayesian methods, see Gelman et al. (2003).

ble to compile the resulting distribution over linkings into the simpler multinomial $\mathrm{P}(\ell|v)$.

More formally, we factor $\mathrm{P}(\ell|v)$ as follows, where $\mathbf{c}$ is the vector of construction operations used to build ℓ:

$$\begin{aligned}\mathrm{P}(\ell|v) &= \sum_{\mathbf{c}} \mathrm{P}(\ell|\mathbf{c})\mathrm{P}(\mathbf{c}|v) \\ &= \sum_{\mathbf{c}} \prod_{i=1}^{|\mathcal{R}|} \mathrm{P}(c_i|v)\end{aligned}$$

Note that in the second step we drop the term $\mathrm{P}(\ell|\mathbf{c})$ since it is always 1 (a sequence of operations leads deterministically to a linking).

Given this derivation process, it is easy to created a structured prior: we just place *pseudocounts* on the operations that are likely *a priori* across all verbs. We place high pseudocounts on the no-operations (which preserve simple intransitive and transitive structure) and low pseudocounts on all the rest. Note that the use of this structured prior has another desired side effect: it breaks the symmetry of the role names (because some linkings more likely than others) which encourages the model to adhere to canonical role naming conventions, at least for commonly occurring roles like $ARG0$ and $ARG1$.

The design of the linking model does incorporate prior knowledge about the structure of verb linkings and diathesis alternations. Indeed, the linking model provides a weak form of Universal Grammar, encoding the kinds of linking patterns that are known to occur in human languages. While not fully developed as a model of cross-linguistic verb argument realization, the model is not very English specific. It provides a not-very-constrained theory of alternations that captures common cross-linguistic patterns. Finally, though we do encode knowledge in the form of the model structure and associated prior distributions, note that we do not provide any verb-specific knowledge; this is left to the learning algorithm.

4 Learning

Our goal in learning is to find parameter settings of our model which are likely given the data. Using θ to represent the vector of all model parameters, if our data were fully observed, we could express our learning problem as

$$\begin{aligned}\theta^* &= \operatorname*{argmax}_\theta \mathrm{P}(\theta|\mathcal{D}) = \operatorname*{argmax}_\theta \prod_{i=1}^{N} \mathrm{P}(d^i;\theta) \\ &= \operatorname*{argmax}_\theta \prod_{i=1}^{N} \mathrm{P}(v^i, \ell^i, o^i, \mathbf{g}^i, \mathbf{r}^i, \mathbf{w}^i;\theta)\end{aligned}$$

Because of the factorization of the joint distribution, this learning task would be trivial, computable in closed form from relative frequency counts. Unfortunately, in our training set the variables ℓ, o and $\mathbf{r}$ are hidden (not observed), leaving us with a much harder optimization problem:

$$\begin{aligned}\theta^* &= \operatorname*{argmax}_\theta \prod_{i=0}^{N} \mathrm{P}(v^i, \mathbf{g}^i, \mathbf{w}^i;\theta) \\ &= \operatorname*{argmax}_\theta \prod_{i=0}^{N} \sum_{\ell^i, o^i, \mathbf{r}^i} \mathrm{P}(v^i, \ell^i, o^i, \mathbf{g}^i, \mathbf{r}^i, \mathbf{w}^i;\theta)\end{aligned}$$

In other words, we want model parameters which maximize the expected likelihood of the observed data, where the expectation is taken over the hidden variables for each instance. Although it is intractable to find exact solutions to optimization problems of this form, the Expectation-Maximization (EM) algorithm is a greedy search procedure over the parameter space which is guaranteed to increase the expected likelihood, and thus find a local maximum of the function.

While the M-step is clearly trivial, the E-step at first looks more complex: there are three hidden variables for each instance, ℓ, o, and $\mathbf{r}$, each of which can take an exponential number of values. Note however, that conditioned on the observed set of syntactic relations $\mathbf{g}$, the variables ℓ and o are completely determined by a choice of roles $\mathbf{r}$ for each dependent. So to represent uncertainty over these variables, we need only to represent a distribution over possible role vectors $\mathbf{r}$. Though in the worst case the set of possible role vectors is still exponential, we only need role vectors that are consistent with both the observed list of syntactic relations and a linking that can be generated by the construction operations. Empirically the number of linkings is small (less than 50) for each of the observed instances in our data sets.

Then for each instance we construct a conditional probability distribution over this set, which is computable in terms of the model parameters:

$$P(\mathbf{r}, \ell_{\mathbf{r}}, o_{\mathbf{r}}, |v, \mathbf{g}, \mathbf{w}) \propto$$
$$P(\ell_{\mathbf{r}}|v)P(o_{\mathbf{r}}|\ell_{\mathbf{r}}) \prod_{j=1}^{M} P(g_j|o_{\mathbf{r}})P(r_j|o_{\mathbf{r}})P(w_j|r_j)$$

We have denoted as $\ell_{\mathbf{r}}$ and $o_{\mathbf{r}}$ the values of ℓ and o that are determined by each choice of $\mathbf{r}$.

To make EM work, there are a few additional subtleties. First, because EM is a hill-climbing algorithm, we must initialize it to a point in parameter space with slope (and without symmetries). We do so by adding a small amount of noise: for each dependent of each verb, we add a fractional count of 10^{-6} to the word distribution of a semantic role selected at random. Second, we must choose when to stop EM: we run until the relative change in data log likelihood is less than 10^{-4}.

A separate but important question is how well EM works for finding "good" models in the space of possible parameter settings. "Good" models are ones which list linkings for each verb that correspond to linguists' judgments about verb linking behavior. Recall that EM is guaranteed only to find a local maximum of the data likelihood function. There are two reasons why a particular maximum might not be a "good" model. First, because it is a greedy procedure, EM might get stuck in local maxima, and be unable to find other points in the space that have much higher data likelihood. We take the traditional approach to this problem, which is to use random restarts; however empirically there is very little variance over runs. A deeper problem is that data likelihood may not correspond well to a linguist's assessment of model quality. As evidence that this is not the case, we have observed a strong correlation between data log likelihood and labeling accuracy.

5 Datasets and Evaluation

We train our models with verb instances extracted from three parsed corpora: (1) the Wall Street Journal section of the Penn Treebank (PTB), which was parsed by human annotators (Marcus et al., 1993), (2) the Brown Laboratory for Linguistic Information Processing corpus of Wall Street Journal text (BLLIP), which was parsed automatically by the Charniak parser (Charniak, 2000), and (3) the Gigaword corpus of raw newswire text (GW), which we parsed ourselves with the Stanford parser. In all cases, when training a model,

	Coarse Roles			**Core Roles**		
Sec. 23	**P**	**R**	**F1**	**P**	**R**	**F1**
ID Only	.957	.802	.873	.944	.843	.891
CL Only						
Baseline	.856	.856	.856	.975	.820	.886
PTB Tr.	.889	.889	.889	.928	.898	.911
1000 Tr.	.897	.897	.897	.947	.898	.920
ID+CL						
Baseline	.819	.686	.747	.920	.691	.789
PTB Tr.	.851	.712	.776	.876	.757	.812
1000 Tr.	.859	.719	.783	.894	.757	.820
Sec. 24	**P**	**R**	**F1**	**P**	**R**	**F1**
ID Only	.954	.788	.863	.941	.825	.879
CL Only						
Baseline	.844	.844	.844	.980	.810	.882
PTB Tr.	.893	.893	.893	.940	.903	.920
1000 Tr.	.899	.899	.899	.956	.898	.925
ID+CL						
Baseline	.804	.665	.729	.922	.668	.775
PTB Tr.	.852	.704	.771	.885	.745	.809
1000 Tr.	.858	.709	.776	.900	.741	.813

Table 3: Summary of results on labeling verb instances in PropBank Section 23 and Section 24 for semantic role. Learned results are averaged over 5 runs.

we specify a set of target verb types (e.g., the ones in the test set), and build a training set by adding a fixed number of instances of each verb type from the PTB, BLLIP, and GW data sets, in that order.

For the semantic role labeling evaluation, we use our system to label the dependents of unseen verb instances for semantic role. We use the sentences in PTB section 23 for testing, and PTB section 24 for development. The development set consists of 2507 verb instances and 833 different verb types, and the test set consists of 4269 verb instances and 1099 different verb types. Free parameters were tuned on the development set, and the test set was only used for final experiments.

Because we do not observe the gold standard semantic roles at training time, we must choose an alignment between the guessed labels and the gold labels. We do so optimistically, by choosing the gold label for each guessed label which maximizes the number of correct guesses. This is a well known approach to evaluation in unsupervised learning: when it is used to compute accuracy, the resulting metric is sometimes called *cluster purity*. While this amounts to "peeking" at the answers before evaluation, the amount of human knowledge that is given to the system is small: it corresponds to the effort required to hand assign a "name" to each label that the system proposes.

As is customary, we divide the problem into two subtasks: *identification* (ID) and *classification* (CL). In the identification task, we identify the set of constituents which fill some role for a

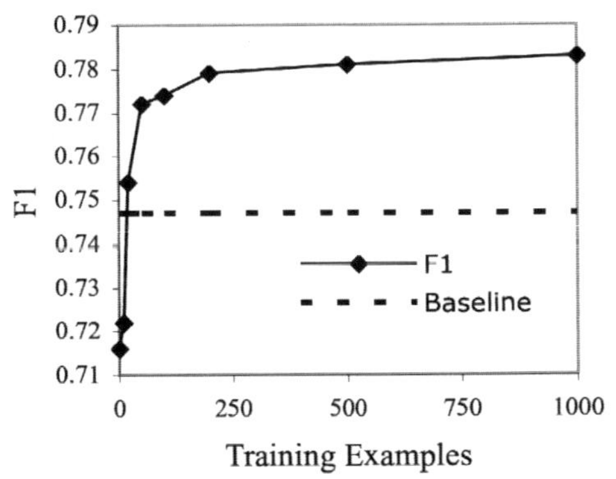

Figure 3: Test set F1 as a function of training set size.

target verb: in our system we use simple rules to extract dependents of the target verb and their grammatical relations. In the classification task, the identified constituents are labeled for their semantic role by the learned probabilistic model. We report results on two variants of the basic classification task: *coarse roles*, in which all of the adjunct roles are collapsed to a single $ARGM$ role (Toutanova, 2005), and *core roles*, in which we evaluate performance on the core semantic roles only (thus collapsing the $ARGM$ and unlabeled categories). We do not report results on the *all roles* task, since our current model does not distinguish between different types of adjunct roles. For each task we report precision, recall, and F1.

6 Results

The semantic role labeling results are summarized in Table 3. Our performance on the identification task is high precision but low recall, as one would expect from a rule-based system. The recall errors stem from constituents which are considered to fill roles by PropBank, but which are not identified as dependents by the extraction rules (such as those external to the verb phrase). The precision errors stem from dependents which are found by the rules, but are not marked by PropBank (such as the expletive "it").

In the classification task, we compare our system to an informed baseline, which is computed by labeling each dependent with a role that is a deterministic function of its syntactic relation. The syntactic relation *subj* is assumed to be $ARG0$, and the syntactic relations *np#1*, *cl#1*, *xcl#1*, and *acomp#1* are mapped to role $ARG1$, and all other dependents are mapped to $ARGM$.

Our best system, trained with 1000 verb instances per verb type (where available), gets an F1 of 0.897 on the coarse roles classification task on the test set (or 0.783 on the combined identification and classification task), compared with an F1 of 0.856 for the baseline (or 0.747 on the combined task), thus reducing 28.5% of the relative error. Similarly, this system reduces 35% of the error on the coarse roles task on development set.

Verb (△ F1)		Learned Linkings
give (+.436)	.57	{0=subj,1=np#2,2=np#1}
	.24	{0=subj,1=np#1}
	.13	{0=subj,1=np#1,2=to}
work (+.206)	.45	{0=subj}
	.09	{0=subj,2=with}
	.09	{0=subj,2=for}
	.09	{0=subj,2=on}
pay (+.178)	.47	{0=subj,1=np#1}
	.21	{0=subj,1=np#1,2=for}
	.10	{0=subj}
	.07	{0=subj,1=np#2,2=np#1}
look (+.170)	.28	{0=subj}
	.18	{0=subj,2=at}
	.16	{0=subj,2=for}
rise (+.160)	.25	{0=subj,1=np#1,2=to}
	.17	{0=subj,1=np#1}
	.14	{0=subj,2=to}
	.12	{0=subj,1=np#1,2=to,3=from}

Table 4: Learned linking models for the most improved verbs. To conserve space, $ARG0$ is abbreviated as 0, and *prep_to* is abbreviated as *to*.

To get a better sense of what is and is not being learned by the model, we compare the performance of individual verbs in both the baseline system and our best learned system. For this analysis, we have restricted focus to verbs for which there are at least 10 evaluation examples, to yield a reliable estimate of performance. Of these, 27 verbs have increased F1 measure, 17 are unchanged, and 8 verbs have decreased F1. We show learned linkings for the 5 verbs which are most and least improved in Tables 4 and 5.

The improvement in the verb *give* comes from the model's learning the ditransitive alternation. The improvements in *work*, *pay*, and *look* stem from the model's recognition that the oblique dependents are generated by a core semantic role. Unfortunately, in some cases it lumps different roles together, so the gains are not as large as they could be. The reason for this conservatism is the relatively high level of smoothing in the word distribution relative to the linking distribution. These smoothing parameters, set to optimize performance on the development set, prevent errors of spurious role formation on other verbs. The improvement in the verb *rise* stems from the model correctly assigning separate roles each for the amount risen, the source, and the destination.

Verb (△ F1)		Learned Linkings
help	.52	{0=subj,1=cl#1}
(−.039)	.25	{0=subj,1=xcl#1}
	.16	{0=subj,1=np#1}
follow	.81	{0=subj,1=np#1}
(−.056)	.13	{0=subj,1=cl#1}
make	.64	{0=subj,1=np#1}
(−.133)	.23	{0=subj,1=cl#1}
leave	.57	{0=subj,1=np#1}
(−.138)	.18	{0=subj}
	.12	{0=subj,1=cl#1}
close	.24	{0=subj,2=in,3=at}
(−.400)	.18	{0=subj,3=at}
	.11	{0=subj,2=in}
	.10	{0=subj,1=np#1,2=in,3=at}

Table 5: Learned linking models for the least improved verbs. To conserve space, $ARG0$ is abbreviated as 0, and *prep_to* is abbreviated as *to*.

The poor performance on the verb *close* stems from its idiosyncratic usage in the WSJ corpus; a typical use is *In national trading, SFE shares closed yesterday at 31.25 cents a share, up 6.25 cents* (wsj_0229). Our unsupervised system finds that the best explanation of this frequent use pattern is to give special roles to the temporal (*yesterday*), locative (*at 31.25 cents*), and manner (*in trading*) modifiers, none of which are recognized as roles by PropBank. The decrease in performance on *leave* stems from its inability to distinguish between its two common senses (*left Mary with the gift* vs. *left Mary alone*), and the fact that PropBank tags Mary as $ARG1$ in the first instance, but $ARG2$ (beneficiary) in the second. The errors in *make* and *help* result from the fact that in a phrase like *make them unhappy* the Penn Treebank chooses to wrap *them unhappy* in a single S, so that our rules show only a single dependent following the verb: a complement clause (cl#1) with head word *unhappy*. Unfortunately, our system calls this clause $ARG1$ (omplement clauses following the verb are usually $ARG1$), but PropBank calls it $ARG2$. The errors in the verb *follow* also stem from a sense confusion: *the second followed the first* vs. *he followed the principles*.

7 Conclusion

We have demonstrated that it is possible to learn a statistical model of verb semantic argument structure directly from unannotated text. More work needs to be done to resolve particular classes of errors; for example, the one reported above for the verb *work*. It is perhaps understandable that the dependents occurring in the obliques *with* and *for* are put in the same role (the head words should refer to *people*), but it is harder to accept that dependents occurring in the oblique *on* are also grouped into the same role (the head words of these should refer to *tasks*). It seems plausible that measures to combat word sparsity might help to differentiate these roles: backing-off to word classes, or even just training with much more data. Nevertheless, semantic role labeling performance improvements demonstrate that on average the technique is learning verb linking models that are correct.

References

C. F. Baker, C. J. Fillmore, and J. B. Lowe. 1998. The Berkeley FrameNet project. In *ACL 1998*, pages 86–90.

T. Briscoe and J. Carroll. 1997. Automatic extraction of subcategorization from corpora. In *Applied NLP 1997*, pages 356–363.

E. Charniak. 2000. A maximum entropy inspired parser. In *NAACL 2002*.

J. M. Eisner. 2001. *Smoothing a probabilistic lexicon via syntactic transformations*. Ph.D. thesis, University of Pennsylvania.

A. Gelman, J. B. Carlin, H. S. Stern, and Donald D. B. Rubin. 2003. *Bayesian Data Analysis*. Chapman & Hall.

D. Gildea and D. Jurafsky. 2002. Automatic labeling of semantic roles. *Computational Linguistics*, 28.

D. Klein and C. Manning. 2003. Accurate unlexicalized parsing. In *ACL 2003*.

A. Korhonen. 2002. *Subcategorization acquisition*. Ph.D. thesis, University of Cambridge.

M. Lapata. 1999. Acquiring lexical generalizations from corpora: A case study for diathesis alternations. In *ACL 1999*, pages 397–404.

B. Levin. 1993. *English Verb Classes and Alternations*. University of Chicago Press.

C. D. Manning. 1993. Automatic acquisition of a large subcategorization dictionary. In *ACL 1993*, pages 235–242.

M. P. Marcus, B. Santorini, and M. A. Marcinkiewicz. 1993. Building a large annotated corpus of English: the Penn Treebank. *Computational Linguistics*, 19:313–330.

C. McCarthy and A. Korhonen. 1998. Detecting verbal participation in diathesis alternations. In *ACL 1998*, pages 1493–1495.

P. Merlo and S. Stevenson. 2001. Automatic verb classification based on statistical distributions of argument structure. *Computational Linguistics*, 27(3):373–408.

M. Palmer, D. Gildea, and P. Kingsbury. 2003. The proposition bank: An annotated corpus of semantic roles. *Computational Linguistics*.

S. Pradhan, W. Ward, K. Hacioglu, J. Martin, and D. Jurafsky. 2005. Semantic role labeling using different syntactic views. In *ACL 2005*.

V. Punyakanok, D. Roth, and W. Yih. 2005. Generalized inference with multiple semantic role labeling systems shared task paper. In *CoNLL 2005*.

S. Schulte im Walde. 2000. Clustering verbs automatically according to their alternation behavior. In *ACL 2000*, pages 747–753.

S. Stevenson and P. Merlo. 1999. Automatic verb classification using distributions of grammatical features. In *EACL 1999*, pages 45–52.

R. S. Swier and S. Stevenson. 2004. Unsupervised semantic role labeling. In *EMNLP 2004*.

K. Toutanova. 2005. *Effective statistical models for syntactic and semantic disambiguation*. Ph.D. thesis, Stanford University.

An Empirical Approach to the Interpretation of Superlatives

Johan Bos
Laboratory for Computational Linguistics
Department of Computer Science
University of Rome "La Sapienza"
bos@di.uniroma1.it

Malvina Nissim
Laboratory for Applied Ontology
Institute for Cognitive Science and Technology
National Research Council (CNR), Rome
malvina.nissim@loa-cnr.it

Abstract

In this paper we introduce an empirical approach to the semantic interpretation of superlative adjectives. We present a corpus annotated for superlatives and propose an interpretation algorithm that uses a wide-coverage parser and produces semantic representations. We achieve F-scores between 0.84 and 0.91 for detecting attributive superlatives and an accuracy in the range of 0.69–0.84 for determining the correct comparison set. As far as we are aware, this is the first automated approach to superlatives for open-domain texts and questions.

1 Introduction

Although superlative noun phrases (*the nation's largest milk producer, the most complex arms-control talks ever attempted*, etc.) received considerable attention in formal linguistics (Szabolcsi, 1986; Gawron, 1995; Heim, 1999; Farkas and Kiss, 2000), this interest is not mirrored in computational linguistics and NLP. On the one hand, this seems remarkable, since superlatives are fairly frequently found in natural language. On the other hand, this is probably not that surprising, given that their semantic complexity requires deep linguistic analysis that most wide-coverage NLP systems do not provide.

But even if NLP systems incorporated linguistic insights for the automatic processing of superlatives, it might not be of help: the formal semantics literature on superlatives focuses on linguistically challenging examples (many of them artificially constructed) which might however rarely occur in real data and would therefore have little impact on the performance of NLP systems. Indeed, no corpus-based studies have been conducted to get a comprehensive picture of the variety of configurations superlatives exhibit, and their distribution in real occurring data.

In this paper we describe our work on the analysis of superlative adjectives, which is empirically grounded and is implemented into an existing wide-coverage text understanding system. To get an overview of the behaviour of superlatives in text, we annotated newswire data, as well as queries obtained from search engines logs. On the basis of this corpus study, we propose, implement and evaluate a syntactic and semantic analysis for superlatives. To the best of our knowledge, this is the first automated approach to the interpretation of superlatives for open-domain texts that is grounded on actual corpus-evidence and thoroughly evaluated. Some obvious applications that would benefit from this work are question answering, recognition of entailment, and more generally relation extraction systems.

2 Syntax and Semantics of Superlatives

2.1 Surface Forms

In English, superlative adjectives appear in a large variety of syntactic and morphological forms. One-syllable adjectives and some two-syllable adjectives are directly inflected with the suffix "-est". Some words of two syllables and all words of three or more syllables are instead introduced by "most" (or "least"). Superlatives can be modified by ordinals, cardinals or adverbs, such as intensifiers or modals, and are normally preceeded by the definite article or a possessive. The examples below illustrate the wide variety and uses of superlative adjectives.

Proceedings of the 2006 Conference on Empirical Methods in Natural Language Processing (EMNLP 2006), pages 9–17,
Sydney, July 2006.

the **tallest** woman

AS Roma's **quickest** player

the Big Board's **most respected** floor traders

France's **third-largest** chemical group

the **most-recent** wave of friendly takeovers

the **two largest** competitors

the **the southern-most** tip of England

its **lowest possible** prices

Superlative adjectives can manifest themselves in predicative ("Mia is the tallest.") or attributive form ("the tallest woman"). Furthermore, there are superlative adverbs, such as "most recently", and idiomatic usages.

2.2 The Comparison Set

It is well known that superlatives can be analysed in terms of comparative constructions (Szabolcsi, 1986; Alshawi, 1992; Gawron, 1995; Heim, 1999; Farkas and Kiss, 2000). Accordingly, "the oldest character" can be interpreted as the character such that there is no older character, in the given context. Therefore, a correct semantic interpretation of the superlative depends on the correct characterisation of the *comparison set*. The comparison set denotes the set of entities that are compared to each other with respect to a certain dimension (see Section 2.3). In "the oldest character in the book", the members of the comparison set are characters in the book, and the dimension of comparison is age.

The computation of the comparison set is complicated by complex syntactic structure involving the superlative. The presence of possessives for example, as in "AS Roma's quickest player", extends the comparison set to players of AS Roma. Prepositional phrases (PPs), gerunds, and relative clauses introduce additional complexity. PPs that are attached to the head noun of the superlative are part of the comparison set — those that modify the entire NP are not. Similarly, restrictive relative clause are included in the comparison set, non-restrictive aren't.

We illustrate this complexity in the following examples, taken from the Wall Street Journal, where the comparison set is underlined:

The **oldest** designer got to work on the dashboard, she recalls. (WSJ02)

A spokesman for Borden Inc., the nation's **largest** milk producer, concedes Goya may be on to something. (WSJ02)

Right now, the **largest** loan the FHA can insure in high-cost housing markets is $101,250. (WSJ03)

With newspapers being the **largest** single component of solid waste in our landfills ... (WSJ02)

... questions being raised by what generally are considered the **most complex** arms-control talks ever attempted. (WSJ02)

Besides syntactic ambiguities, the determination of the comparison set can be further complicated by semantic ambiguities. Some occurrences of superlatives licence a so-called "comparitive" reading, as in the following example discussed in the formal semantics literature (Heim, 1999; Szabolcsi, 1986):

John climbed the **highest** mountain.

Here, in the standard interpretion, the mountain referred to is the highest available in the context. However, another interpretation might arise in a situation where several people climbed several mountains, and John climbed a mountain higher than anyone else did, but not necessarily the highest of all mountains in the context. Our corpus study reveals that these readings are rare, although they tend to be more frequent in questions than in newspaper texts.

2.3 Dimension

Part of the task of semantically interpretating superlative adjectives is the selection of the *dimension* on which entities are compared. In "the highest mountain" we compare mountains with respect to the dimension height, in "the best paper" we compare papers with respect to the dimension quality, and so on. A well-known problem is that some adjectives can be ambiguous or vague in choosing their dimension. Detecting the appropriate dimension is not covered in this paper, but is orthogonal to the analysis we provide.

2.4 Superlatives and Entailment

Superlatives exhibit a non-trivial semantics. Some examples of textual entailment make this very evident. Consider the contrasts in the following entailment tests with indefinite and universally quantified noun phrases:

I bought a blue car $\models$ I bought a car
I bought a car $\not\models$ I bought a blue car

I bought every blue car $\not\models$ I bought every car
I bought every car $\models$ I bought every blue car

Observe that the directions of entailments are mirrorred. Now consider a similar test with superlatives, where the entailments fail in both directions:

I bought the cheapest blue car $\not\models$ I bought the cheapest car
I bought the cheapest car $\not\models$ I bought the cheapest blue car.

These entailment tests underline the point that the meaning of superlatives is rather complicated, and that a shallow semantic representation, say λx.[cheapest(x) $\wedge$ car(x)] for "cheapest car", simply won't suffice. A semantic represention capturing the meaning of a superlative requires a more sophisticated analysis. In particular, it is important to explicitly represent the comparison set of a superlative. In "the cheapest car", the comparison set is formed by the set of cars, whereas in "the cheapest blue car", the comparison set is the set of blue cars. Semantically, we can represent "cheapest blue car" as follows, where the comparison set is made explicit in the antecedent of the conditional:

$$\lambda x.[\mathrm{car}(x) \wedge \mathrm{blue}(x) \wedge \forall y((\mathrm{car}(y) \wedge \mathrm{blue}(y) \wedge x{\neq}y) \rightarrow \mathrm{cheaper}(x,y))]$$

Paraphrased in English, this stipulates that some blue car is cheaper than any other blue car. A meaning representation like this will logically predict the correct entailment relations for superlatives.

3 Annotated Corpus of Superlatives

In order to develop and evaluate our system we manually annotated a collection of newspaper article and questions with occurrences of superlatives. The design of the corpus and its characteristics are described in this section.

3.1 Classification and Annotation Scheme

Instances of superlatives are identified in text and classified into one of four possible classes: *attributive*, *predicative*, *adverbial*, or *idiomatic*:

its rates will be among the **highest** (predicative)

the **strongest** dividend growth (attributive)

free to do the task **most quickly** (adverbial)

who won the TONY for **best featured** actor? (idiom)

For all cases, we annotate the span of the superlative adjective in terms of the position of the tokens in the sentence. For instance, in "its$_1$ rates$_2$ will$_3$ be$_4$ among$_5$ the$_6$ highest$_7$", the superlative span would be 7–7.

Additional information is encoded for the attributive case: type of determiner (possessive, definite, bare, demonstrative, quantifier), number (sg, pl, mass), cardinality (yes, no), modification (adjective, ordinal, intensifier, none). Table 1 shows some examples from the WSJ with annotation values.

Not included in this study are adjectives such as "next", "past", "last", nor the ordinal "first", although they somewhat resemble superlatives in their semantics. Also excluded are adjectives that lexicalise a superlative meaning but are not superlatives morphologically, like "main", "principal", and the like. For etymological reasons we however include "foremost" and "uttermost."

3.2 Data and Annotation

Our corpus consists of a collection of newswire articles from the Wall Street Journal (Sections 00, 01, 02, 03, 04, 10, and 15) and the Glasgow Herald (GH950110 from the CLEF evaluation forum), and a large set of questions from the TREC QA evaluation exercise (years 2002 and 2003) and natural language queries submitted to the Excite search engine (Jansen and Spink, 2000). The data was automatically tokenised, but all typos and extra-grammaticalities were preserved. The corpus was split into a development set used for tuning the system and a test set for evaluation. The size of each sub-corpus is shown in Table 2.

Table 2: Size of each data source (in number of sentences/questions)

source	dev	test	total
WSJ	8,058	6,468	14,526
GH	—	2,553	2,553
TREC	1,025	—	1,025
Excite	—	67,140	67,140
total	9,083	76,161	85,244

The annotation was performed by two trained linguists. One section of the WSJ was annotated by both annotators independently to calculate inter-annotator agreement. All other documents were first annotated by one judge and then checked by the second, in order to ensure maximum correctness. All disagreements were discussed and resolved for the creation of a gold standard corpus.

Inter-annotator agreement was assessed mainly using f-score and percentage agreement as well as

Table 1: Annotation examples of superlative adjectives

example	sup span	det	num	car	mod	comp set
The **third-largest** thrift institution in Puerto Rico also [...]	2–2	def	sg	no	ord	3–7
The Agriculture Department reported that feedlots in the **13 biggest** ranch states held [...]	9–10	def	pl	yes	no	11–12
The failed takeover would have given UAL employees 75 % voting control of the nation 's **second-largest** airline [...]	17–17	pos	sg	no	ord	14–18

the kappa statistics (K), where applicable (Carletta, 1996). In using f-score, we arbitrarily take one of the annotators' decisions (A) as gold standard and compare them with the other annotator's decisions (B). Note that here f-score is symmetric, since precision(A,B) = recall(B,A), and (balanced) f-score is the harmonic mean of precision and recall (Tjong Kim Sang, 2002; Hachey et al., 2005, see also Section 5).

We evaluated three levels of agreement on a sample of 1967 sentences (one full WSJ section). The first level concerns superlative detection: to what extent different human judges can agree on what constitutes a superlative. For this task, f-score was measured at 0.963 with a total of 79 superlative phrases agreed upon.

The second level of agreement is relative to type identification (attributive, predicative, adverbial, idiomatic), and is only calculated on the subset of cases both annotators recognised as superlatives (79 instances, as mentioned). The overall f-score for the classification task is 0.974, with 77 cases where both annotators assigned the same type to a superlative phrase. We also assessed agreement for each class, and the attributive type resulted the most reliable with an f-score of 1 (total agreement on 64 cases), whereas there was some disagreement in classifying predicative and adverbial cases (0.9 and 0.8 f-score, respectively). Idiomatic uses where not detected in this portion of the data. To assess this classification task we also used the kappa statistics which yielded K_{Co}=0.922 (following (Eugenio and Glass, 2004) we report K as K_{Co}, indicating that we calculate K à la Cohen (Cohen, 1960). K_{Co} over 0.9 is considered to signal very good agreement (Krippendorff, 1980).

The third and last level of agreement deals with the span of the comparison set and only concerns attributive cases (64 out of 79). Percentage agreement was used since this is not a classification task and was measured at 95.31%.

The agreement results show that the task appears quite easy to perform for linguists. Despite the limited number of instances compared, this has also emerged from the annotators' perception of the difficulty of the task for humans.

3.3 Distribution

The gold standard corpus comprises a total of 3,045 superlatives, which roughly amounts to one superlative in every 25 sentences/questions. The overwhelming majority of superlatives are attributive (89.1%), and only a few are used in a predicative way (6.9%), adverbially (3.0%), or in idiomatic expressions (0.9%).[1] Table 3 shows the detailed distribution according to data source and experimental sets. Although the corpus also includes annotation about determination, modification, grammatical number, and cardinality of attributive superlatives (see Section 3.1), this information is not used by the system described in this paper.

Table 3: Distribution of superlative types in the development and evaluation sets.

type	dev		test			total
	WSJ	TREC	WSJ	GH	Excite	
att	240	43	218	68	2,145	2,714
pre	40	3	26	17	125	211
adv	17	2	22	9	41	91
idi	6	5	1	2	15	29
total	303	53	267	96	2,326	3,045

4 Automatic Analysis of Superlatives

The system that we use to analyse superlatives is based on two linguistic formalisms: Combinatory Categorial Grammar (CCG), for a theory of syntax; and Discourse Representation Theory (DRT)

[1]Percentages are rounded to the first decimal and do not necessarily sum up to 100%.

for a theory of semantics. In this section we will illustrate how we extend these theories to deal with superlatives and how we implemented this into a working system.

4.1 Combinatory Categorial Grammar (CCG)

CCG is a lexicalised theory of grammar (Steedman, 2001). We used Clark & Curran's wide-coverage statistical parser (Clark and Curran, 2004) trained on CCG-bank, which in turn is derived from the Penn-Treebank (Hockenmaier and Steedman, 2002). In CCG-bank, the majority of superlative adjective of cases are analysed as follows:

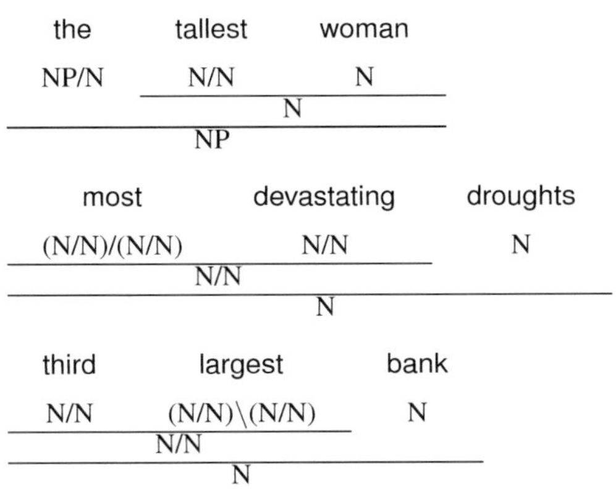

Clark & Curran's parser outputs besides a CCG derivation of the input sentence also a part-of-speech (POS) tag and a lemmatised form for each input token. To recognise attributive superlatives in the output of the parser, we look both at the POS tag and the CCG-category assigned to a word. Words with POS-tag JJS and CCG-category N/N, (N/N)/(N/N), or (N/N)\(N/N) are considered attributive superlatives adjectives, and so are the words "most" and "least" with CCG category (N/N)/(N/N).

However, most hyphenated superlatives are not recognised by the parser as JJ instead of JJS, and are corrected in a post-processing step.[2] Examples that fall in this category are "most-recent wave" and "third-highest".

4.2 Discourse Representation Theory (DRT)

The output of the parser, a CCG derivation of the input sentence, is used to construct a Discourse Representation Structure (DRS, the semantic representation proposed by DRT (Kamp and Reyle, 1993)). We follow (Bos et al., 2004; Bos, 2005) in automatically building semantic representation on the basis of CCG derivations in a compositional fashion. We briefly summarise the approach here.

The semantic representation for a word is determined by its CCG category, POS-tag, and lemma. Consider the following lexical entries:

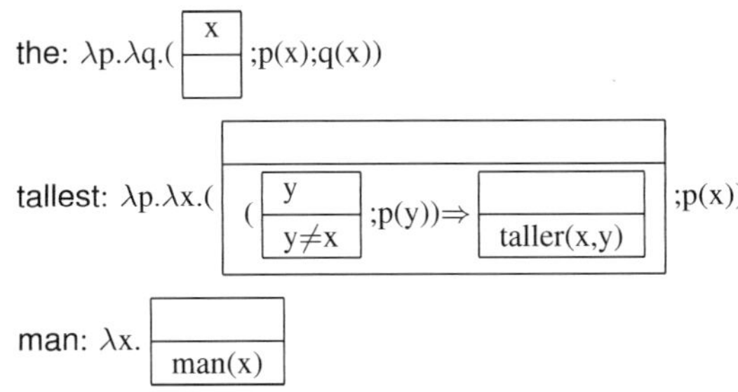

These lexical entries are combined in a compositional fashion following the CCG derivation, using the λ-calculus as a glue language:

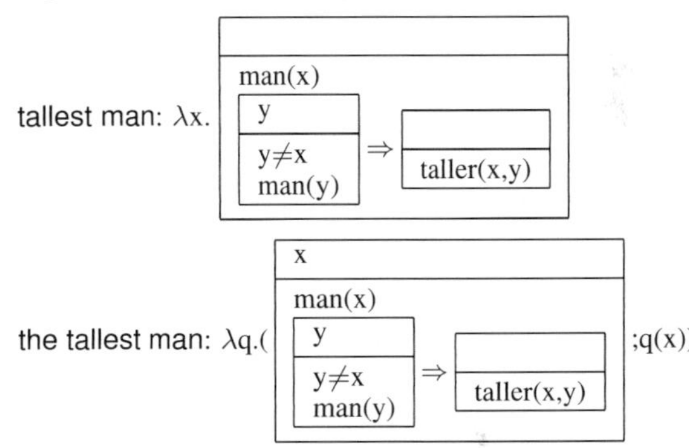

In this way DRSs can be produced in a robust way, achieving high-coverage. An example output representation of the complete system is shown in Figure 1.

As is often the case, the output of the parser is not always what one needs to construct a meaningful semantic representation. There are two cases where we alter the CCG derivation output by the parser in order to improve the resulting DRSs. The first case concerns modifiers following a superlative construction, that are attached to the NP node rather than N. A case in point is

> ... the largest toxicology lab in New England ...

where the PP in New England has the CCG category NP\NP rather than N\N. This would result in a comparison set containing of toxicology labs, rather than a set toxicology labs in New England.

The second case are possessive NPs preceding a superlative construction. An example here is

> ... Jaguar's largest shareholder ...

[2] This is due to the fact that the Penn-Treebank annotation guidelines prescribe that all hyphenated adjectives ought to be tagged as JJ.

```
 ______________________________________________
| x0 x1 x2 x3 x4 x5 x6                         |
|----------------------------------------------|
| acquisition(x1)                              |
| nn(x0,x1)                                    |
| named(x0,georgia-pacific,nam)                |
| named(x2,nekoosa,loc)                        |
| of(x1,x2)                                    |
| company(x5)                                  |
| nn(x3,x5)                                    |
| forest-product(x3)                           |
| nn(x4,x5)                                    |
| named(x4,us,loc)                             |
|   ___________________       _______________  |
|  | x7 x8 x9          |     |               | |
|  |-------------------|     |---------------| |
|  | company(x9)       | ==> | largest(x5,x9)| |
|  | nn(x7,x9)         |     |_______________| |
|  | forest-product(x7)|                       |
|  | nn(x8,x9)         |                       |
|  | named(x8,us,loc)  |                       |
|  |        _________  |                       |
|  |       |         | |                       |
|  |  __   |---------| |                       |
|  |    |  | x5 = x9 | |                       |
|  |       |_________| |                       |
|  |___________________|                       |
| create(x6)                                   |
| agent(x6,x1)                                 |
| patient(x6,x5)                               |
| event(x6)                                    |
|______________________________________________|
```

Figure 1: Example DRS output

where a correct interpretation of the superlative requires a comparison set of shareholders from Jaguar, rather than just any shareholder. However, the parser outputs a derivation where "largest" is combined with "shareholder", and then with the possessive construction, yielding the wrong semantic interpretation. To deal with this, we analyse possessives that interact with the superlative as follows:

```
Rome   's                 oldest   church
NP     ((NP/N)/(N/N))\NP  N/N      N
------------------------
    (NP/N)/(N/N)
----------------------------------
             NP/N
-------------------------------------------
             NP
```

This analysis yields the correct comparison set for superlative that follow a possessive noun phrase, given the following lexical semantics for the genitive:

$$\lambda n.\lambda S.\lambda p.\lambda q.(\boxed{\begin{array}{c}u\\ \hline \\ \end{array}};S(\lambda x.(p(x);n(\lambda y.\boxed{\begin{array}{c} \\ \hline of(y,x)\end{array}})(u);q(u))))$$

For both cases, we apply some simple post-processing rules to the output of the parser to obtain the required derivations. The effect of these rules is reported in the next section, where we assess the accuracy of the semantic representations produced for superlatives by comparing the automatic analysis with the gold standard.

5 Evaluation

The automatic analysis of superlatives we present in the following experiments consists of two sequential tasks: *superlative detection*, and *comparison set determination*.

The first task is concerned with finding a superlative in text and its exact span ("largest", "most beautiful", "10 biggest"). For a found string to to be judged as correct, its whole span must correspond to the gold standard. The task is evaluated using precision (P), recall (R), and f-score (F), calculated as follows:

$$\mathrm{P} = \frac{correct\ assignments\ of\ c}{total\ assignments\ of\ c}$$

$$\mathrm{R} = \frac{correct\ assignments\ of\ c}{total\ corpus\ instances\ of\ c}$$

$$\mathrm{F} = \frac{2P_cR_c}{P_c+R_c}$$

The second task is conditional on the first: once a superlative is found, its comparison set must also be identified ("rarest flower in New Zealand", "New York's tallest building", see Section 2.2). A selected comparison set is evaluated as correct if it corresponds exactly to the gold standard annotation: partial matches are counted as wrong. Assignments are evaluated using accuracy (number of correct decisions made) only on the subset of previously correctly identified superlatives.

For both tasks we developed simple baseline systems based on part-of-speech tags, and a more sophisticated linguistic analysis based on CCG and DRT (i.e. the system described in Section 4). In the remainder of the paper we refer to the latter system as DLA (Deep Linguistic Analysis).

5.1 Superlative Detection

Baseline system For superlative detection we generated a baseline that solely relies on part-of-speech information. The data was tagged using TnT (Brants, 2000), using a model trained on the Wall Street Journal. In the WSJ tagset, superlatives can be marked in two different ways, depending on whether the adjective is inflected or modified by most/least. So, "largest", for instance, is tagged as JJS, whereas "most beautiful" is a sequence of RBS (most) and JJ (beautiful). We also checked that they are followed by a common or proper noun (NN.*), allowing one word to occur in between. To cover more complex cases, we also considered pre-modification by adjectives (JJ), and cardinals (CD). In summary, we matched on sequences found by the following pattern:

```
[(CD || JJ)* (JJS || (RBS JJ)) * NN.*]
```

This rather simple baseline is capable of detecting superlatives such as "100 biggest banks", "fourth largest investors", and "most important element", but will fail on expressions such as "fastest growing segments" or "Scotland 's lowest permitted 1995-96 increase".

DLA system For evaluation, we extrapolated superlatives from the DRSs output by the system. Each superlative introduces an implicational DRS condition, but not all implicational DRS conditions are introduced by superlatives. Hence, for the purposes of this experiment superlative DRS conditions were assigned a special mark. While traversing the DRS, we use this mark to retrieve superlative instances. In order to retrieve the original string that gave rise to the superlative interpretation, we exploit the meta information encoded in each DRS about the relation between input tokens and semantic information. The obtained string position can in turn be evaluated against the gold standard.

Table 4 lists the results achieved by the baseline system and the DLA system on the detection task. The DLA system outperforms the baseline system on precision in all sub-corpora. However, the baseline achieves a higher recall on the Excite queries. This is not entirely surprising given that the coverage of the parser is between 90–95% on unseen data. Moreover, Excite queries are often ungrammatical, thus further affecting the performance of parsing.

Table 4: Detection of Attributive Superlatives, reporting P (precision), R (Recall) and F-score, for WSJ sections, extracts of the Glasgow Herald, TREC questions, and Excite queries. D indicates development data, T test data.

	Baseline			DLA		
Corpus	**P**	**R**	**F**	**P**	**R**	**F**
WSJ (D)	0.93	0.86	0.89	0.96	0.90	0.93
WSJ (T)	0.91	0.83	0.87	0.95	0.87	0.91
GH (T)	0.80	0.76	0.78	0.87	0.81	0.84
TREC (D)	0.76	0.91	0.83	0.85	0.91	0.88
Excite (T)	0.92	0.92	0.92	0.97	0.84	0.90

5.2 Comparison Set Determination

Baseline For comparison set determination we developed two baseline systems. Both use the same match on sequences of part-of-speech tags described above. For Baseline 1, the beginning of the comparison set is the first word following the superlative. The end of the comparison set is the first word tagged as NN.* in that sequence (the same word could be the beginning and end of the comparison set, as it often happens).

The second baseline takes the first word after the superlative as the beginning of the comparison set, and the end of the sentence (or question) as the end (excluding the final punctuation mark). We expect this strategy to perform well on questions, as the following examples show.

Where is the oldest <u>synagogue in the United States</u>?
What was the largest <u>crowd to ever come see Michael Jordan</u>?

This approach is obviously likely to generate comparison sets much wider than required.

More complex examples that neither baseline can tackle involve possessives, since on the surface the comparison set lies at both ends of the superlative adjective:

<u>The nation's</u> largest <u>pension fund</u>
<u>the world's</u> most corrupt <u>organizations</u>

DLA 1 We first extrapolate superlatives from the DRS output by the system (see procedure above). Then, we exploit the semantic representation to select the comparison set: it is determined by the information encoded in the antecedent of the DRS-conditional introduced by the superlative. Again, we exploit meta information to reconstruct the original span, and we match it against the gold standard for evaluation.

DLA 2 DLA 2 builds on DLA 1, to which it adds post-processing rules to the CCG derivation, i.e. before the DRSs are constructed. This set of rules deal with NP post-modification of the superlative (see Section 4).

DLA 3 In this version we include a set of post-processing rules that apply to the CCG derivation to deal with possessives preceding the superlative (see Section 4).

DLA 4 This is a combination of DLA 2 and DLA 3. This system is clearly expected to perform best.

Results for both baseline systems and all versions of DLA are shown in Table 5

On text documents, DLA 2/3/4 outperform the baseline systems. DLA 4 achieves the best performance, with an accuracy of 69–83%. On questions, however, DLA 4 competes with the baseline: whereas it is better on TREC questions, it performs worse on Excite questions. One of the obvious reasons for this is that the parser's model

Table 5: Determination of Comparison Set of Attributive Superlatives (Accuracy) for WSJ sections, extracts of the Glasgow Herald, TREC and Excite questions. D indicates development data, T test data.

Corpus	Base 1	Base 2	DLA 1	DLA 2	DLA3	DLA 4
WSJ (D)	0.29	0.17	0.29	0.52	0.53	0.78
WSJ (T)	0.31	0.22	0.32	0.59	0.53	0.83
GH (T)	0.23	0.31	0.22	0.51	0.38	0.69
TREC (D)	0.10	0.69	0.13	0.69	0.23	0.82
Excite (T)	0.23	0.90	0.32	0.82	0.33	0.84

for questions was trained on TREC data. Additionally, as noted earlier, Excite questions are often ungrammatical and make parsing less likely to succeed. However, the baseline system, by definition, does not output semantic representations, so that its outcome is of little use for further reasoning, as required by question answering or general information extraction systems.

6 Conclusions

We have presented the first empirically grounded study of superlatives, and shown the feasibility of their semantic interpretation in an automatic fashion. Using Combinatory Categorial Grammar and Discourse Representation Theory we have implemented a system that is able to recognise a superlative expression and its comparison set with high accuracy.

For developing and testing our system, we have created a collection of over 3,000 instances of superlatives, both in newswire text and in natural language questions. This very first corpus of superlatives allows us to get a comprehensive picture of the behaviour and distribution of superlatives in real occurring data. Thanks to such broad view of the phenomenon, we were able discover issues previously unnoted in the formal semantics literature, such as the interaction of prenominal possessives and superlatives, which cause problems at the syntax-semantics interface in the determination of the comparison set. Similarly problematic are hyphenated superlatives, which are tagged as normal adjectives in the Penn Treebank.

Moreover, this work provides a concrete way of evaluating the output of a stochastic wide-coverage parser trained on the CCGBank (Hockenmaier and Steedman, 2002). With respect to superlatives, our experiments show that the quality of the raw output is not entirely satisfactory. However, we have also shown that some simple post-processing rules can increase the performance considerably. This might indicate that the way superlatives are annotated in the CCGbank, although consistent, is not fully adequate for the purpose of generating meaningful semantic representations, but probably easy to amend.

7 Future Work

Given the syntactic and semantic complexity of superlative expressions, there is still wide scope for improving the coverage and accuracy of our system. One obvious improvement is to amend CCGbank in order to avoid the need for postprocessing rules, thereby also allowing the creation of more accurate language models. Another aspect which we have neglected in this study but want to consider in future work is the interaction between superlatives and focus (Heim, 1999; Gawron, 1995). Also, only one of the possible types of superlative was considered, namely the attributive case. In future work we will consider the interpretation of predicative and adverbial superlatives, as well as comparative expressions. Finally, we would like to investigate the extent to which existing NLP systems (such as open-domain QA systems) can benefit from a detailed analysis of superlatives.

Acknowledgements

We would like to thank Steve Pulman (for information on the analysis of superlatives in the Core Language Engine), Mark Steedman (for useful suggestions on an earlier draft of this paper), and Jean Carletta (for helpful comments on annotation agreement issues), as well as three anonymous reviewers for their comments. We are extremely grateful to Stephen Clark and James Curran for making their parser available to us. Johan Bos is supported by a "Rientro dei Cervelli" grant (Italian Ministry for Research); Malvina Nissim is supported by the EU FP6 NeOn project.

References

Hiyan Alshawi, editor. 1992. *The Core Language Engine*. The MIT Press, Cambridge, Massachusetts.

J. Bos, S. Clark, M. Steedman, J.R. Curran, and Hockenmaier J. 2004. Wide-Coverage Semantic Representations from a CCG Parser. In *Proceedings of the 20th International Conference on Computational Linguistics (COLING '04)*, Geneva, Switzerland.

Johan Bos. 2005. Towards wide-coverage semantic interpretation. In *Proceedings of Sixth International Workshop on Computational Semantics IWCS-6*, pages 42–53.

Thorsten Brants. 2000. TnT - A Statistical Part-of-Speech Tagger. In *Proceedings of the Sixth Applied Natural Language Processing Conference ANLP-2000, Seattle, WA.*

Jean Carletta. 1996. Assessing agreement on classification tasks: the kappa statistic. *Computational Linguistics*, 22(2):249–254.

S. Clark and J.R. Curran. 2004. Parsing the WSJ using CCG and Log-Linear Models. In *Proceedings of the 42nd Annual Meeting of the Association for Computational Linguistics (ACL '04)*, Barcelona, Spain.

Jacob Cohen. 1960. A coefficient of agreement for nominal scales. *Educational and Psychological Measurements*, 20:37–46.

Barbara Di Eugenio and Michael Glass. 2004. The kappa statistic: a second look. *Computational Linguistics*, 30(1).

Donka F. Farkas and Katalin È. Kiss. 2000. On the comparative and absolute readings of superlatives. *Natural Language and Linguistic Theory*, 18:417–455.

Jean Mark Gawron. 1995. Comparatives, superlatives, and resolution. *Linguistics and Philosophy*, 18:333–380.

Ben Hachey, Beatrice Alex, and Markus Becker. 2005. Investigating the effects of selective sampling on the annotation task. In *Proceedings of the 9th Conference on Computational Natural Language Learning, Ann Arbor, Michigan, USA.*

Irene Heim. 1999. Notes on superlatives. MIT.

J. Hockenmaier and M. Steedman. 2002. Generative Models for Statistical Parsing with Combinatory Categorial Grammar. In *Proceedings of 40th Annual Meeting of the Association for Computational Linguistics*, Philadelphia, PA.

Bernard J. Jansen and Amanda Spink. 2000. The excite research project: A study of searching by web users. *Bulletin of the American Society for Information Science and Technology*, 27(1):5–17.

H. Kamp and U. Reyle. 1993. *From Discourse to Logic; An Introduction to Modeltheoretic Semantics of Natural Language, Formal Logic and DRT.* Kluwer, Dordrecht.

Klaus Krippendorff. 1980. *Content Analysis: An Introduction to Its Methodology.* Sage Publications.

M. Steedman. 2001. *The Syntactic Process.* The MIT Press.

Anna Szabolcsi. 1986. Comparative superlatives. In N. Fukui et al., editor, *Papers in Theoretical Linguistics, MITWPL*, volume 8. MIT.

Erik F. Tjong Kim Sang. 2002. Introduction to the conll-2002 shared task: Language-independent named entity recognition. In *Proceedings of CoNLL-2002*, pages 155–158. Taipei, Taiwan.

Paraphrase Recognition via Dissimilarity Significance Classification

Long Qiu, Min-Yen Kan and **Tat-Seng Chua**
Department of Computer Science
National University of Singapore
Singapore, 117543
{qiul,kanmy,chuats}@comp.nus.edu.sg

Abstract

We propose a supervised, two-phase framework to address the problem of paraphrase recognition (PR). Unlike most PR systems that focus on sentence similarity, our framework detects dissimilarities between sentences and makes its paraphrase judgment based on the significance of such dissimilarities. The ability to differentiate significant dissimilarities not only reveals what makes two sentences a non-paraphrase, but also helps to recall additional paraphrases that contain extra but insignificant information. Experimental results show that while being accurate at discerning non-paraphrasing dissimilarities, our implemented system is able to achieve higher paraphrase recall (93%), at an overall performance comparable to the alternatives.

1 Introduction

The task of sentence-level paraphrase recognition (PR) is to identify whether a set of sentences (typically, a pair) are semantically equivalent. In such a task, "equivalence" takes on a relaxed meaning, allowing sentence pairs with minor semantic differences to still be considered as paraphrases.

PR can be thought of as synonym detection extended for sentences, and it can play an equally important role in natural language applications. As with synonym detection, applications such as summarization can benefit from the recognition and canonicalization of concepts and actions that are shared across multiple documents. Automatic construction of large paraphrase corpora could mine alternative ways to express the same concept, aiding machine translation and natural language generation applications.

In our work on sentence-level PR, we have identified two main issues through observation of sample sentences. The first is to identify all discrete *information nuggets*, or individual semantic content units, shared by the sentences. For a pair of sentences to be deemed a paraphrase, they must share a substantial amount of these nuggets. A trivial case is when both sentences are identical, word for word. However, paraphrases often employ different words or syntactic structures to express the same concept. Figure 1 shows two sentence pairs, in which the first pair is a paraphrase while the second is not. The paraphrasing pair (also denoted as the $+pp$ class) use different words. Focusing just on the matrix verbs, we note differences between "injured" and "hurt". A paraphrase recognition system should be able to detect such semantic similarities (despite the different syntactic structures). Otherwise, the two sentences could look even less similar than two non-paraphrasing sentences, such as the two in the second pair. Also in the paraphrasing pair, the first sentence includes an extra phrase "Authorities said". Human annotators tend to regard the pair as a paraphrase despite the presence of this extra information nugget.

Paraphrase (+pp): Authorities said a young man *injured* Richard Miller. Richard Miller was *hurt* by a young man.
Non-Paraphrase (-pp): The technology-laced Nasdaq Composite Index .IXIC *added* 1.92 points, or 0.12 percent, at 1,647.94. The technology-laced Nasdaq Composite Index .IXIC *dipped* 0.08 of a point to 1,646.

Figure 1: Examples: Paraphrasing & Non-paraphrasing

Proceedings of the 2006 Conference on Empirical Methods in Natural Language Processing (EMNLP 2006), pages 18–26, Sydney, July 2006.

This leads to the second issue: how to recognize when such extra information is extraneous with respect to the paraphrase judgment. Such paraphrases are common in daily life. In news articles describing the same event, paraphrases are widely used, possibly with extraneous information.

We equate PR with solving these two issues, presenting a natural two-phase architecture. In the first phase, the nuggets shared by the sentences are identified by a pairing process. In the second phase, any unpaired nuggets are classified as significant or not (leading to $-pp$ and $+pp$ classifications, respectively). If the sentences do not contain unpaired nuggets, or if all unpaired nuggets are insignificant, then the sentences are considered paraphrases. Experiments on the widely-used MSR corpus (Dolan et al., 2004) show favorable results.

We first review related work in Section 2. We then present the overall methodology and describe the implemented system in Section 3. Sections 4 and 5 detail the algorithms for the two phases respectively. This is followed with our evaluation and discussion of the results.

2 Related Work

Possibly the simplest approach to PR is an information retrieval (IR) based "bag-of-words" strategy. This strategy calculates a cosine similarity score for the given sentence set, and if the similarity exceeds a threshold (either empirically determined or learned from supervised training data), the sentences are paraphrases. PR systems that can be broadly categorized as IR-based include (Corley and Mihalcea, 2005; Brockett and Dolan, 2005). In the former work, the authors defined a *directional similarity* formula reflecting the semantic similarity of one text "with respect to" another. A word contributes to the directional similarity only when its counterpart has been identified in the opposing sentence. The associated word similarity scores, weighted by the word's specificity (represented as inverted document frequency, *idf*), sum to make up the directional similarity. The mean of both directions is the overall similarity of the pair. Brockett and Dolan (2005) represented sentence pairs as a feature vector, including features (among others) for sentence length, edit distance, number of shared words, morphologically similar word pairs, synonym pairs (as suggested by WordNet and a semi-automatically constructed thesaurus). A support vector machine is then trained to learn the $\{+pp, -pp\}$ classifier.

Strategies based on bags of words largely ignore the semantic interactions between words. Weeds et al. (2005) addressed this problem by utilizing parses for PR. Their system for phrasal paraphrases equates paraphrasing as distributional similarity of the partial sub-parses of a candidate text. Wu (2005)'s approach relies on the generative framework of Inversion Transduction Grammar (ITG) to measure how similar two sentences arrange their words based on edit distance.

Barzilay and Lee (2003) proposed to apply multiple-sequence alignment (MSA) for traditional, sentence-level PR. Given multiple articles on a certain type of event, sentence clusters are first generated. Sentences within the same cluster, presumably similar in structure and content, are then used to construct a lattice with "backbone" nodes corresponding to words shared by the majority and "slots" corresponding to different realization of arguments. If sentences from different clusters have shared arguments, the associated lattices are claimed to be paraphrase. Likewise, Shinyama et al. (2002) extracted paraphrases from similar news articles, but use shared named entities as an indication of paraphrasing. It should be noted that the latter two approaches are geared towards acquiring paraphrases rather than detecting them, and as such have the disadvantage of requiring a certain level of repetition among candidates for paraphrases to be recognized.

All past approaches invariably aim at a proper similarity measure that accounts for all of the words in the sentences in order to make a judgment for PR. This is suitable for PR where input sentences are precisely equivalent semantically. However, for many people the notion of paraphrases also covers cases in which minor or irrelevant information is added or omitted in candidate sentences, as observed in the earlier example. Such extraneous content should not be a barrier to PR if the main concepts are shared by the sentences. Approaches that focus only on the similarity of shared contents may fail when the (human) criteria for PR include whether the unmatched content is significant or not. Correctly addressing this problem should increase accuracy. In addition, if extraneous portions of sentences can be identified, their confounding influence on the sentence similarity judgment can be removed, leading to more accurate modeling of semantic similarity for both recognition and acquisition.

3 Methodology

As noted earlier, for a pair of sentences to be a paraphrase, they must possess two attributes:

1. *similarity*: they share a substantial amount of information nuggets;

2. *dissimilarities are extraneous*: if extra information in the sentences exists, the effect of its removal is not significant.

A key decision for our two-phase PR framework is to choose the representation of an information nugget. A simple approach is to use representative words as information nuggets, as is done in the SimFinder system (Hatzivassiloglou et al., 2001).

Instead of using words, we choose to equate information nuggets with *predicate argument tuples*. A predicate argument tuple is a structured representation of a verb predicate together with its arguments. Given a sentence from the example in Figure 1, its predicate argument tuple form in PropBank (Kingsbury et al., 2002) format is:

target(predicate):	hurt
arg0:	a young man
arg1:	Richard Miller

We feel that this is a better choice for the representation of a nugget as it accounts for the action, concepts and their relationships as a single unit. In comparison, using fine-grained units such as words, including nouns and verbs may result in inaccuracy (sentences that share vocabulary may not be paraphrases), while using coarser-grained units may cause key differences to be missed. In the rest of this paper, we use the term *tuple* for conciseness when no ambiguity is introduced.

An overview of our paraphrase recognition system is shown in Figure 2. A pair of sentences is first fed to a syntactic parser (Charniak, 2000) and then passed to a semantic role labeler (ASSERT; (Pradhan et al., 2004)), to label predicate argument tuples. We then calculate normalized tuple similarity scores over the tuple pairs using a metric that accounts for similarities in both syntactic structure and content of each tuple. A thesaurus constructed from corpus statistics (Lin, 1998) is utilized for the content similarity.

We utilize this metric to greedily pair together the most similar predicate argument tuples across sentences. Any remaining unpaired tuples represent extra information and are passed to a dissimilarity classifier to decide whether such information is significant. The dissimilarity classifier uses supervised machine learning to make such a decision.

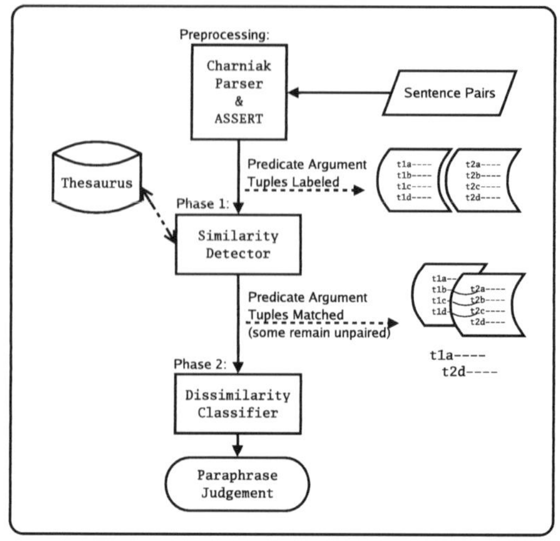

Figure 2: System architecture

4 Similarity Detection and Pairing

We illustrate this advantage of using predicate argument tuples from our running example. In Table 1, one of the model sentences is shown in the middle column. Two edited versions are shown on the left and right columns. While it is clear that the left modification is an example of a paraphrase and the right is not, the version on the left involves more changes in its syntactic structure and vocabulary. Standard word or syntactic similarity measures would assign the right modification a higher similarity score, likely mislabeling one or both modifications.

In contrast, semantic role labeling identifies the dependencies between predicates and their arguments, allowing a more precise measurement of sentence similarity. Assuming that the arguments in predicate argument tuples are assigned the same role when their roles are comparable[1], we define the similarity score of two tuples T_a and T_b as the weighted sum of the pairwise similarities of all their shared constituents $C=\{(c_a, c_b)\}$ (c being either the *target* or one of the *arguments* that both

[1] ASSERT, which is trained on the Propbank, only guarantees consistency of **arg0** and **arg1** slots, but we have found in practice that aligning **arg2** and above arguments do not cause problems.

	Modification 1: **paraphrase**	**Model Sentence**	Modification 2: **non-paraphrase**
Sentence	Richard Miller was hurt by a young man.	Authorities said a young man injured Richard Miller.	Authorities said Richard Miller injured a young man.
(Paired) Tuples		**target**: said **arg0**: Authorities **arg1**: a young man injured Richard Miller	**target**: said **arg0**: Authorities **arg1**: Richard Miller injured a young man
	target: hurt **arg0**: a young man **arg1**: Richard Miller	**target**: injured **arg0**: a young man **arg1**: Richard Miller	**target**: injured **arg0**: Richard Miller **arg1**: a young man

Table 1: Similarity Detection: pairing of predicate argument tuples

tuples have):

$$Sim(T_a, T_b) = \frac{1}{\alpha} \sum_{c=\{target, arg_{shared}\}} Sim(c_a, c_b) * \ w_{target}^{c==target} \quad (1)$$

where normalization factor α is the sum of the weights of constituents in C, *i.e.*:

$$\alpha = \|\{arg_{shared}\}\| + w_{target} \quad (2)$$

In our current implementation we reduce targets and their arguments to their syntactic headwords. These headwords are then directly compared using a corpus-based similarity thesaurus. As we hypothesized that targets are more important for predicate argument tuple similarity, we multiply the target's similarity by a weighting factor w_{target}, whose value we have empirically determined as 1.7, based on a 300-pair development set from the MSR training set.

We then proceed to pair tuples in the two sentences using a greedy iterative algorithm. The algorithm locates the two most similar tuples from each sentence, pairs them together and removes them from futher consideration. The process stops when subsequent best pairings are below the similarity threshold or when all possible tuples are exhausted. If unpaired tuples still exist in a given sentence pair, we further examine the copular constructions and noun phrases in the opposing sentence for possible pairings[2]. This results in a one-to-one mapping with possibly some tuples left unpaired. The curved arrows in Table 1 denote the correct results of similarity pairing: two tuples are paired up if their target and shared arguments are identical or similar respectively, otherwise they remain unpaired even if the "bag of words" they contain are the same.

5 Dissimilarity Significance Classification

If some tuples remain unpaired, they are dissimilar parts of the sentence that need to be labeled by the dissimilarity classifier. Such unpaired information could be extraneous or they could be semantically important, creating a barrier for paraphrase. We frame this as a supervised machine learning problem in which a set of features are used to inform the classifier. A support vector machine, SVM^{Light}, was chosen as the learning model as it has shown to yield good performance over a wide application range. We experimented with a wide set of features of unpaired tuples, including internal counts of *numeric expressions*, *named entities*, *words*, *semantic roles*, whether they are similar to other tuples in the same sentence, and contextual features like *source/target sentence length* and *paired tuple count*. Currently, only two features are correlated in improved classification, which we detail now.

Syntactic Parse Tree Path: This is a series of features that reflect how the unpaired tuple connects with the context: the rest of the sentence. It models the syntactic connection between the constituents on both ends of the path (Gildea and Palmer, 2002; Pradhan et al., 2004). Here, we model the ends of the path as the unpaired tuple and the paired tuple with the closest shared ancestor, and model the path itself as a sequence of constituent category tags and directions to reach the destination (the paired target) from the source (the

[2]Copular constructions are not handled by ASSERT. Such constructions account for a large proportion of the semantic meaning in sentences. Consider the pair "Microsoft rose 50 cents" and "Microsoft was up 50 cents", in which the second is in copular form. Similarly, NPs can often be equivalent to predicate argument tuples when actions are nominalized. Consider an NP that reads "(be blamed for) frequent attacks on soldiers" and a predicate argument tuple: "(be blamed for) attacking soldiers". Again, identical information is conveyed but not captured by semantic role labeling. In such cases, they can be paired if we allow a candidate tuple to pair with the *predicative argument* (e.g., *50 cents*) of a copula, or (the head of) an NP in the opposing sentence. As these heuristic matches may introduce errors, we resort to these methods of matching tuple only in the contingency when there are unpaired tuples.

unpaired target) via the the shared ancestor. When no tuples have been paired in the sentence pair, the destination defaults to the root of the syntactic parse tree. For example, the tuples with target "injured" are unpaired when the model sentence and the non-paraphrasing modification in Table 1 are being compared. A path "$\uparrow_{VBD}, \uparrow_{VP}, \uparrow_{S}, \uparrow_{SBAR}, \uparrow_{VP}, \downarrow_{VBD}$" links a target "injured" to the paired target "said", as shown in Figure 3.

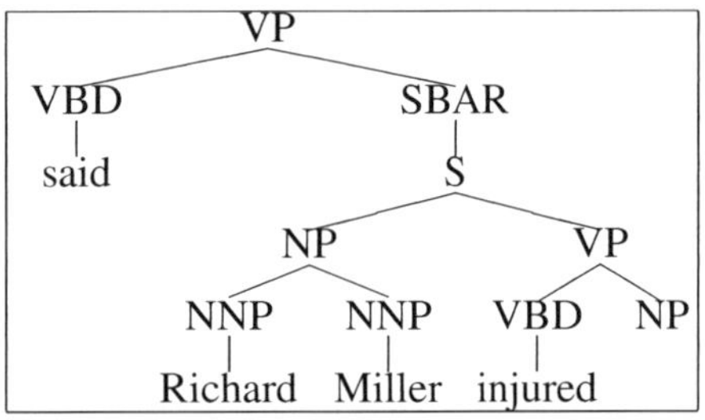

Figure 3: Syntactic parse tree path

The syntactic path can act as partial evidence in significance classification. In the above example, the category tag "$_{VBD}$" assigned to "injured" indicates that the verb is in its past tense. Such a predicate argument tuple bears the main content of the sentence and generally can not be ignored if its meaning is missing in the opposing sentence. Another example is shown in Figure 4. The second sentence has one unpaired target "proposed" while the rest all find their counterpart. The path we get from the syntactic parse tree reads "$\uparrow_{VBN}, \uparrow_{NP}, \uparrow_{S}, ...$", showing that the unpaired tuple (consisting of a single predicate) is a modifier contained in an NP. It can be ignored if there is no contradiction in the opposing sentence.

We represent a syntactic path by a set of n-gram ($n \leq 4$) features of subsequences of category tags found in the path, along with the respective direction. We require these n-gram features to be no more than four category tags away from the unpaired target, as our primary concern is to model what role the target plays in its sentence.

> Sheena Young of Child, the national infertility support network, hoped the guidelines would lead to a more "fair and equitable" service for infertility sufferers.
>
> Sheena Young, a spokesman for Child, the national infertility support network, said the **proposed** guidelines should lead to a more "fair and equitable" service for infertility sufferers.

Figure 4: Unpaired predicate argument tuple as modifier in a paraphrase

Predicate: This is the lexical token of predicate argument tuple's target, as a text feature. As this feature is liable to run into sparse data problems, the semantic category of the target would be a more suitable feature. However, verb similarity is generally regarded as difficult to measure, both in terms of semantic relatedness as well as in finding a consistent granularity for verb categories. We investigated using WordNet as well as Levin's classification (Levin, 1993) as additional features on our validation data, but currently find that using the lexical form of the target works best.

5.1 Classifier Training Set Acquisition

Currently, no training corpus for predicate argument tuple significance exists. Such a corpus is indispensable for training the classifier. Rather than manually annotating training instances, we use an automatic method to construct instances from paraphrase corpora. This is possible as the paraphrase judgments in the corpora can imply which portion of the sentence(s) are significant barriers to paraphrasing or not. Here, we exploit the similarity detector implemented for the first phase for this purpose. If unpaired tuples exist after greedy pairing, we classify them along two dimensions: whether the sentence pair is a (non-)paraphrase, and the source of the unpaired tuples:

1. **[PS] p**araphrasing pairs and unpaired predicate argument tuples are only from a **s**ingle sentence;
2. **[NS] n**on-paraphrasing pairs and only one **s**ingle unpaired predicate argument tuple exists;
3. **[PM] p**araphrasing pairs and unpaired predicate argument tuples are from **m**ultiple (both) sentences;
4. **[NM] n**on-paraphrasing pairs and **m**ultiple unpaired predicate argument tuples (from either one or both sentences) exist.

Assuming that similarity detector pairs tuples correctly, for the first two categories, the paraphrasing judgment is directly linked to the unpaired tuples. PS tuple instances are therefore used as $insignificant$ class instances, and NS as $significant$ ones. The last two categories cannot be used for training data, as it is unclear which of the unpaired tuples is responsible for the (non-) paraphrasing as the similarity measure may mistakenly leave some similar predicate argument tuples unpaired.

6 Evaluation

The goal of our evaluation is to show that our system can reliably determine the cause(s) of non-

MSR Corpus Label	+pp		-pp		
system prediction correct?	T	F	T	F	total
# sentence pairs (*s-ps*)	85	23	**55**	37	200
# labelings (H&C agree)	80	19	53	35	187
# tuple pairs (*t-ps*) (S)	80	6	36	35	**157**
# correct *t-ps* (H&S agree)	74	6	34	30	**144**
# missed *t-ps* (H)	11	10	5	5	**31**
# sig. unpaired tuples(H)	6	4	69	51	130
# sig. unpaired tuples(S)	0	32	70	0	102
# sig. unpaired tuples(H&S)	0	4	**43**	0	47
# -pp for other reasons	0	0	5	2	7

Table 2: (H)uman annotations vs. (C)orpus annotations and (S)ystem output

paraphrase examples, while maintaining the performance level of the state-of-the-art PR systems.

For evaluation, we conduct both component evaluations as well as a holistic one, resulting in three separate experiments. In evaluating the first tuple pairing component, we aim for high precision, so that sentences that have all tuples paired can be safely assumed to be paraphrases. In evaluating the dissimilarity classifier, we simply aim for high accuracy. In our overall system evaluation, we compare our system versus other PR systems on standard corpora.

Experimental Data Set. For these experiments, we utilized two widely-used corpora for paraphrasing evaluation: the MSR and PASCAL RTE corpora. The Microsoft Research Paraphrase coupus (Dolan et al., 2004) consists of 5801 newswire sentence pairs, 3900 of which are annotated as semantically equivalent by human annotators. It reflects ordinary paraphrases that people often encounter in news articles, and may be viewed as a typical domain-general paraphrase recognition task that downstream NLP systems will need to deal with. The corpus comes divided into standard training (70%) and testing (30%) divisions, a partition we follow in our experiments. ASSERT (the semantic role labeler) shows for this corpus a sentence contains 2.24 predicate argument tuples on average. The second corpus is the *paraphrase acquisition* subset of the PASCAL Recognizing Textual Entailment (RTE) Challenge corpus (Dagan et al., 2005). This is much smaller, consisting of 50 pairs, which we employ for testing only to show portability.

To assess the component performance, we need additional ground truth beyond the $\{+pp, -pp\}$ labels provided by the corpora. For the first evaluation, we need to ascertain whether a sentence pair's tuples are correctly paired, misidentified or mispaired. For the second, which tuple(s) (if any) are responsible for a $-pp$ instance. However, creating ground truth by manual annotation is expensive, and thus we only sampled the data set to get an indicative assessment of performance. We sampled 200 random instances from the total MSR testing set, and first processed them through our framework. Then, five human annotators (two authors and three volunteers) annotated the ground truth for tuple pairing and the semantic significance of the unpaired tuples, while checking system output. They also independently came up with their own $\{+pp,-pp\}$ judgment so we could assess the reliability of the provided annotations.

The results of this annotation is shown in Table 2. Examining this data, we can see that the similarity detector performs well, despite its simplicity and assumption of a one-to-one mapping. Out of the 157 predicate argument tuple pairs identified through similarity detection, annotators agreed that 144 (92%) are semantically similar or equivalent. However, 31 similar pairs were missed by the system, resulting in 82% recall. We defer discussion on the other details of this table to Section 7.

To assess the dissimilarity classifier, we focus on the $-pp$ subset of 55 instances recognized by the system. For 43 unpaired tuples from 40 sentence pairs (73% of 55), the annotators' judgments agree with the classifier's claim that they are significant. For these cases, the system is able to both recognize that the sentence pair is not a paraphrase and further correctly establish a cause of the non-paraphrase.

In addition to this ground truth sampled evaluation, we also show the effectiveness of the classifier by examining its performance on PS and NS tuples in the MSR corpus as described in Section 5. The test set consists of 413 randomly selected PS and NS instances among which 145 are significant (leading to non-paraphrases). The classifier predicts predicate argument tuple significance at an accuracy of 71%, outperforms a majority classifier (65%), a gain which is marginally statistically significant ($p < .09$).

significant	insignificant	
112	263	insignificant by classifier
33	5	**significant** by classifier

We can see the classifier classifies the majority of insignificant tuples correctly (by outputting a

Algorithm	709 Sentence Pairs Without Unpaired Tuples (41.1% of Test set)			1016 Sentence Pairs With Unpaired Tuples (58.9% of Test set)			Overall (100% of Test set)			
	Acc	R	P	Acc	R	P	Acc	R	P	F1
Majority Classifier	79.5%	100%	79.5%	57.4%	100%	57.4%	66.5%	100%	66.5%	79.9%
SimFinder	82.2%	92.2%	86.4%	66.3%	84.9%	66.1%	**72.9%**	88.5%	**75.1%**	81.3%
CM05	-	-	-	-	-	-	71.5%	92.5%	72.3%	81.2%
Our System	79.5%	100%	79.5%	66.7%	87.0%	66.0%	72.0%	**93.4%**	72.5%	**81.6%**

Table 3: Results on MSR test set

Algorithm	17 Sentence Pairs Without Unpaired Tuples (34% of Test set)			33 Sentence Pairs With Unpaired Tuples (66% of Test set)			Overall (100% of Test set)			
	Acc	R	P	Acc	R	P	Acc	R	P	F1
Majority Classifier	65%	100%	65%	42%	100%	42%	50%	100%	50%	67%
SimFinder	71%	91%	71%	42%	21%	27%	52%	52%	52%	52%
Our System	65%	100%	65%	48%	64%	43%	54%	80%	53%	64%

Table 4: Results on PASCAL PP test set

score greater than zero), which is effectively a 98% recall of insignificant tuples. However, the precision is less satisfatory. We suspect this is partially due the tuples that fail to be paired up with their counterpart. Such noise is found among the automatically collected PS instances used in training.

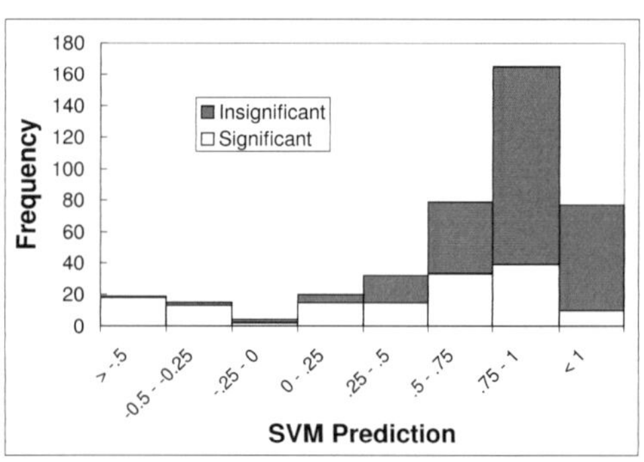

Figure 5: Dissimilarity classifier performance

For the final system-wide evaluation, we implemented two baseline systems: a majority classifier and SimFinder (Hatzivassiloglou et al., 2001), a bag-of-words sentence similarity module incorporating lexical, syntactic and semantic features. In Table 3, precision and recall are measured with respect to the paraphrasing class. The table shows sentence pairs falling under the column "pairs without unpaired tuples" are more likely to be paraphrasing than an arbitrary pair (79.5% versus 66.5%), providing further validation for using predicate argument tuples as information nuggets.

The results for the experiment benchmarking the overall system performance are shown under the "Overall" column: our approach performs comparably to the baselines at both accuracy and paraphrase recall. The system performance reported in (CM05; (Corley and Mihalcea, 2005)), which is among the best we are aware of, is also included for comparison.

We also ran our system (trained on the MSR corpus) on the 50 instances in the PASCAL paraphrase acquisition subset. Again, the system performance (as shown in Table 4) is comparable to the baseline systems.

7 Discussion

We have just shown that when two sentences have perfectly matched predicate argument tuples, they are more likely to be a paraphrase than a random sentence pair drawn from the corpus. Furthermore, in the sampled human evaluation in Table 2, among the 88 non-paraphrasing instances with whose MSR corpus labels our annotators agreed (53 correctly and 35 incorrectly judged by our system), the cause of the $-pp$ is correctly attributed in 81 cases to one or more predicate argument tuples. The remaining 7 cases (as shown in the last row) are caused by phenomenon that are not captured by our tuple representation. We feel this justifies using predicate argument tuples as *information nuggets*, but we are currently considering expanding our representation to account for some of these cases.

The evaluation also confirms the difficulty of making paraphrase judgements. Although the

MSR corpus used strict means of resolving inter-rater disagreements during its construction, the annotators agreed with the MSR corpus labels only 93.5% (187/200) of the time.

One weakness of our system is that we rely on a thesaurus (Lin, 1998) for word similarity information for predicate argument tuple pairing. However, it is designed to provide similarity scores between pairs of individual words (rather than phrases). If a predicate argument tuple's target or one argument is realized as a phrase (*borrow* $\rightarrow$ *check out*, for instance), the thesaurus is unable to provide an accurate similarity score. For similarity between predicate argument tuples, negation and modality have yet to be addressed, although they account for only a tiny fraction of the corpus.

We further estimated how the similarity detector can be affected when the semantic role labeler makes mistakes (by failing to identify arguments or assigning incorrect role names). Checking 94 pairs ground-truth similar tuples, we found that the system mislabels 43 of them. The similarity detector failed to pair around 30% of them. In comparison, all the tuple pairs free of labeling errors are correctly paired. A saving grace is that labeling errors rarely lead to incorrect pairing (one pairing in all the examined sentences). The labeling errors impact the whole system in two ways: 1) they caused similar tuples that should have been paired up to be added as noise in that dissimilarity classifier's training set and 2) paired tuples with labeling errors erroneously increase the target weight in Equation (1).

Some example paraphrasing cases that are problematic for our current system are:

1. Non-literal language issues such as implicature, idiom, metaphor, *etc.* are not addressed in our current system. When predicate argument tuples imply each other, they are less similar than what our system currently is trained for, causing the pairing to fail:

+pp, Later in the day, a standoff developed between French soldiers and a Hema battlewagon that attempted to pass the UN compound.

French soldiers later threatened to open fire on a Hema battlewagon that tried to pass near the UN compound.

2. A paraphrasing pair may exceed the systems' threshold for syntactic difference:

+pp, With the exception of dancing, physical activity did not decrease the risk.

Dancing was the only physical activity associated with a lower risk of dementia.

3. One or more unpaired tuples exist, but their significance is not inferred correctly:

+pp, Inhibited children tend to be timid with new people, objects, and situations, while uninhibited children spontaneously approach them.

Simply put, shy individuals tend to be more timid with new people and situations.

In the MSR corpus, the first error case is more frequent than the other two. We identify these as challenging cases where idiomatic processing is needed.

Below we show some unpaired predicate argument tuples (underlined) that are significant enough to be paraphrase barriers. These examples give an indicative categorization of what significant tuples are and their corpus frequency (when predicate argument tuples are the reasons; we examined 40 such cases for this estimation). There is one thing in common: every case involves substantial information that is difficult to infer from context. Such tuples appear as:

1. (40%) The nucleus of the sentence (often the matrix tuple):

Michael Hill, a Sun reporter who is a member of the Washington-Baltimore Newspaper Guild's bargaining committee, estimated meetings to last late Sunday.

2. (30%) A part of a coordination:

Security lights have also been installed and police have swept the grounds for booby traps.

3. (13%) A predicate of a modifying clause:

Westermayer was 26 then, and a friend and former manager who knew she was unhappy in her job tipped her to another position.

4. (7%) An adjunct:

While waiting for a bomb squad to arrive, the bomb exploded, killing Wells.

5. (7%) An embedded sentence:

Dean told reporters traveling on his 10-city "Sleepless Summer" tour that he considered campaigning in Texas a challenge.

6. (3%) Or factual content that conflicts with the opposing sentence:

Total sales for the period declined 8.0 percent to USD1.99 billion from a year earlier.

Wal-Mart said sales at stores open at least a year rose 4.6 percent from a year earlier.

8 Conclusions

We have proposed a new approach to the paraphrase recognition (PR) problem: a supervised, two-phase framework emphasizing dissimilarity classification. To emulate human PR judgment in which insignificant, extraneous *information nuggets* are generally allowed for a paraphrase, we estimate whether such additional information nuggets affect the final paraphrasing status of a sentence pair. This approach, unlike previous PR approaches, has the key benefit of explaining the cause of a non-paraphrase sentence pair.

In the first, similarity detection module, using predicate argument tuples as the unit for comparison, we pair them up in a greedy manner. Unpaired tuples thus represent additional information unrepresented in the opposing sentence. A second, dissimilarity classification module uses the lexical head of the predicates and the tuples' path of attachment as features to decide whether such tuples are barriers to paraphrase.

Our evaluations show that the system obtains 1) high accuracy for the similarity detector in pairing predicate argument tuples, 2) robust dissimilarity classification despite noisy training instances and 3) comparable overall performance to current state-of-the-art PR systems. To our knowledge this is the first work that tackles the problem of identifying what factors stop a sentence pair from being a paraphrase.

We also presented corpus examples that illustrate the categories of errors that our framework makes, suggesting future work in PR. While we continue to explore more suitable representation of unpaired predicate argument tuples, we plan to augment the similarity measure for phrasal units to reduce the error rate in the first component. Another direction is to detect semantic redundancy in a sentence. Unpaired tuples that are semantically redundant should also be regarded as insignificant.

References

Regina Barzilay and Lillian Lee. 2003. Learning to paraphrase: An unsupervised approach using multiple-sequence alignment. In *Proceedings of HLT-NAACL 2003*.

Chris Brockett and Bill Dolan. 2005. Support vector machines for paraphrase identification and corpus construction. In *Proceedings of the 3rd International Workshop on Paraphrasing*.

Eugene Charniak. 2000. A maximum-entropy-inspired parser. In *Proceedings of the First Annual Meeting of the North American Chapter of the Association for Computational Linguistics (NAACL'2000)*.

Courtney Corley and Rada Mihalcea. 2005. Measuring the semantic similarity of texts. In *Proceedings of the ACL Workshop on Empirical Modeling of Semantic Equivalence and Entailment*, pages 13–18, Ann Arbor, USA.

Ido Dagan, Oren Glickman, and Bernardo Magnini. 2005. The pascal recognising textual entailment challenge. In *PASCAL Proceedings of the First Challenge Workshop–Recognizing Textual Entailment*, Southampton,UK.

Bill Dolan, Chris Quirk, and Chris Brockett. 2004. Unsupervised construction of large paraphrase corpora: Exploiting massively parallel news sources. In *Proceedings of the 20th International Conference on Computational Linguistics*, Geneva, Switzerland.

Daniel Gildea and Martha Palmer. 2002. The necessity of parsing for predicate argument recognition. In *Proceedings of the 40th Annual Meeting of the Association for Computational Linguistics*, Philadelphia, USA.

Vassileios Hatzivassiloglou, Judith Klavans, Melissa Holcombe, Regina Barzilay, Min-Yen Kan, and Kathleen McKeown. 2001. Simfinder: A flexible clustering tool for summarization. In *Proceedings of the NAACL Workshop on Automatic Summarization*, pages 41–49.

Paul Kingsbury, Martha Palmer, and Mitch Marcus. 2002. Adding semantic annotation to the penn treebank. In *Proceedings of the Human Language Technology Conference*, San Diego, USA.

Beth Levin. 1993. English verb classes and alternations: A preliminary investigation. University of Chicago Press.

Dekang Lin. 1998. Automatic retrieval and clustering of similar words. In *Proceedings of COLING-ACL '98*, pages 768–774, Montreal, Canada.

Sameer Pradhan, Wayne Ward, Kadri Hacioglu, James Martin, and Dan Jurafsky. 2004. Shallow semantic parsing using support vector machines. In *Proceedings of HLT/NAACL*, Boston, USA.

Yusuke Shinyama, Satoshi Sekine, Kiyoshi Sudo, and Ralph Grishman. 2002. Automatic paraphrase acquisition from news articles. In *Proceedings of the Human Language Technology Conference*, pages 40–46, San Diego, USA.

Julie Weeds, David Weir, and Bill Keller. 2005. The distributional similarity of sub-parses. In *Proceedings of the ACL Workshop on Empirical Modeling of Semantic Equivalence and Entailment*, pages 7–12, Ann Arbor, USA.

Dekai Wu. 2005. Recognizing paraphrases and textual entailment using inversion transduction grammars. In *Proceedings of the ACL Workshop on Empirical Modeling of Semantic Equivalence and Entailment*, Ann Arbor, USA.

Detecting Parser Errors Using Web-based Semantic Filters

Alexander Yates **Stefan Schoenmackers** **Oren Etzioni**
University of Washington
Computer Science and Engineering
Box 352350
Seattle, WA 98195-2350
{ayates, stef, etzioni} @cs.washington.edu

Abstract

NLP systems for tasks such as question answering and information extraction typically rely on statistical parsers. But the efficacy of such parsers can be surprisingly low, particularly for sentences drawn from heterogeneous corpora such as the Web. We have observed that incorrect parses often result in wildly implausible semantic interpretations of sentences, which can be detected automatically using semantic information obtained from the Web.

Based on this observation, we introduce *Web-based semantic filtering*—a novel, domain-independent method for automatically detecting and discarding incorrect parses. We measure the effectiveness of our filtering system, called WOODWARD, on two test collections. On a set of TREC questions, it reduces error by 67%. On a set of more complex Penn Treebank sentences, the reduction in error rate was 20%.

1 Introduction

Semantic processing of text in applications such as question answering or information extraction frequently relies on statistical parsers. Unfortunately, the efficacy of state-of-the-art parsers can be disappointingly low. For example, we found that the Collins parser correctly parsed just 42% of the list and factoid questions from TREC 2004 (that is, 42% of the parses had 100% precision and 100% recall on labeled constituents). Similarly, this parser produced 45% correct parses on a subset of 100 sentences from section 23 of the Penn Treebank.

Although statistical parsers continue to improve their efficacy over time, progress is slow, particularly for Web applications where training the parsers on a "representative" corpus of hand-tagged sentences is not an option. Because of the heterogeneous nature of text on the Web, such a corpus would be exceedingly difficult to generate.

In response, this paper investigates the possibility of detecting parser errors by using semantic information obtained from the Web. Our fundamental hypothesis is that *incorrect parses often result in wildly implausible semantic interpretations of sentences, which can be detected automatically in certain circumstances.* Consider, for example, the following sentence from the Wall Street Journal: "That compares with per-share earnings from continuing operations of 69 cents." The Collins parser yields a parse that attaches "of 69 cents" to "operations," rather than "earnings." By computing the mutual information between "operations" and "cents" on the Web, we can detect that this attachment is unlikely to be correct.

Our WOODWARD system detects parser errors as follows. First, it maps the tree produced by a parser to a *relational conjunction* (RC), a logic-based representation language that we describe in Section 2.1. Second, WOODWARD employs four distinct methods for analyzing whether a conjunct in the RC is likely to be "reasonable" as described in Section 2.

Our approach makes several assumptions. First, if the sentence is absurd to begin with, then a correct parse could be deemed incorrect. Second, we require a corpus whose content overlaps at least in part with the content of the sentences to be parsed. Otherwise, much of our semantic analysis is impossible.

In applications such as Web-based question answering, these assumptions are quite natural. The

Proceedings of the 2006 Conference on Empirical Methods in Natural Language Processing (EMNLP 2006), pages 27–34,
Sydney, July 2006.

questions are *about* topics that are covered extensively on the Web, and we can assume that most questions link verbs to nouns in reasonable combinations. Likewise, when using parsing for information extraction, we would expect our assumptions to hold as well.

Our contributions are as follows:

1. We introduce *Web-based semantic filtering*—a novel, domain-independent method for detecting and discarding incorrect parses.
2. We describe four techniques for analyzing relational conjuncts using semantic information obtained from the Web, and assess their efficacy both separately and in combination.
3. We find that WOODWARD can filter good parses from bad on TREC 2004 questions for a reduction of 67% in error rate. On a harder set of sentences from the Penn Treebank, the reduction in error rate is 20%.

The remainder of this paper is organized as follows. We give an overview of related work in Section 1.1. Section 2 describes semantic filtering, including our RC representation and the four Web-based filters that constitute the WOODWARD system. Section 3 presents our experiments and results, and section 4 concludes and gives ideas for future work.

1.1 Related Work

The problem of detecting parse errors is most similar to the idea of parse reranking. Collins (2000) describes statistical techniques for reranking alternative parses for a sentence. Implicitly, a reranking method detects parser errors, in that if the reranking method picks a new parse over the original one, it is classifying the original one as less likely to be correct. Collins uses syntactic and lexical features and trains on the Penn Treebank; in contrast, WOODWARD uses semantic features derived from the web. See section 3 for a comparison of our results with Collins'.

Several systems produce a semantic interpretation of a sentence on top of a parser. For example, Bos et al. (2004) build semantic representations from the parse derivations of a CCG parser, and the English Resource Grammar (ERG) (Toutanova et al., 2005) provides a semantic representation using minimal recursion semantics. Toutanova et al. also include semantic features in their parse selection mechanism, although it is mostly syntax-driven. The ERG is a hand-built grammar and thus does not have the same coverage as the grammar we use. We also use the semantic interpretations in a novel way, checking them against semantic information on the Web to decide if they are plausible.

NLP literature is replete with examples of systems that produce semantic interpretations and use semantics to improve understanding. Several systems in the 1970s and 1980s used hand-built augmented transition networks or semantic networks to prune bad semantic interpretations. More recently, people have tried incorporating large lexical and semantic resources like WordNet, FrameNet, and PropBank into the disambiguation process. Allen (1995) provides an overview of some of this work and contains many references. Our work focuses on using statistical techniques over large corpora, reducing the need for hand-built resources and making the system more robust to changes in domain.

Numerous systems, including Question-Answering systems like MULDER (Kwok et al., 2001), PiQASso (Attardi et al., 2001), and Moldovan et al.'s QA system (2003), use parsing technology as a key component in their analysis of sentences. In part to overcome incorrect parses, Moldovan et al.'s QA system requires a complex set of relaxation techniques. These systems would greatly benefit from knowing when parses are correct or incorrect. Our system is the first to suggest using the output of a QA system to classify the input parse as good or bad.

Several researchers have used pointwise mutual information (PMI) over the Web to help make syntactic and semantic judgments in NLP tasks. Volk (2001) uses PMI to resolve preposition attachments in German. Lapata and Keller (2005) use web counts to resolve preposition attachments, compound noun interpretation, and noun countability detection, among other things. And Markert et al. (2003) use PMI to resolve certain types of anaphora. We use PMI as just one of several techniques for acquiring information from the Web.

2 Semantic Filtering

This section describes semantic filtering as implemented in the WOODWARD system. WOODWARD consists of two components: a semantic interpreter that takes a parse tree and converts it to a conjunction of first-order predicates, and a sequence of four increasingly sophisticated methods that check semantic plausibility of conjuncts on the Web. Below, we describe each component in turn.

1. What(NP1) ∧ **are(VP1, NP1, NP2)** ∧ states(NP2) ∧ **producing(VP2, NP2, NP3)** ∧	oil(NP3) ∧ in(PP1, NP2, U.S.)
2. What(NP1) ∧ states(NP2) ∧ **producing(VP1, NP3, NP2, NP1)** ∧	oil(NP3) ∧ in(PP1, NP2, U.S.)

Figure 2: **Example relational conjunctions. The first RC is the correct one for the sentence "What are oil producing states in the U.S.?" The second is the RC derived from the Collins parse in Figure 1. Differences between the two RCs appear in bold.**

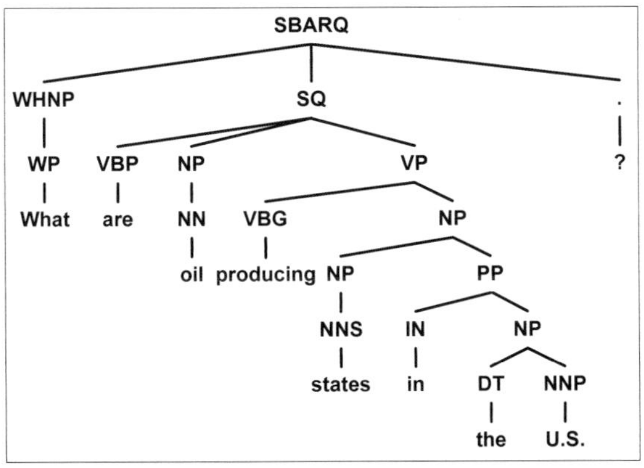

Figure 1: **An *incorrect* Collins Parse of a TREC question. The parser treats "producing" as the main verb in the clause, rather than "are".**

2.1 Semantic Interpreter

The semantic interpreter aims to make explicit the relations that a sentence introduces, and the arguments to each of those relations. More specifically, the interpreter identifies the main verb relations, preposition relations, and semantic type relations in a sentence; identifies the number of arguments to each relation; and ensures that for every argument that two relations share in the sentence, they share a variable in the logical representation. Given a sentence and a Penn-Treebank-style parse of that sentence, the interpreter outputs a conjunction of First-Order Logic predicates. We call this representation a *relational conjunction* (RC). Each relation in an RC consists of a relation name and a tuple of variables and string constants representing the arguments of the relation. As an example, Figure 1 contains a sentence taken from the TREC 2003 corpus, parsed by the Collins parser. Figure 2 shows the correct RC for this sentence and the RC derived automatically from the incorrect parse.

Due to space constraints, we omit details about the algorithm for converting a parse into an RC, but Moldovan et al. (2003) describe a method similar to ours.

2.2 Semantic Filters

Given the RC representation of a parsed sentence as supplied by the Semantic Interpreter, we test the parse using four web-based methods. Fundamentally, the methods all share the underlying principle that some form of co-occurrence of terms in the vast Web corpus can help decide whether a proposed relationship is semantically plausible.

Traditional statistical parsers also use co-occurrence of lexical heads as features for making parse decisions. We expand on this idea in two ways: first, we use a corpus several orders of magnitude larger than the tagged corpora traditionally used to train statistical parses, so that the fundamental problem of data sparseness is ameliorated. Second, we search for targeted patterns of words to help judge specific properties, like the number of complements to a verb. We now describe each of our techniques in more detail.

2.3 A PMI-Based Filter

A number of authors have demonstrated important ways in which search engines can be used to uncover semantic relationships, especially Turney's notion of *pointwise mutual information* (PMI) based on search-engine hits counts (Turney, 2001). WOODWARD's PMI-Based Filter (PBF) uses PMI scores as features in a learned filter for predicates. Following Turney, we use the formula below for the PMI between two terms $t1$ and $t2$:

$$PMI(t1, t2) = log\left(\frac{P(t1 \wedge t2)}{P(t1)P(t2)}\right) \quad (1)$$

We use PMI scores to judge the semantic plausibility of an RC conjunct as follows. We construct a number of different phrases, which we call *discriminator phrases*, from the name of the relation and the head words of each argument. For example, the prepositional attachment "operations of 65 cents" would yield phrases like "operations of" and "operations of * cents". (The '*' character is a wildcard in the Google interface; it can match any single word.) We then collect hitcounts for each discriminator phrase, as well as for the relation name and each argument head word, and compute a PMI score for each phrase, using the phrase's hitcount as the numerator in Equation 1.

Given a set of such PMI scores for a single relation, we apply a learned classifier to decide if the PMI scores justify calling the relation implausible.

This classifier (as well as all of our other ones) is trained on a set of sentences from TREC and the Penn Treebank; our training and test sets are described in more detail in section 3. We parsed each sentence automatically using Daniel Bikel's implementation of the Collins parsing model,[1] trained on sections 2–21 of the Penn Treebank, and then applied our semantic interpreter algorithm to come up with a set of relations. We labeled each relation by hand for correctness. Correct relations are positive examples for our classifier, incorrect relations are negative examples (and likewise for all of our other classifiers). We used the LIBSVM software package[2] to learn a Gaussian-kernel support vector machine model from the PMI scores collected for these relations. We can then use the classifier to predict if a relation is correct or not depending on the various PMI scores we have collected.

Because we require different discriminator phrases for preposition relations and verb relations, we actually learn two different models. After extensive experimentation, optimizing for training set accuracy using leave-one-out cross-validation, we ended up using only two patterns for verbs: "$noun\ verb$" ("$verb\ noun$" for non-subjects) and "$noun * verb$" ("$verb * noun$" for non-subjects). We use the PMI scores from the argument whose PMI values add up to the lowest value as the features for a verb relation, with the intuition being that the relation is correct only if every argument to it is valid.

For prepositions, we use a larger set of patterns. Letting $arg1$ and $arg2$ denote the head words of the two arguments to a preposition, and letting $prep$ denote the preposition itself, we used the patterns "$arg1\ prep$", "$arg1\ prep * arg2$", "$arg1$ $prep$ the $arg2$", "$arg1 * arg2$", and, for verb attachments, "$arg1$ it $prep\ arg2$" and "$arg1$ them $prep\ arg2$". These last two patterns are helpful for preposition attachments to strictly transitive verbs.

2.4 The Verb Arity Sampling Test

In our training set from the Penn Treebank, 13% of the time the Collins parser chooses too many or too few arguments to a verb. In this case, checking the PMI between the verb and each argument independently is insufficient, and there is not enough data to find hitcounts for the verb and all of its arguments at once. We therefore use a different type of filter in order to detect these errors, which we call the Verb Arity Sampling Test (VAST).

Instead of testing a verb to see if it can take a *particular* argument, we test if it can take a certain *number* of arguments. The verb predicate *producing(VP1, NP3, NP2, NP1)* in interpretation 2 of Figure 2, for example, has too many arguments. To check if this predicate can actually take three noun phrase arguments, we can construct a common phrase containing the verb, with the property that *if the verb can take three NP arguments, the phrase will often be followed by a NP in text, and vice versa*. An example of such a phrase is "which it is producing." Since "which" and "it" are so common, this phrase will appear many times on the Web. Furthermore, for verbs like "producing," there will be very few sentences in which this phrase is followed by a NP (mostly temporal noun phrases like "next week"). But for verbs like "give" or "name," which can accept three noun phrase arguments, there will be significantly more sentences where the phrase is followed by a NP.

The VAST algorithm is built upon this observation. For a given verb phrase, VAST first counts the number of noun phrase arguments. The Collins parser also marks clause arguments as being essential by annotating them differently. VAST counts these as well, and considers the sum of the noun and clause arguments as the number of *essential arguments*. If the verb is passive and the number of essential arguments is one, or if the verb is active and the number of essential arguments is two, VAST performs no check. We call these *strictly transitive* verb relations. If the verb is passive and there are two essential arguments, or if the verb is active and there are three, it performs the ditransitive check below. If the verb is active and there is one essential argument, it does the intransitive check described below. We call these two cases collectively *nontransitive* verb relations. In both cases, the checks produce a single real-valued score, and we use a linear kernel SVM to identify an appropriate threshold such that predicates above the threshold have the correct arity.

The ditransitive check begins by querying Google for two hundred documents containing the phrase "which it $verb$" or "which they $verb$". It downloads each document and identifies the sentences containing the phrase. It then POS-tags and NP-chunks the sentences using a maximum entropy tagger and chunker. It filters out any sen-

[1] http://www.cis.upenn.edu/~dbikel/software.html

[2] http://www.csie.ntu.edu.tw/~cjlin/libsvm/

tences for which the word "which" is preceded by a preposition. Finally, if there are enough sentences remaining (more than ten), it counts the number of sentences in which the verb is directly followed by a noun phrase chunk, which we call an extraction. It then calculates the ditransitive score for verb v as the ratio of the number of extractions E to the number of filtered sentences F:

$$ditransitiveScore(v) = \frac{E}{F} \quad (2)$$

The intransitive check performs a very similar set of operations. It fetches up to two hundred sentences matching the phrases "but it $verb$" or "but they $verb$", tags and chunks them, and extracts noun phrases that directly follow the verb. It calculates the intransitive score for verb v using the number of extractions E and sentences S as:

$$intransitiveScore(v) = 1 - \frac{E}{S} \quad (3)$$

2.5 TextRunner Filter

TextRunner is a new kind of web search engine. Its design is described in detail elsewhere (Cafarella et al., 2006), but we utilize its capabilities in WOODWARD. TextRunner provides a search interface to a set of over a billion triples of the form *(object string, predicate string, object string)* that have been extracted automatically from approximately 90 million documents to date. The search interface takes queries of the form $(string1, string2, string3)$, and returns all tuples for which each of the three tuple strings contains the corresponding query string as a substring.

TextRunner's object strings are very similar to the standard notion of a noun phrase chunk. The notion of a predicate string, on the other hand, is loose in TextRunner; a variety of POS sequences will match the patterns for an extracted relation. For example, a search for tuples with a predicate containing the word 'with' will yield the tuple *(risks, associated with dealing with, waste wood)*, among thousands of others.

TextRunner embodies a trade-off with the PMI method for checking the validity of a relation. Its structure provides a much more natural search for the purpose of verifying a semantic relationship, since it has already arranged Web text into predicates and arguments. It is also much faster than querying a search engine like Google, both because we have local access to it and because commercial search engines tightly limit the number of queries an application may issue per day. On the other hand, the TextRunner index is at present still about two orders of magnitude smaller than Google's search index, due to limited hardware.

The TextRunner semantic filter checks the validity of an RC conjunct in a natural way: it asks TextRunner for the number of tuples that match the argument heads and relation name of the conjunct being checked. Since TextRunner predicates only have two arguments, we break the conjunct into trigrams and bigrams of head words, and average over the hitcounts for each. For predicate $P(A_1, \ldots, A_n)$ with $n \geq 2$, the score becomes

$$TextRunnerScore = \frac{1}{n-1}\sum_{i=2}^{n} hits(A_1, P, A_i) + \frac{1}{n}(hits(A_1, P,) + \sum_{i=2}^{n} hits(, P, A_i))$$

As with PBF, we learn a threshold for good predicates using the LIBSVM package.

2.6 Question Answering Filter

When parsing questions, an additional method of detecting incorrect parses becomes available: use a question answering (QA) system to find answers. If a QA system using the parse can find an answer to the question, then the question was probably parsed correctly.

To test this theory, we implemented a lightweight, simple, and fast QA system that directly mirrors the semantic interpretation. It relies on TextRunner and KnowItNow (Cafarella et al., 2005) to quickly find possible answers, given the *relational conjunction* (RC) of the question. KnowItNow is a state of the art Information Extraction system that uses a set of domain independent patterns to efficiently find hyponyms of a class.

We formalize the process as follows: define a question as a set of variables X_i corresponding to noun phrases, a set of noun type predicates $T_i(X_i)$, and a set of relational predicates $P_i(X_{i1}, ..., X_{ik})$ which relate one or more variables and constants. The conjunction of type and relational predicates is precisely the RC.

We define an answer as a set of values for each variable that satisfies all types and predicates

$$ans(x_1, ..., x_n) = \bigwedge_i T_i(x_i) \wedge \bigwedge_j P_j(x_{j1}, ..., x_{jk})$$

The algorithm is as follows:

1. Compute the RC of the question sentence.

2. $\forall i$ find instances of the class T_i for possible values for X_i, using KnowItNow.

3. $\forall j$ find instances of the relation predicate $P_j(x_{j1}, ..., x_{jk})$. We use TextRunner to efficiently find objects that are related by the predicate P_j.

4. Return all tuples that satisfy $ans(x_1, ..., x_n)$

The QA semantic filter runs the Question Answering algorithm described above. If the number of returned answers is above a threshold (1 in our case), it indicates the question has been parsed correctly. Otherwise, it indicates an incorrect parse. This differs from the TextRunner semantic filter in that it tries to find subclasses and instances, rather than just argument heads.

2.7 The WOODWARD Filter

Each of the above semantic filters has its strengths and weaknesses. On our training data, TextRunner had the most success of any of the methods on classifying verb relations that did not have arity errors. Because of sparse data problems, however, it was less successful than PMI on preposition relations. The QA system had the interesting property that when it predicted an interpretation was correct, it was always right; however, when it made a negative prediction, its results were mixed.

WOODWARD combines the four semantic filters in a way that draws on each of their strengths. First, it checks if the sentence is a question that does not contain prepositions. If so, it runs the QA module, and returns true if that module does.

After trying the QA module, WOODWARD checks each predicate in turn. If the predicate is a preposition relation, it uses PBF to classify it. For nontransitive verb relations, it uses VAST. For strictly transitive verb relations, it uses TextRunner. WOODWARD accepts the RC if every relation is predicted to be correct; otherwise, it rejects it.

3 Experiments

In our experiments we tested the ability of WOODWARD to detect bad parses. Our experiments proceeded as follows: we parsed a set of sentences, ran the semantic interpreter on them, and labeled each parse and each relation in the resulting RCs for correctness. We then extracted all of the necessary information from the Web and TextRunner. We divided the sentences into a training and test set, and trained the filters on the labeled RCs from the training sentences. Finally, we ran each of the filters and WOODWARD on the test set to predict which parses were correct. We report the results below, but first we describe our datasets and tools in more detail.

3.1 Datasets and Tools

Because question-answering is a key application, we began with data from the TREC question-answering track. We split the data into a training set of 61 questions (all of the TREC 2002 and TREC 2003 questions), and a test set of 55 questions (all list and factoid questions from TREC 2004). We preprocessed the questions to remove parentheticals (this affected 3 training questions and 1 test question). We removed 12 test questions because the Collins parser did not parse them as questions,[3] and that error was too easy to detect. 25 training questions had the same error, but we left them in to provide more training data.

We used the Penn Treebank as our second data set. Training sentences were taken from section 22, and test sentences from section 23. Because PBF is time-consuming, we took a subset of 100 sentences from each section to expedite our experiments. We extracted from each section the first 100 sentences that did not contain conjunctions, and for which all of the errors, if any, were contained in preposition and verb relations.

For our parser, we used Bikel's implementation of the Collins parsing model, trained on sections 2-21 of the Penn Treebank. We only use the top-ranked parse for each sentence. For the TREC data only, we first POS-tagged each question using Ratnaparkhi's MXPOST tagger. We judged each of the TREC parses manually for correctness, but scored the Treebank parses automatically.

3.2 Results and Discussion

Our semantic interpreter was able to produce the appropriate RC for every parsed sentence in our data sets, except for a few minor cases. Two idiomatic expressions in the WSJ caused the semantic interpreter to find noun phrases outside of a clause to fill gaps that were not actually there. And in several sentences with infinitive phrases, the semantic interpreter did not find the extracted subject of the infinitive expression. It turned out that none of these mistakes caused the filters to reject correct parses, so we were satisfied that our results mainly reflect the performance of the filters, rather than the interpreter.

[3]That is, the root node was neither SBARQ nor SQ.

Relation Type	num. correct	num. incorrect	PBF acc.	VAST acc.	TextRunner acc.
Nontrans. Verb	41	35	0.54	0.66	0.52
Other Verb	126	68	0.72	N/A	0.73
Preposition	183	58	0.73	N/A	0.76

Table 1: **Accuracy of the filters on three relation types in the TREC 2004 questions and WSJ data.**

			Baseline			WOODWARD			
	sents.	parser eff.	filter prec.	filter rec.	F1	filter prec.	filter rec.	F1	red. err.
trec	43	54%	0.54	1.0	0.70	0.82	1.0	0.90	**67%**
wsj	100	45%	0.45	1.0	0.62	0.58	0.88	0.70	**20%**

Table 2: **Performance of WOODWARD on different data sets. Parser efficacy reports the percentage of sentences that the Collins parser parsed correctly. See the text for a discussion of our baseline and the precision and recall metrics. We weight precision and recall equally in calculating F1. Reduction in error rate (red. err.) reports the relative decrease in error (error calculated as 1 − F1) over baseline.**

In Table 1 we report the accuracy of our first three filters on the task of predicting whether a relation in an RC is correct. We break these results down into three categories for the three types of relations we built filters for: strictly transitive verb relations, nontransitive verb relations, and preposition relations. Since the QA filter works at the level of an entire RC, rather than a single relation, it does not apply here. These results show that the trends on the training data mostly held true: VAST was quite effective at verb arity errors, and TextRunner narrowly beat PBF on the remaining verb errors. However, on our training data PBF narrowly beat TextRunner on preposition errors, and the reverse was true on our test data.

Our QA filter predicts whether a full parse is correct with an accuracy of 0.76 on the 17 TREC 2004 questions that had no prepositions. The Collins parser achieves the same level of accuracy on these sentences, so the main benefit of the QA filter for WOODWARD is that it never misclassifies an incorrect parse as a correct one, as was observed on the training set. This property allows WOODWARD to correctly predict a parse is correct whenever it passes the QA filter.

Classification accuracy is important for good performance, and we report it to show how effective each of WOODWARD's components is. However, it fails to capture the whole story of a filter's performance. Consider a filter that simply predicts that every sentence is incorrectly parsed: it would have an overall accuracy of 55% on our WSJ corpus, not too much worse than WOODWARD's classification accuracy of 66% on this data. However, such a filter would be useless because it filters out every correctly parsed sentence.

Let the *filtered set* be the set of sentences that a filter predicts to be correctly parsed. The performance of a filter is better captured by two quantities related to the filtered set: first, how "pure" the filtered set is, or how many good parses it contains compared to bad parses; and second, how wasteful the filter is in terms of losing good parses from the original set. We measure these two quantities using metrics we call *filter precision* and *filter recall*. Filter precision is defined as the ratio of correctly parsed sentences in the filtered set to total sentences in the filtered set. Filter recall is defined as the ratio of correctly parsed sentences in the filtered set to correctly parsed sentences in the unfiltered set. Note that these metrics are quite different from the labeled constituent precision/recall metrics that are typically used to measure statistical parser performance.

Table 2 shows our overall results for filtering parses using WOODWARD. We compare against a baseline model that predicts every sentence is parsed correctly. WOODWARD outperforms this baseline in precision and F1 measure on both of our data sets.

Collins (2000) reports a decrease in error rate of 13% over his original parsing model (the same model as used in our experiments) by performing a discriminative reranking of parses. Our WSJ test set is a subset of the set of sentences used in Collins' experiments, so our results are not directly comparable, but we do achieve a roughly similar decrease in error rate (20%) when we use our filtered precision/recall metrics. We also measured the labeled constituent precision and recall of both the original test set and the filtered set, and found a decrease in error rate of 37% according to this metric (corresponding to a jump in F1 from 90.1 to 93.8). Note that in our case, the error is reduced by throwing out bad parses, rather than trying to fix them. The 17% difference between the two decreases in error rate is probably due to the fact that WOODWARD is more likely to detect the worse parses in the original set, which contribute a proportionally larger share of error in labeled constituent precision/recall in the original test set.

WOODWARD performs significantly better on the TREC questions than on the Penn Treebank data. One major reason is that there are far more clause adjuncts in the Treebank data, and adjunct errors are intrinsically harder to detect. Consider the Treebank sentence: "The S&P pit stayed locked at its 30-point trading limit as the Dow average ground to its final 190.58 point loss Friday." The parser incorrectly attaches the clause beginning "as the Dow ..." to "locked", rather than to "stayed." Our current methods aim to use key words in the clause to determine if the attachment is correct. However, with such clauses there is no single key word that can allow us to make that determination. We anticipate that as the paradigm matures we and others will design filters that can use more of the information in the clause to help make these decisions.

4 Conclusions and Future Work

Given a parse of a sentence, WOODWARD constructs a representation that identifies the key semantic relationships implicit in the parse. It then uses a set of Web-based sampling techniques to check whether these relationships are plausible. If any of the relationships is highly implausible, WOODWARD concludes that the parse is incorrect. WOODWARD successfully detects common errors in the output of the Collins parser including verb arity errors as well as preposition and verb attachment errors. While more extensive experiments are clearly necessary, our results suggest that the paradigm of *Web-based semantic filtering* could substantially improve the performance of statistical parsers.

In future work, we hope to further validate this paradigm by constructing additional semantic filters that detect other types of errors. We also plan to use semantic filters such as WOODWARD to build a large-scale corpus of automatically-parsed sentences that has higher accuracy than can be achieved today. Such a corpus could be used to re-train a statistical parser to improve its performance. Beyond that, we plan to embed semantic filtering into the parser itself. If semantic filters become sufficiently accurate, they could rule out enough erroneous parses that the parser is left with just the correct one.

Acknowledgements

This research was supported in part by NSF grant IIS-0312988, DARPA contract NBCHD030010, ONR grant N00014-02-1-0324 as well as gifts from Google, and carried out at the University of Washington's Turing Center.

References

J. Allen. 1995. *Natural Language Understanding*. Benjamin/Cummings Publishing, Redwood City, CA, 2nd edition.

G. Attardi, A. Cisternino, F. Formica, M. Simi, and A. Tommasi. 2001. PiQASso: Pisa Question Answering System. In *TREC*.

J. Bos, S. Clark, M. Steedman, J. R. Curran, and J. Hockenmaier. 2004. Wide-coverage semantic representations from a CCG parser. In *COLING*.

Michael J. Cafarella, Doug Downey, Stephen Soderland, and Oren Etzioni. 2005. KnowItNow: Fast, scalable information extraction from the web. In *HLT-EMNLP*.

M. J. Cafarella, M. Banko, and O. Etzioni. 2006. Relational web search. *UW Tech Report 06-04-02*.

M. Collins. 2000. Discriminative reranking for natural language parsing. In *ICML*, pages 175–182.

C. C. T. Kwok, O. Etzioni, and D. S. Weld. 2001. Scaling question answering to the web. In *WWW*.

M. Lapata and F. Keller. 2005. Web-based models for natural language processing. *ACM Transactions on Speech and Language Processing*, 2:1–31.

K. Markert, N. Modjeska, and M. Nissim. 2003. Using the web for nominal anaphora resolution. In *EACL Workshop on the Computational Treatment of Anaphora*.

D. Moldovan, C. Clark, S. Harabagiu, and S. Maiorano. 2003. Cogex: A logic prover for question answering. In *HLT*.

K. Toutanova, C. D. Manning, D. Flickinger, and S. Oepen. 2005. Stochastic HPSG parse disambiguation using the Redwoods Corpus. *Journal of Logic and Computation*.

P.D. Turney. 2001. Mining the Web for Synonyms: PMI–IR versus LSA on TOEFL. *Lecture Notes in Computer Science*, 2167:491–502.

M. Volk. 2001. Exploiting the WWW as a corpus to resolve PP attachment ambiguities. In *Corpus Linguistics*.

Distributional Measures of Concept-Distance: A Task-oriented Evaluation

Saif Mohammad and Graeme Hirst
Department of Computer Science
University of Toronto
Toronto, ON M5S 3G4, Canada
{smm,gh}@cs.toronto.edu

Abstract

We propose a framework to derive the distance between concepts from distributional measures of word co-occurrences. We use the categories in a published thesaurus as coarse-grained concepts, allowing all possible distance values to be stored in a concept–concept matrix roughly .01% the size of that created by existing measures. We show that the newly proposed concept-distance measures outperform traditional distributional word-distance measures in the tasks of (1) ranking word pairs in order of semantic distance, and (2) correcting real-word spelling errors. In the latter task, of all the WordNet-based measures, only that proposed by Jiang and Conrath outperforms the best distributional concept-distance measures.

1 Semantic and distributional measures

Measures of distance of meaning are of two kinds. The first kind, which we will refer to as **semantic measures**, rely on the structure of a resource such as WordNet or, in some cases, a semantic network, and hence they measure the distance between the concepts or word-senses that the nodes of the resource represent. Examples include the measure for MeSH proposed by Rada et al. (1989) and those for WordNet proposed by Leacock and Chodorow (1998) and Jiang and Conrath (1997). (Some of the more successful measures, such as Jiang–Conrath, also use information content derived from word frequency.) Typically, these measures rely on an extensive hierarchy of hyponymy relationships for nouns. Therefore, these measures are expected to perform poorly when used to estimate distance between senses of part-of-speech pairs other than noun–noun, not just because the WordNet hierarchies for other parts of speech are less well developed, but also because the hierarchies for the different parts of speech are not well connected.

The second kind of measures, which we will refer to as **distributional measures**, are inspired by the maxim "You shall know a word by the company it keeps" (Firth, 1957). These measures rely simply on raw text, and hence are much less resource-hungry than the semantic measures; but they measure the distance between words rather than word-senses or concepts. In these measures, two words are considered close if they occur in similar contexts. The context (or "company") of a target word is represented by its **distributional profile (DP)**, which lists the strength of association between the target and each of the lexical, syntactic, and/or semantic units that co-occur with it. Commonly used **measures of strength of association** are conditional probability (0 to 1) and pointwise mutual information ($-\infty$ to ∞)[1]. Commonly used units of co-occurrence with the target are other *words*, and so we speak of the **lexical distributional profile of a word (lexical DPW)**. The co-occurring words may be all those in a predetermined window around the target, or may be restricted to those that have a certain syntactic (*e.g.*, verb–object) or semantic (*e.g.*, agent–theme) relation with the target word. We will refer to the former kind of DPs as **relation-free**. Usually in

[1] In our experiments, we set negative PMI values to 0, because Church and Hanks (1990), in their seminal paper on word association ratio, show that negative PMI values are not expected to be accurate unless co-occurrence counts are made from an extremely large corpus.

Proceedings of the 2006 Conference on Empirical Methods in Natural Language Processing (EMNLP 2006), pages 35–43,
Sydney, July 2006.

Table 1: Measures of DP distance and measures of strength of association.

DP distance	Strength of association
α-skew divergence	conditional probability
cosine	pointwise mutual information
Jensen–Shannon divergence	
Lin	

the latter case, separate association values are calculated for each of the different relations between the target and the co-occurring units. We will refer to such DPs as **relation-constrained**.

Typical relation-free DPs are those of Schütze and Pedersen (1997) and Yoshida et al. (2003). Typical relation-constrained DPs are those of Lin (1998) and Lee (2001). Below are contrived, but plausible, examples of each for the word *pulse*; the numbers are conditional probabilities.

> **relation-free DP**
> ***pulse***: *beat* (.28), *racing* (.2), *grow* (.13), *beans* (.09), *heart* (.04), ...
>
> **relation-constrained DP**
> ***pulse***: <*beat*, subject–verb> (.34), <*racing*, noun–qualifying adjective> (.22), <*grow*, subject–verb> (.14), ...

The distance between two words, given their DPs, is calculated using a **measure of DP distance**, such as cosine. While any of the measures of DP distance may be used with any of the measures of strength of association (see Table 1), in practice α-skew divergence (ASD), cosine, and Jensen–Shannon divergence (JSD) are used with conditional probability (CP), whereas Lin is used with PMI, resulting in the distributional measures ASD_{cp} (Lee, 2001), Cos_{cp} (Schütze and Pedersen, 1997), JSD_{cp}, and Lin_{pmi} (Lin, 1998), respectively. ASD_{cp} is a modification of Kullback-Leibler divergence that overcomes the latter's problem of division by zero, which can be caused by data sparseness. JSD_{cp} is another relative entropy–based measure (like ASD_{cp}) but it is symmetric. JSD_{cp} and ASD_{cp} are distance measures that give scores between 0 (identical) and infinity (maximally distant). Lin_{pmi} and Cos_{cp} are similarity measures that give scores between 0 (maximally distant) and 1 (identical). See Mohammad and Hirst (2005) for a detailed study of these and other measures.

2 The distributional hypothesis and its limitations

The distributional hypothesis (Firth, 1957) states that words that occur in similar contexts tend to be semantically similar. It is often suggested, therefore, that a distributional measure can act as a *proxy* for a semantic measure: the distance between the DPs of words will approximate the distance between their senses. But when words have more than one sense, it is not at all clear what semantic distance between them actually means. A word in each of its senses is likely to co-occur with different sets of words. For example, *bank* in the 'financial institution' sense is likely to co-occur with *interest, money, accounts,* and so on, whereas the 'river bank' sense might have words such as *river, erosion,* and *silt* around it. If we define the distance between two words, at least one of which is ambiguous, to be the closest distance between some sense of one and some sense of the other, then distributional distance between words may indeed be used in place of semantic distance between concepts. However, because measures of distributional distance depend on occurrences of the target word in all its senses, this substitution is inaccurate. For example, observe that both DPWs of *pulse* above have words that co-occur with its 'throbbing arteries' sense and words that co-occur with its 'edible seed' sense. Relation-free DPs of *pulse* in its two separate senses might be as follows:

> ***pulse*** 'throbbing arteries': *beat* (.36), *racing* (.27), *heart* (.11), ...
> ***pulse*** 'edible seeds': *grow* (.24), *beans* (.14), ...

Thus, it is clear that different senses of a word have different distributional profiles ("different company"). Using a single DP for the word will mean the union of those profiles. While this might be useful for certain applications, we believe that in a number of tasks (including estimating linguistic distance), acquiring different DPs for the different senses is not only more intuitive, but also, as we will show through experiments in Section 5, more useful. We argue that **distributional profiles of senses or concepts (DPCs)** can be used to infer semantic properties of the senses: "You shall know a sense by the company it keeps."

3 Conceptual grain size and storage requirements

As applications for linguistic distance become more sophisticated and demanding, it becomes attractive to pre-compute and store the distance values between all possible pairs of words or senses. But both kinds of measures have large space requirements to do this, requiring matrices of size $N \times N$, where N is the size of the vocabulary (perhaps 100,000 for most languages) in the case of distributional measures and the number of senses (75,000 just for nouns in WordNet) in the case of semantic measures.

It is generally accepted, however, that WordNet senses are far too fine-grained (Agirre and Lopez de Lacalle Lekuona (2003) and citations therein). On the other hand, published thesauri, such as *Roget's* and *Macquarie*, group near-synonymous and semantically related words into a relatively small number of **categories**—typically between 800 and 1100—that roughly correspond to very coarse concepts or senses (Yarowsky, 1992). Words with more than one sense are listed in more than one category. A published thesaurus thus provides us with a very coarse human-developed set or inventory of **word senses** or **concepts**[2] that are more intuitive and discernible than the "concepts" generated by dimensionality-reduction methods such as latent semantic analysis. Using coarse senses from a known inventory means that the senses can be represented unambiguously by a large number of possibly ambiguous words (conveniently available in the thesaurus)—a feature that we exploited in our earlier work (Mohammad and Hirst, 2006) to determine useful estimates of the strength of association between a concept and co-occurring words.

In this paper, we go one step further and use the idea of a very coarse sense inventory to develop a framework for distributional measures of concepts that can more naturally and more accurately be used in place of semantic measures of word senses. We use the *Macquarie Thesaurus* (Bernard, 1986) as a sense inventory and repository of words pertaining to each sense. It has 812 categories with around 176,000 word tokens and 98,000 word types. This allows us to have much smaller **concept–concept distance matrices** of size just 812×812 (roughly .01% the size of matrices required by existing measures). We evaluate our distributional concept-distance measures on two tasks: ranking word pairs in order of their semantic distance, and correcting real-word spelling errors. We compare performance with distributional word-distance measures and the WordNet-based concept-distance measures.

[2]We use the terms *senses* and *concepts* interchangeably. This is in contrast to studies, such as that of Cooper (2005), that attempt to make a principled distinction between them.

4 Distributional measures of concept-distance

4.1 Capturing distributional profiles of concepts

We use relation-free *lexical* DPs—both DPWs and DPCs—in our experiments, as they allow determination of semantic properties of the target from just its co-occurring words.

Determining lexical DPWs simply involves making word–word co-occurrence counts in a corpus. A direct method to determine lexical DPCs, on the other hand, requires information about which words occur with which concepts. This means that the text from which counts are made has to be sense annotated. Since existing labeled data is minimal and manual annotation is far too expensive, indirect means must be used. In an earlier paper (Mohammad and Hirst, 2006), we showed how this can be done with simple word sense disambiguation and bootstrapping techniques. Here, we summarize the method.

First, we create a **word–category co-occurrence matrix (WCCM)** using the *British National Corpus (BNC)* and the *Macquarie Thesaurus*. The WCCM has the following form:

	c_1	c_2	$\ldots$	c_j	$\ldots$
w_1	m_{11}	m_{12}	$\ldots$	m_{1j}	$\ldots$
w_2	m_{21}	m_{22}	$\ldots$	m_{2j}	$\ldots$
$\vdots$	$\vdots$	$\vdots$	$\ddots$	$\ldots$	$\ldots$
w_i	m_{i1}	m_{i2}	$\ldots$	m_{ij}	$\ldots$
$\vdots$	$\vdots$	$\vdots$	$\vdots$	$\vdots$	$\ddots$

A cell m_{ij}, corresponding to word w_i and category c_j, contains the number of times w_i co-occurs (in a window of ± 5 words in the corpus) with any of the words listed under category c_j in the thesaurus. Intuitively, the cell m_{ij} captures the number of times c_j and w_i co-occur. A contingency table for a single word and single category can be created by simply collapsing all other rows and columns into one and summing their frequencies. Applying a suitable statistic, such as odds

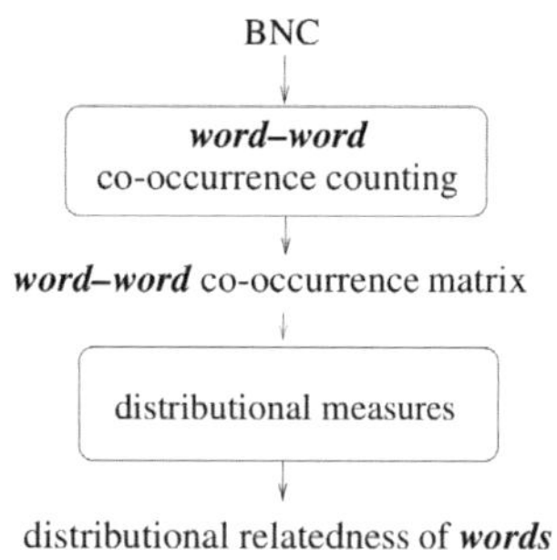

Figure 1: Distributional word-distance.

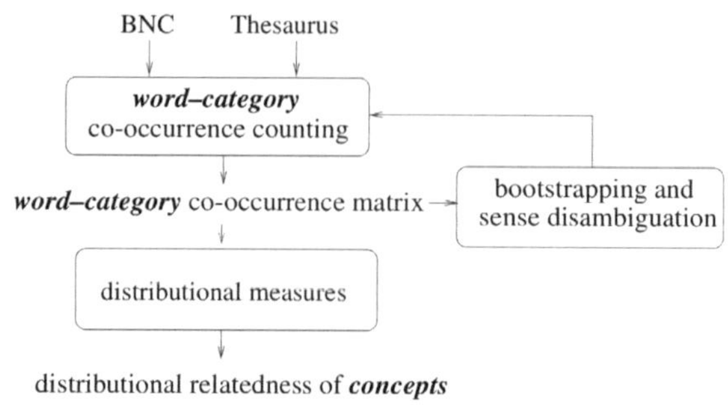

Figure 2: Distributional concept-distance.

ratio, on the contingency table gives the strength of association between a concept (category) and co-occurring word. Therefore, the WCCM can be used to create the lexical DP for any concept.

The matrix that is created after one pass of the corpus, which we call the **base WCCM**, although noisy (as it is created from raw text and not sense-annotated data), captures strong associations between categories and co-occurring words. Therefore the intended sense (thesaurus category) of a word in the corpus can now be determined using frequencies of co-occurring words and its various senses as evidence. A new **bootstrapped WCCM** is created, after a second pass of the corpus, in which the cell m_{ij} contains the number of times *any word used in sense* c_j co-occurs with w_i. We have shown (Mohammad and Hirst, 2006) that the bootstrapped WCCM captures word–category co-occurrences much more accurately than the base WCCM, using the task of determining word sense dominance[3] as a test bed.

4.2 Applying distributional measures to DPCs

Recall that in computing distributional word-distance, we consider two target words to be distributionally similar (less distant) if they occur in similar contexts. The contexts are represented by the DPs of the target words, where a DP gives the strength of association between the target and the co-occurring units. A distributional measure uses a measure of DP distance to determine the distance between two DPs and thereby between the two target words (see Figure 1). The various measures differ in what statistic they use to calculate the strength of association and the measure of DP distance they use (see Mohammad and Hirst (2005) for details). For example, following is the cosine formula for distance between words w_1 and w_2 using relation-free lexical DPWs, with conditional probability of the co-occurring word given the target as the strength of association:

$$Cos_{cp}(w_1, w_2) = \frac{\sum_{w \in C(w_1) \cup C(w_2)} \left(P(w|w_1) \times P(w|w_2)\right)}{\sqrt{\sum_{w \in C(w_1)} P(w|w_1)^2} \times \sqrt{\sum_{w \in C(w_2)} P(w|w_2)^2}}$$

Here, $C(x)$ is the set of words that co-occur with *word* x within a pre-determined window.

In order to calculate distributional *concept-distance*, consider the same scenario, except that the targets are now senses or concepts. Two concepts are closer if their DPs are similar, and these DPCs require the strength of association between the target *concepts* and their co-occurring words. The associations can be estimated from the bootstrapped WCCM, described in Section 4.1 above. Any of the distributional measures used for DPWs can now be used to estimate concept-distance with DPCs. Figure 2 illustrates our methodology. Below is the formula for cosine with conditional probabilities when applied to concepts:

$$Cos_{cp}(c_1, c_2) = \frac{\sum_{w \in C(c_1) \cup C(c_2)} \left(P(w|c_1) \times P(w|c_2)\right)}{\sqrt{\sum_{w \in C(c_1)} P(w|c_1)^2} \times \sqrt{\sum_{w \in C(c_2)} P(w|c_2)^2}}$$

Now, $C(x)$ is the set of words that co-occur with *concept* x within a pre-determined window.

We will refer to such measures as distributional measures of concept-distance ($Distrib_{concept}$), in contrast to the earlier-described distributional measures of word-distance ($Distrib_{word}$) and WordNet-based (or semantic) measures of concept-distance ($WNet_{concept}$). We shall refer

[3]Near-upper-bound results were achieved in the task of determining predominant senses of 27 words in 11 target texts with a wide range of sense distributions over their two most dominant senses.

to these three kinds of distance measures as **measure-types**. Individual measures in each kind will be referred to simply as **measures**.

A distributional measure of concept-distance can be used to populate a small 812 × 812 **concept–concept distance matrix** where a cell m_{ij}, pertaining to concepts c_i and c_j, contains the distance between the two concepts. In contrast, a word–word distance matrix for a conservative vocabulary of 100,000 word types will have a size 100,000 × 100,000, and a WordNet-based concept–concept distance matrix will have a size 75,000 × 75,000 just for nouns. Our concept–concept distance matrix is roughly .01% the size of these matrices.

Note that the DPs we are using are relation-free because (1) we use all co-occurring words (not just those that are related to the target by certain syntactic or semantic relations) and (2) the WCCM, as described in Section 4.1, does not maintain separate counts for the different relations between the target and co-occurring words. Creating a larger matrix with separate counts for the different relations would lead to *relation-constrained* DPs.

5 Evaluation

To evaluate the distributional concept-distance measures, we used them in the tasks of ranking word pairs in order of their semantic distance and of correcting real-word spelling errors, and compared our results to those that we obtained on the same tasks with distributional word-distance measures and those that Budanitsky and Hirst (2006) obtained with WordNet-based semantic measures.

The distributional concept-distance measures used a bootstrapped WCCM created from the *BNC* and the *Macquarie Thesaurus*. The word-distance measures used a word–word co-occurrence matrix created from the *BNC* alone. The *BNC* was not lemmatized, part of speech tagged, or chunked. The vocabulary was restricted to the words present in the thesaurus (about 98,000 word types) both to provide a level evaluation platform and to keep the matrix to a manageable size. Co-occurrence counts less than 5 were reset to 0, and words that co-occurred with more than 2000 other words were stoplisted (543 in all). We used ASD_{cp} ($\alpha = 0.99$), Cos_{cp}, JSD_{cp}, and Lin_{pmi}[4] to populate corresponding concept–concept distance matrices and

[4]Whereas Lin (1998) used relation-constrained DPs, in our experiments all DPs are relation-free.

Table 2: Correlation of distributional measures with human ranking. Best results for each measure-type are shown in boldface.

Measure	Measure-type $Distrib_{word}$	$Distrib_{concept}$ closest	$Distrib_{concept}$ average
ASD_{cp}	.45	.60	–
Cos_{cp}	**.54**	.69	.42
JSD_{cp}	.48	.61	–
Lin_{pmi}	.52	**.71**	**.59**

word–word distance matrices. Applications that require distance values will enjoy a run-time benefit if the distances are precomputed. While it is easy to completely populate the concept–concept co-occurrence matrix, completely populating the word–word distance matrix is a non-trivial task because of memory and time constraints.[5]

5.1 Ranking word pairs

A direct approach to evaluating linguistic distance measures is to determine how close they are to human judgment and intuition. Given a set of word-pairs, humans can rank them in order of their distance—placing near-synonyms on one end of the ranking and unrelated pairs on the other. Rubenstein and Goodenough (1965) provide a "gold-standard" list of 65 human-ranked word-pairs (based on the responses of 51 subjects). One automatic word-distance estimator, then, is deemed to be more accurate than another if its ranking of word-pairs correlates more closely with this human ranking. Measures of concept-distance can perform this task by determining word-distance for each word-pair by finding the concept-distance between all pairs of senses of the two words, and choosing the distance of the closest sense pair. This is based on the assumption that when humans are asked to judge the semantic distance between a pair of words, they implicitly consider its closest senses. For example, most people will agree that *bank* and *interest* are semantically related, even though both have multiple senses—most of which are unrelated. Alternatively, the method could take the average of the distance of all pairs of senses.

[5]As we wanted to perform experiments with both concept–concept and word–word distance matrices, we populated them as and when new distance values were calculated.

Table 3: Hirst and St-Onge metrics for evaluation of real-word spelling correction.

$$\textit{suspect ratio} = \frac{\frac{\text{no. of true-suspects}}{\text{no. of malaps}}}{\frac{\text{no. of false-suspects}}{\text{no. of non-malaps}}}$$

$$\textit{alarm ratio} = \frac{\frac{\text{no. of true-alarms}}{\text{no. of true-suspects}}}{\frac{\text{no. of false-alarms}}{\text{no. of false-suspects}}}$$

$$\textit{detection ratio} = \frac{\frac{\text{no. of true-alarms}}{\text{no. of malaps}}}{\frac{\text{no. of false-alarms}}{\text{no. of non-malaps}}}$$

$$\textit{correction ratio} = \frac{\frac{\text{no. corrected malaps}}{\text{no. of malaps}}}{\frac{\text{no. of false-alarms}}{\text{no. of non-malaps}}}$$

$$\textit{correction accuracy} = \frac{\text{no. of corrected malaps}}{\text{no. of true-alarms}}$$

Table 2 lists correlations of human rankings with those created using distributional measures. Observe that $Distrib_{concept}$ measures give markedly higher correlation values than $Distrib_{word}$ measures. Also, using the distance of the closest sense pair (for Cos_{cp} and Lin_{pmi}) gives much better results than using the average distance of all relevant sense pairs. (We do not report average distance for ASD_{cp} and JSD_{cp} because they give very large distance values when sense-pairs are unrelated—values that dominate the averages, overwhelming the others, and making the results meaningless.) These correlations are, however, notably lower than those obtained by the best WordNet-based measures (not shown in the table), which fall in the range .78 to .84 (Budanitsky and Hirst, 2006).

5.2 Real-word spelling error correction

The set of Rubenstein and Goodenough word pairs is much too small to safely assume that measures that work well on them do so for the entire English vocabulary. Consequently, semantic measures have traditionally been evaluated through applications that use them, such as the work by Hirst and Budanitsky (2005) on correcting **real-word spelling errors** (or **malapropisms**). If a word in a text is not "semantically close" to any other word in its context, then it is considered a **suspect**. If the suspect has a spelling-variant that *is* "semantically close" to a word in its context, then the suspect is declared a probable real-word spelling error and an "**alarm**" is raised; the related spelling-variant is considered its **correction**. Hirst and Budanitsky tested the method on 500 articles from the 1987–89 *Wall Street Journal* corpus for their experiments, replacing every 200th word by a spelling-variant. We adopt this method and this test data, but whereas Hirst and Budanitsky used WordNet-based semantic measures, we use distributional measures $Distrib_{word}$ and $Distrib_{concept}$.

In order to determine whether two words are "semantically close" or not as per any measure of distance, a **threshold** must be set. If the distance between two words is less than the threshold, then they will be considered **semantically close**. Hirst and Budanitsky (2005) pointed out that there is a notably wide band between 1.83 and 2.36 (on a scale of 0–4), such that all Rubenstein and Goodenough word pairs were assigned values either higher than 2.36 or lower than 1.83 by human subjects. They argue that somewhere within this band is a suitable threshold between semantically close and semantically distant, and therefore set thresholds for the WordNet-based measures such that there was maximum overlap in what the measures and human judgments considered semantically close and distant. Following this idea, we use an automatic method to determine thresholds for the various $Distrib_{word}$ and $Distrib_{concept}$ measures. Given a list of Rubenstein and Goodenough word pairs ordered according to a distance measure, we repeatedly consider the mean of all consecutive distance values as **candidate thresholds**. Then we determine the number of word-pairs correctly classified as semantically close or semantically distant for each candidate threshold, considering which side of the band they lie as per human judgments. The candidate threshold with highest accuracy is chosen as the threshold.

We follow Hirst and St-Onge (1998) in the metrics that we use to evaluate real-word spelling correction; they are listed in Table 3. **Suspect ratio** and **alarm ratio** evaluate the processes of identifying suspects and raising alarms, respectively. **Detection ratio** is the product of the two, and measures overall performance in detecting the errors. **Correction ratio** indicates overall correction performance, and is the "bottom-line" statistic that we focus on. Values greater than 1 for each of these ratios indicate results better than random guessing. The ability of the system to determine the intended word, given that it has correctly detected an error, is indicated by the **correction accuracy** (0 to 1).

Table 4: Real-word error correction using distributional word-distance ($Distrib_{word}$), distributional concept-distance ($Distrib_{concept}$), and Hirst and Budanitsky's (2005) results using WordNet-based concept-distance measures ($WNet_{concept}$). Best results for each measure-type are shown in boldface.

Measure	*suspect ratio*	*alarm ratio*	*detection ratio*	*correction accuracy*	***correction ratio***	*detection* P	*detection* R	*detection* F	***correction performance***
$Distrib_{word}$									
ASD_{cp}	3.36	1.78	5.98	0.84	5.03	7.37	45.53	12.69	10.66
Cos_{cp}	2.91	1.64	4.77	0.85	4.06	5.97	37.15	10.28	8.74
JSD_{cp}	3.29	1.77	5.82	0.83	4.88	7.19	44.32	12.37	10.27
$\mathbf{Lin_{pmi}}$	3.63	2.15	7.78	0.84	**6.52**	9.38	58.38	16.16	**13.57**
$Distrib_{concept}$									
$\mathbf{ASD_{cp}}$	4.11	2.54	10.43	0.91	**9.49**	12.19	25.28	16.44	**14.96**
Cos_{cp}	4.00	2.51	10.03	0.90	9.05	11.77	26.99	16.38	14.74
JSD_{cp}	3.58	2.46	8.79	0.90	7.87	10.47	34.66	16.08	14.47
Lin_{pmi}	3.02	2.60	7.84	0.88	6.87	9.45	36.86	15.04	13.24
$WNet_{concept}$									
Hirst–St-Onge	4.24	1.95	8.27	0.93	7.70	9.67	26.33	14.15	13.16
Jiang–Conrath	4.73	2.97	14.02	0.92	**12.91**	14.33	46.22	21.88	**20.13**
Leacock–Chodrow	3.23	2.72	8.80	0.83	7.30	11.56	60.33	19.40	16.10
Lin	3.57	2.71	9.70	0.87	8.48	9.56	51.56	16.13	14.03
Resnik	2.58	2.75	7.10	0.78	5.55	9.00	55.00	15.47	12.07

Notice that the correction ratio is the product of the detection ratio and correction accuracy. The overall (single-point) precision P (no. of true-alarms / no. of alarms), recall R (no. of true-alarms / no. of malapropisms), and F-score ($\frac{2\times P\times R}{P+R}$) of detection are also computed. The product of detection F-score and correction accuracy, which we will call **correction performance**, can also be used as a bottom-line performance metric.

Table 4 details the performance of $Distrib_{word}$ and $Distrib_{concept}$ measures. For comparison, results obtained by Hirst and Budanitsky (2005) with the use of $WNet_{concept}$ measures are also shown. Observe that the correction ratio results for the $Distrib_{word}$ measures are poor compared to $Distrib_{concept}$ measures; the concept-distance measures are clearly superior, in particular ASD_{cp} and Cos_{cp}. Moreover, if we consider correction ratio to be the bottom-line statistic, then the $Distrib_{concept}$ measures outperform all $WNet_{concept}$ measures except the Jiang–Conrath measure. If we consider correction performance to be the bottom-line statistic, then again we see that the distributional concept-distance measures outperform the word-distance measures, except in the case of Lin_{pmi}, which gives slightly poorer results with concept-distance. Also, in contrast to correction ratio values, using the Leacock–Chodorow measure results in relatively higher correction performance values than the best $Distrib_{concept}$ measures. While it is clear that the Leacock–Chodorow measure is relatively less accurate in choosing the right spelling-variant for an alarm (correction accuracy), detection ratio and detection F-score present contrary pictures of relative performance in detection. As correction ratio is determined by the product of a number of ratios, each evaluating the various stages of malapropism correction (identifying suspects, raising alarms, and applying the correction), we believe it is a better indicator of overall performance than correction performance, which is a not-so-elegant product of an F-score and accuracy. However, no matter which of the two is chosen as the bottom-line performance statistic, the results show that the newly proposed distributional concept-distance measures are clearly superior to word-distance measures. Further, of all the WordNet-based measures, only that proposed by Jiang and Conrath outperforms the best distributional concept-distance measures consistently with respect to both bottom-line statistics.

6 Related Work

Patwardhan and Pedersen (2006) create **aggregate co-occurrence vectors** for a WordNet sense by adding the co-occurrence vectors of the words in its WordNet gloss. The distance between two senses is then determined by the cosine of the angle between their aggregate vectors. However, as we pointed out in Mohammad and Hirst (2005), such aggregate co-occurrence vectors are expected to be noisy because they are created from data that is not sense-annotated. Therefore, we employed simple word sense disambiguation and bootstrapping techniques on our base WCCM to create more-accurate co-occurrence vectors, which gave markedly higher accuracies in the task of determining word sense dominance. In the experiments described in this paper, we used these bootstrapped co-occurrence vectors to determine concept-distance.

Pantel (2005) also provides a way to create co-occurrence vectors for WordNet senses. The lexical co-occurrence vectors of words in a leaf node are propagated up the WordNet hierarchy. A parent node inherits those co-occurrences that are shared by its children. Lastly, co-occurrences not pertaining to the leaf nodes are removed from its vector. Even though the methodology attempts at associating a WordNet node or sense with only those co-occurrences that pertain to it, no attempt is made at correcting the frequency counts. After all, *word1–word2* co-occurrence frequency (or association) is likely not the same as SENSE1–*word2* co-occurrence frequency (or association), simply because *word1* may have senses other than SENSE1, as well. The co-occurrence frequency of a parent is the weighted sum of co-occurrence frequencies of its children. The frequencies of the child nodes are used as weights. Sense ambiguity issues apart, this is still problematic because a parent concept (say, BIRD) may co-occur much more frequently (or infrequently) with a word than its children (such as, *hen, archaeopteryx, aquatic bird, trogon,* and others). In contrast, the bootstrapped WCCM we use not only identifies which words co-occur with which concepts, but also has more sophisticated estimates of the co-occurrence frequencies.

7 Conclusion

We have proposed a framework that allows distributional measures to estimate concept-distance using a published thesaurus and raw text. We evaluated them in comparison with traditional distributional word-distance measures and WordNet-based measures through their ability in ranking word-pairs in order of their human-judged linguistic distance, and in correcting real-word spelling errors. We showed that distributional concept-distance measures outperformed word-distance measures in both tasks. They do not perform as well as the best WordNet-based measures in ranking a small set of word pairs, but in the task of correcting real-word spelling errors, they beat all WordNet-based measures except for Jiang–Conrath (which is markedly better) and Leacock-Chodorow (which is slightly better if we consider correction performance as the bottom-line statistic, but slightly worse if we rely on correction ratio). It should be noted that the Rubenstein and Goodenough word-pairs used in the ranking task, as well as all the real-word spelling errors in the correction task are nouns. We expect that the WordNet-based measures will perform poorly when other parts of speech are involved, as those hierarchies of WordNet are not as extensively developed. On the other hand, our DPC-based measures do not rely on any hierarchies (even if they exist in a thesaurus) but on sets of words that unambiguously represent each sense. Further, because our measures are tied closely to the corpus from which co-occurrence counts are made, we expect the use of domain-specific corpora to result in even better results.

All the distributional measures that we have considered in this paper are *lexical*—that is, the distributional profiles of the target word or concept are based on their co-occurrence with words in a text. By contrast, *semantic* DPs would be based on information such as what concepts usually co-occur with the target word or concept. Semantic profiles of words can be obtained from the WCCM itself (using the row entry for the word). It would be interesting to see how distributional measures of word-distance that use these semantic DPs of words perform. We also intend to explore the use of semantic DPs of concepts acquired from a **concept–concept co-occurrence matrix (CCCM)**. A CCCM can be created from the WCCM by setting the row entry for a concept or category to be the average of WCCM row values for all the words pertaining to it.

Both DPW- and WordNet-based measures have large space and time requirements for precomputing and storing all possible distance values for a language. However, by using the categories of a thesaurus as very coarse concepts, precomputing and storing all possible distance values for our DPC-based measures requires a matrix of size only about 800 × 800. This level of concept-coarseness might seem drastic at first glance, but we have shown that distributional measures of distance between these coarse concepts are quite useful. Part of our future work will be to try an intermediate degree of coarseness (still much coarser than WordNet) by using the paragraph subdivisions of the thesaurus instead of its categories to see if this gives even better results.

Acknowledgments

We thank Afsaneh Fazly, Siddharth Patwardhan, and the CL group at the University of Toronto for their valuable feedback. We thank Alex Budanitsky for helping us adapt his malapropism-correction software to work with distributional measures. This research is financially supported by the Natural Sciences and Engineering Research Council of Canada and the University of Toronto.

References

Eneko Agirre and O. Lopez de Lacalle Lekuona. 2003. Clustering WordNet word senses. In *Proceedings of the Conference on Recent Advances in Natural Language Processing (RANLP'03)*, Bulgaria.

J.R.L. Bernard, editor. 1986. *The Macquarie Thesaurus*. Macquarie Library, Sydney, Australia.

Alexander Budanitsky and Graeme Hirst. 2006. Evaluating WordNet-based measures of semantic distance. *Computational Linguistics*, 32(1).

Kenneth Church and Patrick Hanks. 1990. Word association norms, mutual information and lexicography. *Computational Linguistics*, 16(1):22–29.

Martin C. Cooper. 2005. A mathematical model of historical semantics and the grouping of word meanings into concepts. *Computational Linguistics*, 31(2):227–248.

John R. Firth. 1957. A synopsis of linguistic theory 1930–55. In *Studies in Linguistic Analysis (special volume of the Philological Society)*, pages 1–32, Oxford. The Philological Society.

Graeme Hirst and Alexander Budanitsky. 2005. Correcting real-word spelling errors by restoring lexical cohesion. *Natural Language Engineering*, 11(1):87–111.

Graeme Hirst and David St-Onge. 1998. Lexical chains as representations of context for the detection and correction of malapropisms. In Christiane Fellbaum, editor, *WordNet: An Electronic Lexical Database*, chapter 13, pages 305–332. The MIT Press, Cambridge, MA.

Jay J. Jiang and David W. Conrath. 1997. Semantic similarity based on corpus statistics and lexical taxonomy. In *Proceedings of International Conference on Research on Computational Linguistics (ROCLING X)*, Taiwan.

Claudia Leacock and Martin Chodorow. 1998. Combining local context and WordNet similarity for word sense identification. In Christiane Fellbaum, editor, *WordNet: An Electronic Lexical Database*, chapter 11, pages 265–283. The MIT Press, Cambridge, MA.

Lillian Lee. 2001. On the effectiveness of the skew divergence for statistical language analysis. In *Artificial Intelligence and Statistics 2001*, pages 65–72.

Dekang Lin. 1998. Automatic retreival and clustering of similar words. In *Proceedings of the 17th International Conference on Computational Linguistics (COLING-98)*, pages 768–773, Montreal, Canada.

Saif Mohammad and Graeme Hirst. 2005. Distributional measures as proxies for semantic relatedness. *In submission*, http://www.cs.toronto.edu/compling/Publications.

Saif Mohammad and Graeme Hirst. 2006. Determining word sense dominance using a thesaurus. In *Proceedings of the 11th Conference of the European Chapter of the Association for Computational Linguistics (EACL)*, Trento, Italy.

Patrick Pantel. 2005. Inducing ontological co-occurrence vectors. In *Proceedings of the 43rd Annual Meeting of the Association for Computational Linguistics (ACL-05)*, pages 125–132, Ann Arbor, Michigan.

Siddharth Patwardhan and Ted Pedersen. 2006. Using WordNet based context vectors to estimate the semantic relatedness of concepts. In *Proceedings of the EACL 2006 Workshop Making Sense of Sense—Bringing Computational Linguistics and Psycholinguistics Together*, pages 1–8, Trento, Italy.

Roy Rada, Hafedh Mili, Ellen Bicknell, and Maria Blettner. 1989. Development and application of a metric on semantic nets. *IEEE Transactions on Systems, Man, and Cybernetics*, 19(1):17–30.

Herbert Rubenstein and John B. Goodenough. 1965. Contextual correlates of synonymy. *Communications of the ACM*, 8(10):627–633.

Hinrich Schütze and Jan O. Pedersen. 1997. A cooccurrence-based thesaurus and two applications to information retreival. *Information Processing and Management*, 33(3):307–318.

David Yarowsky. 1992. Word-sense disambiguation using statistical models of Roget's categories trained on large corpora. In *Proceedings of the 14th International Conference on Computational Linguistics (COLING-92)*, pages 454–460, Nantes, France.

Sen Yoshida, Takashi Yukawa, and Kazuhiro Kuwabara. 2003. Constructing and examining personalized cooccurrence-based thesauri on web pages. In *Proceedings of the 12th International World Wide Web Conference*, pages 20–24, Budapest, Hungary.

SPMT: Statistical Machine Translation with Syntactified Target Language Phrases

Daniel Marcu, Wei Wang, Abdessamad Echihabi, and Kevin Knight
Language Weaver Inc.
4640 Admiralty Way, Suite 1210
Marina del Rey, CA 90292
{dmarcu,wwang,aechihabi,kknight}@languageweaver.com

Abstract

We introduce SPMT, a new class of statistical Translation Models that use Syntactified target language Phrases. The SPMT models outperform a state of the art phrase-based baseline model by 2.64 Bleu points on the NIST 2003 Chinese-English test corpus and 0.28 points on a human-based quality metric that ranks translations on a scale from 1 to 5.

1 Introduction

During the last four years, various implementations and extentions to phrase-based statistical models (Marcu and Wong, 2002; Koehn et al., 2003; Och and Ney, 2004) have led to significant increases in machine translation accuracy. Although phrase-based models yield high-quality translations for language pairs that exhibit similar word order, they fail to produce grammatical outputs for language pairs that are syntactically divergent. Recent models that exploit syntactic information of the source language (Quirk et al., 2005) have been shown to produce better outputs than phrase-based systems when evaluated on relatively small scale, domain specific corpora. And syntax-inspired formal models (Chiang, 2005), in spite of being trained on significantly less data, have shown promising results when compared on the same test sets with mature phrase-based systems. To our knowledge though, no previous research has demonstrated that a syntax-based statistical translation system could produce better results than a phrase-based system on a large-scale, well-established, open domain translation task. In this paper we present such a system.

Our translation models rely upon and naturally exploit submodels (feature functions) that have been initially developed in phrase-based systems for choosing target translations of source language phrases, and use new, syntax-based translation and target language submodels for assembling target phrases into well-formed, grammatical outputs.

After we introduce our models intuitively, we discuss their formal underpinning and parameter training in Section 2. In Section 3, we present our decoder and, in Section 4, we evaluate our models empirically. In Section 5, we conclude with a brief discussion.

2 SPMT: statistical Machine Translation with Syntactified Phrases

2.1 An intuitive introduction to SPMT

After being exposed to 100M+ words of parallel Chinese-English texts, current phrase-based statistical machine translation learners induce reasonably reliable phrase-based probabilistic dictionaries. For example, our baseline statistical phrase-based system learns that, with high probabilities, the Chinese phrases "ASTRO- -NAUTS", "FRANCE AND RUSSIA" and "COMINGFROM" can be translated into English as "astronauts"/"cosmonauts", "france and russia"/"france and russian" and "coming from"/"from", respectively. [1] Unfortunately, when given as input Chinese sentence 1, our phrase-based system produces the output shown in 2 and not the translation in 3, which correctly orders the phrasal translations into a grammatical sequence. We believe this happens because the distortion/reordering models that are used by state-of-the-art phrase-based systems, which exploit phrase movement and ngram target

[1]To increase readability, in this paper, we represent Chinese words using fully capitalized English glosses and English words using lowercased letters.

Proceedings of the 2006 Conference on Empirical Methods in Natural Language Processing (EMNLP 2006), pages 44–52,
Sydney, July 2006.

language models (Och and Ney, 2004; Tillman, 2004), are too weak to help a phrase-based decoder reorder the target phrases into grammatical outputs.

THESE 7PEOPLE INCLUDE COMINGFROM FRANCE AND RUSSIA p-DE ASTRO- -NAUTS . (1)

the 7 people including those from france and the russian cosmonauts . (2)

these 7 people include astronauts coming from france and russia . (3)

One method for increasing the ability of a decoder to reorder target language phrases is that of decorating them with syntactic constituent information. For example, we may make explicit that the Chinese phrase "ASTRO- -NAUTS" may be translated into English as a noun phrase, NP(NNS(astronauts)); that the phrase FRANCE AND RUSSIA may be translated into a complex noun-phrase, NP(NP(NNP(france)) CC(and) NP(NNP(russia))); that the phrase COMINGFROM may be translated into a partially realized verb phrase that is looking for a noun phrase to its right in order to be fully realized, VP(VBG(coming) PP(IN(from) NP:x0)); and that the Chinese particle p-DE, when occurring between a Chinese string that was translated into a verb phrase to its left and another Chinese string that was translated into a noun phrase to its right, VP:x1 p-DE NP:x0, should be translated to nothing, while forcing the reordering of the two constituents, NP(NP:x0, VP:x1). If all these translation rules (labeled r_1 to r_4 in Figure 1) were available to a decoder that derives English parse trees starting from Chinese input strings, this decoder could produce derivations such as that shown in Figure 2. Because our approach uses translation rules with Syntactified target language Phrases (see Figure 1), we call it SPMT.

2.2 A formal introduction to SPMT

2.2.1 Theoretical foundations

We are interested to model a generative process that explains how English parse trees π and their associated English string yields E, foreign sentences, F, and word-level alignments, A, are produced. We assume that observed (π, F, A) triplets are generated by a stochastic process similar to

r_1 :NP(NNS(astronauts)) → ASTRO- -NAUTS
r_2 :NP(NP(NNP(france)) CC(and) NP(NNP(russia))) →
FRANCE AND RUSSIA
r_3 :VP(VBG(coming) PP(IN(from) NP:x0)) →
COMINGFROM x0
r_4 :NP(NP:x0, VP:x1) → x1 p-DE x0
r_5 :NNP(france) → FRANCE
r_6 :NP(NP(NNP(france)) CC(and) NP:x0) → FRANCE AND x0
r_7 :NNS(astronauts) → ASTRO- -NAUTS
r_8 :NNP(russia) → RUSSIA
r_9 :NP(NNS:x0) → x0
r_{10} :PP(IN:x0 NP:x1) → x0 x1
r_{11} :NP(NP:x0 CC:x1 NP:x2) → x0 x1 x2
r_{12} :NP(NNP:x0) → x0
r_{13} :CC(and) → AND
r_{14} :NP(NP:x0 CC(and) NP:x1) → x0 AND x1
r_{15} :NP(NP:x0 VP(VBG(coming) PP(IN(from) NP:x1))) →
x1 COMINGFROM x0

Figure 1: Examples of xRS rules.

that used in Data Oriented Parsing models (Bonnema, 2002). For example, if we assume that the generative process has already produced the top NP node in Figure 2, then the corresponding partial English parse tree, foreign/source string, and word-level alignment could be generated by the rule derivation $r_4(r_1, r_3(r_2))$, where each rule is assumed to have some probability.

The extended tree to string transducers introduced by Knight and Graehl (2005) provide a natural framework for expressing the tree to string transformations specific to our SPMT models. The transformation rules we plan to exploit are equivalent to one-state xRS top-down transducers with look ahead, which map subtree patterns to strings. For example, rule r_3 in Figure 1 can be applied only when one is in a state that has a VP as its syntactic constituent and the tree pattern VP(VBG(coming) PP(IN(from) NP)) immediately underneath. The rule application outputs the string "COMINGFROM" as the transducer moves to the state co-indexed by x0; the outputs produced from the new state will be concatenated to the right of the string "COMINGFROM".

Since there are multiple derivations that could lead to the same outcome, the probability of a tuple (π, F, A) is obtained by summing over all derivations $\theta_i \in \Theta$ that are consistent with the tu-

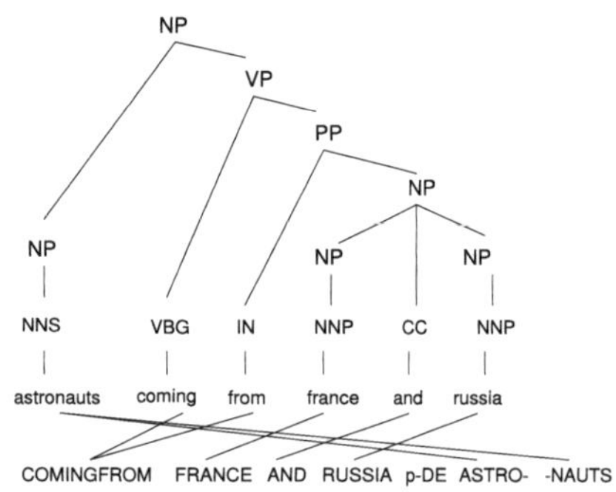

Figure 2: English parse tree derivation of the Chinese string COMINGFROM FRANCE AND RUSSIA p-DE ASTRO- -NAUTS.

ple, $c(\Theta) = (\pi, F, A)$. The probability of each derivation θ_i is given by the product of the probabilities of all the rules $p(r_j)$ in the derivation (see equation 4).

$$Pr(\pi, F, A) = \sum_{\theta_i \in \Theta, c(\Theta)=(\pi,F,A)} \prod_{r_j \in \theta_i} p(r_j) \quad (4)$$

In order to acquire the rules specific to our model and to induce their probabilities, we parse the English side of our corpus with an in-house implementation (Soricut, 2005) of Collins parsing models (Collins, 2003) and we word-align the parallel corpus with the Giza++[2] implementation of the IBM models (Brown et al., 1993). We use the automatically derived ⟨English-parse-tree, English-sentence, Foreign-sentence, Word-level-alignment⟩ tuples in order to induce xRS rules for several models.

2.2.2 SPMT Model 1

In our simplest model, we assume that each tuple (π, F, A) in our automatically annotated corpus could be produced by applying a combination of minimally syntactified, lexicalized, phrase-based compatible xRS rules, and minimal/necessary, non-lexicalized xRS rules. We call a rule non-lexicalized whenever it does not have any directly aligned source-to-target words. Rules r_9–r_{12} in Figure 1 are examples of non-lexicalized rules.

Minimally syntactified, lexicalized, phrase-based-compatible xRS rules are extracted via a simple algorithm that finds for each foreign phrase F_i^j, the smallest xRS rule that is consistent with the foreign phrase F_i^j, the English syntactic tree π, and the alignment A. The algorithm finds for each foreign/source phrase span its projected span on the English side and then traverses the English parse tree bottom up until it finds a node that subsumes the projected span. If this node has children that fall outside the projected span, then those children give rise to rules that have variables. For example, if the tuple shown in Figure 2 is in our training corpus, for the foreign/source phrases FRANCE, FRANCE AND, FRANCE AND RUSSIA, and ASTRO- -NAUTS, we extract the minimally syntactified, lexicalized phrase-based-compatible xRS rules r_5, r_6, r_2, and r_7 in Figure 1, respectively. Because, as in phrase-based MT, all our rules have continuous phrases on both the source and target language sides, we call these phrase-based compatible xRS rules.

Since these lexicalized rules are not sufficient to explain an entire (π, F, A) tuple, we also extract the required minimal/necessary, non-lexicalized xRS rules. The minimal non-lexicalized rules that are licensed by the tuple in Figure 2 are labeled r_4, r_9, r_{10}, r_{11} and r_{12} in Figure 1. To obtain the non-lexicalized xRS rules, we compute the set of all minimal rules (lexicalized and non-lexicalized) by applying the algorithm proposed by Galley et al. (2006) and then remove the lexicalized rules. We remove the Galley et al.'s lexicalized rules because they are either already accounted for by the minimally syntactified, lexicalized, phrase-based-compatible xRS rules or they subsume non-continuous source-target phrase pairs.

It is worth mentioning that, in our framework, a rule is defined to be "minimal" with respect to a foreign/source language phrase, i.e., it is the minimal xRS rule that yields that source phrase. In contrast, in the work of Galley et al. (2004; 2006), a rule is defined to be minimal when it is necessary in order to explain a (π, F, A) tuple.

Under SPMT model 1, the tree in Figure 2 can be produced, for example, by the following derivation: $r_4(r_9(r_7), r_3(r_6(r_{12}(r_8))))$.

2.2.3 SPMT Model 1 Composed

We hypothesize that composed rules, i.e., rules that can be decomposed via the application of a sequence of Model 1 rules may improve the performance of an SPMT system. For example, although the minimal Model 1 rules r_{11} and r_{13} are

[2] http://www.fjoch.com/GIZA++.html

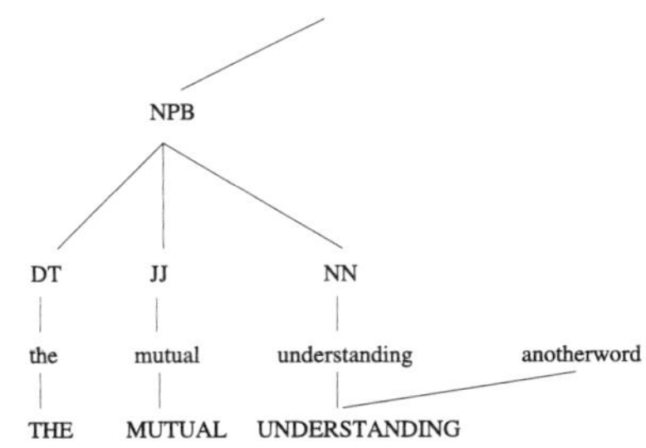

Figure 3: Problematic syntactifications of phrasal translations.

sufficient for building an English NP on top of two NPs separated by the Chinese conjunction AND, the composed rule r_{14} in Figure 1 accomplishes the same result in only one step. We hope that the composed rules could play in SPMT the same role that phrases play in string-based translation models.

To test our hypothesis, we modify our rule extraction algorithm so that for every foreign phrase F_i^j, we extract not only a minimally syntactified, lexicalized xRS rule, but also *one* composed rule. The composed rule is obtained by extracting the rule licensed by the foreign/source phrase, alignment, English parse tree, and the first multi-child ancestor node of the root of the minimal rule. Our intuition is that composed rules that involve the application of more than two minimal rules are not reliable. For example, for the tuple in Figure 2, the composed rule that we extract given the foreign phrases AND and COMINGFROM are respectively labeled as rules r_{14} and r_{15} in Figure 1.

Under the SPMT composed model 1, the tree in Figure 2 can be produced, for example, by the following derivation: $r_{15}(r_9(r_7), r_{14}(r_{12}(r_5), r_{12}(r_8)))$.

2.2.4 SPMT Model 2

In many instances, the tuples (π, F, A) in our training corpus exhibit alignment patterns that can be easily handled within a phrase-based SMT framework, but that become problematic in the SPMT models discussed until now.

Consider, for example, the (π, F, A) tuple fragment in Figure 3. When using a phrase-based translation model, one can easily extract the phrase pair (THE MUTUAL; the mutual) and use it during the phrase-based model estimation phrase and in decoding. However, within the xRS transducer framework that we use, it is impossible to extract an equivalent syntactified phrase translation rule that subsumes the same phrase pair because valid xRS translation rules cannot be multi-headed. When faced with this constraint, one has several options:

- One can label such phrase pairs as non-syntactifiable and ignore them. Unfortunately, this is a lossy choice. On our parallel English-Chinese corpus, we have found that approximately 28% of the foreign/source phrases are non-syntactifiable by this definition.
- One can also traverse the parse tree upwards until one reaches a node that is xRS valid, i.e., a node that subsumes the entire English span induced by a foreign/source phrase and the corresponding word-level alignment. This choice is also inappropriate because phrase pairs that are usually available to phrase-based translation systems are then expanded and made available in the SPTM models only in larger applicability contexts.
- A third option is to create xRS compatible translation rules that overcome this constraint.

Our SPMT Model 2 adopts the third option by rewriting on the fly the English parse tree for each foreign/source phrase and alignment that lead to non-syntactifiable phrase pairs. The rewriting process adds new rules to those that can be created under the SPMT model 1 constraints. The process creates one xRS rule that is headed by a pseudo, non-syntactic nonterminal symbol that subsumes the target phrase and corresponding multi-headed syntactic structure; and one sibling xRS rule that explains how the non-syntactic nonterminal symbol can be combined with other genuine nonterminals in order to obtain genuine parse trees. In this view, the foreign/source phrase THE MUTUAL and corresponding alignment in Figure 3 licenses the rules $\star$NPB$\star$_NN(DT(the) JJ(mutual)) $\rightarrow$ THE MUTUAL and NPB($\star$NPB$\star$_NN:x0 NN:x1) $\rightarrow$ x0 x1 even though the foreign word UNDERSTANDING is aligned to an English word outside the NPB consituent. The name of the non-syntactic nonterminal reflects the intuition that the English phrase "the mutual" corresponds to a partially realized NPB that needs an NN to its right in order to be fully realized.

Our hope is that the rules headed by pseudo nonterminals could make available to an SPMT system all the rules that are typically available to a phrase-based system; and that the sibling rules could provide a sufficiently robust generalization layer for integrating pseudo, partially realized constituents into the overall decoding process.

2.2.5 SPMT Model 2 Composed

The SPMT composed model 2 uses all rule types described in the previous models.

2.3 Estimating rule probabilities

For each model, we extract all rule instances that are licensed by a symmetrized Giza-aligned parallel corpus and the constraints we put on the model. We condition on the root node of each rule and use the rule counts $f(r)$ and a basic maximum likelihood estimator to assign to each rule type a conditional probability (see equation 5).

$$p(r|root(r)) = \frac{f(r)}{\sum_{r':root(r')=root(r)} f(r')} \quad (5)$$

It is unlikely that this joint probability model can be discriminative enough to distinguish between good and bad translations. We are not too concerned though because, in practice, we decode using a larger set of submodels (feature functions).

Given the way all our lexicalized xRS rules have been created, one can safely strip out the syntactic information and end up with phrase-to-phrase translation rules. For example, in string-to-string world, rule r_5 in Figure 1 can be rewritten as "france → FRANCE"; and rule r_6 can be rewritten as "france and → FRANCE AND". When one analyzes the lexicalized xRS rules in this manner, it is easy to associate with them any of the submodel probability distributions that have been proven useful in statistical phrase-based MT. The non-lexicalized rules are assigned probability distributions under these submodels as well by simply assuming a NULL phrase for any missing lexicalized source or target phrase.

In the experiments described in this paper, we use the following submodels (feature functions):

Syntax-based-like submodels:

- $p_{root}(r_i)$ is the root normalized conditional probability of all the rules in a model.
- $p_{cfg}(r_i)$ is the CFG-like probability of the non-lexicalized rules in the model. The lexicalized rules have by definition $p_{cfg} = 1$.
- $is\_lexicalized(r_i)$ is an indicator feature function that has value 1 for lexicalized rules, and value 0 otherwise.
- $is\_composed(r_i)$ is an indicator feature function that has value 1 for composed rules.
- $is\_lowcount(r_i)$ is an indicator feature function that has value 1 for the rules that occur less than 3 times in the training corpus.

Phrase-based-like submodels:

- $lex\_pef(r_i)$ is the direct phrase-based conditional probability computed over the foreign/source and target phrases subsumed by a rule.
- $lex\_pfe(r_i)$ is the inverse phrase-based conditional probability computed over the source and target phrases subsumed by a rule.
- $m1(r_i)$ is the IBM model 1 probability computed over the bags of words that occur on the source and target sides of a rule.
- $m1inv(r_i)$ is the IBM model 1 inverse probability computed over the bags of words that occur on the source and target sides of a rule.
- $lm(e)$ is the language model probability of the target translation under an ngram language model.
- $wp(e)$ is a word penalty model designed to favor longer translations.

All these models are combined log-linearly during decoding. The weights of the models are computed automatically using a variant of the Maximum Bleu training procedure proposed by Och (2003).

The phrase-based-like submodels have been proved useful in phrase-based approaches to SMT (Och and Ney, 2004). The first two syntax-based submodels implement a "fused" translation and lexical grounded distortion model (p_{root}) and a syntax-based distortion model (p_{cfg}). The indicator submodels are used to determine the extent to which our system prefers lexicalized vs. non-lexicalized rules; simple vs. composed rules; and high vs. low count rules.

3 Decoding

3.1 Decoding with one SPMT model

We decode with each of our SPMT models using a straightforward, bottom-up, CKY-style decoder that builds English syntactic constituents on the top of Chinese sentences. The decoder uses a binarized representation of the rules, which is obtained via a syncronous binarization procedure (Zhang et al., 2006). The CKY-style decoder computes the probability of English syntactic constituents in a bottom up fashion, by log-linearly interpolating all the submodel scores described in Section 2.3.

The decoder is capable of producing nbest derivations and nbest lists (Knight and Graehl, 2005), which are used for Maximum Bleu training (Och, 2003). When decoding the test corpus, the decoder returns the translation that has the most probable derivation; in other words, the sum operator in equation 4 is replaced with an argmax.

3.2 Decoding with multiple SPMT models

Combining multiple MT outputs to increase performance is, in general, a difficult task (Matusov et al., 2006) when significantly different engines compete for producing the best outputs. In our case, combining multiple MT outputs is much simpler because the submodel probabilities across the four models described here are mostly identifical, with the exception of the root normalized and CFG-like submodels which are scaled differently – since Model 2 composed has, for example, more rules than Model 1, the root normalized and CFG-like submodels have smaller probabilities for identical rules in Model 2 composed than in Model 1. We compare these two probabilities across the submodels and we scale all model probabilities to be compatible with those of Model 2 composed.

With this scaling procedure into place, we produce 6,000 non-unique nbest lists for all sentences in our development corpus, using all SPMT submodels. We concatenate the lists and we learn a new combination of weights that maximizes the Bleu score of the combined nbest list using the same development corpus we used for tuning the individual systems (Och, 2003). We use the new weights in order to rerank the nbest outputs on the test corpus.

4 Experiments

4.1 Automatic evaluation of the models

We evaluate our models on a Chinese to English machine translation task. We use the same training corpus, 138.7M words of parallel Chinese-English data released by LDC, in order to train several statistical-based MT systems:

- PBMT, a strong state of the art phrase-based system that implements the alignment template model (Och and Ney, 2004); this is the system ISI has used in the 2004 and 2005 NIST evaluations.
- four SPMT systems (M1, M1C, M2, M2C) that implement each of the models discussed in this paper;
- a SPMT system, *Comb*, that combines the outputs of all SPMT models using the procedure described in Section 3.2.

In all systems, we use a rule extraction algorithm that limits the size of the foreign/source phrases to four words. For all systems, we use a Kneser-Ney (1995) smoothed trigram language model trained on 2.3 billion words of English. As development data for the SPMT systems, we used the sentences in the 2002 NIST development corpus that are shorter than 20 words; we made this choice in order to finish all experiments in time for this submission. The PBMT system used all sentences in the 2002 NIST corpus for development. As test data, we used the 2003 NIST test set.

Table 1 shows the number of string-to-string or tree-to-string rules extracted by each system and the performance on both the subset of sentences in the test corpus that were shorter than 20 words and the entire test corpus. The performance is measured using the Bleu metric (Papineni et al., 2002) on lowercased, tokenized outputs/references.

The results show that the SPMT models clearly outperform the phrase-based systems – the 95% confidence intervals computed via bootstrap resampling in all cases are around 1 Bleu point. The results also show that the simple system combination procedure that we have employed is effective in our setting. The improvement on the development corpus transfers to the test setting as well.

A visual inspection of the outputs shows significant differences between the outputs of the four models. The models that use composed rules prefer to produce outputs by using mostly lexicalized

System	# of rules (in millions)	Bleu score on Dev (4 refs) < 20 words	Bleu score on Test (4 refs) < 20 words	Bleu score on Test (4 refs)
PBMT	125.8	34.56	34.83	31.46
SPMT-M1	34.2	37.60	38.18	33.15
SPMT-M1C	75.7	37.30	38.10	32.39
SPMT-M2	70.4	37.77	38.74	33.39
SPMT-M2C	111.1	37.48	38.59	33.16
SPMT-Comb	111.1	39.44	39.56	34.10

Table 1: Automatic evaluation results.

rules; in contrast, the simple M1 and M2 models produce outputs in which content is translated primarily using lexicalized rules and reorderings and word insertions are explained primarily by the non-lexical rules. It appears that the two strategies are complementary, succeeding and failing in different instances. We believe that this complementarity and the overcoming of some of the search errors in our decoder during the model rescoring phase explain the success of the system combination experiments.

We suspect that our decoder still makes many search errors. In spite of this, the SPTM outputs are still significantly better than the PBMT outputs.

4.2 Human-based evaluation of the models

We also tested whether the Bleu score improvements translate into improvements that can be perceived by humans. To this end, we randomly selected 138 sentences of less than 20 words from our development corpus; we expected the translation quality of sentences of this size to be easier to assess than that of sentences that are very long.

We prepared a web-based evaluation interface that showed for each input sentence:

- the Chinese input;
- three English reference translations;
- the output of seven "MT systems".

The evaluated "MT systems" were the six systems shown in Table 1 and one of the reference translations. The reference translation presented as automatically produced output was selected from the set of four reference translations provided by NIST so as to be representative of human translation quality. More precisely, we chose the second best reference translation in the NIST corpus according to its Bleu score against the other three reference translations. The seven outputs were randomly shuffled and presented to three English speakers for assessment.

The judges who participated in our experiment were instructed to carefully read the three reference translations and seven machine translation outputs, and assign a score between 1 and 5 to each translation output on the basis of its quality. Human judges were told that the translation quality assessment should take into consideration both the grammatical fluency of the outputs and their translation adequacy. Table 2 shows the average scores obtained by each system according to each judge. For convenience, the table also shows the Bleu scores of all systems (including the human translations) on three reference translations.

The results in Table 2 show that the human judges are remarkably consistent in preferring the syntax-based outputs over the phrase-based outputs. On a 1 to 5 quality scale, the difference between the phrase-based and syntax-based systems was, on average, between 0.2 and 0.3 points. All differences between the phrase-based baseline and the syntax-based outputs were statistically significant. For example, when comparing the phrase-based baseline against the combined system, the improvement in human scores was significant at $P = 4.04e^{-6}(t = 4.67, df = 413)$.

The results also show that the LDC reference translations are far from being perfect. Although we selected from the four references the second best according to the Bleu metric, this human reference was judged to be at a quality level of only 4.67 on a scale from 1 to 5. Most of the translation errors were fluency errors. Although the human outputs had most of the time the right meaning, the syntax was sometimes incorrect.

In order to give readers a flavor of the types of re-orderings enabled by the SPMT models, we present in Table 3, several translation outputs produced by the phrase-based baseline and the com-

System	Bleu score on Dev (3 refs) < 20 words	Judge 1	Judge 2	Judge 3	Judge avg
PBMT	31.00	3.00	3.34	2.95	3.10
SPMT-M1	33.79	3.28	3.49	3.04	3.27
SPMT-M1C	33.66	3.23	3.43	3.26	3.31
SPMT-M2	34.05	3.24	3.45	3.10	3.26
SPMT-M2C	33.42	3.24	3.48	3.13	3.28
SPMT-Combined	35.33	3.31	3.59	3.25	3.38
Human Ref	40.84	4.64	4.62	4.75	4.67

Table 2: Human-based evaluation results.

bined SPMT system. The outputs were selected to reflect both positive and negative effects of large-scale re-orderings.

5 Discussion

The SPMT models are similar to the models proposed by Chiang (2005) and Galley et al. (2006). If we analyze these three models in terms of expressive power, the Galley et al. (2006) model is more expressive than the SPMT models, which in turn, are more expressive than Chiang's model. The xRS formalism utilized by Galley et al. (2006) allows for the use of translation rules that have multi-level target tree annotations and discontinuous source language phrases. The SPMT models are less general: they use translation rules that have multi-level target tree annotations but require that the source language phrases are continuous. The Syncronous Grammar formalism utilized by Chiang is stricter than SPMT since it allows only for single-level target tree annotations.

The parameters of the SPMT models presented in this paper are easier to estimate than those of Galley et al's (2006) and can easily exploit and expand on previous research in phrase-based machine translation. Also, the SPMT models yield significantly fewer rules that the model of Galley et al. In contrast with the model proposed by Chiang, the SPMT models introduced in this paper are fully grounded in syntax; this makes them good candidates for exploring the impact that syntax-based language models could have on translation performance.

From a machine translation perspective, the SPMT translation model family we have proposed in this paper is promising. To our knowledge, we are the first to report results that show that a syntax-based system can produce results that are better than those produced by a strong phrase-based system in experimental conditions similar to those used in large-scale, well-established independent evaluations, such as those carried out annually by NIST.

Although the number of syntax-based rules used by our models is smaller than the number of phrase-based rules used in our state-of-the-art baseline system, the SPMT models produce outputs of higher quality. This feature is encouraging because it shows that the syntactified translation rules learned in the SPMT models can generalize better than the phrase-based rules.

We were also pleased to see that the Bleu score improvements going from the phrase- to the syntax-based models, as well as the Bleu improvements going from the simple syntax-based models to the combined models system are fully consistent with the human qualitative judgments in our subjective evaluations. This correlation suggests that we can continue to use the Bleu metric to further improve our models and systems.

Acknowledgements. This research was partially supported by the National Institute of Standards and Technology's Advanced Technology Program Award 70NANB4H3050 to Language Weaver Inc.

References

R. Bonnema. 2002. Probability models for DOP. In *Data-Oriented Parsing*. CSLI publications.

Peter F. Brown, Stephen A. Della Pietra, Vincent J. Della Pietra, and Robert L. Mercer. 1993. The mathematics of statistical machine translation: Parameter estimation. *Computational Linguistics*, 19(2):263–311.

David Chiang. 2005. A hierarchical phrase-based model for statistical machine translation. In *Proceedings of the 43rd Annual Meeting of the Association for Computational Linguistics (ACL'05)*, pages 263–270, Ann Arbor, Michigan, June.

System	Output
PBMT	fujian is china 's coastal areas most rapid development of foreign trade of the region .
SPMT-Combined	china 's coastal areas of fujian is one of the areas of the most rapid development of foreign trade and economic cooperation .
PBMT	investment in macao has become the largest foreign investors .
SPMT-Combined	the chinese - funded enterprises have become the largest foreign investor in macao.
PBMT	they are now two people were unaccounted for .
SPMT-Combined	currently , both of them remain unaccounted for .
PBMT	there was no further statement .
SPMT-Combined	the statement did not explain further .

Table 3: Sample translations.

Michael Collins. 2003. Head-driven statistical models for natural language parsing. *Computational Linguistics*, 29(4):589–637, December.

Michel Galley, Mark Hopkins, Kevin Knight, and Daniel Marcu. 2004. What's in a translation rule? In *HLT-NAACL'2004: Main Proceedings*, pages 273–280, Boston, Massachusetts, USA, May 2 - May 7.

Michel Galley, Jonathan Graehl, Kevin Knight, Daniel Marcu, Steve DeNeefe, Wei Wang, and Ignacio Thayer. 2006. Scalable inferences and training of context-rich syntax translation models. In *Proceedings of the Annual Meeting of the Association for Computational Linguistics (ACL'2006)*, Sydney, Australia, July.

Reinhard Kneser and Hermann Ney. 1995. Improved backing-off for m-gram language modeling. In *Proceedings of the International Conference on Acoustics, Speech, and Signal Processing (ICASSP'95)*, volume 1, pages 181–184.

Kevin Knight and Jonathan Graehl. 2005. An overview of probabilistic tree transducers for natural language processing. In *Proc. of the Sixth International Conference on Intelligent Text Processing and Computational Linguistics (CICLing'2005)*, pages 1–25. Springer Verlag.

Philipp Koehn, Franz Joseph Och, and Daniel Marcu. 2003. Statistical phrase-based translation. In *Proceedings of the Human Language Technology and North American Association for Computational Linguistics Conference (HLT-NAACL'2003)*, Edmonton, Canada, May 27–June 1.

Daniel Marcu and William Wong. 2002. A phrase-based, joint probability model for statistical machine translation. In *Proceedings of the Conference on Empirical Methods in Natural Language Processing (EMNLP'2002)*, pages 133–139, Philadelphia, PA, July 6-7.

Evgeny Matusov, Nicola Ueffi ng, and Hermann Ney. 2006. Computing consensus translation from multiple machine translation systems using enhanced hypothesis alignment. In *Proceedings of the Annual Meeting of the European Chapter of the Association for Computational Linguistics (EACL'2006)*, Trento, Italy.

Franz Joseph Och and Hermann Ney. 2004. The alignment template approach to statistical machine translation. *Computational Linguistics*, 30(4), December.

Franz Joseph Och. 2003. Minimum error training in statistical machine translation. In *Proceedings of the Annual Meeting of the Association for Computational Linguistics (ACL'2003)*, pages 160–167, Sapooro, Japan.

Kishore Papineni, Salim Roukos, Todd Ward, John Henderson, and Florence Reeder. 2002. Corpus-based comprehensive and diagnostic MT evaluation: Initial Arabic, Chinese, French, and Spanish results. In *Proceedings of the Human Language Technology Conference (ACL'2002)*, pages 124–127, San Diego, CA, March 24-27.

Chris Quirk, Arul Menezes, and Colin Cherry. 2005. Dependency treelet translation: Syntactically informed phrasal SMT. In *Proceedings of the 43rd Annual Meeting of the Association for Computational Linguistics (ACL'2005)*, pages 271–279, Ann Arbor, Michigan, June.

Radu Soricut. 2005. A reimplementation of Collins's parsing models.

Christoph Tillman. 2004. A unigram orientation model for statistical machine translation. In *HLT-NAACL 2004: Short Papers*, pages 101–104, Boston, Massachusetts, USA, May 2 - May 7.

Hao Zhang, Liang Huang, Daniel Gildea, and Kevin Knight. 2006. Syncronous binarization for machine translation. In *Proceding of the Human Language Technology and North American Chapter of the Association for Computational Linguistics (HLT-NAACL'2006)*, New York, June.

Phrasetable Smoothing for Statistical Machine Translation

George Foster and **Roland Kuhn** and **Howard Johnson**
National Research Council Canada
Ottawa, Ontario, Canada
firstname.lastname@nrc.gc.ca

Abstract

We discuss different strategies for smoothing the phrasetable in Statistical MT, and give results over a range of translation settings. We show that any type of smoothing is a better idea than the relative-frequency estimates that are often used. The best smoothing techniques yield consistent gains of approximately 1% (absolute) according to the BLEU metric.

1 Introduction

Smoothing is an important technique in statistical NLP, used to deal with perennial data sparseness and empirical distributions that overfit the training corpus. Surprisingly, however, it is rarely mentioned in statistical Machine Translation. In particular, state-of-the-art phrase-based SMT relies on a *phrasetable*—a large set of ngram pairs over the source and target languages, along with their translation probabilities. This table, which may contain tens of millions of entries, and phrases of up to ten words or more, is an excellent candidate for smoothing. Yet very few publications describe phrasetable smoothing techniques in detail.

In this paper, we provide the first systematic study of smoothing methods for phrase-based SMT. Although we introduce a few new ideas, most methods described here were devised by others; the main purpose of this paper is not to invent new methods, but to compare methods. In experiments over many language pairs, we show that smoothing yields small but consistent gains in translation performance. We feel that this paper only scratches the surface: many other combinations of phrasetable smoothing techniques remain to be tested.

We define a phrasetable as a set of source phrases (ngrams) $\tilde{s}$ and their translations $\tilde{t}$, along with associated translation probabilities $p(\tilde{s}|\tilde{t})$ and $p(\tilde{t}|\tilde{s})$. These conditional distributions are derived from the joint frequencies $c(\tilde{s}, \tilde{t})$ of source/target phrase pairs observed in a word-aligned parallel corpus.

Traditionally, maximum-likelihood estimation from relative frequencies is used to obtain conditional probabilities (Koehn et al., 2003), eg, $p(\tilde{s}|\tilde{t}) = c(\tilde{s}, \tilde{t}) / \sum_{\tilde{s}} c(\tilde{s}, \tilde{t})$ (since the estimation problems for $p(\tilde{s}|\tilde{t})$ and $p(\tilde{t}|\tilde{s})$ are symmetrical, we will usually refer only to $p(\tilde{s}|\tilde{t})$ for brevity). The most obvious example of the overfitting this causes can be seen in phrase pairs whose constituent phrases occur only once in the corpus. These are assigned conditional probabilities of 1, higher than the estimated probabilities of pairs for which much more evidence exists, in the typical case where the latter have constituents that co-occur occasionally with other phrases. During decoding, overlapping phrase pairs are in direct competition, so estimation biases such as this one in favour of infrequent pairs have the potential to significantly degrade translation quality.

An excellent discussion of smoothing techniques developed for ngram language models (LMs) may be found in (Chen and Goodman, 1998; Goodman, 2001). Phrasetable smoothing differs from ngram LM smoothing in the following ways:

- Probabilities of individual unseen events are not important. Because the decoder only proposes phrase translations that are in the phrasetable (ie, that have non-zero count), it never requires estimates for pairs $\tilde{s}, \tilde{t}$ having

Proceedings of the 2006 Conference on Empirical Methods in Natural Language Processing (EMNLP 2006), pages 53–61,
Sydney, July 2006.

$c(\tilde{s},\tilde{t}) = 0$.[1] However, probability mass is reserved for the *set* of unseen translations, implying that probability mass is subtracted from the seen translations.

- There is no obvious lower-order distribution for backoff. One of the most important techniques in ngram LM smoothing is to combine estimates made using the previous $n-1$ words with those using only the previous $n-i$ words, for $i = 2 \dots n$. This relies on the fact that closer words are more informative, which has no direct analog in phrasetable smoothing.

- The predicted objects are word sequences (in another language). This contrasts to LM smoothing where they are single words, and are thus less amenable to decomposition for smoothing purposes.

We propose various ways of dealing with these special features of the phrasetable smoothing problem, and give evaluations of their performance within a phrase-based SMT system.

The paper is structured as follows: section 2 gives a brief description of our phrase-based SMT system; section 3 presents the smoothing techniques used; section 4 reviews previous work; section 5 gives experimental results; and section 6 concludes and discusses future work.

2 Phrase-based Statistical MT

Given a source sentence $\mathbf{s}$, our phrase-based SMT system tries to find the target sentence $\hat{\mathbf{t}}$ that is the most likely translation of $\mathbf{s}$. To make search more efficient, we use the Viterbi approximation and seek the most likely combination of $\mathbf{t}$ and its alignment $\mathbf{a}$ with $\mathbf{s}$, rather than just the most likely $\mathbf{t}$:

$$\hat{\mathbf{t}} = \operatorname*{argmax}_{\mathbf{t}} p(\mathbf{t}|\mathbf{s}) \approx \operatorname*{argmax}_{\mathbf{t},\mathbf{a}} p(\mathbf{t},\mathbf{a}|\mathbf{s}),$$

where $\mathbf{a} = (\tilde{s}_1,\tilde{t}_1,j_1),...,(\tilde{s}_K,\tilde{t}_K,j_K)$; $\tilde{t}_k$ are target phrases such that $\mathbf{t} = \tilde{t}_1 \dots \tilde{t}_K$; $\tilde{s}_k$ are source phrases such that $\mathbf{s} = \tilde{s}_{j_1} \dots \tilde{s}_{j_K}$; and $\tilde{s}_k$ is the translation of the kth target phrase $\tilde{t}_k$.

[1] This is a first approximation; exceptions occur when different phrasetables are used in parallel, and when rules are used to translate certain classes of entities.

To model $p(\mathbf{t},\mathbf{a}|\mathbf{s})$, we use a standard loglinear approach:

$$p(\mathbf{t},\mathbf{a}|\mathbf{s}) \propto \exp\left[\sum_i \lambda_i f_i(\mathbf{s},\mathbf{t},\mathbf{a})\right]$$

where each $f_i(\mathbf{s},\mathbf{t},\mathbf{a})$ is a feature function, and weights λ_i are set using Och's algorithm (Och, 2003) to maximize the system's BLEU score (Papineni et al., 2001) on a development corpus. The features used in this study are: the length of $\mathbf{t}$; a single-parameter distortion penalty on phrase reordering in $\mathbf{a}$, as described in (Koehn et al., 2003); phrase translation model probabilities; and trigram language model probabilities $\log p(\mathbf{t})$, using Kneser-Ney smoothing as implemented in the SRILM toolkit (Stolcke, 2002).

Phrase translation model probabilities are features of the form:

$$\log p(\mathbf{s}|\mathbf{t},\mathbf{a}) \approx \sum_{k=1}^{K} \log p(\tilde{s}_k|\tilde{t}_k)$$

ie, we assume that the phrases $\tilde{s}_k$ specified by $\mathbf{a}$ are conditionally independent, and depend only on their aligned phrases $\tilde{t}_k$. The "forward" phrase probabilities $p(\tilde{t}|\tilde{s})$ are not used as features, but only as a filter on the set of possible translations: for each source phrase $\tilde{s}$ that matches some ngram in $\mathbf{s}$, only the 30 top-ranked translations $\tilde{t}$ according to $p(\tilde{t}|\tilde{s})$ are retained.

To derive the joint counts $c(\tilde{s},\tilde{t})$ from which $p(\tilde{s}|\tilde{t})$ and $p(\tilde{t}|\tilde{s})$ are estimated, we use the phrase induction algorithm described in (Koehn et al., 2003), with symmetrized word alignments generated using IBM model 2 (Brown et al., 1993).

3 Smoothing Techniques

Smoothing involves some recipe for modifying conditional distributions away from pure relative-frequency estimates made from joint counts, in order to compensate for data sparsity. In the spirit of ((Hastie et al., 2001), figure 2.11, pg. 38) smoothing can be seen as a way of combining the relative-frequency estimate, which is a model with high complexity, high variance, and low bias, with another model with lower complexity, lower variance, and high bias, in the hope of obtaining better performance on new data. There are two main ingredients in all such recipes: some probability distribution that is smoother than relative frequencies (ie, that has fewer parameters and is thus less complex) and some technique for combining that distribution with relative frequency estimates. We will now discuss both these choices: the distribution for carrying out smoothing and the combination technique. In this discussion, we use $\tilde{p}()$ to denote relative frequency distributions.

Choice of Smoothing Distribution

One can distinguish between two approaches to smoothing phrase tables. *Black-box* techniques do not look inside phrases but instead treat them as atomic objects: that is, both the $\tilde{s}$ and the $\tilde{t}$ in the expression $p(\tilde{s}|\tilde{t})$ are treated as units about which nothing is known except their counts. In contrast, *glass-box* methods break phrases down into their component words.

The black-box approach, which is the simpler of the two, has received little attention in the SMT literature. An interesting aspect of this approach is that it allows one to implement phrasetable smoothing techniques that are analogous to LM smoothing techniques, by treating the problem of estimating $p(\tilde{s}|\tilde{t})$ as if it were the problem of estimating a bigram conditional probability. In this paper, we give experimental results for phrasetable smoothing techniques analogous to Good-Turing, Fixed-Discount, Kneser-Ney, and Modified Kneser-Ney LM smoothing.

Glass-box methods for phrasetable smoothing have been described by other authors: see section 3.3. These authors decompose $p(\tilde{s}|\tilde{t})$ into a set of lexical distributions $p(s|\tilde{t})$ by making independence assumptions about the words s in $\tilde{s}$. The other possibility, which is similar in spirit to ngram LM lower-order estimates, is to combine estimates made by replacing words in $\tilde{t}$ with wildcards, as proposed in section 3.4.

Choice of Combination Technique

Although we explored a variety of black-box and glass-box smoothing distributions, we only tried two combination techniques: linear interpolation, which we used for black-box smoothing, and loglinear interpolation, which we used for glass-box smoothing.

For black-box smoothing, we could have used a backoff scheme or an interpolation scheme. Backoff schemes have the form:

$$p(\tilde{s}|\tilde{t}) = \begin{cases} p_h(\tilde{s}|\tilde{t}), & c(\tilde{s},\tilde{t}) \geq \tau \\ p_b(\tilde{s}|\tilde{t}), & \text{else} \end{cases}$$

where $p_h(\tilde{s}|\tilde{t})$ is a higher-order distribution, $p_b(\tilde{s}|\tilde{t})$ is a smooth backoff distribution, and τ is a threshold above which counts are considered reliable. Typically, $\tau = 1$ and $p_h(\tilde{s}|\tilde{t})$ is version of $\tilde{p}(\tilde{s}|\tilde{t})$ modified to reserve some probability mass for unseen events.

Interpolation schemes have the general form:

$$p(\tilde{s}|\tilde{t}) = \alpha(\tilde{s},\tilde{t})\tilde{p}(\tilde{s}|\tilde{t}) + \beta(\tilde{s},\tilde{t})p_b(\tilde{s}|\tilde{t}), \quad (1)$$

where α and β are combining coefficients. As noted in (Chen and Goodman, 1998), a key difference between interpolation and backoff is that the former approach uses information from the smoothing distribution to modify $\tilde{p}(\tilde{s}|\tilde{t})$ for higher-frequency events, whereas the latter uses it only for low-frequency events (most often 0-frequency events). Since for phrasetable smoothing, better prediction of unseen (zero-count) events has no direct impact—only seen events are represented in the phrasetable, and thus hypothesized during decoding—interpolation seemed a more suitable approach.

For combining relative-frequency estimates with glass-box smoothing distributions, we employed loglinear interpolation. This is the traditional approach for glass-box smoothing (Koehn et al., 2003; Zens and Ney, 2004). To illustrate the difference between linear and loglinear interpolation, consider combining two Bernoulli distributions $p_1(x)$ and $p_2(x)$ using each method:

$$\begin{aligned} p_{linear}(x) &= \alpha p_1(x) + (1-\alpha)p_2(x) \\ p_{loglin}(x) &= \frac{p_1(x)^\alpha p_2(x)}{p_1(x)^\alpha p_2(x) + q_1(x)^\alpha q_2(x)} \end{aligned}$$

where $q_i(x) = 1 - p_i(x)$. Setting $p_2(x) = 0.5$ to simulate uniform smoothing gives $p_{loglin}(x) = p_1(x)^\alpha/(p_1(x)^\alpha + q_1(x)^\alpha)$. This is actually *less* smooth than the original distribution $p_1(x)$: it preserves extreme values 0 and 1, and makes intermediate values more extreme. On the other hand, $p_{linear}(x) = \alpha p_1(x) + (1-\alpha)/2$, which has the opposite properties: it moderates extreme values and tends to preserve intermediate values.

An advantage of loglinear interpolation is that we can tune loglinear weights so as to maximize the true objective function, for instance BLEU; recall that our translation model is itself loglinear, with weights set to minimize errors. In fact, a limitation of the experiments described in this paper is that the loglinear weights for the glass-box techniques were optimized for BLEU using Och's algorithm (Och, 2003), while the linear weights for black-box techniques were set heuristically. Obviously, this gives the glass-box techniques an advantage when the different smoothing techniques are compared using BLEU! Implementing an algorithm for optimizing linear weights according to BLEU is high on our list of priorities.

The preceding discussion implicitly assumes a single set of counts $c(\tilde{s}, \tilde{t})$ from which conditional distributions are derived. But, as phrases of different lengths are likely to have different statistical properties, it might be worthwhile to break down the global phrasetable into separate phrasetables for each value of $|\tilde{t}|$ for the purposes of smoothing. Any similar strategy that does not split up $\{\tilde{s}|c(\tilde{s}, \tilde{t}) > 0\}$ for any fixed $\tilde{t}$ can be applied to any smoothing scheme. This is another idea we are eager to try soon.

We now describe the individual smoothing schemes we have implemented. Four of them are black-box techniques: Good-Turing and three fixed-discount techniques (fixed-discount interpolated with unigram distribution, Kneser-Ney fixed-discount, and modified Kneser-Ney fixed-discount). Two of them are glass-box techniques: Zens-Ney "noisy-or" and Koehn-Och-Marcu IBM smoothing. Our experiments tested not only these individual schemes, but also some loglinear combinations of a black-box technique with a glass-box technique.

3.1 Good-Turing

Good-Turing smoothing is a well-known technique (Church and Gale, 1991) in which observed counts c are modified according to the formula:

$$c_g = (c + 1)n_{c+1}/n_c \qquad (2)$$

where c_g is a modified count value used to replace c in subsequent relative-frequency estimates, and n_c is the number of events having count c. An intuitive motivation for this formula is that it approximates relative-frequency estimates made by successively leaving out each event in the corpus, and then averaging the results (Nádas, 1985).

A practical difficulty in implementing Good-Turing smoothing is that the n_c are noisy for large c. For instance, there may be only one phrase pair that occurs exactly $c = 347,623$ times in a large corpus, and no pair that occurs $c = 347,624$ times, leading to $c_g(347,623) = 0$, clearly not what is intended. Our solution to this problem is based on the technique described in (Church and Gale, 1991). We first take the log of the observed (c, n_c) values, and then use a linear least squares fit to $\log n_c$ as a function of $\log c$. To ensure that the result stays close to the reliable values of n_c for large c, error terms are weighted by c, ie: $c(\log n_c - \log n'_c)^2$, where n'_c are the fitted values.

Our implementation pools all counts $c(\tilde{s}, \tilde{t})$ together to obtain n'_c (we have not yet tried separate counts based on length of $\tilde{t}$ as discussed above). It follows directly from (2) that the total count mass assigned to unseen phrase pairs is $c_g(0)n_0 = n_1$, which we approximate by n'_1. This mass is distributed among contexts $\tilde{t}$ in proportion to $c(\tilde{t})$, giving final estimates:

$$p(\tilde{s}|\tilde{t}) = \frac{c_g(\tilde{s}, \tilde{t})}{\sum_s c_g(\tilde{s}, \tilde{t}) + p(\tilde{t})n'_1},$$

where $p(\tilde{t}) = c(\tilde{t}) / \sum_{\tilde{t}} c(\tilde{t})$.

3.2 Fixed-Discount Methods

Fixed-discount methods subtract a fixed discount D from all non-zero counts, and distribute the resulting probability mass according to a smoothing distribution (Kneser and Ney, 1995). We use an interpolated version of fixed-discount proposed by (Chen and Goodman, 1998) rather than the original backoff version. For phrase pairs with non-zero counts, this distribution has the general form:

$$p(\tilde{s}|\tilde{t}) = \frac{c(\tilde{s}, \tilde{t}) - D}{\sum_{\tilde{s}} c(\tilde{s}, \tilde{t})} + \alpha(\tilde{t})p_b(\tilde{s}|\tilde{t}), \qquad (3)$$

where $p_b(\tilde{s}|\tilde{t})$ is the smoothing distribution. Normalization constraints fix the value of $\alpha(\tilde{t})$:

$$\alpha(\tilde{t}) = D\, n_{1+}(*, \tilde{t}) / \sum_{\tilde{s}} c(\tilde{s}, \tilde{t}),$$

where $n_{1+}(*, \tilde{t})$ is the number of phrases $\tilde{s}$ for which $c(\tilde{s}, \tilde{t}) > 0$.

We experimented with two choices for the smoothing distribution $p_b(\tilde{s}|\tilde{t})$. The first is a plain unigram $p(\tilde{s})$, and the second is the Kneser-Ney lower-order distribution:

$$p_b(\tilde{s}) = n_{1+}(\tilde{s}, *) / \sum_{\tilde{s}} n_{1+}(\tilde{s}, *),$$

ie, the proportion of unique target phrases that $\tilde{s}$ is associated with, where $n_{1+}(\tilde{s}, *)$ is defined analogously to $n_{1+}(*, \tilde{t})$. Intuitively, the idea is that source phrases that co-occur with many different target phrases are more likely to appear in new contexts.

For both unigram and Kneser-Ney smoothing distributions, we used a discounting coefficient derived by (Ney et al., 1994) on the basis of a leave-one-out analysis: $D = n_1/(n_1 + 2n_2)$. For the Kneser-Ney smoothing distribution, we also tested the "Modified Kneser-Ney" extension suggested in (Chen and Goodman, 1998), in which specific coefficients D_c are used for small count values c up to a maximum of three (ie D_3 is used for $c \geq 3$). For $c = 2$ and $c = 3$, we used formulas given in that paper.

3.3 Lexical Decomposition

The two glass-box techniques that we considered involve decomposing source phrases with independence assumptions. The simplest approach assumes that all source words are conditionally independent, so that:

$$p(\tilde{s}|\tilde{t}) = \prod_{j=1}^{\tilde{J}} p(s_j|\tilde{t})$$

We implemented two variants for $p(s_j|\tilde{t})$ that are described in previous work. (Zens and Ney, 2004) describe a "noisy-or" combination:

$$\begin{aligned} p(s_j|\tilde{t}) &= 1 - p(\bar{s}_j|\tilde{t}) \\ &\approx 1 - \prod_{i=1}^{\tilde{I}} (1 - p(s_j|t_i)) \end{aligned}$$

where $\bar{s}_j$ is the probability that s_j is *not* in the translation of $\tilde{t}$, and $p(s_j|t_i)$ is a lexical probability. (Zens and Ney, 2004) obtain $p(s_j|t_i)$ from smoothed relative-frequency estimates in a word-aligned corpus. Our implementation simply uses IBM1 probabilities, which obviate further smoothing.

The noisy-or combination stipulates that s_j should not appear in $\tilde{s}$ if it is not the translation of any of the words in $\tilde{t}$. The complement of this, proposed in (Koehn et al., 2005), to say that s_j *should* appear in $\tilde{s}$ if it is the translation of at least one of the words in $\tilde{t}$:

$$p(s_j|\tilde{t}) = \sum_{i \in A_j} p(s_j|t_i)/|A_j|$$

where A_j is a set of likely alignment connections for s_j. In our implementation of this method, we assumed that $A_j = \{1, \ldots, \tilde{I}\}$, ie the set of all connections, and used IBM1 probabilities for $p(s|t)$.

3.4 Lower-Order Combinations

We mentioned earlier that LM ngrams have a naturally-ordered sequence of smoothing distributions, obtained by successively dropping the last word in the context. For phrasetable smoothing, because no word in $\tilde{t}$ is a priori less informative than any others, there is no exact parallel to this technique. However, it is clear that estimates made by replacing particular target (conditioning) words with wildcards will be smoother than the original relative frequencies. A simple scheme for combining them is just to average:

$$p(\tilde{s}|\tilde{t}) = \sum_{i=\tilde{I}} \frac{c_i^*(\tilde{s}, \tilde{t})}{\sum_{\tilde{s}} c_i^*(\tilde{s}, \tilde{t})} / \tilde{I}$$

where:

$$c_i^*(\tilde{s}, \tilde{t}) = \sum_{t_i} c(\tilde{s}, t_1 \ldots t_i \ldots t_{\tilde{I}}).$$

One might also consider progressively replacing the least informative remaining word in the target phrase (using tf-idf or a similar measure).

The same idea could be applied in reverse, by replacing particular source (conditioned) words with wildcards. We have not yet implemented this new glass-box smoothing technique, but it has considerable appeal. The idea is similar in spirit to Collins' backoff method for prepositional phrase attachment (Collins and Brooks, 1995).

4 Related Work

As mentioned previously, (Chen and Goodman, 1998) give a comprehensive survey and evaluation of smoothing techniques for language modeling. As also mentioned previously, there is relatively little published work on smoothing for statistical MT. For the IBM models, alignment probabilities need to be smoothed for combinations of sentence lengths and positions not encountered in training data (García-Varea et al., 1998). Moore (2004) has found that smoothing to correct overestimated IBM1 lexical probabilities for rare words can improve word-alignment performance. Langlais (2005) reports negative results for synonym-based smoothing of IBM2 lexical probabilities prior to extracting phrases for phrase-based SMT.

For phrase-based SMT, the use of smoothing to avoid zero probabilities during phrase induction is reported in (Marcu and Wong, 2002), but no details are given. As described above, (Zens and

Ney, 2004) and (Koehn et al., 2005) use two different variants of glass-box smoothing (which they call "lexical smoothing") over the phrasetable, and combine the resulting estimates with pure relative-frequency ones in a loglinear model. Finally, (Cettollo et al., 2005) describes the use of Witten-Bell smoothing (a black-box technique) for phrasetable counts, but does not give a comparison to other methods. As Witten-Bell is reported by (Chen and Goodman, 1998) to be significantly worse than Kneser-Ney smoothing, we have not yet tested this method.

5 Experiments

We carried out experiments in two different settings: broad-coverage ones across six European language pairs using selected smoothing techniques and relatively small training corpora; and Chinese to English experiments using all implemented smoothing techniques and large training corpora. For the black-box techniques, the smoothed phrase table replaced the original relative-frequency (RF) phrase table. For the glass-box techniques, a phrase table (either the original RF phrase table or its replacement after black-box smoothing) was interpolated in loglinear fashion with the smoothing glass-box distribution, with weights set to maximize BLEU on a development corpus.

To estimate the significance of the results across different methods, we used 1000-fold pairwise bootstrap resampling at the 95% confidence level.

5.1 Broad-Coverage Experiments

In order to measure the benefit of phrasetable smoothing for relatively small corpora, we used the data made available for the WMT06 shared task (WMT, 2006). This exercise is conducted openly with access to all needed resources and is thus ideal for benchmarking statistical phrase-based translation systems on a number of language pairs.

The WMT06 corpus is based on sentences extracted from the proceedings of the European Parliament. Separate sentence-aligned parallel corpora of about 700,000 sentences (about 150MB) are provided for the three language pairs having one of French, Spanish and German with English. SRILM language models based on the same source are also provided for each of the four languages. We used the provided 2000-sentence dev-sets for tuning loglinear parameters, and tested on the 3064-sentence test sets.

Results are shown in table 1 for relative-frequency (RF), Good-Turing (GT), Kneser-Ney with 1 (KN1) and 3 (KN3) discount coefficients; and loglinear combinations of both RF and KN3 phrasetables with Zens-Ney-IBM1 (ZN-IBM1) smoothed phrasetables (these combinations are denoted RF+ZN-IBM1 and KN3+ZN-IBM1).

It is apparent from table 1 that any kind of phrase table smoothing is better than using none; the minimum improvement is 0.45 BLEU, and the difference between RF and all other methods is statistically significant. Also, Kneser-Ney smoothing gives a statistically significant improvement over GT smoothing, with a minimum gain of 0.30 BLEU. Using more discounting coefficients does not appear to help. Smoothing relative frequencies with an additional Zens-Ney phrasetable gives about the same gain as Kneser-Ney smoothing on its own. However, combining Kneser-Ney with Zens-Ney gives a clear gain over any other method (statistically significant for all language pairs except en→es and en→de) demonstrating that these approaches are complementary.

5.2 Chinese-English Experiments

To test the effects of smoothing with larger corpora, we ran a set of experiments for Chinese-English translation using the corpora distributed for the NIST MT05 evaluation (www.nist.gov/speech/tests/mt). These are summarized in table 2. Due to the large size of the out-of-domain UN corpus, we trained one phrasetable on it, and another on all other parallel corpora (smoothing was applied to both). We also used a subset of the English Gigaword corpus to augment the LM training material.

corpus	use	sentences
non-UN	phrasetable1 + LM	3,164,180
UN	phrasetable2 + LM	4,979,345
Gigaword	LM	11,681,852
multi-p3	dev	993
eval-04	test	1788

Table 2: Chinese-English Corpora

Table 3 contains results for the Chinese-English experiments, including fixed-discount with unigram smoothing (FDU), and Koehn-Och-Marcu smoothing with the IBM1 model (KOM-IBM1)

smoothing method	fr ⟶ en	es ⟶ en	de ⟶ en	en ⟶ fr	en ⟶ es	en ⟶ de
RF	25.35	27.25	20.46	27.20	27.18	14.60
GT	25.95	28.07	21.06	27.85	27.96	15.05
KN1	26.83	28.66	21.36	28.62	28.71	15.42
KN3	26.84	28.69	21.53	28.64	28.70	15.40
RF+ZN-IBM1	26.84	28.63	21.32	28.84	28.45	15.44
KN3+ZN-IBM1	**27.25**	**29.30**	**21.77**	**29.00**	**28.86**	**15.49**

Table 1: Broad-coverage results

as described in section 3.3. As with the broad-coverage experiments, all of the black-box smoothing techniques do significantly better than the RF baseline. However, GT appears to work better in the large-corpus setting: it is statistically indistinguishable from KN3, and both these methods are significantly better than all other fixed-discount variants, among which there is little difference.

Not surprisingly, the two glass-box methods, ZN-IBM1 and KOM-IBM1, do poorly when used on their own. However, in combination with another phrasetable, they yield the best results, obtained by RF+ZN-IBM1 and GT+KOM-IBM1, which are statistically indistinguishable. In constrast to the situation in the broad-coverage setting, these are not significantly better than the best black-box method (GT) on its own, although RF+ZN-IBM1 *is* better than all other glass-box combinations.

smoothing method	BLEU score
RF	29.85
GT	30.66
FDU	30.23
KN1	30.29
KN2	30.13
KN3	30.54
ZN-IBM1	29.55
KOM-IBM1	28.09
RF+ZN-IBM1	**30.95**
RF+KOM-IBM1	30.10
GT+ZN-IBM1	30.45
GT+KOM-IBM1	30.81
KN3+ZN-IBM1	30.66

Table 3: Chinese-English Results

A striking difference between the broad-coverage setting and the Chinese-English setting is that in the former it appears to be beneficial to apply KN3 smoothing to the phrasetable that gets combined with the best glass-box phrasetable (ZN), whereas in the latter setting it does not. To test whether this was due to corpus size (as the broad-coverage corpora are around 10% of those for Chinese-English), we calculated Chinese-English learning curves for the RF+ZN-IBM1 and KN3-ZN-IBM1 methods, shown in figure 1. The results are somewhat inconclusive: although the KN3+ZN-IBM1 curve is perhaps slightly flatter, the most obvious characteristic is that this method appears to be highly sensitive to the particular corpus sample used.

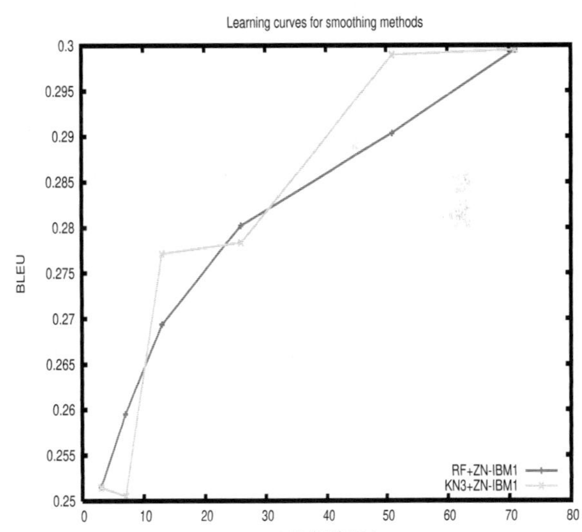

Figure 1: Learning curves for two glass-box combinations.

6 Conclusion and Future Work

We tested different phrasetable smoothing techniques in two different translation settings: European language pairs with relatively small corpora, and Chinese to English translation with large corpora. The smoothing techniques fall into two categories: black-box methods that work only on phrase-pair counts; and glass-box methods that decompose phrase probabilities into lexical probabilities. In our implementation, black-box techniques use linear interpolation to combine relative frequency estimates with smoothing distributions, while glass-box techniques are combined in loglinear fashion with either relative-frequencies or black-box estimates.

All smoothing techniques tested gave statistically significant gains over pure relative-frequency estimates. In the small-corpus setting, the best technique is a loglinear combination of Kneser-Ney count smoothing with Zens-Ney glass-box smoothing; this yields an average gain of 1.6 BLEU points over relative frequencies. In the large-corpus setting, the best technique is a loglinear combination of relative-frequency estimates with Zens-Ney smoothing, with a gain of 1.1 BLEU points. Of the two glass-box smoothing methods tested, Zens-Ney appears to have a slight advantage over Koehn-Och-Marcu. Of the black-box methods tested, Kneser-Ney is clearly better for small corpora, but is equivalent to Good-Turing for larger corpora.

The paper describes several smoothing alternatives which we intend to test in future work:

- Linear versus loglinear combinations (in our current work, these coincide with the black-box versus glass-box distinction, making it impossible to draw conclusions).
- Lower-order distributions as described in section 3.4.
- Separate count-smoothing bins based on phrase length.

7 Acknowledgements

The authors would like to thank their colleague Michel Simard for stimulating discussions. The first author would like to thank all his colleagues for encouraging him to taste a delicacy that was new to him (shredded paper with maple syrup). This material is based upon work supported by the Defense Advanced Research Projects Agency (DARPA) under Contract No. HR0011-06-C-0023. Any opinions, findings and conclusions or recommendations expressed in this material are those of the author(s) and do not necessarily reflect the views of the Defense Advanced Research Projects Agency (DARPA).

References

Peter F. Brown, Stephen A. Della Pietra, Vincent Della J. Pietra, and Robert L. Mercer. 1993. The mathematics of Machine Translation: Parameter estimation. *Computational Linguistics*, 19(2):263–312, June.

M. Cettollo, M. Federico, N. Bertoldi, R. Cattoni, and B. Chen. 2005. A look inside the ITC-irst SMT system. In *Proceedings of MT Summit X*, Phuket, Thailand, September. International Association for Machine Translation.

Stanley F. Chen and Joshua T. Goodman. 1998. An empirical study of smoothing techniques for language modeling. Technical Report TR-10-98, Computer Science Group, Harvard University.

K. Church and W. Gale. 1991. A comparison of the enhanced Good-Turing and deleted estimation methods for estimating probabilities of English bigrams. *Computer speech and language*, 5(1):19–54.

M. Collins and J. Brooks. 1995. Prepositional phrase attachment through a backed-off model. In *Proceedings of the 3rd ACL Workshop on Very Large Corpora (WVLC)*, Cambridge, Massachusetts.

Ismael García-Varea, Francisco Casacuberta, and Hermann Ney. 1998. An iterative, DP-based search algorithm for statistical machine translation. In *Proceedings of the 5th International Conference on Spoken Language Processing (ICSLP) 1998*, volume 4, pages 1135–1138, Sydney, Australia, December.

Joshua Goodman. 2001. A bit of progress in language modeling. *Computer Speech and Language*.

Trevor Hastie, Robert Tibshirani, and Jerome Friedman. 2001. *The Elements of Statistical Learning*. Springer.

Reinhard Kneser and Hermann Ney. 1995. Improved backing-off for m-gram language modeling. In *Proceedings of the International Conference on Acoustics, Speech, and Signal Processing (ICASSP) 1995*, pages 181–184, Detroit, Michigan. IEEE.

Philipp Koehn, Franz Josef Och, and Daniel Marcu. 2003. Statistical phrase-based translation. In Eduard Hovy, editor, *Proceedings of the Human Language Technology Conference of the North American Chapter of the Association for Computational Linguistics*, pages 127–133, Edmonton, Alberta, Canada, May. NAACL.

P. Koehn, A. Axelrod, A. B. Mayne, C. Callison-Burch, M. Osborne, D. Talbot, and M. White. 2005. Edinburgh system description for the 2005 NIST MT evaluation. In *Proceedings of Machine Translation Evaluation Workshop*.

Philippe Langlais, Guihong Cao, and Fabrizio Gotti. 2005. RALI: SMT shared task system description.

In *Proceedings of the 2nd ACL workshop on Building and Using Parallel Texts*, pages 137–140, University of Michigan, Ann Arbor, June.

Daniel Marcu and William Wong. 2002. A phrase-based, joint probability model for statistical machine translation. In *Proceedings of the 2002 Conference on Empirical Methods in Natural Language Processing (EMNLP)*, Philadelphia, PA.

Robert C. Moore. 2004. Improving IBM word-alignment model 1. In *Proceedings of the 42th Annual Meeting of the Association for Computational Linguistics (ACL)*, Barcelona, July.

Hermann Ney, Ute Essen, and Reinhard Kneser. 1994. On structuring probabilistic dependencies in stochastic language modelling. *Computer Speech and Language*, 10:1–38.

Arthur Nádas. 1985. On Turing's formula for word probabilities. *IEEE Transactions on Acoustics, Speech and Signal Processing (ASSP)*, ASSP-33(6):1415–1417, December.

Franz Josef Och. 2003. Minimum error rate training for statistical machine translation. In *Proceedings of the 41th Annual Meeting of the Association for Computational Linguistics (ACL)*, Sapporo, July.

Kishore Papineni, Salim Roukos, Todd Ward, and Wei-Jing Zhu. 2001. BLEU: A method for automatic evaluation of Machine Translation. Technical Report RC22176, IBM, September.

Andreas Stolcke. 2002. SRILM - an extensible language modeling toolkit. In *Proceedings of the 7th International Conference on Spoken Language Processing (ICSLP) 2002*, Denver, Colorado, September.

WMT. 2006. *The NAACL Workshop on Statistical Machine Translation (www.statmt.org/wmt06)*, New York, June.

Richard Zens and Hermann Ney. 2004. Improvements in phrase-based statistical machine translation. In *Proceedings of Human Language Technology Conference / North American Chapter of the ACL*, Boston, May.

The impact of parse quality on syntactically-informed statistical machine translation

Chris Quirk and **Simon Corston-Oliver**
Microsoft Research
One Microsoft Way
Redmond, WA 98052 USA
{chrisq,simonco}@microsoft.com

Abstract

We investigate the impact of parse quality on a syntactically-informed statistical machine translation system applied to technical text. We vary parse quality by varying the amount of data used to train the parser. As the amount of data increases, parse quality improves, leading to improvements in machine translation output and results that significantly outperform a state-of-the-art phrasal baseline.

1 Introduction

The current study is a response to a question that proponents of syntactically-informed machine translation frequently encounter: How sensitive is a syntactically-informed machine translation system to the quality of the input syntactic analysis? It has been shown that phrasal machine translation systems are not affected by the quality of the input word alignments (Koehn et al., 2003). This finding has generally been cast in favorable terms: such systems are robust to poor quality word alignment. A less favorable interpretation of these results might be to conclude that phrasal statistical machine translation (SMT) systems do not stand to benefit from improvements in word alignment.

In a similar vein, one might ask whether contemporary syntactically-informed machine translation systems would benefit from improvements in parse accuracy. One possibility is that current syntactically-informed SMT systems are deriving only limited value from the syntactic analyses, and would therefore not benefit from improved analyses. Another possibility is that syntactic analysis does indeed contain valuable information that could be exploited by machine learning techniques, but that current parsers are not of sufficient quality to be of use in SMT.

With these questions and concerns, let us begin. Following some background discussion we describe a set of experiments intended to elucidate the impact of parse quality on SMT.

2 Background

We trained statistical machine translation systems on technical text. In the following sections we provide background on the data used for training, the dependency parsing framework used to produce treelets, the treelet translation framework and salient characteristics of the target languages.

2.1 Dependency parsing

Dependency analysis is an alternative to constituency analysis (Tesnière, 1959; Melčuk, 1988). In a dependency analysis of syntax, words directly modify other words, with no intervening non-lexical nodes. We use the terms child node and parent node to denote the tokens in a dependency relation. Each child has a single parent, with the lexical root of the sentence dependent on a synthetic ROOT node.

We use the parsing approach described in (Corston-Oliver et al., 2006). The parser is trained on dependencies extracted from the English Penn Treebank version 3.0 (Marcus et al., 1993) by using the head-percolation rules of (Yamada and Matsumoto, 2003).

Given a sentence x, the goal of the parser is to find the highest-scoring parse $\hat{y}$ among all possible parses $y \in Y$:

$$\hat{y} = \arg\max_{y \in Y} s(x, y) \qquad (1)$$

The score of a given parse y is the sum of the

Proceedings of the 2006 Conference on Empirical Methods in Natural Language Processing (EMNLP 2006), pages 62–69,
Sydney, July 2006. ©2006 Association for Computational Linguistics

scores of all its dependency links $(i,j) \in y$:

$$s(x,y) = \sum_{(i,j)\in y} d(i,j) = \sum_{(i,j)\in y} \mathbf{w} \cdot \mathbf{f}(i,j) \quad (2)$$

where the link (i,j) indicates a parent-child dependency between the token at position i and the token at position j. The score $d(i,j)$ of each dependency link (i,j) is further decomposed as the weighted sum of its features $\mathbf{f}(i,j)$.

The feature vector $\mathbf{f}(i,j)$ computed for each possible parent-child dependency includes the part-of-speech (POS), lexeme and stem of the parent and child tokens, the POS of tokens adjacent to the child and parent, and the POS of each token that intervenes between the parent and child. Various combinations of these features are used, for example a new feature is created that combines the POS of the parent, lexeme of the parent, POS of the child and lexeme of the child. Each feature is also conjoined with the direction and distance of the parent, e.g. does the child precede or follow the parent, and how many tokens intervene?

To set the weight vector $\mathbf{w}$, we train twenty averaged perceptrons (Collins, 2002) on different shuffles of data drawn from sections 02–21 of the Penn Treebank. The averaged perceptrons are then combined to form a Bayes Point Machine (Herbrich et al., 2001; Harrington et al., 2003), resulting in a linear classifier that is competitive with wide margin techniques.

To find the optimal parse given the weight vector $\mathbf{w}$ and feature vector $\mathbf{f}(i,j)$ we use the decoder described in (Eisner, 1996).

2.2 Treelet translation

For syntactically-informed translation, we follow the treelet translation approach described in (Quirk et al., 2005). In this approach, translation is guided by treelet translation pairs. Here, a *treelet* is a connected subgraph of a dependency tree. A treelet translation pair consists of a source treelet S, a target treelet T, and a word alignment $A \subset S \times T$ such that for all $s \in S$, there exists a unique $t \in T$ such that $(s,t) \in A$, and if t is the root of T, there is a unique $s \in S$ such that $(s,t) \in A$.

Translation of a sentence begins by parsing that sentence into a dependency representation. This dependency graph is partitioned into treelets; like (Koehn et al., 2003), we assume a uniform probability distribution over all partitions. Each source treelet is matched to a treelet translation pair; together, the target language treelets in those treelet translation pairs will form the target translation. Next the target language treelets are joined to form a single tree: the parent of the root of each treelet is dictated by the source. Let t_r be the root of the target language treelet, and s_r be the source node aligned to it. If s_r is the root of the source sentence, then t_r is made the root of the target language tree. Otherwise let s_p be the parent of s_r, and t_p be the target node aligned to s_p: t_r is attached to t_p. Finally the ordering of all the nodes is determined, and the target tree is specified, and the target sentence is produced by reading off the labels of the nodes in order.

Translations are scored according to a log-linear combination of feature functions, each scoring different aspects of the translation process. We use a beam search decoder to find the best translation T^* according to the log-linear combination of models:

$$T^* = \arg\max_T \left\{ \sum_{f\in F} \lambda_f f(S,T,A) \right\} \quad (3)$$

The models include inverted and direct channel models estimated by relative frequency, lexical weighting channel models following (Vogel et al., 2003), a trigram target language model using modified Kneser-Ney smoothing (Goodman, 2001), an order model following (Quirk et al., 2005), and word count and phrase count functions. The weights for these models are determined using the method described in (Och, 2003).

To estimate the models and extract the treelets, we begin from a parallel corpus. First the corpus is word-aligned using GIZA++ (Och and Ney, 2000), then the source sentence are parsed, and finally dependencies are projected onto the target side following the heuristics described in (Quirk et al., 2005). This word aligned parallel dependency tree corpus provides training material for an order model and a target language tree-based language model. We also extract treelet translation pairs from this parallel corpus. To limit the combinatorial explosion of treelets, we only gather treelets that contain at most four words and at most two gaps in the surface string. This limits the number of mappings to be $O(n^3)$ in the worst case, where n is the number of nodes in the dependency tree.

2.3 Language pairs

In the present paper we focus on English-to-German and English-to-Japanese machine transla-

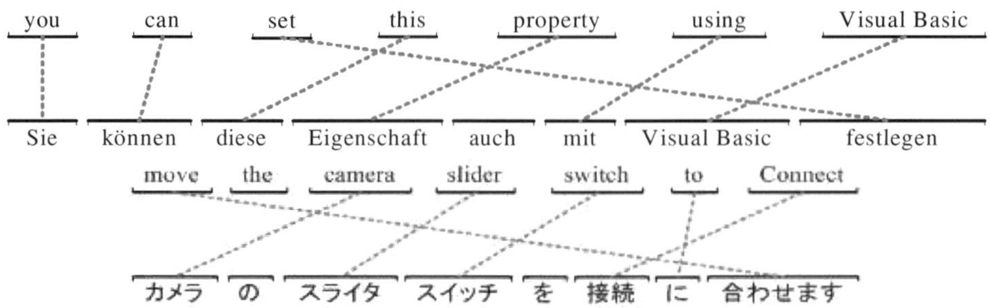

Figure 1: Example German-English and Japanese-English sentence pairs, with word alignments.

tion. Both German and Japanese differ markedly from English in ways that we believe illuminate well the strengths of a syntactically-informed SMT system. We provide a brief sketch of the linguistic characteristics of German and Japanese relevant to the present study.

2.3.1 German

Although English and German are closely related – they both belong to the western branch of the Germanic family of Indo-European languages – the languages differ typologically in ways that are especially problematic for current approaches to statistical machine translation as we shall now illustrate. We believe that these typological differences make English-to-German machine translation a fertile test bed for syntax-based SMT.

German has richer inflectional morphology than English, with obligatory marking of case, number and lexical gender on nominal elements and person, number, tense and mood on verbal elements. This morphological complexity, combined with pervasive, productive noun compounding is problematic for current approaches to word alignment (Corston-Oliver and Gamon, 2004).

Equally problematic for machine translation is the issue of word order. The position of verbs is strongly determined by clause type. For example, in main clauses in declarative sentences, finite verbs occur as the second constituent of the sentence, but certain non-finite verb forms occur in final position. In Figure 1, for example, the English "can" aligns with German "können" in second position and "set" aligns with German "festlegen" in final position.

Aside from verbs, German is usually characterized as a "free word-order" language: major constituents of the sentence may occur in various orders, so-called "separable prefixes" may occur bound to the verb or may detach and occur at a considerable distance from the verb on which they depend, and extraposition of various kinds of subordinate clause is common. In the case of extraposition, for example, more than one third of relative clauses in human-translated German technical text are extraposed. For comparable English text the figure is considerably less than one percent (Gamon et al., 2002).

2.3.2 Japanese

Word order in Japanese is rather different from English. English has the canonical constituent order subject-verb-object, whereas Japanese prefers subject-object-verb order. Prepositional phrases in English generally correspond to postpositional phrases in Japanese. Japanese noun phrases are strictly head-final whereas English noun phrases allow postmodifiers such as prepositional phrases, relative clauses and adjectives. Japanese has little nominal morphology and does not obligatorily mark number, gender or definiteness. Verbal morphology in Japanese is complex with morphological marking of tense, mood, and politeness. Topicalization and subjectless clauses are pervasive, and problematic for current SMT approaches.

The Japanese sentence in Figure 1 illustrates several of these typological differences. The sentence-initial imperative verb "move" in the English corresponds to a sentence-final verb in the Japanese. The Japanese translation of the object noun phrase "the camera slider switch" precedes the verb in Japanese. The English preposition "to" aligns to a postposition in Japanese.

3 Experiments

Our goal in the current paper is to measure the impact of parse quality on syntactically-informed statistical machine translation. One method for producing parsers of varying quality might be to train a parser and then to transform its output, e.g.

by replacing the parser's selection of the parent for certain tokens with different nodes.

Rather than randomly adding noise to the parses, we decided to vary the quality in ways that more closely mimic the situation that confronts us as we develop machine translation systems. Annotating data for POS requires considerably less human time and expertise than annotating syntactic relations. We therefore used an automatic POS tagger (Toutanova et al., 2003) trained on the complete training section of the Penn Treebank (sections 02–21). Annotating syntactic dependencies is time consuming and requires considerable linguistic expertise.[1] We can well imagine annotating syntactic dependencies in order to develop a machine translation system by annotating first a small quantity of data, training a parser, training a system that uses the parses produced by that parser and assessing the quality of the machine translation output. Having assessed the quality of the output, one might annotate additional data and train systems until it appears that the quality of the machine translation output is no longer improving. We therefore produced parsers of varying quality by training on the first *n* sentences of sections 02–21 of the Penn Treebank, where *n* ranged from 250 to 39,892 (the complete training section). At training time, the gold-standard POS tags were used. For parser evaluation and for the machine translation experiments reported here, we used an automatic POS tagger (Toutanova et al., 2003) trained on sections 02–21 of the Penn Treebank.

We trained English-to-German and English-to-Japanese treelet translation systems on approximately 500,000 manually aligned sentence pairs drawn from technical computer documentation. The sentence pairs consisted of the English source sentence and a human-translation of that sentence. Table 1 summarizes the characteristics of this data. Note that German vocabulary and singleton counts are slightly more than double the corresponding English counts due to complex morphology and pervasive compounding (see section 2.3.1).

3.1 Parser accuracy

To evaluate the accuracy of the parsers trained on different samples of sentences we used the traditional blind test section of the Penn Treebank (section 23). As is well-known in the parsing community, parse quality degrades when a parser trained on the Wall Street Journal text in the Penn Treebank is applied to a different genre or semantic domain. Since the technical materials that we were training the translation system on differ from the Wall Street Journal in lexicon and syntax, we annotated a set of 250 sentences of technical material to use in evaluating the parser. Each of the authors independently annotated the same set of 250 sentences. The annotation took less than six hours for each author to complete. Inter-annotator agreement excluding punctuation was 91.8%. Differences in annotation were resolved by discussion, and the resulting set of annotations was used to evaluate the parsers.

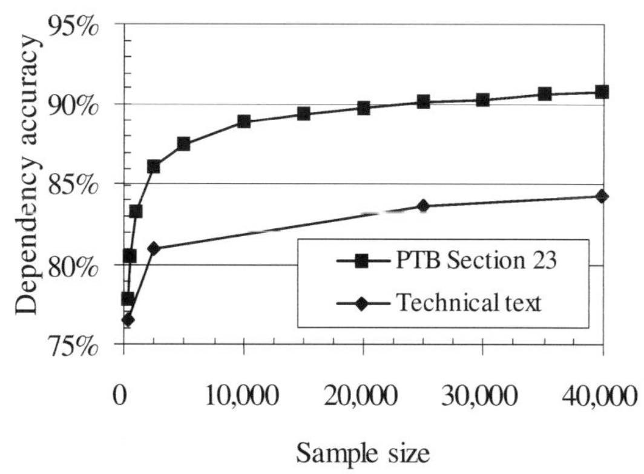

Figure 2: Unlabeled dependency accuracy of parsers trained on different numbers of sentences. The graph compares accuracy on the blind test section of the Penn Treebank to accuracy on a set of 250 sentences drawn from technical text. Punctuation tokens are excluded from the measurement of dependency accuracy.

Figure 2 shows the accuracy of parsers trained on samples of various sizes, excluding punctuation tokens from the evaluation, as is customary in evaluating dependency parsers. When measured against section 23 of the Penn Treebank, the section traditionally used for blind evaluation, the parsers range in accuracy from 77.8% when trained on 250 sentences to 90.8% when trained on all of sections 02–21. As expected, parse accuracy degrades when measured on text that differs greatly from the training text. A parser trained on 250 Penn Treebank sentences has a dependency

[1] Various people have suggested to us that the linguistic expertise required to annotate syntactic dependencies is less than the expertise required to apply a formal theory of constituency like the one that informs the Penn Treebank. We tend to agree, but have not put this claim to the test.

		English	German	English	Japanese
Training	Sentences	515,318		500,000	
	Words	7,292,903	8,112,831	7,909,198	9,379,240
	Vocabulary	59,473	134,829	66,731	68,048
	Singletons	30,452	66,724	50,381	52,911
Test	Sentences	2,000		2,000	
	Words	28,845	31,996	30,616	45,744

Table 1: Parallel data characteristics

accuracy of 76.6% on the technical text. A parser trained on the complete Penn Treebank training section has a dependency accuracy of 84.3% on the technical text.

Since the parsers make extensive use of lexical features, it is not surprising that the performance on the two corpora should be so similar with only 250 training sentences; there were not sufficient instances of each lexical item to train reliable weights or lexical features. As the amount of training data increases, the parsers are able to learn interesting facts about specific lexical items, leading to improved accuracy on the Penn Treebank. Many of the lexical items that occur in the Penn Treebank, however, occur infrequently or not at all in the technical materials so the lexical information is of little benefit. This reflects the mismatch of content. The Wall Street Journal articles in the Penn Treebank concern such topics as world affairs and the policies of the Reagan administration; these topics are absent in the technical materials. Conversely, the Wall Street Journal articles contain no discussion of such topics as the intricacies of SQL database queries.

3.2 Translation quality

Table 2 presents the impact of parse quality on a treelet translation system, measured using BLEU (Papineni et al., 2002). Since our main goal is to investigate the impact of parser accuracy on translation quality, we have varied the parser training data, but have held the MT training data, part-of-speech-tagger, and all other factors constant. We observe an upward trend in BLEU score as more training data is made available to the parser; the trend is even clearer in Japanese.[2] As a baseline, we include right-branching dependency trees, i.e., trees in which the parent of each word is its left neighbor and the root of a sentence is the first word. With this analysis, treelets are simply subsequences of the sentence, and therefore are very similar to the phrases of Phrasal SMT. In English-to-German, this result produces results very comparable to a phrasal SMT system (Koehn et al., 2003) trained on the same data. For English-to-Japanese, however, this baseline performs much worse than a phrasal SMT system. Although phrases and treelets should be nearly identical under this scenario, the decoding constraints are somewhat different: the treelet decoder assumes phrasal cohesion during translation. This constraint may account for the drop in quality.

	EG	EJ
Phrasal decoder	31.7±1.2	32.9±0.9
Treelet decoder		
Right-branching	31.4±1.3	28.0±0.7
250 sentences	32.8±1.4	34.1±0.9
2,500 sentences	33.0±1.4	34.6±1.0
25,000 sentences	33.7±1.5	35.7±0.9
39,892 sentences	33.6±1.5	36.0±1.0

Table 2: BLEU score vs. decoder and parser variants. Here sentences refer to the amount of parser training data, not MT training data.

Since the confidence intervals for many pairs overlap, we ran pairwise tests for each system to determine which differences were significant at the $p < 0.05$ level using the bootstrap method described in (Zhang and Vogel, 2004); Table 3 summarizes this comparison. Neither language pair achieves a statistically significant improvement from increasing the training data from 25,000 pairs to the full training set; this is not surprising since the increase in parse accuracy is quite small (90.2% to 90.8% on Wall Street Journal text).

To further understand what differences in dependency analysis were affecting translation quality, we compared a treelet translation system that

[2]This is particularly encouraging since various people have remarked to us that syntax-based SMT systems may be disadvantaged under n-gram scoring techniques such as BLEU.

	Pharaoh	Right-branching	250	2,500	25,000	39,892
Pharaoh		$\sim$	$>$	$>$	$>$	$>$
Right-branching			$>$	$>$	$>$	$>$
250				$\sim$	$>$	$>$
2,500					$>$	$>$
25,000						$\sim$

(a) English-German

	Pharaoh	Right-branching	250	2,500	25,000	39,892
Pharaoh		$<$	$\sim$	$>$	$>$	$>$
Right-branching			$>$	$>$	$>$	$>$
250				$>$	$>$	$>$
2,500					$>$	$>$
25,000						$\sim$

(b) English-Japanese

Table 3: Pairwise statistical significance tests. $>$ indicates that the system on the top is significantly better than the system on the left; $<$ indicates that the system on top is significantly worse than the system on the left; $\sim$ indicates that difference between the two systems is not statistically significant.

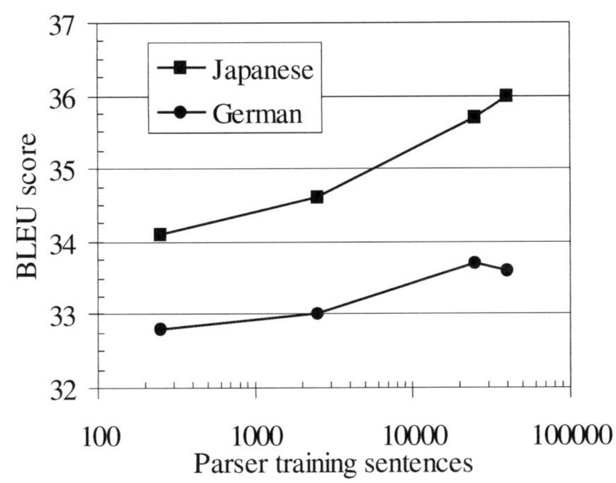

Figure 3: BLEU score vs. number of sentences used to train the dependency parser

used a parser trained on 250 Penn Treebank sentences to a treelet translation system that used a parser trained on 39,892 Treebank sentences. From the test data, we selected 250 sentences where these two parsers produced different analyses. A native speaker of German categorized the differences in machine translation output as either improvements or regressions. We then examined and categorized the differences in the dependency analyses. Table 4 summarizes the results of this comparison. Note that this table simply identifies correlations between parse changes and translation changes; it does not attempt to identify a causal link. In the analysis, we borrow the term "NP [Noun Phrase] identification" from constituency analysis to describe the identification of dependency treelets spanning complete noun phrases.

There were 141 sentences for which the machine translated output improved, 71 sentences for which the output regressed and 38 sentences for which the output was identical. Improvements in the attachment of prepositions, adverbs, gerunds and dependent verbs were common amongst improved translations, but rare amongst regressed translations. Correct identification of the dependent of a preposition[3] was also much more common amongst improvements.

Certain changes, such as improved root identification and final punctuation attachment, were very common across the corpus. Therefore their common occurrence amongst regressions is not very surprising. It was often the case that improvements in root identification or final punctuation attachment were offset by regressions elsewhere in the same sentence.

Improvements in the parsers are cases where the syntactic analysis more closely resembles the analysis of dependency structure that results from applying Yamada and Matsumoto's head-finding rules to the Penn Treebank. Figure 4 shows different parses produced by parsers trained on dif-

[3]In terms of constituency analysis, a prepositional phrase should consist of a preposition governing a single noun phrase

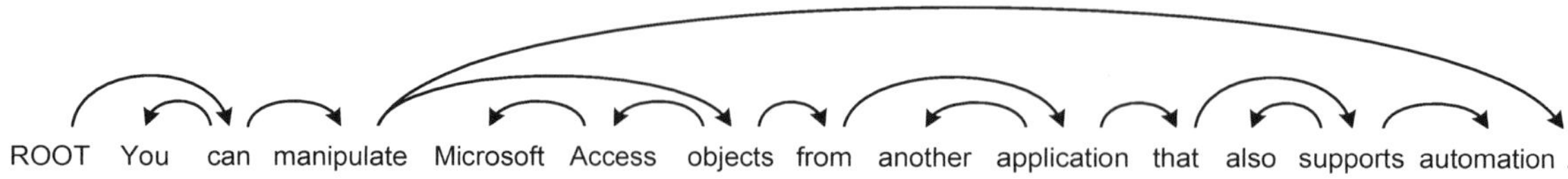

(a) Dependency analysis produced by parser trained on 250 Wall Street Journal sentences.

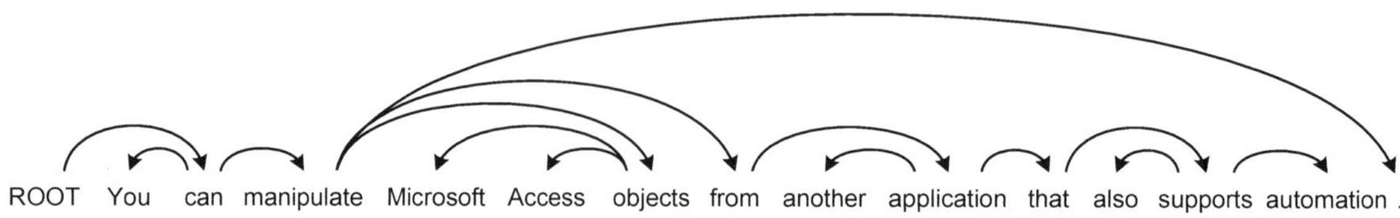

(b) Dependency analysis produced by parser trained on 39,892 Wall Street Journal sentences.

Figure 4: Parses produced by parsers trained on different numbers of sentences.

ferent numbers of sentences. The parser trained on 250 sentences incorrectly attaches the preposition "from" as a dependent of the noun "objects" whereas the parser trained on the complete Penn Treebank training section correctly attaches the preposition as a dependent of the verb "manipulate". These two parsers also yield different analyses of the phrase "Microsoft Access objects". In parse (a), "objects" governs "Office" and "Office" in turn governs "Microsoft". This analysis is linguistically well-motivated, and makes a treelet spanning "Microsoft Office" available to the treelet translation system. In parse (b), the parser has analyzed this phrase so that "objects" directly governs "Microsoft" and "Office". The analysis more closely reflects the flat branching structure of the Penn Treebank but obscures the affinity of "Microsoft" and "Office".

An additional measure of parse utility for MT is the amount of translation material that can be extracted from a parallel corpus. We increased the parser training data from 250 sentences to 39,986 sentences, but held the number of aligned sentence pairs used train other modules constant. The count of treelet translation pairs occurring at least twice in the English-German parallel corpus grew from 1,895,007 to 2,010,451.

4 Conclusions

We return now to the questions and concerns raised in the introduction. First, is a treelet SMT system sensitive to parse quality? We have shown that such a system *is* sensitive to the quality of the input syntactic analyses. With the less accurate parsers that result from training on extremely small numbers of sentences, performance is comparable to state-of-the-art phrasal SMT systems. As the amount of data used to train the parser increases, both English-to-German and English-to-Japanese treelet SMT improve, and produce results that are statistically significantly better than the phrasal baseline.

Error category	Regress	Improve
Attachment of prep	1%	22%
Root identification	13%	28%
Final punctuation	18%	30%
Coordination	6%	16%
Dependent verbs	14%	32%
Arguments of verb	6%	15%
NP identification	24%	33%
Dependent of prep	0%	7%
Other attachment	3%	22%

Table 4: Error analysis, showing percentage of regressed and improved translations exhibiting a parse improvement in each specified category

In the introduction we mentioned the concern that others have raised when we have presented our research: syntax might contain valuable information but current parsers might not be of sufficient quality. It is certainly true that the accuracy of the best parser used here falls well short of what we might hope for. A parser that achieves 90.8% dependency accuracy when trained on the Penn Treebank Wall Street Journal corpus and evaluated on comparable text degrades to 84.3% accuracy when evaluated on technical text. Despite the degradation in parse accuracy caused by the dramatic differences between the Wall Street Journal text and the technical articles, the treelet SMT system was able to extract useful patterns. Research on syntactically-informed SMT is not impeded by the accuracy of contemporary parsers.

One significant finding is that as few as 250 sentences suffice to train a dependency parser for use in the treelet SMT framework. To date our research has focused on translation from English to other languages. One concern in applying the treelet SMT framework to translation from languages other than English has been the expense of data annotation: would we require 40,000 sentences annotated for syntactic dependencies, i.e., an amount comparable to the Penn Treebank, in order to train a parser that was sufficiently accurate to achieve the machine translation quality that we have seen when translating from English? The current study gives hope that source languages can be added with relatively modest investments in data annotation. As more data is annotated with syntactic dependencies and more accurate parsers are trained, we would hope to see similar improvements in machine translation output.

We challenge others who are conducting research on syntactically-informed SMT to verify whether or to what extent their systems are sensitive to parse quality.

References

M. Collins. 2002. Discriminative training methods for hidden markov models: Theory and experiments with perceptron algorithms. In *Proceedings of EMNLP*.

Simon Corston-Oliver and Michael Gamon. 2004. Normalizing German and English inflectional morphology to improve statistical word alignment. In R. E. Frederking and K. B. Taylor, editors, *Machine translation: From real users to research*. Springer Verlag.

Simon Corston-Oliver, Anthony Aue, Kevin Duh, and Eric Ringger. 2006. Multilingual dependency parsing using Bayes Point Machines. In *Proceedings of HLT/NAACL*.

Jason M. Eisner. 1996. Three new probabilistic models for dependency parsing: An exploration. In *Proceedings of COLING*, pages 340–345.

Michael Gamon, Eric Ringger, Zhu Zhang, Robert Moore, and Simon Corston-Oliver. 2002. Extraposition: A case study in German sentence realization. In *Proceedings of COLING*, pages 301–307.

Joshua Goodman. 2001. A bit of progress in language modeling, extended version. Technical Report MSR-TR-2001-72, Microsoft Research.

Edward Harrington, Ralf Herbrich, Jyrki Kivinen, John C. Platt, and Robert C. Williamson. 2003. Online bayes point machines. In *Proc. 7th Pacific-Asia Conference on Knowledge Discovery and Data Mining*, pages 241–252.

Ralf Herbrich, Thore Graepel, and Colin Campbell. 2001. Bayes Point Machines. *Journal of Machine Learning Research*, pages 245–278.

Philipp Koehn, Franz Josef Och, and Daniel Marcu. 2003. Statistical phrase-based translation. In *Proceedings of HLT/NAACL*.

M. Marcus, B. Santorini, and M. Marcinkiewicz. 1993. Building a large annotated corpus of english: The Penn Treebank. *Computational Linguistics*, 19(2):313–330.

Igor A. Melčuk. 1988. *Dependency Syntax: Theory and Practice*. State University of New York Press.

Franz Josef Och and Hermann Ney. 2000. Improved statistical alignment models. In *Proceedings of the ACL*, pages 440–447, Hongkong, China, October.

Franz Josef Och. 2003. Minimum error rate training in statistical machine translation. In *Proceedings of the ACL*.

Kishore Papineni, Salim Roukos, Todd Ward, and Wei-Jing Zhu. 2002. Bleu: a method for automatic evaluation of machine translation. In *Proceedings of the ACL*, pages 311–318, Philadelpha, Pennsylvania.

Chris Quirk, Arul Menezes, and Colin Cherry. 2005. Dependency treelet translation: Syntactically informed phrasal SMT. In *Proceedings of the ACL*.

Lucien Tesnière. 1959. *Éléments de syntaxe structurale*. Librairie C. Klincksieck.

Kristina Toutanova, Dan Klein, Christopher D. Manning, and Yoram Singer. 2003. Feature-rich part-of-speech tagging with a cyclic dependency network. In *Proceedings of HLT/EMNLP*, pages 252–259.

Stephan Vogel, Ying Zhang, Fei Huang, Alicia Tribble, Ashish Venugopal, Bing Zhao, and Alex Waibel. 2003. The CMU statistical machine translation system. In *Proceedings of the MT Summit*.

Hiroyasu Yamada and Yuji Matsumoto. 2003. Statistical dependency analysis with support vector machines. In *Proceedings of IWPT*, pages 195–206.

Ying Zhang and Stephan Vogel. 2004. Measuring confidence intervals for mt evaluation metrics. In *Proceedings of TMI*.

Statistical Machine Reordering

Marta R. Costa-jussà and **José A. R. Fonollosa**
Department of Signal Theory and Communications
TALP Research Center (UPC)
Barcelona 08034, Spain
(mruiz,adrian)@gps.tsc.upc.edu

Abstract

Reordering is currently one of the most important problems in statistical machine translation systems. This paper presents a novel strategy for dealing with it: statistical machine reordering (SMR). It consists in using the powerful techniques developed for statistical machine translation (SMT) to translate the source language (*S*) into a reordered source language (*S'*), which allows for an improved translation into the target language (*T*). The SMT task changes from *S2T* to *S'2T* which leads to a monotonized word alignment and shorter translation units. In addition, the use of classes in SMR helps to infer new word reorderings. Experiments are reported in the EsEn WMT06 tasks and the ZhEn IWSLT05 task and show significant improvement in translation quality.

1 Introduction

During the last few years, SMT systems have evolved from the original word-based approach (Brown et al., 1993) to phrase-based translation systems (Koehn et al., 2003). In parallel to the phrase-based approach, the use of bilingual n-grams gives comparable results, as shown by Crego et al. (2005a). Two basic issues differentiate the n-gram-based system from the phrase-based: training data are monotonously segmented into bilingual units; and, the model considers n-gram probabilities rather than relative frequencies. This translation approach is described in detail by Mariño et al. (2005). The n-gram-based system follows a maximum entropy approach, in which a log-linear combination of multiple models is implemented (Och and Ney, 2002), as an alternative to the source-channel approach.

In both systems, introducing reordering capabilities is of crucial importance for certain language pairs. Recently, new reordering strategies have been proposed in the literature on SMT such as the reordering of each source sentence to match the word order in the corresponding target sentence, see Kanthak et al. (2005) and Crego et al. (2005b). Similarly, Matusov et al. (2006) describe a method for simultaneously aligning and monotonizing the training corpus. The main problems of these approaches are: (1) the fact that the proposed monotonization is based on the alignment and cannot be applied to the test sets, and (2) the lack of reordering generalization.

This paper presents a reordering approach called statistical machine reordering (SMR) which improves the reordering capabilities of SMT systems without incurring any of the problems mentioned above. SMR is a first-pass translation performed on the source corpus, which converts it into an intermediate representation, in which source-language words are presented in an order that more closely matches that of the target language. SMR and SMT are performed using the same modeling tools as n-gram-based systems but using different statistical log-linear models.

In order to be able to infer new reorderings we use word classes instead of words themselves as the input to the SMR system. In fact, the use of classes to help in the reordering is a key difference between our approach and standard SMT systems.

This paper is organized as follows: Section 2 outlines the baseline system. Section 3 describes the reordering strategy in detail. Section 4 presents and discusses the results, and Section 5 presents our conclusions and suggestions for further work.

Proceedings of the 2006 Conference on Empirical Methods in Natural Language Processing (EMNLP 2006), pages 70–76,
Sydney, July 2006.

2 N-gram-based SMT System

This section briefly describes the n-gram-based SMT which uses a translation model based on bilingual n-grams. It is actually a language model of bilingual units, referred to as tuples, which approximates the joint probability between source and target languages by using bilingual n-grams (de Gispert and Mariño, 2002).

Bilingual units (tuples) are extracted from any word alignment according to the following constraints:

1. a monotonous segmentation of each bilingual sentence pairs is produced,
2. no word inside the tuple is aligned to words outside the tuple, and
3. no smaller tuples can be extracted without violating the previous constraints.

As a result of these constraints, only one segmentation is possible for a given sentence pair.

Figure 1 presents a simple example which illustrates the tuple extraction process.

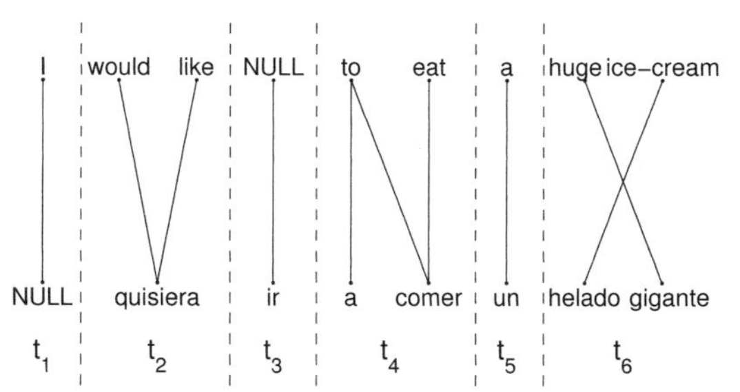

Figure 1: *Example of tuple extraction from an aligned bilingual sentence pair.*

Two important issues regarding this translation model must be considered. First, it often occurs that large number of single-word translation probabilities are left out of the model. This happens for all words that are always embedded in tuples containing two or more words. Consider for example the word "ice-cream" in Figure 1. As seen from the Figure, "ice-cream" is embedded into tuple t_6. If a similar situation is encountered for all occurrences of "ice-cream" in the training corpus, then no translation probability for an independent occurrence of this word will exist.

To overcome this problem, the tuple 4-gram model is enhanced by incorporating 1-gram translation probabilities for all the embedded words detected during the tuple extraction step. These 1-gram translation probabilities are computed from the intersection of both, the source-to-target and the target-to-source alignments.

The second issue has to do with the fact that some words linked to NULL end up producing tuples with NULL source sides. Consider for example the tuple t_3 in Figure 1. Since no NULL is actually expected to occur in translation inputs, this type of tuple is not allowed. Any target word that is linked to NULL is attached either to the word that precedes or the word that follows it. To determine this, we use the $IBM1$ probabilities, see Crego et al. (2005a).

In addition to the bilingual n-gram translation model, the baseline system implements a log-linear combination of four feature functions, which are described as follows:

- A **target language model**. This feature consists of a 4-gram model of words, which is trained from the target side of the bilingual corpus.
- A **word bonus function**. This feature introduces a bonus based on the number of target words contained in the partial-translation hypothesis. It is used to compensate for the system's preference for short output sentences.
- A **source-to-target lexicon model**. This feature, which is based on the lexical parameters of the IBM Model 1 (Brown et al., 1993), provides a complementary probability for each tuple in the translation table. These lexicon parameters are obtained from the source-to-target alignments.
- A **target-to-source lexicon model**. Similarly to the previous feature, this feature is based on the lexical parameters of the IBM Model 1 but, in this case, these parameters are obtained from target-to-source alignments.

All these models are combined in the decoder. Additionally, the decoder allows for a non-monotonous search with the following distorsion model.

- A word distance-based **distorsion model**.

$$P(t_1^K) = exp(-\sum_{k=1}^{K} d_k)$$

where d_k is the distance between the first word of the kth tuple (unit), and the last word+1 of the $(k-1)^{th}$ tuple. Distance are measured in words referring to the units source side.

To reduce the computational cost we place limits on the search using two parameters: the distortion limit (the maximum distance measured in words that a tuple is allowed to be reordered, m) and the reordering limit (the maximum number of reordering jumps in a sentence, j). This feature is independent of the reordering approach presented in this paper, so they can be used simultaneously.

In order to combine the models in the decoder suitably, an optimization tool is needed to compute log-linear weights for each model.

3 Statistical Machine Reordering

As mentioned in the introduction, SMR and SMT are based on the same principles. Here, we give a detailed description of the SMR reordering approach proposed.

3.1 Concept

The aim of SMR consists in using an SMT system to deal with reordering problems. Therefore, the SMR system can be seen as an SMT system which translates from an original source language (*S*) to a reordered source language (*S'*), given a target language (*T*). Then, the translation tasks changes from *S2T* to *S'2T*. The main difference between the two tasks is that the latter allows for: (1) monotonized word alignment, and (2) higher quality monotonized translation.

3.2 Description

Figure 2 shows the SMR block diagram. The input is the initial source sentence (*S*) and the output is the reordered source sentence (*S'*). There three blocks inside SMR: (1) class replacing ; (2) the decoder, which requires the translation model; and, (3) the block which reorders the original sentence using the indexes given by the decoder. The following example specifies the input and output of each block inside the SMR.

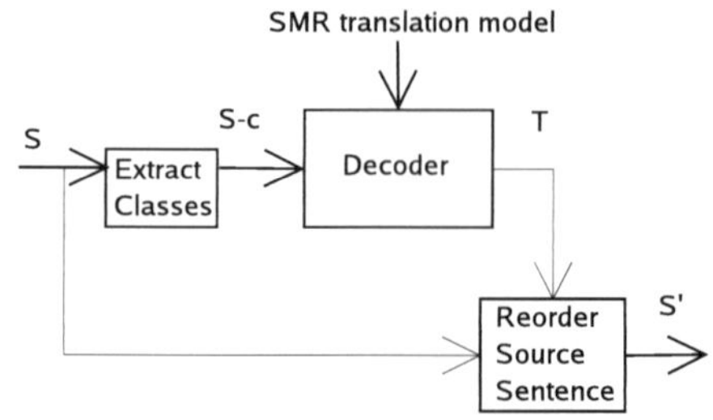

Figure 2: *SMR block diagram.*

1. Source sentence (*S*):

   El compromiso sólo podría mejorar

2. Source sentence classes (*S-c*):

   C38 C43 C49 C42 C22

3. Decoder output (translation, *T*):

   C38#0 | C43 C49 C42#1 2 0 | C22#0

   where | indicates the segmentation into translation units and # divides the source and target. The source part is composed of word classes and the target part is composed of the new positions of the source word classes, starting at 0.

4. SMR output (*S'*). The reordering information inside each translation unit of the decoder output (*T*) is applied to the original source sentence (*S*):

   El sólo podría compromiso mejorar

3.3 Training

For the reordering translation, we used an n-gram-based SMT system (and considered only the translation model). Figure 3 shows the block diagram of the training process of the SMR translation model, which is a bilingual n-gram-based model. The training process uses the training source and target corpora and consists of the following steps:

1. Determine source and target word classes.

2. Align parallel training sentences at the word level in both translation directions. Compute the union of the two alignments to obtain a symmetrized many-to-many word alignment.

3. Extract reordering tuples, see Figure 4.

   (a) From union word alignment, extract bilingual *S2T* tuples (i.e. source and target fragments) while maintaining the

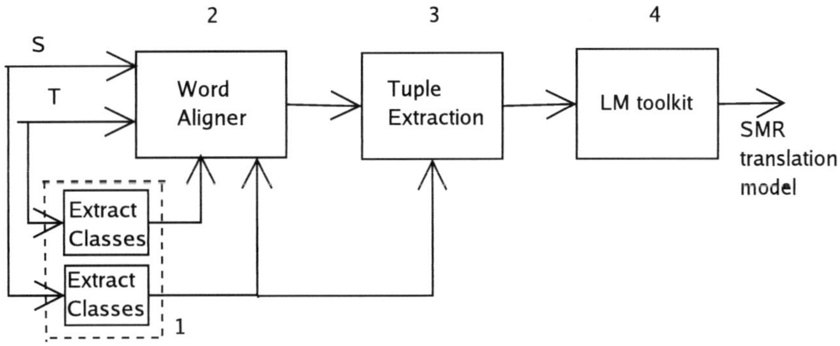

Figure 3: *Block diagram of the training process of the SMR translation model.*

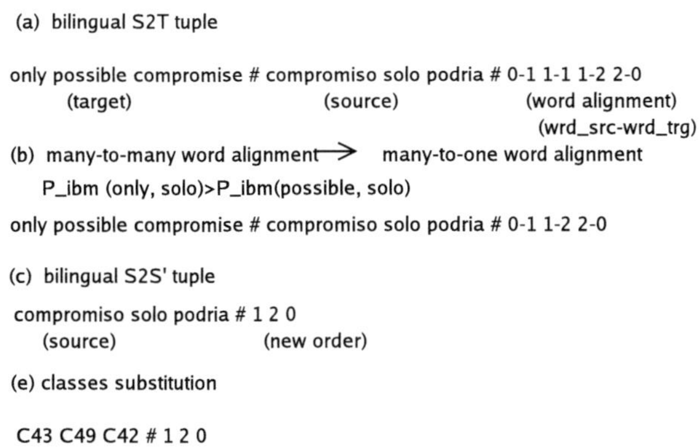

Figure 4: *Example of the extraction of reordering tuples (step 3).*

alignment inside the tuple. As an example of a bilingual *S2T* tuple consider: *only possible compromise # compromiso sólo podría # 0-1 1-1 1-2 2-0*, as shown in Figure 4, where the different fields are separated by # and correspond to: (1) the target fragment; (2) the source fragment; and (3) the word alignment (in this case, the fields that respectively correspond to a target and source word are separated by –).

(b) Modify the many-to-many word alignment from each tuple to many-to-one. If one source word is aligned to two or more target words, the most probable link given IBM Model 1 is chosen, while the other are omitted (i.e. the number of source words is the same before and after the reordering translation). In the above example, the tuple would be changed to: *only possible compromise # compromiso sólo podría # 0-1 1-2 2-0*, as P_{ibm1}(only, sólo) is higher than P_{ibm1}(possible, sólo).

(c) From bilingual *S2T* tuples (with many-to-one inside alignment), extract bilingual *S2S'* tuples (i.e. the source fragment and its reordering). As in the example: *compromiso sólo podría # 1 2 0*, where the first field is the source fragment, and the second is the reordering of these source words.

(d) Eliminate tuples whose source fragment consists of the NULL word.

(e) Replace the words of each tuple source fragment with the classes determined in Step 1.

4. Compute the bilingual language model of the bilingual *S2S'* tuple sequence composed of the source fragment (in classes) and its reorder.

Once the translation model is built, the original source corpus *S* is translated into the reordered source corpus *S'* with the SMR system, see Figure 2. The reordered training source corpus and the original training target corpus are used to train the SMT system (as explained in Section 2). Finally, with this system, the reordered test source corpus is translated.

4 Evaluation Framework

In this section, we present experiments carried out using the EsEn WMT06 and the ZhEn IWSLT05 parallel corpus. We detail the tools which have been used and the corpus statistics.

EuroParl	*Spanish*	*English*
Training Sentences	727.1 k	727.1 k
Words	15.7 M	15.2 M
Vocabulary	108.7 k	72.3 k
Development Sentences	500	500
Words	15.2 k	14.8 k
Vocabulary	3.6 k	3 k
Test Sentences	3064	3064
Words	91.9 k	85.2 k
Vocabulary	11.1 k	9.1 k

Table 1: *Spanish to English task. EuroParl corpus: training, development and test data sets.*

BTEC	*Chinese*	*English*
Training Sentences	20 k	20 k
Words	176.2 k	182.3 k
Vocabulary	8.7 k	7.3 k
Development Sentences	506	506
Words	3.5 k	3.3 k
Vocabulary	870	799
Test Sentences	506	506
Words	4 k	3 k
Vocabulary	916	818

Table 2: *Chinese to English task. BTEC corpus: training, development and test data sets. Development and test data sets have 16 references.*

4.1 Tools

- The word alignments were computed using the GIZA++ tool (Och, 2003).
- The word classes were determined using 'mkcls', a freely-available tool with GIZA++.
- The language model was estimated using the SRILM toolkit (Stolcke, 2002).
- We used MARIE as a decoder (Crego et al., 2005b).
- The optimization tool used for computing log-linear weights (see Section 2) is based on the simplex method (Nelder and Mead, 1965).

4.2 Corpus Statistics

Experiments were carried out on the Spanish and English task of the WMT06 evaluation[1] (EuroParl Corpus) and on the Chinese to English task of the IWSLT05 evaluation[2] (BTEC Corpus). The former is a large corpus, whereas the latter is a small corpus translation task. Table 1 and 2 show the main statistics of the data used, namely the number of sentences, words, vocabulary, and mean sentence lengths for each language.

4.3 Units

In this section different statistics units of both approaches (*S2T* and *S'2T*) are shown (using the ZhEn task). All the experiments in this section were carried out using 100 classes in the SMR step.

Table 3 shows the vocabulary of bilingual n-grams and embedded words in the translation model. Once the reordering translation has been computed, alignment becomes more monotonic. It is commonly known that non-monotonicity poses difficulties for word alignments. Therefore, when the alignment becomes more monotonic, we expect an improvement in the alignment, and, therefore in the translation. Here, we can observe a significant enlargement of the number of translation units, which leads to a growth of the translation vocabulary. We also observe a decrease in the number of embedded words (around 20%). From Section 2, we know that the probability of embedded words is estimated independently of the translation model. Reducing embedded words allows for a better estimation of the translation model.

Figure 5 shows the histogram of the tuple size in the two approaches. We observe that the number of tuples is similar over length 5. However, there are a greater number of shorter units in the case of SMR+NB (shorter units lead to a reduction in data sparseness).

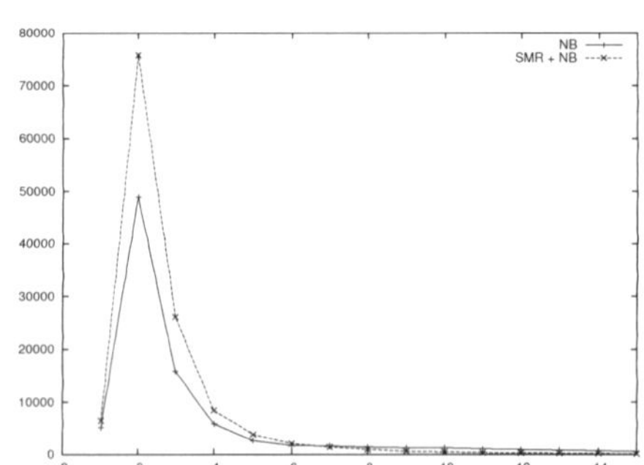

Figure 5: *Comparison of the histogram of the tuple size in the two approaches (NB and SMR+NB).*

[1] www.statmt.org/wmt06/shared-task/

[2] www.slt.atr.jp/IWSLT2005

System	1gr	2gr	3gr	4gr	Embedded
NB	34487	57597	3536	1918	5735
SMR + NB	35638	70947	5894	3412	4632

Table 3: *Vocabulary of n-grams and embedded words in the translation model.*

System	Total	Vocabulary
NB	4460	959
SMR + NB	4628	1052

Table 4: *Tuples used to translate the test set (total number and vocabulary).*

Table 4 shows the tuples used to translate the test set (total number and vocabulary). Note that the number of tuples and vocabulary used to translate the test set is significantly greater after the reordering translation.

4.4 Results

Here, we introduce the experiments that were carried out in order to evaluate the influence of the SMR approach in both tasks EsEn and ZhEn. The log-linear translation model was optimized with the simplex algorithm by maximizing over the BLEU score. The evaluation was carried out using references and translation in lowercase and, in the ZhEn task, without punctuation marks.

We studied the influence of the proposed SMR approach on the n-gram-based SMT system described using a monotonous search (NBm or monotonous baseline configuration) in the two tasks and a non-monotonous search (NBnm or non-monotonous baseline configuration) in the ZhEn task. In allowing for reordering in the SMT decoder, the distortion limit (m) and reordering limit (j) (see Section 2) were empirically set to 5 and 3, as they showed a good trade-off between quality and efficiency. Both systems include the four features explained in Section 2: the language model, the word bonus, and the source-to-target and target-to-source lexicon models.

Tables 5 and 6 show the results in the test set. The former corresponds to the influence of the SMR system on the EsEn task (NBm), whereas the latter corresponds to the influence of the SMR system on the ZhEn task (NBm and NBnm).

4.5 Discussion

Both BLEU and NIST coherently increase after the inclusion of the SMR step when 100 classes are used. The improvement in translation quality can be explained as follows:

- SMR takes advantage of the use of classes and correctly captures word reorderings that are missed in the standard SMT system. In addition, the use of classes allows new reorderings to be inferred.
- The new task *S'2T* becomes more monotonous. Therefore, the translation units tend to be shorter and SMT systems perform better.

The gain obtained in the SMR+NBnm case indicates that the reordering provided by SMR system and the non-monotonous search are complementary. It means that the output of the SMR could still be further monotonized. Note that the ZhEn task has complex word reorderings.

These preliminary results also show that SMR itself provides further improvements to those provided by the non-monotonous search.

5 Conclusions and Further Research

In this paper we have mainly dealt with the reordering problem for an n-gram-based SMT system. However, our approach could be used similarly for a phrase-based system. We have addressed the reordering problem as a translation from the source sentence to a monotonized source sentence. The proposed SMR system is applied before a standard SMT system. The SMR and SMT systems are based on the same principles and share the same type of decoder.

In extracting bilingual units, the change of order performed in the source sentence has allowed the modeling of the translation units to be improved (shorter units mean a reduction in data sparseness). Also, note that the SMR approach allows the coherence between the change of order in the training and test source corpora to be maintained.

System	Classes	BLEU	NIST	WER	PER
NBm	-	27.69	7.31	61.6	45.34
SMR + NBm	-	28.60	7.53	59.89	43.53
SMR + NBm	100	30.89	7.75	55.77	42.85

Table 5: *Results in the test set of the EsEn task using a monotonous search.*

System	Classes	BLEU	NIST	WER	PER
NBm	-	42.42	8.3	42.87	33.44
NBnm	-	43.58	8.9	43.89	34.05
SMR + NBm	100	43.75	8.49	42.45	33.85
SMR + NBnm	100	45.97	9.0	40.92	32.32

Table 6: *Results in the test set of the ZhEn task using a monotonous and a non-monotonous search.*

Performing reordering as a preprocessing step and independently from the SMT system allows for a more efficient final system implementation and a quicker translation. Additionally, using word classes helps to infer unseen reorderings. These preliminary results show consistent and significant improvements in translation quality.

As further research, we would like to add extra features to the SMR system, and study new types of classes for the reordering task.

6 Acknowledgments

This work has been partially funded by the European Union under the integrated project TC-STAR - Technology and Corpora for Speech to Speech Translation - (IST-2002-FP6-506738, http://www.tc-star.org) and the Spanish government under a FPU grant.

References

E. Matusov A. Mauser and H. Ney. 2006. Training a statistical machine translation system without giza++. *5th Int. Conf. on Language Resources and Evaluation, LREC'06*, May.

P. Brown, S. Della Pietra, V. Della Pietra, and R. Mercer. 1993. The mathematics of statistical machine translation. *Computational Linguistics*, 19(2):263–311.

J. M. Crego, M. R. Costa-jussà, J. Mariño, and J. A. Fonollosa. 2005a. Ngram-based versus phrase-based statistical machine translation. *Proc. of the Int. Workshop on Spoken Language Translation, IWSLT'05*, October.

J.M. Crego, J. Mariño, and A. de Gispert. 2005b. An Ngram-based statistical machine translation decoder. *Proc. of the 9th Int. Conf. on Spoken Language Processing, ICSLP'05*.

A. de Gispert and J. Mariño. 2002. Using X-grams for speech-to-speech translation. *Proc. of the 7th Int. Conf. on Spoken Language Processing, ICSLP'02*, September.

S. Kanthak, D. Vilar, E. Matusov, R. Zens, and H. Ney. 2005. Novel reordering approaches in phrase-based statistical machine translation. *Proceedings of the ACL Workshop on Building and Using Parallel Texts: Data-Driven Machine Translation and Beyond*, pages 167–174, June.

P. Koehn, F.J. Och, and D. Marcu. 2003. Statistical phrase-based translation. *Proc. of the Human Language Technology Conference, HLT-NAACL'2003*, May.

J.B. Mariño, R.E. Banchs, J.M. Crego, A. de Gispert, P. Lambert, J.A.R. Fonollosa, and M. Ruiz. 2005. Bilingual n-gram statistical machine translation. In *Proc. of the MT Summit X*, pages 275–82, Pukhet (Thailand), May.

J.A. Nelder and R. Mead. 1965. A simplex method for function minimization. *The Computer Journal*, 7:308–313.

F.J. Och and H. Ney. 2002. Discriminative training and maximum entropy models for statistical machine translation. *40th Annual Meeting of the Association for Computational Linguistics*, pages 295–302, July.

F.J. Och. 2003. Giza++ software. http://www-i6.informatik.rwth-aachen.de/~och/ software/giza++.html.

A. Stolcke. 2002. Srilm - an extensible language modeling toolkit. *Proc. of the 7th Int. Conf. on Spoken Language Processing, ICSLP'02*, September.

Re-evaluating Machine Translation Results with Paraphrase Support

Liang Zhou, Chin-Yew Lin, and Eduard Hovy
University of Southern California
Information Sciences Institute
4676 Admiralty Way
Marina del Rey, CA 90292-6695
{liangz, cyl, hovy} @isi.edu

Abstract

In this paper, we present ParaEval, an automatic evaluation framework that uses paraphrases to improve the quality of machine translation evaluations. Previous work has focused on fixed *n-gram* evaluation metrics coupled with lexical identity matching. ParaEval addresses three important issues: support for paraphrase/synonym matching, recall measurement, and correlation with human judgments. We show that ParaEval correlates significantly better than BLEU with human assessment in measurements for both *fluency* and *adequacy*.

1 Introduction

The introduction of automated evaluation procedures, such as BLEU (Papineni et al., 2001) for machine translation (MT) and ROUGE (Lin and Hovy, 2003) for summarization, have prompted much progress and development in both of these areas of research in Natural Language Processing (NLP). Both evaluation tasks employ a comparison strategy for comparing textual units from machine-generated and gold-standard texts. Ideally, this comparison process would be performed manually, because of humans' abilities to infer, paraphrase, and use world knowledge to relate differently worded pieces of equivalent information. However, manual evaluations are time consuming and expensive, thus making them a bottleneck in system development cycles.

BLEU measures how close machine-generated translations are to professional human translations, and ROUGE does the same with respect to summaries. Both methods incorporate the comparison of a system-produced text to one or more corresponding reference texts. The closeness between texts is measured by the computation of a numeric score based on n-gram co-occurrence statistics. Although both methods have gained mainstream acceptance and have shown good correlations with human judgments, their deficiencies have become more evident and serious as research in MT and summarization progresses (Callison-Burch et al., 2006).

Text comparisons in MT and summarization evaluations are performed at different text granularity levels. Since most of the phrase-based, syntax-based, and rule-based MT systems translate one sentence at a time, the text comparison in the evaluation process is also performed at the single-sentence level. In summarization evaluations, there is no sentence-to-sentence correspondence between summary pairs—essentially a multi-sentence-to-multi-sentence comparison, making it more difficult and requiring a completely different implementation for matching strategies. In this paper, we focus on the intricacies involved in evaluating MT results and address two prominent problems associated with the BLEU-esque metrics, namely their lack of support for paraphrase matching and the absence of recall scoring. Our solution, ParaEval, utilizes a large collection of paraphrases acquired through an unsupervised process—identifying phrase sets that have the same translation in another language—using state-of-the-art statistical MT word alignment and phrase extraction methods. This collection facilitates paraphrase matching, additionally coupled with lexical identity matching which is designed for comparing text/sentence fragments that are not consumed by paraphrase matching. We adopt a unigram counting strategy for contents matched between sentences from peer and reference translations. This unweighted scoring scheme, for both precision and recall computations, allows us to directly examine both the power and limitations of

Proceedings of the 2006 Conference on Empirical Methods in Natural Language Processing (EMNLP 2006), pages 77–84,
Sydney, July 2006.

ParaEval. We show that ParaEval is a more stable and reliable comparison mechanism than BLEU, in both fluency and adequacy rankings.

This paper is organized in the following way: Section 2 shows an overview on BLEU and lexical identity n-gram statistics; we describe ParaEval's implementation in detail in Section 3; the evaluation of ParaEval is shown in Section 4; recall computation is discussed in Section 5; in Section 6, we discuss the differences between BLEU and ParaEval when the numbers of reference translations change; and we conclude and discuss future work in Section 7.

2 N-gram Co-occurrence Statistics

Being an $8 billion industry (Browner, 2006), MT calls for rapid development and the ability to differentiate good systems from less adequate ones. The evaluation process consists of comparing system-generated *peer translations* to human written *reference translations* and assigning a numeric score to each system. While human assessments are still the most reliable evaluation measurements, it is not practical to solicit manual evaluations repeatedly while making incremental system design changes that would only result in marginal performance gains. To overcome the monetary and time constraints associated with manual evaluations, automated procedures have been successful in delivering benchmarks for performance hill-climbing with little or no cost.

While a variety of automatic evaluation methods have been introduced, the underlining comparison strategy is similar—matching based on lexical identity. The most prominent implementation of this type of matching is demonstrated in BLEU (Papineni et al, 2002). The remaining part of this section is devoted to an overview of BLEU, or the BLEU-esque philosophy.

2.1 The BLEU-esque Matching Philosophy

The primary task that a BLEU-esque procedure performs is to compare n-grams from the peer translation with the n-grams from one or more reference translations and count the number of matches. The more matches a peer translation gets, the better it is.

BLEU is a precision-based metric, which is the ratio of the number of n-grams from the peer translation that occurred in reference translations to the total number of n-grams in the peer translation. The notion of *Modified n-gram Precision* was introduced to detect and avoid rewarding false positives generated by translation systems. To gain high precision, systems could potentially over-generate "good" n-grams, which occur multiple times in multiple references. The solution to this problem was to adopt the policy that an n-gram, from both reference and peer translations, is considered exhausted after participating in a match. As a result, the maximum number of matches an n-gram from a peer translation can receive, when comparing to a set of reference translations, is the maximum number of times this n-gram occurred in any single reference translation. Papineni et al. (2002) called this capping technique *clipping*. Figure 1, taken from the original BLEU paper, demonstrates the computation of the modified unigram precision for a peer translation sentence.

Candidate: `the the the the the the the.`
Reference 1: `The cat is on the mat.`
Reference 2: `There is a cat on the mat.`
Modified Unigram Precision = 2/7.[3]

Figure 1. Modified *n*-gram precision from BLEU.

To compute the modified n-gram precision, P_n, for a whole test set, including all translation segments (usually in sentences), the formula is:

$$P_n = \frac{\sum_{C \in \{peers\}} \sum_{n\text{-}gram \in C} Count_{clip}(n-gram)}{\sum_{C \in \{peers\}} \sum_{n\text{-}gram \in C} Count(n-gram)}$$

2.2 Lack of Paraphrasing Support

Humans are very good at finding creative ways to convey the same information. There is no one definitive reference translation in one language for a text written in another. Having acknowledged this phenomenon, however natural it is, human evaluations on system-generated translations are much more preferred and trusted. However, what humans can do with ease puts machines at a loss. BLEU-esque procedures recognize equivalence only when two n-grams exhibit the same surface-level representations, i.e. the same lexical identities. The BLEU implementation addresses its deficiency in measuring semantic closeness by incorporating the comparison with multiple reference translations. The rationale is that multiple references give a higher chance that the n-grams, assuming correct translations, appearing in the peer translation would be rewarded by one of the reference's n-grams. The more reference translations used, the better the matching and overall evaluation quality. Ideally (and to an extreme), we would need to collect a large set of human-written translations to capture all possible combinations of verbalizing variations before the translation comparison procedure reaches its optimal matching ability.

One can argue that an infinite number of references are not needed in practice because any matching procedure would stabilize at a certain number of references. This is true if precision measure is the only metric computed. However, using precision scores alone unfairly rewards systems that "under-generate"—producing unreasonably short translations. Recall measurements would provide more balanced evaluations. When using multiple reference translations, if an n-gram match is made for the peer, this n-gram could appear in any of the references. The computation of recall becomes difficult, if not impossible. This problem can be reversed if there is crosschecking for phrases occurring across references—paraphrase recognition. BLEU uses the calculation of a brevity penalty to compensate the lack of recall computation problem. The brevity penalty is computed as follows:

$$\mathrm{BP} = \begin{cases} 1 & \text{if } c > r \\ e^{(1-r/c)} & \text{if } c \le r \end{cases}$$

Then, the BLEU score for a peer translation is computed as:

$$\mathrm{BLEU} = \mathrm{BP} \cdot \exp\left(\sum_{n=1}^{N} w_n \log p_n\right)$$

BLEU's adoption of the brevity penalty to offset the effect of not having a recall computation has drawn criticism on its crudeness in measuring translation quality. Callison-Burch et al. (2006) point out three prominent factors:

- ``Synonyms and paraphrases are only handled if they are in the set of multiple reference translations [available].
- The scores for words are equally weighted so missing out on content-bearing material brings no additional penalty.
- The brevity penalty is a stop-gap measure to compensate for the fairly serious problem of not being able to calculate recall."

With the introduction of ParaEval, we will address two of these three issues, namely the paraphrasing problem and providing a recall measure.

3 ParaEval for MT Evaluation

3.1 Overview

Reference translations are created from the same source text (written in the foreign language) to the target language. Ideally, they are supposed to be semantically equivalent, i.e. overlap completely. However, as shown in Figure 2, when matching based on lexical identity is used (indicated by links), only half (6 from the left and 5 from the right) of the 12 words from these two sentences are matched. Also, "to" was a mismatch. In applying paraphrase matching for MT evaluation from ParaEval, we aim to match all shaded words from both sentences.

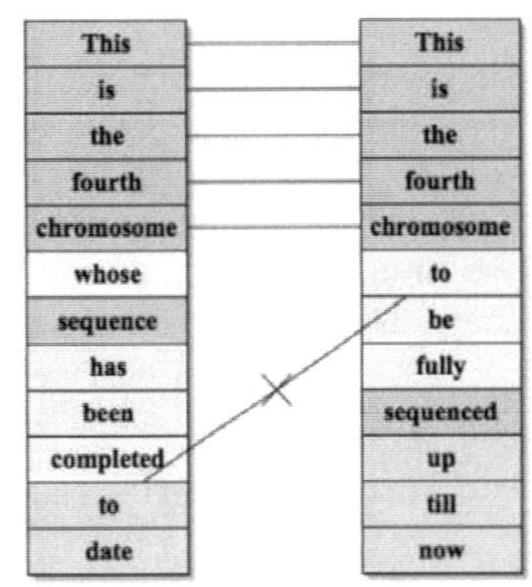

Figure 2. Two reference translations. Grey areas are matched by using BLEU.

3.2 Paraphrase Acquisition

The process of acquiring a large enough collection of paraphrases is not an easy task. Manual corpus analyses produce domain-specific collections that are used for text generation and are application-specific. But operating in multiple domains and for multiple tasks translates into multiple manual collection efforts, which could be very time-consuming and costly. In order to facilitate smooth paraphrase utilization across a variety of NLP applications, we need an unsupervised paraphrase collection mechanism that can be easily conducted, and produces paraphrases that are of adequate quality and can be readily used with minimal amount of adaptation effort.

Our method (Anonymous, 2006), also illustrated in (Bannard and Callison-Burch, 2005), to automatically construct a large domain-independent paraphrase collection is based on the assumption that two different phrases of the same meaning may have the same translation in a

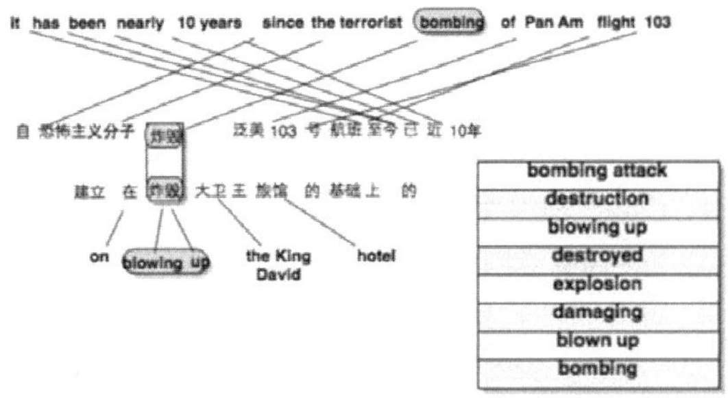

Figure 3. An example of the paraphrase extraction process.

foreign language. Phrase-based Statistical Machine Translation (SMT) systems analyze large quantities of bilingual parallel texts in order to learn translational alignments between pairs of words and phrases in two languages (Och and Ney, 2004). The sentence-based translation model makes word/phrase alignment decisions probabilistically by computing the optimal model parameters with application of the statistical estimation theory. This alignment process results in a corpus of word/phrase-aligned parallel sentences from which we can extract phrase pairs that are translations of each other. We ran the alignment algorithm from (Och and Ney, 2003) on a Chinese-English parallel corpus of 218 million English words, available from the Linguistic Data Consortium (LDC). Phrase pairs are extracted by following the method described in (Och and Ney, 2004) where all contiguous phrase pairs having consistent alignments are extraction candidates. Using these pairs we build paraphrase sets by joining together all English phrases that have the same Chinese translation. Figure 3 shows an example word/phrase alignment for two parallel sentence pairs from our corpus where the phrases "blowing up" and "bombing" have the same Chinese translation. On the right side of the figure we show the paraphrase set which contains these two phrases, which is typical in our collection of extracted paraphrases.

Although our paraphrase extraction method is similar to that of (Bannard and Callison-Burch, 2005), the paraphrases we extracted are for completely different applications, and have a broader definition for what constitutes a paraphrase. In (Bannard and Callison-Burch, 2005), a language model is used to make sure that the paraphrases extracted are direct substitutes, from the same syntactic categories, etc. So, using the example in Figure 3, the paraphrase table would contain only "bombing" and "bombing attack". Paraphrases that are direct substitutes of one another are useful when translating unknown phrases. For instance, if a MT system does not have the Chinese translation for the word "bombing", but has seen it in another set of parallel data (not involving Chinese) and has determined it to be a direct substitute of the phrase "bombing attack", then the Chinese translation of "bombing attack" would be used in place of the translation for "bombing". This substitution technique has shown some improvement in translation quality (Callison-Burch et al., 2006).

3.3 The ParaEval Evaluation Procedure

We adopt a two-tier matching strategy for MT evaluation in ParaEval. At the top tier, a paraphrase match is performed on system-translated sentences and corresponding reference sentences. Then, unigram matching is performed on the words not matched by paraphrases. Precision is measured as the ratio of the total number of words matched to the total number of words in the peer translation.

Running our system on the example in Figure 2, the paraphrase-matching phase consumes the words marked in grey and aligns "have been" and "to be", "completed" and "fully", "to date" and "up till now", and "sequence" and "sequenced". The subsequent unigram-matching aligns words based on lexical identity.

We maintain the computation of *modified unigram precision*, defined by the BLEU-esque Philosophy, in principle. In addition to clipping individual candidate *words* with their corresponding maximum reference counts (only for words not matched by paraphrases), we clip candidate *paraphrases* by their maximum reference paraphrase counts. So two completely different phrases in a reference sentence can be counted as two occurrences of one phrase. For example in Figure 4, candidate phrases "blown up" and "bombing" matched with three phrases from the references, namely "bombing" and two instances of "explosion". Treating these two candidate phrases as one (paraphrase match), we can see its clip is 2 (from Ref 1, where "bombing" and "explosion" are counted as two occurrences of a single phrase). The only word that was matched by its lexical identity is "was". The modified unigram precision calculated by our method is 4/5, where as BLEU gives 2/5.

Candidate: [blown up] [bombing] was happening

Ref 1: the [bombing] resulted in an [explosion]

Ref 2: there was an [explosion]

Modified Unigram Precision

$$= \frac{\text{paraphrase match} + \text{lexical match}}{\text{total number of words in peer}}$$

$$= \frac{(2+1)+1}{5} = \frac{4}{5}$$

Figure 4. ParaEval's matching process.

4 Evaluating ParaEval

To be effective in MT evaluations, an automated procedure should be capable of distinguishing good translation systems from bad ones, human translations from systems', and human translations of differing quality. For a particular evaluation exercise, an evaluation system produces a ranking for system and human translations, and compares this ranking with one created by human judges (Turian et al., 2003). The closer a system's ranking is to the human's, the better the evaluation system is.

4.1 Validating ParaEval

To test ParaEval's ability, NIST 2003 Chinese MT evaluation results were used (NIST 2003). This collection consists of 100 source documents in Chinese, translations from eight individual translation systems, reference translations from four humans, and human assessments (on fluency and adequacy). The Spearman rank-order coefficient is computed as an indicator of how close a system ranking is to gold-standard human ranking. It should be noted that the 2003 MT data is separate from the corpus that we extracted paraphrases from.

For comparison purposes, BLEU[1] was also run. Table 1 shows the correlation figures for the two automatic systems with the NIST rankings on fluency and adequacy. The lower and higher 95% confidence intervals are labeled as "L-CI" and "H-CI". To estimate the significance of the rank-order correlation figures, we applied bootstrap resampling to calculate the confidence intervals. In each of 1000 runs, systems were ranked based on their translations of 100 randomly selected documents. Each ranking was compared with the NIST ranking, producing a correlation score for each run. A t-test was then

	BLEU	ParaEval
Fluency	0.6978	0.7575
95% L-CI	0.6967	0.7553
95% H-CI	0.6989	0.7596
Adequacy	0.6108	0.6918
95% L-CI	0.6083	0.6895
95% H-CI	0.6133	0.694

Table 1. Ranking correlations with human assessments.

performed on the 1000 correlation scores. In both *fluency* and *adequacy* measurements, ParaEval correlates significantly better than BLEU. The ParaEval scores used were precision scores. In addition to distinguishing the quality of MT systems, a reliable evaluation procedure must be able to distinguish system translations from humans' (Lin and Och, 2004). Figure 5 shows the overall system and human ranking. In the upper left corner, human translators are grouped together, significantly separated from the automatic MT systems clustered into the lower right corner.

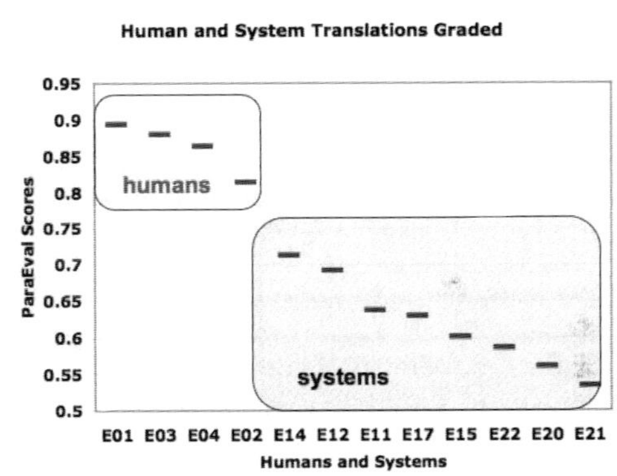

Figure 5. Overall system and human ranking.

4.2 Implications to Word-alignment

We experimented with restricting the paraphrases being matched to various lengths. When allowing only paraphrases of three or more words to match, the correlation figures become stabilized and ParaEval achieves even higher correlation with *fluency* measurement to 0.7619 on the Spearman ranking coefficient.

This phenomenon indicates to us that the bigram and unigram paraphrases extracted using SMT word-alignment and phrase extraction programs are not reliable enough to be applied to evaluation tasks. We speculate that word pairs extracted from (Liang et al., 2006), where a bidirectional discriminative training method was used to achieve consensus for word-alignment

[1] Results shown are from BLEU v.11 (NIST).

(mostly lower n-grams), would help to elevate the level of correlation by ParaEval.

4.3 Implications to Evaluating Paraphrase Quality

Utilizing paraphrases in MT evaluations is also a realistic way to measure the quality of paraphrases acquired through unsupervised channels. If a comparison strategy, coupled with paraphrase matching, distinguishes good and bad MT and summarization systems in close accordance with what human judges do, then this strategy and the paraphrases used are of sufficient quality. Since our underlining comparison strategy is that of BLEU-1 for MT evaluation, and BLEU has been proven to be a good metric for their respective evaluation tasks, the performance of the overall comparison is directly and mainly affected by the paraphrase collection.

5 ParaEval's Support for Recall Computation

Due to the use of multiple references and allowing an n-gram from the peer translation to be matched with its corresponding n-gram from any of the reference translations, BLEU cannot be used to compute recall scores, which are conventionally paired with precision to detect length-related problems from systems under evaluation.

5.1 Using Single References for Recall

The primary goal in using multiple references is to overcome the limitation in matching on lexical identity. More translation choices give more variations in verbalization, which could lead to more matches between peer and reference translations. Since MT results are generated and evaluated at a sentence-to-sentence level (or a segment level, where each segment may contain a small number of sentences) and no text condensation is employed, the number of different and correct ways to state the same sentence is small. This is in comparison to writing generic multi-document summaries, each of which contains multiple sentences and requires significant amount of "rewriting". When using a large collection of paraphrases while evaluating, we are provided with the alternative verbalizations needed. This property allows us to use single references to evaluate MT results and compute recall measurements.

5.2 Recall and Adequacy Correlations

When validating the computed recall scores for MT systems, we correlate with human assessments on *adequacy* only. The reason is that according to the definition of recall, the content coverage in references, and not the fluency reflected from the peers, is being measured. Table 2 shows ParaEval's recall correlation with NIST 2003 Chinese MT evaluation results on systems ranking. We see that ParaEval's correlation with *adequacy* has improved significantly when using recall scores to rank than using precision scores.

	BLEU	ParaEval
Adequacy	0.6108	0.7373
95% L-CI	0.6083	0.7368
95% H-CI	0.6133	0.7377

Table 2. ParaEval's recall ranking correlation.

5.3 Not All Single References are Created Equal

Human-written translations differ not only in word choice, but also in other idiosyncrasies that cannot be captured with paraphrase recognition. So it would be presumptuous to declare that using paraphrases from ParaEval is enough to allow using just one reference translation to evaluate. Using multiple references allow more paraphrase sets to be explored in matching.

In Table 3, we show ParaEval's correlation figures when using single reference translations. E01–E04 indicate the sets of human translations used correspondingly.

	E01	E02	E03	E04
Fluency	0.683	0.6501	0.7284	0.6192
95% L-CI	0.6795	0.6482	0.7267	0.6172
95% H-CI	0.6864	0.6519	0.73	0.6208
Adequacy	0.6308	0.5741	0.6688	0.5858
95% L-CI	0.6266	0.5705	0.665	0.5821
95% H-CI	0.635	0.5777	0.6727	0.5895

Table 3. ParaEval's correlation (precision) while using only single references.

Notice that the correlation figures vary a great deal depending on the set of single references used. How do we differentiate human translations and know which set of references to use? It is difficult to quantify the quality that a human written translation reflects. We can only define "good" human translations as translations that are written not very differently from what other humans would write, and "bad" translations as the ones that are written in an unconventional fashion. Table 4 shows the differences between the four sets of reference translations when comparing one set of references to the other three. The scores here are the raw ParaEval precision scores. E01 and E03 are better, which explains the higher correlations ParaEval has using these two sets of references individually, shown in Table 3.

	ParaEval	95% L-CI	95% H-CI
E01	0.8086	0.8	0.8172
E02	0.7383	0.7268	0.7497
E03	0.7839	0.7754	0.7923
E04	0.7742	0.7617	0.7866

Table 4. Differences among reference translations (raw ParaEval precision scores).

6 Observation of Change in Number of References

When matching on lexical identity, it is the general consensus that using more reference translations would increase the reliability of the MT evaluation (Turian et al., 2003). It is expected that we see an improvement in ranking correlations when moving from using one reference translation to more. However, when running BLEU for the NIST 2003 Chinese MT evaluation, this trend is inverted, and using single reference translation gave higher correlation than using all four references, as illustrated in Table 5.

BLEU	E01	E02	E03	E04	4 refs
Fluency	0.7114	0.701	0.7084	0.7192	0.6978
95% L-CI	0.7099	0.6993	0.7065	0.7177	0.6967
95% H-CI	0.7129	0.7026	0.7102	0.7208	0.6989
Adequacy	0.644	0.6238	0.6535	0.675	0.6108
95% L-CI	0.6404	0.6202	0.6496	0.6714	0.6083
95% H-CI	0.6476	0.6274	0.6574	0.6786	0.6133

Table 5. BLEU's correlating behavior with multi- and single-reference.

Turian et al. (2003) reports the same peculiar behavior from BLEU on Arabic MT evaluations in Figure 5b of their paper. When using three reference translations, as the number of segments (sentences usually) increases, BLEU correlates worse than using single references.

Since the matching and underlining counting mechanisms of ParaEval are built upon the fundamentals of BLEU, we were keen to find out the differences, other than paraphrase matching, between the two methods when the number of reference translation changes. By following the description from the original BLEU paper, three incremental steps were set up for duplicating its implementation, namely modified unigram precision (MUP), geometric mean of MUP (GM), and

MUP	E01	E02	E03	E04	4 refs
Fluency	0.6597	0.6216	0.6923	0.4912	0.692
95% L-CI	0.6568	0.6189	0.6917	0.4863	0.6915
95% H-CI	0.6626	0.6243	0.6929	0.496	0.6925
Adequacy	0.5818	0.5459	0.6141	0.4602	0.6165
95% L-CI	0.5788	0.5432	0.6132	0.4566	0.6156
95% H-CI	0.5847	0.5486	0.6151	0.4630	0.6174

6(a). System-ranking correlation when using modified unigram precision (MUP) scores.

GM	E01	E02	E03	E04	4 refs
Fluency	0.6633	0.6228	0.6925	0.4911	0.6922
95% L-CI	0.6604	0.6201	0.692	0.4862	0.6918
95% H-CI	0.6662	0.6255	0.6931	0.4961	0.6929
Adequacy	0.5817	0.548	0.615	0.4641	0.6159
95% L-CI	0.5813	0.5453	0.614	0.4606	0.615
95% H-CI	0.5871	0.5508	0.616	0.4676	0.6169

6(b). System-ranking correlation when using geometric mean (GM) of MUPs.

BP-BLEU	E01	E02	E03	E04	4 refs
Fluency	0.6637	0.6227	0.6921	0.4947	0.5743
95% L-CI	0.6608	0.62	0.6916	0.4899	0.5699
95% H-CI	0.6666	0.6254	0.6927	0.4996	0.5786
Adequacy	0.5812	0.5486	0.5486	0.5486	0.6671
95% L-CI	0.5782	0.5481	0.5458	0.5458	0.6645
95% H-CI	0.5842	0.5514	0.5514	0.5514	0.6697

6(c). System-ranking correlation when multiplying the brevity penalty with GM.

Table 6. Incremental implementation of BLEU and the correlation behavior at the three steps: MUP, GM, and BP-BLEU.

multiplying brevity penalty with GM to get the final score (BP-BLEU). At each step, correlations were computed for both using single- and multi- references, shown in Table 6a, b, and c.

Given that many small changes have been made to the original BLEU design, our replication would not produce the same scores from the current version of BLEU. Nevertheless, the inverted behavior was observed in *fluency* correlations at the BP-BLEU step, not at MUP and GM. This indicates to us that the multiplication of the brevity penalty to balance precision scores is problematic. According to (Turian et al., 2003), correlation scores computed from using fewer references are inflated because the comparisons exclude the longer n-gram matches that make automatic evaluation procedures diverge from the human judgments. Using a large collection of paraphrases in comparisons allows those longer n-gram matches to happen even if single references are used. This collection also allows ParaEval to directly compute recall scores, avoiding an approximation of recall that is problematic.

7 Conclusion and Future Work

In this paper, we have described ParaEval, an automatic evaluation framework for measuring machine translation results. A large collection of paraphrases, extracted through an unsupervised fashion using SMT methods, is used to improve the quality of the evaluations. We addressed three important issues, the paraphrasing support, the computation of recall measurement, and providing high correlations with human judgments.

Having seen that using paraphrases helps a great deal in evaluation tasks, naturally the next task is to explore the possibility in paraphrase induction. The question becomes how to use contextual information to calculate semantic closeness between two phrases. Can we expand the identification of paraphrases to longer ones, ideally sentences?

The problem in which content bearing words carry the same weights as the non-content bearing ones is not addressed. From examining the paraphrase extraction process, it is unclear how to relate translation probabilities and confidences with semantic closeness. We plan to explore the parallels between the two to enable a weighted implementation of ParaEval.

Reference

Anonymous. 2006. Complete citation omitted due to the blind review process.

Bannard, C. and C. Callison-Burch. 2005. Paraphrasing with bilingual parallel corpora. *Proceedings of ACL-2005.*

Browner, J. 2006. The translator's blues. http://www.slate.com/id/2133922/.

Callison-Burch, P. Koehn, and M. Osborne. 2006. Improved statistical machine translation using paraphrases. In *Proceedings of HLT/NAACL-2006.*

Callison-Burch, C., M. Osborne, and P. Koehn. 2006. Re-evaluating the role of bleu in machine translation research. In *Proceedings of EACL-2006.*

Inkpen, D. Z. and G. Hirst. 2003. Near-synonym choice in natural language generation. *Proceedings of RANLP-2003.*

Leusch, G., N. Ueffing, and H. Ney. 2003. A novel string-to-string distance measure with applications to machine translation evaluation. In *Proceedings of MT Summit IX.*

Liang, P., B. Taskar, and D. Klein. Consensus of simple unsupervised models for word alignment. In *Proceedings in HLT/NAACL-2006.*

Lin, C.Y. and E. Hovy. 2003. Automatic evaluation of summaries using n-gram co-occurrence statistics. *Proceedings of the HLT-2003.*

Lin, C.Y. and F. J. Och. 2004. Automatic evaluation of machine translation quality using longest common subsequence and skip-bigram statistics. *Proceedings of ACL-2004.*

Och, F. J. and H. Ney. 2003. A systematic comparison of various statistical alignment models. *Computational Linguistics*, 29(1): 19—51, 2003.

Och, F. J. and H. Ney. 2004. The alignment template approach to statistical machine translation. *Computational Linguistics*, 30(4), 2004.

Papineni, K., S. Roukos, T. Ward, and W. J. Zhu. 2002. IBM research report Bleu: a method for automatic evaluation of machine translation *IBM Research Division Technical Report*, RC22176, 2001.

Turian, J. P., L. Shen, and I. D. Melamed. 2003. Evaluation of machine translation and its evaluation. *Proceedings of MT Summit IX.*

Exploiting Discourse Structure for Spoken Dialogue Performance Analysis

Mihai Rotaru
University of Pittsburgh
Pittsburgh, USA
mrotaru@cs.pitt.edu

Diane J. Litman
University of Pittsburgh
Pittsburgh, USA
litman@cs.pitt.edu

Abstract

In this paper we study the utility of discourse structure for spoken dialogue performance modeling. We experiment with various ways of exploiting the discourse structure: in isolation, as context information for other factors (correctness and certainty) and through trajectories in the discourse structure hierarchy. Our correlation and PARADISE results show that, while the discourse structure is not useful in isolation, using the discourse structure as context information for other factors or via trajectories produces highly predictive parameters for performance analysis.

1 Introduction

Predictive models of spoken dialogue system (**SDS**) performance are an important tool for researchers and practitioners in the SDS domain. These models offer insights on what factors are important for the success of a SDS and allow researchers to assess the performance of future system improvements without running additional costly user experiments.

One of the most popular models of performance is the PARADISE framework proposed by (Walker et al., 2000). In PARADISE, a set of *interaction parameters* are measured in a SDS corpus, and then used in a multivariate linear regression to predict the target performance metric. A critical ingredient in this approach is the relevance of the interaction parameters for the SDS success. A number of parameters that measure the dialogue efficiency (e.g. number of system/user turns, task duration) and the dialogue quality (e.g. recognition accuracy, rejections, helps) have been shown to be successful in (Walker et al., 2000). An extensive set of parameters can be found in (Möller, 2005a).

In this paper we study the utility of *discourse structure* as an information source for SDS performance analysis. The discourse structure hierarchy has been shown to be useful for other tasks: understanding specific lexical and prosodic phenomena (Hirschberg and Nakatani, 1996; Levow, 2004), natural language generation (Hovy, 1993), predictive/generative models of postural shifts (Cassell et al., 2001), and essay scoring (Higgins et al., 2004).

We perform our analysis on a corpus of speech-based tutoring dialogues. A tutoring SDS (Litman and Silliman, 2004; Pon-Barry et al., 2004) has to discuss concepts, laws and relationships and to engage in complex subdialogues to correct student misconceptions. As a result, dialogues with such systems have a rich discourse structure.

We perform three experiments to measure three ways of exploiting the discourse structure. In our first experiment, we test the predictive utility of the discourse structure in itself. For example, we look at whether the number of pop-up transitions in the discourse structure hierarchy predicts performance in our system.

The second experiment measures the utility of the discourse structure as contextual information for two types of *student states*: correctness and certainty. The intuition behind this experiment is that interaction events should be treated differently based on their position in the discourse structure hierarchy. For example, we test if the number of incorrect answers after a pop-up transition has a higher predictive utility than the total number of incorrect student answers. In contrast, the majority of the previous work either ignores this contextual information (Möller, 2005a; Walker et al., 2000) or makes limited use of the

Proceedings of the 2006 Conference on Empirical Methods in Natural Language Processing (EMNLP 2006), pages 85–93,
Sydney, July 2006.

discourse structure hierarchy by flattening it (Walker et al., 2001) (Section 5).

As another way to exploit the discourse structure, in our third experiment we look at whether specific trajectories in the discourse structure are indicative of performance. For example, we test if two consecutive pushes in the discourse structure are correlated with higher learning.

To measure the predictive utility of our interaction parameters, we focus primarily on *correlations* with our performance metric (Section 4). There are two reasons for this. First, a significant correlation between an interaction parameter and the performance metric is a good indicator of the parameter's relevance for PARADISE modeling. Second, correlations between factors and the performance metric are commonly used in tutoring research to analyze the tutoring/learning process (Chi et al., 2001).

Our correlation and PARADISE results show that, while the discourse structure is not useful in isolation, using the discourse structure as context information for other factors or via trajectories produces highly predictive parameters for performance analysis.

2 Annotation

Our annotation for discourse structure and student state has been performed on a corpus of 95 experimentally obtained spoken tutoring dialogues between 20 students and our system **ITSPOKE** (Litman and Silliman, 2004). ITSPOKE is a speech-enabled version of the text-based Why2-Atlas conceptual physics tutoring system (VanLehn et al., 2002). When interacting with ITSPOKE, students first type an essay answering a qualitative physics problem using a graphical user interface. ITSPOKE then engages the student in spoken dialogue (using head-mounted microphone input and speech output) to correct misconceptions and elicit more complete explanations, after which the student revises the essay, thereby ending the tutoring or causing another round of tutoring/essay revision. Each student went through the same procedure: 1) read a short introductory material, 2) took a pretest to measure the initial physics knowledge, 3) work through a set of 5 problems with ITSPOKE, and 4) took a posttest similar to the pretest. The resulting corpus had 2334 student turns and a comparable number of system turns.

2.1 Discourse structure

We base our annotation of discourse structure on the Grosz & Sidner theory of discourse structure (Grosz and Sidner, 1986). A critical ingredient of this theory is the intentional structure. According to the theory, each discourse has a discourse purpose/intention. Satisfying the main discourse purpose is achieved by satisfying several smaller purposes/intentions organized in a hierarchical structure. As a result, the discourse is segmented in discourse segments each with an associated discourse segment purpose/intention. This theory has inspired several generic dialogue managers for spoken dialogue systems (Bohus and Rudnicky, 2003).

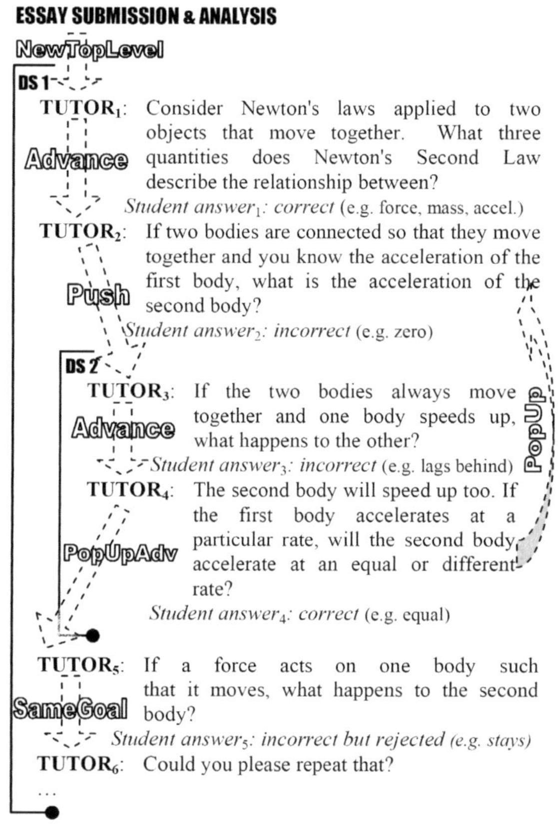

Figure 1. The discourse structure and transition annotation

We automate our annotation of the discourse structure by taking advantage of the structure of the tutored information. A dialogue with ITSPOKE follows a question-answer format (i.e. system initiative): ITSPOKE asks a question, the student provides the answer and then the process is repeated. Deciding what question to ask, in what order and when to stop is hand-authored beforehand in a hierarchical structure that resembles the discourse segment structure (see Figure 1). Tutor questions are grouped in segments which correspond roughly to the discourse segments. Similarly to the discourse segment purpose, each question segment has an associated tutoring goal or purpose. For example, in

ITSPOKE there are question segments discussing about forces acting on the objects, others discussing about objects' acceleration, etc.

In Figure 1 we illustrate ITSPOKE's behavior and our discourse structure annotation. First, based on the analysis of the student essay, ITSPOKE selects a question segment to correct misconceptions or to elicit more complete explanations. This question segment will correspond to the top level discourse segment (e.g. DS1). Next, ITSPOKE asks the student each question in DS1. If the student answer is correct, the system moves on to the next question (e.g. $Tutor_1 \rightarrow Tutor_2$). If the student answer is incorrect, there are two alternatives. For simple questions, the system will simply give out the correct answer and move on to the next question (e.g. $Tutor_3 \rightarrow Tutor_4$). For complex questions (e.g. applying physics laws), ITSPOKE will engage into a *remediation subdialogue* that attempts to remediate the student's lack of knowledge or skills. The remediation subdialogue is specified in another question segment and corresponds to a new discourse segment (e.g DS2). The new discourse segment is dominated by the current discourse segment (e.g. DS2 dominated by DS1). $Tutor_2$ system turn is a typical example; if the student answers it incorrectly, ITSPOKE will enter discourse segment DS2 and go through its questions ($Tutor_3$ and $Tutor_4$). Once all the questions in DS2 have been answered, a heuristic determines whether ITSPOKE should ask the original question again ($Tutor_2$) or simply move on to the next question ($Tutor_5$).

To compute interaction parameters from the discourse structure, we focus on the transitions in the discourse structure hierarchy. For each system turn we define a **transition** feature. This feature captures the position in the discourse structure of the current system turn relative to the previous system turn. We define six labels (see Table 1). **NewTopLevel** label is used for the first question after an essay submission (e.g. $Tutor_1$). If the previous question is at the same level with the current question we label the current question as **Advance** (e.g. $Tutor_{2,4}$). The first question in a remediation subdialogue is labeled as **Push** (e.g. $Tutor_3$). After a remediation subdialogue is completed, ITSPOKE will pop up and it will either ask the original question again or move on to the next question. In the first case, we label the system turn as **PopUp**. Please note that $Tutor_2$ will not be labeled with PopUp because, in such cases, an extra system turn will be created between $Tutor_4$ and $Tutor_5$ with the same content as $Tutor_2$. In addition, variations of "Ok, back to the original question" are also included in the new system turn to mark the discourse segment boundary transition. If the system moves on to the next question after finishing the remediation subdialogue, we label the system turn as **PopUpAdv** (e.g. $Tutor_5$). Note that while the sum of PopUp and PopUpAdv should be equal with Push, it is smaller in our corpus because in some cases ITSPOKE popped up more than one level in the discourse structure hierarchy. In case of rejections, the system question is repeated using variations of "Could you please repeat that?". We label such cases as **SameGoal** (e.g. $Tutor_6$).

Discourse structure transitions	
Advance	53.4%
NewTopLevel	13.5%
PopUp	9.2%
PopUpAdv	3.5%
Push	14.5%
SameGoal	5.9%
Certainty	
Certain	41.3%
Uncertain	19.1%
Mixed	2.4%
Neutral	37.3%
Correctness	
Correct	63.3%
Incorrect	23.3%
Partially Correct	6.2%
Unable to Answer	7.1%

Table 1: Transition and student state distribution.

Please note that each student dialogue has a specific discourse structure based on the dialogue that dynamically emerges based on the correctness of her answers. For this reason, the same system question in terms of content may get a different transition label for different students. For example, in Figure 1, if the student would have answered $Tutor_2$ correctly, the next tutor turn would have had the same content as $Tutor_5$ but the Advance label. Also, while a human annotation of the discourse structure will be more complex but more time consuming (Hirschberg and Nakatani, 1996; Levow, 2004), its advantages are outweighed by the automatic nature of our discourse structure annotation.

We would like to highlight that our transition annotation is *domain independent* and *automatic*. Our transition labels capture behavior like starting a new dialogue (NewTopLevel), crossing discourse segment boundaries (Push, PopUp, PopUpAdv) and local phenomena inside a discourse segment (Advance, SameGoal). If the discourse structure information is available, the transition information can be automatically computed using the procedure described above.

2.2 Student state

Because for our tutoring system student learning is the relevant performance metric, we hypothesize that information about student state in each student turn, in terms of correctness and certainty, will be an important indicator. For example, a student being more correct and certain during her interaction with ITSPOKE might be indicative of a higher learning gain. Also, previous studies have shown that tutoring specific parameters can improve the quality of SDS performance models that model the learning gain (Forbes-Riley and Litman, 2006).

In our corpus, each student turn was manually labeled for *correctness* and *certainty* (Table 1). While our system assigns a correctness label to each student turn to plan its next move, we choose to use a manual annotation of correctness to eliminate the noise introduced by the automatic speech recognition component and the natural language understanding component. A human annotator used the human transcripts and his physics knowledge to label each student turn for various degrees of correctness: correct, partially correct, incorrect and unable to answer. "Unable to Answer" label was used for turns where the student did not answer the system question or used variants of "I don't know".

Previous work has shown that certainty plays an important role in the learning and tutoring process (Pon-Barry et al., 2006; VanLehn et al., 2003). A human annotator listened to the dialogues between students and ITSPOKE and labeled each student turn for its perceived degree of certainness. Four labels were used: certain, uncertain, neutral and mixed (both certain and uncertain). To date, one annotator has labeled all student turns in our corpus[1].

3 Interaction parameters

For each user, interaction parameters measure specific aspects of the dialogue with the system. We use our transition and student state annotation to create two types of interaction parameters: **unigrams** and **bigrams**. The difference between the two types of parameters is whether the discourse structure context is used or not. For each of our 12 labels (4 for correctness, 4 for certainty and 6 for discourse structure), we derive two unigram parameters per student over the 5 dialogues for that student: a *total* parameter and a *percentage* parameter. For example, for the 'Incorrect' unigram we compute, for each student, the total number of student turns labeled with 'Incorrect' (parameter Incorrect) and the percentage of such student turns out of all student turns (parameter Incorrect%). For example, if we consider only the dialogue in Figure 1, Incorrect = 3 ($Student_{2,3,5}$) and Incorrect% = 60% (3 out of 5).

Bigram parameters exploit the discourse structure context. We create two classes of bigram parameters by looking at *transition–student state* bigrams and *transition–transition* bigrams. The transition–student state bigrams combine the information about the student state with the transition information of the previous system turn. Going back to Figure 1, the three incorrect answers will be distributed to three bigrams: Advance–Incorrect ($Tutor_2$–$Student_2$), Push–Incorrect ($Tutor_3$–$Student_3$) and PopUpAdv–Incorrect ($Tutor_5$–$Student_5$). The transition–transition bigram looks at the transition labels of two consecutive system turns. For example, the $Tutor_4$–$Tutor_5$ pair will be counted as an Advance–PopUpAdv bigram.

Similar to the unigrams, we compute a total parameter and a percentage parameter for each bigram. The percentage denominator is number of student turns for the transition–student state bigrams and the number of system turns minus one for the transition–transition bigram. In addition, for each bigram we compute a *relative percentage* parameter (bigram followed by %rel) by computing the percentage relative to the total number of times the transition unigram appears for that student. For example, we will compute the Advance–Incorrect %rel parameter by dividing the number of Advance–Incorrect bigrams with the number of Advance unigrams (1 divided by 2 in Figure 1); this value will capture the percentage of times an Advance transition is followed by an incorrect student answer.

4 Results

We use student learning as our evaluation metric because it is the primary metric for evaluating the performance of tutoring systems. Previous work (Forbes-Riley and Litman, 2006) has suc-

[1] The agreement between the manual correctness annotation and the correctness assigned by ITSPOKE is 90% (kappa of 0.79). In a preliminary agreement study, a second annotator labeled our corpus for a binary version of certainty (uncertainty versus other), resulting in a 90% inter-annotator agreement and a kappa of 0.68.

cessfully used student learning as the performance metric in the PARADISE framework. Two quantities are used to measure student learning: the pretest score and the posttest score. Both tests consist of 40 multiple-choice questions; the test's score is computed as the percentage of correctly answered questions. The average score and standard deviation for each test are: pretest 0.47 (0.17) and posttest 0.68 (0.17).

We focus primarily on correlations between our interaction parameters and student learning. Because in our data the pretest score is significantly correlated with the posttest score, we study *partial* Pearson's correlations between our parameters and the posttest score that account for the pretest score. This correlation methodology is commonly used in the tutoring research (Chi et al., 2001). For each trend or significant correlation we report the unigram/bigram, its average and standard deviation over all students, the Pearson's Correlation Coefficient (R) and the statistical significance of R (p).

First we report significant correlations for unigrams to test our first hypothesis. Next, for our second and third experiment, we report correlations for transition–student state and transition–transition parameters. Finally, we report our preliminary results on PARADISE modeling.

4.1 Unigram correlations

In our first proposed experiment, we want to test the predictive utility of discourse structure in isolation. We compute correlations between our transition unigram parameters and learning. We find no trends or significant correlations. This result suggests that discourse structure in isolation has no predictive utility.

Here we also report all trends and significant correlations for student state unigrams as the baseline for contextual correlations to be presented in Section 4.2. We find only one significant correlation (Table 2): students with a higher percentage of neutral turns (in terms of certainty) are negatively correlated with learning. We hypothesize that this correlation captures the student involvement in the tutoring process: more involved students will try harder thus expressing more certainty or uncertainty. In contrast, less involved students will have fewer certain/uncertain/mixed turns and, in consequence, more neutral turns. Surprisingly, student correctness does not significantly correlate with learning.

Parameter	Mean (SD)	R.	p
Neutral %	37% (8%)	-.47	.04

Table 2: Trend and significant unigram correlations

4.2 Transition–student state correlations

For our second experiment, we need to determine the predictive utility of transition–student state bigram parameters. We find a large number of correlations for both transition–correctness bigrams and transition–certainty bigrams.

Transition–correctness bigrams

This type of bigram informs us whether accounting for the discourse structure transition when looking at student correctness has any predictive value. We find several interesting trends and significant correlations (Table 3).

The student behavior, in terms of correctness, after a PopUp or a PopUpAdv transition is very informative about the student learning process. In both situations, the student has just finished a remediation subdialogue and the system is popping up either by reasking the original question again (PopUp) or by moving on to the next question (PopUpAdv). We find that after PopUp, the number of correct student answers is positively correlated with learning. In contrast, the number, the percentage and the relative percentage of incorrect student answers are negatively correlated with learning. We hypothesize that this correlation indicates whether the student took advantage of the additional learning opportunities offered by the remediation subdialogue. By answering correctly the original system question (PopUp–Correct), the student demonstrates that she has absorbed the information from the remediation dialogue. This bigram is an indication of a successful learning event. In contrast, answering the original system question incorrectly (PopUp–Incorrect) is an indication of a missed learning opportunity; the more events like this happen the less the student learns.

Parameter	Mean (SD)	R.	p
PopUp–Correct	7 (3.3)	.45	.05
PopUp–Incorrect	2 (1.8)	-.42	.07
PopUp–Incorrect %	1.6% (1.2%)	-.46	.05
PopUp–Incorrect %rel	17% (13%)	-.39	.10
PopUpAdv–Correct	2.5 (2)	.43	.06
PopUpAdv–Correct %	2% (1.3%)	.52	.02
NewTopLevel–Incorrect	2.3 (1.8)	.56	.01
NewTopLevel–Incorrect %	1.9% (1.4%)	.49	.03
NewTopLevel–Incorrect %rel	15% (12%)	.51	.02
Advance–Correct	40.5 (9.8)	.45	.05

Table 3: Trend and significant transition–correctness bigram correlations

Similarly, being able to correctly answer the tutor question after popping up from a remediation subdialogue (PopUpAdv–Correct) is positively correlated with learning. Since in many cases, these system questions will make use of the knowledge taught in the remediation subdialogues, we hypothesize that this correlation also captures successful learning opportunities.

Another set of interesting correlations is produced by the NewTopLevel–Incorrect bigram. We find that the number, the percentage and the relative percentage of times ITSPOKE starts a new essay revision dialogue that results in an incorrect student answer is positively correlated with learning. The content of the essay revision dialogue is determined based on ITSPOKE's analysis of the student essay. We hypothesize that an incorrect answer to the first tutor question is indicative of the system's picking of a topic that is problematic for the student. Thus, we see more learning in students for which more knowledge gaps are discovered and addressed by ITSPOKE.

Finally, we find the number of times the student answers correctly after an advance transition is positively correlated with learning (the Advance–Correct bigram). We hypothesize that this correlation captures the relationship between students that advance without having major problems and a higher learning gains.

Transition–certainty bigrams

Next we look at the combination between the transition in the dialogue structure and the student certainty (Table 4). These correlations offer more insight on the negative correlation between the Neutral % unigram parameter and student learning. We find that out of all neutral student answers, those that follow an Advance transitions are negatively correlated with learning. Similar to the Neutral % correlation, we hypothesize that Advance–Neutral correlations capture the lack of involvement of the student in the tutoring process. This might be also due to ITSPOKE engaging in teaching concepts that the student is already familiar with.

Parameter	Mean (SD)	R.	p
Advance–Neutral	27 (8.3)	-.40	.08
Advance–Neutral %	21% (6%)	-.62	.00
Advance–Neutral %rel	38% (10%)	-.73	.00
SameGoal–Neutral %rel	35% (31%)	.46	.05

Table 4: Trend and significant transition–certainty bigram correlations

In contrast, staying neutral in terms of certainty after a system rejection is positively correlated with learning. These correlations show that based on their position in the discourse structure, neutral student answers will be correlated either negatively or positively with learning.

Unlike student state unigram parameters which produce only one significant correlation, transition–student state bigram parameters produce a large number of trend and significant correlations (14). This result suggests that exploiting the discourse structure as a contextual information source can be beneficial for performance modeling.

4.3 Transition–transition bigrams

For our third experiment, we are looking at the transition–transition bigram correlations (Table 5). These bigrams help us find trajectories of length two in the discourse structure that are associated with better student learning. Because our student state is domain dependent, translating the transition–student state bigrams to a new domain will require finding a new set of relevant factors to replace the student state. In contrast, because our transition information is domain independent, transition–transition bigrams can be easily implemented in a new domain.

The Advance–Advance bigram covers situations where the student is covering tutoring material without major knowledge gaps. This is because an Advance transition happens when the student either answers correctly or his incorrect answer can be corrected without going into a remediation subdialogue. Just like with the Advance–Correct correlation (recall Table 3), we hypothesize that these correlations links higher learning gains to students that cover a lot of material without many knowledge gap.

Parameter	Mean (SD)	R.	p
Advance–Advance	35 (9.1)	.47	.04
Push–Push	2.2 (1.7)	.50	.03
Push–Push %	1.8% (1.3%)	.52	.02
Push–Push %rel	11% (7%)	.52	.02
SameGoal–Push %rel	18% (23%)	.49	.03

Table 5: Trend and significant transition–transition bigram correlations

The Push–Push bigrams capture another interesting behavior. In these cases, the student incorrectly answers a question, entering a remediation subdialogue; she also incorrectly answers the first question in the remediation dialogue entering an even deeper remediation subdialogue. We hypothesize that these situations are indicative of big student knowledge gaps. In our corpus, we find that the more such big knowledge gaps are discovered and addressed by the system the higher the learning gain.

The SameGoal–Push bigram captures another type of behavior after system rejections that is positively correlated with learning (recall the SameGoal–Neutral bigram, Table 4). In our previous work (Rotaru and Litman, 2006), we performed an analysis of the rejected student turns and studied how rejections affect the student state. The results of our analysis suggested a new strategy for handling rejections in the tutoring domain: instead of rejecting student answers, a tutoring SDS should make use of the available information. Since the recognition hypothesis for a rejected student turn would be interpreted most likely as an incorrect answer thus activating a remediation subdialogue, the positive correlation between SameGoal–Push and learning suggests that the new strategy will not impact learning.

Similar to the second experiment, the results of our third experiment are also positive: in contrast to transition unigrams, our domain independent trajectories can produce parameters with a high predictive utility.

4.4 PARADISE modeling

Here we present our preliminary results on applying the PARADISE framework to model ITSPOKE performance. A stepwise multivariate linear regression procedure (Walker et al., 2000) is used to automatically select the parameters to be included in the model. Similar to (Forbes-Riley and Litman, 2006), in order to model the learning gain, we use posttest as the dependent variable and force the inclusion of the pretest score as the first variable in the model.

For the first experiment, we feed the model all transition unigrams. As expected due to lack of correlations, the stepwise procedure does not select any transition unigram parameter. The only variable in the model is pretest resulting in a model with a R^2 of .22.

For the second and third experiment, we first build a baseline model using only unigram parameters. The resulting model achieves an R^2 of .39 by including the only significantly correlated unigram parameter: Neutral %. Next, we build a model using all unigram parameters and all significantly correlated bigram parameters. The new model almost doubles the R^2 to 0.75. Besides the pretest, the parameters included in the resulting model are (ordered by the degree of contribution from highest to lowest): Advance–Neutral %rel, and PopUp–Incorrect %. These results strengthen our correlation conclusions: discourse structure used as context information or as trajectories information is useful for performance modeling. Also, note that the inclusion of student certainty in the final PARADISE model provides additional support to a hypothesis that has gained a lot of attention lately: detecting and responding to student emotions has the potential to improve learning (Craig et al., 2004; Forbes-Riley and Litman, 2005; Pon-Barry et al., 2006).

The performance of our best model is comparable or higher than training performances reported in previous work (Forbes-Riley and Litman, 2006; Möller, 2005b; Walker et al., 2001). Since our training data is relatively small (20 data points) and overfitting might be involved here, in the future we plan to do a more in-depth evaluation by testing if our model generalizes on a larger ITSPOKE corpus we are currently annotating.

5 Related work

Previous work has proposed a large number of interaction parameters for SDS performance modeling (Möller, 2005a; Walker et al., 2000; Walker et al., 2001). Several information sources are being tapped to devise parameters classified by (Möller, 2005a) in several categories: dialogue and communication parameters (e.g. dialogue duration, number of system/user turns), speech input parameters (e.g. word error rate, recognition/concept accuracy) and meta-communication parameters (e.g. number of help request, cancel requests, corrections).

But most of these parameters do not take into account the discourse structure information. A notable exception is the DATE dialogue act annotation from (Walker et al., 2001). The DATE annotation captures information on three dimensions: speech acts (e.g. acknowledge, confirm), conversation domain (e.g. conversation- versus task-related) and the task model (e.g. subtasks like getting the date, time, origin, and destination). All these parameters can be linked to the discourse structure but flatten the discourse structure. Moreover, the most informative of these parameters (the task model parameters) are domain dependent. Similar approximations of the discourse structure are also common for other SDS tasks like predictive models of speech recognition problems (Gabsdil and Lemon, 2004).

We extend over previous work in several areas. First, we exploit in more detail the hierarchical information in the discourse structure. We quantify this information by recording the discourse structure transitions. Second, in contrast to previous work, our usage of discourse structure is domain independent (the transitions). Third, we exploit the discourse structure as a contextual information source. To our knowledge, previous work has not employed parameters similar with our transition–student state bigram parameters. Forth, via the transition–transition bigram parameters, we exploit trajectories in the discourse structure as another domain independent source of information for performance modeling. Finally, similar to (Forbes-Riley and Litman, 2006), we are tackling a more problematic performance metric: the student learning gain. While the requirements for a successful information access SDS are easier to spell out, the same can not be said about tutoring SDS due to the current limited understanding of the human learning process.

6 Conclusion

In this paper we highlight the role of discourse structure for SDS performance modeling. We experiment with various ways of using the discourse structure: in isolation, as context information for other factors (correctness and certainty) and through trajectories in the discourse structure hierarchy. Our correlation and PARADISE results show that, while the discourse structure is not useful in isolation, using the discourse structure as context information for other factors or via trajectories produces highly predictive parameters for performance analysis. Moreover, the PARADISE framework selects in the final model only discourse-based parameters ignoring parameters that do not use the discourse structure (certainty and correctness unigrams are ignored).

Our significant correlations also suggest ways we should modify our system. For example, the PopUp–Incorrect negative correlations suggest that after a failed learning opportunity the system should not give out the correct answer but engage in a secondary remediation subdialogue specially tailored for these situations.

In the future, we plan to test the generality of our PARADISE model on other corpora and to compare models built using our interaction parameters against models based on parameters commonly used in previous work (Möller, 2005a). Testing if our results generalize to a human annotation of the discourse structure and automated models of certainty and correctness is also of importance. We also want to see if our results hold for performance metrics based on user satisfaction questionnaires; in the new ITSPOKE corpus we are currently annotating, each student also completed a user satisfaction survey (Forbes-Riley and Litman, 2006) similar to the one used in the DARPA Communicator multi-site evaluation (Walker et al., 2002).

Our work contributes to both the computational linguistics domain and the tutoring domain. For the computational linguistics research community, we show that discourse structure is an important information source for SDS performance modeling. Our analysis can be extended easily to other SDS. First, a similar automatic annotation of the discourse structure can be performed in SDS that rely on dialogue managers inspired by the Grosz & Sidner theory of discourse (Bohus and Rudnicky, 2003). Second, the transition–transition bigram parameters are domain independent. Finally, for the other successful usage of discourse structure (transition–student state bigrams) researchers have only to identify relevant factors and then combine them with the discourse structure information. In our case, we show that instead of looking at the user state in isolation (Forbes-Riley and Litman, 2006), combining it with the discourse structure transition can generate informative interaction parameters.

For the tutoring research community, we show that discourse structure, an important concept in computational linguistics theory, can provide useful insights regarding the learning process. The correlations we observe in our corpus have intuitive interpretations (successful/failed learning opportunities, discovery of deep student knowledge gaps, providing relevant tutoring).

Acknowledgements

This work is supported by NSF Grant No. 0328431. We would like to thank Kate Forbes-Riley, Joel Tetreault and our anonymous reviewers for their helpful comments.

References

D. Bohus and A. Rudnicky. 2003. *RavenClaw: Dialog Management Using Hierarchical Task Decomposition and an Expectation Agenda.* In Proc. of Eurospeech.

J. Cassell, Y. I. Nakano, T. W. Bickmore, C. L. Sidner and C. Rich. 2001. *Non-Verbal Cues for Discourse Structure.* In Proc. of ACL.

M. T. H. Chi, S. A. Siler, H. Jeong, T. Yamauchi and R. G. Hausmann. 2001. Learning from human tutoring. *Cognitive Science, 25.*

S. D. Craig, A. C. Graesser, J. Sullins and B. Gholson. 2004. Affect and learning: an exploratory look into the role affect in learning with AutoTutor. *Journal of Educational Media, 29.*

K. Forbes-Riley and D. Litman. 2005. *Using Bigrams to Identify Relationships Between Student Certainness States and Tutor Responses in a Spoken Dialogue Corpus.* In Proc. of SIGdial.

K. Forbes-Riley and D. Litman. 2006. *Modelling User Satisfaction and Student Learning in a Spoken Dialogue Tutoring System with Generic, Tutoring, and User Affect Parameters.* In Proc. of HLT/NAACL.

M. Gabsdil and O. Lemon. 2004. *Combining Acoustic and Pragmatic Features to Predict Recognition Performance in Spoken Dialogue Systems.* In Proc. of ACL.

B. Grosz and C. L. Sidner. 1986. Attentions, intentions and the structure of discourse. *Computational Lingustics, 12*(3).

D. Higgins, J. Burstein, D. Marcu and C. Gentile. 2004. *Evaluating Multiple Aspects of Coherence in Student Essays.* In Proc. of HLT-NAACL.

J. Hirschberg and C. Nakatani. 1996. *A prosodic analysis of discourse segments in direction-giving monologues.* In Proc. of ACL.

E. Hovy. 1993. Automated discourse generation using discourse structure relations. *Articial Intelligence, 63*(Special Issue on NLP).

G.-A. Levow. 2004. *Prosodic Cues to Discourse Segment Boundaries in Human-Computer Dialogue.* In Proc. of SIGdial.

D. Litman and S. Silliman. 2004. *ITSPOKE: An intelligent tutoring spoken dialogue system.* In Proc. of HLT/NAACL.

S. Möller. 2005a. *Parameters for Quantifying the Interaction with Spoken Dialogue Telephone Services.* In Proc. of SIGDial.

S. Möller. 2005b. *Towards Generic Quality Prediction Models for Spoken Dialogue Systems - A Case Study.* In Proc. of Interspeech.

H. Pon-Barry, B. Clark, E. O. Bratt, K. Schultz and S. Peters. 2004. *Evaluating the effectiveness of Scot:a spoken conversational tutor.* In Proc. of ITS Workshop on Dialogue-based Intelligent Tutoring Systems.

H. Pon-Barry, K. Schultz, E. O. Bratt, B. Clark and S. Peters. 2006. Responding to Student Uncertainty in Spoken Tutorial Dialogue Systems. *International Journal of Artificial Intelligence in Education, 16.*

M. Rotaru and D. Litman. 2006. *Dependencies between Student State and Speech Recognition Problems in Spoken Tutoring Dialogues.* In Proc. of ACL.

K. VanLehn, P. W. Jordan, C. P. Rosé, D. Bhembe, M. Böttner, A. Gaydos, M. Makatchev, U. Pappuswamy, M. Ringenberg, A. Roque, S. Siler and R. Srivastava. 2002. *The Architecture of Why2-Atlas: A Coach for Qualitative Physics Essay Writing.* In Proc. of Intelligent Tutoring Systems (ITS).

K. VanLehn, S. Siler, C. Murray, T. Yamauchi and W. B. Baggett. 2003. Why do only some events cause learning during human tutoring? *Cognition and Instruction, 21*(3).

M. Walker, D. Litman, C. Kamm and A. Abella. 2000. Towards Developing General Models of Usability with PARADISE. *Natural Language Engineering.*

M. Walker, R. Passonneau and J. Boland. 2001. *Quantitative and Qualitative Evaluation of Darpa Communicator Spoken Dialogue Systems.* In Proc. of ACL.

M. Walker, A. Rudnicky, R. Prasad, J. Aberdeen, E. Bratt, J. Garofolo, H. Hastie, A. Le, B. Pellom, A. Potamianos, R. Passonneau, S. Roukos, G. Sanders, S. Seneff and D. Stallard. 2002. *DARPA Communicator: Cross-System Results for the 2001 Evaluation.* In Proc. of ICSLP.

Learning Information Status of Discourse Entities

Malvina Nissim*
Laboratory for Applied Ontology
Institute for Cognitive Science and Technology
National Research Council (ISTC-CNR), Roma, Italy
malvina.nissim@loa-cnr.it

Abstract

In this paper we address the issue of automatically assigning information status to discourse entities. Using an annotated corpus of conversational English and exploiting morpho-syntactic and lexical features, we train a decision tree to classify entities introduced by noun phrases as *old*, *mediated*, or *new*. We compare its performance with hand-crafted rules that are mainly based on morpho-syntactic features and closely relate to the guidelines that had been used for the manual annotation. The decision tree model achieves an overall accuracy of 79.5%, significantly outperforming the hand-crafted algorithm (64.4%). We also experiment with binary classifications by collapsing in turn two of the three target classes into one and retraining the model. The highest accuracy achieved on binary classification is 93.1%.

1 Introduction

Information structure is the way a speaker or writer organises known and new information in text or dialogue. Information structure has been the subject of numerous and very diverse linguistic studies (Halliday, 1976; Prince, 1981; Hajičová, 1984; Vallduví, 1992; Lambrecht, 1994; Steedman, 2000, for instance), thus also yielding a wide range of terms and definitions (see (Vallduví, 1992; Kruijff-Korbayová and Steedman, 2003) for a discussion). In the present study, we adopt the term "Information Status", following the definition employed for the annotation of the corpus we use for our experiments (Nissim et al., 2004). Information status describes to which degree a discourse entity is *available* to the hearer, in terms of the speaker's assumptions about the hearer's knowledge and beliefs. Although there is a fine line in the distinction between Information Status and Information Structure, it is fair to say that whereas the latter models wider discourse coherence, the former focuses mainly on the local level of discourse entities. Section 2 provides more details on how this notion is encoded in our corpus.

Information status has generated large interest among researchers because of its complex interaction with other linguistic phenomena, thus affecting several Natural Language Processing tasks. Since it correlates with word order and pitch accent (Lambrecht, 1994; Hirschberg and Nakatani, 1996), for instance, incorporating knowledge on information status would be helpful for natural language generation, and in particular text-to-speech systems. Stöber and colleagues, for example, ascribe to the lack of such information the lower performance of text-to-speech compared to concept-to-speech generation, where such knowledge could be made directly available to the system (Stöber et al., 2000).

Another area where information status can play an important role is anaphora resolution. A major obstacle in the resolution of definite noun phrases with full lexical heads is that only a small proportion of them is actually anaphoric (ca. 30% (Vieira and Poesio, 2000)). Therefore, in the absence of anaphoricity information, a resolution system will try to find an antecedent also for non-

*The work reported in this paper was carried out while the author was a research fellow at the Institute for Communicating and Collaborative Systems of the University of Edinburgh, United Kingdom, and was supported by a Scottish Enterprise Edinburgh-Stanford Link grant (265000-3102-R36766).

Proceedings of the 2006 Conference on Empirical Methods in Natural Language Processing (EMNLP 2006), pages 94–102,
Sydney, July 2006. ©2006 Association for Computational Linguistics

anaphoric definite noun phrases, thus severely affecting performance. There has been recent interest in determining anaphoricity *before* performing anaphora resolution (Ng and Cardie, 2002; Uryupina, 2003), but results have not been entirely satisfactory. Given that old entities are more likely to be referred to by anaphors, for instance, identification of information status could improve anaphoricity determination.

Postolache et al. (2005) have recently shown that learning information structure with high accuracy is feasible for Czech. However, there are yet no studies that explore such a task for English. Exploiting an existing annotated corpus, in this paper we report experiments on learning a model for the automatic identification of information status in English.

2 Data

For our experiments we annotated a portion of the transcribed Switchboard corpus (Godfrey et al., 1992), consisting of 147 dialogues (Nissim et al., 2004).[1] In the following section we provide a brief description of the annotation categories.

2.1 Annotation

Our annotation of information status mainly builds on (Prince, 1992), and employs a distinction into *old*, *mediated*, and *new* entities similar to the work of (Strube, 1998; Eckert and Strube, 2001).

All noun phrases (NPs) were extracted as markable entities using pre-existing parse information (Carletta et al., 2004). An entity was annotated as *new* if it has not been previously referred to and is yet unknown to the hearer. The tag *mediated* was instead used whenever an entity that is newly mentioned in the dialogue can be inferred by the hearer thanks to prior or general context.[2] Typical examples of mediated entities are generally known objects (such as "the sun", or "the Pope" (Löbner, 1985)), and bridging anaphors (Clark, 1975; Vieira and Poesio, 2000), where an entity is related to a previously introduced one. Whenever an entity was neither new nor mediated, it was considered as *old*.

In order to account for the complexity of the notion of information status, the annotation also includes a sub-type classification for old and mediated entities that provides a finer-grained distinction with information on why a given entity is mediated (e.g., set-relation, bridging) or old (e.g., coreference, generic pronouns). In order to test the feasibility of automatically assigning information status to discourse entities, we took a modular approach and only considered the coarser-grained distinctions for this first study. Information about the finer-grained subtypes will be used in future work.

In addition to the main categories, we used two more annotation classes: a tag *non-applicable*, used for entities that were wrongly extracted in the automatic selection of markables (e.g. "course" in "of course"), for idiomatic occurrences, and expletive uses of "it"; and a tag *not-understood* to be applied whenever an annotator did not fully understand the text. Instances annotated with these two tags, as well as all traces, which were left unannotated, were excluded from all our experiments.

Inter-annotator agreement was measured using the kappa (K) statistics (Cohen, 1960; Carletta, 1996) on 1,502 instances (three Switchboard dialogues) marked by two annotators who followed specific written guidelines. Given that the task involves a fair amount of subjective judgement, agreement was remarkably high. Over the three dialogues, the annotation yielded $K = .845$ for the old/med/new classification ($K = .788$ when including the finer-grained subtype distinction). Specifically, "old" proved to be the easiest to distinguish, with $K = .902$; for "med" and "new" agreement was measured at $K = .800$ and $K = .794$, respectively. A value of $K > .76$ is usually considered good agreement. Further details on the annotation process and corpus description are provided in (Nissim et al., 2004)

2.2 Setup

We split the 147 dialogues into a training, a development and an evaluation set. The training set contains 40,865 NPs distributed over 94 dialogues, the development set consists of 23 dialogues for a total of 10,565 NPs, and the evaluation set comprises 30 dialogues with 12,624 NPs. Instances were randomised, so that occurrences of NPs from the same dialogue were possibly split across the different sets.

[1]Switchboard is a collection of spontaneous phone conversations, averaging six minutes in length, between speakers of American English on predetermined topics. A third of the corpus is syntactically parsed as part of the Penn Treebank (Marcus et al., 1993)

[2]This type corresponds to Prince's (1981; 1992) *inferrables*.

Table 1 reports the distribution of classes for the training, development and evaluation sets. The distributions are similar, with a majority of old entities, followed by mediated entities, and lastly by new ones.

Table 1: Information status distribution of NPs in training, development and evaluation sets

	TRAIN	DEV	EVAL
old	19730 (48.3%)	5181 (49.0%)	6049 (47.9%)
med	15184 (37.1%)	3762 (35.6%)	4644 (36.8%)
new	5951 (14.6%)	1622 (15.4%)	1931 (15.3%)
total	40865 (100%)	10565 (100%)	12624 (100%)

3 Classification with hand-crafted rules

The target classes for our classification experiments are the annotation tags: old, mediated, and new. As baseline, we could take a simple "most-frequent-class" assignment that would classify all entities as old, thus yielding an accuracy of 47.9% on the evaluation set (see Table 1). Although the "all-old" assumption makes a reasonable baseline, it would not provide a particularly interesting solution from a practical perspective, since a dialogue should also contain not-old information. Thus, rather than adopting this simple strategy, we developed a more sophisticated baseline working on a set of hand-crafted rules.

This hand-crafted algorithm is based on rather straightforward, intuitive rules, partially reflecting the instructions specified in the annotation guidelines. As shown in Figure 1, the top split is the NP type: whether the instance to classify is a pronoun, a proper noun, or a common noun. The other information that the algorithm uses is about complete or partial string overlapping with respect to the dialogue's context. For common nouns we also consider the kind of determiner (*def*inite, *indef*inite, *dem*onstrative, *poss*essive, or *bare*).

In order to obtain the NP type information, we exploited the pre-existing morpho-syntactic treebank annotation of Switchboard. Whenever the extraction failed, we assigned a type "other" and always backed-off these cases to old (the most frequent class in training data). Values for the other features were obtained by simple pattern matching and NP extraction.

Evaluation measures The algorithm's performance is evaluated with respect to its general accuracy (Acc): the number of correctly classified instances over all assignments. Moreover, for each

```
case NP is a pronoun
    status := old
case NP is a proper noun
    if first occurrence then
        status := med
    else
        status := old
    endif
case NP is a common noun
    if identical string already mentioned then
        status := old
    else
        if partial string already mentioned then
            status := med
        else
            if determiner is def/dem/poss then
                status := med
            else
                status := new
            endif
        endif
    endif
otherwise
    status := old
```

Figure 1: Hand-crafted rule-based algorithm for the assignment of information status to NPs.

class (c), we report precision (P), recall (R), and f-score (F) thus calculated:

$$P_c = \frac{correct\ assignments\ of\ c}{total\ assignments\ of\ c}$$

$$R_c = \frac{correct\ assignments\ of\ c}{total\ corpus\ instances\ of\ c}$$

$$F_c = \frac{2P_cR_c}{P_c+R_c}$$

The overall accuracy of the rule-based algorithm is 65.8%. Table 2 shows the results for each target class in both the development and evaluation sets. We discuss results on the latter.

Although a very high proportion of old entities is correctly retrieved (93.5%), this is done with relatively low precision (66.7%). Moreover, both precision and recall for the other classes are disappointing. Unsurprisingly, the rules that apply to common nouns (the most ambiguous with respect to information status) generate a large num-

Table 2: Per class performance of hand-crafted rules on the development and evaluation sets

	DEV			EVAL		
	P	R	F	P	R	F
old	.677	.932	.784	.667	.935	.779
med	.641	.488	.554	.666	.461	.545
new	.517	.180	.267	.436	.175	.250

ber of false positives. The rule that predicts an old entity in case of a full previous mention, for example, has a precision of only 39.8%. Better, but not yet satisfactory, is the precision of the rule that predicts a mediated entity for a common noun that has a previous partial mention (64.7%). The worst performing rule is the one that assigns the most frequent class (old) to entities of syntactic type "other", with a precision of 35.4%. To give an idea of the correlation between NP type and information status, in Table 3 we report the distribution observed in the evaluation set.

Table 3: Distribution of information status over NP types in the evaluation set

	old	med	new
pronoun	4465	159	13
proper	107	198	27
common	752	2874	1256
other	725	1413	635

4 Learning Information Status

Our starting point for the automatic assignment of information status are the three already introduced classes: old, mediated and new. Additionally, we experiment with binary classifications, by collapsing mediated entities in turn with old and new ones.

For training, developing and evaluating the model we use the split described in Section 2.2 (see Table 1). Performance is evaluated according to overall accuracy and per class precision, recall, and f-score as described in Section 3. To train a C4.5 decision tree model we use the J48 Weka implementation (Witten and Frank, 2000). The choice of features to build the tree is described in the following section.

4.1 Features

The seven features we use are automatically extracted from the annotated data exploiting preexisting morpho-syntactic markup and using simple pattern matching techniques. They are summarised in Table 4.

Table 4: Feature set for learning experiments

FEATURE	VALUES
full prev mention	numeric
mention time	{first,second,more}
partial prev mention	{yes,no,na}
determiner	{bare,def,dem,indef,poss,na}
NP length	numeric
grammatical role	{subject,subjpass,object,pp,other}
NP type	{pronoun,common,proper,other}

The choice of features is motivated by the following observations. The information coming from partial previous mentions is particularly useful for the identification of mediated entities. This should account specifically for cases of mediation via set-relations; for example, "your children" would be considered a partial previous mention of "my children" or "your four children". The value "na" stands for "non-applicable" and is mainly used for pronouns. Full previous mention is likely to be a good indicator of old entities. Both full and partial previous mentions are calculated within each dialogue without any constraints based on distance.

NP type and determiner type are expected to be helpful for all categories, with pronouns, for instance, tending to be old and indefinite NPs being often new. We included the length of NPs (measured in number of words) since linguistic studies have shown that old entities tend to be expressed with less lexical material (Wasow, 2002). In experiments on the development data we also included the NP string itself, on the grounds that it might be of use in cases of general mediated instances (common knowledge entities), such as "the sun", "people", "Mickey Mouse", and so on. However, this feature turned out to negatively affect performance, and was not included in the final model.

4.2 Results

With an overall final accuracy of 79.5% on the evaluation set, C4.5 significantly outperforms the hand-crafted algorithm (65.8%). Although the identification of old entities is quite successful (F=.928), performance is not entirely satisfactory. This is especially true for the classification of new entities, for which the final f-score is .320, mainly due to extremely low recall (.223). Mediated entities, instead, are retrieved with a fairly low precision but higher recall. Table 5 summarises precision, recall, and f-score for each class.

Table 5: Per class performance of C4.5 on the development and evaluation sets

	DEV			EVAL		
	P	R	F	P	R	F
old	.935	.911	.923	.941	.915	.928
med	.673	.878	.762	.681	.876	.766
new	.623	.234	.341	.563	.223	.320

The major confusion in the classification arises between mediated and new (the most difficult decision to make for human annotators too, see Section 2.1), which are often distinguished on the basis of world knowledge, not available to the classifier. This is clearly shown by the confusion matrix in Table 6: the highest proportion of mistakes is due to 1,453 new instances classified as mediated. Also significant is the wrong assignment of mediated tags to old entities. Such behaviour of the classifier is to be expected, given the 'in-between' nature of mediated entities.

Table 6: Confusion matrix for evaluation set. C=Classifier tag; G=Gold tag

C → G ↓	old	med	new
old	5537	452	60
med	303	4066	275
new	47	1453	431

4.3 Classification with two categories only

Given the above observations, we collapsed mediated entities in turn with old ones (focusing on their non-newness) or new ones (enhancing their non complete givenness), thus reducing the task to a binary classification.

Since it appears to be more difficult to distinguish mediated and new rather than mediated and old (Table 6), we expect the classifier to perform better when mediated is binned with new rather than old. Also, in the case where mediated and old entities are collapsed into one single class as opposed to new ones, the distribution of classes becomes highly skewed towards old entities (84.7%) so that the learner is likely to lack sufficient information for identifying new entities.

Table 7 shows the final accuracy for the two binary classifications (and the three-way one). As expected, when mediated entities are joint with new ones, the classifier performs best (93.1%), with high f-scores for both old and new, and is significantly better than the alternative binary classification (t-test, $p < 0.001$). Indeed, the old+med vs new classification is nearly an all-old assignment and its overall final accuracy (85.5%) is not a significant improvement over the all-old baseline (84.7%). Results suggest that mediated NPs are more similar to new than to old entities and might provide interesting feedback for the theoretical assumptions underlying the corpus annotation.

4.4 Comparison with two categories only

For a fair comparison, we performed a two-way classification using the hand-crafted algorithm, which had to be simplified to account for the lack of a mediated class.

In the case where all mediated instances where collapsed together with the old ones, the decision rules are very simple: pronouns, proper nouns, and common nouns that have been previously fully or partially mentioned are classified as old; first mention common nouns are new; everything else is old. Both precision and recall for old instances are quite high (.868 and .906 respectively), for a resulting f-score of .887. Conversely, the performance on identifying new entities is very poor, with a precision of .337 and a recall of .227, for a combined f-score of .271. The overall accuracy is .803, and this is significantly lower than the performance of C4.5, which achieves an overall accuracy of .850 (t-test, $p < 0.001$).

When mediated entities are collapsed with new ones, rule-based classification is done again with a very basic algorithm derived from the rules in Figure 1: pronouns are old; proper nouns are new if first mention, old otherwise; common nouns that have been fully previously mentioned are old, otherwise new. Everything else is new, which in the training set is now the most frequent class (51.7%). The overall accuracy of .849 is significantly lower than that achieved by C4.5, which is .931 (t-test, $p < 0.001$). Differently from the previous case (mediated collapsed with old), the performance on each class is comparable, with a precision, recall and f-score of .863, .815, and .838 for old and of .838, .881, and .859 for new.

5 Discussion

5.1 Influence of training size

In order to assess the contribution of training size to performance, we experimented with increas-

Table 7: Overview of accuracy for hand-crafted rules and C4.5 on three-way and binary classifications on development and evaluation sets

	DEV		EVAL	
classification	rules	C4.5	rules	C4.5
old vs med vs new	.658	.796	.644	.795
old+med vs new	.810	.861	.803	.855
old vs med+new	.844	.926	.849	.931

ingly larger portions of the training data (from 50 to 30,000 instances). For each training size we ran the classifier 5 times, each with a different randomly picked set of instances. This was done for the three-way and the two binary classifications. Reported results are always averaged over the 5 runs. Figure 2 shows the three learning curves.

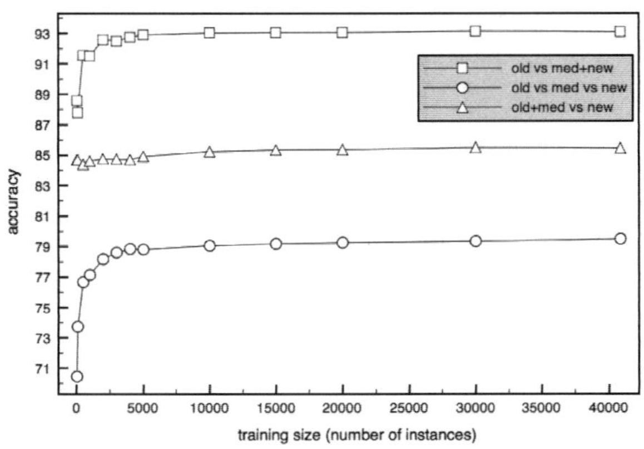

Figure 2: Learning curves for three- and two-way classifications

The curve for the three-way classification shows a slight constant improvement, though it appears to reach a plateau after 5,000 instances. The result obtained training on the full set (40865 instances) is significantly better only if compared to a training set of 4,000 or less (t-test, $p < 0.05$). No other significant difference in accuracy can be observed.

Increasing the training size over 5,000 instances when learning to classify old+mediated vs new leads to a slight improvement due to the learner being able to identify some new entities. With a smaller training set the proportion of new entities is far too small to be of use. However, as said, the overall final accuracy of 85.5% (see Table 7) does not significantly improve over the baseline.

Table 8: Performance of leave-one-out and single-feature classifiers on three-way classification

FEATURE	ACCURACY	
	removed	single
full prev mention	.793	.730
mention time	.795	.730
partial prev mention	.791	.769
determiner	.789	.775
NP length	.793	.733
gram role	.782	.656
NP type	.784	.701
full set	.795	

5.2 Feature contribution

We are also interested in the contribution of each single feature. Therefore, we ran the classifier again, leaving out one feature at a time. No significant drop or gain was observed in any of the runs (t-test, $p < 0.01$), though the worst detriments were yielded by removing the grammatical role and the NP type. These two features, however, also appear to be the least informative in single-feature classification experiments, thus suggesting that such information comes very useful only when combined with other evidence (see also Section 5.4. All results for leave-one-out and single-feature classifiers are shown in Table 8.

5.3 Error Analysis

The overwhelming majority of mistakes (1,453, 56.1% of all errors) in the three-way classification stems from classifying as mediated entities that are in fact new (Table 6). Significant confusion arises from proper nouns, as they are annotated as mediated or new entities, depending on whether they are generally known (such as names of US presidents, for example), or domain/community-specific (such as the name of a local store that only the speaker knows). This inconsistency in the annotation might reflect well the actual status of entities in the dialogues, but it can be misleading for the classifier.

Another large group of errors is formed by old entities classified as mediated (452 cases). This is probably due to the fact that the first node in the decision tree is the "partial mention" feature (see Figure 3). The tree correctly captures the fact that a firstly mentioned entity which has been partially mentioned before is mediated. An entity that has a previous partial mention but also a full previous mention is classified as old only if it is a proper noun or a pronoun, but as mediated if it is a common noun. This yields a large number of mistakes, since many common nouns that have been previously mentioned (both in full and partially) are in fact old. Another problem with previous mentions is the lack of restriction in distance: we consider a previous mention any identical mention of a given NP anywhere in the dialogue, and we have no means of checking that it is indeed the same entity that is referred to. A way to alleviate this problem might be exploiting speaker turn information. Using anaphoric chains could also be of help, but see Section 6.

5.4 Learnt trees meet hand-crafted rules

The learnt trees provide interesting insights on the intuitions behind the choice of hand-crafted rules.

```
partial = yes
|   full <= 1
|   |   det = def: med
|   |   det = indef
|   |   |   length <= 2
|   |   |   |   gramm = subj: med
|   |   |   |   gramm = subjpassive: new
|   |   |   |   gramm = obj: med
|   |   |   |   gramm = pp: med
|   |   |   |   gramm = other
|   |   |   |   |   type = proper: med
|   |   |   |   |   type = common: new
|   |   |   |   |   type = pronoun: new
|   |   |   |   |   type = other: med
|   |   |   length > 2: med
|   |   det = dem
|   |   |   gramm = subj
. . .
```

Figure 3: Top of C.5, full training set, three classes

Figure 3 shows the top of C4.5 (trained on the full training set for the three-way classification), which looks remarkably different from the rules in Figure 1. We had based our decision of emphasising the importance of the NP type on the linguistic evidence that different syntactic realisations reflect different degrees of availability of discourse entities (Givón, 1983; Ariel, 1990; Grosz et al., 1995). In the learnt model, however, knowledge about NP type is only used as subordinate to other features. This is indeed mirrored in the fact that removing NP type information from the feature set causes accuracy to drop, but a classifier building on NP type alone performs poorly (see Table 8).[3] Interestingly, though, more informative knowledge about syntactic form seems to be derived from the determiner type, which helps distinguish degrees of oldness among common nouns.

[3]The NPtype-only classifier assigns old to pronouns and med to all other types; it never assigns new.

5.5 Naive Bayes model

For additional comparison, we also trained a Naive Bayes classifier with the same experimental settings. Results are significantly worse than C4.5's in all three scenarios (t-test, $p < 0.005$), with an accuracy of 74.6% in the three-way classification, 63.3% for old+mediated vs new, and 91.0% for old vs mediated+new. The latter distribution appears again to be the easiest to learn.

6 Related Work

To our knowledge, there are no other studies on the automatic assignment of information status in English. Recently, (Postolache et al., 2005) have reported experiments on learning information structure in the Prague TreeBank. The Czech treebank is annotated following the Topic-Focus articulation theory (Hajičová et al., 1998). The theoretical definitions underlying the Prague Treebank and the corpus we are using are different, with the former giving a more global picture of information structure, and the latter a more entity-specific one. For this reason, and due to the fact that Postolache et al.'s experiments are on Czech (with a freer word order than English), comparing results is not straightforward.

Their best system (C4.5 decision tree) achieves an accuracy of 90.69% on the topic/focus identification task. This result is comparable with the result we obtain when training and testing on the corpus where mediated and new entities are not distinguished (93.1%). Postolache and colleagues also observe a slowly flattening learning curve after a very small amount of data (even 1%, in their case). Therefore, they predict an increase in performance will mainly come from better features rather than more training data. This is likely to be true in our case as well, also because our feature set is currently small and we will further benefit from incorporating additional features. Postolache et al. use a larger feature set, which also includes coreference information. The corpus we use has manually annotated coreference links. However, because we see anaphoricity determination as a task that could benefit from automatic information status assignment, we decided not to exploit this information in the current experiments. Moreover, we did not want our model to rely too heavily on a feature that is not easy to obtain automatically.

7 Conclusions and Future Work

We have presented a model for the automatic assignment of information status in English. On the three-way classification into old, mediated, and new that reflects the corpus annotation tags, the learnt tree outperforms a hand-crafted algorithm and achieves an accuracy of 79.5%, with high precision and recall for old entities, high recall for mediated entities, and a fair precision, but very poor recall, for new ones. When we collapsed mediated and new entities into one category only opposing this to old ones, the classifier performed with an accuracy of 93.1%, with high f-scores for both classes. Binning mediated and old entities together did not produce interesting results, mainly due to the highly skewed distribution of the resulting corpus towards old entities. This suggests that mediated entities are more similar to new than to old ones, and might provide interesting feedback for the theoretical assumptions underlying the annotation. Future work will examine specific cases and investigate how such insights can be used to make the theoretical framework more accurate.

As the first experiments run on English to learn information status, we wanted to concentrate on the task itself and avoid noise introduced by automatic processing. More realistic settings for integrating an information status model in a large-scale NLP system would imply obtaining syntactic information via parsing rather than directly from the treebank. Future experiments will assess the impact of automatic preprocessing of the data.

Results are very promising but there is room for improvement. First, the syntactic category "other" is far too large, and finer distinctions must be made by means of better extraction rules from the trees. Second, and most importantly, we believe that using more features will be the main trigger of higher accuracy. In particular, we plan to use additional lexical and relational features derived from knowledge sources such as WordNet (Fellbaum, 1998) and FrameNet (Baker et al., 1998) which should be especially helpful in distinguishing mediated from new entities, the most difficult decision to make. For example, an entity that is linked in WordNet (within a given depth) and/or FrameNet to a previously introduced one is more likely to be mediated than new.

Additionally, we will attempt to exploit dialogue turns, since knowing which speaker said what is clearly very valuable information. In a similar vein, we will experiment with distance measures, in terms of turns, sentences, or even time, for determining when an introduced entity might stop to be available.

We also plan to run experiments on the automatic classification of old and mediated subtypes (the finer-grained classification) that is included in the corpus but that we did not consider for the present study (see Section 2.1). The major benefit of this would be a contribution to the resolution of bridging anaphora.

References

Mira Ariel. 1990. *Accessing Noun Phrase Antecedents*. Routledge, London-New York.

Collin F. Baker, Charles J. Fillmore, and John B. Lowe. 1998. The Berkeley FrameNet project. In Christian Boitet and Pete Whitelock, editors, *Proceedings of COLING-ACL*, pages 86–90.

Jean Carletta, Shipra Dingare, Malvina Nissim, and Tatiana Nikitina. 2004. Using the NITE XML Toolkit on the Switchboard Corpus to study syntactic choice: a case study. In *Proceedings of the 4th International Conference on Language Resources and Evaluation (LREC2004), Lisbon, May 2004.*

Jean Carletta. 1996. Assessing agreement on classification tasks: the kappa statistic. *Computational Linguistics*, 22(2):249–254.

Herbert H. Clark. 1975. Bridging. In Roger Schank and Bonnie Nash-Webber, editors, *Theoretical Issues in Natural Language Processing*. The MIT Press, Cambridge, MA.

Jacob Cohen. 1960. A coefficient of agreement for nominal scales. *Educational and Psychological Measurements*, 20:37–46.

Miriam Eckert and Michael Strube. 2001. Dialogue acts, synchronising units and anaphora resolution. *Journal of Semantics*, 17(1):51–89.

Christiane Fellbaum, editor. 1998. *WordNet: An Electronic Lexical Database*. The MIT Press, Cambridge, MA.

Talmy Givón. 1983. Introduction. In Talmy Givón, editor, *Topic Continuity in Discourse: A Quantitative Cross-language Study*. John Benjamins, Amsterdam/Philadelphia.

J. Godfrey, E. Holliman, and J. McDaniel. 1992. SWITCHBOARD: Telephone speech corpus for research and development. In *Proceedings of ICASSP-92*, pages 517–520.

Barbara Grosz, Aravind K. Joshi, and Scott Weinstein. 1995. Centering: a framework for modeling the local coherence of discourse. *Computational Linguistics*, 21(2):203–225.

Eva Hajičová, Barbara Partee, and Petr Sgall. 1998. Topic-focus articulation, tripartite structures, and semantic content. In *Studies in Linguistics and Philosophy*, volume 71. Dordrecht.

Eva Hajičová. 1984. Topic and focus. In Petr Sgall, editor, *Contributions to Functional Syntax. Semantics and Language Comprehension (LLSEE 16)*, pages 189–202. John Benjamins, Amsterdam.

M.A.K. Halliday. 1976. Notes on transitivity and theme in English. Part 2. *Journal of Linguistics*, 3(2):199–244.

Julia Hirschberg and Christine H. Nakatani. 1996. A prosodic analysis of discourse segments in direction giving monologues. In *Proceedings of 34th Annual Meeting of the Association for Computational Linguistics*.

Ivana Kruijff-Korbayová and Mark Steedman. 2003. Discourse and information structure. *Journal of Logic, Language, and Information*, 12:249–259.

Knud Lambrecht. 1994. *Information structure and sentence form. Topic, focus, and the mental representation of discourse referents*. Cambridge University Press, Cambridge.

Sebastian Löbner. 1985. Definites. *Journal of Semantics*, 4:279–326.

Mitchell Marcus, Beatrice Santorini, and May Ann Marcinkiewicz. 1993. Building a large annotated corpus of english: The Penn treebank. *Computational Linguistics*, 19:313–330.

Vincent Ng and Claire Cardie. 2002. Identifying anaphoric and non-anaphoric noun phrases to improve coreference resolution. In *Proc of the 19th International Conference on Computational Linguistics; Taipei, Taiwan*, pages 730–736.

Malvina Nissim, Shipra Dingare, Jean Carletta, and Mark Steedman. 2004. An annotation scheme for information status in dialogue. In *Proceedings of the 4th International Conference on Language Resources and Evaluation (LREC2004), Lisbon, May 2004.*

Oana Postolache, Ivana Kruijff-Korbayova, and Geert-Jan Kruijff. 2005. Data-driven approaches for information structure identification. In *Proceedings of Human Language Technology Conference and Conference on Empirical Methods in Natural Language Processing*, pages 9–16, Vancouver, British Columbia, Canada, October. Association for Computational Linguistics.

Ellen F. Prince. 1981. Toward a taxonomy of given-new information. In Peter Cole, editor, *Radical Pragmatics*. Academic Press, New York.

Ellen Prince. 1992. The ZPG letter: subjects, definiteness, and information-status. In Sandra Thompson and William Mann, editors, *Discourse description: diverse analyses of a fund raising text*, pages 295–325. John Benjamins, Philadelphia/Amsterdam.

Mark Steedman. 2000. *The Syntactic Process*. The MIT Press, Cambridge, MA.

K. Stöber, P. Wagner, Jörg Helbig, S. Köster, D. Stall, M. Thomas, J. Blauert, W. Hess, R. Hoffmann, and H. Mangold. 2000. Speech synthesis using multi-level selection and concatenation of units from large speech corpora. In W. Wahlster, editor, *Verbmobil: Foundations of Speech-to-Speech Translation*, pages 519–534. Springer-Verlag, Berlin.

Michael Strube. 1998. Never look back: An alternative to centering. In *Proceedings of the 17th International Conference on Computational Linguistics and 36th Annual Meeting of the Association for Computational Linguistics*, pages 1251–1257, Montréal, Québec, Canada.

Olga Uryupina. 2003. High-precision identification of discourse new and unique noun phrases. In *Proc. of the ACL 2003 Student Workshop*, pages 80–86.

Enric Vallduví. 1992. *The Informational Component*. Garland, New York.

Renata Vieira and Massimo Poesio. 2000. An empirically-based system for processing definite descriptions. *Computational Linguistics*, 26(4).

Thomas Wasow. 2002. *Postverbal Behavior*. CSLI Publications.

Ian H. Witten and Eibe Frank. 2000. *Data Mining: Practical Machine Learning Tools and Techniques with Java Implementations*. Morgan Kaufmann, San Diego, CA.

Automatic classification of citation function

Simone Teufel **Advaith Siddharthan** **Dan Tidhar**
Natural Language and Information Processing Group
Computer Laboratory
Cambridge University, CB3 0FD, UK
{Simone.Teufel,Advaith.Siddharthan,Dan.Tidhar}@cl.cam.ac.uk

Abstract

Citation function is defined as the author's reason for citing a given paper (e.g. acknowledgement of the use of the cited method). The automatic recognition of the rhetorical function of citations in scientific text has many applications, from improvement of impact factor calculations to text summarisation and more informative citation indexers. We show that our annotation scheme for citation function is reliable, and present a supervised machine learning framework to automatically classify citation function, using both shallow and linguistically-inspired features. We find, amongst other things, a strong relationship between citation function and sentiment classification.

1 Introduction

Why do researchers cite a particular paper? This is a question that has interested researchers in discourse analysis, sociology of science, and information sciences (library sciences) for decades (Garfield, 1979; Small, 1982; White, 2004). Many annotation schemes for citation motivation have been created over the years, and the question has been studied in detail, even to the level of in-depth interviews with writers about each individual citation (Hodges, 1972).

Part of this sustained interest in citations can be explained by the fact that bibliometric metrics are commonly used to measure the impact of a researcher's work by how often they are cited (Borgman, 1990; Luukkonen, 1992). However, researchers from the field of discourse studies have long criticised purely quantitative citation analysis, pointing out that many citations are done out of "politeness, policy or piety" (Ziman, 1968), and that criticising citations or citations in passing should not "count" as much as central citations in a paper, or as those citations where a researcher's work is used as the starting point of somebody else's work (Bonzi, 1982). A plethora of manual annotation schemes for citation *motivation* have been invented over the years (Garfield, 1979; Hodges, 1972; Chubin and Moitra, 1975). Other schemes concentrate on citation *function* (Spiegel-Rüsing, 1977; O'Connor, 1982; Weinstock, 1971; Swales, 1990; Small, 1982)). One of the best-known of these studies (Moravcsik and Murugesan, 1975) divides citations in running text into four dimensions: conceptual or operational use (i.e., use of theory vs. use of technical method); evolutionary or juxtapositional (i.e., own work is based on the cited work vs. own work is an alternative to it); organic or perfunctory (i.e., work is crucially needed for understanding of citing article or just a general acknowledgement); and finally confirmative vs. negational (i.e., is the correctness of the findings disputed?). They found, for example, that 40% of the citations were perfunctory, which casts further doubt on the citation-counting approach.

Based on such annotation schemes and hand-analyzed data, different influences on citation behaviour can be determined. Nevertheless, researchers in the field of citation content analysis do not normally cross-validate their schemes with independent annotation studies with other human annotators, and usually only annotate a small number of citations (in the range of hundreds or thousands). Also, automated application of the annotation is not something that is generally considered in the field, though White (2004) sees the future of discourse-analytic citation analysis in automation.

Apart from raw material for bibliometric studies, citations can also be used for search purposes in document retrieval applications. In the library world, printed or electronic citation indexes such as ISI (Garfield, 1979) serve as an orthogonal

Proceedings of the 2006 Conference on Empirical Methods in Natural Language Processing (EMNLP 2006), pages 103–110,
Sydney, July 2006.

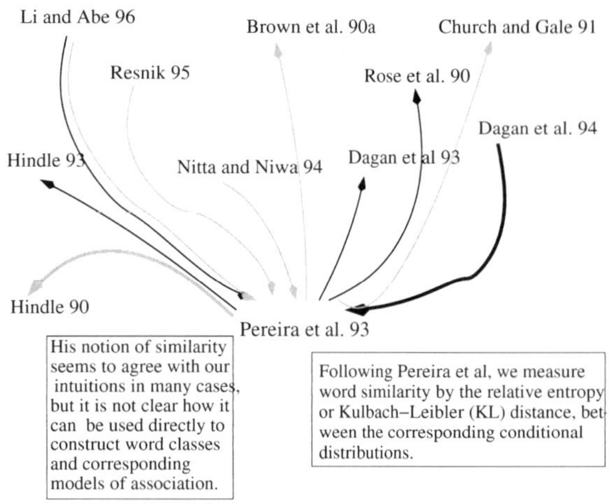

Figure 1: A rhetorical citation map

search tool to find relevant papers, starting from a source paper of interest. With the increased availability of documents in electronic form in recent years, citation-based search and automatic citation indexing have become highly popular, cf. the successful search tools Google Scholar and CiteSeer (Giles et al., 1998).[1]

But not all search needs are fulfilled by current citation indexers. Experienced researchers are often interested in *relations* between articles (Shum, 1998). They want to know if a certain article criticises another and what the criticism is, or if the current work is based on that prior work. This type of information is hard to come by with current search technology. Neither the author's abstract, nor raw citation counts help users in assessing the relation between articles.

Fig. 1 shows a hypothetical search tool which displays differences and similarities between a target paper (here: *Pereira et al., 1993*) and the papers that it cites and that cite it. *Contrastive* links are shown in grey – links to rival papers and papers the current paper contrasts itself to. *Continuative* links are shown in black – links to papers that *use* the methodology of the current paper. Fig. 1 also displays the most characteristic textual sentence about each citation. For instance, we can see which aspect of *Hindle (1990)* our example paper criticises, and in which way the example paper's work was used by *Dagan et al. (1994)*.

Note that not even the CiteSeer text snippet can fulfil the relation search need: it is always centered around the physical location of the citations, but the context is often not informative enough for the searcher to infer the relation. In fact, studies from our annotated corpus (Teufel, 1999) show that 69% of the 600 sentences stating contrast with other work and 21% of the 246 sentences stating research continuation with other work do not contain the corresponding citation; the citation is found in preceding sentences (which means that the sentence expressing the contrast or continuation is outside the CiteSeer snippet). A more sophisticated, discourse-aware citation indexer which finds these sentences and associates them with the citation would add considerable value to the researcher's bibliographic search (Ritchie et al., 2006b).

Our annotation scheme for citations is based on empirical work in content citation analysis. It is designed for information retrieval applications such as improved citation indexing and better bibliometric measures (Teufel et al., 2006). Its 12 categories mark relationships with other works. Each citation is labelled with exactly one category. The following top-level four-way distinction applies:

- Explicit statement of weakness
- Contrast or comparison with other work (4 categories)
- Agreement/usage/compatibility with other work (6 categories), and
- A neutral category.

In this paper, we show that the scheme can be reliably annotated by independent coders. We also report results of a supervised machine learning experiment which replicates the human annotation.

2 An annotation scheme for citations

Our scheme (given in Fig. 2) is adapted from that of Spiegel-Rüsing (1977) after an analysis of a corpus of scientific articles in computational linguistics. We avoid sociologically orientated distinctions ("paying homage to pioneers"), as they can be difficult to operationalise without deep knowledge of the field and its participants (Swales, 1986). Our redefinition of the categories aims at reliably annotation; at the same time, the categories should be informative enough for the document management application sketched in the introduction.

[1]These tools automatically citation-index all scientific articles reached by a web-crawler, making them available to searchers via authors or keywords in the title, and displaying the citation in context of a text snippet.

Category	Description
Weak	Weakness of cited approach
CoCoGM	Contrast/Comparison in Goals or Methods(neutral)
CoCo-	Author's work is stated to be superior to cited work
CoCoR0	Contrast/Comparison in Results (neutral)
CoCoXY	Contrast between 2 cited methods
PBas	Author uses cited work as basis or starting point
PUse	Author uses tools/algorithms/data/definitions
PModi	Author adapts or modifies tools/algorithms/data
PMot	This citation is positive about approach used or problem addressed (used to motivate work in current paper)
PSim	Author's work and cited work are similar
PSup	Author's work and cited work are compatible/provide support for each other
Neut	Neutral description of cited work, or not enough textual evidence for above categories, or unlisted citation function

Figure 2: Annotation scheme for citation function.

Our categories are as follows: One category (Weak) is reserved for weakness of previous research, if it is addressed by the authors. The next four categories describe comparisons or contrasts between own and other work. The difference between them concerns whether the contrast is between methods employed or goals (CoCoGM), or results, and in the case of results, a difference is made between the cited results being worse than the current work (CoCo-), or comparable or better results (CoCoR0). As well as considering differences between the current work and other work, we also mark citations if they are explicitly compared and contrasted with *other* work (i.e. not the work in the current paper). This is expressed in category CoCoXY. While this is not typically annotated in the literature, we expect a potential practical benefit of this category for our application, particularly in searches for differences and rival approaches.

The next set of categories we propose concerns positive sentiment expressed towards a citation, or a statement that the other work is actively used in the current work (which we consider the ultimate praise). We mark statements of use of data and methods of the cited work, differentiating unchanged use (PUse) from use with adaptations (PModi). Work which is stated as the explicit starting point or intellectual ancestry is marked with our category PBas. If a claim in the literature is used to strengthen the authors' argument, or vice versa, we assign the category PSup. We also mark similarity of (an aspect of) the approach to the cited work (PSim), and motivation of approach used or problem addressed (PMot).

Our twelfth category, Neut, bundles truly neutral descriptions of cited work with those cases where the textual evidence for a citation function was not enough to warrant annotation of that category, and all other functions for which our scheme did not provide a specific category.

Citation function is hard to annotate because it in principle requires interpretation of author intentions (what could the author's intention have been in choosing a certain citation?). One of our most fundamental principles is thus to only mark explicitly signalled citation functions. Our guidelines explicitly state that a general linguistic phrase such as "better" or "used by us" must be present; this increases the objectivity of defining citation function. Annotators must be able to point to textual evidence for assigning a particular function (and are asked to type the source of this evidence into the annotation tool for each citation). Categories are defined in terms of certain objective types of statements (e.g., there are 7 cases for PMot, e.g. "Citation claims that or gives reasons for why problem Y is hard"). Annotators can use general text interpretation principles when assigning the categories (such as anaphora resolution and parallel constructions), but are not allowed to use in-depth knowledge of the field or of the authors.

Guidelines (25 pages, $\sim$ 150 rules) describe the categories with examples, provide a decision tree and give decision aids in systematically ambiguous cases. Nevertheless, subjective judgement of the annotators is still necessary to assign a single tag in an unseen context, because of the many difficult cases for annotation. Some of these concern the fact that authors do not always state their purpose clearly. For instance, several earlier studies found that negational citations are rare (Moravcsik and Murugesan, 1975; Spiegel-Rüsing, 1977); MacRoberts and MacRoberts (1984) argue that the reason for this is that they are potentially politically dangerous. In our data we found ample evidence of the "meekness" effect. Other difficulties concern the distinction of the usage of a method from statements of similarity between a method and the own method (i.e., the choice between categories PSim and PUse). This happens in cases where authors do not want to admit (or stress) that they are using somebody else's method. Another difficult distinction concerns the judgement of whether the authors *continue* somebody's research (i.e., consider their research as intellectual ancestry, i.e. `PBas`), or whether they simply *use* the work (`PUse`).

The unit of annotation is a) the full citation (as recognised by our automatic citation processor on our corpus), and b) names of authors of cited papers anywhere in running text outside of a formal citation context (i.e., without date). These latter are marked up, slightly unusually in comparison to other citation indexers, because we believe they function as important referents comparable in importance to formal citations.[2] In principle, there are many other linguistic expressions by which the authors could refer to other people's work: pronouns, abbreviations such as "Mueller and Sag (1990), henceforth M & S", and names of approaches or theories which are associated with particular authors. The fact that in these contexts citation function cannot be annotated (because it is not technically feasible to recognise them well enough) sometimes causes problems with context dependencies.

While there are unambiguous example cases where the citation function can be decided on the basis of the sentence alone, this is not always the case. Most approaches are not criticised in the same sentence where they are also cited: it is more likely that there are several descriptive sentences about a cited approach between its formal citation and the evaluative statement, which is often at the end of the textual segment about this citation. Nevertheless, the annotator must mark the function on the nearest appropriate annotation unit (citation or author name). Our rules decree that context is in most cases constrained to the paragraph boundary. In rare cases, paper-wide information is required (e.g., for `PMot`, we need to know that a praised approach is used by the authors, information which may not be local in the paragraph). Annotators are thus asked to skim-read the paper before annotation.

One possible view on this annotation scheme could consider the first two sets of categories as "negative" and the third set of categories "positive", in the sense of Pang et al. (2002) and Turney (2002). Authors need to make a point (namely, that they have contributed something which is better or at least new (Myers, 1992)), and they thus have a stance towards their citations. But although there is a sentiment aspect to the interpretation of citations, this is not the whole story. Many of our "positive" categories are more concerned with different ways in which the cited work is useful to the current work (which aspect of it is used, e.g., just a definition or the entire solution?), and many of the contrastive statements have no negative connotation at all and simply state a (value-free) difference between approaches. However, if one looks at the distribution of positive and negative adjectives around citations, it is clear that there is a non-trivial connection between our task and sentiment classification.

The data we use comes from our corpus of 360 conference articles in computational linguistics, drawn from the Computation and Language E-Print Archive (http://xxx.lanl.gov/cmp-lg). The articles are transformed into XML format; headlines, titles, authors and reference list items are automatically marked up. Reference lists are parsed using regular patterns, and cited authors' names are identified. Our citation parser then finds citations and author names in running text and marks them up. Ritchie et al. (2006a) report high accuracy for this task (94% of citations recognised, provided the reference list was error-free). On average, our papers contain 26.8 citation instances in running text[3]. For human annotation, we use our own annotation tool based on XML/XSLT technology, which allows us to use a web browser to interactively assign one of the 12 tags (presented as a pull-down list) to each citation.

We measure inter-annotator agreement between three annotators (the three authors), who independently annotated 26 articles with the scheme (containing a total of 120,000 running words and 548 citations), using the written guidelines. The guidelines were developed on a different set of articles from the ones used for annotation.

Inter-annotator agreement was Kappa=.72 (n=12;N=548;k=3)[4]. This is quite high, considering the number of categories and the difficulties

[2]Our citation processor can recognise these after parsing the citation list.

[3]As opposed to reference list items, which are fewer.

[4]Following Carletta (1996), we measure agreement in Kappa, which follows the formula $K = \frac{P(A)-P(E)}{1-P(E)}$ where P(A) is observed, and P(E) expected agreement. Kappa ranges between -1 and 1. K=0 means agreement is only as expected by chance. Generally, Kappas of 0.8 are considered stable, and Kappas of .69 as marginally stable, according to the strictest scheme applied in the field.

(e.g., non-local dependencies) of the task. The relative frequency of each category observed in the annotation is listed in Fig. 3. As expected, the distribution is very skewed, with more than 60% of the citations of category `Neut`.[5] What is interesting is the relatively high frequency of usage categories (`PUse`, `PModi`, `PBas`) with a total of 18.9%. There is a relatively low frequency of clearly negative citations (`Weak`, `CoCo-`, total of 4.1%), whereas the neutral–contrastive categories (`CoCoR0`, `CoCoXY`, `CoCoGM`) are slightly more frequent at 7.6%. This is in concordance with earlier annotation experiments (Moravcsik and Murugesan, 1975; Spiegel-Rüsing, 1977).

3 Features for automatic recognition of citation function

This section summarises the features we use for machine learning citation function. Some of these features were previously found useful for a different application, namely Argumentative Zoning (Teufel, 1999; Teufel and Moens, 2002), some are specific to citation classification.

3.1 Cue phrases

Myers (1992) calls meta-discourse the set of expressions that talk *about* the act of presenting research in a paper, rather than the research itself (which is called object-level discourse). For instance, Swales (1990) names phrases such as *"to our knowledge, no..."* or *"As far as we aware"* as meta-discourse associated with a gap in the current literature. Strings such as these have been used in extractive summarisation successfully ever since Paice's (1981) work.

We model meta-discourse (cue phrases) and treat it differently from object-level discourse. There are two different mechanisms: A finite grammar over strings with a placeholder mechanism for POS and for sets of similar words which can be substituted into a string-based cue phrase (Teufel, 1999). The grammar corresponds to 1762 cue phrases. It was developed on 80 papers which are different to the papers used for our experiments here.

The other mechanism is a POS-based recogniser of agents and a recogniser for specific actions these agents perform. Two main agent types (the authors of the paper, and everybody else) are modelled by 185 patterns. For instance, in a paragraph describing related work, we expect to find references to other people in subject position more often than in the section detailing the authors' own methods, whereas in the background section, we often find general subjects such as *"researchers in computational linguistics"* or *"in the literature"*. For each sentence to be classified, its grammatical subject is determined by POS patterns and, if possible, classified as one of these agent types. We also use the observation that in sentences without meta-discourse, one can assume that agenthood has not changed.

20 different action types model the main verbs involved in meta-discourse. For instance, there is a set of verbs that is often used when the overall scientific goal of a paper is defined. These are the verbs of presentation, such as *"propose, present, report"* and *"suggest"*; in the corpus we found other verbs in this function, but with a lower frequency, namely *"describe, discuss, give, introduce, put forward, show, sketch, state"* and *"talk about"*. There are also specialised verb clusters which co-occur with `PBas` sentences, e.g., the cluster of continuation of ideas (eg. *"adopt, agree with, base, be based on, be derived from, be originated in, be inspired by, borrow, build on,... "*). On the other hand, the semantics of verbs in `Weak` sentences is often concerned with failing (of other researchers' approaches), and often contain verbs such as *"abound, aggravate, arise, be cursed, be incapable of, be forced to, be limited to, ... "*.

We use 20 manually acquired verb clusters. Negation is recognised, but too rare to define its own clusters: out of the $20 \times 2 = 40$ theoretically possible verb clusters, only 27 were observed in our development corpus. We have recently automated the process of verb–object pair acquisition from corpora for two types of cue phrases (Abdalla and Teufel, 2006) and are planning on expanding this work to other cue phrases.

3.2 Cues Identified by annotators

During the annotator training phase, the annotators were encouraged to type in the meta-description cue phrases that justify their choice of category. We went through this list by hand and extracted 892 cue phrases (around 75 per category). The files these cues came from were not part of the test corpus. We included 12 features

[5] Spiegel-Rüsing found that out of 2309 citations she examined, 80% substantiated statements.

Neut	PUse	CoCoGM	PSim	Weak	PMot	CoCoR0	PBas	CoCoXY	CoCo-	PModi	PSup
62.7%	15.8%	3.9%	3.8%	3.1%	2.2%	0.8%	1.5%	2.9%	1.0%	1.6%	1.1%

Figure 3: Distribution of citation categories

	Weak	CoCoGM	CoCoR0	CoCo-	CoCoXY	PBas	PUse	PModi	PMot	PSim	PSup	Neut
P	.78	.81	.77	.56	.72	.76	.66	.60	.75	.68	.83	.80
R	.49	.52	.46	.19	.54	.46	.61	.27	.64	.38	.32	.92
F	.60	.64	.57	.28	.62	.58	.63	.37	.69	.48	.47	.86

Percentage Accuracy	0.77
Kappa (n=12; N=2829; k=2)	0.57
Macro-F	0.57

Figure 4: Summary of Citation Analysis results (10-fold cross-validation; IBk algorithm; k=3).

that recorded the presence of cues that our annotators associated with a particular class.

3.3 Other features

There are other features which we use for this task. We know from Teufel and Moens (2002) that verb tense and voice should be useful for recognizing statements of previous work, future work and work performed in the paper. We also recognise modality (whether or not a main verb is modified by an auxiliary, and which auxiliary it is).

The overall location of a sentence containing a reference should be relevant. We observe that more `PMot` categories appear towards the beginning of the paper, as do `Weak` citations, whereas comparative results (`CoCoR0, CoCoR-`) appear towards the end of articles. More fine-grained location features, such as the location within the paragraph and the section, have also been implemented.

The fact that a citation points to own previous work can be recognised, as we know who the paper authors are. As we have access to the information in the reference list, we also know the last names of *all* cited authors (even in the case where an *et al.* statement in running text obscures the later-occurring authors). With self-citations, one might assume that the probability of re-use of material from previous own work should be higher, and the tendency to criticise lower.

4 Results

Our evaluation corpus for citation analysis consists of 116 articles (randomly drawn from the part of our corpus which was not used for guideline development or cue phrase acquisition). The 116 articles contain 2829 citation instances. Each citation instance was manually tagged as one

	Weakness	Positive	Contrast	Neutral
P	.80	.75	.77	.81
R	.49	.65	.52	.90
F	.61	.70	.62	.86

Percentage Accuracy	0.79
Kappa (n=12; N=2829; k=2)	0.59
Macro-F	0.68

Figure 5: Summary of results (10-fold cross-validation; IBk algorithm; k=3): Top level classes.

	Weakness	Positive	Neutral
P	.77	.75	.85
R	.42	.65	.92
F	.54	.70	.89

Percentage Accuracy	0.83
Kappa (n=12; N=2829; k=2)	0.58
Macro-F	0.71

Figure 6: Summary of results (10-fold cross-validation; IBk algorithm; k=3): Sentiment Analysis.

of {`Weak, CoCoGM, CoCo-, CoCoR0, CoCoXY, PBas, PUse, PModi, PMot, PSim, PSup, Neut`}. The papers are then further processed (e.g. tokenised and POS-tagged). All other features are automatically determined (e.g. self-citations are detected by overlap of citing and cited authors); then, machine learning is applied to the feature vectors.

The 10-fold cross-validation results for citation classification are given in Figure 4, comparing the system to one of the annotators. Results are given in three overall measures: Kappa, percentage accuracy, and Macro-F (following Lewis (1991)). Macro-F is the mean of the F-measures of all twelve categories. We use Macro-F and Kappa because we want to measure success particularly on the rare categories, and because Micro-averaging techniques like percentage accuracy tend to overestimate the contribution of frequent categories in heavily skewed distributions like ours[6].

In the case of Macro-F, each category is treated as one unit, independent of the number of items contained in it. Therefore, the classification success of the individual items in rare categories is given more importance than classification success of frequent category items. However, one should keep in mind that numerical values in macro-averaging are generally lower (Yang and Liu, 1999), due to fewer training cases for the rare categories. Kappa has the additional advantage over Macro-F that it filters out random agreement (random use, but following the observed distribution of categories).

For our task, memory-based learning outperformed other models. The reported results use the IBk algorithm with $k = 3$ (we used the Weka machine learning toolkit (Witten and Frank, 2005) for our experiments). Fig. 7 provides a few examples from one file in the corpus, along with the gold standard citation class, the machine prediction, and a comment.

Kappa is even higher for the top level distinction. We collapsed the obvious similar categories (all `P` categories into one category, and all `CoCo` categories into another) to give four top level categories (`Weak`, `Positive`, `Contrast`, `Neutral`; results in Fig. 5). Precision for all the categories is above 0.75, and K=0.59. For contrast, the human agreement for this situation was K=0.76 (n=3,N=548,k=3).

In a different experiment, we grouped the categories as follows, in an attempt to perform sentiment analysis over the classifications:

Old Categories	New Category
Weak, CoCo-	Negative
PMot, PUse, PBas, PModi, PSim, PSup	Positive
CoCoGM, CoCoR0, CoCoXY, Neut	Neutral

Thus negative contrasts and weaknesses are grouped into `Negative`, while neutral contrasts are grouped into `Neutral`. All positive classes are conflated into `Positive`.

Results show that this grouping raises results to a smaller degree than the top-level distinction did (to K=.58). For contrast, the human agreement for these collapsed categories was K=.75 (n=3,N=548,k=3).

[6]This situation has parallels in information retrieval, where precision and recall are used because accuracy overestimates the performance on irrelevant items.

5 Conclusion

We have presented a new task: annotation of citation function in scientific text, a phenomenon which we believe to be closely related to the overall discourse structure of scientific articles. Our annotation scheme concentrates on weaknesses of other work, and on similarities and contrast between work and usage of other work. In this paper, we present machine learning experiments for replicating the human annotation (which is reliable at K=.72). The automatic result reached K=.57 (acc=.77) for the full annotation scheme; rising to Kappa=.58 (acc=.83) for a three-way classification (Weak, Positive, Neutral).

We are currently performing an experiment to see if citation processing can increase performance in a large-scale, real-world information retrieval task, by creating a test collection of researchers' queries and relevant documents for these (Ritchie et al., 2006a).

6 Acknowledgements

This work was funded by the EPSRC projects CITRAZ (GR/S27832/01, "Rhetorical Citation Maps and Domain-independent Argumentative Zoning") and SCIBORG (EP/C010035/1, "Extracting the Science from Scientific Publications").

References

Rashid M. Abdalla and Simone Teufel. 2006. A bootstrapping approach to unsupervised detection of cue phrase variants. In *Proc. of ACL/COLING-06*.

Susan Bonzi. 1982. Characteristics of a literature as predictors of relatedness between cited and citing works. *JASIS*, 33(4):208–216.

Christine L. Borgman, editor. 1990. *Scholarly Communication and Bibliometrics*. Sage Publications, CA.

Jean Carletta. 1996. Assessing agreement on classification tasks: The kappa statistic. *Computational Linguistics*, 22(2):249–254.

Daryl E. Chubin and S. D. Moitra. 1975. Content analysis of references: Adjunct or alternative to citation counting? *Social Studies of Science*, 5(4):423–441.

Eugene Garfield. 1979. *Citation Indexing: Its Theory and Application in Science, Technology and Humanities*. J. Wiley, New York, NY.

C. Lee Giles, Kurt D. Bollacker, and Steve Lawrence. 1998. Citeseer: An automatic citation indexing system. In *Proc. of the Third ACM Conference on Digital Libraries*, pages 89–98.

T.L. Hodges. 1972. *Citation Indexing: Its Potential for Bibliographical Control*. Ph.D. thesis, University of California at Berkeley.

David D. Lewis. 1991. Evaluating text categorisation. In *Speech and Natural Language: Proceedings of the ARPA Workshop of Human Language Technology*.

Context	Human	Machine	Comment
We have compared four complete and three partial data representation formats for the baseNP recognition task presented in **Ramshaw and Marcus (1995)**.	PUse	PUse	Cues can be weak: *"for.. task... presented in"*
In the version of the algorithm that we have used, IB1-IG, the distances between feature representations are computed as the weighted sum of distances between individual features **(Bosch 1998)**.	Neut	PUse	Human decided citation was for detail in used package, not directly used by paper.
We have used the baseNP data presented in **Ramshaw and Marcus (1995)**.	PUse	PUse	Straightforward case
We will follow **Argamon et al. (1998)** and use a combination of the precision and recall rates: F=(2*precision*recall)/(precision+recall).	PSim	PUse	Human decided F-measure was not attributable to citation. Hence similarity rather than usage.
This algorithm standardly uses the single training item closest to the test i.e. However **Daelemans et al. (1999)** report that for baseNP recognition better results can be obtained by making the algorithm consider the classification values of the three closest training items.	Neut	PUse	Shallow processing by Machine means that it is mislead by the strong cue in preceding sentence.
They are better than the results for section 15 because more training data was used in these experiments. Again the best result was obtained with IOB1 (F=92.37) which is an improvement of the best reported F-rate for this data set **Ramshaw and Marcus 1995** (F=92.03).	CoCo-	PUse	Machine attached citation to the data set being used. Human attached citation to the result being compared.

Figure 7: Examples of classifications by the machine learner.

Terttu Luukkonen. 1992. Is scientists' publishing behaviour reward-seeking? *Scientometrics*, 24:297–319.

Michael H. MacRoberts and Barbara R. MacRoberts. 1984. The negational reference: Or the art of dissembling. *Social Studies of Science*, 14:91–94.

Michael J. Moravcsik and Poovanalingan Murugesan. 1975. Some results on the function and quality of citations. *Social Studies of Science*, 5:88–91.

Greg Myers. 1992. In this paper we report...—speech acts and scientific facts. *Journal of Pragmatics*, 17(4).

John O'Connor. 1982. Citing statements: Computer recognition and use to improve retrieval. *Information Processing and Management*, 18(3):125–131.

Chris D. Paice. 1981. The automatic generation of literary abstracts: an approach based on the identification of self-indicating phrases. In R. Oddy, S. Robertson, C. van Rijsbergen, and P. W. Williams, editors, *Information Retrieval Research*. Butterworth, London, UK.

Bo Pang, Lillian Lee, and Shivakumar Vaithyanathan. 2002. Thumbs up? Sentiment classification using machine learning techniques. In *Proc. of EMNLP-02*.

Anna Ritchie, Simone Teufel, and Stephen Robertson. 2006a. Creating a test collection for citation-based IR experiments. In *Proc. of HLT/NAACL 2006*, New York, US.

Anna Ritchie, Simone Teufel, and Stephen Robertson. 2006b. How to find better index terms through citations. In *Proc. of ACL/COLING workshop "Can Computational Linguistics improve IR"*.

Simon Buckingham Shum. 1998. Evolving the web for scientific knowledge: First steps towards an "HCI knowledge web". *Interfaces, British HCI Group Magazine*, 39.

Henry Small. 1982. Citation context analysis. In P. Dervin and M. J. Voigt, editors, *Progress in Communication Sciences 3*, pages 287–310. Ablex, Norwood, N.J.

Ina Spiegel-Rüsing. 1977. Bibliometric and content analysis. *Social Studies of Science*, 7:97–113.

John Swales. 1986. Citation analysis and discourse analysis. *Applied Linguistics*, 7(1):39–56.

John Swales, 1990. *Genre Analysis: English in Academic and Research Settings. Chapter 7: Research articles in English*, pages 110–176. Cambridge University Press, Cambridge, UK.

Simone Teufel and Marc Moens. 2002. Summarising scientific articles — experiments with relevance and rhetorical status. *Computational Linguistics*, 28(4):409–446.

Simone Teufel, Advaith Siddharthan, and Dan Tidhar. 2006. An annotation scheme for citation function. In *Proc. of SIGDial-06*.

Simone Teufel. 1999. *Argumentative Zoning: Information Extraction from Scientific Text*. Ph.D. thesis, School of Cognitive Science, University of Edinburgh, UK.

Peter D. Turney. 2002. Thumbs up or thumbs down? semantic orientation applied to unsupervised classification of reviews. In *Proc. of ACL-02*.

Melvin Weinstock. 1971. Citation indexes. In *Encyclopedia of Library and Information Science*, volume 5. Dekker, New York, NY.

Howard D. White. 2004. Citation analysis and discourse analysis revisited. *Applied Linguistics*, 25(1):89–116.

Ian H. Witten and Eibe Frank. 2005. *Data Mining: Practical machine learning tools and techniques*. Morgan Kaufmann, San Francisco.

Yiming Yang and Xin Liu. 1999. A re-examination of text categorization methods. In *Proc. of SIGIR-99*.

John M. Ziman. 1968. *Public Knowledge: An Essay Concerning the Social Dimensions of Science*. Cambridge University Press, Cambridge, UK.

Is it Really that Difficult to Parse German?

Sandra Kübler, Erhard W. Hinrichs, Wolfgang Maier
SfS-CL, SFB 441, University of Tübingen
Wilhelmstr. 19
72074 Tübingen, Germany
{kuebler,eh,wmaier}@sfs.uni-tuebingen.de

Abstract

This paper presents a comparative study of probabilistic treebank parsing of German, using the Negra and TüBa-D/Z treebanks. Experiments with the Stanford parser, which uses a factored PCFG and dependency model, show that, contrary to previous claims for other parsers, lexicalization of PCFG models boosts parsing performance for both treebanks. The experiments also show that there is a big difference in parsing performance, when trained on the Negra and on the TüBa-D/Z treebanks. Parser performance for the models trained on TüBa-D/Z are comparable to parsing results for English with the Stanford parser, when trained on the Penn treebank. This comparison at least suggests that German is not harder to parse than its West-Germanic neighbor language English.

1 Introduction

There have been a number of recent studies on probabilistic treebank parsing of German (Dubey, 2005; Dubey and Keller, 2003; Schiehlen, 2004; Schulte im Walde, 2003), using the Negra treebank (Skut et al., 1997) as their underlying data source. A common theme that has emerged from this research is the claim that lexicalization of PCFGs, which has been proven highly beneficial for other languages[1], is detrimental for parsing accuracy of German. In fact, this assumption is by now so widely held that Schiehlen (2004) does not even consider lexicalization as a possible parameter and concentrates instead only on treebank transformations of various sorts in his experiments.

Another striking feature of all studies mentioned above are the relatively low parsing F-scores achieved for German by comparison to the scores reported for English, its West-Germanic neighbor, using similar parsers. This naturally raises the question whether German is just harder to parse or whether it is just hard to parse the Negra treebank.[2]

The purpose of this paper is to address precisely this question by training the Stanford parser (Klein and Manning, 2003b) and the LoPar parser (Schmid, 2000) on the two major treebanks available for German, Negra and TüBa-D/Z, the Tübingen treebank of written German (Telljohann et al., 2005). A series of comparative parsing experiments that utilize different parameter settings of the parsers is conducted, including lexicalization and markovization. These experiments show striking differences in performance between the two treebanks. What makes this comparison interesting is that the treebanks are of comparable size and are both based on a newspaper corpus. However, both treebanks differ significantly in their syntactic annotation scheme. Note, however, that our experiments concentrate on the original (context-free) annotations of the treebank.

The structure of this paper is as follows: section 2 discusses three characteristic grammatical features of German that need to be taken into account in syntactic annotation and in choosing an appropriate parsing model for German. Section 3 introduces the Negra and TüBa-D/Z treebanks and

[1]For English, see Collins (1999).

[2]German is not the first language for which this question has been raised. See Levy and Manning (2003) for a similar discussion of Chinese and the Penn Chinese Treebank.

Proceedings of the 2006 Conference on Empirical Methods in Natural Language Processing (EMNLP 2006), pages 111–119,
Sydney, July 2006.

discusses the main differences between their annotation schemes. Section 4 explains the experimental setup, sections 5-7 the experiments, and section 8 discusses the results.

2 Grammatical Features of German

There are three distinctive grammatical features that make syntactic annotation and parsing of German particularly challenging: its placement of the finite verb, its flexible phrasal ordering, and the presence of discontinuous constituents. These features will be discussed in the following subsections.

2.1 Finite Verb Placement

In German, the placement of finite verbs depends on the clause type. In non-embedded assertion clauses, the finite verb occupies the second position in the clause, as in (1a). In yes/no questions, as in (1b), the finite verb appears clause-initially, whereas in embedded clauses it appears clause finally, as in (1c).

(1) a. Peter wird das Buch gelesen haben.
Peter will the book read have
'Peter will have read the book.'

b. Wird Peter das Buch gelesen haben?
Will Peter the book have read
'Will Peter have read the book?'

c. dass Peter das Buch gelesen haben wird.
that Peter the book read have will
'... that Peter will have read the book.'

Regardless of the particular clause type, any cluster of non-finite verbs, such as *gelesen haben* in (1a) and (1b) or *gelesen haben wird* in (1c), appears at the right periphery of the clause.

The discontinuous positioning of the verbal elements in verb-first and verb-second clauses is the traditional reason for structuring German clauses into so-called *topological fields* (Drach, 1937; Erdmann, 1886; Höhle, 1986). The positions of the verbal elements form the *Satzklammer* (sentence bracket) which divides the sentence into a *Vorfeld* (initial field), a *Mittelfeld* (middle field), and a *Nachfeld* (final field). The Vorfeld and the Mittelfeld are divided by the *linke Satzklammer* (left sentence bracket), which is realized by the finite verb or (in verb-final clauses) by a complementizer field. The *rechte Satzklammer* (right sentence bracket) is realized by the verb complex and consists of verbal particles or sequences of verbs. This right sentence bracket is positioned between the Mittelfeld and the Nachfeld. Thus, the theory of topological fields states the fundamental regularities of German word order.

The topological field structures in (2) for the examples in (1) illustrate the assignment of topological fields for different clause types.

(2) a. [$_{VF}$ [$_{NP}$ Peter]] [$_{LK}$ wird] [$_{MF}$ [$_{NP}$ das Buch]] [$_{RK}$ [$_{VC}$ gelesen haben.]]

b. [$_{LK}$ Wird] [$_{MF}$ [$_{NP}$ Peter] [$_{NP}$ das Buch]] [$_{RK}$ [$_{VC}$ gelesen haben?]]

c. [$_{LK}$ [$_{CF}$ dass]] [$_{MF}$ [$_{NP}$ Peter] [$_{NP}$ das Buch]] [$_{RK}$ [$_{VC}$ gelesen haben wird.]]

(2a) and (2b) are made up of the following fields: LK (for: linke Satzklammer) is occupied by the finite verb. MF (for: Mittelfeld) contains adjuncts and complements of the main verb. RK (for: rechte Satzklammer) is realized by the verbal complex (VC). Additionally, (2a) realizes the topological field VF (for: Vorfeld), which contains the sentence-initial constituent. The left sentence bracket (LK) in (2c) is realized by a complementizer field (CF) and the right sentence bracket (RK) by a verbal complex (VC) that contains the finite verb *wird*.

2.2 Flexible Phrase Ordering

The second noteworthy grammatical feature of German concerns its flexible phrase ordering. In (3), any of the three complements and adjuncts of the main verb *(ge)lesen* can appear sentence-initially.

(3) a. Der Mann hat gestern den Roman
The man has yesterday the novel
gelesen.
read
'The man read the novel yesterday.'

b. Gestern hat der Mann den Roman gelesen

c. Den Roman hat der Mann gestern gelesen

In addition, the ordering of the elements that occur in the Mittelfeld is also free so that there are two possible linearizations for each of the examples in (3a) - (3b), yielding a total of six distinct orderings for the three complements and adjuncts.

Due to this flexible phrase ordering, the grammatical functions of constituents in German, unlike for English, cannot be deduced from the constituents' location in the tree. As a consequence, parsing approaches to German need to be based on treebank data which contain a combination of constituent structure and grammatical functions – for parsing and evaluation.

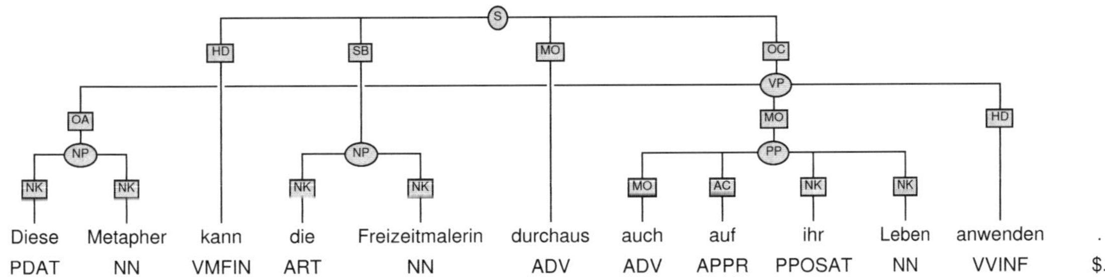

Figure 1: A sample tree from Negra.

2.3 Discontinuous Constituents

A third characteristic feature of German syntax that is a challenge for syntactic annotation and for parsing is the treatment of discontinuous constituents.

(4) Der Mann hat gestern den Roman gelesen,
The man has yesterday the novel read
den ihm Peter empfahl.
which him Peter recommended

'Yesterday the man read the novel which Peter recommended to him.'

(5) Peter soll dem Mann empfohlen haben, den
Peter is to the man recommended have the
Roman zu lesen.
novel to read

'Peter is said to have recommended to the man to read the novel.'

(4) shows an extraposed relative clause which is separated from its head noun *den Roman* by the non-finite verb *gelesen*. (5) is an example of an extraposed non-finite VP complement that forms a discontinuous constituent with its governing verb *empfohlen* because of the intervening non-finite auxiliary *haben*. Such discontinuous structures occur frequently in both treebanks and are handled differently in the two annotation schemes, as will be discussed in more detail in the next section.

3 The Negra and the TüBa-D/Z Treebanks

Both treebanks use German newspapers as their data source: the Frankfurter Rundschau newspaper for Negra and the 'die tageszeitung' (taz) newspaper for TüBa-D/Z. Negra comprises 20 000 sentences, TüBa-D/Z 15 000 sentences. There is evidence that the complexity of sentences in both treebanks is comparable: sentence length as well as the percentage of clause nodes per sentence is comparable. In Negra, a sentence is 17.2 words long, in Tüba-D/Z, 17.5 words. Negra has an average of 1.4 clause nodes per sentence, TüBa-D/Z 1.5 clause nodes.

Both treebanks use an annotation framework that is based on phrase structure grammar and that is enhanced by a level of predicate-argument structure. Annotation for both was performed semi-automatically. Despite all these similarities, the treebank annotations differ in four important aspects: 1) Negra does not allow unary branching whereas TüBa-D/Z does; 2) in Negra, phrases receive a flat annotation whereas TüBa-D/Z uses phrase internal structure; 3) Negra uses crossing branches to represent long-distance relationships whereas TüBa-D/Z uses a pure tree structure combined with functional labels to encode this information; 4) Negra encodes grammatical functions in a combination of structural and functional labeling whereas TüBa-D/Z uses a combination of topological fields functional labels, which results in a flatter structure on the clausal level. The two treebanks also use different notions of grammatical functions: TüBa-D/Z defines 36 grammatical functions covering head and non-head information, as well as subcategorization for complements and modifiers. Negra utilizes 48 grammatical functions. Apart from commonly accepted grammatical functions, such as *SB* (subject) or *OA* (accusative object), Negra grammatical functions comprise a more extended notion, e.g. *RE* (repeated element) or *RC* (relative clause).

(6) Diese Metapher kann die Freizeitmalerin
This metaphor can the amateur painter
durchaus auch auf ihr Leben anwenden.
by all means also to her life apply.

'The amateur painter can by all means apply this metaphor also to her life.'

Figure 1 shows a typical tree from the Negra treebank for sentence (6). The syntactic categories are shown in circular nodes, the grammatical functions as edge labels in square boxes. A major

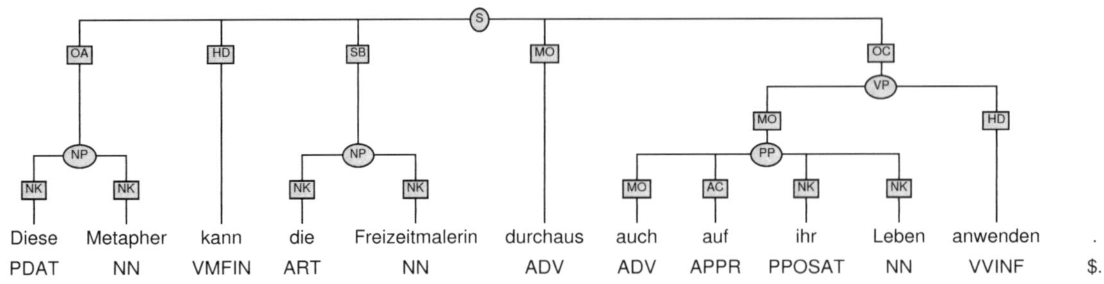

Figure 2: A Negra tree with resolved crossing branches.

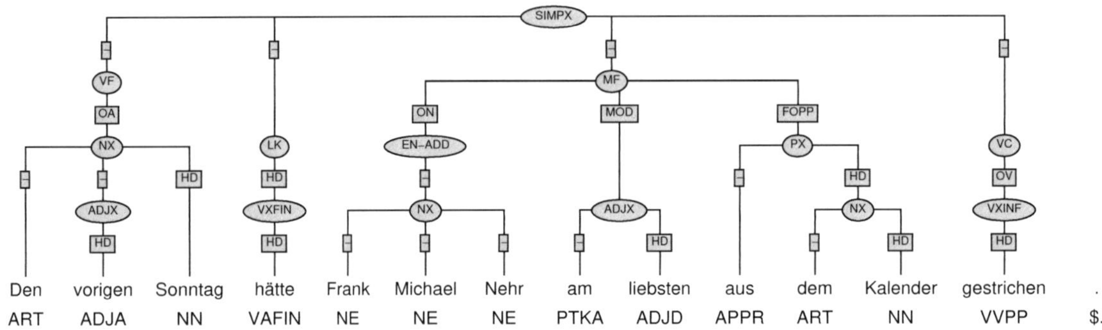

Figure 3: A sample tree from Tüba-D/Z.

phrasal category that serves to structure the sentence as a whole is the verb phrase (VP). It contains non-finite verbs (here: *anwenden*) together with their complements (here: the accusative object *Diese Metapher*) and adjuncts (here: the adverb *durchaus* and the PP modifier *auch auf ihr Leben*). The subject NP (here: *die Freizeitmalerin*) stands outside the VP and, depending on its linear position, leads to crossing branches with the VP. This happens in all cases where the subject follows the finite verb as in Figure 1. Notice also that the PP is completely flat and does not contain an internal NP.

Another phenomenon that leads to the introduction of crossing branches in the Negra treebank are discontinuous constituents of the kind illustrated in section 2.3. Extraposed relative clauses, as in (4), are analyzed in such a way that the relative clause constituent is a sister of its head noun in the Negra tree and crosses the branch that dominates the intervening non-finite verb *gelesen*.

The crossing branches in the Negra treebank cannot be processed by most probabilistic parsing models since such parsers all presuppose a strictly context-free tree structure. Therefore the Negra trees must be transformed into proper trees prior to training such parsers. The standard approach for this transformation is to re-attach crossing non-head constituents as sisters of the lowest mother node that dominates all constituents in question in the original Negra tree.

Figure 2 shows the result of this transformation of the tree in Figure 1. Here, the fronted accusative object *Diese Metapher* is reattached on the clause level. Crossing branches do not only arise with respect to the subject at the sentence level but also in cases of extraposition and fronting of partial constituents. As a result, approximately 30% of all Negra trees contain at least one crossing branch. Thus, tree transformations have a major impact on the type of constituent structures that are used for training probabilistic parsing models. Previous work, such as Dubey (2005), Dubey and Keller (2003), and Schiehlen (2004), uses the version of Negra in which the standard approach to resolving crossing branches has been applied.

(7) Den vorigen Sonntag hätte Frank Michael
The previous Sunday would have Frank Michael
Nehr am liebsten aus dem Kalender gestrichen.
Nehr preferably from the calendar deleted.
'Frank Michael Nehr would rather have deleted the previous Sunday from the calendar.'

Figure 3 shows the TüBa-D/Z annotation for sentence (7), a sentence with almost identical phrasal ordering to sentence (6). Crossing branches are avoided by the introduction of topo-

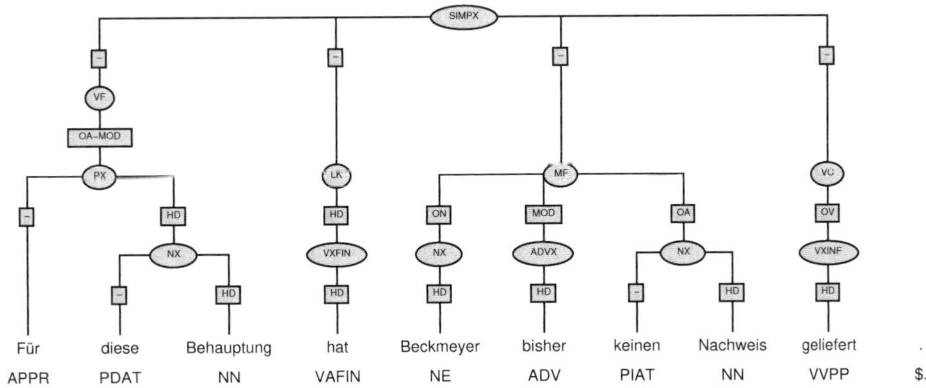

Figure 4: TüBa-D/Z annotation without crossing branches.

logical structures (here: VF, MF and VC) into the tree. Notice also that compared to the Negra annotation, TüBa-D/Z introduces more internal structure into NPs and PPs.

(8) Für diese Behauptung hat Beckmeyer bisher
For this claim has Beckmeyer yet
keinen Nachweis geliefert.
no evidence provided.
'For this claim, Beckmeyer has not provided evidence yet.'

In TüBa-D/Z, long-distance relationships are represented by a pure tree structure and specific functional labels. Figure 4 shows the TüBa-D/Z annotation for sentence (8). In this sentence, the prepositional phrase *Für diese Behauptung* is fronted. Its functional label (*OA-MOD*) provides the information that it modifies the accusative object (*OA*) *keinen Nachweis*.

4 Experimental Setup

The main goals behind our experiments were twofold: (1) to re-investigate the claim that lexicalization is detrimental for treebank parsing of German, and (2) to compare the parsing results for the two German treebanks.

To investigate the first issue, the Stanford Parser (Klein and Manning, 2003b), a state-of-the-art probabilistic parser, was trained with both lexicalized and unlexicalized versions of the two treebanks (Experiment I). For lexicalized parsing, the Stanford Parser provides a factored probabilistic model that combines a PCFG model with a dependency model.

For the comparison between the two treebanks, two types of experiments were performed: a purely constituent-based comparison using both the Stanford parser and the pure PCFG parser LoPar (Schmid, 2000) (Experiment II), and an in-depth evaluation of the three major grammatical functions *subject*, *accusative object*, and *dative object*, using the Stanford parser (Experiment III).

All three experiments use gold POS tags extracted from the treebanks as parser input. All parsing results shown below are averaged over a ten-fold cross-validation of the test data. Experiments I and II used versions of the treebanks that excluded grammatical information, thus only contained constituent labeling. For Experiment III, all syntactic labels were extended by their grammatical function (e.g NX-ON for a subject NP in TüBa-D/Z or NP-SB for a Negra subject). Experiments I and II included all sentences of a maximal length of 40 words. Due to memory limitations (7 GB), Experiment III had to be restricted to sentences of a maximal length of 35 words.

5 Experiment I: Lexicalization

Experiment I investigates the effect of lexicalization on parser performance for the Stanford Parser. The results, summarized in Table 1, show that lexicalization improves parser performance for both the Negra and the TüBa-D/Z treebank in comparison to unlexicalized counterpart models: for labeled bracketing, an F-score improvement from 86.48 to 88.88 for TüBa-D/Z and an improvement from 66.92 to 67.13 for Negra. This directly contradicts the findings reported by Dubey and Keller (2003) that lexicalization has a negative effect on probabilistic parsing models for German. We therefore conclude that these previous claims, while valid for particular configurations of

		Negra			TüBa-D/Z		
		precision	recall	F-score	precision	recall	F-score
Stanford PCFG	unlabeled	71.24	72.68	71.95	93.07	89.41	91.20
	labeled	66.26	67.59	66.92	88.25	84.78	86.48
Stanford lexicalized	unlabeled	71.31	73.12	72.20	91.60	91.21	91.36
	labeled	66.30	67.99	67.13	89.12	88.65	88.88

Table 1: The results of lexicalizing German.

		Negra			TüBa-D/Z		
		precision	recall	F-score	precision	recall	F-score
LoPar	unlabeled	70.84	72.51	71.67	92.62	88.58	90.56
	labeled	65.86	67.41	66.62	87.39	83.57	85.44
Stanford	unlabeled	71.24	72.68	71.95	93.07	89.41	91.20
	labeled	66.26	67.59	66.92	88.25	84.78	86.48
Stanford + markov	unlabeled	74.13	74.12	74.12	92.28	90.90	91.58
	labeled	69.96	69.95	69.95	89.86	88.51	89.18

Table 2: A comparison of unlexicalized parsing of Negra and TüBa-D/Z.

parsers and parameters, should not be generalized to claims about probabilistic parsing of German in general.

Experiment I also shows considerable differences in the overall scores between the two treebanks, with the F-scores for TüBa-D/Z parsing approximating scores reported for English, but with Negra scores lagging behind by an average margin of appr. 20 points. Of course, it is important to note that such direct comparisons with English are hardly possible due to different annotation schemes, different underlying text corpora, etc. Nevertheless, the striking difference in parser performance between the two German treebanks warrants further attention. Experiments II and III will investigate this matter in more depth.

6 Experiment II: Different Parsers

The purpose of Experiment II is to rule out the possibility that the differences in parser performance for the two German treebanks produced by Experiment I may just be due to using a particular parser – in this particular case the hybrid PCFG and dependency model of the Stanford parser. After all, Experiment I also yielded different results concerning the received wisdom about the utility of lexicalization from previously reported results. In order to obtain a broader experimental base, unlexicalized models of the Stanford parser and the pure PCFG parser LoPar were trained on both treebanks. In addition we experimented with two different parameter settings of the Stanford parser, one with and one without markovization. The experiment with markovization used parent information (v=1) and a second order Markov model for horizontal markovization (h=2). The results, summarized in Table 2, show that parsing results for all unlexicalized experiments show roughly the same 20 point difference in F-score that were obtained for the lexicalized models in Experiment I. We can therefore conclude that the difference in parsing performance is robust across two parsers with different parameter settings, such as lexicalization and markovization.

Experiment II also confirms the finding of Klein and Manning (2003a) and of Schiehlen (2004) that horizontal and vertical markovization has a positive effect on parser performance. Notice also that markovization with unlexicalized grammars yields almost the same improvement as lexicalization does in Experiment I.

7 Experiment III: Grammatical Functions

In Experiments I and II, only constituent structure was evaluated, which is highly annotation dependent. It could simply be the case that the TüBa-D/Z annotation scheme contains many local structures that can be easily parsed by a PCFG model or the hybrid Stanford model. Moreover, such easy to parse structures may not be of great importance when it comes to determining the correct macrostructure of a sentence. To empirically verify such a conjecture, a separate evaluation of

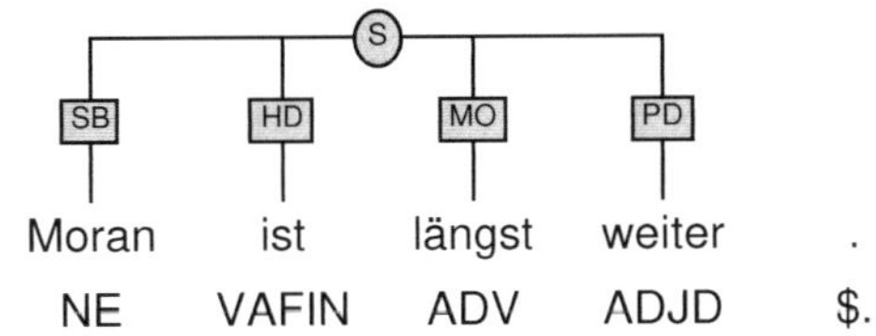

Figure 5: Negra annotation without unary nodes.

	Negra			TüBa-D/Z		
	lab. prec.	lab. rec.	lab. F-score	lab. prec.	lab. rec.	lab. F-score
without gramm. functions	69.96	69.95	69.95	89.86	88.51	89.18
all gramm. functions	47.20	56.43	51.41	75.73	74.93	75.33
subjects	52.50	58.02	55.12	66.82	75.93	71.08
accusative objects	35.14	36.30	35.71	43.84	47.31	45.50
dative objects	8.38	3.58	5.00	24.46	9.96	14.07

Table 3: A comparison of unlexicalized, markovized parsing of constituent structure and grammatical functions in Negra and TüBa-D/Z.

parser performance for different constituent types would be necessary. However, even such an evaluation would only be meaningful if the annotation schemes agree on the defining characteristics of such constituent types. Unfortunately, this is not the case for the two treebanks under consideration. Even for arguably theory-neutral constituents such as NPs, the two treebanks differ considerably. In the Negra annotation scheme, single word NPs directly project from the POS level to the clausal level, while in TüBa-D/Z, they project by a unary rule first to an NP. An extreme case of this Negra annotation is shown in Figure 5 for sentence (9). Here, all the phrases are one word phrases and are thus projected directly to the clause level.

(9) Moran ist längst weiter.
Moran is already further
'Moran is already one step ahead.'

There is an even more important motivation for not focusing on the standard constituent-based parseval measures – at least when parsing German. As discussed earlier in section 2.2, obtaining the correct constituent structure for a German sentence will often not be sufficient for determining its intended meaning. Due to the word order freeness of phrases, a given NP in any one position may in principle fulfill different grammatical functions in the sentence as a whole. Therefore grammatical functions need to be explicitly marked in the treebank and correctly assigned during parsing. Since both treebanks encode grammatical functions, this information is available for parsing and can ultimately lead to a more meaningful comparison of the two treebanks when used for parsing.

The purpose of Experiment III is to investigate parser performance on the treebanks when grammatical functions are included in the trees. For these experiments, the unlexicalized, markovized PCFG version of the Stanford parser was used, with markovization parameters v=1 and h=2, as in Experiment II. The results of this experiment are shown in Table 3. The comparison of the experiments with (line 2) and without grammatical functions (line 1) confirms the findings of Dubey and Keller (2003) that the task of assigning correct grammatical functions is harder than mere constituent-based parsing. When evaluating on all grammatical functions, the results for Negra decrease from 69.95 to 51.41, and for TüBa-D/Z from 89.18 to 75.33. Notice however, that the relative differences between Negra and TüBa-D/Z that were true for Experiments I and II remain more or less constant for this experiment as well.

In order to get a clearer picture of the quality of the parser output for each treebank, it is important to consider individual grammatical functions. As discussed in section 3, the overall inventory of grammatical functions is different for the two treebanks. We therefore evaluated those grammatical functions separately that are crucial for determining function-argument structure and that are at the same time the most comparable for the two treebanks. These are the functions of subject (encoded as *SB* in Negra and as *ON* in TüBa-D/Z), accusative object (*OA*), and dative object (*DA* in Negra and *OD* in TüBa-D/Z). Once again, the results are consistently better for TüBa-D/Z (cf. lines 3-5 in Table 3), with subjects yielding the highest results (71.08 vs. 55.12 F-score) and dative objects the lowest results (14.07 vs. 5.00). The latter results must be attributed to data sparseness, dative object occur only appr. 1 000 times in each treebank while subjects occur more than 15 000 times.

8 Discussion

The experiments presented in sections 5-7 show that there is a difference in results of appr. 20% between Negra and TüBa-D/Z. This difference is consistent throughout, i.e. with different parsers, under lexicalization and markovization. These results lead to the conjecture that the reasons for these differences must be sought in the differences in the annotation schemes of the two treebanks.

In section 3, we showed that one of the major differences in annotation is the treatment of discontinuous constituents. In Negra, such constituents are annotated via crossing branches, which have to be resolved before parsing. In such cases, constituents are extracted from their mother constituents and reattached at higher constituents. In the case of the discontinuous VP in Figure 1, it leads to a VP rule with the following daughters: head (*HD*) and modifier (*MO*), while the accusative object is directly attached at the sentence level as a sister of the VP. This conversion leads to inconsistencies in the training data since the annotation scheme requires that object NPs are daughters of the VP rather than of S. The inconsistency introduced by tree conversion are considerable since they cover appr. 30% of all Negra trees (cf. section 3). One possible explanation for the better performance of Tüba-D/Z might be that it has more information about the correct attachment site of extraposed constituents, which is completely lacking in the context-free version of Negra. For this reason, Kübler (2005) and Maier (2006) tested a version of Negra which contained information of the original attachment site of these discontinuous constituents. In this version of Negra, the grammatical function *OA* in Figure 2 would be changed to *OA*<*VP* to show that it was originally attached to the VP. Experiments with this version showed a decrease in F-score from 52.30 to 49.75. Consequently, adding this information in a similar way to the encoding of discontinuous constituents in Tüba-D/Z harms performance.

By contrast, TüBa-D/Z uses topological fields as the primary structuring principle, which leads to a purely context-free annotation of discontinuous structures. There is evidence that the use of topological fields is advantageous also for other parsing approaches (Frank et al., 2003; Kübler, 2005; Maier, 2006).

Another difference in the annotation schemes concerns the treatment of phrases. Negra phrases are flat, and unary projections are not annotated. TüBa-D/Z always projects to the phrasal category and annotates more phrase-internal structure. The deeper structures in TüBa-D/Z lead to fewer rules for phrasal categories, which allows the parser a more consistent treatment of such phrases. For example, the direct attachment of one word subjects on the clausal level in Negra leads to a high number of different S rules with different POS tags for the subject phrase. An empirical proof for the assumption that flat phrase structures and the omission of unary nodes decrease parsing results is presented by Kübler (2005) and Maier (2006).

We want to emphasize that our experiments concentrate on the original context-free annotations of the treebanks. We did not investigate the influence of treebank refinement in this study. However, we would like to note that by a combination of suffix analysis and smoothing, Dubey (2005) was able to obtain an F-score of 85.2 for Negra. For other work in the area of treebank refinement using the German treebanks see Kübler (2005), Maier (2006), and Ule (2003).

9 Conclusion and Future Work

We have presented a comparative study of probabilistic treebank parsing of German, using the Negra and TüBa-D/Z treebanks. Experiments with the Stanford parser, which uses a factored PCFG and dependency model, show that, contrary to previous claims for other parsers, lexicalization of PCFG models boosts parsing performance for both treebanks. The experiments also show that there is a big difference in parsing performance, when trained on the Negra and on the TüBa-D/Z treebanks. This difference remains constant across lexicalized, unlexicalized (also using the LoPar parser), and markovized models and also extends to parsing of major grammatical functions. Parser performance for the models trained on TüBa-D/Z are comparable to parsing results for English with the Stanford parser, when trained on the Penn treebank. This comparison at least suggests that German is not harder to parse than its West-Germanic neighbor language English.

Additional experiments with the TüBa-D/Z treebank are planned in future work. A new release of the TüBa-D/Z treebank has become available that includes appr. 22 000 trees, instead of the release with 15 000 sentences used for the experiments reported in this paper. This new release also contains morphological information at the POS level, including case and number. With this additional information, we expect considerable improvement in grammatical function assignment for the functions *subject*, *accusative object*, and *dative object*, which are marked by nominative, accusative, and dative case, respectively.

Acknowledgments

We are grateful to Helmut Schmid and to Chris Manning and his group for making their parsers publicly available as well as to Tylman Ule for providing the evaluation scripts. We are also grateful to the anonymous reviewers for many helpful comments. And we are especially grateful to Roger Levy for all the help he gave us in creating the language pack for TüBa-D/Z in the Stanford parser.

References

Michael Collins. 1999. *Head-Driven Statistical Models for Natural Language Parsing*. Ph.D. thesis, University of Pennsylvania.

Erich Drach. 1937. *Grundgedanken der Deutschen Satzlehre*. Diesterweg, Frankfurt/M.

Amit Dubey and Frank Keller. 2003. Probabilistic parsing for German using sister-head dependencies. In *Proceedings of ACL 2003*, pages 96–103, Sapporo, Japan.

Amit Dubey. 2005. What to do when lexicalization fails: Parsing German with suffix analysis and smoothing. In *Proceedings of ACL 2005*, Ann Arbor, MI.

Oskar Erdmann. 1886. *Grundzüge der deutschen Syntax nach ihrer geschichtlichen Entwicklung dargestellt*. Verlag der Cotta'schen Buchhandlung, Stuttgart, Germany.

Anette Frank, Markus Becker, Berthold Crysmann, Bernd Kiefer, and Ulrich Schäfer. 2003. Integrated shallow and deep parsing: TopP meets HPSG. In *Proceedings of ACL 2003*, Sapporo, Japan.

Tilman Höhle. 1986. Der Begriff "Mittelfeld", Anmerkungen über die Theorie der topologischen Felder. In *Akten des Siebten Internationalen Germanistenkongresses 1985*, pages 329–340, Göttingen, Germany.

Dan Klein and Christopher Manning. 2003a. Accurate unlexicalized parsing. In *Proceedings of ACL 2003*, pages 423–430, Sapporo, Japan.

Dan Klein and Christopher Manning. 2003b. Fast exact inference with a factored model for natural language parsing. In *Advances in Neural Information Processing Systems 15 (NIPS 2002)*, pages 3–10, Vancouver, Canada.

Sandra Kübler. 2005. How do treebank annotation schemes influence parsing results? Or how not to compare apples and oranges. In *Proceedings of RANLP 2005*, Borovets, Bulgaria.

Roger Levy and Christopher Manning. 2003. Is it harder to parse Chinese, or the Chinese treebank? In *Proceedings of ACL 2003*, pages 439–446, Sapporo, Japan.

Wolfgang Maier. 2006. Annotation schemes and their influence on parsing results. In *Proceedings of the ACL-2006 Student Research Workshop*, Sydney, Australia.

Michael Schiehlen. 2004. Annotation strategies for probabilistic parsing in German. In *Proceedings of COLING 2004*, Geneva, Switzerland.

Helmut Schmid. 2000. LoPar: Design and implementation. Technical report, Universität Stuttgart, Germany.

Sabine Schulte im Walde. 2003. *Experiments on the Automatic Induction of German Semantic Verb Classes*. Ph.D. thesis, Institut für Maschinelle Sprachverarbeitung, Universität Stuttgart.

Wojciech Skut, Brigitte Krenn, Thorsten Brants, and Hans Uszkoreit. 1997. An annotation scheme for free word order languages. In *Proceedings of ANLP 1997*, Washington, D.C.

Heike Telljohann, Erhard W. Hinrichs, Sandra Kübler, and Heike Zinsmeister, 2005. *Stylebook for the Tübingen Treebank of Written German (TüBa-D/Z)*. Seminar für Sprachwissenschaft, Universität Tübingen, Germany.

Tylman Ule. 2003. Directed treebank refinement for PCFG parsing. In *Proceedings of TLT 2003*, Växjö, Sweden.

Domain Adaptation with Structural Correspondence Learning

John Blitzer **Ryan McDonald** **Fernando Pereira**
{blitzer|ryantm|pereira}@cis.upenn.edu
Department of Computer and Information Science, University of Pennsylvania
3330 Walnut Street, Philadelphia, PA 19104, USA

Abstract

Discriminative learning methods are widely used in natural language processing. These methods work best when their training and test data are drawn from the same distribution. For many NLP tasks, however, we are confronted with new domains in which labeled data is scarce or non-existent. In such cases, we seek to adapt existing models from a resource-rich source domain to a resource-poor target domain. We introduce *structural correspondence learning* to automatically induce correspondences among features from different domains. We test our technique on part of speech tagging and show performance gains for varying amounts of source and target training data, as well as improvements in target domain parsing accuracy using our improved tagger.

1 Introduction

Discriminative learning methods are ubiquitous in natural language processing. Discriminative taggers and chunkers have been the state-of-the-art for more than a decade (Ratnaparkhi, 1996; Sha and Pereira, 2003). Furthermore, end-to-end systems like speech recognizers (Roark et al., 2004) and automatic translators (Och, 2003) use increasingly sophisticated discriminative models, which generalize well to new data that is drawn from the same distribution as the training data.

However, in many situations we may have a *source* domain with plentiful labeled training data, but we need to process material from a *target* domain with a different distribution from the source domain and no labeled data. In such cases, we must take steps to adapt a model trained on the source domain for use in the target domain (Roark and Bacchiani, 2003; Florian et al., 2004; Chelba and Acero, 2004; Ando, 2004; Lease and Charniak, 2005; Daumé III and Marcu, 2006). This work focuses on using unlabeled data from both the source and target domains to learn a common feature representation that is meaningful across both domains. We hypothesize that a discriminative model trained in the source domain using this common feature representation will generalize better to the target domain.

This representation is learned using a method we call structural correspondence learning (SCL). The key idea of SCL is to identify correspondences among features from different domains by modeling their correlations with *pivot* features. Pivot features are features which behave in the same way for discriminative learning in both domains. Non-pivot features from different domains which are correlated with many of the same pivot features are assumed to correspond, and we treat them similarly in a discriminative learner.

Even on the unlabeled data, the co-occurrence statistics of pivot and non-pivot features are likely to be sparse, and we must model them in a compact way. There are many choices for modeling co-occurrence data (Brown et al., 1992; Pereira et al., 1993; Blei et al., 2003). In this work we choose to use the technique of structural learning (Ando and Zhang, 2005a; Ando and Zhang, 2005b). Structural learning models the correlations which are most useful for semi-supervised learning. We demonstrate how to adapt it for transfer learning, and consequently the *structural* part of structural correspondence learning is borrowed from it.[1]

SCL is a general technique, which one can apply to feature based classifiers for any task. Here,

[1] Structural learning is different from learning with structured outputs, a common paradigm for discriminative natural language processing models. To avoid terminological confusion, we refer throughout the paper to a specific structural learning method, alternating structural optimization (ASO) (Ando and Zhang, 2005a).

Proceedings of the 2006 Conference on Empirical Methods in Natural Language Processing (EMNLP 2006), pages 120–128,
Sydney, July 2006.

(a) Wall Street Journal

DT	JJ	VBZ	DT	NN	IN	DT	JJ	NN
The	clash	is	a	sign	of	a	new	toughness
CC	NN	IN	NNP	POS	JJ	JJ	NN	.
and	divisiveness	in	Japan	's	once-cozy	financial	circles	.

(b) MEDLINE

DT	JJ	VBN	NNS	IN	DT	NN	NNS	VBP
The	oncogenic	mutated	forms	of	the	ras	proteins	are
RB	JJ	CC	VBP	IN	JJ	NN	NN	.
constitutively	active	and	interfere	with	normal	**signal**	transduction	.

Figure 1: Part of speech-tagged sentences from both corpora

we investigate its use in part of speech (PoS) tagging (Ratnaparkhi, 1996; Toutanova et al., 2003). While PoS tagging has been heavily studied, many domains lack appropriate training corpora for PoS tagging. Nevertheless, PoS tagging is an important stage in pipelined language processing systems, from information extractors to speech synthesizers. We show how to use SCL to transfer a PoS tagger from the Wall Street Journal (financial news) to MEDLINE (biomedical abstracts), which use very different vocabularies, and we demonstrate not only improved PoS accuracy but also improved end-to-end parsing accuracy while using the improved tagger.

An important but rarely-explored setting in domain adaptation is when we have no labeled training data for the target domain. We first demonstrate that in this situation SCL significantly improves performance over both supervised and semi-supervised taggers. In the case when some in-domain labeled training data is available, we show how to use SCL together with the classifier combination techniques of Florian et al. (2004) to achieve even greater performance.

In the next section, we describe a motivating example involving financial news and biomedical data. Section 3 describes the structural correspondence learning algorithm. Sections 6 and 7 report results on adapting from the Wall Street Journal to MEDLINE. We discuss related work on domain adaptation in section 8 and conclude in section 9.

2 A Motivating Example

Figure 1 shows two PoS-tagged sentences, one each from the Wall Street Journal (hereafter WSJ) and MEDLINE. We chose these sentences for two reasons. First, we wish to visually emphasize the difference between the two domains. The vocabularies differ significantly, and PoS taggers suffer accordingly. Second, we want to focus on the

(a) An ambiguous instance

		JJ vs. NN	
with	normal	**signal**	transduction

(b) MEDLINE occurrences of signal, together with pivot features

the **signal** *required* to
stimulatory **signal** *from*
essential **signal** *for*

(c) Corresponding WSJ words, together with pivot features

of **investment** *required*
of **buyouts** *from* buyers
to **jail** *for* violating

Figure 2: Correcting an incorrect biomedical tag. Corresponding words are in bold, and pivot features are italicized

phrase "with normal signal transduction" from the MEDLINE sentence, depicted in Figure 2(a). The word "signal" in this sentence is a noun, but a tagger trained on the WSJ incorrectly classifies it as an adjective. We introduce the notion of *pivot* features. Pivot features are features which occur frequently in the two domains and behave similarly in both. Figure 2(b) shows some pivot features that occur together with the word "signal" in our biomedical unlabeled data. In this case our pivot features are all of type `<the token on the right>`. Note that "signal" is unambiguously a noun in these contexts. Adjectives rarely precede past tense verbs such as "required" or prepositions such as "from" and "for".

We now search for occurrences of the pivot features in the WSJ. Figure 2(c) shows some words that occur together with the pivot features in the WSJ unlabeled data. Note that "investment", "buy-outs", and "jail" are all common nouns in the financial domain. Furthermore, since we have labeled WSJ data, we expect to be able to label at least some of these nouns correctly.

This example captures the intuition behind structural correspondence learning. We want to use pivot features from our unlabeled data to put domain-specific words in correspondence. That is,

Input: labeled source data $\{(\mathbf{x}_t, y_t)_{t=1}^{T}\}$, unlabeled data from both domains $\{\mathbf{x}_j\}$

Output: predictor $f : X \rightarrow Y$

1. Choose m pivot features. Create m binary prediction problems, $p_\ell(\mathbf{x}),\ \ell = 1 \ldots m$
2. For $\ell = 1$ to m
   $\hat{\mathbf{w}}_\ell = \underset{\mathbf{w}}{\text{argmin}} \left(\sum_j L(\mathbf{w} \cdot \mathbf{x}_j, p_\ell(\mathbf{x}_j)) + \lambda ||\mathbf{w}||^2 \right)$
   end
3. $W = [\hat{\mathbf{w}}_1 | \ldots | \hat{\mathbf{w}}_m], \quad [U\ D\ V^T] = \text{SVD}(W), \quad \theta = U^T_{[1:h,:]}$
4. Return f, a predictor trained on $\left\{ \left(\begin{bmatrix} \mathbf{x}_t \\ \theta \mathbf{x}_i \end{bmatrix}, y_t \right)_{t=1}^{T} \right\}$

Figure 3: SCL Algorithm

we want the pivot features to model the fact that in the biomedical domain, the word *signal* behaves similarly to the words *investments*, *buyouts* and *jail* in the financial news domain. In practice, we use this technique to find correspondences among all features, not just word features.

3 Structural Correspondence Learning

Structural correspondence learning involves a source domain and a target domain. Both domains have ample unlabeled data, but only the source domain has labeled training data. We refer to the task for which we have labeled training data as the *supervised task*. In our experiments, the supervised task is part of speech tagging. We require that the input $\mathbf{x}$ in both domains be a vector of binary features from a finite feature space. The first step of SCL is to define a set of pivot features on the unlabeled data from both domains. We then use these pivot features to learn a mapping θ from the original feature spaces of both domains to a shared, low-dimensional real-valued feature space. A high inner product in this new space indicates a high degree of correspondence.

During supervised task training, we use both the transformed and original features from the source domain. During supervised task testing, we use the both the transformed and original features from the target domain. If we learned a good mapping θ, then the classifier we learn on the source domain will also be effective on the target domain. The SCL algorithm is given in Figure 3, and the remainder of this section describes it in detail.

3.1 Pivot Features

Pivot features should occur frequently in the unlabeled data of both domains, since we must estimate their covariance with non-pivot features accurately, but they must also be diverse enough to adequately characterize the nuances of the supervised task. A good example of this tradeoff are determiners in PoS tagging. Determiners are good pivot features, since they occur frequently in any domain of written English, but choosing *only* determiners will not help us to discriminate between nouns and adjectives. Pivot features correspond to the auxiliary problems of Ando and Zhang (2005a).

In section 2, we showed example pivot features of type `<the token on the right>`. We also use pivot features of type `<the token on the left>` and `<the token in the middle>`. In practice there are many thousands of pivot features, corresponding to instantiations of these three types for frequent words in both domains. We choose m pivot features, which we index with ℓ.

3.2 Pivot Predictors

From each pivot feature we create a binary classification problem of the form "Does pivot feature ℓ occur in this instance?". One such example is "Is `<the token on the right>` *required*?" These binary classification problems can be trained from the unlabeled data, since they merely represent properties of the input. If we represent our features as a binary vector $\mathbf{x}$, we can solve these problems using m linear predictors.

$$f_\ell(\mathbf{x}) = \text{sgn}(\hat{\mathbf{w}}_\ell \cdot \mathbf{x}), \quad \ell = 1 \ldots m$$

Note that these predictors operate on the original feature space. This step is shown in line 2 of Figure 3. Here $L(p, y)$ is a real-valued loss function for binary classification. We follow Ando and Zhang (2005a) and use the modified Huber loss.

Since each instance contains features which are totally predictive of the pivot feature (the feature itself), we never use these features when making the binary prediction. That is, we do not use any feature derived from the right word when solving a right token pivot predictor.

The pivot predictors are the key element in SCL. The weight vectors $\hat{\mathbf{w}}_\ell$ encode the covariance of the non-pivot features with the pivot features. If the weight given to the z'th feature by the ℓ'th pivot predictor is positive, then feature z is positively correlated with pivot feature ℓ. Since pivot features occur frequently in both domains, we expect non-pivot features from both domains to be correlated with them. If two non-pivot features are correlated in the same way with many of the same pivot features, then they have a high degree of correspondence. Finally, observe that $\hat{\mathbf{w}}_\ell$ is a linear projection of the original feature space onto $\mathbb{R}$.

3.3 Singular Value Decomposition

Since each pivot predictor is a projection onto $\mathbb{R}$, we could create m new real-valued features, one for each pivot. For both computational and statistical reasons, though, we follow Ando and Zhang (2005a) and compute a low-dimensional linear approximation to the pivot predictor space. Let W be the matrix whose columns are the pivot predictor weight vectors. Now let $W = UDV^T$ be the singular value decomposition of W, so that $\theta = U^T_{[1:h,:]}$ is the matrix whose rows are the top left singular vectors of W.

The rows of θ are the principal pivot predictors, which capture the variance of the pivot predictor space as best as possible in h dimensions. Furthermore, θ is a projection from the original feature space onto $\mathbb{R}^h$. That is, $\theta\mathbf{x}$ is the desired mapping to the (low dimensional) shared feature representation. This is step 3 of Figure 3.

3.4 Supervised Training and Inference

To perform inference and learning for the supervised task, we simply augment the original feature vector with features obtained by applying the mapping θ. We then use a standard discriminative learner on the augmented feature vector. For training instance t, the augmented feature vector will contain all the original features $\mathbf{x}_t$ plus the new shared features $\theta\mathbf{x}_t$. If we have designed the pivots well, then θ should encode correspondences among features from different domains which are important for the supervised task, and the classifier we train using these new features on the source domain will perform well on the target domain.

4 Model Choices

Structural correspondence learning uses the techniques of alternating structural optimization (ASO) to learn the correlations among pivot and non-pivot features. Ando and Zhang (2005a) describe several free paramters and extensions to ASO, and we briefly address our choices for these here. We set h, the dimensionality of our low-rank representation to be 25. As in Ando and Zhang (2005a), we observed that setting h between 20 and 100 did not change results significantly, and a lower dimensionality translated to faster run-time. We also implemented both of the extensions described in Ando and Zhang (2005a). The first is to only use positive entries in the pivot predictor weight vectors to compute the SVD. This yields a sparse representation which saves both time and space, and it also performs better. The second is to compute block SVDs of the matrix W, where one block corresponds to one feature type. We used the same 58 feature types as Ratnaparkhi (1996). This gave us a total of 1450 projection features for both semisupervised ASO and SCL.

We found it necessary to make a change to the ASO algorithm as described in Ando and Zhang (2005a). We rescale the projection features to allow them to receive more weight from a regularized discriminative learner. Without any rescaling, we were not able to reproduce the original ASO results. The rescaling parameter is a single number, and we choose it using heldout data from our source domain. In all our experiments, we rescale our projection features to have average L_1 norm on the training set five times that of the binary-valued features.

Finally, we also make one more change to make optimization faster. We select only half of the ASO features for use in the final model. This is done by running a few iterations of stochastic gradient descent on the PoS tagging problem, then choosing the features with the largest weight-variance across the different labels. This cut in half training time and marginally improved performance in all our experiments.

5 Data Sets and Supervised Tagger

5.1 Source Domain: WSJ

We used sections 02-21 of the Penn Treebank (Marcus et al., 1993) for training. This resulted in 39,832 training sentences. For the unlabeled data, we used 100,000 sentences from a 1988 subset of the WSJ.

5.2 Target Domain: Biomedical Text

For unlabeled data we used 200,000 sentences that were chosen by searching MEDLINE for abstracts pertaining to cancer, in particular genomic varia-

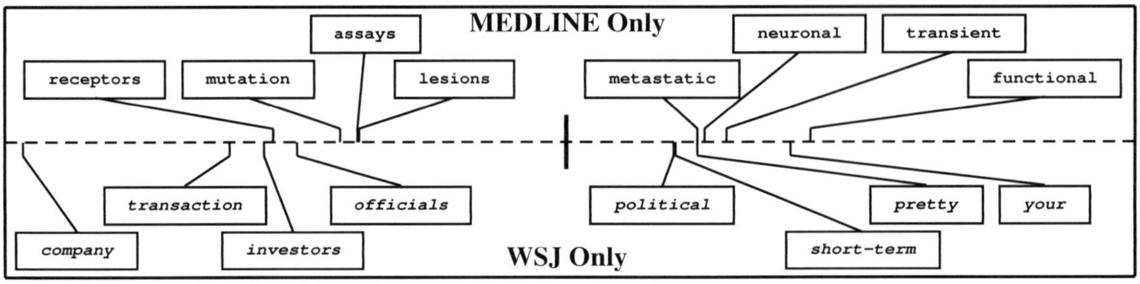

Figure 4: An example projection of word features onto $\mathbb{R}$. Words on the left (negative valued) behave similarly to each other for classification, but differently from words on the right (positive valued). The projection distinguishes nouns from adjectives and determiners in both domains.

tions and mutations. For labeled training and testing purposes we use 1061 sentences that have been annotated by humans as part of the Penn BioIE project (PennBioIE, 2005). We use the same 561-sentence test set in all our experiments. The part-of-speech tag set for this data is a superset of the Penn Treebank's including the two new tags HYPH (for hyphens) and AFX (for common post-modifiers of biomedical entities such as genes). These tags were introduced due to the importance of hyphenated entities in biomedical text, and are used for 1.8% of the words in the test set. Any tagger trained only on WSJ text will automatically predict wrong tags for those words.

5.3 Supervised Tagger

Since SCL is really a method for inducing a set of cross-domain features, we are free to choose any feature-based classifier to use them. For our experiments we use a version of the discriminative online large-margin learning algorithm MIRA (Crammer et al., 2006). MIRA learns and outputs a linear classification score, $s(\mathbf{x}, \mathbf{y}; \mathbf{w}) = \mathbf{w} \cdot \mathbf{f}(\mathbf{x}, \mathbf{y})$, where the feature representation $\mathbf{f}$ can contain arbitrary features of the input, including the correspondence features described earlier. In particular, MIRA aims to learn weights so that the score of correct output, $\mathbf{y_t}$, for input $\mathbf{x}_t$ is separated from the highest scoring incorrect outputs[2], with a margin proportional to their Hamming losses. MIRA has been used successfully for both sequence analysis (McDonald et al., 2005a) and dependency parsing (McDonald et al., 2005b).

As with any structured predictor, we need to factor the output space to make inference tractable. We use a first-order Markov factorization, allowing for an efficient Viterbi inference procedure.

[2]We fix the number of high scoring incorrect outputs to 5.

6 Visualizing θ

In section 2 we claimed that good representations should encode correspondences between words like "signal" from MEDLINE and "investment" from the WSJ. Recall that the rows of θ are projections from the original feature space onto the real line. Here we examine word features under these projections. Figure 4 shows a row from the matrix θ. Applying this projection to a word gives a real value on the horizontal dashed line axis. The words below the horizontal axis occur only in the WSJ. The words above the axis occur only in MEDLINE. The verticle line in the middle represents the value zero. Ticks to the left or right indicate relative positive or negative values for a word under this projection. This projection discriminates between nouns (negative) and adjectives (positive). A tagger which gives high positive weight to the features induced by applying this projection will be able to discriminate among the associated classes of biomedical words, even when it has never observed the words explicitly in the WSJ source training set.

7 Empirical Results

All the results we present in this section use the MIRA tagger from Section 5.3. The ASO and structural correspondence results also use projection features learned using ASO and SCL. Section 7.1 presents results comparing structural correspondence learning with the supervised baseline and ASO in the case where we have no labeled data in the target domain. Section 7.2 gives results for the case where we have some limited data in the target domain. In this case, we use classifiers as features as described in Florian et al. (2004). Finally, we show in Section 7.3 that our SCL PoS

(a)

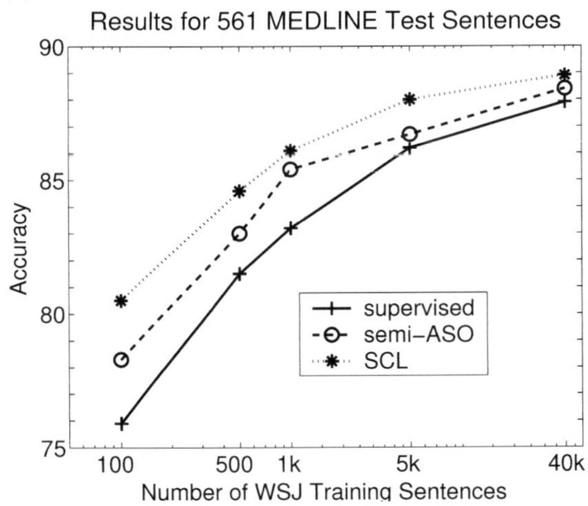

(b) Accuracy on 561-sentence test set

Model	Words: All	Words: Unknown
Ratnaparkhi (1996)	87.2	65.2
supervised	87.9	68.4
semi-ASO	88.4	70.9
SCL	**88.9**	**72.0**

(c) Statistical Significance (McNemar's) for all words

Null Hypothesis	p-value
semi-ASO vs. super	0.0015
SCL vs. super	2.1×10^{-12}
SCL vs. semi-ASO	0.0003

Figure 5: PoS tagging results with no target labeled training data

(a)

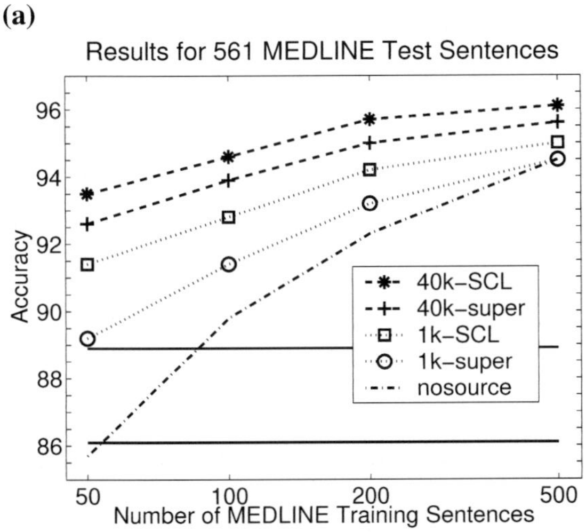

(b) 500 target domain training sentences

Model	Testing Accuracy
nosource	94.5
1k-super	94.5
1k-SCL	**95.0**
40k-super	95.6
40k-SCL	**96.1**

(c) McNemar's Test (500 training sentences)

Null Hypothesis	p-value
1k-super vs. nosource	0.732
1k-SCL vs. 1k-super	0.0003
40k-super vs. nosource	1.9×10^{-12}
40k-SCL vs. 40k-super	6.5×10^{-7}

Figure 6: PoS tagging results with no target labeled training data

tagger improves the performance of a dependency parser on the target domain.

7.1 No Target Labeled Training Data

For the results in this section, we trained a structural correspondence learner with 100,000 sentences of unlabeled data from the WSJ and 100,000 sentences of unlabeled biomedical data. We use as pivot features words that occur more than 50 times in both domains. The supervised baseline does not use unlabeled data. The ASO baseline is an implementation of Ando and Zhang (2005b). It uses 200,000 sentences of unlabeled MEDLINE data but no unlabeled WSJ data. For ASO we used as auxiliary problems words that occur more than 500 times in the MEDLINE unlabeled data.

Figure 5(a) plots the accuracies of the three models with varying amounts of WSJ training data. With one hundred sentences of training data, structural correspondence learning gives a 19.1% relative reduction in error over the supervised baseline, and it consistently outperforms both baseline models. Figure 5(b) gives results for 40,000 sentences, and Figure 5(c) shows corresponding significance tests, with $p < 0.05$ being significant. We use a McNemar paired test for labeling disagreements (Gillick and Cox, 1989). Even when we use all the WSJ training data available, the SCL model significantly improves accuracy over both the supervised and ASO baselines.

The second column of Figure 5(b) gives unknown word accuracies on the biomedical data.

Of thirteen thousand test instances, approximately three thousand were unknown. For unknown words, SCL gives a relative reduction in error of 19.5% over Ratnaparkhi (1996), even with 40,000 sentences of source domain training data.

7.2 Some Target Labeled Training Data

In this section we give results for small amounts of target domain training data. In this case, we make use of the out-of-domain data by using features of the source domain tagger's predictions in training and testing the target domain tagger (Florian et al., 2004). Though other methods for incorporating small amounts of training data in the target domain were available, such as those proposed by Chelba and Acero (2004) and by Daumé III and Marcu (2006), we chose this method for its simplicity and consistently good performance. We use as features the current predicted tag and all tag bigrams in a 5-token window around the current token.

Figure 6(a) plots tagging accuracy for varying amounts of MEDLINE training data. The two horizontal lines are the fixed accuracies of the SCL WSJ-trained taggers using one thousand and forty thousand sentences of training data. The five learning curves are for taggers trained with varying amounts of target domain training data. They use features on the outputs of taggers from section 7.1. The legend indicates the kinds of features used in the target domain (in addition to the standard features). For example, "40k-SCL" means that the tagger uses features on the outputs of an SCL source tagger trained on forty thousand sentences of WSJ data. "nosource" indicates a target tagger that did not use any tagger trained on the source domain. With 1000 source domain sentences and 50 target domain sentences, using SCL tagger features gives a 20.4% relative reduction in error over using supervised tagger features and a 39.9% relative reduction in error over using no source features.

Figure 6(b) is a table of accuracies for 500 target domain training sentences, and Figure 6(c) gives corresponding significance scores. With 1000 source domain sentences and 500 target domain sentences, using supervised tagger features gives no improvement over using no source features. Using SCL features still does, however.

7.3 Improving Parser Performance

We emphasize the importance of PoS tagging in a pipelined NLP system by incorporating our SCL

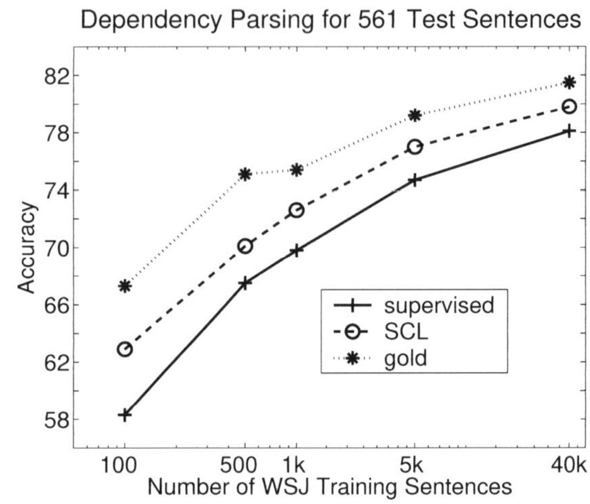

Figure 7: Dependency parsing results using different part of speech taggers

tagger into a WSJ-trained dependency parser and and evaluate it on MEDLINE data. We use the parser described by McDonald et al. (2005b). That parser assumes that a sentence has been PoS-tagged before parsing. We train the parser and PoS tagger on the same size of WSJ data.

Figure 7 shows dependency parsing accuracy on our 561-sentence MEDLINE test set. We parsed the sentences using the PoS tags output by our source domain supervised tagger, the SCL tagger from subsection 7.1, and the gold PoS tags. All of the differences in this figure are significant according to McNemar's test. The SCL tags consistently improve parsing performance over the tags output by the supervised tagger. This is a rather indirect method of improving parsing performance with SCL. In the future, we plan on directly incorporating SCL features into a discriminative parser to improve its adaptation properties.

8 Related Work

Domain adaptation is an important and well-studied area in natural language processing. Here we outline a few recent advances. Roark and Bacchiani (2003) use a Dirichlet prior on the multinomial parameters of a generative parsing model to combine a large amount of training data from a source corpus (WSJ), and small amount of training data from a target corpus (Brown). Aside from Florian et al. (2004), several authors have also given techniques for adapting classification to new domains. Chelba and Acero (2004) first train a classifier on the source data. Then they use maximum a posteriori estimation of the weights of a maximum entropy target domain classifier. The prior is Gaussian with mean equal to the weights of the source domain classifier. Daumé III and Marcu (2006) use an empirical Bayes model to estimate a latent variable model grouping instances into domain-specific or common across both domains. They also jointly estimate the parameters of the common classification model and the domain specific classification models. Our work focuses on finding a common representation for *features* from different domains, not instances. We believe this is an important distinction, since the same instance can contain some features which are common across domains and some which are domain specific.

The key difference between the previous four pieces of work and our own is the use of unlabeled data. We do not require labeled training data in the new domain to demonstrate an improvement over our baseline models. We believe this is essential, since many domains of application in natural language processing have no labeled training data. Lease and Charniak (2005) adapt a WSJ parser to biomedical text without any biomedical treebanked data. However, they assume other labeled resources in the target domain. In Section 7.3 we give similar parsing results, but we adapt a source domain tagger to obtain the PoS resources.

To the best of our knowledge, SCL is the first method to use unlabeled data from both domains for domain adaptation. By using just the unlabeled data from the target domain, however, we can view domain adaptation as a standard semisupervised learning problem. There are many possible approaches for semisupservised learning in natural language processing, and it is beyond the scope of this paper to address them all. We chose to compare with ASO because it consistently outperforms cotraining (Blum and Mitchell, 1998) and clustering methods (Miller et al., 2004). We did run experiments with the *top-k* version of ASO (Ando and Zhang, 2005a), which is inspired by cotraining but consistently outperforms it. This did not outperform the supervised method for domain adaptation. We speculate that this is because biomedical and financial data are quite different. In such a situation, bootstrapping techniques are likely to introduce too much noise from the source domain to be useful.

Structural correspondence learning is most similar to that of Ando (2004), who analyzed a situation with no target domain labeled data. Her model estimated co-occurrence counts from source unlabeled data and then used the SVD of this matrix to generate features for a named entity recognizer. Our ASO baseline uses unlabeled data from the *target* domain. Since this consistently outperforms unlabeled data from only the *source* domain, we report only these baseline results. To the best of our knowledge, this is the first work to use unlabeled data from both domains to find feature correspondences.

One important advantage that this work shares with Ando (2004) is that an SCL model can be easily combined with all other domain adaptation techniques (Section 7.2). We are simply inducing a feature representation that generalizes well across domains. This feature representation can then be used in all the techniques described above.

9 Conclusion

Structural correspondence learning is a marriage of ideas from single domain semi-supervised learning and domain adaptation. It uses unlabeled data and frequently-occurring pivot features from both source and target domains to find correspondences among features from these domains. Finding correspondences involves estimating the correlations between pivot and non-pivot feautres, and we adapt structural learning (ASO) (Ando and Zhang, 2005a; Ando and Zhang, 2005b) for this task. SCL is a general technique that can be applied to any feature-based discriminative learner.

We showed results using SCL to transfer a PoS tagger from the Wall Street Journal to a corpus of MEDLINE abstracts. SCL consistently outperformed both supervised and semi-supervised learning with no labeled target domain training data. We also showed how to combine an SCL tagger with target domain labeled data using the classifier combination techniques from Florian et al. (2004). Finally, we improved parsing performance in the target domain when using the SCL PoS tagger.

One of our next goals is to apply SCL directly to parsing. We are also focusing on other potential applications, including chunking (Sha and Pereira, 2003), named entity recognition (Florian et al., 2004; Ando and Zhang, 2005b; Daumé III and Marcu, 2006), and speaker adaptation (Kuhn et al., 1998). Finally, we are investigating more direct ways of applying structural correspondence learning when we have labeled data from both source and target domains. In particular, the labeled data of both domains, not just the unlabeled data, should influence the learned representations.

Acknowledgments

We thank Rie Kubota Ando and Tong Zhang for their helpful advice on ASO, Steve Carroll and Pete White of The Children's Hospital of Philadelphia for providing the MEDLINE data, and the PennBioIE annotation team for the annotated MEDLINE data used in our test sets. This material is based upon work partially supported by the Defense Advanced Research Projects Agency (DARPA) under Contract No. NBCHD030010. Any opinions, findings, and conclusions or recommendations expressed in this material are those of the author(s) and do not necessarily reflect the views of the DARPA or the Department of Interior-National Business Center (DOI-NBC). Additional support was provided by NSF under ITR grant EIA-0205448.

References

R. Ando and T. Zhang. 2005a. A framework for learning predictive structures from multiple tasks and unlabeled data. *JMLR*, 6:1817–1853.

R. Ando and T. Zhang. 2005b. A high-performance semi-supervised learning method for text chunking. In *ACL*.

R. Ando. 2004. Exploiting unannotated corpora for tagging and chunking. In *ACL. Short paper*.

D. Blei, A. Ng, and M. Jordan. 2003. Latent dirichlet allocation. *JMLR*, 3:993–1022.

A. Blum and T. Mitchell. 1998. Combining labeled and unlabeled data with co-training. In *Workshop on Computational Learning Theory*.

P. Brown, V. Della Pietra, P. deSouza, J. Lai, and R. Mercer. 1992. Class-based n-gram models of natural language. *Computational Linguistics*, 18(4):467–479.

C. Chelba and A. Acero. 2004. Adaptation of maximum entropy capitalizer: Little data can help a lot. In *EMNLP*.

K. Crammer, Dekel O, J. Keshet, S. Shalev-Shwartz, and Y. Singer. 2006. Online passive-aggressive algorithms. *JMLR*, 7:551–585.

H. Daum´e III and D. Marcu. 2006. Domain adaptation for statistical classifi ers. *JAIR*.

R. Florian, H. Hassan, A.Ittycheriah, H. Jing, N. Kambhatla, X. Luo, N. Nicolov, and S. Roukos. 2004. A statistical model for multilingual entity detection and tracking. In *of HLT-NAACL*.

L. Gillick and S. Cox. 1989. Some statistical issues in the comparison of speech recognition algorithms. In *ICASSP*.

R. Kuhn, P. Nguyen, J.C. Junqua, L. Goldwasser, N. Niedzielski, S. Fincke, K. Field, and M. Contolini. 1998. Eigenvoices for speaker adaptation. In *ICSLP*.

M. Lease and E. Charniak. 2005. Parsing biomedical literature. In *IJCNLP*.

M. Marcus, B. Santorini, and M. Marcinkiewicz. 1993. Building a large annotated corpus of English: The Penn Treebank. *Computational Linguistics*, 19(2):313–330.

R. McDonald, K. Crammer, and F. Pereira. 2005a. Flexible text segmentation with structured multilabel classifi cation. In *HLT-EMNLP*.

R. McDonald, K. Crammer, and F. Pereira. 2005b. Online large-margin training of dependency parsers. In *ACL*.

S. Miller, J. Guinness, and A. Zamanian. 2004. Name tagging with word clusters and discriminative training. In *HLT-NAACL*.

F. Och. 2003. Minimum error rate training in statistical machine translation. In *Proc. of ACL*.

PennBioIE. 2005. Mining The Bibliome Project. http://bioie.ldc.upenn.edu/.

F. Pereira, N. Tishby, and L. Lee. 1993. Distributional clustering of english words. In *ACL*.

A. Ratnaparkhi. 1996. A maximum entropy model for part-of-speech tagging. In *EMNLP*.

B. Roark and M. Bacchiani. 2003. Supervised and unsupervised PCFG adaptation to novel domains. In *HLT-NAACL*.

B. Roark, M. Saraclar, M. Collins, and M. Johnson. 2004. Discriminative language modeling with conditional random fi elds and the perceptron algorithm. In *ACL*.

F. Sha and F. Pereira. 2003. Shallow parsing with conditional random fi elds. In *HLT-NAACL*.

K. Toutanova, D. Klein, C. D. Manning, and Y. Singer. 2003. Feature-rich part-of-speech tagging with a cyclic dependency network. In *NAACL*.

Incremental Integer Linear Programming for Non-projective Dependency Parsing

Sebastian Riedel and **James Clarke**
School of Informatics, University of Edinburgh
2 Bucclecuch Place, Edinburgh EH8 9LW, UK
s.r.riedel@sms.ed.ac.uk, jclarke@ed.ac.uk

Abstract

Integer Linear Programming has recently been used for decoding in a number of probabilistic models in order to enforce global constraints. However, in certain applications, such as non-projective dependency parsing and machine translation, the complete formulation of the decoding problem as an integer linear program renders solving intractable. We present an approach which solves the problem incrementally, thus we avoid creating intractable integer linear programs. This approach is applied to Dutch dependency parsing and we show how the addition of linguistically motivated constraints can yield a significant improvement over state-of-the-art.

1 Introduction

Many inference algorithms require models to make strong assumptions of conditional independence between variables. For example, the Viterbi algorithm used for decoding in conditional random fields requires the model to be Markovian. Strong assumptions are also made in the case of McDonald et al.'s (2005b) non-projective dependency parsing model. Here attachment decisions are made independently of one another[1]. However, often such assumptions can not be justified. For example in dependency parsing, if a subject has already been identified for a given verb, then the probability of attaching a second subject to the verb is zero. Similarly, if we find that one coordination argument is a noun, then the other argument cannot be a verb. Thus decisions are often co-dependent.

Integer Linear Programming (ILP) has recently been applied to inference in sequential conditional random fields (Roth and Yih, 2004), this has allowed the use of truly global constraints during inference. However, it is not possible to use this approach directly for a complex task like non-projective dependency parsing due to the exponential number of constraints required to prevent cycles occurring in the dependency graph. To model all these constraints explicitly would result in an ILP formulation too large to solve efficiently (Williams, 2002). A similar problem also occurs in an ILP formulation for machine translation which treats decoding as the Travelling Salesman Problem (Germann et al., 2001).

In this paper we present a method which extends the applicability of ILP to a more complex set of problems. Instead of adding all the constraints we wish to capture to the formulation, we first solve the program with a fraction of the constraints. The solution is then examined and, if required, additional constraints are added. This procedure is repeated until all constraints are satisfied. We apply this dependency parsing approach to Dutch due to the language's non-projective nature, and take the parser of McDonald et al. (2005b) as a starting point for our model.

In the following section we introduce dependency parsing and review previous work. In Section 3 we present our model and formulate it as an ILP problem with a set of linguistically motivated constraints. We include details of an incremental algorithm used to solve this formulation. Our experimental set-up is provided in Section 4 and is followed by results in Section 5 along with runtime experiments. We finally discuss fu-

[1]If we ignore the constraint that dependency trees must be cycle-free (see sections 2 and 3 for details).

Proceedings of the 2006 Conference on Empirical Methods in Natural Language Processing (EMNLP 2006), pages 129–137,
Sydney, July 2006.

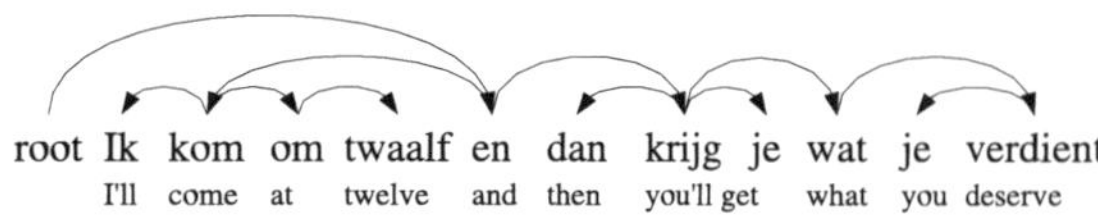

Figure 1: A Dutch dependency tree for "I'll come at twelve and then you'll get what you deserve"

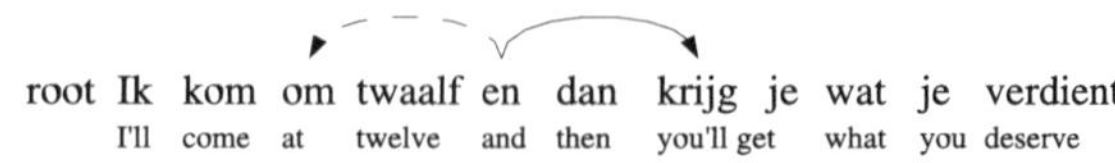

Figure 2: An incorrect partial dependency tree. The verb "krijg" is incorrectly coordinated with the preposition "om".

ture research and potential improvements to our approach.

2 Dependency Parsing

Dependency parsing is the task of attaching words to their arguments. Figure 1 shows a dependency graph for the Dutch sentence "I'll come at twelve and then you'll get what you deserve" (taken from the Alpino Corpus (van der Beek et al., 2002)). In this dependency graph the verb "kom" is attached to its subject "ik". "kom" is referred to as the head of the dependency and "ik" as its child. In labelled dependency parsing edges between words are labelled with the relation captured. In the case of the dependency between "kom" and "ik" the label would be "subject".

In a dependency tree every token must be the child of exactly one other node, either another token or the dummy root node. By definition, a dependency tree is free of cycles. For example, it must not contain dependency chains such as "en" → "kom" → "ik" → "en". For a more formal definition see previous work (Nivre et al., 2004).

An important distinction between dependency trees is whether they are projective or non-projective. Figure 1 is an example of a projective dependency tree, in such trees dependencies do not cross. In Dutch and other flexible word order languages such as German and Czech we also encounter non-projective trees, in these cases the trees contain crossing dependencies.

Dependency parsing is useful for applications such as relation extraction (Culotta and Sorensen, 2004) and machine translation (Ding and Palmer, 2005). Although less informative than lexicalised phrase structures, dependency structures still capture most of the predicate-argument information needed for applications. It has the advantage of being more efficient to learn and parse.

McDonald et al. (2005a) introduce a dependency parsing framework which treats the task as searching for the projective tree that maximises the sum of local dependency scores. This framework is efficient and has also been extended to non-projective trees (McDonald et al., 2005b). It provides a discriminative online learning algorithm which when combined with a rich feature set reaches state-of-the-art performance across multiple languages.

However, within this framework one can only define features over single attachment decisions. This leads to cases where basic linguistic constraints are not satisfied (e.g. verbs with two subjects or incompatible coordination arguments). An example of this for Dutch is illustrated in Figure 2 which was produced by the parser of McDonald et al. (2005b). Here the parse contains a coordination of incompatible word classes (a preposition and a verb).

Our approach is able to include additional constraints which forbid configurations such as those in Figure 2. While McDonald and Pereira (2006) address the issue of local attachment decisions by defining scores over attachment pairs, our solution is more general. Furthermore, it is complementary in the sense that we could formulate their model using ILP and then add constraints.

The method we present is not the only one that can take global constraints into account. Deterministic dependency parsing (Nivre et al., 2004; Yamada and Matsumoto, 2003) can apply global constraints by conditioning attachment decisions on the intermediate parse built. However, for efficiency a greedy search is used which may produce sub-optimal solutions. This is not the case when using ILP.

3 Model

Our underlying model is a modified labelled version[2] of McDonald et al. (2005b):

$$\begin{aligned} s(\mathbf{x}, \mathbf{y}) &= \sum_{(i,j,l) \in \mathbf{y}} s(i,j,l) \\ &= \sum_{(i,j,l) \in \mathbf{y}} \mathbf{w} \cdot \mathbf{f}(i,j,l) \end{aligned}$$

[2]Note that this is not described in the McDonald papers but implemented in his software.

where $\mathbf{x}$ is a sentence, $\mathbf{y}$ is a set of labelled dependencies, $\mathbf{f}(i,j,l)$ is a multidimensional feature vector representation of the edge from token i to token j with label l and $\mathbf{w}$ the corresponding weight vector. For example, a feature f_{101} in $\mathbf{f}$ could be:

$$f_{101}(i,j,l) = \begin{cases} 1 & \text{if } t(i) = \text{“en”} \wedge p(j) = \text{V} \\ & \wedge l = \text{“coordination”} \\ 0 & \text{otherwise} \end{cases}$$

where $t(i)$ is the word at token i and $p(j)$ the part-of-speech tag at token j.

Decoding in this model amounts to finding the $\mathbf{y}$ for a given $\mathbf{x}$ that maximises $s(\mathbf{x}, \mathbf{y})$:

$$y' = \arg\max_{y} s(\mathbf{x}, \mathbf{y})$$

while fulfilling the following constraints:

T1 For every non-root token in $\mathbf{x}$ there exists exactly one head; the root token has no head.

T2 There are no cycles.

Thus far, the formulation follows McDonald et al. (2005b) and corresponds to the Maximum Spanning Tree (MST) problem. In addition to **T1** and **T2**, we include a set of linguistically motivated constraints:

A1 Heads are not allowed to have more than one outgoing edge labelled l for all l in a set of labels U.

C1 In a symmetric coordination there is exactly one argument to the right of the conjunction and at least one argument to the left.

C2 In an asymmetric coordination there are no arguments to the left of the conjunction and at least two arguments to the right.

C3 There must be at least one comma between subsequent arguments to the left of a symmetric coordination.

C4 Arguments of a coordination must have compatible word classes.

P1 Two dependencies must not cross if one of their labels is in a set of labels P.

A1 covers constraints such as “there can only be one subject” if U contains “subject” (see Section 4.4 for more details of U). **C1** applies to configurations which contain conjunctions such as “en”,“of” or “maar” (“and”, “or” and “but”). **C2** will rule-out settings where a conjunction such as “zowel” (translates as “both”) having arguments to its left. **C3** forces coordination arguments to the left of a conjunction to have commas in between. **C4** avoids parses in which incompatible word classes are coordinated, such as nouns and verbs. Finally, **P1** allows *selective projective* parsing: we can, for instance, forbid the crossing of “Noun-Determiner” dependencies if we add the corresponding label type to P(see Section 4.4 for more details of P) . If we extend P to contain all labels we forbid any type of crossing dependencies. This corresponds to projective parsing.

3.1 Decoding

McDonald et al. (2005b) use the Chu-Liu-Edmonds (CLE) algorithm to solve the maximum spanning tree problem. However, global constraints cannot be incorporated into the CLE algorithm (McDonald et al., 2005b). We alleviate this problem by presenting an equivalent Integer Linear Programming formulation which allows us to incorporate global constraints naturally.

Before giving full details of our formulation we first introduce some of the concepts of linear and integer linear programming (for a more thorough introduction see Winston and Venkataramanan (2003)).

Linear Programming (LP) is a tool for solving optimisation problems in which the aim is to maximise (or minimise) a given linear function with respect to a set of linear *constraints*. The function to be maximised (or minimised) is referred to as the *objective function*. A number of *decision variables* are under our control which exert influence on the objective function. Specifically, they have to be optimised in order to maximise (or minimise) the objective function. Finally, a set of constraints restrict the values that the decision variables can take. Integer Linear Programming is an extension of linear programming where all decision variables must take integer values.

There are several explicit formulations of the MST problem as an integer linear program in the literature (Williams, 2002). They are based on the concept of eliminating subtours (cycles), cuts (disconnections) or requiring intervertex flows (paths). However, in practice these formulations cause long solve times — as the first two meth-

Algorithm 1 Incremental Integer Linear Programming

$C \leftarrow B_{\mathbf{x}}$
repeat
  $\mathbf{y} \leftarrow solve(C, O_{\mathbf{x}}, V_{\mathbf{x}})$
  $W \leftarrow violated(\mathbf{y}, I_{\mathbf{x}})$
  $C \leftarrow C \cup W$
until $V = \emptyset$
return $\mathbf{y}$

ods yield an exponential number of constraints. Although the latter scales cubically, it produces non-fractional solutions in its relaxed version; this causes long runtimes for the branch and bound algorithm (Williams, 2002) commonly used in integer linear programming. We found out experimentally that dependency parsing models of this form do not converge on a solution after multiple hours of solving, even for small sentences.

As a workaround for this problem we follow an incremental approach akin to the work of Warme (1998). Instead of adding constraints which forbid all possible cycles in advance (this would result in an exponential number of constraints) we first solve the problem without any cycle constraints. The solution is then examined for cycles, and if cycles are found we add constraints to forbid these cycles; the solver is then run again. This process is repeated until no more violated constraints are found. The same procedure is used for other types of constraints which are too expensive to add in advance (e.g. the constraints of **P1**).

Algorithm 1 outlines our approach. For a sentence $\mathbf{x}$, $B_{\mathbf{x}}$ is the set of constraints that we add in advance and $I_{\mathbf{x}}$ are the constraints we add incrementally. $O_{\mathbf{x}}$ is the objective function and $V_{\mathbf{x}}$ is a set of variables including integer declarations. $solve(C, O, V)$ maximises the objective function O with respect to the set of constraints C and variables V. $violated(\mathbf{y}, I)$ inspects the proposed solution ($\mathbf{y}$) and returns all constraints in I which are violated.

The number of iterations required in this approach is at most polynomial with respect to the number of variables (Grötschel et al., 1981). In practice, this technique converges quickly (less than 20 iterations in 99% of approximately 12,000 sentences), yielding average solve times of less than 0.5 seconds.

Our approach converges quickly due to the quality of the scoring function. Its weights have been trained on cycle free data, thus it is more likely to guide the search to a cycle free solution.

In the following section we present the objective function $O_{\mathbf{x}}$, variables $V_{\mathbf{x}}$ and linear constraints $B_{\mathbf{x}}$ and $I_{\mathbf{x}}$ needed for parsing $\mathbf{x}$ using Algorithm 1.

3.1.1 Variables

$V_{\mathbf{x}}$ contains a set of binary variables to represent labelled edges:

$$e_{i,j,l} \quad \forall i \in 0..n, j \in 1..n, \\ l \in best_k(i,j)$$

where n is the number of tokens and the index 0 represents the root token. $best_k(i,j)$ is the set of k labels with highest $s(i,j,l)$. $e_{i,j,l}$ equals 1 if there is a edge (i.e., a dependency) with the label l between token i (head) and j (child), 0 otherwise. k depends on the type of constraints we want to add. For the plain MST problem it is sufficient to set $k = 1$ and only take the best scoring label for each token pair. However, if we want a constraint which forbids duplicate subjects we need to provide additional labels to fall back on.

$V_{\mathbf{x}}$ also contains a set of binary auxiliary variables:

$$d_{i,j} \quad \forall i \in 0..n, j \in 1..n$$

which represent the existence of a dependency between tokens i and j. We connect these to the $e_{i,j,l}$ variables by the constraint:

$$d_{i,j} = \sum_{l \in best_k(i,j)} e_{i,j,l}$$

3.1.2 Objective Function

Given the above variables our objective function $O_{\mathbf{x}}$ can be represented as (using a suitable k):

$$\sum_{i,j} \sum_{l \in best_k(i,j)} s(i,j,l) \cdot e_{i,j,l}$$

3.1.3 Base Constraints

We first introduce a set of base constraints $B_{\mathbf{x}}$ which we add in advance.

Only One Head (T1) Every token has exactly one head:

$$\sum_i d_{i,j} = 1$$

for non-root tokens $j > 0$ in $\mathbf{x}$. An exception is made for the artificial root node:

$$\sum_i d_{i,0} = 0$$

Label Uniqueness (A1) To enforce uniqueness of children with labels in U we augment our model with the constraint:

$$\sum_j e_{i,j,l} \leq 1$$

for every token i in $\mathbf{x}$ and label l in U.

Symmetric Coordination (C1) For each conjunction token i which forms a symmetric coordination we add:

$$\sum_{j<i} d_{i,j} \geq 1$$

and

$$\sum_{j>i} d_{i,j} = 1$$

Asymmetric Coordination (C2) For each conjunction token i which forms an asymmetric coordination we add:

$$\sum_{j<i} d_{i,j} = 0$$

and

$$\sum_{j>i} d_{i,j} \geq 2$$

3.1.4 Incremental Constraints

Now we present the set of constraints $I_{\mathbf{x}}$ we add incrementally. The constraints are chosen based on the two criteria: (1) adding them to the base constraints (those added in advance) would result in an extremely large program, and (2) it must be efficient to detect whether the constraint is violated in $\mathbf{y}$.

No Cycles (T2) For every possible cycle c for the sentence $\mathbf{x}$ we have a constraint which forbids the case where all edges in c are active simultaneously:

$$\sum_{(i,j)\in c} d_{i,j} \leq |c| - 1$$

Comma Coordination (C3) For each symmetric conjunction token i which forms a symmetric coordination and each set of tokens A in $\mathbf{x}$ to the left of i with no comma between each pair of successive tokens we add:

$$\sum_{a\in A} d_{i,a} \leq |A| - 1$$

which forbids configurations where i has the argument tokens A.

Compatible Coordination Arguments (C4) For each conjunction token i and each set of tokens A in $\mathbf{x}$ with incompatible POS tags, we add a constraint to forbid configurations where i has the argument tokens A.

$$\sum_{a\in A} d_{i,a} \leq |A| - 1$$

Selective Projective Parsing (P1) For each pair of triplets (i, j, l_1) and (m, n, l_2) we add the constraint:

$$e_{i,j,l_1} + e_{m,n,l_2} \leq 1$$

if l_1 or l_2 is in P.

3.2 Training

For training we use single-best MIRA (McDonald et al., 2005a). This is an online algorithm that learns by parsing each sentence and comparing the result with a gold standard. Training is complete after multiple passes through the whole corpus. Thus we decode using the Chu-Liu-Edmonds (CLE) algorithm due to its speed advantage over ILP (see Section 5.2 for a detailed comparison of runtimes).

The fact that we decode differently during training (using CLE) and testing (using ILP) may degrade performance. In the presence of additional constraints weights may be able to capture other aspects of the data.

4 Experimental Set-up

Our experiments were designed to answer the following questions:

1. How much do our additional constraints help improve accuracy?
2. How fast is our generic inference method in comparison with the Chu-Liu-Edmonds algorithm?
3. Can approximations be used to increase the speed of our method while remaining accurate?

Before we try to answer these questions we briefly describe our data, features used, settings for U and P in our parametric constraints, our working environment and our implementation.

4.1 Data

We use the Alpino treebank (van der Beek et al., 2002), taken from the CoNLL shared task of multilingual dependency parsing[3]. The CoNLL data differs slightly from the original Alpino treebank as the corpus has been part-of-speech tagged using a Memory-Based-Tagger (Daelemans et al., 1996). It consists of 13,300 sentences with an average length of 14.6 tokens. The data is non-projective, more specifically 5.4% of all dependencies are crossed by at least one other dependency. It contains approximately 6000 sentences more than the Alpino corpus used by Malouf and van Noord (2004).

The training set was divided into a 10% development set (*dev*) while the remaining 90% is used as a training and cross-validation set (*cross*). Feature sets, constraints and training parameters were selected through training on *cross* and optimising against *dev*.

Our final accuracy scores and runtime evaluations were acquired using a nine-fold cross-validation on *cross*

4.2 Environment and Implementation

All our experiments were conducted on a Intel Xeon with 3.8 Ghz and 4Gb of RAM. We used the open source Mixed Integer Programming library *lp_solve*[4] to solve the Integer Linear Programs. Our code ran in Java and called the JNI-wrapper around the *lp_solve* library.

4.3 Feature Sets

Our feature set was determined through experimentation with the development set. The features are based upon the data provided within the Alpino treebank. Along with POS tags the corpus contains several additional attributes such as gender, number and case.

Our best results on the development set were achieved using the feature set of McDonald et al. (2005a) and a set of features based on the additional attributes. These features combine the attributes of the head with those of the child. For example, if token i has the attributes a_1 and a_2, and token j has the attribute a_3 then we created the features $(a_1 \wedge a_3)$ and $(a_2 \wedge a_3)$.

[3] For details see `http://nextens.uvt.nl/~conll.`

[4] The software is available from `http://www.geocities.com/lpsolve.`

4.4 Constraints

All the constraints presented in Section 3 were used in our model. The set U of unique labels constraints contained *su, obj1, obj2, sup, ld, vc, predc, predm, pc, pobj1, obcomp* and *body*. Here *su* stands for subject and *obj1* for direct object (for full details see Moortgat et al. (2000)).

The set of projective labels P contained *cnj*, for coordination dependencies; and *det*, for determiner dependencies. One exception was added for the coordination constraint: dependencies can cross when coordinated arguments are verbs.

One drawback of hard deterministic constraints is the undesirable effect noisy data can cause. We see this most prominently with coordination argument compatibility. Words ending in "en" are typically wrongly tagged and cause our coordination argument constraint to discard correct coordinations. As a workaround we assigned words ending in "en" a wildcard POS tag which is compatible with all POS tags.

5 Results

In this section we report our results. We not only present our accuracy but also provide an empirical evaluation of the runtime behaviour of this approach and show how parsing can be accelerated using a simple approximation.

5.1 Accuracy

An important question to answer when using global constraints is: How much of a performance boost is gained when using global constraints?

We ran the system without any linguistic constraints as a baseline (*bl*) and compared it to a system with the additional constraints (*cnstr*). To evaluate our systems we use the accuracy over labelled attachment decisions:

$$LAC = \frac{N_l}{N_t}$$

where N_l is the number of tokens with correct head and label and N_t is the total number of tokens. For completeness we also report the unlabelled accuracy:

$$UAC = \frac{N_u}{N_t}$$

where N_u is the number of tokens with correct head.

	LAC	UAC	LC	UC
bl	84.6%	88.9%	27.7%	42.2%
cnstr	85.1%	89.4%	29.7%	43.8%

Table 1: Labelled (*LAC*) and unlabelled (*UAC*) accuracy using nine-fold cross-validation on *cross* for baseline (*bl*) and constraint-based (*constr*) system. *LC* and *UC* are the percentages of sentences with 100% labelled and unlabelled accuracy, respectively.

Table 1 shows our results using nine-fold cross-validation on the *cross* set. The baseline system (no additional constraints) gives an unlabelled accuracy of 84.6% and labelled accuracy of 88.9%. When we add our linguistic constraints the performance increases by 0.5% for both labelled and unlabelled accuracy. This increase is significant ($p < 0.001$) according to Dan Bikel's parse comparison script and using the Sign test ($p < 0.001$).

Now we give a little insight into how our results compare with the rest of the community. The reported state-of-the-art parser of Malouf and van Noord (2004) achieves 84.4% labelled accuracy which is very close numerically to our baseline. However, they use a subset of the CoNLL Alpino treebank with a higher average number of tokens per sentences and also evaluate control relations, thus results are not directly comparable. We have also run our parser on the relatively small (approximately 400 sentences) CoNNL test data. The best performing system (McDonald et al. 2006; note: this system is different to our baseline) achieves 79.2% labelled accuracy while our baseline system achieves 78.6% and our constrained version 79.8%. However, a significant difference is only observed between our baseline and our constraint-based system.

Examining the errors produced using the *dev* set highlight two key reasons why we do not see a greater improvement using our constraint-based system. Firstly, we cannot improve on coordinations that include words ending with "en" based on the workaround present in Section 4.4. This problem can only be solved by improving POS taggers for Dutch or by performing POS tagging within the dependency parsing framework.

Secondly, our system suffers from poor next best solutions. That is, if the best solution violates some constraints, then we find the next best solution is typically worse than the best solution with violated constraints. This appears to be a consequence of inaccurate local score distributions (as opposed to inaccurate best local scores). For example, suppose we attach two subjects, t_1 and t_2, to a verb, where t_1 is the actual subject while t_2 is meant to be labelled as object. If we forbid this configuration (two subjects) and if the score of labelling t_1 object is higher than that for t_2 being labelled subject, then the next best solution will label t_1 incorrectly as object and t_2 incorrectly as subject. This is often the case, and thus results in a drop of accuracy.

5.2 Runtime Evaluation

We now concentrate on the runtime of our method. While we expect a longer runtime than using the Chu-Liu-Edmonds as in previous work (McDonald et al., 2005b), we are interested in how large the increase is.

Table 2 shows the average solve time (*ST*) for sentences with respect to the number of tokens in each sentence for our system with constraints (*cnstr*) and the Chu-Liu-Edmonds (*CLE*) algorithm. All solve times do not include feature extraction as this is identical for all systems. For *cnstr* we also show the number of sentences that could not be parsed after two minutes, the average number of iterations and the average duration of the first iteration.

The results show that parsing using our generic approach is still reasonably fast although significantly slower than using the Chu-Liu-Edmonds algorithm. Also, only a small number of sentences take longer than two minutes to parse. Thus, in practice we would not see a significant degradation in performance if we were to fall back on the CLE algorithm after two minutes of solving.

When we examine the average duration of the first iteration it appears that the majority of the solve time is spent within this iteration. This could be used to justify using the CLE algorithm to find a initial solution as starting point for the ILP solver (see Section 6).

5.3 Approximation

Despite the fact that our parser can parse all sentences in a reasonable amount of time, it is still significantly slower than the CLE algorithm. While this is not crucial during decoding, it does make discriminative online training difficult as training requires several iterations of parsing the whole corpus.

Tokens	1-10	11-20	21-30	31-40	41-50	>50
Count	5242	4037	1835	650	191	60
Avg. ST (CLE)	0.27ms	0.98ms	3.2ms	7.5ms	14ms	23ms
Avg. ST (cnstr)	5.6ms	52ms	460ms	1.5s	7.2s	33s
ST > 120s (cnstr)	0	0	0	0	3	3
Avg. # iter. (cnstr)	2.08	2.87	4.48	5.82	8.40	15.17
Avg. ST 1st iter. (cnstr)	4.2ms	37ms	180ms	540ms	1.3s	2.6s

Table 2: Runtime evaluation for different sentence lengths. Average solve time (*ST*) for our system with constraints (*constr*), the Chu-Liu-Edmonds algorithm (*CLE*), number of sentences with solve times greater than 120 seconds, average number of iterations and first iteration solve time.

	q=5	q=10	all	CLE
LAC	84.90%	85.11%	85.14%	85.14%
ST	351s	760s	3640s	20s

Table 3: Labelled accuracy (*LAC*) and total solve time (*ST*) for the *cross* dataset using varying q values and the Chu-Liu-Edmonds algorithm (*CLE*)

Thus we investigate if it is possible to speed up our inference using a simple approximation. For each token we now only consider the q variables in $V_{\mathbf{x}}$ with the highest scoring edges. For example, if we set $q = 2$ the set of variables for a token j will contain two variables, either both for the same head i but with different labels (variables e_{i,j,l_1} and e_{i,j,l_2}) or two distinct heads i_1 and i_2 (variables e_{i_1,j,l_1} and e_{i_2,j,l_2}) where labels l_1 and l_2 may be identical.

Table 3 shows the effect of different q values on solve time for the full corpus *cross* (roughly 12,000 sentences) and overall accuracy. We see that solve time can be reduced by 80% while only losing a marginal amount of accuracy when we set q to 10. However, we are unable to reach the 20 seconds solve time of the CLE algorithm. Despite this, when we add the time for preprocessing and feature extraction, the CLE system parses a corpus in around 15 minutes whereas our system with $q = 10$ takes approximately 25 minutes[5]. When we view the total runtime of each system we see our system is more competitive.

6 Discussion

While we have presented significant improvements using additional constraints, one may wonder whether the improvements are large enough to justify further research in this direction; especially since McDonald and Pereira (2006) present an approximate algorithm which also makes more global decisions. However, we believe that our approach is complementary to their model. We can model higher order features by using an extended set of variables and a modified objective function. Although this is likely to increase runtime, it may still be fast enough for real world applications. In addition, it will allow exact inference, even in the case of non-projective parsing. Also, we argue that this approach has potential for interesting extensions and applications.

For example, during our runtime evaluations we find that a large fraction of solve time is spent in the first iteration of our incremental algorithm. After the first iteration the solver uses its last state to efficiently search for solutions in the presence of new constraints. Some solvers allow the specification of an initial solution as a starting point, thus it is expected that significant improvements in terms of speed can be made by using the CLE algorithm to provide an initial solution.

Our approach uses a generic algorithm to solve a complex task. Thus other applications may benefit from it. For instance, Germann et al. (2001) present an ILP formulation of the Machine Translation (MT) decoding task in order to conduct exact inference. However, their model suffers from the same type of exponential blow-up we observe when we add all our cycle constraints in advance. In fact, the constraints which cause the exponential explosion in their graphically formulation are of the same nature as our cycle constraints. We hope that the incremental approach will allow exact MT decoding for longer sentences.

[5]Even when caching feature extraction during training McDonald et al. (2005a) still takes approximately 10 minutes to train.

7 Conclusion

In this paper we have presented a novel approach for inference using ILP. While previous approaches which use ILP for decoding have solved each integer linear program in one run, we incrementally add constraints and solve the resulting program until no more constraints are violated. This allows us to efficiently use ILP for dependency parsing and add constraints which provide a significant improvement over the current state-of-the-art parser (McDonald et al., 2005b) on the Dutch Alpino corpus (see *bl* row in Table 1).

Although slower than the baseline approach, our method can still parse large sentences (more than 50 tokens) in a reasonable amount of time (less than a minute). We have shown that parsing time can be significantly reduced using a simple approximation which only marginally degrades performance. Furthermore, we believe that the method has potential for further extensions and applications.

Acknowledgements

Thanks to Ivan Meza-Ruiz, Ruken Çakıcı, Beata Kouchnir and Abhishek Arun for their contribution during the CoNLL shared task and to Mirella Lapata for helpful comments and suggestions.

References

Culotta, Aron and Jeffery Sorensen. 2004. Dependency tree kernels for relation extraction. In *42nd Annual Meeting of the Association for Computational Linguistics*. Barcelona, Spain, pages 423–429.

Daelemans, W., J. Zavrel, and S. Berck. 1996. MBT: A memory-based part of speech tagger-generator. In *Proceedings of the Fourth Workshop on Very Large Corpora*. pages 14–27.

Ding, Yuan and Martha Palmer. 2005. Machine translation using probabilistic synchronous dependency insertion grammars. In *The 43rd Annual Meeting of the Association of Computational Linguistics*. Ann Arbor, MI, USA, pages 541–548.

Germann, Ulrich, Michael Jahr, Kevin Knight, Daniel Marcu, and Kenji Yamada. 2001. Fast decoding and optimal decoding for machine translation. In *Meeting of the Association for Computational Linguistics*. Toulouse, France, pages 228–235.

Grötschel, M., L. Lovász, and A. Schrijver. 1981. The ellipsoid method and its consequences in combina- torial optimization. *Combinatorica* I:169– 197.

Malouf, Robert and Gertjan van Noord. 2004. Wide coverage parsing with stochastic attribute value grammars. In *Proc. of IJCNLP-04 Workshop "Beyond Shallow Analyses"*. Sanya City, Hainan Island, China.

McDonald, R., K. Crammer, and F. Pereira. 2005a. Online large-margin training of dependency parsers. In *43rd Annual Meeting of the Association for Computational Linguistics*. Ann Arbor, MI, USA, pages 91–98.

McDonald, R. and F. Pereira. 2006. Online learning of approximate dependency parsing algorithms. In *11th Conference of the European Chapter of the Association for Computational Linguistics*. Trento, Italy, pages 81–88.

McDonald, R., F. Pereira, K. Ribarov, and J. Hajic. 2005b. Non-projective dependency parsing using spanning tree algorithms. In *Proceedings of Human Language Technology Conference and Conference on Empirical Methods in Natural Language Processing*. Association for Computational Linguistics, Vancouver, British Columbia, Canada, pages 523–530.

McDonald, Ryan, Kevin Lerman, and Fernando Pereira. 2006. Multilingual dependency analysis with a two-stage discriminative parser. In *Proceedings of CoNLL-2006*. New York, USA.

Moortgat, M., I. Schuurman, and T. van der Wouden. 2000. Cgn syntactische annotatie. Internal report Corpus Gesproken Nederlands.

Nivre, J., J. Hall, and J. Nilsson. 2004. Memory-based dependency parsing. In *Proceedings of CoNLL-2004*. Boston, MA, USA, pages 49–56.

Roth, D. and W. Yih. 2004. A linear programming formulation for global inference in natural language tasks. In *Proceedings of CoNLL-2004,*. Boston, MA, USA, pages 1–8.

van der Beek, L., G. Bouma, R. Malouf, G. van Noord, Leonoor van der Beek, Gosse Bouma, Robert Malouf, and Gertjan van Noord. 2002. The Alpino dependency treebank. In *Computational Linguistics in the Netherlands (CLIN)*. Rodopi.

Warme, David Michael. 1998. *Spanning Trees in Hypergraphs with Application to Steiner Trees*. Ph.D. thesis, University of Virginia.

Williams, Justin C. 2002. A linear-size zero - one programming model for the minimum spanning tree problem in planar graphs. *Networks* 39:53–60.

Winston, Wayne L. and Munirpallam Venkataramanan. 2003. *Introduction to Mathematical Programming*. Brooks/Cole.

Yamada, Hiroyasu and Yuji Matsumoto. 2003. Statistical dependency analysis with support vector machines. In *Proceedings of IWPT*. pages 195–206.

Semantic Role Labeling of NomBank: A Maximum Entropy Approach

Zheng Ping Jiang and **Hwee Tou Ng**
Department of Computer Science
National University of Singapore
3 Science Drive 2, Singapore 117543
{jiangzp, nght}@comp.nus.edu.sg

Abstract

This paper describes our attempt at NomBank-based automatic Semantic Role Labeling (SRL). NomBank is a project at New York University to annotate the argument structures for common nouns in the Penn Treebank II corpus. We treat the NomBank SRL task as a classification problem and explore the possibility of adapting features previously shown useful in PropBank-based SRL systems. Various NomBank-specific features are explored. On test section 23, our best system achieves F1 score of 72.73 (69.14) when correct (automatic) syntactic parse trees are used. To our knowledge, this is the first reported automatic NomBank SRL system.

1 Introduction

Automatic Semantic Role Labeling (SRL) systems, made possible by the availability of PropBank (Kingsbury and Palmer, 2003; Palmer et al., 2005), and encouraged by evaluation efforts in (Carreras and Marquez, 2005; Litkowski, 2004), have been shown to accurately determine the argument structure of verb predicates.

A successful PropBank-based SRL system would correctly determine that "Ben Bernanke" is the subject (labeled as ARG0 in PropBank) of predicate "replace", and "Greenspan" is the object (labeled as ARG1):

- Ben Bernanke replaced Greenspan as Fed chair.
- Greenspan was replaced by Ben Bernanke as Fed chair.

The recent release of NomBank (Meyers et al., 2004c; Meyers et al., 2004b), a databank that annotates argument structure for instances of common nouns in the Penn Treebank II corpus, made it possible to develop automatic SRL systems that analyze the argument structures of noun predicates.

Given the following two noun phrases and one sentence, a successful NomBank-based SRL system should label "Ben Bernanke" as the subject (ARG0) and "Greenspan" as the object (ARG1) of the noun predicate "replacement".

- Greenspan's replacement Ben Bernanke
- Ben Bernanke's replacement of Greenspan
- Ben Bernanke was nominated as Greenspan's replacement.

The ability to automatically analyze the argument structures of verb and noun predicates would greatly facilitate NLP tasks like question answering, information extraction, etc.

This paper focuses on our efforts at building an accurate automatic NomBank-based SRL system. We study how techniques used in building PropBank SRL system can be transferred to developing NomBank SRL system. We also make NomBank-specific enhancements to our baseline system. Our implemented SRL system and experiments are based on the September 2005 release of NomBank (NomBank.0.8).

The rest of this paper is organized as follows: Section 2 gives an overview of NomBank, Section 3 introduces the Maximum Entropy classification model, Section 4 introduces our features and feature selection strategy, Section 5 explains the experimental setup and presents the experimental results, Section 6 compares NomBank SRL to

Proceedings of the 2006 Conference on Empirical Methods in Natural Language Processing (EMNLP 2006), pages 138–145, Sydney, July 2006.

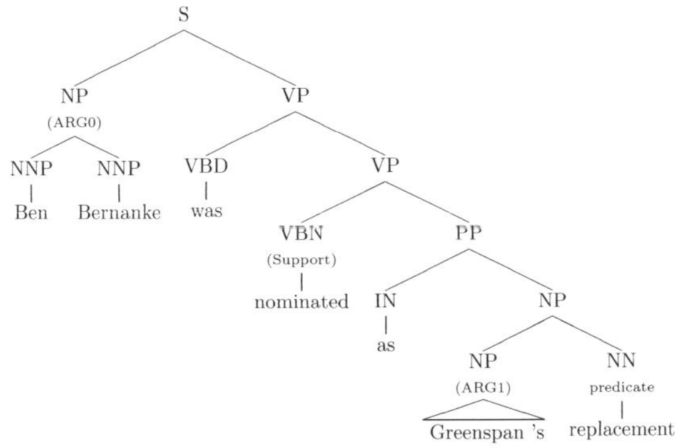

Figure 1: A sample sentence and its parse tree labeled in the style of NomBank

PropBank SRL and discusses possible future research directions.

2 Overview of NomBank

The NomBank (Meyers et al., 2004c; Meyers et al., 2004b) annotation project originated from the NOMLEX (Macleod et al., 1997; Macleod et al., 1998) nominalization lexicon developed under the New York University Proteus Project. NOMLEX lists 1,000 nominalizations and the correspondences between their arguments and the arguments of their verb counterparts. NomBank frames combine various lexical resources (Meyers et al., 2004a), including an extended NOMLEX and PropBank frames, and form the basis for annotating the argument structures of common nouns.

Similar to PropBank, NomBank annotation is made on the Penn TreeBank II (PTB II) corpus. For each common noun in PTB II that takes arguments, its core arguments are labeled with ARG0, ARG1, etc, and modifying arguments are labeled with ARGM-LOC to denote location, ARGM-MNR to denote manner, etc. Annotations are made on PTB II parse tree nodes, and argument boundaries align with the span of parse tree nodes.

A sample sentence and its parse tree labeled in the style of NomBank is shown in Figure 1. For the nominal predicate "replacement", "Ben Bernanke" is labeled as ARG0 and "Greenspan 's" is labeled as ARG1. There is also the special label "Support" on "nominated" which introduces "Ben Bernanke" as an argument of "replacement". The support construct will be explained in detail in Section 4.2.3.

We are not aware of any NomBank-based automatic SRL systems. The work in (Pradhan et al., 2004) experimented with an automatic SRL system developed using a relatively small set of manually selected nominalizations from FrameNet and Penn Chinese TreeBank. The SRL accuracy of their system is not directly comparable to ours.

3 Model training and testing

We treat the NomBank-based SRL task as a classification problem and divide it into two phases: argument identification and argument classification. During the argument identification phase, each parse tree node is marked as either argument or non-argument. Each node marked as argument is then labeled with a specific class during the argument classification phase. The identification model is a binary classifier , while the classification model is a multi-class classifier.

Opennlp maxent[1], an implementation of Maximum Entropy (ME) modeling, is used as the classification tool. Since its introduction to the Natural Language Processing (NLP) community (Berger et al., 1996), ME-based classifiers have been shown to be effective in various NLP tasks. ME modeling is based on the insight that the best model is consistent with the set of constraints imposed and otherwise as uniform as possible. ME models the probability of label l given input x as in Equation 1. $f_i(l, x)$ is a feature function that maps label l and input x to either 0 or 1, while the summation is over all n feature functions and with λ_i as the weight parameter for each feature function $f_i(l, x)$. Z_x is a normalization factor. In the identification model, label l corresponds to either "argument" or "non-argument", and in the classification model, label l corresponds to one of the specific NomBank argument classes. The classification output is the label l with the highest conditional probability $p(l|x)$.

$$p(l|x) = \frac{exp(\sum_{i=1}^{n} \lambda_i f_i(l, x))}{Z_x} \quad (1)$$

To train the ME-based identification model, training data is gathered by treating each parse tree node that is an argument as a positive example and the rest as negative examples. Classification training data is generated from argument nodes only.

During testing, the algorithm of enforcing non-overlapping arguments by (Toutanova et al., 2005) is used. The algorithm maximizes the log-probability of the entire NomBank labeled parse

[1]http://maxent.sourceforge.net/

tree. Specifically, assuming we only have two classes "ARG" and "NONE", the log-probability of a NomBank labeled parse tree is defined by Equation 2.

$$Max(T) = max \begin{cases} NONE(T) + \sum(Max(child)) \\ ARG(T) + \sum(NONETree(child)) \end{cases} \quad (2)$$

$Max(T)$ is the maximum log-probability of a tree T, $NONE(T)$ and $ARG(T)$ are respectively the log-probability of assigning label "NONE" and "ARG" by our argument identification model to tree node T, $child$ ranges through each of T's children, and $NONETree(child)$ is the log-probability of each node that is dominated by node $child$ being labeled as "NONE". Details are presented in Algorithm 1.

Algorithm 1 Maximizing the probability of an SRL tree

```
Input p{syntactic parse tree}
Input m{argument identification model, assigns each constituent in the parse tree log likelihood of being a semantic argument}
Output score{maximum log likelihood of the parse tree p with arguments identified using model m}

MLParse(p, m)
if parse p is a leaf node then
   return max(Score(p, m, ARG), Score(p, m, NONE))
else
   MLscore = 0
   for each node c_i in Children(p) do
      MLscore += MLParse(c_i, m)
   end for
   NONEscore = 0
   for each node c_i in Children(p) do
      NONEscore += NONETree(c_i, m)
   end for
   return max(Score(p, m, NONE)+MLscore,
   Score(p, m, ARG)+NONEscore)
end if

NONETree(p,m)
NONEscore = Score(p, m, NONE)
if parse p is a leaf node then
   return NONEscore
else
   for each node c_i in Children(p) do
      NONEscore += NONETree(c_i, m)
   end for
   return NONEscore
end if

Subroutine:
Children(p) returns the list of children nodes of p.
Score(p, m, state) returns the log likelihood assigned by model m, for parse p with state. state is either ARG or NONE.
```

NomBank sections 02-21 are used as training data, section 24 and 23 are used as development and test data, respectively.

3.1 Training data preprocessing

Unlike PropBank annotation which does not contain overlapping arguments (in the form of parse tree nodes domination) and does not allow predicates to be dominated by arguments, NomBank annotation in the September 2005 release contains such cases. In NomBank sections 02-21, about 0.6% of the argument nodes dominate some other argument nodes or the predicate. To simplify our task, during training example generation, we ignore arguments that dominate the predicate. We also ignore arguments that are dominated by other arguments, so that when argument domination occurs, only the argument with the largest word span is kept. We do *not* perform similar pruning on the test data.

4 Features and feature selection

4.1 Baseline NomBank SRL features

Table 1 lists the baseline features we adapted from previous PropBank-based SRL systems (Pradhan et al., 2005; Xue and Palmer, 2004). For ease of description, related features are grouped, with a specific individual feature given individual reference name. For example, feature b11FW in the group b11 denotes the first word spanned by the constituent and b13LH denotes the left sister's head word. We also experimented with various feature combinations, inspired by the features used in (Xue and Palmer, 2004). These are listed as features b31 to b34 in Table 1.

Suppose the current constituent under identification or classification is "NP-Ben Bernanke" in Figure 1. The instantiations of the baseline features in Table 1 for this example are presented in Table 2. The symbol "NULL" is used to denote features that fail to instantiate.

4.2 NomBank-specific features

4.2.1 NomBank predicate morphology and class

The "NomBank-morph" dictionary provided by the current NomBank release maps the base form of a noun to various morphological forms. Besides singular-plural noun form mapping, it also maps base nouns to hyphenated and compound nouns. For example, "healthcare" and "medical-care" both map to "care". For NomBank SRL fea-

Baseline Features (Pradhan et al., 2005)	
b1	predicate: stemmed noun
b2	subcat: grammar rule that expands the predicate's parent
b3	phrase type: syntactic category of the constituent
b4	head word: syntactic head of the constituent
b5	path: syntactic path from the constituent to the predicate
b6	position: to the left or right of the predicate
b11	first or last word/POS spanned by the constituent (b11FW, b11LW, b11FP, b11LP)
b12	phrase type of the left or right sister (b12L, b12R)
b13	left or right sister's head word/POS (b13LH, b13LP, b13RH, b13RP)
b14	phrase type of parent
b15	parent's head word or its POS (b15H, b15P)
b16	head word of the constituent if its parent has phrase type PP
b17	head word or POS tag of the rightmost NP node, if the constituent is PP (b17H, b17P)
b18	phrase type appended with the length of path
b19	temporal keyword, e.g., "Monday"
b20	partial path from the constituent to the lowest common ancestor with the predicate
b21	projected path from the constituent to the highest NP dominating the predicate
Baseline Combined Features (Xue and Palmer, 2004)	
b31	b1 & b3
b32	b1 & b4
b33	b1 & b5
b34	b1 & b6

Table 1: Baseline features for NomBank SRL

tures, we use this set of more specific mappings to replace the morphological mappings based on WordNet. Specifically, we replace feature b1 in Table 1 with feature a1 in Table 3.

The current NomBank release also contains the "NOMLEX-PLUS" dictionary, which contains the class of nominal predicates according to their origin and the roles they play. For example, "employment" originates from the verb "employ" and is classified as "VERB-NOM", while the nouns "employer" and "employee" are classified as "SUBJECT" and "OBJECT" respectively. Other classes include "ADJ-NOM" for nominalization of adjectives and "NOM-REL" for relational nouns. The class of a nominal predicate is very indicative of the role of its arguments. We would expect a "VERB-NOM" predicate to take both ARG0 and ARG1, while an "OBJECT" predicate to take only ARG0. We incorporated the class of nominal predicates as additional features in our NomBank SRL system. We add feature a2 in Table 3 to use this information.

Baseline Features (Pradhan et al., 2005)	
b1	replacement
b2	NP → NP NN
b3	NP
b4	Bernanke
b5	NP↑S↓VP↓VP↓PP↓NP↓NN
b6	left
b11	Ben, Bernanke, NNP, NNP
b12	NULL, VP
b13	NULL, NULL, was, VBD
b14	S
b15	was, VBD
b16	NULL
b17	NULL, NULL
b18	NP-7
b19	NULL
b20	NP↑S
b21	NP↑S↓VP↓VP↓PP↓NP
Baseline Combined Features (Xue and Palmer, 2004)	
b31	replacement & NP
b32	replacement & Bernanke
b33	replacement & NP↑S↓VP↓VP↓PP↓NP↓NN
b34	replacement & left

Table 2: Baseline feature instantiations, assuming the current constituent is "NP-Ben Bernanke" in Figure 1.

Additional Features Based on NomBank	
a1	Nombank morphed noun stem
a2	Nombank nominal class
a3	identical to predicate?
a4	a DEFREL noun?
a5	whether under the noun phrase headed by the predicate
a6	whether the noun phrase headed by the predicate is dominated by a VP node or has neighboring VP nodes
a7	whether there is a verb between the constituent and the predicate
Additional Combined Features	
a11	a1 & a2
a12	a1 & a3
a13	a1 & a5
a14	a3 & a4
a15	a1 & a6
a16	a1 & a7
Additional Features of Neighboring Arguments	
n1	for each argument already classified, b3-b4-b5-b6-r, where r is the argument class, otherwise b3-b4-b5-b6
n2	backoff version of n1, b3-b6-r or b3-b6

Table 3: Additional NomBank-specific features for NomBank SRL

4.2.2 DEFREL relational noun predicate

About 14% of the argument node instances in NomBank sections 02-21 are identical to their nominal predicate nodes. Most of these nominal predicates are DEFREL relational nouns (Meyers et al., 2004c). Examples of DEFREL relational nouns include "employee", "participant", and "husband", where the nominal predicate itself takes part as an implied argument.

We include in our classification features an indicator of whether the argument coincides with the nominal predicate. We also include a feature testing if the argument is one of the DEFREL nouns we extracted from NomBank training sections 02-21. These two features correspond to a3 and a4 in Table 3.

4.2.3 Support verb

Statistics show that almost 60% of the arguments of nominal predicates occur locally inside the noun phrase headed by the nominal predicate. For the cases where an argument appears outside the local noun phrase, over half of these arguments are introduced by support verbs. Consider our example "Ben Bernanke was nominated as Greenspan's replacement.", the argument "Ben Bernanke" is introduced by the support verb "nominate". The arguments introduced by support verbs can appear syntactically distant from the nominal predicate.

To capture the location of arguments and the existence of support verbs, we add features indicating whether the argument is under the noun phrase headed by the predicate, whether the noun phrase headed by the predicate is dominated by a VP phrase or has neighboring VP phrases, and whether there is a verb between the argument and the predicate. These are represented as features a5, a6, and a7 in Table 3. Feature a7 was also proposed by the system in (Pradhan et al., 2004).

We also experimented with various feature combinations, inspired by the features used in (Xue and Palmer, 2004). These are listed as features a11 to a16 in Table 3.

4.2.4 Neighboring arguments

The research of (Jiang et al., 2005; Toutanova et al., 2005) has shown the importance of capturing information of the global argument frame in order to correctly classify the local argument.

We make use of the features {b3,b4,b5,b6} of the neighboring arguments as defined in Table 1. Arguments are classified from left to right in the textual order they appear. For arguments that are already labeled, we also add their argument class r. Specifically, for each argument to the left of the current argument, we have a feature b3-b4-b5-b6-r. For each argument to the right of the current argument, the feature is defined as b3-b4-b5-b6. We extract features in a window of size 7, centered at the current argument. We also add a backoff version (b3-b6-r or b3-b6) of this specific feature. These additional features are shown as n1 and n2 in Table 3.

Suppose the current constituent under identification or classification is "NP-Ben Bernanke". The instantiations of the additional features in Table 3 are listed in Table 4.

Additional Features based on NomBank	
a1	replacement
a2	VERB-NOM
a3	no
a4	no
a5	no
a6	yes
a7	yes
Additional Combined Features	
a11	replacement & VERB-NOM
a12	replacement & no
a13	replacement & no
a14	no & no
a15	replacement & yes
a16	replacement & yes
Additional Features of Neighboring Arguments	
n1	NP-Greenspan-NP↑NP↓NN-left
n2	NP-left

Table 4: Additional feature instantiations, assuming the current constituent is "NP-Ben Bernanke" in Figure 1.

4.3 Feature selection

Features used by our SRL system are automatically extracted from PTB II parse trees manually labeled in NomBank. Features from Table 1 and Table 3 are selected empirically and incrementally according to their contribution to test accuracy on the development section 24. The feature selection process stops when adding any of the remaining features fails to improve the SRL accuracy on development section 24. We start the selection process with the basic set of features {b1,b2,b3,b4,b5,b6}. The detailed feature selection algorithm is presented in Algorithm 2.

Features for argument identification and argument classification are independently selected. To select the features for argument classification, we assume that all arguments have been correctly identified.

After performing greedy feature selection, the baseline set of features selected for identification is {b1-b6, b11FW, b11LW, b12L, b13RH, b13RP, b14, b15H, b18, b20, b32-b34}, and the baseline

Algorithm 2 Greedy feature selection

Input $F_{candidate}$ {set of all candidate features}
Output F_{select} {set of selected features}
Output M_{select} {selected model}

Initialize:
$F_{select} = \{b1, b2, b3, b4, b5, b6\}$
$F_{candidate} = AllFeatures - F_{select}$

$M_{select} = Train(F_{select})$
$E_{select} = Evaluate(M_{select}, DevData)$
loop
  for each feature f_i in $F_{candidate}$ **do**
    $F_i = F_{select} \bigcup f_i$
    $M_i = Train(F_i)$
    $E_i = Evaluate(M_i, DevData)$
  end for
  $E_{max} = Max(E_i)$
  if $E_{max} > E_{select}$ **then**
    $F_{select} = F_{select} \bigcup f_{max}$
    $M_{select} = M_{max}$
    $E_{select} = E_{max}$
    $F_{candidate} = F_{candidate} - f_{max}$
  end if
  if $F_{candidate} == \phi$ or $E_{max} \leq E_{select}$ **then**
    return F_{select}, M_{select}
  end if
end loop

Subroutine:
$Evaluate(Model, Data)$ returns the accuracy score by evaluating Model on Data.
$Train(FeatureSet)$ returns maxent model trained on the given feature set.

set of features selected for classification is {b1-b6, b11, b12, b13LH, b13LP, b13RP, b14, b15, b16, b17P, b20, b31-b34}. Note that features in {b19, b21} are not selected. For the additional features in Table 3, greedy feature selection chose {a1, a5, a6, a11, a12, a14} for the identification model and {a1, a3, a6, a11, a14, a16, n1, n2} for the classification model.

5 Experimental results

5.1 Scores on development section 24

After applying the feature selection algorithm in Section 4.3, the SRL F1 scores on development section 24 are presented in Table 5. We separately present the F1 score for identification-only and classification-only model. We also apply the classification model on the output of the identification phase (which may contain erroneously identified arguments in general) to obtain the combined accuracy. During the identification-only and combined identification and classification testing, the tree log-probability maximization algorithm based on Equation 2 (and its extension to multi-classes) is used. During the classification-only testing, we classify each correctly identified argument using the classification ME model. The "baseline" row lists the F1 scores when only the baseline features are used, and the "additional" row lists the F1 scores when additional features are added to the baseline features.

	identification	classification	combined
baseline	80.32	84.86	69.70
additional	80.55	87.31	70.12

Table 5: NomBank SRL F1 scores on development section 24, based on correct parse trees

	identification	classification	combined
baseline	82.33	85.85	72.20
additional	82.50	87.80	72.73

Table 6: NomBank SRL F1 scores on test section 23, based on correct parse trees

5.2 Testing on section 23

The identification and classification models based on the chosen features in Section 4.3 are then applied to test section 23. The resulting F1 scores are listed in Table 6. Using additional features, the identification-only, classification-only, and combined F1 scores are 82.50, 87.80, and 72.73, respectively.

Performing chi-square test at the level of significance 0.05, we found that the improvement of the classification model using additional features compared to using just the baseline features is statistically significant, while the corresponding improvements due to additional features for the identification model and the combined model are not statistically significant.

The improved classification accuracy due to the use of additional features does not contribute any significant improvement to the combined identification and classification SRL accuracy. This is due to the noisy arguments identified by the inadequate identification model, since the accurate determination of the additional features (such as those of neighboring arguments) depends critically on an accurate identification model.

5.3 Using automatic syntactic parse trees

So far we have assumed the availability of correct syntactic parse trees during model training and testing. We relax this assumption by using the re-ranking parser presented in (Charniak and

Johnson, 2005) to automatically generate the syntactic parse trees for both training and test data.

The F1 scores of our best NomBank SRL system, when applied to automatic syntactic parse trees, are 66.77 for development section 24 and 69.14 for test section 23. These F1 scores are for combined identification and classification, with the use of additional features. Comparing these scores with those in Table 5 and Table 6, the usage of automatic parse trees lowers the F1 accuracy by more than 3%. The decrease in accuracy is expected, due to the noise introduced by automatic syntactic parsing.

6 Discussion and future work

6.1 Comparison of the composition of PropBank and NomBank

Counting the number of annotated predicates, the size of the September 2005 release of NomBank (NomBank.0.8) is about 83% of PropBank release 1. Preliminary consistency tests reported in (Meyers et al., 2004c) shows that NomBank's inter-annotator agreement rate is about 85% for core arguments and lower for adjunct arguments. The inter-annotator agreement for PropBank reported in (Palmer et al., 2005) is above 0.9 in terms of the Kappa statistic (Sidney and Castellan Jr., 1988). While the two agreement measures are not directly comparable, the current NomBank.0.8 release documentation indicates that only 32 of the most frequently occurring nouns in PTB II have been adjudicated.

We believe the smaller size of NomBank.0.8 and the potential noise contained in the current release of the NomBank data may partly explain our lower SRL accuracy on NomBank, especially in the argument identification phase, as compared to the published accuracies of PropBank-based SRL systems.

6.2 Difficulties in NomBank SRL

The argument structure of nominalization phrases is less fixed (i.e., more flexible) than the argument structure of verbs. Consider again the example given in the introduction, we find the following flexibility in forming grammatical NomBank argument structures for "replacement":

- The positions of the arguments are flexible, so that "Greenspan's replacement Ben Bernanke", "Ben Bernanke's replacement of Greenspan" are both grammatical.
- Arguments can be optional, so that "Greenspan's replacement will assume the post soon", "The replacement Ben Bernanke will assume the post soon", and "The replacement will assume the post soon" are all grammatical.

With the verb predicate "replace", except for "Greenspan was replaced", there is no freedom of forming phrases like "Ben Bernanke replaces" or simply "replaces" without supplying the necessary arguments to complete the grammatical structure.

We believe the flexible argument structure of NomBank noun predicates contributes to the lower automatic SRL accuracy as compared to that of the PropBank SRL task.

6.3 Integrating PropBank and NomBank SRL

Work in (Pustejovsky et al., 2005) discussed the possibility of merging various Treebank annotation efforts including PropBank, NomBank, and others. Future work involves studying ways of concurrently producing automatic PropBank and NomBank SRL, and improving the accuracy by exploiting the inter-relationship between verb predicate-argument and noun predicate-argument structures.

Besides the obvious correspondence between a verb and its nominalizations, e.g., "replace" and "replacement", there is also correspondence between verb predicates in PropBank and support verbs in NomBank. Statistics from NomBank sections 02-21 show that 86% of the support verbs in NomBank are also predicate verbs in PropBank. When they coincide, they share 18,250 arguments of which 63% have the same argument class in PropBank and NomBank.

Possible integration approaches include:

- Using PropBank data as augmentation to NomBank training data.
- Using re-ranking techniques (Collins, 2000) to jointly improve PropBank and NomBank SRL accuracy.

7 Conclusion

We have successfully developed a statistical NomBank-based SRL system. Features that were previously shown to be effective in PropBank SRL are carefully selected and adapted for NomBank SRL. We also proposed new features to address the special predicate-argument structure in NomBank data. To our knowledge, we presented the first result in statistical NomBank SRL.

References

Adam Berger, Stephen Della Pietra, and Vincent Della Pietra. 1996. A Maximum Entropy Approach to Natural Language Processing. *Computational Linguistics*.

Xavier Carreras and Lluis Marquez. 2005. Introduction to the CoNLL-2005 Shared Task: Semantic Role Labeling. In *Proceedings of CoNLL-2005*.

Eugene Charniak and Mark Johnson. 2005. Coarse-to-fine n-Best Parsing and MaxEnt Discriminative Reranking. In *Proceedings of ACL-2005*.

Michael Collins. 2000. Discriminative Reranking for Natural Language Parsing. In *Proceedings of ICML 2000*.

Zheng Ping Jiang, Jia Li, and Hwee Tou Ng. 2005. Semantic Argument Classification Exploiting Argument Interdependence. In *Proceedings of IJCAI 2005*.

Paul Kingsbury and Martha Palmer. 2003. PropBank: the Next Level of TreeBank. In *Proceedings of Treebanks and Lexical Theories*.

Kenneth C. Litkowski. 2004. SENSEVAL-3 Task: Automatic Labeling of Semantic Roles. In *Proceedings of Senseval-3: The Third International Workshop on the Evaluation of Systems for the Semantic Analysis of Text*.

Catherine Macleod, Adam Meyers, Ralph Grishman, Leslie Barrett, and Ruth Reeves. 1997. Designing a Dictionary of Derived Nominals. In *Proceedings of Recent Advances in Natural Language Processing*.

Catherine Macleod, Ralph Grishman, Adam Meyers, Leslie Barrett, and Ruth Reeves. 1998. NOMLEX: A Lexicon of Nominalizations. In *Proceedings of EURALEX'98*.

Adam Meyers, Ruth Reeves, Catherine Macleod, Rachel Szekely, Veronika Zielinska, and Brian Young. 2004a. The Cross-Breeding of Dictionaries. In *Proceedings of LREC-2004*.

Adam Meyers, Ruth Reeves, Catherine Macleod, Rachel Szekely, Veronika Zielinska, Brian Young, and Ralph Grishman. 2004b. Annotating Noun Argument Structure for NomBank. In *Proceedings of LREC-2004*.

Adam Meyers, Ruth Reeves, Catherine Macleod, Rachel Szekely, Veronika Zielinska, Brian Young, and Ralph Grishman. 2004c. The NomBank Project: An Interim Report. In *Proceedings of HLT-NAACL 2004 Workshop on Frontiers in Corpus Annotation*.

Martha Palmer, Daniel Gildea, and Paul Kingsbury. 2005. The Proposition Bank: An Annotated Corpus of Semantic Roles. *Computational Linguistics*.

Sameer S. Pradhan, Honglin Sun, Wayne Ward, James H. Martin, and Dan Jurafsky. 2004. Parsing Arguments of Nominalizations in English and Chinese. In *Proceedings of HLT/NAACL 2004*.

Sameer Pradhan, Kadri Hacioglu, Valerie Krugler, Wayne Ward, James H. Martin, and Daniel Jurafsky. 2005. Support Vector Learning for Semantic Argument Classification. *Machine Learning*.

James Pustejovsky, Adam Meyers, Martha Palmer, and Massimo Poesio. 2005. Merging PropBank, NomBank, TimeBank, Penn Discourse Treebank and Coreference. In *ACL 2005 Workshop on Frontiers in Corpus Annotations II: Pie in the Sky*.

Siegel Sidney and N. John Castellan Jr. 1988. *Nonparametric Statistics for the Behavioral Sciences*. McGraw-Hill, New York.

Kristina Toutanova, Aria Haghighi, and Christopher D. Manning. 2005. Joint Learning Improves Semantic Role Labeling. In *Proceedings of ACL 2005*.

Nianwen Xue and Martha Palmer. 2004. Calibrating Features for Semantic Role Labeling. In *Proceedings of EMNLP-2004*.

Identification of Event Mentions and their Semantic Class

Steven Bethard
Department of Computer Science
University of Colorado at Boulder
430 UCB, Boulder, CO 80309, USA
steven.bethard@colorado.edu

James H. Martin
Department of Computer Science
University of Colorado at Boulder
430 UCB, Boulder, CO 80309, USA
james.martin@colorado.edu

Abstract

Complex tasks like question answering need to be able to identify events in text and the relations among those events. We show that this event identification task and a related task, identifying the semantic class of these events, can both be formulated as classification problems in a word-chunking paradigm. We introduce a variety of linguistically motivated features for this task and then train a system that is able to identify events with a precision of 82% and a recall of 71%. We then show a variety of analyses of this model, and their implications for the event identification task.

1 Introduction

Research in question answering, machine translation and other fields has shown that being able to recognize the important entities in a text is often a critical component of these systems. Such entity information gives the machine access to a deeper level of semantics than words alone can provide, and thus offers advantages for these complex tasks. Of course, texts are composed of much more than just sets of entities, and architectures that rely solely on word and entity-based techniques are likely to have difficulty with tasks that depend more heavily on event and temporal relations. Consider a question answering system that receives the following questions:

- Is Anwar al-Sadat still the president of Egypt?
- How did the linking of the Argentinean peso to the US dollar in 1991 contribute to economic crisis of Argentina in 2003?

Processing such questions requires not only knowing what the important people, places and other entities are, but also what kind of events they are involved in, the roles they play in those events, and the relations among those events. Thus, we suggest that identifying such events in a text should play an important role in systems that attempt to address questions like these.

Of course, to identify events in texts, we must define what exactly it is we mean by "event". In this work, we adopt a traditional linguistic definition of an event that divides words into two aspectual types: states and events. States describe situations that are static or unchanging for their duration, while events describe situations that involve some internal structure. For example, predicates like *know* and *love* would be states because if we *know* (or *love*) someone for a period of time, we *know* (or *love*) that person at each point during the period. Predicates like *run* or *deliver a sermon* would be events because they are built of smaller dissimilar components: *run* includes raising and lowering of legs and *deliver a sermon* includes the various tongue movements required to produce words.

To better explain how we approach the task of identifying such events, we first discuss some past work on related tasks. Then we briefly discuss the characteristics of the TimeBank, a corpus containing event-annotated data. Next we present our formulation of event identification as a classification task and introduce the linguistic features that serve as input to the algorithm. Finally, we show the results of STEP (our "System for Textual Event Parsing") which applies these techniques to the TimeBank data.

2 Related Efforts

Such aspectual distinctions have been alive and well in the linguistic literature since at least the late 60s (Vendler, 1967). However, the use of the

Proceedings of the 2006 Conference on Empirical Methods in Natural Language Processing (EMNLP 2006), pages 146–154,
Sydney, July 2006.

term *event* in natural language processing work has often diverged quite considerably from this linguistic notion. In the Topic Detection and Tracking (TDT) task, events were sets of documents that described "some unique thing that happens at some point in time" (Allan et. al., 1998). In the Message Understanding Conference (MUC), events were groups of phrases that formed a template relating participants, times and places to each other (Marsh and Perzanowski, 1997). In the work of Filatova and Hatzivassiloglou (2003), events consisted of a verb and two named-entities occurring together frequently across several documents on a topic.

Several recent efforts have stayed close to the linguistic definition of events. One such example is the work of Siegel and McKeown (2000) which showed that machine learning models could be trained to identify some of the traditional linguistic aspectual distinctions. They manually annotated the verbs in a small set of texts as either state or event, and then used a variety of linguistically motivated features to train machine learning models that were able to make the event/state distinction with 93.9% accuracy.

Another closely related effort was the Evita system, developed by Saurí et. al. (2005). This work considered a corpus of events called TimeBank, whose annotation scheme was motivated largely by the linguistic definitions of events. Saurí et. al. showed that a linguistically motivated and mainly rule-based algorithm could perform well on this task.

Our work draws from both the Siegel and McKeown and Saurí et. al. works. We consider the same TimeBank corpus as Saurí et. al., but apply a statistical machine learning approach akin to that of Siegel and McKeown. We demonstrate that combining machine learning techniques with linguistically motivated features can produce models from the TimeBank data that are capable of making a variety of subtle aspectual distinctions.

3 Events in the TimeBank

TimeBank (Pustejovsky, et. al. 2003b) consists of just under 200 documents containing 70,000 words; it is drawn from news texts from a variety of different domains, including newswire and transcribed broadcast news. These documents are annotated using the TimeML annotation scheme (Pustejovsky, et. al. 2003a), which aims to identify not just times and dates, but events and the temporal relations between these events.

Of interest here are the EVENT annotations, of which TimeBank 1.1 has annotated 8312. TimeBank annotates a word or phrase as an EVENT if it describes a situation that can "happen" or "occur", or if it describes a "state" or "circumstance" that "participate[s] in an opposition structure in a given text" (Pustejovsky, et. al. 2003b). Note that the TimeBank events are not restricted to verbs; nouns and adjectives denote events as well.

The TimeBank definition of event differs in a few ways from the traditional linguistic definition of event. TimeBank EVENTs include not only the normal linguistic events, but also some linguistic states, depending on the contexts in which they occur. For example[1], in the sentence *None of the people on board the airbus survived the crash* the phrase *on board* would be considered to describe an EVENT because that state changes in the time span covered by the text. Not all linguistic states become TimeBank EVENTs in this manner, however. For example, the state described by *New York is on the east coast* holds true for a time span much longer than the typical newswire document and would therefore not be labeled as an EVENT.

In addition to identifying which words in the TimeBank are EVENTs, the TimeBank also provides a semantic class label for each EVENT. The possible labels include OCCURRENCE, PERCEPTION, REPORTING, ASPECTUAL, STATE, I_STATE, I_ACTION, and MODAL, and are described in more detail in (Pustejovsky, et. al. 2003a).

We consider two tasks on this data:

(1) Identifying which words and phrases are EVENTs, and

(2) Identifying their semantic classes.

The next section describes how we turn these tasks into machine learning problems.

4 Event Identification as Classification

We view event identification as a classification task using a word-chunking paradigm similar to that used by Carreras et. al. (2002). For each word in a document, we assign a label indicating whether the word is inside or outside of an event. We use the standard B-I-O formulation of the word-chunking task that augments each class label with an indicator of whether the given word

[1] These examples are derived from (Pustejovsky, et. al. 2003b)

Word	*Event Label*	*Event Semantic Class Label*
The	O	O
company	O	O
's	O	O
sales	O	O
force	O	O
applauded	B	B_I_ACTION
the	O	O
shake	B	B_OCCURRENCE
up	I	I_OCCURRENCE
.	O	O

Table 1: Event chunks for sentence (1)

is (B)eginning, (I)nside or (O)utside of a chunk (Ramshaw & Marcus, 1995). So, for example, under this scheme, sentence (1) would have its words labeled as in Table 1.

(1) The company's sales force [EVENT(I_ACTION) applauded] the [EVENT(OCCURRENCE) shake up]

The two columns of labels in Table 1 show how the class labels differ depending on our task. If we're interested only in the simple event identification task, it's sufficient to know that *applauded* and *shake* both begin events (and so have the label B), *up* is inside an event (and so has the label I), and all other words are outside events (and so have the label O). These labels are shown in the column labeled Event Label. If in addition to identifying events, we also want to identify their semantic classes, then we need to know that *applauded* begins an intentional action event (B_I_ACTION), *shake* begins an occurrence event (B_OCCURRENCE), *up* is inside an occurrence event (I_OCCURRENCE), and all other words are outside of events (O). These labels are shown in the column labeled Event Semantic Class Label. Note that while the eight semantic class labels in the TimeBank could potentially introduce as many as 8 • 2 + 1 = 17 chunk labels, not all types of events appear as multi-word phrases, so we see only 13 of these labels in our data.

5 Classifier Features

Having cast the problem as a chunking task, our next step is to select and represent a useful set of features. In our case, since each classification instance is a word, our features need to provide the information that we deem important for recognizing whether a word is part of an event or not. We consider a number of such features, grouped into feature classes for the purposes of discussion.

5.1 Text feature

This feature is just the textual string for the word.

5.2 Affix features

These features attempt to isolate the potentially important subsequences of characters in the word. These are intended to identify affixes that have a preference for different types of events.

Affixes: These features identify the first three and four characters of the word, and the last three and four characters of the word.

Nominalization suffix: This feature indicates which of the suffixes typically associated with nominalizations – *ing(s)*, *ion(s)*, *ment(s)*, and *nce(s)* – the word ends with. This overlaps with the Suffixes feature, but allows the classifier to more easily treat nominalizations specially.

5.3 Morphological features

These features identify the various morphological variants of a word, so that, for example, the words *resist*, *resisted* and *resistance* can all be identified as the same basic event type.

Morphological stem: This feature gives the base form of the word, so for example, the stem of *assisted* is *assist* and the stem of *investigations* is *investigation*. Stems are identified with a lookup table from the University of Pennsylvania of around 300,000 words.

Root verb: This feature gives the verb from which the word is derived. For example, *assistance* is derived from *assist* and *investigation* is derived from *investigate*. Root verbs are identified with an in-house lookup table of around 5000 nominalizations.

5.4 Word class features

These features attempt to group the words into different types of classes. The intention here is to identify correlations between classes of words and classes of events, e.g. that events are more likely to be expressed as verbs or in verb phrases than they are as nouns.

Part-of-speech: This feature contains the word's part-of-speech based on the Penn Treebank tag set. Part-of-speech tags are assigned by the MX-POST maximum-entropy based part-of-speech tagger (Ratnaparkhi, 1996).

Syntactic-chunk label: The value of this feature is a B-I-O style label indicating what kind of syntactic chunk the word is contained in, e.g. noun phrase, verb phrase, or prepositional phrase. These are assigned using a word-chunking SVM-based system trained on the CoNLL-2000 data[2] (which uses the lowest nodes of the Penn TreeBank syntactic trees to break sentences into base phrases).

Word cluster: This feature indicates which verb or noun cluster the word is a member of. The clusters were derived from the co-occurrence statistics of verbs and their direct objects, in the same manner as Pradhan et. al. (2004). This produced 128 clusters (half verbs, half nouns) covering around 100,000 words.

5.5 Governing features

These features attempt to include some simple dependency information from the surrounding words, using the dependency parses produced by Minipar[3]. These features aim to identify events that are expressed as phrases or that require knowledge of the surrounding phrase to be identified.

Governing light verb: This feature indicates which, if any, of the light verbs *be*, *have*, *get*, *give*, *make*, *put*, and *take* governs the word. This is intended to capture adjectival predicates such as *may be ready*, and nominal predicates such as *make an offer*, where *ready* and *offer* should be identified as events.

Determiner type: This feature indicates the type of determiner a noun phrase has. If the noun phrase has an explicit determiner, e.g. *a*, *the* or *some*, the value of this feature is the determiner itself. We use the determiners themselves as feature values here because they form a small, closed class of words. For open-class determiner-like modifiers, we instead group them into classes. For noun phrases that are explicitly quantified, like *a million dollars*, the value is CARDINAL, while for noun phrases modified by other possessive noun phrases, like *Bush's real objectives*, the value is GENITIVE. For noun phrases without a determiner-like modifier, the value is PROPER_NOUN, BARE_PLURAL or BARE_SINGULAR, depending on the noun type.

Subject determiner type: This feature indicates for a verb the determiner type (as above) of its subject. This is intended to distinguish generic sentences like *Cats have fur* from non-generics like *The cat has fur*.

5.6 Temporal features

These features try to identify temporal relations between words. Since the duration of a situation is at the core of the TimeBank definition of events, features that can get at such information are particularly relevant.

Time chunk label: The value of this feature is a B-I-O label indicating whether or not this word is contained in a temporal annotation. The temporal annotations are produced by a word-chunking SVM-based system trained on the temporal expressions (TIMEX2 annotations) in the TERN 2004 data[4]. In addition to identifying expressions like *Monday* and *this year*, the TERN data identifies event-containing expressions like *the time she arrived at her doctor's office*.

Governing temporal: This feature indicates which kind of temporal preposition governs the word. Since the TimeBank is particularly interested in which events start or end within the time span of the document, we consider prepositions likely to indicate such a change of state, including *after*, *before*, *during*, *following*, *since*, *till*, *until* and *while*.

Modifying temporal: This feature indicates which kind of temporal expression modifies the word. Temporal expressions are recognized as above, and the type of modification is either the preposition that joins the temporal annotation to the word, or ADVERBIAL for any non-preposition modification. This is intended to capture that modifying temporal expressions often indicate event times, e.g. *He ran the race in an hour*.

5.7 Negation feature

This feature indicates which negative particle, e.g. *not*, *never*, etc., modifies the word. The idea is based Siegel and McKeown's (2000) findings which suggested that in some corpora states occur more freely with negation than events do.

5.8 WordNet hypernym features

These features indicate to which of the WordNet noun and verb sub-hierarchies the word belongs.

[2] http://cnts.uia.ac.be/conll2000/

[3] http://www.cs.ualberta.ca/~lindek/minipar.htm

[4] http://timex2.mitre.org/tern.html

Rather than include all of the thousands of different sub-hierarchies in WordNet, we first selected the most useful candidates by looking at the overlap with WordNet and our training data. For each hierarchy in WordNet, we considered a classifier that labeled all words in that hierarchy as events, and all words outside of that hierarchy as non-events[5]. We then evaluated these classifiers on our training data, and selected the ten with the highest F-measures. This resulted in selecting the following synsets:

- noun: state
- noun: psychological feature
- noun: event
- verb: think, cogitate, cerebrate
- verb: move, displace
- noun: group, grouping
- verb: act, move
- noun: act, human action, human activity
- noun: abstraction
- noun: entity

The values of the features were then whether or not the word fell into the hierarchy defined by each one of these roots. Note that since there are no WordNet senses labeled in our data, we accept a word as falling into one of the above hierarchies if any of its senses fall into that hierarchy.

6 Classifier Parameters

The features described in the previous section give us a way to provide the learning algorithm with the necessary information to make a classification decision. The next step is to convert our training data into sets of features, and feed these classification instances to the learning algorithm. For the learning task, we use the TinySVM[6] support vector machine (SVM) implementation in conjunction with YamCha[7] (Kudo & Matsumoto, 2001), a suite for general-purpose chunking.

YamCha has a number of parameters that define how it learns. The first of these is the window width of the "sliding window" that it uses.

Word	*POS*	*Stem*	*Label*
The	DT	the	O
company	NN	company	O
's	POS	's	O
sales	NNS	sale	O
force	NN	force	O
applauded	VBD	applaud	B
The	DT	the	O
shake	NN	shake	B
up	RP	up	
.	.	.	

Table 2: A window of word features

A sliding window is a way of including some of the context when the classification decision is made for a word. This is done by including the features of preceding and following words in addition to the features of the word to be classified. To illustrate this, we consider our earlier example, now augmented with some additional features in Table 2.

To classify *up* in this scenario, we now look not only at its features, but at the features of some of the neighboring words. For example, if our window width was 1, the feature values we would use for classification would be those in the outlined box, that is, the features of *shake*, *up* and the sentence final period. Note that we do not include the classification labels for either *up* or the period since neither of these classifications is available at the time we try to classify *up*. Using such a sliding window allows YamCha to include important information, like that *up* is preceded by *shake* and that *shake* was identified as beginning an event.

In addition to the window width parameter, YamCha also requires values for the following three parameters: the penalty for misclassification (C), the kernel's polynomial degree, and the method for applying binary classifiers to our multi-class problem, either pair-wise or one-vs-rest. In our experiments, we chose a one-vs-rest multi-class scheme to keep training time down, and then tried different variations of all the other parameters to explore a variety of models.

7 Baseline Models

To be able to meaningfully evaluate the models we train, we needed to establish a reasonable baseline. Because the majority class baseline would simply label every word as a non-event, we introduce two baseline models that should be more reasonable: Memorize and Sim-Evita.

[5] We also considered the reverse classifiers, which classified all words in the hierarchy as non-events and all words outside the hierarchy as events.

[6] http://chasen.org/~taku/software/TinySVM/

[7] http://chasen.org/~taku/software/yamcha/

The Memorize baseline is essentially a lookup table – it memorizes the training data. This system assigns to each word the label with which it occurred most frequently in the training data, or the label O (not an event) if the word never occurred in the training data.

The Sim-Evita model is our attempt to simulate the Evita system (Saurí et. al. 2005). As part of its algorithm, Evita includes a check that determines whether or not a word occurs as an event in TimeBank. It performs this check even when evaluated on TimeBank, and thus though Evita reports 74% precision and 87% recall, these numbers are artificially inflated because the system was trained and tested on the same corpus. Thus we cannot directly compare our results to theirs. Instead, we simulate Evita by taking the information that it encodes as rules, and encoding this instead as features which we provide to a YamCha-based system.

Saurí et. al. (2005) provides a description of Evita's rules, which, according to the text, are based on information from lexical stems, part of speech tags, syntactic chunks, weak stative predicates, copular verbs, complements of copular predicates, verbs with bare plural subjects and WordNet ancestors. We decided that the following features most fully covered the same information:

- Text
- Morphological stem
- Part-of-speech
- Syntactic-chunk label
- Governing light verb
- Subject determiner type
- WordNet hypernyms

We also decided that since Evita does not consider a word-window around the word to be classified, we should set our window size parameter to zero.

Because our approximation of Evita uses a feature-based statistical machine learning algorithm instead of the rule-based Evita algorithm, it cannot predict how well Evita would perform if it had not used the same data for training and testing. However, it can give us an approximation of how well a model can perform using information similar to that of Evita.

8 Results

Having decided on our feature space, our learning model, and the baselines to which we will compare, we now describe the results of our models on the TimeBank. We selected a stratified sample of 90% of the TimeBank data for a training set, and reserved the remaining 10% for testing[8].

We consider three evaluation measures: precision, recall and F-measure. Precision is defined as the number of B and I labels our system identifies correctly, divided by the total number of B and I labels our system predicted. Recall is defined as the number of B and I labels our system identifies correctly, divided by the total number of B and I labels in the TimeBank data. F-measure is defined as the geometric mean of precision and recall[9].

To determine the best parameter settings for the models, we performed cross-validations on our training data, leaving the testing data untouched. We divided the training data randomly into five equally-sized sections. Then, for each set of parameters to be evaluated, we determined a cross-validation F-measure by averaging the F-measures of five runs, each tested on one of the training data sections and trained on the remaining training data sections. We selected the parameters of the model that had the best cross-validation F-measure on the training data as the parameters for the rest of our experiments. For the simple event identification model this selected a window width of 2, polynomial degree of 3 and C value of 0.1, and for the event and class identification model this selected a window width of 1, polynomial degree of 1 and C value 0.1. For the Sim-Evita simple event identification model this selected a degree of 2 and C value of 0.01, and for the Sim-Evita event and class identification model, this selected a degree of 1 and C value of 1.0.

Having selected the appropriate parameters for our learning algorithm, we then trained our SVM models on the training data. Table 3 presents the results of these models on the test data. Our model (named STEP above for "System for Tex-

[8] The testing documents were: APW19980219.0476, APW19980418.0210, NYT19980206.0466, PRI19980303.2000.2550, ea980120.1830.0071, and the wsj_XXXX_orig documents numbered 0122, 0157, 0172, 0313, 0348, 0541, 0584, 0667, 0736, 0791, 0907, 0991 and 1033.

[9] $F = \frac{2 \cdot P \cdot R}{P + R}$

	Event Identification			Event and Class Identification		
Model	*Precision*	*Recall*	*F*	*Precision*	*Recall*	*F*
Memorize	0.806	0.557	0.658	0.640	0.413	0.502
Sim-Evita	0.812	0.659	0.727	0.571	0.459	0.509
STEP	0.820	0.706	0.759	0.667	0.512	0.579

Table 3: Overall results for both tasks

	Event Identification				Event and Class Identification			
	%	*Precision*	*Recall*	*F*	*%*	*Precision*	*Recall*	*F*
Verbs	59	0.864	0.903	0.883	59	0.714	0.701	0.707
Nouns	28	0.729	0.432	0.543	28	0.473	0.261	0.337

Table 4: Results by word class for both tasks

	%	*Precision*	*Recall*	*F*
B	92	0.827	0.737	0.779
I	8	0.679	0.339	0.452
B Occurrence	44	0.633	0.727	0.677
B State	14	0.519	0.136	0.215
B Reporting	11	0.909	0.779	0.839
B Istate	10	0.737	0.378	0.500
B Iaction	10	0.480	0.174	0.255
I State	7	0.818	0.173	0.286
B Aspectual	3	0.684	0.684	0.684

Table 5: Results by label

tual Event Parsing") outperforms both baselines on both tasks. For simple event identification, the main win over both baselines is an increased recall. Our model achieves a recall of 70.6%, about 5% better than our simulation of Evita, and nearly 15% better than the Memorize baseline. For event and class identification, the win is again in recall, though to a lesser degree. Our system achieves a recall of 51.2%, about 5% better than Sim-Evita, and 10% better than Memorize. On this task, we also achieve a precision of 66.7%, about 10% better than the precision of Sim-Evita. This indicates that the model trained with no context window and using the Evita-like feature set was at a distinct disadvantage over the model which had access to all of the features.

Table 4 and Table 5 show the results of our systems on various sub-tasks, with the "%" column indicating what percent of the events in the test data each subtask contained. Table 4 shows that in both tasks, we do dramatically better on verbs than on nouns, especially as far as recall is concerned. This is relatively unsurprising – not only is there more data for verbs (59% of event words are verbs, while only 28% are nouns), but our models generally do better on words they have seen before, and there are many more nouns we have not seen than there are verbs.

Table 5 shows how well we did individually on each type of label. For simple event identification (the top two rows) we can see that we do substantially better on B labels than on I labels, as we would expect since 92% of event words are labeled B. The label-wise performance for the event and class identification (the bottom seven rows) is more interesting. Our best performance is actually on Reporting event words, even though the data is mainly Occurrence event words. One reason for this is that instances of the word *said* make up about 60% of Reporting event words in the TimeBank. The word *said* is relatively easy to get right because it comes with by far the most training data[10], and because it is almost always an event: 98% of the time in the TimeBank, and 100% of the time in our test data.

To determine how much each of the feature sets contributed to our models we also performed a pair of ablation studies. In each ablation study, we trained a series of models on successively fewer feature sets, removing the least important feature set each time. The least important feature set was determined by finding out which feature set's removal caused the smallest drop in F-measure. The result of this process was a list of our feature sets, ordered by importance. These lists are given for both tasks in Table 6, along with the precision, recall and F-measures of the various corresponding models. Each row in Table 6 corresponds to a model trained on the feature sets named in that row and all the rows below it. Thus, on the top row, no feature sets have been removed, and on the bottom row only one feature set remains.

[10] The word "said" has over 600 instances in TimeBank. The word with the next most instances has just over 200

Event Identification

Feature set	Precision	Recall	F
Governing	0.820	0.706	0.759
Negation	0.824	0.713	0.765
Affix	0.826	0.715	0.766
WordNet	0.818	0.723	0.768
Temporal	0.820	0.729	0.772
Morphological	0.816	0.727	0.769
Text	0.816	0.697	0.752
Word class	0.719	0.677	0.697

Event and Class Identification

Feature set	Precision	Recall	F
Governing	0.667	0.512	0.579
Temporal	0.675	0.513	0.583
Negation	0.672	0.510	0.580
Morphological	0.670	0.509	0.579
Text	0.671	0.505	0.576
WordNet	0.679	0.497	0.574
Word class	0.682	0.474	0.559
Affix	0.720	0.421	0.531

Table 6: Ablations for both tasks. For each task, the least important feature sets appear at the top of the table, and most important feature sets appear at the bottom. For each row, the precision, recall and F-measure indicate the scores of a model trained with only the feature sets named in that row and the rows below it.

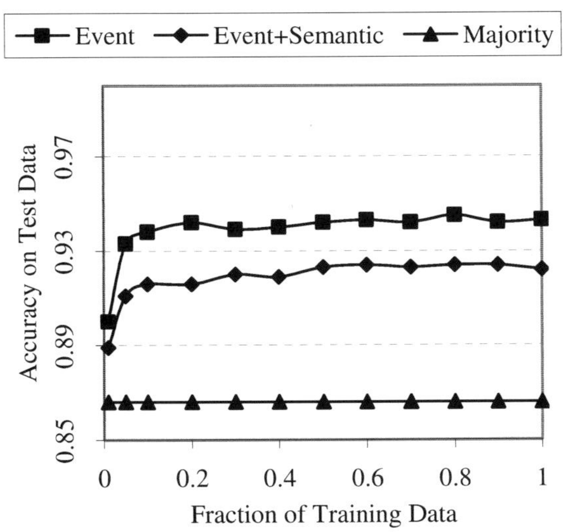

Figure 1: Learning Curves

So, for example, in the simple event identification task, we see that the Governing, Negation, Affix and WordNet features are hurting the classifier somewhat – a model trained without these features performs at an F-measure of 0.772, more than 1% better than a model including these features. In contrast, we can see that for the event and semantic class identification task, the WordNet and Affix features are actually among the most important, with only the Word class features accompanying them in the top three. These ablation results suggest that word class, textual, morphological and temporal information is most useful for simple event identification, and affix, WordNet and negation information is only really needed when the semantic class of an event must also be identified.

The last thing we investigated was the effect of additional training data. To do so, we trained the model on increasing fractions of the training data, and measured the classification accuracy on the testing data of each of the models thus trained. The resulting graph is shown in Figure 1. The Majority line indicates the classifier accuracy when the classifier always guesses majority class, that is, (O)utside of an event. We can see from the two learning curves that even with only the small amount of data available in the TimeBank, our models are already reaching the level part of the learning curve at somewhere around 20% of the data. This suggests that, though additional data may help somewhat in the data sparseness problem, substantial further progress on this task will require new, more descriptive features.

9 Conclusions

In this paper, we showed that statistical machine learning techniques can be successfully applied to the problem of identifying fine-grained events in a text. We formulated this task as a statistical classification task using a word-chunking paradigm, where words are labeled as beginning, inside or outside of an event. We introduced a variety of relevant linguistically-motivated features, and showed that models trained in this way could perform quite well on the task, with a precision of 82% and a recall of 71%. This method extended to the task of identifying the semantic class of an event with a precision of 67% and a recall of 51%. Our analysis of these models indicates that while the simple event identification task can be approached with mostly simple text and word-class based features, identifying the semantic class of an event requires features that encode more of the semantic context of the words. Finally, our training curves suggest that future research in this area should focus primarily on identifying more discriminative features.

10 Acknowledgments

This work was partially supported by a DHS fellowship to the first author and by ARDA under AQUAINT project MDA908-02-C-0008. Computer time was provided by NSF ARI Grant #CDA-9601817, NSF MRI Grant #CNS-0420873, NASA AIST grant #NAG2-1646, DOE SciDAC grant #DE-FG02-04ER63870, NSF sponsorship of the National Center for Atmospheric Research, and a grant from the IBM Shared University Research (SUR) program. Any opinions, findings, or recommendations are those of the authors and do not necessarily reflect the views of the sponsors. Particular thanks go to Wayne Ward and Martha Palmer for many helpful discussions and comments.

References

James Allan, Jaime Carbonell, George Dodding-ton, Jonathan Yamron and Yiming Yang. 1998. Topic Detection and Tracking Pilot Study: Final Report. In: Proceedings of DARPA Broadcast News Transcription and Understanding Workshop.

Xavier Carreras, Lluís Màrquez and Lluís Padró. Named Entity Extraction using AdaBoost. 2002. In Proceedings of CoNNL-2002.

Elena Filatova and Vasileios Hatzivassiloglou. Domain-Independent Detection, Extraction, and Labeling of Atomic Events. 2003. In the Proceedings of Recent Advances in Natural Language Processing Conference, September 2003.

Taku Kudo and Yuji Matsumoto. 2001. Chunking with support vector machines. In Proceedings of NAACL 2001.

Elaine Marsh and Dennis Perzanowski. 1997. MUC-7 evaluation of IE technology: Over-view of results. In Proceedings of the Seventh MUC.

Sameer Pradhan, Wayne Ward, Kadri Hacioglu, James H. Martin and Daniel Jurafsky. 2004. Shallow Semantic Parsing using Support Vector Machines. In Proceedings of HLT/NAACL 2004.

James Pustejovsky, José Castaño, Robert Ingria, Roser Saurí, Robert Gaizauskas, Andrea Setzer and Graham Katz. TimeML: 2003a. Robust Specification of Event and Temporal Expressions in Text. In Proceedings of the Fifth International Workshop on Computational Semantics (IWCS-5)

James Pustejovsky, Patrick Hanks, Roser Saurí, Andrew See, Robert Gaizauskas, Andrea Setzer, Dragomir Radev, Beth Sundheim, David Day, Lisa Ferro and Marcia Lazo. 2003b. The TIMEBANK Corpus. In Proceedings of Corpus Linguistics 2003, 647-656.

Lance A. Ramshaw and Mitchell P. Marcus. 1995. Text Chunking using Transformation-Based Learning. In Proceedings of the ACL Third Workshop on Very Large Corpora. 82-94.

Adwait Ratnaparkhi. 1996. A maximum entropy part-of-speech tagger. In Proceedings of EMNLP 1996.

Roser Saurí, Robert Knippen, Marc Verhagen and James Pustejovsky 2005. Evita: A Robust Event Recognizer For QA Systems. In Proceedings of HLT-EMNLP 2005.

Eric V. Siegel and Kathleen R. McKeown. Learning Methods to Combine Linguistic Indicators: Improving Aspectual Classification and Revealing Linguistic Insights. *Computational Linguistics*, 26(4):595 627.

Zeno Vendler. 1967. Verbs and times. In *Linguistics and Philosophy*. Cornell University Press, Ithaca, New

Extremely Lexicalized Models for Accurate and Fast HPSG Parsing

Takashi Ninomiya
Information Technology Center
University of Tokyo

Takuya Matsuzaki
Department of Computer Science
University of Tokyo

Yoshimasa Tsuruoka
School of Informatics
University of Manchester

Yusuke Miyao
Department of Computer Science
University of Tokyo

Jun'ichi Tsujii
Department of Computer Science, University of Tokyo
School of Informatics, University of Manchester
SORST, Japan Science and Technology Agency
Hongo 7-3-1, Bunkyo-ku, Tokyo, 113-0033, Japan
{ninomi, matuzaki, tsuruoka, yusuke, tsujii}@is.s.u-tokyo.ac.jp

Abstract

This paper describes an extremely lexicalized probabilistic model for fast and accurate HPSG parsing. In this model, the probabilities of parse trees are defined with only the probabilities of selecting lexical entries. The proposed model is very simple, and experiments revealed that the implemented parser runs around four times faster than the previous model and that the proposed model has a high accuracy comparable to that of the previous model for probabilistic HPSG, which is defined over phrase structures. We also developed a hybrid of our probabilistic model and the conventional phrase-structure-based model. The hybrid model is not only significantly faster but also significantly more accurate by two points of precision and recall compared to the previous model.

1 Introduction

For the last decade, accurate and wide-coverage parsing for real-world text has been intensively and extensively pursued. In most of state-of-the-art parsers, probabilistic events are defined over phrase structures because phrase structures are supposed to dominate syntactic configurations of sentences. For example, probabilities were defined over grammar rules in probabilistic CFG (Collins, 1999; Klein and Manning, 2003; Charniak and Johnson, 2005) or over complex phrase structures of head-driven phrase structure grammar (HPSG) or combinatory categorial grammar (CCG) (Clark and Curran, 2004b; Malouf and van Noord, 2004; Miyao and Tsujii, 2005). Although these studies vary in the design of the probabilistic models, the fundamental conception of probabilistic modeling is intended to capture characteristics of phrase structures or grammar rules. Although lexical information, such as head words, is known to significantly improve the parsing accuracy, it was also used to augment information on phrase structures.

Another interesting approach to this problem was using supertagging (Clark and Curran, 2004b; Clark and Curran, 2004a; Wang and Harper, 2004; Nasr and Rambow, 2004), which was originally developed for lexicalized tree adjoining grammars (LTAG) (Bangalore and Joshi, 1999). Supertagging is a process where words in an input sentence are tagged with 'supertags,' which are lexical entries in lexicalized grammars, e.g., elementary trees in LTAG, lexical categories in CCG, and lexical entries in HPSG. Supertagging was, in the first place, a technique to reduce the cost of parsing with lexicalized grammars; ambiguity in assigning lexical entries to words is reduced by the light-weight process of supertagging before the heavy process of parsing. Bangalore and Joshi (1999) claimed that if words can be assigned correct supertags, syntactic parsing is almost trivial. What this means is that if supertags are correctly assigned, syntactic structures are almost de-

Proceedings of the 2006 Conference on Empirical Methods in Natural Language Processing (EMNLP 2006), pages 155–163,
Sydney, July 2006.

termined because supertags include rich syntactic information such as subcategorization frames. Nasr and Rambow (2004) showed that the accuracy of LTAG parsing reached about 97%, assuming that the correct supertags were given. The concept of supertagging is simple and interesting, and the effects of this were recently demonstrated in the case of a CCG parser (Clark and Curran, 2004a) with the result of a drastic improvement in the parsing speed. Wang and Harper (2004) also demonstrated the effects of supertagging with a statistical constraint dependency grammar (CDG) parser. They achieved accuracy as high as the state-of-the-art parsers. However, a supertagger itself was used as an external tagger that enumerates candidates of lexical entries or filters out unlikely lexical entries just to help parsing, and the best parse trees were selected mainly according to the probabilistic model for phrase structures or dependencies with/without the probabilistic model for supertagging.

We investigate an extreme case of HPSG parsing in which the probabilistic model is defined with only the probabilities of lexical entry selection; i.e., the model is never sensitive to characteristics of phrase structures. The model is simply defined as the product of the supertagging probabilities, which are provided by the discriminative method with machine learning features of word trigrams and part-of-speech (POS) 5-grams as defined in the CCG supertagging (Clark and Curran, 2004a). The model is implemented in an HPSG parser instead of the phrase-structure-based probabilistic model; i.e., the parser returns the parse tree assigned the highest probability of supertagging among the parse trees licensed by an HPSG. Though the model uses only the probabilities of lexical entry selection, the experiments revealed that it was as accurate as the previous phrase-structure-based model. Interestingly, this means that accurate parsing is possible using rather simple mechanisms.

We also tested a hybrid model of the supertagging and the previous phrase-structure-based probabilistic model. In the hybrid model, the probabilities of the previous model are multiplied by the supertagging probabilities instead of a *preliminary probabilistic model*, which is introduced to help the process of estimation by filtering unlikely lexical entries (Miyao and Tsujii, 2005). In the previous model, the preliminary probabilistic model is defined as the probability of unigram supertagging. So, the hybrid model can be regarded as an extension of supertagging from unigram to n-gram. The hybrid model can also be regarded as a variant of the statistical CDG parser (Wang, 2003; Wang and Harper, 2004), in which the parse tree probabilities are defined as the product of the supertagging probabilities and the dependency probabilities. In the experiments, we observed that the hybrid model significantly improved the parsing speed, by around three to four times speed-ups, and accuracy, by around two points in both precision and recall, over the previous model. This implies that finer probabilistic model of lexical entry selection can improve the phrase-structure-based model.

2 HPSG and probabilistic models

HPSG (Pollard and Sag, 1994) is a syntactic theory based on lexicalized grammar formalism. In HPSG, a small number of schemata describe general construction rules, and a large number of lexical entries express word-specific characteristics. The structures of sentences are explained using combinations of schemata and lexical entries. Both schemata and lexical entries are represented by typed feature structures, and constraints represented by feature structures are checked with *unification*.

An example of HPSG parsing of the sentence "*Spring has come*" is shown in Figure 1. First, each of the lexical entries for "*has*" and "*come*" is unified with a daughter feature structure of the Head-Complement Schema. Unification provides the phrasal sign of the mother. The sign of the larger constituent is obtained by repeatedly applying schemata to lexical/phrasal signs. Finally, the parse result is output as a phrasal sign that dominates the sentence.

Given a set $\mathcal{W}$ of words and a set $\mathcal{F}$ of feature structures, an HPSG is formulated as a tuple, $G = \langle L, R \rangle$, where

$L = \{l = \langle w, F \rangle | w \in \mathcal{W}, F \in \mathcal{F}\}$ is a set of lexical entries, and

R is a set of schemata; i.e., $r \in R$ is a partial function: $\mathcal{F} \times \mathcal{F} \rightarrow \mathcal{F}$.

Given a sentence, an HPSG computes a set of phrasal signs, i.e., feature structures, as a result of parsing. Note that HPSG is one of the lexicalized grammar formalisms, in which lexical entries determine the dominant syntactic structures.

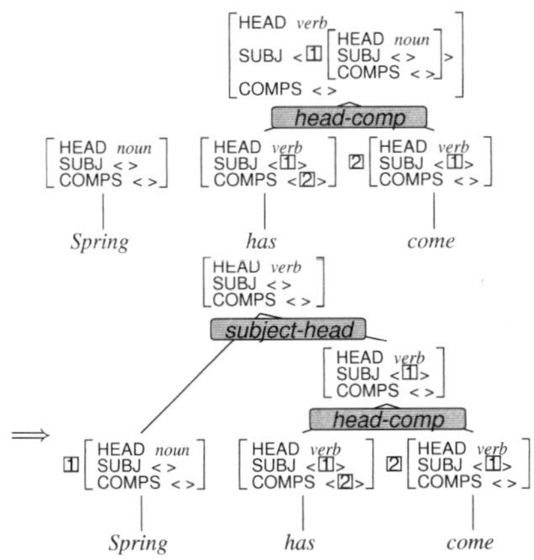

Figure 1: HPSG parsing.

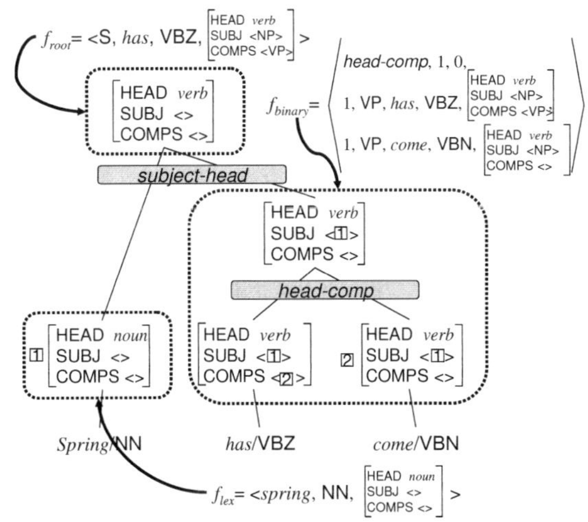

Figure 2: Example of features.

Previous studies (Abney, 1997; Johnson et al., 1999; Riezler et al., 2000; Malouf and van Noord, 2004; Kaplan et al., 2004; Miyao and Tsujii, 2005) defined a probabilistic model of unification-based grammars including HPSG as a *log-linear model* or *maximum entropy model* (Berger et al., 1996). The probability that a parse result T is assigned to a given sentence $\mathbf{w} = \langle w_1, \ldots, w_n \rangle$ is

$$p_{hpsg}(T|\mathbf{w}) = \frac{1}{Z_{\mathbf{w}}} \exp\left(\sum_u \lambda_u f_u(T)\right)$$

$$Z_{\mathbf{w}} = \sum_{T'} \exp\left(\sum_u \lambda_u f_u(T')\right),$$

where λ_u is a model parameter, f_u is a feature function that represents a characteristic of parse tree T, and $Z_{\mathbf{w}}$ is the sum over the set of all possible parse trees for the sentence. Intuitively, the probability is defined as the normalized product of the weights $\exp(\lambda_u)$ when a characteristic corresponding to f_u appears in parse result T. The model parameters, λ_u, are estimated using numerical optimization methods (Malouf, 2002) to maximize the log-likelihood of the training data.

However, the above model cannot be easily estimated because the estimation requires the computation of $p(T|\mathbf{w})$ for all parse candidates assigned to sentence $\mathbf{w}$. Because the number of parse candidates is exponentially related to the length of the sentence, the estimation is intractable for long sentences. To make the model estimation tractable, Geman and Johnson (Geman and Johnson, 2002) and Miyao and Tsujii (Miyao and Tsujii, 2002) proposed a dynamic programming algorithm for estimating $p(T|\mathbf{w})$. Miyao and Tsujii (2005) also introduced a *preliminary probabilistic model* $p_0(T|\mathbf{w})$ whose estimation does not require the parsing of a treebank. This model is introduced as a reference distribution of the probabilistic HPSG model; i.e., the computation of parse trees given low probabilities by the model is omitted in the estimation stage. We have

(Previous probabilistic HPSG)

$$p_{hpsg'}(T|\mathbf{w}) = p_0(T|\mathbf{w}) \frac{1}{Z_{\mathbf{w}}} \exp\left(\sum_u \lambda_u f_u(T)\right)$$

$$Z_{\mathbf{w}} = \sum_{T'} p_0(T'|\mathbf{w}) \exp\left(\sum_u \lambda_u f_u(T')\right)$$

$$p_0(T|\mathbf{w}) = \prod_{i=1}^{n} p(l_i|w_i),$$

where l_i is a lexical entry assigned to word w_i in T and $p(l_i|w_i)$ is the probability of selecting lexical entry l_i for w_i.

In the experiments, we compared our model with the probabilistic HPSG model of Miyao and Tsujii (2005). The features used in their model are combinations of the feature templates listed in Table 1. The feature templates f_{binary} and f_{unary} are defined for constituents at binary and unary branches, f_{root} is a feature template set for the root nodes of parse trees, and f_{lex} is a feature template set for calculating the preliminary probabilistic model. An example of features applied to the parse tree for the sentence "*Spring has come*" is shown in Figure 2.

$$
\begin{aligned}
f_{binary} &= \left\langle \begin{array}{l} r, d, c, \\ sp_l, sy_l, hw_l, hp_l, hl_l, \\ sp_r, sy_r, hw_r, hp_r, hl_r \end{array} \right\rangle \\
f_{unary} &= \langle r, sy, hw, hp, hl \rangle \\
f_{root} &= \langle sy, hw, hp, hl \rangle \\
f_{lex} &= \langle w_i, p_i, l_i \rangle
\end{aligned}
$$

combinations of feature templates for f_{binary}
$\langle r,d,c,hw,hp,hl\rangle$, $\langle r,d,c,hw,hp\rangle$, $\langle r,d,c,hw,hl\rangle$, $\langle r,d,c,sy,hw\rangle$, $\langle r,c,sp,hw,hp,hl\rangle$, $\langle r,c,sp,hw,hp\rangle$, $\langle r,c,sp,hw,hl\rangle$, $\langle r,c,sp,sy,hw\rangle$, $\langle r,d,c,hp,hl\rangle$, $\langle r,d,c,hp\rangle$, $\langle r,d,c,hl\rangle$, $\langle r,d,c,sy\rangle$, $\langle r,c,sp,hp,hl\rangle$, $\langle r,c,sp,hp\rangle$, $\langle r,c,sp,hl\rangle$, $\langle r,c,sp,sy\rangle$

combinations of feature templates for f_{unary}
$\langle r,hw,hp,hl\rangle$, $\langle r,hw,hp\rangle$, $\langle r,hw,hl\rangle$, $\langle r,sy,hw\rangle$, $\langle r,hp,hl\rangle$, $\langle r,hp\rangle$, $\langle r,hl\rangle$, $\langle r,sy\rangle$

combinations of feature templates for f_{root}
$\langle hw,hp,hl\rangle$, $\langle hw,hp\rangle$, $\langle hw,hl\rangle$, $\langle sy,hw\rangle$, $\langle hp,hl\rangle$, $\langle hp\rangle$, $\langle hl\rangle$, $\langle sy\rangle$

combinations of feature templates for f_{lex}
$\langle w_i,p_i,l_i\rangle$, $\langle p_i,l_i\rangle$

r	name of the applied schema
d	distance between the head words of the daughters
c	whether a comma exists between daughters and/or inside daughter phrases
sp	number of words dominated by the phrase
sy	symbol of the phrasal category
hw	surface form of the head word
hp	part-of-speech of the head word
hl	lexical entry assigned to the head word
w_i	i-th word
p_i	part-of-speech for w_i
l_i	lexical entry for w_i

Table 1: Features.

3 Extremely lexicalized probabilistic models

In the experiments, we tested parsing with the previous model for the probabilistic HPSG explained in Section 2 and other three types of probabilistic models defined with the probabilities of lexical entry selection. The first one is the simplest probabilistic model, which is defined with only the probabilities of lexical entry selection. It is defined simply as the product of the probabilities of selecting all lexical entries in the sentence; i.e., the model does not use the probabilities of phrase structures like the previous models.

Given a set of lexical entries, L, a sentence, $\mathbf{w} = \langle w_1, \ldots, w_n \rangle$, and the probabilistic model of lexical entry selection, $p(l_i \in L|\mathbf{w}, i)$, the first model is formally defined as follows:

(Model 1)

$$p_{model1}(T|\mathbf{w}) = \prod_{i=1}^{n} p(l_i|\mathbf{w}, i),$$

where l_i is a lexical entry assigned to word w_i in T and $p(l_i|\mathbf{w}, i)$ is the probability of selecting lexical entry l_i for w_i.

The second model is defined as the product of the probabilities of selecting all lexical entries in the sentence and the root node probability of the parse tree. That is, the second model is also defined without the probabilities on phrase structures:

(Model 2)

$$p_{model2}(T|\mathbf{w}) = \frac{1}{Z_{model2}} p_{model1}(T|\mathbf{w}) \exp\left(\sum_{\substack{u \\ (f_u \in f_{root})}} \lambda_u f_u(T) \right)$$

$$Z_{model2} = \sum_{T'} p_{model1}(T'|\mathbf{w}) \exp\left(\sum_{\substack{u \\ (f_u \in f_{root})}} \lambda_u f_u(T') \right),$$

where Z_{model2} is the sum over the set of all possible parse trees for the sentence.

The third model is a hybrid of model 1 and the previous model. The probabilities of the lexical entries in the previous model are replaced with the probabilities of lexical entry selection:

(Model 3)

$$p_{model3}(T|\mathbf{w}) = \frac{1}{Z_{model3}} p_{model1}(T|\mathbf{w}) \exp\left(\sum_{u} \lambda_u f_u(T) \right)$$

$$Z_{model3} = \sum_{T'} p_{model1}(T'|\mathbf{w}) \exp\left(\sum_{u} \lambda_u f_u(T') \right).$$

In this study, the same model parameters used in the previous model were used for phrase structures.

The probabilities of lexical entry selection, $p(l_i|\mathbf{w}, i)$, are defined as follows:

(Probabilistic Model of Lexical Entry Selection)

$$p(l_i|\mathbf{w}, i) = \frac{1}{Z_w} \exp\left(\sum_{u} \lambda_u f_u(l_i, \mathbf{w}, i) \right)$$

$$f_{exlex} = \left\langle \begin{array}{l} w_{i-1}, w_i, w_{i+1}, \\ p_{i-2}, p_{i-1}, p_i, p_{i+1}, p_{i+2} \end{array} \right\rangle$$

combinations of feature templates
$\langle w_{i-1}\rangle, \langle w_i\rangle, \langle w_{i+1}\rangle,$
$\langle p_{i-2}\rangle, \langle p_{i-1}\rangle, \langle p_i\rangle, \langle p_{i+1}\rangle, \langle p_{i+2}\rangle, \langle p_{i+3}\rangle,$
$\langle w_{i-1}, w_i\rangle, \langle w_i, w_{i+1}\rangle,$
$\langle p_{i-1}, w_i\rangle, \langle p_i, w_i\rangle, \langle p_{i+1}, w_i\rangle,$
$\langle p_i, p_{i+1}, p_{i+2}, p_{i+3}\rangle, \langle p_{i-2}, p_{i-1}, p_i\rangle,$
$\langle p_{i-1}, p_i, p_{i+1}\rangle, \langle p_i, p_{i+1}, p_{i+2}\rangle$
$\langle p_{i-2}, p_{i-1}\rangle, \langle p_{i-1}, p_i\rangle, \langle p_i, p_{i+1}\rangle, \langle p_{i+1}, p_{i+2}\rangle$

Table 2: Features for the probabilities of lexical entry selection.

```
procedure Parsing(⟨w_1, ..., w_n⟩, ⟨L, R⟩, α, β, κ, δ, θ)
  for i = 1 to n
    foreach F' ∈ {F|⟨w_i, F⟩ ∈ L}
      p = Σ_u λ_u f_u(F')
      π[i − 1, i] ← π[i − 1, i] ∪ {F'}
      if (p > ρ[i − 1, i, F']) then
        ρ[i − 1, i, F'] ← p
    LocalThresholding(i − 1, i, α, β)
  for d = 1 to n
    for i = 0 to n − d
      j = i + d
      for k = i + 1 to j − 1
        foreach F_s ∈ φ[i, k], F_t ∈ φ[k, j], r ∈ R
          if F = r(F_s, F_t) has succeeded
            p = ρ[i, k, F_s] + ρ[k, j, F_t] + Σ_u λ_u f_u(F)
            π[i, j] ← π[i, j] ∪ {F}
            if (p > ρ[i, j, F]) then
              ρ[i, j, F] ← p
      LocalThresholding(i, j, κ, δ)
    GlobalThresholding(i, n, θ)
```

```
procedure IterativeParsing(w, G, α_0, β_0, κ_0, δ_0, θ_0, Δα, Δβ, Δκ,
    Δδ, Δθ, α_last, β_last, κ_last, δ_last, θ_last)
  α ← α_0; β ← β_0; κ ← κ_0; δ ← δ_0; θ ← θ_0;
  loop while α ≤ α_last and β ≤ β_last and κ ≤ κ_last and δ ≤ δ_last
  and θ ≤ θ_last
    call Parsing(w, G, α, β, κ, δ, θ)
    if π[1, n] ≠ ∅ then exit
    α ← α + Δα; β ← β + Δβ;
    κ ← κ + Δκ; δ ← δ + Δδ; θ ← θ + Δθ;
```

Figure 3: Pseudo-code of iterative parsing for HPSG.

$$Z_w = \sum_{l'} \exp\left(\sum_u \lambda_u f_u(l', \mathbf{w}, i)\right),$$

where Z_w is the sum over all possible lexical entries for the word w_i. The feature templates used in our model are listed in Table 2 and are word trigrams and POS 5-grams.

4 Experiments

4.1 Implementation

We implemented the iterative parsing algorithm (Ninomiya et al., 2005) for the probabilistic HPSG models. It first starts parsing with a narrow beam. If the parsing fails, then the beam is widened, and parsing continues until the parser outputs results or the beam width reaches some limit. Though the probabilities of lexical entry selection are introduced, the algorithm for the presented probabilistic models is almost the same as the original iterative parsing algorithm.

The pseudo-code of the algorithm is shown in Figure 3. In the figure, the $\pi[i, j]$ represents the set of partial parse results that cover words $w_{i+1}, \ldots, w_j$, and $\rho[i, j, F]$ stores the maximum figure-of-merit (FOM) of partial parse result F at cell (i, j). The probability of lexical entry F is computed as $\sum_u \lambda_u f_u(F)$ for the previous model, as shown in the figure. The probability of a lexical entry for models 1, 2, and 3 is computed as the probability of lexical entry selection, $p(F|\mathbf{w}, i)$. The FOM of a newly created partial parse, F, is computed by summing the values of ρ of the daughters and an additional FOM of F if the model is the previous model or model 3. The FOM for models 1 and 2 is computed by only summing the values of ρ of the daughters; i.e., weights $\exp(\lambda_u)$ in the figure are assigned zero. The terms κ and δ are the thresholds of the number of phrasal signs in the chart cell and the beam width for signs in the chart cell. The terms α and β are the thresholds of the number and the beam width of lexical entries, and θ is the beam width for global thresholding (Goodman, 1997).

4.2 Evaluation

We evaluated the speed and accuracy of parsing with extremely lexicalized models by using Enju 2.1, the HPSG grammar for English (Miyao et al., 2005; Miyao and Tsujii, 2005). The lexicon of the grammar was extracted from Sections 02-21 of the Penn Treebank (Marcus et al., 1994) (39,832 sentences). The grammar consisted of 3,797 lexical entries for 10,536 words[1]. The probabilistic models were trained using the same portion of the treebank. We used beam thresholding, global thresholding (Goodman, 1997), preserved iterative parsing (Ninomiya et al., 2005) and other tech-

[1]An HPSG treebank is automatically generated from the Penn Treebank. Those lexical entries were generated by applying lexical rules to observed lexical entries in the HPSG treebank (Nakanishi et al., 2004). The lexicon, however, included many lexical entries that do not appear in the HPSG treebank. The HPSG treebank is used for training the probabilistic model for lexical entry selection, and hence, those lexical entries that do not appear in the treebank are rarely selected by the probabilistic model. The 'effective' tag set size, therefore, is around 1,361, the number of lexical entries without those never-seen lexical entries.

	No. of tested sentences		Total No. of	Avg. length of tested sentences	
	$\leq$ 40 words	$\leq$ 100 words	sentences	$\leq$ 40 words	$\leq$ 100 words
Section 23	2,162 (94.04%)	2,299 (100.00%)	2,299	20.7	22.2
Section 24	1,157 (92.78%)	1,245 (99.84%)	1,247	21.2	23.0

Table 3: Statistics of the Penn Treebank.

	Section 23 ($\leq$ 40 + Gold POSs)					Section 23 ($\leq$ 100 + Gold POSs)				
	LP (%)	LR (%)	UP (%)	UR (%)	Avg. time (ms)	LP (%)	LR (%)	UP (%)	UR (%)	Avg. time (ms)
previous model	87.65	86.97	91.13	90.42	468	87.26	86.50	90.73	89.93	604
model 1	87.54	86.85	90.38	89.66	111	87.23	86.47	90.05	89.27	129
model 2	87.71	87.02	90.51	89.80	109	87.38	86.62	90.17	89.39	130
model 3	89.79	88.97	92.66	91.81	132	89.48	88.58	92.33	91.40	152
	Section 23 ($\leq$ 40 + POS tagger)					Section 23 ($\leq$ 100 + POS tagger)				
	LP (%)	LR (%)	UP (%)	UR (%)	Avg. time (ms)	LP (%)	LR (%)	UP (%)	UR (%)	Avg. time (ms)
previous model	85.33	84.83	89.93	89.41	509	84.96	84.25	89.55	88.80	674
model 1	85.26	84.31	89.17	88.18	133	85.00	84.01	88.85	87.82	154
model 2	85.37	84.42	89.25	88.26	134	85.08	84.09	88.91	87.88	155
model 3	87.66	86.53	91.61	90.43	155	87.35	86.29	91.24	90.13	183

Table 4: Experimental results for Section 23.

niques for deep parsing[2]. The parameters for beam searching were determined manually by trial and error using Section 22: $\alpha_0 = 4, \Delta\alpha = 4, \alpha_{\text{last}} = 20, \beta_0 = 1.0, \Delta\beta = 2.5, \beta_{\text{last}} = 11.0, \delta_0 = 12, \Delta\delta = 4, \delta_{\text{last}} = 28$, $\kappa_0 = 6.0, \Delta\kappa = 2.25, \kappa_{\text{last}} = 15.0$, $\theta_0 = 8.0, \Delta\theta = 3.0$, and $\theta_{\text{last}} = 20.0$. With these thresholding parameters, the parser iterated at most five times for each sentence.

We measured the accuracy of the predicate-argument relations output of the parser. A predicate-argument relation is defined as a tuple $\langle \sigma, w_h, a, w_a \rangle$, where σ is the predicate type (e.g., adjective, intransitive verb), w_h is the head word of the predicate, a is the argument label (MODARG, ARG1, ..., ARG4), and w_a is the head word of the argument. Labeled precision (LP)/labeled recall (LR) is the ratio of tuples correctly identified by the parser[3]. Unlabeled precision (UP)/unlabeled recall (UR) is the ratio of tuples without the predicate type and the argument label. This evaluation scheme was the same as used in previous evaluations of lexicalized grammars (Hockenmaier, 2003; Clark and Curran, 2004b; Miyao and Tsujii, 2005). The experiments were conducted on an AMD Opteron server with a 2.4-GHz CPU. Section 22 of the Treebank was used as the development set, and the performance was evaluated using sentences of $\leq$ 40 and 100 words in Section 23. The performance of each parsing technique was analyzed using the sentences in Section 24 of $\leq$ 100 words. Table 3 details the numbers and average lengths of the tested sentences of $\leq$ 40 and 100 words in Sections 23 and 24, and the total numbers of sentences in Sections 23 and 24.

The parsing performance for Section 23 is shown in Table 4. The upper half of the table shows the performance using the correct POSs in the Penn Treebank, and the lower half shows the performance using the POSs given by a POS tagger (Tsuruoka and Tsujii, 2005). The left and right sides of the table show the performances for the sentences of $\leq$ 40 and $\leq$ 100 words. Our models significantly increased not only the parsing speed but also the parsing accuracy. Model 3 was around three to four times faster and had around two points higher precision and recall than the previous model. Surprisingly, model 1, which used only lexical information, was very fast and as accurate as the previous model. Model 2 also improved the accuracy slightly without information of phrase structures. When the automatic POS tagger was introduced, both precision and recall dropped by around 2 points, but the tendency towards improved speed and accuracy was again ob-

[2] Deep parsing techniques include quick check (Malouf et al., 2000) and large constituent inhibition (Kaplan et al., 2004) as described by Ninomiya et al. (2005), but hybrid parsing with a CFG chunk parser was not used. This is because we did not observe a significant improvement for the development set by the hybrid parsing and observed only a small improvement in the parsing speed by around 10 ms.

[3] When parsing fails, precision and recall are evaluated, although nothing is output by the parser; i.e., recall decreases greatly.

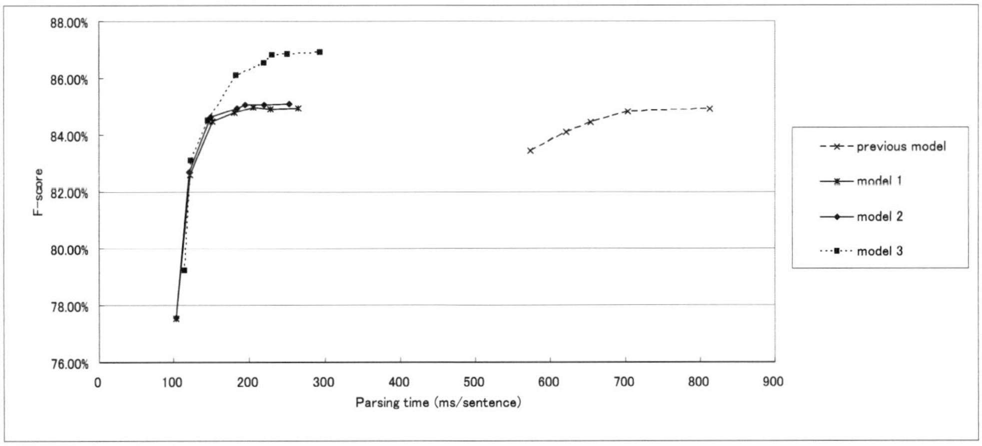

Figure 4: F-score versus average parsing time for sentences in Section 24 of ≤ 100 words.

served.

The unlabeled precisions and recalls of the previous model and models 1, 2, and 3 were significantly different as measured using stratified shuffling tests (Cohen, 1995) with p-values < 0.05. The labeled precisions and recalls were significantly different among models 1, 2, and 3 and between the previous model and model 3, but were not significantly different between the previous model and model 1 and between the previous model and model 2.

The average parsing time and labeled F-score curves of each probabilistic model for the sentences in Section 24 of ≤ 100 words are graphed in Figure 4. The superiority of our models is clearly observed in the figure. Model 3 performed significantly better than the previous model. Models 1 and 2 were significantly faster with almost the same accuracy as the previous model.

5 Discussion

5.1 Supertagging

Our probabilistic model of lexical entry selection can be used as an independent classifier for selecting lexical entries, which is called the supertagger (Bangalore and Joshi, 1999; Clark and Curran, 2004b). The CCG supertagger uses a maximum entropy classifier and is similar to our model.

We evaluated the performance of our probabilistic model as a supertagger. The accuracy of the resulting supertagger on our development set (Section 22) is given in Table 5 and Table 6. The test sentences were automatically POS-tagged. Results of other supertaggers for automatically extracted lexicalized grammars are listed in Table 5. Table 6 gives the average number of supertags assigned to a word, the per-word accuracy, and the sentence accuracy for several values of γ, which is a parameter to determine how many lexical entries are assigned.

	test data	accuracy (%)
HPSG supertagger (this paper)	22	87.51
CCG supertagger (Curran and Clark, 2003)	00/23	91.70 / 91.45
LTAG supertagger (Shen and Joshi, 2003)	22/23	86.01 / 86.27

Table 5: Accuracy of single-tag supertaggers. The numbers under "test data" are the PTB section numbers of the test data.

γ	tags/word	word acc. (%)	sentence acc. (%)
1e-1	1.30	92.64	34.98
1e-2	2.11	95.08	46.11
1e-3	4.66	96.22	51.95
1e-4	10.72	96.83	55.66
1e-5	19.93	96.95	56.20

Table 6: Accuracy of multi-supertagging.

When compared with other supertag sets of automatically extracted lexicalized grammars, the (effective) size of our supertag set, 1,361 lexical entries, is between the CCG supertag set (398 categories) used by Curran and Clark (2003) and the LTAG supertag set (2920 elementary trees) used by Shen and Joshi (2003). The relative order based on the sizes of the tag sets exactly matches the order based on the accuracies of corresponding supertaggers.

5.2 Efficacy of extremely lexicalized models

The implemented parsers of models 1 and 2 were around four times faster than the previous model without a loss of accuracy. However, what surprised us is not the speed of the models, but the fact that they were as accurate as the previous model, though they do not use any phrase-structure-based probabilities. We think that the correct parse is more likely to be selected if the correct lexical entries are assigned high probabilities because lexical entries include specific information about subcategorization frames and syntactic alternation, such as wh-movement and passivization, that likely determines the dominant structures of parse trees. Another possible reason for the accuracy is the constraints placed by unification-based grammars. That is, incorrect parse trees were suppressed by the constraints.

The best performer in terms of speed and accuracy was model 3. The increased speed was, of course, possible for the same reasons as the speeds of models 1 and 2. An unexpected but very impressive result was the significant improvement of accuracy by two points in precision and recall, which is hard to attain by tweaking parameters or hacking features. This may be because the phrase structure information and lexical information complementarily improved the model. The lexical information includes more specific information about the syntactic alternation, and the phrase structure information includes information about the syntactic structures, such as the distances of head words or the sizes of phrases.

Nasr and Rambow (2004) showed that the accuracy of LTAG parsing reached about 97%, assuming that the correct supertags were given. We exemplified the dominance of lexical information in real syntactic parsing, i.e., syntactic parsing without gold-supertags, by showing that the probabilities of lexical entry selection dominantly contributed to syntactic parsing.

The CCG supertagging demonstrated fast and accurate parsing for the probabilistic CCG (Clark and Curran, 2004a). They used the supertagger for eliminating candidates of lexical entries, and the probabilities of parse trees were calculated using the phrase-structure-based model without the probabilities of lexical entry selection. Our study is essentially different from theirs in that the probabilities of lexical entry selection have been demonstrated to dominantly contribute to the disambiguation of phrase structures.

We have not yet investigated whether our results can be reproduced with other lexicalized grammars. Our results might hold only for HPSG because HPSG has strict feature constraints and has lexical entries with rich syntactic information such as wh-movement.

6 Conclusion

We developed an extremely lexicalized probabilistic model for fast and accurate HPSG parsing. The model is very simple. The probabilities of parse trees are defined with only the probabilities of selecting lexical entries, which are trained by the discriminative methods in the log-linear model with features of word trigrams and POS 5-grams as defined in the CCG supertagging. Experiments revealed that the model achieved impressive accuracy as high as that of the previous model for the probabilistic HPSG and that the implemented parser runs around four times faster. This indicates that accurate and fast parsing is possible using rather simple mechanisms. In addition, we provided another probabilistic model, in which the probabilities for the leaf nodes in a parse tree are given by the probabilities of supertagging, and the probabilities for the intermediate nodes are given by the previous phrase-structure-based model. The experiments demonstrated not only speeds significantly increased by three to four times but also impressive improvement in parsing accuracy by around two points in precision and recall.

We hope that this research provides a novel approach to deterministic parsing in which only lexical selection and little phrasal information without packed representations dominates the parsing strategy.

References

Steven P. Abney. 1997. Stochastic attribute-value grammars. *Computational Linguistics*, 23(4):597–618.

Srinivas Bangalore and Aravind Joshi. 1999. Supertagging: An approach to almost parsing. *Computational Linguistics*, 25(2):237–265.

Adam Berger, Stephen Della Pietra, and Vincent Della Pietra. 1996. A maximum entropy approach to natural language processing. *Computational Linguistics*, 22(1):39–71.

Eugene Charniak and Mark Johnson. 2005. Coarse-to-fine n-best parsing and maxent discriminative reranking. In *Proc. of ACL'05*, pages 173–180.

Stephen Clark and James R. Curran. 2004a. The importance of supertagging for wide-coverage CCG parsing. In *Proc. of COLING-04*.

Stephen Clark and James R. Curran. 2004b. Parsing the WSJ using CCG and log-linear models. In *Proc. of ACL'04*, pages 104–111.

Paul R. Cohen. 1995. *Empirical Methods for Artificial Intelligence*. The MIT Press.

Michael Collins. 1999. *Head-Driven Statistical Models for Natural Language Parsing*. Ph.D. thesis, Univ. of Pennsylvania.

James R. Curran and Stephen Clark. 2003. Investigating GIS and smoothing for maximum entropy taggers. In *Proc. of EACL'03*, pages 91–98.

Stuart Geman and Mark Johnson. 2002. Dynamic programming for parsing and estimation of stochastic unification-based grammars. In *Proc. of ACL'02*, pages 279–286.

Joshua Goodman. 1997. Global thresholding and multiple pass parsing. In *Proc. of EMNLP-1997*, pages 11–25.

Julia Hockenmaier. 2003. Parsing with generative models of predicate-argument structure. In *Proc. of ACL'03*, pages 359–366.

Mark Johnson, Stuart Geman, Stephen Canon, Zhiyi Chi, and Stefan Riezler. 1999. Estimators for stochastic "unification-based" grammars. In *Proc. of ACL '99*, pages 535–541.

R. M. Kaplan, S. Riezler, T. H. King, J. T. Maxwell III, and A. Vasserman. 2004. Speed and accuracy in shallow and deep stochastic parsing. In *Proc. of HLT/NAACL'04*.

Dan Klein and Christopher D. Manning. 2003. Accurate unlexicalized parsing. In *Proc. of ACL'03*, pages 423–430.

Robert Malouf and Gertjan van Noord. 2004. Wide coverage parsing with stochastic attribute value grammars. In *Proc. of IJCNLP-04 Workshop "Beyond Shallow Analyses"*.

Robert Malouf, John Carroll, and Ann Copestake. 2000. Efficient feature structure operations without compilation. *Journal of Natural Language Engineering*, 6(1):29–46.

Robert Malouf. 2002. A comparison of algorithms for maximum entropy parameter estimation. In *Proc. of CoNLL-2002*, pages 49–55.

Mitchell P. Marcus, Beatrice Santorini, and Mary Ann Marcinkiewicz. 1994. Building a large annotated corpus of English: The Penn Treebank. *Computational Linguistics*, 19(2):313–330.

Yusuke Miyao and Jun'ichi Tsujii. 2002. Maximum entropy estimation for feature forests. In *Proc. of HLT 2002*, pages 292–297.

Yusuke Miyao and Jun'ichi Tsujii. 2005. Probabilistic disambiguation models for wide-coverage HPSG parsing. In *Proc. of ACL'05*, pages 83–90.

Yusuke Miyao, Takashi Ninomiya, and Jun'ichi Tsujii, 2005. *Keh-Yih Su, Jun'ichi Tsujii, Jong-Hyeok Lee and Oi Yee Kwong (Eds.), Natural Language Processing - IJCNLP 2004 LNAI 3248*, chapter Corpus-oriented Grammar Development for Acquiring a Head-driven Phrase Structure Grammar from the Penn Treebank, pages 684–693. Springer-Verlag.

Hiroko Nakanishi, Yusuke Miyao, and Jun'ichi Tsujii. 2004. An empirical investigation of the effect of lexical rules on parsing with a treebank grammar. In *Proc. of TLT'04*, pages 103–114.

Alexis Nasr and Owen Rambow. 2004. Supertagging and full parsing. In *Proc. of the 7th International Workshop on Tree Adjoining Grammar and Related Formalisms (TAG+7)*.

Takashi Ninomiya, Yoshimasa Tsuruoka, Yusuke Miyao, and Jun'ichi Tsujii. 2005. Efficacy of beam thresholding, unification filtering and hybrid parsing in probabilistic hpsg parsing. In *Proc. of IWPT 2005*, pages 103–114.

Carl Pollard and Ivan A. Sag. 1994. *Head-Driven Phrase Structure Grammar*. University of Chicago Press.

Stefan Riezler, Detlef Prescher, Jonas Kuhn, and Mark Johnson. 2000. Lexicalized stochastic modeling of constraint-based grammars using log-linear measures and EM training. In *Proc. of ACL'00*, pages 480–487.

Libin Shen and Aravind K. Joshi. 2003. A SNoW based supertagger with application to NP chunking. In *Proc. of ACL'03*, pages 505–512.

Yoshimasa Tsuruoka and Jun'ichi Tsujii. 2005. Bidirectional inference with the easiest-first strategy for tagging sequence data. In *Proc. of HLT/EMNLP 2005*, pages 467–474.

Wen Wang and Mary P. Harper. 2004. A statistical constraint dependency grammar (CDG) parser. In *Proc. of ACL'04 Incremental Parsing workshop: Bringing Engineering and Cognition Together*, pages 42–49.

Wen Wang. 2003. *Statistical Parsing and Language Modeling based on Constraint Dependency Grammar*. Ph.D. thesis, Purdue University.

Multilingual Deep Lexical Acquisition for HPSGs via Supertagging

Phil Blunsom and Timothy Baldwin
Computer Science and Software Engineering
University of Melbourne, Victoria 3010 Australia
{pcbl,tim}@csse.unimelb.edu.au

Abstract

We propose a conditional random field-based method for supertagging, and apply it to the task of learning new lexical items for HPSG-based precision grammars of English and Japanese. Using a pseudo-likelihood approximation we are able to scale our model to hundreds of supertags and tens-of-thousands of training sentences. We show that it is possible to achieve start-of-the-art results for both languages using maximally language-independent lexical features. Further, we explore the performance of the models at the type- and token-level, demonstrating their superior performance when compared to a unigram-based baseline and a transformation-based learning approach.

1 Introduction

Over recent years, there has been a resurgence of interest in the use of precision grammars in NLP tasks, due to advances in parsing algorithm development, grammar development tools and raw computational power (Oepen et al., 2002b). **Precision grammars** are defined as implemented grammars of natural language which capture fine-grained linguistic distinctions, and are generative in the sense of distinguishing between grammatical and ungrammatical inputs (or at least have some in-built notion of linguistic "markedness"). Additional characteristics of precision grammars are that they are frequently bidirectional, and output a rich semantic abstraction for each spanning parse of the input string. Examples include DELPH-IN grammars such as the English Resource Grammar (Flickinger, 2002; Uszkoreit, 2002), the various PARGRAM grammars (Butt et al., 1999), and the Edinburgh CCG parser (Bos et al., 2004).

Due to their linguistic complexity, precision grammars are generally hand-constructed and thus restricted in size and coverage. Attempts to (semi-)automate the process of expanding the coverage of precision grammars have focused on either: (a) constructional coverage, e.g. in the form of error mining for constructional expansion (van Noord, 2004; Zhang and Kordoni, 2006), or relaxation of lexico-grammatical constraints to support partial and/or robust parsing (Riezler et al., 2002); or (b) lexical coverage, e.g. in bootstrapping from a pre-existing grammar and lexicon to learn new lexical items (Baldwin, 2005a). Our particular interest in this paper is in the latter of these two, that is the development of methods for automatically expanding the lexical coverage of an existing precision grammar, or more broadly **deep lexical acquisition** (DLA hereafter). In this, we follow Baldwin (2005a) in assuming a semi-mature precision grammar with a fixed inventory of lexical types, based on which we learn new lexical items. For the purposes of this paper, we focus specifically on supertagging as the mechanism for hypothesising new lexical items.

Supertagging can be defined as the process of applying a sequential tagger to the task of predicting the lexical type(s) associated with each word in an input string, relative to a given grammar. It was first introduced as a means of reducing parser ambiguity by Bangalore and Joshi (1999) in the context of the LTAG formalism, and has since been applied in a similar context within the CCG formalism (Clark and Curran, 2004). In both of these cases, supertagging provides the means to perform a beam search over the plausible lexical items for a given string context, and ideally reduces parsing complexity without sacrificing parser accuracy. An alternate application of supertagging is in DLA, in postulating novel lexical items with which to populate the lexicon of a given grammar to boost parser coverage. This can take place

Proceedings of the 2006 Conference on Empirical Methods in Natural Language Processing (EMNLP 2006), pages 164–171,
Sydney, July 2006.

either: (a) off-line for the purposes of rounding out the coverage of a static lexicon, in which case we are generally interested in globally maximising precision over a given corpus and hence predicting the single most plausible lexical type for each word token (**off-line DLA**: Baldwin (2005b)); or (b) on the fly for a given input string to temporarily expand lexical coverage and achieve a spanning parse, in which case we are interested in maximising recall by producing a (possibly weighted) list of lexical item hypotheses to run past the grammar (**on-line DLA**: Zhang and Kordoni (2005)). Our immediate interest in this paper is in the first of these tasks, although we would ideally like to develop an off-line method which is trivially portable to the second task of on-line DLA.

In this research, we focus particularly on the Grammar Matrix-based DELPH-IN family of grammars (Bender et al., 2002), which includes grammars of English, Japanese, Norwegian, Modern Greek, Portuguese and Korean. The Grammar Matrix is a framework for streamlining and standardising HPSG-based multilingual grammar development. One property of Grammar Matrix-based grammars is that they are strongly lexicalist and adhere to a highly constrained lexicon-grammar interface via a unique (terminal) lexical type for each lexical item. As such, lexical item creation in any of the Grammar Matrix-based grammars, irrespective of language, consists predominantly of predicting the appropriate lexical type for each lexical item, relative to the lexical hierarchy for the corresponding grammar. In this same spirit of standardisation and multilinguality, the aim of this research is to develop maximally language-independent supertagging methods which can be applied to any Grammar Matrix-based grammar with the minimum of effort. Essentially, we hope to provide the grammar engineer with the means to semi-automatically populate the lexicon of a semi-mature grammar, hence accelerating the pace of lexicon development and producing a resource of sufficient coverage to be practically useful in NLP tasks.

The contributions of this paper are the development of a pseudo-likelihood conditional random field-based method of supertagging, which we then apply to the task of off-line DLA for grammars of both English and Japanese with only minor language-specific adaptation. We show the supertagger to outperform previously-proposed supertagger-based DLA methods.

The remainder of this paper is structured as follows. Section 2 outlines past work relative to this research, and Section 3 reviews the resources used in our supertagging experiments. Section 4 outlines the proposed supertagger model and reviews previous research on supertagger-based DLA. Section 5 then outlines the set-up and results of our evaluation.

2 Past Research

According to Baldwin (2005b), research on DLA falls into the two categories of *in vitro* methods, where we leverage a secondary language resource to generate an abstraction of the words we hope to learn lexical items for, and *in vivo* methods, where the target resource that we are hoping to perform DLA relative to is used directly to perform DLA. Supertagging is an instance of *in vivo* DLA, as it operates directly over data tagged with the lexical type system for the precision grammar of interest.

Research on supertagging which is relevant to this paper includes the work of Baldwin (2005b) in training a transformation-based learner over data tagged with ERG lexical types. We discuss this method in detail in Section 5.2 and replicate this method over our English data set for direct comparability with this previous research.

As mentioned above, other work on supertagging has tended to view it as a means of driving a beam search to prune the parser search space (Bangalore and Joshi, 1999; Clark and Curran, 2004). In supertagging, token-level annotations (gold-standard, automatically-generated or otherwise) for a given DLR are used to train a sequential tagger, akin to training a POS tagger over POS-tagged data taken from the Penn Treebank.

One related *in vivo* approach to DLA targeted specifically at precision grammars is that of Fouvry (2003). Fouvry uses the grammar to guide the process of learning lexical items for unknown words, by generating underspecified lexical items for all unknown words and parsing with them. Syntactico-semantic interaction between unknown words and pre-existing lexical items during parsing provides insight into the nature of each unknown word. By combining such fragments of information, it is possible to incrementally arrive at a consolidated lexical entry for that word. That is, the precision grammar itself drives the incremental learning process within a parsing context.

An alternate approach is to compile out a set of word templates for each lexical type (with the important qualification that they do not rely on preprocessing of any form), and check for corpus occurrences of an unknown word in such contexts. That is, the morphological, syntactic and/or semantic predictions implicit in each lexical type are made explicit in the form of templates which represent distinguishing lexical contexts of that lexical type. This approach has been shown to be particularly effective over web data, where the sheer size of the data precludes the possibility of linguistic preprocessing but at the same time ameliorates the effects of data sparseness inherent in any lexicalised DLA approach (Lapata and Keller, 2004).

Other work on DLA (e.g. Korhonen (2002), Joanis and Stevenson (2003), Baldwin (2005a)) has tended to take an *in vitro* DLA approach, in extrapolating away from a DLR to corpus or web data, and analysing occurrences of words through the conduit of an external resource (e.g. a secondary parser or POS tagger). *In vitro* DLA can also take the form of resource translation, in mapping one DLR onto another to arrive at the lexical information in the desired format.

3 Task and Resources

In this section, we outline the resources targeted in this research, namely the English Resource Grammar (ERG: Flickinger (2002), Copestake and Flickinger (2000)) and the JACY grammar of Japanese (Siegel and Bender, 2002). Note that our choice of the ERG and JACY as testbeds for experimentation in this paper is somewhat arbitrary, and that we could equally run experiments over any Grammar Matrix-based grammar for which there is treebank data.

Both the ERG and JACY are implemented open-source broad-coverage precision Head-driven Phrase Structure Grammars (HPSGs: Pollard and Sag (1994)). A lexical item in each of the grammars consists of a unique identifier, a lexical type (a leaf type of a type hierarchy), an orthography, and a semantic relation. For example, in the English grammar, the lexical item for the noun *dog* is simply:

```
dog_n1 := n_-_c_le &
 [ STEM < "dog" >,
   SYNSEM [ LKEYS.KEYREL.PRED "_dog_n_1_rel" ] ].
```

in which the lexical type of `n_-_c_le` encodes the fact that *dog* is a noun which does not subcategorise for any other constituents and which is countable, `"dog"` specifies the lexical stem, and `"_dog_n_1_rel"` introduces an ad hoc predicate name for the lexical item to use in constructing a semantic representation. In the context of the ERG and JACY, DLA equates to learning the range of lexical types a given lexeme occurs with, and generating a single lexical item for each.

Recent development of the ERG and JACY has been tightly coupled with treebank annotation, and all major versions of both grammars are deployed over a common set of dynamically-updateable treebank data to help empirically trace the evolution of the grammar and retrain parse selection models (Oepen et al., 2002a; Bond et al., 2004). This serves as a source of training and test data for building our supertaggers, as detailed in Table 1.

In translating our treebank data into a form that can be understood by a supertagger, multiword expressions (MWEs) pose a slight problem. Both the ERG and JACY include multiword lexical items, which can either be **strictly continuous** (e.g. *hot line*) or **optionally discontinuous** (e.g. transitive English verb particle constructions, such as *pick up* as in *Kim picked the book up*).

Strictly continuous lexical items are described by way of a single whitespace-delimited lexical stem (e.g. `STEM < "hot line" >`). When faced with instances of this lexical item, the supertagger must perform two roles: (1) predict that the words *hot* and *line* combine together to form a single lexeme, and (2) predict the lexical type associated with the lexeme. This is performed in a single step through the introduction of the `ditto` lexical type, which indicates that the current word combines (possibly recursively) with the left-adjacent word to form a single lexeme, and shares the same lexical type. This tagging convention is based on that used, e.g., in the CLAWS7 part-of-speech tagset.

Optionally discontinuous lexical items are less of a concern, as selection of each of the discontinuous "components" is done via lexical types. E.g. in the case of *pick up*, the lexical entry looks as follows:

```
pick_up_v1 := v_p-np_le &
 [ STEM < "pick" >,
   SYNSEM [ LKEYS [ --COMPKEY _up_p_sel_rel,
                    KEYREL.PRED "_pick_v_up_rel" ] ] ].
```

in which `"pick"` selects for the `_up_p_sel_rel` predicate, which in turn is associated with the stem `"up"` and lexical type `p_prtcl_le`. In terms of lexical tag mark-up, we can treat these as separate

	ERG	JACY
GRAMMAR		
Language	English	Japanese
Lexemes	16,498	41,559
Lexical items	26,297	47,997
Lexical types	915	484
Strictly continuous MWEs	2,581	422
Optionally discontinuous MWEs	699	0
Proportion of lexemes with more than one lexical item	0.29	0.14
Average lexical items per lexeme	1.59	1.16
TREEBANK		
Training sentences	20,000	40,000
Training words	215,015	393,668
Test sentences	1,013	1,095
Test words	10,781	10,669

Table 1. Make-up of the English Resource Grammar (ERG) and JACY grammars and treebanks

tags and leave the supertagger to model the mutual inter-dependence between these lexical types.

For detailed statistics of the composition of the two grammars, see Table 1.

For morphological processing (including tokenisation and lemmatisation), we use the pre-existing machinery provided with each of the grammars. In the case of the ERG, this consists of a finite state machine which feeds into lexical rules; in the case of JACY, segmentation and lemmatisation is based on a combination of ChaSen (Matsumoto et al., 2003) and lexical rules. That is, we are able to assume that the Japanese data has been pre-segmented in a form compatible with JACY, as we are able to replicate the automatic pre-processing that it uses.

4 Suppertagging

The DLA strategy we adopt in this research is based on supertagging, which is a simple instance of sequential tagging with a larger, more linguistically-diverse tag set than is conventionally the case, e.g., with part-of-speech tagging. Below, we describe the pseudo-likelihood CRF model we base our supertagger on and outline the feature space for the two grammars.

4.1 Pseudo-likelihood CRF-based Supertagging

CRFs are undirected graphical models which define a conditional distribution over a label sequence given an observation sequence. Here we use CRFs to model sequences of lexical types, where each input word in a sentence is assigned a single tag.

The joint probability density of a sequence labelling, $\mathbf{a}$ (a vector of lexical types), given the input sentence, $\mathbf{s}$, is given by:

$$p_\Lambda(\mathbf{a}|\mathbf{s}) = \frac{\exp \sum_t \sum_k \lambda_k h_k(t, a_{t-1}, a_t, \mathbf{s})}{Z_\Lambda(\mathbf{s})} \quad (1)$$

where we make a first order Markov assumption over the label sequence. Here t ranges over the word indices of the input sentence ($\mathbf{s}$), k ranges over the model's features, and $\Lambda = \{\lambda_k\}$ are the model parameters (weights for their corresponding features). The feature functions h_k are predefined real-valued functions over the input sentence coupled with the lexical type labels over adjacent "times" (= sentence locations) t. These feature functions are unconstrained, and may represent overlapping and non-independent features of the data. The distribution is globally normalised by the partition function, $Z_\Lambda(\mathbf{s})$, which sums out the numerator in (1) for every possible labelling:

$$Z_\Lambda(\mathbf{s}) = \sum_{\mathbf{a}} \exp \sum_t \sum_k \lambda_k h_k(t, a_{t-1}, a_t, \mathbf{s})$$

We use a linear chain CRF, which is encoded in the feature functions of (1).

The parameters of the CRF are usually estimated from a fully observed training sample, by maximising the likelihood of these data. I.e. $\Lambda^{ML} = \arg\max_\Lambda p_\Lambda(\mathcal{D})$, where $\mathcal{D} = \{(\mathbf{a}, \mathbf{s})\}$ is the complete set of training data.

However, as calculating $Z_\Lambda(\mathbf{s})$ has complexity quadratic in the number of labels, we need to approximate $p_\Lambda(\mathbf{a}|\mathbf{s})$ in order to scale our model to hundreds of lexical types and tens-of-thousands of training sentences. Here we use the pseudo-likelihood approximation p_Λ^{PL} (Li, 1994) in which the marginals for a node at time t are calculated with its neighbour nodes' labels fixed to those ob-

FEATURE	DESCRIPTION
WORD CONTEXT FEATURES	
$lexeme(\mathbf{s}_t) = x \;\&\; \mathbf{a}_t = l$	lexeme + label
$\mathbf{s}_t = w \;\&\; \mathbf{a}_t = l$	word unigram + label
$\mathbf{s}_{t-1} = w \;\&\; \mathbf{a}_t = l$	previous word unigram + label
$\mathbf{s}_{t+1} = w \;\&\; \mathbf{a}_t = l$	next word unigram + label
$\mathbf{s}_t = w \;\&\; \mathbf{s}_{t-1} = y \;\&\; \mathbf{a}_t = l$	previous word bigram + label
$\mathbf{s}_t = w \;\&\; \mathbf{s}_{t+1} = y \;\&\; \mathbf{a}_t = l$	next word bigram + label
$\mathbf{a}_{t-1} = l \;\&\; \mathbf{a}_t = m$	clique label pair
LEXICAL FEATURES	
$prefix_n(\mathbf{s}_t) \;\&\; \mathbf{a}_t = l$	n-gram prefix + label
$suffix_n(\mathbf{s}_t) = x \;\&\; \mathbf{a}_t = l$	n-gram suffix + label
$contains(\mathbf{s}_t, C_i) \;\&\; \mathbf{a}_t = l$	word contains element of character set C_i + label

Table 2. Extracted feature types for the CRF model

served in the training data:

$$U_\Lambda^{PL}(i, \mathbf{s}, t) = \sum_k \lambda_k (h_k(t, \hat{a}_{t-1}, i, \mathbf{s}) + h_k(t, i, \hat{a}_{t+1}, \mathbf{s})) \quad (2)$$

$$p_\Lambda^{PL}(\mathbf{a}|\mathbf{s}) = \prod_t \frac{\exp(U_\Lambda^{PL}(\mathbf{a}_t, \mathbf{s}, t))}{\sum_l (U_\Lambda^{PL}(l, \mathbf{s}, t))} \quad (3)$$

where $\hat{\mathbf{a}}_t$ is the lexical type label observed in the training data and l ranges over the label set. This approximation removes the need to calculate the partition function, thus reducing the complexity to be linear in the number of labels and training instances.

Because maximum likelihood estimators for log-linear models have a tendency to overfit the training sample (Chen and Rosenfeld, 1999), we define a prior distribution over the model parameters and derive a maximum *a posteriori* (MAP) estimate, $\Lambda^{MAP-PL} = \arg\max_\Lambda p_\Lambda^{PL}(\mathcal{D})p(\Lambda)$. We use a zero-mean Gaussian prior, with the probability density function $p_0(\lambda_k) \propto \exp\left(-\frac{\lambda_k^2}{2\sigma_k^2}\right)$. This yields a log-pseudo-likelihood objective function of:

$$\mathcal{L}^{PL} = \sum_{(\mathbf{a},\mathbf{s}) \in \mathcal{D}} \log p_\Lambda^{PL}(\mathbf{a}|\mathbf{s}) + \sum_k \log p_0(\lambda_k) \quad (4)$$

In order to train the model, we maximize (4). While the log-pseudo-likelihood cannot be maximised for the parameters, Λ, in closed form, it is a convex function, and thus we resort to numerical optimisation to find the globally optimal parameters. We use L-BFGS, an iterative quasi-Newton optimisation method, which performs well for training log-linear models (Malouf, 2002; Sha and Pereira, 2003). Each L-BFGS iteration requires the objective value and its gradient with respect to the model parameters.

As we cannot observe label values for the test data we must use $p_\Lambda(\mathbf{a}|\mathbf{s})$ when decoding. The Viterbi algorithm is used to find the maximum posterior probability alignment for test sentences, $\mathbf{a}^* = \arg\max_\mathbf{a} p_\Lambda(\mathbf{a}|\mathbf{s})$.

4.2 CRF features

One of the strengths of the CRF model is that it supports the use of a large number of non-independent and overlapping features of the input sentence. Table 2 lists the word context and lexical features used by the CRF model (shared across both grammars).

Word context features were extracted from the words and lexemes of the sentence to be labelled combined with a proposed label. A clique label pair feature was also used to model sequences of lexical types.

For the lexical features, we generate a feature for the unigram, bigram and trigram prefixes and suffixes of each word (e.g. for *bottles*, we would generate the prefixes *b*, *bo* and *bot*, and the suffixes *s*, *es* and *les*); for words in the test data, we generate a feature only if that feature-value is attested in the training data. We additionally test each word for the existence of one or more elements of a range of character sets C_i. In the case of English, we focus on five character sets: upper case letters, lower case letters, numbers, punctuation and hyphens. For the Japanese data, we employ six character sets: Roman letters, hiragana, katakana, kanji, (Arabic) numerals and punctuation. For example, カビ臭い "mouldy" would be flagged as containing katakana character(s), kanji character(s) and hiragana character(s) only. Note that the only language-dependent component of

	ERG					JACY				
	ACC	ACC_U	PREC	REC	F-SCORE	ACC	ACC_U	PREC	REC	F-SCORE
Baseline	0.802	0.053	0.184	0.019	0.034	0.866	0.592	0.680	0.323	0.438
FNTBL	0.915	0.236	0.370	0.038	0.068	—	—	—	—	—
$\text{CRF}_{-\text{LEX}}$	0.911	0.427	0.339	0.053	0.092	0.920	0.816	0.548	0.414	0.471
$\text{CRF}_{+\text{LEX}}$	**0.917**	**0.489**	**0.509**	**0.059**	**0.105**	**0.932**	**0.827**	**0.696**	**0.424**	**0.527**

Table 3. Results of supertagging for the ERG and JACY (best result in each column in **bold**)

the lexical features is the character sets, which requires little or no specialist knowledge of the language. Note also that for languages with infixing, such as Tagalog, we may want to include n-gram infixes in addition to n-gram prefixes and suffixes. Here again, however, the decision about what range of affixes is appropriate for a given language requires only superficial knowledge of its morphology.

5 Evaluation

Evaluation is based on the treebank data associated with each grammar, and a random training–test split of 20,000 training sentences and 1,013 test sentences in the case of the ERG, and 40,000 training sentences and 1,095 test sentences in the case of the JACY. This split is fixed for all models tested.

Given that the goal of this research is to acquire novel lexical items, our primary focus is on the performance of the different models at predicting the lexical type of any lexical items which occur only in the test data (which may be either novel lexemes or previously-seen lexemes occurring with a novel lexical type). As such, we identify all unknown lexical items in the test data and evaluate according to: **token accuracy** (the proportion of unknown lexical items which are correctly tagged: ACC_U); **type precision** (the proportion of correctly hypothesised unknown lexical entries: PREC); **type recall** (the proportion of gold-standard unknown lexical entries for which we get a correct prediction: REC); and **type F-score** (the harmonic mean of type precision and type recall: F-SCORE). We also measure the **overall token accuracy** (ACC) across all words in the test data, irrespective of whether they represent known or unknown lexical items.

5.1 Baseline: Unigram Supertagger

As a baseline model, we use a simple unigram supertagger trained based on maximum likelihood estimation over the relevant training data, i.e. the tag t_w for each token instance of a given word w is predicted by:

$$t_w = \arg\max_t p(t|w)$$

In the instance that w was not observed in the training data, we back off to the majority lexical type in the training data.

5.2 Benchmark: fnTBL

In order to benchmark our results with the CRF models, we reimplemented the supertagger model proposed by Baldwin (2005b) which simply takes FNTBL 1.1 (Ngai and Florian, 2001) off the shelf and trains it over our particular training set. FNTBL is a transformation-based learner that is distributed with pre-optimised POS tagging modules for English and other European languages that can be redeployed over the task of supertagging. Following Baldwin (2005b), the only modifications we make to the default English POS tagging methodology are: (1) to set the default lexical types for singular common and proper nouns to `n_-_c_le` and `n_-_pn_le`, respectively; and (2) reduce the threshold score for lexical and context transformation rules to 1. It is important to realise that, unlike our proposed method, the English POS tagger implementation in FNTBL has been fine-tuned to the English POS task, and includes a rich set of lexical templates specific to English.

Note that were only able to run FNTBL over the English data, as encoding issues with the Japanese proved insurmountable. We are thus only able to compare results over the English, although this is expected to be representative of the relative performance of the methods.

5.3 Results

The results for the baseline, benchmark FNTBL method for English and our proposed CRF-based supertagger are presented in Table 3, for each of the ERG and JACY. In order to gauge the impact of the lexical features on the performance of our CRF-based supertagger, we ran the supertagger first without lexical features ($\text{CRF}_{-\text{LEX}}$) and then with the lexical features ($\text{CRF}_{+\text{LEX}}$).

The first finding of note is that the proposed model surpasses both the baseline and FNTBL in all cases. If we look to token accuracy for unknown lexical types, the CRF is far and away the superior method, a result which is somewhat diminished but still marked for type-level precision, recall and F-score. Recall that for the purposes of this paper, our primary interest is in how successfully we are able to learn new lexical items, and in this sense the CRF appears to have a clear edge over the other models. It is also important to recall that our results over both English and Japanese have been achieved with only the bare minimum of lexical feature engineering, whereas those of FNTBL are highly optimised.

Comparing the results for the CRF with and without lexical features ($CRF_{\pm LEX}$), the lexical features appear to have a strong bearing on type precision in particular, for both the ERG and JACY.

Looking to the raw numbers, the type-level performance for all methods is far from flattering. However, it is entirely predictable that the overall token accuracy should be considerably higher than the token accuracy for unknown lexical items. A breakdown of type precision and recall for unknown words across the major word classes for English suggests that the CRF_{+LEX} supertagger is most adept at learning nominal and adjectival lexical items (with an F-score of 0.671 and 0.628, respectively), and has the greatest difficulties with verbs and adverbs (with an F-score of 0.333 and 0.395, respectively). In the case of Japanese, conjugating adjectives and verbs present the least difficulty (with an F-score of 0.933 and 0.886, respectively), and non-conjugating adjectives and adverbs are considerably harder (with an F-score of 0.396 and 0.474, respectively).

It is encouraging to note that type precision is higher than type recall in all cases (a phenomenon that is especially noticeable for the ERG), as this means that while we are not producing the full inventory of lexical items for a given lexeme, over half of the lexical items that we produce are genuine (with CRF_{+LEX}). This suggests that it should be possible to present the grammar developer with a relatively low-noise set of automatically learned lexical items for them to manually curate and feed into the lexicon proper.

One final point of interest is the ability of the CRF to identify multiword expressions (MWEs). There were no unknown multiword expressions in either the English or Japanese data, such that we can only evaluate the performance of the supertagger at identifying known MWEs. In the case of English, CRF_{+LEX} identified strictly continuous MWEs with an accuracy of 0.758, and optionally discontinuous MWEs (i.e. verb particle constructions) with an accuracy of 0.625. For Japanese, the accuracy is considerably lower, at 0.536 for continuous MWEs (recalling that there were no optionally discontinuous MWEs in JACY).

6 Conclusion

In this paper we have explored a method for learning new lexical items for HPSG-based precision grammars through supertagging. Our pseudo-likelihood conditional random field-based approach provides a principled way of learning a supertagger from tens-of-thousands of training sentences and with hundreds of possible tags.

We achieve start-of-the-art results for both English and Japanese data sets with a largely language-independent feature set. Our model also achieves performance at the type- and token-level, over different word classes and at multiword expression identification, superior to a probabilistic baseline and a transformation based learning approach.

Acknowledgements

We would like to thank Dan Flickinger and Francis Bond for support and expert assistance with the ERG and JACY, respectively, and the three anonymous reviewers for their valuable input on this research. The research in this paper has been supported by the Australian Research Council through Discovery Project grant number DP0663879, and also NTT Communication Science Laboratories, Nippon Telegraph and Telephone Corporation

References

Timothy Baldwin. 2005a. Bootstrapping deep lexical resources: Resources for courses. In *Proc. of the ACL-SIGLEX 2005 Workshop on Deep Lexical Acquisition*, pages 67–76, Ann Arbor, USA.

Timothy Baldwin. 2005b. General-purpose lexical acquisition: Procedures, questions and results. In *Proc. of the 6th Meeting of the Pacific Association for Computational Linguistics (PACLING 2005)*, pages 23–32, Tokyo, Japan. (Invited Paper).

Srinivas Bangalore and Aravind K. Joshi. 1999. Supertagging: An approach to almost parsing. *Computational Linguistics*, 25(2):237–65.

Emily M. Bender, Dan Flickinger, and Stephan Oepen. 2002. The grammar Matrix. An open-source starter-kit for the rapid development of cross-linguistically consistent broad-coverage precision grammar. In *Proc. of the Workshop on Grammar Engineering and Evaluation at the 19th International Conference on Computational Linguistics*, Taipei, Taiwan.

Francis Bond, Sanae Fujita, Chikara Hashimoto, Kaname Kasahara, Shigeko Nariyama, Eric Nichols, Akira Ohtani, Takaaki Tanaka, and Shigeaki Amano. 2004. The Hinoki treebank: A treebank for text understanding. In *Proc. of the First International Joint Conference on Natural Language Processing (IJCNLP-04)*, pages 554–9, Hainan Island, China.

Johan Bos, Stephen Clark, Mark Steedman, James R. Curran, and Julia Hockenmaier. 2004. Wide-coverage semantic representations from a CCG parser. In *Proc. of the 20th International Conference on Computational Linguistics (COLING 2004)*, pages 1240–7, Geneva, Switzerland.

Miriam Butt, Tracy Holloway King, Maria-Eugenia Nino, and Frederique Segond. 1999. *A Grammar Writer's Cookbook*. CSLI Publications, Stanford, USA.

Stanley F. Chen and Ronald Rosenfeld. 1999. A survey of smoothing techniques for maximum entropy models. *IEEE Transactions on Speech and Audio Processing*, 8(1):37–50.

Stephen Clark and James R. Curran. 2004. The importance of supertagging for wide-coverage CCG parsing. In *Proc. of the 20th International Conference on Computational Linguistics (COLING 2004)*, pages 282–8, Geneva, Switzerland.

Ann Copestake and Dan Flickinger. 2000. An open-source grammar development environment and broad-coverage English grammar using HPSG. In *Proc. of the 2nd International Conference on Language Resources and Evaluation (LREC 2000)*, Athens, Greece.

Dan Flickinger. 2002. On building a more efficient grammar by exploiting types. In Oepen et al. (Oepen et al., 2002b).

Frederik Fouvry. 2003. *Robust Processing for Constraint-based Grammar Formalisms*. Ph.D. thesis, University of Essex.

Eric Joanis and Suzanne Stevenson. 2003. A general feature space for automatic verb classification. pages 163–70, Budapest, Hungary.

Anna Korhonen. 2002. *Subcategorization Acquisition*. Ph.D. thesis, University of Cambridge.

Mirella Lapata and Frank Keller. 2004. The web as a baseline: Evaluating the performance of unsupervised web-based models for a range of NLP tasks. pages 121–8, Boston, USA.

Stan Z. Li. 1994. Markov random field models in computer vision. In *ECCV (2)*, pages 361–370.

Rob Malouf. 2002. A comparison of algorithms for maximum entropy parameter estimation. In *Proc. of the 6th Conference on Natural Language Learning (CoNLL-2002)*, pages 49–55, Taipei, Taiwan.

Yuji Matsumoto, Akira Kitauchi, Tatsuo Yamashita, Yoshitaka Hirano, Hiroshi Matsuda, Kazuma Takaoka, and Masayuki Asahara. 2003. *Japanese Morphological Analysis System ChaSen Version 2.3.3 Manual*. Technical report, NAIST.

Grace Ngai and Radu Florian. 2001. Transformation-based learning in the fast lane. In *Proc. of the 2nd Annual Meeting of the North American Chapter of Association for Computational Linguistics (NAACL2001)*, pages 40–7, Pittsburgh, USA.

Stephan Oepen, Dan Flickinger, Kristina Toutanova, and Christoper D. Manning. 2002a. LinGO Redwoods: A rich and dynamic treebank for HPSG. In *Proc. of The First Workshop on Treebanks and Linguistic Theories (TLT2002)*, Sozopol, Bulgaria.

Stephan Oepen, Dan Flickinger, Jun'ichi Tsujii, and Hans Uszkoreit, editors. 2002b. *Collaborative Language Engineering*. CSLI Publications, Stanford, USA.

Carl Pollard and Ivan A. Sag. 1994. *Head-driven Phrase Structure Grammar*. The University of Chicago Press, Chicago, USA.

Stefan Riezler, Tracy H. King, Ronald M. Kaplan, Richard Crouch, John T. Maxwell III, and Mark Johnson. 2002. Parsing the Wall Street Journal using a Lexical-Functional Grammar and discriminative estimation techniques. In *Proc. of the 40th Annual Meeting of the ACL and 3rd Annual Meeting of the NAACL (ACL-02)*, Philadelphia, USA.

Fei Sha and Fernando Pereira. 2003. Shallow parsing with conditional random fields. In *Proc. of the 3rd International Conference on Human Language Technology Research and 4th Annual Meeting of the NAACL (HLT-NAACL 2003)*, pages 213–20, Edmonton, Canada.

Melanie Siegel and Emily M. Bender. 2002. Efficient deep processing of Japanese. In *Proc. of the 3rd Workshop on Asian Language Resources and International Standardization*, Taipei, Taiwan.

Hans Uszkoreit. 2002. New chances for deep linguistic processing. In *Proc. of the 19th International Conference on Computational Linguistics (COLING 2002)*, Taipei, Taiwan.

Gertjan van Noord. 2004. Error mining for wide-coverage grammar engineering. In *Proc. of the 42nd Annual Meeting of the ACL*, Barcelona, Spain.

Yi Zhang and Valia Kordoni. 2005. A statistical approach towards unknown word type prediction for deep grammars. In *Proc. of the Australasian Language Technology Workshop 2005*, pages 24–31, Sydney, Australia.

Yi Zhang and Valia Kordoni. 2006. Automated deep lexical acquisition for robust open texts processing. In *Proceedings of the Fifth International Conference on Language Resources and Evaluation (LREC 2006)*, Genoa, Italy.

Lexical Reference: a Semantic Matching Subtask

Oren Glickman and **Eyal Shnarch** and **Ido Dagan**
Computer Science Department
Bar Ilan University
Ramat Gan, Israel
{glikmao, dagan}@cs.biu.ac.il

Abstract

Semantic lexical matching is a prominent subtask within text understanding applications. Yet, it is rarely evaluated in a direct manner. This paper proposes a definition for *lexical reference* which captures the common goals of lexical matching. Based on this definition we created and analyzed a test dataset that was utilized to directly evaluate, compare and improve lexical matching models. We suggest that such decomposition of the global semantic matching task is critical in order to fully understand and improve individual components.

1 Introduction

A fundamental task for text understanding applications is to identify semantically equivalent pieces of text. For example, Question Answering (QA) systems need to match corresponding parts in the question and in the answer passage, even though such parts may be expressed in different terms. Summarization systems need to recognize (redundant) semantically matching parts in multiple sentences that are phrased differently. Other applications, such as information extraction and retrieval, face pretty much the same semantic matching task. The degree of semantic matching found is typically factored into systems' scoring and ranking mechanisms. The recently proposed framework of textual entailment (Dagan et al., 2006) attempts to formulate the generic semantic matching problem in an application independent manner.

The most commonly implemented semantic matching component addresses the lexical level. At this level the goal is to identify whether the meaning of a lexical item of one text is expressed also within the other text. Typically, lexical matching models measure the degree of literal lexical overlap, augmented with lexical substitution criteria based on resources such as Wordnet or the output of statistical similarity methods (see Section 2). Many systems apply semantic matching only at the lexical level, which is used to approximate the overall degree of semantic matching between texts. Other systems incorporate lexical matching as a component within more complex models that examine matching at higher syntactic and semantic levels.

While lexical matching models are so prominent within semantic systems they are rarely evaluated in a direct manner. Typically, improvements to a lexical matching model are evaluated by their marginal contribution to overall system performance. Yet, such global and indirect evaluation does not indicate the absolute performance of the model relative to the sheer lexical matching task for which it was designed. Furthermore, the indirect application-dependent evaluation mode does not facilitate improving lexical matching models in an application dependent manner, and does not allow proper comparison of such models which were developed (and evaluated) by different researchers within different systems.

This paper proposes a generic definition for the lexical matching task, which we term *lexical reference*. This definition is application independent and enables annotating test datasets that evaluate directly lexical matching models. Consequently, we created a dataset annotated for lexical reference, using a sample of sentence pairs (text-hypothesis) from the 1st Recognising Textual Entailment dataset. Further analysis identified sev-

Proceedings of the 2006 Conference on Empirical Methods in Natural Language Processing (EMNLP 2006), pages 172–179,
Sydney, July 2006. ©2006 Association for Computational Linguistics

eral sub-types of lexical reference, pointing at the many interesting cases where lexical reference is derived from a complete context rather than from a particular matching lexical item.

Next, we used the lexical reference dataset to evaluate and compare several state-of-the-art approaches for lexical matching. Having a direct evaluation task enabled us to capture the actual performance level of these models, to reveal their relative strengths and weaknesses, and even to construct a simple combination of two models that outperforms all the original ones. Overall, we suggest that it is essential to decompose global semantic matching and textual entailment tasks into proper subtasks, like lexical reference. Such decomposition is needed in order to fully understand the behavior of individual system components and to guide their future improvements.

2 Background

2.1 Term Matching

Thesaurus-based term expansion is a commonly used technique for enhancing the recall of NLP systems and coping with lexical variability. Expansion consists of altering a given text (usually a query) by adding terms of similar meaning. WordNet is commonly used as a source of related words for expansion. For example, many QA systems perform expansion in the retrieval phase using query related words based on WordNet's lexical relations such as synonymy or hyponymy (e.g (Harabagiu et al., 2000; Hovy et al., 2001)). Lexical similarity measures (e.g. (Lin, 1998)) have also been suggested to measure semantic similarity. They are based on the distributional hypothesis, suggesting that words that occur within similar contexts are semantically similar.

2.2 Textual Entailment

The Recognising Textual Entailment (RTE-1) challenge (Dagan et al., 2006) is an attempt to promote an abstract generic task that captures major semantic inference needs across applications. The task requires to recognize, given two text fragments, whether the meaning of one text can be inferred (entailed) from another text. Different techniques and heuristics were applied on the RTE-1 dataset to specifically model textual entailment. Interestingly, a number of works (e.g. (Bos and Markert, 2005; Corley and Mihalcea, 2005; Jijkoun and de Rijke, 2005; Glickman et al., 2006)) applied or utilized lexical based word overlap measures. Various word-to-word similarity measures where applied, including distributional similarity (such as (Lin, 1998)), web-based co-occurrence statistics and WordNet based similarity measures (such as (Leacock et al., 1998)).

2.3 Paraphrase Acquisition

A substantial body of work has been dedicated to learning patterns of semantic equivalency between different language expressions, typically considered as paraphrases. Recently, several works addressed the task of acquiring paraphrases (semi-) automatically from corpora. Most attempts were based on identifying corresponding sentences in parallel or 'comparable' corpora, where each corpus is known to include texts that largely correspond to texts in another corpus (e.g. (Barzilay and McKeown, 2001)). Distributional Similarity was also used to identify paraphrase patterns from a single corpus rather than from a comparable set of corpora (Lin and Pantel, 2001). Similarly, (Glickman and Dagan, 2004) developed statistical methods that match verb paraphrases within a regular corpus.

3 The Lexical Reference Dataset

3.1 Motivation and Definition

One of the major observations of the 1st Recognizing Textual Entailment (RTE-1) challenge referred to the rich structure of entailment modeling systems and the need to evaluate and optimize individual components within them. When building such a compound system it is valuable to test each component directly during its development, rather than indirectly evaluating the component's performance via the behavior of the entire system. If given tools to evaluate each component independently researchers can target and perfect the performance of the subcomponents without the need of building and evaluating the entire end-to-end system.

A common subtask, addressed by practically all participating systems in RTE-1, was to recognize whether each lexical meaning in the hypothesis is referenced by some meaning in the corresponding text. We suggest that this common goal can be captured through the following definition:

Definition 1 *A word w is **lexically referenced** by a text t if there is an explicit or implied reference* *from a set of words in t to a possible meaning of w.*

Lexical reference may be viewed as a natural extension of textual entailment for sub-sentential hypotheses such as words. In this work we focus on words meanings, however this work can be directly generalized to word compounds and phrases. A concrete version of detailed annotation guidelines for lexical reference is presented in the next section.[1] Lexical Reference is, in some sense, a more general notion than paraphrases. If the text includes a paraphrase for w then naturally it does refer to w's meaning. However, a text need not include a paraphrase for the concrete meaning of the referenced word w, but only an implied reference. Accordingly, the referring part might be a large segment of the text, which captures information different than w's meaning, but still implies a reference to w as part of the text's meaning.

It is typically a necessary, but not sufficient, condition for textual entailment that the lexical concepts in a hypothesis h are referred in a given text t. For example, in order to infer from a text the hypothesis "*a dog bit a man*," it is a necessary that the concepts of *dog*, *bite* and *man* must be referenced by the text, either directly or in an implied manner. However, for proper entailment it is further needed that the right relations would hold between these concepts[2]. Therefore lexical entailment should typically be a component within a more complex entailment modeling (or semantic matching) system.

3.2 Dataset Creation and Annotation Process

We created a lexical reference dataset derived from the RTE-1 development set by randomly choosing 400 out of the 567 text-hypothesis examples. We then created sentence-word examples for all content words in the hypotheses which do not appear in the corresponding sentence and are not a morphological derivation of a word in it (since a simple morphologic module could easily identify these cases). This resulted in a total of 708 lexical reference examples. Two annotators annotated these examples as described in the next section. Taking the same approach as of the RTE-1 dataset creation (Dagan et al., 2006), we limited our experiments to the resulting 580 examples that the two annotators agreed upon[3].

3.2.1 Annotation guidelines

We asked two annotators to annotate the sentence-word examples according to the following guidelines. Given a sentence and a target word the annotators were asked to decide whether the target word is referred by the sentence (true) or not (false). Annotators were guided to mark the pair as true in the following cases:

Word: if there is a word in the sentence which, in the context of the sentence, implies a meaning of the target word (e.g. a synonym or hyponym), or which implies a reference to the target word's meaning (e.g. blind→see, sight). See examples 1-2 in Table 1 where the word that implies the reference is emphasized in the text. Note that in example 2 murder is not a synonym of died nor does it share the same meaning of died; however it is clear from its presence in the sentence that it refers to a death. Also note that in example 8 although home is a possible synonym for house, in the context of the text it does not appear in that meaning and the example should be annotated as false.

Phrase: if there is a multi-word independent expression in the sentence that implies the target (implication in the same sense that a Word does). See examples 3-4 in Table 1.

Context: if there is a clear reference to the meaning of the target word by the overall meaning of some part(s) of the sentence (possibly all the sentence), though it is not referenced by any single word or phrase. The reference is derived from the complete context of the relevant sentence part. See examples 5-7 in Table 1.

If there is no reference from the sentence to the target word the annotators were instructed to choose false. In example 9 in Table 1 the target word "HIV-positive" should be considered as one word that cannot be broken down from its unit and although both the general term "HIV status" and the more specific term "HIV negative" are referred to, the target word cannot be understood or derived from the text. In example 10 although the year 1945 may refer to a specific war, there is no "war" either specifically or generally understood by the text.

[1] These terms should not be confused with the use of *lexical entailment* in WordNet, which is used to describe an entailment relationship between verb lexical types, nor with the related notion of *reference* in classical linguistics, generally describing the relation between nouns or pronouns and objects that are named by them (Frege, 1892)

[2] or quoting the known journalism saying – "*Dog bites man*" isn't news, but "*Man bites dog*" is.

[3] dataset avaiable at `http://ir-srv.cs.biu.ac.il:64080/emnlp06_dataset.zip`

ID	TEXT	TARGET	VALUE
1	Oracle had fought to keep the **forms** from being released.	document	word
2	The court found two men guilty of **murdering** Shapour Bakhtiar.	died	word
3	The new information prompted them to **call off** the search.	cancelled	phrase
4	Milan, **home of** the famed La Scala opera house,...	located	phrase
5	Successful **plaintiffs** recovered **punitive damages** in Texas discrimination **cases** 53	legal	context
6	Recreational marijuana smokers are no more **likely to develop oral cancer** than nonusers.	risk	context
7	A bus ticket **cost nowadays 5.2 NIS whereas last year it cost 4.9**.	increase	context
8	Pakistani officials announced that two South African men in their custody had confessed to planning attacks at popular tourist spots in their home country.	house	false
9	For women who are HIV negative or who do not know their HIV status, breastfeeding should be promoted for six months.	HIV-positive	false
10	On Feb. 1, 1945, the Polish government made Warsaw its capital, and an office for urban reconstruction was set up.	war	false

Table 1: Lexical Reference Annotation Examples

3.2.2 Annotation results

We measured the agreement on the lexical reference binary task (in which Word, Phrase and Context are conflated to true). The resulting kappa statistic of 0.63 is regarded as substantial agreement (Landis and Koch, 1997). The resulting dataset is not balanced in terms of true and false examples and a straw-baseline for accuracy is 0.61, representing a system which predicts all examples as true.

3.3 Dataset Analysis

In a similar manner to (Bar-Haim et al., 2005; Vanderwende et al., 2005) we investigated the relationship between lexical reference and textual entailment. We checked the performance of a textual entailment system which relies solely on an ideal lexical reference component which makes no mistakes and asserts that a hypothesis is entailed from a text if and only if all content words in the hypothesis are referred in the text. Based on the lexical reference dataset annotations, such an "ideal" system would obtain an accuracy of 74% on the corresponding subset of the textual entailment task. The corresponding precision is 68% and a recall of 82%. This is significantly higher than the results of the best performing systems that participated in the challenge on the RTE-1 test set. This suggests that lexical reference is a valuable subtask for entailment. Interestingly, a similar entailment system based on a lexical reference component which doesn't account for the contextual lexical reference (i.e. all Context annotations are regarded as false) would achieve an accuracy of only 63% with 41% precision and a recall of 63%. This suggests that lexical reference in general and contextual entailment in particular, play an important (though not sufficient) role in entailment recognition.

Further, we wanted to investigate the validity of the assumption that for entailment relationship to hold all content words in the hypothesis must be referred by the text. We examined the examples in our dataset which were derived from text-hypothesis pairs that were annotated as true (entailing) in the RTE dataset. Out of 257 such examples only 34 were annotated as false by both annotators. Table 2 lists a few such examples in which entailment at whole holds, however, there exists a word in the hypothesis (highlighted in the table) which is not lexically referenced by the text. In many cases, the target word was part of a non compositional compound in the hypothesis, and therefore should not be expected to be referenced by the text (see examples 1-2). This finding indicates that the basic assumption is a reasonable approximation for entailment. We could not have revealed this fact without the dataset for the subtask of lexical reference.

4 Lexical Reference Models

The lexical reference dataset facilitates qualitative and quantitative comparison of various lexical models. This section describes four state-of-the-art models that can be applied to the lexical reference task. The performance of these models was tested and analyzed, as described in the next section, using the lexical reference dataset. All models assign a $[0, 1]$ score to a given pair of text t and target word u which can be interpreted as the confidence that u is lexically referenced in t.

ID	TEXT	HYPOTHESIS	ENTAIL-MENT	REFER-ENCE
1	Iran is said to give up al Qaeda members.	Iran **hands** over al Qaeda members.	true	false
2	It would help the economy by putting people back to work and more money in the hands of consumers.	More money in the hands of consumers means more money can be spent to get the economy **going**.	true	false
3	The Securities and Exchange Commission's new rule to beef up the independence of mutual fund boards represents an industry defeat.	The SEC's new rule will **give** boards independence.	true	false
4	Texas Data Recovery is also successful at retrieving lost data from notebooks and laptops, regardless of age, make or model.	In the event of a **disaster** you could use Texas Data Recovery and you will have the capability to restore lost data.	true	false

Table 2: examples demonstrating cases when lexical entailment does not correlate with entailment. Target word is shown in bold.

4.1 WordNet

Following the common practice in NLP applications (see Section 2.1) we evaluated the performance of a straight-forward utilization of WordNet's lexical information. Our wordnet model first lemmatizes the text and target word. It then assigns a score of 1 if the text contains a synonym, hyponym or derived form of the target word and a score of 0 otherwise.

4.2 Similarity

As a second measure we used the distributional similarity measure of (Lin, 1998). For a text t and a word u we assign the max similarity score as follows:

$$similarity(t, u) = \max_{v \in t} sim(u, v) \qquad (1)$$

where $sim(u, v)$ is the similarity score for u and v[4].

4.3 Alignment model

(Glickman et al., 2006) was among the top scoring systems on the RTE-1 challenge and supplies a probabilistically motivated lexical measure based on word co-occurrence statistics. It is defined for a text t and a word u as follows:

$$align(t, u) = \max_{v \in t} \mathrm{P}(u|v) \qquad (2)$$

where $\mathrm{P}(u|v)$ is simply the co-occurrence probability – the probability that a sentence containing v also contains u. The co-occurrence statistics were collected from the Reuters Corpus Volume 1.

[4]the scores were obtained from the following online resource: `http://www.cs.ualberta.ca/~lindek/downloads.htm`

4.4 Baysean model

(Glickman et al., 2005) provide a contextual measure which takes into account the whole context of the text rather than from a single word in the text as do the previous models. This model is the only model which addresses contextual reference rather than just word-to-word matching. The model is based on a Naïve Bayes text classification approach in which corpus sentences serve as documents and the class is the reference of the target word u. Sentences containing the word u are used as positive examples while all other sentences are considered as negative examples. It is defined for a text t and a word u as follows:

$$bayes(t, u) = \frac{\mathrm{P}(u) \prod_{v \in t} \mathrm{P}(v|u)^{n(v,t)}}{\mathrm{P}(\neg u) \prod_{v \in t} \mathrm{P}(v|\neg u)^{n(v,t)} + \mathrm{P}(u) \prod_{v \in t} \mathrm{P}(v|u)^{n(v,t)}} \qquad (3)$$

where $n(w, t)$ is the number of times word w appears in t, $\mathrm{P}(u)$ is the probability that a sentence contains the word u and $\mathrm{P}(v|\neg u)$ is the probability that a sentence NOT containing u contains v. In order to reduce data size and to account for zero probabilities we applied smoothing and information gain based feature selection on the data prior to running the model. The co-occurrence probabilities were collected from sentences from the Reuters corpus in a similar manner to the alignment model.

4.5 Combined Model

The WordNet and Bayesian models are derived from quite different motivations. One would expect the WordNet model to be better in identifying the word-to-word explicit reference examples while the Bayesian model is expected to model the contextualy implied references. For this reason we tried to combine forces by evaluating a naïve linear interpolation of the two models (by simply averaging the score of the two models). This model have not been previously suggested and to the best of our knowledge this type of combination is novel.

5 Empirical Evaluation and Analysis

5.1 Results

In order to evaluate the scores produced by the various models as a potential component in an entailment system we compared the recall-precision graphs. In addition we compared the *average precision* which is a single number measure equivalent to the area under an uninterpolated recall-precision curve and is commonly used to evaluate a systems ranking ability (Voorhees and Harman, 1999). On our dataset an average precision greater than 0.65 is better than chance at the 0.05 level and an average precision greater than 0.66 is significant at the 0.01 level.

Figure 1 compares the average precision and recall-precision results for the various models. As can be seen, the combined wordnet+bayes model performs best. In terms of average precision, the similarity and wordnet models are comparable and are slightly better than bayes. The alignment model, however, is not significantly better than random guessing. The recall-precision figure indicates that the baysian model succeeds to rank quite well both within the the positively scored wordnet examples and within the negatively scored wordnet examples and thus resulting in improved average precision of the combined model. A better understanding of the systems' performance is evident from the following analysis.

5.2 Analysis

Table 3 lists a few examples from the lexical reference dataset along with their gold-standard annotation and the Bayesian model score. Manual inspection of the data shows that the Bayesian model commonly assigns a low score to correct examples which have an entailing trigger word or phrase in the sentence but yet the context of the sentence as a whole is not typical for the target hypothesized entailed word. For example, in example 5 the entailing phrase 'set in place' and in example 6 the entailing word 'founder' do appear in the text however the contexts of the sentences are not typical news domain contexts of issued or founded. An interesting future work would be to change the generative story and model to account for such cases.

The WordNet model identified a matching word in the text for 99 out of the 580 examples. This corresponds to a somewhat low recall of 25% and a quite high precision of 90%. Table 4 lists typical mistakes of the wordnet model. Examples 1-3 are false positive examples in which there is a word in the text (emphasized in the table) which is a synonym or hyponym of the target word for some sense in WordNet, however in the context of the text it is not of such a sense. Examples 4-6 show false negative examples, in which the annotators identified a trigger word in the text (emphasized in the table) but yet it or no other word in the text is a synonym or hyponym of the target word.

5.3 Subcategory analysis

	word	phrase	context	false
word	178	16	59	32
phrase	4	12	9	4
context	15	5	56	25
false	24	5	38	226

Table 5: inter-annotator confusion matrix for the auxiliary annotation.

As seen above, the combined model outperforms the others since it identifies both word-to-word lexical reference as well as context-to-word lexical reference. These are quite different cases. We asked the annotators to state the subcategory when they annotated an example as true (as described in the annotation guidelines in Section 3.2.1). The *Word* subcategory corresponds to a word-to-word match and *Phrase* and *Context* subcategories correspond to more than one word to word match. As can be expected, the agreement on such a task resulted in a lower Kappa of 0.5 which corresponds to moderate agreement (Landis and Koch, 1997). the confusion matrix between the two annotators is presented in Table 5. This decomposition enables the evaluation of the strength and weakness of different lexical reference modules, free from the context of the bigger entailment system.

We used the subcategories dataset to test the performances of the different models. Table 6 lists for each subcategory the recall of correctly identified examples for each model's 25% recall level. The table shows that the wordnet and similarity models' strength is in identifying examples where lexical reference is triggered by a dominant word in the sentence. The bayes model, however,

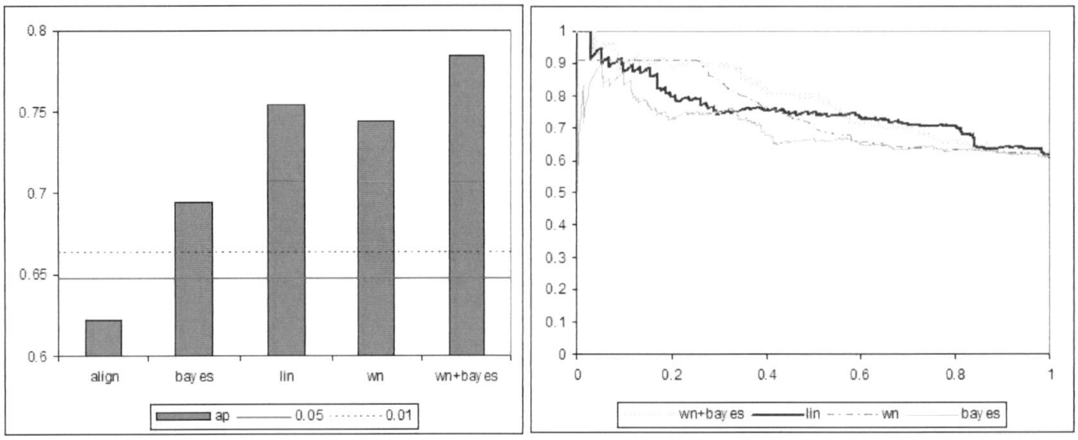

Figure 1: comparison of average precision (left) and recall-precision (right) results for the various models

id	text	token	annotation	score
1	*QNX Software Systems Ltd., a leading provider of real-time software and services to the embedded computing market, is pleased to announce the appointment of Mr. Sachin Lawande to the position of vice president, engineering services.*	named	PHRASE	0.98
2	*NIH's FY05 budget request of $28.8 billion includes $2 billion for the National Institute of General Medical Sciences, a 3.4-percent increase, and $1.1 billion for the National Center for Research Resources, and a 7.2-percent decrease from FY04 levels.*	reduced	WORD	0.91
3	*Pakistani officials announced that two South African men in their custody had confessed to planning attacks at popular tourist spots in their home country.*	security	CONTEXT	0.80
4	*With $549 million in cash as of June 30, Google can easily afford to make amends.*	shares	FALSE	0.03
5	*In the year 538, Cyrus set in place a policy which demanded the return of the various gods to their proper places.*	issued	PHRASE	7e-4
6	*The black Muslim activist said that he had relieved Muhammad of his duties "until he demonstrates that he is willing to conform to the manner of representing Allah and the honorable Elijah Muhammad (founder of the Nation of Islam)".*	founded	WORD	3e-6

Table 3: A sample from the lexical reference dataset along with the Bayesian model's score

id	text	token	annotation
1	*Kerry **hit** Bush hard on his conduct on the war in Iraq*	shot	FALSE
2	*Pakistani officials announced that two South African **men** in their custody had confessed to planning attacks at popular tourist spots in their home country*	forces	FALSE
3	*It would help the economy by putting people back to **work** and more money in the hands of consumers*	get	FALSE
4	*Eating lots of foods that are a good source of fiber may keep your blood **glucose** from rising too fast after you eat*	sugar	WORD
5	*Hippos do come into conflict with **people** quite often*	human	WORD
6	*Weinstock painstakingly reviewed dozens of studies for evidence of any link between sunscreen use and either an increase or decrease in **melanoma***	cancer	WORD

Table 4: A few erroneous examples of WordNet model

is better at identifying phrase and context examples. The combined WordNet and Bayesian models' strength can be explained by the quite different behaviors of the two models - the WordNet model seems to be better in identifying the word-to-word explicit reference examples while the Bayesian model is better in modeling the contextual implied references.

6 Conclusions

This paper proposed an explicit task definition for *lexical reference*. This task captures directly the goal of common lexical matching models, which typically operate within more complex systems

method	word	disagreement	phrase/context
wordnet	38%	9%	17%
similarity	39%	7%	17%
bayes	22%	21%	37%

Table 6: Breakdown of recall of correctly identified example types at an overall system's recall of 25%. Disagreement refers to examples for which the annotators did not agree on the subcategory annotation (word vs. phrase/context).

that address more complex tasks. This definition enabled us to create an annotated dataset for the lexical reference task, which provided insights into interesting sub-classes that require different types of modeling. The dataset enabled us to make a direct evaluation and comparison of lexical matching models, reveal insightful differences between them, and create a simple improved model combination. In the long run, we believe that the availability of such datasets will facilitate improved models that consider the various sub-cases of lexical reference, as well as applying supervised learning to optimize model combination and performance.

References

[Bar-Haim et al.2005] Roy Bar-Haim, Idan Szpecktor, and Oren Glickman. 2005. Definition and analysis of intermediate entailment levels. In *Proceedings of the ACL Workshop on Empirical Modeling of Semantic Equivalence and Entailment*, pages 55–60, Ann Arbor, Michigan, June. Association for Computational Linguistics.

[Barzilay and McKeown2001] Regina Barzilay and Kathleen McKeown. 2001. Extracting paraphrases from a parallel corpus. In *ACL*, pages 50–57.

[Bos and Markert2005] Johan Bos and Katja Markert. 2005. Recognising textual entailment with logical inference techniques. In *EMNLP*.

[Corley and Mihalcea2005] Courtney Corley and Rada Mihalcea. 2005. Measuring the semantic similarity of texts. In *Proceedings of the ACL Workshop on Empirical Modeling of Semantic Equivalence and Entailment*, pages 13–18.

[Dagan et al.2006] Ido Dagan, Oren Glickman, and Bernardo Magnini, editors. 2006. *The PASCAL Recognising Textual Entailment Challenge*, volume 3944. Lecture Notes in Computer Science.

[Frege1892] Gottlob Frege. 1892. On sense and reference. Reprinted in P. Geach and M. Black, eds., Translations from the Philosophical Writings of Gottlob Frege. 1960.

[Glickman and Dagan2004] Oren Glickman and Ido Dagan, 2004. *Recent Advances in Natural Language Processing III*, chapter Acquiring lexical paraphrases from a single corpus, pages 81–90. John Benjamins.

[Glickman et al.2005] Oren Glickman, Ido Dagan, and Moshe Koppel. 2005. A probabilistic classification approach for lexical textual entailment. In *AAAI*, pages 1050–1055.

[Glickman et al.2006] Oren Glickman, Ido Dagan, and Moshe Koppel. 2006. A lexical alignment model for probabilistic textual entailment, volume 3944. In *Lecture Notes in Computer Science*, pages 287 – 298. Springer.

[Harabagiu et al.2000] Sanda M. Harabagiu, Dan I. Moldovan, Marius Pasca, Rada Mihalcea, Mihai Surdeanu, Razvan C. Bunescu, Roxana Girju, Vasile Rus, and Paul Morarescu. 2000. Falcon: Boosting knowledge for answer engines. In *TREC*.

[Hovy et al.2001] Eduard H. Hovy, Ulf Hermjakob, and Chin-Yew Lin. 2001. The use of external knowledge of factoid QA. In *Text REtrieval Conference*.

[Jijkoun and de Rijke2005] Valentin Jijkoun and Maarten de Rijke. 2005. Recognizing textual entailment using lexical similarity. Proceedings of the PASCAL Challenges Workshop on Recognising Textual Entailment (and forthcoming LNAI book chapter).

[Landis and Koch1997] J. R. Landis and G. G. Koch. 1997. The measurements of observer agreement for categorical data. *Biometrics*, 33:159–174.

[Leacock et al.1998] Claudia Leacock, George A. Miller, and Martin Chodorow. 1998. Using corpus statistics and wordnet relations for sense identification. *Comput. Linguist.*, 24(1):147–165.

[Lin and Pantel2001] Dekang Lin and Patrik Pantel. 2001. Discovery of inference rules for question answering. *Natural Language Engineering*, 4(7):343–360.

[Lin1998] Dekang Lin. 1998. Automatic retrieval and clustering of similar words. In *Proceedings of the 17th international conference on Computational linguistics*, pages 768–774, Morristown, NJ, USA. Association for Computational Linguistics.

[Vanderwende et al.2005] Lucy Vanderwende, Deborah Coughlin, and Bill Dolan. 2005. What syntax can contribute in entailment task. Proceedings of the PASCAL Challenges Workshop on Recognising Textual Entailment.

[Voorhees and Harman1999] Ellen M. Voorhees and Donna Harman. 1999. Overview of the seventh text retrieval conference. In *Proceedings of the Seventh Text REtrieval Conference (TREC-7)*. NIST Special Publication.

Semantic Role Labeling via Instance-Based Learning

Chi-San Althon Lin
Department of Computer Science
Waikato University
Hamilton, New Zealand
cl123@cs.waikato.ac.nz

Tony C. Smith
Department of Computer Science
Waikato University
Hamilton, New Zealand
tcs@cs.waikato.ac.nz

Abstract

This paper demonstrates two methods to improve the performance of instance-based learning (IBL) algorithms for the problem of Semantic Role Labeling (SRL). Two IBL algorithms are utilized: k-Nearest Neighbor (kNN), and Priority Maximum Likelihood (PML) with a modified back-off combination method. The experimental data are the WSJ23 and Brown Corpus test sets from the CoNLL-2005 Shared Task. It is shown that applying the Tree-Based Predicate-Argument Recognition Algorithm (PARA) to the data as a preprocessing stage allows kNN and PML to deliver F_1: 68.61 and 71.02 respectively on the WSJ23, and F_1: 56.96 and 60.55 on the Brown Corpus; an increase of 8.28 in F_1 measurement over the most recent published PML results for this problem (Palmer et al., 2005). Training times for IBL algorithms are very much faster than for other widely used techniques for SRL (e.g. parsing, support vector machines, perceptrons, etc); and the feature reduction effects of PARA yield testing and processing speeds of around 1.0 second per sentence for kNN and 0.9 second per sentence for PML respectively, suggesting that IBL could be a more practical way to perform SRL for NLP applications where it is employed; such as real-time Machine Translation or Automatic Speech Recognition.

1 Introduction

The proceedings from CoNLL2004 and CoNLL2005 detail a wide variety of approaches to Semantic Role Labeling (SRL). Many research efforts utilize machine learning (ML) approaches; such as support vector machines (Moschitti et al., 2004; Pradhan et al., 2004), perceptrons (Carreras et al., 2004), the SNoW learning architecture (Punyakanok et al., 2004), EM-based clustering (Baldewein et al., 2004), transformation-based learning (Higgins, 2004), memory-based learning (Kouchnir, 2004), and inductive learning (Surdeanu et al., 2003). This paper compares two instance-based learning approaches, kNN and PML. The PML method used here utilizes a modification of the backoff lattice method used by Gildea & Jurafsky (2002) to use a set of basic features—specifically, the features employed for learning in this paper are Predicate (pr), Voice (vo), Phrase Type (pt), Distance (di), Head Word (hw), Path (pa), Preposition in a PP (pp), and an "Actor" heuristic.

The general approach presented here is an example of memory-based learning. Many existing SRL systems are also memory-based (Bosch et al., 2004;Kouchnir, 2004), implemented using TiMBL software (http://ilk.kub.nl/software.html) with advanced methods such as Feature Weighting, and so forth. This paper measures the performance of kNN and PML for comparison in terms of accuracy and processing speed, both against each other and against previously published results.

2 Related Work

Features
Most of the systems outlined in CoNLL2004 and CoNLL2005 utilize as many as 30 features for learning approaches to SRL. The research presented here uses only seven of these:

Proceedings of the 2006 Conference on Empirical Methods in Natural Language Processing (EMNLP 2006), pages 180–188,
Sydney, July 2006.

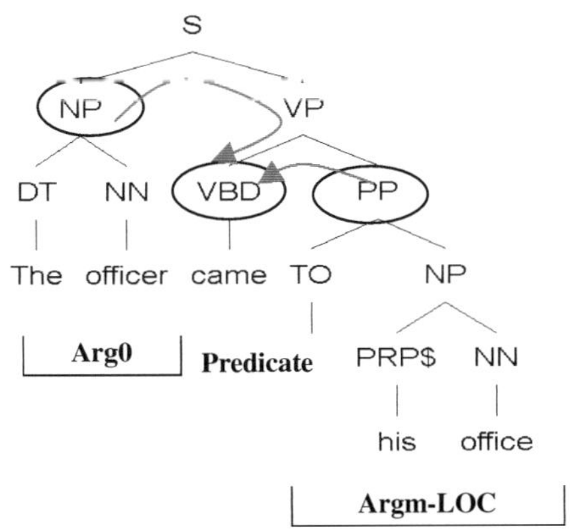

Figure 1. Illustration of path "NP ↑ S ↓ VP ↓ VBD" from a constituent "The officer" to the predicate "came"

.

Predicate – the given predicate lemma
Voice – whether the predicate is realized as an active or passive construction (Pradhan et al., 2004, claim approximately 11% of the sentences in PropBank use a passive instantiation)
Phrase Type – the syntactic category (NP, PP, S, etc.) of the phrase corresponding to the semantic argument
Distance – the relative displacement from the predicate, measured in intervening constituents (negative if the constituent appears prior to the predicate, positive if it appears after it)
Head Word – the syntactic head of the phrase, calculated by finding the last noun of a Noun Phrase
Path – the syntactic path through the parse tree, from the parse constituent to the predicate being classified (for example, in Figure 1, the path from Arg0 – "The officer" to the predicate "came", is represented with the string NP ↑ S ↓ VP ↓ VBD" represent upward and downward movements in the tree respectively)
Preposition – the preposition of an argument in a PP, such as "during", "at", "with", etc (for example, in Figure 1, the preposition for the PP with Argm-Loc label is "to").

In addition, an **actor heuristic** is adopted: where an instance can be labeled as A0 (actor) only if the argument is a subject before the predicate in active voice, or if the preposition "by" appears prior to this argument but after the predicate in a passive voice sentence. For example, if there is a set of labels, A0 (subject or actor) V (active) A0 (non actor), then the latter "A0" after V is skipped and labeled to another suitable role by this heuristic; such as the label with the second highest probability for this argument according to the PML estimate, or with the second shortest distance estimate by kNN.

2.1 k Nearest Neighbour (kNN) Algorithm

One instance-based learning algorithm is k-Nearest Neighbour (kNN), which is suitable when 1) instances can be mapped to points/classifications in n-dimensional feature dimension, 2) fewer than 20 features are utilized, and 3) training data is sufficiently abundant. One advantage of kNN is that training is very fast; one disadvantage is it is generally slow at testing. The implementation of kNN is described as following

1. **Instance base:**
   All the training data is stored in a format similar to Bosch et al., (2004)—specifically, "Role, Predicate, Voice, Phrase type, Distance, Head Word, Path". As an example instance, the second argument of a predicate "take" in the training data is stored as:
   A0 take active NP –1 classics NP ↑ S ↓ VP ↓ VBD
   This format maps each argument to six feature dimensions + one classification.
2. **Distance metric** (Euclidean distance) is defined as:

   $$D(x_i, x_j) = \sqrt{\Sigma(a_r(x_i))-a_r(x_j))^2}$$

   where r=1 to n (n = number of different classifications), and $a_r(x)$ is the r-th feature of instance x. If instances x_i and x_j are identical, then $D(x_i, x_j)=0$ otherwise $D(x_i, x_j)$ represents the vector distance between x_i and x_j.
3. **Classification function**
   Given a query/test instance x_q to be classified, let $x_1, \dots x_k$ denote the k instances from the training data that are nearest to x_q. The classification function is

   $$F\hat{}(x_q) \leftarrow \text{argmax} \, \Sigma \, \delta(v, f(x_i))$$

   where i =1 to k, v =1 to m (m = size of training data), $\delta(a,b)=1$ if a=b, 0 otherwise; and v denotes a semantic role for each instance of training data.

Computational complexity for kNN is linear, such that $T_{kNN} \to O(m * n)$, which is proportional to the product of the number of features (m) and the number of training instances (n).

2.2 Priority Maximum Likelihood (PML) Estimation

Gildea & Jurafsky (2002), Gildea & Hockenmaier (2003) and Palmer et al., (2005) use a statistical approach based on Maximum Likelihood method for SRL, with different backoff combination methods in which selected probabilities are combined with linear interpolation. The probability estimation or Maximum Likelihood is based on the number of known features available. If the full feature set is selected the probability is calculated by

$$P(r \mid pr, vo, pt, di, hw, pa, pp) = \#(r, pr, vo, pt, di, hw, pa, pp) \,/\, \#(pr, vo, pt, di, hw, pa, pp)$$

Gildea & Jurafsky (2002) claims "*there is a trade-off between more-specific distributions, which have higher accuracy but lower coverage, and less-specific distributions, which have lower accuracy but higher coverage*" and that the selection of feature subsets is exponential; and that selection of combinations of different feature subsets is doubly exponential, which is NP-complete. Gildea & Jurafsky (2002) propose the backoff combination in a linear interpolation for both coverage and precision. Following their lead, the research presented here uses Priority Maximum Likelihood Estimation modified from the backoff combination as follows:

$$P'(r \mid pr, vo, pt, di, hw, pa, pp) = \lambda_1{*}P(r \mid pr, pp) + \lambda_2{*}P(r \mid pt, pr, pp) + \lambda_3{*}P(r \mid pt, pa, pr, pp) + \lambda_4{*}P(r \mid pt, di, vo, pp) + \lambda_5{*}P(r \mid pt, di, vo, pr, pp) + \lambda_6{*}P(r \mid hw, pp) + \lambda_7{*}P(r \mid hw, pr, pp) + \lambda_8{*}P(r \mid hw, pt, pr, pp)$$

where $\Sigma_i \lambda_i = 1$.

Figure 2 depicts a graphic organization of the priority combination with more-specific distribution toward the top, similar to Palmer et al. (2005) but adding another preposition feature. The backoff lattice is consulted to calculate probabilities for whichever subset of features is available to combine. As Gildea & Jurasksy (2002) state, "*the less-specific distributions were used only when no data were present for any more-specific distribution. Thus, the distributions selected are arranged in a cut across the lattice representing the most-specific distributions for which data are available.*"

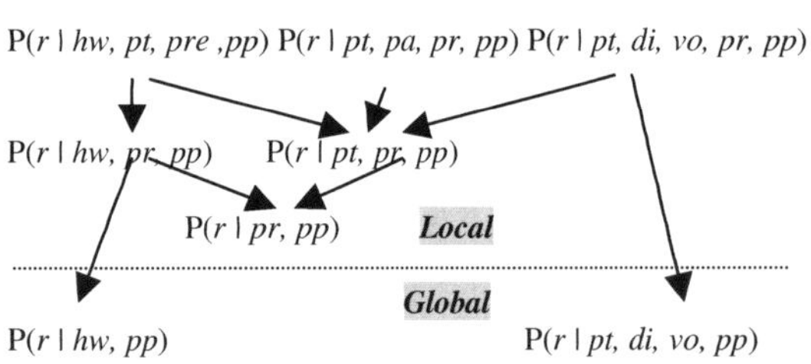

Figure 2. Combination of Priority Estimation for PML system originated from Gildea et al., (2002)

The classification decision is made by the following calculation for each argument in a sentence: $\arg\max_{r_{1..n}} P(r_{1...n} \mid f_{1...n})$ This approach is described in more detail in Gildea and Jurasky (2002).

The computational complexity of PML is hard to calculate due to the many different distributions at each priority level. In Figure 2, the two calculations $P(r \mid hw, pp)$, and $P(r \mid pt, di, vo, pp)$ belong to the global search, while the rest belong to a local search which can reduce the computational complexity. Examination of the details of execution time (described in the results section of this paper) show that a plot of the execution time exhibits logarithmic characteristics, implying that the computational complexity for PML is log-linear, such that $T_{PML} \rightarrow O(m * \log n)$ where m denotes the size of features and n denotes the size of training data.

2.3 Predicate-Argument Recognition Algorithm (PARA)

Lin & Smith (2005; 2006) describe a tree-based predicate-argument recognition algorithm (PARA). PARA simply finds all boundaries for given predicates by browsing input parse-trees, such as given by Charniak's parser or hand-corrected parses. There are three major types of phrases including given predicates, which are VP, NP, and PP. Boundaries can be recognized within boundary areas or from the top levels of clauses (as in Xue & Palmer, 2004). Figure 3 shows the basic algorithm of PARA, and more details can be found in Lin & Smith (2006). The best state-of-the-art ML technique using the same syntactic information (Moschitti, 2005) only just outperforms a preliminary version of PARA in F_1 from 80.72 to 81.52 for boundary recognition tasks. But PARA is much faster than all other existing techniques, and is therefore used for preprocessing in this study to minimize query time when applying instance-based learning to SRL. The computational complexity of PARA is constant.

3 System Architecture

There are two stages to this system: the building stage (comparable to training for inductive systems) and testing (or classification). The building stage shown in Figure 4 just stores all feature representations of training instances in memory without any calculations. All instances are stored in memory in the format described earlier, denoting {Role (r), Predicate (pr), Voice (vo),

Phrase Type (pt), Path (pa), Distance (di), Head Word (hw), Preposition in a PP (pp) }. Figure 5 characterizes the testing stage, where new instances are classified by matching their feature representation to all instances in memory in order to find the most similar instances. There are two tasks during the testing stage: Argument Identification (or Boundary recognition) performed by PARA, and Argument Classification (or Role Labeling) performed using either kNN or PML. This approach is thus a "lazy learning" strategy applied to SRL because no calculations occur during the building stage.

4 Data, Evaluation, and Parsers

The research outlined here uses the dataset released by the CoNLL-05 Shared Task (http://www.lsi.upc.edu/~srlconll/soft.html). It includes several Wall Street Journal sections with parse-trees from both Charniak's (2000) parser and Collins' (1999) parser. These sections are also part of the PropBank corpus (http://www.cis.upenn.edu/~treebank). WSJ sections 20 and 21 (with Charniak's parses) were used as test data. PARA operates directly on the parse tree. Evaluation is carried out using precision, recall and F_1 measures of assignment-accuracy of predicated arguments. Precision (p) is the proportion of arguments predicated by the system that are correct. Recall (r) is the proportion of correct arguments in the dataset that are predicated by the system.

Finally, the F_1 measure computes the harmonic mean of precision and recall, such that $F_1 = 2*p*r / (p+r)$, and is the most commonly used primary measure when comparing different SRL systems. For consistency, the performance of PARA for boundary recognition is tested using the official evaluation script from CoNLL 2005, *srl-eval.pl* (http://www.lsi.upc.edu/~srlconll/soft.html) in all experiments presented in this paper. Related statistics of training data and testing data are outlined in Table 1. The average number of predicates in a sentence for WSJ02-21 is 2.27, and each predicate comes with an average of 2.64 arguments.

Create_Boundary(*predicate*, *tree*)

If the phrase type of the ***predicate*** == VP

- find the boundary area (the closest S clause)
- find NP before ***predicate***
- If there is no NP, then find the closest NP from Ancestors.
- find if WHNP in it's siblings of the boundary area,

  if found // for what, which, that , who,...

  - if the word of the first WP's family is "what" then
    - add WHNP to boundary list

  else // not what, such as who which,...

  - find the closest NP from Ancestors
  - add the NP to the boundary list and add this WHNP to boundary list as reference of NP

- add valid boundaries of the rest of constituents to boundary list.

If phrase type of the ***predicate*** ==NP

- find the boundary area (the NP clause)
- find RB(POS) before ***predicate*** and add to boundary list.
- Add this ***predicate*** to boundary list.
- Add the rest of word group after the ***predicate*** and before the end of the NP clause as a whole boundary to boundary list.

If phrase type of the ***predicate*** ==PP

- find the boundary area (the PP clause)
- find the closet NP from Ancestors if the lemma of the ***predicate*** is "include", and add this NP to boundary list.(special for PropBank)
- Add this ***predicate*** to boundary list.
-

Add the rest of children of this ***predicate*** to boundary list or add one closest NP outside the boundary area to boundary list if there is no child after this ***predicate***.

Figure 3. Outline of the Predicate Argument Recognition Algorithm (PARA)

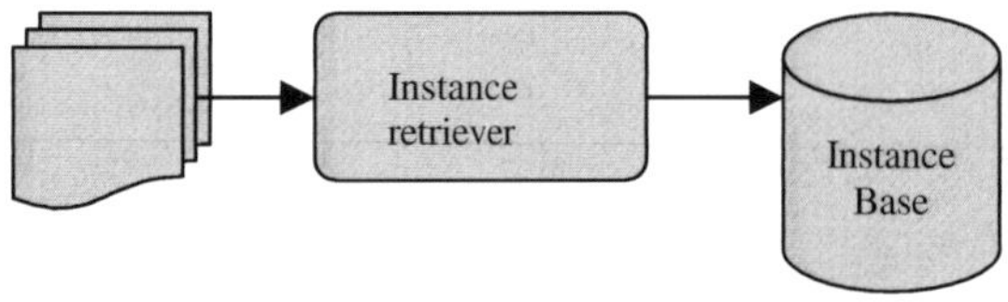

Figure 4. Illustration of System Architecture for the building stage

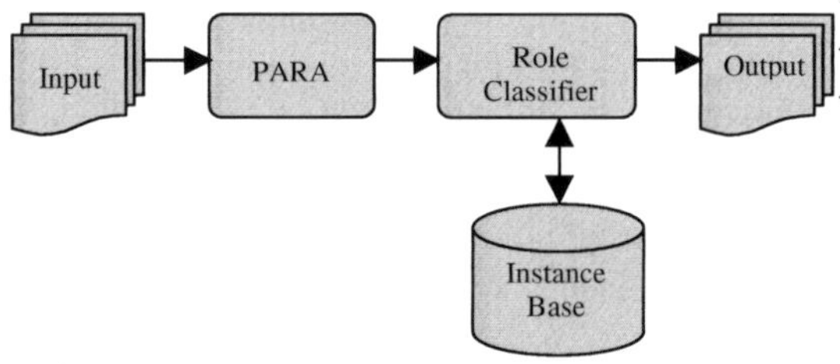

Figure 5. Illustration of System Architecture for the testing stage

5 Experiments and Results

Experimental results were obtained for part of the Brown corpus (the part provided by CoNLL-2005) and for Wall Street Journal (WSJ) Sections 21, 23, and 24 using different training data sets (WSJ 21, WSJ 15 to 18, and WSJ 02 to 21) shown in Table 1. There are two tasks, Role classification with known arguments as input, and Boundary recognition & Role classification with gold (hand-corrected) parses or auto (Charniak's) parses. In addition, execution speed, the learning curve, and some further results for exploration of kNN and PML are also included below.

5.1 WSJ 24 with known arguments

Table 2 shows the results from kNN and PML with known boundaries/arguments (i.e. the systems are given the correct arguments for role classification). All training datasets (WSJ02-21) include Charniak's parse trees. The table shows that PML achieves F1: 2.69 better than kNN.

5.2 Features & Heuristic on WSJ 24 with known arguments

Table 3 shows the contribution of each feature and the actor heuristic by excluding one feature or heuristic. It indicates that Head Word, Preposition, and Distance are the three features that contribute most to system accuracy, and the additional Actor heuristic is fourth. Path, Phrase type and Voice are the three features contibuting the least for both classification algorithms.

	W02-21	W15-18	W21	W23	W24	Brown
Sent	39,832	8,936	1,671	2,416	1,346	426
Tok	950,028	211,727	40,039	56,684	32,853	7,159
Pred	90,750	19,098	3,627	5,267	3,248	804
Verb	3,101	1,838	855	982	860	351
Args	239,858	50,182	9,598	14,077	8,346	2,177

Table 1. Counts on the data sets used in this paper from CoNLL 2005 Shared Task

Known Boundary on WSJ 24

Algorithm	P	R	F1	Lacc
kNN	83.71	83.73	83.72	85.03
PML	86.29	86.52	86.41	87.20

Table 2. Illustration of results by kNN (k=1) and PML on WSJ Section 24 with known arguments

5.3 Learning Curve

Table 4 shows that performance improves as more training data is provided; and that PML outperforms kNN by about F_1:2.8 on average for WSJ 24 for the three different training sets, mainly because the backoff lattice improves both recall and precision. The table shows that it is not always beneficial to include all features for labeling all roles. While $P(r \mid hw, pt, pre, pp)$ is mainly for adjunctive roles (e.g. AM-TMP), $P(r \mid pt, di, vo, pr, pp)$ is mainly for core roles (e.g. A0).

5.4 Performance of Execution Time

Building (or training) time is about 2.5 minutes for both PML and kNN, whereas it takes anywhere from about 10 hours to 60 hours for other ML-based architectures (according to the data presented by McCracken http://www.lsi.upc.es/~srlconll/st05/slides/mccracken.pdf). Table 5 shows average execution time (in seconds) per sentence for the two algorithms. PML runs faster than kNN when all 20 training datasets are used (i.e. WSJ 02 to 21). A graphic illustration of execution speed is shown in Figure 6. The simulation formulas for PML and kNN are "$y = 0.1734\mathrm{Ln}(x) - 0.9046$" and "$y = 2.441*10^{-5} x + 0.0129$" respectively. "$x$" denotes numbers of training sentences, and "y" denotes second per sentence related to "x" training sentences. The execution time for PML is about 8 times longer than kNN for 1.7k training sentences, but PML ultimately runs faster than kNN on all 39.8K training sentences (and, extrapolating from the graph in Figure 6, on any larger datasets). Thus PML seems generally more suitable for large training data.

Training sets	KNN	PML
WSJ 21	0.050	0.396
WSJ 15 - 18	0.241	0.687
WSJ 02 - 21	1.000	0.941

Table 5. Illustration of results for execution time by kNN and PML on WSJ 24 with known arguments

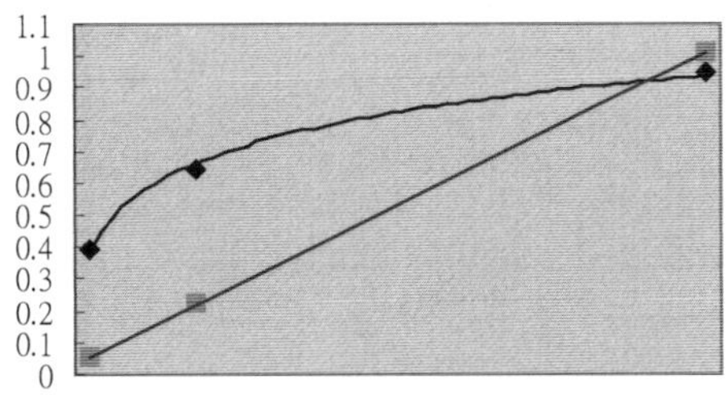

Figure 6. Curve of execution time for kNN (k=1) and PML on WSJ 24 with known arguments

5.5 WSJ 24 with Gold parses and PARA

Table 6 shows performance for both systems when gold (hand-corrected) parses are supplied and PARA preprocessing is employed. Compared to the results in Table 4, the performance on the combined training sets (WSJ 02 to 21) drops F_1:9.24 and Lacc (label accuracy):2.4 for kNN; and drops F_1:8.02 and Lacc:0.66 for PML respectively. This may indicate that PML is more error tolerant in labeling accuracy. However, both systems perform worse due largely to an idiosyncratic problem in the PARA-preprocessor when dealing with hand-corrected parses—ultimately due to a particular parsing error.

5.6 WSJ 24 with Charniak's parses and PARA

Table 7 shows the performance of both systems using auto-parsing (i.e. Charniak's parser) and PARA argument recognition. Compared to the results in Table 4, the performance on all training sets (WSJ 02 to 21) drops F_1:17.25 and Lacc:0.65 for kNN, and F_1:16.78 and Lacc:-0.78 (i.e. increasing Lacc) for PML respectively. Both systems drop a lot in F_1 due to errors caused by the auto-parser (in particular errors relating to punctuation), whose effects are subsequently exacerbated by PARA. Even so, the label accuracy (Lacc) is more or less similar because the training dataset are parsed by Charniak's parser instead of gold parses.

5.7 WSJ 23 with Charniak's parses and PARA

Table 8 shows the results for WSJ 23, where the performance of PML exceeds kNN by about F_1:3.8. WSJ 23 is used as a comparison dataset in SRL. More comparisons with other systems are shown in Table 12.

5.8 Brown corpus with Charniak's parses and PARA

Table 9 shows the results when moving to a different language domain—the Brown corpus. Both systems drop a lot in F_1 . Compared to WSJ 23, MPL drops 10.47 in F_1 and kNN, 11.65 in F_1. These drops are caused partially by PARA, and partially by classifiers. PARA in Lin & Smith (2006) drops about 3.1 in F_1 when moving to the Brown Corpus; but more research is required to uncover the cause.

5.9 Further results on kNN with all training data

Table 10 shows different results for various values of k in kNN. Both systems, GP (gold-parse) & PARA and CP (Charniak's parse) & PARA, perform best (as measured by F_1) when K is set as one. But when the system is labeling a known argument, selection of k=5 is better in terms of both F_1 and Label accuracy (Lacc).

5.10 Further results on PML with all training data

Table 11 shows results for PML with different methods of calculating probabilities. "L+G" means the basic probability distribution (from Figure 2). "L only" and "G only" mean all probability is calculated only as either "local" or "global", respectively. "L>>G" means that probabilities are calculated globally only when the local probability is zero. "L only" is the fastest approach, and "G only" the slowest (about five seconds per sentence). Both are poor in performance. "L+G" has the best result and "L>>G" is rated as intermediate in performance and execution time.

5.11 Comparison with other systems

Table 12 shows results from other existing systems. In the second row (PARA+PML) is trained on all datasets (WSJ 02 to 21) for the "BR+RL" task (to recognize argument boundaries and label arguments) on the test data WSJ 23, with an improvement of F_1:8.28 in comparison to the result of Palmer et al., (2005) given in the first row. The basic kNN in the fourth row, trained by four datasets (WSJ 15 to 18 in CoNLL 2004) for the RL" task (to label arguments by giving the known arguments) on the test data WSJ 21, increases F_1:6.68 compared to the result of Kouchnir (2004) in the third row. Execution time for our own re-implementation of Palmer (2005) is about 3.785 sec per sentence. Instead of calculating each node in a parse tree like the Palmer (2005) model, PARA+PML can only focus on essential nodes from the output of PARA, which helps to reduce the execution time as 0.941 second per sentence. Execution time by Palmer (2005) is about 4 times longer than PARA+PML on the same machine (n.b. execution times are for a computer running Linux on a P4 2.6GHz CPU with 1G MBRAM).

More details from different systems and combinations of systems are described in the proceedings of CoNLL-2005.

	kNN k=1			PML		
	P	R	F1	P	R	F1
ALL	83.71	83.73	83.72	86.29	86.52	86.41
- *Voice*	81.69	81.60	81.64	85.64	85.90	85.77
- *Phrase Type*	82.79	82.79	82.79	85.68	85.96	85.82
- ***Distance***	76.53	76.42	**76.47**	83.76	83.97	**83.86**
- ***Head Word***	78.26	78.05	**78.15**	81.84	81.96	**81.90**
- *Path*	83.67	83.63	83.65	85.44	85.72	85.58
- ***Preposition***	79.40	79.29	**79.33**	82.02	82.12	**82.07**
- ***Actor***	80.38	80.64	**80.51**	84.74	85.01	**84.81**

Table 3. Illustration of contribution for each feature and the Actor heuristic by kNN (k=1) and PML on WSJ 24 with known arguments

	kNN k=1				PML			
Training sets	P	R	F1	Lacc	P	R	F1	Lacc
WSJ 21	76.76	77.02	76.89	78.03	79.20	79.26	79.23	80.40
WSJ 15 - 18	80.40	80.18	80.29	81.85	83.61	83.70	83.66	84.61
WSJ 02 - 21	83.71	83.73	83.72	85.03	86.29	86.52	86.41	87.20

Table 4. Illustration of results with different training datasets by kNN (k=1) and PML on WSJ 24 with known arguments

	kNN k=1				PML			
Training sets	P	R	F1	Lacc	P	R	F1	Lacc
WSJ 21	67.96	67.90	67.93	75.61	70.51	70.57	70.54	78.17
WSJ 15 - 18	72.42	72.25	72.34	80.66	75.64	75.62	75.63	83.55
WSJ 02 - 21	74.48	74.48	74.48	82.63	78.39	78.40	78.39	86.54

Table 6. Illustration of results with different training datasets by kNN (k=1) and PML on WSJ 24 with gold (Hand corrected) parses and PARA

	kNN k=1				PML			
Training sets	P	R	F1	Lacc	P	R	F1	Lacc
WSJ 21	61.05	60.90	60.98	77.45	63.75	63.43	63.59	80.70
WSJ 15 - 18	64.66	64.11	64.38	82.13	67.55	67.15	67.35	85.23
WSJ 02 - 21	66.62	66.32	66.47	84.38	69.81	69.45	69.63	87.98

Table 7. Illustration of results with different training datasets by kNN (k=1) and PML on WSJ 24 with Charniak's parses and PARA

	kNN k=1				PML			
Training sets	P	R	F1	Lacc	P	R	F1	Lacc
WSJ 21	62.87	62.55	62.71	78.85	64.94	64.49	64.71	81.31
WSJ 15 - 18	66.66	65.96	66.31	83.60	69.05	68.52	68.79	86.14
WSJ 02 - 21	68.92	68.31	68.61	86.20	71.24	70.79	71.02	88.77

Table 8. Illustration of results with different training datasets by kNN (k=1) and PML on WSJ 23 with Charniak's parses and PARA

	kNN k=1				PML			
Training sets	P	R	F1	Lacc	P	R	F1	Lacc
WSJ 21	52.56	51.40	51.97	67.70	55.17	53.88	54.52	70.15
WSJ 15 - 18	55.58	54.20	54.88	71.56	59.10	57.56	58.32	75.53
WSJ 02 - 21	57.71	56.22	56.96	74.14	61.26	59.85	60.55	78.26

Table 9. Illustration of results with different training datasets by kNN (k=1) and PML on Brown Corpus with Charniak's parses and PARA

	Known boundary		GP & PARA		CP & PARA	
K	F1	Lacc	F1	Lacc	F1	Lacc
1	83.72	85.03	**74.48**	82.63	**66.47**	**84.38**
3	83.67	85.13	74.33	**82.70**	65.94	84.03
5	**83.89**	**85.16**	74.14	82.28	65.89	83.81
7	83.27	84.66	73.43	81.59	65.52	83.54
9	82.86	84.25	73.00	81.22	65.13	82.99

Table 10. Illustration of results by kNN with different K values on WSJ 24 with known arguments, Gold (Hand-corrected) parses & PARA and Charniak's parses & PARA

	Known boundary on WSJ 24				
Method	P	R	F1	Lacc	T (Sec/Sen)
L+G	86.29	86.52	86.41	87.20	0.941
L only	80.78	80.73	80.76	81.70	0.027
G only	75.60	76.35	75.97	77.52	5.094
L>>G	82.44	82.42	82.43	83.29	0.128

Table 11. Illustration of results by PML with different methods on WSJ 24 with known arguments

System	Train	Test	Tasks	P	R	F1	Lacc	T
Palmer (2005)	W02-21	W23	BR+RL	68.60	57.80	62.74	81.70	3.785
PARA+PML	W02-21	W23	BR+RL	71.24	70.79	71.02	88.77	0.941
Kouchnir (2004)	W15-18	W21	RL	75.71	74.60	75.15		
kNN	W15-18	W21	RL	81.86	81.79	81.83	83.57	0.242

Table 12. Illustration of results for different tasks by different systems and training datasets on different testing datasets

6 Summary and Remarks

This paper has shown that basic syntactic information is useful for Semantic role labeling using instance-based learning techniques. Specifically, the following have been demonstrated:

1. It is possible to achieve acceptable F_1 scores with considerably faster execution times (compared to Gildea & Jurasky, 2002) for the Semantic role labeling problem using the Priority Maximum Likelihood instance-based learning algorithm and the Tree-based Predicate-Argument Algorithm (PARA) as a preprocessing step, without any training given a state-of-the-art parser such as Charniak's parser. The overall performance on WSJ 23 dataset is 71.02 in F_1 score. Performance drops to 60.55 for the Brown corpus, but this appears to be similar to performance drops experienced by other systems reported in CoNLL-2005.
2. F_1 performance is better for PML than for kNN, where the computational complexity for PML is O(m * log n) as opposed to O(m * n) for kNN, where m denotes the number of features and n denotes the number of training instances.
3. Execution time for the instance-based learning presented here is about four times faster for SRL than the comparable approach used by Palmer, (2005). That is, PARA plays an important role reducing the overhead during classification when using instance-based learning.
4. Using PARA, and other modifications such as the preposition feature and Actor heuristic, improves the accuracy of both kNN and PML in comparison to similar approaches.

5. The best system developed for this paper (PML & PARA) is still outperformed by some of the best systems from CoNLL-2005 when it comes to accuracy, but it is much simpler and is many orders-of-magnitude faster at delivering acceptable performance.

With the latest revised and optimized PML, the performance on WSJ 23 is 71.22 in F_1, and the speed is 0.623 second per sentence with 3.0G CPU and 1 G RAM. Koomen et al. (2006), with more than 25 features, achieved the best results reported in CoNLL2005 on WSJ 24; but PML's performance (using PARA as a preprocessor, and seven features) achieves an F_1 measure 5.10 less than Kooman's system (74.76) on WSJ 24 utilising Charniak-1 parses, and 4.07 less when using Kooman's test result (WSJ 23) as known-boundary input. In this experiment, with the Actor heuristic, PML delivers better accuracy for A0 (89.96%) than Kooman's (88.22%), but the recall (83.53%) is 4.35 % lower than Kooman's (87.88%). There are some spaces to improve PML such as low accuracy on AM-MOD, and AM-NEG, and duplicate core roles, and forth. Future work will investigate using more features, new heuristics and/or other ML approaches to improve the performance of instance-based learning algorithms at the SRL task.

References

Baldewein, U, Erk, K, Padó, S. and Prescher, D. (2004). Semantic role labelling with similarity-based generalization using EM-based clustering In *Proceedings of Senseval-3* pp. 64-68

Bosch, A. V. D., Canisius, S., Daelemans, W., and Sang, E. T. K. (2004). Memory-based semantic role labeling: Optimizing features, algorithm and output. In *Proceeding of CoNLL'2004 Shared Task.*

Carreras, X., Màrquez, L. and Chrupała, G. (2004). Hierarchical Recognition of Propositional Arguments with Perceptrons. In *Proceeding of CoNLL'2004 Shared Task.*

Charniak, E. (2000). A Maximum-Entropy-Inspired Parser. In *Proceedings of NAACL-2000.*

Collins, M. (1999). Head-Driven Statistical Models for Natural Language Parsing. *PhD Dissertation, University of Pennsylvania.*

Gildea, D. and Jurafsky, D. (2002). Automatic Labeling of Semantic Roles. *Computational Linguistics*, 28(3):245-288.

Gildea, D. and Hockenmaier, J. (2003). Identifying Semantic Roles Using Combinatory Categorial Grammar . In *Proceedings of EMNLP-2003*, Sapporo, Japan.

Higgins, D. (2004). A transformation-based approach to argument labeling. In *Proceeding of CoNLL'2004 Shared Task.*

Kouchnir, B. (2004). A Memory-Based Approach for Semantic Role Labeling. In *Proceeding of CoNLL'2004 Shared Task.*

Kooman, P., Punyakanok, V., Roth, D., and Yih, W. (2005). Generalized Inference with Multiple Semantic Role Labeling Systems. In *Proceedings of CoNLL-2005.*

Lin, C.S. A. and Smith, T. C. (2005). Semantic role labeling via Consensus in Pattern-matching. In *Proceedings of CoNLL-2005.*

Lin, C.S. A. and Smith, T. C. (2006). A Tree-based Algorithm for Predicate-Argument Recognition. In *Bulletin of Association for Computing Machinery New Zealand (ACM_NZ), volumn 2, issue 1.*

Moschitti, A., Giuglea, A. M., Coppola, B., and Basili, R. (2005). Semantic role labeling using support vector machines. In *Proceedings of CoNLL-2005.*

Palmer, M., Gildea, D., and Kingsbury, P., (2005). The Propostin Bank: An Annotated Corpus of Semantic Roles. In *Proceedings of ACL: Volume 31, Number 1. p72-105.*

Pradhan, S., Ward, W., Hacioglu, K., Martin, J. H., Jurafsky, D. (2004). Shallow Semantic Parsing using Support Vector Machines, in *Proceedings of the Human Language Technology Conference/North American chapter of the Association for Computational Linguistics annual meeting (HLT/NAACL-2004)*, Boston, MA.

Punyakanok, V., Roth, D., Yih, W., and Zimak, D. (2004). Semantic Role Labeling via Integer Linear Programming Inference . In *Proceedings of. the International Conference on Computational Linguistics (COLING),2004.*

Surdeanu, M., Harabagiu, S., Williams, J., and Aarseth, P. (2003). Using Predicate-Argument Structures for Information Extraction. In *Proceedings of ACL 2003*, Sapporo, Japan.

Inducing Temporal Graphs

Philip Bramsen
MIT CSAIL
bramsen@mit.edu

Pawan Deshpande
MIT CSAIL
pawan@mit.edu

Yoong Keok Lee
DSO National Laboratories
lyoongke@dso.org.sg

Regina Barzilay
MIT CSAIL
regina@csail.mit.edu

Abstract

We consider the problem of constructing a directed acyclic graph that encodes temporal relations found in a text. The unit of our analysis is a temporal segment, a fragment of text that maintains temporal coherence. The strength of our approach lies in its ability to simultaneously optimize pairwise ordering preferences and global constraints on the graph topology. Our learning method achieves 83% F-measure in temporal segmentation and 84% accuracy in inferring temporal relations between two segments.

1 Introduction

Understanding the temporal flow of discourse is a significant aspect of text comprehension. Consequently, temporal analysis has been a focus of linguistic research for quite some time. Temporal interpretation encompasses levels ranging from the syntactic to the lexico-semantic (Reichenbach, 1947; Moens and Steedman, 1987) and includes the characterization of temporal discourse in terms of rhetorical structure and pragmatic relations (Dowty, 1986; Webber, 1987; Passonneau, 1988; Lascarides and Asher, 1993).

Besides its linguistic significance, temporal analysis has important practical implications. In multidocument summarization, knowledge about the temporal order of events can enhance both the content selection and the summary generation processes (Barzilay et al., 2002). In question answering, temporal analysis is needed to determine when a particular event occurs and how events relate to each other. Some of these needs can be addressed by emerging technologies for temporal analysis (Wilson et al., 2001; Mani et al., 2003; Lapata and Lascarides, 2004; Boguraev and Ando, 2005).

This paper characterizes the temporal flow of discourse in terms of *temporal segments* and their ordering. We define a temporal segment to be a fragment of text that does not exhibit abrupt changes in temporal focus (Webber, 1988). A segment may contain more than one event or state, but the key requirement is that its elements maintain temporal coherence. For instance, a medical case summary may contain segments describing a patient's admission, his previous hospital visit, and the onset of his original symptoms. Each of these segments corresponds to a different time frame, and is clearly delineated as such in a text.

Our ultimate goal is to automatically construct a graph that encodes ordering between temporal segments. The key premise is that in a coherent document, temporal progression is reflected in a wide range of linguistic features and contextual dependencies. In some cases, clues to segment ordering are embedded in the segments themselves. For instance, given a pair of adjacent segments, the temporal adverb *next day* in the second segment is a strong predictor of a precedence relation. In other cases, we can predict the right order between a pair of segments by analyzing their relation to other segments in the text. The interaction between pairwise ordering decisions can easily be formalized in terms of constraints on the graph topology. An obvious example of such a constraint is prohibiting cycles in the ordering graph. We show how these complementary sources of information can be incorporated in a model using global inference.

We evaluate our temporal ordering algorithm on a corpus of medical case summaries. Temporal

Proceedings of the 2006 Conference on Empirical Methods in Natural Language Processing (EMNLP 2006), pages 189–198,
Sydney, July 2006.

analysis in this domain is challenging in several respects: a typical summary exhibits no significant tense or aspect variations and contains few absolute time markers. We demonstrate that humans can reliably mark temporal segments and determine segment ordering in this domain. Our learning method achieves 83% F-measure in temporal segmentation and 84% accuracy in inferring temporal relations between two segments.

Our contributions are twofold:

Temporal Segmentation We propose a fully automatic, linguistically rich model for temporal segmentation. Most work on temporal analysis is done on a finer granularity than proposed here. Our results show that the coarse granularity of our representation facilitates temporal analysis and is especially suitable for domains with sparse temporal anchors.

Segment Ordering We introduce a new method for learning temporal ordering. In contrast to existing methods that focus on pairwise ordering, we explore strategies for global temporal inference. The strength of the proposed model lies in its ability to simultaneously optimize pairwise ordering preferences and global constraints on graph topology. While the algorithm has been applied at the segment level, it can be used with other temporal annotation schemes.

2 Related Work

Temporal ordering has been extensively studied in computational linguistics (Passonneau, 1988; Webber, 1988; Hwang and Schubert, 1992; Lascarides and Asher, 1993; Lascarides and Oberlander, 1993). Prior research has investigated a variety of language mechanisms and knowledge sources that guide interpretation of temporal ordering, including tense, aspect, temporal adverbials, rhetorical relations and pragmatic constraints. In recent years, the availability of annotated corpora, such as TimeBank (Pustejovsky et al., 2003), has triggered the use of machine-learning methods for temporal analysis (Mani et al., 2003; Lapata and Lascarides, 2004; Boguraev and Ando, 2005). Typical tasks include identification of temporal anchors, linking events to times, and temporal ordering of events.

Since this paper addresses temporal ordering, we focus our discussion on this task. Existing ordering approaches vary both in terms of the ordering unit — it can be a clause, a sentence or an event — and in terms of the set of ordering relations considered by the algorithm. Despite these differences, most existing methods have the same basic design: each pair of ordering units (i.e., clauses) is abstracted into a feature vector and a supervised classifier is employed to learn the mapping between feature vectors and their labels. Features used in classification include aspect, modality, event class, and lexical representation. It is important to note that the classification for each pair is performed independently and is not guaranteed to yield a globally consistent order.

In contrast, our focus is on globally optimal temporal inference. While the importance of global constraints has been previously validated in symbolic systems for temporal analysis (Fikes et al., 2003; Zhou et al., 2005), existing corpus-based approaches operate at the local level. These improvements achieved by a global model motivate its use as an alternative to existing pairwise methods.

3 TDAG: A representation of temporal flow

We view text as a linear sequence of temporal segments. Temporal focus is retained within a segment, but radically changes between segments. The length of a segment can range from a single clause to a sequence of adjacent sentences. Figure 1 shows a sample of temporal segments from a medical case summary. Consider as an example the segment S13 of this text. This segment describes an examination of a patient, encompassing several events and states (i.e., an abdominal and neurological examination). All of them belong to the same time frame, and temporal order between these events is not explicitly outlined in the text.

We represent ordering of events as a temporal directed acyclic graph (TDAG). An example of the transitive reduction[1] of a TDAG is shown in Figure 1. Edges in a TDAG capture temporal precedence relations between segments. Because the graph encodes an order, cycles are prohibited. We do not require the graph to be fully connected — if the precedence relation between two nodes is not specified in the text, the corresponding nodes will not be connected. For instance, consider the segments S5 and S7 from Figure 1, which describe her previous tests and the history of eczema. Any

[1]The transitive reduction of a graph is the smallest graph with the same transitive closure.

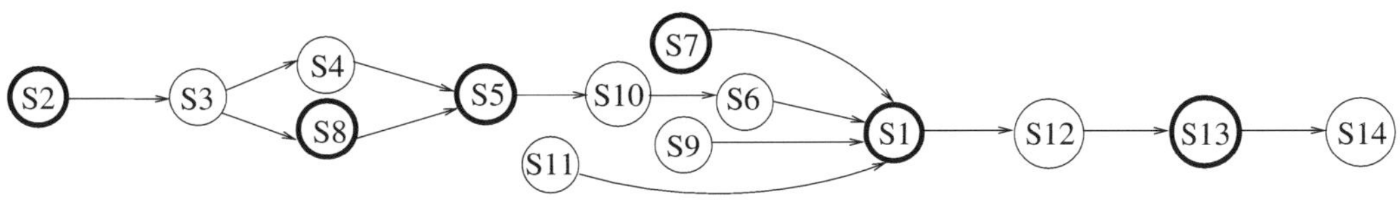

S1	A 32-year-old woman was admitted to the hospital because of left subcostal pain...
S2	The patient had been well until four years earlier,
S5	Three months before admission an evaluation elsewhere included an ultrasonographic examination, a computed tomographic (CT) scan of the abdomen...
S7	She had a history of eczema and of asthma...
S8	She had lost 18 kg in weight during the preceding 18 months.
S13	On examination the patient was slim and appeared well. An abdominal examination revealed a soft systolic bruit... and a neurologic examination was normal...

Figure 1: An example of the transitive reduction of a TDAG for a case summary. A sample of segments corresponding to the nodes marked in bold is shown in the table.

order between the two events is consistent with our interpretation of the text, therefore we cannot determine the precedence relation between the segments S5 and S7.

In contrast to many existing temporal representations (Allen, 1984; Pustejovsky et al., 2003), TDAG is a coarse annotation scheme: it does not capture interval overlap and distinguishes only a subset of commonly used ordering relations. Our choice of this representation, however, is not arbitrary. The selected relations are shown to be useful in text processing applications (Zhou et al., 2005) and can be reliably recognized by humans. Moreover, the distribution of event ordering links under a more refined annotation scheme, such as TimeML, shows that our subset of relations covers a majority of annotated links (Pustejovsky et al., 2003).

4 Method for Temporal Segmentation

Our first goal is to automatically predict shifts in temporal focus that are indicative of segment boundaries. Linguistic studies show that speakers and writers employ a wide range of language devices to signal change in temporal discourse (Bestgen and Vonk, 1995). For instance, the presence of the temporal anchor *last year* indicates the lack of temporal continuity between the current and the previous sentence. However, many of these predictors are heavily context-dependent and, thus, cannot be considered independently. Instead of manually crafting complex rules controlling feature interaction, we opt to learn them from data.

We model temporal segmentation as a binary classification task. Given a set of candidate boundaries (e.g., sentence boundaries), our task is to select a subset of the boundaries that delineate temporal segment transitions. To implement this approach, we first identify a set of potential boundaries. Our analysis of the manually-annotated corpus reveals that boundaries can occur not only between sentences, but also within a sentence, at the boundary of syntactic clauses. We automatically segment sentences into clauses using a robust statistical parser (Charniak, 2000). Next, we encode each boundary as a vector of features. Given a set of annotated examples, we train a classifier[2] to predict boundaries based on the following feature set:

Lexical Features Temporal expressions, such as *tomorrow* and *earlier*, are among the strongest markers of temporal discontinuity (Passonneau, 1988; Bestgen and Vonk, 1995). In addition to a well-studied set of domain-independent temporal markers, there are a variety of domain-specific temporal markers. For instance, the phrase *initial hospital visit* functions as a time anchor in the medical domain.

To automatically extract these expressions, we provide a classifier with n-grams from each of the candidate sentences preceding and following the candidate segment boundary.

Topical Continuity Temporal segmentation is closely related to topical segmentation (Chafe, 1979). Transitions from one topic to another may indicate changes in temporal flow and, therefore,

[2] BoosTexter package (Schapire and Singer, 2000).

identifying such transitions is relevant for temporal segmentation.

We quantify the strength of a topic change by computing a cosine similarity between sentences bordering the proposed segmentation. This measure is commonly used in topic segmentation (Hearst, 1994) under the assumption that change in lexical distribution corresponds to topical change.

Positional Features Some parts of the document are more likely to exhibit temporal change than others. This property is related to patterns in discourse organization of a document as a whole. For instance, a medical case summary first discusses various developments in the medical history of a patient and then focuses on his current conditions. As a result, the first part of the summary contains many short temporal segments. We encode positional features by recording the relative position of a sentence in a document.

Syntactic Features Because our segment boundaries are considered at the clausal level, rather than at the sentence level, the syntax surrounding a hypothesized boundary may be indicative of temporal shifts. This feature takes into account the position of a word with respect to the boundary. For each word within three words of the hypothesized boundary, we record its part-of-speech tag along with its distance from the boundary. For example, NNP_{+1} encodes the presence of a proper noun immediately following the proposed boundary.

5 Learning to Order Segments

Our next goal is to automatically construct a graph that encodes ordering relations between temporal segments. One possible approach is to cast graph construction as a standard binary classification task: predict an ordering for each pair of distinct segments based on their attributes alone. If a pair contains a temporal marker, like *later*, then accurate prediction is feasible. In fact, this method is commonly used in event ordering (Mani et al., 2003; Lapata and Lascarides, 2004; Boguraev and Ando, 2005). However, many segment pairs lack temporal markers and other explicit cues for ordering. Determining their relation out of context can be difficult, even for humans. Moreover, by treating each segment pair in isolation, we cannot guarantee that all the pairwise assignments are consistent with each other and yield a valid TDAG.

Rather than ordering each pair separately, our ordering model relies on global inference. Given the pairwise ordering predictions of a local classifier[3], our model finds a globally optimal assignment. In essence, the algorithm constructs a graph that is maximally consistent with individual ordering preferences of each segment pair and at the same time satisfies graph-level constraints on the TDAG topology.

In Section 5.2, we present three global inference strategies that vary in their computational and linguistic complexity. But first we present our underlying local ordering model.

5.1 Learning Pairwise Ordering

Given a pair of segments (i, j), our goal is to assign it to one of three classes: forward, backward, and null (not connected). We generate the training data by using all pairs of segments (i, j) that belong to the same document, such that i appears before j in the text.

The features we consider for the pairwise ordering task are similar to ones used in previous research on event ordering (Mani et al., 2003; Lapata and Lascarides, 2004; Boguraev and Ando, 2005). Below we briefly summarize these features.

Lexical Features This class of features captures temporal markers and other phrases indicative of order between two segments. Representative examples in this category include domain-independent cues like *years earlier* and domain-specific markers like *during next visit*. To automatically identify these phrases, we provide a classifier with two sets of n-grams extracted from the first and the second segments. The classifier then learns phrases with high predictive power.

Temporal Anchor Comparison Temporal anchors are one of the strongest cues for the ordering of events in text. For instance, medical case summaries use phrases like *two days before admission* and *one day before admission* to express relative order between events. If the two segments contain temporal anchors, we can determine their ordering by comparing the relation between the two anchors. We identified a set of temporal anchors commonly used in the medical domain and devised a small set of regular expressions for their comparison.[4] The corresponding feature has three

[3]The perceptron classifi er.

[4]We could not use standard tools for extraction and analysis of temporal anchors as they were developed on the newspaper corpora, and are not suitable for analysis of medical

values that encode preceding, following and incompatible relations.

Segment Adjacency Feature Multiple studies have shown that two subsequent sentences are likely to follow a chronological progression (Bestgen and Vonk, 1995). To encode this information, we include a binary feature that captures the adjacency relation between two segments.

5.2 Global Inference Strategies for Segment Ordering

Given the scores (or probabilities) of all pairwise edges produced by a local classifier, our task is to construct a TDAG. In this section, we describe three inference strategies that aim to find a consistent ordering between *all* segment pairs. These strategies vary significantly in terms of linguistic motivation and computational complexity. Examples of automatically constructed TDAGs derived from different inference strategies are shown in Figure 2.

5.2.1 Greedy Inference in Natural Reading Order (NRO)

The simplest way to construct a consistent TDAG is by adding segments in the order of their appearance in a text. Intuitively speaking, this technique processes segments in the same order as a reader of the text. The motivation underlying this approach is that the reader incrementally builds temporal interpretation of a text; when a new piece of information is introduced, the reader knows how to relate it to already processed text.

This technique starts with an empty graph and incrementally adds nodes in order of their appearance in the text. When a new node is added, we greedily select the edge with the highest score that connects the new node to the existing graph, without violating the consistency of the TDAG. Next, we expand the graph with its transitive closure. We continue greedily adding edges and applying transitive closure until the new node is connected to all other nodes already in the TDAG. The process continues until all the nodes have been added to the graph.

5.2.2 Greedy Best-first Inference (BF)

Our second inference strategy is also greedy. It aims to optimize the score of the graph. The score of the graph is computed by summing the scores of its edges. While this greedy strategy is not guaranteed to find the optimal solution, it finds a reasonable approximation (Cohen et al., 1999).

This method begins by sorting the edges by their score. Starting with an empty graph, we add one edge at a time, without violating the consistency constraints. As in the previous strategy, at each step we expand the graph with its transitive closure. We continue this process until all the edges have been considered.

5.2.3 Exact Inference with Integer Linear Programming (ILP)

We can cast the task of constructing a globally optimal TDAG as an optimization problem. In contrast to the previous approaches, the method is not greedy. It computes the optimal solution within the Integer Linear Programming (ILP) framework.

For a document with N segments, each pair of segments (i, j) can be related in the graph in one of three ways: forward, backward, and null (not connected). Let $s_{i\to j}$, $s_{i\leftarrow j}$, and $s_{i\nleftrightarrow j}$ be the scores assigned by a local classifier to each of the three relations respectively. Let $I_{i\to j}$, $I_{i\leftarrow j}$, and $I_{i\nleftrightarrow j}$ be indicator variables that are set to 1 if the corresponding relation is active, or 0 otherwise.

The objective is then to optimize the score of a TDAG by maximizing the sum of the scores of all edges in the graph:

$$\max \sum_{i=1}^{N} \sum_{j=i+i}^{N} s_{i\to j} I_{i\to j} + s_{i\leftarrow j} I_{i\leftarrow j} + s_{i\nleftrightarrow j} I_{i\nleftrightarrow j} \quad (1)$$

subject to:

$$I_{i\to j}, I_{i\leftarrow j}, I_{i\nleftrightarrow j} \in \{0,1\} \quad \forall\, i,j = 1,\ldots N, i<j \quad (2)$$

$$I_{i\to j} + I_{i\leftarrow j} + I_{i\nleftrightarrow j} = 1 \quad \forall\, i,j = 1,\ldots N, i<j \quad (3)$$

We augment this basic formulation with two more sets of constraints to enforce validity of the constructed TDAG.

Transitivity Constraints The key requirement on the edge assignment is the transitivity of the resulting graph. Transitivity also guarantees that the graph does not have cycles. We enforce transitivity by introducing the following constraint for every triple (i, j, k):

$$I_{i\to j} + I_{j\to k} - 1 \le I_{i\to k} \quad (4)$$

If both indicator variables on the left side of the inequality are set to 1, then the indicator variable

text (Wilson et al., 2001).

on the right side must be equal to 1. Otherwise, the indicator variable on the right can take any value.

Connectivity Constraints The connectivity constraint states that each node i is connected to at least one other node and thereby enforces connectivity of the generated TDAG. We introduce these constraints because manually-constructed TDAGs do not have any disconnected nodes. This observation is consistent with the intuition that the reader is capable to order a segment with respect to other segments in the TDAG.

$$(\sum_{j=1}^{i-1} I_{i \nleftrightarrow j} + \sum_{j=i+1}^{N} I_{j \nleftrightarrow i}) < N - 1 \qquad (5)$$

The above constraint rules out edge assignments in which node i has null edges to the rest of the nodes.

Solving ILP Solving an integer linear program is NP-hard (Cormen et al., 1992). Fortunately, there exist several strategies for solving ILPs. We employ an efficient Mixed Integer Programming solver *lp_solve*[5] which implements the Branch-and-Bound algorithm. It takes less than five seconds to decode each document on a 2.8 GHz Intel Xeon machine.

6 Evaluation Set-Up

We first describe the corpora used in our experiments and the results of human agreement on the segmentation and the ordering tasks. Then, we introduce the evaluation measures that we use to assess the performance of our model.

6.1 Corpus Characteristics

We applied our method for temporal ordering to a corpus of medical case summaries. The medical domain has been a popular testbed for methods for automatic temporal analyzers (Combi and Shahar, 1997; Zhou et al., 2005). The appeal is partly due to rich temporal structure of these documents and the practical need to parse this structure for meaningful processing of medical data.

We compiled a corpus of medical case summaries from the online edition of The New England Journal of Medicine.[6] The summaries are written by physicians of Massachusetts General Hospital. A typical summary describes an admission status, previous diseases related to the current conditions and their treatments, family history, and the current course of treatment. For privacy protection, names and dates are removed from the summaries before publication.

The average length of a summary is 47 sentences. The summaries are written in the past tense, and a typical summary does not include instances of the past perfect. The summaries do not follow a chronological order. The ordering of information in this domain is guided by stylistic conventions (i.e., symptoms are presented before treatment) and the relevance of information to the current conditions (i.e., previous onset of the same disease is summarized before the description of other diseases).

6.2 Annotating Temporal Segmentation

Our approach for temporal segmentation requires annotated data for supervised training. We first conducted a pilot study to assess the human agreement on the task. We employed two annotators to manually segment a portion of our corpus. The annotators were provided with two-page instructions that defined the notion of a temporal segment and included examples of segmented texts. Each annotator segmented eight summaries which on average contained 49 sentences. Because annotators were instructed to consider segmentation boundaries at the level of a clause, there were 877 potential boundaries. The first annotator created 168 boundaries, while the second — 224 boundaries. We computed a Kappa coefficient of 0.71 indicating a high inter-annotator agreement and thereby confirming our hypothesis about the reliability of temporal segmentation.

Once we established high inter-annotator agreement on the pilot study, one annotator segmented the remaining 52 documents in the corpus.[7] Among 3,297 potential boundaries, 1,178 (35.7%) were identified by the annotator as segment boundaries. The average segment length is three sentences, and a typical document contains around 20 segments.

6.3 Annotating Temporal Ordering

To assess the inter-annotator agreement, we asked two human annotators to construct TDAGs from

[5] http://groups.yahoo.com/group/lp_solve

[6] http://content.nejm.org

[7] It took approximately 20 minutes to segment a case summary.

five manually segmented summaries. These summaries consist of 97 segments, and their transitive closure contain a total of 1,331 edges. We computed the agreement between human judges by comparing the transitive closure of the TDAGs. The annotators achieved a surprisingly high agreement with a Kappa value of 0.98.

After verifying human agreement on this task, one of the annotators constructed TDAGs for another 25 summaries.[8] The transitive reduction of a graph contains on average 20.9 nodes and 20.5 edges. The corpus consists of 72% forward, 12% backward and 16% null segment edges inclusive of edges induced by transitive closure. At the clause level, the distribution is even more skewed — forward edges account for 74% edges, equal for 18%, backward for 3% and null for 5%.

6.4 Evaluation Measures

We evaluate temporal segmentation by considering the ratio of correctly predicted boundaries. We quantify the performance using F-measure, a commonly used binary classification metric. We opt not to use the P_k measure, a standard topical segmentation measure, because the temporal segments are short and we are only interested in the identification of the exact boundaries.

Our second evaluation task is concerned with ordering manually annotated segments. In these experiments, we compare an automatically generated TDAG against the annotated reference graph. In essence, we compare edge assignment in the transitive closure of two TDAGs, where each edge can be classified into one of the three types: forward, backward, or null.

Our final evaluation is performed at the clausal level. In this case, each edge can be classified into one of the four classes: forward, backward, equal, or null. Note that the clause-level analysis allows us to compare TDAGs based on the automatically derived segmentation.

7 Results

We evaluate temporal segmentation using leave-one-out cross-validation on our corpus of 60 summaries. The segmentation algorithm achieves a performance of 83% F-measure, with a recall of 78% and a precision of 89%.

[8] It took approximately one hour to build a TDAG for each segmented document.

To evaluate segment ordering, we employ leave-one-out cross-validation on 30 annotated TDAGs that overall contain 13,088 edges in their transitive closure. In addition to the three global inference algorithms, we include a majority baseline that classifies all edges as forward, yielding a chronological order.

Our results for ordering the manually annotated temporal segments are shown in Table 1. All inference methods outperform the baseline, and their performance is consistent with the complexity of the inference mechanism. As expected, the ILP strategy, which supports exact global inference, achieves the best performance — 84.3%.

An additional point of comparison is the accuracy of the pairwise classification, prior to the application of global inference. The accuracy of the local ordering is 81.6%, which is lower than that of ILP. The superior performance of ILP demonstrates that accurate global inference can further refine local predictions. Surprisingly, the local classifier yields a higher accuracy than the two other inference strategies. Note, however, the local ordering procedure is not guaranteed to produce a consistent TDAG, and thus the local classifier cannot be used on its own to produce a valid TDAG.

Table 2 shows the ordering results at the clausal level. The four-way classification is computed using both manually and automatically generated segments. Pairs of clauses that belong to the same segment stand in the equal relation, otherwise they have the same ordering relation as the segments to which they belong.

On the clausal level, the difference between the performance of ILP and BF is blurred. When evaluated on manually-constructed segments, ILP outperforms BF by less than 1%. This unexpected result can be explained by the skewed distribution of edge types — the two hardest edge types to classify (see Table 3), backward and null, account only for 7.4% of all edges at the clause level.

When evaluated on automatically segmented text, ILP performs slightly worse than BF. We hypothesize that this result can be explained by the difference between training and testing conditions for the pairwise classifier: the classifier is trained on manually-computed segments and is tested on automatically-computed ones, which negatively affects the accuracy on the test set. While all the strategies are negatively influenced by this discrepancy, ILP is particularly vulnerable as it relies

Algorithm	Accuracy
Integer Linear Programming (ILP)	**84.3**
Best First (BF)	78.3
Natural Reading Order (NRO)	74.3
Baseline	72.2

Table 1: Accuracy for 3-way ordering classification over manually-constructed segments.

Algorithm	Manual Seg.	Automatic Seg.
ILP	**91.9**	84.8
BF	91.0	**85.0**
NRO	87.8	81.0
Baseline	73.6	73.6

Table 2: Results for 4-way ordering classification over clauses, computed over manually and automatically generated segments.

on the score values for inference. In contrast, BF only considers the rank between the scores, which may be less affected by noise.

We advocate a two-stage approach for temporal analysis: we first identify segments and then order them. A simpler alternative is to directly perform a four-way classification at the clausal level using the union of features employed in our two-stage process. The accuracy of this approach, however, is low — it achieves only 74%, most likely due to the sparsity of clause-level representation for four-way classification. This result demonstrates the benefits of a coarse representation and a two-stage approach for temporal analysis.

8 Conclusions

This paper introduces a new method for temporal ordering. The unit of our analysis is a temporal segment, a fragment of text that maintains temporal coherence. After investigating several inference strategies, we concluded that integer linear programming and best first greedy approach are valuable alternatives for TDAG construction.

In the future, we will explore a richer set of constraints on the topology on the ordering graph. We will build on the existing formal framework (Fikes et al., 2003) for the verification of ordering consistency. We are also interested in expanding our framework for global inference to other temporal annotation schemes. Given a richer set of temporal relations, the benefits from global inference can be even more significant.

Algorithm	Forward	Backward	Null
ILP	**92.5**	**45.6**	**76.0**
BF	91.4	42.2	74.7
NRO	87.7	43.6	66.4

Table 3: Per class accuracy for clause classification over manually computed segments.

Acknowledgments

The authors acknowledge the support of the National Science Foundation and National Institute of Health (CAREER grant IIS-0448168, grant IIS-0415865). Thanks to Terry Koo, Igor Malioutov, Zvika Marx, Benjamin Snyder, Peter Szolovits, Luke Zettlemoyer and the anonymous reviewers for their helpful comments and suggestions. Any opinions, findings, conclusions or recommendations expressed above are those of the authors and do not necessarily reflect the views of the NSF or NIH.

References

James F. Allen. 1984. Towards a general theory of action and time. *Artificial Intelligence*, 23(2):123–154.

Regina Barzilay, Noemie Elhadad, and Kathleen McKeown. 2002. Inferring strategies for sentence ordering in multidocument news summarization. *Journal of Artificial Intelligence Research*, 17:35–55.

Yves Bestgen and Wietske Vonk. 1995. The role of temporal segmentation markers in discourse processing. *Discourse Processes*, 19:385–406.

Branimir Boguraev and Rie Kubota Ando. 2005. Timeml-compliant text analysis for temporal reasoning. In *Proceedings of IJCAI*, pages 997–1003.

Wallace Chafe. 1979. The fbw of thought and the fbw of language. In Talmy Givon, editor, *Syntax and Semantics: Discourse and Syntax*, volume 12, pages 159–182. Academic Press.

Eugene Charniak. 2000. A maximum-entropy-inspired parser. In *Proceedings of the NAACL*, pages 132–139.

William Cohen, Robert Schapire, and Yoram Singer. 1999. Learning to order things. *Journal of Artificial Intelligence*, 10:243–270.

Carlo Combi and Yuval Shahar. 1997. Temporal reasoning and temporal data maintenance in medicine: Issues and challenges. *Computers in Biology and Medicine*, 27(5):353–368.

Thomas H. Cormen, Charles E. Leiserson, and Ronald L. Rivest. 1992. *Intoduction to Algorithms*. The MIT Press.

David R. Dowty. 1986. The effects of aspectual class on the temporal structure of discourse: Semantics or Pragmatics? *Linguistics and Philosophy*, 9:37–61.

R. Fikes, J. Jenkins, and G. Frank. 2003. A system architecture and component library for hybrid reasoning. Technical report, Stanford University.

Marti Hearst. 1994. Multi-paragraph segmentation of expository text. In *Proceedings of the ACL*, pages 9–16.

Chung Hee Hwang and Lenhart K. Schubert. 1992. Tense trees as the "fi ne structure" of discourse. In *Proceedings of the ACL*, pages 232–240.

Mirella Lapata and Alex Lascarides. 2004. Inferring sentence-internal temporal relations. In *Proceedings of HLT-NAACL*, pages 153–160.

Alex Lascarides and Nicholas Asher. 1993. Temporal interpretation, discourse relations, and commonsense entailment. *Linguistics and Philosophy*, 16:437–493.

Alex Lascarides and John Oberlander. 1993. Temporal connectives in a discourse context. In *Proceeding of the EACL*, pages 260–268.

Inderjeet Mani, Barry Schiffman, and Jianping Zhang. 2003. Inferring temporal ordering of events in news. In *Proceeding of HLT-NAACL*, pages 55–57.

Mark Moens and Mark J. Steedman. 1987. Temporal ontology in natural language. In *Proceedings of the ACL*, pages 1–7.

Rebecca J. Passonneau. 1988. A computational model of the semantics of tense and aspect. *Computational Linguistics*, 14(2):44–60.

James Pustejovsky, Patrick Hanks, Roser Sauri, Andrew See, David Day, Lissa Ferro, Robert Gaizauskas, Marcia Lazo, Andrea Setzer, and Beth Sundheim. 2003. The timebank corpus. *Corpus Linguistics*, pages 647–656.

Hans Reichenbach. 1947. *Elements of Symbolic Logic*. Macmillan, New York, NY.

Robert E. Schapire and Yoram Singer. 2000. Boostexter: A boosting-based system for text categorization. *Machine Learning*, 39(2/3):135–168.

Bonnie L. Webber. 1987. The interpretation of tense in discourse. In *Proceedings of the ACL*, pages 147–154.

Bonnie L. Webber. 1988. Tense as discourse anaphor. *Computational Linguistics*, 14(2):61–73.

George Wilson, Inderjeet Mani, Beth Sundheim, and Lisa Ferro. 2001. A multilingual approach to annotating and extracting temporal information. In *Proceedings of the ACL 2001 Workshop on Temporal and Spatial Information Processing*, pages 81–87.

Li Zhou, Carol Friedman, Simon Parsons, and George Hripcsak. 2005. System architecture for temporal information extraction, representation and reasoning in clinical narrative reports. In *Proceedings of AMIA*, pages 869–873.

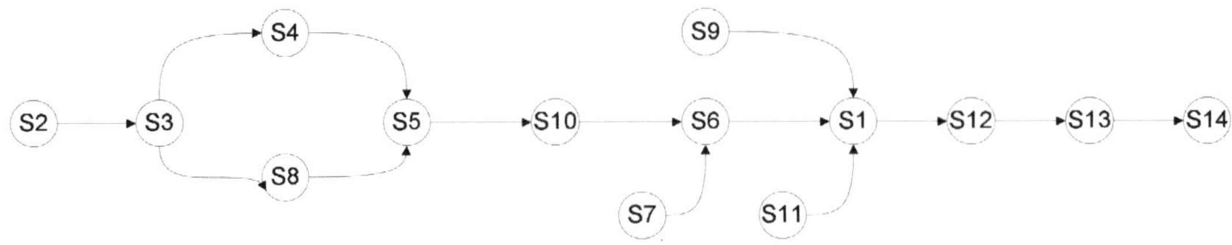

(a) Reference TDAG

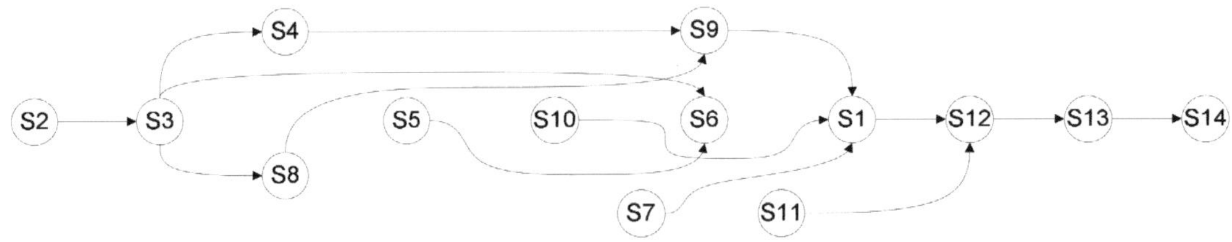

(b) ILP generated TDAG with an accuracy of 84.6%

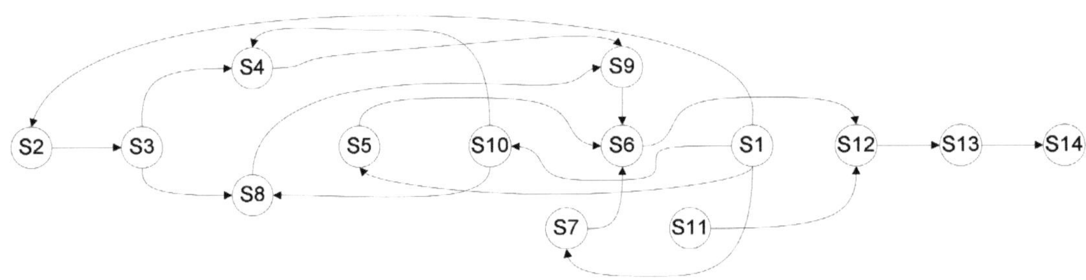

(b) BF generated TDAG with an accuracy of 71.4%; NRO produces the same graph for this example.

S1	A 32-year-old woman was admitted to the hospital because of left subcostal pain. . .
S2	The patient had been well until four years earlier,
S3	when she began to have progressive, constant left subcostal pain, with an intermittent increase in the temperature to 39.4°C, anorexia, and nausea. The episodes occurred approximately every six months and lasted for a week or two;
S4	they had recently begun to occur every four months.
S5	Three months before admission an evaluation elsewhere included an ultrasonographic examination, a computed tomographic (CT) scan of the abdomen. . .
S6	Because of worsening pain she came to this hospital.
S7	The patient was an unemployed child-care worker. She had a history of eczema and of asthma. . .
S8	She had lost 18 kg in weight during the preceding 18 months.
S9	Her only medications were an albuterol inhaler, which was used as needed,
S10	and an oral contraceptive, which she had taken during the month before admission.
S11	There was no history of jaundice, dark urine, light stools, intravenous drug abuse, hypertension, diabetes mellitus, tuberculosis, risk factors for infection with the human immunodeficiency virus, or a change in bowel habits. She did not smoke and drank little alcohol.
S12	The temperature was 36.5°C, the pulse was 68, and the respirations were 16. . .
S13	On examination the patient was slim and appeared well. . . An abdominal examination revealed a soft systolic bruit. . . and a neurologic examination was normal. . .
S14	A diagnostic procedure was performed.

(d) An example of a case summary

Figure 2: Examples of automatically constructed TDAGs with the reference TDAG and text.

A Weakly Supervised Learning Approach for Spoken Language Understanding

Wei-Lin Wu, Ru-Zhan Lu, Jian-Yong Duan,
Hui Liu, Feng Gao, Yu-Quan Chen
Department of Computer Science and Engineering
Shanghai Jiao Tong University
Shanghai, 200030, P. R. China
{wu-wl,lu-rz,duan-jy,liuhui,gaofeng,chen-yq}
@cs.sjtu.edu.cn

Abstract

In this paper, we present a weakly supervised learning approach for spoken language understanding in domain-specific dialogue systems. We model the task of spoken language understanding as a successive classification problem. The first classifier (topic classifier) is used to identify the topic of an input utterance. With the restriction of the recognized target topic, the second classifier (semantic classifier) is trained to extract the corresponding slot-value pairs. It is mainly data-driven and requires only minimally annotated corpus for training whilst retaining the understanding robustness and deepness for spoken language. Most importantly, it allows the employment of weakly supervised strategies for training the two classifiers. We first apply the training strategy of combining active learning and self-training (Tur et al., 2005) for topic classifier. Also, we propose a practical method for bootstrapping the topic-dependent semantic classifiers from a small amount of labeled sentences. Experiments have been conducted in the context of Chinese public transportation information inquiry domain. The experimental results demonstrate the effectiveness of our proposed SLU framework and show the possibility to reduce human labeling efforts significantly.

1 Introduction

Spoken Language Understanding (SLU) is one of the key components in spoken dialogue systems. Its task is to identify the user's goal and extract from the input utterance the information needed to complete the query. Traditionally, there are mainly two mainstreams in the SLU researches: knowledge-based approaches, which are based on robust parsing or template matching techniques (Sneff, 1992; Dowding et al., 1993; Ward and Issar, 1994); and data-driven approaches, which are generally based on stochastic models (Pieraccini and Levin, 1993; Miller et al., 1995). Both approaches have their drawbacks, however. The former approach is cost-expensive to develop since its grammar development is time-consuming, laboursome and requires linguistic skills. It is also strictly domain-dependent and hence difficult to be adapted to new domains. On the other hand, although addressing such drawbacks associated with knowledge-based approaches, the latter approach often suffers the data sparseness problem and hence needs a fully annotated corpus in order to reliably estimate an accurate model. More recently, some new variation methods are proposed through certain trade-offs, such as the semi-automatically grammar learning approach (Wang and Acero, 2001) and Hidden Vector State (HVS) model (He and Young, 2005). The two methods require only minimally annotated data (only the semantic frames are annotated).

This paper proposes a novel weakly supervised spoken language understanding approach. Our SLU framework mainly includes two successive classifiers: topic classifier and semantic classifier. The main advantage of the proposed approach is that it is mainly data-driven and requires only minimally annotated corpus for training whilst retaining the understanding robustness and deepness for spoken language. In particular, the two classifiers are trained using weakly supervised strategies: the former one is trained through the combination of active learning and self-training (Tur et al., 2005), and the latter one

Proceedings of the 2006 Conference on Empirical Methods in Natural Language Processing (EMNLP 2006), pages 199–207,
Sydney, July 2006.

is trained using a practical bootstrapping technique.

2 The System Architecture

The semantic representation of an application domain is usually defined in terms of the semantic frame, which contains a frame type representing the topic of the input sentence, and some slots representing the constraints the query goal has to satisfy. Then, the goal of the SLU system is to translate an input utterance into a semantic frame. Besides the two key components, i.e., topic classifier and semantic classifier, our system also contains a preprocessor and a slot-value merger. Figure 1 illustrates the overall system architecture. It also describes the whole SLU procedure using an example sentence.

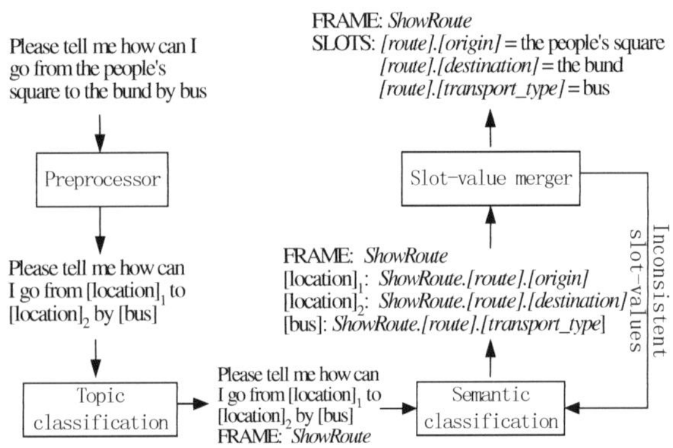

Figure 1: The System architecture[1]

2.1 The Preprocessor

Usually, the preprocessor is to look for the substrings in a sentence that correspond to a semantic class or matching a regular expression and to replace them with the class label, e.g., "Huashan Road" and "1954" are replaced with two class labels [road_name] and [number] respectively. In our system, the preprocessor can recognize more complex word sequences, e.g., "1954 Huashan Road" can be recognized as [address] through matching a rule like "[address] → [number] [road_name]". The preprocessor is implemented with a local chart parser, which is a variation of the robust parser introduced in (Wang, 1999). The robust local parser can skip noise words in the sentence, which ensures that the system has the low level robustness. For example, "1954 of the Huashan Road)" can also be recognized as [address] by skipping the words "of the". However, the robust local parser possibly skips the words in the sentence by mistake and produces an incorrect class label. To avoid this side-effect, this local parser exploits an embedded decision tree for pruning, of which the details can be seen in (Wu et al., 2005). According to our experience, it is fairly easy for a general developer with good understanding of the application to author the small grammar used by the local chart parser and annotate the training cases for the embedded decision tree. The work can be finished in several hours.

2.2 Topic Classification

Given the representation of semantic frame, topic classification can be regarded as identifying the frame type. It is suited to be dealt using pattern recognition techniques. The application of statistical pattern techniques to topic classification can improve the robustness of the whole understanding system. Also, in our system, topic classification can greatly reduce the search space and hence improve the performance of subsequent semantic classification. For example, the total number of slots into which the concept [location] can be filled in all topics is 33 and the corresponding maximum number of slots in a single topic is decreased to 10.

Many statistical pattern recognition techniques have been applied to similar tasks, such as Naïve Bayes, N-Gram and Support Vector Machines (SVMs) (Wang et al., 2002). According to the literature (Wang et al., 2002) and our experiments, the SVMs showed the best performance among many other statistical classifiers. Also, it has been showed that active learning can be effectively applied to the SVMs (Schohn and Cohn, 2000; Tong and Koller, 2000). Therefore, we choose the SVMs as the topic classifier. We resorted to the LIBSVM toolkit (Chang and Lin, 2001) to construct the SVMs for our experiments. Following the practice in (Wang et al., 2002), the SVMs use a binary valued features vector. If the simplest feature (Chinese character) is used, each query is converted into a feature vector $\overline{ch} = < ch_1, \ldots, ch_{|\overline{ch}|} >$ ($|\overline{ch}|$ is the total number of Chinese characters occur in the corpus) with binary valued elements: 1 if a given Chinese character is in this input sentence or 0 otherwise. Due to the existence of the preprocessor, we can also include semantic class labels (e.g., [location]) as features for topic classification. Intuitively, the class label features are more informative than the

[1] Because the length is limited, in this paper we only illustrate all the example sentences in English, which are Chinese sentences, in fact.

Chinese character features. At the same time, including class labels as features can also relieve the data sparseness problem.

2.3 Topic-dependent Semantic Classification

The job of semantic classification is to assign the concepts with the most likely slots. It can also be modeled as a classification problem since the number of possible slot names for each concept is limited. Let's consider the example sentence in Figure 1. After the preprocessing and topic classification, we get the preprocessed result "*Please tell me how can I go from [location]$_1$ to [location]$_2$ by [bus]?*" and the topic **ShowRoute**. We have to work out which slots are to be filled with the values such as [location]$_2$. The first clue is the surrounding literal context. Intuitively, we can infer that it is a [destination] since a [destination] indicator "to" is before it. If [location]$_1$ has already been recognized as a [origin], it is another clue to imply that [location]$_2$ is a [destina tion]. Since initially the slot context is not available, the slot context is only employed for the semantic re-classification, which will be described in latter section.

To learn the topic-dependent semantic classifiers, the training sentences need to be annotated against the semantic frame. Our annotating scenario is relatively simple and can be performed by general developers. For example, for the sentence "*Please tell me how can I go from the people's square to the bund by bus?*", the annotated results are like the following:

FRAME: **ShowRoute**
Slots: [route].[origin].[location].(the people's square)
[route].[destination].[location].(the bund)
[route].[transport_type].[by_bus].(bus)

The corresponding slot names can be automatically extracted from the domain model. A domain model is usually a hierarchical structure of the relevant concepts in the application domain. For every occurrence of a concept in the domain model graph, we list all the concept names along the path from the root to its occurrence position and regard their concatenation as a slot name. Thus, the slot name is not flat since it inherits the hierarchy from the domain model.

With provision of the annotated data, we can collect all the literal and slot context features related to each concept. The examples of features for the concept [location] are illustrated as follows:

(1) *to* within the –3 windows
(2) *from _ to*
(3) *ShowRoute.[route].[origin]* within the ±2 windows

The former two are literal context features. Feature (1) is a context-word that tends to indicate ShowRoute.[route].[destination]. Feature (2) is a collocation that checks for the pattern "from" and "to" immediately before and after the concept [location] respectively, and tends to indicate ShowRoute.[route].[origin]. The third one is a slot context feature, which tends to imply the target concept [location] is of type ShowRoute.[route].[destination]. In nature, these features are equivalent to the rules in the semantic grammar used by the robust rule-based parser. For example, the feature (2) has the same function as the semantic rule "[origin] → from [location] to". The advantage of our approach is that we can automatically learn the semantic "rules" from the training data rather than manually authoring them. Also, the learned "rules" are intrinsically robust since they may involves gaps, for example, feature (1) allows skipping some noise words between "to" and [location].

The next problem is how to apply these features when predicting a new case since the active features for a new case may make opposite predictions. One simple and effective strategy is employed by the decision list (Rivest, 1987), i.e., always applying the strongest features. In a decision list, all the features are sorted in order of descending confidence. When a new target concept is classified, the classifier runs down the list and compares the features against the contexts of the target concept. The first matched feature is applied to make a predication. Obviously, how to measure the confidence of features is a very important issue for the decision list. We use the metric described in (Yarowsky, 1994; Golding, 1995). Provided that $P(s_1 \mid f) > 0$ for all i:

$$confidence(f) = \max_i P(s_i \mid f) \quad (1)$$

This value measures the extent to which the context is unambiguously correlated with one particular slot s_i.

2.4 Slot-value merging and semantic re-classification

The slot-value merger is to combine the slots assigned to the concepts in an input sentence. Another simultaneous task of the slot-value merger is to check the consistency among the identified slot-values. Since the topic-dependent classifiers corresponding to different concepts are training and running independently, it possibly results in inconsistent predictions. Considering the preprocessed word sequence "*Please tell me how can I go from [location]$_1$ to [location]$_2$ by [bus]*", they are semantically clashed if [location]$_1$ and [location]$_2$ are both classified as ShowRoute.[route].[origin]. To relieve this problem, we can use the semantic classifier based on the slot context feature. We apply the context features like, for example, "ShowRoute.[route].[origin] within the $\pm k$ windows", which tends to imply ShowRoute.[route].[destination]. The literal contexts reflect the local lexical semantic dependency. The slot contexts, however, are good at capturing the long distance dependency. Therefore, when the slot-value merger finds that two or more slot-value pairs clash, it first anchors the one with the highest confidence. Then, it extracts the slot contexts for the other concepts and passes them to the semantic classification module for re-classification. If the re- classification results still clash, the dialog system can involve the user in an interactive dialog for clarity.

The idea of semantic classification and re-classification can be understood as follows: it first finds the concept or slot islands (like partial parsing) and then links them together. This mechanism is well-suited for SLU since the spoken utterance usually consists of several phrases and noises (restart, repeats and filled pauses, etc) are most often between them (Ward and Issar, 1994). Especially, this phenomena and the out-of-order structures are very frequent in the spoken Chinese utterances.

3 Weakly Supervised Training of the Topic Classifier and Topic-dependent Semantic Classifiers

As stated before, to train the classifiers for topic identification and slot-filling, we need to label each sentence in the training set against the semantic frame. Although this annotating scenario is relatively minimal, the labeling process is still time-consuming and costly. Meanwhile unlabeled sentences are relatively easy to collect. Therefore, to reduce the cost of labeling training utterances, we employ weakly supervised techniques for training the topic and semantic classifiers.

The weakly supervised training of the two classifiers is successive. Assume that a small amount of seed sentences are manually labeled against the semantic frame. We first exploit the labeled frame types (e.g. **ShowRoute**) of the seed sentences to train a topic classifier through the combination of active learning and self-training. The resulting topic classifier is used to label the remaining training sentences with the corresponding topic, which are not selected by active learning. Then, we use all the sentences annotated against the semantic frame (including the seed sentences and sentences labeled by active learning) and the remaining training sentences labeled the topic to train the semantic classifiers using a practical bootstrapping technique.

3.1 Combining Active Learning and Self-training for Topic Classification

We employ the strategy of combining active learning and self-training for training the topic classifier, which was firstly proposed in (Tur et al., 2005) and applied to a similar task.

One way to reduce the number of labeling examples is active learning, which have been applied in many domains (McCallum and Nigam, 1998; Tang et al., 2002; Tur et al., 2005). Usually, the classifier is trained by randomly sampling the training examples. However, in active learning, the classifier is trained by selectively sampling the training examples (Cohn et al., 1994). The basic idea is that the most informative ones are selected from the unlabeled examples for a human to label. That is to say, this strategy tries to always select the examples, which will have the largest improvement on performance, and hence minimizes the human labeling effort whilst keeping performance (Tur et al., 2005). According to the strategy of determining the informative level of an example, the active learning approaches can be divided into two categories: uncertainty-based and committee-based. Here, we employ the uncertainty-based strategy for selective sampling. It is assumed that a small amount of labeled examples is initially available, which is used to train a basic classifier. Then the classifier is applied to the unannotated examples. Typically the most unconfident examples are selected for a human to label and then added to the training set. The classifier is re-trained and the procedure is repeated until the system performance converges.

Another alternative for reducing human labeling effort is self-training. In self-training, an initial classifier is built using a small amount of annotated examples. The classifier is then used to label the unannotated training examples. The examples with classification confidence scores over a certain threshold, together with their predicted labels, are added to the training set to retrain the classifier. This procedure repeated until the system performance converges.

These two strategies are complementary and hence can be combined. The combination strategy is quite straightforward for pool-based training. At each iteration, the current classifier is applied to the examples in the current pool. The most unconfident examples in the pool are selected by active learning and labeled by a human. The remaining examples in the pool are automatically labeled by the current classifier. Then, these two parts of labeled examples are both added into the training set and used for retraining the classifier. Since the LIBSVM toolkit provides the class probability, we directly use the class probability as the confidence score. Our dynamic pool-based (the pool size is n) algorithm of combining active learning and self-training for training the topic classifier is as follows:

1. Given a small amount of human-labeled training set S_t (n sentences) and a larger amount of unlabeled set S_u , build the initial classifier using S_t .
2. While labelers/ sentences are available
   (a) Get n unlabeled sentences from S_u
   (b) Apply the current classifier to n unlabeled sentences
   (c) Select m examples which are most informative to the current classifier and manually label the selected m examples
   (d) Add the m human-labeled examples and the remaining $n-m$ machine-labeled examples to the training set S_t
   (e) Train a new classifier on all labeled examples

3.2 Bootstrapping the Topic-dependent Semantic Classifiers

Bootstrapping refers to a problem of inducing a classifier given a small set of labeled data and a large set of unlabeled data (Abney, 2002). It has been applied to problems such as word-sense disambiguation (Yarowsky, 1995), web-page classification (Blum and Mitchell, 1998), named-entity recognition (Collins and Singer, 1999) and automatic construction of semantic lexicon (Thelen and Riloff, 2003). The key to the bootstrapping methods is to exploit the redundancy in the unlabeled data (Collins and Singer, 1999). Thus, many language processing problems can be dealt using the bootstrapping methods since language is highly redundant (Yarowsky, 1995). The semantic classification problem here also exhibits the redundancy. In the example "*Please tell me how can I go from [location]$_1$ to [location]$_2$ by [bus]?*", there are multiple literal context features which all indicate that [location]$_1$ is of type ShowRoute.[route].[origin], such as:

(1) *from* within the –1 windows;
(2) *from _ to* ;
(3) *to* within the +1 windows.

If the [location]$_2$ has already be recognized as ShowRoute.[route].[destination], thus the slot context feature "ShowRoute.[route].[origin] within the ± 2 windows" is also a strong evidence that [location]$_1$ is of type ShowRoute.[route].[origin]. That is to say, the literal context and slot context features above effectively overdetermine the slot of a concept in the input sentence. Especially, the literal and slot context features can be seen as two natural "views" of an example from the respective of "Co-Training" (Blum and Mitchell, 1998). Our bootstrapping algorithm exploits the property of redundancy to incrementally identify the features for assigning slots of a concept, given a few annotated seed sentences.

The bootstrapping algorithm is performed on each topic T_i ($1 \le i \le n$, n is the number of topic) as follows:

1. For each concept C_j in T_i ($1 \le j \le m$, m is the number of concepts appears in the sentences of topic T_i):

(1.1) Build the two initial classifiers based on literal and slot context features respectively using a small amount of labeled seed sentences.

(1.2) Apply the current classifier based on the literal context feature to the remaining unlabeled concepts in the training sentences belong to topic T_i . Keep those classified slots with confidence score above a certain threshold (In this paper, the threshold is fixed on 0.5).

2. Check the consistency of the classified slots in each sentence. If some slots in a sentence clashed, take the one with the highest confidence score among them and leave the others unlabeled.
3. For each concept C_j in T_i, apply the current classifier based on the slot context to the residual unlabeled concepts. Keep those classi-

fied slots with confidence score above a certain threshold. Repeat Step 3.

4. Augment the new classified cases into the training set and retrain the two classifiers based on literal and slot context features respectively.
5. If new slots are classified from the training data, return to step 2. Otherwise, repeat 2-5 to label training data and keep all new classified slots regardless of the confidence score. Train the two final semantic classifiers based on the literal and context features respectively using the new labeled training data.

4 Experiments and Results

4.1 Data Collection and Experimental Setting

Our experiments were carried out in the context of Chinese public transportation information inquiry domain. We collected two kinds of corpus for our domain using different ways. Firstly, a natural language corpus was collected through a specific website which simulated a dialog system. The user can conduct some mixed-initiative conversational dialogues with it by typing Chinese queries. Then we collected 2,286 natural language utterances through this way. It was divided into two parts: the training set contained 1,800 sentences (TR), and the test set contained 486 sentences (TS1). Also, a spoken language corpus was collected through the deployment of a preliminary version of telephone-based dialog system, of which the speech recognizer is based on the speaker-independent Chinese dictation system of IBM ViaVoice Telephony and the SLU component is a robust rule-based parser. The spoken utterances corpus contained 363 spoken utterances. Then we obtained two test set from this corpus: one consisted of the recognized text (TS2); the other consisted of the corresponding transcription (TS3). The Chinese character error rate and concept error rate of TS2 are 35.6% and 41.1% respectively. We defined ten types of topic for our domain: **ListStop**, **ShowFare**, **ShowRoute**, **ShowRouteTime**, etc. The first corpus covers all the ten topic types and the second corpus only covers four topic types. The total number of Chinese characters appear in the data set is 923. All the sentences were annotated against the semantic frame. In our experiments, the topic classifier and semantic classifiers were trained on the natural language training set (TR) and tested on three test sets (TS1, TS2 and TS3).

The performance of topic classification and semantic classification are measured in terms of topic error rate and slot error rate respectively. Topic performance is measured by comparing the topic of a sentence predicated by the topic classifier with the reference topic. The slot error rate is measured by counting the insertion, deletion and substitution errors between the slots generated by our system and these in the reference annotation.

4.2 Supervised Training Experiments

Firstly, in order to validate the effectiveness of our proposed SLU system using successive learners, we compared our system with a rule-based robust semantic parser. The parsing algorithm of this parser is same as the local chart parser used by the preprocessor. The handcrafted grammar for this semantic parser took a linguistic expert one month to develop, which consists of 798 rules (except the lexical rules for named entities such as [loc_name]). In our SLU system, we first use the SVMs to identify the topic and then apply the semantic classifier (decision list) related to the identified topic to assign the slots to the concepts. The SVMs used the augmented binary features (923 Chinese characters and 20 semantic class labels). A general developer independently annotated the TR set against the semantic frame, which took only four days. Through feature extraction from the TR set and feature pruning, we obtained 2,259 literal context features and 369 slot context features for 20 kinds of concepts in our domain. Table 1 Shows that our SLU method has better performance than the rule-based robust parser in both topic classification and slot identification. Due to the high concept error rate of recognized utterances, the performance of semantic classification on the TS2 is relatively poor. However, if considering only the correctly identified concepts on TS2, the slot error rate is 9.2%. Note that, since the TS2 (recognized speech) covers only four types of topic but TS1 (typed utterance) covers ten topics, the topic error on the TS2 (recognized speech) is lower than that on TS1.

Table 1 also compares our system with the two-stage classification with the reversed order. Another alternative for our system is to reverse the two main processing stages, i.e., finding the roles for the concepts prior to identifying the topic. For instance, in the example sentence in Fig.1, the concept (e.g., [location]) in the preprocessed sequence is first recognized as slots (e.g., [route].[origin]) before topic classification.

Therefore, the slots like [route].[origin] can be included as features for topic classification, which is deeper than the concepts like [location] and potential to achieve improvement on performance of topic classification. This strategy was adopted in some previous works (He and Young, 2003; Wutiwiwatchai and Furui, 2003). However, the results indicate that, at least in our two-stage classification formwork, the strategy of identifying the topic before assigning the slots to the concepts is more optimal. According to our error analysis, the unsatisfied performance of the reversed two-stage classification system can be explained as follows: (1) Since the semantic classification is performed on all topics, the search space is much bigger and the ambiguities increase. This deteriorates the performance of semantic classification. (2) In the case that the slots and Chinese characters are included as features, the topic classifier relies heavily on the slot features. Then, the errors of semantic classification have serious negative effect on the topic classification.

Table 1: Performance comparsion of the rule-based robust semantic parser, the reversed two-stage classification system and our SLU systems (TER: Topic Error Rate; SER: Slot Error Rate; DL: Decision List)

	TS1		TS2		TS3	
	TER (%)	SER (%)	TER (%)	SER (%)	TER (%)	SER (%)
Rule-based semantic parser	6.8	11.6	4.1	47.9	3.0	5.4
Reversed two-stage classification system	4.9	11.1	3.6	47.4	2.5	4.9
Our system	2.9	8.4	2.2	45.6	1.4	4.6

4.3 Weakly Supervised Training Experiments

4.3.1 Active Learning and Self-training Experiments for Topic Classification

In order to evaluate the performance of active learning and self-training, we compared three sampling strategies: random sampling, active learning only, active learning and self-training. At each iteration of pool-based active learning and self-training, we get 200 sentences (i.e., the pool size is set as 200) and select 50 most unconfident sentences from them for manually labeling and exploit the remaining sentences using self-training. All the experiments were repeated ten times with different randomly selected seed sentences and the results were averaged. Figure 1 plots the learning curves of three strategies trained on TR and tested on the TS1 set. It is evident that active learning significantly reduces the need for labeled data. For instance, it requires 1600 examples if they are randomly chosen to achieve a topic error rate of 3.2% on TS1, but only 600 actively selected examples, a saving of 62.5%. The strategy of combing active learning and self-training can further improve the performance of topic classification compared with active learning only with the same amount of labeled data.

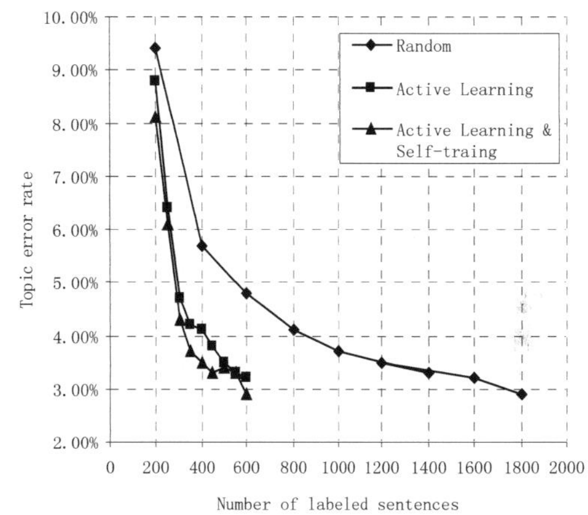

Figure 2: Learning curves using different sampling strategies.

We also evaluated the performance of topic classification using active learning and self-training with the pool size of 200 on the three test sets. Table 2 shows that active learning and self-training with the pool size of 200 achieves almost the same performance on three test sets as random sampling, but requires only 33.3% data.

Table 2: The topic error rate using active learning and self-training with pool size of 200 on the three test sets (AL: Active Learning)

	TS1 (%)	TS2 (%)	TS3 (%)	Labeled Sent.(#)
Random	2.9	2.2	1.4	1,800
AL	3.2	2.5	1.7	600
AL & self-training	2.9	2.5	1.4	600

4.3.2 Bootstrapping Experiments for Semantic Classification

As stated before, the bootstrapping procedure begins with a small amount of sentences annotated against the semantic frame, which is the initial seed sentence or annotated by active learning, and the remaining training sentences, the topics of which are machine-labeled by the resulting topic classifier. For example, in the weakly supervised training scenario with the pool size of 200, the active learning and self-training procedure ran 8 iterations. At each iteration, 50 sentences were selected by active learning. So the total number of labeled sentences is 600. We compared our bootstrapping methods with supervised training for semantic classification. We tried two bootstrapping methods: using only the literal context features (Bootstrapping 1) and using the literal and slot context features (Bootstrapping 2). If the step 4 of the bootstrapping algorithm in Section 3.2 is canceled, the new bootstrapping variation corresponds to Bootstrapping 2. Also, we repeated the experiments ten times with different labeled sentences and the results were averaged. Figure 3 plots the learning curves of bootstrapping and supervised training with different number of labeled sentences on the TS1 set. The results indicate that bootstrapping methods can effectively make use of the unlabeled data to improve the semantic classification performance. In particular, the learning curve of bootstrapping 1 achieves more significant improvement than the curve of bootstrapping 2. It can be explained as follows: including the slot context features further increases the redundancy of data and hence corrects the initial misclassified cases by the semantic classifier using only literal context features or provides new cases.

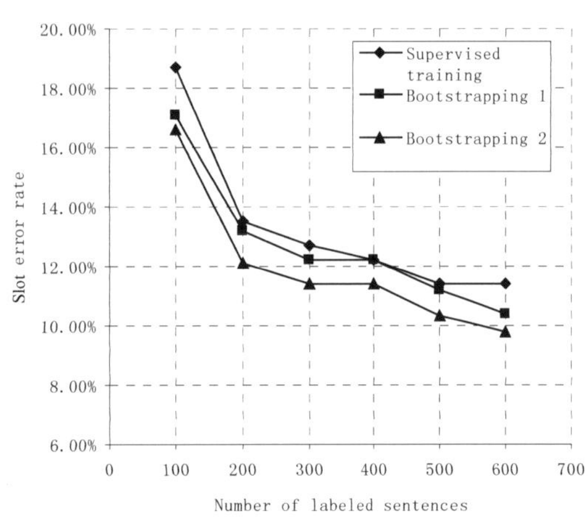

Figure 3: Learning curves of bootstrapping methods for semantic classification on TS1.

Finally, we compared two SLU systems through weakly supervised and supervised training respectively. The supervised one was trained using all the annotated sentences in TR (1800 sentences). In the weakly supervised training scenario (the pool size is still 200), The topic classifier and semantic classifiers were both trained using only 600 labeled sentences. Table 3 shows that the weakly supervised scenario achieves comparable performance to the supervised one, but requires only 33.3% labeled data.

Table 3: Performance comparison of two SLU systems through weakly supervised and supervised training on the three test sets (TER: Topic Error Rate; SER: Slot Error Rate)

	TS1		TS2		TS3	
	TER (%)	SER (%)	TER (%)	SER (%)	TER (%)	SER (%)
Supervised	2.9	8.4	2.2	45.6	1.4	4.6
Weakly Supervised	2.9	9.7	2.5	44.8	1.4	5.7

5 Conclusion and Future work

We have presented a new SLU framework using two successive classifiers. The proposed framework exhibits the advantages as follows.

- It has good robustness on processing spoken language: (1) The preprocessor provides the low level robustness. (2) It inherits the robustness of topic classification using statistical pattern recognition techniques. It can also make use of topic classification to guide slot filling. (3) The strategy of first finding the concepts or slot islands and then linking them is suited for processing spoken language.
- It also keeps the understanding deepness: (1) The class of semantic classification is the slot name, which inherits the hierarchy from the domain model. (2) The semantic re-classification mechanism ensures the consistency among the identified slot-value pairs.
- It is mainly data-driven and requires only minimally annotated corpus for training. Most importantly, our proposed SLU framework allows the employment of weakly supervised strategies for training the two classifiers, which can reduce the cost of annotating labeled sentences.

The future work includes further evaluation of our approach in other application domains and languages. We also plan to integrate this understanding system into a whole dialog system. Then, high level knowledges, such as the dialog context, can also be included as the features of topic and semantic classifiers. Moreover, currently, the topics are manually defined through examination of the example sentences by human. Then, it is worthwhile to investigate how to appropriately define topics and the probability of exploiting the sentence clustering techniques to facilitate the topic (frame) designment.

6 Acknowledgements

The authors would like to thank three anonymous reviewers for their careful reading and helpful suggestions. This work is supported by National Natural Science Foundation of China (NSFC, No. 60496326) and 863 project of China (No. 2001AA114210-11).

References

S. Abney. 2002. *Bootstrapping*. In Proc. of ACL, pp. 360-367, Philadelphia, PA.

A. Blum and T. Mitchell. 1998. *Combining labeled and unlabeled data with co-training*. In Proc. of COLT, Madison, WI.

C. Chang and C. Lin. 2001. *LIBSVM: a library for support vector machines*. Software available at http://www.csie.ntu.edu.tw/~cjlin/libsvm.

D. Cohn, L. Atlas and R. Ladner. 1994. *Improving generalization with active learning*. Machine Learning 15, pp.201-221.

M. Collins and Y. Singer.1999. *Unsupervised models for named entity classification*. In Proc. of EMNLP.

J. Dowding, J. M. Gawron, D. Appelt, J. Bear, L. Cherny, R. Moore, and D. Moran. 1993. *GEMINI: A natural language system for spoken-language understanding*. In Proc. of ACL, Columbus, Ohio, pp. 54-61.

R. Golding. 1995. *A Bayesian Hybrid Method for Context-sensitive Spelling Correction*. In Proc. 3rd Workshop on Very Large Corpora, Boston, MA.

Y. He and S.J. Young. 2003. *A Data-Driven Spoken Language Understanding System*. IEEE Workshop on Automatic Speech Recognition and Understanding, US Virgin Islands.

Y. He and S. Young. 2005. *Semantic Processing using the Hidden Vector State Model*. Computer Speech and Language 19(1): 85-106.

A. McCallum and K. Nigam.1998. *Employing EM and pool-based active learning for text classification*. In Proc. of ICML.

S. Miller, R. Bobrow, R. Ingria, and R. Schwartz. 1994. *Hidden Understanding Models of Natural Language*. In Proc. of ACL, pp. 25-32.

R. Pieraccini and E. Levin. 1993. *A learning approach to natural language understanding*. NATO-ASI, New Advances & Trends in Speech Recognition and Coding, Springer-Verlag, Bubion, Spain.

R. L. Rivest. 1987. *Learning decision lists*. Machine Learning, 2(3):229--246, 1987.

S. Seneff. 1992. *TINA: A natural language system for spoken language applications*. Computational Linguistics, vol. 18, no. 1., pp. 61-86.

G. Schohn and D. Cohn. 2000. *Less Is More: Active Learning with Support Vector Machines*. In Proc. of ICML, pp. 839-846.

M. Tang, X. Luo, S. Roukos.2002. *Active learning for statistical natural language parsing*. In Proc. of ACL, Philadelphia, Pennsylvania.

M. Thelen and E. Riloff. 2002. *A Bootstrapping Method for Learning Semantic Lexicons using Extraction Pattern Contexts*. In Proc. of EMNLP'02.

S. Tong and D. Koller. 2000. *Support Vector Machine Active Learning with Applications to Text Classification*. In Proc. of ICML, pp. 999-1006.

G. Tur, D. Hakkani-Tür, Robert E. Schapire. *Combining Active and Semi-Supervised Learning for Spoken Language Understanding*. Speech Communication, Vol. 45, No. 2, pp. 171-186, 2005.

Y. Wang. 1999. *A Robust Parser for Spoken Language Understanding*. In Proc. of EUROSPEECH. Budapest, Hungary.

Y. Wang and A Acero. 2001.*Grammar learning for spoken language understanding*. In Proc. of ASRU Workshop, Madonna di Campiglio, Italy.

Y. Wang, A. Acero, C. Chelba, B. Frey and L. Wong. 2002. *Combination of Statistical and Rule-based Approaches for Spoken Language Understanding*, In ICSLP. Denver, Colorado.

W. Ward and S. Issar. 1994. *Recent Improvements in the CMU Spoken Language Understanding System*. In Proc. of ARPA Workshop on HLT, March, 1994.

W Wu, J Duan, R Lu, F Gao. 2005. *Embedded machine learning systems for Robust Spoken Language Parsing*. In Proc. of IEEE NLP-KE, Wuhan, China.

C. Wutiwiwatchai and S. Furui. 2003. *Combination of Finite State Automata and Neural Network for Spoken Language Understanding*. In Proc. of EUROSPEECH2003, Geneva, Switzerland.

D. Yarowsky. 1994. *Decision Lists for Lexical Ambiguity Resolution: Application to Accent Restoration in Spanish and French*. In Proc. of ACL 1994, pp. 88-95.

Humor: Prosody Analysis and Automatic Recognition for F * R * I * E * N * D * S *

Amruta Purandare and Diane Litman
Intelligent Systems Program
University of Pittsburgh
{amruta,litman}@cs.pitt.edu

Abstract

We analyze humorous spoken conversations from a classic comedy television show, FRIENDS, by examining acoustic-prosodic and linguistic features and their utility in automatic humor recognition. Using a simple annotation scheme, we automatically label speaker turns in our corpus that are followed by *laughs* as humorous and the rest as non-humorous. Our humor-prosody analysis reveals significant differences in prosodic characteristics (such as pitch, tempo, energy etc.) of humorous and non-humorous speech, even when accounted for the gender and speaker differences. Humor recognition was carried out using standard supervised learning classifiers, and shows promising results significantly above the baseline.

1 Introduction

As conversational systems are becoming prevalent in our lives, we notice an increasing need for adding social intelligence in computers. There has been a considerable amount of research on incorporating affect (Litman and Forbes-Riley, 2004) (Alm et al., 2005) (D'Mello et al., 2005) (Shroder and Cowie, 2005) (Klein et al., 2002) and personality (Gebhard et al., 2004) in computer interfaces, so that, for instance, user frustrations can be recognized and addressed in a graceful manner. As (Binsted, 1995) correctly pointed out, one way to alleviate user frustrations, and to make human-computer interaction more natural, personal and interesting for the users, is to model HUMOR.

Research in computational humor is still in very early stages, partially because humorous language often uses complex, ambiguous and incongruous syntactic and semantic expressions (Attardo, 1994) (Mulder and Nijholt, 2002) which require deep semantic interpretation. Nonetheless, recent studies have shown a feasibility of automatically recognizing (Mihalcea and Strapparava, 2005) (Taylor and Mazlack, 2004) and generating (Binsted and Ritchie, 1997) (Stock and Strapparava, 2005) humor in computer systems. The state of the art research in computational humor (Binsted et al., 2006) is, however, limited to text (such as humorous *one-liners*, *acronyms* or *wordplays*), and to our knowledge, there has been no work to date on automatic humor recognition in spoken conversations.

Before we can model humor in real application systems, we must first analyze features that characterize humor. Computational approaches to humor recognition so far primarily rely on lexical and stylistic cues such as alliteration, antonyms, adult slang (Mihalcea and Strapparava, 2005). The focus of our study is, on the other hand, on analyzing acoustic-prosodic cues (such as pitch, intensity, tempo etc.) in humorous conversations and testing if these cues can help us to automatically distinguish between humorous and non-humorous (normal) utterances in speech. We hypothesize that not only the lexical content but also the prosody (or how the content is expressed) makes humorous expressions *humorous*.

The following sections describe our data collection and pre-processing, followed by the discussion of various acoustic-prosodic as well as other types of features used in our humorous-speech analysis and classification experiments. We then present our experiments, results, and finally end with conclusions and future work.

Proceedings of the 2006 Conference on Empirical Methods in Natural Language Processing (EMNLP 2006), pages 208–215,
Sydney, July 2006.

2 FRIENDS Corpus

(Scherer, 2003) discuss a number of pros and cons of using *real* versus *acted* data, in the context of emotional speech analysis. His main argument is that while real data offers natural expressions of emotions, it is not only hard to collect (due to ethical issues) but also very challenging to annotate and analyze, as there are very few instances of strong expressions and the rest are often very subtle. Acted data (also referred to as *portrayed* or *simulated*), on the other hand, offers ample of prototypical examples, although these are criticized for not being *natural* at times. To achieve some balance between naturalness and strength/number of humorous expressions, we decided to use dialogs from a comedy television show FRIENDS, which provides classical examples of casual, humorous conversations between friends who often discuss very real-life issues, such as job, career, relationships etc.

We collected a total of 75 dialogs (scenes) from six episodes of FRIENDS, four from Season I (Monica Gets a New Roommate, The One with Two Parts: Part 1 and 2, All the Poker) and two from Season II (Ross Finds Out, The Prom Video), all available on *The Best of Friends Volume I* DVD. This gave us approximately 2 hrs of audio. Text transcripts of these episodes were obtained from: *http://www.friendscafe.org/scripts.shtml*, and were used to extract lexical features (used later in classification).

Figure 1 shows an excerpt from one of the dialogs in our corpus.

[1] Rachel: Guess what?
[2] Ross: You got a job?
[3] Rachel: Are you kidding? I am trained for nothing!
[4] <Laughter>
[5] Rachel: I was laughed out of twelve interviews today.
[6] Chandler: And yet you're surprisingly upbeat.
[7] Rachel: You would be too if you found John and David boots on sale, fifty percent off!
[8] <Laughter>
[9] Chandler: Oh, how well you know me...
[10] <Laughter>
[11] Rachel: They are my new, I don't need a job, I don't need my parents, I got great boots, boots!
[12] <Laughter>
[13] Monica: How'd you pay for them?
[14] Rachel: Uh, credit card.
[15] Monica: And who pays for that?
[16] Rachel: Um... my... father.
[17] <Laughter>

Figure 1: Dialog Excerpt

3 Audio Segmentation and Annotation

We segmented each audio file (manually) by marking speaker turn boundaries, using Wavesurfer (http://www.speech.kth.se/wavesurfer). We apply a fairly straightforward annotation scheme to automatically identify humorous and non-humorous turns in our corpus. Speaker turns that are followed by artificial laughs are labeled as *Humorous*, and all the rest as *Non-Humorous*. For example, in the dialog excerpt shown in figure 1, turns 3, 7, 9, 11 and 16 are marked as *humorous*, whereas turns 1, 2, 5, 6, 13, 14, 15 are marked as *non-humorous*. Artificial laughs, silences longer than 1 second and segments of audio that contain purely non-verbal sounds (such as phone rings, door bells, music etc.) were excluded from the analysis. By considering only speaker turns that are followed by laughs as humorous, we also automatically eliminate cases of pure visual comedy where humor is expressed using only gestures or facial expressions. In short, non-verbal sounds or silences followed by laughs are not treated as humorous. Henceforth, by *turn*, we mean proper speaker turns (and not non-verbal turns). We currently do not apply any special filters to remove non-verbal sounds or background noise (other than laughs) that overlap with speaker turns. However, if artificial laughs overlap with a speaker turn (there were only few such instances), the speaker turn is chopped by marking a turn boundary exactly before/after the laughs begin/end. This is to ensure that our prosody analysis is fair and does not catch any cues from the laughs. In other words, we make sure that our speaker turns are *clean* and not garbled by laughs.

After segmentation, we got a total of 1629 speaker turns, of which 714 (43.8%) are humorous, and 915 (56.2%) are non-humorous. We also made sure that there is a 1-to-1 correspondence between speaker turns in text transcripts that were obtained online and our audio segments, and corrected few cases where there was a mis-match (due to turn-chopping or errors in online transcripts).

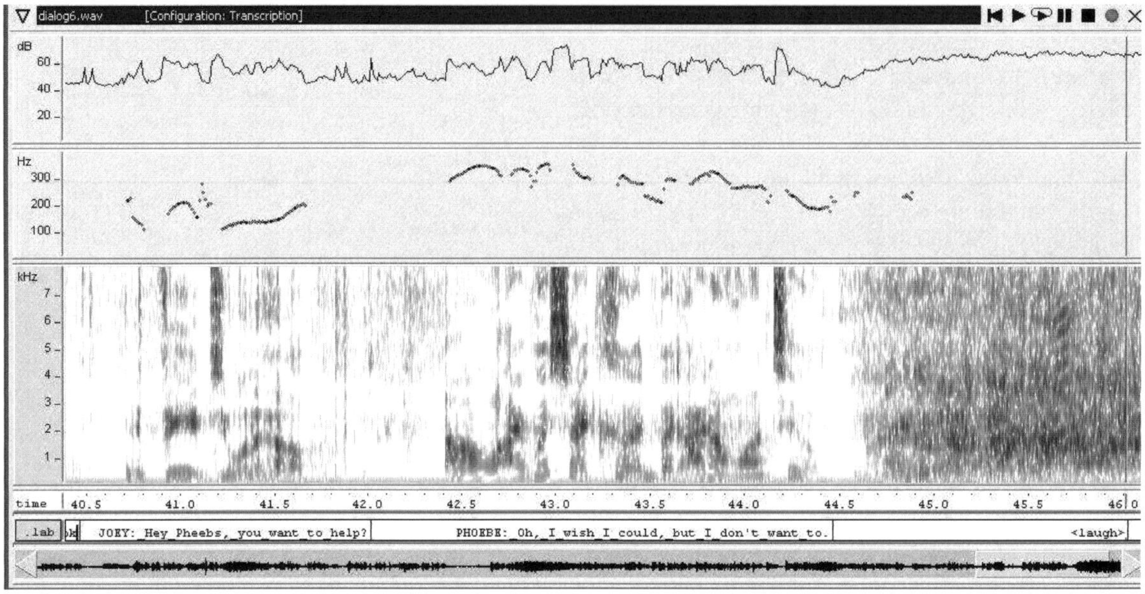

Figure 2: Audio Segmentation, Transcription and Feature Extraction using Wavesurfer

4 Speaker Distributions

There are 6 *main* actors/speakers (3 male and 3 female) in this show, along with a number of (in our data 26) guest actors who appear briefly and rarely in some of our dialogs. As the number of guest actors is quite large, and their individual contribution is less than 5% of the turns in our data, we decided to group all the guest actors together in one *GUEST* class.

As these are *acted* (not real) conversations, there were only few instances of speaker turn-overlaps, where multiple speakers speak together. These turns were given a speaker label *MULTI*. Table 1 shows the total number of turns and humorous turns for each speaker, along with their percentages in braces. Percentages for the Humor column show, out of the total (714) humorous turns, how many are by each speaker. As one can notice, the distribution of turns is fairly balanced among the six main speakers. We also notice that even though each guest actors' individual contribution is less than 5% in our data, their combined contribution is fairly large, almost 16% of the total turns.

Table 2 shows that the six main actors together form a total of 83% of our data. Also, of the total 714 humorous turns, 615 (86%) turns are by the main actors. To study if prosody of humor differs across males and females, we also grouped the main actors into two gender classes. Table 2 shows that the gender distribution is fairly balanced among the main actors, with 50.5% male and 49.5% female turns. We also see that of the 685 male turns, 347 turns (almost 50%) are humorous, and of the 672 female turns, 268 (approximately 40%) are humorous. Guest actors and multi-speaker turns are not considered in the gender analysis.

Speaker	#Turns(%)	#Humor (%)
Chandler (M)	244 (15)	163 (22.8)
Joey (M)	153 (9.4)	57 (8)
Monica (F)	219 (13.4)	74 (10.4)
Phoebe (F)	180 (11.1)	104 (14.6)
Rachel (F)	273 (16.8)	90 (12.6)
Ross (M)	288 (17.7)	127 (17.8)
GUEST (26)	263 (16.1)	95 (13.3)
MULTI	9 (0.6)	4 (0.6)

Table 1: Speaker Distribution

Speaker	#Turns	#Humor
Male	685 (50.5% of Main)	347 (50.6% of Male)
Female	672 (49.5% Of Main)	268 (39.9% of Female)
Total Main	1357 (83.3% of Total)	615 (86.1% of Humor)

Table 2: Gender Distribution for Main Actors

5 Features

Literature in emotional speech analysis (Liscombe et al., 2003)(Litman and Forbes-Riley, 2004) (Scherer, 2003)(Ang et al., 2002) has shown that prosodic features such as pitch, energy, speaking rate (tempo) are useful indicators of emotional states, such as joy, anger, fear, boredom etc. While humor is not necessarily considered as an emotional state, we noticed that most humorous utterances in our corpus (and also in general) often make use of hyper-articulations, similar to those found in emotional speech.

For this study, we use a number of acoustic-prosodic as well as some non acoustic-prosodic features as listed below:

Acoustic-Prosodic Features:

- Pitch (F0): Mean, Max, Min, Range, Standard Deviation
- Energy (RMS): Mean, Max, Min, Range, Standard Deviation
- Temporal: Duration, Internal Silence, Tempo

Non Acoustic-Prosodic Features:

- Lexical
- Turn Length (#Words)
- Speaker

Our acoustic-prosodic features make use of the pitch, energy and temporal information in the speech signal, and are computed using Wavesurfer. Figure 2 shows Wavesurfer's energy (dB), pitch (Hz), and transcription (.lab) panes. The transcription interface shows text corresponding to the dialog turns, along with the turn boundaries. All features are computed at the turn level, and essentially measure the mean, maximum, minimum, range (maximum-minimum) and standard deviation of the feature value (F0 or RMS) over the entire turn (ignoring zeroes). Duration is measured in terms of time in seconds, from the beginning to the end of the turn including pauses (if any) in between. Internal silence is measured as the percentage of zero F0 frames, and essentially account for the amount of silence in the turn. Tempo is computed as the total number of syllables divided by the duration of the turn. For computing the number of syllables per word, we used the General Inquirer database (Stone et al., 1966).

Our lexical features are simply all words (alphanumeric strings including apostrophes and stopwords) in the turn. The value of these features is integral and essentially counts the number of times a word is repeated in the turn. Although this indirectly accounts for alliterations, in the future studies, we plan to use more *stylistic* lexical features like (Mihalcea and Strapparava, 2005).

Turn length is measured as the number of words in the turn. For our classification study, we consider eight speaker classes (6 Main actors, 1 for Guest and Multi) as shown in table 1, whereas for the gender study, we consider only two speaker categories (male and female) as shown in table 2.

6 Humor-Prosody Analysis

Feature	Humor	Non-Humor
Mean-F0	206.9	208.9
Max-F0*	299.8	293.5
Min-F0*	121.1	128.6
Range-F0*	178.7	164.9
StdDev-F0	41.5	41.1
Mean-RMS*	58.3	57.2
Max-RMS*	76.4	75
Min-RMS*	44.2	44.6
Range-RMS*	32.16	30.4
StdDev-RMS*	7.8	7.5
Duration*	3.18	2.66
Int-Sil*	0.452	0.503
Tempo*	3.21	3.03
Length*	10.28	7.97

Table 3: Humor Prosody: Mean feature values for Humor and Non-Humor groups

Table 3 shows mean values of various acoustic-prosodic features over all speaker turns in our data, across humor and non-humor groups. Features that have statistically ($p<=0.05$ as per independent samples t-test) different values across the two groups are marked with asterisks. As one can see, all features except Mean-F0 and StdDev-F0 show significant differences across humorous and non-humorous speech. Table 3 shows that humorous turns in our data are longer, both in terms of the time duration and the number of words, than non-humorous turns. We also notice that humorous turns have smaller internal silence, and hence rapid tempo. Pitch (F0) and energy (RMS) features have higher maximum, but lower minimum values, for humorous turns. This in turn gives higher values for range and standard deviation for humor compared to the non-humor group. This result is somewhat consistent with previous findings of (Liscombe et al., 2003) who found that most of these features are largely associated with positive and active emotional states such as happy, encouraging, confident etc. which are likely to appear in our humorous turns.

7 Gender Effect on Humor-Prosody

To analyze prosody of humor across two genders, we conducted a 2-way ANOVA test, using speaker gender (male/female) and humor (yes/no) as our fixed factors, and each of the above acoustic-prosodic features as a dependent variable. The test tells us the effect of humor on prosody adjusted for gender, the effect of gender on prosody adjusted for humor and also the effect of interaction between gender and humor on prosody (i.e. if the effect of humor on prosody differs according to gender). Table 4 shows results of 2-way ANOVA, where Y shows significant effects, and N shows non-significant effects. For example, the result for tempo shows that tempo differs significantly only across humor and non-humor groups, but not across the two gender groups, and that there is no effect of interaction between humor and gender on tempo. As before, all features except Mean-F0 and StdDev-F0 show significant differences across humor and no-humor conditions, even when adjusted for gender differences. The table also shows that all features except internal silence and tempo show significant differences across two genders, although only pitch features (Max-F0, Min-F0, and StdDev-F0) show the effect of interaction between gender and humor. In other words, the effect of humor on these pitch features is dependent on gender. For instance, if male speakers raise their pitch while expressing humor, female speakers might lower. To confirm this, we computed means values of various features for males and females separately (See Tables 5 and 6). These tables indeed suggest that male speakers show higher values for pitch features (Mean-F0, Min-F0, StdDev-F0), while expressing humor, whereas females show lower. Also for male speakers, differences in Min-F0 and Min-RMS values are not statistically significant across humor and non-humor groups, whereas for female speakers, features Mean-F0, StdDev-F0 and tempo do not show significant differences across the two groups. One can also notice that the differences in the mean pitch feature values (specifically Mean-F0, Max-F0 and Range-F0) between humor and non-humor groups are much higher for males than for females.

In summary, our gender analysis shows that although most acoustic-prosodic features are different for males and females, the prosodic style of expressing humor by male and female speakers differs only along some pitch-features (both in magnitude and direction).

Feature	Humor	Gender	Humor x Gender
Mean-F0	N	Y	N
Max-F0	Y	Y	Y
Min-F0	Y	Y	Y
Range-F0	Y	Y	N
StdDev-F0	N	Y	Y
Mean-RMS	Y	Y	N
Max-RMS	Y	Y	N
Min-RMS	Y	Y	N
Range-RMS	Y	Y	N
StdDev-RMS	Y	Y	N
Duration	Y	Y	N
Int-Sil	Y	N	N
Tempo	Y	N	N
Length	Y	Y	N

Table 4: Gender Effect on Humor Prosody: 2-Way ANOVA Results

8 Speaker Effect on Humor-Prosody

We then conducted similar ANOVA test to account for the speaker differences, i.e. by considering humor (yes/no) and speaker (8 groups as shown in table 1) as our fixed factors and each of the acoustic-prosodic features as a dependent variable for a 2-Way ANOVA. Table 7 shows results of this analysis. As before, the table shows the effect of humor adjusted for speaker, the effect of speaker adjusted for humor and also the effect of interaction between humor and speaker, on each of the acoustic-prosodic features. According to table 7, we no longer see the effect of humor on features Min-F0, Mean-RMS and Tempo (in addition to Mean-F0 and StdDev-F0), in presence of the speaker variable. Speaker, on the other hand, shows significant effect on prosody for all features. But

Feature	Humor	Non-Humor
Mean-F0*	188.14	176.43
Max-F0*	276.94	251.7
Min-F0	114.54	113.56
Range-F0*	162.4	138.14
StdDev-F0*	37.83	34.27
Mean-RMS*	57.86	56.4
Max-RMS*	75.5	74.21
Min-RMS	44.04	44.12
Range-RMS*	31.46	30.09
StdDev-RMS*	7.64	7.31
Duration*	3.1	2.57
Int-Sil*	0.44	0.5
Tempo*	3.33	3.1
Length*	10.27	8.1

Table 5: Humor Prosody for Male Speakers

Feature	Humor	Non-Humor
Mean-F0	235.79	238.75
Max-F0*	336.15	331.14
Min-F0*	133.63	143.14
Range-F0*	202.5	188
StdDev-F0	46.33	46.6
Mean-RMS*	58.44	57.64
Max-RMS*	77.33	75.57
Min-RMS*	44.08	44.74
Range-RMS*	33.24	30.83
StdDev-RMS*	8.18	7.59
Duration*	3.35	2.8
Int-Sil*	0.47	0.51
Tempo	3.1	3.1
Length*	10.66	8.25

Table 6: Humor Prosody for Female Speakers

surprisingly, again only pitch features Mean-F0, Max-F0 and Min-F0 show the interaction effect, suggesting that the effect of humor on these pitch features differs from speaker to speaker. In other words, different speakers use different pitch variations while expressing humor.

9 Humor Recognition by Supervised Learning

We formulate our humor-recognition experiment as a classical supervised learning problem, by automatically classifying spoken turns into humor and non-humor groups, using standard machine learning classifiers. We used the decision tree algorithm ADTree from Weka, and ran a 10-fold cross validation experiment on all 1629 turns in our data[1]. The baseline for these experiments is 56.2% for the majority class (non-humorous). Table 8 reports classification results for six feature categories: lexical alone, lexical + speaker, prosody alone, prosody + speaker, lexical + prosody and lexical + prosody + speaker (all). Numbers in braces show the number of features in each category. There are total 2025 features which include 2011 lexical (all word types plus turn length), 13 acoustic-prosodic and 1 for the speaker information. Feature *Length* was included in the lexical feature group, as it counts the number of lexical items (words) in the turn.

All results are significantly above the baseline (as measured by a pair-wise t-test) with the best accuracy of 64% (8% over the baseline) obtained using all features. We notice that the classification accuracy improves on adding speaker information to both lexical and prosodic features. Although these results do not show a strong evidence that prosodic features are better than lexical, it is interesting to note that the performance of just a few (13) prosodic features is comparable to that of 2011 lexical features. Figure 3 shows the decision tree produced by the classifier in 10 iterations. Numbers indicate the order in which the nodes are created, and indentations mark parent-child relations. We notice that the classifier primarily selected speaker and prosodic features in the first 10 iterations, whereas lexical features were selected only in the later iterations (not shown here). This seems consistent with our original hypothesis that speech features are better at discriminating between humorous and non-humorous utterances in speech than lexical content.

Although (Mihalcea and Strapparava, 2005) obtained much higher accuracies using lexical features alone, it might be due to the fact that our data is *homogeneous* in the sense that both humorous and non-humorous turns are extracted from the same source, and involve same speakers, which makes the two groups highly alike and hence challenging to distinguish. To make sure that the lower accuracy we get is not simply due to using smaller data compared to (Mihalcea and Strappar-

[1]We also tried other classifiers like Naive Bayes and AdaBoost, although since the results were equivalent to ADTree, we do not report those here.

Feature	Humor	Speaker	Humor x Speaker
Mean-F0	N	Y	Y
Max-F0	Y	Y	Y
Min-F0	N	Y	Y
Range-F0	Y	Y	N
StdDev-F0	N	Y	N
Mean-RMS	N	Y	N
Max-RMS	Y	Y	N
Min-RMS	Y	Y	N
Range-RMS	Y	Y	N
StdDev-RMS	Y	Y	N
Duration	Y	Y	N
Int-Sil	Y	Y	N
Tempo	N	Y	N
Length	Y	Y	N

Table 7: Speaker Effect on Humor Prosody: 2-Way ANOVA Results

Feature	-Speaker	+Speaker
Lex	61.14 (2011)	63.5 (2012)
Prosody	60 (13)	63.8 (14)
Lex + Prosody	62.6 (2024)	64 (2025)

Table 8: Humor Recognition Results (% Correct)

ava, 2005), we looked at the learning curve for the classifier (see figure 4) and found that the classifier performance is not sensitive to the amount of data.

Table 9 shows classification results by gender, using all features. For the male group, the baseline is 50.6%, as the majority class *humor* is 50.6% (See Table 2). For females, the baseline is 60% (for non-humorous) as only 40% of the female turns are humorous.

Gender	Baseline	Classifier
Male	50.6	64.63
Female	60.1	64.8

Table 9: Humor Recognition Results by Gender

As Table 9 shows, the performance of the classifier is somewhat consistent cross-gender, although for male speakers, the relative improvement is much higher (14% above the baseline), than for females (only 5% above the baseline). Our earlier observation (from tables 5 and 6) that differences in pitch features between humor and non-humor

```
| (1)SPEAKER = chandler: 0.469
| (1)SPEAKER != chandler: -0.083
| | (4)SPEAKER = phoebe: 0.373
| | (4)SPEAKER != phoebe: -0.064
| (2)DURATION < 1.515: -0.262
| | (5)SILENCE < 0.659: 0.115
| | (5)SILENCE >= 0.659: -0.465
| | (8)SD_F0 < 9.919: -1.11
| | (8)SD_F0 >= 9.919: 0.039
| (2)DURATION >= 1.515: 0.1
| | (3)MEAN_RMS < 56.117: -0.274
| | (3)MEAN_RMS >= 56.117: 0.147
| | | (7)come < 0.5: -0.056
| | | (7)come >= 0.5: 0.417
| | (6)SD_F0 < 57.333: 0.076
| | (6)SD_F0 >= 57.333: -0.285
| | (9)MAX_RMS < 86.186: 0.011
| | | (10)MIN_F0 < 166.293: 0.047
| | | (10)MIN_F0 >= 166.293: -0.351
| | (9)MAX_RMS >= 86.186: -0.972
Legend: +ve = humor, -ve = non-humor
```

Figure 3: Decision Tree (only the first 10 iterations are shown)

groups are quite higher for males than for females, may explain why we see higher improvement for male speakers.

10 Conclusions

In this paper, we presented our experiments on humor-prosody analysis and humor recognition in spoken conversations, collected from a classic television comedy, FRIENDS. Using a simple automated annotation scheme, we labeled speaker turns in our corpus that are followed by artificial laughs as humorous, and the rest as non-humorous. We then examined a number of acoustic-prosodic features based on pitch, energy and temporal information in the speech signal, that have been found useful by previous studies in emotion recognition.

Our prosody analysis revealed that humorous and non-humorous turns indeed show significant differences in most of these features, even when accounted for the speaker and gender differences. Specifically, we found that humorous turns tend to have higher tempo, smaller internal silence, and higher peak, range and standard deviation for pitch and energy, compared to non-humorous turns.

On the humor recognition task, our classifier

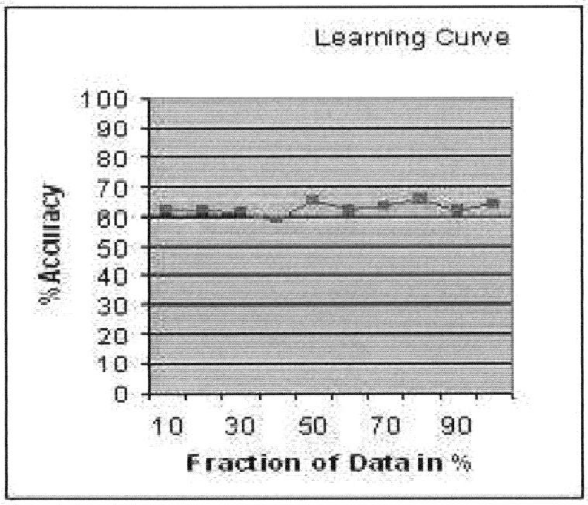

Figure 4: Learning Curve: %Accuracy versus %Fraction of Data

achieved the best performance when acoustic-prosodic features were used in conjunction with lexical and other types of features, and in all experiments attained the accuracy statistically significant over the baseline. While prosody of humor shows some differences due to gender, the performance on the humor recognition task is equivalent for males and females, although the relative improvement over the baseline is much higher for males than for females.

Our current study focuses only on lexical and speech features, primarily because these features can be computed automatically. In the future, we plan to explore more sophisticated semantic and pragmatic features such as incongruity, ambiguity, expectation-violation etc. We also like to investigate if our findings generalize to other types of corpora besides TV-show dialogs.

References

C. Alm, D. Roth, and R. Sproat. 2005. Emotions from text: Machine learning for text-based emotion prediction. In *Proceedings of HLT/EMNLP*, Vancouver, CA.

J. Ang, R. Dhillon, A. Krupski, E. Shriberg, and A. Stolcke. 2002. Prosody-based automatic detection of annoyance and frustration in human-computer dialog. In *Proceedings of ICSLP*.

S. Attardo. 1994. *Linguistic Theory of Humor*. Mounton de Gruyter, Berlin.

K. Binsted and G. Ritchie. 1997. Computational rules for punning riddles. *Humor*, 10(1).

K. Binsted, B. Bergen, S. Coulson, A. Nijholt, O. Stock, C. Strapparava, G. Ritchie, R. Manurung, H. Pain, A. Waller, and D. O'Mara. 2006. Computational humor. *IEEE Intelligent Systems*, March-April.

K. Binsted. 1995. Using humour to make natural language interfaces more friendly. In *Proceedings of the AI, ALife and Entertainment Workshop*, Montreal, CA.

S. D'Mello, S. Craig, G. Gholson, S. Franklin, R. Picard, and A. Graesser. 2005. Integrating affect sensors in an intelligent tutoring system. In *Proceedings of Affective Interactions: The Computer in the Affective Loop Workshop*.

P. Gebhard, M. Klesen, and T. Rist. 2004. Coloring multi-character conversations through the expression of emotions. In *Proceedings of Affective Dialog Systems*.

J. Klein, Y. Moon, and R. Picard. 2002. This computer responds to user frustration: Theory, design, and results. *Interacting with Computers*, 14.

J. Liscombe, J. Venditti, and J. Hirschberg. 2003. Classifying subject ratings of emotional speech using acoustic features. In *Proceedings of Eurospeech*, Geneva, Switzerland.

D. Litman and K. Forbes-Riley. 2004. Predicting student emotions in computer-human tutoring dialogues. In *Proceedings of ACL*, Barcelona, Spain.

R. Mihalcea and C. Strapparava. 2005. Making computers laugh: Investigations in automatic humor recognition. In *Proceedings of HLT/EMNLP*, Vancouver, CA.

M. Mulder and A. Nijholt. 2002. Humor research: State of the art. Technical Report 34, CTIT Technical Report Series.

Scherer. 2003. Vocal communication of emotion: A review of research paradigms. *Speech Communication*, 40(1-2):227–256.

M. Shroder and R. Cowie. 2005. Toward emotion-sensitive multimodal interfaces: the challenge of the european network of excellence humaine. In *Proceedings of User Modeling Workshop on Adapting the Interaction Style to Affective Factors*.

O. Stock and C. Strapparava. 2005. Hahaacronym: A computational humor system. In *Proceedings of ACL Interactive Poster and Demonstration Session*, pages 113–116, Ann Arbor, MI.

P. Stone, D. Dunphy, M. Smith, and D. Ogilvie. 1966. *The General Inquirer: A Computer Approach to Content Analysis*. MIT Press, Cambridge, MA.

J. Taylor and L. Mazlack. 2004. Computationally recognizing wordplay in jokes. In *Proceedings of the CogSci 2004*, Chicago, IL.

Distributed Language Modeling for N-best List Re-ranking

Ying Zhang **Almut Silja Hildebrand** **Stephan Vogel**
Language Technologies Institute, Carnegie Mellon University
5000 Forbes Ave. Pittsburgh, PA 15213, U.S.A.
{joy+, silja+, vogel+}@cs.cmu.edu

Abstract

In this paper we describe a novel distributed language model for N-best list re-ranking. The model is based on the client/server paradigm where each server hosts a portion of the data and provides information to the client. This model allows for using an arbitrarily large corpus in a very efficient way. It also provides a natural platform for relevance weighting and selection. We applied this model on a 2.97 billion-word corpus and re-ranked the N-best list from Hiero, a state-of-the-art phrase-based system. Using BLEU as a metric, the re-ranked translation achieves a relative improvement of 4.8%, significantly better than the model-best translation.

1 Introduction

Statistical language modeling has been widely used in natural language processing applications such as Automatic Speech Recognition (ASR), Statistical Machine Translation (SMT) (Brown et al., 1993) and Information Retrieval (IR) (Ponte and Croft, 1998).

Conventional n-gram language modeling counts the frequency of all the n-grams in a corpus and calculates the conditional probabilities of a word given its history of $n-1$ words $P(w_i|w_{i-n+1}^{i-1})$. As the corpus size increases, building a high order language model offline becomes very expensive if it is still possible (Goodman, 2000).

In this paper, we describe a new approach of language modeling using a distributed computing paradigm. Distributed language modeling can make use of arbitrarily large training corpora and provides a natural way for language model adaptation.

We applied the distributed LM to the task of re-ranking the N-best list in statistical machine translation and achieved significantly better translation quality when measured by the BLEU metric (Papineni et al., 2001).

2 N-best list re-ranking

When translating a source language sentence $\mathbf{f}$ into English, the SMT decoder first builds a translation lattice over the source words by applying the translation model and then explores the lattice and searches for an optimal path as the best translation. The decoder uses different models, such as the translation model, n-gram language model, fertility model, and combines multiple model scores to calculate the objective function value which favors one translation hypothesis over the other (Och et al., 2004).

Instead of outputting the top hypothesis $\mathbf{e}^{(1)}$ based on the decoder model, the decoder can output N (usually $N = 1000$) alternative hypotheses $\{\mathbf{e}^{(r)}|r = 1, \ldots, N\}$ for one source sentence and rank them according to their model scores.

Figure 1 shows an example of the output from a SMT system. In this example, alternative hypothesis $\mathbf{e}^{(2)}$ is a better translations than $\mathbf{e}^{(1)}$ according to the reference (Ref) although its model score is lower.

SMT models are not perfect, it is unavoidable to have a sub-optimal translation output as the model-best by the decoder. The objective of N-best list re-ranking is then to re-rank the translation hypotheses using features which are not used during decoding so that better translations can emerge as "optimal" translations. Our exper-

Proceedings of the 2006 Conference on Empirical Methods in Natural Language Processing (EMNLP 2006), pages 216–223,
Sydney, July 2006.

f: 自从 2001 年 美国 遭受 恐怖 攻击 的 事件 之后

Ref: Since the terrorist attacks on the United States in 2001

$\mathbf{e}^{(1)}$: since 200 year , the united states after the terrorist attacks in the incident

$\mathbf{e}^{(2)}$: since 2001 after the incident of the terrorist attacks on the united states

$\mathbf{e}^{(3)}$: since the united states 2001 threats of terrorist attacks after the incident

$\mathbf{e}^{(4)}$: since 2001 the terrorist attacks after the incident

$\mathbf{e}^{(5)}$: since 200 year , the united states after the terrorist attacks in the incident

Figure 1: An example of N-best list.

iments (section 5.1) have shown that the oracle-best translation from a typical N-best list could be 6 to 10 BLEU points better than the model-best translation.

In this paper we use the distributed language model on very large data to re-rank the N-best list.

2.1 Sentence likelihood

The goal of a language model is to determine the probability, or in general the "likelihood" of a word sequence $w_1 \dots w_m$ (w_1^m for short) given some training data. The standard language modeling approach breaks the sentence probability down into:

$$P(w_1^m) = \prod_i P(w_i | w_1^{i-1}) \tag{1}$$

Under the Markov or higher order Markov process assumption that only the closest $n-1$ words have real impact on the choice of w_i, equation 1 is approximated to:

$$P(w_1^m) = \prod_i P(w_i | w_{i-n+1}^{i-1}) \tag{2}$$

The probability of a word given its history can be approximated with the maximum likelihood estimate (MLE) without any smoothing:

$$P(w_i | w_{i-n+1}^{i-1}) \approx \frac{C(w_{i-n+1}^{i})}{C(w_{i-n+1}^{i-1})} \tag{3}$$

In addition to the standard n-gram probability estimation, we propose 3 sentence likelihood metrics.

- L_0: Number of n-grams matched.

The simplest metric for sentence likelihood is to count how many n-grams in this sentence can be found in the corpus.

$$L_0(w_1^m) = \sum_{\substack{i,j \\ i \leq j}} \delta(w_i^j) \tag{4}$$

$$\delta(w_i^j) = \begin{cases} 1 & : \ C(w_i^j) > 0 \\ 0 & : \ C(w_i^j) = 0 \end{cases} \tag{5}$$

For example, L_0 for sentence in figure 2 is 52 because 52 n-grams have non-zero counts.

- L_1^n: Average interpolated n-gram conditional probability.

$$L_1^n(w_1^m) = \left(\prod_{i=1}^{m} \sum_{k=1}^{n} \lambda_k P(w_i | w_{i-k+1}^{i-1}) \right)^{\frac{1}{m}} \tag{6}$$

$P(w_i | w_{i-k+1}^{i-1})$ is approximated from the n-gram counts (Eq. 3) without any smoothing. λ_k is the weight for k-gram conditional probability, $\sum \lambda_k = 1$.

L_1^n is similar to the standard n-gram LM except the probability is averaged over the words in the sentence to prevent shorter sentences being favored unfairly.

- L_2: Sum of n-gram's non-compositionality

For each matched n-gram, we consider all the possibilities to cut/decompose it into two short n-grams, for example "the terrorist attacks on the united states" could be decomposed into ("the", "terrorist attacks on the united states") or ("the terrorist", "attacks on the united states"), ... , or ("the terrorist attacks on the united", "states"). For each cut, calculate the point-wise mutual information (PMI) between the two short n-grams. The one with the minimal PMI is the most "natural" cut for this n-gram. The PMI over the natural cut quantifies the *non-compositionality* I_{nc} of an n-gram w_i^j. The higher the value of $I_{nc}(w_i^j)$ the more likely w_i^j is a meaningful constituent, in other words, it is less likely that w_i^j is composed from two short n-grams just by chance (Yamamoto and Church, 2001).

Define L_2 formally as:

$$L_2(w_1^m) = \sum_{\substack{i,j \\ i \leq j}} I_{nc}(w_i^j) \tag{7}$$

$$I_{nc}(w_i^j) = \begin{cases} \min_k I(w_i^k; w_{k+1}^j) & : C(w_i^j) > 0 \\ 0 & : C(w_i^j) = 0 \end{cases} \quad (8)$$

$$I(w_i^k; w_{k+1}^j) = log \frac{P(w_i^j)}{P(w_i^k)P(w_{k+1}^j)} \quad (9)$$

3 Distributed language model

The fundamental information required to calculate the likelihood of a sentence is the frequency of n-grams in the corpus. In conventional LM training, all the counts are collected from the corpus $\mathcal{D}$ and saved to disk for probability estimation. When the size of $\mathcal{D}$ becomes large and/or n is increased to capture more context, the count file can be too large to be processed.

Instead of collecting n-gram counts offline, we index $\mathcal{D}$ using a suffix array (Manber and Myers, 1993) and count the occurrences of w_{i-n+1}^i in $\mathcal{D}$ on the fly.

3.1 Calculate n-gram frequency using suffix array

For a corpus $\mathcal{D}$ with $\mathcal{N}$ words, locating all the occurrences of w_{i-n+1}^i takes $O(log\mathcal{N})$. Zhang and Vogel (2005) introduce a search algorithm which locates all the $m(m+1)/2$ embedded n-grams in a sentence of m words within $O(m \cdot log\mathcal{N})$ time.

Figure 2 shows the frequencies of all the embedded n-grams in sentence "since 2001 after the incident of the terrorist attacks on the united states" matched against a 26 million words corpus. For example, unigram "after" occurs 4.43×10^4 times, trigram "after the incident" occurs 106 times. The longest n-gram that can be matched is the 8-gram "of the terrorist attacks on the united states" which occurs 7 times in the corpus.

3.2 Client/Server paradigm

To load the corpus and its suffix array index into the memory, each word token needs 8 bytes. For example, if the corpus has 50 million words, 400MB memory is required. For the English[1] GigaWord[2] corpus which has 2.7 billion words, the total memory required is 22GB. It is practically impossible to fit such data into the memory of any single machine.

To make use of the large amount of data, we developed a distributed client/server architecture for language modeling. Client/server is the most common paradigm of distributed computing at present (Leopold, 2001). The paradigm describes an asymmetric relationship between two type of processes, of which one is the client, and the other is the server. The server process manages some resources and offers a service which can be used by other processes. The client is a process that needs the service in order to accomplish its task. It sends a request to the server and asks for the execution of a task that is covered by the service.

We split the large corpus $\mathcal{D}$ into d non-overlapping chunks. One can easily verify that for any n-gram w_{i-n+1}^i the count of its occurrences in $\mathcal{D}$ is the sum of its occurrences in all the chunks, i.e.,

$$C(w_{i-n+1}^i)|\mathcal{D} = \sum_d C(w_{i-n+1}^i)|\mathcal{D}_d \quad (10)$$

Each server[3] loads one chunk of the corpus with its suffix array index. The client sends an English sentence $w_1 \dots w_m$ to each of the servers and requests for the count information of all the n-grams in the sentence. The client collects the count information from all the servers, sums up the counts for each n-gram and then calculates the likelihood of the sentence.

The client communicates with the servers via TCP/IP sockets. In our experiments, we used 150 servers running on 26 computers to serve one client. Multiple clients can be served at the same time if needed. The process of collecting counts and calculating the sentence probabilities takes about 1 to 2 ms for each English sentence (average length 23.5 words). With this architecture, we can easily make use of larger corpora by adding additional data servers. In our experiments, we used all the 2.7 billion word data in the English Gigaword corpus without any technical difficulties.

[1] Though we used English data for our experiments in this paper, the approach described here is language independent.

[2] http://www.ldc.upenn.edu/Catalog/CatalogEntry.jsp?catalogId=LDC2005T12

[3] A server is a special program that provides services to client processes. It runs on a physical computer but the concept of server should not be confused with the actual machine that runs it. In practice, one computer usually hosts multiple servers at the same time.

n	since	2001	after	the	incident	of	the	terrorist	attacks	on	the	united	states
1	2.19×10^4	7559	4.43×10^4	1.67×10^6	2989	6.9×10^5	1.67×10^6	6160	9278	2.7×10^5	1.67×10^6	5.1×10^4	3.78×10^4
2		165	105	1.19×10^4	1892	34	2.07×10^5	807	1398	1656	5.64×10^4	3.72×10^4	3.29×10^4
3			6	56	106	6	3	162	181	216	545	605	2.58×10^4
4				0	0	0	1	0	35	67	111	239	424
5					0	0	0	0	0	15	34	77	232
6						0	0	0	0	0	10	23	76
7							0	0	0	0	0	7	23
8								0	0	0	0	0	7

Figure 2: Frequencies of all the embedded n-grams in sentence "since 2001 after the incident of the terrorist attacks on the united states."

4 "More data is better data" or "Relevant data is better data"

Although statistical systems usually improve with more data, performance can decrease if additional data does not fit the test data. There have been debates in the data-driven NLP community as to whether "more data is better data" or "relevant data is better data". For N-best list re-ranking, the question becomes: "should we use all the data to re-rank the hypotheses for one source sentence, or select some corpus chunks that are believed to be relevant to this sentence?"

Various relevance measures are proposed in (Iyer and Ostendorf, 1999) including content-based relevance criteria and style-based criteria. In this paper, we use a very simple relevance metric. Define corpora $\mathcal{D}_d$'s relevance to a source sentence $\mathbf{f}_t$ as:

$$R(\mathcal{D}_d, \mathbf{f}_t) = \sum_{r=1}^{N} L_0(\mathbf{e}_t^{(r)})|\mathcal{D}_d \qquad (11)$$

$R(\mathcal{D}_d, \mathbf{f}_t)$ estimates how well a corpus $\mathcal{D}_d$ can cover the n-grams in the N-best list of a source sentence. The higher the coverage, the more relevant $\mathcal{D}_d$ is.

In the distributed LM architecture, the client first sends N translations of $\mathbf{f}_t$ to all the servers. From the returned n-gram matching information, client calculates $R(\mathcal{D}_d, \mathbf{f}_t)$ for each server, and choose the most relevant (e.g., 20) servers for $\mathbf{f}_t$. The n-gram counts returned from these relevant servers are summed up for calculating the likelihood of $\mathbf{f}_t$. One could also assign weights to the n-gram counts returned from different servers during the summation so that the relevant data has more impact than the less-relevant ones.

5 Experiments

We used the N-best list generated by the Hiero SMT system (Chiang, 2005). Hiero is a statistical phrase-based translation model that uses hierarchical phrases. The decoder uses a trigram language model trained with modified Kneser-Ney smoothing (Kneser and Ney, 1995) on a 200 million words corpus. The 1000-best list was generated on 919 sentences from the MT03 Chinese-English evaluation set.

All the data from the English Gigaword corpus plus the English side of the Chinese-English bilingual data available from LDC are used. The 2.97 billion words data is split into 150 chunks, each has about 20 million words. The original order is kept so that each chunk contains data from the same news source and a certain period of time. For example, chunk *Xinhua2003* has all the Xinhua News data from year 2003 and *NYT9499_038* has the last 20 million words from the New York Times 1994-1999 corpus. One could split the data into larger(smaller) chunks which will require less(more) servers. We choose 20 million words as the size for each chunk because it can be loaded by our smallest machine and it is a reasonable granularity for selection.

In total, 150 corpus information servers run on 26 machines connected by the standard Ethernet LAN. One client sends each English hypothesis translations to all 150 servers and uses the returned information to re-rank. The whole process takes about 600 seconds to finish.

We use BLEU scores to measure the translation accuracy. A bootstrapping method is used to calculate the 95% confidence intervals for BLEU (Koehn, 2004; Zhang and Vogel, 2004).

5.1 Oracle score of the N-best list

Because of the *spurious ambiguity*, there are only 24,612 unique hypotheses in the 1000-best list, on average 27 per source sentence. This limits the potential of N-best re-ranking. *Spurious ambiguity* is created by the decoder where two hypotheses generated from different decoding path are considered different even though they have identical word sequences. For example, "the terrorist attacks on the united states" could be the output of decoding path [the terrorist attacks][on the united states] and [the terrorist attacks on] [the united states].

We first calculate the oracle score from the N-best list to verify that there are alternative hypotheses better than the model-best translation. The oracle best translations are created by selecting the hypothesis which has the highest sentence BLEU score for each source sentence. Yet a critical problem with BLEU score is that it is a function of the entire test set and does not give meaningful scores for single sentences. We followed the approximation described in (Collins et al., 2005) to get around this problem. Given a test set with T sentences, N hypotheses are generated for each source sentence $\mathbf{f}_t$. Denote $\mathbf{e}_t^{(r)}$ as the r-th ranked hypothesis for $\mathbf{f}_t$. $\mathbf{e}_t^{(1)}$ is the model-best hypothesis for this sentence. The baseline BLEU scores are calculated based on the model-best translation set $\{\mathbf{e}_t^{(1)} | t = 1, \ldots, T\}$.

Define the BLEU sentence-level gain for $\mathbf{e}_t^{(r)}$ as:

$$\begin{aligned} G_{BLEU}\mathbf{e}_t^{(r)} = \\ & BLEU\{\mathbf{e}_1^{(1)}, \mathbf{e}_2^{(1)}, \ldots, \mathbf{e}_t^{(r)}, \ldots, \mathbf{e}_T^{(r)}\} \\ - & BLEU\{\mathbf{e}_1^{(1)}, \mathbf{e}_2^{(1)}, \ldots, \mathbf{e}_t^{(1)}, \ldots, \mathbf{e}_T^{(r)}\} \end{aligned}$$

$G_{BLEU}\mathbf{e}_t^{(r)}$ calculates the gain if we switch the model-best hypothesis $\mathbf{e}_t^{(1)}$ using $\mathbf{e}_t^{(r)}$ for sentence $\mathbf{f}_t$ and keep the translations for the rest of the test set untouched.

With the estimated sentence level gain for each hypothesis, we can construct the oracle best translation set by selecting the hypotheses with the highest BLEU gain for each sentence. Oracle best BLEU translation set is: $\{\mathbf{e}_t^{(r_t^*)} | t = 1, \ldots, T\}$ where $r_t^* = \arg\max_r G_{BLEU}\mathbf{e}_t^{(r)}$.

	Model-best		Oracle
	Score	Confidence Interval	
BLEU	31.44	[30.49, 32.33]	37.48

Table 1: BLEU scores for the model-best and oracle-best translations.

Table 1 shows the BLEU score of the approximated oracle best translation. The oracle score is 7 points higher than the model-best scores even though there are only 27 unique hypotheses for each sentence on average. This confirms our observation that there are indeed better translations in the N-best list.

5.2 Training standard n-gram LM on large data for comparison

Besides comparing the distributed language model re-ranked translations with the model-best translations, we also want to compare the distributed LM with the the standard 3-gram and 4-gram language models on the N-best list re-ranking task.

Training a standard n-gram model for a 2.9 billion words corpora is much more complicated and tedious than setting up the distributed LM. Because of the huge size of the corpora, we could only manage to train a test-set specific n-gram LM for this experiment.

First, we split the corpora into smaller chunks and generate n-gram count files for each chunk. Each count file is then sub-sampled to entries where all the words are listed in the vocabulary of the N-best list (5,522 word types). We merge all the sub-sampled count files into one and train the standard language model based on it.

We manage to train a 3-gram LM using the 2.97 billion-word corpus. Resulting LM requires 2.3GB memory to be loaded for the re-ranking experiment.

A 4-gram LM for this N-best list is of 13 GB in size and can not be fit into the memory. We split the N-best list into 9 parts to reduce the vocabulary size of each sub N-best list to be around 1000 words. The 4-gram LM tailored for each sub N-best list is around 1.5 to 2 GB in size.

Training higher order standard n-gram LMs with this method requires even more partitions of the N-best list to get smaller vocabularies. When the vocabulary becomes too small, the smoothing could fail and results in unreliable LM probabilities.

Adapting the standard n-gram LM for each individual source sentence is almost infeasible given our limited computing resources. Thus we do not have equivalent n-gram LMs to be compared with the distributed LM for conditions where the most relevant data chunks are used to re-rank the N-best list for a particular source sentence.

5.3 Results

Table 2 lists results of the re-ranking experiments under different conditions. The re-ranked translation improved the BLEU score from 31.44 to

32.64, significantly better than the model-best translation.

Different metrics are used under the same data situation for comparison. L_0, though extremely simple, gives quite nice results on N-best list re-ranking. With only one corpus chunk (the most relevant one) for each source sentence, L_0 improved the BLEU score to 32.22. We suspect that L_0 works well because it is inline with the nature of BLEU score. BLEU measures the similarity between the translation hypothesis and human reference by counting how many n-grams in MT can be found in the references.

Instead of assigning weights 1 to all the matched n-grams in L_0, L_2 weights each n-gram by its *non-compositionality*. For all data conditions, L_2 consistently gives the best results.

Metric family L_1 is close to the standard n-gram LM probability estimation. Because no smoothing is used, L_1^3 performance (32.00) is slightly worse than the standard 3-gram LM result (32.22). On the other hand, increasing the length of the history in L_1 generally improves the performance.

Figure 3 shows the BLEU score of the re-ranked translation when using different numbers of relevant data chunks for each sentence. The selected data chunks may differ for each sentences. For example, the 2 most relevant corpora for sentence 1 are *Xinhua2002* and *Xinhua2003* while for sentence 2 *APW2003A* and *NYT2002D* are more relevant. When we use the most relevant data chunk (about 20 million words) to re-rank the N-best list, 36 chunks of data will be used at least once for 919 different sentences, which accounts for about 720 million words in total. Thus the x-axis in figure 3 should not be interpreted as the total amount of data used but the number of the most relevant corpora used for each sentence.

All three metrics in figure 3 show that using all data together (150 chunks, 2.97 billion words) does not give better discriminative powers than using only some relevant chunks. This supports our argument in section 4 that relevance selection is helpful in N-best list re-ranking. In some cases the re-ranked N-best list has a higher BLEU score after adding a supposedly "less-relevant" corpus chunk and a lower BLEU score after adding a "more-relevant" chunk. This indicates that the relevance measurement (Eq. 11) is not fully reflecting the real "relevance" of a data chunk for a sentence. With a better relevance measurement one would expect to see the curves in figure 3 to be much smoother.

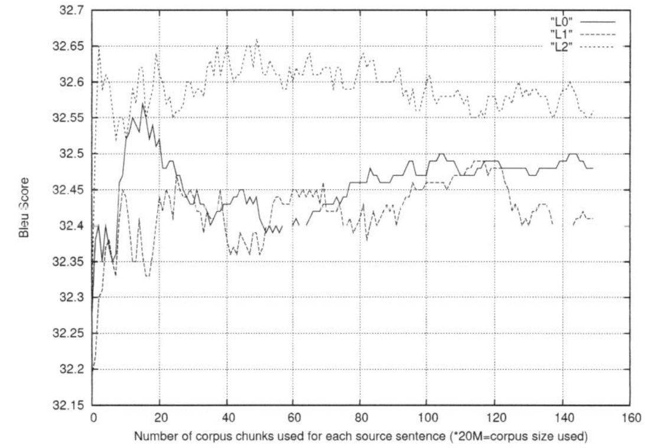

Figure 3: BLEU score of the re-ranked best hypothesis vs. the number of the most relevant corpus chunks used to re-rank the n-best list for each sentences. L_0: number of n-grams matched; L_1: average interpolated n-gram conditional probability; L_2: sum of n-grams' non-compositionality.

6 Related work and discussion

Yamamoto and Church (2001) used suffix arrays to compute the frequency and location of an n-gram in a corpus. The frequencies are used to find "interesting" substrings which have high mutual information.

Soricut et al. (2002) build a Finite State Acceptor (FSA) to compactly represent all possible English translations of a source sentence according to the translation model. All sentences in a big monolingual English corpus are then scanned by this FSA and those accepted by the FSA are considered as possible translations for the source sentence. The corpus is split into hundreds of chunks for parallel processing. All the sentences in one chunk are scanned by the FSA on one processor. Matched sentences from all chunks are then used together as possible translations. The assumption of this work that possible translations of a source sentence can be found as exact match in a big monolingual corpus is weak even for very large corpus. This method can easily fail to find any possible translation and return zero proposed translations.

Kirchhoff and Yang (2005) used a factored 3-gram model and a 4-gram LM (modified KN smoothing) together with seven system scores to re-rank an SMT N-best. They improved the translation quality of their best baseline (Spanish-

# of Relevant Chunks per. Sent	1	2	5	10	20	150
3-gram KN	32.22					32.08
4-gram KN	32.22					32.53
L_0	32.27	32.38	32.40	32.47	32.51	32.48
L_1^3	32.00	32.14	32.14	32.15	32.16	
L_1^4	32.18	32.36	32.28	32.44	32.41	
L_1^5	32.21	32.33	32.35	32.41	32.37	
L_1^6	32.19	32.22	32.37	32.45	32.40	32.41
L_1^7	32.22	32.29	32.37	32.44	32.40	
L_2	32.29	32.52	**32.61**	32.55	**32.64**	32.56

Table 2: BLEU scores of the re-ranked translations. Baseline score = 31.44

English) from BLEU 30.5 to BLEU 31.0.

Iyer and Ostendorf (1999) select and weight data to train language modeling for ASR. The data is selected based on its relevance for a topic or the similarity to data known to be in the same domain as the test data. Each additional document is classified to be in-domain or out-of-domain according to cosine distance with TF-IDF term weights, POS-tag LM and a 3-gram word LM. n-gram counts from the in-domain and the additionally selected out-of-domain data are then combined with an weighting factor. The combined counts are used to estimate a LM with standard smoothing.

Hildebrand et al. (2005) use information retrieval to select relevant data to train adapted translation and language models for an SMT system.

Si et al. (2002) use unigram distribution similarity to select the document collection which is most relevant to the query documents. Their work is mainly focused on information retrieval application.

7 Conclusion and future work

In this paper, we presented a novel distributed language modeling solution. The distributed LM is capable of using an arbitrarily large corpus to estimate the n-gram probability for arbitrarily long histories. We applied the distributed language model to N-best re-ranking and improved the translation quality by 4.8% when evaluated by the BLEU metric. The distributed LM provides a flexible architecture for relevance selection, which makes it possible to select data for each individual test sentence. Our experiments have shown that relevant data has better discriminative power than using all the data.

We will investigate different relevance weighting schemes to better combine n-gram statistics from different data sources. We are planning to integrate the distributed LM in the statistical machine translation decoder in the near future.

8 Acknowledgement

We would like to thank Necip Fazil Ayan and Philip Resnik for providing Hiero system's N-best list and allowing us to use it for this work.

References

Peter F. Brown, Vincent J. Della Pietra, Stephen A. Della Pietra, and Robert L. Mercer. 1993. The mathematics of statistical machine translation: parameter estimation. *Comput. Linguist.*, 19(2):263–311.

David Chiang. 2005. A hierarchical phrase-based model for statistical machine translation. In *Proceedings of ACL 2005*, pages 263–270, Ann Arbor, MI, June 2005. ACL.

Michael Collins, Philipp Koehn, and Ivona Kucerova. 2005. Clause restructuring for statistical machine translation. In *Proceedings of ACL 2005*, pages 531–540, Ann Arbor, MI, June.

J. Goodman. 2000. A bit of progress in language modeling. Technical report, Microsoft Research, 56 Fuchun Peng.

Almut Silja Hildebrand, Matthias Eck, Stephan Vogel, and Alex Waibel. 2005. Adaptation of the translation model for statistical machine translation based on information retrieval. In *Proceedings of the 10th EAMT conference "Practical applications of machine translation"*, pages 133–142, Budapest, May.

R. Iyer and M. Ostendorf. 1999. Relevance weighting for combining multi-domain data for n-gram language modeling. *Comptuer Speech and Language*, 13(3):267–282.

Katrin Kirchhoff and Mei Yang. 2005. Improved language modeling for statistical machine translation. In *Proceedings of the ACL Workshop on Building and Using Parallel Texts*, pages 125–128, Ann Arbor, Michigan, June. Association for Computational Linguistics.

Reinhard Kneser and Hermann Ney. 1995. Improved backing-off for m-gram language modeling. In *Proceedings of the IEEE International Conference on Acoustics, Speech and Signal Processing, volume 1*, pages 181–184.

Philipp Koehn. 2004. Statistical significance tests for machine translation evaluation. In *Proceedings of EMNLP 2004*, Barcelona, Spain, July.

Claudia Leopold. 2001. *Parallel and Distributed Computing: A Survey of Models, Paradigms and Approaches*. John Wiley & Sons, Inc., New York, NY, USA.

Udi Manber and Gene Myers. 1993. Suffix arrays: a new method for on-line string searches. *SIAM J. Comput.*, 22(5):935–948.

Franz Josef Och, Daniel Gildea, Sanjeev Khudanpur, Anoop Sarkar, Kenji Yamada, Alex Fraser, Shankar Kumar, Libin Shen, David Smith, Katherine Eng, Viren Jain, Zhen Jin, and Dragomir Radev. 2004. A smorgasbord of features for statistical machine translation. In *Proceedings of the 2004 Meeting of the North American chapter of the Association for Computational Linguistics (NAACL-04)*, Boston.

K. Papineni, S. Roukos, T. Ward, and W. Zhu. 2001. Bleu: a method for automatic evaluation of machine translation. Technical Report RC22176(W0109-022), IBM Research Division, Thomas J. Watson Research Center.

Jay M. Ponte and W. Bruce Croft. 1998. A language modeling approach to information retrieval. In *Research and Development in Information Retrieval*, pages 275–281.

Luo Si, Rong Jin, Jamie Callan, and Paul Ogilvie. 2002. A language modeling framework for resource selection and results merging. In *CIKM '02: Proceedings of the eleventh international conference on Information and knowledge management*, pages 391–397, New York, NY, USA. ACM Press.

Radu Soricut, Kevin Knight, and Daniel Marcu. 2002. Using a large monolingual corpus to improve translation accuracy. In *AMTA '02: Proceedings of the 5th Conference of the Association for Machine Translation in the Americas on Machine Translation: From Research to Real Users*, pages 155–164, London, UK. Springer-Verlag.

Mikio Yamamoto and Kenneth W. Church. 2001. Using suffix arrays to compute term frequency and document frequency for all substrings in a corpus. *Comput. Linguist.*, 27(1):1–30.

Ying Zhang and Stephan Vogel. 2004. Measuring confidence intervals for the machine translation evaluation metrics. In *Proceedings of The 10th International Conference on Theoretical and Methodological Issues in Machine Translation*, October.

Ying Zhang and Stephan Vogel. 2005. An efficient phrase-to-phrase alignment model for arbitrarily long phrase and large corpora. In *Proceedings of the Tenth Conference of the European Association for Machine Translation (EAMT-05)*, Budapest, Hungary, May. The European Association for Machine Translation.

Efficient Search for Inversion Transduction Grammar

Hao Zhang and **Daniel Gildea**
Computer Science Department
University of Rochester
Rochester, NY 14627

Abstract

We develop admissible A* search heuristics for synchronous parsing with Inversion Transduction Grammar, and present results both for bitext alignment and for machine translation decoding. We also combine the dynamic programming hook trick with A* search for decoding. These techniques make it possible to find optimal alignments much more quickly, and make it possible to find optimal translations for the first time. Even in the presence of pruning, we are able to achieve higher BLEU scores with the same amount of computation.

1 Introduction

The Inversion Transduction Grammar (ITG) of Wu (1997) is a syntactically motivated algorithm for producing word-level alignments of pairs of translationally equivalent sentences in two languages. The algorithm builds a synchronous parse tree for both sentences, and assumes that the trees have the same underlying structure but that the ordering of constituents may differ in the two languages. ITG imposes constraints on which alignments are possible, and these constraints have been shown to be a good match for real bitext data (Zens and Ney, 2003).

A major motivation for the introduction of ITG was the existence of polynomial-time algorithms both for alignment and translation. Alignment, whether for training a translation model using EM or for finding the Viterbi alignment of test data, is $O(n^6)$ (Wu, 1997), while translation (decoding) is $O(n^7)$ using a bigram language model, and $O(n^{11})$ with trigrams. While polynomial-time algorithms are a major improvement over the NP-complete problems posed by the alignment models of Brown et al. (1993), the degree of these polynomials is high, making both alignment and decoding infeasible for realistic sentences without very significant pruning. In this paper, we explore use of the "hook trick" (Eisner and Satta, 1999; Huang et al., 2005) to reduce the asymptotic complexity of decoding, and the use of heuristics to guide the search.

Our search heuristics are a conservative estimate of the outside probability of a bitext cell in the complete synchronous parse. Some estimate of this outside probability is a common element of modern statistical (monolingual) parsers (Charniak et al., 1998; Collins, 1999), and recent work has developed heuristics that are *admissible* for A* search, guaranteeing that the optimal parse will be found (Klein and Manning, 2003). We extend this type of outside probability estimate to include both word translation and n-gram language model probabilities. These measures have been used to guide search in word- or phrase-based MT systems (Wang and Waibel, 1997; Och et al., 2001), but in such models optimal search is generally not practical even with good heuristics. In this paper, we show that the same assumptions that make ITG polynomial-time can be used to efficiently compute heuristics which guarantee us that we will find the optimal alignment or translation, while significantly speeding the search.

2 Inversion Transduction Grammar

An Inversion Transduction Grammar can generate pairs of sentences in two languages by recursively applying context-free bilingual production rules. Most work on ITG has focused on the 2-normal form, which consists of unary production rules that are responsible for generating word pairs:

$$X \rightarrow e/f$$

Proceedings of the 2006 Conference on Empirical Methods in Natural Language Processing (EMNLP 2006), pages 224–231,
Sydney, July 2006.

and binary production rules in two forms that are responsible for generating syntactic subtree pairs:

$$X \to [YZ]$$

and

$$X \to \langle YZ \rangle$$

The rules with square brackets enclosing the right hand side expand the left hand side symbol into the two symbols on the right hand side in the same order in the two languages, whereas the rules with pointed brackets expand the left hand side symbol into the two right hand side symbols in reverse order in the two languages.

3 A* Viterbi Alignment Selection

A* parsing is a special case of agenda-based chart parsing, where the priority of a node $X[i, j]$ on the agenda, corresponding to nonterminal X spanning positions i through j, is the product of the node's current inside probability with an estimate of the outside probability. By the current inside probability, we mean the probability of the so-far-most-probable subtree rooted on the node $X[i, j]$, with leaves being ${}_iw_j$, while the outside probability is the highest probability for a parse with the root being $S[0, N]$ and the sequence ${}_0w_iX_jw_n$ forming the leaves. The node with the highest priority is removed from the agenda and added to the chart, and then explored by combining with all of its neighboring nodes in the chart to update the priorities of the resulting nodes on the agenda. By using estimates close to the actual outside probabilities, A* parsing can effectively reduce the number of nodes to be explored before putting the root node onto the chart. When the outside estimate is both admissible and monotonic, whenever a node is put onto the chart, its current best inside parse is the Viterbi inside parse.

To relate A* parsing with A* search for finding the lowest cost path from a certain source node to a certain destination node in a graph, we view the forest of all parse trees as a hypergraph. The source node in the hypergraph fans out into the nodes of unit spans that cover the individual words. From each group of children to their parent in the forest, there is a hyperedge. The destination node is the common root node for all the parse trees in the forest. Under the mapping, a parse is a hyperpath from the source node to the destination node. The Viterbi parse selection problem thus becomes finding the lowest-cost hyperpath from the source node to the destination node. The cost in this scenario is thus the negative of log probability. The inside estimate and outside estimate naturally correspond to the $\hat{g}$ and $\hat{h}$ for A* searching, respectively.

A stochastic ITG can bc thought of as a stochastic CFG extended to the space of bitext. A node in the ITG chart is a bitext cell that covers a source substring and a target substring. We use the notion of $X[l, m, i, j]$ to represent a tree node in ITG parse. It can potentially be combined with any bitext cells at the four corners, as shown in Figure 1(a).

Unlike CFG parsing where the leaves are fixed, the Viterbi ITG parse selection involves finding the Viterbi alignment under ITG constraint. Good outside estimates have to bound the outside ITG Viterbi alignment probability tightly.

3.1 A* Estimates for Alignment

Under the ITG constraints, each source language word can be aligned with at most one target language word and vice versa. An ITG constituent $X[l, m, i, j]$ implies that the words in the source substring in the span $[l, m]$ are aligned with the words in the target substring $[i, j]$. It further implies that the words outside the span $[l, m]$ in the source are aligned with the words outside the span $[i, j]$ in the target language. Figure 1(b) displays the tic-tac-toe pattern for the inside and outside components of a particular cell. To estimate the upper bound of the ITG Viterbi alignment probability for the outside component with acceptable complexity, we need to relax the ITG constraint. Instead of ensuring one-to-one in both directions, we use a many-to-one constraint in one direction, and we relax all constraints on reordering within the outside component.

The many-to-one constraint has the same dynamic programming structure as IBM Model 1, where each target word is supposed to be translated from any of the source words or the NULL symbol. In the Model 1 estimate of the outside probability, source and target words can align using any combination of points from the four outside corners of the tic-tac-toe pattern. Thus in Figure 1(b), there is one solid cell (corresponding to the Model 1 Viterbi alignment) in each column, falling either in the upper or lower outside shaded corner. This can be also be thought of as squeezing together the four outside corners, creat-

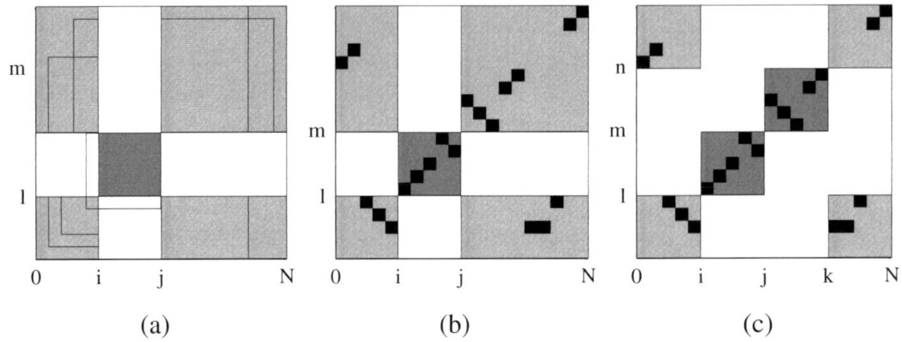

Figure 1: (a) A bitext cell $X[l, m, i, j]$ (shaded) for ITG parsing. The inside cell can be combined with adjacent cells in the four outside corners (lighter shading) to expand into larger cells. One possible expansion to the lower left corner is displayed. (b) The tic-tac-toe pattern of alignments consistent with a given cell. If the inner box is used in the final synchronous parse, all other alignments must come from the four outside corners. (c) Combination of two adjacent cells shown with region for new outside heuristic.

ing a new cell whose probability is estimated using IBM Model 1. In contrast, the inside Viterbi alignment satisfies the ITG constraint, implying only one solid cell in each column and each row. Mathematically, our Model 1 estimate for the outside component is:

$$h_{\mathrm{M1}}(l, m, i, j) = \prod_{\substack{t<i,\\ t>j}} \max_{\substack{s<l,\\ s>m}} P(f_t, e_s)$$

This Model 1 estimate is admissible. Maximizing over each column ensures that the translation probability for each target word is greater than or equal to the corresponding word translation probability under the ITG constraint. Model 1 virtually assigns a probability of 1 for deleting any source word. As a product of word-to-word translation probabilities including deletions and insertions, the ITG Viterbi alignment probability cannot be higher than the product of maximal word-to-word translation probabilities using the Model 1 estimate.

The Model 1 estimate is also monotonic, a property which is best understood geometrically. A successor state to cell (l, m, i, j) in the search is formed by combining the cell with a cell which is adjacent at one of the four corners, as shown in Figure 1(c). Of the four outside corner regions used in calculating the search heuristic, one will be the same for the successor state, and three will be a subset of the old corner region. Without loss of generality, assume we are combining a cell (m, n, j, k) that is adjacent to (l, m, i, j) to the upper right. We define

$$H_{\mathrm{M1}}(l, m, i, j) = -\log h_{\mathrm{M1}}(l, m, i, j)$$

as the negative log of the heuristic in order to correspond to an estimated cost or distance in search terminology. Similarly, we speak of the cost of a chart entry $c(X[l, m, i, j])$ as its negative log probability, and the cost of a cell $c(l, m, i, j)$ as the cost of the best chart entry with the boundaries (l, m, i, j). The cost of the cell (m, n, j, k) which is being combined with the old cell is guaranteed to be greater than the contribution of the columns j through k to the heuristic $H_{\mathrm{M1}}(l, m, i, j)$. The contribution of the columns k through N to the new heuristic $H_{\mathrm{M1}}(l, n, i, k)$ is guaranteed to be greater in cost than their contribution to the old heuristic. Thus,

$$H_{\mathrm{M1}}(l, m, i, j) \leq c(m, n, j, k) + c(X \rightarrow YZ) + H_{\mathrm{M1}}(l, n, i, k)$$

meaning that the heuristic is monotonic or consistent.

The Model 1 estimate can be applied in both translation directions. The estimates from both directions are an upper bound of the actual ITG Viterbi probability. By taking the minimum of the two, we can get a tighter upper bound.

We can precompute the Model 1 outside estimate for all bitext cells before parsing starts. A naïve implementation would take $O(n^6)$ steps of computation, because there are $O(n^4)$ cells, each of which takes $O(n^2)$ steps to compute its Model 1 probability. Fortunately, exploiting the recursive

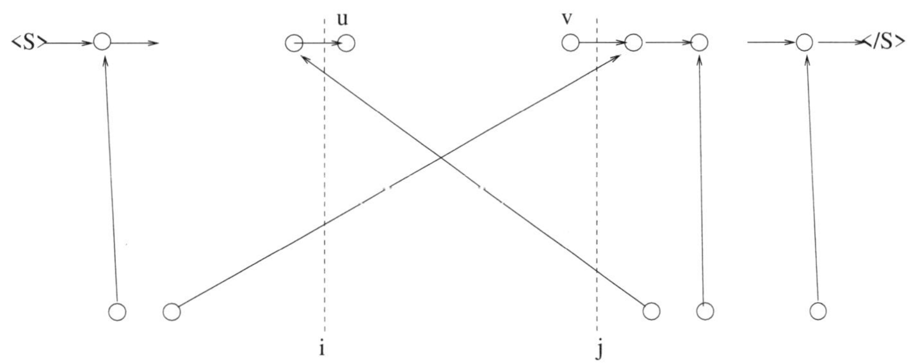

Figure 2: The region within the dashed lines is the translation hypothesis $X[i, j, u, v]$. The word sequence on the top is the Viterbi translation of the sentence on the bottom. Wide range word order change may happen.

nature of the cells, we can compute values for the inside and outside components of each cell using dynamic programming in $O(n^4)$ time (Zhang and Gildea, 2005).

4 A* Decoding

The of ITG decoding algorithm of Wu (1996) can be viewed as a variant of the Viterbi parsing algorithm for alignment selection. The task of standard alignment is to find word level links between two fixed-order strings. In the decoding situation, while the input side is a fixed sequence of words, the output side is a bag of words to be linked with the input words and then reordered. Under the ITG constraint, if the target language substring $[i, j]$ is translated into s_1 in the source language and the target substring $[j, k]$ is translated into s_2, then s_1 and s_2 must be consecutive in the source language as well and two possible orderings, $s_1 s_2$ and $s_2 s_1$, are allowed. Finding the best translation of the substring of $[i, k]$ involves searching over all possible split points j and two possible reorderings for each split. In theory, the inversion probabilities associated with the ITG rules can do the job of reordering. However, a language model as simple as bigram is generally stronger. Using an n-gram language model implies keeping at least $n - 1$ boundary words in the dynamic programming table for a hypothetical translation of a source language substring. In the case of a bigram ITG decoder, a translation hypothesis for the source language substring $[i, j]$ is denoted as $X[i, j, u, v]$, where u and v are the left boundary word and right boundary word of the target language counterpart.

As indicated by the similarity of parsing item notation, the dynamic programming property of the Viterbi decoder is essentially the same as the bitext parsing for finding the underlying Viterbi alignment. By permitting translation from the null target string of $[i, i]$ into source language words as many times as necessary, the decoder can translate an input sentence into a longer output sentence. When there is the null symbol in the bag of candidate words, the decoder can choose to translate a word into null to decrease the output length. Both insertions and deletions are special cases of the bitext parsing items.

Given the similarity of the dynamic programming framework to the alignment problem, it is not surprising that A* search can also be applied in a similar way. The initial parsing items on the agenda are the basic translation units: $X[i, i+1, u, u]$, for normal word-for-word translations and deletions (translations into nothing), and also $X[i, i, u, u]$, for insertions (translations from nothing). The goal item is $S[0, N, \langle s \rangle, \langle /s \rangle]$, where $\langle s \rangle$ stands for the beginning-of-sentence symbol and $\langle /s \rangle$ stands for the end-of-sentence symbol. The exploration step of the A* search is to expand the translation hypothesis of a substring by combining with neighboring translation hypotheses. When the outside estimate is admissible and monotonic, the exploration is optimal in the sense that whenever a hypothesis is taken from the top of the agenda, it is a Viterbi translation of the corresponding target substring. Thus, when $S[0, N, \langle s \rangle, \langle /s \rangle]$ is added to the chart, we have found the Viterbi translation for the entire sentence.

$$\beta(X[i,j,u,v]) = \max\left\{\beta_{\langle\rangle}(X[i,j,u,v]), \beta_{[]}(X[i,j,u,v])\right\}$$

$$\beta_{[]}(X[i,j,u,v]) = \max_{k,v_1,u_2,Y,Z}\left[\beta(Y[i,k,u,v_1])\cdot\beta(Z[k,j,u_2,v])\cdot P(X\to[YZ])\cdot P_{lm}(u_2\mid v_1)\right]$$

$$= \max_{k,u_2,Y,Z}\left[\max_{v_1}\left[\beta(Y[i,k,u,v_1])\cdot P_{lm}(u_2\mid v_1)\right]\cdot P(X\to[YZ])\cdot\beta(Z[k,j,u_2,v])\right]$$

Figure 3: Top: An ITG decoding constituent can be built with either a straight or an inverted rule. Bottom: An efficient factorization for straight rules.

4.1 A* Estimates for Translation

The key to the success of A* decoding is an outside estimate that combines word-for-word translation probabilities and n-gram probabilities. Figure 2 is the picture of the outside translations and bigrams of a particular translation hypothesis $X[i,j,u,v]$.

Our heuristic involves precomputing two values for each word in the input string, involving forward- and backward-looking language model probabilities. For the forward looking value h_f at input position n, we take a maximum over the set of words S_n that the input word t_n can be translated as:

$$h_f(n) = \max_{s\in S_n}\left[P_t(s\mid t_n)\max_{s'\in S} P_{lm}(s'\mid s)\right]$$

where:

$$S = \bigcup_n S_n$$

is the set of all possible translations for all words in the input string. While h_f considers language model probabilities for words following s, the backward-looking value h_b considers language model probabilities for s given possible preceding words:

$$h_b(n) = \max_{s\in S_n}\left[P_t(s\mid t_n)\max_{s'\in S} P_{lm}(s\mid s')\right]$$

Our overall heuristic for a partial translation hypothesis $X[i,j,u,v]$ combines language model probabilities at the boundaries of the input substring with backward-looking values for the preceding words, and forward-looking values for the following words:

$$h(i,j,u,v) = \left[\max_{s\in S} P_{lm}(u\mid s)\right]\left[\max_{s\in S} P_{lm}(s\mid v)\right] \cdot \prod_{\substack{n<i,\\ n>j}} \max\left[h_b(n), h_f(n)\right]$$

Because we don't know whether a given input word will appear before or after the partial hypothesis in the final translation, we take the maximum of the forward and backward values for words outside the span $[i,j]$.

4.2 Combining the Hook Trick with A*

The hook trick is a factorization technique for dynamic programming. For bilexical parsing, Eisner and Satta (1999) pointed out we can reduce the complexity of parsing from $O(n^5)$ to $O(n^4)$ by combining the non-head constituents with the bilexical rules first, and then combining the resultant hook constituents with the head constituents. By doing so, the maximal number of interactive variables ranging over n is reduced from 5 to 4. For ITG decoding, we can apply a similar factorization trick. We describe the bigram-integrated decoding case here, and refer to Huang et al. (2005) for more detailed discussion. Figure 3 shows how to decompose the expression for the case of straight rules; the same method applies to inverted rules. The number of free variables on the right hand side of the second equation is 7: i, j, k, u, v, v_1, and u_2.[1] After factorization, counting the free variables enclosed in the innermost max operator, we get five: i, k, u, v_1, and u_2. The decomposition eliminates one free variable, v_1. In the outermost level, there are six free variables left. The maximum number of interacting variables is six overall. So, we reduced the complexity of ITG decoding using bigram language model from $O(n^7)$ to $O(n^6)$. If we visualize an ITG decoding constituent Y extending from source language position i to k and target language boundary words u and v_1 with a diagram:

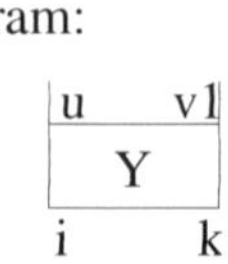

[1] X, Y, and Z range over grammar nonterminals, of which there are a constant number.

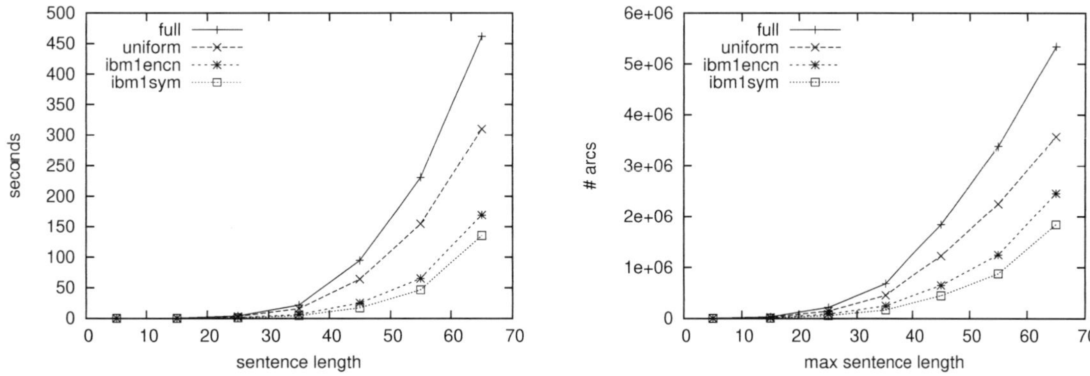

Figure 4: Speed of various techniques for finding the optimal alignment.

the hook corresponding to the innermost $\max$ operator in the equation can be visualized as follows:

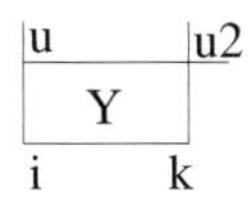

with the expected language model state u_2 "hanging" outside the target language string.

The trick is generic to the control strategies of actual parsing, because the hooks can be treated as just another type of constituent. Building hooks is like applying special unary rules on top of non-hooks. In terms of of outside heuristic for hooks, there is a slight difference from that for non-hooks:

$$h(i, j, u, v) = \left[\max_{s \in S} P_{lm}(s \mid v) \right] \cdot \prod_{\substack{n<i, \\ n>j}} \max \left[h_b(n), h_f(n) \right]$$

That is, we do not need the backward-looking estimate for the left boundary word u.

5 Experiments

We tested the performance of our heuristics for alignment on a Chinese-English newswire corpus. Probabilities for the ITG model were trained using Expectation Maximization on a corpus of 18,773 sentence pairs with a total of 276,113 Chinese words and 315,415 English words. For EM training, we limited the data to sentences of no more than 25 words in either language. Here we present timing results for finding the Viterbi alignment of longer sentences using this fixed translation model with different heuristics. We compute alignments on a total of 117 test sentences, which are broken down by length as shown in Table 1.

Length	# sentences
0-9	5
10–19	26
20–29	29
30–39	22
40–49	24
50–59	10
60	1

Table 1: Length of longer sentence in each pair from test data.

method	*time*	*speedup*
full	815s	–
uniform	547s	1.4
ibm1encn	269s	3.0
ibm1sym	205s	3.9

Table 2: Total time for each alignment method.

Results are presented both in terms of time and the number of arcs added to the chart before the optimal parse is found. *Full* refers to exhaustive parsing, that is, building a complete chart with all n^4 arcs. *Uniform* refers to a best-first parsing strategy that expands the arcs with the highest inside probability at each step, but does not incorporate an estimate of the outside probability. *Ibm1encn* denotes our heuristic based on IBM model 1, applied to translations from English to Chinese, while *ibm1sym* applies the Model 1 heuristic in both translation directions and takes the minimum. The factor by which times were decreased was found to be roughly constant across different length sentences. The alignment times for the entire test set are shown in Table 2, the best heuristic is 3.9 times faster than exhaustive

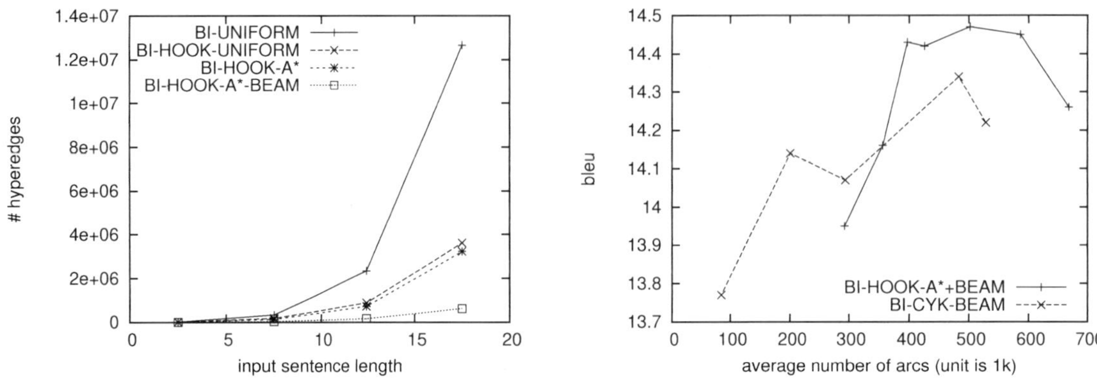

Figure 5: On the left, we compare decoding speed for uniform outside estimate best-first decoding with and without the hook trick, as well as results using our heuristic (labeled A*) and with beam pruning (which no longer produces optimal results). On the right, we show the relationship between computation time and BLEU scores as the pruning threshold is varied for both A* search and bottom-up CYK parsing.

dynamic programming.

We did our ITG decoding experiments on the LDC 2002 MT evaluation data set for translation of Chinese newswire sentences into English. The evaluation data set has 10 human translation references for each sentence. There are a total of 371 Chinese sentences of no more than 20 words in the data set. These sentences are the test set for our different versions of ITG decoders using both a bigram language model and a trigram language model. We evaluate the translation results by comparing them against the reference translations using the BLEU metric. The word-for-word translation probabilities are from the translation model of IBM Model 4 trained on a 160-million-word English-Chinese parallel corpus using GIZA++. The language model is trained on a 30-million-word English corpus. The rule probabilities for ITG are from the same training as in the alignment experiments described above.

We compared the BLEU scores of the A* decoder and the ITG decoder that uses beam ratio pruning at each stage of bottom-up parsing. In the case of bigram-integrated decoding, for each input word, the best 2 translations are put into the bag of output words. In the case of trigram-integrated decoding, top 5 candidate words are chosen. The A* decoder is guaranteed to find the Viterbi translation that maximizes the product of n-grams probabilities, translation probabilities (including insertions and deletions) and inversion rule probabilities by choosing the right words and the right word order subject to the ITG constraint.

Figure 5 (left) demonstrates the speedup obtained through the hook trick, the heuristic, and pruning, all based on A* search. Table 3 shows the improvement of BLEU score after applying the A* algorithm to find the optimal translation under the model. Figure 5 (right) investigates the relationship between the search effort and BLEU score for A* and bottom-up CYK parsing, both with pruning. Pruning for A* works in such a way that we never explore a low probability hypothesis falling out of a certain beam ratio of the best hypothesis within the bucket of $X[i, j, *, *]$, where $*$ means any word. Table 4 shows results for trigram-integrated decoding. However, due to time constraint, we have not explored time/performance tradeoff as we did for bigram decoding.

The number of combinations in the table is the average number of hyperedges to be explored in searching, proportional to the total number of

Decoder	Combinations	BLEU
BI-UNIFORM	8.02M	14.26
BI-HOOK-A*	2.10M	14.26
BI-HOOK-A*-BEAM	0.40M	14.43
BI-CYK-BEAM	0.20M	14.14

Table 3: Decoder speed and BLEU scores for bigram decoding.

Decoder	Cbns	BLEU
TRI-A*-BEAM(10^{-3})	213.4M	17.83
TRI-A*-BEAM(10^{-2})	20.7M	17.09
TRI-CYK-BEAM(10^{-3})	21.2M	16.86

Table 4: Results for trigram decoding.

computation steps.

6 Conclusion

A* search for Viterbi alignment selection under ITG is efficient using IBM Model 1 as an outside estimate. The experimental results indicate that despite being a more relaxed word-for-word alignment model than ITG, IBM Model 1 can serve as an efficient and reliable approximation of ITG in terms of Viterbi alignment probability. This is more true when we apply Model 1 to both translation directions and take the minimum of both. We have also tried to incorporate estimates of binary rule probabilities to make the outside estimate even sharper. However, the further improvement was marginal.

We are able to find the ITG Viterbi translation using our A* decoding algorithm with an outside estimate that combines outside bigrams and translation probabilities for outside words. The hook trick gave us a significant further speedup; we believe this to be the first demonstrated practical application of this technique.

Interestingly, the BLEU score for the optimal translations under the probabilistic model is lower than we achieve with our best bigram-based system using pruning. However, this system makes use of the A* heuristic, and our speed/performance curve shows that the heuristic allows us to achieve higher BLEU scores with the same amount of computation. In the case of trigram integrated decoding, there is 1 point of BLEU score improvement by moving from a typical CYK plus beam search decoder to a decoder using A* plus beam search.

However, without knowing what words will appear in the output language, a very sharp outside estimate to further bring down the number of combinations is difficult to achieve.

The brighter side of the move towards optimal decoding is that the A* search strategy leads us to the region of the search space that is close to the optimal result, where we can more easily find good translations.

Acknowledgments This work was supported by NSF ITR IIS-09325646 and NSF ITR IIS-0428020.

References

Peter F. Brown, Stephen A. Della Pietra, Vincent J. Della Pietra, and Robert L. Mercer. 1993. The mathematics of statistical machine translation: Parameter estimation. *Computational Linguistics*, 19(2):263 311.

Eugene Charniak, Sharon Goldwater, and Mark Johnson. 1998. Edge-based best-first chart parsing. In *Proceedings of the Sixth Workshop on Very Large Corpora*.

Michael John Collins. 1999. *Head-driven Statistical Models for Natural Language Parsing*. Ph.D. thesis, University of Pennsylvania, Philadelphia.

Jason Eisner and Giorgio Satta. 1999. Efficient parsing for bilexical context-free grammars and head automaton grammars. In *37th Annual Meeting of the Association for Computational Linguistics*.

Liang Huang, Hao Zhang, and Daniel Gildea. 2005. Machine translation as lexicalized parsing with hooks. In *International Workshop on Parsing Technologies (IWPT05)*, Vancouver, BC.

Dan Klein and Christopher D. Manning. 2003. A* parsing: Fast exact viterbi parse selection. In *Proceedings of the 2003 Meeting of the North American chapter of the Association for Computational Linguistics (NAACL-03)*.

Franz Josef Och, Nicola Ueffing, and Herman Ney. 2001. An efficient a* search algorithm for statistical machine translation. In *Proceedings of the ACL Workshop on Data-Driven Machine Translation*, pages 55–62, Toulouse, France.

Ye-Yi Wang and Alex Waibel. 1997. Decoding algorithm in statistical machine translation. In *35th Annual Meeting of the Association for Computational Linguistics*.

Dekai Wu. 1996. A polynomial-time algorithm for statistical machine translation. In *34th Annual Meeting of the Association for Computational Linguistics*.

Dekai Wu. 1997. Stochastic inversion transduction grammars and bilingual parsing of parallel corpora. *Computational Linguistics*, 23(3):377–403.

Richard Zens and Hermann Ney. 2003. A comparative study on reordering constraints in statistical machine translation. In *Proceedings of the 40th Annual Meeting of the Association for Computational Linguistics*, Sapporo, Japan.

Hao Zhang and Daniel Gildea. 2005. Stochastic lexicalized inversion transduction grammar for alignment. In *Proceedings of the 43rd Annual Conference of the Association for Computational Linguistics (ACL-05)*, Ann Arbor, MI.

A Discriminative Model for Tree-to-Tree Translation

Brooke Cowan
MIT CSAIL
brooke@csail.mit.edu

Ivona Kučerová
MIT Linguistics Department
kucerova@mit.edu

Michael Collins
MIT CSAIL
mcollins@csail.mit.edu

Abstract

This paper proposes a statistical, tree-to-tree model for producing translations. Two main contributions are as follows: (1) a method for the extraction of syntactic structures with alignment information from a parallel corpus of translations, and (2) use of a discriminative, feature-based model for prediction of these target-language syntactic structures—which we call *aligned extended projections*, or AEPs. An evaluation of the method on translation from German to English shows similar performance to the phrase-based model of Koehn et al. (2003).

1 Introduction

Phrase-based approaches (Och and Ney, 2004) to statistical machine translation (SMT) have recently achieved impressive results, leading to significant improvements in accuracy over the original IBM models (Brown et al., 1993). However, phrase-based models lack a direct representation of syntactic information in the source or target languages; this has prompted several researchers to consider various approaches that make use of syntactic information.

This paper describes a framework for *tree-to-tree* based statistical translation. Our goal is to learn a model that maps parse trees in the source language to parse trees in the target language. The model is learned from a corpus of translation pairs, where each sentence in the source or target language has an associated parse tree. We see two major benefits of tree-to-tree based translation. First, it is possible to explicitly model the syntax of the target language, thereby improving grammaticality. Second, we can build a detailed model of the correspondence between the source and target parse trees, with the aim of constructing translations that preserve the meaning of source language sentences.

Our translation framework involves a process where the target-language parse tree is broken down into a sequence of clauses, and each clause is then translated separately. A central concept we introduce in the translation of clauses is that of an *aligned extended projection* (AEP). AEPs are derived from the concept of an *extended projection* in lexicalized tree adjoining grammars (LTAG) (Frank, 2002), with the addition of alignment information that is based on work in synchronous LTAG (Shieber and Schabes, 1990). A key contribution of this paper is a method for learning to map German clauses to AEPs using a feature-based model with a perceptron learning algorithm.

We performed experiments on translation from German to English on the Europarl data set. Evaluation in terms of both BLEU scores and human judgments shows that our system performs similarly to the phrase-based model of Koehn et al. (2003).

1.1 A Sketch of the Approach

This section provides an overview of the translation process. We will use the German sentence *wir wissen daß das haupthemmnis der vorhersehbare widerstand der hersteller war* as a running example. For this example we take the desired translation to be *we know that the main obstacle has been the predictable resistance of manufacturers.*

Translation of a German sentence proceeds in the following four steps:

Step 1: The German sentence is parsed and then broken down into separate parse structures for a sequence of clauses. For example, the German example above is broken into a parse structure for the clause *wir wissen* followed by a parse structure for the subordinate clause *daß. . .war.* Each of these clauses is then translated separately, using steps 2–3 below.

Step 2: An *aligned extended projection* (AEP) is predicted for each German clause. To illustrate this step, consider translation of the second German clause, which has the following parse structure:

Proceedings of the 2006 Conference on Empirical Methods in Natural Language Processing (EMNLP 2006), pages 232–241,
Sydney, July 2006.

```
s-oc kous-cp daß
      np-sb[1] art das
               nn haupthemmnis
      np-pd[2] art der
               adja vorhersehbare
               nn widerstand
               np-ag art der
                     nn hersteller
      vafin-hd war
```

Note that we use the symbols [1] and [2] to identify the two modifiers (arguments or adjuncts) in the clause, in this case a subject and an object.

A major part of the AEP is a parse-tree fragment, that is similar to a TAG elementary tree (see also Figure 2):

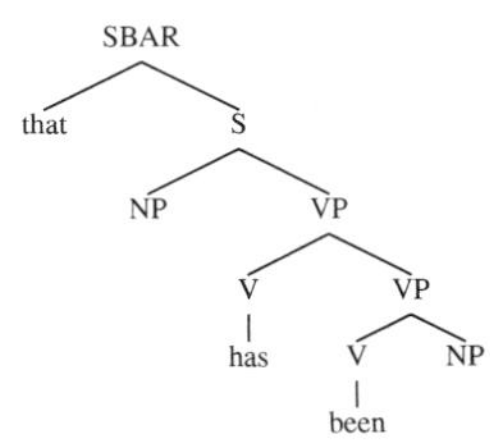

Following the work of Frank (2002), we will refer to a structure like this as an *extended projection* (EP). The EP encapsulates the core syntactic structure in the English clause. It contains the main verb *been*, as well as the function words *that* and *has*. It also contains a parse tree "spine" which has the main verb *been* as one of its leaves, and has the clause label `SBAR` as its root. In addition, it specifies positions for arguments in the clause—in this case NPs corresponding to the subject and object.

An AEP contains an EP, as well as *alignment information* about where the German modifiers should be placed in the extended projection. For example, the AEP in this case would contain the tree fragment shown above, together with an alignment specifying that the modifiers [1] and [2] from the German parse will appear in the EP as subject and object, respectively.

Step 3: The German modifiers are translated and placed in the appropriate positions within the AEP. For example, the modifiers *das haupthemmnis* and *der vorhersehbare widerstand der hersteller* would be translated as *the main obstacle*, and *the predictable resistance of manufacturers*, respectively, and then placed into the subject and object positions in the AEP.

Step 4: The individual clause translations are combined to give a final translation. For example, the translations *we know* and *that the main obstacle has been* ... would be concatenated to give *we know that the main obstacle has been* ....

The main focus of this paper will be Step 2: the prediction of AEPs from German clauses. AEPs are detailed structural objects, and their relationship to the source-language clause can be quite complex. We use a discriminative feature-based model, trained with the perceptron algorithm, to incrementally predict the AEP in a sequence of steps. At each step we define features that allow the model to capture a wide variety of dependencies within the AEP itself, or between the AEP and the source-language clause.

1.2 Motivation for the Approach

Our approach to tree-to-tree translation is motivated by several observations. Breaking the source-language tree into clauses (Step 1) considerably simplifies the difficult problem of defining an alignment between source and target trees. Our impression is that high-quality translations can be produced in a clause-by-clause fashion.[1] The use of a feature-based model for AEP prediction (Step 2) allows us to capture complex syntactic correspondences between English and German, as well as grammaticality constraints on the English side.

In this paper, we implement the translation of modifiers (Step 3) with the phrase-based system of Koehn et al. (2003). The modifiers in our data set are generally small chunks of text such as NPs, PPs, and ADJPs, which by definition do not include clauses or verbs. In our approach, we use the phrase-based system to generate n-best lists of candidate translations and then rerank the translations based on grammaticality, i.e., using criteria that judge how well they fit the position in the AEP. In future work, we might use finite state machines in place of a reranking approach, or recursively apply the AEP approach to the modifiers.

Stitching translated clauses back together (Step 4) is a relatively simple task: in a substantial majority of cases, the German clauses are not embedded, but instead form a linear sequence that accounts for the entire sentence. In these cases we can simply concatenate the English clause translations to form the full translation. Embedded clauses in German are slightly more complicated, but it is not difficult to form embedded structures in the English translations.

Section 5.2 of this paper describes the features

[1]Note that we do not assume that all of the translations in the training data have been produced in a clause-by-clause fashion. Rather, we assume that good translations for test examples can be produced in this way.

we use for AEP prediction in translation from German to English. Many of the features of the AEP prediction model are specifically tuned to the choice of German and English as the source and target languages. However, it should be easy to develop new feature sets to deal with other languages or treebanking styles. We see this as one of the strengths of the feature-based approach.

In the work presented in this paper, we focus on the prediction of clausal AEPs, i.e., AEPs associated with main verbs. One reason for this is that clause structures are particularly rich and complex from a syntactic perspective. This means that there should be considerable potential in improving translation quality if we can accurately predict these structures. It also means that clause-level AEPs are a good test-bed for the discriminative approach to AEP prediction; future work may consider applying these methods to other structures such as NPs, PPs, ADJPs, and so on.

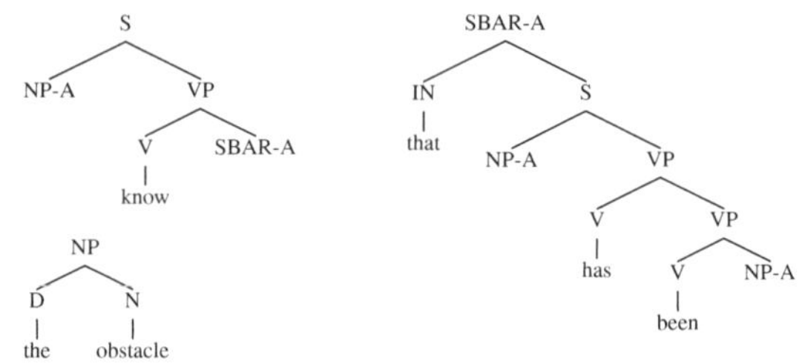

Figure 1: Extended projections for the verbs *know* and *been*, and for the noun *obstacle*. The EPs were taken from the parse tree for the sentence *We know that the main obstacle has been the predictable resistance of manufacturers*.

2 Related Work

There has been a substantial amount of previous work on approaches that make use of syntactic information in statistical machine translation. Wu (1997) and Alshawi (1996) describe early work on formalisms that make use of transductive grammars; Graehl and Knight (2004) describe methods for training tree transducers. Melamed (2004) establishes a theoretical framework for generalized synchronous parsing and translation. Eisner (2003) discusses methods for learning synchronized elementary tree pairs from a parallel corpus of parsed sentences. Chiang (2005) has recently shown significant improvements in translation accuracy, using synchronous grammars. Riezler and Maxwell (2006) describe a method for learning a probabilistic model that maps LFG parse structures in German into LFG parse structures in English.

Yamada and Knight (2001) and Galley et al. (2004) describe methods that make use of syntactic information in the target language alone; Quirk et al. (2005) describe similar methods that make use of dependency representations. Syntactic parsers in the target language have been used as language models in translation, giving some improvement in accuracy (Charniak et al., 2001). The work of Gildea (2003) involves methods that make use of syntactic information in both the source and target languages.

Other work has attempted to incorporate syntactic information through reranking approaches applied to n-best output from phrase-based systems (Och et al., 2004). Another class of approaches has shown improvements in translation through reordering, where source language strings are parsed and then reordered, in an attempt to recover a word order that is closer to the target language (Collins et al., 2005; Xia and McCord, 2004).

Our approach is closely related to previous work on synchronous tree adjoining grammars (Shieber and Schabes, 1990; Shieber, 2004), and the work on TAG approaches to syntax described by Frank (2002). A major departure from previous work on synchronous TAGs is in our use of a discriminative model that incrementally predicts the information in the AEP. Note also that our model may include features that take into account any part of the German clause.

3 A Translation Architecture Based on Aligned Extended Projections

3.1 Background: Extended Projections (EPs)

Extended projections (EPs) play a crucial role in the lexicalized tree adjoining grammar (LTAG) (Joshi, 1985) approach to syntax described by Frank (2002). In this paper we focus almost exclusively on extended projections associated with main verbs; note, however, that EPs are typically associated with all content words (nouns, adjectives, etc.). As an example, a parse tree for the sentence *we know that the main obstacle has been the predictable resistance of manufacturers* would make use of EPs for the words *we, know, main, obstacle, been, predictable, resistance*, and *manufacturers*. Function words (in this sentence *that, the, has*, and *of*) do not have EPs; instead, as we describe shortly, each function word is incorporated in an EP of some content word.

Figure 1 has examples of EPs. Each one is an LTAG elementary tree which contains a single content word as one of its leaves. Substitution nodes (such as NP-A or SBAR-A) in the elementary trees specify the positions of arguments of the content words. Each EP may contain one or more function words that are associated with the content word. For verbs, these function words include items such as modal verbs and auxiliaries (e.g., *should* and *has*); complementizers (e.g., *that*); and wh-words (e.g., *which*). For nouns, function words include determiners and prepositions.

Elementary trees corresponding to EPs form the basic units in the LTAG approach described by Frank (2002). They are combined to form a full parse tree for a sentence using the TAG operations of substitution and adjunction. For example, the EP for *been* in Figure 1 can be substituted into the SBAR-A position in the EP for *know*; the EP for *obstacle* can be substituted into the subject position of the EP for *been*.

3.2 Aligned Extended Projections (AEPs)

We now build on the idea of extended projections to give a detailed description of AEPs. Figure 2 shows examples of German clauses paired with the AEPs found in training data.[2] The German clause is assumed to have n (where $n \geq 0$) modifiers. For example, the first German parse in Figure 2 has two arguments, indexed as 1 and 2. Each of these modifiers must either have a translation in the corresponding English clause, or must be deleted.

An AEP consists of the following parts:

STEM: A string specifying the stemmed form of the main verb in the clause.

SPINE: A syntactic structure associated with the main verb. The structure has the symbol V as one of its leaf nodes; this is the position of the main verb. It includes higher projections of the verb such as VPs, Ss, and SBARs. It also includes leaf nodes NP-A in positions corresponding to noun-phrase arguments (e.g., the subject or object) of the main verb. In addition, it may contain leaf nodes labeled with categories such as WHNP or WHADVP where a wh-phrase may be placed. It may include leaf nodes corresponding to one or more complementizers (common examples being *that*, *if*, *so that*, and so on).

VOICE: One of two alternatives, active or passive, specifying the voice of the main verb.

SUBJECT: This variable can be one of three types. If there is no subject position in the SPINE variable, then the value for SUBJECT is NULL. Otherwise, SUBJECT can either be a string, for example *there*,[3] or an index of one of the n modifiers in the German clause.

OBJECT: This variable is similar to SUBJECT, and can also take three types: NULL, a specific string, or an index of one of the n German modifiers. It is always NULL if there is no object position in the SPINE; it can never be a modifier index that has already been assigned to SUBJECT.

WH: This variable is always NULL if there is no wh-phrase position within the SPINE; it is always a non-empty string (such as *which*, or *in which*) if a wh-phrase position does exist.

MODALS: This is a string of verbs that constitute the modals that appear within the clause. We use NULL to signify an absence of modals.

INFL: The inflected form of the verb.

MOD(i): There are n modifier variables MOD(1), MOD(2), ..., MOD(n) that specify the positions for German arguments that have not already been assigned to the SUBJECT or OBJECT positions in the spine. Each variable MOD(i) can take one of five possible values:

- null: This value is chosen if and only if the modifier has already been assigned to the subject or object position.
- deleted: This means that a translation of the i'th German modifier is not present in the English clause.
- pre-sub: The modifier appears after any complementizers or wh-phrases, but before the subject of the English clause.
- post-sub: The modifier appears after the subject of the English clause, but before the modals.
- in-modals: The modifier appears after the first modal in the sequence of modals, but before the second modal or the main verb.
- post-verb: The modifier appears somewhere after the main verb.

[2]Note that in this paper we consider translation from German to English; in the remainder of the paper we take *English* to be synonymous with the target language in translation and *German* to be synonymous with the source language.

[3]This happens in the case where there exists a subject in the English clause which is not aligned to a modifier in the German clause. See, for instance, the second example in Figure 2.

German Clause	English AEP
s-oc kous-cp daß np-sb[1] art das nn haupthemmnis np-pd[2] art der adja vorhersehbare nn widerstand np-ag art der nn hersteller vafin-hd war Paraphrase: *that [np-sb the main obstacle] [np-pd the predictable resistance of manufacturers] was*	STEM: be SPINE: SBAR-A IN that S NP-A VP V NP-A VOICE: active SUBJECT: [1] OBJECT: [2] WH: NULL MODALS: has INFL: been MOD1: null MOD2: null
s pp-mo[1] appr zwischen piat beiden nn gesetzen vvfin-hd bestehen adv-mo[2] also np-sb[3] adja erhebliche adja rechtliche $, , adja praktische kon und adja wirtschaftliche nn unterschiede Paraphrase: *[pp-mo between the two pieces of legislation] exist so [np-sb significant legal, practical and economic differences]*	STEM: be SPINE: S NP-A VP V NP-A VOICE: active SUBJECT: "there" OBJECT: [3] WH: NULL MODALS: NULL INFL: are MOD1: post-verb MOD2: pre-sub MOD3: null
s-rc prels-sb die vp pp-mo[1] appr an pdat jenem nn tag pp-mo[2] appr in ne tschernobyl vvpp-hd gezündet vafin-hd wurde Paraphrase: *which [pp-mo on that day] [pp-mo in chernobyl] released were*	STEM: release SPINE: SBAR WHNP SG-A VP V VOICE: passive SUBJECT: NULL OBJECT: NULL WH: which MODALS: was INFL: released MOD1: post-verb MOD2: post-verb

Figure 2: Three examples of German parse trees, together with their aligned extended projections (AEPs) in the training data. Note that in the second example the correspondence between the German clause and its English translation is not entirely direct. The subject in the English is the expletive *there*; the subject in the German clause becomes the object in English. This is a typical pattern for the German verb *bestehen*. The German PP *zwischen ...* appears at the start of the clause in German, but is post-verbal in the English. The modifier *also*—whose English translation is *so*—is in an intermediate position in the German clause, but appears in the `pre-subject` position in the English clause.

4 Extracting AEPs from a Corpus

A crucial step in our approach is the extraction of training examples from a translation corpus. Each training example consists of a German clause paired with an English AEP (see Figure 2).

In our experiments, we used the Europarl corpus (Koehn, 2005). For each sentence pair from this data, we used a version of the German parser described by Dubey (2005) to parse the German component, and a version of the English parser described by Collins (1999) to parse the English component. To extract AEPs, we perform the following steps:

NP and PP Alignment To align NPs and PPs, first all German and English nouns, personal and possessive pronouns, numbers, and adjectives are identified in each sentence and aligned using GIZA++ (Och and Ney, 2003). Next, each NP in an English tree is aligned to an NP or PP in the corresponding German tree in a way that is *consistent* with the word-alignment information. That is, the words dominated by the English node must be aligned only to words dominated by the German node, and vice versa. Note that if there is more than one German node that is consistent, then the one rooted at the minimal subtree is selected.

Clause alignment, and AEP Extraction The next step in the training process is to identify German/English clause pairs which are translations of each other. We first break each English or German parse tree into a set of clauses; see Appendix A for a description of how we identify clauses. We retain only those training examples where the English and German sentences have the same number of clauses. For these retained examples, define the English sentence to contain the clause sequence $\langle e_1, e_2, \ldots, e_n \rangle$, and the German sentence to contain the clause sequence $\langle g_1, g_2, \ldots, g_n \rangle$. The clauses are ordered according to the position of their main verbs in the original sentence. We create n candidate pairs $\langle (e_1, g_1), (e_2, g_2), \ldots, (e_n, g_n) \rangle$ (i.e., force a one-to-one correspondence between the two clause sequences). We then discard any clause pairs (e, g) which are inconsistent with the NP/PP alignments for that sentence.[4]

[4]A clause pair is inconsistent with the NP/PP alignments if it contains an NP/PP on either the German or English side which is aligned to another NP/PP which is not within the clause pair.

Note that this method is deliberately conservative (i.e., high precision, but lower recall), in that it discards sentence pairs where the English/German sentences have different numbers of clauses. In practice, we have found that the method yields a large number of training cxamples, and that these training examples are of relatively high quality. Future work may consider improved methods for identifying clause pairs, for example methods that make use of labeled training examples.

An AEP can then be extracted from each clause pair. The EP for the English clause is first extracted, giving values for all variables except for `SUBJECT`, `OBJECT`, and `MOD(1)`, ..., `MOD(n)`. The values for the `SUBJECT`, `OBJECT`, and `MOD(i)` variables are derived from the alignments between NPs/PPs, and an alignment of other clauses (ADVPs, ADJPs, etc.) derived from GIZA++ alignments. If the English clause has a subject or object which is not aligned to a German modifier, then the value for `SUBJECT` or `OBJECT` is taken to be the full English string.

5 The Model

5.1 Beam search and the perceptron

In this section we describe linear history-based models with beam search, and the perceptron algorithm for learning in these models. These methods will form the basis for our model that maps German clauses to AEPs.

We have a training set of n examples, (x_i, y_i) for $i = 1 \dots n$, where each x_i is a German parse tree, and each y_i is an AEP. We follow previous work on history-based models, by representing each y_i as a series of N decisions $\langle d_1, d_2, \dots d_N \rangle$. In our approach, N will be a fixed number for any input x: we take the N decisions to correspond to the sequence of variables `STEM, SPINE, ..., MOD(1), MOD(2), ..., MOD(n)` described in section 3. Each d_i is a member of a set $\mathcal{D}_i$ which specifies the set of allowable decisions at the i'th point (for example, $\mathcal{D}_2$ would be the set of all possible values for `SPINE`). We assume a function ADVANCE$(x, \langle d_1, d_2, \dots, d_{i-1} \rangle)$ which maps an input x together with a prefix of decisions $d_1 \dots d_{i-1}$ to a subset of $\mathcal{D}_i$. ADVANCE is a function that specifies which decisions are allowable for a past history $\langle d_1, \dots, d_{i-1} \rangle$ and an input x. In our case the ADVANCE function implements hard constraints on AEPs (for example, the constraint that the `SUBJECT` variable must be `NULL` if no subject position exists in the `SPINE`). For any input x, a *well-formed* decision sequence for x is a sequence $\langle d_1, \dots, d_N \rangle$ such that for $i = 1 \dots n$, $d_i \in$ ADVANCE$(x, \langle d_1, \dots, d_{i-1} \rangle)$. We define GEN$(x)$ to be the set of all decision sequences (or AEPs) which are well-formed for x.

The model that we will use is a discriminatively-trained, feature-based model. A significant advantage to feature-based models is their flexibility: it is very easy to sensitize the model to dependencies in the data by encoding new features. To define a feature-based model, we assume a function $\bar{\phi}(x, \langle d_1, \dots, d_{i-1} \rangle, d_i) \in \mathbb{R}^d$ which maps a decision d_i in context $(x, \langle d_1, \dots, d_{i-1} \rangle)$ to a *feature vector*. We also assume a vector $\bar{\alpha} \in \mathbb{R}^d$ of parameter values. We define the *score* for any partial or complete decision sequence $y = \langle d_1, d_2, \dots, d_m \rangle$ paired with x as:

$$\text{SCORE}(x, y) = \Phi(x, y) \cdot \bar{\alpha} \quad (1)$$

where $\Phi(x, y) = \sum_{i=1}^{m} \bar{\phi}(x, \langle d_1, \dots, d_{i-1} \rangle, d_i)$. In particular, given the definitions above, the output structure $F(x)$ for an input x is the highest–scoring well–formed structure for x:

$$F(x) = \arg \max_{y \in \text{GEN}(x)} \text{SCORE}(x, y) \quad (2)$$

To decode with the model we use a beam-search method. The method incrementally builds an AEP in the decision order $d_1, d_2, \dots, d_N$. At each point, a beam contains the top M highest–scoring partial paths for the first m decisions, where M is taken to be a fixed number. The score for any partial path is defined in Eq. 1. The ADVANCE function is used to specify the set of possible decisions that can extend any given path in the beam.

To train the model, we use the averaged perceptron algorithm described by Collins (2002). This combination of the perceptron algorithm with beam-search is similar to that described by Collins and Roark (2004).[5] The perceptron algorithm is a convenient choice because it converges quickly — usually taking only a few iterations over the training set (Collins, 2002; Collins and Roark, 2004).

5.2 The Features of the Model

The model's features allow it to capture dependencies between the AEP and the German clause, as well as dependencies between different parts of the AEP itself. The features included in $\bar{\phi}$

[5] Future work may consider alternative algorithms, such as those described by Daumé and Marcu (2005).

1	main verb
2	any verb in the clause
3	all verbs, in sequence
4	spine
5	tree
6	preterminal label of left-most child of subject
7	terminal label of left-most child of subject
8	suffix of terminal label of right-most child of subject
9	preterminal label of left-most child of object
10	terminal label of left-most child of object
11	suffix of terminal label of right-most child of object
12	preterminal label of the negation word *nicht* (*not*)
13	is either of the strings *es gibt* (*there is/are*) or *es gab* (*there was/were*) present?
14	complementizers and wh-words
15	labels of all wh-nonterminals
16	terminal labels of all wh-words
17	preterminal label of a verb in first position
18	terminal label of a verb in first position
19	terminal labels of all words in any relative pronoun under a PP
20	are all of the verbs at the end?
21	nonterminal label of the root of the tree
22	terminal labels of all words constituting the subject
23	terminal labels of all words constituting the object
24	the leaves dominated by each node in the tree
25	each node in the context of a CFG rule
26	each node in the context of the RHS of a CFG rule
27	each node with its left and right sibling
28	the number of leaves dominated by each node in the tree

Table 1: Functions of the German clause used for making features in the AEP prediction model.

can consist of any function of the decision history $\langle d_1, \ldots, d_{i-1} \rangle$, the current decision d_i, or the German clause. In defining features over AEP/clause pairs, we make use of some basic functions which look at the German clause and the AEP (see Tables 1 and 2). We use various combinations of these basic functions in the prediction of each decision d_i, as described below.

STEM: Features for the prediction of `STEM` conjoin the value of this variable with each of the functions in lines 1–13 of Table 1. For example, one feature is the value of `STEM` conjoined with the main verb of the German clause. In addition, $\bar{\phi}$ includes features sensitive to the rank of a candidate stem in an externally-compiled lexicon.[6]

SPINE: Spine prediction features make use of the values of the variables `SPINE` and `STEM` from the AEP, as well as functions of the spine in lines 1–7 of Table 2, conjoined in various ways with the functions in lines 4, 12, and 14–21 of Table 1. Note that the functions in Table 2 allow us to look

[6]The lexicon is derived from GIZA++ and provides, for a large number of German main verbs, a ranked list of possible English translations.

1	does the `SPINE` have a subject?
2	does the `SPINE` have an object?
3	does the `SPINE` have any wh-words?
4	the labels of any complementizer nonterminals in the `SPINE`
5	the labels of any wh-nonterminals in the `SPINE`
6	the nonterminal labels `SQ` or `SBARQ` in the `SPINE`
7	the nonterminal label of the root of the `SPINE`
8	the grammatical category of the finite verbal form `INFL` (i.e., infinitive, 1st-, 2nd-, or 3rd-person pres, pres participle, sing past, plur past, past participle)

Table 2: Functions of the English AEP used for making features in the AEP prediction model.

at substructure in the spine. For instance, one of the features for `SPINE` is the label `SBARQ` or `SQ`, if it exists in the candidate spine, conjoined with a verbal preterminal label if there is a verb in the first position of the German clause. This feature captures the fact that German yes/no questions begin with a verb in the first position.

VOICE: Voice features in general combine values of `VOICE`, `SPINE`, and `STEM`, with the functions in lines 1–5, 22, and 23 of Table 1.

SUBJECT: Features used for subject prediction make use of the AEP variables `VOICE` and `STEM`. In addition, if the value of `SUBJECT` is an index i (see section 3), then $\bar{\phi}$ looks at the nonterminal label of the German node indexed by i as well as the surrounding context in the German clausal tree. Otherwise, $\bar{\phi}$ looks at the value of `SUBJECT`. These basic features are combined with the functions in lines 1, 3, and 24–27 of Table 1.

OBJECT: We make similar features to those for the prediction of `SUBJECT`. In addition, $\bar{\phi}$ can look at the value predicted for `SUBJECT`.

WH: Features for `WH` look at the values of `WH` and `SPINE`, conjoined with the functions in lines 1, 15, and 19 of Table 1.

MODALS: For the prediction of `MODALS`, $\bar{\phi}$ looks at `MODALS`, `SPINE`, and `STEM`, conjoined with the functions in lines 2–5 and 12 of Table 1.

INFL: The features for `INFL` include the values of `INFL`, `MODALS`, and `SUBJECT`, and `VOICE`, and the function in line 8 of Table 2.

MOD(i): For the `MOD(i)` variables, $\bar{\phi}$ looks at the value of `MODALS`, `SPINE` and the current `MOD(i)`, as well as the nonterminal label of the root node of the German modifier being placed, and the functions in lines 24 and 28 of Table 1.

6 Deriving Full Translations

As we described in section 1.1, the translation of a full German sentence proceeds in a series of steps: a German parse tree is broken into a sequence of clauses; each clause is individually translated; and finally, the clause-level translations are combined to form the translation for a full sentence. The first and last steps are relatively straightforward. We now show how the second step is achieved—i.e., how AEPs can be used to derive English clause translations from German clauses.

We will again use the following translation pair as an example: *daß das haupthemmnis der vorhersehbare widerstand der hersteller war./that the main obstacle has been the predictable resistance of manufacturers.*

First, an AEP like the one at the top of Figure 2 is predicted. Then, for each German modifier which does not have the value `deleted`, an English translation is predicted. In the example, the modifiers *das haupthemmnis* and *der vorhersehbare widerstand der hersteller* would be translated to *the main obstacle*, and *the predictable resistance of manufacturers*, respectively.

A number of methods could be used for translation of the modifiers. In this paper, we use the phrase-based system of Koehn et al. (2003) to generate n-best translations for each of the modifiers, and we then use a discriminative reranking algorithm (Bartlett et al., 2004) to choose between these modifiers. The features in the reranking model can be sensitive to various properties of the candidate English translation, for example the words, the part-of-speech sequence or the parse tree for the string. The reranker can also take into account the original German string. Finally, the features can be sensitive to properties of the AEP, such as the main verb or the position in which the modifier appears (e.g., subject, object, `pre-sub`, `post-verb`, etc.) in the English clause. See Appendix B for a full description of the features used in the modifier translation model. Note that the reranking stage allows us to filter translation candidates which do not fit syntactically with the position in the English tree. For example, we can parse the members of the n-best list, and then learn a feature which strongly disprefers prepositional phrases if the modifier appears in subject position.

Finally, the full string is predicted. In our example, the AEP variables `SPINE`, `MODALS`, and `INFL` in Figure 2 give the ordering `<that SUBJECT has been OBJECT>`. The AEP and modifier translations would be combined to give the final English string. In general, any modifiers assigned to `pre-sub`, `post-sub`, `in-modals` or `post-verb` are placed in the corresponding position within the spine. For example, the second AEP in Figure 2 has a spine with ordering `<SUBJECT are OBJECT>`; modifiers 1 and 2 would be placed in positions `pre-sub` and `post-verb`, giving the ordering `<MOD2 SUBJECT are OBJECT MOD1>`. Note that modifiers assigned `post-verb` are placed after the object. If multiple modifiers appear in the same position (e.g., `post-verb`), then they are placed in the order seen in the original German clause.

7 Experiments

We applied the approach to translation from German to English, using the Europarl corpus (Koehn, 2005) for our training data. This corpus contains over 750,000 training sentences; we extracted over 441,000 training examples for the AEP model from this corpus, using the method described in section 4. We reserved 35,000 of these training examples as development data for the model. We used a set of features derived from the those described in section 5.2. This set was optimized using the development data through experimentation with several different feature subsets.

Modifiers within German clauses were translated using the phrase-based model of Koehn et al. (2003). We first generated n-best lists for each modifier. We then built a reranking model—see section 6—to choose between the elements in the n-best lists. The reranker was trained using around 800 labeled examples from a development set.

The test data for the experiments consisted of 2,000 sentences, and was the same test set as that used by Collins et al. (2005). We use the model of Koehn et al. (2003) as a baseline for our experiments. The AEP-driven model was used to translate all test set sentences where all clauses within the German parse tree contained at least one verb and there was no embedding of clauses—there were 1,335 sentences which met these criteria. The remaining 665 sentences were translated with the baseline system. This set of 2,000 translations had a BLEU score of 23.96. The baseline system alone achieved a BLEU score of 25.26 on the same set of 2,000 test sentences. We also obtained judgments from two human annotators on

100 randomly-drawn sentences on which the baseline and AEP-based outputs differed. For each example the annotator viewed the reference translation, together with the two systems' translations presented in a random order. Annotator 1 judged 62 translations to be equal in quality, 16 translations to be better under the AEP system, and 22 to be better for the baseline system. Annotator 2 judged 37 translations to be equal in quality, 32 to be better under the baseline, and 31 to be better under the AEP-based system.

8 Conclusions and Future Work

We have presented an approach to tree-to-tree based translation which models a new representation—aligned extended projections—within a discriminative, feature-based framework. Our model makes use of an explicit representation of syntax in the target language, together with constraints on the alignments between source and target parse trees.

The current system presents many opportunities for future work. For example, improvement in accuracy may come from a tighter integration of modifier translation into the overall translation process. The current method—using an n-best reranking model to select the best candidate—chooses each modifier independently and then places it into the translation. We intend to explore an alternative method that combines finite-state machines representing the n-best output from the phrase-based system with finite-state machines representing the complementizers, verbs, modals, and other substrings of the translation derived from the AEP. Selecting modifiers using this representation would correspond to searching the finite-state network for the most likely path. A finite-state representation has many advantages, including the ability to easily incorporate an n-gram language model.

Future work may also consider expanded definitions of AEPs. For example, we might consider AEPs that include larger chunks of phrase structure, or we might consider AEPs that contain more detailed information about the relative ordering of modifiers. There is certainly room for improvement in the accuracy with which AEPs are predicted in our data; the feature-driven approach allows a wide range of features to be tested. For example, it would be relatively easy to incorporate a syntactic language model (i.e., a prior distribution over AEP structures) induced from a large amount of English monolingual data.

Appendix A: Identification of Clauses

In the English parse trees, we identify clauses as follows. Any non-terminal labeled by the parser of (Collins, 1999) as `SBAR` or `SBAR-A` is labeled as a clause root. Any node labeled by the parser as `S` or `S-A` is also labeled as the root of a clause, unless it is directly dominated by a non-terminal labeled `SBAR` or `SBAR-A`. Any node labeled `SG` or `SG-A` by the parser is labeled as a clause root, unless (1) the node is directly dominated by `SBAR` or `SBAR-A`; or (2) the node is directly dominated by a VP, and the node is directly preceded by a verb (POS tag beginning with `V`) or modal (POS tag beginning with `M`). Any node labeled `VP` is marked as a clause root if (1) the node is not directly dominated by a `VP`, `S`, `S-A`, `SBAR`, `SBAR-A`, `SG`, or `SG-A`; or (2) the node is directly preceded by a coordinating conjunction (i.e., a POS tag labeled as `CC`).

In German parse trees, we identify any nodes labeled as `S` or `CS` as clause roots. In addition, we mark any node labeled as `VP` as a clause root, provided that (1) it is preceded by a coordinating conjunction, i.e., a POS tag labeled as `KON`; or (2) it has one of the functional tags `-mo`, `-re` or `-sb`.

Appendix B: Reranking Modifier Translations

The n-best reranking model for the translation of modifiers considers a list of candidate translations. We hand-labeled 800 examples, marking the element in each list that would lead to the best translation. The features of the n-best reranking algorithm are combinations of the basic features in Tables 3 and 4.

Each list contained the n-best translations produced by the phrase-based system of Koehn et al. (2003). The lists also contained a supplementary candidate "DELETED", signifying that the modifier should be deleted from the English translation. In addition, each candidate derived from the phrase-based system contributed one new candidate to the list signifying that the first word of the candidate should be deleted. These additional candidates were motivated by our observation that the optimal candidate in the n-best list produced by the phrase-based system often included an unwanted preposition at the beginning of the string.

1	candidate string
2	should the first word of the candidate be deleted?
3	POS tag of first word of candidate
4	POS tag of last word of candidate
5	top nonterminal of parse of candidate
6	modifier deleted from English translation?
7	first candidate on n-best list
8	first word of candidate
9	last word of candidate
10	rank of candidate in n-best list
11	is there punctuation at the beginning, middle, or end of the string?
12	if the first word of the candidate should be deleted, what is the string that is deleted?
13	if the first word of the candidate should be deleted, what is the POS tag of the word that is deleted?

Table 3: Functions of the candidate modifier translations used for making features in the n-best reranking model.

1	the position of the modifier (0–4) in AEP
2	main verb
3	voice
4	subject prediction
5	German input string

Table 4: Functions of the German input string and predicted AEP output used for making features in the n-best reranking model.

Acknowledgements

We would like to thank Luke Zettlemoyer, Regina Barzilay, Ed Filisko, and Ben Snyder for their valuable comments and help during the writing of this paper. Thanks also to Jason Rennie and John Barnett for providing human judgments of the translation output. This work was funded by NSF grants IIS-0347631, IIS-0415030, and DMS-0434222, as well as a grant from NTT, Agmt. Dtd. 6/21/1998.

References

H. Alshawi. 1996. Head automata and bilingual tiling: translation with minimal representations. *ACL 96*.

P. Bartlett, M. Collins, B. Taskar, and D. McAllester. 2004. Exponentiated gradient algorithms for large-margin structured classification. *Proceedings of NIPS 2004*.

P. Brown, S. Della Pietra, V. Della Pietra, and R. Mercer. 1993. The mathematics of statistical machine translation. *Computational Linguistics*, 22(1):39–69.

E. Charniak, K. Knight, and K. Yamada. 2001. Syntax-based language models for statistical machine translation. *ACL 01*.

D. Chiang. 2005. A hierarchical phrase-based model for statistical machine translation. *ACL 05*.

M. Collins. 1999. Head-Driven Statistical Models for Natural Language Parsing. University of Pennsylvania.

M. Collins. 2002. Discriminative training methods for hidden markov models: theory and experiments with perceptron algorithms. *EMNLP 02*.

M. Collins and B. Roark. 2004. Incremental parsing with the perceptron algorithm. *ACL 04*.

M. Collins, P. Koehn, and I. Kučerová. 2005. Clause restructuring for statistical machine translation. *ACL 05*.

H. Daumé III and D. Marcu. 2005. Learning as search optimization: approximate large margin methods for structured prediction. *ICML 05*.

A. Dubey. 2005. What to do when lexicalization fails: parsing German with suffix analysis and smoothing. *ACL 05*.

J. Eisner. 2003. Learning non-isomorphic tree mappings for machine translation. *ACL 03, Companion Volume*.

R. Frank. 2002. *Phrase Structure Composition and Syntactic Dependencies*. Cambridge, MA: MIT Press.

M. Galley, M. Hopkins, K. Knight, and D. Marcu. 2004. What's in a translation rule? *HLT-NAACL 04*.

D. Gildea. 2003. Loosely tree-based alignment for machine translation. *ACL 03*.

J. Graehl and K. Knight. 2004. Training tree transducers. *NAACL-HLT 04*.

A. Joshi. 1985. How much context-sensitivity is necessary for characterizing structural descriptions – tree-adjoining grammar. Cambridge University Press.

P. Koehn, F. J. Och, and D. Marcu. 2003. Statistical phrase based translation. *HLT-NAACL 03*.

P. Koehn. 2005. Europarl: A parallel corpus for statistical machine translation. *MT Summit 05*.

I. D. Melamed 2004. Statistical machine translation by parsing. *ACL 04*.

F. J. Och, D. Gildea, S. Khudanpur, A. Sarkar, K. Yamada, A. Fraser, S. Kumar, L. Shen, D. Smith, K. Eng, V. Jain, Z. Jin, D. Radev. 2004. A smorgasbord of features for statistical machine translation. *HLT/NAACL 04*

F. J. Och and H. Ney. 2004. The alignment template approach to statistical machine translation. *Computational Linguistics*, 30(4):417–449.

F. J. Och and H. Ney. 2003. A systematic comparison of various statistical alignment models. *Computational Linguistics*, 29(1):19–51.

C. Quirk, A. Menezes, and C. Cherry. 2005. Dependency tree translation: syntactically informed phrasal SMT. *EACL 05*.

S. Riezler and J. Maxwell. 2006. Grammatical machine translation. In *NLT-NAACL 06*.

S. Shieber. 2004. Synchronous grammars as tree transducers. In *Proceedings of the Seventh International Workshop on Tree Adjoining Grammar and Related Formalisms*.

S. Shieber and Y. Schabes. 1990. Synchronous tree-adjoining grammars. In *Proceedings of the 13th International Conference on Computational Linguistics*.

D. Wu. 1997. Stochastic inversion transduction grammars and bilingual parsing of parallel corpora. *Computational Linguistics*, 23(3):377–403.

F. Xia and M. McCord. 2004. Improving a statistical MT system with automatically learned rewrite patterns. *COLING 04*.

K. Yamada and K. Knight. 2001. A syntax-based statistical translation model. *ACL 01*.

Modeling Impression in Probabilistic Transliteration into Chinese

LiLi Xu* **Atsushi Fujii**
Graduate School of Library,
Information and Media Studies
University of Tsukuba
1-2 Kasuga, Tsukuba, 305-8550, Japan
fujii@slis.tsukuba.ac.jp

Tetsuya Ishikawa
The Historiographical Institute
The University of Tokyo
3-1 Hongo 7-chome, Bunkyo-ku
Tokyo, 133-0033, Japan
ishikawa@hi.u-tokyo.ac.jp

Abstract

For transliterating foreign words into Chinese, the pronunciation of a source word is spelled out with Kanji characters. Because Kanji comprises ideograms, an individual pronunciation may be represented by more than one character. However, because different Kanji characters convey different meanings and impressions, characters must be selected carefully. In this paper, we propose a transliteration method that models both pronunciation and impression, whereas existing methods do not model impression. Given a source word and impression keywords related to the source word, our method derives possible transliteration candidates and sorts them according to their probability. We evaluate our method experimentally.

1 Introduction

Reflecting the rapid growth of science, technology, and economies, new technical terms and product names have progressively been created. These new words have also been imported into different languages. There are three fundamental methods for importing foreign words into a language.

In the first method—*translation*—the meaning of the source word in question is represented by an existing or new word in the target language.

In the second method—*transliteration*—the pronunciation of the source word is represented by using the phonetic alphabet of the target language, such as Katakana in Japanese and Hangul in Korean.

In the third method, the source word is spelled out as it is. However, the misuse of this method decreases the understandability and readability of the target language.

While translation is time-consuming, requiring selection of an existing word or generation of a new word that correctly represents the meaning of the source word, transliteration can be performed rapidly. However, the situation is complicated for Chinese, where a phonetic alphabet is not used and Kanji is used to spell out both conventional Chinese words and foreign words.

Because Kanji comprises ideograms, an individual pronunciation can potentially be represented by more than one character. However, if several Kanji strings are related to the same pronunciation of the source word, their meanings will be different and will therefore convey different impressions.

For example, "Coca-Cola" can be represented by different Kanji strings in Chinese. The official transliteration is "可口可乐", which comprises "可口 (tasty)" and "可乐 (pleasant)", and is therefore associated with a positive connotation.

However, there are a number of Kanji strings that represent similar pronunciations to that of "Coca-Cola", but which are associated with inappropriate impressions for a beverage, such as "口卡口拉". This word includes "口卡", which is associated with choking.

Therefore, Kanji characters must be selected carefully during transliteration into Chinese. This is especially important when foreign companies intend to introduce their names and products into China.

In this paper, we propose a method that models both impression and pronunciation for transliteration into Chinese.

* This work was done when the first author was a graduate student at University of Tsukuba, who currently works for Hitachi Construction Machinery Co., Ltd.

Proceedings of the 2006 Conference on Empirical Methods in Natural Language Processing (EMNLP 2006), pages 242–249,
Sydney, July 2006.

Section 2 surveys previous research into automatic transliteration, in order to clarify the meaning and contribution of our research. Section 3 elaborates on our transliteration method. Section 4 evaluates the effectiveness of our method.

2 Related Work

In a broad sense, the term "transliteration" has been used to refer to two tasks.

The first task is transliteration in the strict sense, which creates new words in a target language (Haizhou et al., 2004; Wan and Verspoor, 1998).

The second task is back-transliteration (Fujii and Ishikawa, 2001; Jeong et al., 1999; Knight and Graehl, 1998; Qu et al., 2003), which identifies the source word corresponding to an existing transliterated word. Back-transliteration is intended mainly for cross-lingual information retrieval and machine translation.

Both transliteration tasks require methods that model pronunciation in the source and target languages.

However, by definition, in back-transliteration, the word in question has already been transliterated and the meaning or impression of the source word does not have to be considered. Thus, back-transliteration is outside the scope of this paper.

In the following, we use the term "transliteration" to refer to transliteration in the strict sense.

Existing transliteration methods for Chinese (Haizhou et al., 2004; Wan and Verspoor, 1998) aim to spell out foreign names of people and places, and do not model impression.

However, as exemplified by "Coca-Cola" in Section 1, the impression of words needs to be modeled in the transliteration of proper names, such as companies and products. The contribution of our research is to incorporate a model of impression into automatic transliteration.

3 Methodology

3.1 Overview

Figure 1 shows our transliteration method, which models both pronunciation and impression when transliterating foreign words into Chinese. We will explain the entire process of our transliteration method in terms of Figure 1.

The input for our method is twofold. First, a source word to be transliterated into Chinese is requested. Second, one or more words that describe

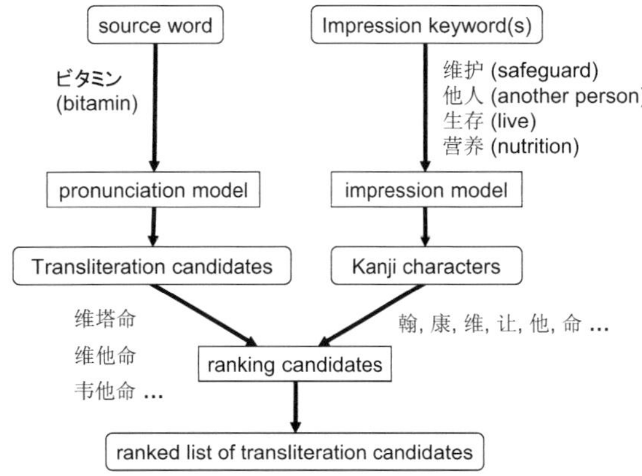

Figure 1: Overview of our transliteration method for Chinese.

the impression of the source word, which we call "impression keywords", are requested. Currently, impression keywords must be provided manually in Chinese. The output of our method is one or more Kanji strings.

In an example scenario using our method, a user has a good command of Chinese and intends to introduce something (e.g., a company or product) into China. It is reasonable to assume that this user can provide one or more Chinese impression keywords to associate with the target object.

Using the pronunciation model, the source word is converted into a set of Kanji strings whose pronunciation is similar to that of the source word. Each of these Kanji strings is a transliteration candidate.

Currently, we use Japanese Katakana words as source words, because Katakana words can easily be converted into pronunciations using the Latin alphabet. However, in principle, any language that uses phonetic script can be a source language for our method. In Figure 1, the Katakana word "*bitamin* (vitamin)" is used as an example source word.

Using the impression model, impression keywords are converted into a set of Kanji characters. A simple implementation is to segment each impression keyword into characters.

However, because it is difficult for a user to provide an exhaustive list of appropriate keywords and characters, our impression model derives characters that are not included in the impression keywords.

Because of the potentially large number of selected candidates, we need to rank the candidates. We model both pronunciation and impression in a probabilistic framework, so that transliteration candidates are sorted according to their probability score.

Transliteration candidates that include many characters derived from the impression model are preferred. In other words, the Kanji characters derived via the impression model are used to re-rank the candidates derived via the pronunciation model.

We elaborate on our probabilistic transliteration model in Section 3.2. We then discuss the pronunciation and impression models in Sections 3.3 and 3.4, respectively.

3.2 Probabilistic Transliteration Model

Given a romanized Japanese Katakana word R and a set of impression keywords W, our purpose is to select the Kanji string K that maximizes $P(K|R,W)$, which is evaluated as shown in Equation (1), using Bayes' theorem.

$$\begin{aligned} P(K|R,W) &= \frac{P(R,W|K)\cdot P(K)}{P(R,W)} \\ &\approx \frac{P(R|K)\cdot P(W|K)\cdot P(K)}{P(R,W)} \\ &\propto P(R|K)\cdot P(W|K)\cdot P(K) \end{aligned} \quad (1)$$

In the second line of Equation (1), we assume the conditional independence of R and W given K. In the third line, we omit $P(R,W)$, which is independent of K. This does not affect the relative rank of Kanji strings, when ranked in terms of $P(K|R,W)$.

In Figure 1, R and W are "bitamin" and "维护 他人 生存 营养", respectively, and a K candidate is "维塔命".

If a user intends to select more than one Kanji string, those Ks associated with higher probabilities should be selected.

As shown in Equation (1), $P(K|R,W)$ can be approximated by the product of $P(R|K)$, $P(W|K)$, and $P(K)$. We call these three factors the pronunciation, impression, and language models, respectively.

The language model, $P(K)$, models the probability of K irrespective of R and W. In probabilistic natural language processing, $P(K)$ is usually realized by a word or character N-gram model, and therefore a K that appears frequently in a corpus is assigned a high probability.

However, because our purpose is to generate new words, the use of statistics obtained from existing corpora is not effective. Therefore, we consider $P(K)$ to be constant for every K.

In summary, $P(K|R,W)$ is approximated by a product of $P(R|K)$ and $P(W|K)$. The quality of our transliteration method will depend on the implementation of the pronunciation and impression models.

3.3 Pronunciation Model

The pronunciation model, $P(R|K)$, models the probability that a roman representation R is selected, given a Kanji string K.

In Japanese, the Hepburn and *Kunrei* systems are commonly used for romanization purposes. We use the Hepburn system. We use Pinyin as a representation for Kanji characters. We decompose K into Kanji characters and associate K with R on a character-by-character basis. We calculate $P(R|K)$ as shown in Equation (2).

$$\begin{aligned} P(R|K) &\approx P(R|Y)\cdot P(Y|K) \\ &\approx \prod_{i=1}^{N} P(r_i|y_i)\cdot \prod_{j=1}^{N} P(y_j|k_j) \end{aligned} \quad (2)$$

Y denotes the Pinyin strings representing the pronunciation of K. k_i denotes a single Kanji character. r_i and y_i denote substrings of R and Y, respectively. R, Y, and K are decomposed into the same number of elements, namely N. We calculate $P(r_i|y_i)$ and $P(y_i|k_i)$ as shown in Equation (3).

$$\begin{aligned} P(r_i|y_i) &= \frac{F(r_i,y_i)}{\sum_r F(r,y_i)} \\ P(y_i|k_i) &= \frac{F(y_i,k_i)}{\sum_y F(y,k_i)} \end{aligned} \quad (3)$$

$F(x,y)$ denotes the co-occurrence frequency of x and y. We need the co-occurrence frequencies of r_i and y_i and the co-occurrence frequencies of y_i and k_i in order to calculate $P(R|K)$.

We used a bilingual dictionary comprising 1 140 Katakana words, most of which are technical terms and proper nouns, and their transliterations into Chinese, which are annotated with Pinyin. We manually corresponded 151 pairs of Katakana and roman characters on a mora-by-mora basis, and romanized Katakana characters in the dictionary automatically.

We obtained 1 140 tuples, of the form $< R,Y,K >$. Because the number of tuples was manageable, we obtained the element-by-element R, Y, and K correspondences manually. Finally, we calculated $F(r_i, y_i)$ and $F(y_i, k_i)$.

If there are many tuples, and the process of manual correspondence is expensive, we can automate the process as performed in existing transliteration methods, such as the EM algorithm (Knight and Graehl, 1998) or DP matching (Fujii and Ishikawa, 2001).

The above calculations are performed off-line. In the online process, we consider all possible segmentations of a single Katakana word. For example, the romanized Katakana word "*bitamin* (vitamin)" corresponds to two Pinyin strings and is segmented differently, as follows:

- bi-ta-min: wei-ta-ming,
- bi-ta-mi-n: wei-ta-mi-an.

3.4 Impression Model

The impression model, $P(W|K)$, models the probability that W is selected as a set of impression keywords, given Kanji string K. As in the calculation of $P(R|K)$ in Equation (2), we decompose W and K into elements, in calculating $P(W|K)$.

W is decomposed into a set of words, w_i, and K is decomposed into a set of Kanji characters, k_j. We calculate $P(W|K)$ as a product of $P(w_i|k_j)$, which is the probability that w_i is selected as an impression keyword given k_j.

However, unlike Equation (2), the numbers of w_i and k_j derived from W and K are not always the same, because users are allowed to provide an arbitrary number of impression keywords. Therefore, for each k_j we select the w_i that maximizes $P(w_i|k_j)$ and approximate $P(W|K)$ as shown in Equation (4).

$$P(W|K) \approx \prod_{j} \max_{w_i} P(w_i|k_j) \qquad (4)$$

Figure 2 shows an example in which the four Chinese words in the "w_i" column are also used in Figure 1.

We calculate $P(w_i|k_j)$ by Equation (5).

$$P(w_i|k_j) = \frac{F(w_i, k_j)}{\sum_{w} F(w, k_j)} \qquad (5)$$

As in Equation (3), $F(x, y)$ denotes the co-occurrence frequency of x and y.

w_i \ k_j	维	他	命
维护	0.5	—	—
他人	0.3	0.4	—
生存	—	—	0.6
营养	0.1	—	—

P(维护 他人 生存 营养|维他命)
= P(维护|维)×P(他人|他)×P(生存|命)
= 0.5×0.4×0.6

Figure 2: Example calculation of $P(W|K)$.

In summary, we need co-occurrences of each word and character in Chinese.

These co-occurrences can potentially be collected from existing language resources, such as corpora in Chinese.

However, it is desirable to collect an *association* between a word and a character, not simply their co-occurrence in corpora. Therefore, we used a dictionary of Kanji in Chinese, in which each Kanji character entry is explained via sentences, and often exemplified by one or more words that include that character.

We selected 599 entry characters that are often used to spell out foreign words. Then we collected the frequencies with which each word is used to explain each entry character.

Because Chinese sentences lack lexical segmentation, we used SuperMorpho[1] to perform a morphological analysis of explanation sentences and example words. As a result, 16 943 word types were extracted. We used all of these words to calculate the co-occurrence frequencies, irrespective of the parts of speech.

Table 1 shows examples of Kanji characters, Chinese words, and their co-occurrence frequencies in the dictionary.

However, $P(w_i|k_j)$ cannot be calculated for the Kanji characters not modeled in our method (i.e., the Kanji characters not included in the 599 entry characters). Thus, for smoothing purposes, we experimentally set $P(w_i|k_j)$ at 0.001 for those k_j not modeled.

4 Experiments

4.1 Method

We evaluated our transliteration method experimentally. Because the contribution of our research is the incorporation of the impression model in a transliteration method, we used a method that uses only the pronunciation model as a control.

[1]http://www.omronsoft.com/

Table 1: Example of characters, words, and their co-occurrence frequencies.

k_j	w_i	$F(w_i,k_j)$	k_j	w_i	$F(w_i,k_j)$	k_j	w_i	$F(w_i,k_j)$
高	高	39	好	美	3	乐	喜悦	2
高	高大	8	好	貌美	2	乐	愉快	1
高	远	4	好	好	43	乐	快乐	5
高	下	4	好	好看	2	乐	幸福	2
高	距离	2	好	美丽	2	乐	乐	51
高	大	1	好	好不	2	乐	笑	5
高	俗	2	好	好吃	2	乐	喜	3
高	崇高	2	好	表示	4	乐	音乐	11
高	高尚	2	好	同意	2	乐	乐意	2
高	加高	3	好	喜好	1	乐	安乐	7
高	增高	1	好	喜爱	2	乐	乐于	5

From a Japanese–Chinese dictionary, we selected 210 Katakana words that had been transliterated into Chinese, and used these Katakana words as test words. Each test word can be classified into one of the following five categories: products, companies, places, persons, or general words. Details of the categories of test inputs are shown in Table 2.

Three Chinese graduate students who had a good command of Japanese served as assessors and produced reference data. None of the assessors was an author of this paper. The assessors performed the same task for the same test words independently, in order to enhance the objectivity of the results.

We produced the reference data via the following procedure.

First, for each test word, each assessor provided one or more impression keywords in Chinese. We did not restrict the number of impression keywords per test word, which was determined by each assessor.

If an assessor provided more than one impression keyword for a single test word, he/she was requested to sort them in order of preference, so that we could investigate the effect of the number of impression keywords on the evaluation results, by changing the number of top keywords used for transliteration purposes.

We provided the assessors with the descriptions for the test words from the source dictionary, so that the assessors could understand the meaning of each test word.

Second, for each test word, we applied the control method and our method independently, which produced two lists of ranked transliteration candidates. Because the impression keywords provided by the assessors were used only in our method, the ranked list produced by the control was the same for all assessors.

Table 2: Categories of test words.

Category	# Words	Example word		
		Japanese	Chinese	English
Product	63	アウディ	奥迪	Audi
Company	49	エプソン	爱普生	Epson
Place	36	オハイオ	俄亥俄	Ohio
Person	21	ショパン	肖邦	Chopin
General	41	エンジェル	安琪儿	angel

Third, for each test word, each assessor identified one or more correct transliterations, according to their impression of the test word. It was important not to reveal to the assessors which method produced which candidates.

By these means, we selected the top 100 transliteration candidates from the two ranked lists for the control and our method. We merged these candidates, removed duplications, and sorted the remaining candidates by the character code.

As a result, the assessors judged the correctness of up to 200 candidates for each test word. However, for some test words, assessors were not able to find correct transliterations in the candidate list.

The resultant reference data was used to evaluate the accuracy of a test method in ranking transliteration candidates. We used the average rank of correct answers in the list as the evaluation measure. If more than one correct answer was found for a single test word, we first averaged the ranks of these answers and then averaged the ranks over the test words.

Although we used the top 100 candidates for judgment purposes, the entire ranked list was used to evaluate each method. Therefore, the average rank of correct answers can potentially be over 100. The average number of candidates per test word was 31 779.

Because our method uses the impression model to re-rank the candidates produced by the pronunciation model, the lists for the control and our method comprise the same candidates. Therefore, it is fair to compare these two methods by the average rank of the correct answers.

For each test word, there is more than one type of "correct answer", as follows:

(a) transliteration candidates judged as correct by the assessors independently (transliteration candidates judged as correct by at least one assessor);

(b) transliteration candidates judged as correct by all assessors;

(c) transliterations defined in the source dictionary.

In (a), the coverage of correct answers is the largest, whereas the objectivity of the judgment is the lowest.

In (c), the objectivity of the judgment is the largest, whereas the coverage of correct answers is the lowest. Although for each Katakana word the source dictionary gives only one transliteration that is commonly used, there are a number of appropriate out-of-dictionary transliterations.

In (b), where the assessors did not disagree about the correctness, the coverage of correctness and the objectivity are both middle ranked.

Because none of the above answer types is perfect, we used all three types independently.

4.2 Results and Analyses

Tables 3–5 show the results of comparative experiments using the answer types (a)–(c) above, respectively.

In Tables 3–5, the column "# of test words" denotes the number of test words for which at least one correct answer exists. While the values in the second column of Table 3 are different depending on the assessor, in Tables 4 and 5 the values of the second column are the same for all assessors.

The columns "Avg. # of KW" and "Avg. # of answers" denote the number of impression keywords and the number of correct answers per test word, respectively. While the values in the fourth column of Table 3 are different depending on the assessor, in Tables 4 and 5 the values of the fourth column are the same for all assessors.

In Tables 4 and 5, the average rank of correct answers for the control is the same for all assessors. However, the average rank of correct answers for our method is different depending on the assessor, because the impression keywords used depended on the assessor.

The two columns in "Avg. rank" denote the average ranks of correct answers for the control and for our method, respectively. Looking at Tables 3–5, it can be seen that our method outperformed the control in ranking transliteration candidates, irrespective of the assessor and the answer type.

The average rank of correct answers for our method in Table 5 was lower than those in Tables 3 and 4. One reason is that the correct answers in the source dictionary are not always related to the impression keywords provided by the assessors.

Table 6 presents the results in Table 3 on a category-by-category basis. Because the results were similar for answer types (b) and (c), we show only the answer type (a) results, for the sake of conciseness. Looking at Table 6, it can be seen that our method outperformed the control in ranking transliteration candidates, irrespective of the category of test words.

Our method was effective for transliterating names of places and people, although these types of words are usually transliterated independently of their impressions, compared with the names of products and companies.

One reason is that, in the dictionary of Kanji used to produce the impression model, the explanation of an entry sometimes includes a phrase, such as "this character is often used for a person's name". Assessors provided the word "person" in Chinese as an impression keyword for a number of person names. As a result, transliteration candidates that included characters typically used for a person's name were highly ranked.

It may be argued that, because the impression model was produced using Kanji characters that are often used for transliteration purposes, the impression model could possibly rank correct answers better than the pronunciation model. However, the pronunciation model was also produced from Kanji characters used for transliteration purposes.

Figure 3 shows the distribution of correct answers for different ranges of ranks, using answer type (a). The number of correct answers in the top 10 for our method is approximately twice that of the control. In addition, by our method, most of the correct answers can be found in the top 100 candidates. Because the results were similar for answer types (b) and (c), we show only the answer type (a) results, for the sake of conciseness.

As explained in Section 4.1, for each test word, the assessors were requested to sort the impression keywords in order of preference. We analyzed the relation between the number of impression keywords used for the transliteration and the average rank of correct answers, by varying the threshold for the number of top impression keywords used.

Table 3: Results obtained with answer type (a).

Assessor	# of test words	Avg. # of KW	Avg. # of answers	Avg. rank Control	Avg. rank Our method
A	205	5.1	3.8	706	82
B	204	5.8	3.8	728	44
C	199	3.5	2.6	1 130	28
Avg.	203	4.8	3.4	855	51

Table 4: Results obtained with answer type (b).

Assessor	# of test words	Avg. # of KW	Avg. # of answers	Avg. rank Control	Avg. rank Our method
A	108	5.1	1.1	297	22
B	108	5.8	1.1	297	23
C	108	3.5	1.1	297	18
Avg.	108	4.8	1.1	297	21

Table 5: Results obtained with answer type (c).

Assessor	# of test words	Avg. # of KW	Avg. # of answers	Avg. rank Control	Avg. rank Our method
A	210	5.1	1	1 738	260
B	210	5.8	1	1 738	249
C	210	3.5	1	1 738	103
Avg.	210	4.8	1	1 738	204

Table 6: Results obtained with answer type (a) on a category-by-category basis.

Category	# of test words	Avg. # of KW	Avg. # of answers	Avg. rank Control	Avg. rank Our method
Product	144	4.8	3.5	1 527	64
Company	186	4.7	3.6	742	54
Place	102	4.8	3.7	777	46
Person	61	5.0	3.4	766	51
General	115	4.7	2.6	280	38
Avg.	122	4.8	3.4	818	51

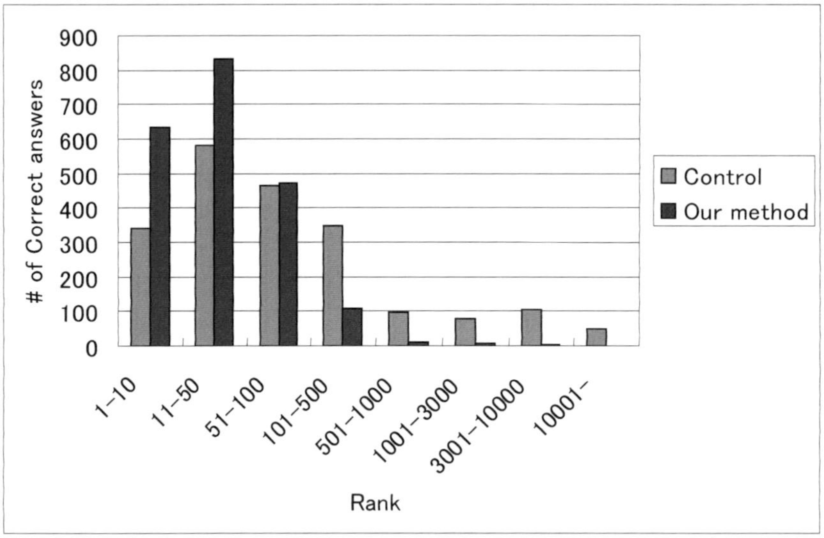

Figure 3: Distribution of average rank for correct answers.

Table 7 shows the average rank of correct answers for different numbers of impression keywords, on an assessor-by-assessor basis. By comparing Tables 3 and 7, we see that even if a single impression keyword was provided, the average rank of correct answers was higher than that for the control. In addition, the average rank of correct answers was generally improved by increasing the number of impression keywords.

Finally, we investigated changes in the rank of correct answers caused by our method. Table 8 shows the results, in which "Higher" and "Lower" denote the number of correct answers whose ranks determined by our method were higher or lower, respectively, than those determined by the control.

For approximately 30% of the correct answers, our method decreased the control's rank. Errors were mainly caused by correct answers containing Kanji characters that were not modeled in the impression model. Although we used a smoothing technique for characters not in the model, the result was not satisfactory. To resolve this problem, the number of characters in the impression model should be increased.

In summary, our method, which uses both the impression and pronunciation models, ranked correct transliterations more highly than a method that used only the pronunciation model. We conclude that the impression model is effective for transliterating foreign words into Chinese. At the same time, we concede that there is room for improvement in the impression model.

5 Conclusion

For transliterating foreign words into Chinese, the pronunciation of a source word is spelled out with Kanji characters. Because Kanji characters are ideograms, a single pronunciation can be represented by more than one character. However, because different Kanji characters convey different meanings and impressions, characters must be selected carefully.

In this paper, we proposed a transliteration method that models both pronunciation and impression, compared to existing methods that do not model impression. Given a source word and impression keywords related to the source word, our method derives possible transliteration candidates, and sorts them according to their probability. We showed the effectiveness of our method experimentally.

Table 7: Relation between the number of impression keywords and average rank of correct answers with answer type (a).

	# of KW		
Assessor	1	2	3
A	103	94	92
B	64	60	52
C	113	73	34

Table 8: Changes in ranks of correct answers caused by our method.

		Avg. rank	
Answer type	# of answers	Higher	Lower
(a)	2070	1431	639
(b)	360	250	110
(c)	630	422	208

Future work will include collecting impression keywords automatically, and adapting the language model to the category of source words.

References

Atsushi Fujii and Tetsuya Ishikawa. 2001. Japanese/English cross-language information retrieval: Exploration of query translation and transliteration. *Computers and the Humanities*, 35(4):389–420.

Li Haizhou, Zhang Min, and Su Jian. 2004. A joint source-channel model for machine transliteration. In *Proceedings of the 42nd Annual Meeting of the Association for Computational Linguistics*, pages 160–167.

Kil Soon Jeong, Sung Hyon Myaeng, Jae Sung Lee, and Key-Sun Choi. 1999. Automatic identification and back-transliteration of foreign words for information retrieval. *Information Processing & Management*, 35:523–540.

Kevin Knight and Jonathan Graehl. 1998. Machine transliteration. *Computational Linguistics*, 24(4):599–612.

Yan Qu, Gregory Grefenstette, and David A. Evans. 2003. Automatic transliteration for Japanese-to-English text retrieval. In *Proceedings of the 26th Annual International ACM SIGIR Conference on Research and Development in Information Retrieval*, pages 353–360.

Stephen Wan and Cornelia Maria Verspoor. 1998. Automatic English-Chinese name transliteration for development of multilingual resources. In *Proceedings of the 36th Annual Meeting of the Association for Computational Linguistics and the 17th International Conference on Computational Linguistics*, pages 1352–1356.

Unsupervised Named Entity Transliteration Using Temporal and Phonetic Correlation

Tao Tao, Su-Youn Yoon, Andrew Fister, Richard Sproat and ChengXiang Zhai
University of Illinois at Urbana-Champaign
{syoon9,afister2,rws}@uiuc.edu, {taotao,czhai}@cs.uiuc.edu

Abstract

In this paper we investigate *unsupervised* name transliteration using *comparable corpora*, corpora where texts in the two languages deal in some of the same topics — and therefore share references to named entities — but are not translations of each other. We present two distinct methods for transliteration, one approach using an unsupervised phonetic transliteration method, and the other using the temporal distribution of candidate pairs. Each of these approaches works quite well, but by combining the approaches one can achieve even better results. We believe that the novelty of our approach lies in the phonetic-based scoring method, which is based on a combination of carefully crafted phonetic features, and empirical results from the pronunciation errors of second-language learners of English. Unlike previous approaches to transliteration, this method can in principle work with any pair of languages in the absence of a training dictionary, provided one has an estimate of the pronunciation of words in text.

1 Introduction

As a part of a on-going project on multilingual named entity identification, we investigate unsupervised methods for transliteration across languages that use different scripts. Starting from paired comparable texts that are about the same topic, but are not in general translations of each other, we aim to find the transliteration correspondences of the paired languages. For example, if there were an English and Arabic newspaper on the same day, each of the newspapers would likely contain articles about the same important international events. From these comparable articles across the two languages, the same named entities such as persons and locations would likely be found. For at least some of the English named entities, we would therefore expect to find Arabic equivalents, many of which would in fact be transliterations.

The characteristics of transliteration differ according to the languages involved. In particular, the exact transliteration of say, an English name is highly dependent on the language since this will be influenced by the difference in the phonological systems of the language pairs. In order to show the reliability of a multi-lingual transliteration model, it should be tested with a variety of different languages. We have tested our transliteration methods with three unrelated target languages — Arabic, Chinese and Hindi, and a common source language — English. Transliteration from English to Arabic and Chinese is complicated (Al-Onaizan and Knight, 2002). For example, while Arabic orthography has a conventional way of writing long vowels using selected consonant symbols — basically <w>, <y> and <?>, in ordinary text short vowels are rarely written. When transliterating English names there is the option of representing the vowels as either short (i.e. unwritten) or long (i.e. written with one of the above three mentioned consonant symbols). For example *London* is transliterated as لندن *lndn*, with no vowels; *Washington* often as واشنطون *wSnjTwn*, with <w> representing the final <o>. Transliterations in Chinese are very different from the original English pronunciation due to the limited syllable structure and phoneme inventory of Chinese. For example, Chinese does not allow consonant clusters or coda consonants except [n, N], and this results in deletion, substitution of consonants or insertion of vowels. Thus while a syllable initial /d/ may surface as in *Baghdad* 巴格达 *ba-ge-da*, note that the syllable final /d/ is not represented.

Proceedings of the 2006 Conference on Empirical Methods in Natural Language Processing (EMNLP 2006), pages 250–257,
Sydney, July 2006.

Hindi transliteration is not well-studied, but it is in principle easier than Arabic and Chinese since Hindi phonotactics is much more similar to that of English.

2 Previous Work

Named entity transliteration is the problem of producing, for a name in a source language, a set of one or more transliteration candidates in a target language. Previous work — e.g. (Knight and Graehl, 1998; Meng et al., 2001; Al-Onaizan and Knight, 2002; Gao et al., 2004) — has mostly assumed that one has a training lexicon of transliteration pairs, from which one can learn a model, often a source-channel or MaxEnt-based model.

Comparable corpora have been studied extensively in the literature — e.g.,(Fung, 1995; Rapp, 1995; Tanaka and Iwasaki, 1996; Franz et al., 1998; Ballesteros and Croft, 1998; Masuichi et al., 2000; Sadat et al., 2004), but transliteration in the context of comparable corpora has not been well addressed. The general idea of exploiting time correlations to acquire word translations from comparable corpora has been explored in several previous studies — e.g., (Fung, 1995; Rapp, 1995; Tanaka and Iwasaki, 1996). Recently, a Pearson correlation method was proposed to mine word pairs from comparable corpora (Tao and Zhai, 2005); this idea is similar to the method used in (Kay and Roscheisen, 1993) for sentence alignment. In our work, we adopt the method proposed in (Tao and Zhai, 2005) and apply it to the problem of transliteration; note that (Tao and Zhai, 2005) compares several different metrics for time correlation, as we also note below — and see (Sproat et al., 2006).

3 Transliteration with Comparable Corpora

We start from comparable corpora, consisting of newspaper articles in English and the target languages for the same time period. In this paper, the target languages are Arabic, Chinese and Hindi. We then extract named-entities in the English text using the named-entity recognizer described in (Li et al., 2004), which is based on the SNoW machine learning toolkit (Carlson et al., 1999). To perform transliteration, we use the following general approach: **1** Extract named entities from the English corpus for each day; **2** Extract candidates from the same day's newspapers in the target language; **3** For each English named entity, score and rank the target-language candidates as potential transliterations. We apply two unsupervised methods — time correlation and pronunciation-based methods — independently, and in combination.

3.1 Candidate scoring based on pronunciation

Our phonetic transliteration score uses a standard string-alignment and alignment-scoring technique based on (Kruskal, 1999) in that the distance is determined by a combination of substitution, insertion and deletion costs. These costs are computed from a language-universal cost matrix based on phonological features and the degree of phonetic similarity. (Our technique is thus similar to other work on phonetic similarity such as (Frisch, 1996) though details differ.) We construct a single cost matrix, and apply it to English and all target languages. This technique requires the knowledge of the phonetics and the sound change patterns of the language, but it does not require a transliteration-pair training dictionary. In this paper we assume the WorldBet transliteration system (Hieronymus, 1995), an ASCII-only version of the IPA.

The cost matrix is constructed in the following way. All phonemes are decomposed into standard phonological features. However, phonological features alone are not enough to model the possible substution/insertion/deletion patterns of languages. For example, /h/ is more frequently deleted than other consonants, whereas no single phonological feature allows us to distinguish /h/ from other consonants. Similarly, stop and fricative consonants such as /p, t, k, b, d, g, s, z/ are frequently deleted when they appear in the coda position. This tendency is very salient when the target languages do not allow coda consonants or consonant clusters. So, Chinese only allows [n, N] in coda position, and stop consonants in coda position are frequently lost; *Stanford* is transliterated as *sitanfu*, with the final /d/ lost. Since phonological features do not consider the position in the syllable, this pattern cannot be captured by conventional phonological features alone. To capture this, an additional feature "deletion of stop/fricative consonant in the coda position" is added. We base these observations, and the concomitant *pseudofeatures* on pronunciation error data of learners of English as a second language, as reported in (Swan and Smith, 2002). Errors in second language pronunciation are determined by the difference in the phonological system of learner's first and second language. The same substitution/deletion/insertion patterns in the second language learner's errors appear also in the transliteration of foreign names. For example, if the learner's first language does not have a particular phoneme found in English, it is substituted by the most similar phoneme in their first language. Since Chinese does not have /v/, it is frequently substituted by /w/ or /f/. This substitution occurs frequently in the transliteration of foreign names in Chinese. Swan & Smith's study covers 25 languages, and includes Asian languages such as Thai, Korean, Chinese and Japanese, European languages such as German, Italian, French, and Polish and Middle Eastern languages such as Arabic and Farsi. Frequent substitution/insertion/deletion patterns of phonemes are collected from these data. Some examples are presented in Table 1.

Twenty phonological features and 14 pseudofeatures are used for the construction of the cost matrix. All features are classified into 5 classes. There are 4 classes of consonantal features — place, manner, laryngeality and major (consonant, sonorant, syllabicity), and a separate class of vocalic features. The purpose of these classes is to define groups of features which share the same substitution/insertion/deletion costs. Formally, given a class $\mathcal{C}$, and a cost $C_{\mathcal{C}}$, for each feature $f \in \mathcal{C}$, $C_{\mathcal{C}}$ defines the cost of substituting a different value for f than the one present in the source phoneme. Among manner features, the feature *continuous* is classified separately, since the substitution between stop and fricative consonants is very frequent; but between, say, nasals and fricatives such substitution is much less common. The cost for frequent sound change patterns should be low. Based on our intuitions, our pseudofeatures are classified into one or another of the above-mentioned five classes. The substitution/deletion/insertion cost for a pair of phonemes is the sum of the individual costs of the features which are different between the two phonemes. For example, /n/ and /p/ are different in sonorant, labial and coronal features. Therefore, the substitution cost of /n/ for /p/ is the sum of the sonorant, labial and coronal cost (20+10+10 = 40). Features and associated costs are shown in Table 2. Sample substitution, insertion, and deletion costs for /g/ are presented in Table 3.

The resulting cost matrix based on these principles is then used to calculate the edit distance between two phonetic strings. Pronunciations for English words are obtained using the Festival text-to-speech system (Taylor et al., 1998), and the target language words are automatically converted into their phonemic level transcriptions by various language-dependent means. In the case of Mandarin Chinese this is based on the standard pinyin transliteration system. For Arabic this is based on the orthography, which works reasonably well given that (apart from the fact that short vowels are no represented) the script is fairly phonemic. Similarly, the pronunciation of Hindi can be reasonably well-approximated based on the standard Devanagari orthographic representation. The edit cost for the pair of strings is normalized by the number of phonemes. The resulting score ranges from zero upwards; the score is used to rank candidate transliterations, with the candidate having the lowest cost being considered the most likely transliteration. Some examples of English words and the top three ranking candidates among all of the potential target-language candidates are given in Table 4.[1] Starred entries are correct.

3.2 Candidate scoring based on time correlation

Names of the same entity that occur in different languages often have correlated frequency patterns due to common triggers such as a major event. For example, the 2004 tsunami disaster was covered in news articles in many different languages. We would thus expect to see a peak of frequency of names such as *Sri Lanka*, *India*, and *Indonesia* in news articles published in multiple languages in the same time period. In general, we may expect topically related names in different languages to tend to co-occur together over time. Thus if we have comparable news articles over a sufficiently long time period, it is possible to exploit such correlations to learn the associations of names in different languages.

The idea of exploiting time correlation has been well studied. We adopt the method proposed in (Tao and Zhai, 2005) to represent the source name and each name candidate with a frequency vector and score each candidate by the similarity of the

[1] We describe candidate selection for each of the target languages later.

Input	Output	Position
D	D, d, z	everywhere
T	T, t, s	everywhere
N	N, n, g	everywhere
p/t/k	**deletion**	coda

Table 1: Substitution/insertion/deletion patterns for phonemes based on English second-language learner's data reported in (Swan and Smith, 2002). Each row shows an input phoneme class, possible output phonemes (including null), and the positions where the substitution (or deletion) is likely to occur.

Class	Feature	Cost
Major features and Consonant Del	consonant	20
	sonorant	
	consonant deletion	
Place features and Vowel Del	coronal	10
	vowel del/ins	
	stop/fricative consonant del at coda position	
	h del/ins	
Manner features	nasal	5
	dorsal feature for palatal consonants	
Vowel features and Exceptions	vowel height	3
	vowel place	
	exceptional	
Manner/ Laryngeal features	continuous	1.5
	voicing	

Table 2: Examples of features and associated costs. Pseudofeatures are shown in boldface. **Exceptional** denotes a situation such as the semivowel [j] substituting for the affricate [dZ]. Substitutions between these two sounds actually occur frequently in second-language error data.

two frequency vectors. This is very similar to the case in information retrieval where a query and a document are often represented by a term vector and documents are ranked by the similarity between their vectors and the query vector (Salton and McGill, 1983). But the vectors are very different and should be constructed in quite different ways. Following (Tao and Zhai, 2005), we also normalize the raw frequency vector so that it becomes a frequency distribution over all the time points. In order to compute the similarity between two distribution vectors $\vec{x} = (x_1, ..., x_T)$ and $\vec{y} = (y_1, ..., y_T)$, the Pearson correlation coefficient was used in (Tao and Zhai, 2005). We also consider two other commonly used measures – **cosine** (Salton and McGill, 1983), and **Jensen-Shannon divergence** (Lin, 1991), though our results show that Pearson correlation coefficient performs better than these two other methods. Since the time correlation method and the phonetic correspondence method exploit *distinct* resources, it makes sense to combine them. We explore two approaches to combining these two methods, namely *score combination* and *rank combination*. These will be defined below in Section 4.2.

4 Experiments

We evaluate our algorithms on three comparable corpora: English/Arabic, English/Chinese, and English/Hindi. Data statistics are shown in Table 5.

From each data set in Table 5, we picked out all news articles from seven randomly selected days. We identified about 6800 English names using the entity recognizer from (Carlson et al., 1999), and chose the most frequent 200 names as our English named entity candidates. Note that we chose the most frequent names because the reliability of the statistical correlation depends on the size of sample data. When a name is rare in a collection,

Source	Target	*Cost*	Target	*Cost*
g	g	0	r	40.5
	kh	2.5	e	44.5
	cCh	5.5	**del**	24
	tsh	17.5	**ins**	20
	N	26.5		

Table 3: Substitution/deletion/insertion costs for /g/.

English		Candidate	
		Script	Worldbet
Philippines	1	فلبين	f l b y n
	*2	فلبينية	f l b y n y t
	3	فلبينَى	f l b y n a
Megawati	*1	محَافظ	m h a f th
	2	ميجَاوَاتَى	m i j a w a t a
	3	مَاكوزَا	m a k w z a

English		Candidate		
		Script	Romanization	Worldbet
Belgium	*1	बेल्जियम	beljiyam	b e l j i y a m
	2	बेरहम	beraham	b e 9 a h a m
	3	फोरम	phoram	ph o 9 a m
Paraguay	1	परिचय	paricay	p a 9 i c a y
	*2	पैराग्वे	pairaagve	p a i 9 a g v e
	3	भिड़ेगी	bhir.egii	bh i rr e g i

English		Candidate		
		Script	Pinyin	Worldbet
Angola	*1	安哥拉	an-ge-la	a n k & l a
	1	安格拉	an-ge-la	a n k & l a
	2	阿格拉	a-ge-la	a k & l a
Megawati	*1	梅加瓦蒂	me-jia-wa-ti	m & i cC j a w a t i
	2	米九几	mi-jie-ji	m i cC j & u cC i
	3	马哈蒂尔	ma-ha-ti-er	m a x a t i & r

Table 4: Examples of the three top candidates in the transliteration of English/Arabic, English/Hindi and English/Chinese. The second column is the rank.

one can either only use the phonetic model, which does not depend on the sample size; or else one must expand the data set and hope for more occurrence. To generate the Hindi and Arabic candidates, all words from the same seven days were extracted. The words were stemmed all possible ways using simple hand-developed affix lists: for example, given a Hindi word $c_1c_2c_3$, if both c_3 and c_2c_3 are in our suffix and ending list, then this single word generates three possible candidates: c_1, c_1c_2, and $c_1c_2c_3$. In contrast, Chinese candidates were extracted using a list of 495 characters that are frequently used for foreign names (Sproat et al., 1996). A sequence of three or more such characters from the list is taken as a possible name. The number of candidates for each target language is presented in the last column of Table 5.

We measured the accuracy of transliteration by Mean Reciprocal Rank (MRR), a measure commonly used in information retrieval when there is precisely one correct answer (Kantor and Voorhees, 2000).

We attempted to create a complete set of answers for 200 English names in our test set, but a small number of English names do not seem to have any standard transliteration in the target language according to the resources that we looked at, and these names we removed from the evaluation set. Thus, we ended up having a list of less than 200 English names, shown in the second column of Table 6 (**All**). Furthermore some correct transliterations are not found in our candidate list for the second language, for two reasons: (1) The answer does not occur at all in the target news articles; (Table 6 # Missing 1) (2) The answer is there, but our candidate generation method has missed it. (Table 6 # Missing 2) Thus this results in an even smaller number of candidates to evaluate (**Core**); this smaller number is given in the fifth column of Table 6. We compute MRRs on the two sets

Languages	News Agency	Period	# days	# Words	# Cand.
Eng/Arab	Xinhua/Xinhua	08/06/2001–11/07/2001	150	12M/1.8M	12466
Eng/Chin	Xinhua/Xinhua	08/06/2001– 11/07/2001	150	12M/21M	6291
Eng/Hind	Xinhua/Naidunia	08/01/1997–08/03/1998	380	24M/5.5M	10169

Table 5: Language-pair datasets.

Language	# All	# missing 1	# missing 2	# Core
Arabic	192	113	9	70
Chinese	186	83	1	82
Hindi	147	82	0	62

Table 6: Number of evaluated English NEs.

of candidates — those represented by the count in column 2, and the smaller set represented by the count in column 5; we term the former MRR "AllMRR" and the latter "CoreMRR".[2] It is worth noting that the major reason for not finding a candidate transliteration of an English name in the target language is almost always because it is really not there, rather than because our candidate generation method has missed it. Presumably this reflects the fact that the corpora are merely comparable, rather than parallel. But the important point is that the true performance of the system would be closer to what we report below for CoreMRR, if we were working with truly parallel data where virtually all source language names would have target-language equivalents.

4.1 Performance of phonetic method and time correlation method

The performance of the phonetic method and the time correlation method are reported in Table 7, top and middle panels, respectively. In addition to the MRR scores, we also report another metric — CorrRate, namely the proportion of times the first candidate is the correct one.

Each of the two methods has advantages and disadvantages. The time correlation method relies more on the quality of the comparable corpora. It is perhaps not surprising that the time correlation method performs the best on English/Chinese, since these data come from the same source (Xinhua). Because the English and Hindi corpora are from different new agencies (Xinhua and Naidunia), the method performs relatively poorly. On the other hand, the phonetic method is less affected by corpus quality, but is sensitive to differences between languages. As discussed in the introduction, Hindi is relatively easy, and so we see the best MRR scores there. The performance is worse on Chinese and Arabic. It makes sense then to consider combining the two methods.

[2]We are aware that the resulting test set is very small, but we believe that it is large enough to demonstrate that the method is effective.

4.2 Method combination

In this section, we evaluate the performance of such a combination. We first use the phonetic method to filter out unlikely candidates, and then apply both the phonetic method and the time correlation method to rank the candidates.

We explore two combination methods: *score combination* and *rank combination*. In score combination, since the scores of two methods are not on the same scale, we first normalize them into the range [0,1] where the 1 is the best transliteration score and 0 the worst. Given a phonetic score p and a time correlation score t on the same transliteration pairs, the final combination score f would be: $f = \alpha \times p + (1-\alpha) \times t$, where $\alpha \in [0, 1]$ is a linear combination parameter. For the rank combination, we take the *unnormalized* rankings of each candidate pair by the two methods and combine as follows: $r_{combined} = \alpha \times r_p + (1-\alpha) \times r_t$, where r_p and r_t are the phonetic and temporal rankings, respectively.

The bottom panel of Table 7 shows the CoreMRR scores for these combination methods. In the second and third column, we repeat the phonetic and time correlation scores for ease of comparison. The fourth column and the sixth column represent the combination results with $\alpha = 0.5$ for both combination methods. The fifth column and the last column are the best MRR scores that we can achieve through tuning α's. Score combination, in particular, significantly outperforms the individual phonetic and time correlation methods alone.

Figure 1 plots the performance for all three languages with a variety of α's for the score combination method. Note that a higher α puts more weight on the phonetic model. As we have noted above, favoring the phonetic model is an advantage in our English/Hindi evaluation where the

Language	AllMRR	ALLCorrRate	CoreMRR	CoreCorrRate
Arabic	0.226	0.120	0.599	0.320
Chinese	0.281	0.203	0.637	0.462
Hindi	0.309	0.259	0.727	0.610

Language	AllMRR	AllCorrRate	CoreMRR	CoreCorrRate
Arabic	0.246	0.164	0.676	0.450
Chinese	0.363	0.292	0.824	0.662
Hindi	0.212	0.158	0.499	0.372

Language	Phonetic	Time Correlation	ScoreComb $\alpha = 0.5$	ScoreComb best α	RankComb $\alpha = 0.5$	RankComb best α
Arabic	0.599	0.676	0.733	0.788	0.733	0.754
Chinese	0.637	0.824	0.864	0.875	0.811	0.843
Hindi	0.727	0.499	0.749	0.761	0.689	0.765

Table 7: MRRs and CorrRate for the pronunciation method (top) and time correlation method (middle). The bottom table shows the scores for the combination (CoreMRR).

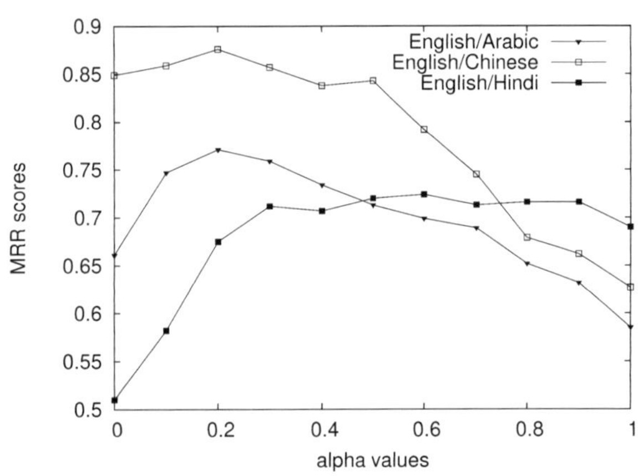

Figure 1: CoreMRR scores with different α values using score combination. A higher α puts more weight on the phonetic model.

phonetic correspondence between the two languages is fairly close, but the data sources are quite different; whereas for Arabic and Chinese we observe the opposite tendency. This suggests that one can balance the α scores according to whether one trusts one's data source versus whether one trusts in the similarity of the two languages' phonotactics.[3]

[3] A reviewer notes that we have not compared our method to state-of-the-art supervised transliteration models. This is true, but in the absence of a common evaluation set for transliteration, such a comparison would be meaningless. Certainly there are no standard databases, so far as we know, for the three language pairs we have been considering.

5 Conclusions and Future Work

In this paper we have discussed the problem of name transliteration as one component of a system for finding matching names in comparable corpora. We have proposed two unsupervised methods for transliteration, one that is based on carefully designed measures of phonetic correspondence and the other that is based on the temporal distribution of words. We have shown that both methods yield good results, and that even better results can be achieved by combining the methods.

One particular area that we will continue to work on is phonetic distance. We believe our hand-assigned costs are a reasonable starting point if one knows nothing about the particular pair of languages in question. However one could also train such costs, either from an existing list of known transliterations, or as part of an iterative bootstrapping method as, for example, in Yarowsky and Wicentowski's (2000) work on morphological induction.

The work we report is ongoing and is part of a larger project on multilingual named entity recognition and transliteration. One of the goals of this project is to develop tools and resources for under-resourced languages. Insofar as the techniques we have proposed have been shown to work on three language pairs involving one source language (English) and three unrelated and quite different target languages, one can reasonably claim that the techniques are language-independent. Furthermore, as the case of Hindi shows, even with data from completely different news agencies we are able to extract useful correspondences.

6 Acknowledgments

This work was funded by Dept. of the Interior contract NBCHC040176 (REFLEX). We thank three EMNLP reviewers for useful feedback.

References

Y. Al-Onaizan and K. Knight. 2002. Machine transliteration of names in Arabic text. In *Proceedings of the ACL Workshop on Computational Approaches to Semitic Languages*, Philadelphia, PA.

Lisa Ballesteros and W. Bruce Croft. 1998. Resolving ambiguity for cross-language retrieval. In *Research and Development in Information Retrieval*, pages 64–71.

A. Carlson, C. Cumby, J. Rosen, and D. Roth. 1999. The SNoW learning architecture. Technical Report UIUCDCS-R-99-2101, UIUC CS Dept.

Martin Franz, J. Scott McCarley, and Salim Roukos. 1998. Ad hoc and multilingual information retrieval at IBM. In *Text REtrieval Conference*, pages 104–115.

S. Frisch. 1996. *Similarity and Frequency in Phonology*. Ph.D. thesis, Northwestern University, Evanston, IL.

Pascale Fung. 1995. A pattern matching method for finding noun and proper noun translations from noisy parallel corpora. In *Proceedings of ACL 1995*, pages 236–243.

W. Gao, K.-F. Wong, and W. Lam. 2004. Phoneme-based transliteration of foreign names for OOV problem. In *IJCNLP*, pages 374–381, Sanya, Hainan.

James Hieronymus. 1995. Ascii phonetic symbols for the world's languages: Worldbet. http://www.ling.ohio-state.edu/ edwards/worldbet.pdf.

P. Kantor and E. Voorhees. 2000. The TREC-5 confusion track: Comparing retrieval methods for scanned text. *Information Retrieval*, 2:165–176.

M. Kay and M. Roscheisen. 1993. Text translation alignment. *Computational Linguistics*, 19(1):75–102.

K. Knight and J. Graehl. 1998. Machine transliteration. *Computational Linguistics*, 24(4).

J. Kruskal. 1999. An overview of sequence comparison. In D. Sankoff and J. Kruskal, editors, *Time Warps, String Edits, and Macromolecules*, chapter 1, pages 1–44. CSLI, 2nd edition.

X. Li, P. Morie, and D. Roth. 2004. Robust reading: Identification and tracing of ambiguous names. In *NAACL-2004*.

J. Lin. 1991. Divergence measures based on the shannon entropy. *IEEE Transactions on Information Theory*, 37(1):145–151.

H. Masuichi, R. Flournoy, S. Kaufmann, and S. Peters. 2000. A bootstrapping method for extracting bilingual text pairs.

H.M. Meng, W.K Lo, B. Chen, and K. Tang. 2001. Generating phonetic cognates to handle named entities in English-Chinese cross-languge spoken document retrieval. In *Proceedings of the Automatic Speech Recognition and Understanding Workshop*.

R. Rapp. 1995. Identifying word translations in non-parallel texts. In *Proceedings of ACL 1995*, pages 320–322.

F. Sadat, M. Yoshikawa, and S. Uemura. 2004. Bilingual terminology acquisition from comparable corpora and phrasal translation to cross-language information retrieval. http://acl.ldc.upenn.edu/P/P03/P03-2025.pdf.

G. Salton and M. McGill. 1983. *Introduction to Modern Information Retrieval*. McGraw-Hill.

R. Sproat, C. Shih, W. Gale, and N. Chang. 1996. A stochastic finite-state word-segmentation algorithm for Chinese. *Computational Linguistics*, 22(3).

Richard Sproat, Tao Tao, and ChengXiang Zhai. 2006. Named entity transliteration with comparable corpora. In *Proceedings of COLING-ACL 2006*, Sydney, July.

Michael Swan and Bernard Smith. 2002. *Learner English*. Cambridge University Press, Cambridge.

K. Tanaka and H. Iwasaki. 1996. Extraction of lexical translation from non-aligned corpora. In *Proceedings of COLING 1996*.

Tao Tao and ChengXiang Zhai. 2005. Mining comparable bilingual text corpora for cross-language information integration. In *Proceeding of the eleventh ACM SIGKDD international conference on Knowledge discovery in data mining*, pages 691–696.

P. Taylor, A. Black, and R. Caley. 1998. The architecture of the Festival speech synthesis system. In *Proceedings of the Third ESCA Workshop on Speech Synthesis*, pages 147–151, Jenolan Caves, Australia.

D. Yarowsky and R. Wicentowski. 2000. Minimally supervised morphological analysis by multimodal alignment. In K. Vijay-Shanker and Chang-Ning Huang, editors, *Proceedings of the 38th Meeting of the Association for Computational Linguistics*, pages 207–216, Hong Kong, October.

Capturing Out-of-Vocabulary Words in Arabic Text

Abdusalam F.A. Nwesri S.M.M. Tahaghoghi Falk Scholer
School of Computer Science and Information Technology
RMIT University, GPO Box 2476V, Melbourne 3001, Australia
{nwesri,saied,fscholer}@cs.rmit.edu.au

Abstract

The increasing flow of information between languages has led to a rise in the frequency of non-native or loan words, where terms of one language appear transliterated in another. Dealing with such out of vocabulary words is essential for successful cross-lingual information retrieval. For example, techniques such as stemming should not be applied indiscriminately to all words in a collection, and so before any stemming, foreign words need to be identified. In this paper, we investigate three approaches for the identification of foreign words in Arabic text: lexicons, language patterns, and n-grams and present that results show that lexicon-based approaches outperform the other techniques.

1 Introduction

Arabic words are derived from roots having three, four, or, in rare instances, five characters. The derivation process consistently follows patterns that are based on the three letter verb فَعَلَ (/faʕala/ to do)[1]. Each root word matches a base pattern. Characters are added at the beginning, the middle, or end of the root, but the base characters that match the pattern remain unchanged.

The pronunciation of Arabic characters is associated with short vowels; these are represented by diacritics, and attached to other characters to show how the characters should be pronounced. An Arabic character can be pronounced in several different ways. For example, the letter ب with the diacritic Fatha بَ is pronounced /ba/, with the diacritic Kasra بِ is pronounced /bɪ/, and with having the diacritic Damma بُ is pronounced /bʊ/. Diacritics are not shown in general written Arabic, and the reader must rely on the context to determine the implicit diacritics and therefore the pronunciation of each word. For example, the word ذهب can represent ذَهَبَ (/ðahaba/ = went), ذَهَبْ (/ðahab/ = gold).

Pure Arabic words follow restricted rules in their construction to keep them short and easy to pronounce. Their sounds usually follow the CVCV pattern, where C stands for a consonant and V stands for a Vowel. An Arabic word never has two consecutive consonants nor four consecutive vowels (Al-Shanti, 1996).

Foreign words are words that are borrowed from other languages. Some are remodelled to conform with Arabic word paradigms, and become part of the Arabic lexicon; others are transliterated into Arabic as they are pronounced by different Arabic speakers, with some segmental and vowel changes. The latter are called Out-Of-Vocabulary (OOV) words as they are not found in a standard Arabic lexicon. Such OOV words are increasingly common due to the inflow of information from foreign sources, and include terms that are either new and have yet to be translated into native equivalents, or proper nouns that have had their phonemes replaced by Arabic ones. Examples include words such as مارغرت /margrɪt/ (Margaret) or لينكس /linɪks/ (Linux). This process often results in different Arabic spellings for the same word.

Current Arabic Information Retrieval (AIR) systems do not handle the problem of retrieving the different versions of the same foreign

[1]We represent phonetics using the International Phonetic Alphabet (http://www.arts.gla.ac.uk/IPA/ipachart.html)

Proceedings of the 2006 Conference on Empirical Methods in Natural Language Processing (EMNLP 2006), pages 258–266, Sydney, July 2006.

word (Abdelali et al., 2004), and instead typically retrieve only the documents containing the same spelling of the word as used in the query.

One solution to this problem has been used in cross-lingual information retrieval, where OOV words in the query are transliterated into their possible equivalents. Transliterating terms in English queries into multiple Arabic equivalents using an English-Arabic dictionary has been shown to have a positive impact on retrieval results (Abduljaleel and Larkey, 2003). However, we are aware of no work on handling OOV terms in Arabic queries.

For this, proper identification of foreign words is essential. Otherwise, query expansion for such words is not likely to be effective: many Arabic words could be wrongly expanded, resulting in long queries with many false transliterations of Arabic words. Furthermore, proper identification of foreign words would be helpful because such words could then be treated differently using techniques such as approximate string matching (Zobel and Dart, 1995).

In this paper, we examine possible techniques to identify foreign words in Arabic text. In the following sections we categorise and define foreign words in Arabic, and follow in section 2 with a discussion of possible different approaches that can identify them in Arabic text. In section 3 we present an initial evaluation of these approaches, and describe improvements in section 4 that we then explore in a second experiment in section 5. We discuss results in section 6 and finally conclude our work in section 7.

1.1 Foreign words in Arabic

Arabic has many foreign words, with varying levels of assimilation into the language. Words borrowed from other languages usually have different style in writing and construction, and Arabic linguists have drawn up rules to identify them. For example, any root Arabic word that has four or more characters should have one or more of the "Dalaga" letters (ف, ر, م, ن, ل, ب). Those that have no such letters are considered foreign (Al-Shanti, 1996). However, while such rules could be useful for linguistic purposes, they have limited application in Information Retrieval (IR); based on rules, many foreign words that have long been absorbed into the language and are spelled consistently would be considered to be OOV. From the IR perspective, foreign words can be split into two

ميليسوفيتش	ميلوسيفيتيش	ميلوشفيتش
مليوسيفيتش	ميليسيفيتش	ميلوشيفيتش
ميلو يسفيتش	ميلسيفيتش	مليشيفيتش
ميلسوفيتش	ميلوسيوفيتش	ميليشفيتش
ميليوسيفيتش	ميلوسيفيتس	ميليشيفتش
مليوسوفيتش	ميلوسوفيتس	ميلوزيفيتش
مليوسفيتش	ميلوشيفيتس	ميلوزفيتش
ميلوسوفيتش	ميلوسيفتيش	ميلوسيفيتش
ميلوسفيتيش	ميلوسفيتش	ميلوسيفتش
		ميلوسفتيش

Table 1: Different spelling versions for the name Milosevic

general categories: translated and transliterated.

Translated: These are foreign words that are modified or remodelled to conform with Arabic word paradigms; they are well assimilated into Arabic, and are sometimes referred to as Arabicised words (Aljlayl and Frieder, 2002). This process includes changes in the structure of the borrowed word, including segmental and vowel changes, and the addition, deletion, and modification of stress patterns (Al-Qinal, 2002). This category of foreign words usually has a single spelling version that is used consistently. Examples include words such as بستان (/bʊstæn/ = garden), برج (/bʊrʒ/ = tower), راديو (/ræduʊ/ = radio), and قنبلة (/qʊnbula = bomb).

Transliterated: Words in this category are transliterated into Arabic by replacing phonemes with their nearest Arabic equivalents. Although Arabic has a broad sound system that contains most phonemes used in other languages, not all phonemes have Arabic equivalents. In practice, such phonemes may be represented in different ways by different persons, resulting in several spelling versions for the same foreign word. For example, we observed 28 transliterated versions for the name of the former Serbian leader (Milosevic) in the TREC 2002 Arabic collection; these are shown in Table 1.

Transliteration has become more common than translation due to the need for instant access to new foreign terms. It can take considerable time for a new foreign term to be included in reference dictionaries. However, users often need to immediately use a particular term, and cannot wait until a standard form of the word is created; news agencies form an important category of such users. This transliteration process often results in multiple spellings in common usage.

1.2 Related work

In the context of information retrieval, most work on foreign words in Arabic has been based on transliteration, and carried out under machine translation and cross-lingual information retrieval (CLIR) tasks, where English queries are used to search for Arabic documents, or vice versa. This often involves the use of a bilingual dictionary to translate queries and transliterate OOV words into their equivalents in Arabic.

Expanding a foreign word to its possible variants in a query has been shown to increase the precision of search results (Abduljaleel and Larkey, 2003). However, OOV words in the query are easily recognised based on English rules and an English-Arabic dictionary: capitalised words are marked as nouns, and the remaining words are translated using the dictionary. Words not found in the dictionary are marked as OOV and are transliterated into probable Arabic forms. In contrast, we aim to identify foreign words as a within Arabic text which is made difficult by the absence of such easily perceptible difference.

Stalls and Knight (1998) describe research to determine the original foreign word from its Arabic version; this is known as *back transliteration*. However, rather than using automatic methods to identify foreign words, they used a list of 2 800 names to test the accuracy of the back transliteration algorithm. Of these, only 900 names were successfully transliterated to their source names. While this approach can be used to identify transliterated foreign words, its effectiveness is not known on normal Arabic words as only names were used to test the algorithm.

Jeong et al. (1999) used statistical differences in syllable unigram and bigram patterns between pure Korean words and foreign words to identify foreign words in Korean documents. This approach was later enhanced by Kang and Choi (2002) to incorporate word segmentation.

A related area is language identification, where statistics derived from a language model are used to automatically identify languages (Dunning, 1994). Using N-gram counting produces good accuracy for long strings with 50 or more characters, and moderately well with 10-character-long strings. It is unclear how well this approach would work on individual words with five characters on average.

2 Identifying foreign words

We categorise three general approaches for recognising foreign words in Arabic text:

Arabic lexicon

OOV words can be easily captured by checking whether they exist in an Arabic lexicon. However, the lexicon is unlikely to include all Arabic words, while at the same time it could contain some foreign words. Moreover, this approach will identify misspelled Arabic words as foreign.

Arabic patterns system

Arabic uses a pattern system to derive words from their roots. Roots are three, four or sometimes five letters long. The reference pattern فَعَلَ (/faʕala/ = to do) is often used to represent three-letter root words. For example, the word بَحَثَ (/bн θa/ = searched) can be represented by this pattern through mapping بَـ to فَـ, ـحَـ to ـعَـ, and ـثَ to ـلَ.

Many stems can be generated from this root using standard patterns. For instance, فَاعِلْ (/fæʕɪl/ = doer) , and يَفْعَلُ (/yfʕlʊ/ = is doing) are two different patterns that respectively represent the active participle, and present tense verb from the pattern فَعَلَ. By placing the appropriate core letters and adding additional letters in each pattern, we can generate words such as بَاحِثْ (/bæнɪθ/ = researcher), يَبْحَثُ (/ybнθʊ/ = does search) respectively. New words can further accept prefixes and suffixes.

We can recognise whether a word is an Arabic or foreign word by reversing the process and testing the different patterns. If, after all possible affixes have been removed, the remaining stem matches an Arabic pattern, the word is likely to be an Arabic word. For example, to check whether the word وَالْبَاحِثْ (/walbæнɪθ/ = and the researcher) is a foreign word, we first remove the prefixes و and ال to get the stem بَاحِثْ; we find that this word matches the pattern فَاعِلْ — it has the same length, and the letter ـا is in the same position — and conclude that it is therefore an Arabic word. Note that we must perform this determination without relying on diacritics.

This approach is not perfect, as general Arabic text does not include explicit diacritics; if parts of a foreign word match a pattern, it will be marked as being Arabic. Similarly, misspelled words may be classified as foreign words if no matching pattern is found.

N-gram approach

Transliterated foreign words exhibit construction patterns that are often different from Arabic patterns. By counting the N-grams of a sample of foreign words, a profile can be constructed to identify similar words. This approach has been used in language identification, although it is reported to have only moderate effectiveness in identifying short strings (Cavnar and Trenkle, 1994; Dunning, 1994).

2.1 Resources

For the lexicon approach, we used three lexicons: the Khoja root lexicon (Khoja and Garside, 1999), the Buckwalter Lexicon (Buckwalter, 2002), and the Microsoft office 2003 lexicon (Microsoft Corporation, 2002).

The Khoja stemmer has an associated compressed language dictionary that contains well-known roots. The stemmer strips prefixes and suffixes and matches the remaining stem with a list of Arabic patterns. If a match is found, the root is extracted and checked against the dictionary of root words. If no entry is found, the word is considered to be a non-Arabic word. We call this the Khoja Lexicon Approach (KLA).

The Buckwalter morphological analyser is a lexicon that uses three tables and an algorithm to check possible affixes. The algorithm checks a word and analyses its possible prefixes and suffixes to determine possible segmentation for an Arabic word. If the algorithm fails to find any possible segmentation, the word is considered not found in the lexicon. We name this approach the Buckwalter Lexicon Approach (BLA).

The Microsoft office lexicon is the one used in the Microsoft Office 2003 spell-checker. We test whether an Arabic word is found in this lexicon, and classify those that are not in the lexicon to be foreign words. We call this approach the Office Lexicon Approach (OLA).

افعلل	افعلاء	افعلال	افعلة	افعوعل
افعولل	افعيل	تستفعل	تفاعيل	تفعال
تفعلة	تفعلل	فاعلة	فاعول	فعالا
فعالل	فعالى	فعاليل	فعلة	فعللة
فعيلا	فعيلة	فواعيل	فياعل	فياعيل
مفاعلة	مفعالة	مفعلا	مفعلة	مفعلل
تفعل	افعول	فعالة	فعولة	متفعلل
			مفعيل	مفعيلا

Table 2: Patterns added to the Khoja modified stemmer to implement the KPA approach

To use Arabic patterns, we modified the Khoja stemmer to check whether there is a match between a word and a list of patterns after stemming without further checking against the root dictionary. If there is no match, the word is considered a foreign word. This approach is similar to the approach used by Taghva et al. (2005). We adopted the patterns of the Khoja stemmer and added 37 patterns compiled from Arabic grammar books, these are shown in Table 2. We call these approaches the Khoja Pattern Approach (KPA), and Modified Khoja Pattern Approach (MKP) respectively. A word is also considered to be an Arabic word if the remaining stem has three or fewer letters.

We evaluate the effectiveness of the n-gram method in two ways. First, we extend the n-gram text categorisation method presented by Cavnar and Trenkle (1994). The method uses language profiles where, for each language, all n-grams that occur in a training corpus are sorted in order of decreasing frequency of occurrence, for n ranging from 1 to 5. To classify a text t, we build its n-gram frequency profile, and compute the distance between each n-gram in the text and in each language profile l_j. The total distance is computed by summing up all differences between the position of the n-gram in the text profile and the position of the same n-gram in the language profile:

$$D_j = \sum_{i=1}^{N_i} \mid \frac{rank(t_i, text)}{N_i} - \frac{rank(t_i, l_j)}{N_j} \mid$$

where D_j is the total distance between a text t with N_i n-grams, and a language profile l_j with N_j n-grams; and $rank$ is the position of the n-gram in the frequency-sorted list of all n-grams for either the text or language profile.

In our work, we build two language profiles, one

for native Arabic words and another for foreign words. We compare the n-grams in each word in our list against these two profiles. If the total distance between the word and the foreign words profile is smaller than the total distance between the word and the Arabic words profile, then it is classified as a foreign word. As the two language profiles are not in same size, we compute the relative position of each n-gram by dividing its position in the list by the number of the n-grams in the language profile. We call this approach the n-gram approach (NGR).

We also tried a simpler approach based on the construction of two trigram models: one from Arabic words, and another from foreign words. The probability that a string is a foreign word is determined by comparing the frequency of its trigrams with each language model. A word is considered foreign if the sum of the relative frequency of its trigrams in the foreign words profile is higher than the sum of the relative frequency of its trigrams in the Arabic words profile. We call this approach trigram (TRG).

3 Training Experiments

In this section, we describe how we formed a development data set using Arabic text from the Web, and how we evaluated and improved techniques for identification of foreign words.

3.1 Data

To form our development data set, we crawled the Arabic web sites of the Al-Jazeera news channel[1], the Al-Anwar[2] and El-Akhbar[3] newspapers. A list of 285 482 Arabic words was extracted. After removing Arabic stop words such as pronouns and prepositions, the list had 246 281 Arabic words with 25 492 unique words.

In the absence of diacritics, we decided to remove words with three or fewer characters, as these words could be interpreted as being either Arabic or foreign in different situations. For example, the word بي (/bi/) could be interpreted as the Arabic word meaning "in me", or the English letter B. After this step, 24 218 unique words remained.

We examined these words and categorised each of them either as Arabic word (AW), or a transliterated foreign word (FW). We also had to classify some terms as misspelled Arabic word (MW). We used the Microsoft Office spell-checker as a first-pass filter to identify misspelled words, and then manually inspected each word to identify any that were actually correct; the spell-checker fails to recognise some Arabic words, especially those with some complex affixes. The list also had some local Arabic dialect spellings that we chose to classify as misspelled.

The final list had three categories: 22 295 correct Arabic words, 1 218 foreign words and 705 misspelled words.

To build language models for the trigram approaches (NRG and TRG), we used the TREC 2001 Arabic collection (Gey and Oard, 2001). We manually selected 3 046 foreign words out of the OOV words extracted from the collection using the Microsoft office spell-checker. These foreign words are transliterated foreign words. We built the Arabic language model using 100 000 words extracted from the TREC collection using the same spell-checker. However, we excluded any word that could be a proper noun, to avoid involving foreign words. We used an algorithm to exclude any word that does not accept the suffix haa (ـه), as transliterated proper nouns can not accept Arabic affixes.

3.2 Evaluation

We measure the accuracy of each approach by examining the number of foreign words correctly identified, and the number of incorrect classifications. The precision of each approach is calculated as the ratio of correctly identified foreign words to the total number of words identified as foreign The latter could be correct or misspelled Arabic words identified as foreign plus the actual foreign words identified. The recall is calculated as the ratio of correctly identified foreign words to the number of words marked manually as foreign. Although there is generally a compromise between precision and recall, we consider precision to be more important, since incorrectly classifying Arabic words as foreign would be more likely to harm general retrieval performance. The left-hand side of Table 3 shows the results of our experiments. We have included the MW results to illustrate the effects of misspelled words on each approach

The results show that the n-gram approach (NGR) has the highest precision, while the

[1] `http://www.aljazeera.net`

[2] `http://www.alanwar.com`

[3] `http://www.elkhabar.com`

	AW	MW	FW		
Appr.	#	#	#	R	P
OLA	614	698	1 017	0.834	0.437
BLA	384	404	628	0.515	0.443
KLA	1 732	215	745	0.612	0.277
KPA	1 034	135	590	0.480	0.340
MKP	940	126	573	0.470	0.350
NGR	718	95	726	0.596	0.471
TRG	1 591	118	737	0.605	0.301

	AW	MW	FW		
Appr.	#	#	#	R	P
OLA	145	248	866	0.711	0.687
BLA	88	149	534	0.438	0.693
KLA	420	83	642	0.527	0.508
KPA	302	52	520	0.430	0.590
MKP	269	51	507	0.416	0.613
NGR	411	69	669	0.549	0.582
TRG	928	85	642	0.527	0.387

Table 3: Identification of foreign words: initial results (left) and results after improvements (right)

lexicon-based OLA approach gives the highest recall. The pattern approaches (KPA) and (MKP) perform well compared to the combination of patterns and the root lexicon (KLA), although the latter produces higher recall. There is a slight improvement in precision when adding more patterns, but recall is sightly reduced. The KLA approach produces the poorest precision, but has better recall rate than the NGR approach.

The results show that many Arabic native words are mistakenly caught in the foreign words net. Our intention is to handle foreign words differently from Arabic native words. Our approach is based on normalising the different forms of the same foreign word to one form at the index level rather than expanding the foreign word to its possible variants at the query level. Retrieval precision will be negatively affected by incorrect classification of native and foreign words. Consequently, we consider that keeping the proportion of false positives — correct Arabic words identified as foreign (precision) — low to be more important than correctly identifying a higher number of foreign words (recall).

Some of the Arabic words categorised as foreign are in fact misspelled; we believe that these have limited effect on retrieval precision, and there is limited value in identifying such words in a query unless the retrieval system incorporates a correction process.

4 Enhanced rules

To reduce the false identification rate of foreign words, we analysed the lists of foreign words, correct Arabic words identified as foreign, and Arabic misspelled words identified as foreign. We noticed that some Arabic characters rarely exist in transliterated foreign words, and used these to separate Arabic words — correctly or incorrectly spelled – from true foreign words. Table 4 shows the count of each character in the sample of 3 046 foreign words; foreign words tend to have vowels inserted between consonants to maintain the CVCV paradigm. We also noticed that most of transliterated foreign words do not start with the definite article ال, or end with the Taa Marbuta ـة. Foreign words also rarely end with two Arabic suffixes.

Letter	count	letter	count	letter	count
ي	3 839	م	632	ح	2
ا	3 599	د	559	ع	2
و	2 453	ش	514	ص	1
ن	1 660	ج	458	ء	0
س	1 587	ز	334	ؤ	0
ت	1 544	ه	171	أ	0
ر	1 244	خ	84	إ	0
ك	1 070	ث	23	آ	0
ب	900	ق	20	ض	0
ل	863	ط	12	ظ	0
ف	769	ئ	7	ى	0
غ	728	ذ	3	ة	0

Table 4: Frequency of Arabic letters in a sample of 3 046 foreign words

We also noticed that lexicon based approaches fail to recognise some correct Arabic words for the following reasons:

- Words with the letter ا (Alef) with or without the diacritics Hamza (أ, إ), or the diacritic Madda (آ) are not recognised as correct in many cases. Many words are also categorised incorrectly if the Hamza is wrongly placed above or below the initial Alef or the Madda is absent. In modern Arabic text, the Alef often appears without the Hamza diacritic and the Madda is sometimes dropped.

- Correct Arabic words are not recognised with particular suffixes. For example, words that have the object suffix, such as the suffix كها in يعلمونكها (/yʊʕalımunakaha/ = they teach it to you).
- Some Arabic words are compound words, written attached to each other most of the time. For example, compound nouns such as عبدالقادر (/ʕbdulqadır/), although composed of two words that are individually identified as being correct, are flagged as incorrect when combined.
- Some common typographical shortcuts result in words being written without white space between them. Where a character that always terminates a word (for example ة) is found in the apparent middle of a word, it is clear that this problem has occurred.

From these observations, we constructed the following rules. Whenever one of the following conditions is met, a word is not classified as foreign:

1. the word contains any of the Arabic characters:

   ة, ى, ض, ظ, آ, إ, أ, ؤ, ص, ح, ذ, ء, ئ;

2. the word starts with the definite article (الـ);
3. the word has more than one Arabic suffix (pronouns attached at the end of the word);
4. the word has no vowels between the second and penultimate character (inclusive); or
5. the word contains one of the strings: ة, ى, ء, اا, يال, رال, زال, دال, ذال, وال, اال, and when split into two parts at the first character of any sequence, the first part is three characters or longer, and the second part is four characters or longer.

The right-hand side of Table 3 shows the improvements achieved using these rules. It can be seen that they have a large positive impact. Overall, OLA performs the best, with precision at 69% and recall at 71%. Figure 1 shows the precision obtained before and after applying these rules. Improvement is consistent across all approaches, with an increase in precision between 10% and 25%.

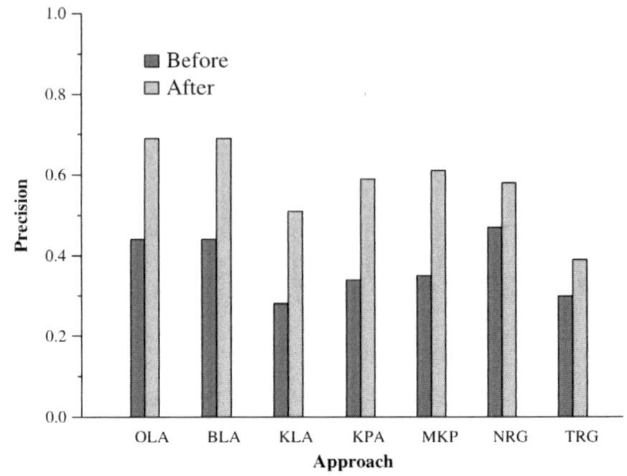

Figure 1: Precision of different approaches before and after Improvements

5 Verification Experiments

To verify our results, we used another data set of similar size to the first to verify our approach. We collected a list of 23 466 unique words from the Dar-al-Hayat newspaper[4]. Words, and classified and marked words in the same way as for the first data set (described in Section 3.1). We determined this new set to comprise 22 800 Arabic words (AW), 536 Foreign words (FW), and 130 Misspelled words (MW). Table 5 shows the initial results and improvements using the enhanced rules obtained by each approach using this data set.

The results on this unseen data are relatively consistent with the previous experiment, but precision in this sample is expectedly lower.

6 Discussion

We have seen that foreign words are not easily recognised in Arabic text, and a large number of Arabic words are affected when we try to exclude foreign words.

We found the lexicon approach to be the best in identifying foreign words. However, current lexicons are relatively small, and the variety of Arabic inflection makes it very difficult to include all correct word forms. Furthermore, current lexicons include many foreign words; for example when using OLA approach, 1 017 foreign words out of 1 218 are OOV, indicating that about 200 foreign words are present in that lexicon. The pattern approach is more efficient but the lack of diacritics in general written Arabic makes it very difficult to precisely match a pattern with a

[4] http://www.daralhayat.com

	AW	MW	FW		
Appr.	#	#	#	R	P
OLA	1 189	112	417	0.777	0.242
BLA	780	96	267	0.498	0.234
KLA	1 684	55	312	0.582	0.152
KPA	992	29	238	0.440	0.189
MKP	901	26	231	0.431	0.199
NGR	740	22	286	0.533	0.272
TRG	1 655	19	308	0.575	0.155

	AW	MW	FW		
Appr.	#	#	#	R	P
OLA	302	38	307	0.572	0.474
BLA	149	33	184	0.343	0.502
KLA	350	16	216	0.403	0.371
KPA	238	9	166	0.310	0.402
MKP	202	8	162	0.302	0.435
NGR	401	8	245	0.457	0.374
TRG	972	11	235	0.438	0.193

Table 5: Identification of foreign words on the test set: initial results (left) and results after improvements (right)

word, resulting in many foreign words being incorrectly identified as Arabic. Passing the list of all 3 046 manually judged foreign words to the pattern approach, some 2 017 words of this list were correctly judged as foreign, and about one third (1 029) were incorrectly judged to be Arabic. The n-gram method produced reasonable precision compared to the lexicon-based methods. In contrast, TRG had the worst results. This could be due to the limited size of the training corpus. However, we expect that improvements to this approach will remain limited due to the fact that many Arabic and foreign words share the same trigrams. It is clear that all the approaches are improved dramatically when applying the enhancement rules. The improvements of the NGR wasn't as equal as other approaches. This is because some of the rules are implicitly applied within the n-gram approach. The lack of diacritics also makes it very difficult to distinguish between certain foreign and Arabic words. For example, without diacritics, the word كلينتين could be كْلِيْنْتِيْن (/klınton/ = Clinton), or كَلِيْنَتَيْن (/kalinatin/ = as two date trees). The pronunciation is different in the two cases, but only context or diacritics can make it clear which word is being used.

7 Conclusion

Identifying foreign words in Arabic text is an important problem for cross-lingual information retrieval, since commonly-used techniques such as stemming should not be applied indiscriminately to all words in a collection.

We have presented three approaches for identifying foreign words in Arabic text: lexicons, patterns, and n-grams. We have presented results that show that the lexicon approach outperforms the other approaches, and have described improvements to minimise the false identification of foreign words. These rules result in improved precision, but have a small negative impact on recall. Overall, the results are relatively low for practical applications, and more work is needed to deal with this problem. As foreign words are characterised by having different versions, an algorithm that collapse those versions to one form could be useful in identifying foreign words. We are presently exploring algorithms to normalise foreign words in Arabic text. This will allow us to identify normalised forms for foreign words and use a single consistent version for indexing and retrieval.

8 Acknowledgements

We thank Microsoft Corporation for providing us with a copy of Microsoft Office Proofing Tools 2003.

References

Ahmed Abdelali, Jim Cowie, and Hamdy S. Soliman. 2004. Arabic information retrieval perspectives. In *Proceedings of the 11th Conference on Natural Language Processing, Journes d'Etude sur la Parole - Traitement Automatique des Langues Naturelles (JEP-TALN)*, Fez, Morocco.

Nasreen Abduljaleel and Leah S. Larkey. 2003. Statistical transliteration for English-Arabic cross-language information retrieval. In *Proceedings of the International Conference on Information and Knowledge Management*, pages 139–146. ACM Press.

Jamal B. S. Al-Qinal. 2002. Morphophonemics of loanwords in translation. *Journal of King Saud University*, 13:1–132.

Mohamed Saleh Al-Shanti. 1996. *Al Maharat Allughawia*. Al Andalus for publishing and distribution. 4th edition.

Mohammed Aljlayl and Ophir Frieder. 2002. On Arabic search: improving the retrieval effectiveness via a light stemming approach. In *Proceedings of the International Conference on Information and Knowledge Management*, pages 340–347. ACM Press.

Tim Buckwalter. 2002. Buckwalter Arabic morphological analyzer version 1.0. LDC Catalog No. LDC2002L49.

William B. Cavnar and John M. Trenkle. 1994. N-gram-based text categorization. In *Proceedings of 3rd Annual Symposium on Document Analysis and Information Retrieval, SDAIR-94,*, pages 161–175, Las Vegas, US.

Ted Dunning. 1994. Statistical identification of language. Technical Report MCCS-94-273, Computing Research Lab (CRL), New Mexico State University.

Fredric C. Gey and Douglas W. Oard. 2001. The TREC-2001 cross-language information retrieval track: Searching Arabic using English, French or Arabic queries. In *TREC-2001*, volume NIST Special Publication:SP 500-250. National Institute of Standards and Technology.

Kil S. Jeong, Sung Hyon Myaeng, Jae S. Lee, and Key-Sun Choi. 1999. Automatic identification and back-transliteration of foreign words for information retrieval. *Information Processing and Management*, 35(4):523–540.

Byung-Ju Kang and Key-Sun Choi. 2002. Effective foreign word extraction for Korean information retrieval. *Information Processing and Management*, 38(1):91–109.

Shereen Khoja and Roger Garside. 1999. Stemming Arabic text. Technical report, Computing Department, Lancaster University, Lancaster.

Microsoft Corporation. 2002. Arabic proofing tools in Office 2003.
URL: `http://www.microsoft.com/middleeast/arabicdev/office/office2003/Proofing.asp`.

Bonnie Glover Stalls and Kevin Knight. 1998. Translating names and technical terms in Arabic text. In *COLING/ACL Workshop on Computational Approaches to Semitic Languages*, pages 34–41.

Kazem Taghva, Rania Elkhoury, and Jeffrey Coombs. 2005. Arabic stemming without a root dictionary. In *Proceedings of ITCC 2005 Intlernational Conference on Information Technology: Coding and Computing*.

Justin Zobel and Philip Dart. 1995. Finding approximate matches in large lexicons. *Software - Practice and Experience*, 25(3):331–345.

Using Linguistically Motivated Features for Paragraph Boundary Identification

Katja Filippova and **Michael Strube**
EML Research gGmbH
Schloss-Wolfsbrunnenweg 33
69118 Heidelberg, Germany
http://www.eml-research.de/nlp

Abstract

In this paper we propose a machine-learning approach to paragraph boundary identification which utilizes linguistically motivated features. We investigate the relation between paragraph boundaries and discourse cues, pronominalization and information structure. We test our algorithm on German data and report improvements over three baselines including a reimplementation of Sporleder & Lapata's (2006) work on paragraph segmentation. An analysis of the features' contribution suggests an interpretation of what paragraph boundaries indicate and what they depend on.

1 Introduction

Our work is concerned with multi-document summarization, namely with the merging of multiple documents about the same topic taken from the web. We view summarization as extraction of important sentences from the text. As a consequence of the merging process the layout of the documents is lost. In order to create the layout of the output, the document structure (Power et al., 2003) has to be regenerated. One aspect of this structure is of particular importance for our work: the paragraph structure. In web documents paragraph boundaries are used to anchor figures and illustrations, so that the figures are always aligned with the same paragraph even when the font size or the window size is changed. Since we want to include figures in the generated summaries, paragraph segmentation is an important subtask in our application.

Besides multi-document summarization of web documents, paragraph boundary identification (PBI) could be useful for a number of different applications, such as producing the layout for transcripts provided by speech recognizers and optical character recognition systems, and determining the layout of documents generated for output devices with different screen size.

Though related to the task of topic segmentation which stimulated a large number of studies (Hearst, 1997; Choi, 2000; Galley et al., 2003, inter alia), paragraph segmentation has not been thoroughly investigated so far. We explain this by the fact that paragraphs are considered a stylistic phenomenon and that there is no unanimous opinion on what the function of the paragraph is. Some authors (Irmscher (1972) as cited by Stark (1988)) suggest that paragraph structure is arbitrary and can not be determined based solely on the properties of the text. Still, psycholinguistic studies report that humans agree, at least to some extent, on placing boundaries between paragraphs. These studies also note that paragraph boundaries are informative and make the reader perceive paragraph-initial sentences as being important (Stark, 1988). In contrast to topic segmentation, paragraph segmentation has the advantage that large amounts of annotated data are readily availabe for supervised learning.

In this paper we describe our approach to paragraph segmentation. Previous work (Sporleder & Lapata, 2004; 2006) mainly focused on superficial and easily obtainable surface features like punctuation, quotes, distance and words in the sentence. Their approach was claimed to be domain- and language-independent. Our hypothesis, however, is that linguistically motivated features, which we compute automatically, provide a better paragraph segmentation than Sporleder & Lapata's surface ones, though our approach may loose some of the

Proceedings of the 2006 Conference on Empirical Methods in Natural Language Processing (EMNLP 2006), pages 267–274,
Sydney, July 2006.

domain-independence. We test our hypothesis on a corpus of biographies downloaded from the German Wikipedia[1]. The results we report in this paper indicate that linguistically motivated features outperform surface features significantly. It turned out that pronominalization and information structure contribute to the determination of paragraph boundaries while discourse cues have a negative effect.

The paper is organized as follows: First, we describe related work in Section 2, then in Section 3 our data is introduced. The baselines, the machine learners, the features and the experimental setup are given in Section 4. Section 5 reports and discusses the results.

2 Related Work

Compared to other text segmentation tasks, e.g. topic segmentation, PBI has received relatively little attention. We are aware of three studies which approach the problem from different perspectives. Bolshakov & Gelbukh (2001) assume that splitting text into paragraphs is determined by text cohesion: The link between a paragraph initial sentence and the preceding context is weaker than the links between sentences within a paragraph. They evaluate text cohesion using a database of collocations and semantic links and insert paragraph boundaries where the cohesion is low.

The algorithm of Sporleder & Lapata (2004, 2006) uses surface, syntactic and language model features and is applied to three different languages and three domains (fiction, news, parliament). This study is of particular interest to us since one of the languages the algorithm is tested on is German. They investigate the impact of different features and data size, and report results significantly better than a simple baseline. However, their results vary considerably between the languages and the domains. Also, the features determined important is different for each setting. So, it may be possible that Sporleder & Lapata do not provide conclusive results.

Genzel (2005) considers lexical and syntactic features and reports accuracy obtained from English fiction data as well as from the WSJ corpus. He points out that lexical coherence and structural features turn out to be the most useful for his algorithm. Unfortunately, the only evaluation measure he provides is accuracy which, for the PBI task, does not describe the performance of a system sufficiently.

In comparison to the mentioned studies, our goal is to examine the influence of cohesive features on the choice of paragraph boundary insertion. Unlike Bolshakov & Gelbukh (2001), who have similar motivation but measure cohesion by collocations, we explore the role of discourse cues, pronominalization and information structure.

The task of topic segmentation is closely related to the task of paragraph segmentation. If there is a topic boundary, it is very likely that it coincides with a paragraph boundary. However, the reverse is not true and one topic can extend over several paragraphs. So, if determined reliably, topic boundaries could be used as high precision, low recall predictors for paragraph boundaries. Still, there is an important difference: While work on topic segmentation mainly depends on content words (Hearst, 1997) and relations between them which are computed using lexical chains (Galley et al., 2003), paragraph segmentation as a stylistic phenomenon may depend equally likely on function words. Hence, paragraph segmentation is a task which encompasses the traditional borders between content and style.

3 Data

The data we used is a collection of biographies from the German version of Wikipedia. We selected all biographies under the Wikipedia categories of physicists, chemists, mathematicians and biologists and obtained 970 texts with an average length of 20 sentences and 413,776 tokens in total.

Although our corpus is substantially smaller than the German corpora of Sporleder & Lapata (2006), it should be big enough for a fair comparison between their algorithm and the algorithm proposed here. Having investigated the effect of the training size, Sporleder & Lapata (2006) came to the conclusion that their system performs well being trained on a small data set. In particular, the learning curve for German shows an improvement of only about 2% when the amount of training data is increased from 20%, which in case of German fiction approximately equals 370,000 tokens, to 100%.

Fully automatic preprocessing in our system comprises the following stages: First, a list of people of a certain Wikipedia category is taken and for every person an article is extracted The text

[1]http://de.wikipedia.org

	training	development	test
tokens	347,763	39,228	19,943
sentences	15,583	1,823	922
paragraphs	5,323	654	362

Table 1: Number of tokens and sentences per set

is purged from Wiki tags and comments, the information on subtitles and paragraph structure is preserved. Second, sentence boundaries are identified with a Perl CPAN module[2] whose performance we improved by extending the list of abbreviations and modifying the output format. Next, the sentences are split into tokens. The TnT tagger (Brants, 2000) and the TreeTagger (Schmid, 1997) are used for tagging and lemmatizing. Finally, the texts are parsed with the CDG dependency parser (Foth & Menzel, 2006). Thus, the text is split on three levels: paragraphs, sentences and tokens, and morphological and syntactic information is provided.

A publicly available list of about 300 discourse connectives was downloaded from the Internet site of the Institute for the German Language[3] (Institut für Deutsche Sprache, Mannheim) and slightly extended. These are identified in the text and annotated automatically as well. Named entities are classified according to their type using information from Wikipedia: *person, location, organization* or *undefined*. Given the peculiarity of our corpus, we are able to identify all mentions of the biographee in the text by simple string matching. We also annotate different types of referring expressions (*first, last, full name*) and resolve anaphora by linking personal pronouns to the biographee provided that they match in number and gender.

The annotated corpus is split into training (85%), development (10%) and testing (5%) sets. Distribution of data among the three sets is presented in Table 1. Sentences which serve as subtitles in a text are filtered out because they make identifying a paragraph boundary for the following sentence trivial.

4 Experiments

4.1 Machine Learners

The PBI task was reformulated as a binary classification problem: every training instance representing a sentence was classified either as paragraph-initial or not.

We used two machine learners: BoosTexter (Schapire & Singer, 2000) and TiMBL (Daelemans et al., 2004). BoosTexter was developed for text categorization, and combines simple rules (decision stumps) in a boosting manner. Sporleder & Lapata used this learner because it has the ability to combine many only moderately accurate hypotheses. TiMBL is a memory-based learner which classifies every test instance by finding the most similar examples in the training set, hence it does not abstract from the data and is well suited to handle features with many values, e.g. the list of discourse cues. For both classifiers, all experiments were run with the default settings.

4.2 Baselines

We compared the performance of our algorithm against three baselines. The first one (**distance**) trivially inserts a paragraph break after each third sentence, which is the average number of sentences in a paragraph. The second baseline (**Galley**) hypothesizes that paragraph breaks coincide with topic boundaries and utilizes Galley et al.'s (2003) topic boundary identification tool LCseg. The third baseline (**Sporleder**) is a reimplementation of Sporleder & Lapata's 2006 algorithm with the following features:

Word and **Sentence Distances** from the current sentence to the previous paragraph break;

Sentence Length and **Relative Position (relPos)** of the sentence in a text;

Quotes encodes whether this and the previous sentences contain a quotation, and whether the quotation is continued in the current sentence or not;

Final Punctuation of the previous sentence;

Words – the first (**word1**), the first two (**word2**), the first three and all words from the sentence;

Parsed has positive value in case the sentence is parsed, negative otherwise;

Number of S, VP, NP and **PP** nodes in the sentence;

Signature is the sequence of PoS tags with and without punctuation;

[2] http://search.cpan.org/~holsten/Lingua-DE-Sentence-0.07/Sentence.pm

[3] http://hypermedia.ids-mannheim.de/index.html

Children of Top-Level Nodes are two features representing the sequence of syntactic labels of the children of the root of the parse tree and the children of the highest S-node;

Branching Factor features express the average number of children of S, VP, NP and PP nodes in the parse;

Tree Depth is the average length of the path from the root to the leaves;

Per-word Entropy is a feature based on Genzel & Charniak's (2003) observation that paragraph-initial sentences have lower entropy than non-initial ones;

Sentence Probability according to a language model computed from the training data;

Character-level *n*-gram models are built using the CMU toolkit (Clarkson & Rosenfeld, 1997).

Since the parser we used produces dependency trees as an output, we could not distinguish between such features as **children of the root of the tree** and **children of the top-level S-node**. Apart from this minor change, we reimplemented the algorithm in every detail.

4.3 Our Features

For our algorithm we first selected the features of Sporleder & Lapata's (2006) system which performed best on the development set. These are relative position, the first and the first two words (**relPos, word1, word2**). Quote and final punctuation features, which were particularly helpful in Sporleder & Lapata's experiments on the German fiction data, turned out to be superfluous given the infrequency of quotations and the prevalent use of the period as sentence delimiter in our data.

We experimented with *text cohesion* features assuming that the paragraph structure crucially depends on cohesion and that paragraph breaks are likely to occur between sentences where cohesive links are weak. In order to estimate the degree of cohesion, we looked at lexical cohesion, pronominalization, discourse cues and information structure.

4.3.1 Lexical Cohesion

nounOver, verbOver: Similar to Sporleder & Lapata (2006), we introduced an overlap feature, but measured the degree of overlap as a number of common noun and verb lemmas between two adjacent sentences. We preferred lemmas over words in order to match all possible forms of the same word in German.

LCseg: Apart from the overlap, a boolean feature based on LCseg (Galley et al., 2003) marked whether the tool suggests that a new topic begins with the current sentence. This feature, relying on lexical chains, was supposed to provide more fine-grained information on the degree of similarity between two sentences.

4.3.2 Pronominalization

As Stark (1988) points out, humans tend to interpret over-reference as a clue for the beginning of a new paragraph: In a sentence, if a non-pronominal reference is preferred over a pronominal one where the pronoun would be admissible, humans are likely to mark this sentence as a paragraph-initial one. In order to check whether over-reference indeed correlates with paragraph-initial sentences, we described the way the biographee is referred to in the current and the previous sentences.

prevSPerson, currSPerson: This feature[4] with the values *NA, biographee, other* indicates whether there is a reference to the biographee or some other person in the sentence.

prevSRE, currSRE: This feature describes the biographee's referring expression and has three possible values: *NA, name, pronoun.*

Although our annotation distinguishes between first, last and full names, we found out that, for the PBI task, the distinction is spurious and unifying these three under the same category improves the results.

REchange: Since our classifiers assume feature independence and can not infer the information on the change in referring expression, we explicitly encoded that information by merging the values of the previous feature for the current and the preceding sentences into one, which has nine possible values (*name-name, NA-name, pronoun-name*, etc.).

[4] Prefixes **prevS-**, **currS-** stand for the previous and the current sentences respectively.

4.3.3 Discourse Cues

The intuition behind these features is that cue words and phrases are used to signal the relation between the current sentence and the preceding sentence or context (Mann & Thompson, 1988). Such connectives as *endlich (finally), abgesehen davon (apart from that), danach (afterwards)* explicitly mark a certain relation between the sentence they occur in and the preceding context. We hypothesize that the relations which hold across paragraph boundaries should differ from those which hold within paragraphs and that the same is true for the discourse cues. Absence of a connective is supposed to be informative as well, being more typical for paragraph-initial sentences.

Three features describe the connective of the current sentence. Another three features describe the one from the preceding sentence.

prevSCue, currSCue: This feature is the connective itself (*NA* in case of none).

prevSCueClass, currSCueClass: This feature represents the semantic class of the cue word or phrase as assigned by the IDS Mannheim. There are 25 values, including *NA* in case of no connective, altogether, with the most frequent values being *temporal, concessive, conclusive*, etc.

prevSProCue, currSProCue: The third binary feature marks whether the connective is proadverbial or not (*NA* if there is no connective). Being anaphors, proadverbials, such as *deswegen (because of that), darüber (about that)* explicitly link a sentence to the preceding one(s).

4.3.4 Information Structure

Information structure, which is in German to a large extent expressed by word order, provides additional clues to the degree of connectedness between two sentences. In respect to the PBI task, Stark (1988) reports that paragraph-initial sentences are often *theme-marking* which means that the subject of such sentences is not the first element. Given the lower frequency of paragraph-initial sentences, this feature can not be considered reliable, but in combination with others it provides an additional clue. In German, the first element best corresponds to the *prefield* (Vorfeld) – normally, the single constituent placed before the finite verb in the main clause.

currSVF encodes whether the constituent in the prefield is a *NP, PP, ADV, CARD*, or *Sub.Clause*. Values different from *NP* unambiguously represent theme-marking sentences, whereas the *NP* value may stand for both: theme-marking as well as not theme-marking sentence.

4.4 Discussion

Note, that we did not exclude text-initial sentences from the study because the encoding we used does not make such cases trivial for classification. Although some of the features refer to the previous sentence, none of them has to be necessarily realized and therefore none of them explicitly indicates the absence of the preceding sentence. For example, the label *NA* appears in cases where there is no discourse cue in the preceding sentence as well as in cases where there is no preceding sentence. The same holds for all other features prefixed with **prevS-**.

Another point concerns the use of pronominalization-based features. Sporleder & Lapata (2006) waive using such features because they consider pronominalization dependent on the paragraph structure and not the other way round. At the same time they mention speech and optical character recognition tasks as possible application domains for the PBI. There, pronouns are already given and need not be regenerated, hence for such applications features which utilize pronouns are absolutely appropriate. Unlike the recognition tasks, for multi-document summarization both decisions have to be made, and the order of the two tasks is not self-evident. The best decision would probably be to decide simultaneously on both using optimization methods (Roth & Yih, 2004; Marciniak & Strube, 2005). Generating pronouns before inserting boundaries seems as reasonable as doing it the other way round.

4.5 Feature Selection

We determine the relevant feature set and evaluate which features from this set contribute most to the performance of the system by the following procedures.

First, we follow an iterative algorithm similar to the wrapper approach for feature selection (Kohavi & John, 1997) using the development data and TiMBL. The feature subset selection algorithm performs a hill-climbing search along the

Feature set	F-measure
all	58.85%
–prevSCue	0.78%
–currSCue	0.32%
–currSCueClass	0.38%
–prevSCueClass	0.37%
–prevSProCue	1.02%
best	61.72%

Table 2: Removed features

Feature set	F-measure
relPos, word1, word2	48.06%
+currSRE	+10.50%
+currSVF	+0.49%
+currSPerson	+0.57%
+prevSPerson	+1.32%
best	60.94%

Table 3: Best features

feature space. We start with a model based on all available features. Then we train models obtained by removing one feature at a time. We choose the worst performing feature, namely the one whose removal gives the largest improvement based on the F-measure, and remove it from the model. We then train classifiers removing each of the remaining features separately from the enhanced model. The process is iteratively run as long as significant improvement is observed.

To measure the contribution of the relevant features we start with the three best features from Sporleder & Lapata (2006) (see Section 4.3) and train TiMBL combining the current feature set with each feature in turn. We then choose the best performing feature based on the F-measure and add it to the model. We iterate the process until all features are added to the three-feature system.

Thus, we optimize the default setting and obtain the information on what the paragraph structure crucially depends.

5 Results

Having trained our algorithm on the development data, we then determined the optimal feature combination and finally evaluated the performance on the previously unseen test data.

Table 2 and Table 3 present the ranking of the least and of the most beneficial features respectively. Somewhat surprising to us, Table 2 shows that basically *all* features capturing information on discourse cues actually worsened the performance of the classifier. The bad performance of the *prevSCue* and *currSCue* features may be caused by their extreme sparseness. To test these features reasonably, we plan to increase the data set size by an order of magnitude. Then, at least, it should be possible to determine which discourse cues, if any, are correlated with paragraph boundaries. The bad performance of the *prevSCueClass* and *currSCueClass* features may be caused by the categorization provided by the IDS. This question also requires further investigation, maybe with a different categorization.

Table 3 also provides interesting insights in the feature set. First, with only the three features *relPos, word1* and *word2* the baseline performs almost as well as the full feature set used by Sporleder & Lapata. Then, as expected, *currSRE* provides the largest gain in performance, followed by *currSVF, currSPerson* and *prevSPerson*. This result confirms our hypothesis that linguistically motivated features capturing information on pronominalization and information structure play an important role in determining paragraph segmentation.

The results of our system and the baselines for different classifiers (BT stands for BoosTexter and Ti for TiMBL) are summarized in Table 4. Accuracy is calculated by dividing the number of matches over the total number of test instances. Precision, recall and F-measure are obtained by considering true positives, false positives and false negatives. The latter metric, WindowDiff (Pevzner & Hearst, 2002), is supposed to overcome the disadvantage of the F-measure which penalizes near misses as harsh as more serious mistakes. The value of WindowDiff varies between 0 and 1, where a lesser count corresponds to better performance.

The significance of our results was computed using the χ^2 test. All results are significantly better (on the $p < 0.01$ level or below) than both baselines and the reimplemented version of Sporleder & Lapata's (2006) algorithm whose performance on our data is comparable to what the authors reported on their corpus of German fiction. Interestingly, TiMBL does much better than BoosTexter on Sporleder & Lapata's feature set. Apparently, Sporleder & Lapata's presupposition, that they would rely on many weak hypotheses,

	Accuracy	Precision	Recall	F-measure	WindowDiff
distance	52.16	37.98	31.88	34.66	.426
Galley	56.83	43.04	26.15	32.54	.416
development					
Sporleder_BT	71.96	80.15	30.46	44.15	.327
Sporleder_Ti	62.36	48.65	62.89	54.86	.338
all_BT	74.93	72.10	50.67	59.52	.286
all_Ti	70.54	59.81	57.91	58.85	.302
best_Ti	73.39	64.73	58.97	61.72	.280
test					
Sporleder_BT	68.76	80.15	28.61	42.16	.341
Sporleder_Ti	60.62	50.46	59.67	54.68	.345
all_BT	72.12	71.31	50.13	58.88	.286
all_Ti	67.13	59.14	56.40	57.74	.303
best_Ti	68.00	60.46	56.67	58.50	.302

Table 4: Results for the development and test sets with the two classifiers

does not hold. This is also confirmed by the results reported in Table 3 where only three of their features perform surprisingly strong. In contrast, on our feature set TiMBL and BoosTexter perform almost equally. However, BoosTexter achieves in all cases a much higher precision which is preferable over the higher recall provided by TiMBL.

6 Conclusion

In this paper, we proposed a novel approach to paragraph boundary identification based on linguistic features such as pronominalization, discourse cues and information structure. The results are significantly higher than all baselines and a reimplementation of Sporleder & Lapata's (2006) system and achieve an F-measure of about 59%.

We investigated to what extent the paragraph structure is determined by each of the three factors and came to the conclusion that it crucially depends on the use of pronouns and information structure. Surprisingly, discourse cues did not turn out to be useful for this task and even negatively affected the results which we explain by the extremely sparseness of the cues in our data.

It turned out that the best results could be achieved by a combination of surface features (*relPos, word1, word2*) and features capturing text cohesion. This indicates that paragraph boundary identification requires features usually used for style analysis and ones describing cohesive relations. Therefore, paragraph boundary identification is in fact a task which crosses the borders between content and style.

An obvious limitation of our study is that we trained and tested the algorithm on one-genre domain where pronouns are used extensively. Experimenting with different genres should shed light on whether our features are in fact domain-dependent. In the future, we also want to experiment with a larger data set for determining whether discourse cues really do not correlate with paragraph boundaries. Then, we will move on towards multi-document summarization, the application which motivates the research described here.

Acknowledments: This work has been funded by the Klaus Tschira Foundation, Heidelberg, Germany. The first author has been supported by a KTF grant (09.009.2004). We would also like to thank the three anonymous reviewers for their comments.

References

Bolshakov, Igor A. & Alexander Gelbukh (2001). Text segmentation into paragraph based on local text cohesion. In *Text, Speech and Dialogue*, pp. 158–166.

Brants, Thorsten (2000). TnT – A statistical Part-of-Speech tagger. In *Proceedings of the 6th Conference on Applied Natural Language Processing,* Seattle, Wash., 29 April – 4 May 2000, pp. 224–231.

Choi, Freddy Y. Y. (2000). Advances in domain independent linear text segmentation. In *Pro-*

ceedings of the 1st Conference of the North American Chapter of the Association for Computational Linguistics, Seattle, Wash., 29 April – 3 May, 2000, pp. 26–33.

Clarkson, Philip & Roni Rosenfeld (1997). Statistical language modeling. In *Proceedings of ESCA, EuroSpeech'97.* Rhodes, pp. 2707–2710.

Daelemans, Walter, Jakub Zavrel, Ko van der Sloot & Antal van den Bosch (2004). *TiMBL: Tilburg Memory Based Learner, version 5.1, Reference Guide.* Technical Report ILK 04-02: ILK Tilburg.

Foth, Kilian & Wolfgang Menzel (2006). Robust parsing: More with less. In *Proceedings of the 11th Conference of the European Chapter of the Association for Computational Linguistics,* Trento, Italy, 3–7 April 2006, pp. 25–32.

Galley, Michel, Kathleen R. McKeown, Eric Fosler-Lussier & Hongyan Jing (2003). Discourse segmentation of multi-party conversation. In *Proceedings of the 41st Annual Meeting of the Association for Computational Linguistics,* Sapporo, Japan, 7–12 July 2003, pp. 562–569.

Genzel, Dmitriy (2005). A paragraph boundary detection system. In *Proceedings of the Sixth International Conference on Intelligent Text Processing and Computational Linguistics,* Mexico City, Mexico.

Genzel, Dmitriy & Eugene Charniak (2003). Variation of entropy and parse trees of sentences as a function of the sentence number. In *Proceedings of the 2003 Conference on Empirical Methods in Natural Language Processing,* Sapporo, Japan, 11–12 July 2003, pp. 65–72.

Hearst, Marti A. (1997). TextTiling: Segmenting text into multi-paragraph subtopic passages. *Computational Linguistics*, 23(1):33–64.

Irmscher, William F. (1972). *The Holt Guide to English.* New-York: Holt, Rinehart Winston.

Kohavi, Ron & George H. John (1997). Wrappers for feature subset selection. *Artificial Intelligence Journal*, 97(1-2):273–324.

Mann, William C. & Sandra A. Thompson (1988). Rhetorical structure theory. Toward a functional theory of text organization. *Text*, 8(3):243–281.

Marciniak, Tomacz & Michael Strube (2005). Beyond the pipeline: Discrete optimization in NLP. In *Proceedings of the 9th Conference on Computational Natural Language Learning,* Ann Arbor, Mich., USA, 29–30 June 2005, pp. 136–145.

Pevzner, Lev & Marti Hearst (2002). A critique and improvement of an evaluation metric for text segmentation. *Computational Linguistics*, 28(1):19–36.

Power, Richard, Donia Scott & Nadjet Bouayad-Agha (2003). Document structure. *Computational Linguistics*, 29(2):211–260.

Roth, Dan & Wen-tau Yih (2004). A linear programming formulation for global inference in natural language tasks. In *Proceedings of the 8th Conference on Computational Natural Language Learning,* Boston, Mass., USA, 6–7 May 2004, pp. 1–8.

Schapire, Robert E. & Yoram Singer (2000). BoosTexter: A boosting-based system for text categorization. *Machine Learning*, 39(2/3):135–168.

Schmid, Helmut (1997). Probabilistic part-of-speech tagging using decision trees. In Daniel Jones & Harold Somers (Eds.), *New Methods in Language Processing*, pp. 154–164. London, UK: UCL Press.

Sporleder, Caroline & Mirella Lapata (2004). Automatic paragraph identification: A study across languages and domains. In *Proceedings of the 2004 Conference on Empirical Methods in Natural Language Processing,* Barcelona, Spain, 25–26 July 2004, pp. 72–79.

Sporleder, Caroline & Mirella Lapata (2006). Broad coverage paragraph segmentation across languages and domains. *ACM Transactions in Speech and Language Processing*. To appear.

Stark, Heather (1988). What do paragraph markings do? *Discourse Processes*, (11):275–303.

BESTCUT: A Graph Algorithm for Coreference Resolution

Cristina Nicolae and Gabriel Nicolae
Human Language Technology Research Institute
Department of Computer Science
University of Texas at Dallas
Richardson, TX 75083-0688
{cristina, gabriel}@hlt.utdallas.edu

Abstract

In this paper we describe a coreference resolution method that employs a classification and a clusterization phase. In a novel way, the clusterization is produced as a graph cutting algorithm, in which nodes of the graph correspond to the mentions of the text, whereas the edges of the graph constitute the confidences derived from the coreference classification. In experiments, the graph cutting algorithm for coreference resolution, called BESTCUT, achieves state-of-the-art performance.

1 Introduction

Recent coreference resolution algorithms tackle the problem of identifying coreferent mentions of the same entity in text as a two step procedure: (1) a classification phase that decides whether pairs of noun phrases corefer or not; and (2) a clusterization phase that groups together all mentions that refer to the same entity. An **entity** is an object or a set of objects in the real world, while a **mention** is a textual reference to an entity[1]. Most of the previous coreference resolution methods have similar classification phases, implemented either as decision trees (Soon et al., 2001) or as maximum entropy classifiers (Luo et al., 2004). Moreover, these methods employ similar feature sets. The clusterization phase is different across current approaches. For example, there are several linking decisions for clusterization. (Soon et al., 2001) advocate the link-first decision, which links a mention to its closest candidate referent, while (Ng and Cardie, 2002) consider instead the link-best decision, which links a mention to its most confident candidate referent. Both these clustering decisions are locally optimized. In contrast, globally optimized clustering decisions were reported in (Luo et al., 2004) and (DaumeIII and Marcu, 2005a), where all clustering possibilities are considered by searching on a Bell tree representation or by using the *Learning as Search Optimization (LaSO)* framework (DaumeIII and Marcu, 2005b) respectively, but the first search is partial and driven by heuristics and the second one only looks back in text. We argue that a more adequate clusterization phase for coreference resolution can be obtained by using a graph representation.

In this paper we describe a novel representation of the coreference space as an undirected edge-weighted graph in which the nodes represent all the mentions from a text, whereas the edges between nodes constitute the confidence values derived from the coreference classification phase. In order to detect the entities referred in the text, we need to partition the graph such that all nodes in each subgraph refer to the same entity. We have devised a graph partitioning method for coreference resolution, called BESTCUT, which is inspired from the well-known graph-partitioning algorithm Min-Cut (Stoer and Wagner, 1994). BESTCUT has a different way of computing the cut weight than Min-Cut and a different way of stopping the cut[2]. Moreover, we have slightly modified the Min-Cut procedures. BESTCUT replaces the bottom-up search in a tree representation (as it was performed in (Luo et al., 2004)) with the top-down problem of obtaining the best partitioning of a graph. We start by assuming that all mentions refer to a single entity; the graph cut splits the mentions into subgraphs and the split-

[1]This definition was introduced in (NIST, 2003).

[2]Whenever a graph is split in two subgraphs, as defined in (Cormen et al., 2001), a cut of the graph is produced.

Proceedings of the 2006 Conference on Empirical Methods in Natural Language Processing (EMNLP 2006), pages 275–283,
Sydney, July 2006.

ting continues until each subgraph corresponds to one of the entities. The cut stopping decision has been implemented as an SVM-based classification (Cortes and Vapnik, 1995).

The classification and clusterization phases assume that all mentions are detected. In order to evaluate our coreference resolution method, we have (1) implemented a mention detection procedure that has the novelty of employing information derived from the word senses of common nouns as well as selected lexico-syntactic information; and (2) used a maximum entropy model for coreference classification. The experiments conducted on MUC and ACE data indicate state-of-the-art results when compared with the methods reported in (Ng and Cardie, 2002) and (Luo et al., 2004).

The remainder of the paper is organized as follows. In Section 2 we describe the coreference resolution method that uses the BESTCUT clusterization; Section 3 describes the approach we have implemented for detecting mentions in texts; Section 4 reports on the experimental results; Section 5 discusses related work; finally, Section 6 summarizes the conclusions.

2 BESTCUT Coreference Resolution

For each entity type (PERSON, ORGANIZATION, LOCATION, FACILITY or GPE[3]) we create a graph in which the nodes represent all the mentions of that type in the text, the edges correspond to all pairwise coreference relations, and the edge weights are the confidences of the coreference relations. We will divide this graph repeatedly by cutting the links between subgraphs until a stop model previously learned tells us that we should stop the cutting. The end result will be a partition that approximates the correct division of the text into entities.

We consider this graph approach to clustering a more accurate representation of the relations between mentions than a tree-based approach that treats only anaphora resolution, trying to connect mentions with candidate referents that appear in text before them. We believe that a correct resolution has to tackle cataphora resolution as well, by taking into account referents that appear in the text after the anaphors. Furthermore, we believe that a graph representation of mentions in a text is more adequate than a tree representation because the coreference relation is symmetrical in addition to being transitive. A greedy bottom-up approach does not make full use of this property. A graph-based clusterization starts with a complete overall view of all the connections between mentions, therefore local errors are much less probable to influence the correctness of the outcome. If two mentions are strongly connected, and one of them is strongly connected with the third, all three of them will most probably be clustered together even if the third edge is not strong enough, and that works for any order in which the mentions might appear in the text.

[3]Entity types as defined by (NIST, 2003).

2.1 Learning Algorithm

The coreference confidence values that become the weights in the starting graphs are provided by a maximum entropy model, trained on the training datasets of the corpora used in our experiments. For maximum entropy classification we used a *maxent*[4] tool. Based on the data seen, a maximum entropy model (Berger et al., 1996) offers an expression (1) for the probability that there exists coreference C between a mention m_i and a mention m_j.

$$P(C|m_i, m_j) = \frac{e^{(\sum_k \lambda_k g_k(m_i, m_j, C))}}{Z(m_i, m_j)} \quad (1)$$

where $g_k(m_i, m_j, C)$ is a feature and λ_k is its weight; $Z(m_i, m_j)$ is a normalizing factor.

We created the training examples in the same way as (Luo et al., 2004), by pairing all mentions of the same type, obtaining their feature vectors and taking the outcome (coreferent/non-coreferent) from the key files.

2.2 Feature Representation

We duplicated the statistical model used by (Luo et al., 2004), with three differences. First, no feature combination was used, to prevent long running times on the large amount of ACE data. Second, through an analysis of the validation data, we implemented seven new features, presented in Table 1. Third, as opposed to (Luo et al., 2004), who represented all numerical features quantized, we translated each numerical feature into a set of binary features that express whether the value is in certain intervals. This transformation was necessary because our maximum entropy tool performs better on binary features. (Luo et al., 2004)'s features were not reproduced here from lack of space; please refer to the relevant paper for details.

[4]http://homepages.inf.ed.ac.uk/s0450736/maxent_toolkit.html

Category	*Feature name*	*Feature description*
lexical	*head-match*	**true** if the two heads are identical
	type-pair	for each mention: name → its type, noun → _NOUN_, pronoun → its spelling
	name-alias	**true** if a mention is an alias of the other one
syntactic	*same-governing-category*	**true** if both mentions are covered by the same type of node, e.g. NP, VP, PP
	path	the parse tree path from m_2 to m_1
	coll-comm	**true** if either mention collocates with a communication verb
grammatical	*gn-agree*	**true** if the two mentions agree in gender and number

Table 1: The added features for the coreference model.

2.3 Clusterization Method: BESTCUT

We start with five initial graphs, one for each entity type, each containing all the mentions of that type and their weighted connections. This initial division is correct because no mentions of different entity types will corefer. Furthermore, by doing this division we avoid unnecessary confusion in the program's decisions and we decrease its running time. Each of these initial graphs will be cut repeatedly until the resulting partition is satisfactory. In each cut, we eliminate from the graph the edges between subgraphs that have a very weak connection, and whose mentions are most likely not part of the same entity.

Formally, the graph model can be defined as follows. Let $M = \{m_i : 1..n\}$ be n mentions in the document and $E = \{e_j : 1..m\}$ be m entities. Let $g : M \rightarrow E$ be the map from a mention $m_i \in M$ to an entity $e_j \in E$. Let $c : M\text{x}M \rightarrow [0,1]$ be the confidence the learning algorithm attaches to the coreference between two mentions $m_i, m_j \in M$. Let $T = \{t_k : 1..p\}$ be the set of entity types or classes. Then we attach to each entity class t_k an undirected, edge-weighted graph $G_k(V_k, E_k)$, where $V_k = \{m_i | g(m_i).type = t_k\}$ and $E_k = \{(m_i, m_j, c(m_i, m_j)) | m_i, m_j \in V_k\}$.

The partitioning of the graph is based at each step on the cut weight. As a starting point, we used the Min-Cut algorithm, presented and proved correct in (Stoer and Wagner, 1994). In this simple and efficient method, the weight of the cut of a graph into two subgraphs is the sum of the weights of the edges crossing the cut. The partition that minimizes the cut weight is the one chosen. The main procedure of the algorithm computes cuts-of-the-phase repeatedly and selects the one with the minimum cut value (cut weight). We adapted this algorithm to our coreference situation.

To decide the minimum cut (from here on called the BESTCUT), we use as cut weight the number of mentions that are correctly placed in their set. The method for calculating the correctness score is presented in Figure 1. The BESTCUT at one stage is the cut-of-the-phase with the highest correctness score.

```
cut-weight(Graph G, Cut C = (S,T))
corrects-avg ← corrects-max ← 0
foreach m ∈ G.V
  if m ∈ S.V then setm ← S
  else setm ← T
  if avg_{n∈setm.V,n≠m} weight(m,n) >
       avg_{n∈G.V\setm.V} weight(m,n)
  then corrects-avg++
  if max_{n∈setm.V,n≠m} weight(m,n) >
       max_{n∈G.V\setm.V} weight(m,n)
  then corrects-max++
return (corrects-avg +
        corrects-max) / 2
```

Figure 1: Computing the cut-weight.

An additional learning model was trained to decide if cutting a set of mentions is better or worse than keeping the mentions together. The model was optimized to maximize the ECM-F score[5]. We will denote by S the larger part of the cut and T the smaller one. $C.E$ is the set of edges crossing the cut, and G is the current graph before the cut. $S.V$ and $T.V$ are the set of vertexes in S and in T, respectively. $S.E$ is the set of edges from S, while $T.E$ is the set of edges from T. The features for stopping the cut are presented in Table 2. The model was trained using 10-fold cross-validation on the training set. In order to learn when to stop the cut, we generated a list of positive and negative examples from the training files. Each training example is associated with a certain cut (S, T). Since we want to learn a stop function, the positive examples must be examples that describe when the cut must not be done, and the negative examples are examples that present situations when the cut must be performed. Let us consider that the list of entities from a text is $E = \{e_j : 1..m\}$ with $e_j = \{m_{i_1}, m_{i_2}, ...m_{i_k}\}$ the list of mentions that refer to e_j. We generated a negative example for each pair $(S = \{e_i\}, T = \{e_j\})$ with $i \neq j$ – each entity must be separated from any other en-

[5]As introduced by (Luo et al., 2004).

Feature name	*Feature description*
st-ratio	$\lvert S.V\rvert/\lvert T.V\rvert$ – the ratio between the cut parts
ce-ratio	$\lvert C.E\rvert/\lvert G.E\rvert$ – the proportion of the cut from the entire graph
c-min	$min(C.E)$ – the smallest edge crossing the cut
c-max	$max(C.E)$ – the largest edge crossing the cut
c-avg	$avg(C.E)$ – the average of the edges crossing the cut
c-hmean	$hmean(C.E)$ – the harmonic mean of the edges crossing the cut
c-hmeax	$hmeax(C.E)$ – a variant of the harmonic mean. $hmeax(C.E) = 1 - hmean(C.E')$ where each edge from E' has the weight equal to 1 minus the corresponding edge from E
lt-c-avg-ratio	how many edges from the cut are less than the average of the cut (as a ratio)
lt-c-hmean-ratio	how many edges from the cut are less than the harmonic mean of the cut (as a ratio)
st-avg	$avg(S.E + T.E)$ – the average of the edges from the graph when the edges from the cut are not considered
g-avg	$avg(G.E)$ – the average of the edges from the graph
st-wrong-avg-ratio	how many vertexes are in the wrong part of the cut using the average measure for the 'wrong' (as a ratio)
st-wrong-max-ratio	how many vertexes are in the wrong part of the cut using the max measure for the 'wrong' (as a ratio)
lt-c-avg-ratio $<$ *st-lt-c-avg-ratio*	1 if $r_1 < r_2$, 0 otherwise; r_1 is the ratio of the edges from $C.E$ that are smaller than the average of the cut; r_2 is the ratio of the edges from $S.E + T.E$ that are smaller than the average of the cut
g-avg $>$ *st-avg*	1 if the $avg(G.E) > avg(S.E + T.E)$, and 0 otherwise

Table 2: The features for stopping the cut.

tity. We also generated negative examples for all pairs $(S = \{e_i\}, T = E \setminus S)$ – each entity must be separated from all the other entities considered together. To generate positive examples, we simulated the cut on a graph corresponding to a single entity e_j. Every partial cut of the mentions of e_j was considered as a positive example for our stop model.

We chose not to include pronouns in the BESTCUT initial graphs, because, since most features are oriented towards Named Entities and common nouns, the learning algorithm (*maxent*) links pronouns with very high probability to many possible antecedents, of which not all are in the same chain. Thus, in the clusterization phase the pronouns would act as a bridge between different entities that should not be linked. To prevent this, we solved the pronouns separately (at the end of

```
BESTCUT(Graph G_i)
1  entities.clear()
2  queue.push_back(G_i)
3  while not queue.empty()
4    G ← queue.pop_front()
5    (S,T) ← ProposeCut(G)
6    if StopTheCut(G,S,T)
7    then
8      entities.add(NewEntity(G))
9    else
10     queue.push_back(S)
11     queue.push_back(T)
12 return entities
```

Figure 2: The general algorithm for BESTCUT.

the BESTCUT algorithm) by linking them to their antecedent with the best coreference confidence.

Figure 2 details the main procedure of the BESTCUT algorithm. The algorithm receives as input a weighted graph having a vertex for each mention considered and outputs the list of entities created. In each stage, a cut is proposed for all subgraphs in the queue. In case StopTheCut decides that the cut must be performed on the subgraph, the two sides of the cut are added to the queue (lines 10-11); if the graph is well connected and breaking the graph in two parts would be a bad thing, the current graph will be used to create a single entity (line 8). The algorithm ends when the queue becomes empty. ProposeCut (Fig-

```
ProposeCut(Graph G)
while |G.V| > 1
  (S,T) ← ProposeCutPhase(G)
  if the cut-of-the-phase (S,T)
     is-lighter than the current
     best cut (S_b,T_b)
  then store the cut-of-the-phase
       as (S_b,T_b)
return (S_b,T_b)
```

Figure 3: The algorithm for ProposeCut.

ure 3) returns a cut of the graph obtained with an algorithm similar to the Min-Cut algorithm's procedure called MinimumCut. The differences between our algorithm and the Min-Cut procedure are that **the most tightly connected vertex** in each step of the ProposeCutPhase procedure, z, is found using expression 2:

$$z = argmax_{y \notin A} w_a(A, y) \quad (2)$$

where $w_a(A, y) = \frac{1}{|A|} \sum_{x \in A} w(x, y)$, and the **is-lighter** test function uses the correctness score presented before: the partial cut with the larger correctness score is better. The ProposeCutPhase function is presented in Figure 4.

```
ProposeCutPhase(Graph G)
A ← {G.V.first}
while |A| < |G.V|
  last ← the most tightly
        connected vertex
  add last to A
store the cut-of-the-phase and
  shrink G by merging the two
  vertexes added last
return (G.V \ {last}, last)
```

Figure 4: The algorithm for ProposeCutPhase.

2.4 An Example

Let us consider an example of how the BESTCUT algorithm works on two simple sentences (Figure 5). The entities present in this example are: $\{Mary_1$, *the* $girl_5\}$ and $\{a\ brother_2$, $John_3$, *The* $boy_4\}$. Since they are all PERSONs, the algorithm

Mary$_1$ *has* ***a brother***$_2$*,* ***John***$_3$*.* ***The boy***$_4$ *is older than* ***the girl***$_5$*.*

Figure 5: An example.

will be applied on a single graph, corresponding to the class PERSON and composed of all these mentions.

The initial graph is illustrated in Figure 6, with the coreference relation marked through a different coloring of the nodes. Each node number corresponds to the mention with the same index in Figure 5.

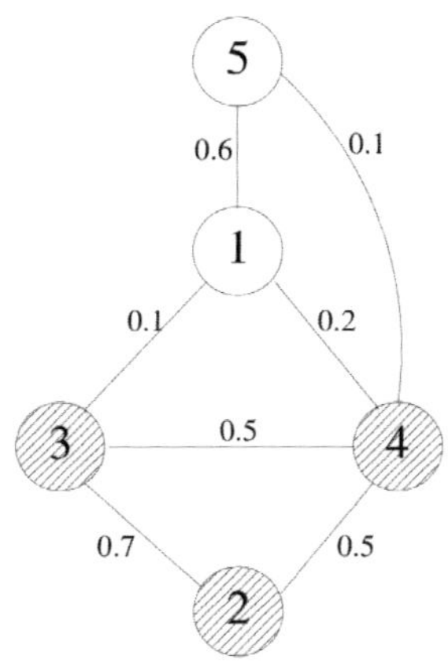

Figure 6: The initial graph

The strongest confidence score is between *a* $brother_2$ and $John_3$, because they are connected through an apposition relation. The graph was simplified by eliminating the edges that have an insignificant weight, e.g. the edges between $John_3$ and *the* $girl_5$ or between $Mary_1$ and *a* $brother_2$.

Function BESTCUT starts with the whole graph. The first cut of the phase, obtained by function ProposeCutPhase, is the one in Figure 7.a. This

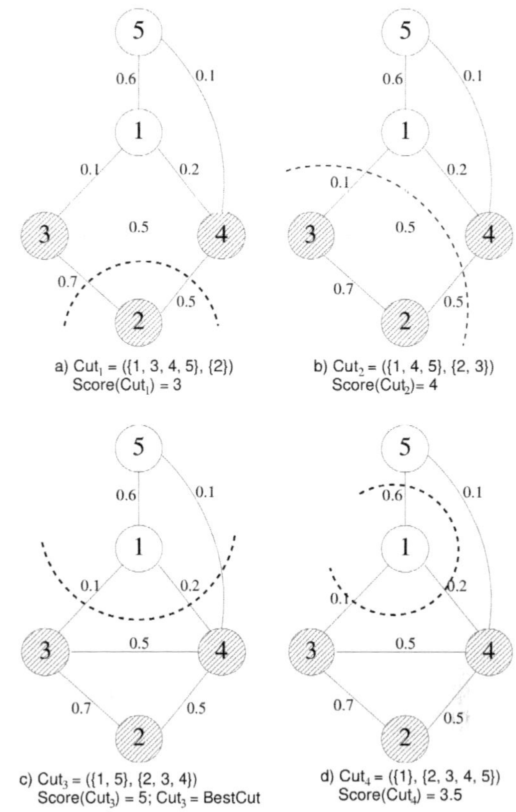

Figure 7: Cuts-of-the-phase

cut separates node 2 from the rest of the graph. In calculating the score of the cut (using the algorithm from Figure 1), we obtain an average number of three correctly placed mentions. This can be verified intuitively on the drawing: mentions 1, 2 and 5 are correctly placed, while 3 and 4 are not. The score of this cut is therefore 3. The second, the third and the fourth cuts of the phase, in Figures 7.b, 7.c and 7.d, have the scores 4, 5 and 3.5 respectively. An interesting thing to note at the fourth cut is that the score is no longer an integer. This happens because it is calculated as an average between *corrects-avg = 4* and *corrects-max = 3*. The methods disagree about the placement of mention 1. The average of the outgoing weights of mention 1 is 0.225, less than 0.5 (the default weight assigned to a single mention) therefore the first method declares it is correctly placed. The second considers only the maximum; 0.6 is greater than 0.5, so the mention appears to be more strongly connected with the outside than the inside. As we can see, the contradiction is because of the uneven distribution of the weights of the outgoing edges.

The first proposed cut is the cut with the great-

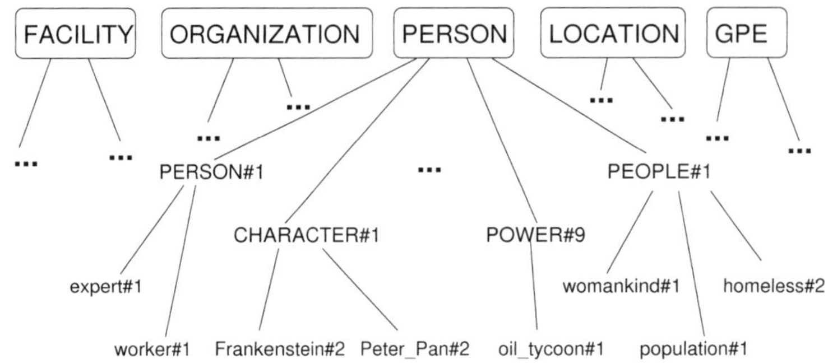

Figure 8: Part of the hierarchy containing 42 WordNet equivalent concepts for the five entity types, with all their synonyms and hyponyms. The hierarchy has 31,512 word-sense pairs in total

est score, which is Cut_3 (Figure 7.c). Because this is also the correct cut, all cuts proposed after this one will be ignored– the machine learning algorithm that was trained when to stop a cut will always declare against further cuts. In the end, the cut returned by function BESTCUT is the correct one: it divides mentions $Mary_1$ and *the* $girl_5$ from mentions *a* $brother_2$, $John_3$ and *The* boy_4.

3 Mention Detection

Because our BESTCUT algorithm relies heavily on knowing entity types, we developed a method for recognizing entity types for nominal mentions. Our statistical approach uses maximum entropy classification with a few simple lexical and syntactic features, making extensive use of WordNet (Fellbaum, 1998) hierarchy information. We used the ACE corpus, which is annotated with mention and entity information, as data in a supervised machine learning method to detect nominal mentions and their entity types. We assigned six entity types: PERSON, ORGANIZATION, LOCATION, FACILITY, GPE and UNK (for those who are in neither of the former categories) and two genericity outcomes: GENERIC and SPECIFIC. We only considered the intended value of the mentions from the corpus. This was motivated by the fact that we need to classify mentions according to the context in which they appear, and not in a general way. Only contextual information is useful further in coreference resolution. We have experimentally discovered that the use of word sense disambiguation improves the performance tremendously (a boost in score of 10%), therefore all the features use the word senses from a previously-applied word sense disambiguation program, taken from (Mihalcea and Csomai, 2005).

For creating training instances, we associated an outcome to each markable (NP) detected in the training files: the markables that were present in the key files took their outcome from the key file annotation, while all the other markables were associated with outcome UNK. We then created a training example for each of the markables, with the feature vector described below and as target function the outcome. The aforementioned outcome can be of three different types. The first type of outcome that we tried was the entity type (one member of the set PERSON, ORGANIZATION, LOCATION, FACILITY, GPE and UNK); the second type was the genericity information (GENERIC or SPECIFIC), whereas the third type was a combination between the two (pairwise combinations of the entity types set and the genericity set, e.g. PERSON_SPECIFIC).

The feature set consists of WordNet features, lexical features, syntactic features and intelligent context features, briefly described in Table 3. With the WordNet features we introduce the *WordNet equivalent concept*. A WordNet equivalent concept for an entity type is a word-sense pair from WordNet whose gloss is compatible with the definition of that entity type. Figure 8 enumerates a few WordNet equivalent concepts for entity class PERSON (e.g. CHARACTER#1), with their hierarchy of hyponyms (e.g. Frankenstein#2). The lexical feature is useful because some words are almost always of a certain type (e.g. *"company"*). The intelligent context set of features are an improvement on basic context features that use the stems of the words that are within a window of a certain size around the word. In addition to this set of features, we created more features by combining them into pairs. Each pair contains two features from two different classes. For instance, we will have features like: *is-a-*

Category	Feature name	Feature description
WordNet	is-a-TYPE	**true** if the mention is of entity type TYPE; five features
	WN-eq-concept-hyp	**true** if the mention is in hyponym set of WN-*eq-concept*; 42 features
	WN-eq-concept-syn	**true** if the mention is in synonym set of WN-*eq-concept*; 42 features
lexical	*stem-sense*	pair between the stem of the word and the WN sense of the word by the WSD
syntactic	*pos*	part of speech of the word by the POS tagger
	is-modifier	**true** if the mention is a modifier in another noun phrase
	*modifier-to-*TYPE	**true** if the mention is a modifier to a TYPE mention
	in-apposition-with	TYPE of the mention our mention is in apposition with
intelligent context	*all-mods*	the nominal, adjectival and pronominal modifiers in the mention's parse tree
	preps	the prepositions right before and after the mention's parse tree

Table 3: The features for the mention detection system.

PERSON~*in-apposition-with(*PERSON*)*.

All these features apply to the "true head" of a noun phrase, i.e. if the noun phrase is a partitive construction (*"five students"*, *"a lot of companies"*, *"a part of the country"*), we extract the "true head", the whole entity that the part was taken out of (*"students"*, *"companies"*, *"country"*), and apply the features to that "true head" instead of the partitive head.

For combining the mention detection module with the BESTCUT coreference resolver, we also generated classifications for Named Entities and pronouns by using the same set of features minus the WordNet ones (which only apply to nominal mentions). For the Named Entity classifier, we added the feature *Named-Entity-type* as obtained by the Named Entity Recognizer. We generated a list of all the markable mentions and their entity types and presented it as input to the BESTCUT resolver instead of the list of perfect mentions. Note that this mention detection does not contain complete anaphoricity information. Only the mentions that are a part of the five considered classes are treated as anaphoric and clustered, while the UNK mentions are ignored, even if an outside anaphoricity classifier might categorize some of them as anaphoric.

4 Experimental Results

The clusterization algorithms that we implemented to evaluate in comparison with our method are (Luo et al., 2004)'s Belltree and Link-Best (best-first clusterization) from (Ng and Cardie, 2002). The features used were described in section 2.2. We experimented on the ACE Phase 2 (NIST, 2003) and MUC6 (MUC-6, 1995) corpora. Since we aimed to measure the performance of coreference, the metrics used for evaluation are the ECM-F (Luo et al., 2004) and the MUC P, R and F scores (Vilain et al., 1995).

In our first experiment, we tested the three coreference clusterization algorithms on the development-test set of the ACE Phase 2 corpus, first on true mentions (i.e. the mentions annotated in the key files), then on detected mentions (i.e. the mentions output by our mention detection system presented in section 3) and finally without any prior knowledge of the mention types. The results obtained are tabulated in Table 4. As can be observed, when it has prior knowledge of the mention types BESTCUT performs significantly better than the other two systems in the ECM-F score and slightly better in the MUC metrics. The more knowledge it has about the mentions, the better it performs. This is consistent with the fact that the first stage of the algorithm divides the graph into subgraphs corresponding to the five entity types. If BESTCUT has no information about the mentions, its performance ranks significantly under the Link-Best and Belltree algorithms in ECM-F and MUC R. Surprisingly enough, the Belltree algorithm, a globally optimized algorithm, performs similarly to Link-Best in most of the scores.

Despite not being as dramatically affected as BESTCUT, the other two algorithms also decrease in performance with the decrease of the mention information available, which empirically proves that mention detection is a very important module for coreference resolution. Even with an F-score of 77.2% for detecting entity types, our mention detection system boosts the scores of all three algorithms when compared to the case where no information is available.

It is apparent that the MUC score does not vary significantly between systems. This only shows that none of them is particularly poor, but it is not a relevant way of comparing methods– the MUC metric has been found too indulgent by researchers ((Luo et al., 2004), (Baldwin et al., 1998)). The MUC scorer counts the common links between the

Clusterization algorithm	*Mentions*	ECM-F%	MUC *score*		
			MUC P%	MUC R%	MUC F%
BESTCUT	key	**82.7**	**91.1**	88.2	**89.63**
	detected	**73.0**	**88.3**	75.1	**81.17**
	undetected	41.2	**52.0**	82.4	**63.76**
Belltree (Luo et al., 2004)	key	77.9	88.5	89.3	88.90
	detected	70.8	86.0	76.6	81.03
	undetected	**52.6**	40.3	87.1	55.10
Link-Best (Ng and Cardie, 2002)	key	77.9	88.0	**90.0**	88.99
	detected	70.7	85.1	**77.3**	81.01
	undetected	51.6	39.6	**88.5**	54.72

Table 4: Comparison of results between three clusterization algorithms on ACE Phase 2. The learning algorithms are *maxent* for coreference and SVM for stopping the cut in BESTCUT. In turn, we obtain the mentions from the key files, detect them with our mention detection algorithm or do not use any information about them.

annotation keys and the system output, while the ECM-F metric aligns the detected entities with the key entities so that the number of common mentions is maximized. The ECM-F scorer overcomes two shortcomings of the MUC scorer: not considering single mentions and treating every error as equally important (Baldwin et al., 1998), which makes the ECM-F a more adequate measure of coreference.

Our second experiment evaluates the impact that the different categories of our added features have on the performance of the BESTCUT system. The experiment was performed with a maxent classifier on the MUC6 corpus, which was priorly converted into ACE format, and employed mention information from the key annotations.

Model	ECM-F%	MUC *score*		
		P%	R%	F%
baseline	78.3	89.5	91.5	90.49
+grammatical	78.4	89.2	92.5	90.82
+lexical	83.1	92.4	91.6	92.00
+syntactic	**85.1**	**92.7**	**92.4**	**92.55**

Table 5: Impact of feature categories on BESTCUT on MUC6. Baseline system has the (Luo et al., 2004) features. The system was tested on key mentions.

From Table 5 we can observe that the lexical features (*head-match*, *type-pair*, *name-alias*) have the most influence on the ECM-F and MUC scores, succeeded by the syntactic features (*same-governing-category*, *path*, *coll-comm*). Despite what intuition suggests, the improvement the grammatical feature *gn-agree* brings to the system is very small.

5 Related Work

It is of interest to discuss why our implementation of the Belltree system (Luo et al., 2004) is comparable in performance to Link-Best (Ng and Cardie, 2002). (Luo et al., 2004) do the clusterization through a beam-search in the Bell tree using either a mention-pair or an entity-mention model, the first one performing better in their experiments. Despite the fact that the Bell tree is a complete representation of the search space, the search in it is optimized for size and time, while potentially losing optimal solutions– similarly to a Greedy search. Moreover, the fact that the two implementations are comparable is not inconceivable once we consider that (Luo et al., 2004) never compared their system to another coreference resolver and reported their competitive results on true mentions only.

(Ng, 2005) treats coreference resolution as a problem of ranking candidate partitions generated by a set of coreference systems. The overall performance of the system is limited by the performance of its best component. The main difference between this approach and ours is that (Ng, 2005)'s approach takes coreference resolution one step further, by comparing the results of multiple systems, while our system is a single resolver; furthermore, he emphasizes the global optimization of ranking clusters obtained locally, whereas our focus is on globally optimizing the clusterization method inside the resolver.

(DaumeIII and Marcu, 2005a) use the *Learning as Search Optimization* framework to take into account the non-locality behavior of the coreference features. In addition, the researchers treat mention detection and coreference resolution as a joint problem, rather than a pipeline approach like we do. By doing so, it may be easier to detect the entity type of a mention once we have additional clues (expressed in terms of coreference features) about its possible antecedents. For example, labeling *Washington* as a PERSON is more probable after encountering *George Washington* previously in the text. However, the coreference problem does not immediately benefit from the joining.

6 Conclusions

We have proposed a novel coreference clusterization method that takes advantage of the efficiency and simplicity of graph algorithms. The approach is top-down and globally optimized, and takes into account cataphora resolution in addition to anaphora resolution. Our system compares favorably to two other implemented coreference systems and achieves state-of-the-art performance on the ACE Phase 2 corpus on true and detected mentions. We have also briefly described our mention detection system whose output we used in conjunction with the BESTCUT coreference system to achieve better results than when no mention information was available.

Acknowledgments

We would like to thank the three anonymous reviewers for their very helpful suggestions and comments on the early draft of our paper.

References

B. Baldwin, T. Morton, A. Bagga, J. Baldridge, R. Chandraseker, A. Dimitriadis, K. Snyder, and M. Wolska. 1998. Description of the university of pennsylvania camp system as used for coreference. In *Proceedings of the 7th Message Understanding Conference (MUC-7)*.

A. L. Berger, S. A. D. Pietra, and V. J. D. Pietra. 1996. A maximum entropy approach to natural language processing. *Computational Linguistics*, 1(22):39–71.

T. H. Cormen, C. E. Leiserson, R. L. Rivest, and C. Stein. 2001. *Introduction to Algorithms, Second Edition*. MIT.

C. Cortes and V. Vapnik. 1995. Support-vector networks. *Machine Learning*, 20(3):273–297.

H. DaumeIII and D. Marcu. 2005a. A large-scale exploration of effective global features for a joint entity detection and tracking model. pages 97–104, Vancouver.

H. DaumeIII and D. Marcu. 2005b. Learning as search optimization: Approximate large margin methods for structured prediction. In *The International Conference on Machine Learning (ICML)*.

C. Fellbaum, editor. 1998. *WordNet: An Electronic Lexical Database and Some of its Applications*. MIT Press.

X. Luo, A. Ittycheriah, H. Jing, N. Kambhatla, and S. Roukos. 2004. A mention-synchronous coreference resolution algorithm based on the bell tree. In *Proceedings of the 42nd Meeting of the Association for Computational Linguistics*, Barcelona, Spain.

R. Mihalcea and A. Csomai. 2005. Senselearner: Word sense disambiguation for all words in unrestricted text. In *Proceedings of the 43rd Meeting of the Association for Computational Linguistics*, Ann Arbor, MI.

MUC-6. 1995. Coreference task definition.

V. Ng and C. Cardie. 2002. Improving machine learning approaches to coreference resolution. In *Proceedings of the 40th Meeting of the Association for Computational Linguistics*, Philadelphia, Pennsylvania.

V. Ng. 2004. Learning noun phrase anaphoricity to improve conference resolution: Issues in representation and optimization. In *Proceedings of the 42nd Meeting of the Association for Computational Linguistics*, Barcelona, Spain.

V. Ng. 2005. Machine learning for coreference resolution: From local classification to global ranking. In *Proceedings of the 43rd Meeting of the Association for Computational Linguistics*, pages 157–164, Ann Arbor, MI.

NIST. 2003. Entity detection and tracking - phase 1; edt and metonymy annotation guidelines. version 2.5.1 20030502.

M. Pasca and S. Harabagiu. 2001. High performance question/answering. In *Proceedings of the 24th Annual International ACM SIGIR Conference on Research and Development in Information Retrieval*, pages 366–374, New Orleans, LA.

W. M. Soon, H. T. Ng, and D. C. Y. Lim. 2001. A machine learning approach to coreference resolution of noun phrases. *Computational Linguistics*, 4(27):521–544.

M. Stoer and F. Wagner. 1994. A simple min cut algorithm. In Jan van Leeuwen, editor, *Proceedings of the 1994 European Symposium on Algorithms*, pages 141–147, New York. Springer-Verlag.

M. Vilain, J.Burger, J. Aberdeen, D. Connolly, and L. Hirschman. 1995. A model-theoretic coreference scoring scheme. In *Proceedings of the Sixth Message Understanding Conference (MUC-6)*, pages 45–52.

Automatic Construction of Predicate-argument Structure Patterns for Biomedical Information Extraction

Akane Yakushiji[*†] **Yusuke Miyao**[*] **Tomoko Ohta**[*] **Yuka Tateisi**[*‡] **Jun'ichi Tsujii**[*§]
[*] Department of Computer Science, University of Tokyo
Hongo 7-3-1, Bunkyo-ku, Tokyo 113-0033 JAPAN
[§] School of Informatics, University of Manchester
POBox 88, Sackville St, MANCHESTER M60 1QD, UK
{akane, yusuke, okap, yucca, tsujii}@is.s.u-tokyo.ac.jp

Abstract

This paper presents a method of automatically constructing information *extraction patterns* on predicate-argument structures (PASs) obtained by full parsing from a smaller training corpus. Because PASs represent generalized structures for syntactical variants, patterns on PASs are expected to be more generalized than those on surface words. In addition, patterns are divided into components to improve recall and we introduce a Support Vector Machine to learn a prediction model using pattern matching results. In this paper, we present experimental results and analyze them on how well protein-protein interactions were extracted from MEDLINE abstracts. The results demonstrated that our method improved accuracy compared to a machine learning approach using surface word/part-of-speech patterns.

1 Introduction

One primitive approach to Information Extraction (IE) is to manually craft numerous extraction patterns for particular applications and this is presently one of the main streams of biomedical IE (Blaschke and Valencia, 2002; Koike et al., 2003). Although such IE attempts have demonstrated near-practical performance, the same sets of patterns cannot be applied to different kinds of information. A real-world task requires several kinds of IE, thus manually engineering extraction patterns, which is tedious and time-consuming process, is not really practical.

Techniques based on machine learning (Zhou et al., 2005; Hao et al., 2005; Bunescu and Mooney, 2006) are expected to alleviate this problem in manually crafted IE. However, in most cases, the cost of manually crafting patterns is simply transferred to that for constructing a large amount of training data, which requires tedious amount of manual labor to annotate text.

To systematically reduce the necessary amount of training data, we divided the task of constructing extraction patterns into a subtask that general natural language processing techniques can solve and a subtask that has specific properties according to the information to be extracted. The former subtask is of full parsing (i.e. recognizing syntactic structures of sentences), and the latter subtask is of constructing specific extraction patterns (i.e. finding clue words to extract information) based on the obtained syntactic structures.

We adopted full parsing from various levels of parsing, because we believe that it offers the best utility to generalize sentences into normalized syntactic relations. We also divided patterns into components to improve recall and we introduced machine learning with a Support Vector Machine (SVM) to learn a prediction model using the matching results of extraction patterns. As an actual IE task, we extracted pairs of interacting protein names from biomedical text.

2 Full Parsing

2.1 Necessity for Full Parsing

A technique that many previous approaches have used is shallow parsing (Koike et al., 2003; Yao et al., 2004; Zhou et al., 2005). Their assertion is

Current Affiliation:
† FUJITSU LABORATORIES LTD.
‡ Faculty of Informatics, Kogakuin University

Proceedings of the 2006 Conference on Empirical Methods in Natural Language Processing (EMNLP 2006), pages 284–292,
Sydney, July 2006.

Distance	Count	(%)	Sum (%)
−1	54	5.0	5.0
0	8	0.7	5.7
1	170	15.7	21.4
2–5	337	31.1	52.5
6–10	267	24.6	77.1
11–	248	22.9	100.0

Distance −1 means protein word has been annotated as interacting with itself (e.g. "actin polymerization"). Distance 0 means words of the interacting proteins are directly next to one another. Multi-word protein names are concatenated as long as they do not cross tags to annotate proteins.

Table 1: Distance between Interacting Proteins

that shallow parsers are more robust and would be sufficient for IE. However, their claims that shallow parsers are sufficient, or that full parsers do not contribute to application tasks, have not been fully proved by experimental results.

Zhou et al. (2005) argued that most information useful for IE derived from full parsing was shallow. However, they only used dependency trees and paths on full parse trees in their experiment. Such structures did not include information of semantic subjects/objects, which full parsing can recognize. Additionally, most relations they extracted from the ACE corpus (Linguistic Data Consortium, 2005) on broadcasts and newswires were within very short word-distance (70% where two entities are embedded in each other or separated by at most one word), and therefore shallow information was beneficial. However, Table 1 shows that the word distance is long between interacting protein names annotated on the AImed corpus (Bunescu and Mooney, 2004), and we have to treat long-distance relations for information like protein-protein interactions.

Full parsing is more effective for acquiring generalized data from long-length words than shallow parsing. The sentences at left in Figure 1 exemplify the advantages of full parsing. The gerund "activating" in the last sentence takes a non-local semantic subject "*ENTITY1*", and shallow parsing cannot recognize this relation because "*ENTITY1*" and "activating" are in different phrases. Full parsing, on the other hand, can identify both the subject of the whole sentence and the semantic subject of "activating" have been shared.

2.2 Predicate-argument Structures

We applied Enju (Tsujii Laboratory, 2005a) as a full parser which outputs predicate-argument structures (PASs). PASs are well normalized forms that represent syntactic relations. Enju is based on Head-driven Phrase Structure Grammar (Sag and Wasow, 1999), and it has been trained on the Penn Treebank (PTB) (Marcus et al., 1994) and a biomedical corpus, the GENIA Treebank (GTB) (Tsujii Laboratory, 2005b). We used a part-of-speech (POS) tagger trained on the GENIA corpus (Tsujii Laboratory, 2005b) as a preprocessor for Enju. On predicate-argument relations, Enju achieved 88.0% precision and 87.2% recall on PTB, and 87.1% precision and 85.4% recall on GTB.

The illustration at right in Figure 1 is a PAS example, which represents the relation between "activate", "*ENTITY1*" and "*ENTITY2*" of all sentences to the left. The predicate and its arguments are words converted to their base forms, augmented by their POSs. The arrows denote the connections from predicates to their arguments and the types of arguments are indicated as arrow labels, i.e., ARGn ($n = 1, 2, \ldots$), MOD. For example, the semantic subject of a transitive verb is ARG1 and the semantic object is ARG2.

What is important here is, thanks to the strong normalization of syntactic variations, that we can expect that the construction algorithm for extracting patterns that works on PASs will need a much smaller training corpus than those working on surface-word sequences. Furthermore, because of the reduced diversity of surface-word sequences at the PAS level, any IE system at this level should demonstrate improved recall.

3 Related Work

Sudo et al. (2003), Culotta and Sorensen (2004) and Bunescu and Mooney (2005) acquired substructures derived from dependency trees as extraction patterns for IE in general domains. Their approaches were similar to our approach using PASs derived from full parsing. However, one problem with their systems is that they could not treat non-local dependencies such as semantic subjects of gerund constructions (discussed in Section 2), and thus rules acquired from the constructions were partial.

Bunescu and Mooney (2006) also learned extraction patterns for protein-protein interactions by SVM with a generalized subsequence kernel. Their patterns are sequences of words, POSs, entity types, etc., and they heuristically restricted length and word positions of the patterns. Al-

ENTITY1 recognizes and **activates** *ENTITY2*.
ENTITY2 **activated** by *ENTITY1* are not well characterized.
The herpesvirus encodes a functional *ENTITY1* that **activates** human *ENTITY2*.
ENTITY1 can functionally cooperate to synergistically **activate** *ENTITY2*.
The *ENTITY1* plays key roles by **activating** *ENTITY2*.

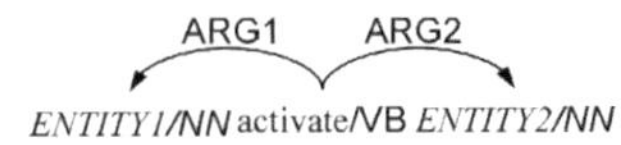

Figure 1: Syntactical Variations of "activate"

though they achieved about 60% precision and about 40% recall, these heuristic restrictions could not be guaranteed to be applied to other IE tasks.

Hao et al. (2005) learned extraction patterns for protein-protein interactions as sequences of words, POSs, entity tags and gaps by dynamic programming, and reduced/merged them using a minimum description length-based algorithm. Although they achieved 79.8% precision and 59.5% recall, sentences in their test corpus have too many positive instances and some of the patterns they claimed to have been successfully constructed went against linguistic or biomedical intuition. (e.g. "*ENTITY1* and interacts with *ENTITY2*" should be replaced by a more general pattern because they aimed to reduce the number of patterns.)

4 Method

We automatically construct patterns to extract protein-protein interactions from an annotated training corpus. The corpus needs to be tagged to denote which protein words are interacting pairs.

We follow five steps in constructing extraction patterns from the training corpus. (1) Sentences in the training corpus are parsed into PASs and we extract raw patterns from the PASs. (2) We divide the raw patterns to generate both *combination* and *fragmental patterns.* Because obtained patterns include inappropriate ones (wrongly generated or too general), (3) we apply both kinds of patterns to PASs of sentences in the training corpus, (4) calculate the scores for matching results of combination patterns, and (5) make a prediction model with SVM using these matching results and scores.

We extract pairs of interacting proteins from a target text in the actual IE phase, in three steps. (1) Sentences in the target corpus are parsed into PASs. (2) We apply both kinds of extraction patterns to these PASs and (3) calculate scores for combination pattern matching. (4) We use the prediction model to predict interacting pairs.

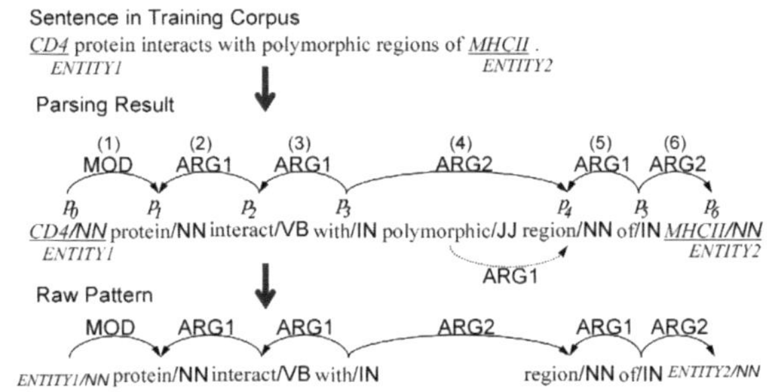

Figure 2: Extraction of Raw Pattern

4.1 Full Parsing and Extraction of Raw Patterns

As the first step in both the construction phase and application phase of extraction patterns, we parse sentences into PASs using Enju.[1] We label all PASs of the protein names as protein PASs.

After parsing, we extract the smallest set of PASs, which *connect* words that denote interacting proteins, and make it a raw pattern. We take the same method to extract and refine raw patterns as Yakushiji et al. (2005). *Connecting* means we can trace predicate-argument relations from one protein word to the other in an interacting pair. The procedure to obtain a raw pattern $(p_0, \ldots, p_n)$ is as follows:

$predicate(p)$: PASs that have p as their argument
$argument(p)$: PASs that p has as its arguments

1. $p_i = p_0$ is the PAS of a word correspondent to one of interacting proteins, and we obtain candidates of the raw pattern as follows:
   - 1-1. If p_i is of the word of the other interacting protein, $(p_0, \ldots, p_i)$ is a candidate of the raw pattern.
   - 1-2. If not, make pattern candidates for each $p_{i+1} \in predicate(p_i) \cup argument(p_i) - \{p_0, \ldots, p_i\}$ by returning to 1-1.
2. Select the pattern candidate of the smallest set as the raw pattern.

[1]Before parsing, we concatenate each multi-word protein name into the one word as long as the concatenation does not cross name boundaries.

3. Substitute variables (*ENTITY1*, *ENTITY2*) for the predicates of PASs correspondent to the interacting proteins.

The lower part of Figure 2 shows an example of the extraction of a raw pattern. "*CD4*" and "*MHCII*" are words representing interacting proteins. First, we set the PAS of "*CD4*" as p_0. $argument(p_0)$ includes the PAS of "protein", and we set it as p_1 (in other words, tracing the arrow (1)). Next, $predicate(p_1)$ includes the PAS of "interact" (tracing the arrow (2) back), so we set it as p_2. We continue similarly until we reach the PAS of "*MHCII*" (p_6). The result of the extracted raw pattern is the set of $p_0, \ldots, p_6$ with substituting variables *ENTITY1* and *ENTITY2* for "*CD4*" and "*MHCII*".

There are some cases where an extracted raw pattern is not appropriate and we need to refine it. One case is when unnecessary coordinations/parentheses are included in the pattern, e.g. two interactions are described in a combined representation ("*ENTITY1* binds this protein and *ENTITY2*"). Another is when two interacting proteins are connected directly by a conjunction or only one protein participates in an interaction. In such cases, we refine patterns by unfolding of coordinations/parentheses and extension of patterns, respectively. We have omitted detailed explanations because of space limitations. The details are described in the work of Yakushiji et al. (2005).

4.2 Division of Patterns

Division for generating combination patterns is based on observation of Yakushiji et al. (2005) that there are many cases where combinations of verbs and certain nouns form IE patterns. In the work of Yakushiji et al. (2005), we divided only patterns that include only one verb. We have extended the division process to also treat nominal patterns or patterns that include more than one verb.

Combination patterns are not appropriate for utilizing individual word information because they are always used in rather strictly combined ways. Therefore we have newly introduced fragmental patterns which consist of independent PASs from raw patterns, in order to use individual word information for higher recall.

4.2.1 Division for Generating Combination Patterns

Raw patterns are divided into some components and the components are combined to construct combination patterns according to types of the division. There are three types of division of raw patterns for generating combination patterns. These are:

(a) Two-entity Division
    (a-1) Entity-Main-Entity Division
    (a-2) Main-Entity-Entity Division
(b) Single-entity Division, and
(c) No Division (Naive Patterns).

Most raw patterns, where entities are at both ends of the patterns, are divided into Entity-Main-Entity. Main-Entity-Entity are for the cases where there are PASs other than entities at the ends of the patterns (e.g. "interaction between *ENTITY1* and *ENTITY2*"). Single-entity is a special Main-Entity-Entity for interactions with only one participant (e.g. "*ENTITY1* dimerization").

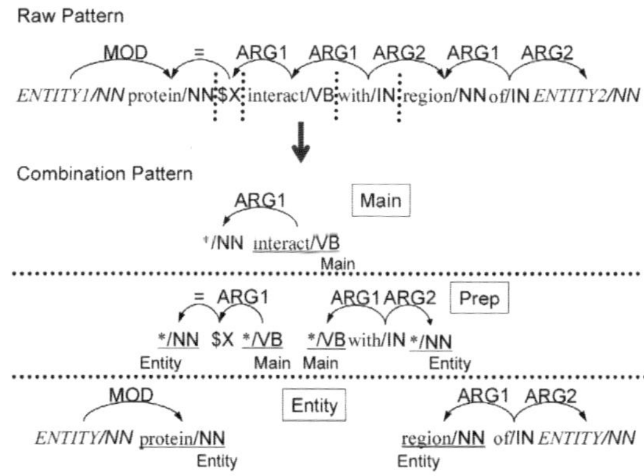

Figure 3: Division of Raw Pattern into Combination Pattern Components (Entity-Main-Entity)

There is an example of Entity-Main-Entity division in Figure 3. First, the *main component* from the raw pattern is the syntactic head PAS of the raw pattern. If the raw pattern corresponds to a sentence, the syntactic head PAS is the PAS of the main verb. We underspecify the arguments of the main component, to enable them to unify with the PASs of any words with the same POSs. Next, if there are PASs of prepositions connecting to the main component, they become *prep components*. If there is no PAS of a preposition next to the main component on the connecting link from the main component to an entity, we make the *pseudo PAS* of a *null preposition* the prep component. The left prep component ($X) in Figure 3 is a pseudo PAS of a null preposition. We also underspecify the arguments of prep components. Finally, the remaining two parts, which are typically noun phrases, of the raw pattern become *entity components*. PASs corresponding to the entities of the original pair are labeled as only unifiable with the entities of other pairs.

Main-Entity-Entity division is similar, except we distinguish only one prep component as a *double-prep component* and the PAS of the coordinate conjunction between entities becomes the *coord component*. Single-entity division is similar to Main-Entity-Entity division and the difference is that single-entity division produces no coord and one entity component. *Naive patterns* are patterns without division, where no division can be applied (e.g. "*ENTITY1/NN* in/IN complexes/NN with/IN *ENTITY2/NN*").

All PASs on boundaries of components are labeled to determine which PAS on a boundary of another component can be unified. Labels are represented by subscriptions in Figure 3. These restrictions on component connection are used in the step of constructing combination patterns.

Constructing combination patterns by combining components is equal to reconstructing original raw patterns with the original combination of components, or constructing new raw patterns with new combinations of components. For example, an Entity-Main-Entity pattern is constructed by combination of any main, any two prep and any two entity components. Actually, this construction process by combination is executed in the pattern matching step. That is, we do not off-line construct all possible combination patterns from the components and only construct the combination patterns that are able to match the target.

4.2.2 Division for Generating Fragmental Patterns

A raw pattern is splitted into individual PASs and each PAS becomes a fragmental pattern. We also prepare underspecified patterns where one or more of the arguments of the original are underspecified, i.e., are able to match any words of the same POSs and the same label of protein/not-protein. We underspecify the PASs of entities in fragmental patterns to enable them to unify with any PASs with the same POSs and a protein label, although in combination patterns we retain the PASs of entities as only unifiable with entities of pairs. This is because fragmental patterns are designed to be less strict than combination patterns.

4.3 Pattern Matching

Matching of combination patterns is executed as a process to match and combine combination pattern components according to their division types (Entity-Main-Entity, Main-Entity-Entity, Single-entity and No Division). Fragmental matching is matching all fragmental patterns to PASs derived from sentences.

4.4 Scoring for Combination Matching

We next calculate the score of each combination matching to estimate the adequacy of the combination of components. This is because new combination of components may form inadequate patterns. (e.g. "*ENTITY1* be *ENTITY2*" can be formed of components from "*ENTITY1* be *ENTITY2* receptor".) Scores are derived from the results of combination matching to the source training corpus.

We apply the combination patterns to the training corpus, and count pairs of True Positives (TP) and False Positives (FP). The scores are calculated basically by the following formula:

$$Score = TP/(TP + FP) + \alpha \times TP$$

This formula is based on the precision of the pattern on the training corpus, i.e., an estimated precision on a test corpus. α works for smoothing, that is, to accept only patterns of large TP when $FP = 0$. α is set as 0.01 empirically. The formula is similar to the Apriori algorithm (Agrawal and Srikant, 1995) that learns association rules from a database. The first term corresponds to the confidence of the algorithm, and the second term corresponds to the support.

For patterns where $TP = FP = 0$, which are not matched to PASs in the training corpus (i.e., newly produced by combinations of components), we estimates TP' and FP' by using the confidence of the main and entity components. This is because main and entity components tend to contain pattern meanings, whereas prep, double-prep and coord components are rather functional. The formulas to calculate the scores for all cases are:

$$Score = \begin{cases} TP/(TP+FP) + \alpha \times TP \\ \quad (TP+FP \neq 0) \\ TP'/(TP'+FP') \\ \quad (TP=FP=0, TP'+FP' \neq 0) \\ 0 \quad (TP=FP=TP'=FP'=0) \end{cases}$$

Combination Pattern	
(1)	Combination of components in combination matching
(2)	Main component in combination matching
(3)	Entity components in combination matching
(4)	Score for combination matching (SCORE)
Fragmental Pattern	
(5)	Matched fragmental patterns
(6)	Number of PASs of example that are not matched in fragmental matching
Raw Pattern	
(7)	Length of raw pattern derived from example

Table 2: Features for SVM Learning of Prediction Model

$$TP' = \begin{cases} TP'_{main} + TP'_{entity1}(+TP'_{entity2}) \\ \quad \text{(for Two-entity, Single-entity)} \\ 0 \quad \text{(for Naive)} \end{cases}$$

$$FP' = (\text{similar to } TP' \text{ but } TP'_x \text{ is replaced by } FP'_x)$$

$$TP'_{main} = \begin{cases} TP_{main:two}/(TP_{main:two} + FP_{main:two}) \\ \quad \left(\begin{array}{l} TP_{main:two} + FP_{main:two} \neq 0, \\ \text{for Two-entity} \end{array} \right) \\ TP_{main:single}/(TP_{main:single} + FP_{main:single}) \\ \quad \left(\begin{array}{l} TP_{main:single} + FP_{main:single} \neq 0, \\ \text{for Single-entity} \end{array} \right) \\ 0 \quad \text{(other cases)} \end{cases}$$

$$TP'_{entityi} = \begin{cases} TP_{entityi}/(TP_{entityi} + FP_{entityi}) \\ \quad \left(TP_{entityi} + FP_{entityi} \neq 0 \right) \\ 0 \quad \text{(other cases)} \end{cases}$$

$$FP'_x = \left(\begin{array}{l} \text{similar to } TP'_x \text{ but } TP'_y \text{ in the} \\ \text{numerators is replaced by } FP'_y \end{array} \right)$$

- TP: number of TPs by the combination of components
- $TP_{main:two}$: sum of TPs by two-entity combinations that include the same main component
- $TP_{main:single}$: sum of TPs by single-entity combinations that include the same main component
- $TP_{entityi}$: sum of TPs by combinations that include the same entity component which is not the straight entity component
- FP_x: similar to TP_x but TP is replaced by FP

The entity component "*ENTITY/NN*", which only consists of the PAS of an entity, adds no information to combinations of components. We call this component a *straight entity component* and exclude its effect from the scores.

4.5 Construction of Prediction Model

We use an SVM to learn a prediction model to determine whether a new protein pair is interacting. We used SVM^{light} (Joachims, 1999) with an rbf kernel, which is known as the best kernel for most tasks. The prediction model is based on the features of Table 2.

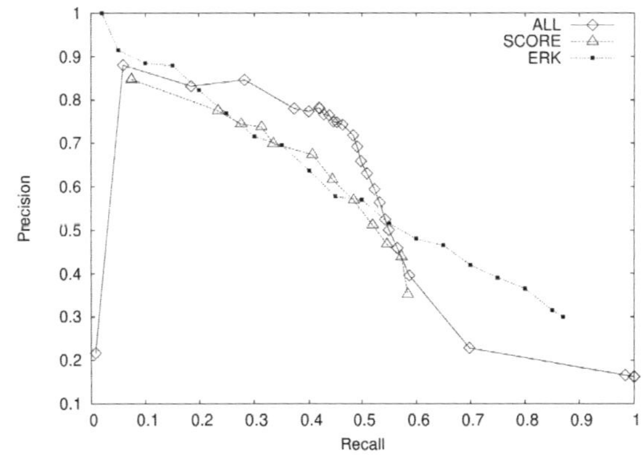

Figure 4: Results of IE Experiment

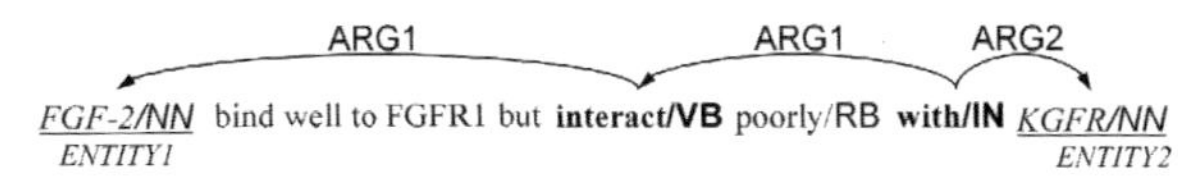

Figure 5: Example Demonstrating Advantages of Full Parsing

5 Results and Discussion

5.1 Experimental Results on the AImed Corpus

To evaluate extraction patterns automatically constructed with our method, we used the AImed corpus, which consists of 225 MEDLINE (U.S. National Library of Medicine, 2006) abstracts (1969 sentences) annotated with protein names and protein-protein interactions, for the training/test corpora. We used tags for the protein names given.

We measured the accuracy of the IE task using the same criterion as Bunescu and Mooney (2006), who used an SVM to construct extraction patterns on word/POS/type sequences from the AImed corpus. That is, an extracted interaction from an abstract is correct if the proteins are tagged as interacting with each other *somewhere* in that abstract (document-level measure).

Figure 4 plots our 10-fold cross validation and the results of Bunescu and Mooney (2006). The line ALL represents results when we used all features for SVM learning. The line SCORE represents results when we extracted pairs with higher combination matching scores than various threshold values. And the line ERK represents results by Bunescu and Mooney (2006).

The line ALL obtained our best overall F-measure 57.3%, with 71.8% precision and 48.4% recall. Our method was significantly better than Bunescu and Mooney (2006) for precision between 50% and 80%. It also needs to be noted that SCORE, which did not use SVM learning and only used the combination patterns, achieved performance comparable to that by Bunescu and Mooney (2006) for the precision range from 50% to 80%. And for this range, introducing the fragmental patterns with SVM learning raised the recall. This range of precision is practical for the IE task, because precision is more important than recall for significant interactions that tend to be described in many abstracts (as shown by the next experiment), and too-low recall accompanying too-high precision requires an excessively large source text.

Figure 5 shows the advantage of introducing full parsing. "FGF-2" and "KGFR" is an interacting protein pair. The pattern "*ENTITY1* interact with *ENTITY2*" based on PASs successfully extracts this pair. However, it is difficult to extract this pair with patterns based on surface words, because there are 5 words between "FGF-2" and "interact".

5.2 Experimental Results on Abstracts of MEDLINE

We also conducted an experiment to extract interacting protein pairs from a large amount of biomedical text, i.e. about 14 million titles and 8 million abstracts in MEDLINE. We constructed combination patterns from all 225 abstracts of the AImed corpus, and calculated a threshold value of combination scores that produced about 70% precision and 30% recall on the training corpus. We extracted protein pairs with higher combination scores than the threshold value. We excluded single-protein interactions to reduce time consumption and we used a protein name recognizer in this experiment[2].

We compared the extracted pairs with a manually curated database, Reactome (Joshi-Tope et al., 2005), which published 16,564 human protein interaction pairs as pairs of Entrez Gene IDs (U.S. National Library of Medicine, 2006). We converted our extracted protein pairs into pairs of Entrez Gene IDs by the protein name recognizer.[3] Because there may be pairs missed by Reactome or pairs that our processed text did not include, we excluded extracted pairs of IDs that are not included in Reactome and excluded Reactome pairs of IDs that do not co-occur in the sentences of our processed text.

[2]Because protein names were recognized after the parsing, multi-word protein names were not concatenated.

[3]Although the same protein names are used for humans and other species, these are considered to be human proteins without checking the context. This is a fair assumption because Reactome itself infers human interaction events from experiments on model organisms such as mice.

Total	89
Parsing Error/Failure	35
(Related to coordinations)	(14)
Lack of Combination Pattern Component	33
Requiring Anaphora Resolution	9
Error in Prediction Model	8
Requiring Attributive Adjectives	5
Others	10

More than one cause can occur in one error, thus the sum of all causes is larger than the total number of False Negatives.

Table 3: Causes of Error for FNs

After this postprocessing, we found that we had extracted 7775 human protein pairs. Of them, 155 pairs were also included in Reactome ([a] pseudo TPs) and 7620 pairs were not included in Reactome ([b] pseudo FPs). 947 pairs of Reactome were not extracted by our system ([c] pseudo False Negatives (FNs)). However, these results included pairs that Reactome missed or those that only co-occurred and were not interacting pairs in the text. There may also have been errors with ID assignment.

To determine such cases, a biologist investigated 100 pairs randomly selected from pairs of pseudo TPs, FPs and FNs retaining their ratio of numbers. She also checked correctness of the assigned IDs. 2 pairs were selected from pseudo TPs, 88 pairs were from pseudo FPs and 10 pairs were from pseudo FNs. The biologist found that 57 pairs were actual TPs (2 pairs of pseudo TPs and 55 pairs of pseudo FPs) and 32 pairs were actual FPs of the pseudo FPs. Thus, the precision was 64.0% in this sample set. Furthermore, even if we assume that all pseudo FNs are actual FNs, the recall can be estimated by actual TPs / (actual TPs + pseudo FNs) $\times$ 100 = 83.8%.

These results mean that the recall of an IE system for interacting proteins is improved for a large amount of text even if it is low for a small corpus. Thus, this justifies our assertion that a high degree of precision in the low-recall range is important.

5.3 Error Analysis

Tables 3 and 4 list causes of error for FNs/FPs on a test set of the AImed corpus using the prediction model with the best F-measure with all the

Total	35
Requiring Attributive Adjectives	13
Corpus Error	11
Error in Prediction Model	5
Requiring Negation Words	2
Parsing Error	1
Others	3

Table 4: Causes of Error for FPs

features. Different to Subsection 5.1, we individually checked each occurring pair of interacting proteins. The biggest problems were parsing error/failure, lack of necessary patterns and learning of inappropriate patterns.

5.3.1 Parsing Error

As listed in Table 3, 14 (40%) of the 35 parsing errors/failures were related to coordinations. Many of these were caused by differences in the characteristics of the PTB/GTB, the training corpora for Enju, and the AImed Corpus. For example, Enju failed to obtain the correct structure for "the *ENTITY1 / ENTITY1* complex" because words in the PTB/GTB are not segmented with "/" and Enju could not be trained on such a case. One method to solve this problem is to avoid segmenting words with "/" and introducing extraction patterns based on surface characters, such as "*ENTITY1/ENTITY2* complex".

Parsing errors are intrinsic problems to IE methods using parsing. However, from Table 3, we can conclude that the key to gaining better accuracy is refining of the method with which the PAS patterns are constructed (there were 46 related FNs) rather than improving parsing (there were 35 FNs).

5.3.2 Lack of Necessary Patterns and Learning of Inappropriate Patterns

There are two different reasons causing the problems with the lack of necessary patterns and the learning of inappropriate patterns: (1) the training corpus was not sufficiently large to saturate IE accuracy and (2) our method of pattern construction was too limited.

Effect of Training Corpus Size To investigate whether the training corpus was large enough to maximize IE accuracy, we conducted experiments on training corpora of various sizes. Figure 6 plots graphs of F-measures by SCORE and Figure 7 plots the number of combination patterns on training corpora of various sizes. From Figures 6 and 7, the training corpus (207 abstracts at a maximum)

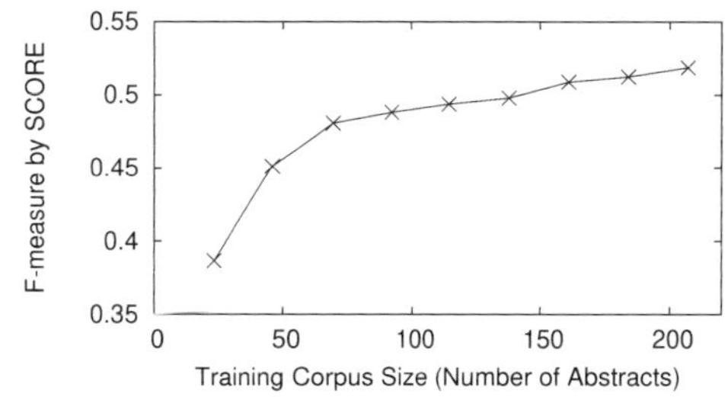

Figure 6: Effect of Training Corpus Size (1)

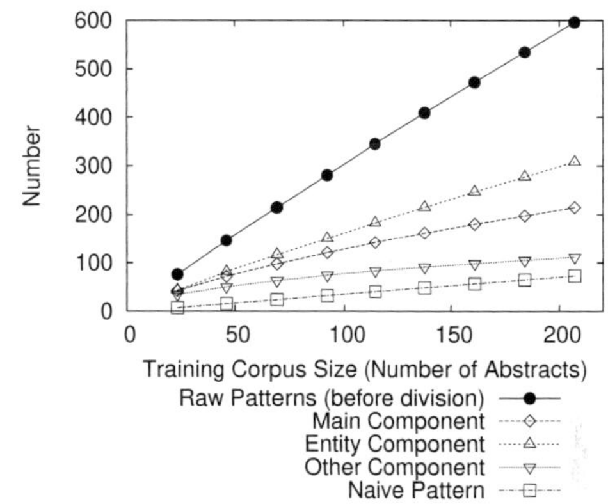

Figure 7: Effect of Training Corpus Size (2)

is not large enough. Thus increasing corpus size will further improve IE accuracy.

Limitation of the Present Pattern Construction The limitations with our pattern construction method are revealed by the fact that we could not achieve a high precision like Bunescu and Mooney (2006) within the high-recall range. Compared to theirs, one of our problems is that our method could not handle attributives. One example is "binding property of *ENTITY1* to *ENTITY2*". We could not obtain "binding" because the smallest set of PASs connecting "*ENTITY1*" and "*ENTITY2*" includes only the PASs of "property", "of" and "to". To handle these attributives, we need distinguish necessary attributives from those that are general[4] by semantic analysis or bootstrapping.

Another approach to improve our method is to include local information in sentences, such as surface words between protein names. Zhao and Grishman (2005) reported that adding local information to deep syntactic information improved IE results. This approach is also applicable to IE in other domains, where related entities are in a short

[4]Consider the case where a source sentence for a pattern is "*ENTITY1* is an important homodimeric protein." ("homodimeric" represents that two molecules of "*ENTITY1*" interact with each other.)

distance like the work of Zhou et al. (2005).

6 Conclusion

We proposed the use of PASs to construct patterns as extraction rules, utilizing their ability to abstract syntactical variants with the same relation. In addition, we divided the patterns for generalization, and used matching results for SVM learning. In experiments on extracting of protein-protein interactions, we obtained 71.8% precision and 48.4% recall on a small corpus and 64.0% precision and 83.8% recall estimated on a large text, which demonstrated the obvious advantages of our method.

Acknowledgement

This work was partially supported by Grant-in-Aid for Scientific Research on Priority Areas "Systems Genomics" (MEXT, Japan) and Solution-Oriented Research for Science and Technology (JST, Japan).

References

R. Agrawal and R Srikant. 1995. Mining Sequential Patterns. In *Proc. the 11th International Conference on Data Engineering*, pages 3–14.

Christian Blaschke and Alfonso Valencia. 2002. The Frame-Based Module of the SUISEKI Information Extraction System. *IEEE Intelligent Systems*, 17(2):14–20.

Razvan Bunescu and Raymond J. Mooney. 2004. Collective information extraction with relational markov networks. In *Proc. ACL'04*, pages 439–446.

Razvan C. Bunescu and Raymond J. Mooney. 2005. A Shortest Path Dependency Kernel for Relation Extraction. In *Proc. HLT/EMNLP 2005*, pages 724–731.

Razvan Bunescu and Raymond Mooney. 2006. Subsequence kernels for relation extraction. In *Advances in Neural Information Processing Systems 18*, pages 171–178. MIT Press.

Aron Culotta and Jeffrey Sorensen. 2004. Dependency tree kernels for relation extraction. In *Proc. ACL'04*, pages 423–429.

Yu Hao, Xiaoyan Zhu, Minlie Huang, and Ming Li. 2005. Discovering patterns to extract protein-protein interactions from the literature: Part II. *Bioinformatics*, 21(15):3294–3300.

Thorsten Joachims. 1999. Making Large-Scale SVM Learning Practical. In *Advances in Kernel Methods – Support Vector Learning*. MIT-Press.

G Joshi-Tope, M Gillespie, I Vastrik, P D'Eustachio, E Schmidt, B de Bono, B Jassal, GR Gopinath, GR Wu, L Matthews, S Lewis, E Birney, and Stein L. 2005. Reactome: a knowledgebase of biological pathways. *Nucleic Acids Research*, 33(Database Issue):D428–D432.

Asako Koike, Yoshiyuki Kobayashi, and Toshihisa Takagi. 2003. Kinase Pathway Database: An Integrated Protein-Kinase and NLP-Based Protein-Interaction Resource. *Genome Research*, 13:1231–1243.

Linguistic Data Consortium. 2005. ACE Program. http://projects.ldc.upenn.edu/ace/.

Mitchell Marcus, Grace Kim, Mary Ann Marcinkiewicz, Robert MacIntyre, Ann Bies, Mark Ferguson, Karen Katz, and Britta Schasberger. 1994. The Penn Treebank: Annotating predicate argument structure. In *Proc. AAI '94*.

Ivan A. Sag and Thomas Wasow. 1999. *Syntactic Theory*. CSLI publications.

Kiyoshi Sudo, Satoshi Sekine, and Ralph Grishman. 2003. An improved extraction pattern representation model for automatic IE pattern acquisition. In *Proc. ACL 2003*, pages 224–231.

Tsujii Laboratory. 2005a. Enju - A practical HPSG parser. http://www-tsujii.is.s.u-tokyo.ac.jp/enju/.

Tsujii Laboratory. 2005b. GENIA Project. http://www-tsujii.is.s.u-tokyo.ac.jp/GENIA/.

U.S. National Library of Medicine. 2006. PubMed. http://www.pubmed.gov.

Akane Yakushiji, Yusuke Miyao, Yuka Tateisi, and Jun'ichi Tsujii. 2005. Biomedical information extraction with predicate-argument structure patterns. In *Proc. SMBM 2005*, pages 60–69.

Daming Yao, Jingbo Wang, Yanmei Lu, Nathan Noble, Huandong Sun, Xiaoyan Zhu, Nan Lin, Donald G. Payan, Ming Li, and Kunbin Qu. 2004. PathwayFinder: Paving The Way Towards Automatic Pathway Extraction. In *Bioinformatics 2004: Proc. the 2nd APBC*, volume 29 of *CRPIT*, pages 53–62.

Shubin Zhao and Ralph Grishman. 2005. Extracting relations with integrated information using kernel methods. In *Proc. ACL'05*, pages 419–426.

GuoDong Zhou, Jian Su, Jie Zhang, and Min Zhang. 2005. Exploring various knowledge in relation extraction. In *Proc. ACL'05*, pages 427–434.

Protein folding and chart parsing

Julia Hockenmaier **Aravind K. Joshi**
Institute for Research in Cognitive Science
University of Pennsylvania
Philadelphia, PA 19104, USA
{juliahr, joshi}@cis.upenn.edu

Ken A. Dill
Dept. of Pharmaceutical Chemistry
University of California, San Francisco
San Francisco, CA 94143, USA
dill@maxwell.compbio.ucsf.edu

Abstract

How can proteins fold so quickly into their unique native structures? We show here that there is a natural analogy between parsing and the protein folding problem, and demonstrate that CKY can find the native structures of a simplified lattice model of proteins with high accuracy.

1 Introduction

In statistical parsing, the task is to find the most likely syntactic structure for an input string of words, given a grammar and a probability model over the analyses defined by that grammar. Proteins are sequences of amino acids (polypeptide chains) that form unique, sequence-specific three-dimensional structures. The structure into which a particular protein folds has a lower energy than all other possible structures. In protein structure prediction, the task is thus to find the lowest-energy physical structure for an input sequence of amino acids, given a representation of possible structures and a function that assigns an energy score to these structures. There is therefore a natural analogy between these two seemingly unrelated computational problems. Based on this analogy, we propose an adaptation of the CKY chart parsing algorithm to protein structure prediction, using a well-known simplified model of proteins as proof of concept.

Models of protein folding additionally aim to explain the process by which this structure formation takes place, and their validity depends not only on the accuracy of the predicted structures, but also on their physical plausibility. One common proposal in the biophysical literature is that the folding process is hierarchical, and that folding routes are tree-shaped. CKY provides an explicit computational recipe to efficiently search (and return) all possible folding routes. This sets it apart from existing folding algorithms, which are typically based on Monte Carlo simulations, and can only sample one possible trajectory.

Since we believe that there is much scope for future work in applying statistical parsing techniques to more detailed models of proteins, a secondary aim of this paper is to provide an introduction to the research questions that arise in protein folding to the NLP community.

Proteins are essential components of the cells of any living organism, and their biological function (eg. as enzymes that catalyze certain reactions) depends on their three-dimensional structure. However, genes only specify the linear, sequence of the amino acids, and the ribosome (the cell's "protein factory") uses this information to assemble the polypeptide chain. Under "natural" conditions, these polypeptide chains then fold rapidly and spontaneously into their unique final structures, or native states. Therefore, protein folding is often referred to as the second half of the genetic code, and the ability to predict the native state for a primary sequence is great practical importance, eg. in drug design, or in our understanding of the genome.

Levinthal (1968), who was the first to frame the folding process as a search problem, showed that folding cannot be guided by a random, exhaustive search: he argued that a chain of 150 amino acids has on the order of 10^{300} possible structures, but since folding takes only a few seconds, not more 10^8 of these structures can be searched. Under the assumption that a better understanding of the physical folding process will ultimately be required to design accurate structure prediction techniques, this observation has lead researchers to try to identify sequence-specific pathways along which folding may proceed or a general mechanism that makes this process so fast and reliable.

Our aim of understanding the folding process is different from a number of approaches which have

Proceedings of the 2006 Conference on Empirical Methods in Natural Language Processing (EMNLP 2006), pages 293–300,
Sydney, July 2006.

used formal grammars to represent the structure of biological molecules such as RNAs or proteins (Searls, 2002; Durbin et al., 1998; Chiang, 2004). These studies have typically focused on a specific classes of protein folds, and are not generally applicable yet. Our folding algorithm restricts the possible order of folding events, but places no explicit restrictions on the structures it can account for (other than those imposed by the spatial model used to represent them, and those that are implied by the hierarchical nature of the folding process).

2 A brief introduction to protein folding

2.1 Protein structure

The *primary structure* describes the linear sequence of amino acids that are linked via peptide bonds (and form the backbone of the polypeptide chain). Each amino acid has one side chain which branches off the backbone. Proteins contain twenty different kinds of amino acids, which differ only in the size and chemical properties of their side-chains. One important distinction is that between hydrophobic (water-repelling) and hydrophillic (polar) amino acids.

The *secondary structure* refers to patterns of local structures such as α-helices or β-sheets, which occur in many different folded structures. These secondary structure elements often assemble into larger *domains*. The *tertiary structure* represents the fully folded three-dimensional conformation of a single-chain protein, and typically consists of multiple domains. Since proteins in the cell are surrounded by water, hydrophobic side-chains are typically inside this structure and in close contact to each other, forming a *hydrophobic core*, whereas polar side-chains are more likely to be on the surface of this structure. This *hydrophobic effect* is known to be the main driving force for the folding process.

Computational models of protein folding often use a very simplified representation of these structures. Ultimately, models which explicitly capture all atoms and their physical interactions are required to study the folding of real proteins. However, since such models often require huge computational resources such as supercomputers or distributed systems, novel search strategies and other general properties of the folding problem are usually first studied with coarse-grained, simplified representations, such as the HP model (Lau and Dill, 1989; Dill et al., 1995) used here.

2.2 Folding and thermodynamics

As first shown by Anfinsen (1973), protein folding is a reversible process: under "denaturing" conditions, proteins typically unfold into a random state (which still preserves the chain connectivity of the primary amino acid sequence), and refold again into their unique native state if the natural folding conditions are restored. Thus, all the information that is necessary to determine the folded structure has to be encoded in the primary sequence. This is analogous to natural language, where the meaning of sentences such as *I drink coffee with milk* vs. *I drink coffee with friends* is also determined by their words.

Since folding occurs spontaneously, the native state has to be the thermodynamically optimal structure (under folding conditions), ie. the structure that results in the lowest *free energy*. The free energy $G = H - TS$ of a system depends on its energy H, its entropy S (the amount of disorder in the system), and the temperature T. A computational model therefore requires an *energy function* $\phi : R^n \to R$, which maps n-dimensional vectors that describe the structure of a polypeptide chain (eg. in terms of the coordinates of its atoms) to the free energies of the corresponding structures. The native state is assumed to be the global minimum of this function. This is again analogous to statistical parsing, where the correct analysis is assumed to be the structure with the highest probability. In the case of proteins, we can use the laws of physics to determine the energy function, whereas in language, the "energies" have to be estimated from corpora.[1]

The energy H of a single protein structure depends essentially on the interactions (*contacts*) between side-chains and on the bond angles along the backbone, whereas the entropy S also depends on the surrounding solvent (water). It is this impact on S which creates the hydrophobic effect. For simplicity's sake most computational models use an *implicit solvent* energy function, which captures the hydrophobic effect by assuming that the contact energies between hydrophobic side-chains are particularly favorable. Since bond angles alone cannot capture the hydrophobic effect (Dill, 1999), simplified models typically ignore their impact and represent the energy of a conformation only

[1] We note, however, that so-called "knowledge-based" or "statistical potentials", whose parameters are also estimated from known structures, are often used as well.

in terms of the side chain contacts. One particularly well-known example is the Miyazawa-Jernigan (1996) energy function, a 20x20 matrix of contact potentials whose parameters are estimated from the Protein Data Bank, a database of experimentally verified protein structures. These simplified energy functions are therefore very similar to the bi-lexical dependency models that are commonly used in statistical parsing.

It is this similarity between inter-residue contacts and word-word dependencies that grammar-based approaches (Searls, 2002) exploit. The set of contacts for a given structure can be represented as a *polymer graph*, although often only the edges of this graph are given in the form of a *contact map* (a triangular matrix whose entry C_{ij} corresponds to the contact between the ith and jth residue). The edges in this graph are inherently undirected. In α-helices and parallel β-sheets, the edges are crossing. Although grammars that capture the "dependencies" in specific kinds of protein structures have been written (Chiang, 2004), it is at present unclear whether such an approach can be generalized. The difficulty for all approximations to structural representations (grammar-based or otherwise) lies in accounting for *excluded volume* or *steric clashes* (the fact that no two amino acids can occupy the same point in space).

The so-called "New View" of protein folding (Dill and Chan, 1997) assumes that the speed of the folding process can be explained by the shape of the *energy landscape* (ie. the surface of the energy function for all possible structures of a given chain). Folding is fastest if the landscape is funnel-shaped (ie. has no local minima, and there is a direct downward path from all points to the native state). If the energy landscape is rugged (ie. has many local minima) or golf-course shaped (ie. all structures except for the native state have the same, high, energy), folding is slow. In the first case, energetic barriers slow down the folding process: the chain gets stuck in local minima, or kinetic traps. Such traps correspond to structures that contain "incorrect" (non-native) contacts which have to be broken (thus increasing the energy) before the native state can be reached. In the case of a plateau in the landscape, the search for the native state is slowed down by entropic barriers, i.e. a situation where a large number of equivalent structures with the same energy are accessible. Implicit in the landscape perspective is

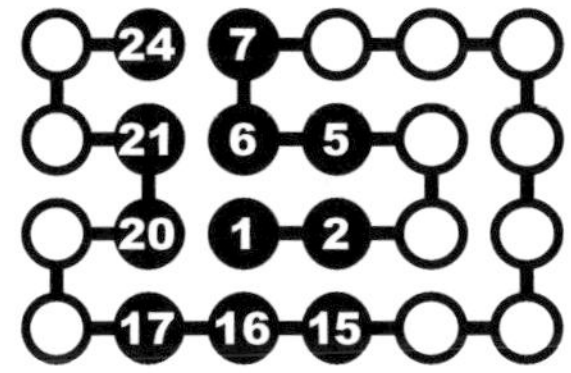

Figure 1: A conformation in the HP model with a "Greek key" β-sheet (1-17) and α-helix (17-24)

the assumption that folding is a greedy search – that local moves in the landscape can successfully identify the global minimum. Not all amino acid sequences have such landscapes, and in fact, most random amino acid sequences are unlikely to fold into a unique structure. This is again similar to language, where random sequences of words are also unlikely to form a grammatical sentence.

Computational simulations of the folding process are typically based on Monte Carlo or related techniques. These approaches require an energy function as well as a "move set" (a set of rules which describe how one conformation can be transformed into another). However, since each individual simulation can only capture the folding trajectory of a single chain, many runs are typically required to sample the entire landscape to a sufficient degree.

2.3 The HP model

The HP model (Lau and Dill, 1989; Dill et al., 1995) is one of the most simplified protein models. Here, proteins are short chains that are placed onto a 2-dimensional square lattice (Figure 1). Each HP sequence consists of two kinds of monomers, hydrophobic (H) and polar (P), and each monomer is represented as a single bead on a lattice site. The chain is placed onto the lattice such that each lattice site is occupied by at most one bead, and beads that are adjacent in the sequence are on adjacent lattice sites, so that it forms a self-avoiding walk (SAW) on the lattice. Such lattice models are commonly used in polymer physics, since they capture excluded volume effects, and the properties of such SAWs on different types of lattices are a well-studied problem in combinatorics.

Each distinct SAW corresponds to one "conformation", or possible structure. The energy of a conformation is determined by the contacts between two H monomers i and j that are not adjacent in the sequence. Contacts arise if the chain is in a configuration such that monomers i and j

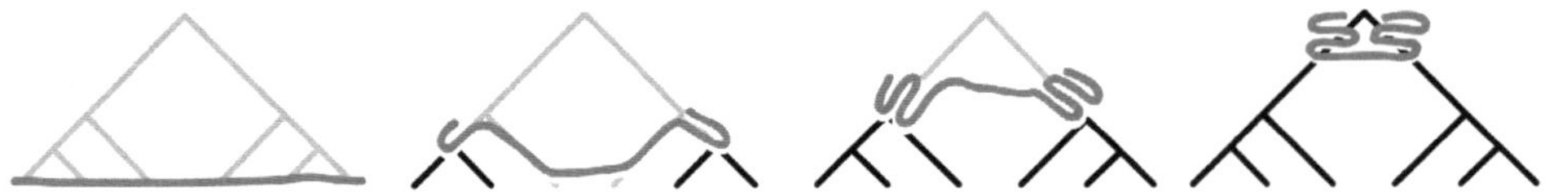

Figure 2: Trees describe folding routes. Tree cuts describe the state of the chain at any point in time.

($i < j$) are located on adjacent lattice sites. Each HH-contact contributes -1 to the energy. The energy $E(c)$ of a conformation c with n HH contacts is therefore $-n$. We consider only sequences that have a single lowest-energy conformation (native state), since these are the most protein-like. All unique-folding sequences up to a length of 25 monomers and their natives states are known (Irbäck and Troein, 2002). In our experiments, we will concentrate on the set of all unique-folding HP sequences of length 20, of which there are 24,900. These 20-residue chains have 41,889,578 viable conformations on the 2D lattice.

Despite its simplicity, the HP model is commonly used to test protein folding algorithms, since it captures essential physical properties of proteins such as chain connectivity and the hydrophobic effect, and since finding the lowest energy conformation is an NP-complete problem (Crescenzi et al., 1998; Berger and Leighton, 1998), as in real proteins.

3 Folding as hierarchical search

3.1 Evidence for hierarchical folding

There is substantial evidence in the experimental literature (starting with Crippen (1978) and Rose (1979); but see also Baldwin and Rose (1999a; 1999b)) that the folding process is guided by a hierarchical search strategy, whereby folding begins simultaneously and independently in different parts of the chain, leading initially to the formation of local structures which either grow larger, or assemble with other local structure. Folded protein structures can typically be recursively decomposed, and in many proteins, small, contiguous parts of the chain form near-native structures during early stages of the folding process. On the theoretical side, Dill et al. (1993) demonstrate that local contacts are easiest to form when the chain is unfolded, and facilitate the subsequent formation of less local contacts, leading to a "zipping" effect, where small, local structures grow larger before being assembled.

3.2 Folding routes as trees

Folding routes describe how individual chains move from the unfolded to the native state. If protein folding is a recursive, parallel process, as assumed here, folding routes are trees whose leaf nodes represent substrings of the primary sequence, and whose root represents the folded structure of the entire chain (Figure 2). The nodes in between the leaves and root correspond to chain segments whose length lies between that of the shortest initial segments and the final complete chain. Folding begins independently and simultaneously at each of the leaves, and moves toward the root. Each internal node of a folding route tree represents a set of partially folded conformations of the corresponding chain segment that is found by combining conformations of smaller pieces formed in previous steps.

Figure 2 also shows that the state of the entire chain at different stages during the folding process is given by a horizontal treecut, a set of nodes whose segments span the entire chain, but do not overlap.

Because we assume that folding routes are trees, contacts between two adjacent segments A and B can only be formed when A and B are combined to form their parent C. Our assumption also implies that in a sequence uvw, contacts between v and w or between v and u have to be formed before or at the same time as contacts between u and w.

Trees provide a unified representation of the growth and assembly process assumed by hierarchical folding theories: A growth step corresponds to a local tree in which a non-terminal node and a leaf node are combined, whereas an assembly step corresponds to a local tree in which two non-terminal nodes are combined.

Folding route trees thus play a very different role from the traditional phrase structure trees in natural language, since they represent merely the process by which the desired structure was formed, and not the structure itself. This is more akin to the role of syntactic derivations in formalisms such as CCG (Steedman, 2000): in CCG, syntactic derivation trees do not constitute an autonomous level of representation, but only specify how the semantic interpretation of a sentence is constructed. We will see below that proteins, like sentences in CCG, have a "flexible" constituent structure, with multiple folding routes leading to the native state.

4 Protein folding as chart parsing

Here, we show how the CKY algorithm (Kasami, 1965; Younger, 1967) can be adapted to protein folding in the HP model. Although we use a simplified lattice model, our technique is sufficiently general to be applicable to other representations. As in standard CKY, structures for substrings $i..j$ are formed from pairs of previously identified structures for substrings $i...k$ and $k+1..j$, and, as in standard probabilistic CKY, we use a pruning strategy akin to Viterbi search, and only retain the lowest energy structures in each cell.

The complexity of standard CKY is $O(n^3|G|)$, where n is the length of the input string and $|G|$ the "size" of the grammar. Since we do not have a grammar with a fixed set of nonterminals, which would allow us to compactly represent all possible structures for a given substring, the constant factor $|G|$ is replaced by an exponential factor n^c, representing the number of possible conformations of a chain of length n. Our pruning strategy captures the physical assumption that only locally optimal structures are stable enough not to unfold before further contacts can be made. With a larger set of amino acids and a corresponding energy function, a beam search strategy (with threshold pruning) may be more appropriate. Pruning is an essential part of our algorithm – without it, it would amount to exhaustive enumeration, repeated $O(n^3)$ times.

The chart Since only HH contacts contribute to the energy of a conformation, the dimensions of the chart are determined by the number of H monomers in the sequence. We segment every HP sequence into h substrings that contain one H each (splitting long substrings of Ps in the middle). For efficiency reasons, non-empty prefixes or suffixes of P monomers (eg. in sequences of the form $PPPH.....HP$) may also be split off as additional substrings (and are then only combined with the rest of the chain once the substring from the first to the last H monomer has been analyzed). These substrings correspond to the leaf nodes in the folding trees. Other regimes are also conceivable. Since no adjacent H monomers can form a contact, up to three consecutive Hs may be kept in the same substring. While this typically leads to an increase in efficiency, it comes at a slight cost in accuracy with our current pruning strategy. Long substrings of Ps could also be treated as separate substrings in a manner similar to P pre- and suffixes.

Chart items The items in our chart represent the lowest-energy conformations that are found for the corresponding substring. Unlike in standard CKY, each cell contains the full set of structures for its substring (which leads to the exponential worst-case behavior observed above). Therefore, the chart does not need to be unpacked to obtain the desired output structure. Backpointers from items in $chart[i][j]$ to pairs of items in $chart[i][k]$ and $chart[k+1][j]$ represent the folding route trees, and thus record the history of the folding process. Each item can only have at most $j-i$ pairs of backpointers, since it can only be constructed from one pair of conformations in each pair of cells.

Initializing the chart The chart is initialized by filling the cells $chart[i][i]$ which correspond to the ith substring. Since each initial substring has at most one H, all its conformations are equivalent (and the size of $chart[i][i]$ is thus exponential in the length of its substring). This exhaustive enumeration can be performed off-line.

Filling the chart As in standard CKY, the internal cells $chart[i][j]$ are filled by combining the entries of cells $chart[i][k]$ and $chart[k+1][j]$ for $i \leq k < j$. Two conformations $l \in chart[i][k]$ and $r \in chart[i][k]$ are combined like two pieces of a jigsaw puzzle where the only constraint is that two pieces may not overlap. That is, we append all (rotational and translational) variants of r to any free site adjacent to the site of l's last monomer, and add all resulting viable conformations c (ie. those where no two monomers occupy the same lattice site) into $chart[i][j]$.

With our current pruning strategy, only the lowest-energy conformations in each cell are kept.

CKY terminates when the top cell, $chart[1][n]$, is filled. It has succeeded if the top cell contains an item with only one conformation, the native state.

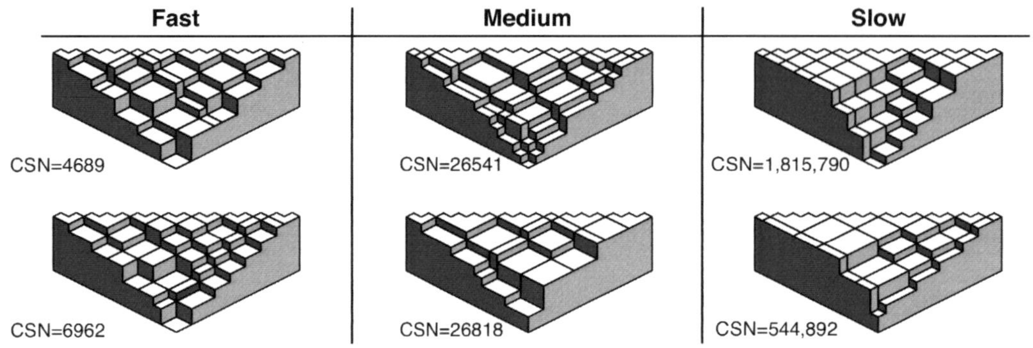

Figure 3: The amount of search depends on the shape of the "chart energy landscapes"

Contact maps as node labels We have also developed a variant of this algorithm where the entries in a cell correspond to contact maps (sets of HH-contacts), and where each entry corresponds in turn to the set of conformations that corresponds to this contact map. Conformations that have the same contact map are assumed to be physically equivalent. While the number of possible contact maps is also exponential in the length of the substring (Vendruscolo et al., 1999), it is obviously much smaller than the number of actual conformations. In our current implementation, the amount of search required is identical in both variants; but in extending this approach beyond the lattice, it may be possible to use a more efficient sampling approach to speed up the combination of conformations in two cells.

5 Results

5.1 Folding accuracy

With our current pruning strategy, CKY finds the native state of 96.7% of all 24,900 unique-folding 20mers, confirming our hypothesis that the hierarchical greedy search that is implemented in CKY is a viable strategy. With exhaustive search, the "conformational search number" (CSN), ie. total number of conformations searched per sequence (summed over all cells), corresponds on average to 2.5% of all possible conformations for a sequence of length 20. We have also explored restrictions where an initial contact is only allowed between H monomers whose distance along the backbone is smaller than or equal to a given threshold Δ. For $\Delta = 7$, accuracy drops slightly to 95.2%, but the number of searched conformations corresponds to only 1% of the search space.

5.2 The chart landscape

Since we employ a beam search strategy, all conformations that remain in a cell after pruning have the same energy level. Therefore, CKY identifies the substring or *chart energy landscape* of each sequence, a function $f(i, j)$ which maps substrings (i, j) to their lowest accessible energy level. Since the energy of a conformation in the HP model is determined by the number of HH contacts, $f(i, j) \leq f(i', j')$ for all $i' \leq i, j \leq j'$. That is, unlike standard energy functions, f has no local minima. As shown in figure 3 (where the size of the cells is adjusted to reflect the length of the corresponding substrings), the "slope" of f determines the amount of search required to fold a sequence. Sequence that require little search have a steep funnel, whereas sequence that require a lot of search have a flat, golf-course like landscape. HH contacts impoose constraints on the number of conformations, therefore a cell with lower energy will also have fewer entries than a cell with higher energy that spans a string of the same length. This is analogous to standard energy landscapes (Dill and Chan, 1997), where a plateau corrresponds to an *entropic* barrier, which requires a lot of search.

5.3 The "constituent structure" of proteins

We can extract the set of all folding routes (all trees which lead to the native state) from the chart, visualize the ensemble-averaged "constituent structure" of a chain by coloring each cell in the (adjusted) chart by the posterior probability that native routes go through it (here black:p=1 and white:p=0). A probability of one corresponds to a structure that has to be formed by all routes, whereas a probability of zero represents a set of misfolded structures. Misfolding arises if the lowest energy structures contain non-native (incor-

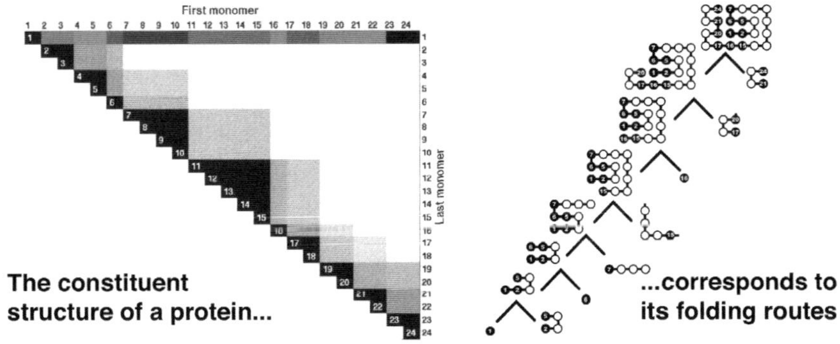

Figure 4: CKY identifies the "constituent structures" of proteins, which correspond to their folding routes

rect) contacts. Since these contacts have to be broken before the native state can be reached, requiring an uphill step in energy, they correspond to *energetic* barriers.

Figure 4 shows the "constituent structure" of the conformation shown in Figure 1, and one of its corresponding folding routes. Many sequences show very specific patterns of folding routes, as in the example given here, where the β-strands 7-10 and 11-16 and the α-helix from 17-24 "grow" onto the hairpin from 1-5.

A number of proteins are known to form so-called "foldons" (Maity et al., 2005). These are substrings of the chain which can be found in their near-native conformation before the entire chain is completely folded. In our parsing perspective on protein folding, these foldons correspond to nodes that are shared by sufficiently many native routes that they can be detected experimentally.

6 Conclusions and future work

This paper has demonstrated that an adaptation of the CKY chart parsing algorithm can be successfully applied to protein folding in the 2D HP model, a commonly used simplified lattice model which captures essential physical and computational properties of the real folding process. Both syntactic parsing and protein folding algorithms search for the globally optimal structure for a given input string. And any given sentence has a large number of possible interpretations, just as any amino acid sequence has an astronomical number of possible spatial conformations. Therefore it is not surprising if similar techniques can be applied to both tasks. In both cases, it seems to be possible to exploit locally available information with a greedy, hierarchical search strategy, which starts with local, independent searches for small substrings (to first determine which small phrases might make sense, or to find partially stable peptide structures) and then either: (a) 'grows' one substring into a larger substring, or (b) 'assembles' two substrings together into a larger substring. More interestingly, in the protein folding case, such recursive hierarchical search strategies, which imply tree-shaped folding routes, have been postulated independently for biological and biophysical reasons. This may indicate a deeper, natural connection between these two processes.

Given that hierarchical search strategies for protein folding have been proposed in the biological literature, our primary interest here has been the question of whether a greedy, hierarchical search as implemented in CKY is able to identify the native state of proteins in the HP model. The research presented here aims to verify these predictions with an explicit computational model. Therefore, we were less concerned with improving efficiency, and more with the properties of this algorithm, which we consider a baseline method upon which more sophisticated techniques such as best-first parsing (Caraballo and Charniak, 1998) or A* search (Klein and Manning, 2003) may well be able to improve.

We also plan to adapt this technique to other, more realistic, representations of proteins, and to longer sequences. For longer sequences, we will take advantage of the fact that CKY is easily parallelizable, since any operation which combines the entries of two cells $chart[i][k]$ and $chart[k+1][j]$ is completely independent of other parts of the chart.

If the routes by which proteins fold really are trees, a dynamic programming technique such as CKY is inherently suited to model this process, since it is the most efficient way to search all possible trees. This distinguishes it from more established techniques such as Monte Carlo, which can only follow one trajectory at a time, and require multiple runs to sample the underlying landscape to a sufficient degree. What CKY by itself does not give us is an accurate prediction of the rates that govern the folding process, including misfolding and unfolding events. However, we believe that it is possible to obtain this information from the chart by extracting all tree cuts (which corresond to the states of the chain at different stages during the folding process) and calculating folding rates between them.

Our work is only the beginning of a larger research program: eventually we would like to be able to model the folding process of real proteins. One aim of this paper was therefore to point out the fundamental similarities between statistical parsing and protein folding. We believe that this is a fertile area for future work where other natural language processing techniques may also prove to be useful.

Acknowledgements

This research is supported by NSF ITR grant 0205456. We would like to thank our colleagues at Penn and UCSF, in particular Vince Voelz, Banu Ozkan, John Chodera, David Chiang, Liang Huang, Fernando Pereira and Mitch Marcus,F for many comments and conversations.

References

Christian B. Anfinsen. 1973. Principles that govern the folding of protein chains. *Science*, 181(96):223–230, July.

Anonymous. in submission. Routes are trees: the parsing perspective on protein folding. *Proteins*.

Robert L. Baldwin and George D. Rose. 1999a. Is protein folding hierarchic? I. local structure and peptide folding. *Trends Biochem. Sci.*, 24(1):26–33, January.

Robert L. Baldwin and George D. Rose. 1999b. Is protein folding hierarchic? II. folding intermediates and transition states. *Trends Biochem. Sci.*, 24(1):77–83, February.

Bonnie Berger and Frank Thomson Leighton. 1998. Protein folding in the hydrophobic-hydrophilic(HP) model is NP-complete. *Journal of Computational Biology 5(1): 27-40*, 5(1):27–40.

Sharon A. Caraballo and Eugene Charniak. 1998. New figures of merit for best-first probabilistic chart parsing. *Computational Linguistics*, 24(2):275–298.

David Chiang. 2004. *Evaluation of Grammar Formalisms for Applications to Natural Language Processing and Biological Sequence Analysis*. Ph.D. thesis, University of Pennsylvania.

Pierluigi Crescenzi, Deborah Goldman, Christos H. Papadimitriou, Antonio Piccolboni, and Mihalis Yannakakis. 1998. On the complexity of protein folding. *Journal of Computational Biology*, 5(3):423–466.

Gordon M. Crippen. 1978. The tree structural organization of proteins. *J. Mol. Biol.*, 126(3):315–32, December.

Ken A. Dill and Hue Sun Chan. 1997. From Levinthal to pathways to funnels. *Nature Structural Biology*, 4(1):10–19, January.

Ken A. Dill, Klaus M. Fiebig, and Hue Sun Chan. 1993. Cooperativity in protein folding kinetics. *Proc. Natl. Acad. Sci.*, 90:1942–1946, March.

Ken A. Dill, Sarina Bromberg, Kaizhi Yue, Klaus M. Fiebig, David P. Yee, Paul D. Thomas, and Hue Sun Chan. 1995. Principles of protein folding – a perspective from simple exact models. *Protein Science*, 4:561–602.

Ken A. Dill. 1999. Polymer principles and protein folding. *Protein Science*, 8:1166–1180.

Richard Durbin, Sean R. Eddy, Anders Krogh, and Graeme Mitchison. 1998. *Biological sequence analysis*. Cambridge University Press.

Anders Irbäck and Carl Troein. 2002. Enumerating designing sequences in the HP model. *Journal of Biological Physics*, 28:1–15.

T. Kasami. 1965. An efficient recognition and syntax algorithm for context-free languages. Scientific Report AFCRL-65-758, Air Force Cambridge Research Laboratory, Bedford MA.

Dan Klein and Christopher D. Manning. 2003. A* parsing: Fast exact Viterbi parse selection. In *Proceedings of HLT-NAACL '03*.

KF Lau and KA. Dill. 1989. A lattice statistical mechanics model of the conformational and sequence spaces of proteins. *Macromolecules*, 22:638–642.

Cyrus Levinthal. 1968. Are there pathways for protein folding? *J. Chim. Phys*, 65:44–45.

H. Maity, M. Maity, M. Krishna, L. Mayne, and S. W. Englander. 2005. Protein folding: The stepwise assembly of foldon units. *Proc. Natl. Acad. Sci.*, 102:4741–4746.

Sanzo Miyazawa and Robert L. Jernigan. 1996. Residue-residue potentials with a favorable contact pair term and an unfavorable high packing density term, for simulation and threading. *Journal of Molecular Biology*, pages 623–644.

George D. Rose. 1979. Hierarchic organization of domains in globular proteins. *J. Mol. Biol.*, 134:447–470.

David B. Searls. 2002. The language of genes. *Nature*, 420:211–217, November.

Mark Steedman. 2000. *The Syntactic Process*. MIT Press, Cambridge, MA.

Michele Vendruscolo, Balakrishna Subramanian, Ido Kanter, Eytan Domany, and Joel Lebowitz. 1999. Statistical properties of contact maps. *Physical Review*, 59:977–984.

D. H. Younger. 1967. Recognition and parsing of context-free languages in time $O(n^3)$. *Information and Control*, 10(2):189–208.

Learning Phrasal Categories

William P. Headden III, Eugene Charniak and Mark Johnson
Brown Laboratory for Linguistic Information Processing (BLLIP)
Brown University
Providence, RI 02912
{headdenw|ec|mj}@cs.brown.edu

Abstract

In this work we learn clusters of contextual annotations for non-terminals in the Penn Treebank. Perhaps the best way to think about this problem is to contrast our work with that of Klein and Manning (2003). That research used tree-transformations to create various grammars with different contextual annotations on the non-terminals. These grammars were then used in conjunction with a CKY parser. The authors explored the space of different annotation combinations by hand. Here we try to automate the process — to learn the "right" combination automatically. Our results are not quite as good as those carefully created by hand, but they are close (84.8 vs 85.7).

1 Introduction and Previous Research

It is by now commonplace knowledge that accurate syntactic parsing is not possible given only a context-free grammar with standard Penn Treebank (Marcus et al., 1993) labels (e.g., S, NP, etc.) (Charniak, 1996). Instead researchers condition parsing decisions on many other features, such as parent phrase-marker, and, famously, the lexical-head of the phrase (Magerman, 1995; Collins, 1996; Collins, 1997; Johnson, 1998; Charniak, 2000; Henderson, 2003; Klein and Manning, 2003; Matsuzaki et al., 2005) (and others).

One particularly perspicuous way to view the use of extra conditioning information is that of tree-transformation (Johnson, 1998; Klein and Manning, 2003). Rather than imagining the parser roaming around the tree for picking up the information it needs, we rather relabel the nodes to directly encode this information. Thus rather than have the parser "look" to find out that, say, the parent of some NP is an S, we simply relabel the NP as an $NP[S]$.

This viewpoint is even more compelling if one does not intend to smooth the probabilities. For example, consider $p(NP \rightarrow PRN \mid NP[S])$ If we have no intention of backing off this probability to $p(NP \rightarrow PRN \mid NP)$ we can treat $NP[S]$ as an uninterpreted phrasal category and run all of the standard PCFG algorithms without change. The result is a vastly simplified parser. This is exactly what is done by Klein and Manning (2003).

Thus the "phrasal categories" of our title refer to these new, hybrid categories, such as $NP[S]$. We hope to learn which of these categories work best given that they cannot be made too specific because that would create sparse data problems.

The Klein and Manning (2003) parser is an unlexicalized PCFG with various carefully selected context annotations. Their model uses some parent annotations, and marks nodes which initiate or in certain cases conclude unary productions. They also propose linguistically motivated annotations for several tags, including VP, IN, CC,NP and S. This results in a reasonably accurate unlexicalized PCFG parser.

The downside of this approach is that their features are very specific, applying different annotations to different treebank nonterminals. For instance, they mark right-recursive NPs and not VPs (i.e., an NP which is the right-most child of another NP). This is because data sparsity issues preclude annotating the nodes in the treebank too liberally. The goal of our work is to automate the process a bit, by annotating with more general features that apply broadly, and by learning clus-

Proceedings of the 2006 Conference on Empirical Methods in Natural Language Processing (EMNLP 2006), pages 301–307,
Sydney, July 2006.

ters of these annotations.

Mohri and Roark (2006) tackle this problem by searching for what they call "structural zeros"or sets of events which are individually very likely, but are unlikely to coincide. This is to be contrasted with sets of events that do not appear together simply because of sparse data. They consider a variety of statistical tests to decide whether a joint event is a structural zero. They mark the highest scoring nonterminals that are part of these joint events in the treebank, and use the resulting PCFG.

Coming to this problem from the standpoint of tree transformation, we naturally view our work as a descendent of Johnson (1998) and Klein and Manning (2003). In retrospect, however, there are perhaps even greater similarities to that of (Magerman, 1995; Henderson, 2003; Matsuzaki et al., 2005). Consider the approach of Matsuzaki et al. (2005). They posit a series of latent annotations for each nonterminal, and learn a grammar using an EM algorithm similar to the inside-outside algorithm. Their approach, however, requires the number of annotations to be specified ahead of time, and assigns the same number of annotations to each treebank nonterminal. We would like to infer the number of annotations for each nonterminal automatically.

However, again in retrospect, it is in the work of Magerman (1995) that we see the greatest similarity. Rather than talking about clustering nodes, as we do, Magerman creates a decision tree, but the differences between clustering and decision trees are small. Perhaps a more substantial difference is that by not casting his problem as one of learning phrasal categories Magerman loses all of the free PCFG technology that we can leverage. For instance, Magerman must use heuristic search to find his parses and incurs search errors because of it. We use an efficient CKY algorithm to do exhaustive search in reasonable time.

Belz (2002) considers the problem in a manner more similar to our approach. Beginning with both a non-annotated grammar and a parent annotated grammar, using a beam search they search the space of grammars which can be attained via merging nonterminals. They guide the search using the performance on parsing (and several other tasks) of the grammar at each stage in the search. In contrast, our approach explores the space of grammars by starting with few nonterminals and splitting them. We also consider a much wider range of contextual information than just parent phrase-markers.

2 Background

A PCFG is a tuple $(V, M, \mu_0, R, q : R \to [0,1])$, where V is a set of terminal symbols; $M = \{\mu_i\}$ is a set of nonterminal symbols; μ_0 is a start or root symbol; R is a set of productions of the form $\mu_i \to \rho$, where ρ is a sequence of terminals and nonterminals; and q is a family of probability distributions over rules conditioned on each rule's left-hand side.

As in (Johnson, 1998) and (Klein and Manning, 2003), we annotate the Penn treebank nonterminals with various context information. Suppose μ is a Treebank non-terminal. Let $\lambda = \mu[\alpha]$ denote the non-terminal category annotated with a vector of context features α. A PCFG is derived from the trees in the usual manner, with production rules taken directly from the annotated trees, and the probability of an annotated rule $q(\lambda \to \rho) = \frac{C(\lambda \to \rho)}{C(\lambda)}$ where $C(\lambda \to \rho)$ and $C(\lambda)$ are the number of observations of the production and its left hand side, respectively.

We refer to the grammar resulting from extracting annotated productions directly out of the treebank as the base grammar.

Our goal is to partition the set of annotated nonterminals into clusters $\Phi = \{\phi_i\}$. Each possible clustering corresponds to a PCFG, with the set of non-terminals corresponding to the set of clusters. The probability of a production under this PCFG is

$$p(\phi_i \to \phi_j \phi_k) = \frac{C(\phi_i \to \phi_j \phi_k)}{C(\phi_i)}$$

where ϕs $\in$ Φ are clusters of annotated nonterminals and where:

$$C(\phi_i \to \phi_j \phi_k \ldots) = \sum_{(\lambda_i, \lambda_j, \lambda_k \ldots) \in \phi_i \times \phi_j \times \phi_k \ldots} C(\lambda_i \to \lambda_j \lambda_k \ldots)$$

We refer to the PCFG of some clustering as the clustered grammar.

2.1 Features

Most of the features we use are fairly standard. These include the label of the parent and grandparent of a node, its lexical head, and the part of speech of the head.

Klein and Manning (2003) find marking nonterminals which have unary rewrites to be helpful.

They also find useful annotating two preterminals (DT,RB) if they are the product of a unary production. We generalize this via two width features: the first marking a node with the number of nonterminals to which it rewrites; the second marking each preterminal with the width of its parent.

Another feature is the span of a nonterminal, or the number of terminals it dominates, which we normalize by dividing by the length of the sentence. Hence preterminals have normalized spans of 1/(length of the sentence), while the root has a normalized span of 1.

Extending on the notion of a Base NP, introduced by Collins (1996), we mark any nonterminal that dominates only preterminals as Base. Collins inserts a unary NP over any base NPs without NP parents. However, Klein and Manning (2003) find that this hurts performance relative to just marking the NPs, and so our Base feature does not insert.

We have two features describing a node's position in the expansion of its parent. The first, which we call the inside position, specifies the nonterminal's position relative to the heir of its parent's head, (to the left or right) or whether the nonterminal is the heir. (By "heir" we mean the constituent donates its head, e.g. the heir of an S is typically the VP under the S.) The second feature, outside position, specifies the nonterminal's position relative to the boundary of the constituent: it is the leftmost child, the rightmost child, or neither.

Related to this, we further noticed that several of Klein & Manning's (2003) features, such as marking NPs as right recursive or possessive have the property of annotating with the label of the rightmost child (when they are NP and POS respectively). We generalize this by marking all nodes both with their rightmost child and (an analogous feature) leftmost child.

We also mark whether or not a node borders the end of a sentence, save for ending punctuation. (For instance, in this sentence, all the constituents with the second "marked" rightmost in their span would be marked).

Another Klein and Manning (2003) feature we try includes the temporal NP feature, where TMP markings in the treebank are retained, and propagated down the head inheritance path of the tree.

It is worth mentioning that all the features here come directly from the treebank. For instance, the part of speech of the head feature has values only from the raw treebank tag set. When a preterminal cluster is split, this assignment does not change the value of this feature.

3 Clustering

The input to the clusterer is a set of annotated grammar productions and counts. Our clustering algorithm is a divisive one reminiscent of (Martin et al., 1995). We start with a single cluster for each Treebank nonterminal and one additional cluster for intermediate nodes, which are described in section 3.2.

The clustering method has two interleaved parts: one in which candidate splits are generated, and one in which we choose a candidate split to enact.

For each of the initial clusters, we generate a candidate split, and place that split in a priority queue. The priority queue is ordered by the Bayesian Information Criterion (BIC), e.g.(Hastie et al., 2003).

The BIC of a model M is defined as -2*(log likelihood of the data according to M) $+d_M$*(log number of observations). d_M is the number of degrees of freedom in the model, which for a PCFG is the number of productions minus the number of nonterminals. Thus in this context BIC can be thought of as optimizing the likelihood, but with a penalty against grammars with many rules.

While the queue is nonempty, we remove a candidate split to reevaluate. Reevaluation is necessary because, if there is a delay between when a split is proposed and when a split is enacted, the grammar used to score the split will have changed. However, we suppose that the old score is close enough to be a reasonable ordering measure for the priority queue. If the reevaluated candidate is no longer better than the second candidate on the queue, we reinsert it and continue. However, if it is still the best on the queue, and it improves the model, we enact the split; otherwise it is discarded.

When a split is enacted, the old cluster is removed from the set of nonterminals, and is replaced with the two new nonterminals of the split. A candidate split for each of the two new clusters is generated, and placed on the priority queue.

This process of reevaluation, enacting splits, and generating new candidates continues until the priority queue is empty of potential splits.

We select a candidate split of a particular cluster as follows. For each context feature we generate

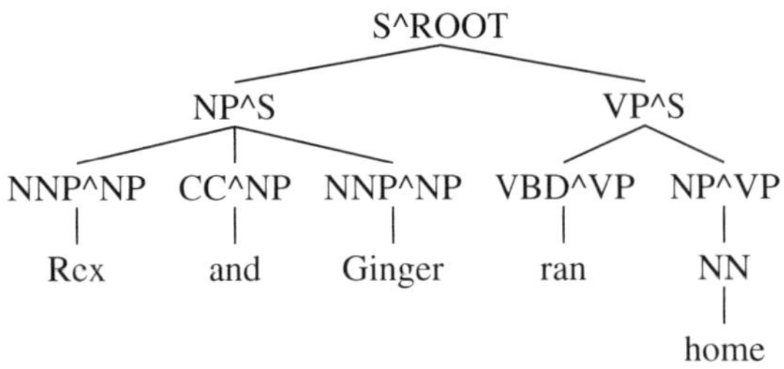

Figure 1: A Parent annotated tree.

a potential nominee split. To do this we first partition randomly the values for the feature into two buckets. We then repeatedly try to move values from one bucket to the other. If doing so results in an improvement to the likelihood of the training data, we keep the change, otherwise we reject it. The swapping continues until moving no individual value results in an improvement in likelihood.

Suppose we have a grammar derived from a corpus of a single tree, whose nodes have been annotated with their parent as in Figure 1. The base productions for this corpus are:

$S[ROOT] \rightarrow$	$NP[S]\ VP[S]$	$1/1$
$VP[S] \rightarrow$	$VBD[VP]\ NP[VP]$	$1/1$
$NP[S] \rightarrow$	$NP[NP]\ CC[NP]\ NP[NP]$	$1/1$
$NP[VP] \rightarrow$	$NN[NP]$	$1/1$
$NP[NP] \rightarrow$	$NNP[NP]$	$2/2$

Suppose we are in the initial state, with a single cluster for each treebank nonterminal. Consider a potential split of the NP cluster on the parent feature, which in this example has three values: S, VP, and NP. If the S and VP values are grouped together in the left bucket, and the NP value is alone in the right bucket, we get cluster nonterminals $NP_L = \{NP[S], NP[VP]\}$ and $NP_R = \{NP[NP]\}$. The resulting grammar rules and their probabilities are:

S	$\rightarrow$	$NP_L\ VP$	$1/1$
VP	$\rightarrow$	$VBD\ NP_L$	$1/1$
NP_L	$\rightarrow$	$NP_R\ CC\ NP_R$	$1/2$
NP_L	$\rightarrow$	NN	$1/2$
NP_R	$\rightarrow$	NNP	$2/2$

If however, VP is swapped to the right bucket with NP, the rules become:

S	$\rightarrow$	$NP_L\ VP$	$1/1$
VP	$\rightarrow$	$VBD\ NP_R$	$1/1$
NP_L	$\rightarrow$	$NP_R\ CC\ NP_R$	$1/1$
NP_R	$\rightarrow$	NN	$1/3$
NP_R	$\rightarrow$	NNP	$2/3$

The likelihood of the tree in Figure 1 is $1/4$ under the first grammar, but only $4/27$ under the second. Hence in this case we would reject the swap of VP from the right to the left buckets.

The process of swapping continues until no improvement can be made by swapping a single value.

The likelihood of the training data according to the clustered grammar is

$$\prod_{r \in R} p(r)^{C(r)}$$

for R the set of observed productions $r = \phi_i \rightarrow \phi_j \ldots$ in the clustered grammar. Notice that when we are looking to split a cluster ϕ, only productions that contain the nonterminal ϕ will have probabilities that change. To evaluate whether a change increases the likelihood, we consider the ratio between the likelihood of the new model, and the likelihood of the old model.

Furthermore, when we move a value from one bucket to another, only a fraction of the rules will have their counts change. Suppose we are moving value x from the left bucket to the right when splitting ϕ_i. Let $\phi_x \subseteq \phi_i$ be the set of base nonterminals in ϕ_i that have value x for the feature being split upon. Only clustered rules that contain base grammar rules which use nonterminals in ϕ_x will have their probability change. These observations allow us to process only a relatively small number of base grammar rules.

Once we have generated a potential nominee split for each feature, we select the partitioning which leads to the greatest improvement in the BIC as the candidate split of this cluster. This candidate is placed on the priority queue.

One odd thing about the above is that in the local search phase of the clustering we use likelihood, while in the candidate selection phase we use BIC. We tried both measures in each phase, but found that this hybrid measure outperformed using only one or the other.

3.1 Model Selection

Unfortunately, the grammar that results at the end of the clustering process seems to overfit the training data. We resolve this by simply noting periodically the intermediate state of the grammar, and using this grammar to parse a small tuning set (we use the first 400 sentences of WSJ section 24, and parse this every 50 times we enact a split). At the conclusion of clustering, we select the grammar

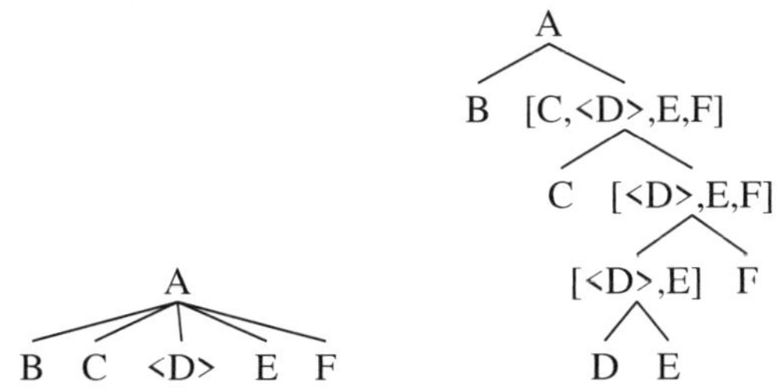

(a) (b)

Figure 2: (a) A production. (b) The production, binarized.

with the highest f-score on this tuning set as the final model.

3.2 Binarization

Since our experiments make use of a CKY (Kasami, 1965) parser [1] we must modify the treebank derived rules so that each expands to at most two labels. We perform this in a manner similar to Klein and Manning (2003) and Matsuzaki et al. (2005) through the creation of intermediate nodes, as in Figure 2. In this example, the nonterminal heir of A's head is D, indicated in the figure by marking D with angled brackets. The square brackets indicate an intermediate node, and the labels inside the brackets indicate that the node will eventually be expanded into those labels.

Klein and Manning (2003) employ Collins' (1999) horizontal markovization to desparsify their intermediate nodes. This means that given an intermediate node such as $[C\,\langle D\rangle\, EF]$ in Figure 2, we forget those labels which will not be expanded past a certain horizon. Klein and Manning (2003) use a horizon of two (or less, in some cases) which means only the next two labels to be expanded are retained. For instance in in this example $[C\,\langle D\rangle\, EF]$ is markovized to $[C\,\langle D\rangle \ldots F]$, since C and F are the next two non-intermediate labels.

Our mechanism lays out the unmarkovized intermediate rules in the same way, but we mostly use our clustering scheme to reduce sparsity. We do so by aligning the labels contained in the intermediate nodes in the order in which they would be added when increasing the markovization horizon from zero to three. We also always keep the heir label as a feature, following Klein and Manning (2003). So for instance, $[C\,\langle D\rangle\, EF]$ is represented as having Treebank label "INTERMEDIATE", and would have feature vector (D, C, F, E, D),while $[\langle D\rangle\, EF]$ would have feature vector $(D, F, E, D, -)$, where the first item is the heir of the parent's head. The "-" indicates that the fourth item to be expanded is here non-existent. The clusterer would consider each of these five features as for a single possible split. We also incorporate our other features into the intermediate nodes in two ways. Some features, such as the parent or grandparent, will be the same for all the labels in the intermediate node, and hence only need to be included once. Others, such as the part of speech of the head, may be different for each label. These features we align with those of corresponding label in the Markov ordering. In our running example, suppose each child node N has part of speech of its head P_N, and we have a parent feature. Our aligned intermediate feature vectors then become $(A, D, C, P_C, F, P_F, E, P_E, D, P_D)$ and $(A, D, F, P_F, E, P_E, D, P_D, -, -)$. As these are somewhat complicated, let us explain them by unpacking the first, the vector for $[C\,\langle D\rangle\, EF]$. Consulting Figure 2 we see that its parent is A. We have chosen to put parents first in the vector, thus explaining $(A, ...)$. Next comes the heir of the constituent, D. This is followed by the first constituent that is to be unpacked from the binarized version, C, which in turn is followed by its head part-of-speech P_C, giving us $(A, D, C, P_C, ...)$. We follow with the next non-terminal to be unpacked from the binarized node and its head part-of-speech, etc.

It might be fairly objected that this formulation of binarization loses the information of whether a label is to the left, right, or is the heir of the parent's head. This is solved by the inside position feature, described in Section 2.1 which contains exactly this information.

3.3 Smoothing

In order to ease comparison between our work and that of Klein and Manning (2003), we follow their lead in smoothing no production probabilities save those going from preterminal to nonterminal. Our smoothing mechanism runs roughly along the lines of theirs.

[1]The implementation we use was created by Mark Johnson and used for the research in (Johnson, 1998). It is available at his homepage.

	LP	LR	F_1	CB	0CB
Klein & Manning	86.3	85.1	85.7	1.31	57.2
Matsuzaki et al.	86.1	86.0	86.1	1.39	58.3
This paper	84.8	84.8	84.8	1.47	57.1

Table 1: Parsing results on final test set (Section 23).

Run	LP	LR	F_1	CB	0CB
1	85.3	85.6	85.5	1.29	59.5
2	85.8	85.9	85.9	1.29	59.4
3	85.1	85.5	85.3	1.36	58.0
4	85.3	85.7	85.5	1.30	59.9

Table 2: Parsing results for grammars generated using clusterer with different random seeds. All numbers here are on the development test set (Section 22).

Preterminal rules are smoothed as follows. We consider several classes of unknown words, based on capitalization, the presence of digits or hyphens, and the suffix. We estimate the probability of a tag T given a word (or unknown class) W, as $p(T \mid W) = \frac{C(T,W)+hp(T|unk)}{C(W)+h}$, where $p(T \mid unk) = C(T, unk)/C(unk)$ is the probability of the tag given any unknown word class. In order to estimate counts of unknown classes,we let the clusterer see every tree twice: once unmodified, and once with the unknown class replacing each word seen less than five times. The production probability $p(W \mid T)$ is then $p(T \mid W)p(W)/p(T)$ where $p(W)$ and $p(T)$ are the respective empirical distributions.

The clusterer does not use smoothed probabilities in allocating annotated preterminals to clusters, but simply the maximum likelihood estimates as it does elsewhere. Smoothing is only used in the parser.

4 Experiments

We trained our model on sections 2-21 of the Penn Wall Street Journal Treebank. We used the first 400 sentences of section 24 for model selection. Section 22 was used for testing during development, while section 23 was used for the final evaluation.

5 Discussion

Our results are shown in Table 1. The first three columns show the labeled precision, recall and f-measure, respectively. The remaining two show the number of crossing brackets per sentence, and the percentage of sentences with no crossing brackets.

Unfortunately, our model does not perform quite as well as those of Klein and Manning (2003) or Matsuzaki et al. (2005). It is worth noting that Matsuzaki's grammar uses a different parse evaluation scheme than Klein & Manning or we do.

We select the parse with the highest probability according to the annotated grammar. Matsuzaki, on the other hand, argues that the proper thing to do is to find the most likely unannotated parse. The probability of this parse is the sum over the probabilities of all annotated parses that reduce to that unannotated parse. Since calculating the parse that maximizes this quantity is NP hard, they try several approximations. One is what Klein & Manning and we do. However, they have a better performing approximation which is used in their reported score. They do not report their score on section 23 using the most-probable-annotated-parse method. They do however compare the performance of different methods using development data, and find that their better approximation gives an absolute improvement in f-measure in the .5-1 percent range. Hence it is probable that even with their better method our grammar would not outperform theirs.

Table 2 shows the results on the development test set (Section 22) for four different initial random seeds. Recall that when splitting a cluster, the initial partition of the base grammar nonterminals is made randomly. The model from the second run was used for parsing the final test set (Section 23) in Table 1.

One interesting thing our method allows is for us to examine which features turn out to be useful in which contexts. We noted for each trereebank nonterminal, and for each feature, how many times that nonterminal was split on that feature, for the grammar selected in the model selection stage. We ran the clustering with these four different random seeds.

We find that in particular, the clusterer only found the head feature to be useful in very specific circumstances. It was used quite a bit to split preterminals; but for phrasals it was only used to split $ADJP$,$ADVP$,NP,PP,VP,QP, and $SBAR$. The part of speech of the head was only used to split NP and VP.

Furthermore, the grandparent tag appears to be of importance primarily for VP and PP nonterminals, though it is used once out of the four runs for NPs.

This indicates that perhaps lexical parsers might be able to make do by only using lexical head and grandparent information in very specific instances, thereby shrinking the sizes of their models, and speeding parsing. This warrants further investigation.

6 Conclusion

We have presented a scheme for automatically discovering phrasal categories for parsing with a standard CKY parser. The parser achieves 84.8% precision-recall f-measure on the standard test-section of the Penn WSJ-Treebank (section 23). While this is not as accurate as the hand-tailored grammar of Klein and Manning (2003), it is close, and we believe there is room for improvement. For starters, the particular clustering scheme is only one of many. Our algorithm splits clusters along particular features (e.g., parent, head-part-of-speech, etc.). One alternative would be to cluster simultaneously on all the features. It is not obvious which scheme should be better, and they could be quite different. Decisions like this abound, and are worth exploring.

More radically, it is also possible to grow many decision trees, and thus many alternative grammars. We have been impressed by the success of random-forest methods in language modeling (Xu and Jelinek, 2004). In these methods many trees (the forest) are grown, each trying to predict the next word. The multiple trees together are much more powerful than any one individually. The same might be true for grammars.

Acknowledgement

The research presented here was funded in part by DARPA GALE contract HR 0011-06-20001.

References

Anja Belz. 2002. Learning grammars for different parsing tasks by partition search. In *Proceedings of the 19th international conference on Computational Linguistics*, pages 1–7.

Eugene Charniak. 1996. Tree-bank grammars. In *Proceedings of the Thirteenth National Conference on Artificial Intelligence*, pages 1031–1036. AAAI Press/MIT Press.

Eugene Charniak. 2000. A maximum-entropy-inspired parser. In *Proceedings of NAACL*, pages 132–139.

Michael J. Collins. 1996. A new statistical parser based on bigram lexical dependencies. In *The Proceedings of the 34th Annual Meeting of the Association for Computational Linguistics*, pages 184–191.

Michael Collins. 1997. Three generative, lexicalised models for statistical parsing. In *The Proceedings of the 35th Annual Meeting of the Association for Computational Linguistics*.

Michael Collins. 1999. *Head-driven Statistical Models for Natural Language Parsing*. Ph.D. thesis, The University of Pennsylvania.

Trevor Hastie, Robert Tibshirani, and Jerome Friedman. 2003. *The Elements of Statistical Learning*. Springer, New York.

James Henderson. 2003. Inducing history representations for broad coverage statistical parsing. In *Proceedings of HLT-NAACL 2003*, pages 25–31.

Mark Johnson. 1998. PCFG models of linguistic tree representations. *Computational Linguistics*, 24(4):613–632.

Tadao Kasami. 1965. An efficient recognition and syntax algorithm for context-free languages. Technical Report AF-CRL-65-758, Air Force Cambridge Research Laboratory.

Dan Klein and Christopher Manning. 2003. Accurate unlexicalized parsing. In *Proceedings of the 41st Annual Meeting of the Association for Computational Linguistics*.

David M. Magerman. 1995. Statistical decision-tree models for parsing. In *The Proceedings of the 33rd Annual Meeting of the Association for Computational Linguistics*, pages 276–283.

Michell P. Marcus, Beatrice Santorini, and Mary Ann Marcinkiewicz. 1993. Building a large annotated corpus of English: The Penn Treebank. *Computational Linguistics*, 19(2):313–330.

Sven Martin, Jörg Liermann, and Hermann Ney. 1995. Algorithms for bigram and trigram word clustering. In *Proceedings of the European Conference on Speech, Communication and Technology*, pages 1253–1256.

Takuya Matsuzaki, Yusuke Miyao, and Jun'ichi Tsujii. 2005. Probabilistic CFG with latent annotations. In *Proceedings of the 2005 Meeting of the Association for Computational Linguistics*.

Mehryar Mohri and Brian Roark. 2006. Effective self-training for parsing. In *Proceedings of HLT-NAACL 2006*.

Peng Xu and Fred Jelinek. 2004. Random forests in language modeling. In *Proceedings of EMNLP 2004*.

Priming Effects in Combinatory Categorial Grammar

David Reitter
School of Informatics
University of Edinburgh
2 Buccleuch Place
Edinburgh EH8 9LW, UK
dreitter@inf.ed.ac.uk

Julia Hockenmaier
Inst. for Res. in Cognitive Science
University of Pennsylvania
3401 Walnut Street
Philadelphia PA 19104, USA
juliahr@cis.upenn.edu

Frank Keller
School of Informatics
University of Edinburgh
2 Buccleuch Place
Edinburgh EH8 9LW, UK
keller@inf.ed.ac.uk

Abstract

This paper presents a corpus-based account of structural priming in human sentence processing, focusing on the role that syntactic representations play in such an account. We estimate the strength of structural priming effects from a corpus of spontaneous spoken dialogue, annotated syntactically with Combinatory Categorial Grammar (CCG) derivations. This methodology allows us to test a range of predictions that CCG makes about priming. In particular, we present evidence for priming between lexical and syntactic categories encoding partially satisfied subcategorization frames, and we show that priming effects exist both for incremental and normal-form CCG derivations.

1 Introduction

In psycholinguistics, *priming* refers to the fact that speakers prefer to reuse recently encountered linguistic material. Priming effects typically manifest themselves in shorter processing times or higher usage frequencies for reused material compared to non-reused material. These effects are attested both in language comprehension and in language production. *Structural priming* occurs when a speaker repeats a syntactic decision, and has been demonstrated in numerous experiments over the past two decades (e.g., Bock, 1986; Branigan et al., 2000). These experimental findings show that subjects are more likely to choose, e.g., a passive voice construction if they have previously comprehended or produced such a construction.

Recent studies have used syntactically annotated corpora to investigate structural priming. The results have demonstrated the existence of priming effects in corpus data: they occur for specific syntactic constructions (Gries, 2005; Szmrecsanyi, 2005), consistent with the experimental literature, but also generalize to syntactic rules across the board, which repeated more often than expected by chance (Reitter et al., 2006b; Dubey et al., 2006). In the present paper, we build on this corpus-based approach to priming, but focus on the role of the underlying *syntactic representations*. In particular, we use priming to evaluate claims resulting from a particular syntactic theory, which is a way of testing the representational assumptions it makes.

Using priming effects to inform syntactic theory is a novel idea; previous corpus-based priming studies have simply worked with uncontroversial classes of constructions (e.g., passive/active). The contribution of this paper is to overcome this limitation by defining a computational model of priming with a clear interface to a particular syntactic framework. The general assumption we make is that priming is a phenomenon relating to grammatical constituents – these constituents determine the syntactic choices whose repetition can lead to priming. Crucially, grammatical frameworks differ in the grammatical constituents they assume, and therefore predict different sets of priming effects.

We require the following ingredients to pursue this approach: a syntactic theory that identifies a set of constituents, a corpus of linguistic data annotated according to that syntactic theory, and a statistical model that estimates the strength of priming based on a set of external factors. We can then derive predictions for the influence of these factors from the syntactic theory, and test them using the statistical model. In this paper, we use regression models to quantify structural priming effects and to verify predictions made by Combinatory Categorial Grammar (CCG, Steedman (2000)), a syntactic framework that has the theoretical potential to elegantly explain some of the phenomena discovered in priming experiments.

Proceedings of the 2006 Conference on Empirical Methods in Natural Language Processing (EMNLP 2006), pages 308–316,
Sydney, July 2006.

CCG is distinguished from most other grammatical theories by the fact that its rules are *type-dependent*, rather than structure-dependent like classical transformations. Such rules adhere strictly to the constituent condition on rules, i.e., they apply to and yield constituents. Moreover, the syntactic types that determine the applicability of rules in derivations are transparent to (i.e., are determined, though not necessarily uniquely, by) the semantic types that they are associated with. As a consequence, syntactic types are more expressive and more numerous than standard parts of speech: there are around 500 highly frequent CCG types, against the standard 50 or so Penn Treebank POS tags. As we will see below, these properties allow CCG to discard a number of traditional assumptions concerning surface constituency. They also allow us to make a number of testable predictions concerning priming effects, most importantly (a) that priming effects are type-driven and independent of derivation, and, as a corollary; (b) that lexical and derived constituents of the same type can prime each other. These effects are not expected under more traditional views of priming as structure-dependent.

This paper is organized as follows: Section 2 explains the relationship between structural priming and CCG, which leads to a set of specific predictions, detailed in Section 3. Sections 4 and 5 present the methodology employed to test these predictions, describing the corpus data and the statistical analysis used. Section 6 then presents the results of three experiments that deal with priming of lexical vs. phrasal categories, priming in incremental vs. normal form derivations, and frequency effects in priming. Section 7 provides a discussion of the implications of these findings.

2 Background

2.1 Structural Priming

Previous studies of structural priming (Bock, 1986; Branigan et al., 2000) have made few theoretical assumptions about syntax, regardless of whether the studies were based on planned experiments or corpora. They leverage the fact that alternations such as *He gave Raquel the car keys* vs. *He gave the car keys to Raquel* are nearly equivalent in semantics, but differ in their syntactic structure (double object vs. prepositional object). In such experiments, subjects are first exposed to a *prime*, i.e., they have to comprehend or produce either the double object or the prepositional object structure. In the subsequent trial, the *target*, they are the free to produce or comprehend either of the two structures, but they tend to prefer the one that has been primed. In corpus studies, the frequencies of the alternative constructions can be compared in a similar fashion (Gries, 2005; Szmrecsanyi, 2005).

Reitter et al. (2006b) present a different method to examine priming effects in the general case. Rather than selecting specific syntactic alternations, general syntactic units are identified. This method detects syntactic repetition in corpora and correlates its probability with the distance between prime and target, where at great distance, any repetition can be attributed to chance. The size of the priming effect is then estimated as the difference between the repetition probability close to the prime and far away from the prime. This is a way of factoring out chance repetition (which is required if we do not deal with syntactic alternations). By relying on syntactic units, the priming model includes implicit assumptions about the particular syntactic framework used to annotate the corpus under investigation.

2.2 Priming and Lexicalized Grammar

Previous work has demonstrated that priming effects on different linguistic levels are not independent (Pickering and Branigan, 1998). Lexical repetition makes repetition on the syntactic level more likely. For instance, suppose we have two verbal phrases (prime, target) produced only a few seconds apart. Priming means that the target is more likely to assume the same syntactic form (e.g., a passive) as the prime. Furthermore, if the head verbs in prime and target are identical, experiments have demonstrated a stronger priming effect. This effect seems to indicate that lexical and syntactic representations in the grammar share the same information (e.g., subcategorization information), and therefore these representations can prime each other.

Consequently, we treat subcategorization as coterminous with syntactic type, rather than as a feature exclusively associated with lexemes. Such types determine the context of a lexeme or phrase, and are determined by derivation. Such an analysis is exactly what categorial grammars suggest. The rich set of syntactic types that categories afford may be just sufficient to describe all and only the units that can show priming effects during syntactic processing. That is to say that syntactic priming is categorial *type-priming*, rather than structural priming.

Consistent with this view, Pickering and Branigan (1998) assume that morphosyntactic features such as tense, aspect or number are represented independently from combinatorial properties which specify the contextual requirements of a lexical item. Property groups are represented centrally and shared between lexicon entries, so that they may – separately – prime each other. For example, the pre-nominal adjective *red* in *the red book* primes other pre-nominal adjectives, but not a post-nominal relative clause (*the book that's red*) (Cleland and Pickering, 2003; Scheepers, 2003).

However, if a lexical item can prime a phrasal constituent of the same type, and vice versa, then a type-driven grammar formalism like CCG can provide a simple account of the effect, because lexical and derived syntactic types have the same combinatory potential, which is completely specified by the type, whereas in structure-driven theories, this information is only implicitly given in the derivational process.

2.3 Combinatory Categorial Grammar

CCG (Steedman, 2000) is a mildly context-sensitive, lexicalized grammar formalism with a transparent syntax-semantics interface and a flexible constituent structure that is of particular interest to psycholinguistics, since it allows the construction of incremental derivations. CCG has also enjoyed the interest of the NLP community, with high-accuracy wide-coverage parsers(Clark and Curran, 2004; Hockenmaier and Steedman, 2002) and generators[1] available (White and Baldridge, 2003).

Words are associated with lexical categories which specify their subcategorization behaviour, eg. ((S[dcl]\NP)/NP)/NP is the lexical category for (tensed) ditransitive verbs in English such as *gives* or *send*, which expect two NP objects to their right, and one NP subject to their left. Complex categories X/Y or X\Y are functors which yield a constituent with category X, if they are applied to a constituent with category Y to their right (/Y) or to their left (\Y).

Constituents are combined via a small set of combinatory rule schemata:

Forward Application:	X/Y Y	$\Rightarrow_{>}$ X
Backward Application:	Y X\Y	$\Rightarrow_{>}$ X
Forward Composition:	X/Y Y/Z	$\Rightarrow_{\mathbf{B}}$ X/Z
Backward Composition:	Y\Z X\Y	$\Rightarrow_{\mathbf{B}}$ X\Z
Backw. Crossed Composition:	Y/Z X\Y	$\Rightarrow_{\mathbf{B}}$ X/Z
Forward Type-raising:	X	$\Rightarrow_{\mathbf{T}}$ T/(T\X)
Coordination:	X conj X	$\Rightarrow_{\Phi}$ X

Function application is the most basic operation (and used by all variants of categorial grammar):

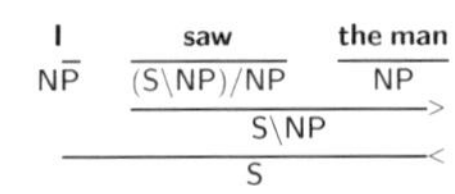

Composition (**B**) and type-raising (**T**) are necessary for the analysis of long-range dependencies and for incremental derivations. CCG uses the same lexical categories for long-range dependencies that arise eg. in wh-movement or coordination as for local dependencies, and does not require traces:

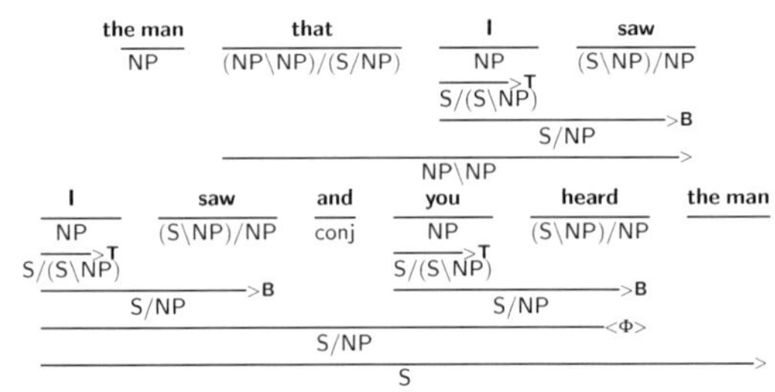

The combinatory rules of CCG allow multiple, semantically equivalent, syntactic derivations of the same sentence. This *spurious ambiguity* is the result of CCG's flexible constituent structure, which can account for long-range dependencies and coordination (as in the above example), and also for interaction with information structure.

CCG parsers often limit the use of the combinatory rules (in particular: type-raising) to obtain a single right-branching *normal form* derivation (Eisner, 1996) for each possible semantic interpretation. Such normal form derivations only use composition and type-raising where syntactically necessary (eg. in relative clauses).

3 Predictions

3.1 Priming Effects

We expect priming effects to apply to CCG *categories*, which describe the type of a constituent including the arguments it expects. Under our assumption that priming manifests itself as a tendency for repetition, repetition probability should be higher for short distances from a prime (see Section 5.2 for details).

[1] http://opennlp.sourceforge.net/

3.2 Terminal and Non-terminal Categories

In categorial grammar, lexical categories specify the subcategorization behavior of their heads, capturing local and non-local arguments, and a small set of rule schemata defines how constituents can be combined.

Phrasal constituents may have the same categories as lexical items. For example, the verb *saw* might have the (lexical) category $(\mathsf{S}\backslash\mathsf{NP})/\mathsf{NP}$, which allows it to combine with an NP to the right. The resulting constituent for *saw Johanna* would be of category $\mathsf{S}\backslash\mathsf{NP}$ – a constituent which expects an NP (the subject) to its left, and also the lexical category of an intransitive verb. Similarly, the constituent consisting of a ditransitive verb and its object, *gives the money*, has the same category as *saw*. Under the assumption that priming occurs for these categories, we proceed to test a hypothesis that follows from the fact that categories merely encode *unsatisfied* subcategorized arguments.

Given that a transitive verb has the same category as the constituent formed by a ditransitive verb and its direct object, we would expect that both categories can prime each other, if they are cognitive units. More generally, we would expect that lexical (terminal) and phrasal (non-terminal) categories of the same syntactic type may prime each other. The interaction of such conditions with the priming effect can be quantified in the statistical model.

3.3 Incrementality of Analyses

Type-raising and composition allow derivations that are mostly left-branching, or *incremental*. Adopting a left-to-right processing order for a sentence is important, if the syntactic theory is to make psycholinguistically viable predictions (Niv, 1994; Steedman, 2000).

Pickering et al. (2002) present priming experiments that suggest that, in production, structural dominance and linearization do not take place in different stages. Their argument involves verbal phrases with a shifted prepositional object such as *showed to the mechanic a torn overall*. At a dominance-only level, such phrases are equivalent to non-shifted prepositional constructions *(showed a torn overall to the mechanic)*, but the two variants may be differentiated at a linearization stage. Shifted primes do not prime prepositional objects in their canonical position, thus priming must occur at a linearized level, and a separate dominance level seems unlikely (unless priming is selective). CCG is compatible with one-stage formulations of syntax, as no transformation is assumed and categories encode linearization together with subcategorization.

CCG assumes that the processor may produce syntactically different, but semantically equivalent derivations.[2] So, while neither the incremental analysis we generate, nor the normal-form, represent one single correct derivation, they are two extremes of a 'spectrum' of derivations. We hypothesize that priming effects predicted on the basis of incremental CCG analyses will be as strong than those predicted on the basis of their normal-form equivalents.

4 Corpus Data

4.1 The Switchboard Corpus

The Switchboard (Marcus et al., 1994) corpus contains transcriptions of spoken, spontaneous conversation annotated with phrase-structure trees. Dialogues were recorded over the telephone among randomly paired North American speakers, who were just given a general topic to talk about. 80,000 utterances of the corpus have been annotated with syntactic structure. This portion, included in the Penn Treebank, has been time-aligned (per word) in the Paraphrase project (Carletta et al., 2004).

Using the same regression technique as employed here, Reitter et al. (2006b) found a marked structural priming effect for Penn-Treebank style phrase structure rules in Switchboard.

4.2 Disfluencies

Speech is often disfluent, and speech repairs are known to repeat large portions of the preceding context (Johnson and Charniak, 2004). The original Switchboard transcripts contains these disfluencies (marked up as `EDITED`):

```
( (S >>>(EDITED
      (RM (-DFL- \bs [) )
      (EDITED
        (RM (-DFL- \bs [) )
        (CC And)
        (, ,)
        (IP (-DFL- \bs +) ))
      (CC and)
      (, ,)
      (RS (-DFL- \bs ]) )
      (IP (-DFL- \bs +) ))<<<
```

[2] Selectional criteria such as information structure and intonation allow to distinguish between semantically different analyses.

```
(CC and)
>>>(RS (-DFL- \bs ]) )<<<
(NP-SBJ (PRP I) )
(VP (VBP guess)
  (SBAR (-NONE- 0)
    (S (NP-SBJ (DT that) )
      (VP (BES 's)
        (SBAR-NOM-PRD
          (WHNP-1 (WP what) )
          (S (NP-SBJ (PRP I) )
             (ADVP (RB really) )
             (VP (VBP like)
               (NP (-NONE- *T*-1) ))))))))
(. .) (-DFL- E_S) ))
```

It is unclear to what extent these repetitions are due to priming rather than simple correction. In disfluent utterances, we therefore eliminate reparanda and only keep repairs (the portions marked with `>...<` are removed). Hesitations (`uh`, etc.), and utterances with unfinished constituents are also ignored.

4.3 Translating Switchboard to CCG

Since the Switchboard annotation is almost identical to the one of the Penn Treebank, we use a similar translation algorithm to Hockenmaier and Steedman (2005). We identify heads, arguments and adjuncts, binarize the trees, and assign categories in a recursive top-down fashion. Nonlocal dependencies that arise through wh-movement and right node raising (`*T*` and `*RNR*` traces) are captured in the resulting derivation. Figure 1 (left) shows the rightmost normal form CCG derivation we obtain for the above tree. We then transform this normal form derivation into the most incremental (i.e., left-branching) derivation possible, as shown in Figure 1 (right).

This transformation is done by a top-down recursive procedure, which changes each tree of depth two into an equivalent left-branching analysis if the combinatory rules allow it. This procedure is run until no further transformation can be executed. The lexical categories of both derivations are identical.

5 Statistical Analysis

5.1 Priming of Categories

CCG assumes a minimal set of combinatory rule schemata. Much more than in those rules, syntactic decisions are evident from the *categories* that occur in the derivation.

Given the categories for each utterance, we can identify their repeated use. A certain amount of repetition will obviously be coincidental. But structural priming predicts that a target category will occur more frequently closer to a potential prime of the same category. Therefore, we can correlate the probability of repetition with the distance between prime and target. Generalized Linear Mixed Effects Models (GLMMs, see next section) allow us to evaluate and quantify this correlation.

Every syntactic category is counted as a potential prime and (almost always) as a target for priming. Because interlocutors tend to stick to a topic during a conversation for some time, we exclude cases of syntactic repetition that are a results of the repetition of a whole phrase.

Previous work points out that priming is sensitive to frequency (Scheepers (2003) for high/low relative clause attachments, (Reitter et al., 2006a) for phrase structure rules). Highly frequent items do not receive (as much) priming. We include the logarithm of the raw frequency of the syntactic category in Switchboard (LNFREQ) to approximate the effect that frequency has on accessibility of the category.

5.2 Generalized Linear Mixed Effects Regression

We use generalized linear mixed effects regression models (GLMM, Venables and Ripley (2002)) to predict a response for a number of given categorial ('factor') or continuous ('predictor') explanatory variables (features). Our data is made up of instances of repetition examples and non-repetition examples from the corpus. For each target instance of a syntactic category c occurring in a derivation and spanning a constituent that begins at time t, we look back for possible instances of constituents with the same category (the prime) in a time frame of $[t-d-0.5; t-d+0.5]$ seconds. If such instances can be found, we have a positive example of repetition. Otherwise, c is included as a data point with a negative outcome. We do so for a range of different distances d, commonly $1 \leq d \leq 15$ seconds.[3] For each data point, we include the logarithm of the distance d between *priming period* and *target* as an explanatory variable LNDIST. (See Reitter et al. (2006b) for a worked example.)

In order to eliminate cases of lexical repetition of a phrase, e.g., names or lexicalized noun

[3]This approach uses a number of data points per target, looking backwards for primes. The opposite way – looking forwards for targets – would make similar predictions.

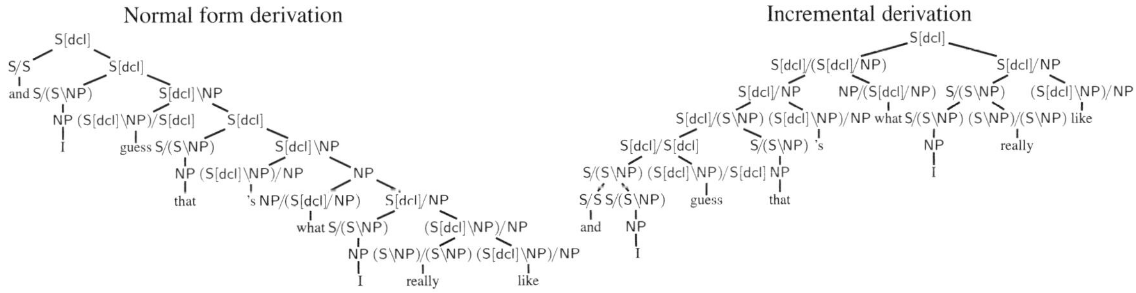

Figure 1: Two derivations (normal form: left), incremental: right) for the sentence fragment *and I guess that's what I really like* from Switchboard.

phrases, which we consider topic-dependent or instances of lexical priming, we only collect syntactic repetitions with at least one differing word.

Without syntactic priming, we would assume that there is no correlation between the probability that a data point is positive (repetition occurs) and distance d. With priming, we would expect that the probability is inversely proportional to d. Our model uses $\ln d$ as predictor LNDIST, since memory effects usually decay exponentially.

The regression model fitted is then simply a choice of coefficients β_i, among them one for each explanatory variable i. β_i expresses the contribution of i to the probability of the outcome event, that is, in our case, successful priming. The coefficient of interest is the one for the time correlation, i.e. β_{lnDist}. It specifies the strength of decay of repetition probability over time. If no other variables are present, a model estimates the repetition probability for a data point i as

$$\hat{p}_i = \beta_0 + \beta_{lnDist} \ln \mathrm{DIST}_i$$

Priming is present if the estimated parameter is negative, i.e. the repetition probability decreases with increasing distance between prime and target.

Other explanatory variables, such as ROLE, which indicates whether priming occurs within a speaker (production-production priming, PP) or in between speakers (comprehension-production priming, CP), receive an interaction coefficient that adds linearly to β_{lnDist}. Additional interaction variables are included depending on the experimental question.[4]

[4]Lastly, we identify the target utterance in a random factor in our model, grouping the several measurements (15 for the different distances from each target) as *repeated measurements*, since they depend on the same target category occurrence and are partially inter-dependent.

From the data produced, we include all cases of reptition and a an equal number of randomly sampled non-repetition cases.[5]

6 Experiments

6.1 Experiment 1: Priming in Incremental and Normal-form Derivations

Hypothesis CCG assumes a multiplicity of semantically equivalent derivations with different syntactic constituent structures. Here, we investigate whether two of these, the normal-form and the most incremental derivation, differ in the strength with which syntactic priming occurs.

Method A joint model was built containing repetition data from both types of derivations. Since we are only interested in cases where the two derivations differ, we excluded all constituents where a string of words was analyzed as a constituent in both derivations. This produced a data set where the two derivations could be contrasted.

A factor DERIVATION in the model indicates whether the repetition occurred in a normal-form (NF) or an incremental derivation (INC).

Results Significant and substantial priming is present in both types of derivations, for both PP and CP priming. There is no significant difference in priming strength between normal-form and incremental derivations ($\beta_{lnDist:NF} = 0.008, p = 0.95$). The logarithm of the raw category frequency is negatively correlated with the priming strength ($\beta_{lnDist:lnFreq} = 0.151, p < 0.0001$. Note that a negative coefficient for LNDIST indicates

[5]We trained our models using Penalized Quasi-Likelihood (Venables and Ripley, 2002). This technique works best if data is balanced, i.e. we avoid having very rare positive examples in the data. Experiment 2 was conducted on a subset of the data.

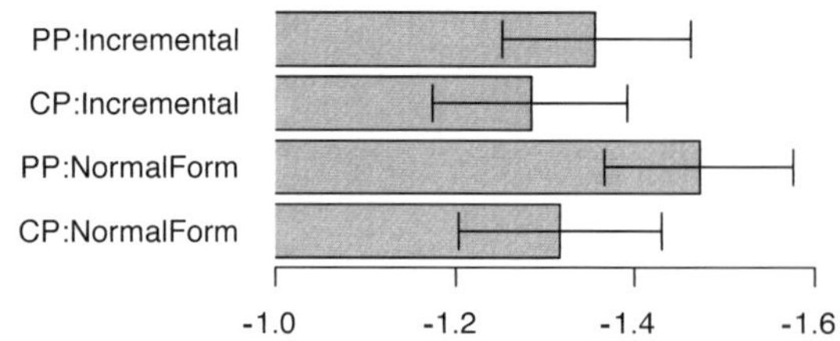

Figure 2: Decay effect sizes in Experiment 1 for combinations of comprehension-production or production-production priming and in incremental or normal-form derivations. Error bars show (non-simultaneous) 95% confidence intervals.

decay. The lower this coefficient, the more decay, hence priming).

If there was no priming of categories for incrementally formed constituents, we would expect to see a large effect of DERIVATION. In the contrary, we see no effect at a high *p*, where the that the regression method used is demonstrably powerful enough to detect even small changes in the priming effect. We conclude that there is no detectable difference in priming between the two derivation types. In Fig. 2, we give the estimated priming effect sizes for the four conditions.[6]

The result is compatible with CCG's separation of derivation structure and the type of the result of derivation. It is not the derivation structure that primes, but rather the type of the result. It is also compatible with the possibility of a non-traditional constituent structure (such as the incremental analysis), even though it is clear that neither incremental nor normal-form derivations necessarily represent the ideal analysis.

The category sets occurring in both derivation variants was largely disjunct, making testing for actual overlap between different derivations impossible.

6.2 Experiment 2: Priming between Lexical and Phrasal Categories

Hypothesis Since CCG categories simply encode unsatisfied subcategorization constraints, constituents which are very different from a traditional linguistic perspective can receive the same category. This is, perhaps, most evident in phrasal

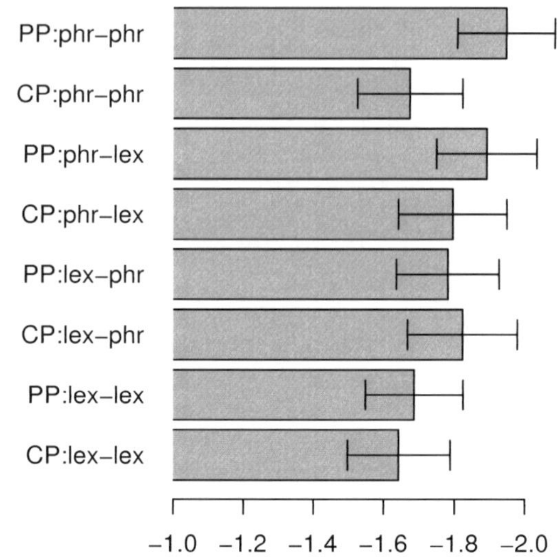

Figure 3: Decay effect sizes in Experiment 2, for combinations of comprehension-production or production-production priming and lexical or phrasal primes and targets, e.g. the third bar denotes the decay in repetition probability of a phrasal category as prime and a lexical one as target, where prime and target occurred in utterances by the same speaker. Error bars show (non-simultaneous) 95% confidence intervals.

and lexical categories (where, e.g., an intransitive verb is indistinguishable from a verb phrase).

Bock and Loebell (1990)'s experiments suggest that priming effects are independent of the subcategorization frame. There, an active voice sentence primed a passive voice one with the same phrase structure, but a different subcategorization. If we find priming from lexical to phrasal categories, then our model demonstrates priming of subcategorization frames.

From a processing point of view, phrasal categories are distinct from lexical ones. Lexical categories are bound to the lemma and thereby linked to the lexicon, while phrasal categories are the result of a structural composition or decomposition process. The latter ones represent temporary states, encoding the syntactic *process*.

Here, we test whether lexical and phrasal categories can prime each other, and if so, contrast the strength of these priming effects.

Method We built a model which allowed lexical and phrasal categories to prime each other. A factor, STRUCTURAL LEVEL was introduced

[6]Note that Figures 2 and 3 stem from nested models that estimate the effect of LNDIST within the four/eight conditions. Confidence intervals will be larger, as fewer datapoints are available than when the overall effect of a single factor is compared.

to distinguish the four cases: priming in between phrasal categories and in between lexical ones, from lexical ones to phrasal ones and from phrasal ones to lexical ones.

Recall that each data point encodes a possibility to repeat a CCG category, referring to a particular instance of a target category at time t and a time span of duration of one second $[t-d-0.5, t-d+0.5]$ in which a priming instance of the same category could occur. If it occurred at least once, the data point was counted as a possible example of priming (response variable: true), otherwise it was included as a counter-example (response variable: false). For the target category, its type (lexical or phrasal) was clear. For the category of the prime, we included two data points, one for each type, with a response indicating whether a prime of the category of such a type occurred in the time window. We built separate models for incremental and normal form derivations. Models were fitted to a balanced subset, including all repetitions and a randomly sampled subset of non-repetitions.

Results Both the normal-form and the incremental model show qualitatively the same results. STRUCTURALLEVEL has a significant influence on priming strength (LN DIST) for the cases where a lexical item serves as prime (e.g., normal-form PP: $\beta_{lnDist:lex-lex} = 0.261$, $p < 0.0001$; $\beta_{lnDist:lex-phr} = 0.166$, $p < 0.0001$; $\beta_{lnDist:phr-lex} = 0.056, p < 0.05$; as compared to the baseline $phr - phr$. N.B. higher values denote less decay & priming). Phrasal categories prime other phrasal and lexical categories, but there is a lower priming effect to be seen from lexical categories. Figure 3 presents the resulting effect sizes.

Albeit significant, we assume the effect of prime type is attributable to processing differences rather than the strong difference that would indicate that there is no priming of, e.g., lexical subcategorization frames. As the analysis of effect sizes shows, we can see priming from and in between both lexical and phrasal categories.

Additionally, there is no evidence suggesting that, once frequency is taken into account, syntactic processes happening high up in derivation trees show more priming (see Scheepers 2003).

7 Discussion

We can confirm the syntactic priming effect for CCG categories. Priming occurs in incremental as well as in normal-form CCG derivations, and at different syntactic levels in those derivations: we demonstrated that priming effects persists across syntactic stages, from the lowest one (lexical categories) up to higher ones (phrasal categories). This is what CCG predicts if priming of categories is assumed.

Linguistic data is inherently noisy. Annotations contain errors, and conversions such as the one to CCG may add further error. However, since noise is distributed across the corpus, it is unlikely to affect priming effect strength or its interaction with the factors we used: priming, in this study, is defined as *decay* of repetition probability. We see the lack of control in the collection of a corpus like Switchboard not only as a challenge, but also as an advantage: it means that realistic data is present in the corpus, allowing us to conduct a controlled experiments to validate a claim about a specific theory of competence grammar.

The fact that CCG categories prime could be explained in a model that includes a basic form of subcategorization. All categories, if lexical or phrasal, contain a subcategorization frame, with only those categories present that have yet to be satisfied. Our CCG based models make predictions for experimental studies, e.g., that specific heads with open subcategorization slots (such as transitive verbs) will be primed by phrases that require the same kinds of arguments (such as verbal phrases with a ditransitive verb and an argument).

The models presented take the frequency of the syntactic category into account, reducing noise, especially in the conditions with lower numbers of (positive) reptition examples (e.g., CP and incremental derivations in Experiment 1). Whether there are significant qualitative and quantitative differences of PP and CP priming with respect to choice of derivation type – which would point out processing differences in comprehension vs. production priming – will be a matter of future work.

At this point, we do not explicitly discriminate different syntactic frameworks. Comparing priming effects in a corpus annotated in parallel according to different theories will be a matter of future work.

8 Conclusions

We have discussed an empirical, corpus-based approach to use priming effects in the validation of general syntactic models. The analysis we presented is compatible with the reality of a lexicalized, categorial grammar such as CCG as a component of the human sentence processor. CCG is unusual in allowing us to compare different types of derivational analyses within the same grammar framework. Focusing on CCG allowed us to contrast priming under different conditions, while still making a statistical and general statement about the priming effects for *all* syntactic phenomena covered by the grammar.

Acknowledgements

We would like to thank Mark Steedman, Roger Levy, Johanna Moore and three anonymous reviewers for their comments. The authors are grateful for being supported by the following grants: DR by The Edinburgh Stanford Link, JH by NSF ITR grant 0205456, FK by The Leverhulme Trust (grant F/00 159/AL – Syntactic Parallelism).

References

J. Kathryn Bock. 1986. Syntactic persistence in language production. *Cognitive Psychology*, 18:355–387.

J. Kathryn Bock and Helga Loebell. 1990. Framing sentences. *Cognition*, 35:1–39.

Holly P. Branigan, Martin J. Pickering, and Alexandra A. Cleland. 2000. Syntactic co-ordination in dialogue. *Cognition*, 75:B13–25.

Jean Carletta, S. Dingare, Malvina Nissim, and T. Nikitina. 2004. Using the NITE XML toolkit on the Switchboard corpus to study syntactic choice: a case study. In *Proc. 4th Language Resources and Evaluation Conference*. Lisbon, Portugal.

Stephen Clark and James R. Curran. 2004. Parsing the WSJ using CCG and log-linear models. In *Proc. of the 42nd Annual Meeting of the Association for Computational Linguistics*. Barcelona, Spain.

A. A. Cleland and M. J. Pickering. 2003. The use of lexical and syntactic information in language production: Evidence from the priming of noun-phrase structure. *Journal of Memory and Language*, 49:214–230.

Amit Dubey, Frank Keller, and Patrick Sturt. 2006. Integrating syntactic priming into an incremental probabilistic parser, with an application to psycholinguistic modeling. In *Proc. of the 21st International Conference on Computational Linguistics and 44th Annual Mtg of the Association for Computational Linguistics*. Sydney, Australia.

Jason Eisner. 1996. Efficient normal-form parsing for combinatory categorial grammar. In *Proceedings of the 34th Annual Meeting of the Association for Computational Linguistics*, pages 79–86. Santa Cruz,CA.

Stefan Th. Gries. 2005. Syntactic priming: A corpus-based approach. *Journal of Psycholinguistic Research*, 34(4):365–399.

Julia Hockenmaier and Mark Steedman. 2002. Generative models for statistical parsing with Combinatory Categorial Grammar. In *Proc. 40th Annual Meeting of the Association for Computational Linguistics*. Philadelphia, PA.

Julia Hockenmaier and Mark Steedman. 2005. CCGbank: Users' manual. Technical Report MS-CIS-05-09, Computer and Information Science, University of Pennsylvania.

Mark Johnson and Eugene Charniak. 2004. A tag-based noisy channel model of speech repairs. In *Proc. 42nd Annual Meeting of the Association for Computational Linguistics*, pages 33–39. Barcelona, Spain.

M. Marcus, G. Kim, M. Marcinkiewicz, R. MacIntyre, A. Bies, M. Ferguson, K. Katz, and B. Schasberger. 1994. The Penn treebank: Annotating predicate argument structure. In *Proc. ARPA Human Language Technology Workshop*. Plainsboro, NJ.

Michael Niv. 1994. A psycholinguistically motivated parser for CCG. In *Mtg. of the Association for Computational Linguistics*, pages 125–132.

Martin J. Pickering and Holly P. Branigan. 1998. The representation of verbs: Evidence from syntactic priming in language production. *Journal of Memory and Language*, 39:633–651.

Martin J. Pickering, Holly P. Branigan, and Janet F. McLean. 2002. Constituent structure is formulated in one stage. *Journal of Memory and Language*, 46:586–605.

David Reitter, Frank Keller, and Johanna D. Moore. 2006a. Computational modelling of structural priming in dialogue. In *Proc. Human Language Technology conference - North American chapter of the Association for Computational Linguistics annual mtg*. New York City.

David Reitter, Johanna D. Moore, and Frank Keller. 2006b. Priming of syntactic rules in task-oriented dialogue and spontaneous conversation. In *Proc. 28th Annual Conference of the Cognitive Science Society*.

Christoph Scheepers. 2003. Syntactic priming of relative clause attachments: Persistence of structural configuration in sentence production. *Cognition*, 89:179–205.

Mark Steedman. 2000. *The Syntactic Process*. MIT Press.

Benedikt Szmrecsanyi. 2005. Creatures of habit: A corpus-linguistic analysis of persistence in spoken english. *Corpus Linguistics and Linguistic Theory*, 1(1):113–149.

William N. Venables and Brian D. Ripley. 2002. *Modern Applied Statistics with S. Fourth Edition*. Springer.

Mike White and Jason Baldridge. 2003. Adapting chart realization to CCG. In *Proc. 9th European Workshop on Natural Language Generation*. Budapest, Hungary.

Better Informed Training of Latent Syntactic Features

Markus Dreyer and **Jason Eisner**
Department of Computer Science / Center for Language and Speech Processing
Johns Hopkins University
3400 North Charles Street, Baltimore, MD 21218 USA
{markus, jason}@clsp.jhu.edu

Abstract

We study unsupervised methods for learning refinements of the nonterminals in a treebank. Following Matsuzaki et al. (2005) and Prescher (2005), we may for example split NP without supervision into NP[0] and NP[1], which behave differently. We first propose to learn a PCFG that adds such features to nonterminals in such a way that they respect patterns of linguistic feature passing: each node's nonterminal features are either identical to, or independent of, those of its parent. This linguistic constraint reduces runtime and the number of parameters to be learned. However, it did not yield improvements when training on the Penn Treebank. An orthogonal strategy was more successful: to improve the performance of the EM learner by treebank preprocessing and by annealing methods that split nonterminals selectively. Using these methods, we can maintain high parsing accuracy while dramatically reducing the model size.

1 Introduction

Treebanks never contain enough information; thus PCFGs estimated straightforwardly from the Penn Treebank (Bies et al., 1995) work only moderately well (Charniak, 1996). To address this problem, researchers have used heuristics to add more information. Eisner (1996), Charniak (1997), Collins (1997), and many subsequent researchers[1] annotated every node with lexical features passed up from its "head child," in order to more precisely reflect the node's "inside" contents. Charniak (1997) and Johnson (1998) annotated each node with its parent and grandparent nonterminals, to more precisely reflect its "outside" context. Collins (1996) split the sentence label S into two versions, representing sentences with and without subjects. He also modified the treebank to contain different labels for standard and for base noun phrases. Klein and Manning (2003) identified nonterminals that could valuably be split into fine-grained ones using hand-written linguistic rules. Their unlexicalized parser combined several such heuristics with rule markovization and reached a performance similar to early lexicalized parsers.

In all these cases, choosing which nonterminals to split, and how, was a matter of art. Ideally such splits would be learned automatically from the given treebank itself. This would be less costly and more portable to treebanks for new domains and languages. One might also hope that the automatically learned splits would be more effective.

Matsuzaki et al. (2005) introduced a model for such learning: PCFG-LA.[2] They used EM to induce fine-grained versions of a given treebank's nonterminals and rules. We present models that similarly learn to propagate fine-grained features through the tree, but only in certain linguistically motivated ways. Our models therefore allocate a supply of free parameters differently, allowing more fine-grained nonterminals but less fine-grained control over the probabilities of rewriting them. We also present simple methods for deciding selectively (during training) which nonterminals to split and how.

Section 2 describes previous work in finding hidden information in treebanks. Section 3 describes automatically induced feature grammars. We start by describing the PCFG-LA model, then introduce new models that use specific agreement patterns to propagate features through the tree. Section 4 describes annealing-like procedures for training latent-annotation models. Section 5 describes the motivation and results of our experiments. We finish by discussing future work and conclusions in sections 6–7.

[1] Not to mention earlier *non*-PCFG lexicalized statistical parsers, notably Magerman (1995) for the Penn Treebank.

[2] Probabilistic context-free grammar with latent annotations.

Proceedings of the 2006 Conference on Empirical Methods in Natural Language Processing (EMNLP 2006), pages 317–326,
Sydney, July 2006.

Citation	Observed data	Hidden data
Collins (1997)	Treebank tree with head child annotated on each nonterminal	*No hidden data. Degenerate EM case.*
Lari and Young (1990)	Words	Parse tree
Pereira and Schabes (1992)	Words and partial brackets	Parse tree
Klein and Manning (2001)	Part-of-speech tags	Parse tree
Chiang and Bikel (2002)	Treebank tree	Head child on each nonterminal
Matsuzaki et al. (2005)	Treebank tree	Integer feature on each nonterminal
INHERIT model (this paper)	Treebank tree and head child heuristics	Integer feature on each nonterminal

Table 1: Observed and hidden data in PCFG grammar learning.

2 Partially supervised EM learning

The parameters of a PCFG can be learned with or without supervision. In the supervised case, the complete tree is observed, and the rewrite rule probabilities can be estimated directly from the observed rule counts. In the unsupervised case, only the words are observed, and the learning method must induce the whole structure above them. (See Table 1.)

In the *partially* supervised case we will consider, some part of the tree is observed, and the remaining information has to be induced. Pereira and Schabes (1992) estimate PCFG parameters from partially bracketed sentences, using the inside-outside algorithm to induce the missing brackets and the missing node labels. Some authors define a complete tree as one that specifies not only a label but also a "head child" for each node. Chiang and Bikel (2002) induces the missing head-child information; Prescher (2005) induces both the head-child information and the latent annotations we will now discuss.

3 Feature Grammars

3.1 The PCFG-LA Model

Staying in the partially supervised paradigm, the PCFG-LA model described in Matsuzaki et al. (2005) observe whole treebank trees, but learn an "annotation" on each nonterminal token—an unspecified and uninterpreted integer that distinguishes otherwise identical nonterminals. Just as Collins manually split the S nonterminal label into S and SG for sentences with and without subjects, Matsuzaki et al. (2005) split S into S[1], S[2], ..., S[L] where L is a predefined number—but they do it automatically and systematically, and not only for S but for every nonterminal. Their partially supervised learning procedure observes trees that are fully bracketed and fully labeled, except for the integer subscript used to annotate each node. After automatically inducing the annotations with EM, their resulting parser performs just as well as one learned from a treebank whose nonterminals were manually refined through linguistic and error analysis (Klein and Manning, 2003).

In Matsuzaki's PCFG-LA model, rewrite rules take the form

$$X[\alpha] \rightarrow Y[\beta]\ Z[\gamma] \qquad (1)$$

in the binary case, and

$$X[\alpha] \rightarrow w \qquad (2)$$

in the lexical case. The probability of a tree consisting of rules $r_1, r_2, \ldots$ is given by the probability of its root symbol times the conditional probabilities of the rules. The annotated tree T_1 in Fig. 1, for example, has the following probability:

$$\begin{aligned} P(T_1) = \; & P(\texttt{ROOT} \rightarrow \texttt{S}[2]) \\ & \times P(\texttt{S}[2] \rightarrow \texttt{NP}[1]\ \texttt{VP}[3]) \\ & \times P(\texttt{NP}[1] \rightarrow^* \texttt{He}) \\ & \times P(\texttt{VP}[3] \rightarrow^* \texttt{loves cookies}) \end{aligned}$$

where, to simplify the notation, we use $P(X \rightarrow Y\ Z)$ to denote the conditional probability $P(Y\ Z \mid X)$ that a given node with label X will have children $Y\ Z$.

Degrees of freedom. We will want to compare models that have about the same size. Models with more free parameters have an inherent advantage on modeling copious data because of their greater

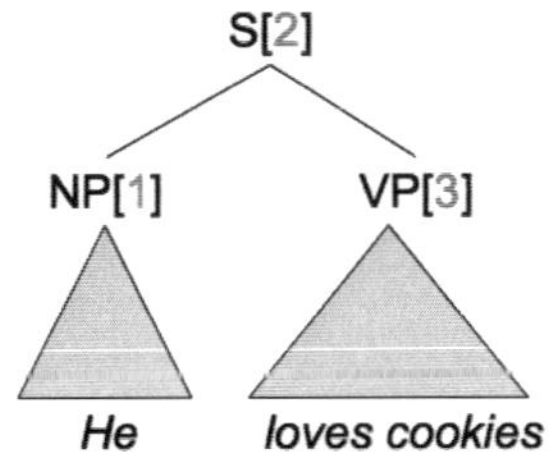

Figure 1: Treebank tree with annotations.

expressiveness. Models with fewer free parameters are easier to train accurately on sparse data, as well as being more efficient in space and often in time. Our question is therefore what can be accomplished with a given number of parameters.

How many free parameters in a PCFG-LA model? Such a model is created by annotating the nonterminals of a standard PCFG (extracted from the given treebank) with the various integers from 1 to L. If the original, "backbone" grammar has R_3 binary rules of the form $X \to Y\ Z$, then the resulting PCFG-LA model has $L^3 \times R_3$ such rules: $X[1] \to Y[1]\ Z[1]$, $X[1] \to Y[1]\ Z[2]$, $X[1] \to Y[2]\ Z[1], \ldots, X[L] \to Y[L]\ Z[L]$. Similarly, if the backbone grammar has R_2 rules of the form $X \to Y$ the PCFG-LA model has $L^2 \times R_2$ such rules.[3] The number of R_1 terminal rules $X \to w$ is just multiplied by L.

The PCFG-LA has as many parameters to learn as rules: one probability per rule. However, not all these parameters are free, as there are $L \times N$ sum-to-one constraints, where N is the number of backbone nonterminals. Thus we have

$$L^3 R_3 + L^2 R_2 + L R_1 - LN \qquad (3)$$

degrees of freedom.

We note that Goodman (1997) mentioned possible ways to factor the probability 1, making independence assumptions in order to reduce the number of parameters.

Runtime. Assuming there are no unary rule cycles in the backbone grammar, bottom-up chart parsing of a length-n sentence at test time takes time proportional to $n^3 L^3 R_3 + n^2 L^2 R_2 + nLR_1$, by attempting to apply each rule everywhere in the sentence. (The dominating term comes from equation (4) of Table 2: we must loop over all n^3 triples i, j, k and all R_3 backbone rules $X \to YZ$ and all L^3 triples α, β, γ.) As a function of n and L only, this is $O(n^3 L^3)$.

At training time, to induce the annotations on a given backbone tree with n nodes, one can run a constrained version of this algorithm that loops over only the n triples i, j, k that are consistent with the given tree (and considers only the single consistent backbone rule for each one). This takes time $O(nL^3)$, as does the inside-outside version we actually use to collect expected PCFG-LA rule counts for EM training.

We now introduce a model that is smaller, and has a lower runtime complexity, because it adheres to specified ways of propagating features through the tree.

3.2 Feature Passing: The INHERIT Model

Many linguistic theories assume that features get passed from the mother node to their children or some of their children. In many cases it is the head child that gets passed its feature value from its mother (e.g., Kaplan and Bresnan (1982), Pollard and Sag (1994)). In some cases the feature is passed to both the head and the non-head child, or perhaps even to the non-head alone.

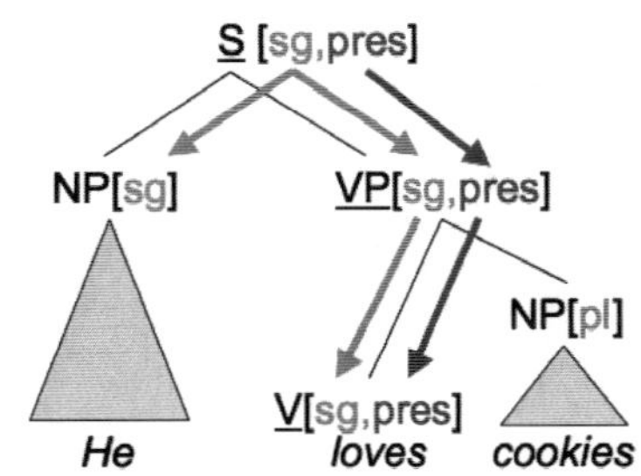

Figure 2: Features are passed to different children at different positions in the tree.

In the example in Fig. 2, the tense feature (*pres*) is always passed to the head child (underlined). How the number feature (*sg/pl*) is passed depends on the rewrite rule: S $\to$ NP VP passes it to both children, to enforce subject-verb agreement, while VP $\to$ V NP only passes it to the head child, since the object NP is free not to agree with the verb.

A feature grammar can incorporate such patterns of feature passing. We introduce additional parameters that define the probability of passing a feature to certain children. The head child of each node is given deterministically by the head rules of (Collins, 1996).

Under the INHERIT model that we propose, the

[3] We use unary rules of this form (e.g. the Treebank's S $\to$ NP) in our reimplementation of Matsuzaki's algorithm.

Model	Runtime and d.f.	Simplified equation for inside probabilities (ignores unary rules)
Matsuzaki et al. (2005)	test: $O(n^3L^3)$ train: $O(nL^3)$ d.f.: $L^3R_3 + L^2R_2 + LR_1 - LN$	$B_{X[\alpha]}(i,k) = \sum_{Y,\beta,Z,\gamma,j} P(X[\alpha] \to Y[\beta]\ Z[\gamma]) \times B_{Y[\beta]}(i,j) \times B_{Z[\gamma]}(j,k)$ (4)
INHERIT model (this paper)	test: $O(n^3L)$ train: $O(nL)$ d.f.: $L(R_3 + R_2 + R_1) + 3R_3 - N$	$B_{X[\alpha]}(i,k) = \sum_{Y,Z,j} P(X[\alpha] \to Y\ Z) \times \left(\begin{array}{l} P(\textbf{neither} \mid X,Y,Z) \times B_Y(i,j) \times B_Z(j,k)) \\ + P(\textbf{left} \mid X,Y,Z) \times B_{Y[\alpha]}(i,j) \times B_Z(j,k)) \\ + P(\textbf{right} \mid X,Y,Z) \times B_Y(i,j) \times B_{Z[\alpha]}(j,k)) \\ + P(\textbf{both} \mid X,Y,Z) \times B_{Y[\alpha]}Y(i,j) \times B_{Z[\alpha]}(j,k)) \end{array} \right)$ (5) $B_X(i,j) = \sum_{\alpha} P_{ann}(\alpha \mid X) \times B_{X[\alpha]}(i,j)$ (6) $P(\textbf{left} \mid X,Y,Z) = \begin{cases} P(\textbf{head} \mid X,Y,Z) & \text{if } Y \text{ heads } X \to \mathbf{Y}\ Z \\ P(\textbf{nonhead} \mid X,Y,Z) & \text{otherwise} \end{cases}$ (7) $P(\textbf{right} \mid X,Y,Z) = \begin{cases} P(\textbf{head} \mid X,Y,Z) & \text{if } Z \text{ heads } X \to Y\ \mathbf{Z} \\ P(\textbf{nonhead} \mid X,Y,Z) & \text{otherwise} \end{cases}$ (8)

Table 2: Comparison of the PCFG-LA model with the INHERIT model proposed in this paper. "d.f." stands for "degrees of freedom" (i.e., free parameters). The B terms are inside probabilities; to compute Viterbi parse probabilities instead, replace summation by maximization. Note the use of the intermediate quantity $B_X(i,j)$ to improve runtime complexity by moving some summations out of the inner loop; this is an instance of a "folding transformation" (Blatz and Eisner, 2006).

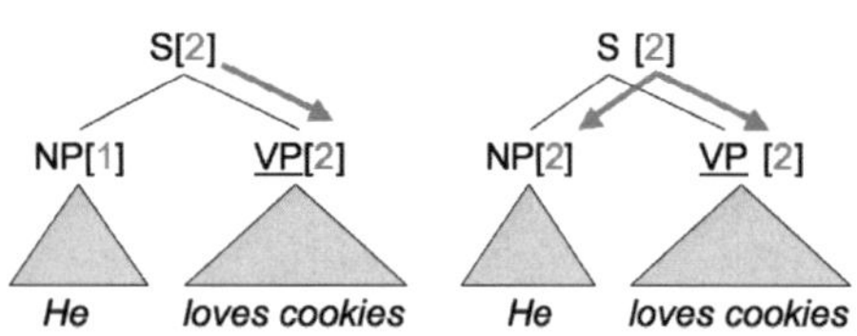

Figure 3: Two passpatterns. Left: T_2. The feature is passed to the head child (underlined). Right: T_3. The feature is passed to both children.

probabilities of tree T_2 in Fig. 3 are calculated as follows, with $P_{ann}(1 \mid NP)$ being the probability of annotating an NP with feature 1 if it does *not* inherit its parent's feature. The VP is boldfaced to indicate that it is the head child of this rule.

$$\begin{aligned} P(T_2) = \ & P(\texttt{ROOT} \to \texttt{S}[2]) \\ & \times P(\texttt{S}[2] \to \texttt{NP}\ \textbf{VP}) \\ & \times P(\textbf{pass to head} \mid \texttt{S} \to \texttt{NP}\ \textbf{VP}) \\ & \times P_{ann}(1 \mid \texttt{NP}) \times P(\texttt{NP}[1] \to^* \texttt{He}) \\ & \times P(\texttt{VP}[2] \to^* \texttt{loves cookies}) \end{aligned}$$

Tree T_3 in Fig. 3 has the following probability:

$$\begin{aligned} P(T_3) = \ & P(\texttt{ROOT} \to \texttt{S}[2]) \\ & \times P(\texttt{S}[2] \to \texttt{NP}\ \textbf{VP}) \\ & \times P(\textbf{pass to both} \mid \texttt{S} \to \texttt{NP}\ \textbf{VP}) \\ & \times P(\texttt{NP}[2] \to^* \texttt{He}) \\ & \times P(\texttt{VP}[2] \to^* \texttt{loves cookies}) \end{aligned}$$

In T_2, the subject NP chose feature 1 or 2 independent of its parent S, according to the distribution $P_{ann}(\cdot \mid \texttt{NP})$. In T_3, it was constrained to inherit its parent's feature 2.

Degrees of freedom. The INHERIT model may be regarded as containing all the same rules (see (1)) as the PCFG-LA model. However, these rules' probabilities are now collectively determined by a smaller set of shared parameters.[4] That is because the distribution of the child features β and γ no longer depends arbitrarily on the rest of the rule. β is either equal to α, or chosen independently of everything but Y.

The model needs probabilities for $L \times R_3$ binary-rule parameters like $P(\texttt{S}[2] \to \texttt{NP}\ \textbf{VP})$ above, as well as $L \times R_2$ unary-rule and $L \times R_1$ lexical-rule parameters. None of these consider the annotations on the children. They are subject to $L \times N$ sum-to-one constraints.

The model also needs $4 \times R_3$ passpattern probabilities like $P(\textbf{pass to head} \mid X \to YZ)$ above, with R_3 sum-to-one constraints, and $L \times N$ non-inherited annotation parameters $P_{ann}(\alpha|X)$, with N sum-to-one constraints.

Adding these up and canceling the two $L \times N$

[4]The reader may find it useful to write out the probability $P(X[\alpha] \to Y[\beta]\ Z[\gamma])$ in terms of the parameters described below. Like equation (5), it is $P(X[\alpha] \to Y\ Z)$ times a sum of up to 4 products, corresponding to the 4 passpattern cases.

terms, the INHERIT model has

$$L(R_3 + R_2 + R_1) + 3R_3 - N \quad (9)$$

degrees of freedom. Thus for a typical grammar where R_3 dominates, we have reduced the number of free parameters from about $L^3 R_3$ to only about LR_3.

Runtime. We may likewise reduce an L^3 factor to L in the runtime. Table 2 shows dynamic programming equations for the INHERIT model. By exercising care, they are able to avoid summing over all possible values of β and γ within the inner loop. This is possible because when they are not inherited, they do not depend on X, Y, Z, or α.

3.3 Multiple Features

The INHERIT model described above is linguistically naive in several ways. One problem (see section 6 for others) is that each nonterminal has only a single feature to pass. Linguists, however, usually annotate each phrase with multiple features. Our example tree in Fig. 2 was annotated with both tense and number features, with different inheritance patterns.

As a step up from INHERIT, we propose an INHERIT2 model where each nonterminal carries two features. Thus, we will have $L^6 R_3$ binary rules instead of $L^3 R_3$. However, we assume that the two features choose their passpatterns independently, and that when a feature is not inherited, it is chosen independently of the other feature. This keeps the number of parameters down. In effect, we are defining

$$\begin{aligned} & P(X[\alpha][\rho] \to Y[\beta][\sigma]\ Z[\gamma][\tau]) \\ &= P(X[\alpha][\rho] \to Y\ Z) \\ &\quad \times P_1(\beta, \gamma \mid X[\alpha] \to Y\ Z) \\ &\quad \times P_2(\sigma, \tau \mid X[\rho] \to Y\ Z) \end{aligned}$$

where P_1 and P_2 choose child features as if they were separate single-feature INHERIT models.

We omit discussion of dynamic programming speedups for INHERIT2. Empirically, the hope is that the two features when learned with the EM algorithm will pick out different linguistic properties of the constituents in the treebank tree.

4 Annealing-Like Training Approaches

Training latent PCFG models, like training most other unsupervised models, requires non-convex optimization. To find good parameter values, it is often helpful to train a simpler model first and use its parameters to derive a starting guess for the harder optimization problem. A well-known example is the training of the IBM models for statistical machine translation (Berger et al., 1994).

In this vein, we did an experiment in which we gradually increased L during EM training of the PCFG-LA and INHERIT models. Whenever the training likelihood began to converge, we *manually* and *globally* increased L, simply doubling or tripling it (see "clone all" in Table 3 and Fig. 5). The probability of $X[\alpha] \to Y[\beta]Z[\gamma]$ under the new model was initialized to be proportional to the probability of $X[\alpha \bmod L] \to Y[\beta \bmod L]Z[\gamma \bmod L]$ (where L refers to the old L),[5] times a random "jitter" to break symmetry.

In a second annealing experiment ("clone some") we addressed a weakness of the PCFG-LA and INHERIT models: They give every nonterminal the same number of latent annotations. It would seem that different coarse-grained nonterminals in the original Penn Treebank have different degrees of impurity (Klein and Manning, 2003). There are linguistically many kinds of NP, which are differentially selected for by various contexts and hence are worth distinguishing. By contrast, -LRB- is almost always realized as a left parenthesis and may not need further refinement. Our "clone some" annealing starts by training a model with L=2 to convergence. Then, instead of cloning all nonterminals as in the previous annealing experiments, we clone only those that have seemed to benefit most from their previous refinement. This benefit is measured by the Jensen-Shannon divergence of the two distributions $P(X[0] \to \cdots)$ and $P(X[1] \to \cdots)$. The

[5] Notice that as well as cloning $X[\alpha]$, this procedure multiplies by 4, 2, and 1 the number of binary, unary, and lexical rules that rewrite $X[\alpha]$. To leave the backbone grammar unchanged, we should have scaled down the probabilities of such rules by 1/4, 1/2, and 1 respectively. Instead, we simply scaled them all down by the same proportion. While this temporarily changes the balance of probability among the three kinds of rules, EM immediately corrects this balance on the next training iteration to match the observed balance on the treebank trees—hence the one-iteration downtick in Figure 5).

Jensen-Shannon divergence is defined as

$$D(q,r) = \frac{1}{2}\left(D\left(q \,||\, \frac{q+r}{2}\right) + D\left(r \,||\, \frac{q+r}{2}\right)\right)$$

These experiments are a kind of "poor man's version" of the deterministic annealing clustering algorithm (Pereira et al., 1993; Rose, 1998), which gradually increases the number of clusters during the clustering process. In deterministic annealing, one starts in principle with a very large number of clusters, but maximizes likelihood only under a constraint that the joint distribution $p(point, cluster)$ must have very high entropy. This drives all of the cluster centroids to coincide exactly, redundantly representing just one effective cluster. As the entropy is permitted to decrease, some of the cluster centroids find it worthwhile to drift apart.[6] In future work, we would like to apply this technique to split nonterminals gradually, by initially requiring high-entropy parse forests on the training data and slowly relaxing this constraint.

5 Experiments

5.1 Setup

We ran several experiments to compare the INHERIT with the PCFG-LA model and look into the effect of different Treebank preprocessing and the annealing-like procedures.

We used sections 2–20 of the Penn Treebank 2 Wall Street Journal corpus (Marcus et al., 1993) for training, section 22 as development set and section 23 for testing. Following Matsuzaki et al. (2005), words occurring fewer than 4 times in the training corpus were replaced by unknown-word symbols that encoded certain suffix and capitalization information.

All experiments used simple add-lambda smoothing (λ=0.1) during the reestimation step (M step) of training.

Binarization and Markovization. Before extracting the backbone PCFG and running the constrained inside-outside (EM) training algorithm, we preprocessed the Treebank using center-parent binarization Matsuzaki et al. (2005). Besides making the rules at most binary, this preprocessing also helpfully enriched the backbone nonterminals. For all but the first ("Basic") experiments, we also enriched the nonterminals with order-1 horizontal and order-2 vertical markovization (Klein and Manning, 2003).[7] Figure 4 shows what a multiple-child structure $X \rightarrow A\ B\ \boldsymbol{H}\ C\ D$ looks like after binarization and markovization. The binarization process starts at the head of the sentence and moves to the right, inserting an auxiliary node for each picked up child, then moving to the left. Each auxiliary node consists of the parent label, the direction (L or R) and the label of the child just picked up.

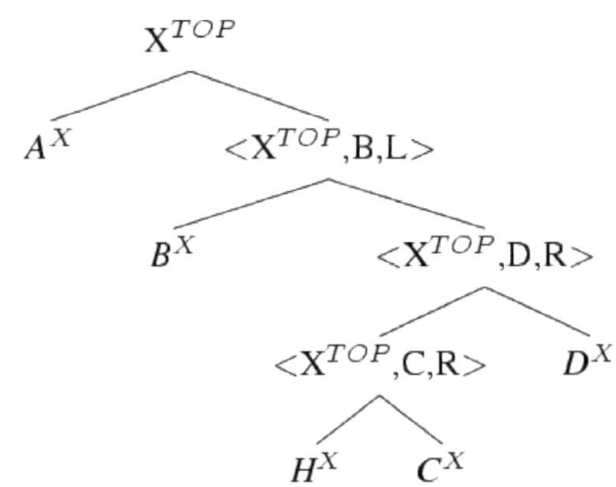

Figure 4: Horizontal and vertical markovization and center-parent binarization of the rule $X \rightarrow A\ B\ \boldsymbol{H}\ C\ D$ where H is the head child.

Initialization. The backbone PCFG grammar was read off the altered Treebank, and the initial annotated grammar was created by creating several versions of every rewrite rule. The probabilities of these newly created rules are uniform and proportional to the original rule, multiplied by a random epsilon factor uniformly sampled from [.9999,1.0001] to break symmetry.

5.2 Decoding

To test the PCFG learned by a given method, we attempted to recover the *unannotated* parse of each sentence in the development set. We then scored these parses by debinarizing or demarkovizing them, then measuring their precision and recall of the labeled constituents from the gold-standard Treebank parses.

[6]In practice, each very large group of centroids (effective cluster) is represented by just two, until such time as those two drift apart to represent separate effective clusters—then each is cloned.

[7]The vertical markovization was applied *before* binarization. – Matsuzaki et al. (2005) used a markovized grammar to get a better unannotated parse forest during decoding, but they did not markovize the training data.

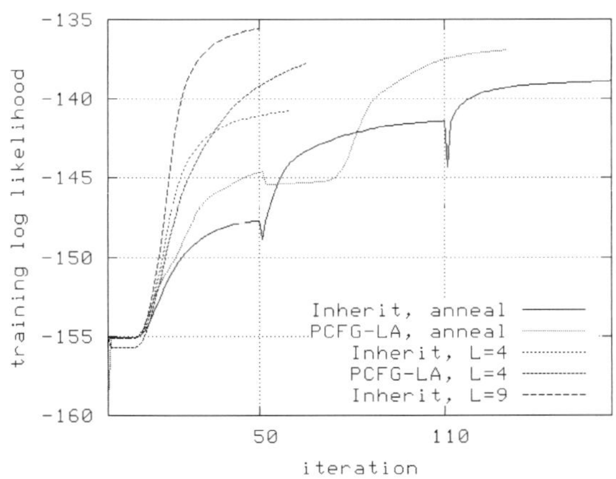

Figure 5: Log_e-likelihood during training. The two "anneal" curves use the "clone all" method. We increased L after iteration 50 and, for the INHERIT model, iteration 110. The downward spikes in the two annealed cases are due to perturbation of the model parameters (footnote 5).

An unannotated parse's probability is the total probability, under our learned PCFG, of all of its annotated refinements. This total can be efficiently computed by the constrained version of the inside algorithm in Table 2.

How do we obtain the unannotated parse whose *total* probability is greatest? It does not suffice to find the single best annotated parse and then strip off the annotations. Matsuzaki et al. (2005) note that the best annotated parse is in fact NP-hard to find. We use their reranking approximation. A 1000-best list for each sentence in the decoding set was created by parsing with our markovized *un*annotated grammar and extracting the 1000 best parses using the k-best algorithm 3 described in Huang and Chiang (2005). Then we chose the most probable of these 1000 unannotated parses under our PCFG, first finding the total probability of each by using the the constrained inside algorithm as explained above.[8]

5.3 Results and Discussion

Table 3 summarizes the results on development and test data. [9] Figure 5 shows the training log-likelihoods.

First, markovization of the Treebank leads to striking improvements. The "Basic" block of experiments in Table 3 used non-markovized grammars, as in Matsuzaki et al. (2005). The next block of experiments, introducing markovized grammars, shows a considerable improvement. This is not simply because markovization increases the number of parameters: markovization with $L = 2$ already beats basic models that have much higher L and far more parameters.

Evidently, markovization pre-splits the labels in the trees in a reasonable way, so EM has less work to do. This is not to say that markovization eliminates the need for hidden annotations: with markovization, going from L=1 to L=2 increases the parsing accuracy even more than without it.

Second, our "clone all" training technique (shown in the next block of Table 3) did not help performance and may even have hurt slightly. Here we initialized the L=2x2 model with the trained L=2 model for PCFG-LA, and the L=3x3 model with the L=3 and the L=3x3x3 model with the L=3x3 model.

Third, our "clone some" training technique appeared to work. On PCFG-LA, the L<2x2 condition (i.e., train with L=2 and then clone some) matched the performance of L=4 with 30% fewer parameters. On INHERIT, L<2x2 beat L=4 with 8% fewer parameters. In these experiments, we used the average divergence as a threshold: X[0] and X[1] are split again if the divergence of their rewrite distributions is higher than average.

Fourth, our INHERIT model was a disappointment. It generally performed slightly worse than PCFG-LA when given about as many degrees of freedom. This was also the case on some cursory experiments on smaller training corpora. It is tempting to conclude that INHERIT simply adopted overly strong linguistic constraints, but relaxing those constraints by moving to the INHERIT2 model did not seem to help. In our one experiment with INHERIT2 (not shown in Table 3), using 2 features that can each take L=2 values (d.f.: 212,707) obtains an F_1 score of only 83.67—worse than 1 feature taking L=4 values.

5.4 Analysis: What was learned by INHERIT?

INHERIT did seem to discover "linguistic" features, as intended, even though this did not improve parse accuracy. We trained INHERIT and PCFG-LA models (both L=2, non-markovized) and noticed the following.

[8] For the first set of experiments, in which the models were trained on a simple non-markovized grammar, the 1000-best trees had to be "demarkovized" before our PCFG was able to rescore them.

[9] All results are reported on sentences of 40 words or less.

	PCFG-LA					INHERIT				
	L	d.f.	LP	LR	F_1	L	d.f.	LP	LR	F_1
Basic	1	24,226	76.99	74.51	75.73	1	35,956	76.99	74.51	75.73
	2	72,392	81.22	80.67	80.94	2	60,902	79.42	77.58	78.49
	4	334,384	83.53	83.39	83.46	12	303,162	82.41	81.55	81.98
	8	2,177,888	85.43	85.05	85.24	80	1,959,053	83.99	83.02	83.50
Markov.	1	41,027	79.95	78.43	79.18	1	88,385	79.95	78.43	79.18
						2	132,371	83.85	82.23	83.03
	2	178,264	85.70	84.37	85.03	3	176,357	85.04	83.60	84.31
						4	220,343	85.30	84.06	84.68
	3	506,427	86.44	85.19	85.81	9	440,273	86.16	85.12	85.64
	4	1,120,232	87.09	85.71	86.39	26	1,188,035	86.55	85.55	86.05
Clone all	2	178,264	85.70	84.37	85.03	3	176,357	85.04	83.60	84.31
						3x3	440,273	85.99	84.88	85.43
	2x2	1,120,232	87.06	85.49	86.27	3x3x3	1,232,021	86.65	85.70	86.17
Cl.some	2	178,264	85.70	84.37	85.03	2	132,371	83.85	82.23	83.03
	<2x2	789,279	**87.17**	**85.71**	**86.43**	<2x2	203,673	85.49	84.45	84.97
						<2x2x2	314,999	85.57	84.60	85.08

Table 3: Results on the development set: labeled precision (LP), labeled recall (LR), and their harmonic mean (F_1). "Basic" models are trained on a non-markovized treebank (as in Matsuzaki et al. (2005)); all others are trained on a markovized treebank. The best model (PCFG-LA with "clone some" annealing, F_1=86.43) has also been decoded on the final test set, reaching P/R=86.94/85.40 (F_1=86.17).

We used both models to assign the most-probable annotations to the gold parses of the development set. Under the INHERIT model, NP[0] vs. NP[1] constituents were 21% plural vs. 41% plural. Under PCFG-LA this effect was weaker (30% vs. 39%), although it was significant in both (Fisher's exact test, $p < 0.001$). Strikingly, under the INHERIT model, the NP's were 10 times more likely to pass this feature to both children (Fisher's, $p < 0.001$)—just as we would expect for a number feature, since the determiner and head noun of an NP must agree.

The INHERIT model also learned to use feature value 1 for "tensed auxiliary." The VP[1] nonterminal was far more likely than VP[0] to expand as V VP, where V represents any of the tensed verb preterminals VBZ, VBG, VBN, VBD, VBP. Furthermore, these expansion rules had a very strong preference for "pass to head," so that the left child would also be annotated as a tensed auxiliary, typically causing it to expand as a form of be, have, or do. In short, the feature ensured that it was genuine auxiliary verbs that subcategorized for VP$'s$.

(The PCFG-LA model actually arranged the same behavior, e.g. similarly preferring VBZ[1] in the auxiliary expansion rule VP $\rightarrow$ VBZ VP. The difference is that the PCFG-LA model was able to express this preference directly without propagating the [1] up to the VP parent. Hence neither VP[0] nor VP[1] became strongly associated with the auxiliary rule.)

Many things are equally learned by both models: They learn the difference between subordinating conjunctions (*while, if*) and prepositions (*under, after*), putting them in distinct groups of the original IN tag, which typically combine with sentences and noun phrases, respectively. Both models also split the conjunction CC into two distinct groups: a group of conjunctions starting with an upper-case letter at the beginning of the sentence and a group containing all other conjunctions.

6 Future Work: Log-Linear Modeling

Our approach in the INHERIT model made certain strict independence assumptions, with no backoff. The choice of a particular passpattern, for example, depends on all and only the three nonterminals X, Y, Z. However, given sparse training data, sometimes it is advantageous to back off to smaller amounts of contextual information; the nonterminal X or Y might alone be sufficient to predict the passpattern.

A very reasonable framework for handling this issue is to model $P(X[\alpha] \rightarrow Y[\beta]\ Z[\gamma])$ with a log-linear model.[10] Feature functions would consider the values of variously sized, overlapping subsets of $X, Y, Z, \alpha, \beta, \gamma$. For example, a certain feature might fire when $X[\alpha] = \text{NP}[1]$ **and** $Z[\gamma] = \text{N}[2]$. This approach can be extended to the multi-feature case, as in INHERIT2.

Inheritance as in the INHERIT model can then be expressed by features like $\alpha = \beta$, or $\alpha = \beta$ **and** $X = \text{VP}$. During early iterations, we could use a prior to encourage a strong positive weight on these inheritance features, and gradually relax this bias—akin to the "structural annealing" of (Smith and Eisner, 2006).

When modeling the lexical rule $P(X[\alpha] \rightarrow w)$, we could use features that consider the spelling of the word w in conjunction with the value of α. Thus, we might learn that $V[1]$ is particularly likely to rewrite as a word ending in `-s`. Spelling features that are predictable from string context are important clues to the existence and behavior of the hidden annotations we wish to induce.

A final remark is that "inheritance" does not necessarily have to mean that $\alpha = \beta$. It is enough that α and β should have high mutual information, so that one can be predicted from the other; they do not actually have to be represented by the same integer. More broadly, we might like α to have high mutual information with the pair (β, γ). One might try using this sort of intuition directly in an unsupervised learning procedure (Elidan and Friedman, 2003).

7 Conclusions

We have discussed "informed" techniques for inducing latent syntactic features. Our INHERIT model tries to constrain the way in which features are passed through the tree. The motivation for this approach is twofold: First, we wanted to capture the linguistic insight that features follow certain patterns in propagating through the tree. Second, we wanted to make it statistically feasible and computationally tractable to increase L to higher values than in the PCFG-LA model. The hope was that the learning process could then make finer distinctions and learn more fine-grained information. However, it turned out that the higher values of L did not compensate for the perhaps overly constrained model. The results on English parsing rather suggest that it is the similarity in degrees of freedom (e.g., INHERIT with L=3x3x3 and PCFG-LA with L=2x2) that produces comparable results.

Substantial gains were achieved by using markovization and splitting only selected nonterminals. With these techniques we reach a parsing accuracy similar to Matsuzaki et al. (2005), but with an order of magnitude less parameters, resulting in more efficient parsing. We hope to get more wins in future by using more sophisticated annealing techniques and log-linear modeling techniques.

[10] This affects EM training only by requiring a convex optimization at the M step (Riezler, 1998).

Acknowledgments

This paper is based upon work supported by the National Science Foundation under Grant No. 0313193. We are grateful to Takuya Matsuzaki for providing details about his implementation of PCFG-LA, and to Noah Smith and the anonymous reviewers for helpful comments.

References

A. Berger, P. Brown, S. Pietra, V. Pietra, J. Lafferty, H. Printz, and L. Ures. 1994. The CANDIDE system for machine translation.

Ann Bies, Mark Ferguson, Karen Katz, Robert MacIntyre, Victoria Tredinnick, Grace Kim, Mary Ann Marcinkiewicz, and Britta Schasberger. 1995. Bracketing guidelines for Treebank II style: Penn Treebank project. Technical Report MS-CIS-95-06, University of Pennsylvania, January.

John Blatz and Jason Eisner. 2006. Transforming parsing algorithms and other weighted logic programs. In *Proceedings of the 11th Conference on Formal Grammar.*

Eugene Charniak. 1996. Tree-bank grammars. In *Proceedings of the 13th National Conference on Artificial Intelligence.*

Eugene Charniak. 1997. Statistical parsing with a context-free grammar and word statistics. In *Proceedings of the Fourteenth National Conference on Artificial Intelligence*, pages 598–603.

David Chiang and Daniel M. Bikel. 2002. Recovering latent information in treebanks. In *COLING 2002: The 17th International Conference on Computational Linguistics*, Taipei.

Michael John Collins. 1996. A new statistical parser based on bigram lexical dependencies. In *ACL-96*, pages 184–191, Santa Cruz, CA. ACL.

Michael Collins. 1997. Three generative, lexicalised models for statistical parsing. In *Proceedings of the 35th Annual Meeting of the Association for Computational Linguistics and 8th Conference of the European Chapter of the Association for Computational Linguistics*, pages 16–23, Madrid. Association for Computational Linguistics.

Jason Eisner, Eric Goldlust, and Noah A. Smith. 2005. Compiling comp ling: Weighted dynamic programming and the Dyna language. In *Proceedings of Human Language Technology Conference and Conference on Empirical Methods in Natural Language Processing*, pages 281–290, Vancouver, October.

Jason Eisner. 1996. Three new probabilistic models for dependency parsing: An exploration. In *COLING96: Proceedings of the 16th International Conference on Computational Linguistics*, pages 340–345, Copenhagen. Center for Sprogteknologi.

Gal Elidan and Nir Friedman. 2003. The information bottleneck EM algorithm. In *Proceedings of UAI*.

Joshua Goodman. 1997. Probabilistic feature grammars. In *Proceedings of the 5th International Workshop on Parsing Technologies*, pages 89–100, MIT, Cambridge, MA, September.

L. Huang and D. Chiang. 2005. Parsing and k-best algorithms. In *Proc. of IWPT*.

Mark Johnson. 1998. PCFG models of linguistic tree representations. *Computational Linguistics*, 24(4):613–632.

Ronald M. Kaplan and Joan Bresnan. 1982. Lexical-functional grammar: A formal system for grammatical representation. In Joan Bresnan, editor, *The Mental Representation of Grammatical Relations*, pages 173–281. MIT Press, Cambridge, MA.

Dan Klein and Christopher D. Manning. 2001. Distributional phrase structure induction. In *The Fifth Conference on Natural Language Learning*.

Dan Klein and Christopher D. Manning. 2003. Accurate unlexicalized parsing. In Erhard Hinrichs and Dan Roth, editors, *Proceedings of the 41st Annual Meeting of the Association for Computational Linguistics*, pages 423–430, Sapporo, Japan.

K. Lari and S. Young. 1990. The estimation of stochastic context-free grammars using the inside-outside algorithm. *Computer Speech and Language*, 4:35–56.

David M. Magerman. 1995. Statistical Decision-Tree models for parsing. In *Proceedings of the 33rd Annual Meeting of the Association for Computational Linguistics*, pages 276–283, Cambridge, Mass.

Mitchell P. Marcus, Beatrice Santorini, and Mary Ann Marcinkiewicz. 1993. Building a large annotated corpus of English: The Penn treebank. *Computational Linguistics*, 19(2):313–330, June.

Takuya Matsuzaki, Yusuke Miyao, and Junichi Tsujii. 2005. Probabilistic CFG with latent annotations. In *Proceedings of the 43rd Annual Meeting of the Association for Computational Linguistics (ACL'05)*, University of Michigan.

Fernando Pereira and Yves Schabes. 1992. Inside-Outside reestimation from partially bracketed corpora. In *Proceedings of the 30th Meeting of the Association for Computational Linguistics*, pages 128–135, Newark. University of Delaware.

Fernando Pereira, Naftali Tishby, and Lillian Lee. 1993. Distributional clustering of English words. In *Proceedings of ACL*, Ohio State University.

Carl Pollard and Ivan A. Sag. 1994. *Head-Driven Phrase Structure Grammar*. University of Chicago Press, Chicago.

Detlef Prescher. 2005. Head-driven PCFGs with latent-head statistics. In *Proceedings of the 9th International Workshop on Parsing Technologies*, pages 115–124, Vancouver, BC, Canada, October.

Stefan Riezler. 1998. Statistical inference and probabilistic modeling for constraint-based NLP. In B. Schröder, W. Lenders, W. Hess, and T. Portele, editors, *Computers, Linguistics, and Phonetics between Language and Speech: Proceedings of the 4th Conference on Natural Language Processing (KONVENS'98)*, pages 111–124, Bonn. Lang.

Kenneth Rose. 1998. Deterministic annealing for clustering, compression, classification, regression, and related optimization problems. *Proceedings of the IEEE*, 80:2210–2239, November.

Noah A. Smith and Jason Eisner. 2006. Annealing structural bias in multilingual weighted grammar induction. In *Proceedings of ACL*.

Get out the vote: Determining support or opposition from Congressional floor-debate transcripts

Matt Thomas, Bo Pang, and Lillian Lee
Department of Computer Science, Cornell University
Ithaca, NY 14853-7501
mattthomas84@gmail.com, pabo@cs.cornell.edu, llee@cs.cornell.edu

Abstract

We investigate whether one can determine from the transcripts of U.S. Congressional floor debates whether the speeches represent support of or opposition to proposed legislation. To address this problem, we exploit the fact that these speeches occur as part of a discussion; this allows us to use sources of information regarding relationships between discourse segments, such as whether a given utterance indicates agreement with the opinion expressed by another. We find that the incorporation of such information yields substantial improvements over classifying speeches in isolation.

1 Introduction

> *One ought to recognize that the present political chaos is connected with the decay of language, and that one can probably bring about some improvement by starting at the verbal end.* — Orwell, "Politics and the English language"

We have entered an era where very large amounts of politically oriented text are now available online. This includes both official documents, such as the full text of laws and the proceedings of legislative bodies, and unofficial documents, such as postings on weblogs (blogs) devoted to politics. In some sense, the availability of such data is simply a manifestation of a general trend of "everybody putting their records on the Internet".[1] The online accessibility of politically oriented texts in particular, however, is a phenomenon that some have gone so far as to say will have a potentially society-changing effect.

In the United States, for example, governmental bodies are providing and soliciting political documents via the Internet, with lofty goals in mind: *electronic rulemaking* (eRulemaking) initiatives involving the "electronic collection, distribution, synthesis, and analysis of public commentary in the regulatory rulemaking process", may "[alter] the citizen-government relationship" (Shulman and Schlosberg, 2002). Additionally, much media attention has been focused recently on the potential impact that Internet sites may have on politics[2], or at least on political journalism[3]. Regardless of whether one views such claims as clear-sighted prophecy or mere hype, it is obviously important to help people understand and analyze politically oriented text, given the importance of enabling informed participation in the political process.

Evaluative and persuasive documents, such as a politician's speech regarding a bill or a blogger's commentary on a legislative proposal, form a particularly interesting type of politically oriented text. People are much more likely to consult such evaluative statements than the actual text of a bill or law under discussion, given the dense nature of legislative language and the fact that (U.S.) bills often reach several hundred pages in length (Smith et al., 2005). Moreover, political opinions are ex-

[1] It is worth pointing out that the United States' Library of Congress was an extremely early adopter of Web technology: the THOMAS database (http://thomas.loc.gov) of congressional bills and related data was launched in January 1995, when Mosaic was not quite two years old and Altavista did not yet exist.

[2] E.g., "Internet injects sweeping change into U.S. politics", Adam Nagourney, *The New York Times*, April 2, 2006.

[3] E.g., "The End of News?", Michael Massing, *The New York Review of Books*, December 1, 2005.

Proceedings of the 2006 Conference on Empirical Methods in Natural Language Processing (EMNLP 2006), pages 327–335,
Sydney, July 2006.

plicitly solicited in the eRulemaking scenario.

In the analysis of evaluative language, it is fundamentally necessary to determine whether the author/speaker supports or disapproves of the topic of discussion. In this paper, we investigate the following specific instantiation of this problem: we seek to determine from the transcripts of U.S. Congressional floor debates whether each "speech" (continuous single-speaker segment of text) represents support for or opposition to a proposed piece of legislation. Note that from an experimental point of view, this is a very convenient problem to work with because we can automatically determine ground truth (and thus avoid the need for manual annotation) simply by consulting publicly available voting records.

Task properties Determining whether or not a speaker supports a proposal falls within the realm of *sentiment analysis*, an extremely active research area devoted to the computational treatment of subjective or opinion-oriented language (early work includes Wiebe and Rapaport (1988), Hearst (1992), Sack (1994), and Wiebe (1994); see Esuli (2006) for an active bibliography). In particular, since we treat each individual speech within a debate as a single "document", we are considering a version of *document-level sentiment-polarity classification*, namely, automatically distinguishing between positive and negative documents (Das and Chen, 2001; Pang et al., 2002; Turney, 2002; Dave et al., 2003).

Most sentiment-polarity classifiers proposed in the recent literature categorize each document independently. A few others incorporate various measures of inter-document similarity between the texts to be labeled (Agarwal and Bhattacharyya, 2005; Pang and Lee, 2005; Goldberg and Zhu, 2006). Many interesting opinion-oriented documents, however, can be linked through certain relationships that occur in the context of evaluative *discussions*. For example, we may find textual[4] evidence of a high likelihood of *agreement* between two speakers, such as explicit assertions ("I second that!") or quotation of messages in emails or postings (see Mullen and Malouf (2006) but cf. Agrawal et al. (2003)). Agreement evidence can be a powerful aid in our classification task: for example, we can easily categorize a complicated (or overly terse) document if we find within it indications of agreement with a clearly positive text.

Obviously, incorporating agreement information provides additional benefit only when the input documents are relatively difficult to classify individually. Intuition suggests that this is true of the data with which we experiment, for several reasons. First, U.S. congressional debates contain very rich language and cover an extremely wide variety of topics, ranging from flag burning to international policy to the federal budget. Debates are also subject to digressions, some fairly natural and others less so (e.g., "Why are we discussing this bill when the plight of my constituents regarding this other issue is being ignored?")

Second, an important characteristic of persuasive language is that speakers may spend more time presenting evidence in support of their positions (or attacking the evidence presented by others) than directly stating their attitudes. An extreme example will illustrate the problems involved. Consider a speech that describes the U.S. flag as deeply inspirational, and thus contains only positive language. If the bill under discussion is a proposed flag-burning ban, then the speech is *supportive*; but if the bill under discussion is aimed at rescinding an existing flag-burning ban, the speech may represent *opposition* to the legislation. Given the current state of the art in sentiment analysis, it is doubtful that one could determine the (probably topic-specific) relationship between presented evidence and speaker opinion.

Qualitative summary of results The above difficulties underscore the importance of enhancing standard classification techniques with new information sources that promise to improve accuracy, such as inter-document relationships between the documents to be labeled. In this paper, we demonstrate that the incorporation of agreement modeling can provide substantial improvements over the application of support vector machines (SVMs) in isolation, which represents the state of the art in the individual classification of documents. The enhanced accuracies are obtained via a fairly primitive automatically-acquired "agreement detector"

[4]Because we are most interested in techniques applicable across domains, we restrict consideration to NLP aspects of the problem, ignoring external problem-specific information. For example, although most votes in our corpus were almost completely along party lines (and despite the fact that same-party information is easily incorporated via the methods we propose), we did not use party-affiliation data. Indeed, in other settings (e.g., a movie-discussion listserv) one may not be able to determine the participants' political leanings, and such information may not lead to significantly improved results even if it were available.

	total	train	test	development
speech segments	3857	2740	860	257
debates	53	38	10	5
average number of speech segments per debate	72.8	72.1	86.0	51.4
average number of speakers per debate	32.1	30.9	41.1	22.6

Table 1: Corpus statistics.

and a conceptually simple method for integrating isolated-document and agreement-based information. We thus view our results as demonstrating the potentially large benefits of exploiting sentiment-related discourse-segment relationships in sentiment-analysis tasks.

2 Corpus

This section outlines the main steps of the process by which we created our corpus (download site: www.cs.cornell.edu/home/llee/data/convote.html).

GovTrack (http://govtrack.us) is an independent website run by Joshua Tauberer that collects publicly available data on the legislative and fund-raising activities of U.S. congresspeople. Due to its extensive cross-referencing and collating of information, it was nominated for a 2006 "Webby" award. A crucial characteristic of GovTrack from our point of view is that the information is provided in a very convenient format; for instance, the floor-debate transcripts are broken into separate HTML files according to the subject of the debate, so we can trivially derive long sequences of speeches guaranteed to cover the same topic.

We extracted from GovTrack all available transcripts of U.S. floor debates in the House of Representatives for the year 2005 (3268 pages of transcripts in total), together with voting records for all roll-call votes during that year. We concentrated on debates regarding "controversial" bills (ones in which the losing side generated at least 20% of the speeches) because these debates should presumably exhibit more interesting discourse structure.

Each debate consists of a series of *speech segments*, where each segment is a sequence of uninterrupted utterances by a single speaker. Since speech segments represent natural discourse units, we treat them as the basic unit to be classified. Each speech segment was labeled by the vote ("yea" or "nay") cast for the proposed bill by the person who uttered the speech segment.

We automatically discarded those speech segments belonging to a class of formulaic, generally one-sentence utterances focused on the yielding of time on the house floor (for example, "Madam Speaker, I am pleased to yield 5 minutes to the gentleman from Massachusetts"), as such speech segments are clearly off-topic. We also removed speech segments containing the term "amendment", since we found during initial inspection that these speeches generally reflect a speaker's opinion on an amendment, and this opinion may differ from the speaker's opinion on the underlying bill under discussion.

We randomly split the data into training, test, and development (parameter-tuning) sets representing roughly 70%, 20%, and 10% of our data, respectively (see Table 1). The speech segments remained grouped by debate, with 38 debates assigned to the training set, 10 to the test set, and 5 to the development set; we require that the speech segments from an individual debate all appear in the same set because our goal is to examine classification of speech segments in the context of the surrounding discussion.

3 Method

The support/oppose classification problem can be approached through the use of standard classifiers such as support vector machines (SVMs), which consider each text unit in isolation. As discussed in Section 1, however, the conversational nature of our data implies the existence of various relationships that can be exploited to improve cumulative classification accuracy for speech segments belonging to the same debate. Our classification framework, directly inspired by Blum and Chawla (2001), integrates both perspectives, optimizing its labeling of speech segments based on both individual speech-segment classification scores and preferences for groups of speech segments to receive the same label. In this section, we discuss the specific classification framework that we adopt and the set of mechanisms that we propose for modeling specific types of relationships.

3.1 Classification framework

Let $s_1, s_2, \ldots, s_n$ be the sequence of speech segments within a given debate, and let $\mathcal{Y}$ and $\mathcal{N}$ stand for the "yea" and "nay" class, respectively. Assume we have a non-negative function $ind(s, C)$ indicating the degree of preference that an individual-document classifier, such as an SVM, has for placing speech-segment s in class C. Also, assume that some pairs of speech segments have *weighted links* between them, where the non-negative *strength* (weight) $str(\ell)$ for a link ℓ indicates the degree to which it is preferable that the linked speech segments receive the same label. Then, any class assignment $c = c(s_1), c(s_2), \ldots, c(s_n)$ can be assigned a *cost*

$$\sum_s ind(s, \bar{c}(s)) + \sum_{s,s':\, c(s) \neq c(s')} \sum_{\ell \text{ between } s,s'} str(\ell),$$

where $\bar{c}(s)$ is the "opposite" class from $c(s)$. A *minimum-cost* assignment thus represents an optimum way to classify the speech segments so that each one tends not to be put into the class that the individual-document classifier disprefers, but at the same time, highly associated speech segments tend not to be put in different classes.

As has been previously observed and exploited in the NLP literature (Pang and Lee, 2004; Agarwal and Bhattacharyya, 2005; Barzilay and Lapata, 2005), the above optimization function, unlike many others that have been proposed for graph or set partitioning, can be solved *exactly* in an provably efficient manner via methods for finding minimum cuts in graphs. In our view, the contribution of our work is the examination of new types of relationships, not the method by which such relationships are incorporated into the classification decision.

3.2 Classifying speech segments in isolation

In our experiments, we employed the well-known classifier SVM^{light} to obtain individual-document classification scores, treating $\mathcal{Y}$ as the positive class and using plain unigrams as features.[5] Following standard practice in sentiment analysis (Pang et al., 2002), the input to SVM^{light} consisted of normalized presence-of-feature (rather than frequency-of-feature) vectors. The *ind* value for each speech segment s was based on the signed distance $d(s)$ from the vector representing s to the trained SVM decision plane:

$$ind(s, \mathcal{Y}) \stackrel{\text{def}}{=} \begin{cases} 1 & d(s) > 2\sigma_s; \\ \left(1 + \frac{d(s)}{2\sigma_s}\right)/2 & |d(s)| \leq 2\sigma_s; \\ 0 & d(s) < -2\sigma_s \end{cases}$$

where σ_s is the standard deviation of $d(s)$ over all speech segments s in the debate in question, and $ind(s, \mathcal{N}) \stackrel{\text{def}}{=} 1 - ind(s, \mathcal{Y})$.

We now turn to the more interesting problem of representing the preferences that speech segments may have for being assigned to the same class.

3.3 Relationships between speech segments

A wide range of relationships between text segments can be modeled as positive-strength links. Here we discuss two types of constraints that are considered in this work.

Same-speaker constraints: In Congressional debates and in general social-discourse contexts, a single speaker may make a number of comments regarding a topic. It is reasonable to expect that in many settings, the participants in a discussion may be convinced to change their opinions midway through a debate. Hence, in the general case we wish to be able to express "soft" preferences for all of an author's statements to receive the same label, where the strengths of such constraints could, for instance, vary according to the time elapsed between the statements. Weighted links are an appropriate means to express such variation.

However, if we assume that most speakers do not change their positions in the course of a discussion, we can conclude that all comments made by the same speaker must receive the same label. This assumption holds by fiat for the ground-truth labels in our dataset because these labels were derived from the single vote cast by the speaker on the bill being discussed.[6] We can implement this assumption via links whose weights are essentially infinite. Although one can also implement this assumption via concatenation of same-speaker speech segments (see Section 4.3), we view the fact that our graph-based framework incorporates

[5] SVM^{light} is available at svmlight.joachims.org. Default parameters were used, although experimentation with different parameter settings is an important direction for future work (Daelemans and Hoste, 2002; Munson et al., 2005).

[6] We are attempting to determine whether a speech segment represents support or not. This differs from the problem of determining what the speaker's actual opinion is, a problem that, as an anonymous reviewer put it, is complicated by "grandstanding, backroom deals, or, more innocently, plain change of mind ('I voted for it before I voted against it')".

both hard and soft constraints in a principled fashion as an advantage of our approach.

Different-speaker agreements In House discourse, it is common for one speaker to make reference to another in the context of an agreement or disagreement over the topic of discussion. The systematic identification of instances of agreement can, as we have discussed, be a powerful tool for the development of intelligently selected weights for links between speech segments.

The problem of agreement identification can be decomposed into two sub-problems: identifying references and their targets, and deciding whether each reference represents an instance of agreement. In our case, the first task is straightforward because we focused solely on by-name references.[7] Hence, we will now concentrate on the second, more interesting task.

We approach the problem of classifying references by representing each reference with a word-presence vector derived from a window of text surrounding the reference.[8] In the training set, we classify each reference connecting two speakers with a positive or negative label depending on whether the two voted the same way on the bill under discussion[9]. These labels are then used to train an SVM classifier, the output of which is subsequently used to create weights on *agreement links* in the test set as follows.

Let $d(r)$ denote the distance from the vector representing reference r to the agreement-detector SVM's decision plane, and let σ_r be the standard deviation of $d(r)$ over all references in the debate in question. We then define the strength *agr* of the *agreement link* corresponding to the reference as:

$$agr(r) \stackrel{\text{def}}{=} \begin{cases} 0 & d(r) < \theta_{\text{agr}}; \\ \alpha \cdot d(r)/4\sigma_r & \theta_{\text{agr}} \leq d(r) \leq 4\sigma_r; \\ \alpha & d(r) > 4\sigma_r. \end{cases}$$

The free parameter α specifies the relative importance of the *agr* scores. The threshold θ_{agr} controls the precision of the agreement links, in that values of θ_{agr} greater than zero mean that greater confidence is required before an agreement link can be added.[10]

Agreement classifier ("reference⇒agreement?")	Devel. set	Test set
majority baseline	81.51	80.26
Train: no amdmts; $\theta_{\text{agr}} = 0$	84.25	81.07
Train: with amdmts; $\theta_{\text{agr}} = 0$	**86.99**	**80.10**

Table 2: Agreement-classifier accuracy, in percent. "Amdmts"="speech segments containing the word 'amendment'". Recall that boldface indicates results for development-set-optimal settings.

4 Evaluation

This section presents experiments testing the utility of using speech-segment relationships, evaluating against a number of baselines. All reported results use values for the free parameter α derived via tuning on the development set. In the tables, **boldface** indicates the development- and test-set results for the *development-set-optimal* parameter settings, as one would make algorithmic choices based on development-set performance.

4.1 Preliminaries: Reference classification

Recall that to gather inter-speaker agreement information, the strategy employed in this paper is to classify by-name references to other speakers as to whether they indicate agreement or not.

To train our agreement classifier, we experimented with undoing the deletion of amendment-related speech segments in the training set. Note that such speech segments were *never* included in the development or test set, since, as discussed in Section 2, their labels are probably noisy; however, including them in the *training* set allows the classifier to examine more instances even though some of them are labeled incorrectly. As Table 2 shows, using more, if noisy, data yields better agreement-classification results on the development set, and so we use that policy in all subsequent experiments.[11]

[7]One subtlety is that for the purposes of mining agreement cues (but *not* for evaluating overall support/oppose classification accuracy), we temporarily re-inserted into our dataset previously filtered speech segments containing the term "yield", since the yielding of time on the House floor typically indicates agreement even though the yield statements contain little relevant text on their own.

[8]We found good development-set performance using the 30 tokens before, 20 tokens after, and the name itself.

[9]Since we are concerned with references that potentially represent relationships between speech segments, we ignore references for which the target of the reference did not speak in the debate in which the reference was made.

[10]Our implementation puts a link between just one arbitrary pair of speech segments among all those uttered by a given pair of apparently agreeing speakers. The "infinite-weight" same-speaker links propagate the agreement information to all other such pairs.

[11]Unfortunately, this policy leads to inferior *test-set* agree-

Agreement classifier	Precision (in percent): Devel. set	Test set
$\theta_{\text{agr}} = 0$	86.23	82.55
$\theta_{\text{agr}} = \mu$	**89.41**	**88.47**

Table 3: Agreement-classifier precision.

An important observation is that precision may be more important than accuracy in deciding which agreement links to add: false positives with respect to agreement can cause speech segments to be incorrectly assigned the same label, whereas false negatives mean only that agreement-based information about other speech segments is not employed. As described above, we can raise agreement precision by increasing the threshold θ_{agr}, which specifies the required confidence for the addition of an agreement link. Indeed, Table 3 shows that we can improve agreement precision by setting θ_{agr} to the (positive) mean agreement score μ assigned by the SVM agreement-classifier over all references in the given debate[12]. However, this comes at the cost of greatly reducing agreement accuracy (development: 64.38%; test: 66.18%) due to lowered recall levels. Whether or not better speech-segment classification is ultimately achieved is discussed in the next sections.

4.2 Segment-based speech-segment classification

Baselines The first two data rows of Table 4 depict baseline performance results. The #("support") − #("oppos") baseline is meant to explore whether the speech-segment classification task can be reduced to simple lexical checks. Specifically, this method uses the signed difference between the number of words containing the stem "support" and the number of words containing the stem "oppos" (returning the majority class if the difference is 0). No better than 62.67% test-set accuracy is obtained by either baseline.

Using relationship information Applying an SVM to classify each speech segment in isolation leads to clear improvements over the two baseline methods, as demonstrated in Table 4. When we impose the constraint that all speech segments uttered by the same speaker receive the same label via "same-speaker links", both test-set and development-set accuracy increase even more, in the latter case quite substantially so.

ment classification. Section 4.5 contains further discussion.

[12] We elected not to explicitly tune the value of θ_{agr} in order to minimize the number of free parameters to deal with.

Support/oppose classifer ("speech segment⇒yea?")	Devel. set	Test set
majority baseline	54.09	58.37
#("support") − #("oppos")	59.14	62.67
SVM [speech segment]	70.04	66.05
SVM + same-speaker links	79.77	67.21
SVM + same-speaker links ...		
+ agreement links, $\theta_{\text{agr}} = 0$	**89.11**	**70.81**
+ agreement links, $\theta_{\text{agr}} = \mu$	87.94	71.16

Table 4: Segment-based speech-segment classification accuracy, in percent.

Support/oppose classifer ("speech segment⇒yea?")	Devel. set	Test set
SVM [speaker]	71.60	70.00
SVM + agreement links ...		
with $\theta_{\text{agr}} = 0$	**88.72**	**71.28**
with $\theta_{\text{agr}} = \mu$	84.44	76.05

Table 5: Speaker-based speech-segment classification accuracy, in percent. Here, the initial SVM is run on the concatenation of all of a given speaker's speech segments, but the results are computed over speech segments (not speakers), so that they can be compared to those in Table 4.

The last two lines of Table 4 show that the best results are obtained by incorporating agreement information as well. The highest test-set result, 71.16%, is obtained by using a high-precision threshold to determine which agreement links to add. While the development-set results would induce us to utilize the standard threshold value of 0, which is sub-optimal on the test set, the $\theta_{\text{agr}} = 0$ agreement-link policy still achieves noticeable improvement over not using agreement links (test set: 70.81% vs. 67.21%).

4.3 Speaker-based speech-segment classification

We use speech segments as the unit of classification because they represent natural discourse units. As a consequence, we are able to exploit relationships at the speech-segment level. However, it is interesting to consider whether we really need to consider relationships specifically between speech segments themselves, or whether it suffices to simply consider relationships between the *speakers* of the speech segments. In particular, as an alternative to using same-speaker links, we tried a *speaker-based* approach wherein the way we determine the initial individual-document classification score for each speech segment uttered by a person p in a given debate is to run an SVM on the concatenation of *all* of p's speech segments within that debate. (We also ensure that agreement-link information is propagated from speech-segment to speaker pairs.)

How does the use of same-speaker links compare to the concatenation of each speaker's speech segments? Tables 4 and 5 show that, not surprisingly, the SVM individual-document classifier works better on the concatenated speech segments than on the speech segments in isolation. However, the effect on overall classification accuracy is less clear: the development set favors same-speaker links over concatenation, while the test set does not.

But we stress that the most important observation we can make from Table 5 is that once again, the addition of agreement information leads to substantial improvements in accuracy.

4.4 "Hard" agreement constraints

Recall that in in our experiments, we created finite-weight agreement links, so that speech segments appearing in pairs flagged by our (imperfect) agreement detector can potentially receive different labels. We also experimented with *forcing* such speech segments to receive the same label, either through infinite-weight agreement links or through a speech-segment concatenation strategy similar to that described in the previous subsection. Both strategies resulted in clear degradation in performance on both the development and test sets, a finding that validates our encoding of agreement information as "soft" preferences.

4.5 On the development/test set split

We have seen several cases in which the method that performs best on the development set does not yield the best test-set performance. However, we felt that it would be illegitimate to change the train/development/test sets in a post hoc fashion, that is, after seeing the experimental results.

Moreover, and crucially, it is very clear that using agreement information, encoded as preferences within our graph-based approach rather than as hard constraints, yields substantial improvements on both the development and test set; this, we believe, is our most important finding.

5 Related work

Politically-oriented text Sentiment analysis has specifically been proposed as a key enabling technology in eRulemaking, allowing the automatic analysis of the opinions that people submit (Shulman et al., 2005; Cardie et al., 2006; Kwon et al., 2006). There has also been work focused upon determining the political leaning (e.g., "liberal" vs. "conservative") of a document or author, where most previously-proposed methods make no direct use of relationships between the documents to be classified (the "unlabeled" texts) (Laver et al., 2003; Efron, 2004; Mullen and Malouf, 2006). An exception is Grefenstette et al. (2004), who experimented with determining the political orientation of websites essentially by classifying the concatenation of all the documents found on that site.

Others have applied the NLP technologies of near-duplicate detection and topic-based text categorization to politically oriented text (Yang and Callan, 2005; Purpura and Hillard, 2006).

Detecting agreement We used a simple method to learn to identify cross-speaker references indicating agreement. More sophisticated approaches have been proposed (Hillard et al., 2003), including an extension that, in an interesting reversal of our problem, makes use of sentiment-polarity indicators within speech segments (Galley et al., 2004). Also relevant is work on the general problems of dialog-act tagging (Stolcke et al., 2000), citation analysis (Lehnert et al., 1990), and computational rhetorical analysis (Marcu, 2000; Teufel and Moens, 2002).

We currently do not have an efficient means to encode *disagreement* information as hard constraints; we plan to investigate incorporating such information in future work.

Relationships between the unlabeled items Carvalho and Cohen (2005) consider sequential relations between different types of emails (e.g., between requests and satisfactions thereof) to classify messages, and thus also explicitly exploit the structure of conversations.

Previous sentiment-analysis work in different domains has considered inter-document similarity (Agarwal and Bhattacharyya, 2005; Pang and Lee, 2005; Goldberg and Zhu, 2006) or explicit inter-document references in the form of hyperlinks (Agrawal et al., 2003).

Notable early papers on graph-based semi-supervised learning include Blum and Chawla (2001), Bansal et al. (2002), Kondor and Lafferty (2002), and Joachims (2003). Zhu (2005) maintains a survey of this area.

Recently, several alternative, often quite sophisticated approaches to *collective classification* have been proposed (Neville and Jensen, 2000; Lafferty et al., 2001; Getoor et al., 2002; Taskar et al., 2002; Taskar et al., 2003; Taskar et al., 2004; McCallum and Wellner, 2004). It would be interesting to investigate the application of such methods to our problem. However, we also believe that our approach has important advantages, including conceptual simplicity and the fact that it is based on an underlying optimization problem that is provably and in practice easy to solve.

6 Conclusion and future work

In this study, we focused on very general types of cross-document classification preferences, utilizing constraints based only on speaker identity and on direct textual references between statements. We showed that the integration of even very limited information regarding inter-document relationships can significantly increase the accuracy of support/opposition classification.

The simple constraints modeled in our study, however, represent just a small portion of the rich network of relationships that connect statements and speakers across the political universe and in the wider realm of opinionated social discourse. One intriguing possibility is to take advantage of (readily identifiable) information regarding interpersonal relationships, making use of speaker/author affiliations, positions within a social hierarchy, and so on. Or, we could even attempt to model relationships between topics or concepts, in a kind of extension of collaborative filtering. For example, perhaps we could infer that two speakers sharing a common opinion on evolutionary biologist Richard Dawkins (a.k.a. "Darwin's rottweiler") will be likely to agree in a debate centered on Intelligent Design. While such functionality is well beyond the scope of our current study, we are optimistic that we can develop methods to exploit additional types of relationships in future work.

Acknowledgments We thank Claire Cardie, Jon Kleinberg, Michael Macy, Andrew Myers, and the six anonymous EMNLP referees for valuable discussions and comments. We also thank Reviewer 1 for generously providing additional *post hoc* feedback, and the EMNLP chairs Eric Gaussier and Dan Jurafsky for facilitating the process (as well as for allowing authors an extra proceedings page...). This paper is based upon work supported in part by the National Science Foundation under grant no. IIS-0329064. Any opinions, findings, and conclusions or recommendations expressed are those of the authors and do not necessarily reflect the views or official policies, either expressed or implied, of any sponsoring institutions, the U.S. government, or any other entity.

References

A. Agarwal, P. Bhattacharyya. 2005. Sentiment analysis: A new approach for effective use of linguistic knowledge and exploiting similarities in a set of documents to be classified. In *Proceedings of the International Conference on Natural Language Processing (ICON)*.

R. Agrawal, S. Rajagopalan, R. Srikant, Y. Xu. 2003. Mining newsgroups using networks arising from social behavior. In *Proceedings of WWW*, 529–535.

N. Bansal, A. Blum, S. Chawla. 2002. Correlation clustering. In *Proceedings of the Symposium on Foundations of Computer Science (FOCS)*, 238–247. Journal version in *Machine Learning Journal*, special issue on theoretical advances in data clustering, 56(1-3):89–113 (2004).

R. Barzilay, M. Lapata. 2005. Collective content selection for concept-to-text generation. In *Proceedings of HLT/EMNLP*, 331–338.

A. Blum, S. Chawla. 2001. Learning from labeled and unlabeled data using graph mincuts. In *Proceedings of ICML*, 19–26.

C. Cardie, C. Farina, T. Bruce, E. Wagner. 2006. Using natural language processing to improve eRulemaking. In *Proceedings of Digital Government Research (dg.o)*.

V. Carvalho, W. W. Cohen. 2005. On the collective classification of email "speech acts". In *Proceedings of SIGIR*, 345–352.

W. Daelemans, V. Hoste. 2002. Evaluation of machine learning methods for natural language processing tasks. In *Proceedings of the Third International Conference on Language Resources and Evaluation (LREC)*, 755–760.

S. Das, M. Chen. 2001. Yahoo! for Amazon: Extracting market sentiment from stock message boards. In *Proceedings of the Asia Pacific Finance Association Annual Conference (APFA)*.

K. Dave, S. Lawrence, D. M. Pennock. 2003. Mining the peanut gallery: Opinion extraction and semantic classification of product reviews. In *Proceedings of WWW*, 519–528.

M. Efron. 2004. Cultural orientation: Classifying subjective documents by cociation [sic] analysis. In *Proceedings of the AAAI Fall Symposium on Style and Meaning in Language, Art, Music, and Design*, 41–48.

A. Esuli. 2006. Sentiment classification bibliography. liinwww.ira.uka.de/bibliography/Misc/Sentiment.html.

M. Galley, K. McKeown, J. Hirschberg, E. Shriberg. 2004. Identifying agreement and disagreement in conversational speech: Use of Bayesian networks to model pragmatic dependencies. In *Proceedings of the 42nd ACL*, 669–676.

L. Getoor, N. Friedman, D. Koller, B. Taskar. 2002. Learning probabilistic models of relational structure. *Journal of Machine Learning Research*, 3:679–707. Special issue on the Eighteenth ICML.

A. B. Goldberg, J. Zhu. 2006. Seeing stars when there aren't many stars: Graph-based semi-supervised learning for sentiment categorization. In *TextGraphs: HLT/NAACL Workshop on Graph-based Algorithms for Natural Language Processing*.

G. Grefenstette, Y. Qu, J. G. Shanahan, D. A. Evans. 2004. Coupling niche browsers and affect analysis for an opinion mining application. In *Proceedings of RIAO*.

M. Hearst. 1992. Direction-based text interpretation as an information access refinement. In P. Jacobs, ed., *Text-Based Intelligent Systems*, 257–274. Lawrence Erlbaum Associates.

D. Hillard, M. Ostendorf, E. Shriberg. 2003. Detection of agreement vs. disagreement in meetings: Training with unlabeled data. In *Proceedings of HLT-NAACL*.

T. Joachims. 2003. Transductive learning via spectral graph partitioning. In *Proceedings of ICML*, 290–297.

R. I. Kondor, J. D. Lafferty. 2002. Diffusion kernels on graphs and other discrete input spaces. In *Proceedings of ICML*, 315–322.

N. Kwon, S. Shulman, E. Hovy. 2006. Multidimensional text analysis for eRulemaking. In *Proceedings of Digital Government Research (dg.o)*.

J. Lafferty, A. McCallum, F. Pereira. 2001. Conditional random fields: Probabilistic models for segmenting and labeling sequence data. In *Proceedings of ICML*, 282–289.

M. Laver, K. Benoit, J. Garry. 2003. Extracting policy positions from political texts using words as data. *American Political Science Review*.

W. Lehnert, C. Cardie, E. Riloff. 1990. Analyzing research papers using citation sentences. In *Program of the Twelfth Annual Conference of the Cognitive Science Society*, 511–18.

D. Marcu. 2000. *The theory and practice of discourse parsing and summarization*. MIT Press.

A. McCallum, B. Wellner. 2004. Conditional models of identity uncertainty with application to noun coreference. In *Proceedings of NIPS*.

T. Mullen, R. Malouf. 2006. A preliminary investigation into sentiment analysis of informal political discourse. In *Proceedings of the AAAI Symposium on Computational Approaches to Analyzing Weblogs*, 159–162.

A. Munson, C. Cardie, R. Caruana. 2005. Optimizing to arbitrary NLP metrics using ensemble selection. In *Proceedings of HLT-EMNLP*, 539–546.

J. Neville, D. Jensen. 2000. Iterative classification in relational data. In *Proceedings of the AAAI Workshop on Learning Statistical Models from Relational Data*, 13–20.

B. Pang, L. Lee. 2004. A sentimental education: Sentiment analysis using subjectivity summarization based on minimum cuts. In *Proceedings of the ACL*, 271–278.

B. Pang, L. Lee. 2005. Seeing stars: Exploiting class relationships for sentiment categorization with respect to rating scales. In *Proceedings of the ACL*.

B. Pang, L. Lee, S. Vaithyanathan. 2002. Thumbs up? Sentiment classification using machine learning techniques. In *Proceedings of EMNLP*, 79–86.

S. Purpura, D. Hillard. 2006. Automated classification of congressional legislation. In *Proceedings of Digital Government Research (dg.o)*.

W. Sack. 1994. On the computation of point of view. In *Proceedings of AAAI*, pg. 1488. Student abstract.

S. Shulman, D. Schlosberg. 2002. Electronic rulemaking: New frontiers in public participation. Prepared for the Annual Meeting of the American Political Science Association.

S. Shulman, J. Callan, E. Hovy, S. Zavestoski. 2005. Language processing technologies for electronic rulemaking: A project highlight. In *Proceedings of Digital Government Research (dg.o)*, 87–88.

S. S. Smith, J. M. Roberts, R. J. Vander Wielen. 2005. *The American Congress*. Cambridge University Press, fourth edition.

A. Stolcke, N. Coccaro, R. Bates, P. Taylor, C. Van Ess-Dykema, K. Ries, E. Shriberg, D. Jurafsky, R. Martin, M. Meteer. 2000. Dialogue act modeling for automatic tagging and recognition of conversational speech. *Computational Linguistics*, 26(3):339–373.

B. Taskar, P. Abbeel, D. Koller. 2002. Discriminative probabilistic models for relational data. In *Proceedings of UAI*, Edmonton, Canada.

B. Taskar, C. Guestrin, D. Koller. 2003. Max-margin Markov networks. In *Proceedings of NIPS*.

B. Taskar, V. Chatalbashev, D. Koller. 2004. Learning associative Markov networks. In *Proceedings of ICML*.

S. Teufel, M. Moens. 2002. Summarizing scientific articles: Experiments with relevance and rhetorical status. *Computational Linguistics*, 28(4):409–445.

P. Turney. 2002. Thumbs up or thumbs down? Semantic orientation applied to unsupervised classification of reviews. In *Proceedings of the ACL*, 417–424.

J. M. Wiebe, W. J. Rapaport. 1988. A computational theory of perspective and reference in narrative. In *Proceedings of the ACL*, 131–138.

J. M. Wiebe. 1994. Tracking point of view in narrative. *Computational Linguistics*, 20(2):233–287.

H. Yang, J. Callan. 2005. Near-duplicate detection for eRulemaking. In *Proceedings of Digital Government Research (dg.o)*.

J. Zhu. 2005. Semi-supervised learning literature survey. Computer Sciences Technical Report TR 1530, University of Wisconsin-Madison. Available at http://www.cs.wisc.edu/~jerryzhu/pub/ssl_survey.pdf; has been updated since the initial 2005 version.

Partially Supervised Coreference Resolution for Opinion Summarization through Structured Rule Learning

Veselin Stoyanov and **Claire Cardie**
Department of Computer Science
Cornell University
Ithaca, NY 14850, USA
{ves,cardie}@cs.cornell.edu

Abstract

Combining fine-grained opinion information to produce opinion summaries is important for sentiment analysis applications. Toward that end, we tackle the problem of source coreference resolution – linking together source mentions that refer to the same entity. The partially supervised nature of the problem leads us to define and approach it as the novel problem of partially supervised clustering. We propose and evaluate a new algorithm for the task of source coreference resolution that outperforms competitive baselines.

1 Introduction

Sentiment analysis is concerned with extracting attitudes, opinions, evaluations, and sentiment from text. Work in this area has been motivated by the desire to provide information analysis applications in the arenas of government, business, and politics (e.g. Coglianese (2004)). Additionally, sentiment analysis can augment existing NLP applications such as question answering, information retrieval, summarization, and clustering by providing information about sentiment (e.g. Stoyanov et al. (2005), Riloff et al. (2005)). To date, research in the area (see Related Work section) has focused on the problem of extracting sentiment both at the document level (*coarse-grained sentiment information*), and at the level of sentences, clauses, or individual expressions (*fine-grained sentiment information*).

In contrast, our work concerns the *summarization* of fine-grained information about *opinions*. In particular, while recent research efforts have shown that fine-grained opinions (e.g. Riloff and Wiebe (2003), Bethard et al. (2004), Wiebe and Riloff (2005)) as well as their sources (e.g. Bethard et al. (2004), Choi et al. (2005), Kim and Hovy (2005)) can be extracted automatically, little has been done to create *opinion summaries*, where opinions from the same source/target are combined, statistics are computed for each source/target and multiple opinions from the same source to the same target are aggregated. A simple opinion summary is shown in figure 1.[1] We expect that this type of opinion summary, based on fine-grained opinion information, will be important for information analysis applications in any domain where the analysis of opinions is critical.

This paper addresses the problem of opinion summarization by considering the creation of simple opinion summaries like those of figure 1. We propose *source coreference resolution* — the task of determining which mentions of opinion sources refer to the same entity — as the primary mechanism for identifying the set of opinions attributed to each real-world source. For this type of summary, source coreference resolution constitutes an integral step in the process of generating full opinion summaries. For example, given the opinion expressions of figure 1, their polarity, and the associated opinion sources and targets, the bulk of the resulting summary can be produced by recognizing that source mentions "Zacarias Moussaoui", "he", "my", and "Mr. Moussaoui" all refer to the same person; and that source mentions "Mr. Zerkin" and "Zerkin" refer to the same person.[2]

[1] For simplicity, the example summary does not contain any source/target statistics.

[2] In addition, the summary would require the closely related task of target coreference resolution and a means for aggregating the conflicting opinions from *Zerkin* toward *Moussaoui*.

Proceedings of the 2006 Conference on Empirical Methods in Natural Language Processing (EMNLP 2006), pages 336–344,
Sydney, July 2006.

At first glance, source coreference resolution appears equivalent to the task of noun phrase coreference resolution and therefore amenable to traditional coreference resolution techniques (e.g. Ng and Cardie (2002), Morton (2000)). We hypothesize in Section 3, however, that the task is likely to succumb to a better solution by treating it in the context of a new machine learning setting that we refer to as *partially supervised clustering*. In particular, due to high coreference annotation costs, data sets that are annotated with opinion information (like ours) do not typically include supervisory coreference information for *all* noun phrases in a document (as would be required for the application of traditional coreference resolution techniques), but only for noun phrases that act as opinion sources (or targets).

As a result, we define the task of *partially supervised clustering*, the goal of which is to learn a clustering function from a set of partially specified clustering examples (Section 4). We are not aware of prior work on the problem of partially supervised clustering and argue that it differs substantially from that of semi-supervised clustering. We propose an algorithm for partially supervised clustering that extends a rule learner with structure information and is generally applicable to problems that fit the partially supervised clustering definition (Section 5). We apply the algorithm to the source coreference resolution task and evaluate its performance on a standard sentiment analysis data set that includes source coreference chains (Section 6). We find that our algorithm outperforms highly competitive baselines by a considerable margin – B^3 score of 83.2 vs. 81.8 and 67.1 vs. 60.9 F1 score for the identification of positive source coreference links.

2 Related Work

Work relevant to our problem can be split into three main areas – sentiment analysis, traditional noun phrase coreference resolution, and supervised and weakly supervised clustering. Related work in the former two areas is summarized briefly below. Supervised and weakly supervised clustering approaches are discussed in Section 4.

Sentiment analysis. Much of the relevant research in sentiment analysis addresses sentiment classification, a text categorization task of extracting opinion at the coarse-grained document level. The goal in sentiment classification is to assign to

[$_{Source}$ Zacarias Moussaoui] [$_-$ *complained*] at length today about [$_{Target}$ his own lawyer], telling a federal court jury that [$_{Target}$ he] was [$_-$ *more interested in achieving fame than saving Moussaoui's life*].

Mr. Moussaoui said he was appearing on the witness stand to tell the truth. And one part of the truth, [$_{Source}$ he] said, is that [$_{Target}$ sending him to prison for life] would be "[$_-$ *a greater punishment*] than being sentenced to death."

"[$_-$ [$_{Target}$ *You*] *have put your interest ahead of* [$_{Source}$ *my*] *life*]," [$_{Source}$ Mr. Moussaoui] told his court-appointed lawyer Gerald T. Zerkin.

...

But, [$_{Source}$ Mr. Zerkin] pressed [$_{Target}$ Mr. Moussaoui], was it [$_-$ *not true*] that he told his lawyers earlier not to involve any Muslims in the defense, not to present any evidence that might persuade the jurors to spare his life?

...

[$_{Source}$ Zerkin] seemed to be trying to show the jurors that while [$_{Target}$ the defendant] is generally [$_+$ *an honest individual*], his conduct shows [$_{Target}$ he] is [$_-$ *not stable mentally*], and thus [$_-$ *undeserving*] of [$_{Target}$ the ultimate punishment].

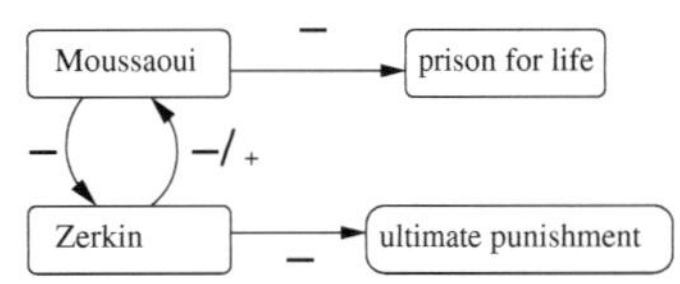

Figure 1: Example text containing opinions (above) and a summary of the opinions (below). Sources and targets of opinions are bracketed; opinion expressions are shown in italics and bracketed with associated polarity, either positive (+) or negative (-). The underlined phrase will be explained later in the paper.

a document either positive ("thumbs up") or negative ("thumbs down") polarity (e.g. Das and Chen (2001), Pang et al. (2002), Turney (2002), Dave et al. (2003)). Other research has concentrated on analyzing fine-grained opinions at, or below, the sentence level. Recent work, for example, indicates that systems can be trained to recognize opinions and their polarity, strength, and sources to a reasonable degree of accuracy (e.g. Dave et al. (2003), Riloff and Wiebe (2003), Bethard et al. (2004), Wilson et al. (2004), Yu and Hatzivassiloglou (2003), Choi et al. (2005), Kim and Hovy (2005), Wiebe and Riloff (2005)). Our work extends research on fine-grained opinion extraction by augmenting the opinions with additional information that allows the creation of concise opinion summaries. In contrast to the opinion extracts produced by Pang and Lee (2004), our summaries are not text extracts, but rather explicitly identify and characterize the relations between opinions and their sources.

Coreference resolution. Coreference resolution is a relatively well studied NLP problem (e.g. Morton (2000), Ng and Cardie (2002), Iida et al. (2003), McCallum and Wellner (2003)). Coreference resolution is defined as the problem of deciding which noun phrases in the text (*mentions*) refer to the same real world entities (*are coreferent*). Generally, successful approaches to coreference resolution have relied on supervised classification followed by clustering. For supervised classification these approaches learn a pairwise function to predict whether a pair of noun phrases is coreferent. Subsequently, when making coreference resolution decisions on unseen documents, the learnt pairwise NP coreference classifier is run, followed by a clustering step to produce the final clusters (coreference chains) of coreferent NPs. For both training and testing, coreference resolution algorithms rely on feature vectors for pairs of noun phrases that encode linguistic information about the NPs and their local context. Our general approach to source coreference resolution is inspired by the state-of-the-art performance of one such approach to coreference resolution, which relies on a rule learner and single-link clustering as described in Ng and Cardie (2002).

3 Source Coreference Resolution

In this section we introduce the problem of source coreference resolution in the context of opinion summarization and argue for the need for novel methods for the task.

The task of *source coreference resolution* is to decide which mentions of opinion sources refer to the same entity. Much like traditional coreference resolution, we employ a learning approach; however, our approach differs from traditional coreference resolution in its definition of the learning task. Motivated by the desire to utilize unlabeled examples (discussed later), we define training as an integrated task in which pairwise NP coreference decisions are learned together with the clustering function as opposed to treating each NP pair as a training example. Thus, our training phase takes as input a set of documents with manually annotated opinion sources together with coreference annotations for the sources; it outputs a classifier that can produce source coreference chains for previously unseen documents containing marked (manually or automatically) opinion sources. More specifically, the source coreference resolution training phase proceeds through the following steps:

1. **Source-to-NP mapping:** We preprocess each document by running a tokenizer, sentence splitter, POS tagger, parser, and an NP finder. Subsequently, we augment the set of NPs found by the NP finder with the help of a system for named entity detection. We then map the sources to the NPs. Since there is no one-to-one correspondence, we use a set of heuristics to create the mapping. More details about why heuristics are needed and the process used to map sources to NPs can be found in Stoyanov and Cardie (2006).

2. **Feature vector creation:** We extract a feature vector for every pair of NPs from the preprocessed corpus. We use the features introduced by Ng and Cardie (2002) for the task of coreference resolution.

3. **Classifier construction:** Using the feature vectors from step 2, we construct a training set containing one training example per document. Each training example consists of the feature vectors for all pairs of NPs in the document, including those that do not map to sources, together with the available coreference information for the *source noun phrases* (i.e. the noun phrases to which sources are mapped). The training instances are provided as input to a learning algorithm (see Section 5), which constructs a classifier that can take the instances associated with a new (previously unseen) document and produce a clustering over all NPs in the document.

The testing phase employs steps 1 and 2 as described above, but replaces step 3 by a straightforward application of the learnt classifier. Since we are interested in coreference information only for the source NPs, we simply discard the non-source NPs from the resulting clustering.

The approach to source coreference resolution described here would be identical to traditional coreference resolution when provided with training examples containing coreference information for all NPs. However, opinion corpora in general, and our corpus in particular, contain no coreference information about general NPs. Nevertheless, after manual sources are mapped to NPs in step 1 above, our approach can rely on the available coreference information for the source NPs. Due to the high cost of coreference annotation, we desire methods that can work in the presence of only this limited amount of coreference information.

A possible workaround the absence of full NP coreference information is to train a traditional coreference system only on the labeled part of the data (indeed that is one of the baselines against which we compare). However, we believe that an effective approach to source coreference resolution has to utilize the unlabeled noun phrases because links between sources might be realized through non-source mentions. This problem is illustrated in figure 1. The underlined *Moussaoui* is coreferent with all of the Moussaoui references marked as sources, but, because it is used in an objective sentence rather than as the source of an opinion, the reference would be omitted from the *Moussaoui* source chain. Unfortunately, this proper noun phrase might be critical in establishing the coreference of the final source reference *he* with the other mentions of the source *Moussaoui*.

As mentioned previously, in order to utilize the unlabeled data, our approach differs from traditional coreference resolution, which uses NP pairs as training instances. We instead follow the framework of supervised clustering (Finley and Joachims, 2005; Li and Roth, 2005) and consider each document as a training example. As in supervised clustering, this framework has the additional advantage that the learning algorithm can consider the clustering algorithm when making decisions about pairwise classification, which could lead to improvements in the classifier. In the next section we describe our approach to classifier construction for step 3 and compare our problem to traditional weakly supervised clustering, characterizing it as an instance of the novel problem of partially supervised clustering.

4 Partially Supervised Clustering

In our desire to perform effective source coreference resolution we arrive at the following learning problem – the learning algorithm is presented with a set of partially specified examples of clusterings and acquires a function that can cluster accurately an unseen set of items, while taking advantage of the unlabeled information in the examples.

This setting is to be contrasted with semi-supervised clustering (or clustering with constraints), which has received much research attention (e.g. Demiriz et al. (1999), Wagstaff and Cardie (2000), Basu (2005), Davidson and Ravi (2005)). Semi-supervised clustering can be defined as the problem of clustering a set of items in the presence of limited supervisory information such as pairwise constraints (e.g. two items must/cannot be in the same cluster) or labeled points. In contrast to our setting, in the semi-supervised case there is no training phase – the algorithm receives all examples (labeled and unlabeled) at the same time together with some distance or cost function and attempts to find a clustering that optimizes a given measure (usually based on the distance or cost function).

Source coreference resolution might alternatively be approached as a supervised clustering problem. Traditionally, approaches to supervised clustering have treated the pairwise link decisions as a classification problem. These approaches first learn a distance metric that optimizes the pairwise decisions; and then follow the pairwise classification with a clustering step. However, these traditional approaches have no obvious way of utilizing the available unlabeled information.

In contrast, we follow recent approaches to supervised clustering that propose ways to learn the distance measure in the context of the clustering decisions (Li and Roth, 2005; Finley and Joachims, 2005; McCallum and Wellner, 2003). This provides two advantages for the problem of source coreference resolution. First, it allows the algorithm to take advantage of the complexity of the rich structural dependencies introduced by the clustering problem. Viewed traditionally as a hurdle, the structural complexity of clustering may be beneficial in the partially supervised case. We believe that provided with a few partially specified clustering examples, an algorithm might be able to generalize from the structural dependencies to infer correctly the whole clustering of the items. In addition, considering pairwise decisions in the context of the clustering can arguably lead to more accurate classifiers.

Unfortunately, none of the supervised clustering approaches is readily applicable to the partially supervised case. However, by adapting the formal supervised clustering definition, which we do next, we can develop approaches to partially supervised clustering that take advantage of the unlabeled portions of the data.

Formal definition. For partially supervised clustering we extend the formal definition of supervised clustering given by Finley and Joachims (2005). In the fully supervised setting, an algorithm is given a set S of n training examples $(x_1, y_1), ..., (x_n, y_n) \in X \times Y$, where X is the set of all possible sets of items and Y is the set of all possible clusterings of these sets. For a training example (x, y), $x = \{x_1, x_2, ..., x_k\}$ is a set of k items and $y = \{y_1, y_2, ..., y_r\}$ is a clustering of the items in x with each $y_i \subseteq x$. Additionally, each item can be in no more than one cluster ($\forall i, j. y_i \cap y_j = \emptyset$) and in the fully supervised case each item is in at least one cluster ($x = \bigcup y_i$). The goal of the learning algorithm is to acquire a function $h : X \rightarrow Y$ that can accurately cluster a (previously unseen) set of items.

In the context of source coreference resolution the training set contains one example for each document. The items in each training example are the NPs and the clustering over the items is the equivalence relation defined by the coreference information. For source coreference resolution, however, clustering information is unavailable for the non-source NPs. Thus, to be able to deal with this unlabeled component of the data we arrive to the setting of partially supervised clustering, in which we relax the condition that each item is in at least one cluster ($x = \bigcup y_i$) and replace it with the condition $x \supseteq \bigcup y_i$. The items with no linking information (items in $x \setminus \bigcup y_i$) constitute the unlabeled (unsupervised) component of the partially supervised clustering.

5 Structured Rule Learner

We develop a novel method for partially supervised clustering, which is motivated by the success of a rule learner (RIPPER) for coreference resolution (Ng and Cardie, 2002). We extend RIPPER so that it can learn rules in the context of single-link clustering, which both suits our task (i.e. pronouns link to their single antecedent) and has exhibited good performance for coreference resolution (Ng and Cardie, 2002). We begin with a brief overview of RIPPER followed by a description of the modifications that we implemented. For ease of presentation, we assume that we are in the fully supervised case. We end this section by describing the changes for the partially supervised case.

```
procedure StRip(TrainData){
  GrowData, PruneData = Split(TrainData);
  //Keep instances from the same document together
  while(there are positive uncovered instances) {
    r = growRule(GrowData);
    r = pruneRule(r, PruneData);
    DL = relativeDL(Ruleset);
    if(DL ≤ minDL + d bits)
      Ruleset.add(r);
      Mark examples covered by r as +;
    else
      exit loop with Ruleset
  }
}
procedure growRule(growData){
  r = empty rule;
  for(every unused feature f){
    if (f is nominal feature) {
      for(every possible value v of f) {
        mark all instances that have values of v for f with +;
        compute the transitive closure of the positive instances
        //(including instances marked + from previous rules);
        compute the infoGain for the future/value combination;
      }
    } else{ //Numeric feature
      create one bag for each feature value and split the instances into bags;
      do a forward and a backward pass over the bags keeping a running
      clustering and compute the information gain for each value;
    }
  }
  add the future/value pair with the best infoGain to r;
  growData = growData - all negative instances;
  return r;
}
procedure pruneRule(r, pruneData){
  for(all antecedents a in the rule){
    apply all antecedents in r up to a to pruneData;
    compute the transitive closure of the positive instances;
    compute A(a) – the accuracy of the rule up to antecedent a;
  }
  Remove all antecedents after the antecedent for which A(a) is maximum.
}
```

Figure 2: The StRip algorithm. Additions to RIPPER are shown in bold.

5.1 The RIPPER Algorithm

RIPPER (for Repeated Incremental Pruning to Produce Error Reduction) was introduced by Cohen (1995) as an extension of an existing rule induction algorithm. Cohen (1995) showed that RIPPER produces error rates competitive with C4.5, while exhibiting better running times. RIPPER consists of two phases – a ruleset is grown and then optimized.

The ruleset creation phase begins by randomly splitting the training data into a rule-growing set (2/3 of the training data) and a pruning set (the remaining 1/3). A rule is then grown on the former set by repeatedly adding the *antecedent* (the feature value test) with the largest information gain until the accuracy of the rule becomes 1.0 or there are no remaining potential antecedents. Next the rule is applied to the pruning data and any rule-final sequence that reduces the accuracy of the rule is removed.

The optimization phase uses the full training

set to first grow a replacement rule and a revised rule for each rule in the ruleset. For each rule, the algorithm then considers the original rule, the replacement rule, and the revised rule, and keeps the rule with the smallest description length in the context of the ruleset. After all rules are considered, RIPPER attempts to grow residual rules that cover data not already covered by the ruleset. Finally, RIPPER deletes any rules from the ruleset that reduce the overall minimum description length of the data plus the ruleset. RIPPER performs two rounds of this optimization phase.

5.2 The StRip Algorithm

The property of partially supervised clustering that we want to explore is the structured nature of the decisions. That is, each decision of whether two items (say a and b) belong to the same cluster has an implication for all items a' that belong to a's cluster and all items b' that belong to b's cluster.

We target modifications to RIPPER that will allow StRip (for Structured RIPPER) to learn rules that produce good clusterings in the context of single-link clustering. We extend RIPPER so that every time it makes a decision about a rule, it considers the effect of the rule on the overall clustering of items (as opposed to considering the instances that the rule classifies as positive/negative in isolation). More precisely, we precede every computation of rule performance (e.g. information gain or description length) by a transitive closure (i.e. single link clustering) of the data w.r.t. to the pairwise classifications. Following the transitive closure, all pairs of items that are in the same cluster are considered covered by the rule for performance computation.

The StRip algorithm is given in figure 2, with modifications to the original RIPPER algorithm shown in bold. Due to space limitations the optimization stage of the algorithm is omitted. Our modifications to the optimization stage of RIPPER are in the spirit of the rest of the StRip algorithm.

Partially supervised case. So far we described StRip only for the fully supervised case. We use a very simple modification to handle the partially supervised setting: we exclude the unlabeled pairs when computing the performance of the rules. Thus, the unlabeled items do not count as correct or incorrect classifications when acquiring or pruning a rule, although they do participate in the transitive closure. Links in the unlabeled data are inferred entirely through the indirect links between items in the labeled component that they introduce. In the example of figure 1, the two problematic unlabeled links are the link between the source mention "he" and the underlined non-source NP "Mr. Moussaoui" and the link between the underlined "Mr. Moussaoui" to any source mention of *Moussaoui*. While StRip will not reward any rule (or rule set) that covers these two links directly, such rules will be rewarded indirectly since they put the source *he* in the chain for the source *Moussaoui*.

StRip running time. StRip's running time is generally comparable to that of RIPPER. We compute transitive closure by using a Union-Find structure, which runs in time $O(log^*n)$, which for practical purposes can be considered linear ($O(n)$) [3]. However, when computing the best information gain for a nominal feature, StRip has to make a pass over the data for each value that the feature takes, while RIPPER can split the data into bags and perform the computation in one pass.

6 Evaluation and Results

This section describes the source coreference data set, the baselines, our implementation of StRip, and the results of our experiments.

6.1 Data set

For evaluation we use the MPQA corpus (Wiebe et al., 2005).[4] The corpus consists of 535 documents from the world press. All documents in the collection are manually annotated with phrase-level opinion information following the annotation scheme of Wiebe et al. (2005). Discussion of the annotation scheme is beyond the scope of this paper; for our purposes it suffices to say that the annotations include the source of each opinion and coreference information for the sources (e.g. source coreference chains). The corpus contains no additional noun phrase coreference information.

For our experiments, we randomly split the data set into a training set consisting of 400 documents and a test set consisting of the remaining 135 documents. We use the same test set for all experi-

[3]For the transitive closure, n is the number of items in a document, which is $O(\sqrt{k})$, where k is the number of NP pairs. Thus, transitive closure is sublinear in the number of training instances.

[4]The MPQA corpus is available at `http://nrrc.mitre.org/NRRC/publications.htm`.

ments, although some learning runs were trained on 200 training documents (see next Subsection). The test set contains a total of 4736 source NPs (average of 35.34 source NPs per document) split into 1710 total source NP chains (average of 12.76 chains per document) for an average of 2.77 source NPs per chain.

6.2 Implementation

We implemented the StRip algorithm by modifying JRip – the java implementation of RIPPER included in the WEKA toolkit (Witten and Frank, 2000). The WEKA implementation follows the original RIPPER specification. We changed the implementation to incorporate the modifications suggested by the StRip algorithm; we also modified the underlying data representations and data handling techniques for efficiency. Also due to efficiency considerations, we train StRip only on the 200-document training set.

6.3 Competitive baselines

We compare the results of the new method to three fully supervised baseline systems, each of which employs the same traditional coreference resolution approach. In particular, we use the aforementioned algorithm proposed by Ng and Cardie (2002), which combines a pairwise NP coreference classifier with single-link clustering.

For one baseline, we train the coreference resolution algorithm on the *MPQA src* corpus — the labeled portion of the MPQA corpus (i.e. NPs from the source coreference chains) with unlabeled instances removed.

The second and third baselines investigate whether the source coreference resolution task can benefit from NP coreference resolution training data *from a different domain*. Thus, we train the traditional coreference resolution algorithm on the *MUC6* and *MUC7* coreference-annotated corpora[5] that contain documents similar in style to those in the MPQA corpus (e.g. newspaper articles), but emanate from different domains.

For all baselines we targeted the best possible systems by trying two pairwise NP classifiers (RIPPER and an SVM in the SVM^{light} implementation (Joachims, 1998)), many different parameter settings for the classifiers, two different feature sets, two different training set sizes (the full training set and a smaller training set consisting of half of the documents selected at random), and three different instance selection algorithms[6]. This variety of classifier and training data settings was motivated by reported differences in performance of coreference resolution approaches w.r.t. these variations (Ng and Cardie, 2002). More details on the different parameter settings and instance selection algorithms as well as trends in the performance of different settings can be found in Stoyanov and Cardie (2006). In the experiments below we report the best performance of each of the two learning algorithms on the MPQA test data.

6.4 Evaluation

In addition to the baselines described above, we evaluate StRip both with and without unlabeled data. That is, we train on the MPQA corpus StRip using either all NPs or just opinion source NPs.

We use the B^3 (Bagga and Baldwin, 1998) evaluation measure as well as precision, recall, and F1 measured on the (positive) pairwise decisions. B^3 is a measure widely used for evaluating coreference resolution algorithms. The measure computes the precision and recall for each NP mention in a document, and then averages them to produce combined results for the entire output. More precisely, given a mention i that has been assigned to chain c_i, the precision for mention i is defined as the number of correctly identified mentions in c_i divided by the total number of mentions in c_i. Recall for i is defined as the number of correctly identified mentions in c_i divided by the number of mentions in the gold standard chain for i.

Results are shown in Table 1. The first six rows of results correspond to the fully supervised baseline systems trained on different corpora — *MUC6*, *MUC7*, and *MPQA src*. The seventh row of results shows the performance of StRip using only labeled data. The final row of the table shows the results for partially supervised learning **with** unlabeled data. The table lists results from the best performing run for each algorithm.

Performance among the baselines trained on the *MUC* data is comparable. However, the two baseline runs trained on the *MPQA src* corpus (i.e. results rows five and six) show slightly better performance on the B^3 metric than the baselines trained

[5]We train each baseline using both the development set and the test set from the corresponding MUC corpus.

[6]The goal of the instance selection algorithms is to balance the data, which contains many more negative than positive instances

ML Framework	Training set	Classifier	B^3	precision	recall	F1
Fully supervised	MUC6	SVM	81.2	*72.6*	*52.5*	60.9
		RIPPER	80.7	*57.4*	*63.5*	60.3
	MUC7	SVM	81.7	*65.6*	*55.9*	60.4
		RIPPER	79.7	*71.6*	*48.5*	57.9
	MPQA src	SVM	81.8	*57.5*	*62.9*	60.2
		RIPPER	81.8	*72.0*	*52.5*	60.6
		StRip	82.3	*76.5*	*56.1*	64.6
Partially supervised	MPQA all	StRip	**83.2**	*77.1*	*59.4*	**67.1**

Table 1: Results for Source Coreference. *MPQA src* stands for the MPQA corpus limited to only source NPs, while *MPQA full* contains the unlabeled NPs.

on the *MUC* data, which indicates that for our task the similarity of the documents in the training and test sets appears to be more important than the presence of complete supervisory information. (Improvements over the RIPPER runs trained on the MUC corpora are statistically significant[7], while improvements over the SVM runs are not.)

Table 1 also shows that StRip outperforms the baselines on both performance metrics. StRip's performance is better than the baselines when trained on *MPQA src* (improvement not statistically significant, $p > 0.20$) and even better when trained on the full MPQA corpus, which includes the unlabeled NPs (improvement over the baselines and the former StRip run statistically significant). These results confirm our hypothesis that StRip improves due to two factors: first, considering pairwise decisions in the context of the clustering function leads to improvements in the classifier; and, second, StRip can take advantage of the unlabeled portion of the data.

StRip's performance is all the more impressive considering the strength of the SVM and RIPPER baselines, which which represent the best runs across the 336 different parameter settings tested for SVM^{light} and 144 different settings tested for RIPPER. In contrast, all four of the StRip runs using the full MPQA corpus (we vary the loss ratio for false positive/false negative cost) outperform those baselines.

7 Future Work

Source coreference resolution is only one aspect of opinion summarization. Additionally, an opinion summarization system will need to handle the closely related task of target coreference resolution in order to cluster targets of opinions[8] and combine multiple conflicting opinions from a source to the same targets. Furthermore, a fully automatic opinion summarizer requires automatic source and opinion extractors. While we anticipate that target coreference resolution will be subject to error rates similar to those of source coreference resolution, incorporating these imperfect opinions and sources will further impair the performance of the opinion summarizer. We are not aware of any measure that can be directly used to assess the goodness of opinion summaries, but plan to develop such in future work in conjunction with the development of methods for creating opinion summaries completely automatically. The evaluation metrics will likely have to depend on the task for which the summaries are used.

A limitation of our approach to partially supervised clustering is that we do not directly optimize for the performance measure (e.g. B^3). Other efforts in the area of supervised clustering (Finley and Joachims, 2005; Li and Roth, 2005) have suggested ways to learn distance measures that can optimize directly for a desired performance measure. We plan to investigate algorithms that can directly optimize for complex measures (such as B^3) for the problem of partially supervised clustering. Unfortunately, a measure as complex as B^3 makes extending existing approaches far from trivial due to the difficulty of establishing the connection between individual pairwise decisions (the distance metric) and the score of the clustering algorithm.

Acknowledgements

The authors would like to thank Vincent Ng and Art Munson for providing coreference resolution

[7]Statistical significance is measured using both a 2-tailed paired t-test and the Wilcoxon matched-pairs signed-ranks test ($p < 0.05$). The two tests agreed on all significance judgements, so we will not report them separately.

[8]We did not tackle the task of target coreference resolution in this paper because the MPQA corpus did not contain target annotations at the time of publication.

code, members of the Cornell NLP group (especially Yejin Choi and Art Munson) for many helpful discussions, and the anonymous reviewers for their insightful comments. This work was supported by the Advanced Research and Development Activity (ARDA), by NSF Grants IIS-0535099 and IIS-0208028, by gifts from Google and the Xerox Foundation, and by an NSF Graduate Research Fellowship to the first author.

References

A. Bagga and B. Baldwin. 1998. Entity-based cross-document coreferencing using the vector space model. In *In Proceedings of COLING/ACL*.

S. Basu. 2005. *Semi-supervised Clustering: Probabilistic Models, Algorithms and Experiments*. Ph.D. thesis, Department of Computer Sciences, UT at Austin.

S. Bethard, H. Yu, A. Thornton, V. Hativassiloglou, and D. Jurafsky. 2004. Automatic extraction of opinion propositions and their holders. In *2004 AAAI Spring Symposium on Exploring Attitude and Affect in Text*.

Y. Choi, C. Cardie, E. Riloff, and S. Patwardhan. 2005. Identifying sources of opinions with conditional random fields and extraction patterns. In *Proceedings of EMNLP*.

C. Coglianese. 2004. E-rulemaking: Information technology and regulatory policy: New directions in digital government research. Technical report, Harvard University, J. F. Kennedy School of Government.

W. Cohen. 1995. Fast effective rule induction. In *Proceedings of ICML*.

S. Das and M. Chen. 2001. Yahoo for amazon: Extracting market sentiment from stock message boards. In *Proceedings of APFAAC*.

K. Dave, S. Lawrence, and D. Pennock. 2003. Mining the peanut gallery: Opinion extraction and semantic classification of product reviews. In *Proceedings of IWWWC*.

I. Davidson and S. Ravi. 2005. Clustering with constraints: Feasibility issues and the k-means algorithm. In *Proceedings of SDM*.

A. Demiriz, K. P. Bennett, and M. J. Embrechts. 1999. Semi-supervised clustering using genetic algorithms. In *Proceeding of ANNIE*.

T. Finley and T. Joachims. 2005. Supervised clustering with support vector machines. In *Proceedings of ICML*.

R. Iida, K. Inui, H. Takamura, and Y. Matsumoto. 2003. Incorporating contextual cues in trainable models for coreference resolution. In *Proceedings of the EACL Workshop on The Computational Treatment of Anaphora*.

T. Joachims. 1998. Making large-scale support vector machine learning practical. In A. Smola B. Schölkopf, C. Burges, editor, *Advances in Kernel Methods: Support Vector Machines*. MIT Press, Cambridge, MA.

S. Kim and E. Hovy. 2005. Identifying opinion holders for question answering in opinion texts. In *Proceedings of AAAI Workshop on Question Answering in Restricted Domains*.

X. Li and D. Roth. 2005. Discriminative training of clustering functions: Theory and experiments with entity identification. In *Proceedings of CoNLL*.

A. McCallum and B. Wellner. 2003. Toward conditional models of identity uncertainty with application to proper noun coreference. In *Proceedings of the IJCAI Workshop on Information Integration on the Web*.

T. Morton. 2000. Coreference for NLP applications. In *Proceedings of ACL*.

V. Ng and C. Cardie. 2002. Improving machine learning approaches to coreference resolution. In *In Proceedings of ACL*.

B. Pang and L. Lee. 2004. A sentimental education: Sentiment analysis using subjectivity summarization based on minimum cuts. In *Proceedings of ACL*.

B. Pang, L. Lee, and S. Vaithyanathan. 2002. Thumbs up? Sentiment classification using machine learning techniques. In *Proceedings of EMNLP*.

E. Riloff and J. Wiebe. 2003. Learning extraction patterns for subjective expressions. In *Proceesings of EMNLP*.

E. Riloff, J. Wiebe, and W. Phillips. 2005. Exploiting subjectivity classification to improve information extraction. In *Proceedings of AAAI*.

V. Stoyanov and C. Cardie. 2006. Toward opinion summarization: Linking the sources. In *Proceedings of the ACL Workshop on Sentiment and Subjectivity in Text*.

V. Stoyanov, C. Cardie, and J. Wiebe. 2005. Multi-Perspective question answering using the OpQA corpus. In *Proceedings of EMNLP*.

P. Turney. 2002. Thumbs up or thumbs down? Semantic orientation applied to unsupervised classification of reviews. In *Proceedings of ACL*.

K. Wagstaff and C. Cardie. 2000. Clustering with instance-level constraints. In *Proceedings of the 17-th National Conference on Artificial Intelligence and 12-th Conference on Innovative Applications of Artificial Intelligence*.

J. Wiebe and E. Riloff. 2005. Creating subjective and objective sentence classifiers from unannotated texts. In *Proceedings of CICLing*.

J. Wiebe, T. Wilson, and C. Cardie. 2005. Annotating expressions of opinions and emotions in language. *Language Resources and Evaluation*, 1(2).

T. Wilson, J. Wiebe, and R. Hwa. 2004. Just how mad are you? Finding strong and weak opinion clauses. In *Proceedings of AAAI*.

I.H. Witten and E. Frank. 2000. *Data Mining: Practical machine learning tools with Java implementations*. Morgan Kaufmann, San Francisco.

H. Yu and V. Hatzivassiloglou. 2003. Towards answering opinion questions: Separating facts from opinions and identifying the polarity of opinion sentences. In *Proceedings of EMNLP*.

Sentiment Retrieval using Generative Models

Koji Eguchi
National Institute of Informatics
Tokyo 101-8430, Japan
eguchi@nii.ac.jp

Victor Lavrenko
Department of Computer Science
University of Massachusetts
Amherst, MA 01003, USA
lavrenko@cs.umass.edu

Abstract

Ranking documents or sentences according to both topic and sentiment relevance should serve a critical function in helping users when topics and sentiment polarities of the targeted text are not explicitly given, as is often the case on the web. In this paper, we propose several sentiment information retrieval models in the framework of probabilistic language models, assuming that a user both inputs query terms expressing a certain topic and also specifies a sentiment polarity of interest in some manner. We combine sentiment relevance models and topic relevance models with model parameters estimated from training data, considering the topic dependence of the sentiment. Our experiments prove that our models are effective.

1 Introduction

The recent rapid expansion of access to information has significantly increased the demands on retrieval or classification of sentiment information from a large amount of textual data. The field of *sentiment classification* has recently received considerable attention, where the polarities of sentiment, such as positive or negative, were identified from unstructured text (Shanahan et al., 2005). A number of studies have investigated sentiment classification at document level, e.g., (Pang et al., 2002; Dave et al., 2003), and at sentence level, e.g., (Hu and Liu, 2004; Kim and Hovy, 2004; Nigam and Hurst, 2005); however, the accuracy is still less than desirable. Therefore, ranking according to the likelihood of containing sentiment information is expected to serve a crucial function in helping users. We believe that our work is the first attempt at *sentiment retrieval* that aims at finding sentences containing information with a specific sentiment polarity on a certain topic.

Intuitively, the expression of sentiment in text is dependent on the topic. For example, a negative view for some voting event may be expressed using 'flaw', while a negative view for some politician may be expressed using 'reckless'. Moreover, sentiment polarities are also dependent on topics or domains. For example, the adjective 'unpredictable' may have a negative orientation in an automotive review, in a phrase such as 'unpredictable steering', but it could have a positive orientation in a movie review, in a phrase such as 'unpredictable plot', as mentioned in (Turney, 2002) in the context of his sentiment word detection.

We propose sentiment retrieval models in the framework of generative language modeling, not only assuming query terms expressing a certain topic, but also assuming that the polarity of sentiment interest is specified by the user in some manner, where the topic dependence of the sentiment is considered. To the best of our knowledge, there have been no other studies on a retrieval model unifying both topic and sentiment, and further, there have been no other studies on sentiment retrieval. The sentiment information often appears as local in a document, and therefore focusing on finer levels, i.e., sentence or passage levels rather than document level, is crucial. We thus experiment on sentiment retrieval at the sentence level in this paper.

The rest of this paper is structured as follows. Section **2** introduces the work related to this study. Section **3** describes a generative model of sentiment, which is proposed here as a theoretical framework for our work. Section **4** describes the task definition and our sentiment retrieval model.

Proceedings of the 2006 Conference on Empirical Methods in Natural Language Processing (EMNLP 2006), pages 345–354,
Sydney, July 2006.

Section **5** explains the data we used for our experiments, and gives our experimental results. Section **6** concludes the paper.

2 Related Work

Some efforts for the TREC Novelty Track were related to our work. Although some of the topics used in the Novelty Track in 2003 and 2004 (Soboroff and Harman, 2003; Soboroff, 2004) were related to opinions, most of the efforts were focused on topic, such as studies using term distribution within each sentence, e.g., (Allan et al., 2003; Losada, 2005; Murdock and Croft, 2005). Amongst the participants in the TREC Novelty Track, only (Kim et al., 2004) proposed a method specialized to opinion-bearing sentence retrieval, by making use of lists of words with positive or negative polarities. They aimed to find opinions on a given topic but did not distinguish or did not care about sentiment polarities that should be represented in some sentences (hereafter, *opinion retrieval*). We focus on finding positive views or negative views according to a given topic and sentiment of interest (hereafter, *sentiment retrieval*). Our work is the first work on sentiment retrieval, to the best of our knowledge.

In the context of *sentiment classification*, some researchers have conducted studies on the topic dependence of sentiment polarities. (Nasukawa and Yi, 2003) and (Yi et al., 2003) extracted positive or negative expressions on a given product name using handmade lexicons. (Engström, 2004) studied how the topic dependence influences the accuracy of sentiment classification and attempted to reduce the influence to improve the accuracy. (Wilson et al., 2005) investigated how context influences sentiment polarity at the phrase level in a corpus, beginning with a predefined list of words with polarities. Their focus on the phenomena of topic dependence of sentiment can be shared with our work; however, their work is not directly related to ours, because we focus on a different task, sentiment retrieval, where different approaches are required.

3 A Generative Model of Sentiment

In this section we will provide a formal underpinning for our approach to sentiment retrieval. The approach is based on the *generative* paradigm: we describe a statistical process that could be viewed, hypothetically, as a source of every statement of interest to our system. We stress that this generative process is to be treated as purely hypothetical; the process is only intended to reflect those aspects of human discourse that are pertinent to the problem of retrieving affectively appropriate and topic-relevant texts in response to a query posed by our user.

Before giving a formal specification of our model, we will provide a high-level overview of the main ideas. We are trying to model a collection of natural-language statements, some of which are relevant to a user's query. In our experiments, these statements are individual sentences, but the model can be applied to textual chunks of any length. We assume that the content of an individual statement can be modeled independently of all other statements in the collection. Each statement consists of some topic-bearing and some sentiment-bearing words. We assume that the topic-bearing words represent exchangeable samples from some underlying topic language model. Exchangeability means that the relative order of the words is irrelevant, but the words are not independent of each other—the idea often stated as a *bag-of-words* assumption. Similarly, sentiment-bearing words are viewed as an order-invariant 'bag', sampled from the underlying sentiment language model. We will explicitly model dependency between the topic and sentiment language models, and will demonstrate that treating them independently leads to sub-optimal retrieval performance. When a *sentiment polarity* value is observed for a given statement, we will treat it as a ternary variable influencing the topic and sentiment language models.

We represent a user's query as just another statement, consisting of topic and sentiment parts, subject to all the independence assumptions stated above. We will use the query to estimate the topic and sentiment language models that are representative of the user's interests. Following (Lavrenko and Croft, 2001), we will use the term *relevance models* to describe these models, and will use them to rank statements in order of their relevance to the query.

3.1 Definitions

We start by providing a set of definitions that will be used in the remainder of this section. The task of our model is to *generate* a collection of statements $\mathbf{w}_1 \ldots \mathbf{w}_n$. A statement $\mathbf{w}_i$ is a string of words $\mathbf{w}_{i1} \ldots \mathbf{w}_{in_i}$, drawn from a common vocabulary $\mathcal{V}$. We introduce a binary variable $b_{ij} \in \{S, T\}$ as an indicator of whether the word in the jth position of the ith statement will be a topic word or a sentiment word. For our purposes, b_{ij} is either provided by a human annotator (*manual annotation*), or determined heuristically (*automatic annotation*).

The sentiment polarity x_i for a given statement is a discrete random variable with three outcomes: $\{-1, 0, +1\}$, representing negative, neutral and positive polarity values, respectively. As a matter of convenience we will often denote a statement as a triple $\{\mathbf{w}_i^s, \mathbf{w}_i^t, x_i\}$, where $\mathbf{w}_i^s$ contains the sentiment words and $\mathbf{w}_i^t$ contains the topic words. As we mentioned above, the user's query is treated as just another statement. It will be denoted as a triple $\{\mathbf{q}^s, \mathbf{q}^t, \mathbf{q}^x\}$, corresponding to sentiment words, topic keywords, and the desired polarity value. We will use $\mathbf{p}$ to denote a unigram language model, i.e., a function that assigns a number $\mathbf{p}(v) \in [0, 1]$ to every word v in our vocabulary $\mathcal{V}$, such that $\Sigma_v \mathbf{p}(v) = 1$. The set of all possible unigram language models is the probability simplex $\mathbb{P}$. Similarly, $\mathbf{p}_x$ will denote a distribution over the three possible polarity values, and $\mathbb{P}_x$ is the corresponding ternary probability simplex. We define $\pi : \mathbb{P} \times \mathbb{P} \times \mathbb{P}_x \rightarrow [0, 1]$ to be a measure function that assigns a probability $\pi(\mathbf{p}_1, \mathbf{p}_2, \mathbf{p}_x)$ to a pair of language models $\mathbf{p}_1$ and $\mathbf{p}_2$ together with a polarity model $\mathbf{p}_x$.

3.2 Generative model

Using the definitions presented above, and assuming that $\pi()$ is given, we hypothesize that a new statement $\mathbf{w}_i$ containing words $\mathbf{w}_{i1} \ldots \mathbf{w}_{im}$ with sentiment polarity x_i can be generated according to the following mechanism.

1. Draw $\mathbf{p}_t, \mathbf{p}_s$ and $\mathbf{p}_x$ from $\pi(\cdot, \cdot, \cdot)$.
2. Sample x_i from a polarity distribution $\mathbf{p}_x(\cdot)$.
3. For each position $j = 1 \ldots m$:
   (a) if $b_{ij} = T$: draw $\mathbf{w}_{ij}$ from $\mathbf{p}_t(\cdot)$;
   (b) if $b_{ij} = S$: draw $\mathbf{w}_{ij}$ from $\mathbf{p}_s(\cdot)$.

The probability of observing the new statement $\mathbf{w}_{i1} \ldots \mathbf{w}_{im}$ under this mechanism is given by:

$$\sum_{\mathbf{p}_t, \mathbf{p}_s, \mathbf{p}_x} \pi(\mathbf{p}_t, \mathbf{p}_s, \mathbf{p}_x) \mathbf{p}_x(x_i) \prod_{j=1}^{m} \begin{cases} \mathbf{p}_t(\mathbf{w}_{ij}) & \text{if } b_{ij} = T \\ \mathbf{p}_s(\mathbf{w}_{ij}) & \text{otherwise} \end{cases} \quad (1)$$

The summation in equation (1) goes over all possible pairs of language models $\mathbf{p}_t, \mathbf{p}_s$, but we can avoid integration by specifying a mass function $\pi()$ that assigns nonzero probabilities to a finite subset of points in $\mathbb{P} \times \mathbb{P} \times \mathbb{P}_x$. We accomplish this by using a nonparametric estimate for $\pi()$, the details of which are provided below.

3.2.1 A nonparametric generative mass function

We use a nonparametric estimate for $\pi(\cdot, \cdot, \cdot)$, which makes our generative model similar to *kernel-based* density estimators or *Parzen-window* classifiers (Silverman, 1986). The primary difference is that our model operates over discrete events (strings of words), and accordingly the mass function is defined over the space of distributions, rather than directly over the data points. Our estimate relies on a collection of paired observations $C = \{\mathbf{w}_i^t, \mathbf{w}_i^s, x_i : i = 1..n\}$, which represent statements for which we know which words are topic words ($\mathbf{w}_i^t$), and which are sentiment words ($\mathbf{w}_i^s$). Each of these observations corresponds to a unique point $\mathbf{p}_{ti}, \mathbf{p}_{si}, \mathbf{p}_{xi}$ in the space of paired distributions $\mathbb{P} \times \mathbb{P} \times \mathbb{P}_x$, defined by the following coordinates:

$$\begin{aligned} \mathbf{p}_{ti}(v) &= \lambda_t \#(v, \mathbf{w}_i^t) / \#(\mathbf{w}_i^t) + (1 - \lambda_t) c_{tv} \\ \mathbf{p}_{si}(v) &= \lambda_s \#(v, \mathbf{w}_i^s) / \#(\mathbf{w}_i^s) + (1 - \lambda_s) c_{sv} \\ \mathbf{p}_{xi}(x) &= \lambda_x 1_{x = x_i} + (1 - \lambda_x). \end{aligned} \quad (2)$$

Here, $\#(v, \mathbf{w}_i^t)$ represents the number of times the word v was observed in the topic part of statement i, the length of which is denoted by $\#(\mathbf{w}_i^t)$. c_{tv} stands for the relative frequency of v in the topic part of the collection. The same definitions apply to the sentiment parameters $\#(v, \mathbf{w}_i^s)$, $\#(\mathbf{w}_i^s)$ and c_{sv}. The Boolean indicator function 1_y returns one when the predicate y is true and zero otherwise. Metaparameters λ_t, λ_s and λ_x specify the amount of Dirichlet smoothing (Zhai and Lafferty, 2001) applied to the topic, sentiment and polarity estimates respectively; values for these parameters are determined empirically.

We define $\pi(\mathbf{p}_t, \mathbf{p}_s, \mathbf{p}_x)$ to have mass $\frac{1}{n}$ when its argument $\mathbf{p}_t, \mathbf{p}_s, \mathbf{p}_x$ corresponds to some observation $\mathbf{p}_{ti}, \mathbf{p}_{si}, \mathbf{p}_{xi}$, and zero otherwise:

$$\pi(\mathbf{p}_t, \mathbf{p}_s, \mathbf{p}_x) = \frac{1}{n} \sum_{i=1}^{n} 1_{\mathbf{p}_t = \mathbf{p}_{ti}} \times 1_{\mathbf{p}_s = \mathbf{p}_{si}} \times 1_{\mathbf{p}_x = \mathbf{p}_{xi}}. \quad (3)$$

Equation (3) maintains empirical dependencies between the topic language model $\mathbf{p}_t$ and the sentiment model $\mathbf{p}_s$, because we assign nonzero probability mass only to pairs of models that actually *co-occur* in our observations.

3.2.2 Limitations of the model

Our model represents each statement $\mathbf{w}_i$ as a *bag of words*, or more formally an order-invariant sequence. This representation is often confused with *word independence*, which is a much stronger assumption. The generative model defined by equation (1) ignores the relative ordering of the words, but it does allow arbitrarily strong *unordered dependencies* among them. To illustrate, consider the probability of observing the words 'unpredictable' and 'plot' in the same statement. Suppose we set $\lambda_t, \lambda_s{=}1$ in equation (2), reducing the effects of smoothing. It should be evident that $P(\text{unpredictable,plot})$ will be non-zero only when the two words actually co-occur in the training data. By carefully selecting the smoothing parameters, the model can preserve dependencies between topic and sentiment words, and is quite capable of distinguishing the positive sentiment of 'unpredictable plot' from the negative sentiment of 'unpredictable steering'. On the other hand, the model does ignore the ordering of the words, so it will not be able to differentiate the negative phrase 'gone from good to bad' from its exact opposite. Furthermore, our model is not well suited for modeling adjacency effects: the phrase 'unpredictable plot' is treated in the same way as two separate words, 'unpredictable' and 'plot', co-occurring in the same sentence.

3.3 Using the model for retrieval

The generative model presented above can be applied to sentiment retrieval in the following fashion. We start with a collection of statements C and a query $\{\mathbf{q}^s, \mathbf{q}^t, \mathbf{q}^x\}$ supplied by the user. We use the machinery outlined in Section **3.2** to estimate the topic and sentiment relevance models corresponding to the user's information need, and then determine which statements in our collection most closely correspond to these models of relevance. The topic relevance model R_t and sentiment relevance model R_s are estimated as follows. We assume that our query $\mathbf{q}^s, \mathbf{q}^t, \mathbf{q}^x$ is a random sample from a distribution defined by equation (1), and then for each word v we estimate the likelihood that v would be observed if we sampled one more topic or sentiment word:

$$R_t(v){=}\frac{P(\mathbf{q}^s, \mathbf{q}^t{\circ}v, \mathbf{q}^x)}{P(\mathbf{q}^s, \mathbf{q}^t, \mathbf{q}^x)},\ R_s(v){=}\frac{P(\mathbf{q}^s{\circ}v, \mathbf{q}^t, \mathbf{q}^x)}{P(\mathbf{q}^s, \mathbf{q}^t, \mathbf{q}^x)}. \quad (4)$$

Both the numerator and denominator are computed according to equation (1), with the mass function $\pi()$ given by equations (3) and (2). We use the notation $\mathbf{q}{\circ}v$ to denote appending word v to the string $\mathbf{q}$. Estimation is done over the training corpus, which may or may not include numeric values of sentiment polarity.[1] Once we have estimates for the topic and sentiment relevance models, we can rank testing statements $\mathbf{w}$ by their similarity to R_t and R_s. We rank statements using a variation of cross-entropy, which was proposed by (Zhai, 2002):

$$\alpha \sum_v R_t(v) \log \mathbf{p}_t(v) + (1-\alpha) \sum_v R_s(v) \log \mathbf{p}_s(v). \quad (5)$$

Here the summations extend over all words v in the vocabulary, R_t and R_s are given by equation (4), while $\mathbf{p}_t$ and $\mathbf{p}_s$ are computed according to equation (2). A weighting parameter α allows us to change the balance of topic and sentiment in the final ranking formula; its value is selected empirically.

4 Sentiment Retrieval Task

4.1 Task definition

We define two variations of the sentiment retrieval task. In one, the user supplies us with a numeric value for the desired polarity $\mathbf{q}^x$. In the other, the user supplies a set of *seed words* $\mathbf{q}^s$, reflecting the desired sentiment. The first task requires us to have polarity observations x_i in our training data, while the second does not.

Task with training data:

Input: (1) a set of topic keywords $\mathbf{q}^t$ and (2) a sentiment specification $\mathbf{q}^x \in \{-1, 1\}$. In this case we assume $\mathbf{q}^s$ to be the empty string.

Output: a ranked list of topic-relevant and sentiment-relevant sentences from the test data.

Task with seed words:

Input: (1) a set of topic keywords $\mathbf{q}^t$ and (2) a set of sentiment seed words $\mathbf{q}^s$. In this case our model ignores $\mathbf{q}^x$ and x_i.

[1] When the training corpus does not contain numeric polarity values x_i, we assume $\pi(\mathbf{p}_t, \mathbf{p}_s, \mathbf{p}_x){=}\pi(\mathbf{p}_t, \mathbf{p}_s)$ and force $\mathbf{p}_x(x_i)$ to be a constant.

Output: a ranked list of topic-relevant and sentiment-relevant sentences from the test data.

In the first task, we split our corpus into three parts: (i) the training set, which was used for estimating the relevance models R_s and R_t; (ii) the development set, which was used for tuning the model parameters λ_t, λ_s and α; and (iii) the testing set, from which we retrieved sentences in response to the query. In the second task, we split the corpus into two parts: (i) the training set, which was used for tuning the model parameters; and (ii) the testing set, which was used for constructing R_s and R_t and from which we retrieved sentences in response to queries.[2] The testing set was identical in both tasks. Note that the sentiment relevance model R_s can be constructed in a topic-dependent fashion for both tasks.

4.2 Variations of the retrieval model

slm: the retrieval model as described in Section **3.3**.

lmt: the standard language modeling approach (Ponte and Croft, 1998; Song and Croft, 1999) on the topic keywords $\mathbf{q}^t$ for the topic part of the text $\mathbf{w}^t$.

lms: the standard language modeling approach on the sentiment keywords $\mathbf{q}^s$ for the sentiment part of the text $\mathbf{w}^s$.

base: the weighted linear combination of *lmt* and *lms*.

rmt: only the topic relevance model was used for ranking using $\mathbf{q}^t$ and for $\mathbf{w}^t$.[3]

rms: only the sentiment relevance model was used for ranking using $\mathbf{q}^s$ and for $\mathbf{w}^s$.

rmt-base: the *slm* model with $\alpha = 1$, ignoring the sentiment relevance model.

rms-base: the *slm* model with $\alpha = 0$, ignoring the topic relevance model.

rmt-rms: the *rmt* and *rms* models are treated independently.

rmt-slm: the *rmt* and *rms-base* models are combined.

lmtf: the standard language modeling approach using $\mathbf{q}^t$ for the nonsplit text, as baseline.

rmtf: the conventional relevance model was used for ranking using $\mathbf{q}^t$ for the nonsplit text, as baseline.

lmtsf: the standard language modeling approach using both $\mathbf{q}^t$ and $\mathbf{q}^s$ for the nonsplit text, for reference.

rmtsf: the conventional relevance model was used for ranking using both $\mathbf{q}^t$ and $\mathbf{q}^s$ for the nonsplit text, for reference.

Note that the relevance models are constructed using training data for the training-based task, but are constructed using test data for the seed-based task, as mentioned in Section **4.1**. Therefore, the *base* model is only used for the training data, not for the test data, in the training-based task, while it can be performed for the test data in the case of the seed-based task. Moreover, the *lms*, *lmtsf* and *rmtsf* models are based on the premise of using seed words to specify sentiments, and so they are only applicable to the seed-based task.

In the models described in this subsection, λ_t and λ_s in equation (2) were set to Dirichlet estimates (Zhai and Lafferty, 2001), $\#(\mathbf{w}_i^t)/(\#(\mathbf{w}_i^t) + \mu_t)$ and $\#(\mathbf{w}_i^s)/(\#(\mathbf{w}_i^s) + \mu_s)$ for the relevance models R_t and R_s, respectively, in equation (4), and were fixed at 0.9 for ranking as in equation (5) for our experiments in Section **5**. Here, μ_t and μ_s were selected empirically according to the tasks described in Section **4.1**. The model parameter α in equation (5) was also selected empirically in the same manner. The number of ranked documents used in the relevance models R_t and R_s, in equation (4), was selected empirically in the same manner as above; however, we fixed the number of terms used in the relevance models as 1000.

5 Experiments

5.1 Data set and evaluation measure

We used the MPQA Opinion Corpus version 1.2 (Wilson et al., 2005; Wiebe et al., 2005) to measure the effectiveness of our sentiment re-

[2] Because the training set was used for tuning the model parameters, no development set was required for this task.

[3] When we use the automatic annotation that is described in Section **5.2.2**, we use the whole text instead of the topic part of the text, for the reasons given in that section. This treatment is applied to the *base*, *rmt-base*, *rms-base*, *rmt-rms*, *rmt-slm* and *slm* models that are described in this section for using the automatic annotation. However, we distinguish the *lmt* and *rmt* models using the topic part of the text and the *lmtf* and *rmtf* models, as baselines, using the whole text, respectively, even in the experiments using the automatic annotation.

trieval models. We summarize this data set as follows.

- This corpus contains news articles collected from 187 different foreign and U.S. news sources from June 2001 to May 2002. The corpus contains 535 documents, a total of 11,114 sentences.
- The majority of the articles are on 10 different topics, which are labeled at document level, but, in addition to these, a number of additional articles were randomly selected from a larger corpus of 270,000 documents.
- Each article was manually annotated using an annotation scheme for opinions and other private states at phrase level. We only used the annotations for sentiments that included some attributes such as polarity and strength.

In this data set, the topic relevance for the 10 topics is known at the document level, but unknown at the sentence level. We assumed that all the sentences in a relevant document could be considered relevant to the topic.[4]

This data set was annotated with sentiment polarities at the phrase level, but not explicitly annotated at the sentence level. Therefore, we provided sentiment polarities at the sentence level to prepare training data and data for evaluation. We set the sentence-level sentiment polarity equal to the polarity with the highest strength in each sentence.[5]

Queries were expressed using the title of one of the 10 topics and specified as positive or negative. Thus, we had 20 types of queries for our experiments. Because the supposed relevance judgments in this setting are imperfect at sentence level, we used *bpref* (Buckley and Voorhees, 2004), in both the training and testing phases, as it is known to be tolerant of imperfect judgments. Bpref uses binary relevance judgments to define the preference relation (i.e., any relevant document is preferred over any nonrelevant document for a given topic), while other measures, such as mean average precision, depend only on the ranks of the relevant documents.

[4]This is a strong assumption to make and may not be true in all cases. A larger, more complete data set is required to perform a more detailed analysis, which is left as future work.

[5]We disregarded 'neutral' and 'both' if other polarities appeared. We can also set the sentence-level sentiment polarity according to the presence of polarity in each sentence, but we did not consider this setting here.

5.2 Extracting sentiment expressions

5.2.1 Using manual annotation

Because the MPQA corpus was annotated with phrase-level sentiments, we can use these annotations to split a sentence into a topic part $\mathbf{w}^t$ and a sentiment part $\mathbf{w}^s$. The Krovetz stemmer (Krovetz, 1993) was applied to the topic part, the sentiment part and to the query terms[6] and, for the retrieval experiments in Sections **5.3** and **5.4**, a total of 418 stopwords from a standard stopword list were removed when they appeared.

5.2.2 Using automatic annotation

In automatic extraction of sentiment expressions in this study, we detected sentiment-bearing words using lists of words with established polarities. At this stage, topic dependence was not considered; however, at the stage of sentiment modeling, the topic dependence can be reflected, as described in Sections **3** and **4**.

We first prepared a list of words indicating sentiments. We used Hatzivassiloglou and McKeown's sentiment word list (Hatzivassiloglou and McKeown, 1997), which consists of 657 positive and 679 negative adjectives, and The General Inquirer (Stone et al., 1966), which contains 1621 positive and 1989 negative words.[7] By merging these lists, we obtained 1947 positive and 2348 negative words. After stemming these words in the same manner as in Section **5.2.1**, we were left with 1667 positive and 2129 negative words, which we will use hereafter in this paper.

The sentiment polarities are sometimes sensitive to the structural information, for instance, a negation expression reverses the following sentiment polarity. To handle negation, every sentiment-bearing word was rewritten with a 'NEG' suffix, such as 'good_NEG', if an odd number of negation expressions was found within the five preceding words in the sentence. To detect negation expressions, we used a predefined negation expression list. This negation handling is similar to that used in (Das and Chen, 2001; Pang et al., 2002). We extracted sentiment-bearing expressions using the list of words with established po-

[6]We used the topic labels attached to the MPQA corpus as the topic query terms $\mathbf{q}^t$ in all the experiments in Sections **5.3** and **5.4**.

[7]We extracted positive and negative words from the General Inquirer basically in the same manner as in (Turney and Littman, 2003); however, we did not exclude any words, unlike (Turney and Littman, 2003), where some seed words were excluded for the evaluation of their work.

Table 1: Sample probabilities from the sentiment relevance models

Topic-independent		Topic-independent		Reaction to President Bush's 2002 State of the Union Address				2002 presidential election in Zimbabwe				Israeli settlements in Gaza and West Bank			
w/ manual annot.		w/ automatic annot.		w/ manual annot.		w/ automatic annot.		w/ manual annot.		w/ automatic annot.		w/ manual annot.		w/ automatic annot.	
$P(w\|Q)$	w	$P(w\|Q)$	w	$P(w\|Q)$	w	$P(w\|Q)$	w	$P(w\|Q)$	w	$P(w\|Q)$	w	$P(w\|Q)$	w	$P(w\|Q)$	w
0.047	demand	0.029	state	0.030	support	0.067	state	0.042	support	0.039	support	0.041	ask	0.097	settle
0.031	expect	0.026	support	0.016	promise	0.034	support	0.033	legitimate	0.033	legitimate	0.036	agreed	0.032	peace
0.031	defend	0.014	lead	0.014	call	0.024	call	0.031	free	0.033	lead	0.036	call	0.025	state
0.031	invite	0.013	call	0.014	excellent	0.019	meet	0.029	congratulate	0.025	free	0.033	aim	0.022	secure
0.031	humane	0.013	minister	0.013	goal	0.017	minister	0.028	fair	0.025	fair	0.028	immediate	0.015	call
0.031	safeguard	0.011	right	0.013	express	0.015	promise	0.023	please	0.018	state	0.025	aware	0.014	conflict
0.031	nutritious	0.010	foreign	0.013	best	0.014	white	0.017	confident	0.017	congratulate	0.024	key	0.013	support
0.031	helpful	0.009	hope	0.012	count	0.013	foreign	0.017	call	0.015	call	0.022	expect	0.012	right
0.016	time	0.009	meet	0.012	cooperate	0.012	success	0.012	hopeful	0.015	meet	0.018	justify	0.011	attack
0.016	say	0.008	interest	0.011	proposal	0.011	defense	0.012	express	0.013	unity	0.018	honoure	0.011	minister
0.091	evil	0.037	state	0.065	evil	0.098	state	0.029	flaw	0.028	flaw	0.018	palestinian	0.100	settle
0.080	axis	0.022	evil	0.049	axis	0.051	evil	0.018	condemn	0.026	critic	0.013	protest	0.031	state
0.045	threat	0.015	right	0.022	critic	0.028	critic	0.015	true	0.023	state	0.012	decide	0.019	peace
0.033	qualify	0.015	prison	0.011	prepare	0.017	call	0.014	critic	0.022	opposition	0.011	peace	0.014	secure_NEG
0.030	wrote	0.013	critic	0.010	recognize	0.012	interest	0.012	expect	0.019	reject	0.011	fatten	0.013	critic
0.020	particular	0.010	human	0.010	reckless	0.011	move	0.011	reject	0.017	condemn	0.011	believe	0.012	force
0.020	word	0.008	support	0.010	country	0.011	reject	0.011	s	0.016	legal	0.009	plan	0.012	attack
0.018	harsh	0.008	protest	0.009	upset	0.010	slam	0.011	fair	0.015	move	0.009	fear	0.012	war
0.015	reject	0.008	war	0.009	pick	0.010	right	0.011	free	0.015	democratic	0.009	mistake	0.011	believe
0.015	dangerous	0.008	force	0.009	eyesore	0.010	attack	0.010	angry	0.014	support	0.009	continue	0.011	minister

The upper and lower tables correspond to positive and negative sentiments, respectively. The topic-independent sentiment relevance models (in the left two columns) correspond to *rms*, and the topic-dependent models (in the rest of the columns) correspond to *rms-base*, which is used for *slm*.

larities, considering negation, as described above. Note that we used the list of words with sentiments to extract sentiment expressions, but we did not use the predefined sentiments to model sentiment relevance.

Some expressions are sometimes used to express a certain topic, such as *settlements* in "Israeli *settlements* in Gaza and West Bank"; but at other times are used to express a certain sentiment, such as the same word in "All parties signed court-mediated compromise *settlements*". Therefore, we will use whole sentences to model topic relevance, while we will use the automatically extracted sentiment expressions to model sentiment relevance, in Sections **5.3** and **5.4**.

5.3 Experiments on training-based task

We conducted experiments on the training-based task described in Section **4.1**, using either manual annotation as described in Section **5.2.1** or automatic annotation as described in Section **5.2.2**. **Table 1** contrasts sample probabilities from topic-independent sentiment relevance models and those from topic-dependent sentiment relevance models. In the left two columns of this table, two sets of sample probabilities using the topic-independent model are presented. One was computed from the manual annotation and the other was computed from the automatic annotation. In the remaining columns, samples using the topic-dependent model are shown according to the three topics: (1) "reaction to President Bush's 2002 State of the Union Address", (2) "2002 presidential election in Zimbabwe", and (3) "Israeli settlements in Gaza and West Bank". A number of positive expressions appeared topic dependent, such as 'promise' (stemmed from 'promising' or not) and 'support' for Topic (1), 'legitimate' and 'congratulate' for Topic (2) and 'justify' and 'secure' for Topic (3); while negative expressions appeared topic-dependent, such as 'critic' (stemmed from 'criticism') and 'eyesore' for Topic (1), 'flaw' and 'condemn' for Topic (2) and 'mistake' and 'secure_NEG' (i.e., 'secure' was negated) for Topic (3).

Some expressions were unexpectedly generated regardless of the types of annotation, e.g., 'palestinian' for Topic (3); however, we found some characteristics in the results using automatic annotation. Some expressions on opinions that did not convey sentiments, such as 'state', frequently appeared regardless of topic. This sort of expression may effectively function as degrading sentences only conveying facts, but may function harmfully by catching sentences conveying opinions without sentiments in the task of sentiment retrieval. Some topic expressions, such as 'settle' (stemmed from 'settlement' or not) for Topic (3), were generated, because such words convey positive sentiments in some other contexts and thus they were contained in the list of sentiment-bearing words that we used for automatic annotation. This will not cause a topic relevance model to drift, because we modeled the topic relevance using whole sentences, as described in Section **5.2.2**; however, it may harm the sentiment relevance model to some extent.

Table 2: Experimental results of training-based task using manually annotated data

	10%		25%		40%	
Models	Bpref	(AvgP)	Bpref	(AvgP)	Bpref	(AvgP)
lmtf	0.1389	(0.1135)	0.1389	(0.1135)	0.1386	(0.1145)
lmt	0.1499	(0.1164)	0.1499	(0.1164)	0.1444	(0.1148)
rmtf	0.1811	(0.1706)	0.1887	(0.1770)	0.1841	(0.1691)
rmt	0.1712	(0.1619)	0.1712	(0.1619)	0.1922	(0.1705)
rmt-base	0.1922	(0.1723)	0.2005	(0.1812)	0.2100*	(0.1951)
rms	0.0464	(0.0384)	0.0452	(0.0394)	0.0375	(0.0320)
rms-base	0.0772	(0.0640)	0.0869	(0.0704)	0.0865	(0.0724)
rmt-rms	0.2025	(0.1413)	0.2210	(0.1925)	0.2117	(0.2003)
rmt-slm	0.2278*	(0.1715)	0.2249	(0.1676)	0.1999	(0.1819)
slm	0.2006	(0.1914)	0.2247	(0.1824)	0.2441*	(0.2427)

'*' indicates statistically significant improvement over *rmtf* where $p < 0.05$ with the two-sided Wilcoxon signed-rank test.

Table 3: Experimental results of training-based task using automatically annotated data

	10%		25%		40%	
Models	Bpref	(AvgP)	Bpref	(AvgP)	Bpref	(AvgP)
lmtf	0.1389	(0.1135)	0.1389	(0.1135)	0.1386	(0.1145)
lmt	0.1325	(0.0972)	0.1315	(0.0976)	0.1325	(0.0972)
rmtf	0.1811	(0.1706)	0.1887	(0.1770)	0.1841	(0.1691)
rmt	0.1490	(0.1418)	0.1762	(0.1584)	0.1695	(0.1485)
rmt-base	0.2076*	(0.1936)	0.2252*	(0.2139)	0.2302*	(0.2196)
rms	0.0347	(0.0287)	0.0501	(0.0408)	0.0501	(0.0408)
rms-base	0.0943	(0.0733)	0.1196	(0.0896)	0.1241	(0.0979)
rmt-rms	0.1690	(0.1182)	0.2063	(0.1938)	0.1603	(0.1591)
rmt-slm	0.1980	(0.1426)	0.2013	(0.1835)	0.2148	(0.1882)
slm	0.2011	(0.1537)	0.2261*	(0.1716)	0.2318*	(0.1802)

'*' indicates statistically significant improvement over *rmtf* where $p < 0.05$ with the two-sided Wilcoxon signed-rank test.

We performed retrieval experiments in the steps described in Section **4.1**. For this purpose, we split the data into three parts: (i) $x\%$ as the training data, (ii) $(50 - x)\%$ as the evaluation data, and (iii) 50% as the test data.

The test results of training-based task using manually annotated data and automatically annotated data are shown in **Tables 2** and **3**, respectively. The scores were computed according to the *bpref* evaluation measure (Buckley and Voorhees, 2004), as mentioned in Section **5.1**. In addition to the bpref, mean average precision values are presented as 'AvgP' in the tables, for reference.[8] In these tables, the top row indicates the percentages of the training data x. It turned out that in all our experiments the appropriate fraction of training data was 40%. In this setting, our *slm* model worked 76.1% better than the query likelihood model and 32.6% better than the conventional relevance model, when using manual annotation, and both improvements were statistically significant according to the Wilcoxon signed-rank test.[9] When using automatic annotation, the *slm* model worked 67.2% better than the query likelihood model and 25.9% better than the conventional relevance model, where both improvements were statistically significant. The *rmt-base* model also worked well with automatic annotation.

5.4 Experiments on seed-based task

For experiments on the seed-based task that was described in Section **4.1**, we used three groups of seed words: KAM, TUR and ORG. Each group consists of a positive word set $\mathbf{q}^s_{(+)}$ and a negative word set $\mathbf{q}^s_{(-)}$, as follows:

KAM: $\mathbf{q}^s_{(+)} = \{$good$\}$, and $\mathbf{q}^s_{(-)} = \{$bad$\}$.

TUR: $\mathbf{q}^s_{(+)} = \{$good, nice, excellent, positive, fortunate, correct, superior$\}$, and $\mathbf{q}^s_{(-)} = \{$bad, nasty, poor, negative, unfortunate, wrong, inferior$\}$.

ORG: $\mathbf{q}^s_{(+)} = \{$support, demand, promise, want, hope$\}$, and $\mathbf{q}^s_{(-)} = \{$refuse, accuse, criticism, fear, reject$\}$.

KAM and TUR were used in (Kamps and Marx, 2002) and (Turney and Littman, 2003), respectively. We constructed ORG considering sentiment-bearing words that may frequently appear in newspaper articles.

We experimented with the seed-based task, making use of each of these seed word groups, in the steps described in Section **4.1**. For this purpose, we split the data into two parts: (i) 50% as the estimation data and (ii) 50% as the test data.

The test results using manually annotated data and automatically annotated data are shown in **Tables 4** and **5**, respectively, where the scores were computed according to the bpref evaluation measure. Mean average precision values are also presented as 'AvgP' in the tables, for reference.

When using the manually annotated approach, our *slm* model worked well, especially with the seed word group ORG, as shown in **Table 4**. Using ORG, the *slm* model worked 61.2% better than the query likelihood model and 15.2% better than the conventional relevance model, where both improvements were statistically significant according to the Wilcoxon signed-rank test. Even

[8] As mentioned in Section **5.1**, the bpref is more appropriate for the evaluation of our experiments than the mean average precision.

[9] Significance tests involved only 20 queries, which makes it difficult to achieve statistical significance.

Table 4: Experimental results of seed-based task using manually annotated data

	ORG		TUR		KAM	
Models	Bpref	(AvgP)	Bpref	(AvgP)	Bpref	(AvgP)
lmtf	0.1385	(0.1119)	0.1385	(0.1119)	0.1385	(0.1119)
lmtsf	0.1182	(0.1035)	0.1061	(0.0884)	0.1330	(0.1062)
lmt	0.1501	(0.1171)	0.1501	(0.1171)	0.1501	(0.1171)
base	0.1615	(0.1319)	0.1531	(0.1217)	0.1514	(0.1180)
rmtf	0.1938	(0.1776)	0.1938	(0.1776)	0.1938	(0.1776)
rmtsf	0.1884	(0.1775)	0.1661	(0.1412)	0.1927	(0.1754)
rmt	0.1974	(0.1826)	0.1974	(0.1826)	0.1974	(0.1826)
rmt-base	0.1960	(0.1918)	0.1931	(0.1703)	0.1837	(0.1721)
rms	0.0434	(0.0262)	0.0295	(0.0205)	0.0280	(0.0170)
rms-base	0.1142	(0.1022)	0.1144	(0.0841)	0.1226	(0.0973)
rmt-rms	0.1705	(0.1117)	0.1403	(0.1424)	0.1405	(0.0842)
rmt-slm	0.2266*	(0.2034)	0.2272*	(0.2012)	0.2264*	(0.2016)
slm	0.2233*	(0.2048)	0.2160	(0.1945)	0.2072	(0.1929)

'*' indicates statistically significant improvement over *rmtf* where $p < 0.05$ with the two-sided Wilcoxon signed-rank test.

Table 5: Experimental results of seed-based task using automatically annotated data

	ORG		TUR		KAM	
Models	Bpref	(AvgP)	Bpref	(AvgP)	Bpref	(AvgP)
lmtf	0.1385	(0.1119)	0.1385	(0.1119)	0.1385	(0.1119)
lmtsf	0.1182	(0.1035)	0.1061	(0.0884)	0.1330	(0.1062)
lmt	0.1325	(0.0972)	0.1325	(0.0972)	0.1325	(0.0972)
basef	0.1550	(0.1369)	0.1451	(0.1188)	0.1416	(0.1142)
rmtf	0.1938	(0.1776)	0.1938	(0.1776)	0.1938	(0.1776)
rmtsf	0.1884	(0.1775)	0.1661	(0.1412)	0.1927	(0.1754)
rmt	0.1757	(0.1578)	0.1757	(0.1578)	0.1757	(0.1578)
rmt-base	0.1957	(0.1862)	0.1976	(0.1882)	0.1825	(0.1704)
rms	0.0421	(0.0236)	0.0364	(0.0205)	0.0217	(0.0147)
rms-base	0.1268	(0.1096)	0.1301	(0.1148)	0.1326	(0.1158)
rmt-rms	0.1465	(0.1514)	0.1390	(0.1393)	0.1252	(0.0757)
rmt-slm	0.1977	(0.1811)	0.2008	(0.1649)	0.1959	(0.1677)
slm	0.2031	(0.1714)	0.2055*	(0.1668)	0.2044*	(0.1698)

'*' indicates statistically significant improvement over *rmtf* where $p < 0.05$ with the two-sided Wilcoxon signed-rank test.

using the other seed word groups, the *slm* model worked 49–56% better than the query likelihood model and 6–12% better than the conventional relevance model; however, the latter improvement was not statistically significant. The *rmt-slm* model also worked well with manual annotation.

When using automatic annotation, the *slm* model worked 46–48% better than the query likelihood model and 4–6% better than the conventional relevance model, as shown in **Table 5**. The improvements over the conventional relevance model were statistically significant only when using TUR or KAM; however, the score when using ORG is almost comparable with the others.

6 Conclusion

We propose sentiment retrieval models in the framework of probabilistic generative models, not only assuming that a user inputs query terms expressing a certain topic, but also assuming that the user specifies a sentiment polarity of interest either as a sentiment specification $\mathbf{q}^x \in \{-1, 1\}$ or as a set of sentiment seed words $\mathbf{q}^s$. For this purpose, we combine sentiment relevance models and topic relevance models, considering the topic dependence of the sentiment. In our experiments, our model worked significantly better than standard language modeling approaches, both when using $\mathbf{q}^x$ and $\mathbf{q}^s$, and with both manual and automatic annotation of the fragments expressing sentiments in text. With $\mathbf{q}^s$ and automatic annotation, our model still worked significantly better than the standard approaches; however, the performance did not reach that achieved with other settings. We believe the performance can be improved with larger-scale data.

We experimented to find sentences that were relevant to a given topic and were appropriate to a given sentiment; however, our models can also be applied to textual chunks of any length, such as at document level or passage level. Our model can be easily extended to *opinion retrieval*, if the opinion retrieval is defined as retrieving sentences or documents that contain either positive or negative sentiments. This issue is worth pursuing in future work. Approaches considering polarity strength or continuous values for the polarity specification, rather than using $\{-1, 1\}$, can also be considered in future work.

Acknowledgments

We thank James Allan, W. Bruce Croft and the anonymous reviewers for valuable discussions and comments. This work was supported in part by the Overseas Research Scholars Program and the Grant-in-Aid for Scientific Research (#17680011) from the Ministry of Education, Culture, Sports, Science and Technology, Japan, in part by the Telecommunications Advancement Foundation, Japan, in part by the Center for Intelligent Information Retrieval, and in part by the Defense Advanced Research Projects Agency (DARPA), USA under contract number HR0011-06-C-0023. Any opinions, findings and conclusions or recommendations expressed in this material are those of the author(s) and do not necessarily reflect those of the sponsor.

References

James Allan, Courtney Wade, and Alvaro Bolivar. 2003. Retrieval and novelty detection at the sentence level. In *Proc. of the 26th Annual International ACM SIGIR Conference*, pages 314–321, Toronto, Canada.

Chris Buckley and Ellen M. Voorhees. 2004. Retrieval evaluation with incomplete information. In *Proc. of the 27th Annual International ACM SIGIR Conference*, pages 25–32, Sheffield, United Kingdom.

Sanjiv R. Das and Mike Y. Chen. 2001. Yahoo! for Amazon: Sentiment parsing from small talk on the Web. In *Proc. of the 2001 European Finance Association Annual Conference*, Barcelona, Spain.

Kushal Dave, Steve Lawrence, and David M. Pennock. 2003. Mining the peanut gallery: Opinion extraction and semantic classification of product reviews. In *Proc. of the 12th International Conference on the World Wide Web*, pages 519–528, Budapest, Hungary.

Charlotta Engström. 2004. Topic dependence in sentiment classification. Master's thesis, University of Cambridge.

Vasileios Hatzivassiloglou and Kathleen R. McKeown. 1997. Predicting the semantic orientation of adjectives. In *Proc. of the 35th Annual Meeting of the Association for Computational Linguistics*, pages 174–181, Madrid, Spain.

Minqing Hu and Bing Liu. 2004. Mining and summarizing customer reviews. In *Proc. of the 10th ACM SIGKDD International Conference on Knowledge Discovery and Data Mining*, pages 168–177, Seattle, USA.

Jaap Kamps and Maarten Marx. 2002. Words with attitude. In *Proc. of the 1st International Conference on Global WordNet*, pages 332–341, Mysore, India.

Soo-Min Kim and Eduard Hovy. 2004. Determining the sentiment of opinions. In *Proc. of the 20th International Conference on Computational Linguistics*, Geneva, Czech Republic.

Soo-Min Kim, Deepak Ravichandran, and Eduard Hovy. 2004. ISI Novelty Track system for TREC 2004. In *Proc. of the 13th Text Retrieval Conference*. NIST Special Publication 500-261.

Robert Krovetz. 1993. Viewing morphology as an inference process. In *Proc. of the 16th Annual International ACM SIGIR Conference*, pages 191–202, Pittsburgh, Pennsylvania, USA.

Victor Lavrenko and W. Bruce Croft. 2001. Relevance-based language models. In *Proc. of the 24th Annual International ACM-SIGIR Conference*, pages 120–127, New Orleans, Louisiana, USA.

David E. Losada. 2005. Language modeling for sentence retrieval: A comparison between multiple-Bernoulli and multinomial models. In *Information Retrieval and Theory Workshop*, Glasgow, United Kingdom.

Vanessa Murdock and W. Bruce Croft. 2005. A translation model for sentence retrieval. In *Proc. of HLT/EMNLP 2005*, pages 684–691, Vancouver, Canada.

Tetsuya Nasukawa and Jeonghee Yi. 2003. Sentiment analysis: Capturing favorability using natural language processing. In *Proc. of the 2nd International Conference on Knowledge Capture*, pages 70–77, Sanibel Island, Florida, USA.

Kamal Nigam and Matthew Hurst, 2005. *Computing Attitude and Affect in Text: Theory and Applications*, chapter Towards a Robust Metric of Opinion. Springer.

Bo Pang, Lillian Lee, and Shivakumar Vaithyanathan. 2002. Thumbs up? Sentiment classification using machine learning techniques. In *Proc. of the 2002 Conference on Empirical Methods in Natural Language Processing*, pages 79–86, Philadelphia, Pennsylvania, USA.

Jay M. Ponte and W. Bruce Croft. 1998. A language modeling approach to information retrieval. In *Proc. of the 21st Annual International ACM-SIGIR Conference*, pages 275–281, Melbourne, Australia.

James Shanahan, Yan Qu, and Janyce Wiebe, editors. 2005. *Computing attitude and affect in text*. Springer.

B. W. Silverman, 1986. *Density Estimation for Statistics and Data Analysis*, pages 75–94. CRC Press.

Ian Soboroff and Donna Harman. 2003. Overview of the TREC 2003 Novelty Track. In *Proc. of the 12th Text Retrieval Conference*, pages 38–53. NIST Special Publication 500-255.

Ian Soboroff. 2004. Overview of the TREC 2004 Novelty Track. In *Proc. of the 13th Text Retrieval Conference*. NIST Special Publication 500-261.

Fei Song and W. Bruce Croft. 1999. A general language model for information retrieval. In *Proc. of the 8th International Conference on Information and Knowledge Management*, pages 316–321, Kansas City, Missouri, USA.

Philip J. Stone, Dexter C. Dunphy, Marshall S. Smith, and Daniel M. Ogilvie. 1966. *The General Inquirer: A Computer Approach to Content Analysis*. MIT Press.

Peter D. Turney and Michael L. Littman. 2003. Measuring praise and criticism: Inference of semantic orientation from association. *ACM Transactions on Information Systems*, 21(4):315–346.

Peter D. Turney. 2002. Thumbs up or thumbs down? Semantic orientation applied to unsupervised classification of reviews. In *Proc. of the 40th Annual Meeting of the Association for Computational Linguistics*, pages 417–424, Philadelphia, Pennsylvania, USA.

Janyce Wiebe, Theresa Wilson, and Claire Cardie. 2005. Annotating expressions of opinions and emotions in language. *Language Resources and Evaluation*, 1(2):0–0.

Theresa Wilson, Janyce Wiebe, and Paul Hoffmann. 2005. Recognizing contextual polarity in phrase-level sentiment analysis. In *Proc. of HLT/EMNLP 2005*, Vancouver, Canada.

Jeonghee Yi, Tetsuya Nasukawa, Razvan Bunescu, and Wayne Niblack. 2003. Sentiment analyzer: Extracting sentiments about a given topic using natural language processing techniques. In *Proc. of the 3rd IEEE International Conference on Data Mining*, pages 427– 434, Melbourne, Florida, USA.

Chengxiang Zhai and John Lafferty. 2001. A study of smoothing methods for language models applied to ad hoc information retrieval. In *Proc. of the 24th Annual International ACM-SIGIR Conference*, pages 334–342, New Orleans, Louisiana, USA.

Chengxiang Zhai. 2002. *Risk Minimization and Language Modeling in Text Retrieval*. PhD dissertation, Carnegie Mellon University.

Fully Automatic Lexicon Expansion for Domain-oriented Sentiment Analysis

Hiroshi Kanayama **Tetsuya Nasukawa**
Tokyo Research Laboratory, IBM Japan, Ltd.
1623-14 Shimotsuruma, Yamato-shi, Kanagawa-ken, 242-8502 Japan
{hkana,nasukawa}@jp.ibm.com

Abstract

This paper proposes an unsupervised lexicon building method for the detection of *polar clauses*, which convey positive or negative aspects in a specific domain. The lexical entries to be acquired are called *polar atoms*, the minimum human-understandable syntactic structures that specify the polarity of clauses. As a clue to obtain candidate polar atoms, we use *context coherency*, the tendency for same polarities to appear successively in contexts. Using the overall density and precision of coherency in the corpus, the statistical estimation picks up appropriate polar atoms among candidates, without any manual tuning of the threshold values. The experimental results show that the precision of polarity assignment with the automatically acquired lexicon was 94% on average, and our method is robust for corpora in diverse domains and for the size of the initial lexicon.

1 Introduction

Sentiment Analysis (SA) (Nasukawa and Yi, 2003; Yi et al., 2003) is a task to recognize writers' feelings as expressed in positive or negative comments, by analyzing unreadably large numbers of documents. Extensive syntactic patterns enable us to detect sentiment expressions and to convert them into semantic structures with high precision, as reported by Kanayama et al. (2004). From the example Japanese sentence (1) in the digital camera domain, the SA system extracts a sentiment representation as (2), which consists of a predicate and an argument with positive (+) polarity.

(1) *Kono kamera-ha subarashii-to omou.*
'I think this camera is splendid.'

(2) [+] splendid(camera)

SA in general tends to focus on subjective sentiment expressions, which explicitly describe an author's preference as in the above example (1). Objective (or factual) expressions such as in the following examples (3) and (4) may be out of scope even though they describe desirable aspects in a specific domain. However, when customers or corporate users use SA system for their commercial activities, such domain-specific expressions have a more important role, since they convey strong or weak points of the product more directly, and may influence their choice to purchase a specific product, as an example.

(3) *Kontorasuto-ga kukkiri-suru.*
'The contrast is sharp.'

(4) *Atarashii kishu-ha zuumu-mo tsuite-iru.*
'The new model has a zoom lens, too.'

This paper addresses the Japanese version of *Domain-oriented Sentiment Analysis*, which identifies *polar clauses* conveying goodness and badness in a specific domain, including rather objective expressions. Building domain-dependent lexicons for many domains is much harder work than preparing domain-independent lexicons and syntactic patterns, because the possible lexical entries are too numerous, and they may differ in each domain. To solve this problem, we have devised an unsupervised method to acquire domain-dependent lexical knowledge where a user has only to collect unannotated domain corpora.

The knowledge to be acquired is a domain-dependent set of *polar atoms*. A polar atom is a minimum syntactic structure specifying polarity in a predicative expression. For example, to detect polar clauses in the sentences (3)

Proceedings of the 2006 Conference on Empirical Methods in Natural Language Processing (EMNLP 2006), pages 355–363,
Sydney, July 2006.

and (4)[1], the following polar atoms (5) and (6) should appear in the lexicon:

(5) [+] *kukkiri-suru*
'to be sharp'

(6) [+] *tsuku* ← *zuumu-ga*
'to have ← zoom lens-NOM'

The polar atom (5) specified the positive polarity of the verb *kukkiri-suru*. This atom can be generally used for this verb regardless of its arguments. In the polar atom (6), on the other hand, the nominative case of the verb *tsuku* ('have') is limited to a specific noun *zuumu* ('zoom lens'), since the verb *tsuku* does not hold the polarity in itself. The automatic decision for the scopes of the atoms is one of the major issues.

For lexical learning from unannotated corpora, our method uses *context coherency* in terms of polarity, an assumption that polar clauses with the same polarity appear successively unless the context is changed with adversative expressions. Exploiting this tendency, we can collect candidate polar atoms with their tentative polarities as those adjacent to the polar clauses which have been identified by their domain-independent polar atoms in the initial lexicon. We use both intra-sentential and inter-sentential contexts to obtain more candidate polar atoms.

Our assumption is intuitively reasonable, but there are many non-polar (neutral) clauses adjacent to polar clauses. Errors in sentence delimitation or syntactic parsing also result in false candidate atoms. Thus, to adopt a candidate polar atom for the new lexicon, some threshold values for the frequencies or ratios are required, but they depend on the type of the corpus, the size of the initial lexicon, etc.

Our algorithm is *fully automatic* in the sense that the criteria for the adoption of polar atoms are set automatically by statistical estimation based on the distributions of coherency: *coherent precision* and *coherent density*. No manual tuning process is required, so the algorithm only needs unannotated domain corpora and the initial lexicon. Thus our learning method can be used not only by the developers of the system, but also by end-users. This feature is very helpful for users to analyze documents in new domains.

In the next section, we review related work, and Section 3 describes our runtime SA system. In Section 4, our assumption for unsupervised learning, *context coherency* and its key metrics, *coherent precision* and *coherent density* are discussed. Section 5 describes our unsupervised learning method. Experimental results are shown in Section 6, and we conclude in Section 7.

2 Related Work

Sentiment analysis has been extensively studied in recent years. The target of SA in this paper is wider than in previous work. For example, Yu and Hatzivassiloglou (2003) separated facts from opinions and assigned polarities only to opinions. In contrast, our system detects factual polar clauses as well as sentiments.

Unsupervised learning for sentiment analysis is also being studied. For example, Hatzivassiloglou and McKeown (1997) labeled adjectives as positive or negative, relying on *semantic orientation*. Turney (2002) used collocation with "excellent" or "poor" to obtain positive and negative clues for document classification. In this paper, we use contextual information which is wider than for the contexts they used, and address the problem of acquiring lexical entries from the noisy clues.

Inter-sentential contexts as in our approach were used as a clue also for subjectivity analysis (Riloff and Wiebe, 2003; Pang and Lee, 2004), which is two-fold classification into subjective and objective sentences. Compared to it, this paper solves a more difficult problem: three-fold classification into positive, negative and non-polar expressions using imperfect coherency in terms of sentiment polarity.

Learning methods for phrase-level sentiment analysis closely share an objective of our approach. Popescu and Etzioni (2005) achieved high-precision opinion phrases extraction by using *relaxation labeling*. Their method iteratively assigns a polarity to a phrase, relying on semantic orientation of co-occurring words in specific relations in a sentence, but the scope of semantic orientation is limited to within a sentence. Wilson et al. (2005) proposed supervised learning, dividing the resources into

[1]The English translations are included only for convenience.

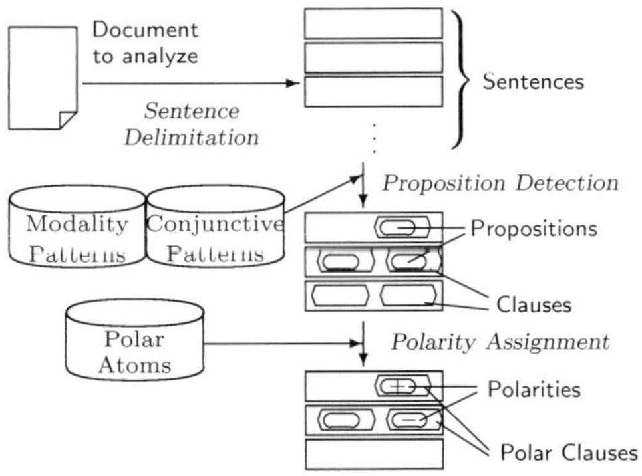

Figure 1: The flow of the clause-level SA.

prior polarity and *context polarity*, which are similar to polar atoms and syntactic patterns in this paper, respectively. Wilson et al. prepared prior polarities from existing resources, and learned the context polarities by using prior polarities and annotated corpora. Therefore the prerequisite data and learned data are opposite from those in our approach. We took the approach used in this paper because we want to acquire more domain-dependent knowledge, and context polarity is easier to access in Japanese[2]. Our approach and their work can complement each other.

3 Methodology of Clause-level SA

As Figure 1 illustrates, the flow of our sentiment analysis system involves three steps. The first step is *sentence delimitation*: the input document is divided into sentences. The second step is *proposition detection*: propositions which can form polar clauses are identified in each sentence. The third step is *polarity assignment*: the polarity of each proposition is examined by considering the polar atoms. This section describes the last two processes, which are based on a deep sentiment analysis method analogous to machine translation (Kanayama et al., 2004) (hereafter "the MT method").

3.1 Proposition Detection

Our basic tactic for clause-level SA is the high-precision detection of polar clauses based on deep syntactic analysis. 'Clause-level' means that only predicative verbs and adjectives such as in (7) are detected, and adnominal (attributive) usages of verbs and adjectives as in (8) are ignored, because *utsukushii* ('beautiful') in (8) does not convey a positive polarity.

(7) *E-ga utsukushii.*
'The picture is beautiful.'

(8) *Utsukushii hito-ni aitai.*
'I want to meet a beautiful person.'

Here we use the notion of a *proposition* as a clause without modality, led by a predicative verb or a predicative adjective. The propositions detected from a sentence are subject to the assignment of polarities.

Basically, we detect a proposition only at the head of a syntactic tree[3]. However, this limitation reduces the recall of sentiment analysis to a very low level. In the example (7) above, *utsukushii* is the head of the tree, while those initial clauses in (9) to (11) below are not. In order to achieve higher recall while maintaining high precision, we apply two types of syntactic patterns, *modality patterns* and *conjunctive patterns*[4], to the tree structures from the full-parsing.

(9) *Sore-ha utsukushii-to omou.*
'I think it is beautiful.'

(10) *Sore-ha utsukushiku-nai.*
'It is not beautiful.'

(11) *Sore-ga utsukushii-to yoi.*
'I hope it is beautiful.'

Modality patterns match some auxiliary verbs or corresponding sentence-final expressions, to allow for specific kinds of modality and negation. One of the typical patterns is [[v] *to omou*] ('I think [v]')[5], which allows *utsukushii* in (9) to be a proposition. Also negation is handled with a modality pattern, such as [[v] *nai*] ('not [v]'). In this case a neg feature is attached to the proposition to identify *utsukushii* in (10) as a negated proposition. On the other hand, no proposition is identified in (11) due to the deliberate absence of a pattern [[v] *to yoi*] ('I hope [v]'). We used a total of 103 domain-independent modality patterns, most of which are derived from the

[2]For example, indirect negation such as caused by a subject "nobody" or a modifier "seldom" is rare in Japanese.

[3]This is same as the rightmost part of the sentence since all Japanese modification is directed left to right.

[4]These two types of patterns correspond to *auxiliary patterns* in the MT method, and can be applied independent of domains.

[5][v] denotes a verb or an adjective.

coordinative (roughly 'and')	
	-te, -shi, -ueni, -dakedenaku, -nominarazu
causal (roughly 'because')	
	-tame, -kara, -node
adversative (roughly 'but')	
	-ga, -kedo, -keredo, - monono, -nodaga

Table 1: Japanese conjunctions used for conjunctive patterns.

MT method, and some patterns are manually added for this work to achieve higher recall.

Another type of pattern is conjunctive patterns, which allow multiple propositions in a sentence. We used a total of 22 conjunctive patterns also derived from the MT method, as exemplified in Table 1. In such cases of coordinative clauses and causal clauses, both clauses can be polar clauses. On the other hand, no proposition is identified in a conditional clause due to the absence of corresponding conjunctive patterns.

3.2 Polarity Assignment Using Polar Atoms

To assign a polarity to each proposition, *polar atoms* in the lexicon are compared to the proposition. A polar atom consists of polarity, verb or adjective, and optionally, its arguments. Example (12) is a *simple polar atom*, where no argument is specified. This atom matches any proposition whose head is *utsukushii*. Example (13) is a *complex polar atom*, which assigns a negative polarity to any proposition whose head is the verb *kaku* and where the accusative case is *miryoku*.

(12) [+] *utsukushii*
'to be beautiful'

(13) [−] *kaku* ← *miryoku-wo*
'to lack ← attraction-ACC'

A polarity is assigned if there exists a polar atom for which verb/adjective and the arguments coincide with the proposition, and otherwise no polarity is assigned. The opposite polarity of the polar atom is assigned to a proposition which has the neg feature.

We used a total of 3,275 polar atoms, most of which are derived from an English sentiment lexicon (Yi et al., 2003).

According to the evaluation of the MT method (Kanayama et al., 2004), high-precision sentiment analysis had been achieved using the polar atoms and patterns, where the system never took positive sentiment for negative and vice versa, and judged positive or negative to neutral expressions in only about 10% cases. However, the recall is too low, and most of the lexicon is for domain-independent expressions, and thus we need more lexical entries to grasp the positive and negative aspects in a specific domain.

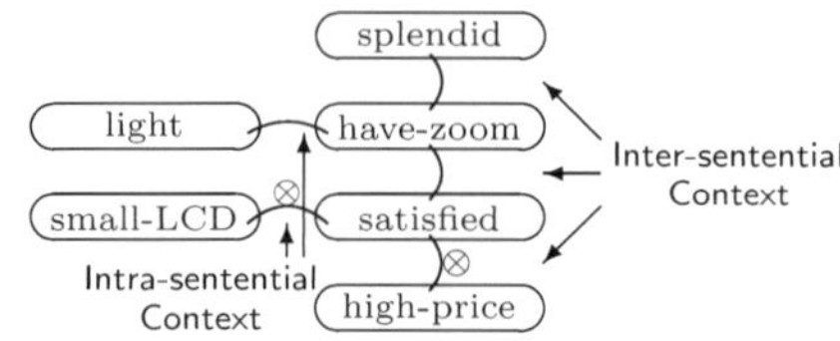

Figure 2: The concept of the intra- and inter-sentential contexts, where the polarities are perfectly coherent. The symbol '⊗' denotes the existence of an adversative conjunction.

4 Context Coherency

This section introduces the intra- and inter-sentential contexts in which we assume *context coherency* for polarity, and describes some preliminary analysis of the assumption.

4.1 Intra-sentential and Inter-sentential Context

The identification of propositions described in Section 3.1 clarifies our viewpoint of the contexts. Here we consider two types of contexts: *intra-sentential context* and *inter-sentential context*. Figure 2 illustrates the context coherency in a sample discourse (14), where the polarities are perfectly coherent.

(14) *Kono kamera-ha subarashii-to omou.*
'I think this camera is splendid.'
Karui-shi, zuumu-mo tsuite-iru.
'It's light and has a zoom lens.'
Ekishou-ga chiisai-kedo, manzoku-da.
'Though the LCD is small, I'm satisfied.'
Tada, nedan-ga chotto takai.
'But, the price is a little high.'

The intra-sentential context is the link between propositions in a sentence, which are detected as coordinative or causal clauses. If there is an adversative conjunction such as *-kedo* ('but') in the third sentence in (14), a flag is attached to the relation, as denoted with '⊗' in Figure 2. Though there are differences in syntactic phenomena, this is sim-

shikashi ('however'), *demo* ('but'), *sorenanoni* ('even though'), *tadashi* ('on condition that'), *dakedo* ('but'), *gyakuni* ('on the contrary'), *tohaie* ('although'), *keredomo* ('however'), *ippou* ('on the other hand')

Table 2: Inter-sentential adversative expressions.

Domain	Post.	Sent.	Len.
digital cameras	263,934	1,757,917	28.3
movies	163,993	637,054	31.5
mobile phones	155,130	609,072	25.3
cars	159,135	959,831	30.9

Table 3: The corpora from four domains used in this paper. The "Post." and "Sent." columns denote the numbers of postings and sentences, respectively. "Len." is the average length of sentences (in Japanese characters).

ilar to the semantic orientation proposed by Hatzivassiloglou and McKeown (1997).

The inter-sentential context is the link between propositions in the main clauses of pairs of adjacent sentences in a discourse. The polarities are assumed to be the same in the inter-sentential context, unless there is an adversative expression as those listed in Table 2. If no proposition is detected as in a nominal sentence, the context is split. That is, there is no link between the proposition of the previous sentence and that of the next sentence.

4.2 Preliminary Study on Context Coherency

We claim these two types of context can be used for unsupervised learning as clues to assign a tentative polarity to unknown expressions. To validate our assumption, we conducted preliminary observations using various corpora.

4.2.1 Corpora

Throughout this paper we used Japanese corpora from discussion boards in four different domains, whose features are shown in Table 3. All of the corpora have clues to the boundaries of postings, so they were suitable to identify the discourses.

4.2.2 Coherent Precision

How strong is the coherency in the context proposed in Section 4.1? Using the polar clauses detected by the SA system with the initial lexicon, we observed the *coherent precision* of domain d with lexicon L, defined as:

$$cp(d, L) = \frac{\#(\text{Coherent})}{\#(\text{Coherent})+\#(\text{Conflict})} \quad (15)$$

where #(Coherent) and #(Conflict) are occurrence counts of the same and opposite polarities observed between two polar clauses as observed in the discourse. As the two polar clauses, we consider the following types:

Window. A polar clause and the nearest polar clause which is found in the preceding n sentences in the discourse.

Context. Two polar clauses in the intra-sentential and/or inter-sentential context described in Section 4.1. This is the viewpoint of context in our method.

Table 4 shows the frequencies of coherent pairs, conflicting pairs, and the coherent precision for half of the digital camera domain corpus. "Baseline" is the percentage of positive clauses among the polar clauses[6].

For the "Window" method, we tested for n=0, 1, 2, and ∞. "0" means two propositions within a sentence. Apparently, the larger the window size, the smaller the *cp* value. When the window size is "∞", implying anywhere within a discourse, the ratio is larger than the baseline by only 2.7%, and thus these types of coherency are not reliable even though the number of clues is relatively large.

"Context" shows the coherency of the two types of context that we considered. The *cp* values are much higher than those in the "Window" methods, because the relationships between adjacent pairs of clauses are handled more appropriately by considering syntactic trees, adversative conjunctions, etc. The *cp* values for inter-sentential and intra-sentential contexts are almost the same, and thus both contexts can be used to obtain 2.5 times more clues for the intra-sentential context. In the rest of this paper we will use both contexts.

We also observed the coherent precision for each domain corpus. The results in the center column of Table 5 indicate the number is slightly different among corpora, but all of them are far from perfect coherency.

[6] If there is a polar clause whose polarity is unknown, the polarity is correctly predicted with at least 57.0% precision by assuming "positive".

Model		Coherent	Conflict	$cp(d, L)$
Baseline				57.0%
Window	$n = 0$	3,428	1,916	64.1%
	$n = 1$	11,448	6,865	62.5%
	$n = 2$	16,231	10,126	61.6%
	$n = \infty$	26,365	17,831	59.7%
Context	intra.	2,583	996	72.2%
	inter.	3,987	1,533	72.2%
	both	6,570	2,529	72.2%

Table 4: Coherent precision with various viewpoints of contexts.

Domain	$cp(d, L)$	$cd(d, L)$
digital cameras	72.2%	7.23%
movies	76.7%	18.71%
mobile phones	72.9%	7.31%
cars	73.4%	7.36%

Table 5: Coherent precision and coherent density for each domain.

4.2.3 Coherent Density

Besides the conflicting cases, there are many more cases where a polar clause does not appear in the polar context. We also observed the *coherent density* of the domain d with the lexicon L defined as:

$$cd(d, L) = \frac{\#(\text{Coherent})}{\#(\text{Polar})} \qquad (16)$$

This indicates the ratio of polar clauses that appear in the coherent context, among all of the polar clauses detected by the system.

The right column of Table 5 shows the coherent density in each domain. The movie domain has notably higher coherent density than the others. This indicates the sentiment expressions are more frequently used in the movie domain.

The next section describes the method of our unsupervised learning using this imperfect context coherency.

5 Unsupervised Learning for Acquisition of Polar Atoms

Figure 3 shows the flow of our unsupervised learning method. First, the runtime SA system identifies the polar clauses, and the candidate polar atoms are collected. Then, each candidate atom is validated using the two metrics in the previous section, *cp* and *cd*, which are calculated from all of the polar clauses found in the domain corpus.

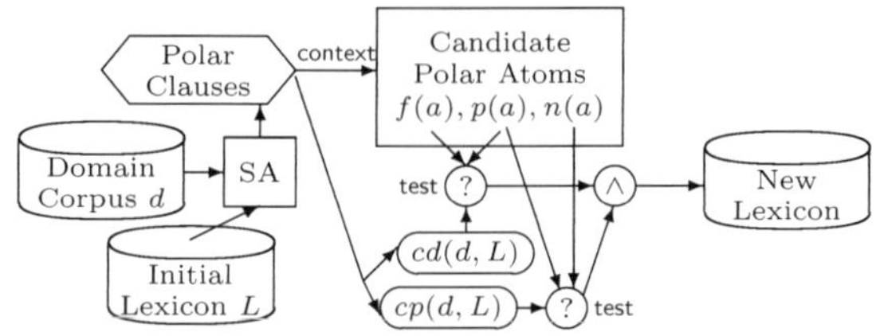

Figure 3: The flow of the learning process.

ID	Candidate Polar Atom	$f(a)$	$p(a)$	$n(a)$
1*	*chiisai* 'to be small'	3,014	226	227
2	*shikkari-suru* 'to be firm'	246	54	10
3	*chiisai* ← *bodii-ga* 'to be small ← body-NOM'	11	4	0
4*	*todoku* ← *mokuyou-ni* 'to be delivered←on Thursday'	2	0	2

Table 6: Examples of candidate polar atoms and their frequencies. '*' denotes that it should not be added to the lexicon. $f(a)$, $p(a)$, and $n(a)$ denote the frequency of the atom and in positive and negative contexts, respectively.

5.1 Counts of Candidate Polar Atoms

From each proposition which does not have a polarity, *candidate polar atoms* in the form of simple atoms (just a verb or adjective) or complex atoms (a verb or adjective and its rightmost argument consisting of a pair of a noun and a postpositional) are extracted. For each candidate polar atom a, the total appearances $f(a)$, and the occurrences in positive contexts $p(a)$ and negative contexts $n(a)$ are counted, based on the context of the adjacent clauses (using the method described in Section 4.1). If the proposition has the neg feature, the polarity is inverted. Table 6 shows examples of candidate polar atoms with their frequencies.

5.2 Determination for Adding to Lexicon

Among the located candidate polar atoms, how can we distinguish *true polar atoms*, which should be added to the lexicon, from *fake polar atoms*, which should be discarded?

As shown in Section 4, both the coherent precision (72-77%) and the coherent density (7-19%) are so small that we cannot rely on each single appearance of the atom in the polar context. One possible approach is to set the threshold values for frequency in a polar context, $\max(p(a), n(a))$ and for the ratio of appearances in polar contexts among the total appearances, $\frac{\max(p(a),n(a))}{f(a)}$. However, the optimum threshold values should depend on the corpus and the initial lexicon.

In order to set general criteria, here we assume that a true positive polar atom a should have higher $\frac{p(a)}{f(a)}$ than its average *i.e.* coherent density, $cd(d, L_{+a})$, and also have higher $\frac{p(a)}{p(a)+n(a)}$ than its average *i.e.* coherent precision, $cp(d, L_{+a})$ and these criteria should be met with 90% confidence, where L_{+a} is the initial lexicon with a added. Assuming the binomial distribution, a candidate polar atom is adopted as a positive polar atom[7] if both (17) and (18) are satisfied[8].

$$q > cd(d, L), \text{ where } \sum_{k=0}^{p(a)} {}_{f(a)}C_k q^k (1-q)^{f(a)-k} = 0.9 \quad (17)$$

$$r > cp(d, L) \text{ or } n(a) = 0, \text{ where } \sum_{k=0}^{p(a)} {}_{p(a)+n(a)}C_k r^k (1-r)^{p(a)+n(a)-k} = 0.9 \quad (18)$$

We can assume $cd(d, L_{+a}) \simeq cd(d, L)$, and $cp(d, L_{+a}) \simeq cp(d, L)$ when L is large. We compute the confidence interval using approximation with the F-distribution (Blyth, 1986).

These criteria solve the problems in minimum frequency and scope of the polar atoms simultaneously. In the example of Table 6, the simple atom *chiisai* (ID=1) is discarded because it does not meet (18), while the complex atom *chiisai* ← *bodii-ga* (ID=3) is adopted as a positive atom. *shikkari-suru* (ID=2) is adopted as a positive simple atom, even though 10 cases out of 64 were observed in the negative context. On the other hand, *todoku* ← *mokuyou-ni* (ID=4) is discarded because it does not meet (17), even though $\frac{n(a)}{f(a)} = 1.0$, *i.e.* always observed in negative contexts.

6 Evaluation

6.1 Evaluation by Polar Atoms

First we propose a method of evaluation of the lexical learning.

[7] The criteria for the negative atoms are analogous.

[8] ${}_nC_r$ notation is used here for combination (n choose k).

		Annotator B		
		Positive	Neutral	Negative
Annotator A	Positive	65	11	3
	Neutral	3	72	0
	Negative	1	4	41

Table 7: Agreement of two annotators' judgments of 200 polar atoms. κ=0.83.

It is costly to make consistent and large 'gold standards' in multiple domains, especially in identification tasks such as clause-level SA (*cf.* classification tasks). Therefore we evaluated the learning results by asking human annotators to classify the acquired polar atoms as positive, negative, and neutral, instead of the instances of polar clauses detected with the new lexicon. This can be done because the polar atoms themselves are informative enough to imply to humans whether the expressions hold positive or negative meanings in the domain.

To justify the reliability of this evaluation method, two annotators[9] evaluated 200 randomly selected candidate polar atoms in the digital camera domain. The agreement results are shown in Table 7. The manual classification was agreed upon in 89% of the cases and the Kappa value was 0.83, which is high enough to be considered consistent.

Using manual judgment of the polar atoms, we evaluated the performance with the following three metrics.

Type Precision. The coincidence rate of the polarity between the acquired polar atom and the human evaluators' judgments. It is always false if the evaluators judged it as 'neutral.'

Token Precision. The coincidence rate of the polarity, weighted by its frequency in the corpus. This metric emulates the precision of the detection of polar clauses with newly acquired poler atoms, in the runtime SA system.

Relative Recall. The estimated ratio of the number of detected polar clauses with the expanded lexicon to the number of detected polar clauses with the initial lex-

[9] For each domain, we asked different annotators who are familiar with the domain. They are not the authors of this paper.

Domain	#	Type Prec.	Token Prec.	Relative Recall
digital cameras	708	65%	96.5%	1.28
movies	462	75%	94.4%	1.19
mobile phones	228	54%	92.1%	1.13
cars	487	68%	91.5%	1.18

Table 8: Evaluation results with our method. The column '#' denotes the number of polar atoms acquired in each domain.

icon. Relative recall will be 1 when no new polar atom is acquired. Since the precision was high enough, this metric can be used for approximation of the recall, which is hard to evaluate in extraction tasks such as clause-/phrase-level SA.

6.2 Robustness for Different Conditions

6.2.1 Diversity of Corpora

For each of the four domain corpora, the annotators evaluated 100 randomly selected polar atoms which were newly acquired by our method, to measure the precisions. Relative recall is estimated by comparing the numbers of detected polar clauses from randomly selected 2,000 sentences, with and without the acquired polar atoms. Table 8 shows the results. The token precision is higher than 90% in all of the corpora, including the movie domain, which is considered to be difficult for SA (Turney, 2002). This is extremely high precision for this task, because the correctness of both the extraction and polarity assignment was evaluated simultaneously. The relative recall 1.28 in the digital camera domain means the recall is increased from 43%[10] to 55%. The difference was smaller in other domains, but the domain-dependent polar clauses are much informative than general ones, thus the high-precision detection significantly enhances the system.

To see the effects of our method, we conducted a control experiment which used preset criteria. To adopt the candidate atom a, the frequency of polarity, $\max(p(a), n(a))$ was required to be 3 or more, and the ratio of polarity, $\frac{\max(p(a),n(a))}{f(a)}$ was required to be higher than the threshold θ. Varying θ from 0.05 to 0.8, we evaluated the token precision and the relative recall in the domains of digital cameras and movies. Figure 4 shows the results.

[10]The human evaluation result for digital camera domain (Kanayama et al., 2004).

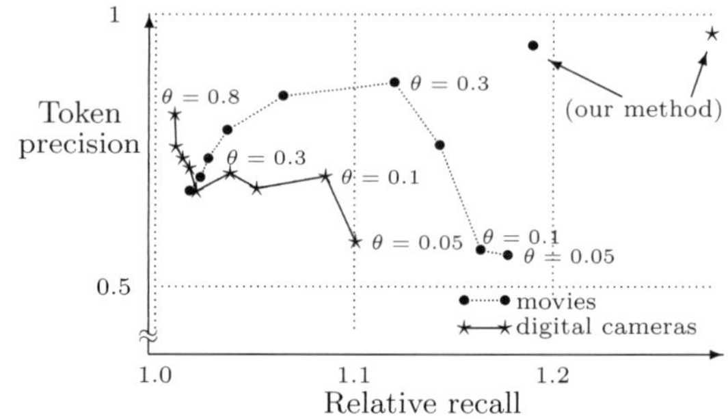

Figure 4: Relative recall vs. token precision with various preset threshold values θ for the digital camera and movie domains. The rightmost star and circle denote the performance of our method.

The results showed both relative recall and token precision were lower than in our method for every θ, in both corpora. The optimum θ was 0.3 in the movie domain and 0.1 in the digital camera domain. Therefore, in this preset approach, a tuning process is necessary for each domain. Our method does not require this tuning, and thus fully automatic learning was possible.

Unlike the normal precision-recall tradeoff, the token precision in the movie domain got lower when the θ is strict. This is due to the frequent polar atoms which can be acquired at the low ratios of the polarity. Our method does not discard these important polar atoms.

6.2.2 Size of the Initial Lexicon

We also tested the performance while varying the size of the initial lexicon L. We prepared three subsets of the initial lexicon, $L_{0.8}$, $L_{0.5}$, and $L_{0.2}$, removing polar atoms randomly. These lexicons had 0.8, 0.5, 0.2 times the polar atoms, respectively, compared to L. Table 9 shows the precisions and recalls using these lexicons for the learning process. Though the *cd* values vary, the precision was stable, which means that our method was robust even for different sizes of the lexicon. The smaller the initial lexicon, the higher the relative recall, because the polar atoms which were removed from L were recovered in the learning process. This result suggests the possibility of

lexicon	cd	Token Prec.	Relative Rec.
L	7.2%	96.5%	1.28
$L_{0.8}$	6.1%	97.5%	1.41
$L_{0.5}$	3.9%	94.2%	2.10
$L_{0.2}$	3.6%	84.8%	3.55

Table 9. Evaluation results for various sizes of the initial lexicon (the digital camera domain).

the bootstrapping method from a small initial lexicon.

6.3 Qualitative Evaluation

As seen in the agreement study, the polar atoms used in our study were intrinsically meaningful to humans. This is because the atoms are predicate-argument structures derived from predicative clauses, and thus humans could imagine the meaning of a polar atom by generating the corresponding sentence in its predicative form.

In the evaluation process, some interesting results were observed. For example, a negative atom *nai* ← *kerare-ga* ('to be free from vignetting') was acquired in the digital camera domain. Even the evaluator who was familiar with digital cameras did not know the term *kerare* ('vignetting'), but after looking up the dictionary she labeled it as negative. Our learning method could pick up such technical terms and labeled them appropriately.

Also, there were discoveries in the error analysis. An evaluator assigned positive to *aru* ← *kamera-ga* ('to have camera') in the mobile phone domain, but the acquired polar atom had the negative polarity. This was actually an insight from the recent opinions that many users want phones without camera functions[11].

7 Conclusion

We proposed an unsupervised method to acquire polar atoms for domain-oriented SA, and demonstrated its high performance. The lexicon can be expanded automatically by using unannotated corpora, and tuning of the threshold values is not required. Therefore even end-users can use this approach to improve the sentiment analysis. These features allow them to do on-demand analysis of more narrow domains, such as the domain of digital cameras of a specific manufacturer, or the domain of mobile phones from the female users' point of view.

[11]Perhaps because cameras tend to consume battery power and some users don't need them.

Rcferences

C. R. Blyth. 1986. Approximate binomial confidence limits. *Journal of the American Statistical Asscoiation*, 81(395):843–855.

Vasileios Hatzivassiloglou and Kathleen R. McKeown. 1997. Predicting the semantic orientation of adjectives. In *Proceedings of the 35th ACL and the 8th EACL*, pages 174–181.

Hiroshi Kanayama, Tetsuya Nasukawa, and Hideo Watanabe. 2004. Deeper sentiment analysis using machine translation technology. In *Proceedings of the 20th COLING*, pages 494–500.

Tetsuya Nasukawa and Jeonghee Yi. 2003. Sentiment analysis: Capturing favorability using natural language processing. In *Proceedings of the Second K-CAP*, pages 70–77.

Bo Pang and Lillian Lee. 2004. A sentimental education: Sentiment analysis using subjectivity summarization based on minimum cuts. In *Proceedings of the 42nd ACL*, pages 271–278.

Ana-Maria Popescu and Oren Etzioni. 2005. Extracting product features and opinions from reviews. In *Proceedings of HLT/EMNLP-05*, pages 339–346.

Ellen Riloff and Janyee Wiebe. 2003. Learning extraction patterns for subjective expressions. In *Proceedings of EMNLP-03*, pages 105–112.

Peter D. Turney. 2002. Thumbs up or thumbs down? Semantic orientation applied to unsupervised classification of reviews. In *Proceedings of the 40th ACL*, pages 417–424.

Theresa Wilson, Janyce Wiebe, and Paul Hoffmann. 2005. Recognizing contextual polarity in phrase-level sentiment analysis. In *Proceedings of HLT/EMNLP-05*, pages 347–354.

Jeonghee Yi, Tetsuya Nasukawa, Razvan Bunescu, and Wayne Niblack. 2003. Sentiment analyzer: Extracting sentiments about a given topic using natural language processing techniques. In *Proceedings of the Third IEEE International Conference on Data Mining*, pages 427–434.

Hong Yu and Vasileios Hatzivassiloglou. 2003. Towards answering opinion questions: Separating facts from opinions and identifying the polarity of opinion sentences. In *Proceedings of EMNLP-2003*, pages 129–136.

A Skip-Chain Conditional Random Field for Ranking Meeting Utterances by Importance*

Michel Galley
Columbia University
Department of Computer Science
New York, NY 10027, USA
galley@cs.columbia.edu

Abstract

We describe a probabilistic approach to content selection for meeting summarization. We use *skip-chain Conditional Random Fields* (CRF) to model non-local pragmatic dependencies between paired utterances such as QUESTION-ANSWER that typically appear together in summaries, and show that these models outperform linear-chain CRFs and Bayesian models in the task. We also discuss different approaches for ranking all utterances in a sequence using CRFs. Our best performing system achieves 91.3% of human performance when evaluated with the Pyramid evaluation metric, which represents a 3.9% absolute increase compared to our most competitive non-sequential classifier.

1 Introduction

Summarization of meetings faces many challenges not found in texts, i.e., high word error rates, absence of punctuation, and sometimes lack of grammaticality and coherent ordering. On the other hand, meetings present a rich source of structural and pragmatic information that makes summarization of multi-party speech quite unique. In particular, our analyses of patterns in the verbal exchange between participants found that *adjacency pairs* (AP), a concept drawn from the conversational analysis literature (Schegloff and Sacks, 1973), have particular relevance to summarization. APs are pairs of utterances such as QUESTION-ANSWER or OFFER-ACCEPT, in which the second utterance is said to be conditionally relevant on the first. We show that there is a strong correlation between the two elements of an AP in summarization, and that one is unlikely to be included if the other element is not present in the summary.

Most current statistical sequence models in natural language processing (NLP), such as hidden Markov models (HMMs) (Rabiner, 1989), are linear chains that only encode local dependencies between utterances to be labeled. In multi-party speech, the two elements of an AP are generally arbitrarily distant, and such models can only poorly account for dependencies underlying APs in summarization. We use instead skip-chain sequence models (Sutton and McCallum, 2004), which allow us to explicitly model dependencies between distant utterances, and turn out to be particularly effective in the summarization task.

In this paper, we compare two types of network structures—linear-chain and skip-chain—and two types of network semantics—Bayesian Networks (BNs) and Conditional Random Fields (CRFs). We discuss the problem of estimating the class posterior probability of each utterance in a sequence in order to extract the N most probable ones, and show that the cost assigned by a CRF to each utterance needs to be locally normalized in order to outperform BNs. After analyzing the predictive power of a large set of durational, acoustical, lexical, structural, and information retrieval features, we perform feature selection to have a competitive set of predictors to test the different models. Empirical evaluations using two standard summarization metrics—the Pyramid method (Nenkova and Passonneau, 2004b) and ROUGE (Lin, 2004)—show that the best performing system is a CRF incorporating both order-2 Markov dependencies and skip-chain dependencies, which achieves 91.3% of human performance in Pyramid score, and outperforms our best-performing non-sequential model by 3.9%.

2 Corpus

The work presented here was applied to the ICSI Meeting Corpus (Janin et al., 2003), a corpus of "naturally-occurring" meetings, i.e. meetings that would have taken place anyway. Their style is quite informal, and topics are primarily concerned with speech, natural language, artificial

*This material is based on research supported in part by the U.S. National Science Foundation (NSF) under Grants No. IIS-0121396 and IIS-05-34871, and the Defense Advanced Research Projects Agency (DARPA) under Contract No. HR0011-06-C-0023. Any opinions, findings and conclusions or recommendations expressed in this material are those of the author and do not necessarily reflect the views of the NSF or DARPA.

Proceedings of the 2006 Conference on Empirical Methods in Natural Language Processing (EMNLP 2006), pages 364–372,
Sydney, July 2006. ©2006 Association for Computational Linguistics

intelligence, and networking research. The corpus contains 75 meetings, which are 60 minutes long on average, and involve a number of participants ranging from 3 to 10 (6 on average). The total number of unique speakers is 60, including 26 non-native English speakers. Experiments in this paper are based either on human orthographic transcriptions or automatic speech recognition output, which were available for all meetings. For automatic recognition, we used the ICSI-SRI-UW speech recognition system (Mirghafori et al., 2004), a state-of-the-art conversational telephone speech (CTS) recognizer whose language and acoustic models were adapted to the meeting domain. It achieves 34.8% WER on the ICSI corpus, which is indicative of the difficulty involved in processing meetings automatically.

We also used additional annotation that has been developed to support higher-level analyses of meeting structure, in particular the ICSI Meeting Recorder Dialog act (MRDA) corpus (Shriberg et al., 2004). Dialog act (DA) labels describe the pragmatic function of utterances, e.g. a STATEMENT or a BACKCHANNEL. This auxiliary corpus consists of over 180,000 human-annotated dialog act labels ($\kappa = .8$), for which so-called *adjacency pair* (AP) relations (e.g., APOLOGY-DOWNPLAY) were also labeled. This latter annotation was used to train an AP classifier that is instrumental in automatically determining the structure of our sequence models. Note that, in the case of three or more speakers, *adjacency pair* is admittedly an unfortunate term, since labeled APs are generally not adjacent (e.g., see Table 1), but we will nevertheless use the same terminology to enforce consistency with previous work.

To train and evaluate our summarizer, we used a corpus of extractive summaries produced at the University of Edinburgh (Murray et al., 2005). For each of the 75 meetings, human judges were asked to select transcription utterances segmented by DA to include in summaries, resulting in an average compression ratio of 6.26% (though no strict limit was imposed). Inter-labeler agreement was measured using six meetings that were summarized by multiple coders (average $\kappa = .323$). While this level of agreement is quite low, this situation is not uncommon to summarization, since there may be many good summaries for a given document; a main challenge lies in using evaluation schemes that properly accounts for this diversity.

3 Content selection

State sequence Markov models such as hidden Markov models (Rabiner, 1989) have been highly successful in many speech and natural language processing applications, including summarization. Following an intuition that the probability of a given sentence may be locally conditioned on the previous one, Conroy (2004) built a HMM-based summarizer that consistently ranked among the top systems in recent Document Understanding Conference (DUC) evaluations.

Inter-sentential influences become more complex in the case of dialogues or correspondences, especially when they involve multiple parties. In the case of summarization of conversational speech, Zechner (2002) found, for instance, that a simple technique consisting of linking together questions and answers in summaries—and thus preventing the selection of orphan questions or answers—significantly improved their readability according to various human summary evaluations. In email summarization (Rambow et al., 2004), Shrestha and McKeown (2004) obtained good performance in automatic detection of questions and answers, which can help produce summaries that highlight or focus on the question and answer exchange. In a combined chat and email summarization task, a technique (Zhou and Hovy, 2005) consisting of identifying APs and appending any relevant responses to topic initiating messages was instrumental in outperforming two competitive summarization baselines.

The need to model pragmatic influences, such as between a question and an answer, is also prevalent in meeting summarization. In fact, question-answer pairs are not the only discourse relations that we need to preserve in order to create coherent summaries, and, as we will see, most instances of APs would need to be preserved together, either inside or outside the summary. Table 1 displays an AP construction with one statement (A part) and three respondents (B parts). This example illustrates that the number of turns between constituents of APs is variable and thus difficult to model with standard sequence models. This example also illustrates some of the predictors investigated in this paper. First, many speakers respond to A's utterance, which is generally a strong indicator that the A utterance should be included. Secondly, while APs are generally characterized in terms of pre-defined dialog acts, such

Time	Speaker	AP	Transcript
1480.85-1493.91	1	A	are - are those d- delays adjustable? see a lot of people who actually build stuff with human computer interfaces understand that delay, and - and so when you - by the time you click it it'll be right on because it'll go back in time to put the -
1489.71-1489.94	2		*yeah.*
1493.95-1495.41	3	B	*yeah, uh, not in this case.*
1494.31-1495.83	2	B	*it could do that, couldn't it.*
1495.1-1497.07	4	B	we could program that pretty easily , couldn't we?

Table 1: Snippet of a meeting displaying an AP construction, where a question (A) initiates three responses (B). Sentences in *italic* are not present in the reference summary.

as OFFER-ACCEPT, we found that the type of dialog act has much less importance than the existence of the AP connection itself (APs in the data represent a great variety of DA pairs, including many that are not characterized as APs in the litterature—e.g., STATEMENT-STATEMENT in the table). Since DAs seem to matter less than adjacency pairs, the aim will be to build techniques to automatically identify such relations and exploit them in utterance selection.

In the current work, we use skip-chain sequence models (Sutton and McCallum, 2004) to represent dependencies between both contiguous utterances and paired utterances appearing in the same AP constructions. The graphical representations of skip-chain models, such as the CRF represented in Figure 1, are composed of two types of edges: linear-chain and skip-chain edges. The latter edges model AP links, which we represent as a set of (s, d) index pairs (note that no more than one AP may share the same second element d).

The intuition that the summarization labels (-1 or 1) are highly correlated with APs is confirmed in Table 2. While contiguous labels y_{t-1} and y_t seem to seldom influence each other, the correlation between AP elements y_s and y_d is particularly strong, and they have a tendency to be either both included or both excluded. Note that the second table is not symmetric, because the data allows an A part to be linked to multiple B parts, but not vice-versa. While counts in Table 2 reflect human labels, we only use automatically predicted (s, d) pairs in the experiments of the remaining part of this paper. To find these pairs automatically, we trained a non-sequential log-linear model that achieves a .902 accuracy (Galley et al., 2004).

4 Skip-Chain Sequence Models

In this paper, we investigate conditional models for paired sequences of observations and labels. In the case of utterance selection, the observation sequence $\mathbf{x} = \mathbf{x}_{1:T} = (x_1, \ldots, x_T)$ represents local

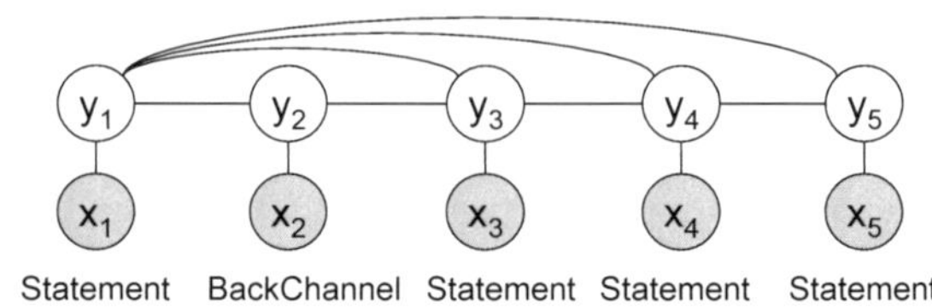

Figure 1: A skip-chain CRF with pragmatic-level links.

Linear-chain edges	$y_t = 1$	$y_t = -1$
$y_{t-1} = 1$	529	7742
$y_{t-1} = -1$	7742	116040
Skip-chain edges	$y_d = 1$	$y_d = -1$
$y_s = 1$	6792	2191
$y_s = -1$	1479	121591

Table 2: Contingency tables: while the correlation between adjacent labels y_{t-1} and y_t is not significant ($\chi^2 = 2.3$, $p > .05$), empirical evidence clearly shows that y_s and y_d influence each other ($\chi^2 = 78948$, $p < .001$).

summarization predictors (see Section 6), and the binary sequence $\mathbf{y} = \mathbf{y}_{1:T} = (y_1, \ldots, y_T)$ (where $y_t \in \{-1, 1\}$) determines which utterances must be included in the summary. In a discriminative framework, we concentrate our modeling effort on estimating $p(\mathbf{y}|\mathbf{x})$ from data, and do not explicitly model the prior probability $p(\mathbf{x})$, since $\mathbf{x}$ is fixed during testing anyway.

Many probabilistic approaches to modeling sequences have relied on directed graphical models, also known as Bayesian networks (BN),[1] in particular hidden Markov models (Rabiner, 1989) and conditional Markov models (McCallum et al., 2000). However, prominent recent approaches have focused on undirected graphical models, in particular conditional random fields (CRF) (Lafferty et al., 2001), and provided state-of-the-art performance in many NLP tasks. In our work, we will provide empirical results for state sequence models of both semantics, and we will now de-

[1]In the existing literature, sequence models that satisfy the Markovian condition—i.e., the state of the system at time t depend only on its immediate past $t - k{:}t - 1$ (typically just $t - 1$)—are generally termed dynamic Bayesian networks (DBN). Since the particular models under investigation, i.e. skip-chain models, do not have this property, we will simply refer to them as Bayesian networks.

scribe skip-chain models for both BNs and CRFs.

In a BN, the probability of the sequence $\mathbf{y}$ factorizes as a product of probabilities of local predictions y_t conditioned on their parents $\pi(y_t)$ (Equation 1). In a CRF, the probability of the sequence $\mathbf{y}$ factorizes according to a set of clique potentials $\{\Phi_c\}_{c \in C}$, where C is represents the cliques of the underlying graphical model (Equation 2).

$$p_{\text{BN}}(\mathbf{y}|\mathbf{x}) = \prod_{i=1}^{T} p_{\text{BN}}(y_t|\mathbf{x}, \pi(y_t)) \quad (1)$$

$$p_{\text{CRF}}(\mathbf{y}|\mathbf{x}) \propto \prod_{c \in C} \Phi_c(\mathbf{x}_c, \mathbf{y}_c) \quad (2)$$

We parameterize these BNs and CRFs as log-linear models, and factorize both BN's local prediction probabilities and CRF's clique potentials using two types of feature functions. *Linear-chain* feature functions $f_j(\mathbf{y}_{t-k:t}, \mathbf{x}, t)$ represent local dependencies that are consistent with an order-k Markov assumption. For instance, one such function could be a predicate that is true if and only if $y_{t-1} = 1$, $y_t = -1$, and (x_{t-1}, x_t) indicates that both utterances are produced by the same speaker. Given a set of skip edges $\mathcal{S} = \{(s_t, t)\}$ specifying source and destination indices, *skip-chain* feature functions $g_j(y_{s_t}, y_t, \mathbf{x}, s_t, t)$ exploit dependencies between variables that are arbitrarily distant in the chain. For instance, the finding that OFFER-REJECT pairs are often linked in summaries might be encoded as a skip-chain feature predicate that is true if and only if $y_{s_t} = 1$, $y_t = 1$, and the first word of the t-th utterance is "no".

Log-linear models for skip-chain sequence models are defined in terms of weights $\{\lambda_k\}$ and $\{\mu_k\}$, one for each feature function. In the case of BNs, we write:

$$\log p_{\text{BN}}(y_t|\mathbf{x}, \pi(y_t)) \propto \sum_{j=1}^{J} \lambda_j f_j(\mathbf{x}, \mathbf{y}_{t-k:t}, t) + \sum_{j=1}^{J'} \mu_j g_j(\mathbf{x}, y_{s_t}, y_t, s_t, t)$$

We can reduce a particular skip-chain CRF to represent only the set of cliques along (y_{t-1}, y_t) adjacency edges and (y_{s_t}, y_t) skip edges, resulting in only two potential functions:

$$\log \Phi_{\text{LIN}}(\mathbf{x}, \mathbf{y}_{t-k:t}, t) = \sum_{j=1}^{J} \lambda_j f_j(\mathbf{x}, \mathbf{y}_{t-k:t}, t)$$

$$\log \Phi_{\text{SKIP}}(\mathbf{x}, y_{s_t}, y_t, t) = \sum_{j=1}^{J'} \mu_j g_j(\mathbf{x}, y_{s_t}, y_t, s_t, t)$$

4.1 Inference and Parameter Estimation

Our CRF and BN models were designed using MALLET (McCallum, 2002), which provides tools for training log-linear models with L-BFGS optimization techniques and maximize the log-likelihood of our training data $\mathcal{D} = (\mathbf{x}^{(i)}, \mathbf{y}^{(i)})_{i=1}^{N}$, and provides probabilistic inference algorithms for linear-chain BNs and CRFs.

Most previous work with CRFs containing non-local dependencies used approximate probabilistic inference techniques, including TRP (Sutton and McCallum, 2004) and Gibbs sampling (Finkel et al., 2005). Approximation is needed when the junction tree of a graphical model is associated with prohibitively large cliques. For example, the worse case reported in (Sutton and McCallum, 2004) is a clique of 61 nodes. In the case of skip-chain models representing APs, the inference problem is somewhat simpler: loops in the graph are relatively short, 98% of AP edges span no more than 5 time slices, and the maximum clique size in the entire data is 5. While exact inference might be possible in our case, we used the simpler approach of adapting standard inference algorithms for linear-chain models.

Specifically, to account for skip-edges, we used a technique inspired by (Sha and Pereira, 2003), in which multiple state dependencies, such as an order-2 Markov model, are encoded using auxiliary tags. For instance, an order-2 Markov model is parameterized using state triples $y_{t-2:t}$, and each possible triple is converted to a label $z_t = y_{t-2:t}$. Using these auxiliary labels only, we can then use the standard forward-backward algorithm for computing marginal distributions in linear-chain CRFs, and Viterbi decoding in linear-chain CRFs and BNs. The only requirement is to ensure that a transition between z_t and z_{t+1} is forbidden if the sub-states $y_{t-1:t}$ common to both states differ, i.e., is assigned an infinite cost. This approach can be extended to the case of skip-chain transitions. For instance, an order-1 Markov model with skip-edges can be constructed using $z_t = (y_{s_t}, y_{t-1}, y_t)$ triples, where the first element y_{s_t} represents the label at the source of the skip-edge. Similarly to the case of order-2 Markov models, we need to ensure that only valid sequences of labels are considered, which is trivial to enforce if we assume that no skip edge ranges more than a predefined threshold of k time slices.

While this approach is not exact, it still provides

competitive performance as we will see in Section 8. In future work, we plan to explore more accurate probabilistic inference techniques.

5 Ranking Utterances by Importance

As we will see in Section 8, using the actual $\{-1, 1\}$ label predictions of our BNs and CRFs leads to significantly sub-optimal results, which might be explained by the following reasons. First, our models are optimized to maximize the conditional log-likelihood of the training data, a measure that does not correlate well with utility measures generally used in retrieval oriented tasks such as summarization, especially when faced with a significant class imbalance (only 6.26% of reference instances are positive). Second, the MAP decision rule doesn't give us the freedom to select an arbitrary number of sentences in order to satisfy any constraint on length. Instead of using actual predictions, it seems more reasonable to compute the posterior probability of each local prediction y_t, and extract the N most probable summary sentences $(y_{r_1}, \ldots, y_{r_k})$, where N may depend on a length expressed in number of words, as it is the case in our evaluation in Section 7.

BNs assign probability distributions over entire sequences by estimating the probability of each individual instance y_t in the sequence (Equation 1), and seem thus particularly suited for ranking utterances. A first approach is then to rank utterances according to the cost of predicting $y_t = 1$ at each time step on the Viterbi path. While these costs are well-formed (negative log) probabilities in the case of BNs, they cannot be interpreted as such in the case of CRFs, and turn out to produce poor results with CRFs. Indeed, the set of CRF potentials associated with each time step have no immediate probabilistic interpretation, and cannot be used directly to rank sentences. Since BNs and CRFs are here parameterized as log-linear models and rely on the same set of feature functions, a second approach is to use CRF-trained model parameters to build a BN classifier that assigns a probability to each y_t. Specifically, the CRF model is first used to generate label predicitons $\hat{\mathbf{y}}$, from which the locally-normalized model estimates the cost of predicting $\hat{y}_t = 1$ given a label history $\hat{\mathbf{y}}_{1:t-1}$. This ensures that we have a well-formed probability distribution at each time slice, while capitalizing on the good performance of CRF models.

Lexical features:
- n-grams ($n \leq 3$)
- number of words
- number of digits
- number of consecutive repeats

Information retrieval features:
- max/sum/mean frequency of all terms in u_t
- max/sum/mean *idf* score
- max/sum/mean $tf \cdot idf$ score
- cosine similarity between word vector of u_t with centroid of of the meeting
- scores of LSA with 5, 10, 50, 100, 200, 300 concepts

Acoustic features:
- seconds of silence before/during/after the turn
- speech rate
- min/max/mean/median/stddev/onset/outset f0 of utterance t, and of first and last word
- min/max/mean/stddev energy
- .05, .25, .5, .75, .95 quantiles of f0 and energy
- pitch range
- f0 mean absolute slope

Durational and structural features:
- duration of the previous/current/next utterance
- relative position within meeting (i.e., index t)
- relative position within speaker turn
- large number of structural predicates, i.e. "is the previous utterance of the same speaker?"
- number of APs initiated in y_t

Discourse features:
- lexical cohesion score (for topic shifts) (Hearst, 1994)
- first and second word of utterance, if in cue word list
- number of pronouns
- number of fillers and fluency devices (e.g., "uh", "um")
- number of backchannel and acknowledgment tokens (e.g., "uh-huh", "ok", "right")

Table 3: Features for extractive summarization. Unless otherwise mentioned, we refer to features of utterance t whose label y_t we are trying to predict.

6 Features for extractive summarization

We started our analyses with a large collection of features found to be good predictors in either speech (Inoue et al., 2004; Maskey and Hirschberg, 2005; Murray et al., 2005) or text summarization (Mani and Maybury, 1999). Our goal is to build a very competitive feature set that capitalizes on recent advances in summarization of both genres. Table 3 lists some important features.

There is strong evidence that lexical cues such as "significant" and "great" are strong predictors in many summarization tasks (Edmundson, 1968). Such cues are admittedly quite genre specific, so we did not want to commit ourselves to any specific list, which may not carry over well to our specific speech domain, and we automatically selected a list of n-grams ($n \leq 3$) using cross-validation on the training data. More specifically, we computed the mutual information of each n-

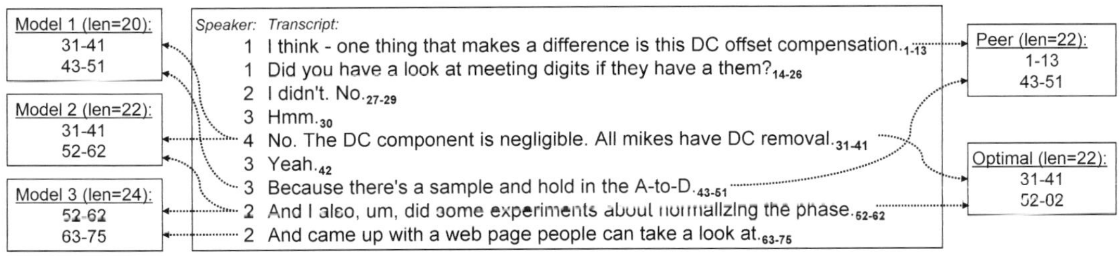

Figure 2: Model, peer, and "optimal" summaries are all extracts taken from the same transcription.

gram with the class variable, and selected for each n the 200 best scoring n-grams. Other lexical features include: the number of digits, which is helpful for identifying sections of the meetings where participants collect data by recording digits; the number of repeats, which may indicate the kind of hesitations and disfluencies that negatively correlates with what is included in the summary.

The information retrieval feature set contains many features that are generally found helpful in summarization, in particular $tf \cdot idf$ and scores derived from centroid methods. In particular, we used the latent semantic analysis (LSA) feature discussed in (Murray et al., 2005), which attempts to determine sentence importance through singular value decomposition, and whose resulting singular values and singular vectors can be exploited to associate each utterance a degree of relevance to one of the top-n concepts of the meetings (where n represents the number of dimensions in the LSA). We used the same scoring mechanism as (Murray et al., 2005), though we extracted features for many different n values.

Acoustic features extracted with Praat (Boersma and Weenink, 2006) were normalized by channel and speaker, including many raw features such as f0 and energy. Structural features listed in the table are those computed from the sequence model before decoding, e.g., the duration that separates the two elements of an AP. Finally, discourse features represent predictors that may substitute to DA labels. While DA tagging is not directly our concern, it is presumably helpful to capitalize on discourse characteristics of utterances involved in adjacency pairs, since different types of dialog acts may be unequally likely to appear in a summary.

7 Evaluation

Evaluating summarization is a difficult problem and there is no broad consensus on how to best perform this task. Two metrics have become quite popular in multi-document summarization, namely the Pyramid method (Nenkova and Passonneau, 2004b) and ROUGE (Lin, 2004). Pyramid and ROUGE are techniques looking for content units repeated in different model summaries, i.e., summary content units (SCUs) such as clauses and noun phrases for the Pyramid method, and n-grams for ROUGE. The underlying hypothesis is that different model sentences, clauses, or phrases may convey the same meaning, which is a reasonable assumption when dealing with reference summaries produced by different authors, since it is quite unlikely that any two abstractors would use the exact same words to convey the same idea.

Our situation is however quite different, since all model summaries of a given document are utterance extracts of that same document, as this can been seen in the excerpt of Figure 2. In our own annotation of three meetings with SCUs defined as in (Nenkova and Passonneau, 2004a), we found that repetitions and reformulation of the same information are particularly infrequent, and that textual units that express the same content among model summaries are generally originating from the same document sentence (e.g., in the figure, the first sentence in model 1 and 2 emanate from the same document sentence). Very short SCUs (e.g., base noun phrases) sometimes appeared in different locations of a meeting, but we think it is problematic to assume that connections between such short units are indicative of any similarity of sentential meaning: the contexts are different, and words may be uttered by different speakers, which may lead to unrelated or conflicting pragmatic forces. For instance, an SCU realized as "DC offset" and "DC component" appears in two different sentences in the figure, i.e. those identified as 1-13 and 31-41. However, the two sentences have contradictory meanings, and it would be unfortunate to increase the score of a peer summary containing the former sentence because the latter is included in some model summaries.

For all these reasons, we believe that summarization evaluation in our case should rely on the following restrictive matching: two summary units should be considered equivalent if and only if they are extracted from the *same location* in the original document (e.g., the "DC" appearing in models 1 and 2 is not the same as the "DC" in the peer summary, since they are extracted from different sentences). This constraint on the matching is reflected in our Pyramid evaluation, and we define an SCU as a word and its document position, which lets us distinguish ("DC",11) from ("DC",33). While this restriction on SCUs forces us to disregard scarcely occurring paraphrases and repetitions of the same information, it provides the benefit of automated evaluation.

Once all SCUs have been identified, the Pyramid method is applied as in (Nenkova and Passonneau, 2004b): we compute a score $\mathcal{D}$ by adding for each SCU present in the summary a score equal to the number of model summaries in which that SCU appears. The Pyramid score $\mathcal{P}$ is computed by dividing $\mathcal{D}$ by the maximum $\mathcal{D}^*$ value that is obtainable given the constraint on length. For instance, the peer summary in the figure gets a score $\mathcal{D} = 9$ (since the 9 SCUs in range 43-51 occur in one model), and the maximum obtainable score is $\mathcal{D}^* = 44$ (all SCUs of the optimal summary appear in exactly two model summaries), hence the peer summary's score is $\mathcal{P} = .204$.

While our evaluation scheme is similar to comparing the binary predictions of model and peer summaries—each prediction determining whether a given transcription word is included or not—and averaging precision scores over all peer-model pairs, the Pyramid evaluation differs on an important point, which makes us prefer the Pyramid evaluation method: the maximum possible Pyramid score is always guaranteed to be 1, but average precision scores can become arbitrarily low as the consensus between summary annotators decreases. For instance, the average precision score of the optimal summary in the figure is $PR = \frac{2}{3}$.[2]

[2]Precision scores of the optimal summary compared against the the three model summaries are .5, 1, and .5, respectively, and hence average $\frac{2}{3}$. We can show that $\mathcal{P} = PR/PR^*$, where PR^* is the average precision of the optimal summary. Lack of space prevent us from providing a proof, so we will just show that the equality holds in our example: since the peer summary's precision scores against the three model summaries are respectively $\frac{9}{22}$, 0, and 0, we have $PR/PR^* = (\frac{9}{66})/(\frac{2}{3}) = \frac{9}{44} = \mathcal{P}$.

	FEATURE	$F_{\beta=1}$
1	utterance duration	.246
2	100-dimension LSA	.268
3	duration of utterance $t-1$	.275
4	time between utterances s and $d = t$	.281
5	IDF mean	.284
6	meeting position	.286
7	number of APs initiated in t	.288
8	duration of utterance $t+1$	.288
9	number of fillers	.289
10	.25-quantile of energy	.290
11	number of lexical repeats	.292
12	lexical cohesion score	.294
13	f0 mean of last word of utterance t	.294
14	LSA 50 dimensions	.295
15	utterances $(t,t+1)$ by same speaker	.298
16	speech rate	.302
17	"is that"	.303
18	"for the"	.303
19	(u_{t-1},u_t) by same speaker	.305
20	"to try"	.305
21	"meetings"	.305
22	utterance starts with "and"	.306
23	"we have"	.306
24	"new"	.307
25	utterance starts with "what"	.307

Table 4: Forward feature selection.

In the case of the six test meetings, which all have either 3 or 4 model summaries, the maximum possible average precision is .6405.

8 Experiments

We follow (Murray et al., 2005) in using the same six meetings as test data, since each of these meetings has multiple reference summaries. The remaining 69 meetings were used for training, which represent in total more than 103,000 training instances (or DA units), of which 6,464 are positives (6.24%). The multi-reference test set contains more than 28,000 instances.

The goal of a preliminary experiment was to devise a set of useful predictors from a full set of 1171. We performed feature selection by incrementally growing a log-linear model with order-0 features $f(\mathbf{x}, y_t)$ using a forward feature selection procedure similar to (Berger et al., 1996). Probably due to the imbalance between positive and negative samples, we found it more effective to rank candidate features by gains in F-measure (through 5-fold cross validation on the entire training set). The increase in F_1 by adding new features to the model is displayed in Table 4; this greedy search resulted in a set $\mathcal{S}$ of 217 features.

We now analyze the performance of different sequence models on our test set. The target length of each summary was set to 12.7% of the number of words of the full document, which is the average on the entire training data (the average on the test data is 12.9%). In Table 5, we use an order-0 CRF to compare $\mathcal{S}$ against all features and various categorical groupings. Overall, we notice lexical predictors and statistics derived from them (e.g. LSA features) represent the most helpful feature group (.497), though all other features combined achieve a competitive performance (.476).

FEATURE SET	$\mathcal{P}$
lexical	.471
IR	.415
lexical + IR	.497
acoustic	.407
structural/durational	.478
acoustic + structural/durational	.476
all features	.507
selected features ($\mathcal{S}$)	.515

Table 5: Pyramid score for each feature set.

Table 6 displays performance for sequence models incorporating linear-chain features of increasing order k. Its second column indicates what criterion was used to rank utterances. In the case of 'pred', we used actual model $\{-1, 1\}$ predictions, which in all cases generated summaries much shorted than the allowable length, and produced poor performance. 'Costs' and 'norm-CRF' refer to the two ranking criteria presented in Section 5, and it is clear that the performance of CRFs degrades with increasing orders without local normalization. While the contingency counts in Table 2 only hinted a limited benefit of linear-chain features, empirical results show the contrary—especially for order $k = 2$. However, the further increase of k causes overfitting, and skip-chain features seem a better way to capture non-local dependencies while keeping the number of model parameters relatively small. Overall, the addition of skip-chain edges to linear-chain models provide noticeable improvement in Pyramid scores. Our system that performed best on cross-validation data is an order-2 CRF with skip-chain transitions, which achieves a Pyramid score of $\mathcal{P} = .554$.

MODEL	RANKING	$k = 1$	2	3
linear-chain BN	pred	.241	.267	.269
linear-chain BN	costs	.512	.519	.525
skip-chain BN	costs	.543	.549	.542
linear-chain CRF	pred	.326	.36	.348
linear-chain CRF	costs	.508	.475	.447
linear-chain CRF	norm-CRF	.53	.548	.54
skip-chain CRF	norm-CRF	.541	**.554**	.559

Table 6: Pyramid scores for different sequence models, where k stands for the order of linear-chain features. The value in bold is the performance of the model that was selected after a 5-fold cross validation on the training data, which obtained the highest F_1 score.

We now assess the significance of our results by comparing our best system against: (1) a lead summarizer that always selects the first N utterances to match the predefined length; (2) human performance, which is obtained by leave-one-out comparisons among references (Table 7); (3) "optimal" summaries generated using the procedure explained in (Nenkova and Passonneau, 2004b) by ranking document utterances by the number of model summaries in which they appear. It appears that our system is considerably better than the baseline, and achieves 91.3% of human performance in terms of Pyramid scores, and 83% if using ASR transcription. This last result is particularly positive if we consider our strong reliance on lexical features.

SUMMARIZER	$\mathcal{P}$	R-1	R-2	R-L
baseline	.188	.501	.210	.495
skip-chain CRF (transcript)	.554	.715	.442	.709
skip-chain CRF (ASR)	.504	.714	.42	.706
human	.607	.720	.477	.715
optimal	1	.791	.648	.788

Table 7: Pyramid, and average ROUGE scores for summaries produces by a baseline (lead summarizer), our best system, humans, and the optimal summarizer.

For completeness, we also included standard ROUGE (1, 2, and L) scores in Table 7, which were obtained using parameters defined for the DUC-05 evaluation. Since system summaries have on average approximately the same length as references, we only report recall measures of ROUGE (precision and F averages are within $\pm$ .002).[3] It may come as a surprise that our best system (both with ASR and true words) performs almost as well as humans; it seems more reasonable to conclude that, in our case, ROUGE has trouble discriminating between systems with moderately close performance. This seems to confirm our impression that content evaluation in our task should be based on exact matches.

We performed a last experiment to compare our best system against Murray et al. (2005), who used the same test data, but constrained summary sizes in terms of number of DA units instead of words. In their experiments, 10% of DAs had to be selected. Our system achieves .91 recall, .5 precision, and .64 F_1 with the same length constraint.

[3]Human performance with ROUGE was assessed by cross-validating reference summaries of each meeting (i.e., n references for a given meeting resulted in n evaluations against the other references). We used the same leave-one-out procedure with other summarizers, in order to get results comparable to humans.

The discrepancy between recall and precision is largely due to the fact that generated summaries are on average much longer than model summaries (10% vs. 6.26% of DAs), which explains why our precision is relatively low in this last evaluation. The best ROUGE-1 measure reported in (Murray et al., 2005) is .69 recall, which is significantly lower than ours according to confidence intervals.

9 Conclusion

An order-2 CRF with skip-chain dependencies derived from the automatic analysis of participant interaction was shown to outperform linear-chain BNs and CRFs, despite the incorporation in all cases of the same competitive set of predictors resulting from cross-validated feature selection. Compared to an order-0 CRF model, the absolute increase in performance is 3.9% (7.5% relative increase), which indicates that it is helpful to use skip-chain sequence models in the summarization task. Our best performing system reaches 91.3% of human performance, and scales relatively well on automatic speech recognition output.

Acknowledgments

This work has benefited greatly from suggestions and advice from Kathleen McKeown. I also would like to thank Jean Carletta, Steve Renals and Gabriel Murray for giving me access to their summarization corpus, Ani Nenkova for helpful discussions about summarization evaluation, Michael Collins, Daniel Ellis, Julia Hirschberg, and Owen Rambow for useful preliminary discussions, and three anonymous reviewers for their insightful comments on an earlier version of this paper.

References

A. Berger, S. Della Pietra, and V. Della Pietra. 1996. A maximum entropy approach to natural language processing. *Computational Linguistics*, 22(1):39–72.

P. Boersma and D. Weenink. 2006. Praat: doing phonetics by computer. `http://www.praat.org/`.

J. Conroy, J. Schlesinger, J. Goldstein, and D. O'Leary. 2004. Left-brain/right-brain multi-document summarization. In *DUC 04 Conference Proceedings*.

H.P. Edmundson. 1968. New methods in automatic extracting. *Journal of the ACM*, 16(2):264–285.

J. Finkel, T. Grenager, and C. Manning. 2005. Incorporating non-local information into information extraction systems by gibbs sampling. In *Proc. of ACL*, pages 363–370.

M. Galley, K. McKeown, J. Hirschberg, and E. Shriberg. 2004. Identifying agreement and disagreement in conversational speech: Use of bayesian networks to model pragmatic dependencies. In *Proc. of ACL*, pages 669–676.

M. Hearst. 1994. Multi-paragraph segmentation of expository text. In *Proc. of ACL*, pages 9–16.

A. Inoue, T. Mikami, and Y. Yamashita. 2004. Improvement of speech summarization using prosodic information. In *Proc. of Speech Prosody*.

A. Janin, D. Baron, J. Edwards, D. Ellis, D. Gelbart, N. Morgan, B. Peskin, T. Pfau, E. Shriberg, A. Stolcke, and C. Wooters. 2003. The ICSI meeting corpus. In *Proc. of ICASSP*.

J. Lafferty, A. McCallum, and F. Pereira. 2001. Conditional random fields: Probabilistic models for segmenting and labeling sequence data. In *Proc. of ICML*, pages 282–289.

C.-Y. Lin. 2004. ROUGE: a package for automatic evaluation of summaries. In *Proc. of workshop on text summarization, ACL-04*.

I. Mani and M. Maybury. 1999. *Advances in Automatic Text Summarization*. MIT Press.

S. Maskey and J. Hirschberg. 2005. Comparing lexial, acoustic/prosodic, discourse and structural features for speech summarization. In *Proc. of Eurospeech*.

A. McCallum, D. Freitag, and F. Pereira. 2000. Maximum entropy markov models for information extraction and segmentation. In *Proc. of ICML*.

A. McCallum. 2002. MALLET: A machine learning for language toolkit. `http://mallet.cs.umass.edu`.

N. Mirghafori, A. Stolcke, C. Wooters, T. Pirinen, I. Bulyko, D. Gelbart, M. Graciarena, S. Otterson, B. Peskin, and M. Ostendorf. 2004. From switchboard to meetings: Development of the 2004 ICSI-SRI-UW meeting recognition system. In *Proc. of ICSLP*.

G. Murray, S. Renals, J. Carletta, and J. Moore. 2005. Evaluating automatic summaries of meeting recordings. In *Proc. of the ACL Workshop on Intrinsic and Extrinsic Evaluation Measures for MT and/or Summarization*.

A. Nenkova and R. Passonneau. 2004a. Evaluating content selection in human- or machine-generated summaries: The pyramid scoring method. Technical Report CUCS-025-03, Columbia University, CS Department.

A. Nenkova and R. Passonneau. 2004b. Evaluating content selection in summarization: The pyramid method. In *Proc. of HLT/NAACL*, pages 145–152.

L. Rabiner. 1989. A tutorial on hidden markov models and selected applications in speech recogntion. *Proc. of the IEEE*, 77(2):257–286.

O. Rambow, L. Shrestha, J. Chen, and C. Lauridsen. 2004. Summarizing email threads. In *Proc. of HLT-NAACL*.

E. Schegloff and H. Sacks. 1973. Opening up closings. *Semiotica*, 7-4:289–327.

F. Sha and F. Pereira. 2003. Shallow parsing with conditional random fields. In *Proc. of NAACL*, pages 134–141.

L. Shrestha and K. McKeown. 2004. Detection of question-answer pairs in email conversations. In *Proc. of COLING*, pages 889–895.

E. Shriberg, R. Dhillon, S. Bhagat, J. Ang, and H. Carvey. 2004. The ICSI meeting recorder dialog act (MRDA) corpus. In *SIGdial Workshop on Discourse and Dialogue*, pages 97–100.

C. Sutton and A. McCallum. 2004. Collective segmentation and labeling of distant entities in information extraction. Technical Report TR # 04-49, University of Massachusetts.

K. Zechner. 2002. Automatic summarization of open domain multi-party dialogues in diverse genres. *Computational Liguistics*, 28(4):447–485.

L. Zhou and E. Hovy. 2005. Digesting virtual "geek" culture: The summarization of technical internet relay chats. In *Proc. of ACL*, pages 298–305.

Style & Topic Language Model Adaptation Using HMM-LDA

Bo-June (Paul) Hsu, James Glass
MIT Computer Science and Artificial Intelligence Laboratory
32 Vassar Street, Cambridge, MA 02139, USA
{bohsu,glass}@mit.edu

Abstract

Adapting language models across styles and topics, such as for lecture transcription, involves combining generic style models with topic-specific content relevant to the target document. In this work, we investigate the use of the Hidden Markov Model with Latent Dirichlet Allocation (HMM-LDA) to obtain syntactic state and semantic topic assignments to word instances in the training corpus. From these context-dependent labels, we construct style and topic models that better model the target document, and extend the traditional bag-of-words topic models to n-grams. Experiments with static model interpolation yielded a perplexity and relative word error rate (WER) reduction of 7.1% and 2.1%, respectively, over an adapted trigram baseline. Adaptive interpolation of mixture components further reduced perplexity by 9.5% and WER by a modest 0.3%.

1 Introduction

With the rapid growth of audio-visual materials available over the web, effective language modeling of the diverse content, both in style and topic, becomes essential for efficient access and management of this information. As a prime example, successful language modeling for academic lectures not only enables the initial transcription via automatic speech recognition, but also assists educators and students in the creation and navigation of these materials through annotation, retrieval, summarization, and even translation of the embedded content.

Compared with other types of audio content, lecture speech often exhibits a high degree of spontaneity and focuses on narrow topics with specific terminology (Furui, 2003; Glass et al, 2004). Unfortunately, training corpora available for language modeling rarely match the target lecture in both style and topic. While transcripts from other lectures better match the style of the target lecture than written text, it is often difficult to find transcripts on the target topic. On the other hand, although topic-specific vocabulary can be gleaned from related text materials, such as the textbook and lecture slides, written language is a poor predictor of how words are actually spoken. Furthermore, given that the precise topic of a target lecture is often unknown a priori and may even shift over time, it is generally difficult to identify topically related documents. Thus, an effective language model (LM) need to not only account for the casual speaking style of lectures, but also accommodate the topic-specific vocabulary of the subject matter. Moreover, the ability of the language model to dynamically adapt over the course of the lecture could prove extremely useful for both increasing transcription accuracy, as well as providing evidence for lecture segmentation and information retrieval.

In this paper, we investigate the application of the syntactic state and semantic topic assignments from the Hidden Markov Model with Latent Dirichlet Allocation model to the problem of language modeling. We explore the use of these context-dependent labels to identify style and learn topics from both a large number of spoken lectures as well as written text. By dynamically interpolating lecture style models with topic-specific models, we obtain language models that better describe the subtopic structure within a lecture. Initial experiments demonstrate a 16.1% perplexity reduction and a 2.4% WER reduction over an adapted trigram baseline.

Proceedings of the 2006 Conference on Empirical Methods in Natural Language Processing (EMNLP 2006), pages 373–381,
Sydney, July 2006.

In the following sections, we first summarize related research on adaptive and topic-mixture language models, and describe previous work on the HMM-LDA model. We then examine the ability of the model to learn syntactic classes as well as topics from textbook materials and lecture transcripts. Next, we describe a variety of language model experiments we performed to combine style and topic models constructed from the state and topic labels with conventional trigram models trained from both spoken and written materials. We also demonstrate the use of the combined model in an on-line adaptive mode. Finally, we summarize the results of this research and suggest future opportunities for related modeling techniques in spoken lecture and other content processing research.

2 Adaptive and Topic-Mixture LMs

The concept of adaptive and topic-mixture language models has been previously explored by many researchers. Adaptive language modeling exploits the property that words appearing earlier in a document are likely to appear again. Cache language models (Kuhn and De Mori, 1990; Clarkson and Robinson, 1997) leverage this observation and increase the probability of previously observed words in a document when predicting the next word. By interpolating with a conditional trigram cache model, Goodman (2001) demonstrated up to 34% decrease in perplexity over a trigram baseline for small training sets.

The cache intuition has been extended by attempting to increase the probability of unobserved but topically related words. Specifically, given a mixture model with topic-specific components, we can increase the mixture weights of the topics corresponding to previously observed words to better predict the next word. Some of the early work in this area used a maximum entropy language model framework to trigger increases in likelihood of related words (Lau et al., 1993; Rosenfeld, 1996).

A variety of methods has been used to explore topic-mixture models. To model a mixture of topics within a document, the sentence mixture model (Iyer and Ostendorf, 1999) builds multiple topic models from clusters of training sentences and defines the probability of a target sentence as a weighted combination of its probability under each topic model. Latent Semantic Analysis (LSA) has been used to cluster topically related words and has demonstrated significant reduction in perplexity and word error rate (Bellegarda, 2000). Probabilistic LSA (PLSA) has been used to decompose documents into component word distributions and create unigram topic models from these distributions. Gildea and Hofmann (1999) demonstrated noticeable perplexity reduction via dynamic combination of these unigram topic models with a generic trigram model.

To identify topics from an unlabeled corpus, (Blei et al., 2003) extends PLSA with the Latent Dirichlet Allocation (LDA) model that describes each document in a corpus as generated from a mixture of topics, each characterized by a word unigram distribution. Hidden Markov Model with LDA (HMM-LDA) (Griffiths et al., 2004) further extends this topic mixture model to separate syntactic words from content words whose distributions depend primarily on local context and document topic, respectively.

In the specific area of lecture processing, previous work in language model adaptation has primarily focused on customizing a fixed n-gram language model for each lecture by combining n-gram statistics from general conversational speech, other lectures, textbooks, and other resources related to the target lecture (Nanjo and Kawahara, 2002, 2004; Leeuwis et al., 2003; Park et al., 2005).

Most of the previous work on topic-mixture models focuses on in-domain adaptation using large amounts of matched training data. However, most, if not all, of the data available to train a lecture language model are either cross-domain or cross-style. Furthermore, although adaptive models have been shown to yield significant perplexity reduction on clean transcripts, the improvements tend to diminish when working with speech recognizer hypotheses with high WER.

In this work, we apply the concept of dynamic topic adaptation to the lecture transcription task. Unlike previous work, we first construct a style model and a topic-domain model using the classification of word instances into syntactic states and topics provided by HMM-LDA. Furthermore, we leverage the context-dependent labels to extend topic models from unigrams to n-grams, allowing for better prediction of transitions involving topic words. Note that although this work focuses on the use of HMM-LDA to generate the state and topic labels, any method that yields such labels suffices for the purpose of the language modeling experiments. The following section describes the HMM-LDA framework in more detail.

3 HMM-LDA

3.1 Latent Dirichlet Allocation

Discrete Principal Component Analysis describes a family of models that decompose a set of feature vectors into its principal components (Buntine and Jakulin, 2005). Describing feature vectors via their components reduces the number of parameters required to model the data, hence improving the quality of the estimated parameters when given limited training data. LSA, PLSA, and LDA are all examples from this family.

Given a predefined number of desired components, LSA models feature vectors by finding a set of orthonormal components that maximize the variance using singular value decomposition (Deerwester et al., 1990). Unfortunately, the component vectors may contain non-interpretable negative values when working with word occurrence counts as feature vectors. PLSA eliminates this problem by using non-negative matrix factorization to model each document as a weighted combination of a set of non-negative feature vectors (Hofmann, 1999). However, because the number of parameters grows linearly with the number of documents, the model is prone to overfitting. Furthermore, because each training document has its own set of topic weight parameters, PLSA does not provide a generative framework for describing the probability of an unseen document (Blei et al., 2003).

To address the shortcomings of PLSA, Blei et al. (2003) introduced the LDA model, which further imposes a Dirichlet distribution on the topic mixture weights corresponding to the documents in the corpus. With the number of model parameters dependent only on the number of topic mixtures and vocabulary size, LDA is less prone to overfitting and is capable of estimating the probability of unobserved test documents.

Empirically, LDA has been shown to outperform PLSA in corpus perplexity, collaborative filtering, and text classification experiments (Blei et al., 2003). Various extensions to the basic LDA model have since been proposed. The Author Topic model adds an additional dependency on the author(s) to the topic mixture weights of each document (Rosen-Zvi et al., 2005). The Hierarchical Dirichlet Process is a nonparametric model that generalizes distribution parameter modeling to multiple levels. Without having to estimate the number of mixture components, this model has been shown to match the best result from LDA on a document modeling task (Teh et al., 2004).

3.2 Hidden Markov Model with LDA

HMM-LDA model proposed by Griffiths et al. (2004) combines the HMM and LDA models to separate syntactic words with local dependencies from topic-dependent content words without requiring any labeled data. Similar to HMM-based part-of-speech taggers, HMM-LDA maps each word in the document to a hidden syntactic state. Each state generates words according to a unigram distribution except the special topic state, where words are modeled by document-specific mixtures of topic distributions, as in LDA. Figure 1 describes this generative process in more detail.

For each document d in the corpus:

1. Draw topic weights θ^d from Dirichlet(α)
2. For each word w_i in document d:
   a. Draw topic z_i from Multinomial(θ^d)
   b. Draw state s_i from Multinomial$(\pi^{s_{i-1}})$
   c. Draw word w_i from:

$$\begin{cases} \text{Multinomial}(\beta^{z_i}) & s_i = \text{s}_{\text{topic}} \\ \text{Multinomial}(\gamma^{s_i}) & \textit{otherwise} \end{cases}$$

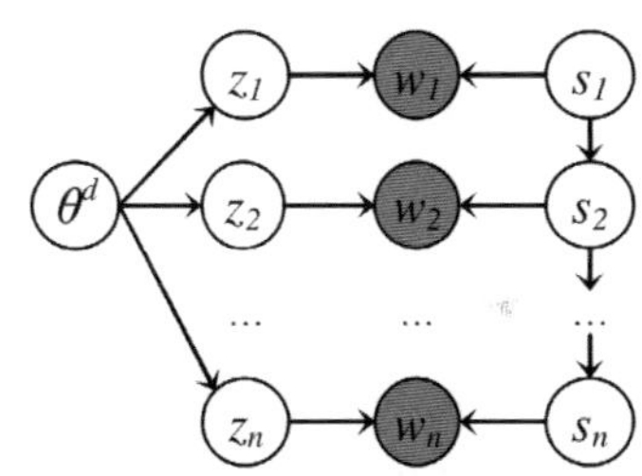

Figure 1: Generative framework and graphical model representation of HMM-LDA. The number of states and topics are pre-specified. The topic mixture for each document is modeled with a Dirichlet distribution. Each word w_i in the n-word document is generated from its hidden state s_i or hidden topic z_i if s_i is the special topic state.

Unlike vocabulary selection techniques that separate domain-independent words from topic-specific keywords using word collocation statistics, HMM-LDA classifies each word instance according to its context. Thus, an instance of the word "*return*" may be assigned to a syntactic state in "to *return* a", but classified as a topic keyword in "expected *return* for". By labeling each word in the training set with its syntactic state and mixture topic, HMM-LDA not only separates stylistic words from content words in a context-dependent manner, but also decomposes the corpus into a set of topic word distributions. This form of soft, context-dependent classification has many potential uses for language modeling, topic segmentation, and indexing.

3.3 Training

To train an HMM-LDA model, we employ the MATLAB Topic Modeling Toolbox 1.3 (Griffiths and Steyvers, 2004; Griffiths et al., 2004). This particular implementation performs Gibbs sampling, a form of Markov chain Monte Carlo (MCMC), to estimate the optimal model parameters fitted to the training data. Specifically, the algorithm creates a Markov chain whose stationary distribution matches the expected distribution of the state and topic labels for each word in the training corpus. Starting from random labels, Gibbs sampling sequentially samples the label for each hidden variable conditioned on the current value of all other variables. After a sufficient number of iterations, the Markov chain converges to the stationary distribution. We can easily compute the posterior word distribution for each state and topic from a single sample by averaging over the label counts and prior parameters. With a sufficiently large training set, we will have enough words assigned to each state and topic to yield a reasonable approximation to the underlying distribution.

In the following sections, we examine the application of models derived from the HMM-LDA labels to the task of spoken lecture transcription and explore techniques on adaptive topic modeling to construct a better lecture language model.

4 HMM-LDA Analysis

Our language modeling experiments have been conducted on high-fidelity transcripts of approximately 168 hours of lectures from three undergraduate subjects in math, physics, and computer science (CS), as well as 79 seminars covering a wide range of topics (Glass et al., 2004). For evaluation, we withheld the set of 20 CS lectures and used the first 10 lectures as a development set and the last 10 lectures for the test set. The remainder of these data was used for training and will be referred to as the *Lectures* dataset.

To supplement the out-of-domain lecture transcripts with topic-specific textual resources, we added the CS course textbook (*Textbook*) as additional training data for learning the target topics. To create topic-cohesive documents, the textbook is divided at every section heading to form 271 documents. Next, the text is heuristically segmented at sentence-like boundaries and normalized into the words corresponding to the spoken form of the text. Table 1 summarizes the data used in this evaluation.

Dataset	Documents	Sentences	Vocabulary	Words
Lectures	150	58,626	25,654	1,390,039
Textbook	271	6,762	4,686	131,280
CS Dev	10	4,102	3,285	93,348
CS Test	10	3,595	3,357	87,518

Table 1: Summary of evaluation datasets.

In the following analysis, we ran the Gibbs sampler against the *Lectures* dataset for a total of 2800 iterations, computing a model every 10 iterations, and took the model with the lowest perplexity as the final model. We built the model with 20 states and 100 topics based on preliminary experiments. We also trained an HMM-LDA model on the *Textbook* dataset using the same model parameters. We ran the sampler for a total of 2000 iterations, computing the perplexity every 100 iterations. Again, we selected the lowest perplexity model as the final model.

4.1 Semantic Topics

HMM-LDA extracts words whose distributions vary across documents and clusters them into a set of components. In Figure 2, we list the top 10 words from a random selection of 10 topics computed from the *Lectures* dataset. As shown, the words assigned to the LDA topic state are representative of content words and are grouped into broad semantic topics. For example, topic 4, 8, and 9 correspond to machine learning, linear algebra, and magnetism, respectively.

Since the *Lectures* dataset consists of speech transcripts with disfluencies, it is interesting to

1	2	3	4	5	6	7	8	9	10
center	work	rights	system	<laugh>	<partial>	class	basis	magnetic	light
world	research	human	things	her	memory	people	v	current	red
and	right	U.	robot	children	ah	tax	<eh>	field	water
ideas	people	S.	systems	book	brain	wealth	vector	loop	colors
new	computing	government	work	Cambridge	animal	social	matrix	surface	white
technology	network	international	example	books	okay	American	transformation	direction	angle
innovation	system	countries	person	street	eye	power	linear	e	blue
community	information	president	robots	city	synaptic	world	eight	law	here
place	software	world	learning	library	receptors	<unintelligible>	output	flux	rainbow
building	computers	support	machine	brother	mouse	society	t	m	sun

Figure 2: The top 10 words from 10 randomly selected topics computed from the *Lectures* dataset.

observe that "*<laugh>*" is the top word in a topic corresponding to childhood memories. Cursory examination of the data suggests that the speakers talking about children tend to laugh more during the lecture. Although it may not be desirable to capture speaker idiosyncrasies in the topic mixtures, HMM-LDA has clearly demonstrated its ability to capture distinctive semantic topics in a corpus. By leveraging all documents in the corpus, the model yields smoother topic word distributions that are less vulnerable to overfitting.

Since HMM-LDA labels the state and topic of each word in the training corpus, we can also visualize the results by color-coding the words by their topic assignments. Figure 3 shows a color-coded excerpt from a topically coherent paragraph in the *Textbook* dataset. Notice how most of the content words (uppercase) are assigned to the same topic/color. Furthermore, of the 7 instances of the words *"and"* and *"or"* (underlined), 6 are correctly classified as syntactic or topic words, demonstrating the context-dependent labeling capabilities of the HMM-LDA model. Moreover, from these labels, we can identify multi-word topic key phrases (e.g. *output signals*, *input signal*, *"and" gate*) in addition to standalone keywords, an observation we will leverage later on with n-gram topic models.

> We draw an INVERTER SYMBOLICALLY as in Figure 3.24. An AND GATE, also shown in Figure 3.24, is a PRIMITIVE FUNCTION box with two INPUTS and ONE OUTPUT. It drives its OUTPUT SIGNAL to a value that is the LOGICAL AND of the INPUTS. That is, if both of its INPUT SIGNALS BECOME 1. Then ONE and GATE DELAY time later the AND GATE will force its OUTPUT SIGNAL TO be 1; otherwise the OUTPUT will be 0. An OR GATE is a SIMILAR two INPUT PRIMITIVE FUNCTION box that drives its OUTPUT SIGNAL to a value that is the LOGICAL OR of the INPUTS. That is, the OUTPUT will BECOME 1 if at least ONE of the INPUT SIGNALS is 1; otherwise the OUTPUT will BECOME 0.

Figure 3: Color-coded excerpt from the *Textbook* dataset showing the context-dependent topic labels. Syntactic words appear black in lowercase. Topic words are shown in uppercase with their respective topic colors. All instances of the words *"and"* and *"or"* are underlined.

4.2 Syntactic States

Since the syntactic states are shared across all documents, we expect words associated with the syntactic states when applying HMM-LDA to the *Lectures* dataset to reflect the lecture style vocabulary.

In Figure 4, we list the top 10 words from each of the 19 syntactic states (state 20 is the topic state). Note that each state plays a clear syntactic role. For example, state 2 contains prepositions while state 7 contains verbs. Since the model is trained on transcriptions of spontaneous speech, hesitation disfluencies (*<uh>*, *<um>*, *<partial>*) are all grouped in state 3 along with other words (*so*, *if*, *okay*) that frequently indicate hesitation. While many of these hesitation words are conjunctions, the words in state 6 show that most conjunctions are actually assigned to a different state representing different syntactic behavior from hesitations. As demonstrated with spontaneous speech, HMM-LDA yields syntactic states that have a good correspondence to part-of-speech labels, without requiring any labeled training data.

4.3 Discussions

Although MCMC techniques converge to the global stationary distribution, we cannot guarantee convergence from observation of the perplexity alone. Unlike EM algorithms, random sampling may actually temporarily decrease the model likelihood. Thus, in the above analysis, the number of iterations was chosen to be at least double the point at which the perplexity first appeared to converge.

In addition to the number of iterations, the choice of the number of states and topics, as well as the values of the hyper-parameters on the Dirichlet prior, also impact the quality and effectiveness of the resulting model. Ideally, we run the algorithm with different combinations of the parameter values and perform model selection to choose the model with the best complexity-penalized likelihood. However, given finite computing resources, this approach is often im-

1	2	3	4	5	6	7	8	9	10	11	12	13	14	15	16	17	18	19
the	of	so	know	I	and	is	it's	it	a	way	it	two	going	that	can	very	to	have
this	in	<uh>	see	you	but	are	not	you	an	time	this	one	doing	what	will	more	just	be
a	for	if	do	we	or	was	that's	out	some	thing	that	three	one	how	would	little	longer	want
that	on	<um>	think	they	because	has	I'm	up	one	lot	there	hundred	looking	where	don't	much	doesn't	had
these	with	<partial>	go	let	as	were	just	them	no	question	which	m	sort	when	could	good	never	get
my	at	now	get	let's	that	goes	there's	that	in	kind	he	t	done	if	do	different	go	like
our	from	then	say	he	where	had	<uh>	me	two	point	here	five	able	why	just	than	physically	got
your	by	okay	make	I'll	thank	comes	we're	about	any	case	course	d	coming	which	me	important	that'll	need
those	about	well	look	people	which	means	also	here	this	idea	who	years	talking	as	should	long	anybody's	try
their	as	but	take	I'd	is	says	you're	all	another	problem	they	four	trying	because	may	as	with	take

Figure 4: The top 10 words from the 19 syntactic states computed from the *Lectures* dataset.

practical. As an alternative for future work, we would like to perform Gibbs sampling on the hyper-parameters (Griffiths et al., 2004) and apply the Dirichlet process to estimate the number of states and topics (Teh et al., 2004).

Despite the suboptimal choice of parameters and potential lack of convergence, the labels derived from HMM-LDA are still effective for language modeling applications, as described next.

5 Language Modeling Experiments

To evaluate the effectiveness of models derived from the separation of syntax from content, we performed experiments that compare the perplexities and WERs of various model combinations. For a baseline, we used an adapted model (L+T) that linearly interpolates trigram models trained on the *Lectures* (L) and *Textbook* (T) datasets. In all models, all interpolation weights and additional parameters are tuned on a development set consisting of the first half of the CS lectures and tested on the second half. Unless otherwise noted, modified Kneser-Ney discounting (Chen and Goodman, 1998) is applied with the respective training set vocabulary using the SRILM Toolkit (Stolcke, 2002).

To compute the word error rates associated with a specific language model, we used a speaker-independent speech recognizer (Glass, 2003). The lectures were pre-segmented into utterances by forced alignment of the reference transcription.

5.1 Lecture Style

In general, an n-gram model trained on a limited set of topic-specific documents tends to overemphasize words from the observed topics instead of evenly distributing weights over all potential topics. Specifically, given the list of words following an n-gram context, we would like to deemphasize the observed occurrences of topic words and ideally redistribute these counts to all potential topic words. As an approximation, we can build such a topic-deemphasized style trigram model (S) by using counts of only n-gram sequences that do not end on a topic word, smoothed over the *Lectures* vocabulary. Figure 5 shows the n-grams corresponding to an utterance used to build the style trigram model. Note that the counts of topic to style word transitions are not altered as these probabilities are mostly independent of the observed topic distribution.

By interpolating the style model (S) from above with the smoothed trigram model based on the *Lectures* dataset (L), the combined model (L+S) achieves a 3.6% perplexity reduction and 1.0% WER reduction over (L), as shown in Table 2. Without introducing topic-specific training data, we can already improve the generic lecture LM performance using the HMM-LDA labels.

<s> for the SPATIAL MEMORY </s>	
unigrams:	for, the, spatial, memory, </s>
bigrams:	<s> for, for the, ~~the spatial~~, ~~spatial memory~~, memory </s>
trigrams:	<s> <s> for, <s> for the, ~~for the spatial~~, ~~the spatial memory~~, spatial memory </s>

Figure 5: Style model n-grams. Topic words in the utterance are in uppercase.

5.2 Topic Domain

Unlike *Lectures*, the *Textbook* dataset contains content words relevant to the target lectures, but in a mismatched style. Commonly, the *Textbook* trigram model is interpolated with the generic model to improve the probability estimates of the transitions involving topic words. The interpolation weight is chosen to best fit the probabilities of these n-gram sequences while minimizing the mismatch in style. However, with only one parameter, all n-gram contexts must share the same mixture weight. Because transitions from contexts containing topic words are rarely observed in the off-topic *Lectures*, the *Textbook* model (T) should ideally have higher weight in these contexts than contexts that are more equally observed in both datasets.

One heuristic approach for adjusting the weight in these contexts is to build a topic-domain trigram model (D) from the *Textbook* n-gram counts with Witten-Bell smoothing (Chen and Goodman, 1998) where we emphasize the sequences containing a topic word in the context by doubling their counts. In effect, this reduces the smoothing on words following topic contexts with respect to lower-order models without significantly affecting the transitions from non-topic words. Figure 6 shows the adjusted counts for an utterance used to build the domain trigram model.

<s> HUFFMAN CODE can be represented as a BINARY TREE …	
unigrams:	huffman, code, can, be, represented, as, binary, tree, …
bigrams:	<s> huffman, huffman code (2×), code can (2×), can be, be represented, represented as, a binary, binary tree (2×), …
trigrams:	<s> <s> hufmann, <s> hufmann code (2×), hufmann code can (2×), code can be (2×), can be represented, be represented as, represented as a, as a binary, a binary tree (2×), …

Figure 6: Domain model n-grams. Topic words in the utterance are in uppercase.

Empirically, interpolating the lectures, textbook, and style models with the domain model (L+T+S+D) further decreases the perplexity by 1.4% and WER by 0.3% over (L+T+S), validating our intuition. Overall, the addition of the style and domain models reduces perplexity and WER by a noticeable 7.1% and 2.1%, respectively, as shown in Table 2.

Model	Perplexity Development	Perplexity Test
L: Lectures Trigram	180.2 (0.0%)	199.6 (0.0%)
T: Textbook Trigram	291.7 (+61.8%)	331.7 (+66.2%)
S: Style Trigram	207.0 (+14.9%)	224.6 (+12.5%)
D: Domain Trigram	354.1 (+96.5%)	411.6 (+106.3%)
L+S	174.2 (–3.3%)	192.4 (–3.6%)
L+T: Baseline	138.3 (0.0%)	154.4 (0.0%)
L+T+S	131.0 (–5.3%)	145.6 (–5.7%)
L+T+S+D	128.8 (–6.9%)	**129.5 (–16.1%)**
L+T+S+D+Topic100		
• Static Mixture (cheat)	118.1 (–14.6%)	
• Dynamic Mixture	**115.7 (–16.4%)**	

Model	Word Error Rate Development	Word Error Rate Test
L: Lectures Trigram	49.5% (0.0%)	50.2% (0.0%)
L+S	49.2% (–0.7%)	49.7% (–1.0%)
L+T: Baseline	46.6% (0.0%)	46.7% (0.0%)
L+T+S	46.0% (–1.2%)	45.8% (–1.8%)
L+T+S+D	45.8% (–1.8%)	**45.6% (–2.4%)**
L+T+S+D+Topic100		
• Static Mixture (cheat)	45.5% (–2.4%)	
• Dynamic Mixture	**45.4% (–2.6%)**	

Table 2: Perplexity (top) and WER (bottom) performance of various model combinations. Relative reduction is shown in parentheses.

5.3 Textbook Topics

In addition to identifying content words, HMM-LDA also assigns words to a topic based on their distribution across documents. Thus, we can apply HMM-LDA with 100 topics to the *Textbook* dataset to identify representative words and their associated contexts for each topic. From these labels, we can build unsmoothed trigram language models (Topic100) for each topic from the counts of observed n-gram sequences that end in a word assigned to the respective topic.

Figure 7 shows a sample of the word n-grams identified via this approach for a few topics. Note that some of the n-grams are key phrases for the topic while others contain a mixture of syntactic and topic words. Unlike bag-of-words models that only identify the unigram distribution for each topic, the use of context-dependent labels enables the construction of n-gram topic models that not only characterize the frequencies of topic words, but also describe the transition contexts leading up to these words.

Huffman tree	Monte Carlo	time segment	assoc key
relative frequency	rand update	the agenda	the table
relative frequencies	random numbers	segment time	local table
the tree	trials remaining	current time	a table
one hundred	trials passed	first agenda	of records

Figure 7: Sample of n-grams from select topics.

5.4 Topic Mixtures

Since each target lecture generally only covers a subset of the available topics, it will be ideal to identify the specific topics corresponding to a target lecture and assign those topic models more weight in a linearly interpolated mixture model. As an ideal case, we performed a cheating experiment to measure the best performance of a statically interpolated topic mixture model (L+T+S+D+Topic100) where we tuned the mixture weights of all mixture components, including the lectures, textbook, style, domain, and the 100 individual topic trigram models on individual target lectures.

Table 2 shows that by weighting the component models appropriately, we can reduce the perplexity and WER by an additional 7.9% and 0.7%, respectively, over the (L+T+S+D) model even with simple linear interpolation for model combination.

To gain further insight into the topic mixture model, we examine the breakdown of the normalized topic weights for a specific lecture. As shown in Figure 8, of the 100 topic models, 15 of them account for over 90% of the total weight. Thus, lectures tend to show a significant topic skew which topic adaptation approaches can model effectively.

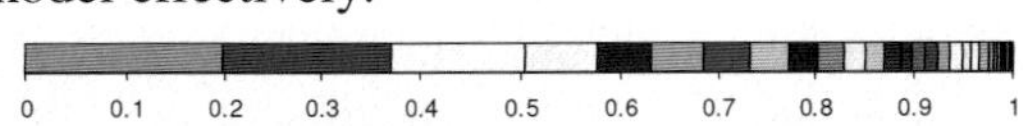

Figure 8: Topic mixture weight breakdown.

5.5 Topic Adaptation

Unfortunately, since different lectures cover different topics, we generally cannot tune the topic mixture weights ahead of time. One approach, without any a priori knowledge of the target lecture, is to adaptively estimate the optimal mixture weights as we process the lecture (Gildea and Hofmann, 1999). However, since the topic distribution shifts over a long lecture, modeling a lecture as an interpolation of components with fixed weights may not be the most optimal. Instead, we employ an exponential decay strategy where we update the current mixture distribution by linearly interpolating it with the posterior topic distribution given the current word. Specifically, applying Bayes' rule, the probability of topic t generating the current word w is given by:

$$P(t \mid w) = \frac{P(w|t)P(t)}{\sum_{t'} P(w|t')P(t')}$$

To achieve the exponential decay, we update the topic distribution after each word according to $P^{i+1}(t) = (1 - \alpha) \cdot P^i(t) + \alpha \cdot P(t \mid w^i)$, where α is the adaptation rate.

We evaluated this approach of dynamic mixture weight adaptation on the (L+T+S+D+Topic 100) model, with the same set of components as the cheating experiment with static weights. As shown in Table 2, the dynamic model actually outperforms the static model by more than 1% in perplexity, by better modeling the dynamic topic substructure within the lecture.

To run the recognizer with a dynamic LM, we rescored the top 100 hypotheses generated with the (L+T+S+D) model using the dynamic LM. The WER obtained through such n-best rescoring yielded noticeable improvements over the (L+T+S+D) model without a priori knowledge of the topic distribution, but did not beat the optimal static model on the test set.

To further gain an intuition for mixture weight adaptation, we plotted the normalized adapted weights of the topic models across the first lecture of the test set in Figure 9. Note that the topic mixture varies greatly across the lecture. In this particular lecture, the lecturer starts out with a review of the previous lecture. Subsequently, he shows an example of computation using accumulators. Finally, he focuses the lecture on stream as a data structure, with an intervening example that finds pairs of i and j that sum up to a prime. By comparing the topic labels in Figure 9 with the top words from the corresponding topics in Figure 10, we observe that the topic weights obtained via dynamic adaptation match the subject matter of the lecture fairly closely.

Finally, to assess the effect that word error rate has on adaptation performance, we applied the adaptation algorithm to the corresponding transcript from the automatic speech recognizer (ASR). Traditional cache language models tend to be vulnerable to recognition errors since incorrect words in the history negatively bias the prediction of the current word. However, by adapting at a topic level, which reduces the number of dynamic parameters, the dynamic topic model is less sensitive to recognition errors. As seen in Figure 9, even with a word error rate around 40%, the normalized topic mixture weights from the ASR transcript still show a strong resemblance to the original weights from the manual reference transcript.

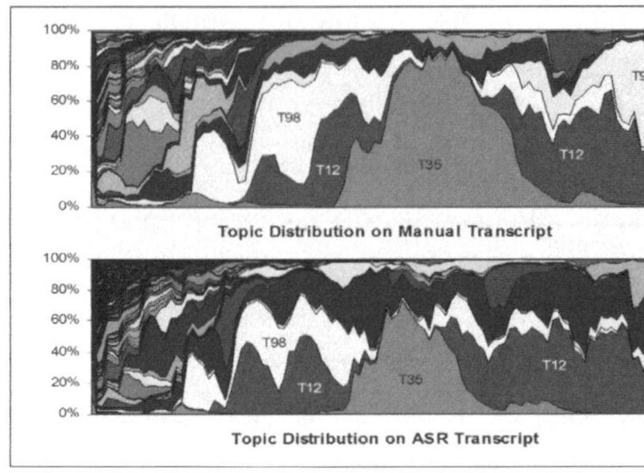

Figure 9: Adaptation of topic model weights on manual and ASR transcription of a single lecture.

T12	T35	T98	T99
stream	pairs	sequence	of
s	i	enumerate	see
streams	j	accumulate	and
integers	k	map	in
series	pair	interval	for
prime	s	filter	vs
filter	integers	sequences	register
delayed	sum	operations	data
interleave	queens	odd	as
infinite	t	nil	make

Figure 10: Top 10 words from select *Textbook* topics appearing in Figure 9.

6 Summary and Conclusions

In this paper, we have shown how to leverage context-dependent state and topic labels, such as the ones generated by the HMM-LDA model, to construct better language models for lecture transcription and extend topic models beyond traditional unigrams. Although the WER of the top recognizer hypotheses exceeds 45%, by dynamically updating the mixture weights to model the topic substructure within individual lectures, we are able to reduce the test set perplexity and WER by over 16% and 2.4%, respectively, relative to the combined *Lectures* and *Textbook* (L+T) baseline.

Although we primarily focused on lecture transcription in this work, the techniques extend to language modeling scenarios where exactly matched training data are often limited or nonexistent. Instead, we have to rely on appropriate combination of models derived from partially matched data. HMM-LDA and related techniques show great promise for finding structure in unlabeled data, from which we can build more sophisticated models.

The experiments in this paper combine models primarily through simple linear interpolation. As motivated in section 5.2, allowing for context-dependent interpolation weights based on topic labels may yield significant improvement for both perplexity and WER. Thus, in future work, we would like to study algorithms for automatically learning appropriate context-dependent interpolation weights. Furthermore, we hope to improve the convergence properties of the dynamic adaptation scheme at the start of lectures and across topic transitions. Lastly, we would like to extend the LDA framework to support speaker-specific adaptation and apply the resulting topic distributions to lecture segmentation.

Acknowledgements

We would like to thank the anonymous reviewers for their useful comments and feedback. Support for this research was provided in part by the National Science Foundation under grant #IIS-0415865. Any opinions, findings, and conclusions, or recommendations expressed in this material are those of the authors and do not necessarily reflect the views of the NSF.

Reference

Y. Akita and T. Kawahara. 2004. Language Model Adaptation Based on PLSA of Topics and Speakers. In *Proc. ICSLP.*

J. Bellegarda. 2000. Exploiting Latent Semantic Information in Statistical Language Modeling. In *Proc. IEEE*, 88(8):1279-1296.

D. Blei, A. Ng, and M. Jordan. 1993. Latent Dirichlet Allocation. *Journal of Machine Learning Research*, 3:993-1022.

W. Buntine and A. Jakulin. 2005. Discrete Principal Component Analysis. Technical Report, Helsinki Institute for Information Technology.

S. Chen and J. Goodman. 1996. An Empirical Study of Smoothing Techniques for Language Modeling. In *Proc. ACL*, 310-318.

P. Clarkson and A. Robinson. 1997. Language Model Adaptation Using Mixtures and an Exponentially Decaying Cache. In *Proc. ICASSP.*

S. Deerwester, S. Dumais, G. Furnas, T. Landauer, R. Harshman. 1990. Indexing by Latent Semantic Analysis. *Journal of the American Society for Information Science*, 41(6):391-407.

S. Furui. 2003. Recent Advances in Spontaneous Speech Recognition and Understanding. In *Proc. IEEE Workshop on Spontaneous Speech Proc. and Rec*, 1-6.

D. Gildea and T. Hofmann. 1999. Topic-Based Language Models Using EM. In *Proc. Eurospeech.*

J. Glass. 2003. A Probabilistic Framework for Segment-based Speech Recognition. *Computer, Speech and Language*, 17:137-152.

J. Glass, T.J. Hazen, L. Hetherington, and C. Wang. 2004. Analysis and Processing of Lecture Audio Data: Preliminary Investigations. In *Proc. HLT-NAACL Workshop on Interdisciplinary Approaches to Speech Indexing and Retrieval*, 9-12.

J. Goodman. 2001. A Bit of Progress in Language Modeling (Extended Version). Technical Report, Microsoft Research.

T. Griffiths and M. Steyvers. 2004. Finding Scientific Topics. In *Proc. National Academy of Science*, 101(Suppl. 1):5228-5235.

T. Griffiths, M. Steyvers, D. Blei, and J. Tenenbaum. 2004. Integrating Topics and Syntax. *Adv. in Neural Information Processing Systems*, 17:537-544.

R. Iyer and M. Ostendorf. 1999. Modeling Long Distance Dependence in Language: Topic Mixtures Versus Dynamic Cache. In *IEEE Transactions on Speech and Audio Processing*, 7:30-39.

R. Kuhn and R. De Mori. 1990. A Cache-Based Natural Language Model for Speech Recognition. In *IEEE Transactions on Pattern Analysis and Machine Intelligence*, 12:570-583.

R. Lau, R. Rosenfeld, S. Roukos. 1993. Trigger-Based Language Models: a Maximum Entropy Approach. In *Proc. ICASSP.*

E. Leeuwis, M. Federico, and M. Cettolo. 2003. Language Modeling and Transcription of the TED Corpus Lectures. In *Proc. ICASSP.*

H. Nanjo and T. Kawahara. 2002. Unsupervised Language Model Adaptation for Lecture Speech Recognition. In *Proc. ICSLP.*

H. Nanjo and T. Kawahara. 2004. Language Model and Speaking Rate Adaptation for Spontaneous Presentation Speech Recognition. In *IEEE Trans. SAP*, 12(4):391-400.

A. Park, T. Hazen, and J. Glass. 2005. Automatic Processing of Audio Lectures for Information Retrieval: Vocabulary Selection and Language Modeling. In *Proc. ICASSP.*

M. Rosen-Zvi, T. Griffiths, M. Steyvers, and P. Smyth. 2004. The Author-Topic Model for Authors and Documents. *20th Conference on Uncertainty in Artificial Intelligence.*

R. Rosenfeld. 1996. A Maximum Entropy Approach to Adaptive Statistical Language Modeling. *Computer, Speech and Language*, 10:187-228.

A. Stolcke. 2002. SRILM – An Extensible Language Modeling Toolkit. In *Proc. ICSLP.*

Y. Teh, M. Jordan, M. Beal, and D. Blei. 2006. Hierarchical Dirichlet Processes. To appear in *Journal of the American Statistical Association.*

Text data acquisition for domain-specific language models

Abhinav Sethy, Panayiotis G. Georgiou, Shrikanth Narayanan
Speech Analysis and Interpretation Lab
Integrated Media Systems Center
Viterbi School of Engineering
Department of Electrical Engineering-Systems
University of Southern California

Abstract

The language modeling community is showing a growing interest in using large collections of text mined from the World Wide Web (WWW) to supplement sparse in-domain text resources. However, in most cases the style and content of the text harvested from these corpora differs significantly from the specific nature of these domains. In this paper we present a relative entropy (r.e.) based method to select *relevant subsets* of sentences whose distribution in an *n-gram* sense matches the domain of interest. Using simulations, we provide an analysis of how the proposed scheme outperforms filtering techniques proposed in recent language modeling literature on mining text from the web. A comparative study is presented using a text collection of over 800M words collected from the WWW. Experimental results show that by using the proposed subset selection scheme we can get performance improvement in both Word Error Rate (WER) and Perplexity (PPL) over the models built from the entire collection by using just 10% of the data. Improvements in data selection also translated to a significant reduction in the vocabulary size as well as the number of estimated parameters in the adapted language model.

1 Introduction

State of the art speech and Natural Language Processing (NLP) systems are data-driven, relying on learning patterns from large amounts of data. A key step in creating such systems for different domains and applications is to identify the appropriate text resources for building language models matched to that application or domain. In most cases, this data is not readily available and needs to be collected manually, which is an expensive and time consuming process.

This has naturally led to a growing interest in using the World Wide Web (WWW) as a corpus for building statistical models (Lapata, 2005; Lapata, 2002; Resnik, 2003). Text harvested from the web combined with other large text collections such as GigaWord provides a good resource to supplement the in-domain data for a variety of applications. However, text gathered from such generic sources rarely fits the demands or the nature of the domain of interest completely. Even with the best queries and web crawling schemes, both the style and content of the data will usually differ significantly from the specific nature of the domain of interest. For example, a speech recognition system requires conversational style text whereas most of the data on the web is literary.

In most cases we have available to us a set of in-domain example sentences which we can use in a semi-supervised (Nigam, 2000; Zhu, 2005) fashion to refine our selection of text. Recent literature on building language models with text acquired from the web addresses the issue of mismatch, partly by using various rank-and-select schemes for identifying sentences from the web-data[1] which match the in-domain data (Ostendorf, 2005; Sarikaya, 2005). The central idea behind these schemes is to rank order sentences in terms of their match to the seed in-domain set, and then select the top sentences.

[1] We will use web-data to refer to text harvested from web and other generic sources.

Proceedings of the 2006 Conference on Empirical Methods in Natural Language Processing (EMNLP 2006), pages 382–389,
Sydney, July 2006. ©2006 Association for Computational Linguistics

Research in semi-supervised learning for classification (Zhu (2005) presents a good survey) has shown the need to balance the unlabeled data. We believe that similar to the question of balance in semi-supervised learning for classification, we need to address the question of distributional similarity while selecting the appropriate sentences for building a language model from noisy data. Rank-and-select filtering schemes select individual sentences on the merit of their match to the in-domain model. As a result, even though individual sentences might be good in-domain examples, the overall distribution of the selected set will focus solely on the high probability regions of the distribution. This will be made more clear in simulation results described in section 4.

To address the issue of distributional similarity we present an incremental selection algorithm which compares the distribution of the selected set and the in-domain examples by using a relative entropy (r.e.) criterion at each step. Some ranking schemes, which provide baseline for performance comparison are reviewed in section 2. The proposed algorithm is described in section 3. Section 4 will provide an analysis of how the proposed algorithm improves upon rank and select schemes. Experimental results are provided in section 5. We conclude with a summary of this work and directions for future research.

2 Rank and select methods for text cleaning

In recent literature, the central idea behind text cleanup schemes for using web-data to build language models, has been to use a scoring function that measures the similarity of each observed sentence in the web-data to the in-domain set and assign an appropriate score. The subsequent step is to set a threshold in terms of either the minimum score or the number of top scoring sentences. The threshold can usually be fixed using a held-out set. Ostendorf (2005) use perplexity from an in-domain n-gram language model as a scoring function. More recently, a modified version of the BLEU metric which measures sentence similarity in machine translation has been proposed by Sarikaya (2005) as a scoring function. Instead of explicit ranking and thresholding it is also possible to design a classifier to learn from positive and unlabeled examples (LPU) (Liu, 2003). In this system, a subset of the unlabeled set is selected as the negative or noise set **N**. A binary classifier is then trained using the in-domain set **I** and the negative set. The classifier is then used to label sentences in the web-data. The classifier can then be iteratively refined by using a better and larger subset of the **I/N** sentences selected in each iteration.

Rank ordering schemes do not address the issue of distributional similarity and select many sentences which already have a high probability in the in-domain text. Adapting models on such data has the tendency to skew the distribution even further towards the center. For example, in our doctor-patient interaction task, short sentences containing the word 'okay' such as 'okay','yes okay', 'okay okay' were very frequent in the in-domain data. Perplexity and other similarity measures assign a high score to all such examples in the web-data, increasing the probability of these words even further. In contrast other pertinent sentences seen rarely in the in-domain data such as 'Can you stand up please?' receive a low rank and are more likely to be rejected.

3 Incremental Selection

To address the shortcomings of the rank-and-select schemes we need to ensure that the set of sentences that we select from web-data has a distribution similar to the in-domain distribution. Thus we need to move from selecting sentences on the basis of individual score to selecting a set of sentences as a group. We propose an incremental greedy sentence selection algorithm based on relative entropy which selects a sentence if adding it to the already selected set of sentences reduces the relative entropy with respect to the in-domain data distribution. To describe our algorithm we will employ unigram probabilities though the method generalizes to higher order n-grams also.

3.1 The Basic Algorithm

Let us denote the language model built from in-domain data by P. We also need a language model P_{init} to initialize our selection algorithm . We experimented with two methods for selecting the initial model. The first is to use a uniform distribution over the vocabulary. The second approach is to sample with replacement the in-domain data and get a bagged estimate of the in-domain model. The results from both approaches were very close with the bagging approach being slightly better in all cases. For reasons of implementation simplicity, we prefer the use of a uniform distribution. We convert the model P_{init} into a set of counts $W(i)$ for words i in the vocabulary V by multiplying with the vocabulary size V_n. Thus the total initial counts $\sum_i W(i) = V_n$.

Our selection algorithm considers every sentence in the corpus sequentially. Suppose we are at the jth sentence s_j. We denote the count of word i in s_j with m_{ij}. Let $n_j = \sum_i m_{ij}$ be the number of words in the sentence and $N = \sum_i W(i)$ be the total number of words already selected. The relative entropy of the maximum likelihood estimate of the language model of the selected sentences to the initial model P is given by

$$H(j) = -\sum_i P(i) \ln \frac{P(i)}{W(i)/N}$$

The model parameters and the r.e. remain unchanged if sentence s_j is not selected. If we select s_j , the updated r.e. is given by

$$H^+(j) = -\sum_i P(i) \ln \frac{P(i)}{(W(i) + m_{ij})/(N + n_j)}$$

Direct computation of r.e. using the above expressions for every sentence in the web-data will have a very high computational cost since $O(V)$ computations per sentence in the web-data are required. The number of sentences in the web-data can be very large, easily on the order 10^8 to 10^9. The total computation cost for even moderate vocabularies (around 10^5) would be large.

However given the fact that m_{ij} is sparse, we can split the summation $H^+(j)$ into

$$\begin{aligned} H^+(j) &= -\sum_i P(i) \ln P(i) + \\ &\quad + \sum_i P(i) \ln \frac{W(i) + m_{ij}}{N + n_j} \\ &= H(j) - \underbrace{\ln \frac{N + n_j}{N}}_{T1} \\ &\quad + \underbrace{\sum_{i, m_{ij} \neq 0} P(i) \ln \frac{(W(i) + m_{ij})}{W(i)}}_{T2} \end{aligned}$$

Intuitively, the term $T1$ measures the decrease in probability mass because of the addition of n_j words to the corpus, and the term $T2$ measures the in-domain distribution P weighted increase in probability for words with non-zero m_{ij}.

We will select the sentence s_j if including it decreases the r.e. with the in-domain distribution, i.e $H^+(j) < H(j)$. Thus s_j is selected if $T1 > T2$. To make the selection more refined we can impose a condition $T1 > T2 + thr(j)$ where $thr(j)$ is a function of j. A good choice for $thr(j)$ based on empirical studies is a function that declines at the same rate as the ratio $\ln \frac{(N+n_j)}{N} \approx n_j/N \approx 1/kj$ where k is the average number of words for every sentence. The counts W and N are updated with the selection of a sentence, and $H(j)$ is set to $H^+(j)$.

3.2 Text permutations and resequencing

The proposed algorithm is sequential and greedy in nature and can benefit from randomization of the order in which it scans the corpus. We generate permutations of the corpus by scanning through the corpus and randomly swapping sentences. Next we do sequential selection on each permutation and merge the selected sets.

As more sentences are selected, the r.e. $H(j)$ decreases and the distribution of the selected set gets closer to the in-domain distribution. The sentence selection becomes more refined as it becomes harder to improve $H(j)$ further. This motivated us to use a simple heuristic to ensure that the sentences selected in the initial stage are useful. At the end of a scan through the corpus we take the list of selected sentences and reverse it. We then scan the corpus again with the reversed list at the top. The sentences which were selected in the initial stages of the algorithm are retained only if they contribute to r.e. improvement even when they are in the latter part of the scan sequence.

3.3 Smoothing

The choice of maximum likelihood estimation for estimating the intermediate language models for $W(j)$ is motivated by a simplification in the entropy calculation which reduces the computation effort significantly. However, maximum likelihood estimation of language models is poor when compared to smoothing based estimation. To balance the computation cost and estimation accuracy, we modify the counts $W(j)$ using Good-Turing smoothing periodically, after a fixed number of sentences. The choice of the number of sentences to wait before smoothing depends on computation time constraints.

In the next section we provide an intuitive analysis of the advantages of iterative selection over rank-and-select schemes using simulated data.

4 Some intuition from simulations

A measure of the relevancy of the selected adaptation data is the Kullback-Leibler distance between the estimated n-gram model and the true n-gram distribution for that domain[2]. By comparing the two distributions we can identify the convergence properties of the data selection methods and also explain how the selection affects the estimated probability mass distribution compared to the true distribution.

To compare the n-gram language models we developed a fast r.e. computation scheme for tree based n-gram models. The description of this computation scheme is given in Appendix A. The fast scheme makes it possible to compute the r.e. between two LMs in $O(L)$ computations where L is the number of language model terms actually present in the two LMs, compared to V^n computations required in a direct implementation. This helps to reduce the computation effort by a factor of 10^4 or more.

We cannot use KL distance to judge relevance with real world data since the true distribution for real world data is unknown. However for analysis purposes, we can substitute the true distribution with a known distribution and then sample from it to get examples of in-domain text (with reference to the known distribution). We can then mix the known distribution with a noise model to simulate a generic text corpus, such as text acquired from web.

For simulation purposes, the language model used to generate the equivalent of in-domain text becomes the true distribution P_{true}. To complete the analogy with our data selection problem, text samples D_{ind} generated from P_{true} serve as the equivalent of in-domain data. The equivalent of the large generic corpus $D_{generic}$ can be generated from the noisy model. The simulation equivalent of the in-domain language model will be the language model P_{ind} estimated from the clean data D_{ind} .

We use a P_{true} with a vocabulary of 3K words estimated from a real world medical dialog task. The noise model is a language model of vocabulary 20K estimated from 1M words collected from webpages identified by Google using medical domain queries (Section 5.1). We used a D_{ind} set (generated from P_{true}) of 200K words and a generic set $D_{generic}$ of size 20M words or 3.8M sentences. The vocabulary sizes were kept small to efficiently generate text samples from the language models. The goal of the simulations is solely to gain an insight into the differences between iterative selection and rank-and-select scheme. Results on real world data are presented in the next section where the vocabulary size is more realistic.

[2]We restrict ourselves to the n-gram approach for modeling the distribution of word sequences.

	Rand	PPLSel	ItSel
200K	32.2	**9.1**	16.1
400K	34.2	**13.3**	24.3
800K	31.1	**22**	27.3
1200K	33.7	**28**	29.5
2400K	32.9	**31**	31

Table 1: Perplexity of data selected with respect to P_{ind} for varying number of selected sentences

4.1 Simulation results

The first question that we address is whether it is useful to select all data from the generic corpus $D_{generic}$ which scores high in perplexity terms with the in-domain model P_{ind}. In Table 1, we compare the perplexity of the data selected by different methods. *Rand* selects n sentences randomly, *PPLSel* selects the top n sentences ranked by perplexity and *ItSel* is the proposed iterative method. We build language models with the selected data and merge it with P_{ind} using weights determined from the heldout set. Table 2 shows the relative entropy of the adapted models with the true distribution. Our goal is to select the adaptation data cleverly to reduce the r.e. between the adapted model and the true distribution P_{true}. It can be seen that selecting data with lowest perplexity does not lead to a better language model. The perplexity of the data selected by *ItSel*, which is the most beneficial in improving the language model lies between the perplexity of random selection and *PPLSel*. It should be noted that by design, as the number of selected sentences approaches the size of the generic corpus, the selected data for all methods will be similar (identical if all the data is selected). Thus all methods essentially give same performance when selecting high percentages of data.

	Rand	PPLSel	ItSel
200K	12.1	15.2	**9.2**
400K	11.3	13.2	**8.3**
800K	10.5	11.1	**10.1**
1200K	9.7	9.5	**9.4**
2400K	9.3	8.9	**8.9**

Table 2: Relative entropy of models built from the selected data with the reference P_{true} distribution for varying number of sentences

Next we verify our hypothesis that use of ranking methods skews the distribution by focusing solely on the high probability regions. We selected the top 10% words which have the highest probability in P_{ind} and 10% words with the smallest probability. Then we computed the partial sums

$$H_{bias}^{high} = - \sum_{w \in top} P_{true}(w) \ln \frac{P_{true}(w)}{P_{sel}(w)}$$

$$H_{bias}^{low} = - \sum_{w \in bottom} P_{true}(w) \ln \frac{P_{true}(w)}{P_{sel}(w)}$$

for the language models P_{sel} estimated from the selected data. Note that the summation involves the true density P_{true}. If the selected data is imbalanced with respect to the true distribution P_{true} and unnecessarily biased towards the high probability regions of P_{base} the separation of the partial sums

$$H_{imbalance} = H_{bias}^{high} - H_{bias}^{low}$$

will be large. However, if the bias towards high probability regions of P_{base} is justified, $H_{imbalance}$ will be low.

In Figure 1, we plot $H_{imbalance}$ with increasing number of selected sentences for *PPlSel* and *ItSel*. High $H_{imbalance}$ for *PPLSel* especially when number of sentences selected is low confirms our hypothesis that selection using perplexity ranking skews the distribution by focusing solely on the high probability regions.

The simulation results provide an easy and intuitive way to understand how the proposed algorithm scores over rank-and-select scheme. Perplexity and WER results on real world tasks are hard to interpret because the underlying distributions are unknown. For example, our claim of skew towards high probability regions is hard to justify by looking at perplexity of test sets. However we do need to ensure that our algorithm indeed improves over the baseline methods on real world applications. We proceed to do so in the next section.

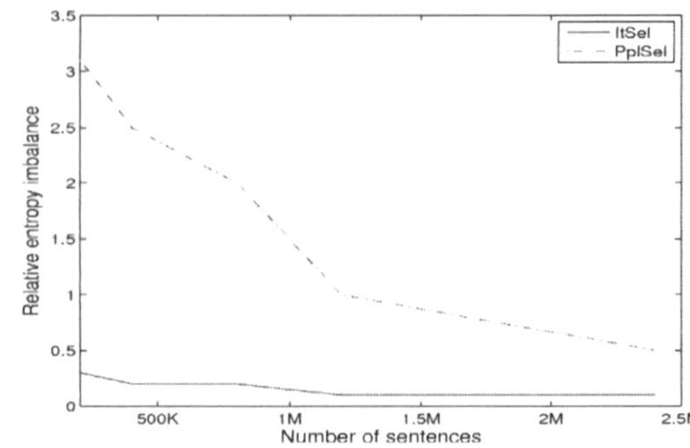

Figure 1: Relative entropy imbalance with number of selected sentences

5 Experiments

Our experiments were conducted on medical domain data collected as part of the English ASR of an English-Persian speech to speech translation project. We have 50K in-domain sentences for this task. A generic conversational-speech language model was built from the WSJ, Fisher and SWB corpora interpolated with the CMU LM. All language models built from web-data and in-domain data were interpolated with this language model with the interpolation weight determined on the heldout set. The test set for perplexity evaluations consists of 5000 sentences (35K words) and the heldout set had 2000 sentences (12K words). The test set for word error rate evaluation consists of 520 utterances.

5.1 Data collection from web

We downloaded around 100GB data from the web using automatically generated queries. Candidate query terms were generated by comparing the probabilities of word n-grams in the in-domain text with a background model of conversational speech. The prominent unigram, bigram and trigram word sequences were selected and combined to form queries for Google. The top 20 URLs returned by Google for each such conjunction of queries were downloaded and converted to text. The converted data from HTML typically does not have well defined sentence boundaries. We piped the text through a maximum entropy based sentence boundary detector to insert better sentence boundary marks. Sentences and documents with high OOV rates were rejected as noise to keep the

	10K	20K	40K
No Web	60.0	49.6	39.7
AllWeb	57.1	48.1	38.2
PPL	56.1	48.1	38.2
BLEU	56.3	48.2	38.3
LPU	56.3	48.2	38.3
Proposed	**54.8**	**46.8**	**38.1**

Table 3: Perplexity of testdata with the web adapted model for different number of initial sentences. Corpus size=150M

converted text clean. After filtering and normalization the downloaded data amounted to 320M words. We use a 150M word subset of this downloaded data for our initial experiments.

5.2 Experiments on 150M web-data

We first compare our proposed algorithm against baselines based on perplexity (PPL), BLEU and LPU classification (Section 2) in terms of test set perplexity. As the comparison shows, the proposed algorithm outperforms the rank and select schemes with just 10% of data. Table 3 shows the test set perplexity with different amounts of initial in-domain data. Table 4 shows the number of sentences selected for the best perplexity on the held-out set by the above schemes. *No Web* refers to the language model built from just in-domain data with no web-data. *AllWeb* refers to the case where the entire web-data was used.

The WER results are shown in Table 5. The average reduction in WER is close to 3% (relative). It can be seen that adding data from the web without proper filtering can actually harm the performance of the speech recognition system when the initial in-domain data size increases. This can be attributed to the large increase in vocabulary size which increases the acoustic decoder perplexity.

	10K	20K	40K
PPL	93	92	91
BLEU	91	90	89
LPU	90	88	87
Proposed	**12**	**11**	**12**

Table 4: Percentage of web-data selected for different number of initial sentences. Corpus size=150M

	10K	20K	40K
No Web	19.8	18.9	17.9
AllWeb	19.5	19.1	17.9
PPL	19.2	18.8	17.9
BLEU	19.3	18.8	17.9
LPU	19.2	18.8	17.8
Proposed	**18.3**	**18.2**	**17.3**

Table 5: Word Error Rate (WER) with web adapted models for different number of initial sentences. Corpus size=150M

5.3 Final results

To test how the performance of our algorithm scales with increasing data, we conducted experiments on a larger data set of 850M words which consisted of the medical domain collection of 320M words collected from the web and a 525M word collection published by the University of Washington for the Fisher corpus (Cetin, 2005). We will provide comparison with only the perplexity based rank-and-select system, as LPU and the BLEU based system are hard to scale to large text collections. Also, our results on the 150M set suggest that the performance of these systems is comparable to perplexity based selection.

The results on PPL and WER (Table 6, Table 7) follow the same trend as in the 150M data set. The importance of proper data selection is highlighted by the fact that there was little to no improvement in the unfiltered case (*AllWeb*) by adding the extra data, whereas there were consistent improvements when the proposed iterative selection algorithm was used. Perplexity reduction in relative terms was 7%,5% and 4% for the 10K,20K and 40K in-domain set, respectively. Corresponding WER improvements in relative terms were 6% ,4% and 4%. It is interesting to note that for our data selection scheme the perplexity improvments correlate surprisingly well with WER improvments. A plausible explanation is that the perplexity improvments are accompanied by a significant reduction in the number of language model parameters.

Table 8 shows the percentage of data selected using the proposed scheme and PPL based rank-and-select. We are able to achieve around a factor of 9 reduction in the selected data size. This translates to (Table 9) a factor of 7 reduction in the number of estimated language model parameters (bigram+trigram) and a 30% reduction in the vocabulary size.

	10K	20K	40K
No Web	60.0	49.6	39.7
AllWeb	56.9	47.7	38.2
PPL	55.8	47.4	38.2
Proposed	**52.6**	**45.3**	**37.1**

Table 6: Perplexity of testdata with the web adapted model for different number of initial sentences. Corpus size=850M

	10K	20K	40K
No Web	19.8	18.9	17.9
AllWeb	19.3	19.1	17.9
PPL	19.1	18.7	17.9
Proposed	**18.0**	**17.9**	**17.1**

Table 7: Word Error Rate (WER) with web adapted models for different number of initial sentences. Corpus size=850M

6 Conclusion

6.1 Contribution

In this paper we presented a novel and computationally efficient scheme for selecting *relevant* subsets of sentences from large collections of text acquired from the web. Our results indicate that with this scheme, we can identify significantly smaller sets of sentences such that the models built from the selected data have a substantially sparser representation and yet perform better (in terms of both perplexity and WER) than models built from the entire corpus. On our medical domain task we were able to achieve around 3% improvment in WER with a factor of 7 reduction in language model parameters while selecting a set of sentences 10% the size of the original web-data. The proposed method clearly outperforms text cleaning methods described in recent language modeling literature by moving from individual ranking to (greedy) group selection of sentences. Although our focus in this paper was on data acquired from the web, we believe the proposed method can be used for adaptation of domain specific models from other large generic corpora.

	10K	20K	40K
PPL	88.5%	87.8%	87.3%
Proposed	**9.5%**	**10.1%**	**8.9%**

Table 8: Percentage of web-data selected for different number of initial sentences. Corpus size=850M

	unigram	bigram	trigram
NoWeb	70K	1.5M	2.7M
AllWeb	105K	25.3M	36.2M
PPL	99K	22.1M	32.4M
Proposed	**70K**	**3.2M**	**8.2M**

Table 9: Number of estimated n-grams with web adapted models for different number of initial sentences for the case with 40K in-domain sentences. Corpus size=850M

We also present new analysis techniques (Section 4) based on simulated data and relative entropy which help us to gain valuable insight into the nature of different data selection algorithms.

6.2 Scope of this work

The research effort presented in this paper is directed towards selecting relevant domain specific data from large collections of generic text. We make no assumptions on how the data was collected or the use of specific web crawling and querying techniques. The methods we have developed can be seen to supplement the research effort by the machine translation community on identifying web resources (Resnik, 2003; Huang, 2005) or using web counts (Lapata, 2002) for language modeling.

6.3 Directions for future work

The proposed method can be combined with rank-and-select schemes described in Section 2. We are exploring the use of ranking to reorder the data such that the sequential selection process gives better results. Another idea we are currently investigating is to use multiple instances of the selection algorithm with different initial language models P_{init} generated by bagging. Sentence selection can then be improved by considering the composite entropy for all the models.

References

Bing Liu, Xiaoli Li, Yang Dai, Wee Sun Lee and Philip Yu. Building Text Classifiers Using Positive and Unlabeled Examples. Proceedings of ICDM. 2003.

Fei Huang, Ying Zhang and Stephan Vogel. Mining Key Phrase Translations from Web Corpora. Proceedings of EMNLP. 2005

Frank Keller, Maria Lapata and Olga Ourioupina. Using the Web to Overcome Data Sparseness. Proceedings of EMNLP. 2002.

Kamal Nigam, Andrew Kachites McCallum, Sebastian Thrun and Tom Mitchell. Text Classification from Labeled and Unlabeled Documents using EM. Journal of Machine Learning. 39(2:3)103–134. 2000.

Mirella Lapata and Frank Keller. Web-based models for natural language processing. ACM Transactions on Speech and Language Processing. 2(1),2005.

O.Cetin and Andreas Stolcke. Language Modeling in the ICSI-SRI Spring 2005 Meeting Speech Recognition Evaluation. ICSI Technical Report TR-05-006. 2005.

Philip Resnik and Noah A. Smith. The Web as a parallel corpus. Computational Linguistics. 29(3),2003.

Ruhi Sarikaya, Agustin Gravano and Yuqing Gao. Rapid Language Model Development Using External Resources For New Spoken Dialog Domains. Proceedings of ICASSP. 2005.

Tim Ng, Mari Ostendorf, Mei-Yuh Hwang, Manhung Siu, Ivan Bulyko and Xin Lei. Web-data Augmented Language Model for Mandarin Speech Recognition. Proceedings of ICASSP. 2005.

Xiaojin Zhu. Semi-Supervised Learning Literature Survey. Computer Science, University of Wisconsin-Madison.

R. C. Carrasco. Accurate computation of the relative entropy between stochastic regular grammars. RAIRO (Theoretical Informatics and Applications). 1997.

Appendix A: Fast Computation of Relative Entropy

We define the following symbols for the purpose of describing the r.e. computation:

x: The current word
h: The history $w_1..w_{n-1}$
h': The back off history $w_2..w_{n-1}$
b_h: The back-off weight for p distribution for history h
b'_h: The back-off weight for the q distribution
W: The vocabulary of the language model

Consider two n-gram language models $p(x|h)$ and $q(x|h)$.

r.e. at level n

$$D_n = \sum_{h \in H} p_h \sum_{x \in W} p(x|h) \ln \frac{p(x|h)}{q(x|h)} \tag{1}$$

We can divide the set of histories (H) at level n into H_s for all h which exist as $n-1$ gram and have a back-off weight$\neq 1$ in the p or the q distribution. The complement set ($H_{s'}$) will contain histories with a back-off 1. $H_{s'}$ corresponds to histories not seen in either language model. We define

$$D_h = \sum_{x \in W} p(x|h) \ln \frac{p(x|h)}{q(x|h)} \tag{2}$$

Then r.e. at level n D_n can be expressed as

$$\begin{aligned} D_n &= \sum_{h \in H_s} p_h D_h + \sum_{h \in H_{s'}} p_h D_h \\ &= \sum_{h \in H} p_h D_{h'} + \sum_{h \in H_s} p_h D_h - \sum_{h \in H_s} p_h D_{h'} \end{aligned}$$

Marginalizing w_1

$$D_n = D_{n-1} + \sum_{h \in H_s} p_h \left(D_h - D_{h'} \right) \tag{3}$$

D_h can be split into four terms depending on whether x/h is defined in the p or the q distribution

$$\begin{aligned} D_h &= T_1 + T_2 + T_3 + T_4 \\ T_1 &= \sum_{x \in X_1} p(x|h) \ln \frac{p(x|h)}{q(x|h)} \\ T_2 &= b_h \ln b_h \sum_{x \in X_2} p(x|h') \\ &\quad + b_h \sum_{x \in X_2} p(x|h') \ln \frac{p(x|h')}{q(x|h)} \\ T_3 &= \sum_{x \in X_3} p(x|h) \ln \frac{p(x|h)}{q(x|h')} - \ln b'_h \sum_{x \in X_3} p(x|h) \\ T_4 &= \sum_{x \in X_4} b_h p(x|h') \ln \frac{b_h p(x|h')}{b'_h q(x|h')} \\ &= b_h \ln \frac{b_h}{b'_h} \left(1 - \sum_{x \in X'_4} p(x|h') \right) + b_h D_{h'} \\ &\quad - b_h \sum_{x \in X'_4} p(x|h') \ln \frac{p(x|h')}{q(x|h')} \end{aligned} \tag{4}$$

Thus we are able to express D_h, in terms of the LM terms actually seen. Using D_h computed in this fashion in (3) we get a recursive formulation for r.e. at level n using LM densities actually seen. An alternative method for r.e. computation between finite state automata can be seen in (Carrasco, 1997).

Corrective Models for Speech Recognition of Inflected Languages

Izhak Shafran and **Keith Hall**
Center for Language and Speech Processing
Johns Hopkins University
Baltimore, MD 21218
{zakshafran,keith_hall}@jhu.edu

Abstract

This paper presents a corrective model for speech recognition of inflected languages. The model, based on a discriminative framework, incorporates word n-grams features as well as factored morphological features, providing error reduction over the model based solely on word n-gram features. Experiments on a large vocabulary task, namely the Czech portion of the MALACH corpus, demonstrate performance gain of about 1.1–1.5% absolute in word error rate, wherein morphological features contribute about a third of the improvement. A simple feature selection mechanism based on χ^2 statistics is shown to be effective in reducing the number of features by about 70% without any loss in performance, making it feasible to explore yet larger feature spaces.

1 Introduction

N-gram models have long been the stronghold of statistical language modeling approaches. Within the n-gram paradigm, straightforward approaches for increasing accuracy include using larger training sets and augmenting the contextual information within the n-gram window. Incorporating syntactic features into the context has been at the forefront of recent research (Collins et al., 2005; Rosenfeld et al., 2001; Chelba and Jelinek, 2000; Hall and Johnson, 2004). However, much of the previous work has focused on English language syntax. This paper addresses syntax as captured by the inflectional morphology of highly inflected language.

High inflection in a language is generally correlated with some level of word-order flexibility. Morphological features either directly identify or help disambiguate the syntactic participants of a sentence. Inflectional morphology works as a proxy for structured syntax in a language. Modeling morphological features in these languages not only provides an additional source of information but can also alleviate data sparsity problems.

Czech speech recognition needs to deal with two sources of errors which are absent in English, namely, the inflectional morphology and the differences in the formal (written) and colloquial (spoken) forms. Table 1 presents an example output of our speech recognizer on an utterance from a Holocaust survivor, who is recounting General Romel's desert campaign during the Second World War. In this example, the feminine past-tense form of the Czech verb for *to be* is chosen mistakenly, which is followed by a sequence of incorrect words chosen primarily to maintain agreement with the feminine form of the verb. This is an example of what we refer to as the morphological *grouping* effect. When the acoustic model prefers a word with an incorrect inflection, the language model effectively propagates the error to later words. A language model based on word-forms prefers sequences observed in the training data, which will implicitly force an agreement with the inflections of preceding words, making it difficult to stop propagating errors. Although this analysis is anecdotal in nature, the *grouping* effect appears to be prevalent in the Czech dataset used in this work. The proposed corrective model with morphological features is expected to alleviate the *grouping* effect as well as to improve the recognition of inflected languages in general.

In the following section, we present a brief review of related work on morphological language modeling and discriminative language mod-

Proceedings of the 2006 Conference on Empirical Methods in Natural Language Processing (EMNLP 2006), pages 390–398,
Sydney, July 2006.

REF	no	Ježíš	to	už	byl	Romel	hnedle	před	Alexandrií
gloss	well	Jesus	by that time	already	was	Romel	just	in front of	Alexandria
translation	oh Jesus, Romel was already just in front of Alexandria by that time								
HYP	no	Ježíš	to	už	byla	sama	hned	lepší	Alexandrie
gloss	well	Jesus	by that time	already	(she) was	herself	just	better	Alexandria
translation	oh Jesus, she was herself just better Alexandria by that time								

Table 1: An example of the *grouping* effect. The incorrect form of the verb *to be* begins a group of incorrect words in the hypothesis, but these words agree in their morphological inflection.

els. We begin the description of our work in section 3 with the type of morphological features modeled as well as their computation from the output word-lattices of a speech recognizer. Section 4 presents the corrective model and the training approach explored in the current work. A simple and effective feature selection mechanism is described in section 5. In section 6, the proposed framework is evaluated on a large vocabulary Czech speech recognition task. Results show that the morphological features provide a significant improvement over models lacking these features; subsequently, two different analyses are provided to understand the contribution of different morphological features.

2 Related Work

It has long been assumed that incorporating morphological features into a language models should help improve the performance of speech recognition systems. Early models for German showed little improvements over bigram language models and almost no improvement over trigram models (Geutner, 1995). More recently, morphology-based models have been shown to help reduce error rate for out-of-vocabulary words (Carki et al., 2000; Podvesky and Machek, 2005).

Much of the early work on morphological language modeling was focused on utilizing composite morphological tags, largely due to the difficulty in teasing apart the intricate interdependencies of the morphological features. Apart from a few exceptions, there has been little work done in exploring the morphological systems of highly inflected languages.

Kirchhoff and colleagues (2004) successfully incorporated morphological features for Arabic using a factored language model. In their approach, morphological inflections are modeled in a generative framework, and the space of factored morphological tags is explored using a genetic algorithm.

Adopting a different tactic, Choueiter and colleagues (2006) exploited morphological constraints to prune illegal morpheme sequences from ASR output. They noticed that the gains obtained from the application of such constraints in Arabic depends on the size of the vocabulary – an absolute gain of 2.4% in word error rate (WER) reduced to 0.2% when the size was increased from 64k to 800k.

Our approach to modeling morphology differs from that of Vergyri et al. (2004) and Choueiter et al. (2006). By choosing a discriminative framework and maximum entropy based estimation, we allow arbitrary features or constraints and their combinations without the need for explicit elaboration of the factored space and its backoff architecture. Thus, morphological features can be incorporated in the absence of knowledge about their interdependencies.

Several researchers have investigated techniques for improving automatic speech recognition (ASR) results by modeling the errors (Collins et al., 2005; Shafran and Byrne, 2004). Collins et al. (2005) present a corrective language model based on a discriminative framework. Initially, a set of hypotheses is generated by a baseline decoder with standard acoustic and language models. A corrective model is estimated such that it scores desired or oracle hypotheses higher than competing hypotheses. The parameters are learned via the perceptron algorithm which shifts weight away from features associated with poor hypotheses and towards those associated with better hypotheses. By the appropriate choice of desired hypotheses, the model parameters can be estimated to minimize WER in speech recognition. During decoding, the model can then be used to rerank a set of hypotheses, and hence, it is also known as a *reranking* framework. This paradigm allows modeling arbitrary input features, even syntactic features obtained from a parser. We adopt a variant of this framework where the corrective model is based on a conditional model estimated by the maximum entropy procedure (Charniak and Johnson, 2005) and we investigate its effectiveness in modeling morphological features for highly inflected languages, in particular, Czech.

3 Inflectional Morphology

Inflectional abundance in a language generally corresponds to some flexibility in word order. In a free word-order language, the order of sentential participants is relatively unconstrained. This does not mean a speaker of the language can arbitrarily choose an order. Word-order choice may change the semantic and/or pragmatic interpretation of an utterance. Czech is known as a free word-order language allowing for subject, object, and verbal components to come in any order. Morphological inflection in these languages must include a syntactic *case* marker to allow the determination of which participants are subjects (nominative case), objects (accusative or dative) and other such entities. Additionally, morphological inflection encodes features such as gender and number. The agreement of these features between sentential components (adjectives with nouns, subjects with verbs, etc.) may further disambiguate the target of a modifier (e.g., identifying the noun that is modified by a particular adjective).

The increased flexibility in word order aggravates the data sparsity of standard n-gram language model for two reasons: first, the number of valid configurations of a group of words increases with the free order; and second, lexical items are decorated with the inflectional morphemes, multiplying the number of word-forms that appear.

In addition to modeling sequences of word-forms, we model sequences of morphologically reduced *lemmas*, sequence of morphological *tags* and sequences of various factored representations of the morphological tags. Factoring a word into the semantics-bearing lemma and syntax-bearing morphological tag alleviates the data sparsity problem to some extent. However, the number of possible factorizations of n-grams is large. The approach adopted in this work is to provide a rich class of features and defer the modeling of their interaction to the learning procedure.

3.1 Extracting Morphological Features

The extraction of reliable morphological features critically effects further morphological modeling. Here, we first select the most likely morphological analysis for each word using a morphological tagger. In particular, we use the Czech feature-based tagger distributed with the Prague Dependency Treebank (Hajič et al., 2005). The tagger is based on a morphological analyzer which uses a lexicon and a rule-based tag guesser for words not found in the lexicon. Trained by the maximum entropy procedure, the tagger uses left and right contextual features from the input string. Currently, this is the best available Czech-language tagger. See Hajič and Vidová-Hladká (1998) for further details on the tagger.

Label	Description	# Values
lemma	Reduced lexeme	$< \|vocab\|$
POS	Coarse part-of-speech	12
D-POS	Detailed part-of-speech	65
gen	Grammatical Gender	10
num	Grammatical Number	5
case	Grammatical Case	8

Table 2: Czech morphological features used in the current work. The # Values field indicates the size of the closed set of possible values. Not all values are used in the annotated data.

A disadvantage of such an approach is that the tagger works on strings rather than the word-lattices that we expect from an ASR system. Therefore, we must extract a set of strings from the lattices prior to tagging. An alternative approach is to hypothesize all morphological analyses for each word in the lattice, thereby considering the entire set of analyses as features in the model. In the current implementation we have chosen to use a tagger to reduce the complexity of the model by limiting the number of active features while still obtaining relatively reliable features. Moreover, systematic errors in tagging can be potentially compensated by the corrective model.

The initial stage of feature extraction begins with an analysis of the data on which we train and test our models. The process follows:

1. Extract the n-best hypotheses according to a baseline model, where n varies from 50 to 1000 in the current work.

2. Tag each of the hypotheses with the morphological tagger.

3. Re-encode the original word strings along with their tagged morphological analysis in a weighted finite state transducer to allow

Word-form	to	období	bylo	poměrné	krátké
gloss	that	period	was	relatively	short
lemma	ten	období	být	poměrně	krátký
tag	PDNS1	NNNS1	VpNS-	Dg—	AAFS2

Table 3: A morphological analysis of Czech. This analyses was generated by the Hajič tagger.

form	to	období	bylo	poměrné	krátké
	to_období	období_bylo	bylo_poměrné	poměrné_krátké	
lemma	ten	období	být	poměrně	krátký
	ten_období	období_být	být_poměrně	poměrně_krátký	
tag	PDNS1	NNNS1	VpNS-	Dg—	AAFS2
	PDNS1_NNNS1	NNNS1_VpNS-	VpNS-_Dg—	Dg—_AAFS2	
POS	P	N	V	D	A
	P_N	N_V	V_D	D_A	
...			...		
case	1	1	-	-	2
	1_1	1_-	-_0	-_2	
num/case	S1	S1	S-	–	S2
	S1_S1	S1_S-	S-_–	–_S2	
...			...		

Table 4: Examples of the n-grams extracted from the Czech sentence *To období bylo poměrně krátké.* A subset of the feature classes is presented here. The morphological feature values are those assigned by the Hajič tagger.

an efficient means of projecting the hypotheses from word-form to morphology and vice versa.

4. Extract appropriately factored n-gram features for each hypothesis as described below.

Each word state in the original lattice has an associated lemma/tag from which a variety of n-gram features can be extracted.

From the morphological features assigned by the tagger, we chose to retain only a subset and discard the less reliable features which are semantic in nature. The basic morphological features used are detailed in Table 2. In the tag-based model, a string of 5 characters representing the 5 morphological fields is used as a unique identifier. The derived features include n-grams of POS, D-POS, gender (gen), number (num), and case features as well as their combinations.

POS, D-POS Captures the sub-categorization of the part-of-speech tags.

gen, num Captures complex gender-number agreement features.

num, case Captures number agreement between specific case markers.

POS, case Captures associated POS/Case features (e.g., adjectives associated with nominative elements).

The paired features allow for complex inflectional interactions and are less sparse than the composite 5-component morphological tags. Additionally, the morphologically reduced lemma and n-grams of lemmas are used as features in the models.

Table 3 presents a morphological analysis of the Czech sentence *To období bylo poměrně krátké.* The encoded tags represent the first 5 fields of the Prague Dependency Treebank morphological encoding and correspond to the last 5 rows of Table 2. Features for this sentence include the word-form, lemma, and composite tag features as well as the components of each tag and the above mentioned concatenation of tag fields. Additionally, n-grams of each of these features are included. Bigram features extracted from an example sentence are illustrated in Table 4.

The following section describes how the features extracted above are modeled in a discriminative framework to reduce word error rate.

4 Corrective Model and Estimation

In this work, we adopt the reranking framework of Charniak and Johnson (2005) for incorporating morphological features. The model scores each test hypothesis y using a linear function, $v_\theta(y)$, of features extracted from the hypothesis $f_j(y)$ and model parameters θ_j, i.e., $v_\theta(y) = \sum_j \theta_j f_j(y)$. The hypothesis with the highest score is then chosen as the output.

The model parameters, θ, are learned from a training set by maximum entropy estimation of the following conditional model:

$$\prod_s \sum_{y_i \in Y_s : g(y_i) = max_j g(y_j)} P_\theta(y_i|Y_s)$$

Here, $Y_s = \{y_j\}$ is the set of hypotheses for each training utterance s and the function g returns an extrinsic evaluation score, which in our case is the WER of the hypothesis. $P_\theta(y_i|Y_s)$ is modeled by a maximum entropy distribution of the form, $P_\theta(y_i|Y_s) = \exp v_\theta(y_i) / \sum_j \exp v_\theta(y_j)$. This choice simplifies the numerical estimation procedure since the gradient of the log-likelihood with respect to a parameter, say θ_j, reduces to difference in expected counts of the associated feature, $E_\theta[f_j|Y_s] - E_\theta[f_j|y_i \in Y_s : g(y_i) = max_j g(y_j)]$. To allow good generalization properties, a Gaussian regularization term is also included in the cost function.

A set of hypotheses Y_s is generated for each training utterance using a baseline ASR system. Care is taken to reduce the bias in decoding the training set by following a jack-knife procedure. The training set is divided into 20 subsets and each subset is decoded after excluding the transcripts of that subset from the language model of the decoder.

The model allows the exploration of a large feature space, including n-grams of words, morphological tags, and factored tags. In a large vocabulary system, this could be an enormous space. However, in a discriminative maximum entropy framework, only the observed features are considered. Among the observed features, those associated with words that are correct in all hypotheses do not provide any additional discrimination capability. Mathematically, the gradient of the log-likelihood with respect to the parameters of these features tends to zero and they may be discarded. Additionally, the parameters associated with features that are rarely observed in the training set are difficult to learn reliably and may be discarded.

To avoid redundant features, we focus on words which are frequently incorrect; this is the *error region* we aim to model. In the training utterance, the error regions of a hypothesis are identified using the alignment corresponding to the minimum edit distance from the reference, akin to computing word error rate. To mark all the error regions in an ASR lattice, the minimum edit distance alignment is obtained using equivalent finite state machine operations (Mohri, 2002). From amongst all the error regions in the training lattices, the most frequent 12k words in error are shortlisted. Features are computed in the corrective model only if they involve words for the shortlist. The parameters, θ, are estimated by numerical optimization as in (Charniak and Johnson, 2005).

5 Feature Selection

The space of features spanned by the cross-product space of words, lemmas, tags, factored-tags and their n-gram can potentially be overwhelming. However, not all of these features are equally important and many of the features may not have a significant impact on the word error rate. The maximum entropy framework affords the luxury of discarding such irrelevant features without much bookkeeping, unlike maximum likelihood models. In the context of modeling morphological features, we investigate the efficacy of simple feature selection based on the χ^2 statistics, which has been shown to effective in certain text categorization problems. e.g. (Yang and Pedersen, 1997).

The χ^2 statistics measures the lack of independence by computing the deviation of the observed counts O_i from the expected counts E_i.

$$\chi^2 = \sum_i (O_i - E_i)^2 / E_i$$

In our case, there are two classes – oracle hypotheses c and competing hypotheses $\bar{c}$. The expected count is the count marginalized over classes.

$$\begin{aligned} \chi^2(f,c) &= \frac{(P(f,c) - P(f))^2}{P(f)} + \frac{(P(f,\bar{c}) - P(f))^2}{P(f)} \\ &+ \frac{(P(\bar{f},c) - P(\bar{f}))^2}{P(\bar{f})} + \frac{(P(\bar{f},\bar{c}) - P(\bar{f}))^2}{P(\bar{f})} \end{aligned}$$

This can be simplified using a two-way contingency table of feature and class, where A is the number of times f and c co-occur, B is the number of times f occurs without c, C is the number of times c occurs without f, and D is the number of times neither f nor c occurs, and N is the total number of examples. Then, the χ^2 is defined to be:

$$\chi^2(f,c) = \frac{N \times (AD - CB)^2}{(A+C) \times (B+D) \times (A+B) \times (C+D)}$$

The χ^2 statistics are computed for all the features and the features with larger value are retained. Alternatives feature selection mechanisms such as those based on mutual information and information gain are less reliable than χ^2 statistics for heavy-tailed distributions. More complex feature selection mechanism would entail computing higher order interaction between features which is computationally expensive and so is not explored in this work.

6 Empirical Evaluation

The corrective model presented in this work is evaluated on a large vocabulary task consisting of spontaneous spoken testimonies in Czech language, which is a subset of the multilingual MALACH corpus (Psutka et al., 2003).

6.1 Task

For acoustic model training, transcripts are available for about 62 hours of speech from 336 speakers, amounting to 507k spoken words from a vocabulary of 79k. A portion of this data containing speech from 44 speakers, about 21k words in all is treated as development set (dev). The test set (eval) consists of about 2 hours of speech from 10 new speakers and contains about 15k words.

6.2 Baseline ASR System

The baseline ASR system uses perceptual linear prediction (PLP) features which is computed on 44KHz input speech at the rate of 10 frames per second, and is normalized to have zero mean and unit variance per speaker. The acoustic models are made of 3-state HMM triphones, whose observation distributions are clustered into about 4500 allophonic (triphone) states. Each state is modeled by a 16 component Gaussian mixture with diagonal covariances. The parameters of the acoustic models are initially estimated by maximum likelihood and then refined by five iterations of maximum mutual information estimation (MMI).

Unlike other comparable corpora, this corpus contains a relatively high percentage of colloquial words – about 9% of the vocabulary and 7% of the tokens. For the sake of downstream application, the colloquial variants are subsumed in the lexicon. As a result, common words contain several pronunciation variants, and a few have as many as 14 variants.

For the first pass decoding, a language model was created by interpolating the in-domain model (weight=0.75), estimated from 600k words of transcripts with an out-of-domain model, estimated from 15M words of Czech National Corpus (Psutka et al., 2003). Both models are parameterized by a trigram language model with Katz back-off. The decoding graph was built by composing the language model, the lexical transducer and the context-dependent transducer (phones to triphones) into a single compact finite state machine.

The baseline ASR system decodes test utterance in two passes. A first pass decoding is performed with MMIE acoustic models, whose output transcripts are bootstrapped to estimate two maximum likelihood linear regression transforms for each speaker using five iterations. A second pass decoding is then performed with the new speaker adapted acoustic models. The resulting performance is given in Table 5. The performance reflects the difficulty of transcribing spontaneous speech from the elderly speakers whose speech is also heavily accented and emotional in this corpus.

	1-best	1000-best
Dev	29.9	21.5
Eval	35.9	22.4

Table 5: The performance of the baseline ASR system is reported, showing the word error rate of 1-best MAP hypothesis and the oracle in 1000-best hypotheses for dev and eval sets.

6.3 Experiments With Morphology

We present a set of contrastive experiments to gauge the performance of the corrective models and the contribution of morphological features. For training the corrective models, 50 best hypotheses are generated for each utterance using the

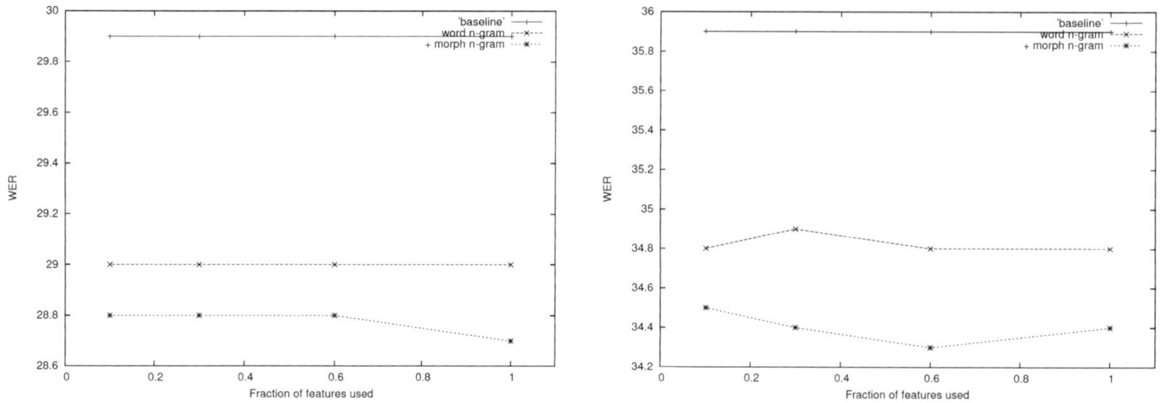

$(a) Devel$ $(b) Eval$

Figure 1: Feature selection via χ^2 statistics helps reduce the number of parameters by 70% without any loss in performance, as observed in dev (a) and eval (b) sets.

jack-knife procedure mentioned earlier. For each hypothesis, bigram and unigram features are computed which consist of word-forms, lemmas, morphologoical tags, factored morphological tags, and the likelihood from the baseline ASR system. For testing, the baseline ASR system is used to generate 1000 best hypotheses for each utterance. These are then evaluated using the corrective models and the best scored hypothesis is chosen as the output.

Table 6 summarizes the results on two test sets – the dev and the eval set. A corrective model with word bigram features improve the word error rate by about an absolute 1% over the baseline. Morphological features provide a further gain on both the test sets consistently.

Features	Dev	Eval
Baseline	29.9	35.9
Word bigram	29.0	34.8
+ Morph bigram	28.7	34.4

Table 6: The word error rate of the corrective model is compared with that of the baseline ASR system, illustrating the improvement in performance with morphological features.

The gains on the dev set are significant at the level of $p < 0.001$ for three standard NIST tests, namely, matched pair sentence segment, signed pair comparison, and Wilcoxon signed rank tests. For the smaller eval set the significant levels were lower for morphological features. The relative gains observed are consistent over a variety of conditions that we have tested including the ones reported below.

Subsequently, we investigated the impact of reducing the number of features using χ^2 statistics, as described in section 5. The experiments with bigram features of word-forms and morphology were repeated using reduced feature sets, and the performance was measured at 10%, 30% and 60% of their original features. The results, as illustrated in Figure 1, show that the word error rate does not change significantly even after the number of features are reduced by 70%. We have also observed that most of the gain can be achieved by evaluating 200 best hypotheses from the baseline ASR system, which could further reduce the computational cost for time-sensitive applications.

6.4 Analysis of Feature Classes

The impact of feature classes can be analyzed by excluding all features from a particular class and evaluating the performance of the resulting model without re-estimation. Figure 2 illustrates the effectiveness of different features class. The y-axis shows the gain in F-score, which is monotonic with the word error rate, on the entire development dataset. In this analysis, the likelihood score from the baseline ASR system was omitted since our interest is in understanding the effectiveness of categorical features such as words, lemmas and tags.

The most independently influential feature class is the factored tag features. This corresponds with

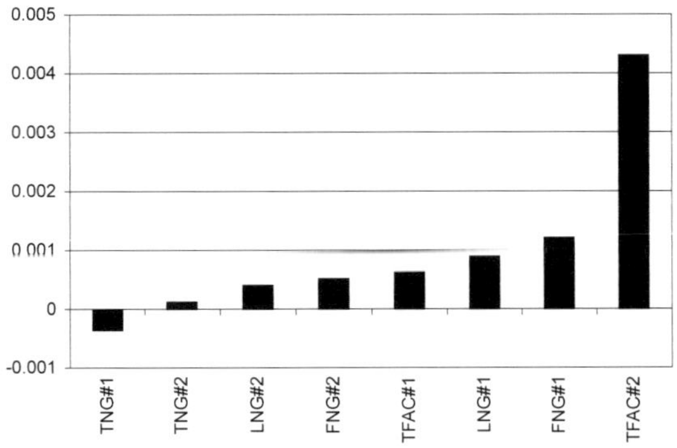

Figure 2: Analysis of features classes for a bigram form, lemma, tag, and factored tag model. Y-axis is the contribution of this feature if added to an otherwise complete model. Feature classes are labeled: TNG – tag n-gram, LNG – lemma n-gram, FNG – form n-gram and TFAC – factored tag n-grams. The number following the # represents the order of the n-gram.

our belief that modeling morphological features requires detailed models of the morphology; in this model the composite morphological tag n-gram features (TNG) offer little contribution in the presence of the factored features.

Analysis of feature reduction by the χ^2 statistics reveals a similar story. When features are ranked according to their χ^2 statistics, about 57% of the factored tag n-grams occur in the top 10% while only 7% of the word n-grams make it. The lemma and composite tag n-grams give about 6.2% and 19.2% respectively. Once again, the factored tag is the most influential feature class.

7 Conclusion

We have proposed a corrective modeling framework for incorporating inflectional morphology into a discriminative language model. Empirical results on a difficult Czech speech recognition task support our claim that morphology can help improve speech recognition results for these types of languages. Additionally, we present a feature selection method that effectively reduces the model size by about 70% while having little or no impact on recognition accuracy. Model size reduction greatly reduces training time which can often be prohibitively expensive for maximum entropy training.

Analysis of the models learned on our task show that factored morphological tags along with word-forms provide most of the discriminative power; and, in the presence of these features, composite morphological tags are of little use.

The corrective model outlined here operates on the word lattices produced by an ASR system. The morphological tags are inferred from the word sequences in the lattice. Alternatively, by employing an ASR system that models the morphological constraints in the acoustics as in (Chung and Seneff, 1999), the corrective model could be applied directly to a lattice with morphological tags.

When dealing with ASR word lattices, the efficacy of the proposed feature selection mechanism can be exploited to eliminate the intermediate tagger, a potential source of errors. Instead of considering the best morphological analysis, the model could consider all possible analyses of the words. Further, the feature space could be enriched with syntactic features which are known to be useful (Collins et al., 2005). The task of modeling is then tackled by feature selection and the maximum entropy training procedure.

8 Acknowledgements

The authors would like to thank William Byrne for discussions on modeling aspects, and Jan Hajič, Petr Němec, and Vaclav Novák for discussions regarding Czech morphology and tagging. This work was supported by the NSF (U.S.A) under the Information Technology Research (ITR) program, NSF IIS Award No. 0122466.

References

Kenan Carki, Petra Geutner, and Tanja Schultz. 2000. Turkish LVCSR: towards better speech recognition for agglutinative languages. In *Proceedings of the 2000 IEEE International Conference on Acoustics, Speech, and Signal Processing*, pages 3688–3691.

Eugene Charniak and Mark Johnson. 2005. Coarse-to-fine n-best parsing and MaxEnt discriminative reranking. In *Proceedings of the 43rd Annual Meeting of the Association for Computational Linguistics*.

Ciprian Chelba and Frederick Jelinek. 2000. Structured language modeling. *Computer Speech and Language*, 14(4):283–332.

Ghinwa Choueiter, Daniel Povey, Stanley Chen, and Geoffrey Zweig. 2006. Morpheme-based language modeling for Arabic LVCSR. In *Proceedings of the 2006 IEEE International Conference on Acoustics, Speech, and Signal Processing*, Toulouse, France.

Grace Chung and Stephanie Seneff. 1999. A hierarchical duration model for speech recognition based on the ANGIE framework. *Speech Communication*, 27:113–134.

Michael Collins, Brian Roark, and Murat Saraclar. 2005. Discriminative syntactic language modeling for speech recognition. In *Proceedings of the 43rd Annual Meeting of the Association for Computational Linguistics (ACL'05)*, pages 507–514, Ann Arbor, Michigan, June. Association for Computational Linguistics.

Petra Geutner. 1995. Using morphology towards better large-vocabulary speech recognition systems. In *Proceedings of the 1995 IEEE International Conference on Acoustics, Speech, and Signal Processing*, pages 445–448, Detroit, MI.

Jan Hajič and Barbora Vidová-Hladká. 1998. Tagging inflective languages: Prediction of morphological categories for a rich, structured tagset. In *Proceedings of the COLING-ACL Conference*, pages 483–490, Montreal, Canada.

Jan Hajič, Eva Hajičová, Petr Pajas, Jarmila Panevová, Petr Sgall, and Barbora Vidová Hladká. 2005. The prague dependency treebank 2.0. http://ufal.mff.cuni.cz/pdt2.0.

Keith Hall and Mark Johnson. 2004. Attention shifting for parsing speech. In *Proceedings of the 42nd Annual Meeting of the Association for Computational Linguistics*, pages 41–47, Barcelona.

Mehryar Mohri. 2002. Edit-distance of weighted automata. In *Proceedings of the 7th International Conference on Implementation and Application of Automata, Jean-Marc Champarnaud and Denis Maurel, Eds.*

Petr Podvesky and Pavel Machek. 2005. Speech recognition of Czech—inclusion of rare words helps. In *Proceedings of the ACL Student Research Workshop*, pages 121–126, Ann Arbor, Michigan, June. Association for Computational Linguistics.

Josef Psutka, Pavel Ircing, Josef V. Psutka, Vlasta Radovic, William Byrne, Jan Hajič, Jiri Mirovsky, and Samuel Gustman. 2003. Large vocabulary ASR for spontaneous Czech in the MALACH project. In *Proceedings of the 8th European Conference on Speech Communication and Technology*, Geneva, Switzerland.

Roni Rosenfeld, Stanley F. Chen, and Xiaojin Zhu. 2001. Whole-sentence exponential language models: a vehicle for linguistic-statistical integration. *Computers Speech and Language*, 15(1).

Izhak Shafran and William Byrne. 2004. Task-specific minimum Bayes-risk decoding using learned edit distance. In *Proceedings of the 7th International Conference on Spoken Language Processing*, volume 3, pages 1945–48, Jeju Islands, Korea.

Dimitra Vergyri, Katrin Kirchhoff, Kevin Duh, and Andreas Stolcke. 2004. Morphology-based language modeling for arabic speech recognition. In *Proceedings of the International Conference on Spoken Language Processing (ICSLP/Interspeech 2004).*

Yiming Yang and Jan 0. Pedersen. 1997. A comparative study on feature selection in text categorization. In *Proceedings of the 14th International Conference on Machine Learning*, pages 412 – 420, San Francisco, CA, USA.

Lexicon Acquisition for Dialectal Arabic Using Transductive Learning

Kevin Duh
Dept. of Electrical Engineering
University of Washington
Seattle, WA, USA
duh@ee.washington.edu

Katrin Kirchhoff
Dept. of Electrical Engineering
University of Washington
Seattle, WA, USA
katrin@ee.washington.edu

Abstract

We investigate the problem of learning a part-of-speech (POS) lexicon for a resource-poor language, dialectal Arabic. Developing a high-quality lexicon is often the first step towards building a POS tagger, which is in turn the front-end to many NLP systems. We frame the lexicon acquisition problem as a transductive learning problem, and perform comparisons on three transductive algorithms: Transductive SVMs, Spectral Graph Transducers, and a novel Transductive Clustering method. We demonstrate that lexicon learning is an important task in resource-poor domains and leads to significant improvements in tagging accuracy for dialectal Arabic.

1 Introduction

Due to the rising importance of globalization and multilingualism, there is a need to build natural language processing (NLP) systems for an increasingly wider range of languages, including those languages that have traditionally not been the focus of NLP research. The development of NLP technologies for a new language is a challenging task since one needs to deal not only with language-specific phenomena but also with a potential lack of available resources (e.g. lexicons, text, annotations). In this study we investigate the problem of learning a part-of-speech (POS) lexicon for a resource-poor language, dialectal Arabic.

Developing a high-quality POS lexicon is the first step towards training a POS tagger, which in turn is typically the front end for other NLP applications such as parsing and language modeling. In the case of resource-poor languages (and dialectal Arabic in particular), this step is much more critical than is typically assumed: a lexicon with too few constraints on the possible POS tags for a given word can have disastrous effects on tagging accuracy. Whereas such constraints can be obtained from large hand-labeled corpora or high-quality annotation tools in the case of resource-rich languages, no such resources are available for dialectal Arabic. Instead, constraints on possible POS tags must be inferred from a small amount of tagged words, or imperfect analysis tools. This can be seen as the problem of learning complex, structured outputs (multi-class labels, with a different number of classes for different words and dependencies among the individual labels) from partially labeled data.

Our focus is on investigating several machine learning techniques for this problem. In particular, we argue that lexicon learning in resource-poor languages can be best viewed as transductive learning. The main contribution of this work are: (1) a comprehensive evaluation of three transductive algorithms (Transductive SVM, Spectral Graph Transducer, and a new technique called Transductive Clustering) as well as an inductive SVM on this task; and (2) a demonstration that lexicon learning is a worthwhile investment and leads to significant improvements in the tagging accuracy for dialectal Arabic.

The outline of the paper is as follows: Section 2 describes the problem in more detail and discusses the situation in dialectal Arabic. The transductive framework and algorithms for lexicon learning are elaborated in Section 3. Sections 4 and 5 describe the data and system. Experimental results are presented in Section 6. We discuss some related work in Section 7 before concluding in Section 8.

Proceedings of the 2006 Conference on Empirical Methods in Natural Language Processing (EMNLP 2006), pages 399–407,
Sydney, July 2006.

2 The Importance of Lexicons in Resource-poor POS Tagging

2.1 Unsupervised Tagging

The lack of annotated training data in resource-poor languages necessitates the use of unsupervised taggers. One commonly-used unsupervised tagger is the Hidden Markov model (HMM), which models the joint distribution of a word sequence $w_{0:M}$ and tag sequence $t_{0:M}$ as:

$$P(t_{0:M}, w_{0:M}) = \prod_{i=0}^{M} p(w_i|t_i)p(t_i|t_{i-1}, t_{i-2}) \tag{1}$$

This is a trigram HMM. Unsupervised learning is performed by running the Expectation-Maximization (EM) algorithm on raw text. In this procedure, the tag sequences are unknown, and the probability tables $p(w_i|t_i)$ and $p(t_i|t_{i-1}, t_{i-2})$ are iteratively updated to maximize the likelihood of the observed word sequences.

Although previous research in unsupervised tagging have achieved high accuracies rivaling supervised methods (Kupiec, 1992; Brill, 1995), much of the success is due to the use of artificially *constrained* lexicons. Specifically, the lexicon is a wordlist where each word is annotated with the set of all its possible tags. (We will call the set of possible tags of a given word the *POS-set* of that word; an example: POS-set of the English word `bank` may be {`NN`, `VB`}.) Banko and Moore (2004) showed that unsupervised tagger accuracies on English degrade from 96% to 77% if the lexicon is not constrained such that only high frequency tags exist in the POS-set for each word.

Why is the lexicon so critical in unsupervised tagging? The answer is that it provides additional knowledge about word-tag distributions that may otherwise be difficult to glean from raw text alone. In the case of unsupervised HMM taggers, the lexicon provides constraints on the probability tables $p(w_i|t_i)$ and $p(t_i|t_{i-1}, t_{i-2})$. Specifically, the lexical probability table is initialized such that $p(w_i|t_i) = 0$ if and only if tag t_i is not included in the POS-set of word w_i. The transition probability table is initialized such that $p(t_i|t_{i-1}, t_{i-2}) = 0$ if and only if the tag sequence (t_i, t_{i-1}, t_{i-2}) never occurs in the tag lattice induced by the lexicon on the raw text. The effect of these zero-probability initialization is that they will always stay zero throughout the EM procedure (modulo the effects of smoothing). This therefore acts as hard constraints and biases the EM algorithm to avoid certain solutions when maximizing likelihood. If the lexicon is accurate, then the EM algorithm can learn very good predictive distributions from raw text only; conversely, if the lexicon is poor, EM will be faced with more confusability during training and may not produce a good tagger. In general, the addition of rare tags, even if they are correct, creates a harder learning problem for EM.

Thus, a critical aspect of resource-poor POS tagging is the acquisition of a high-quality lexicon. This task is challenging because the lexicon learning algorithm must not be resource-intensive. In practice, one may be able to find analysis tools or incomplete annotations such that only a partial lexicon is available. The focus is therefore on effective machine learning algorithms for inferring a full high-quality lexicon from a partial, possibly noisy initial lexicon. We shall now discuss this situation in the context of dialectal Arabic.

2.2 Dialectal Arabic

The Arabic language consist of a collection of spoken dialects and a standard written language (Modern Standard Arabic, or MSA). The dialects of Arabic are of considerable importance since they are used extensively in almost all everyday conversations. NLP technology for dialectal Arabic is still in its infancy, however, due to the lack of data and resources. Apart from small amounts of written dialectal material in e.g. plays, novels, chat rooms, etc., data can only be obtained by recording and manually transcribing actual conversations. Annotated corpora are scarce because annotation requires another stage of manual effort beyond transcription work. In addition, basic resources such as lexicons, morphological analyzers, tokenizers, etc. have been developed for MSA, but are virtually non-existent for dialectal Arabic.

In this study, we address lexicon learning for Levantine Colloquial Arabic. We assume that only two resources are available during training: (1) raw text transcriptions of Levantine speech and (2) a morphological analyzer developed for MSA.

The lexicon learning task begins with a partial lexicon generated by applying the MSA analyzer to the Levantine wordlist. Since MSA differs from Levantine considerably in terms of syntax, morphology, and lexical choice, not all Levantine words receive an analysis. In our data, 23% of the words are un-analyzable. Thus, the goal of lexicon learning is to infer the POS-sets of the un-analyzable words, given the partially-annotated lexicon and raw text.

Details on the Levantine data and overall system are provided in Sections 4 and 5. We discuss the learning algorithms in the next section.

3 Learning Frameworks and Algorithms

Let us formally define the lexicon learning problem. We have a wordlist of size $m + u$. A portion of these words (m) are annotated with POS-set labels, which may be acquired by manual annotation or an automatic analysis tool. The set of labeled words $\{X_m\}$ is the training set, also referred to as the partial lexicon. The task is to predict the POS-sets of the remaining u unlabeled words $\{X_u\}$, the test set. The goal of lexicon learning is to label $\{X_u\}$ with low error. The final result is a full lexicon that contains POS-sets for all $m + u$ words.

3.1 Transductive Learning with Structured Outputs

We argue that the above problem formulation lends itself to a transductive learning framework. Standard *inductive learning* uses a training set of fully labeled samples in order to learn a classification function. After completion of the training phase, the learned model is then used to classify samples from a new, previously unseen test set. *Semi-supervised* inductive learning exploits unlabeled data in addition to labeled data to better learn a classification function. *Transductive learning*, first described by Vapnik (Vapnik, 1998) also describes a setting where both labeled and unlabeled data are used *jointly* to decide on a label assignment to the unlabeled data points. However, the goal here is not to learn a general classification function that can be applied to new test sets multiple times but to achieve a high-quality one-time labeling of a particular data set. Transductive learning and inductive semi-supervised learning are sometimes confused in the literature. Both approaches use unlabeled data in learning – the key difference is that a transductive classifier only optimizes the performance on the given unlabeled data while an inductive semi-supervised classifier is trained to perform well on any new unlabeled data.

Lexicon learning fits in the transductive learning framework as follows: The test set $\{X_u\}$, i.e. the unlabeled words, is static and known during learning time; we are not interested in inferring POS-sets for any words outside the word list.

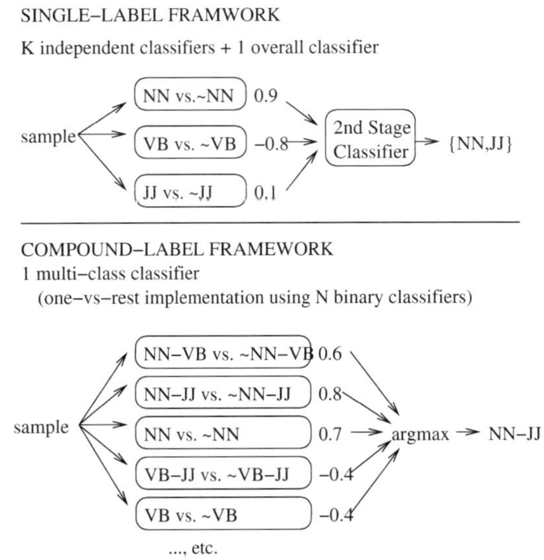

Figure 1: Learning with Structured Outputs using single or compound labels

An additional characterization of the lexicon learning problem is that it is a problem of learning with complex, structured outputs. The label for each word is its POS-set, which may contain one to K POS tags (where K is the size of the tagset, K=20 in our case). This differs from traditional classification tasks where the output is a single scalar variable.

Structured output problems like lexicon learning can be characterized by the granularity of the basic unit of labels. We define two cases: single-label and compound-label. In the single-label framework (see Figure 1), each individual POS tag is the target of classification and we have K binary classifiers each hypothesizing whether a word has a POS tag k ($k = 1, \ldots, K$). A second-stage classifier takes the results of the K individual classifiers and outputs a POS-set. This classifier can simply take all POS tags hypothesized positive by the individual binary classifiers to form the POS-set, or use a more sophisticated scheme for determining the number of POS tags (Elisseeff and Weston, 2002).

The alternative compound-label framework treats each POS-set as an atomic label for classification. A POS-set such as {"NN", "VB"} is "compounded" into one label "NN-VB", which results in a different label than, say, "NN" or "NN-JJ". Suppose there exist N distinct POS-sets in the training data; then we have N atomic units for labeling. Thus a (N-ary) multi-class classifier is employed to directly predict the POS-set of a word. If only binary classifiers are available (i.e. in the case of Support Vector Machines), one can use one-vs-rest, pairwise, or error correcting code schemes to implement the multi-class classification.

The single-label framework is potentially ill-suited for capturing the dependencies between POS tags. Dependencies between POS tags arise since some tags, such as "NN" and "NNP" can often be tagged to the same word and therefore co-occur in the POS-set label. The compound-label framework implicitly captures tag co-occurrence, but potentially suffers from training data fragmentation as well as the inability to hypothesize POS-sets that do not already exist in the training data. In our initial experiments, the compound-label framework gave better classification results; thus we implemented all of our algorithms in the multi-class framework (using the one-vs-rest scheme and choosing the argmax as the final decision).

3.2 Transductive Clustering

How does a transductive algorithm effectively utilize unlabeled samples in the learning process? One popular approach is the application of the so-called *cluster assumption*, which intuitively states that samples close to each other (i.e. samples that form a cluster) should have similar labels.

Transductive clustering (TC) is a simple algorithm that directly implements the cluster assumption. The algorithm clusters labeled and unlabeled samples jointly, then uses the labels of labeled samples to infer the labels of unlabeled words in the same cluster. This idea is relatively straightforward, yet what is needed is a principled way of deciding the correct number of clusters and the precise way of label transduction (e.g. based on majority vote vs. probability thresholds). Typically, such parameters are decided heuristically (e.g. (Duh and Kirchhoff, 2005a)) or by tuning on a labeled development set; for resource-poor languages, however, no such set may be available.

As suggested by (El-Yaniv and Gerzon, 2005), the TC algorithm can utilize a theoretical error bound as a principled way of determining the parameters. Let $\hat{R}_h(X_m)$ be the empirical risk of a given hypothesis (i.e. classifier) on the training set; let $R_h(X_u)$ be the test risk. (Derbeko et al., 2004) derive an error bound which states that, with probability $1-\delta$, the risk on the test samples is bounded by:

$$R_h(X_u) \leq \hat{R}_h(X_m) + \sqrt{\left(\frac{m+u}{u}\right)\left(\frac{u+1}{u}\right)\left(\frac{\ln\frac{1}{p(h)}+\ln\frac{1}{\delta}}{2m}\right)} \quad (2)$$

i.e. the test risk is bounded by the empirical risk on the labeled data, $\hat{R}_h(X_m)$, plus a term that varies with the prior $p(h)$ of the hypothesis or classifier. This is a PAC-Bayesian bound (McAllester, 1999). The prior $p(h)$ indicates ones prior belief on the hypothesis h over the set of all possible hypotheses. If the prior is low or the empirical risk is high, then the bound is large, implying that test risk may be large. A good hypothesis (i.e. classifier) will ideally have a small value for the bound, thus predicting a small expected test risk.

The PAC-Bayesian bound is important because it provides a theoretical guarantee on the quality of a hypothesis. Moreover, the bound in Eq. 2 is particularly useful because it is easily computable on any hypothesis h, assuming that one is given the value of $p(h)$. Given two hypothesized labelings of the test set, h_1 and h_2, the one with the lower PAC-Bayesian bound will achieve a lower expected test risk. Therefore, one can use the bound as a principled way of choosing the parameters in the Transductive Clustering algorithm: First, a large number of different clusterings is created; then the one that achieves the lowest PAC-Bayesian bound is chosen. The pseudo-code is given in Figure 2.

(El-Yaniv and Gerzon, 2005) has applied the Transductive Clustering algorithm successfully to binary classification problems and demonstrated improvements over the current state-of-the-art Spectral Graph Transducers (Section 3.4). We use the algorithm as described in (Duh and Kirchhoff, 2005b), which adapts the algorithm to structured output problems. In particular, the modification involves a different estimate of the priors $p(h)$, which was assumed to be uniform in (El-Yaniv and Gerzon, 2005). Since there are many possible h, adopting a uniform prior will lead to small values of $p(h)$ and thus a loose bound for all h. Probability mass should only be spent on POS-sets that are possible, and as such, we calculate $p(h)$ based on frequencies of compound-labels in the training data (i.e. an empirical prior).

3.3 Transductive SVM

Transductive SVM (TSVM) (Joachims, 1999) is an algorithm that implicitly implements the cluster

For $\tau = 2 : C$ (C is set arbitrarily to a large number)
  Apply a clustering algorithm to generate τ clusters on X_{m+u}.
  Generate label hypothesis h_τ (by labeling each cluster with the most frequent label among its labeled samples)
  Calculate the bound for h_τ as defined in Eq. 2.
Choose the hypothesis h_τ with the lowest bound; output the corresponding classification of X_u.

Figure 2. Pseudo-code for transductive clustering.

assumption. In standard inductive SVM (ISVM), the learning algorithm seeks to maximize the margin subject to misclassification constraints on the training samples. In TSVM, this optimization is generalized to include additional constraints on the unlabeled samples. The resulting optimization algorithm seeks to maximize the margin on both labeled and unlabeled samples and creates a hyperplane that avoids high-density regions (e.g. clusters).

3.4 Spectral Graph Transducer

Spectral Graph Transducer (SGT) (Joachims, 2003) achieves transduction via an extension of the normalized mincut clustering criterion. First, a data graph is constructed where the vertices are labeled or unlabeled samples and the edge weights represent similarities between samples. The mincut criteria seeks to partition the graph such that the sum of cut edges is minimized. SGT extends this idea to transductive learning by incorporating constraints that require samples of the same label to be in the same cluster. The resulting partitions decide the label of unlabeled samples.

4 Data

4.1 Corpus

The dialect addressed in this work is Levantine Colloquial Arabic (LCA), primarily spoken in Jordan, Lebanon, Palestine, and Syria. Our development/test data comes from the Levantine Arabic CTS Treebank provided by LDC. The training data comes from the Levantine CTS Audio Transcripts. Both are from the Fisher collection of conversational telephone speech between Levantine speakers previously unknown to each other. The LCA data was transcribed in standard MSA script and transliterated into ASCII characters using the Buckwalter transliteration scheme[1]. No diacritics are used in either the training or development/test data. Speech effects such as disfluencies and noises were removed prior to our experiments.

The training set consists of 476k tokens and 16.6k types. It is not annotated with POS tags – this is the raw text we use to train the unsupervised HMM tagger. The test set consists of 15k tokens and 2.4k types, and is manually annotated with POS tags. The development set is also POS-annotated, and contains 16k tokens and 2.4k types. We used the reduced tagset known as the Bies tagset (Maamouri et al., 2004), which focuses on major part-of-speech and excludes detailed morphological information.

Using the compound-label framework, we observe 220 and 67 distinct compound-labels (i.e. POS-sets) in the training and test sets, respectively. As mentioned in Section 3.1, a classifier in the compound-label framework can never hypothesize POS-sets that do not exist in the training data: 43% of the test vocabulary (and 8.5% by token frequency) fall under this category.

4.2 Morphological Analyzer

We employ the LDC-distributed Buckwalter analyzer for morphological analyses of Arabic words. For a given word, the analyzer outputs all possible morphological analyses, including stems, POS tags, and diacritizations. The information regarding possible POS tags for a given word is crucial for constraining the unsupervised learning process in HMM taggers.

The Buckwalter analyzer is based on an internal stem lexicon combined with rules for affixation. It was originally developed for the MSA, so only a certain percentage of Levantine words can be correctly analyzed. Table 1 shows the percentages of words in the LCA training text that received N possible POS tags from the Buckwalter analyzer. Roughly 23% of types and 28% of tokens received no tags (N=0) and are considered un-analyzable.

5 System

Our overall system looks as follows (see Figure 3): In Step 1, the MSA (Buckwalter) analyzer is applied to the word list derived from the raw training text. The result is a partial POS lexicon,

[1] http://www.ldc.upenn.edu/myl/morph/buckwalter.html

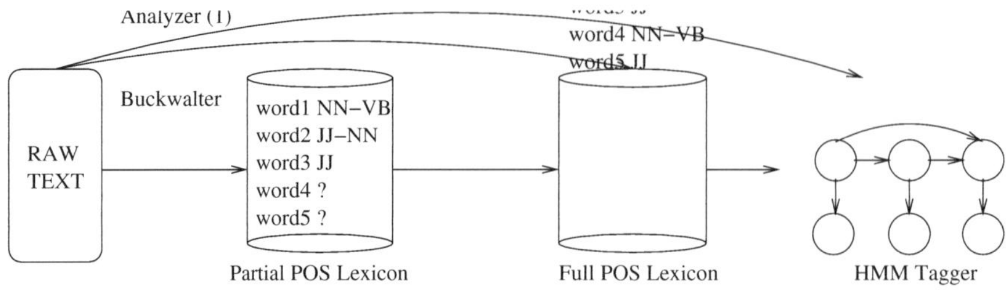

Figure 3: Overall System: (1) Apply Buckwalter Analyzer to dialectal Arabic raw text, obtaining a partial POS lexicon. (2) Use Transductive Learning to infer missing POS-sets. (3) Unsupervised training of HMM Tagger using both raw text and inferred lexicon.

N	Type	Token
0	23.3	28.2
1	52.5	40.4
2	17.7	19.9
3	5.2	10.5
4	1.0	2.3
5	0.1	0.6

Table 1: Percentage of word types/tokens with N possible tags, as determined by the Buckwalter analyzer. Words with 0 tags are un-analyzable.

which lists the set of possible POS tags for those words for which the analyzer provided some output. All possibilities suggested by the analyzer are included.

The focus of Step 2 is to infer the POS-sets of the remaining, unannotated words using one of the automatic learning procedures described in Section 3. Finally, Step 3 involves training an HMM tagger using the learned lexicon. This is the standard unsupervised learning component of the system. We use a trigram HMM, although modifications such as the addition of affixes and variables modeling speech effects may improve tagging accuracy. Our concern here is the evaluation of the lexicon learning component in Step 2.

An important problem in this system setup is the possibility of error propagation. In Step 1, the MSA analyzer may give incorrect POS-sets to analyzable words. It may not posit the correct tag (low recall), or it may give too many tags (low precision). Both have a negative effect on lexicon learning and EM training. For lexicon learning, Step 1 errors represent corrupt training data; For EM training, Step 1 error may cause the HMM tagger to never hypothesize the correct tag (low recall) or have too much confusibility during training (low precision). We attempted to measure the extent of this error by calculating the tag precision/recall on words that occur in the test set: Among the 12k words analyzed by the analyzer, 1483 words occur in the test data. We used the annotations in the test data and collected all the "oracle" POS-sets for each of these 1483 words.[2] The average precision of the analyzer-generated POS-sets against the oracle is 56.46%. The average recall is 81.25%. Note that precision is low–this implies that the partial lexicon is not very constrained. The recall of 81.25% means that 18.75% of the words may never receive the correct tag in tagging. In the experiments, we will investigate to what extent this kind of error affects lexicon learning and EM training.

6 Experiments

6.1 Lexicon learning experiments

We seek to answer the following three questions in our experiments:

- How useful is the lexicon learning step in an end-to-end POS tagging system? Do the machine learning algorithms produce lexicons that result in higher tagging accuracies, when compared to a baseline lexicon that simply hypothesizes all POS tags for un-analyzable words? The answer is a definitive **yes**.

- What machine learning algorithms perform the best on this task? Do transductive learning outperform inductive learning? The empirical answer is that TSVM performs best, SGT performs worst, and TC and ISVM are in the middle.

[2]Since the test set is small, these "oracle" POS-sets may be missing some tags. Thus the true precision may be higher (and recall may be lower) than measured.

Orthographic features:
w_i matches `/^pre/`, `pre` = {set of data-derived prefixes}
w_i matches `/suf$/`, `suf` = {set of data-derived suffixes}
Contextual features:
w_{i-1} = `voc`, `voc` = {set of words in lexicon}
t_{i-1} = `tag`, `tag` = {set of POS tags}
t_{i+1} = `tag`, `tag` = {set of POS tags}
w_{i-1} is an un-analyzable word
w_{i+1} is an un-analyzable word

Table 2: Binary features used for predicting POS-sets of un-analyzable words.

- What is the relative impact of errors from the MSA analyzer on lexicon learning and EM training? The answer is that Step 1 errors affect EM training more, and lexicon learning is comparably robust to these errors.

In our problem, we have 12k labeled samples and 3970 unlabeled samples. We define the feature of each sample as listed in Table 2. The contextual features are generated by co-occurrence statistics gleaned from the training data. For instance, for a word `foo`, we collect all bigrams consisting of `foo` from the raw text; all features [w_{t-1} = `voc`] that correspond to the bigrams (`voc`, `foo`) are set to 1. The idea is that words with similar orthographic and/or contextual features should receive similar POS-sets.

All results, unless otherwise noted, are tagging accuracies on the test set given by training a HMM tagger on a specific lexicon. Table 3 gives tagging accuracies of the four machine learning methods (TSVM, TC, ISVM, SGT) as well as two baseline approaches for generating a lexicon: (all tags) gives all 20 possible tags to the un-analyzable words, whereas (open class) gives only the subset of open-class POS tags.[3] The results are given in descending order of overall tagging accuracy.[4] With the exception of TSVM (63.54%) vs. TC (62.89%), all differences are statistically significant. As seen in the table, applying a machine learning step for lexicon learning is a worthwhile effort since it always leads to better tagging accuracies than the baseline methods.

[3] Not all un-analyzable words are open-class. Close-class words may be un-analyzable due to dialectal spelling variations.

[4] Note that the unknown word accuracies do not follow the same trend and are generally quite low. This might be due to the fact that POS tags of unknown words are usually best predicted by the HMM's transition probabilities, which may not be as robust due to the noisy lexicon.

Method	Accuracy	UnkAcc
TSVM	63.54	26.19
TC	62.89	26.71
ISVM	61.53	27.68
SGT	59.68	25.82
open class	57.39	27.08
all tags	55.64	25.00

Table 3: Tagging Accuracies for lexicons derived by machine learning (TSVM, TC, ISVM, SGT) and baseline methods. Accuracy=Overall accuracy; UnkAcc=Accuracy of unknown words.

The poor performance of SGT is somewhat surprising since it is contrary to results presented in other papers. We attributed this to the difficulty in constructing the data graph. For instance, we constructed k-nearest-neighbor graphs based on the cosine distance between feature vectors, but it is difficult to decide the best distance metric or number of neighbors. Finally, we note that besides the performance of SGT, transductive learning methods (TSVM, TC) outperform the inductive ISVM.

We also compute precision/recall statistics of the final lexicon on the test set words (similar to Section 5) and measure the average size of the POS-sets (||POSset||). As seen in Table 4, POS-set sizes of machine-learned lexicon is a factor of 2 or 3 smaller than that of the baseline lexicons. On the other hand, recall is better for the baseline lexicons. These observations, combined with the fact that machine-learned lexicons gave better tagging accuracy, suggests that we have a *constrained* lexicon effect here: i.e. for EM training, it is better to constrain the lexicon with small POS-sets than to achieve high recall.

Method	Precision	Recall	||POSset||
TSVM	58.15	88.85	1.89
TC	59.19	87.88	1.80
ISVM	58.09	88.44	1.87
SGT	53.98	82.60	1.87
open class	54.03	96.77	3.39
all tags	53.31	98.53	5.17

Table 4: Statistics of the Lexicons in Table 3.

Next, we examined the effects of error propagation from the MSA analyzer in Step 1. We attempted to correct these errors by using POS-sets of words derived from the development data. In particular, of the 1562 partial lexicon words that also occur in the development set, we found 1044 words without entirely matching POS-sets. These POS-sets are replaced with the oracle POS-sets derived from the development data, and the result is treated as the (corrected) partial lexicon of Step 1. In this procedure, the average POS-set size of the partial lexicon decreased from 2.13 to 1.10, recall increased from 82.44% to 100%, and precision increased from 57.15% to 64.31%. We apply lexicon learning to this corrected partial lexicon and evaluate tagging results, shown in Table 5. The fact that all numbers in Table 5 represent significant improvements over Table 3 implies that error propagation is not a trivial problem, and automatic error correction methods may be desired.

Method	Accuracy	UnkAcc
TSVM	66.54	27.38
ISVM	65.08	26.86
TC	64.05	28.20
SGT	63.78	27.23
all tags	62.96	27.91
open class	61.26	27.83

Table 5: Tag accuracies by correcting mistakes in the partial lexicon prior to lexicon learning. Interestingly, we note ISVM outperforms TC here, which differs from Table 3.

Finally, we determine whether error propagation impacts lexicon learning (Step 2) or EM training (Step 3) more. Table 6 shows the results of TSVM for four scenarios: correcting analyzer errors in the the lexicon: (A) prior to lexicon learning, (B) prior to EM training, (C) both, or (D) none. As seen in Table 6, correcting the lexicon at Step 3 (EM training) gives the most improvements, indicating that analyzer errors affects EM training more than lexicon learning. This implies that lexicon learning is relatively robust to training data corruption, and that one can mainly focus on improved estimation techniques for EM training (Wang and Schuurmans, 2005) if the goal is to alleviate the impact of analyzer errors. The same evaluation on the other machine learning methods (TC, ISVM, SGT) show similar results.

6.2 Comparison experiments: Expert lexicon and supervised learning

Our approach to building a resource-poor POS tagger involves (a) lexicon learning, and (b) unsupervised training. In this section we examine cases where (a) an expert lexicon is available, so that lexicon learning is not required, and (b) sentences are annotated with POS information, so that supervised training is possible. The goal of these experiments is to determine when alternative approaches involving additional human annotations become worthwhile in this task.

Scenario	Step2	Step3	TSVM
(B)	N	Y	66.70
(C)	Y	Y	66.54
(A)	Y	N	64.93
(D)	N	N	63.54

Table 6: Effect of correcting the lexicon in different steps. Y=yes, lexicon corrected; N=no, POS-set remains the same as analyzer's output.

(a) Expert lexicon: First, we build an expert lexicon by collecting all tags per word in the development set (i.e. "oracle" POS-sets). Then, the tagger is trained using EM by treating the development set as raw text (i.e. ignoring the POS annotations). This achieves an accuracy of 74.45% on the test set. Note that this accuracy is significantly higher than the ones in Table 3, which represent unsupervised training on more raw text (the training set), but with non-expert lexicons derived from the MSA analyzer and a machine learner. This result further demonstrates the importance of obtaining an accurate lexicon in unsupervised training. If one were to build this expert lexicon by hand, one would need an annotator to label the POS-sets of 2450 distinct lexicon items.

(b) Supervised training: We build a supervised tagger by training on the POS annotations of the development set, which achieves 82.93% accuracy. This improved accuracy comes at the cost of annotating 2.2k sentences (16k tokens) with complete POS information.

Finally, we present the same results with reduced data, taking first 50, 100, 200, etc. sentences in the development set for lexicon or POS annotation. The learning curve is shown in Table 7. One may be tempted to draw conclusions regarding supervised vs. unsupervised approaches by directly comparing this table with the results in Section 6.1; we avoid doing so since taggers in Sections 6.1 and 6.2 are trained on different data sets (training vs. development set) and the accuracy differences are compounded by issues such

Supervised		Unsupervised, Expert	
#Sentence	Acc	#Vocab	Acc
50	47.82	123	47.13
100	55.32	188	54.65
200	61.17	299	57.37
400	69.17	497	64.36
800	76.92	953	70.36
1600	81.73	1754	72.99
2200	82.93	2450	74.45

Table 7: (1) Supervised training accuracies with varying numbers of sentences. (2) Accuracies of unsupervised training using a expert lexicon of different vocabulary sizes.

as ngram coverage, data-set selection, and the way annotations are done.

7 Related Work

There is an increasing amount of work in NLP tools for Arabic. In supervised POS tagging, (Diab et al., 2004) achieves high accuracy on MSA with the direct application of SVM classifiers. (Habash and Rambow, 2005) argue that the rich morphology of Arabic necessitates the use of a morphological analyzer in combination with POS tagging. This can be considered similar in spirit to the learning of lexicons for unsupervised tagging.

The work done at a recent JHU Workshop (Rambow and others, 2005) is very relevant in that it investigates a method for improving LCA tagging that is orthogonal to our approach. They do not use the raw LCA text as we have done. Instead, they train a MSA supervised tagger and adapt it to LCA by a combination of methods, such using a MSA-LCA translation lexicon and redistributing the probabibility mass of MSA words to LCA.

8 Conclusion

In this study, we investigated several machine learning algorithms on the task of lexicon learning and demonstrated its impact on dialectal Arabic tagging. We achieve a POS tagging accuracy of 63.54% using a transductively-learned lexicon (TSVM), outperforming the baseline (57.39%). This result brings us one step closer to the accuracies of unsupervised training with expert lexicon (74.45%) and supervised training (82.93%), both of which require significant annotation effort. Future work includes a more detailed analysis of transductive learning in this domain and possible solutions to alleviating error propagation.

Acknowledgments

We would like to thank Rebecca Hwa for discussions regarding the JHU project. This work is funded in part by NSF Grant IIS-0326276 and an NSF Graduate Fellowship for the 1st author. Any opinions, findings, and conclusions expressed in this material are those of the authors and do not necessarily reflect the views of these agencies.

References

M. Banko and R. Moore. 2004. Part-of-speech tagging in context. In *Proc. of COLING 2004*.

E. Brill. 1995. Unsupervised learning of disambiguation rules for part of speech tagging. In *Proc. of the Third Workshop on Very Large Corpora*.

P. Derbeko, R. El-Yaniv, and R. Meir. 2004. Explicit learning curves for transduction and application to clustering and compression algorithms. *Journal of Artificial Intelligence Research*, 22:117-142.

M. Diab, K. Hacioglu, and D. Jurafsky. 2004. Automatic tagging of Arabic text: from raw text to base phrase chunks. In *Proceedings of HLT/NAACL*.

K. Duh and K. Kirchhoff. 2005a. POS tagging of dialectal arabic: a minimally-supervised approach. In *ACL 2005, Semitic Languages Workshop*.

K. Duh and K. Kirchhoff. 2005b. Structured multi-label transductive learning. In *NIPS Workshop on Advances in Structured Learning for Text/Speech Processing*.

R. El-Yaniv and L. Gerzon. 2005. Effective transductive learning via objective model selection. *Pattern Recognition Letters*, 26(13):2104-2115.

A. Elisseeff and J. Weston. 2002. Kernel methods for multi-labeled classification. In *NIPS*.

N. Habash and O. Rambow. 2005. Arabic tokenization, morphological analysis, and part-of-speech tagging in one fell swoop. In *ACL*.

T. Joachims. 1999. Transductive inference for text classification using support vector machines. In *ICML*.

T. Joachims. 2003. Transductive learning via spectral graph partitioning. In *ICML*.

J. Kupiec. 1992. Robust part-of-speech tagging using a hidden Markov model. *Computer Speech and Language*, 6.

M. Maamouri, A. Bies, and T. Buckwalter. 2004. The Penn Arabic Treebank: Building a large-scale annotated Arabic corpus. In *NEMLAR Conf. on Arabic Language Resources and Tools*.

D. McAllester. 1999. Some PAC-Bayesian theorems. *Machine Learning*, 37(3):255-36.

O. Rambow et al. 2005. Parsing Arabic dialects. Technical report, Final Report, 2005 JHU Summer Workshop.

V. Vapnik. 1998. *Statistical Learning Theory*. Wiley Interscience.

Q. Wang and D. Schuurmans. 2005. Improved estimation for unsupervised part-of-speech tagging. In *IEEE NLP-KE*.

Arabic OCR Error Correction Using Character Segment Correction, Language Modeling, and Shallow Morphology

Walid Magdy and Kareem Darwish
IBM Technology Development Center
P.O. Box 166 El-Ahram, Giza, Egypt
{wmagdy,darwishk}@eg.ibm.com

Abstract

This paper explores the use of a character segment based character correction model, language modeling, and shallow morphology for Arabic OCR error correction. Experimentation shows that character segment based correction is superior to single character correction and that language modeling boosts correction, by improving the ranking of candidate corrections, while shallow morphology had a small adverse effect. Further, given sufficiently large corpus to extract a dictionary and to train a language model, word based correction works well for a morphologically rich language such as Arabic.

1 Introduction

Recent advances in printed document digitization and processing led to large scale digitization efforts of legacy printed documents producing document images. To enable subsequent processing and retrieval, the document images are often transformed to character-coded text using Optical Character Recognition (OCR). Although OCR is fast, OCR output typically contains errors. The errors are even more pronounced in OCR'ed Arabic text due to Arabic's orthographic and morphological properties. The introduced errors adversely affect linguistic processing and retrieval of OCR'ed documents. This paper explores the effectiveness post-OCR error correction. The correction uses an improved character segment based noisy channel model, language modeling, and shallow morphological processing to correct OCR errors. The paper will be organized as follows: Section 2 provides background information on Arabic OCR and OCR error correction; Section 3 presents the error correction methodology; Section 4 reports and discusses experimental results; and Section 5 concludes the paper and provides possible future directions.

2 Background

This section reviews prior work on Arabic OCR for Arabic and OCR error correction.

2.1 Arabic OCR

The goal of OCR is to transform a document image into character-coded text. The usual process is to automatically segment a document image into character images in the proper reading order using image analysis heuristics, apply an automatic classifier to determine the character codes that most likely correspond to each character image, and then exploit sequential context (e.g., preceding and following characters and a list of possible words) to select the most likely character in each position. The character error rate can be influenced by reproduction quality (e.g., original documents are typically better than photocopies), the resolution at which a document was scanned, and any mismatch between the instances on which the character image classifier was trained and the rendering of the characters in the printed document. Arabic OCR presents several challenges, including:

• Arabic's cursive script in which most characters are connected and their shape vary with position in the word.

• The optional use of word elongations and ligatures, which are special forms of certain letter sequences.

• The presence of dots in 15 of the 28 letters to distinguish between different letters and the optional use of diacritic which can be confused with dirt, dust, and speckle (Darwish and Oard, 2002).

• The morphological complexity of Arabic, which results in an estimated 60 billion possible

Proceedings of the 2006 Conference on Empirical Methods in Natural Language Processing (EMNLP 2006), pages 408–414, Sydney, July 2006.

surface forms, complicates dictionary-based error correction. Arabic words are built from a closed set of about 10,000 root forms that typically contain 3 characters, although 4-character roots are not uncommon, and some 5-character roots do exist. Arabic stems are derived from these root forms by fitting the root letters into a small set of regular patterns, which sometimes includes addition of "infix" characters between two letters of the root (Ahmed, 2000).

There is a number of commercial Arabic OCR systems, with Sakhr's Automatic Reader and Shonut's Omni Page being perhaps the most widely used. Retrieval of OCR degraded text documents has been reported for many languages, including English (Harding et al., 1997), Chinese (Tseng and Oard, 2001), and Arabic (Darwish and Oard, 2002).

2.2 OCR Error Correction

Much research has been done to correct recognition errors in OCR-degraded collections. There are two main categories of determining how to correct these errors. They are word-level and passage-level post-OCR processing. Some of the kinds of word level post-processing include the use of dictionary lookup, probabilistic relaxation, character and word n-gram frequency analysis (Hong, 1995), and morphological analysis (Oflazer, 1996). Passage-level post-processing techniques include the use of word n-grams, word collocations, grammar, conceptual closeness, passage level word clustering, linguistic context, and visual context. The following introduces some of the error correction techniques.

• Dictionary Lookup: Dictionary Lookup, which is the basis for the correction reported in this paper, is used to compare recognized words with words in a term list (Church and Gale, 1991; Hong, 1995; Jurafsky and Martin, 2000). If a word is found in the dictionary, then it is considered correct. Otherwise, a checker attempts to find a dictionary word that might be the correct spelling of the misrecognized word.

Jurafsky and Martin (2000) illustrate the use of a noisy channel model to find the correct spelling of misspelled or misrecognized words. The model assumes that text errors are due to edit operations namely insertions, deletions, and substitutions. Given two words, the number of edit operations required to transform one of the words to the other is called the Levenshtein edit distance (Baeza-Yates and Navarro, 1996). To capture the probabilities associated with different edit operations, confusion matrices are employed. Another source of evidence is the relative probabilities that candidate word corrections would be observed. These probabilities can be obtained using word frequency in text corpus (Jurafsky and Martin, 2000). However, the dictionary lookup approach has the following problems (Hong, 1995):

a) A correctly recognized word might not be in the dictionary. This problem could surface if the dictionary is small, if the correct word is an acronym or a named entity that would not normally appear in a dictionary, or if the language being recognized is morphologically complex. In a morphological complex language such as Arabic, German, and Turkish the number of valid word surface forms is arbitrarily large which complicates building dictionaries for spell checking.

b) A word that is misrecognized is in the dictionary. An example of that is the recognition of the word "tear" instead of "fear". This problem is particularly acute in a language such as Arabic where a large fraction of three letters sequences are valid words.

• Character N-Grams: Character n-grams maybe used alone or in combination with dictionary lookup (Lu et al., 1999; Taghva et al., 1994). The premise for using n-grams is that some letter sequences are more common than others and other letter sequences are rare or impossible. For example, the trigram "xzx" is rare in the English language, while the trigram "ies" is common. Using this method, an unusual sequence of letters can point to the position of an error in a misrecognized word. This technique is employed by BBN's Arabic OCR system (Lu et al., 1999).

• Using Morphology: Many morphologically complex languages, such as Arabic, Swedish, Finnish, Turkish, and German, have enormous numbers of possible words. Accounting for and listing all the possible words is not feasible for purposes of error correction. Domeij proposed a method to build a spell checker that utilizes a stem lists and orthographic rules, which govern how a word is written, and morphotactic rules, which govern how morphemes (building blocks of meanings) are allowed to combine, to accept legal combinations of stems (Domeij et al., 1994). By breaking up compound words, dictionary lookup can be applied to individual constituent stems. Similar work was done for Turkish in which an error tolerant finite state recognizer was employed (Oflazer, 1996). The finite state recognizer tolerated a maximum number of edit operations away from correctly spelled candidate words. This approach was initially developed to perform morphological analysis for Turkish and was extended to perform spelling correction. The techniques used for Swedish and Turkish can potentially be applied to Arabic. Much work has been done on Arabic morphology and can be potentially extended for spelling correction.

• Word Clustering: Another approach tries to cluster different spellings of a word based on a weighted Levenshtein edit distance. The insight is that an important word, specially acronyms and named-entities, are likely to appear more than once in a passage. Taghva described an English recognizer that identifies acronyms and named-entities, clusters them, and then treats the words in each cluster as one word (Taghva, 1994). Applying this technique for Arabic requires accounting for morphology, because prefixes or suffixes might be affixed to instances of named entities. DeRoeck introduced a clustering technique tolerant of Arabic's complex morphology (De Roeck and Al-Fares, 2000). Perhaps the technique can be modified to make it tolerant of errors.

• Using Grammar: In this approach, a passage containing spelling errors is parsed based on a language specific grammar. In a system described by Agirre (1998), an English grammar was used to parse sentences with spelling mistakes. Parsing such sentences gives clues to the expected part of speech of the word that should replace the misspelled word. Thus candidates produced by the spell checker can be filtered. Applying this technique to Arabic might prove challenging because the work on Arabic parsing has been very limited (Moussa et al., 2003).

• Word N-Grams (Language Modeling): A Word n-gram is a sequence of *n* consecutive words in text. The word n-gram technique is a flexible method that can be used to calculate the likelihood that a word sequence would appear (Tillenius, 1996). Using this method, the candidate correction of a misspelled word might be successfully picked. For example, in the sentence "I bought a peece of land," the possible corrections for the word peece might be "piece" and "peace". However, using the n-gram method will likely indicate that the word trigram "piece of land" is much more likely than the trigram "peace of land." Thus the word "piece" is a more likely correction than "peace".

3 Error Correction Methodology

This section describes the character level modeling, the language modeling, and shallow morphological analysis.

3.1 OCR Character Level Model

A noisy channel model was used to learn how OCR corrupts single characters or character segments, producing a character level confusion model. To train the model, 6,000 OCR corrupted words were obtained from a modern printing of a medieval religious Arabic book (called "The Provisions of the Return" or "Provisions" for short by *Ibn Al-Qayim*). The words were then manually corrected, and the corrupted and manually corrected versions were aligned. The Provisions book was scanned at 300x300 dots per inch (dpi), and Sakhr's Automatic Reader was used to OCR the scanned pages. From the 6,000 words, 4,000 were used for training and the remaining words were set aside for later testing. The Word Error Rate (WER) for the 2,000 testing words was 39%. For all words (in training and testing), the different forms of *alef* (*hamza*, *alef*, *alef maad*, *alef with hamza on top*, *hamza on wa*, *alef with hamza on the bottom*, and *hamza on ya*) were normalized to *alef*, and *ya* and *alef maqsoura* were normalized to *ya*. Subsequently, the characters in the aligned words can aligned in two different ways, namely: *1:1* (one-to-one) character alignment, where each character is mapped to no more than one character (Church and Gale, 1991); or using *m:n* alignment, where a character segment of length *m* is aligned to a character segment of length *n* (Brill and Moore, 2000). The second method is more general and potentially more accurate especially for Arabic where a character can be confused with as many as three or four characters. The following example highlights the difference between the *1:1* and the *m:n* alignment approaches. Given the training pair (rnacle, made):

1:1 alignment :

r	n	a	c	l	e
|	|	|	|	|	|
m	ε	a	d	ε	e

m:*n* alignment:

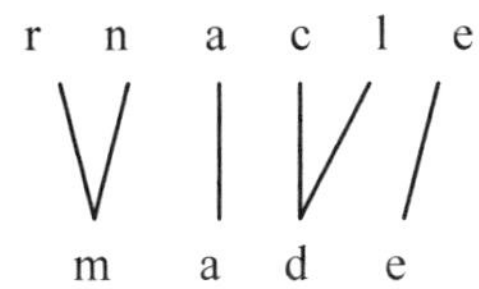

For alignment, Levenstein dynamic programming minimum edit distance algorithm was used to produce *1*:*1* alignments. The algorithm computes the minimum number of edit operations required to transform one string into another. Given the output alignments of the algorithm, properly aligned characters (such as a → a and e → e) are used as anchors, ε's (null characters) are combined to misaligned adjacent characters producing *m*:*n* alignments, and ε's between correctly aligned characters are counted as deletions or insertions.

To formalize the error model, given a clean word $\chi = \#C_1..C_k..\ C_l..C_n\#$ and the resulting OCR degraded word $\delta = \#D_1..D_x..\ D_y..D_m\#$, where $D_x..\ D_y$ resulted from $C_k..\ C_l$, ε representing the null character, and # marking word boundaries, the probability estimates for the three edit operations for the models are:

$$P_{\text{substitution}}\ (C_k..C_l \rightarrow D_x..\ D_y) = \frac{count(C_k..C_l \rightarrow D_x..D_y)}{count(C_k..C_l)}$$

$$P_{\text{deletion}}\ (C_k..C_l \rightarrow \varepsilon) = \frac{count(C_k..C_l \rightarrow \varepsilon)}{count(C_k..C_l)}$$

$$P_{\text{insertion}}\ (\varepsilon \rightarrow D_x..\ D_y) = \frac{count(\varepsilon \rightarrow D_x..D_y)}{count(C)}$$

When decoding a corrupted string δ composed of the characters $D_1..D_x..\ D_y..D_m$, the goal is to find a string χ composed of the characters $C_1..C_k..\ C_l..C_n$ such that $P(\delta|\chi)\cdot P(\chi)$ is maximum. $P(\chi)$ is the prior probability of observing χ in text and $P(\delta|\chi)$ is the probability of producing δ from χ.

$P(\chi)$ was computed from a web-mined collection of religious text by *Ibn Taymiya*, the main teacher of the medieval author of the "Provisions" book. The collection contained approximately 16 million words, with 278,877 unique surface forms.

$P(\delta|\chi)$ is calculated using the trained model, as follows:

$$P(\delta \mid \chi) = \prod_{all:D_x..D_y} P(D_x..D_y \mid C_k..C_l)$$

The segments $D_x..\ D_y$ are generated by finding all possible 2^{n-1} segmentations of the word δ. For example, given "macle" then all possible segmentations are (m,a,c,l,e), (ma,c,l,e), (m,ac,l,e), (mac,l,e), (m,a,cl,e), (ma,cl,e), (m,acl,e), (macl,e), (m,a,c,le), (ma,c,le), (m,ac,le), (mac,le), (m,a,cle), (ma,cle), (m,acle), (macle).

All segment sequences $C_k..\ C_l$ known to produce $D_x..\ D_y$ for each of the possible segmentations are produced. If a sequence of $C_1..\ C_n$ segments generates a valid word χ which exists in the web-mined collection, then $\text{argmax}_\chi\ P(\delta|\chi)\cdot P(\chi)$ is computed, otherwise the sequence is discarded. Possible corrections are subsequently ranked. For all the experiments reported in this paper, the top 10 corrections are generated. Note that error correction reported in this paper does not assume that a word is correct because it exists in the web-mined collection and assumes that all words are possibly incorrect.

The effect of two modifications to the *m*:*n* character model mentioned above were examined.

The first modification involved making the character model account for the position of letters in a word. The intuition for this model is that since Arabic letters change their shape based on their positions in words and would hence affect the letters with which they would be confused. Formally, given *L* denoting the positions of the letter at the boundaries of character segments, whether start, middle, end, or isolated, the character model would be:

$$P_{\text{substitution}}\ (C_k..C_l \rightarrow D_x..\ D_y \mid L) = \frac{count(C_k..C_l \rightarrow D_x..D_y \mid L)}{count(C_k..C_l \mid L)}$$

$$P_{\text{deletion}}\ (C_k..C_l \rightarrow \varepsilon \mid L) = \frac{count(C_k..C_l \rightarrow \varepsilon \mid L)}{count(C_k..C_l \mid L)}$$

$$P_{\text{insertion}}\ (\varepsilon \rightarrow D_x..\ D_y) = \frac{count(\varepsilon \rightarrow D_x..D_y \mid L)}{count(C \mid L)}$$

The second modification involved giving a small uniform probability to single character substiutions that are unseen in the training data. This was done in accordance to Lidstone's law to smooth probabilities. The probability was set to be 100 times smaller than the probability of the smallest seen single character substitution*.

* Other uniform probability estimates were examined for the training data and the one reported here seemed to work best

3.2 Language Modeling

For language modeling, a trigram language model was trained on the same web-mined collection that was mentioned in the previous subsection without any kind of morphological processing. Like the text extracted from the "Provisions" book, *alef* and *ya* letter normalizations were performed. The language model was built using SRILM toolkit with Good-Turing smoothing and default backoff.

Given a corrupted word sequence $\Delta = \{\delta_1 .. \delta_i .. \delta_n\}$ and $\Xi = \{X_1 .. X_i .. X_n\}$, where $X_i = \{\chi_{i0} .. \chi_{im}\}$ are possible corrections of δ_i ($m = 10$ for all the experiments reported in the paper), the aim was to find a sequence $\Omega = \{\omega_1 .. \omega_i .. \omega_n\}$, where $\omega_i \in X_i$, that maximizes:

$$\underbrace{\left(\prod_{i=1..n,j=1..m} P\left(\chi_{ij} \mid \chi_{i-1,j}, \chi_{i-2,j}\right)\right)}_{LanguageModel} \cdot \underbrace{P(\delta_i \mid \chi_{ij})}_{CharacterModel}$$

3.3 Language Modeling and Shallow Morphological Analysis

Two paths were pursued to explore the combined effect of language modeling and shallow morphological analysis.

In the first, a 6-gram language model was trained on the same web-mined collection after each of the words in the collection was segmented into its constituent prefix, stem, and suffix (in this order) using language model based stemmer (Lee et al., 2003). For example, "وكتابهم – wktAbhm" was replaced by "w# ktAb +hm" where # and + were used to mark prefixes and suffixes respectively and to distinguish them from stems. Like before, *alef* and *ya* letter normalizations were performed and the language model was built using SRILM toolkit with the same parameters.

Formally, the only difference between this model and the one before is that $X_i = \{\chi_{i0} .. \chi_{im}\}$ are the {prefix, stem, suffix} tuples of the possible corrections of δ_i (a tuple is treated as a block). Otherwise everything else is identical.

In the second, a trigram language model was trained on the same collection after the language modeling based stemming was used on all the tokens in the collection (Lee et al., 2003). The top *n* generated corrections were subsequently stemmed and the stems were reranked using the language model. The top resulting stem was compared to the condition in which language modeling was used without morphological analysis (as in the previous subsection) and then the top resulting correction were stemmed. This path was pursued to examine the effect of correction on applications where stems are more useful than words such as Arabic information retrieval (Darwish et al., 2005; Larkey et al., 2002).

3.4 Testing the Models

The *1:1* and *m:n* character mapping models were tested while enabling or disabling character position training (CP), smoothing by the assignment of small probabilities to unseen single character substitutions (UP), language modeling (LM), and shallow morphological processing (SM) using the 6-gram model.

As mentioned earlier, all models were tested using sentences containing 2,000 words in total.

4 Experimental Results

Table 1 reports on the percentage of words for which a proper correction was found in the top *n* generated corrections using different models. The percentage of words for which a proper correction exists in the top 10 proposed correction is the upper limit accuracy we can achieve given than we can rerank the correction using language modeling. Table 2 reports the word error rate for the *1:1* and *m:n* models with and without CP, UP, LM, and SM. Further, the before and after stemming error rates are reported for setups that use language modeling. Table 3 reports on the stem error rate when using the stem trigram language model.

The best model was able to find the proper correction within the top 10 proposed correction for 90% of the words. The failure to find a proper correction within the proposed corrections was generally due to grossly misrecognized words and was rarely due to words that do not exist in web-mined collection. Perhaps, more training examples for the character based models would improve correction.

Corrections	1	2	3	4	5	10
1:1	75.3	80.3	83.1	84.5	85	86.5
1:1 + CP	76.9	82.1	83.5	83.2	85	86
1:1 + UP	76	81	83.6	84.6	85.2	86.7
m:n	78.3	83.5	85.4	86.7	87.1	88.5
m:n + CP	79.9	83.9	84.0	85.5	85.9	86.8
m:n + UP	78.4	83.7	85.6	84.1	87.0	90.0

Table 1: Percentage of words for which a proper correction was found in the top n generated corrections

Model	*1:1*		*m:n*	
	Word	Stem	Word	Stem
No Correction	39.0%	-	39.0%	-
Base Model	24.7%	-	21.8%	-
+ CP	23.1%	-	21.5%	-
+ UP	24%	-	21.6%	-
+ LM	**15.8%**	**14.6%**	**13.3%**	**12.1%**
+ LM + CP	16.5%	15.1%	15.5%	14.7%
+ LM + UP	**15.4%**	**14.3%**	**11.7%**	**10.8%**
+ SM + UP	27.8%	26.5%	24.5%	23.0%

Table 2: Word/stem error rate for correction with the different models

Model	*1:1*	*m:n*
Stem 3-gram	16.1%	12.9%

Table 3: Stem error rate for top correction using stem trigram language model

The results indicate that the *m:n* character model is better than the *1:1* model in two ways. The first is that the *m:n* model yielded a greater percentage of proper corrections in the top 10 generated corrections, and the second is that the scores of the top 10 corrections were better which led to better results compared to the *1:1* model when used in combination with language modeling. For the *m:n* model with language modeling, the language model properly picked the proper correction from the proposed correction 98% of the time (for the cases where a proper correction was within the proposed corrections).

Also the use of smoothing, UP, produced better corrections, while accounting for character positions had an adverse effect on correction. This might be an indication that the character segment correction training data was sparse. Using the 6-gram language model on the segmented words had a severely negative impact on correction accuracy. Perhaps is due to insufficient training data for the model. This situation lends itself to using a factored language model using the surface form of words as well as other linguistic features of the word such as part of speech tags, prefixes, and suffixes.

As for training a language model on words versus stems, the results suggest that word based correction is slightly better than stem based correction. The authors' intuition is that this resulted from having a sufficiently large corpus to train the language model and that this might have been reversed if the training corpus for the language model was smaller. Perhaps further investigation would prove or disprove the authors' intuition.

5 Conclusion and Future Work

The paper examined the use of single character and character segment models based correction of Arabic OCR text combined with language modeling and shallow morphological analysis. Further, character position and smoothing issues were also examined. The results show the superiority of the character segment based model compared to the single character based model. Further, the use of language modeling yielded improved error correction particularly for the character segment based model. Accounting for character position and shallow morphological analysis had a negative impact on correction, while smoothing had a positive impact. Lastly, given a large in-domain corpus to extract a correction dictionary and to train a language model is a sufficient strategy for correcting a morphologically rich language such as Arabic with a 70% reduction in word error rate.

For future work, a factor language model might prove beneficial to incorporate morphological information and other factors such as part of speech tags while overcoming training data sparseness problems. Also, determining the size of a sufficiently large corpus to generate a correction dictionary and to train a language model is desirable. Finally, word prediction might prove useful for cases where OCR grossly misrecognized words.

Reference

Agirre, E., K. Gojenola, K. Sarasola, and A. Voutilainen. Towards a Single Proposal in Spelling Correction. *In COLING-ACL'98* (1998).

Ahmed, M. A Large-Scale Computational Processor of Arabic Morphology and Applications. *MSc. Thesis, in Faculty of Engineering Cairo University: Cairo, Egypt.* (2000).

Baeza-Yates, R. and G. Navarro. A Faster Algorithm for Approximate String Matching. *In Combinatorial Pattern Matching (CPM'96), Springer-Verlag LNCS* (1996).

Brill, E. and R. Moore. An improved error model for noisy channel spelling correction. *In the proceedings of the 38th Annual Meeting on Association for Computational Linguistics*, pages 286 – 293 (2000).

Church, K. and W. Gale. "Probability Scoringfor Spelling Correction." *Statistics and Computing*, 1: 93-103 (1991).

Darwish, K. and D. Oard. Term Selection for Searching Printed Arabic. *In SIGIR-2002* (2002).

Darwish, K., H. Hassan, and O. Emam. Examining the Effect of Improved Context Sensitive Morphology on Arabic Information Retrieval. *In ACL Workshop on Computation Approaches to Semitic Languages*, Ann Arbor, (2005).

De Roeck, A. and W. Al-Fares. A Morphologically Sensitive Clustering Algorithm for Identifying Arabic Roots. *In the 38th Annual Meeting of the ACL*, Hong Kong, (2000).

Domeij, R., J. Hollman, V. Kann. Detection of spelling errors in Swedish not using a word list en clair. *Journal of Quantitative Linguistics* (1994) 195-201.

Harding, S., W. Croft, and C. Weir. Probabilistic Retrieval of OCR-degraded Text Using N-Grams. *In European Conference on Digital Libraries* (1997).

Hong, T. Degraded Text Recognition Using Visual and Linguistic Context. *Ph.D. Thesis, Computer Science Department, SUNY Buffalo: Buffalo* (1995).

Jurafsky, D. and J. Martin. Speech and Language Processing. Chapter 5: pages 141-163. *Prentice Hall* (2000).

Larkey, L., L. Ballesteros, and M. Connell. Improving stemming for Arabic information retrieval: light stemming and cooccurrence analysis. *In proceedings of the 25th annual international ACM SIGIR conference*, pages 275-282 (2002).

Lee, Y., K. Papineni, S. Roukos, O. Emam, and H. Hassan. Language Model Based Arabic Word Segmentation. *In the Proceedings of the 41st Annual Meeting of the Association for Computational Linguistics*, pages 399 - 406 (2003).

Lu, Z., I. Bazzi, A. Kornai, J. Makhoul, P. Natarajan, and R. Schwartz. A Robust, Language-Independent OCR System. *In the 27th AIPR Workshop: Advances in Computer Assisted Recognition, SPIE* (1999).

Moussa B., M. Maamouri, H. Jin, A. Bies, X. Ma. Arabic Treebank: Part 1 - 10Kword English Translation. *Linguistic Data Consortium* (2003).

Oflazer, K. Error-Tolerant Finite State Recognition with Applications to Morphological Analysis and Spelling Correction. *Computational Linguistics 22(1)*, 73-90 (1996).

Taghva, K., J. Borsack, and A. Condit. An Expert System for Automatically Correcting OCR Output. *In SPIE - Document Recognition* (1994).

Tillenius, M., Efficient generation and ranking of spelling error corrections. *NADA* (1996).

Tseng, Y. and D. Oard. Document Image Retrieval Techniques for Chinese. *In Symposium on Document Image Understanding Technology, Columbia, MD* (2001).

Partially Supervised Sense Disambiguation by Learning Sense Number from Tagged and Untagged Corpora

Zheng-Yu Niu, Dong-Hong Ji
Institute for Infocomm Research
21 Heng Mui Keng Terrace
119613 Singapore
{zniu, dhji}@i2r.a-star.edu.sg

Chew Lim Tan
Department of Computer Science
National University of Singapore
3 Science Drive 2
117543 Singapore
tancl@comp.nus.edu.sg

Abstract

Supervised and semi-supervised sense disambiguation methods will mis-tag the instances of a target word if the senses of these instances are not defined in sense inventories or there are no tagged instances for these senses in training data. Here we used a model order identification method to avoid the misclassification of the instances with undefined senses by discovering new senses from mixed data (tagged and untagged corpora). This algorithm tries to obtain a natural partition of the mixed data by maximizing a stability criterion defined on the classification result from an extended label propagation algorithm over all the possible values of the number of senses (or sense number, model order). Experimental results on SENSEVAL-3 data indicate that it outperforms SVM, a one-class partially supervised classification algorithm, and a clustering based model order identification algorithm when the tagged data is incomplete.

1 Introduction

In this paper, we address the problem of partially supervised word sense disambiguation, which is to disambiguate the senses of occurrences of a target word in untagged texts when given incomplete tagged corpus [1].

Word sense disambiguation can be defined as associating a target word in a text or discourse with a definition or meaning. Many corpus based methods have been proposed to deal with the sense disambiguation problem when given definition for each possible sense of a target word or a tagged corpus with the instances of each possible sense, e.g., supervised sense disambiguation (Leacock et al., 1998), and semi-supervised sense disambiguation (Yarowsky, 1995).

Supervised methods usually rely on the information from previously sense tagged corpora to determine the senses of words in unseen texts. Semi-supervised methods for WSD are characterized in terms of exploiting unlabeled data in the learning procedure with the need of predefined sense inventories for target words. The information for semi-supervised sense disambiguation is usually obtained from bilingual corpora (e.g. parallel corpora or untagged monolingual corpora in two languages) (Brown et al., 1991; Dagan and Itai, 1994), or sense-tagged seed examples (Yarowsky, 1995).

Some observations can be made on the previous supervised and semi-supervised methods. They always rely on hand-crafted lexicons (e.g., WordNet) as sense inventories. But these resources may miss domain-specific senses, which leads to incomplete sense tagged corpus. Therefore, sense taggers trained on the incomplete tagged corpus will misclassify some instances if the senses of these instances are not defined in sense inventories. For example, one performs WSD in information technology related texts using WordNet [2] as sense inventory. When disambiguating the word "boot" in the phrase "boot sector", the sense tagger will assign this instance with one of the senses of "boot" listed in WordNet. But the correct sense

[1] "incomplete tagged corpus" means that tagged corpus does not include the instances of some senses for the target word, while these senses may occur in untagged texts.

[2] Online version of WordNet is available at http://wordnet.princeton.edu/cgi-bin/webwn2.0

Proceedings of the 2006 Conference on Empirical Methods in Natural Language Processing (EMNLP 2006), pages 415–422,
Sydney, July 2006.

"loading operating system into memory" is not included in WordNet. Therefore, this instance will be associated with an incorrect sense.

So, in this work, we would like to study the problem of partially supervised sense disambiguation with an incomplete sense tagged corpus. Specifically, given an incomplete sense-tagged corpus and a large amount of untagged examples for a target word [3], we are interested in (1) labeling the instances in the untagged corpus with sense tags occurring in the tagged corpus; (2) trying to find undefined senses (or new senses) of the target word [4] from the untagged corpus, which will be represented by instances from the untagged corpus.

We propose an automatic method to estimate the number of senses (or sense number, model order) of a target word in mixed data (tagged corpus+untagged corpus) by maximizing a stability criterion defined on classification result over all the possible values of sense number. At the same time, we can obtain a classification of the mixed data with the optimal number of groups. If the estimated sense number in the mixed data is equal to the sense number of the target word in tagged corpus, then there is no new sense in untagged corpus. Otherwise new senses will be represented by groups in which there is no instance from the tagged corpus.

This partially supervised sense disambiguation algorithm may help enriching manually compiled lexicons by inducing new senses from untagged corpora.

This paper is organized as follows. First, a model order identification algorithm will be presented for partially supervised sense disambiguation in section 2. Section 3 will provide experimental results of this algorithm for sense disambiguation on SENSEVAL-3 data. Then related work on partially supervised classification will be summarized in section 4. Finally we will conclude our work and suggest possible improvements in section 5.

2 Partially Supervised Word Sense Disambiguation

The partially supervised sense disambiguation problem can be generalized as a model order identification problem. We try to estimate the sense number of a target word in mixed data (tagged corpus+untagged corpus) by maximizing a stability criterion defined on classification results over all the possible values of sense number. If the estimated sense number in the mixed data is equal to the sense number in the tagged corpus, then there is no new sense in the untagged corpus. Otherwise new senses will be represented by clusters in which there is no instance from the tagged corpus. The stability criterion assesses the agreement between classification results on full mixed data and sampled mixed data. A partially supervised classification algorithm is used to classify the full or sampled mixed data into a given number of classes before the stability assessment, which will be presented in section 2.1. Then we will provide the details of the model order identification procedure in section 2.2.

2.1 An Extended Label Propagation Algorithm

Table 1: Extended label propagation algorithm.

	Function: ELP(D_L, D_U, k, $Y^0_{D_L+D_U}$)
	Input: labeled examples D_L, unlabeled examples D_U, model order k, initial labeling matrix $Y^0_{D_L+D_U}$;
	Output: the labeling matrix Y_{D_U} on D_U;
1	If $k < k_{X_L}$ then
	Y_{D_U}=NULL;
2	Else if $k = k_{X_L}$ then
	Run plain label propagation algorithm on D_U with Y_{D_U} as output;
3	Else then
3.1	Estimate the size of tagged data set of new classes;
3.2	Generate tagged examples from D_U for ($k_{X_L} + 1$)-th to k-th new classes;
3.3	Run plain label propagation algorithm on D_U with augmented tagged dataset as labeled data;
3.4	Y_{D_U} is the output from plain label propagation algorithm;
	End if
4	Return Y_{D_U};

Let $X_{L+U} = \{x_i\}_{i=1}^n$ be a set of contexts of occurrences of an ambiguous word w, where x_i represents the context of the i-th occurrence, and n is the total number of this word's occurrences. Let

[3] Untagged data usually includes the occurrences of all the possible senses of the target word

[4] "undefined senses" are the senses that do not appear in tagged corpus.

$S_L = \{s_j\}_{j=1}^c$ denote the sense tag set of w in X_L, where X_L denotes the first l examples $x_g (1 \leq g \leq l)$ that are labeled as y_g ($y_g \in S_L$). Let X_U denote other u ($l + u = n$) examples $x_h (l + 1 \leq h \leq n)$ that are unlabeled.

Let $Y^0_{X_{L+U}} \in N^{|X_{L+U}| \times |S_L|}$ represent initial soft labels attached to tagged instances, where $Y^0_{X_{L+U},ij} = 1$ if y_i is s_j and 0 otherwise. Let $Y^0_{X_L}$ be the top l rows of $Y^0_{X_{L+U}}$ and $Y^0_{X_U}$ be the remaining u rows. $Y^0_{X_L}$ is consistent with the labeling in labeled data, and the initialization of $Y^0_{X_U}$ can be arbitrary.

Let k denote the possible value of the number of senses in mixed data X_{L+U}, and k_{X_L} be the number of senses in initial tagged data X_L. Note that $k_{X_L} = |S_L|$, and $k \geq k_{X_L}$.

The classification algorithm in the order identification process should be able to accept labeled data D_L [5], unlabeled data D_U [6] and model order k as input, and assign a class label or a cluster index to each instance in D_U as output. Previous supervised or semi-supervised algorithms (e.g. SVM, label propagation algorithm (Zhu and Ghahramani, 2002)) cannot classify the examples in D_U into k groups if $k > k_{X_L}$. The semi-supervised k-means clustering algorithm (Wagstaff et al., 2001) may be used to perform clustering analysis on mixed data, but its efficiency is a problem for clustering analysis on a very large dataset since multiple restarts are usually required to avoid local optima and multiple iterations will be run in each clustering process for optimizing a clustering solution.

In this work, we propose an alternative method, an extended label propagation algorithm (ELP), which can classify the examples in D_U into k groups. If the value of k is equal to k_{X_L}, then ELP is identical with the plain label propagation algorithm (LP) (Zhu and Ghahramani, 2002). Otherwise, if the value of k is greater than k_{X_L}, we perform classification by the following steps:

(1) estimate the dataset size of each new class as $size_{new\_class}$ by identifying the examples of new classes using the "Spy" technique [7] and assuming that new classes are equally distributed;

(2) $D'_L = D_L$, $D'_U = D_U$;

(3) remove tagged examples of the m-th new class ($k_{X_L} + 1 \leq m \leq k$) from D'_L [8] and train a classifier on this labeled dataset without the m-th class;

(4) the classifier is then used to classify the examples in D'_U;

(5) the least confidently unlabeled point $x_{class\_m} \in D'_U$, together with its label m, is added to the labeled data $D'_L = D'_L + x_{class\_m}$, and $D'_U = D'_U - x_{class\_m}$;

(6) steps (3) to (5) are repeated for each new class till the augmented tagged data set is large enough (here we try to select $size_{new\_class}/4$ examples with their sense tags as tagged data for each new class);

(7) use plain LP algorithm to classify remaining unlabeled data D'_U with D'_L as labeled data.

Table 1 shows this extended label propagation algorithm.

Next we will provide the details of the plain label propagation algorithm.

Define $W_{ij} = exp(-\frac{d_{ij}^2}{\sigma^2})$ if $i \neq j$ and $W_{ii} = 0$ ($1 \leq i, j \leq |D_L + D_U|$), where d_{ij} is the distance (e.g., Euclidean distance) between the example x_i and x_j, and σ is used to control the weight W_{ij}.

Define $|D_L + D_U| \times |D_L + D_U|$ probability transition matrix $T_{ij} = P(j \rightarrow i) = \frac{W_{ij}}{\sum_{k=1}^n W_{kj}}$, where T_{ij} is the probability to jump from example x_j to example x_i.

Compute the row-normalized matrix $\overline{T}$ by $\overline{T}_{ij} = T_{ij} / \sum_{k=1}^n T_{ik}$.

The classification solution is obtained by $Y_{D_U} = (I - \overline{T}_{uu})^{-1} \overline{T}_{ul} Y^0_{D_L}$. I is $|D_U| \times |D_U|$ identity matrix. $\overline{T}_{uu}$ and $\overline{T}_{ul}$ are acquired by splitting matrix $\overline{T}$ after the $|D_L|$-th row and the $|D_L|$-th column into 4 sub-matrices.

2.2 Model Order Identification Procedure

For achieving the model order identification (or sense number estimation) ability, we use a cluster validation based criterion (Levine and Domany, 2001) to infer the optimal number of senses of w in X_{L+U}.

[5] D_L may be the dataset X_L or a subset sampled from X_L.

[6] D_U may be the dataset X_U or a subset sampled from X_U.

[7] The "Spy" technique was proposed in (Liu et al., 2003). Our re-implementation of this technique consists of three steps: (1) sample a small subset D^s_L with the size $15\% \times |D_L|$ from D_L; (2) train a classifier with tagged data $D_L - D^s_L$; (3) classify D_U and D^s_L, and then select some examples from D_U as the dataset of new classes, which have the classification confidence less than the average of that in D^s_L. Classification confidence of the example x_i is defined as the absolute value of the difference between two maximum values from the i-th row in labeling matrix.

[8] Initially there are no tagged examples for the m-th class in D'_L. Therefore we do not need to remove tagged examples for this new class, and then directly train a classifier with D'_L.

Table 2: Model order evaluation algorithm.

	Function: CV(X_{L+U}, k, q, $Y^0_{X_{L+U}}$)
	Input: data set X_{L+U}, model order k, and sampling frequency q;
	Output: the score of the merit of k;
1	Run the extended label propagation algorithm with X_L, X_U, k and $Y^0_{X_{L+U}}$;
2	Construct connectivity matrix C_k based on above classification solution on X_U;
3	Use a random predictor ρ_k to assign uniformly drawn labels to each vector in X_U;
4	Construct connectivity matrix C_{ρ_k} using above classification solution on X_U;
5	For $\mu = 1$ to q do
5.1	Randomly sample a subset X^{μ}_{L+U} with the size $\alpha\|X_{L+U}\|$ from X_{L+U}, $0 < \alpha < 1$;
5.2	Run the extended label propagation algorithm with X^{μ}_L, X^{μ}_U, k and $Y^{0\mu}$;
5.3	Construct connectivity matrix C^{μ}_k using above classification solution on X^{μ}_U;
5.4	Use ρ_k to assign uniformly drawn labels to each vector in X^{μ}_U;
5.5	Construct connectivity matrix $C^{\mu}_{\rho_k}$ using above classification solution on X^{μ}_U;
	Endfor
6	Evaluate the merit of k using following formula: $M_k = \frac{1}{q}\sum_{\mu}(M(C^{\mu}_k, C_k) - M(C^{\mu}_{\rho_k}, C_{\rho_k}))$, where $M(C^{\mu}, C)$ is given by equation (2);
7	Return M_k;

Then this model order identification procedure can be formulated as:

$$\hat{k}_{X_{L+U}} = argmax_{K_{min} \leq k \leq K_{max}} \{CV(X_{L+U}, k, q, Y^0_{X_{L+U}})\}. \quad (1)$$

$\hat{k}_{X_{L+U}}$ is the estimated sense number in X_{L+U}, K_{min} (or K_{max}) is the minimum (or maximum) value of sense number, and k is the possible value of sense number in X_{L+U}. Note that $k \geq k_{X_L}$. Then we set $K_{min} = k_{X_L}$. K_{max} may be set as a value greater than the possible ground-truth value. CV is a cluster validation based evaluation function. Table 2 shows the details of this function. We set q, the resampling frequency for estimation of stability score, as 20. α is set as 0.90. The random predictor assigns uniformly distributed class labels to each instance in a given dataset. We run this CV procedure for each value of k. The value of k that maximizes this function will be selected as the estimation of sense number. At the same time, we can obtain a partition of X_{L+U} with $\hat{k}_{X_{L+U}}$ groups.

The function $M(C^{\mu}, C)$ in Table 2 is given by (Levine and Domany, 2001):

$$M(C^{\mu}, C) = \frac{\sum_{i,j} 1\{C^{\mu}_{i,j} = C_{i,j} = 1, x_i, x_j \in X^{\mu}_U\}}{\sum_{i,j} 1\{C_{i,j} = 1, x_i, x_j \in X^{\mu}_U\}}, \quad (2)$$

where X^{μ}_U is the untagged data in X^{μ}_{L+U}, X^{μ}_{L+U} is a subset with the size $\alpha|X_{L+U}|$ $(0 < \alpha < 1)$ sampled from X_{L+U}, C or C^{μ} is $|X_U| \times |X_U|$ or $|X^{\mu}_U| \times |X^{\mu}_U|$ connectivity matrix based on classification solutions computed on X_U or X^{μ}_U respectively. The connectivity matrix C is defined as: $C_{i,j} = 1$ if x_i and x_j belong to the same cluster, otherwise $C_{i,j} = 0$. C^{μ} is calculated in the same way.

$M(C^{\mu}, C)$ measures the proportion of example pairs in each group computed on X_U that are also assigned into the same group by the classification solution on X^{μ}_U. Clearly, $0 \leq M \leq 1$. Intuitively, if the value of k is identical with the true value of sense number, then classification results on the different subsets generated by sampling should be similar with that on the full dataset. In the other words, the classification solution with the true model order as parameter is robust against resampling, which gives rise to a local optimum of $M(C^{\mu}, C)$.

In this algorithm, we normalize $M(C^{\mu}_k, C_k)$ by the equation in step 6 of Table 2, which makes our objective function different from the figure of merit (equation (2)) proposed in (Levine and Domany, 2001). The reason to normalize $M(C^{\mu}_k, C_k)$ is that $M(C^{\mu}_k, C_k)$ tends to decrease when increasing the value of k (Lange et al., 2002). Therefore for avoiding the bias that the smaller value of k is to be selected as the model order, we use the cluster validity of a random predictor to normalize $M(C^{\mu}_k, C_k)$.

If $\hat{k}_{X_{L+U}}$ is equal to k_{X_L}, then there is no new sense in X_U. Otherwise ($\hat{k}_{X_{L+U}} > k_{X_L}$) new senses of w may be represented by the groups in which there is no instance from X_L.

3 Experiments and Results

3.1 Experiment Design

We evaluated the ELP based model order identification algorithm on the data in English lexical sample task of SENSEVAL-3 (including all

Table 3: Description of The percentage of official training data used as tagged data when instances with different sense sets are removed from official training data.

	The percentage of official training data used as tagged data
$S_{subset} = \{s_1\}$	42.8%
$S_{subset} = \{s_2\}$	76.7%
$S_{subset} = \{s_3\}$	89.1%
$S_{subset} = \{s_1, s_2\}$	19.6%
$S_{subset} = \{s_1, s_3\}$	32.0%
$S_{subset} = \{s_2, s_3\}$	65.9%

the 57 English words) [9], and further empirically compared it with other state of the art classification methods, including SVM [10] (the state of the art method for supervised word sense disambiguation (Mihalcea et al., 2004)), a one-class partially supervised classification algorithm (Liu et al., 2003) [11], and a semi-supervised k-means clustering based model order identification algorithm.

The data for English lexical samples task in SENSEVAL-3 consists of 7860 examples as official training data, and 3944 examples as official test data for 57 English words. The number of senses of each English word varies from 3 to 11.

We evaluated these four algorithms with different sizes of incomplete tagged data. Given official training data of the word w, we constructed incomplete tagged data X_L by removing the all the tagged instances from official training data that have sense tags from S_{subset}, where S_{subset} is a subset of the ground-truth sense set S for w, and S consists of the sense tags in official training set for w. The removed training data and official test data of w were used as X_U. Note that $S_L = S - S_{subset}$. Then we ran these four algorithm for each target word w with X_L as tagged data and X_U as untagged data, and evaluated their performance using the accuracy on official test data of all the 57 words. We conducted six experiments for each target word w by setting S_{subset} as $\{s_1\}$, $\{s_2\}$, $\{s_3\}$, $\{s_1, s_2\}$, $\{s_1, s_3\}$, or $\{s_2, s_3\}$, where s_i is the i-th most frequent sense of w. S_{subset} cannot be set as $\{s_4\}$ since some words have only three senses. Table 3 lists the percentage of official training data used as tagged data (the number of examples in incomplete tagged data divided by the number of examples in official training data) when we removed the instances with sense tags from S_{subset} for all the 57 words. If $S_{subset} = \{s_3\}$, then most of sense tagged examples are still included in tagged data. If $S_{subset} = \{s_1, s_2\}$, then there are very few tagged examples in tagged data. If no instances are removed from official training data, then the value of percentage is 100%.

Given an incomplete tagged corpus for a target word, SVM does not have the ability to find the new senses from untagged corpus. Therefore it labels all the instances in the untagged corpus with sense tags from S_L.

Given a set of positive examples for a class and a set of unlabeled examples, the one-class partially supervised classification algorithm, LPU (Learning from Positive and Unlabeled examples) (Liu et al., 2003), learns a classifier in four steps:

Step 1: Identify a small set of reliable negative examples from unlabeled examples by the use of a classifier.

Step 2: Build a classifier using positive examples and automatically selected negative examples.

Step 3: Iteratively run previous two steps until no unlabeled examples are classified as negative ones or the unlabeled set is null.

Step 4: Select a good classifier from the set of classifiers constructed above.

For comparison, LPU [12] was run to perform classification on X_U for each class in X_L. The label of each instance in X_U was determined by maximizing the classification score from LPU output for each class. If the maximum score of an instance is negative, then this instance will be labeled as a new class. Note that LPU classifies X_{L+U} into $k_{X_L} + 1$ groups in most of cases.

The clustering based partially supervised sense disambiguation algorithm was implemented by replacing ELP with a semi-supervised k-means clustering algorithm (Wagstaff et al., 2001) in the model order identification procedure. The label information in labeled data was used to guide the semi-supervised clustering on X_{L+U}. Firstly, the labeled data may be used to determine initial cluster centroids. If the cluster number is greater

[9] Available at http://www.senseval.org/senseval3

[10] we used a linear SVM^{light}, available at http://svmlight.joachims.org/.

[11] Available at http://www.cs.uic.edu/~liub/LPU/LPU-download.html

[12] The three parameters in LPU were set as follows: "-s1 spy -s2 svm -c 1". It means that we used the spy technique for step 1 in LPU, the SVM algorithm for step 2, and selected the first or the last classifier as the final classifier. It is identical with the algorithm "Spy+SVM IS" in Liu et al. (2003).

than k_{X_L}, the initial centroids of clusters for new classes will be assigned as randomly selected instances. Secondly, in the clustering process, the instances with the same class label will stay in the same cluster, while the instances with different class labels will belong to different clusters. For better clustering solution, this clustering process will be restarted three times. Clustering process will be terminated when clustering solution converges or the number of iteration steps is more than 30. $K_{min} = k_{X_L} = |S_L|$, $K_{max} = K_{min} + m$. m is set as 4.

We used Jensen-Shannon (JS) divergence (Lin, 1991) as distance measure for semi-supervised clustering and ELP, since plain LP with JS divergence achieves better performance than that with cosine similarity on SENSEVAL-3 data (Niu et al., 2005).

For the LP process in ELP algorithm, we constructed connected graphs as follows: two instances u, v will be connected by an edge if u is among v's 10 nearest neighbors, or if v is among u's 10 nearest neighbors as measured by cosine or JS distance measure (following (Zhu and Ghahramani, 2002)).

We used three types of features to capture the information in all the contextual sentences of target words in SENSEVAL-3 data for all the four algorithms: part-of-speech of neighboring words with position information, words in topical context without position information (after removing stop words), and local collocations (as same as the feature set used in (Lee and Ng, 2002) except that we did not use syntactic relations). We removed the features with occurrence frequency (counted in both training set and test set) less than 3 times.

If the estimated sense number is more than the sense number in the initial tagged corpus X_L, then the results from order identification based methods will consist of the instances from clusters of unknown classes. When assessing the agreement between these classification results and the known results on official test set, we will encounter the problem that there is no sense tag for each instance in unknown classes. Slonim and Tishby (2000) proposed to assign documents in each cluster with the most dominant class label in that cluster, and then conducted evaluation on these labeled documents. Here we will follow their method for assigning sense tags to unknown classes from LPU, clustering based order identification process, and ELP based order identification process. We assigned the instances from unknown classes with the dominant sense tag in that cluster. The result from LPU always includes only one cluster of the unknown class. We also assigned the instances from the unknown class with the dominant sense tag in that cluster. When all instances have their sense tags, we evaluated the their results using the accuracy on official test set.

3.2 Results on Sense Disambiguation

Table 4 summarizes the accuracy of SVM, LPU, the semi-supervised k-means clustering algorithm with correct sense number $|S|$ or estimated sense number $\hat{k}_{X_{L+U}}$ as input, and the ELP algorithm with correct sense number $|S|$ or estimated sense number $\hat{k}_{X_{L+U}}$ as input using various incomplete tagged data. The last row in Table 4 lists the average accuracy of each algorithm over the six experimental settings. Using $|S|$ as input means that we do not perform order identification procedure, while using $\hat{k}_{X_{L+U}}$ as input is to perform order identification and obtain the classification results on X_U at the same time.

We can see that ELP based method outperforms clustering based method in terms of average accuracy under the same experiment setting, and these two methods outperforms SVM and LPU. Moreover, using the correct sense number as input helps to improve the overall performance of both clustering based method and ELP based method.

Comparing the performance of the same system with different sizes of tagged data (from the first experiment to the third experiment, and from the fourth experiment to the sixth experiment), we can see that the performance was improved when given more labeled data. Furthermore, ELP based method outperforms other methods in terms of accuracy when rare senses (e.g. s_3) are missing in the tagged data. It seems that ELP based method has the ability to find rare senses with the use of tagged and untagged corpora.

LPU algorithm can deal with only one-class classification problem. Therefore the labeled data of other classes cannot be used when determining the positive labeled data for current class. ELP can use the labeled data of all the known classes to determine the seeds of unknown classes. It may explain why LPU's performance is worse than ELP based sense disambiguation although LPU can correctly estimate the sense number in X_{L+U}

Table 4: This table summarizes the accuracy of SVM, LPU, the semi-supervised k-means clustering algorithm with correct sense number $|S|$ or estimated sense number $\hat{k}_{X_{L+U}}$ as input, and the ELP algorithm with correct sense number $|S|$ or estimated sense number $\hat{k}_{X_{L+U}}$ as input on the official test data of ELS task in SENSEVAL-3 when given various incomplete tagged corpora.

	SVM	LPU	Clustering algorithm with $\|S\|$ as input	ELP algorithm with $\|S\|$ as input	Clustering algorithm with $\hat{k}_{X_{L+U}}$ as input	ELP algorithm with $\hat{k}_{X_{L+U}}$ as input
$S_{subset} = \{s_1\}$	30.6%	22.3%	43.9%	47.8%	40.0%	38.7%
$S_{subset} = \{s_2\}$	59.7%	54.6%	44.0%	62.4%	48.5%	62.6%
$S_{subset} = \{s_3\}$	67.0%	53.4%	48.7%	67.2%	52.4%	69.1%
$S_{subset} = \{s_1, s_2\}$	14.6%	13.1%	44.4%	40.2%	35.6%	33.0%
$S_{subset} = \{s_1, s_3\}$	25.7%	21.1%	48.5%	37.9%	39.8%	31.0%
$S_{subset} = \{s_2, s_3\}$	56.2%	53.1%	47.3%	59.4%	46.6%	58.7%
Average accuracy	42.3%	36.3%	46.1%	52.5%	43.8%	48.9%

Table 5: These two tables provide the mean and standard deviation of absolute values of the difference between ground-truth results $|S|$ and sense numbers estimated by clustering or ELP based order identification procedure respectively.

	Clustering based method	ELP based method
$S_{subset} = \{s_1\}$	1.3±1.1	2.2±1.1
$S_{subset} = \{s_2\}$	2.4±0.9	2.4±0.9
$S_{subset} = \{s_3\}$	2.6±0.7	2.6±0.7
$S_{subset} = \{s_1, s_2\}$	1.2±0.6	1.6±0.5
$S_{subset} = \{s_1, s_3\}$	1.4±0.6	1.8±0.4
$S_{subset} = \{s_2, s_3\}$	1.8±0.5	1.8±0.5

when only one sense is missing in X_L.

When very few labeled examples are available, the noise in labeled data makes it difficult to learn the classification score (each entry in Y_{D_U}). Therefore using the classification confidence criterion may lead to poor performance of seed selection for unknown classes if the classification score is not accurate. It may explain why ELP based method does not outperform clustering based method with small labeled data (e.g., $S_{subset} = \{s_1\}$).

3.3 Results on Sense Number Estimation

Table 5 provides the mean and standard deviation of absolute difference values between ground-truth results $|S|$ and sense numbers estimated by clustering or ELP based order identification procedures respectively. For example, if the ground truth sense number of the word w is k_w, and the estimated value is $\hat{k}_w$, then the absolute value of the difference between these two values is $|k_w - \hat{k}_w|$. Therefore we can have this value for each word. Then we calculated the mean and deviation on this array of absolute values. LPU does not have the order identification capability since it always assumes that there is at least one new class in unlabeled data, and does not further differentiate the instances from these new classes. Therefore we do not provide the order identification results of LPU.

From the results in Table 5, we can see that estimated sense numbers are closer to ground truth results when given less labeled data for clustering or ELP based methods. Moreover, clustering based method performs better than ELP based method in terms of order identification when given less labeled data (e.g., $S_{subset} = \{s_1\}$). It seems that ELP is not robust to the noise in small labeled data, compared with the semi-supervised k-means clustering algorithm.

4 Related Work

The work closest to ours is partially supervised classification or building classifiers using positive examples and unlabeled examples, which has been studied in machine learning community (Denis et al., 2002; Liu et al., 2003; Manevitz and Yousef, 2001; Yu et al., 2002). However, they cannot group negative examples into meaningful clusters. In contrast, our algorithm can find the occurrence of negative examples and further group these negative examples into a "natural" number of clusters. Semi-supervised clustering (Wagstaff et al., 2001) may be used to perform classification by the use of labeled and unlabeled examples, but it encounters the same problem of partially supervised classification that model order cannot be automatically estimated.

Levine and Domany (2001) and Lange et al. (2002) proposed cluster validation based criteria for cluster number estimation. However, they showed the application of the cluster validation method only for unsupervised learning. Our work can be considered as an extension of their methods in the setting of partially supervised learning.

In natural language processing community, the work that is closely related to ours is word sense discrimination which can induce senses by grouping occurrences of a word into clusters (Schütze, 1998). If it is considered as unsupervised methods to solve sense disambiguation problem, then our method employs partially supervised learning technique to deal with sense disambiguation problem by use of tagged and untagged texts.

5 Conclusions

In this paper, we present an order identification based partially supervised classification algorithm and investigate its application to partially supervised word sense disambiguation problem. Experimental results on SENSEVAL-3 data indicate that our ELP based model order identification algorithm achieves better performance than other state of the art classification algorithms, e.g., SVM, a one-class partially supervised algorithm (LPU), and a semi-supervised k-means clustering based model order identification algorithm.

References

Brown P., Stephen, D.P., Vincent, D.P., & Robert, Mercer.. 1991. Word Sense Disambiguation Using Statistical Methods. *Proceedings of ACL.*

Dagan, I. & Itai A.. 1994. Word Sense Disambiguation Using A Second Language Monolingual Corpus. *Computational Linguistics*, Vol. 20(4), pp. 563-596.

Denis, F., Gilleron, R., & Tommasi, M.. 2002. Text Classification from Positive and Unlabeled Examples. *Proceedings of the 9th International Conference on Information Processing and Management of Uncertainty in Knowledge-Based Systems.*

Lange, T., Braun, M., Roth, V., & Buhmann, J. M. 2002. Stability-Based Model Selection. *NIPS 15.*

Leacock, C., Miller, G.A. & Chodorow, M.. 1998. Using Corpus Statistics and WordNet Relations for Sense Identification. *Computational Linguistics*, 24:1, 147–165.

Lee, Y.K. & Ng, H.T.. 2002. An Empirical Evaluation of Knowledge Sources and Learning Algorithms for Word Sense Disambiguation. *Proceedings of EMNLP*, (pp. 41-48).

Levine, E., & Domany, E. 2001. Resampling Method for Unsupervised Estimation of Cluster Validity. *Neural Computation*, Vol. 13, 2573–2593.

Lin, J. 1991. Divergence Measures Based on the Shannon Entropy. *IEEE Transactions on Information Theory*, 37:1, 145–150.

Liu, B., Dai, Y., Li, X., Lee, W.S., & Yu, P.. 2003. Building Text Classifiers Using Positive and Unlabeled Examples. *Proceedings of IEEE ICDM.*

Manevitz, L.M., & Yousef, M.. 2001. One Class SVMs for Document Classification. *Journal of Machine Learning*, 2, 139-154.

Mihalcea R., Chklovski, T., & Kilgariff, A.. 2004. The SENSEVAL-3 English Lexical Sample Task. *SENSEVAL-2004.*

Niu, Z.Y., Ji, D.H., & Tan, C.L.. 2005. Word Sense Disambiguation Using Label Propagation Based Semi-Supervised Learning. *Proceedings of ACL.*

Schütze, H.. 1998. Automatic Word Sense Discrimination. *Computational Linguistics*, 24:1, 97–123.

Wagstaff, K., Cardie, C., Rogers, S., & Schroedl, S.. 2001. Constrained K-Means Clustering with Background Knowledge. *Proceedings of ICML.*

Yarowsky, D.. 1995. Unsupervised Word Sense Disambiguation Rivaling Supervised Methods. *Proceedings of ACL.*

Yu, H., Han, J., & Chang, K. C.-C.. 2002. PEBL: Positive example based learning for web page classification using SVM. *Proceedings of ACM SIGKDD.*

Zhu, X. & Ghahramani, Z.. 2002. Learning from Labeled and Unlabeled Data with Label Propagation. *CMU CALD tech report CMU-CALD-02-107.*

Automatically Assessing Review Helpfulness

Soo-Min Kim[†]**, Patrick Pantel**[†]**, Tim Chklovski**[†]**, Marco Pennacchiotti**[‡]

[†]Information Sciences Institute
University of Southern California
4676 Admiralty Way
Marina del Rey, CA 90292
{skim,pantel,timc}@isi.edu

[‡]ART Group - DISP
University of Rome "Tor Vergata"
Viale del Politecnico 1
Rome, Italy
pennacchiotti@info.uniroma2.it

Abstract

User-supplied reviews are widely and increasingly used to enhance e-commerce and other websites. Because reviews can be numerous and varying in quality, it is important to assess how *helpful* each review is. While review helpfulness is currently assessed manually, in this paper we consider the task of automatically assessing it. Experiments using SVM regression on a variety of features over Amazon.com product reviews show promising results, with rank correlations of up to 0.66. We found that the most useful features include the length of the review, its unigrams, and its product rating.

1 Introduction

Unbiased user-supplied reviews are solicited ubiquitously by online retailers like Amazon.com, Overstock.com, Apple.com and Epinions.com, movie sites like imdb.com, traveling sites like citysearch.com, open source software distributors like cpanratings.perl.org, and countless others. Because reviews can be numerous and varying in quality, it is important to rank them to enhance customer experience.

In contrast with ranking search results, assessing *relevance* when ranking reviews is of little importance because reviews are directly associated with the relevant product or service. Instead, a key challenge when ranking reviews is to determine which reviews the customers will find helpful.

Most websites currently rank reviews by their recency or product rating (e.g., number of *stars* in Amazon.com reviews). Recently, more sophisticated ranking schemes measure reviews by their *helpfulness*, which is typically estimated by having users manually assess it. For example, on Amazon.com, an interface allows customers to vote whether a particular review is helpful or not. Unfortunately, newly written reviews and reviews with few votes cannot be ranked as several assessments are required in order to properly estimate helpfulness. For example, for all MP3 player products on Amazon.com, 38% of the 20,919 reviews received three or fewer helpfulness votes. Another problem is that low-traffic items may never gather enough votes. Among the MP3 player reviews that were authored at least three months ago on Amazon.com, still only 31% had three or fewer helpfulness votes.

It would be useful to assess review helpfulness automatically, as soon as the review is written. This would accelerate determining a review's ranking and allow a website to provide rapid feedback to review authors.

In this paper, we investigate the task of automatically predicting review helpfulness using a machine learning approach. Our main contributions are:

- **A system for automatically ranking reviews according to *helpfulness***; using state of the art SVM regression, we empirically evaluate our system on a real world dataset collected from Amazon.com on the task of reconstructing the helpfulness ranking; and
- **An analysis of different classes of features most important to capture review helpfulness**; including *structural* (e.g., html tags, punctuation, review length), *lexical* (e.g., *n*-grams), *syntactic* (e.g., percentage of verbs and nouns), *semantic* (e.g., product feature mentions), and *meta-data* (e.g., star rating).

2 Relevant Work

The task of automatically assessing product review helpfulness is related to these broader areas

Proceedings of the 2006 Conference on Empirical Methods in Natural Language Processing (EMNLP 2006), pages 423–430,
Sydney, July 2006.

of research: automatic analysis of product reviews, opinion and sentiment analysis, and text classification.

In the thriving area of research on automatic analysis and processing of product reviews (Hu and Liu 2004; Turney 2002; Pang and Lee 2005), little attention has been paid to the important task studied here – assessing review helpfulness. Pang and Lee (2005) have studied prediction of product ratings, which may be particularly relevant due to the correlation we find between product rating and the helpfulness of the review (discussed in Section 5). However, a user's overall rating for the product is often already available. Helpfulness, on the other hand, is valuable to assess because it is not explicitly known in current approaches until many users vote on the helpfulness of a review.

In opinion and sentiment analysis, the focus is on distinguishing between statements of fact vs. opinion, and on detecting the polarity of sentiments being expressed. Many researchers have worked in various facets of opinion analysis. Pang et al. (2002) and Turney (2002) classified sentiment polarity of reviews at the document level. Wiebe et al. (1999) classified sentence level subjectivity using syntactic classes such as adjectives, pronouns and modal verbs as features. Riloff and Wiebe (2003) extracted subjective expressions from sentences using a bootstrapping pattern learning process. Yu and Hatzivassiloglou (2003) identified the polarity of opinion sentences using semantically oriented words. These techniques were applied and examined in different domains, such as customer reviews (Hu and Liu 2004) and news articles (TREC novelty track 2003 and 2004).

In text classification, systems typically use bag-of-words models, although there is some evidence of benefits when introducing relevant semantic knowledge (Gabrilovich and Markovitch, 2005). In this paper, we explore the use of some semantic features for review helpfulness ranking. Another potential relevant classification task is academic and commercial efforts on detecting email spam messages[1], which aim to capture a much broader notion of helpfulness. For an SVM-based approach, see (Drucker et al 1999).

Finally, a related area is work on automatic essay scoring, which seeks to rate the quality of an essay (Attali and Burstein 2006; Burstein et al. 2004). The task is important for reducing the human effort required in scoring large numbers of student essays regularly written for standard tests such as the GRE. The exact scoring approaches developed in commercial systems are often not disclosed. However, more recent work on one of the major systems, e-rater 2.0, has focused on systematizing and simplifying the set of features used (Attali and Burstein 2006). Our choice of features to test was partially influenced by the features discussed by Attali and Burstein. At the same time, due to differences in the tasks, we did not use features aimed at assessing essay structure such as discourse structure analysis features. Our observations suggest that even helpful reviews vary widely in their discourse structure. We present the features which we have used below, in Section 3.2.

3 Modeling Review Helpfulness

In this section, we formally define the learning task and we investigate several features for assessing review helpfulness.

3.1 Task Definition

Formally, given a set of reviews R for a particular product, our task is to rank the reviews according to their *helpfulness*. We define a review *helpfulness* function, h, as:

$$h(r \in R) = \frac{rating_+(r)}{rating_+(r) + rating_-(r)} \quad (1)$$

where $rating_+(r)$ is the number of people that will find a review helpful and $rating_-(r)$ is the number of people that will find the review unhelpful. For evaluation, we resort to estimates of h from manual review assessments on websites like Amazon.com, as described in Section 4.

3.2 Features

One aim of this paper is to investigate how well different classes of features capture the helpfulness of a review. We experimented with various features organized in five classes: *Structural*, *Lexical*, *Syntactic*, *Semantic*, and *Meta-data*. Below we describe each feature class in turn.

Structural Features

Structural features are observations of the document structure and formatting. Properties such as review length and average sentence length are hypothesized to relate structural complexity to helpfulness. Also, HTML formatting tags could help in making a review more readable, and consequently more helpful. We experimented with the following features:

[1] See http://www.ceas.cc/, http://spamconference.org/

- *Length* (LEN): The total number of tokens in a syntactic analysis[2] of the review.
- *Sentential* (SEN): Observations of the sentences, including the number of sentences, the average sentence length, the percentage of question sentences, and the number of exclamation marks.
- *HTML* (HTM): Two features for the number of bold tags <b> and line breaks <br>.

Lexical Features

Lexical features capture the words observed in the reviews. We experimented with two sets of features:

- *Unigram* (UGR): The *tf-idf* statistic of each word occurring in a review.
- *Bigram* (BGR): The *tf-idf* statistic of each bigram occurring in a review.

For both unigrams and bigrams, we used lemmatized words from a syntactic analysis of the reviews and computed the *tf-idf* statistic (Salton and McGill 1983) using the following formula:

$$tf\ idf = \frac{tf \times \log(idf)}{N}$$

where N is the number of tokens in the review.

Syntactic Features

Syntactic features aim to capture the linguistic properties of the review. We grouped them into the following feature set:

- *Syntax* (SYN): Includes the percentage of parsed tokens that are open-class (i.e., nouns, verbs, adjectives and adverbs), the percentage of tokens that are nouns, the percentage of tokens that are verbs, the percentage of tokens that are verbs conjugated in the first person, and the percentage of tokens that are adjectives or adverbs.

Semantic Features

Most online reviews are fairly short; their sparsity suggests that bigram features will not perform well (which is supported by our experiments described in Section 5.3). Although semantic features have rarely been effective in many text classification problems (Moschitti and Basili 2004), there is reason here to hypothesize that a specialized vocabulary of *important* words might help with the sparsity. We hypothesized that good reviews will often contain: i) references to the features of a product (e.g., the *LCD* and *resolution* of a digital camera), and ii) mentions of sentiment words (i.e., words that express an opinion such as "*great* screen"). Below we describe two families of features that capture these semantic observations within the reviews:

- *Product-Feature* (PRF): The features of products that occur in the review, e.g., *capacity* of MP3 players and *zoom* of a digital camera. This feature counts the number of lexical matches that occur in the review for each product feature. There is no trivial way of obtaining a list of all the features of a product. In Section 5.1 we describe a method for automatically extracting product features from *Pro/Con* listings from Epinions.com. Our assumption is that pro/cons are the features that are important for customers (and hence should be part of a helpful review).
- *General-Inquirer* (GIW): Positive and negative sentiment words describing products or product features (e.g., "*amazing* sound quality" and "*weak* zoom"). The intuition is that reviews that analyze product features are more helpful than those that do not. We try to capture this analysis by extracting sentiment words using the publicly available list of positive and negative sentiment words from the General Inquirer Dictionaries[3].

Meta-Data Features

Unlike the previous four feature classes, meta-data features capture observations which are independent of the text (i.e., unrelated with linguistic features). We consider the following feature:

- *Stars* (STR): Most websites require reviewers to include an overall rating for the products that they review (e.g., star ratings in Amazon.com). This feature set includes the rating score (STR1) as well as the absolute value of the difference between the rating score and the average rating score given by all reviewers (STR2).

We differentiate meta-data features from semantic features since they require *external* knowledge that may not be available from certain review sites. Nowadays, however, most sites that collect user reviews also collect some form of product rating (e.g., Amazon.com, Overstock.com, and Apple.com).

---

[2] Reviews are analyzed using the Minipar dependency parser (Lin 1994).

[3] http://www.wjh.harvard.edu/~inquirer/homecat.htm

Table 1. Sample of 4 out of 43 reviews for the *iPod Photo 20GB* product from Amazon.com along with their ratings as well as their helpfulness ranks (from both the gold standard from Amazon.com and the SVM prediction of our best performing system described in Section 5.2).

Review Title	*Helpful Votes*	*Unhelpful Votes*	Rank(h)	
			Gold Standard	SVM Prediction
"iPod Moves to All-color Line-up"	215	11	7	1
"iPod: It's NOT Music to My Ears"	11	13	25	30
"The best thing I ever bought"	22	32	26	27
"VERY disappointing"	1	18	40	40

4 Ranking System

In this paper, we estimate the *helpfulness* function in Equation 1 using user ratings extracted from Amazon.com, where $rating_+(r)$ is the number of unique users that rated the review r as helpful and $rating_-(r)$ is the number of unique users that rated r as unhelpful.

Reviews from Amazon.com form a gold standard labeled dataset of $\{review, h(review)\}$ pairs that can be used to train a supervised machine learning algorithm. In this paper, we applied an SVM (Vapnik 1995) package on the features extracted from reviews to learn the function h.

Two natural options for learning helpfulness according to Equation 1 are SVM Regression and SVM Ranking (Joachims 2002). Though learning to rank according to *helpfulness* requires only SVM Ranking, the helpfulness function provides non-uniform differences between ranks in the training set. Also, in practice, many products have only one review, which can serve as training data for SVM Regression but not SVM Ranking. Furthermore, in large sites such as Amazon.com, when new reviews are written it is inefficient to re-rank all previously ranked reviews. We therefore choose SVM Regression in this paper. We describe the exact implementation in Section 5.1.

After the SVM is trained, for a given product and its set of reviews R, we rank the reviews of R in decreasing order of $h(r)$, $r \in R$.

Table 1 shows four sample reviews for the *iPod Photo 20GB* product from Amazon.com, their total number of helpful and unhelpful votes, as well as their rank according to the helpfulness score h from both the gold standard from Amazon.com and using the SVM prediction of our best performing system described in Section 5.2.

5 Experimental Results

We empirically evaluate our review model and ranking system, described in Section 3 and Section 4, by comparing the performance of various feature combinations on products mined from Amazon.com. Below, we describe our experimental setup, present our results, and analyze system performance.

5.1 Experimental Setup

We describe below the datasets that we extracted from Amazon.com, the implementation of our SVM system, and the method we used for extracting features of reviews.

Extraction and Preprocessing of Datasets

We focused our experiments on two products from Amazon.com: *MP3 Players* and *Digital Cameras*.

Using Amazon Web Services API, we collected reviews associated with all products in the *MP3 Players* and *Digital Cameras* categories. For *MP3 Players*, we collected 821 products and 33,016 reviews; for *Digital Cameras*, we collected 1,104 products and 26,189 reviews.

In most retailer websites like Amazon.com, duplicate reviews, which are quite frequent, skew statistics and can greatly affect a learning algorithm. Looking for exact string matches between reviews is not a sufficient filter since authors of duplicated reviews often make small changes to the reviews to avoid detection. We built a simple filter that compares the distribution of word bigrams across each pair of reviews. A pair is deemed a duplicate if more than 80% of their bigrams match.

Also, whole products can be duplicated. For different product versions, such as iPods that can come in black or white models, reviews on Amazon.com are duplicated between them. We filter

Table 2. Overview of filtered datasets extracted from Amazon.com.

	MP3 PLAYERS	*DIGITAL CAMERAS*
Total Products	736	1066
Total Reviews	11,374	14,467
Average Reviews/Product	15.4	13.6
Min/MaxReviews/Product	1 / 375	1 / 168

out complete products where each of its reviews is detected as a duplicate of another product (i.e., only one iPod version is retained).

The filtering of duplicate products and duplicate reviews discarded 85 products and 12,097 reviews for *MP3 Players* and 38 products and 3,692 reviews for *Digital Cameras*.

In order to have accurate estimates for the helpfulness function in Equation 1, we filtered out any review that did not receive at least five user ratings (i.e., reviews where less than five users voted it as helpful or unhelpful are filtered out). This filtering was performed before duplicate detection and discarded 45.7% of the *MP3 Players* reviews and 32.7% of the *Digital Cameras* reviews.

Table 2 describes statistics for the final datasets after the filtering steps. 10% of products for both datasets were withheld as development corpora and the remaining 90% were randomly sorted into 10 sets for 10-fold cross validation.

SVM Regression

For our regression model, we deployed the state of the art SVM regression tool SVM^{light} (Joachims 1999). We tested on the development sets various kernels including linear, polynomial (degrees 2, 3, and 4), and radial basis function (RBF). The best performing kernel was RBF and we report only these results in this paper (performance was measured using Spearman's correlation coefficient, described in Section 5.2).

We tuned the RBF kernel parameters C (the penalty parameter) and γ (the kernel width hyperparameter) performing full grid search over the 110 combinations of exponentially spaced parameter pairs (C,γ) following (Hsu et al. 2003).

Feature Extraction

To extract the features described in Section 3.2, we preprocessed each review using the Minipar dependency parser (Lin 1994). We used the parser tokenization, sentence breaker, and syntactic categorizations to generate the *Length*, *Sentential*, *Unigram*, *Bigram*, and *Syntax* feature sets.

In order to count the occurrences of product features for the *Product-Feature* set, we developed an automatic way of mining references to product features from Epinions.com. On this website, user-generated product reviews include explicit lists of *pros* and *cons*, describing the best and worst aspects of a product. For example, for MP3 players, we found the pro *"belt clip"* and the con *"Useless FM tuner"*. Our assumption is that the *pro/con* lists tend to contain references to the product features that are important to customers, and hence their occurrence in a review may correlate with review helpfulness. We filtered out all single-word entries which were infrequently seen (e.g., *hold*, *ever*). After splitting and filtering the *pro/con* lists, we were left with a total of 9,110 unique features for *MP3 Players* and 13,991 unique features for *Digital Cameras.*

The *Stars* feature set was created directly from the star ratings given by each author of an Amazon.com review.

For each feature measurement f, we applied the following standard transformation:

$$\ln(f+1)$$

and then scaled each feature between [0, 1] as suggested in (Hsu et al. 2003).

We experimented with various combinations of feature sets. Our results tables use the abbreviations presented in Section 3.2. For brevity, we report the combinations which contributed to our best performing system and those that help assess the power of the different feature classes in capturing helpfulness.

5.2 Ranking Performance

Evaluating the quality of a particular ranking is difficult since certain ranking intervals can be more important than others (e.g., top-10 versus bottom-10) We adopt the Spearman correlation coefficient ρ (Spearman 1904) since it is the most commonly used measure of correlation between two sets of ranked data points[4].

For each fold in our 10-fold cross-validation experiments, we trained our SVM system using 9 folds. For the remaining test fold, we ranked each product's reviews according to the SVM prediction (described in Section 4) and computed the ρ

[4] We used the version of Spearman's correlation coefficient that allows for ties in rankings. See Siegel and Castellan (1988) for more on alternate rank statistics such as Kendall's *tau*.

Table 3. Evaluation of the feature combinations that make up our best performing system (in bold), for ranking reviews of Amazon.com *MP3 Players* and *Digital Cameras* according to *helpfulness*.

FEATURE COMBINATIONS	*MP3 PLAYERS*		*DIGITAL CAMERAS*	
	SPEARMAN†	*PEARSON*†	*SPEARMAN*†	*PEARSON*†
LEN	0.575 ± 0.037	0.391 ± 0.038	0.521 ± 0.029	0.357 ± 0.029
UGR	0.593 ± 0.036	0.398 ± 0.038	0.499 ± 0.025	0.328 ± 0.029
STR1	0.589 ± 0.034	0.326 ± 0.038	0.507 ± 0.029	0.266 ± 0.030
UGR+STR1	0.644 ± 0.033	0.436 ± 0.038	0.490 ± 0.032	0.324 ± 0.032
LEN+UGR	0.582 ± 0.036	0.401 ± 0.038	0.553 ± 0.028	0.394 ± 0.029
LEN+STR1	0.652 ± 0.033	0.470 ± 0.038	0.577 ± 0.029	0.423 ± 0.031
LEN+UGR+STR1	**0.656 ± 0.033**	**0.476 ± 0.038**	**0.595 ± 0.028**	**0.442 ± 0.031**

LEN=*Length*; UGR=*Unigram*; STR=*Stars*

†95% confidence bounds are calculated using 10-fold cross-validation.

correlation between the ranking and the gold standard ranking from the test fold[5].

Although our task definition is to learn review rankings according to *helpfulness*, as an intermediate step the SVM system learns to predict the absolute helpfulness score for each review. To test the correlation of this score against the gold standard, we computed the standard Pearson correlation coefficient.

Results show that the highest performing feature combination consisted of the *Length*, the *Unigram*, and the *Stars* feature sets. Table 3 reports the evaluation results for every combination of these features with 95% confidence bounds. Of the three features alone, neither was statistically more significant than the others. Examining each pair combination, only the combination of *length* with *stars* outperformed the others. Surprisingly, adding *unigram* features to this combination had little effect for the *MP3 Players*.

Given our list of features defined in Section 3.2, helpfulness of reviews is best captured with a combination of the *Length* and *Stars* features. Training an RBF-kernel SVM regression model does not necessarily make clear the exact relationship between input and output variables. To investigate this relationship between length and helpfulness, we inspected their Pearson correlation coefficient, which was 0.45. Users indeed tend to find short reviews less helpful than longer ones: out of the 5,247 reviews for *MP3 Players* that contained more than 1000 characters, the average gold standard helpfulness score was 82%; the 204 reviews with fewer than 100 characters had on average a score of 23%. The explicit product rating, such as *Stars* is also an indicator of review helpfulness, with a Pearson correlation coefficient of 0.48.

The low Pearson correlations of Table 3 compared to the Spearman correlations suggest that we can learn the ranking without perfectly learning the function itself. To investigate this, we tested the ability of SVM regression to recover the target helpfulness score, given the score itself as the only feature. The Spearman correlation for this test was a perfect 1.0. Interestingly, the Pearson correlation was only 0.798, suggesting that the RBF kernel does learn the *helpfulness* ranking without learning the function exactly.

5.3 Results Analysis

Table 3 shows only the feature combinations of our highest performing system. In Table 4, we report several other feature combinations to show why we selected certain features and what was the effect of our five feature classes presented in Section 3.2.

In the first block of six feature combinations in Table 4, we show that the *unigram* features outperform the *bigram* features, which seem to be suffering from the data sparsity of the short reviews. Also, *unigram* features seem to subsume the information carried in our semantic features *Product-Feature* (PRF) and *General-Inquirer* (GIW). Although both PRF and GIW perform well as standalone features, when combined with unigrams there is little performance difference (for *MP3 Players* we see a small but insignificant decrease in performance whereas for *Digital Cameras* we see a small but insignificant improvement). Recall that PRF and GIW are simply subsets of review words that are found to be *product features* or *sentiment words*. The learning algorithm seems to discover on its own which

[5] Recall that the gold standard is extracted directly from user helpfulness votes on Amazon.com (see Section 4).

Table 4. Performance evaluation of various feature combinations for ranking reviews of *MP3 Players* and *Digital Cameras* on Amazon.com according to *helpfulness*. The first six lines suggest that unigrams subsume the semantic features; the next two support the use of the raw counts of product ratings (stars) rather than the distance of this count from the average rating; the final six investigate the importance of auxiliary feature sets.

Feature Combinations	*MP3 Players*		*Digital Cameras*	
	Spearman†	*Pearson*†	*Spearman*†	*Pearson*†
UGR	0.593 ± 0.036	0.398 ± 0.038	0.499 ± 0.025	0.328 ± 0.029
BGR	0.499 ± 0.040	0.293 ± 0.038	0.434 ± 0.032	0.242 ± 0.029
PRF	0.591± 0.037	0.400 ± 0.039	0.527 ± 0.030	0.316 ± 0.028
GIW	0.571 ± 0.036	0.381 ± 0.038	0.524 ± 0.030	0.333 ± 0.028
UGR+PRF	0.570 ± 0.037	0.375 ± 0.038	0.546 ± 0.029	0.348 ± 0.028
UGR+GIW	0.554 ± 0.037	0.358 ± 0.038	0.568 ± 0.031	0.324 ± 0.029
STR1	0.589 ± 0.034	0.326 ± 0.038	0.507 ± 0.029	0.266 ± 0.030
STR2	0.556 ± 0.032	0.303 ± 0.038	0.504 ± 0.027	0.229 ± 0.027
LEN+UGR+STR1	**0.656 ± 0.033**	**0.476 ± 0.038**	0.595 ± 0.028	0.442 ± 0.031
LEN+UGR+STR1+SEN	0.653 ± 0.033	0.470 ± 0.038	**0.599 ± 0.028**	**0.448 ± 0.030**
LEN+UGR+STR1+HTM	0.640 ± 0.035	0.459 ± 0.039	0.594 ± 0.028	0.442 ± 0.031
LEN+UGR+STR1+SYN	0.645 ± 0.034	0.469 ± 0.039	0.595 ± 0.028	0.447 ± 0.030
LEN+UGR+STR1+SEN+HTM+SYN	0.631 ± 0.035	0.453 ± 0.039	0.600 ± 0.028	0.452 ± 0.030
LEN+UGR+STR1+SEN+HTM+SYN+PRF+GIW	0.601 ± 0.035	0.396 ± 0.038	0.604 ± 0.027	0.460 ± 0.030

LEN=*Length*; SEN=*Sentential*; HTM=*HTML*; UGR=*Unigram*; BGR=*Bigram*; SYN=*Syntax*; PRF=*Product-Feature*; GIW=*General-Inquirer*; STR=*Stars*

†95% confidence bounds are calculated using 10-fold cross-validation.

words are most important in a review and does not use additional knowledge about the meaning of the words (at least not the semantics contained in PRF and GIW).

We tested two different versions of the *Stars* feature: i) the number of star ratings, *STR1*; and ii) the difference between the star rating and the average rating of the review, *STR2*. The second block of feature combinations in Table 4 shows that neither is significantly better than the other so we chose *STR1* for our best performing system.

Our experiments also revealed that our *structural* features *Sentential* and *HTML*, as well as our syntactic features, *Syntax*, did not show any significant improvement in system performance. In the last block of feature combinations in Table 4, we report the performance of our best performing features (*Length*, *Unigram*, and *Stars*) along with these other features. Though none of the features cause a performance deterioration, neither of them significantly improves performance.

5.4 Discussion

In this section, we discuss the broader implications and potential impacts of our work, and possible connections with other research directions.

The usefulness of the *Stars* feature for determining review helpfulness suggests the need for developing automatic methods for assessing product ratings, e.g., (Pang and Lee 2005).

Our findings focus on predictors of helpfulness of reviews of tangible consumer products (consumer electronics). Helpfulness is also solicited and tracked for reviews of many other types of entities: restaurants (citysearch.com), films (imdb.com), reviews of open-source software modules (cpanratings.perl.org), and countless others. Our findings of the importance of *Length*, *Unigrams*, and *Stars* may provide the basis of comparison for assessing helpfulness of reviews of other entity types.

Our work represents an initial step in assessing helpfulness. In the future, we plan to investigate other possible indicators of helpfulness such as a reviewer's reputation, the use of comparatives (e.g., *more* and *better than*), and references to other products.

Taken further, this work may have interesting connections to work on personalization, social networks, and recommender systems, for instance by identifying the reviews that a particular user would find helpful.

Our work on helpfulness of reviews also has potential applications to work on automatic generation of review information, by providing a way to assess helpfulness of automatically generated reviews. Work on generation of reviews includes review summarization and extraction of useful reviews from blogs and other mixed texts.

6 Conclusions

Ranking reviews according to user *helpfulness* is an important problem for many online sites such as Amazon.com and Ebay.com. To date, most websites measure helpfulness by having users manually assess how helpful each review is to them. In this paper, we proposed an algorithm for automatically assessing helpfulness and ranking reviews according to it. Exploiting the multitude of user-rated reviews on Amazon.com, we trained an SVM regression system to learn a helpfulness function and then applied it to rank unlabeled reviews. Our best system achieved Spearman correlation coefficient scores of 0.656 and 0.604 against a gold standard for MP3 players and digital cameras.

We also performed a detailed analysis of different features to study the importance of several feature classes in capturing helpfulness. We found that the most useful features were the length of the review, its unigrams, and its product rating. Semantic features like mentions of product features and sentiment words seemed to be subsumed by the simple unigram features. Structural features (other than length) and syntactic features had no significant impact.

It is our hope through this work to shed some light onto what people find helpful in user-supplied reviews and, by automatically ranking them, to ultimately enhance user experience.

References

Attali, Y. and Burstein, J. 2006. Automated Essay Scoring With e-rater® V.2. *Journal of Technology, Learning, and Assessment, 4*(3).

Burstein, J., Chodorow, M., and Leacock, C. 2004. Automated essay evaluation: the criterion online writing service. *AI Magazine*. 25(3), pp 27–36.

Drucker,H., Wu,D. and Vapnik,V. 1999. Support vector machines for spam categorization. *IEEE Trans. Neural Netw.*, 10, 1048–1054.

Gabrilovich, E. and Markovitch, S. 2005. Feature Generation for Text Categorization Using World Knowledge. In *Proceedings of IJCAI-2005*.

Hsu, C.-W.; Chang, C.-C.; and Lin, C.-J. 2003. A practical guide to SVM classification. *Technical report*, Department of Computer Science and Information Technology, National Taiwan University.

Hu, M. and Liu, B. 2004. *Mining and summarizing customer reviews*. KDD'04. pp.168 – 177

Kim, S. and Hovy, E. 2004. Determining the Sentiment of Opinions. *Proceedings of COLING-04*.

Joachims, T. 1999. Making Large-Scale SVM Learning Practical. In B. Schölkopf, C. Burges, and A. Smola (eds), *Advances in Kernel Methods: Support Vector Learning*. MIT Press. Cambridge, MA.

Joachims, T. 2002. Optimizing Search Engines Using Clickthrough Data. In Proceedings of ACM KDD-02.

Moschitti, A. and Basili R. 2004. Complex Linguistic Features for Text Classification: A Comprehensive Study. In *Proceedings of ECIR 2004*. Sunderland, U.K.

Pang, B, L. Lee, and S. Vaithyanathan. 2001. Thumbs up? Sentiment Classification using Machine Learning Techniques. *Proceedings of EMNLP 2002*.

Pang, B. and Lee, L. 2005. Seeing stars: Exploiting class relationships for sentiment categorization with respect to rating scales. In *Proceedings of the ACL*, 2005.

Riloff , E. and J. Wiebe. 2003. Learning Extraction Patterns for Subjective Expressions. In *Proc. of EMNLP-03*.

Riloff, E., J. Wiebe, and T. Wilson. 2003. Learning Subjective Nouns Using Extraction Pattern Bootstrapping. *Proceedings of CoNLL-03*

Rose, C., Roque, A., Bhembe, D., and Vanlehn, K. 2003. A Hybrid Text Classification Approach for Analysis of Student Essays. In *Proc. of the HLT-NAACL*, 2003.

Salton, G. and McGill, M. J. 1983. *Introduction to Modern Information Retrieval*. McGraw Hill.

Siegel, S. and Castellan, N.J. Jr. 1988. *Nonparametric Statistics for the Behavioral Sciences*. McGraw-Hill.

Spearman C. 1904. The Proof and Measurement of Association Between Two Things. *American Journal of Psychology*, 15:72–101.

Turney, P. 2002. Thumbs Up or Thumbs Down? Semantic Orientation Applied to Unsupervised Classification of Reviews. *Proceedings of the 40th Annual Meeting of the ACL*, Philadelphia, 417–424.

Vapnik, V.N. 1995. *The Nature of Statistical Learning Theory*. Springer.

Wiebe, J, R. Bruce, and T. O'Hara. 1999. Development and use of a gold standard data set for subjectivity classifications. *Proc. of the 37th Annual Meeting of the Association for Computational Linguistics(ACL-99)*, 246–253.

Yu, H. and Hatzivassiloglou, V. 2003. Towards Answering Opinion Questions: Separating Facts from Opinions and Identifying the Polarity of Opinion Sentences. *Proceedings of EMNLP 2003*.

Joint Extraction of Entities and Relations for Opinion Recognition

Yejin Choi and Eric Breck and Claire Cardie
Department of Computer Science
Cornell University
Ithaca, NY 14853
{ychoi,ebreck,cardie}@cs.cornell.edu

Abstract

We present an approach for the joint extraction of entities and relations in the context of opinion recognition and analysis. We identify two types of opinion-related entities — expressions of opinions and sources of opinions — along with the linking relation that exists between them. Inspired by Roth and Yih (2004), we employ an integer linear programming approach to solve the joint opinion recognition task, and show that global, constraint-based inference can significantly boost the performance of both relation extraction and the extraction of opinion-related entities. Performance further improves when a semantic role labeling system is incorporated. The resulting system achieves F-measures of 79 and 69 for entity and relation extraction, respectively, improving substantially over prior results in the area.

1 Introduction

Information extraction tasks such as recognizing entities and relations have long been considered critical to many domain-specific NLP tasks (e.g. Mooney and Bunescu (2005), Prager et al. (2000), White et al. (2001)). Researchers have further shown that *opinion-oriented information extraction* can provide analogous benefits to a variety of practical applications including product reputation tracking (Morinaga et al., 2002), opinion-oriented question answering (Stoyanov et al., 2005), and opinion-oriented summarization (e.g. Cardie et al. (2004), Liu et al. (2005)). Moreover, much progress has been made in the area of opinion extraction: it is possible to identify sources of opinions (i.e. the opinion holders) (e.g. Choi et al. (2005) and Kim and Hovy (2005b)), to determine the polarity and strength of opinion expressions (e.g. Wilson et al. (2005)), and to recognize propositional opinions and their sources (e.g. Bethard et al. (2004)) with reasonable accuracy. To date, however, there has been no effort to simultaneously identify arbitrary opinion expressions, their sources, and the relations between them. Without progress on the *joint extraction of opinion entities **and** their relations*, the capabilities of opinion-based applications will remain limited.

Fortunately, research in machine learning has produced methods for global inference and joint classification that can help to address this deficiency (e.g. Bunescu and Mooney (2004), Roth and Yih (2004)). Moreover, it has been shown that exploiting dependencies among entities and/or relations via global inference not only solves the joint extraction task, but often boosts performance on the individual tasks when compared to classifiers that handle the tasks independently — for semantic role labeling (e.g. Punyakanok et al. (2004)), information extraction (e.g. Roth and Yih (2004)), and sequence tagging (e.g. Sutton et al. (2004)).

In this paper, we present a global inference approach (Roth and Yih, 2004) to the extraction of opinion-related entities and relations. In particular, we aim to identify two types of entities (i.e. spans of text): entities that express opinions and entities that denote sources of opinions. More specifically, we use the term *opinion expression* to denote all direct expressions of subjectivity including opinions, emotions, beliefs, sentiment, etc., as well as all speech expressions that introduce subjective propositions; and use the term *source* to denote the person or entity (e.g. a re-

Proceedings of the 2006 Conference on Empirical Methods in Natural Language Processing (EMNLP 2006), pages 431–439,
Sydney, July 2006.

port) that holds the opinion.[1] In addition, we aim to identify the relations between opinion expression entities and source entities. That is, for a given opinion expression O_i and source entity S_j, we determine whether the relation $L_{i,j} \stackrel{\text{def}}{=} (S_j \text{ expresses } O_i)$ obtains, i.e. whether S_j is the source of opinion expression O_i. We refer to this particular relation as the *link* relation in the rest of the paper. Consider, for example, the following sentences:

S1. [*Bush*]$^{(1)}$ intends$^{(1)}$ to curb the increase in harmful gas emissions and is counting on$^{(1)}$ the good will$^{(2)}$ of [*US industrialists*]$^{(2)}$.

S2. By questioning$^{(3)}$ [*the Imam*]$^{(4)}$'s edict$^{(4)}$ [*the Islamic Republic of Iran*]$^{(3)}$ made [*the people of the world*]$^{(5)}$ understand$^{(5)}$...

The underlined phrases above are opinion expressions and phrases marked with square brackets are source entities. The numeric superscripts on entities indicate link relations: a source entity and an opinion expression with the same number satisfy the link relation. For instance, the source entity *"Bush"* and the opinion expression *"intends"* satisfy the link relation, and so do *"Bush"* and *"counting on."* Notice that a sentence may contain more than one link relation, and link relations are not one-to-one mappings between sources and opinions. Also, the pair of entities in a link relation may not be the closest entities to each other, as is the case in the second sentence, between *"questioning"* and *"the Islamic Republic of Iran."*

We expect the extraction of opinion relations to be critical for many opinion-oriented NLP applications. For instance, consider the following question that might be given to a question-answering system:

- What is *the Imam*'s opinion toward *the Islamic Republic of Iran*?

Without in-depth opinion analysis, the question-answering system might mistake example S2 as relevant to the query, even though S2 exhibits the opinion of the Islamic Republic of Iran toward Imam, not the other way around.

Inspired by Roth and Yih (2004), we model our task as global, constraint-based inference over separately trained entity and relation classifiers. In particular, we develop three base classifiers: two sequence-tagging classifiers for the extraction of opinion expressions and sources, and a binary classifier to identify the link relation. The global inference procedure is implemented via integer linear programming (ILP) to produce an optimal and coherent extraction of entities and relations.

Because many (60%) opinion-source relations appear as predicate-argument relations, where the predicate is a verb, we also hypothesize that semantic role labeling (SRL) will be very useful for our task. We present two baseline methods for the joint opinion-source recognition task that use a state-of-the-art SRL system (Punyakanok et al., 2005), and describe two additional methods for incorporating SRL into our ILP-based system.

Our experiments show that the global inference approach not only improves relation extraction over the base classifier, but does the same for individual entity extractions. For source extraction in particular, our system achieves an F-measure of 78.1, significantly outperforming previous results in this area (Choi et al., 2005), which obtained an F-measure of 69.4 on the same corpus. In addition, we achieve an F-measure of 68.9 for link relation identification and 82.0 for opinion expression extraction; for the latter task, our system achieves human-level performance.[2]

2 High-Level Approach and Related Work

Our system operates in three phases.

Opinion and Source Entity Extraction We begin by developing two separate token-level sequence-tagging classifiers for opinion expression extraction and source extraction, using linear-chain Conditional Random Fields (CRFs) (Lafferty et al., 2001). The sequence-tagging classifiers are trained using only local syntactic and lexical information to extract each type of entity without knowledge of any nearby or neighboring entities or relations. We collect n-best sequences from each sequence tagger in order to boost the recall of the final system.

Link Relation Classification We also develop a relation classifier that is trained and tested on all pairs of opinion and source entities extracted from the aforementioned n-best opinion expression and source sequences. The relation classifier is modeled using Markov order-0 CRFs(Lafferty

[1] See Wiebe et al. (2005) for additional details.

[2] Wiebe et al. (2005) reports human annotation agreement for opinion expression as 82.0 by F1 measure.

et al., 2001), which are equivalent to maximum entropy models. It is trained using only local syntactic information potentially useful for connecting a pair of entities, but has no knowledge of nearby or neighboring extracted entities and link relations.

Integer Linear Programming Finally, we formulate an integer linear programming problem for each sentence using the results from the previous two phases. In particular, we specify a number of soft and hard constraints among relations and entities that take into account the confidence values provided by the supporting entity and relation classifiers, and that encode a number of heuristics to ensure coherent output. Given these constraints, global inference via ILP finds the optimal, coherent set of opinion-source pairs by exploiting mutual dependencies among the entities and relations.

While good performance in entity or relation extraction can contribute to better performance of the final system, this is not always the case. Punyakanok et al. (2004) notes that, in general, it is better to have high recall from the classifiers included in the ILP formulation. For this reason, it is not our goal to directly optimize the performance of our opinion and source entity extraction models or our relation classifier.

The rest of the paper is organized as follows. Related work is outlined below. Section 3 describes the components of the first phase of our system, the opinion and source extraction classifiers. Section 4 describes the construction of the link relation classifier for phase two. Section 5 describes the ILP formulation to perform global inference over the results from the previous two phases. Experimental results that compare our ILP approach to a number of baselines are presented in Section 6. Section 7 describes how SRL can be incorporated into our global inference system to further improve the performance. Final experimental results and discussion comprise Section 8.

Related Work The definition of our source-expresses-opinion task is similar to that of Bethard et al. (2004); however, our definition of opinion and source entities are much more extensive, going beyond single sentences and propositional opinion expressions. In particular, we evaluate our approach with respect to (1) a wide variety of opinion expressions, (2) explicit and implicit[3] sources, (3) multiple opinion-source link relations per sentence, and (4) link relations that span more than one sentence. In addition, the link relation model explicitly exploits mutual dependencies among entities and relations, while Bethard et al. (2004) does not directly capture the potential influence among entities.

Kim and Hovy (2005b) and Choi et al. (2005) focus only on the extraction of sources of opinions, without extracting opinion expressions. Specifically, Kim and Hovy (2005b) assume a priori existence of the opinion expressions and extract a single source for each, while Choi et al. (2005) do not explicitly extract opinion expressions nor link an opinion expression to a source even though their model implicitly learns approximations of opinion expressions in order to identify opinion sources. Other previous research focuses only on the extraction of opinion expressions (e.g. Kim and Hovy (2005a), Munson et al. (2005) and Wilson et al. (2005)), omitting source identification altogether.

There have also been previous efforts to simultaneously extract entities and relations by exploiting their mutual dependencies. Roth and Yih (2002) formulated global inference using a Bayesian network, where they captured the influence between a relation and a pair of entities via the conditional probability of a relation, given a pair of entities. This approach however, could not exploit dependencies between relations. Roth and Yih (2004) later formulated global inference using integer linear programming, which is the approach that we apply here. In contrast to our work, Roth and Yih (2004) operated in the domain of factual information extraction rather than opinion extraction, and assumed that the exact boundaries of entities from the gold standard are known a priori, which may not be available in practice.

3 Extraction of Opinion and Source Entities

We develop two separate sequence tagging classifiers for opinion extraction and source extraction, using linear-chain Conditional Random Fields (CRFs) (Lafferty et al., 2001). The sequence tagging is encoded as the typical 'BIO' scheme.[4] Each training or test instance represents a sentence, encoded as a linear chain of tokens and their

[3] *Implicit* sources are those that are not explicitly mentioned. See Section 8 for more details.

[4] 'B' is for the token that **b**egins an entity, 'I' is for tokens that are **i**nside an entity, and 'O' is for tokens **o**utside an entity.

associated features. Our feature set is based on that of Choi et al. (2005) for source extraction[5], but we include additional lexical and WordNet-based features. For simplicity, we use the same features for opinion entity extraction and source extraction, and let the CRFs learn appropriate feature weights for each task.

3.1 Entity extraction features

For each token x_i, we include the following features. For details, see Choi et al. (2005).

word: words in a [-4, +4] window centered on x_i.

part-of-speech: POS tags in a [-2, +2] window.[6]

grammatical role: grammatical role (subject, object, prepositional phrase types) of x_i derived from a dependency parse.[7]

dictionary: whether x_i is in the opinion expression dictionary culled from the training data and augmented by approximately 500 opinion words from the MPQA Final Report[8]. Also computed for tokens in a [-1, +1] window and for x_i's parent "chunk" in the dependency parse.

semantic class: x_i's semantic class.[9]

WordNet: the WordNet hypernym of x_i.[10]

4 Relation Classification

We also develop a maximum entropy binary classifier for opinion-source *link* relation classification. Given an opinion-source pair, O_i-S_j, the relation classifier decides whether the pair exhibits a valid link relation, $L_{i,j}$. The relation classifier focuses only on the syntactic structure and lexical properties between the two entities of a given pair, without knowing whether the proposed entities are correct. Opinion and source entities are taken from the n-best sequences of the entity extraction models; therefore, some are invariably incorrect.

From each sentence, we create training and test instances for all possible opinion-source pairings that do not overlap: we create an instance for $L_{i,j}$ only if the span of O_i and S_j do not overlap.

For training, we also filter out instances for which neither the proposed opinion nor source entity overlaps with a correct opinion or source entity per the gold standard. This training instance filtering helps to avoid confusion between examples like the following (where entities marked in bold are the gold standard entities, and entities in square brackets represent the n-best output sequences from the entity extraction classifiers):

(1) [**The president**]$_{-S1}$ walked away from [the meeting]$_{-O1}$, [[**revealing**]$_{-O2}$ **his disappointment**]$_{-O3}$ with the deal.

(2) [The monster]$_{-S2}$ walked away, [revealing]$_{-O4}$ a little box hidden underneath.

For these sentences, we construct training instances for $L_{1,1}$, $L_{1,2}$, and $L_{1,3}$, but not $L_{2,4}$, which in fact has very similar sentential structure as $L_{1,2}$, and hence could confuse the learning algorithm.

4.1 Relation extraction features

The training and test instances for each (potential) link $L_{i,j}$ (with opinion candidate entity O_i and source candidate entity S_j) include the following features.

opinion entity word: the words contained in O_i.

phrase type: the syntactic category of the constituent in which the entity is embedded, e.g. NP or VP. We encode separate features for O_i and S_j.

grammatical role: the grammatical role of the constituent in which the entity is embedded. Grammatical roles are derived from dependency parse trees, as done for the entity extraction classifiers. We encode separate features for O_i and S_j.

position: a boolean value indicating whether S_j precedes O_i.

distance: the distance between O_i and S_j in numbers of tokens. We use four coarse categories: adjacent, very near, near, far.

dependency path: the path through the dependency tree from the head of S_j to the head of O_i. For instance, 'subj↑verb' or 'subj↑verb↓obj'.

voice: whether the voice of O_i is passive or active.

syntactic frame: key intra-sentential relations between O_i and S_j. The syntactic frames that we use are:

- [E_1:role]_[distance]_[E_2:role], where distance $\in$ {adjacent, very near, near, far}, and E_i:role is the grammatical role of E_i. Either E_1 is an opinion entity and E_2 is a source, or vice versa.
- [E_1:phrase]_[distance]_[E_2:phrase], where E_i:phrase is the phrasal type of entity E_i.

[5] We omit only the extraction pattern features.

[6] Using GATE: http://gate.ac.uk/

[7] Provided by Rebecca Hwa, based on the Collins parser: ftp://ftp.cis.upenn.edu/pub/mcollins/PARSER.tar.gz

[8] https://rrc.mitre.org/pubs/mpqaFinalReport.pdf

[9] Using SUNDANCE: (http://www.cs.utah.edu/~riloff/publications.html#sundance)

[10] http://wordnet.princeton.edu/

- ∘ $[E_1$:phrase]_$[E_2$:headword], where E_2 must be the opinion entity, and E_1 must be the source entity (i.e. no lexicalized frames for sources). E_1 and E_2 can be contiguous.
- ∘ $[E_1$:role]_$[E_2$:headword], where E_2 must be the opinion entity, and E_1 must be the source entity.
- ∘ $[E_1$:phrase]_NP_$[E_2$:phrase] indicates the presence of specific syntactic patterns, e.g. 'VP_NP_VP' depending on the possible phrase types of opinion and source entities. The three phrases do not need to be contiguous.
- ∘ $[E_1$:phrase]_VP_$[E_2$:phrase] (See above.)
- ∘ $[E_1$:phrase]_[wh-word]_$[E_2$:phrase] (See above.)
- ∘ Src_[distance]_[x]_[distance]_Op, where $x \in$ {by, of, from, for, between, among, and, have, be, will, not,], ", ... }.

When a syntactic frame is matched to a sentence, the bracketed items should be instantiated with particular values corresponding to the sentence. Pattern elements without square brackets are constants. For instance, the syntactic frame '$[E_1$:phrase]_NP_$[E_2$:phrase]' may be instantiated as 'VP_NP_VP'. Some frames are lexicalized with respect to the head of an opinion entity to reflect the fact that different verbs expect source entities in different argument positions (e.g. SOURCE *blamed* TARGET vs. TARGET *angered* SOURCE).

5 Integer Linear Programming Approach

As noted in the introduction, we model our task as global, constraint-based inference over the separately trained entity and relation classifiers, and implement the inference procedure as binary integer linear programming (ILP) ((Roth and Yih, 2004), (Punyakanok et al., 2004)). ILP consists of an objective function which is a dot product between a vector of variables and a vector of weights, and a set of equality and inequality constraints among variables. Given an objective function and a set of constraints, LP finds the optimal assignment of values to variables, i.e. one that minimizes the objective function. In binary ILP, the assignments to variables must be either 0 or 1. The variables and constraints defined for the opinion recognition task are summarized in Table 1 and explained below.

Entity variables and weights For each opinion entity, we add two variables, O_i and $\bar{O}_i$, where $O_i = 1$ means to extract the opinion entity, and $\bar{O}_i = 1$ means to discard the opinion entity. To ensure coherent assignments, we add equality constraints $\forall i,\ O_i + \bar{O}_i = 1$. The weights w_{o_i} and $\bar{w}_{o_i}$ for O_i and $\bar{O}_i$ respectively, are computed as a negative conditional probability of the span of an entity to be extracted (or suppressed) given the labelings of the adjacent variables of the CRFs:

$$w_{o_i} \stackrel{\text{def}}{=} -\text{P}\,(x_k, x_{k+1}, ..., x_l | x_{k-1}, x_{l+1}) \quad \text{where } x_k = \text{'B'} \ \&\ x_m = \text{'I' for } m \in [k+1, l]$$

$$\bar{w}_{o_i} \stackrel{\text{def}}{=} -\text{P}\,(x_k, x_{k+1}, ..., x_l | x_{k-1}, x_{l+1}) \quad \text{where } x_m = \text{'O' for } m \in [k, l]$$

where x_i is the value assigned to the random variable of the CRF corresponding to an entity O_i. Likewise, for each source entity, we add two variables S_j and $\bar{S}_j$ and a constraint $S_j + \bar{S}_j = 1$. The weights for source variables are computed in the same way as opinion entities.

Relation variables and weights For each link relation, we add two variables $L_{i,j}$ and $\bar{L}_{i,j}$, and a constraint $L_{i,j} + \bar{L}_{i,j} = 1$. By the definition of a link, if $L_{i,j} = 1$, then it is implied that $O_i = 1$ and $S_j = 1$. That is, if a link is extracted, then the pair of entities for the link must be also extracted. Constraints to ensure this coherency are explained in the following subsection. The weights for link variables are based on probabilities from the binary link classifier.

Constraints for link coherency In our corpus, a source entity can be linked to more than one opinion entity, but an opinion entity is linked to only

Objective function f
$= \sum_i (w_{o_i} O_i) + \sum_i (\bar{w}_{o_i} \bar{O}_i)$ $+ \sum_j (w_{s_j} S_j) + \sum_j (\bar{w}_{s_j} \bar{S}_j)$ $+ \sum_{i,j} (w_{l_{i,j}} L_{i,j}) + \sum_i (\bar{w}_{l_{i,j}} \bar{L}_{i,j})$
$\forall i,\ O_i + \bar{O}_i = 1$ $\forall j,\ S_j + \bar{S}_j = 1$ $\forall i,j,\ L_{i,j} + \bar{L}_{i,j} = 1$ $\forall i,\ O_i = \sum_j L_{i,j}$ $\forall j,\ S_j + A_j = \sum_i L_{i,j}$ $\forall j,\ A_j - S_j \leq 0$ $\forall i,j,i<j,\ X_i + X_j = 1, X \in \{S, O\}$

Table 1: Binary ILP formulation

one source. Nonetheless, the majority of opinion-source pairs involve one-to-one mappings, which we encode as hard and soft constraints as follows:

For each opinion entity, we add an equality constraint $O_i = \sum_j L_{i,j}$ to enforce that only one link can emanate from an opinion entity. For each source entity, we add an equality constraint and an inequality constraint that together allow a source to link to at most two opinions: $S_j + A_j = \sum_i L_{i,j}$ and $A_j - S_j \leq 0$, where A_j is an auxiliary variable, such that its weight is some positive constant value that suppresses A_j from being assigned to 1. And A_j can be assigned to 1 only if S_j is already assigned to 1. It is possible to add more auxiliary variables to allow more than two opinions to link to a source, but for our experiments two seemed to be a reasonable limit.

Constraints for entity coherency When we use n-best sequences where $n > 1$, proposed entities can overlap. Because this should not be the case in the final result, we add an equality constraint $X_i + X_j = 1$, $X \in \{S, O\}$ for all pairs of entities with overlapping spans.

Adjustments to weights To balance the precision and recall, and to take into account the performance of different base classifiers, we apply adjustments to weights as follows.

1) We define six coefficients c_x and $\bar{c}_x$, where $x \in \{O, S, L\}$ to modify a group of weights as follows.
 $\forall i, x,\ w_{x_i} := w_{x_i} * c_x$;
 $\forall i, x,\ \bar{w}_{x_i} := \bar{w}_{x_i} * \bar{c}_x$;
 In general, increasing c_x will promote recall, while increasing $\bar{c}_x$ will promote precision. Also, setting $c_o > c_s$ will put higher confidence on the opinion extraction classifier than the source extraction classifier.
2) We also define one constant c_A to set the weights for auxiliary variable A_i. That is, $\forall i,\ w_{A_i} := c_A$.
3) Finally, we adjust the confidence of the link variable based on n-th-best sequences of the entity extraction classifiers as follows.
 $\forall i,\ w_{L_{i,j}} := w_{L_{i,j}} * d$
 where $d \stackrel{\text{def}}{=} 4/(3 + min(m, n))$, when O_i is from an m-th sequence and S_j is from a n-th sequence.[11]

[11] This will smoothly degrade the confidence of a link based on the entities from higher n-th sequences. Values of d decrease as $4/4$, $4/5$, $4/6$, $4/7$....

6 Experiments–I

We evaluate our system using the NRRC Multi-Perspective Question Answering (MPQA) corpus that contains 535 newswire articles that are manually annotated for opinion-related information. In particular, our gold standard opinion entities correspond to *direct subjective expression* annotations and *subjective speech event* annotations (i.e. speech events that introduce opinions) in the MPQA corpus (Wiebe et al., 2005). Gold standard source entities and link relations can be extracted from the *agent* attribute associated with each opinion entity. We use 135 documents as a development set and report 10-fold cross validation results on the remaining 400 documents in all experiments below.

We evaluate entity and link extraction using both an *overlap* and *exact* matching scheme.[12] Because the exact start and endpoints of the manual annotations are somewhat arbitrary, the overlap scheme is more reasonable for our task (Wiebe et al., 2005). We report results according to both matching schemes, but focus our discussion on results obtained using overlap matching.[13]

We use the Mallet[14] implementation of CRFs. For brevity, we will refer to the opinion extraction classifier as CRF-OP, the source extraction classifier as CRF-SRC, and the link relation classifier as CRF-LINK. For ILP, we use Matlab, which produced the optimal assignment in a matter of few seconds for each sentence. The weight adjustment constants defined for ILP are based on the development data.[15]

The link-nearest baselines For baselines, we first consider a *link-nearest* heuristic: for each opinion entity extracted by CRF-OP, the link-nearest heuristic creates a link relation with the closest source entity extracted by CRF-SRC. Recall that CRF-SRC and CRF-OP extract entities from n-best sequences. We test the link-nearest heuristic with $n = \{1, 2, 10\}$ where larger n will boost recall at the cost of precision. Results for the

[12] Given two links $L_{1,1} = (O_1, S_1)$ and $L_{2,2} = (O_2, S_2)$, exact matching requires the spans of O_1 and O_2, and the spans of S_1 and S_2, to match exactly, while overlap matching requires the spans to overlap.

[13] Wiebe et al. (2005) also reports the human annotation agreement study via the overlap scheme.

[14] Available at http://mallet.cs.umass.edu

[15] $c_o = 2.5, \bar{c}_o = 1.0, c_s = 1.5, \bar{c}_s = 1.0, c_L = 2.5, \bar{c}_L = 2.5, c_A = 0.2$. Values are picked so as to boost recall while reasonably suppressing incorrect links.

	Overlap Match			Exact Match		
	r(%)	p(%)	f(%)	r(%)	p(%)	f(%)
NEAREST-1	51.6	71.4	59.9	26.2	36.9	30.7
NEAREST-2	60.7	45.8	52.2	29.7	19.0	23.1
NEAREST-10	66.3	20.9	31.7	28.2	00.0	00.0
SRL	59.7	36.3	45.2	32.6	19.3	24.2
SRL+CRF-OP	45.6	83.2	58.9	27.6	49.7	35.5
ILP-1	51.6	80.8	63.0	26.4	42.0	32.4
ILP-10	64.0	72.4	68.0	31.0	34.8	32.8

Table 2: Relation extraction performance

NEAREST-n : link-nearest heuristic w/ n-best
SRL : all V-A0 frames from SRL
SRL+CRF-OP : all V-A0 filtered by CRF-OP
ILP-n : ILP applied to n-best sequences

link-nearest heuristic on the full source-expresses-opinion relation extraction task are shown in the first three rows of table 2. NEAREST-1 performs the best in overlap-match F-measure, reaching 59.9. NEAREST-10 has higher recall (66.3%), but the precision is really low (20.9%). Performance of the opinion and source entity classifiers will be discussed in Section 8.

SRL baselines Next, we consider two baselines that use a state-of-the-art SRL system (Punyakanok et al., 2005). In many link relations, the opinion expression entity is a verb phrase and the source entity is in an agent argument position. Hence our second baseline, SRL, extracts all verb(V)-agent(A0) frames from the output of the SRL system and provides an upper bound on recall (59.7%) for systems that use SRL in isolation for our task. A more sophisticated baseline, SRL+CRF-OP, extracts only those V-A0 frames whose verb overlaps with entities extracted by the opinion expression extractor, CRF-OP. As shown in table 2, filtering out V-A0 frames that are incompatible with the opinion extractor boosts precision to 83.2%, but the F-measure (58.9) is lower than that of NEAREST-1.

ILP results The ILP-n system in table 2 denotes the results of the ILP approach applied to the n-best sequences. ILP-10 reaches an F-measure of 68.0, a significant improvement over the highest performing baseline[16], and also a substantial improvement over ILP-1. Note that the performance of NEAREST-10 was much worse than that

[16]Statistically significant by paired-t test, where $p < 0.001$.

	Overlap Match			Exact Match		
	r(%)	p(%)	f(%)	r(%)	p(%)	f(%)
ILP-1	51.6	80.8	63.0	26.4	42.0	32.4
ILP-10	64.0	72.4	68.0	31.0	34.8	32.8
ILP+SRL-f-1	51.7	81.5	63.3	26.6	42.5	32.7
ILP+SRL-f-10	65.7	72.4	68.9	31.5	34.3	32.9
ILP+SRL-fc-10	64.0	73.5	68.4	28.4	31.3	29.8

Table 3: Relation extraction with ILP and SRL

ILP-n : ILP applied to n-best sequences
ILP+SRL-f-n : ILP w/ SRL features, n-best
ILP+SRL-fc-n : ILP w/ SRL features, and SRL constraints, n-best

of NEAREST-1, because the 10-best sequences include many incorrect entities whereas the corresponding ILP formulation can discard the bad entities by considering dependencies among entities and relations.[17]

7 Additional SRL Incorporation

We next explore two approaches for more directly incorporating SRL into our system.

Extra SRL Features for the Link classifier We incorporate SRL into the link classifier by adding extra features based on SRL. We add boolean features to check whether the span of an SRL argument and an entity matches exactly. In addition, we include **syntactic frame** features as follows:

- [E_1:srl-arg]_[E_2:srl-arg], where E_i:srl-arg indicates the SRL argument type of entity E_i.
- [E_1.srl-arg]_[E_1:headword]_[E_2:srl-arg], where E_1 must be an opinion entity, and E_2 must be a source entity.

Extra SRL Constraints for the ILP phase We also incorporate SRL into the ILP phase of our system by adding extra constraints based on SRL. In particular, we assign very high weights for links that match V-A0 frames generated by SRL, in order to force the extraction of V-A0 frames.

[17]A potential issue with overlap precision and recall is that the measures may drastically overestimate the system's performance as follows: a system predicting a single link relation whose source and opinion expression both overlap with every token of a document would achieve 100% overlap precision and recall. We can ensure this does not happen by measuring the average number of (source, opinion) pairs to which each correct or predicted pair is aligned (excluding pairs not aligned at all). In our data, this does not exceed 1.08, (except for baselines), so we can conclude these evaluation measures are behaving reasonably.

		Opinion			Source			Link		
		r(%)	p(%)	f(%)	r(%)	p(%)	f(%)	r(%)	p(%)	f(%)
Before ILP	CRF-OP/SRC/LINK with 1 best	76.4	88.4	81.9	67.3	81.9	73.9	60.5	50.5	55.0
	merged 10 best	95.7	31.2	47.0	95.3	24.5	38.9	N/A		
After ILP	ILP-SRL-f-10	75.1	82.9	78.8	80.6	75.7	78.1	65.7	72.4	68.9
	ILP-SRL-f-10 $\cup$ CRF-OP/SRC with 1 best	82.3	81.7	82.0	81.5	73.4	77.3	N/A		

Table 4: Entity extraction performance (by overlap-matching)

8 Experiments–II

Results using SRL are shown in Table 3 (on the previous page). In the table, ILP+SRL-f denotes the ILP approach using the link classifier with the extra SRL 'f'eatures, and ILP+SRL-fc denotes the ILP approach using both the extra SRL 'f'eatures and the SRL 'c'onstraints. For comparison, the ILP-1 and ILP-10 results from Table 2 are shown in rows 1 and 2.

The F-measure score of ILP+SRL-f-10 is 68.9, about a 1 point increase from that of ILP-10, which shows that extra SRL features for the link classifier further improve the performance over our previous best results.[18] ILP+SRL-fc-10 also performs better than ILP-10 in F-measure, although it is slightly worse than ILP+SRL-f-10. This indicates that the link classifier with extra SRL features already makes good use of the V-A0 frames from the SRL system, so that forcing the extraction of such frames via extra ILP constraints only hurts performance by not allowing the extraction of non-V-A0 pairs in the neighborhood that could have been better choices.

Contribution of the ILP phase In order to highlight the contribution of the ILP phase for our task, we present 'before' and 'after' performance in Table 4. The first row shows the performance of the individual CRF-OP, CRF-SRC, and CRF-LINK classifiers before the ILP phase. Without the ILP phase, the 1-best sequence generates the best scores. However, we also present the performance with merged 10-best entity sequences[19] in order to demonstrate that using 10-best sequences without ILP will only hurt performance. The precision of the merged 10-best sequences system is very low, however the recall level is above 95% for both CRF-OP and CRF-SRC, giving an upper bound for recall for our approach. The third row presents results after the ILP phase is applied for the 10-best sequences, and we see that, in addition to the improved link extraction described in Section 7, the performance on source extraction is substantially improved, from F-measure of 73.9 to 78.1. Performance on opinion expression extraction decreases from F-measure of 81.9 to 78.8. This decrease is largely due to *implicit* links, which we will explain below. The fourth row takes the union of the entities from ILP-SRL-f-10 and the entities from the best sequences from CRF-OP and CRF-SRC. This process brings the F-measure of CRF-OP up to 82.0, with a different precision-recall break down from those of 1-best sequences without ILP phase. In particular, the recall on opinion expressions now reaches 82.3%, while maintaining a high precision of 81.7%.

	Overlap Match			Exact Match		
	r(%)	p(%)	f(%)	r(%)	p(%)	f(%)
DEV.CONF	65.7	72.4	68.9	31.5	34.3	32.9
NO.CONF	63.7	76.2	69.4	30.9	36.7	33.5

Table 5: Relation extraction with ILP weight adjustment. (All cases using ILP+SRL-f-10)

Effects of ILP weight adjustment Finally, we show the effect of weight adjustment in the ILP formulation in Table 5. The DEV.CONF row shows relation extraction performance using a weight configuration based from the development data. In order to see the effect of weight adjustment, we ran an experiment, NO.CONF, using fixed default weights.[20] Not surprisingly, our weight adjustment tuned from the development set is not the optimal choice for cross-validation set. Nevertheless, the weight adjustment helps to balance the precision and recall, i.e. it improves recall at the

[18] Statistically significant by paired-t test, where $p < 0.001$.

[19] If an entity E_i extracted by the ith-best sequence overlaps with an entity E_j extracted by the jth-best sequence, where $i < j$, then we discard E_j. If E_i and E_j do not overlap, then we extract both entities.

[20] To be precise, $c_x = 1.0, \bar{c}_x = 1.0$ for $x \in \{O, S, L\}$, but $c_A = 0.2$ is the same as before.

cost of precision. The weight adjustment is more effective when the gap between precision and recall is large, as was the case with the development data.

Implicit links A good portion of errors stem from the *implicit* link relation, which our system did not model directly. An implicit link relation holds for an opinion entity without an associated source entity. In this case, the opinion entity is linked to an *implicit* source. Consider the following example.

- Anti-Soviet hysteria was firmly oppressed.

Notice that opinion expressions such as *"Anti-Soviet hysteria"* and *"firmly oppressed"* do not have associated source entities, because sources of these opinion expressions are not explicitly mentioned in the text. Because our system forces each opinion to be linked with an explicit source entity, opinion expressions that do not have explicit source entities will be dropped during the global inference phase of our system. Implicit links amount to 7% of the link relations in our corpus, so the upper bound for recall for our ILP system is 93%. In the future we will extend our system to handle implicit links as well. Note that we report results against a gold standard that includes implicit links. Excluding them from the gold standard, the performance of our final system ILP+SRL-f-10 is 72.6% in recall, 72.4% in precision, and 72.5 in F-measure.

9 Conclusion

This paper presented a global inference approach to jointly extract entities and relations in the context of opinion oriented information extraction. The final system achieves performance levels that are potentially good enough for many practical NLP applications.

Acknowledgments We thank the reviewers for their many helpful comments and Vasin Punyakanok for running our data through his SRL system. This work was supported by the Advanced Research and Development Activity (ARDA), by NSF Grants IIS-0535099 and IIS-0208028, and by gifts from Google and the Xerox Foundation.

References

S. Bethard, H. Yu, A. Thornton, V. Hativassiloglou and D. Jurafsky 2004. Automatic Extraction of Opinion Propositions and their Holders. In *AAAI Spring Symposium on Exploring Attitude and Affect in Text.*

R. Bunescu and R. J. Mooney 2004. Collective Information Extraction with Relational Markov Networks. In *ACL.*

C. Cardie, J. Wiebe, T. Wilson and D. Litman 2004. Low-Level Annotations and Summary Representations of Opinions for Multi-Perspective Question Answering. *New Directions in Question Answering.*

Y. Choi, C. Cardie, E. Riloff and S. Patwardhan 2005. Identifying Sources of Opinions with Conditional Random Fields and Extraction Patterns. In *HLT-EMNLP.*

S. Kim and E. Hovy 2005. Automatic Detection of Opinion Bearing Words and Sentences. In *IJCNLP.*

S. Kim and E. Hovy 2005. Identifying Opinion Holders for Question Answering in Opinion Texts. In *AAAI Workshop on Question Answering in Restricted Domains.*

J. Lafferty, A. K. McCallum and F. Pereira 2001 Conditional Random Fields: Probabilistic Models for Segmenting and Labeling Sequence Data. In *ICML.*

B. Liu, M. Hu and J. Cheng 2005 Opinion Observer: Analyzing and Comparing Opinions on the Web. In *WWW.*

R. J. Mooney and R. Bunescu 2005 Mining Knowledge from Text Using Information Extraction. In *SIGKDD Explorations.*

S. Morinaga, K. Yamanishi, K. Tateishi and T. Fukushima 2002. Mining product reputations on the Web. In *KDD.*

M. A. Munson, C. Cardie and R. Caruana. 2005. Optimizing to arbitrary NLP metrics using ensemble selection. In *HLT-EMNLP.*

J. Prager, E. Brown, A. Coden and D. Radev 2000. Question-answering by predictive annotation. In *SIGIR.*

V. Punyakanok, D. Roth and W. Yih 2005. Generalized Inference with Multiple Semantic Role Labeling Systems (Shared Task Paper). In *CoNLL.*

V. Punyakanok, D. Roth, W. Yih and D. Zimak 2004. Semantic Role Labeling via Integer Linear Programming Inference. In *COLING.*

D. Roth and W. Yih 2004. A Linear Programming Formulation for Global Inference in Natural Language Tasks. In *CoNLL.*

D. Roth and W. Yih 2002. Probabilistic Reasoning for Entity and Relation Recognition. In *COLING.*

V. Stoyanov, C. Cardie and J. Wiebe 2005. Multi-Perspective Question Answering Using the OpQA Corpus. In *HLT-EMNLP.*

C. Sutton, K. Rohanimanesh and A. K. McCallum 2004. Dynamic Conditional Random Fields: Factorized Probabilistic Models for Labeling and Segmenting Sequence Data. In *ICML.*

M. White, T. Korelsky, C. Cardie, V. Ng, D. Pierce and K. Wagstaff 2001. Multi-document Summarization via Information Extraction In *HLT.*

J. Wiebe and T. Wilson and C. Cardie 2005. Annotating Expressions of Opinions and Emotions in Language. In *Language Resources and Evaluation, volume 39, issue 2-3.*

T. Wilson, J. Wiebe and P. Hoffmann 2005. Recognizing Contextual Polarity in Phrase-Level Sentiment Analysis. In *HLT-EMNLP.*

Feature Subsumption for Opinion Analysis

Ellen Riloff and Siddharth Patwardhan
School of Computing
University of Utah
Salt Lake City, UT 84112
{riloff,sidd}@cs.utah.edu

Janyce Wiebe
Department of Computer Science
University of Pittsburgh
Pittsburgh, PA 15260
wiebe@cs.pitt.edu

Abstract

Lexical features are key to many approaches to sentiment analysis and opinion detection. A variety of representations have been used, including single words, multi-word Ngrams, phrases, and lexico-syntactic patterns. In this paper, we use a *subsumption hierarchy* to formally define different types of lexical features and their relationship to one another, both in terms of representational coverage and performance. We use the subsumption hierarchy in two ways: (1) as an analytic tool to automatically identify complex features that outperform simpler features, and (2) to reduce a feature set by removing unnecessary features. We show that reducing the feature set improves performance on three opinion classification tasks, especially when combined with traditional feature selection.

1 Introduction

Sentiment analysis and opinion recognition are active research areas that have many potential applications, including review mining, product reputation analysis, multi-document summarization, and multi-perspective question answering. Lexical features are key to many approaches, and a variety of representations have been used, including single words, multi-word Ngrams, phrases, and lexico-syntactic patterns. It is common for different features to overlap representationally. For example, the unigram "happy" will match all of the texts that the bigram "very happy" matches. Since both features represent a positive sentiment and the bigram matches fewer contexts than the unigram, it is probably sufficient just to have the unigram. However, there are many cases where a feature captures a subtlety or non-compositional meaning that a simpler feature does not. For example, "basket case" is a highly opinionated phrase, but the words "basket" and "case" individually are not. An open question in opinion analysis is how often more complex feature representations are needed, and which types of features are most valuable. Our first goal is to devise a method to automatically identify features that are representationally subsumed by a simpler feature but that are better opinion indicators. These subjective expressions could then be added to a subjectivity lexicon (Esuli and Sebastiani, 2005), and used to gain understanding about which types of complex features capture meaningful expressions that are important for opinion recognition.

Many opinion classifiers are created by adopting a "kitchen sink" approach that throws together a variety of features. But in many cases adding new types of features does not improve performance. For example, Pang et al. (2002) found that unigrams outperformed bigrams, and unigrams outperformed the combination of unigrams plus bigrams. Our second goal is to automatically identify features that are unnecessary because similar features provide equal or better coverage and discriminatory value. Our hypothesis is that a reduced feature set, which selectively combines unigrams with only the most valuable complex features, will perform better than a larger feature set that includes the entire "kitchen sink" of features.

In this paper, we explore the use of a *subsumption hierarchy* to formally define the subsumption relationships between different types of textual features. We use the subsumption hierarchy in two ways. First, we use subsumption as an an-

Proceedings of the 2006 Conference on Empirical Methods in Natural Language Processing (EMNLP 2006), pages 440–448,
Sydney, July 2006.

alytic tool to compare features of different complexities and automatically identify complex features that substantially outperform their simpler counterparts. Second, we use the subsumption hierarchy to reduce a feature set based on representational overlap and on performance. We conduct experiments with three opinion data sets and show that the reduced feature sets can improve classification performance.

2 The Subsumption Hierarchy

2.1 Text Representations

We analyze two feature representations that have been used for opinion analysis: Ngrams and Extraction Patterns. *Information extraction (IE) patterns* are lexico-syntactic patterns that represent expressions which identify role relationships. For example, the pattern *"<subj> ActVP(recommended)"* extracts the subject of active-voice instances of the verb "recommended" as the recommender. The pattern *"<subj> PassVP(recommended)"* extracts the subject of passive-voice instances of "recommended" as the object being recommended.

(Riloff and Wiebe, 2003) explored the idea of using extraction patterns to represent more complex subjective expressions that have non-compositional meanings. For example, the expression *"drive (someone) up the wall"* expresses the feeling of being annoyed, but the meanings of the words "drive", "up", and "wall" have no emotional connotations individually. Furthermore, this expression is not a fixed word sequence that can be adequately modeled by Ngrams. Any noun phrase can appear between the words "drive' and "up", so a flexible representation is needed to capture the general pattern *"drives <NP> up the wall"*.

This example represents a general phenomenon: many expressions allow intervening noun phrases and/or modifying terms. For example:

> "stepped on <mods> toes"
> Ex: *stepped on the boss' toes*
>
> "dealt <np> <mods> blow"
> Ex: *dealt the company a decisive blow*
>
> "brought <np> to <mods> knees"
> Ex: *brought the man to his knees*

(Riloff and Wiebe, 2003) also showed that syntactic variations of the same verb phrase can behave very differently. For example, they found that passive-voice constructions of the verb "ask" had a 100% correlation with opinion sentences, but active-voice constructions had only a 63% correlation with opinions.

Pattern Type	Example Pattern
<subj> PassVP	<subj> is satisfied
<subj> ActVP	<subj> complained
<subj> ActVP Dobj	<subj> dealt blow
<subj> ActInfVP	<subj> appear to be
<subj> PassInfVP	<subj> is meant to be
<subj> AuxVP Dobj	<subj> has position
<subj> AuxVP Adj	<subj> is happy
ActVP <dobj>	endorsed <dobj>
InfVP <dobj>	to condemn <dobj>
ActInfVP <dobj>	get to know <dobj>
PassInfVP <dobj>	is meant to be <dobj>
Subj AuxVP <dobj>	fact is <dobj>
NP Prep <np>	opinion on <np>
ActVP Prep <np>	agrees with <np>
PassVP Prep <np>	is worried about <np>
InfVP Prep <np>	to resort to <np>
<possessive> NP	<noun>'s speech

Figure 1: Extraction Pattern Types

Our goal is to use the subsumption hierarchy to identify Ngram and extraction pattern features that are more strongly associated with opinions than simpler features. We used three types of features in our research: unigrams, bigrams, and IE patterns. The Ngram features were generated using the *Ngram Statistics Package* (NSP) (Banerjee and Pedersen, 2003).[1] The extraction patterns (EPs) were automatically generated using the Sundance/AutoSlog software package (Riloff and Phillips, 2004). AutoSlog relies on the Sundance shallow parser and can be applied exhaustively to a text corpus to generate IE patterns that can extract every noun phrase in the corpus. AutoSlog has been used to learn IE patterns for the domains of terrorism, joint ventures, and microelectronics (Riloff, 1996), as well as for opinion analysis (Riloff and Wiebe, 2003). Figure 1 shows the 17 types of extraction patterns that AutoSlog generates. PassVP refers to passive-voice verb phrases (VPs), ActVP refers to active-voice VPs, InfVP refers to infinitive VPs, and AuxVP refers

[1] NSP is freely available for use under the GPL from http://search.cpan.org/dist/Text-NSP. We discarded Ngrams that consisted entirely of stopwords. We used a list of 281 stopwords.

to VPs where the main verb is a form of "to be" or "to have". Subjects (subj), direct objects (dobj), PP objects (np), and possessives can be extracted by the patterns.[2]

2.2 The Subsumption Hierarchy

We created a *subsumption hierarchy* that defines the representational scope of different types of features. We will say that feature A *representationally subsumes* feature B if the set of text spans that match feature A is a superset of the set of text spans that match feature B. For example, the unigram "happy" subsumes the bigram "very happy" because the set of text spans that match "happy" includes the text spans that match "very happy".

First, we define a hierarchy of valid subsumption relationships, shown in Figure 2. The 2Gram node, for example, is a child of the 1Gram node because a 1Gram can subsume a 2Gram. Ngrams may subsume extraction patterns as well. Every extraction pattern has at least one corresponding 1Gram that will subsume it.[3]. For example, the 1Gram "recommended" subsumes the pattern "<subj> ActVP(recommended)" because the pattern only matches active-voice instances of "recommended". An extraction pattern may also subsume another extraction pattern. For example, "<subj> ActVP(recommended)" subsumes "<subj> ActVP(recommended) Dobj(movie)".

To compare specific features we need to formally define the representation of each type of feature in the hierarchy. For example, the hierarchy dictates that a 2Gram can subsume the pattern "ActInfVP <dobj>", but this should hold only if the words in the bigram correspond to adjacent words in the pattern. For example, the 2Gram "to fish" subsumes the pattern "ActInfVP(like to fish) <dobj>". But the 2Gram "like fish" should not subsume it. Similarly, consider the pattern "InfVP(plan) <dobj>", which represents the infinitive "to plan". This pattern subsumes the pattern "ActInfVP(want to plan) <dobj>", but it should not subsume the pattern "ActInfVP(plan to start)".

To ensure that different features truly subsume each other representationally, we formally define each type of feature based on words, sequential dependencies, and syntactic dependencies. A *sequential dependency* between words w_i and w_{i+1} means that w_i and w_{i+1} must be adjacent, and that w_i must precede w_{i+1}. Figure 3 shows the formal definition of a bigram (2Gram) node. The bigram is defined as two words with a sequential dependency indicating that they must be adjacent.

Name = **2Gram**
Constituent[0] = WORD1
Constituent[1] = WORD2
Dependency = Sequential(0, 1)

Figure 3: 2Gram Definition

A *syntactic dependency* between words w_i and w_{i+1} means that w_i has a specific syntactic relationship to w_{i+1}, and w_i must precede w_{i+1}. For example, consider the extraction pattern "NP Prep <np>", in which the object of the preposition attaches to the NP. Figure 4 shows the definition of this extraction pattern in the hierarchy. The pattern itself contains three components: the NP, the attaching preposition, and the object of the preposition (which is the NP that the pattern extracts). The definition also includes two syntactic dependencies: the first dependency is between the NP and the preposition (meaning that the preposition syntactically attaches to the NP), while the second dependency is between the preposition and the extraction (meaning that the extracted NP is the syntactic object of the preposition).

Name = **NP Prep <np>**
Constituent[0] = NP
Constituent[1] = PREP
Constituent[2] = NP_EXTRACTION
Dependency = Syntactic(0, 1)
Dependency = Syntactic(1, 2)

Figure 4: "NP Prep <np>" Pattern Definition

Consequently, the bigram "affair with" will not subsume the extraction pattern "affair with <np>" because the bigram requires the noun and preposition to be adjacent but the pattern does not. For example, the extraction pattern matches the text *"an affair in his mind with Countess Olenska"* but the bigram does not. Conversely, the extraction pattern does not subsume the bigram either because the pattern requires syntactic attachment but the bigram does not. For example, the bigram matches

[2]However, the items extracted by the patterns are not actually used by our opinion classifiers; only the patterns themselves are matched against the text.

[3]Because every type of extraction pattern shown in Figure 1 contains at least one word (not including the extracted phrases, which are not used as part of our feature representation).

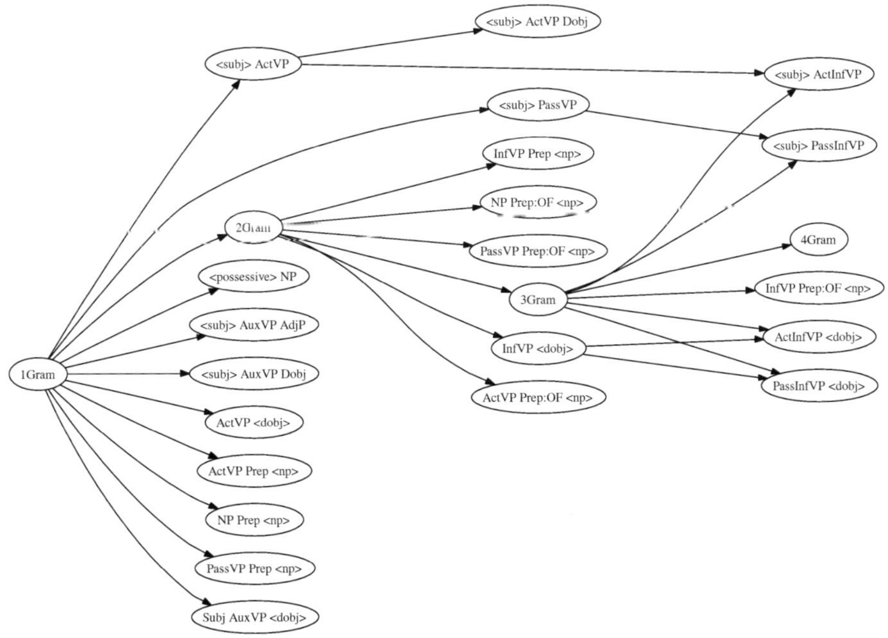

Figure 2: The Subsumption Hierarchy

the sentence *"He ended the affair with a sense of relief"*, but the extraction pattern does not.

Figure 5 shows the definition of another extraction pattern, "InfVP <dobj>", which includes both syntactic and sequential dependencies. This pattern would match the text *"to protest high taxes"*. The pattern definition has three components: the infinitive "to", a verb, and the direct object of the verb (which is the NP that the pattern extracts). The definition also shows two syntactic dependencies. The first dependency indicates that the verb syntactically attaches to the infinitive "to". The second dependency indicates that the extracted NP syntactically attaches to the verb (i.e., it is the direct object of that particular verb).

The pattern definition also includes a sequential dependency, which specifies that "to" must be adjacent to the verb. Strictly speaking, our parser does not require them to be adjacent. For example, the parser allows intervening adverbs to split infinitives (e.g., *"to strongly protest high taxes"*), and this does happen occasionally. But split infinitives are relatively rare, so in the vast majority of cases the infinitive "to" will be adjacent to the verb. Consequently, we decided that a bigram (e.g., *"to protest"*) should representationally subsume this extraction pattern because the syntactic flexibility afforded by the pattern is negligible. The sequential dependency link represents this judgment call that the infinitive "to" and the verb are adjacent in most cases.

For all of the node definitions, we used our best judgment to make decisions of this kind. We tried to represent major distinctions between features, without getting caught up in minor differences that were likely to be negligible in practice.

Name = **InfVP <dobj>**
Constituent[0] = INFINITIVE_TO
Constituent[1] = VERB
Constituent[2] = DOBJ_EXTRACTION
Dependency = Syntactic(0, 1)
Dependency = Syntactic(1, 2)
Dependency = Sequential(0, 1)

Figure 5: "InfVP <dobj>" Pattern Definition

To use the subsumption hierarchy, we assign each feature to its appropriate node in the hierarchy based on its type. Then we perform a top-down breadth-first traversal. Each feature is compared with the features at its ancestor nodes. If a feature's words and dependencies are a superset of an ancestor's words and dependencies, then it is subsumed by the (more general) ancestor and discarded.[4] When the subsumption process is finished, a feature remains in the hierarchy only if

[4]The words that they have in common must also be in the same relative order.

there are no features above it that subsume it.

2.3 Performance-based Subsumption

Representational subsumption is concerned with whether one feature is more general than another. But the purpose of using the subsumption hierarchy is to identify more complex features that outperform simpler ones. Applying the subsumption hierarchy to features without regard to performance would simply eliminate all features that have a more general counterpart in the feature set. For example, all bigrams would be discarded if their component unigrams were also present in the hierarchy.

To estimate the quality of a feature, we use Information Gain (IG) because that has been shown to work well as a metric for feature selection (Forman, 2003). We will say that feature A *behaviorally subsumes* feature B if two criteria are met: (1) A representationally subsumes B, and (2) IG(A) $\geq$ IG(B) - δ, where δ is a parameter representing an acceptable margin of performance difference. For example, if δ=0 then condition (2) means that feature A is just as valuable as feature B because its information gain is the same or higher. If δ>0 then feature A is allowed to be a little worse than feature B, but within an acceptable margin. For example, δ=.0001 means that A's information gain may be up to .0001 lower than B's information gain, and that is considered to be an acceptable performance difference (i.e., A is good enough that we are comfortable discarding B in favor of the more general feature A).

Note that based on the subsumption hierarchy shown in Figure 2, all 1Grams will always survive the subsumption process because they cannot be subsumed by any other types of features. Our goal is to identify complex features that are worth adding to a set of unigram features.

3 Data Sets

We used three opinion-related data sets for our analyses and experiments: the *OP data set* created by (Wiebe et al., 2004), the *Polarity data set*[5] created by (Pang and Lee, 2004), and the *MPQA data set* created by (Wiebe et al., 2005).[6] The OP and Polarity data sets involve document-level opinion classification, while the MPQA data set involves sentence-level classification.

The OP data consists of 2,452 documents from the Penn Treebank (Marcus et al., 1993). Metadata tags assigned by the Wall Street Journal define the opinion/non-opinion classes: the class of any document labeled *Editorial, Letter to the Editor, Arts & Leisure Review*, or *Viewpoint* by the Wall Street Journal is *opinion*, and the class of documents in all other categories (such as *Business* and *News*) is *non-opinion*. This data set is highly skewed, with only 9% of the documents belonging to the opinion class. Consequently, a trivial (but useless) opinion classifier that labels all documents as non-opinion articles would achieve 91% accuracy.

The Polarity data consists of 700 positive and 700 negative reviews from the Internet Movie Database (IMDb) archive. The positive and negative classes were derived from author ratings expressed in stars or numerical values. The MPQA data consists of English language versions of articles from the world press. It contains 9,732 sentences that have been manually annotated for subjective expressions. The opinion/non-opinion classes are derived from the lower-level annotations: a sentence is an opinion if it contains a subjective expression of medium or higher intensity; otherwise, it is a non-opinion sentence. 55% of the sentences belong to the opinion class.

4 Using the Subsumption Hierarchy for Analysis

In this section, we illustrate how the subsumption hierarchy can be used as an analytic tool to automatically identify features that substantially outperform simpler counterparts. These features represent specialized usages and expressions that would be good candidates for addition to a subjectivity lexicon. Figure 6 shows pairs of features, where the first is more general and the second is more specific. These feature pairs were identified by the subsumption hierarchy as being representationally similar but behaviorally different (so the more specific feature was retained). The *IGain* column shows the information gain values produced from the training set of one cross-validation fold. The *Class* column shows the class that the more specific feature is correlated with (the more general feature is usually not strongly correlated with either class).

The top table in Figure 6 contains examples for the opinion/non-opinion classification task from

[5] Version v2.0, which is available at: http://www.cs.cornell.edu/people/pabo/movie-review-data/

[6] Available at http://www.cs.pitt.edu/mpqa/databaserelease/

Opinion/Non-Opinion Classification

ID	Feature	IGain	Class	Example
A_1	line	.0016	-	...issue consists of notes backed by credit *line* receivables
A_2	the line	.0075	opin	...lays it on *the line*; ...steps across *the line*
B_1	nation	.0046	-	...has 750,000 cable-tv subscribers around the *nation*
B_2	a nation	.0080	opin	It's not that we are spawning *a nation* of ascetics ...
C_1	begin	.0006	-	Campeau buyers will *begin* writing orders...
C_2	begin with	.0036	opin	To *begin with*, we should note that in contrast...
D_1	benefits	.0040	-	...earlier period included $235,000 in tax *benefits*.
D_{EP}	NP Prep(benefits to)	.0090	opin	...boon to the rich with no proven *benefits to* the economy
E_1	due	.0001	-	...an estimated $ 1.23 billion in debt *due* next spring
E_{EP}	ActVP Prep(due to)	.0038	opin	It's all *due to* the intense scrutiny...

Positive/Negative Sentiment Classification

ID	Feature	IGain	Class	Example
F_1	short	.0014	-	to make a long story *short*...
F_2	nothing short	.0039	pos	*nothing short* of spectacular
G_1	ugly	.0008	-	...an *ugly* monster on a cruise liner
G_2	and ugly	.0054	neg	it's a disappointment to see something this dumb *and ugly*
H_1	disaster	.0010	-	...rated pg-13 for *disaster* related elements
H_{EP}	AuxVP Dobj(be disaster)	.0048	neg	...this *is* such a confused *disaster* of a film
I_1	work	.0002	-	the next day during the drive to *work*...
I_{EP}	ActVP(work)	.0062	pos	the film *will work* just as well...
J_1	manages	.0003	-	he still *manages* to find time for his wife
J_{EP}	ActInfVP(manages to keep)	.0054	pos	this film *manages to keep* up a rapid pace

Figure 6: Sample features that behave differently, as revealed by the subsumption hierarchy. (1 $\Rightarrow$ unigram; 2 $\Rightarrow$ bigram; EP $\Rightarrow$ extraction pattern)

the OP data. The more specific features are more strongly correlated with opinion articles. Surprisingly, simply adding a determiner can dramatically change behavior. Consider A_2. There are many subjective idioms involving *"the line"* (two are shown in the table; others include *"toe the line"* and *"draw the line"*), while objective language about credit lines, phone lines, etc. uses the determiner less often. Similarly, consider B_2. Adding *"a"* to *"nation"* often corresponds to an abstract reference used when making an argument (e.g., *"a nation of ascetics"*), whereas other instances of "nation" are used more literally (e.g., *"the 6th largest in the nation"*). 21% of feature B_1's instances appear in opinion articles, while 70% of feature B_2's instances are in opinion articles.

"Begin with" (C_2) captures an adverbial phrase used in argumentation (*"To begin with..."*) but does not match objective usages such as *"will begin"* an action. The word *"benefits"* alone (D_1) matches phrases like *"tax benefits"* and *"employee benefits"* that are not opinion expressions, while D_{EP} typically matches positive senses of the word *"benefits"*. Interestingly, the bigram *"benefits to"* is not highly correlated with opinions because it matches infinitive phrases such as *"tax benefits to provide"* and *"health benefits to cut"*. In this case, the extraction pattern "NP Prep(benefits to)" is more discriminating than the bigram for opinion classification. The extraction pattern E_{EP} is also highly correlated with opinions, while the unigram *"due"* and the bigram *"due to"* are not.

The bottom table in Figure 6 shows feature pairs identified for their behavioral differences on the Polarity data set, where the task is to distinguish positive reviews from negative reviews. F_2 and G_2 are bigrams that behave differently from their component unigrams. The expression *"nothing short (of)"* is typically used to express positive sentiments, while *"nothing"* and *"short"* by themselves are not. The word *"ugly"* is often used as a descriptive modifier that is not expressing a sentiment per se, while *"and ugly"* appears in predicate adjective constructions that are expressing a negative sentiment. The extraction pattern H_{EP} is more discriminatory than H_1 because it distinguishes negative sentiments (*"the film is a disaster!"*) from plot descriptions (*"the disaster movie..."*). I_{EP} shows that active-voice usages of "work" are strong positive indicators, while the unigram *"work"* appears in a variety of both positive and negative contexts. Finally, J_{EP} shows that the expression *"manages to keep"* is a strong positive indicator, while *"manages"* by itelf is much less discriminating.

These examples illustrate that the subsumption hierarchy can be a powerful tool to better understand the behaviors of different kinds of features, and to identify specific features that may be desirable for inclusion in specialized lexical resources.

5 Using the Subsumption Hierarchy to Reduce Feature Sets

When creating opinion classifiers, people often throw in a variety of features and trust the machine learning algorithm to figure out how to make the best use of them. However, we hypothesized that classifiers may perform better if we can proactively eliminate features that are not necesary because they are subsumed by other features. In this section, we present a series of experiments to explore this hypothesis. First, we present the results for an SVM classifier trained using different sets of unigram, bigram, and extraction pattern features, both before and after subsumption. Next, we evaluate a standard feature selection approach as an alternative to subsumption and then show that combining subsumption with standard feature selection produces the best results of all.

5.1 Classification Experiments

To see whether feature subsumption can improve classification performance, we trained an SVM classifier for each of the three opinion data sets. We used the SVM^{light} (Joachims, 1998) package with a linear kernel. For the Polarity and OP data we discarded all features that have frequency < 5, and for the MPQA data we discarded features that have frequency < 2 because this data set is substantially smaller. All of our experimental results are averages over 3-fold cross-validation.

First, we created 4 baseline classifiers: a *1Gram* classifier that uses only the unigram features; a *1+2Gram* classifier that uses unigram and bigram features; a *1+EP* classifier that uses unigram and extraction pattern features, and a *1+2+EP* classifier that uses all three types of features. Next, we created analogous 1+2Gram, 1+EP, and 1+2+EP classifiers but applied the subsumption hierarchy first to eliminate unnecessary features before training the classifier. We experimented with three delta values for the subsumption process: δ=.0005, .001, and .002.

Figures 7, 8, and 9 show the results. The subsumption process produced small but consistent improvements on all 3 data sets. For example, Figure 8 shows the results on the OP data, where all of the accuracy values produced after subsumption (the rightmost 3 columns) are higher than the accuracy values produced without subsumption (the Base[line] column). For all three data sets, the best overall accuracy (shown in boldface) was always achieved after subsumption.

Features	**Base**	**δ=.0005**	**δ=.001**	**δ=.002**
1Gram	79.8			
1+2Gram	81.2	81.0	81.3	81.0
1+EP	81.7	81.4	81.4	82.0
1+2+EP	81.7	82.3	82.3	**82.7**

Figure 7: Accuracies on Polarity Data

Features	**Base**	**δ=.0005**	**δ=.001**	**δ=.002**
1Gram	97.5	-	-	-
1+2Gram	98.0	**98.7**	98.6	**98.7**
1+EP	97.2	97.8	97.9	97.9
1+2+EP	97.8	98.6	**98.7**	**98.7**

Figure 8: Accuracies on OP Data

Features	**Base**	**δ=.0005**	**δ=.001**	**δ=.002**
1Gram	74.8			
1+2Gram	74.3	**74.9**	74.6	74.8
1+EP	74.4	74.6	74.6	74.6
1+2+EP	74.4	**74.9**	74.7	74.6

Figure 9: Accuracies on MPQA Data

We also observed that subsumption had a dramatic effect on the F-measure scores on the OP data, which are shown in Figure 10. The OP data set is fundamentally different from the other data sets because it is so highly skewed, with 91% of the documents belonging to the non-opinion class. Without subsumption, the classifier was conservative about assigning documents to the opinion class, achieving F-measure scores in the 82-88 range. After subsumption, the overall accuracy improved but the F-measure scores increased more dramatically. These numbers show that the subsumption process produced not only a more accurate classifier, but a more useful classifier that identifies more documents as being opinion articles.

For the MPQA data, we get a very small improvement of 0.1% (74.8% $\rightarrow$ 74.9%) using subsumption. But note that without subsumption the performance actually decreased when bigrams and

Features	Base	δ=.0005	δ=.001	δ=.002
1Gram	84.5			
1+2Gram	88.0	**92.5**	92.0	92.3
1+EP	82.4	86.9	87.4	87.4
1+2+EP	86.7	91.8	**92.5**	92.3

Figure 10: F-measures on OP Data

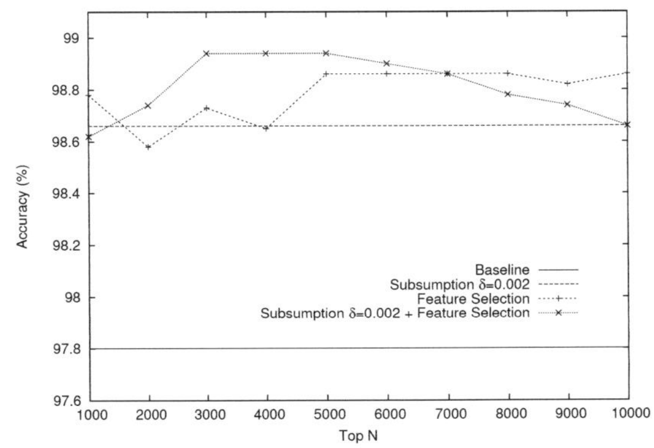

Figure 11: Feature Selection on OP Data

extraction patterns were added! The subsumption process counteracted the negative effect of adding the more complex features.

5.2 Feature Selection Experiments

We conducted a second series of experiments to determine whether a traditional feature selection approach would produce the same, or better, improvements as subsumption. For each feature, we computed its information gain (IG) and then selected the N features with the highest scores.[7] We experimented with values of N ranging from 1,000 to 10,000 in increments of 1,000.

We hypothesized that applying subsumption before traditional feature selection might also help to identify a more diverse set of high-performing features. In a parallel set of experiments, we explored this hypothesis by first applying subsumption to reduce the size of the feature set, and then selecting the best N features using information gain.

Figures 11, 12, and 13 show the results of these experiments for the 1+2+EP classifiers. Each graph shows four lines. One line corresponds to the baseline classifier with no subsumption, and another line corresponds to the baseline classifier with subsumption using the best δ value for that data set. Each of these two lines corresponds to

[7]In the case of ties, we included all features with the same score as the Nth-best as well.

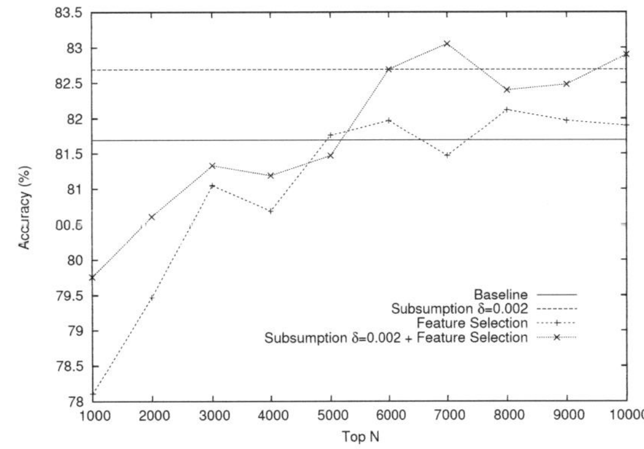

Figure 12: Feature Selection on Polarity Data

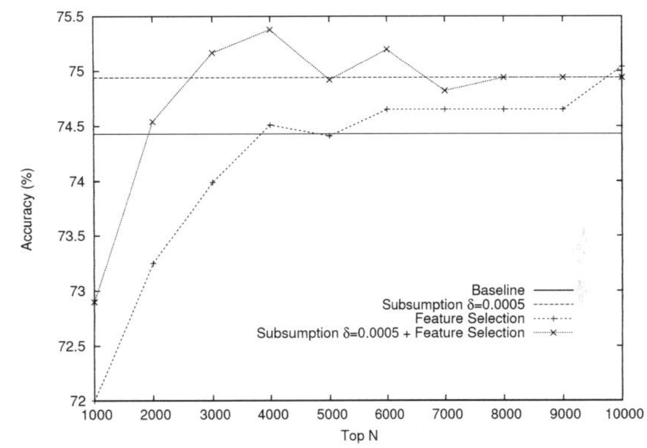

Figure 13: Feature Selection on MPQA Data

just a single data point (accuracy value), but we drew that value as a line across the graph for the sake of comparison. The other two lines on the graph correspond to (a) feature selection for different values of N (shown on the x-axis), and (b) subsumption followed by feature selection for different values of N.

On all 3 data sets, traditional feature selection performs worse than the baseline in some cases, and it virtually never outperforms the best classifier trained after subsumption (but without feature selection). Furthermore, the combination of subsumption plus feature selection generally performs best of all, and nearly always outperforms feature selection alone. For all 3 data sets, our best accuracy results were achieved by performing subsumption prior to feature selection. The best accuracy results are 99.0% on the OP data, 83.1% on the Polarity data, and 75.4% on the MPQA data. For the OP data, the improvement over baseline for both accuracy and F-measure are statistically significant at the $p < 0.05$ level (paired t-test). For the MPQA data, the improvement over baseline is statistically significant at the $p < 0.10$ level.

6 Related Work

Many features and classification algorithms have been explored in sentiment analysis and opinion recognition. Lexical cues of differing complexities have been used, including single words and Ngrams (e.g., (Mullen and Collier, 2004; Pang et al., 2002; Turney, 2002; Yu and Hatzivassiloglou, 2003; Wiebe et al., 2004)), as well as phrases and lexico-syntactic patterns (e.g, (Kim and Hovy, 2004; Hu and Liu, 2004; Popescu and Etzioni, 2005; Riloff and Wiebe, 2003; Whitelaw et al., 2005)). While many of these studies investigate combinations of features and feature selection, this is the first work that uses the notion of subsumption to compare Ngrams and lexico-syntactic patterns to identify complex features that outperform simpler counterparts and to reduce a combined feature set to improve opinion classification.

7 Conclusions

This paper uses a *subsumption hierarchy* of feature representations as (1) an analytic tool to compare features of different complexities, and (2) an automatic tool to remove unnecessary features to improve opinion classification performance. Experiments with three opinion data sets showed that subsumption can improve classification accuracy, especially when combined with feature selection.

Acknowledgments

This research was supported by NSF Grants IIS-0208798 and IIS-0208985, the ARDA AQUAINT Program, and the Institute for Scientific Computing Research and the Center for Applied Scientific Computing within Lawrence Livermore National Laboratory.

References

S. Banerjee and T. Pedersen. 2003. The Design, Implementation, and Use of the Ngram Statistics Package. In *Proc. Fourth Int'l Conference on Intelligent Text Processing and Computational Linguistics*.

A. Esuli and F. Sebastiani. 2005. Determining the semantic orientation of terms through gloss analysis. In *Proc. CIKM-05*.

G. Forman. 2003. An Extensive Empirical Study of Feature Selection Metrics for Text Classification. *J. Mach. Learn. Res.*, 3:1289–1305.

M. Hu and B. Liu. 2004. Mining and summarizing customer reviews. In *Proc. KDD-04*.

T. Joachims. 1998. Making Large-Scale Support Vector Machine Learning Practical. In A. Smola B. Schölkopf, C. Burges, editor, *Advances in Kernel Methods: Support Vector Machines*. MIT Press, Cambridge, MA.

S-M. Kim and E. Hovy. 2004. Determining the sentiment of opinions. In *Proc. COLING-04*.

M. Marcus, B. Santorini, and M. Marcinkiewicz. 1993. Building a Large Annotated Corpus of English: The Penn Treebank. *Computational Linguistics*, 19(2):313–330.

T. Mullen and N. Collier. 2004. Sentiment Analysis Using Support Vector Machines with Diverse Information Sources. In *Proc. EMNLP-04*.

B. Pang and L. Lee. 2004. A sentimental education: Sentiment analysis using subjectivity summarization based on minimum cuts. In *Proc. ACL-04*.

B. Pang, L. Lee, and S. Vaithyanathan. 2002. Thumbs up? Sentiment Classification using Machine Learning Techniques. In *Proc. EMNLP-02*.

A-M. Popescu and O. Etzioni. 2005. Extracting product features and opinions from reviews. In *Proc. HLT-EMNLP-05*.

E. Riloff and W. Phillips. 2004. An Introduction to the Sundance and AutoSlog Systems. Technical Report UUCS-04-015, School of Computing, University of Utah.

E. Riloff and J. Wiebe. 2003. Learning Extraction Patterns for Subjective Expressions. In *Proc. EMNLP-03*.

E. Riloff. 1996. An Empirical Study of Automated Dictionary Construction for Information Extraction in Three Domains. *Artificial Intelligence*, 85:101–134.

P. Turney. 2002. Thumbs up or thumbs down? Semantic orientation applied to unsupervised classification of reviews. In *Proc. ACL-02*.

C. Whitelaw, N. Garg, and S. Argamon. 2005. Using appraisal groups for sentiment analysis. In *Proc. CIKM-05*.

J. Wiebe, T. Wilson, R. Bruce, M. Bell, and M. Martin. 2004. Learning subjective language. *Computational Linguistics*, 30(3):277–308.

J. Wiebe, T. Wilson, and C. Cardie. 2005. Annotating expressions of opinions and emotions in language. *Language Resources and Evaluation*, 39(2/3).

H. Yu and V. Hatzivassiloglou. 2003. Towards answering opinion questions: Separating facts from opinions and identifying the polarity of opinion sentences. In *Proc. EMNLP-03*.

Relevance Feedback Models for Recommendation

Masao Utiyama
National Institute of Information and Communications Technology
3-5 Hikari-dai, Soraku-gun, Kyoto 619-0289 Japan
mutiyama@nict.go.jp

Mikio Yamamoto
University of Tsukuba, 1-1-1 Tennodai, Tsukuba, 305-8573 Japan
myama@cs.tsukuba.ac.jp

Abstract

We extended language modeling approaches in information retrieval (IR) to combine collaborative filtering (CF) and content-based filtering (CBF). Our approach is based on the analogy between IR and CF, especially between CF and relevance feedback (RF). Both CF and RF exploit users' preference/relevance judgments to recommend items. We first introduce a multinomial model that combines CF and CBF in a language modeling framework. We then generalize the model to another multinomial model that approximates the Polya distribution. This generalized model outperforms the multinomial model by 3.4% for CBF and 17.4% for CF in recommending English Wikipedia articles. The performance of the generalized model for three different datasets was comparable to that of a state-of-the-art item-based CF method.

1 Introduction

Recommender systems (Resnick and Varian, 1997) help users select particular items (e.g, movies, books, music, and TV programs) that match their taste from a large number of choices by providing recommendations. The systems either recommend a set of N items that will be of interest to users (*top-N recommendation problem*) or predict the degree of users' preference for items (*prediction problem*).

For those systems to work, they first have to aggregate users' evaluations of items explicitly or implicitly. Users may explicitly evaluate certain movies as rating five stars to express their preference. These evaluations are used by the systems as *explicit ratings (votes)* of items or the systems infer the evaluations of items from the behavior of users and use these inferred evaluations as *implicit ratings*. For example, systems can infer that users may like certain items if the systems learn which books they buy, which articles they read, or which TV programs they watch.

Collaborative filtering (CF) (Resnick et al., 1994; Breese et al., 1998) and *content-based (or adaptive) filtering* (CBF) (Allan, 1996; Schapire et al., 1998) are two of the most popular types of algorithms used in recommender systems. A CF system makes recommendations to current (*active*) users by exploiting their ratings in the database. *User-based CF* (Resnick et al., 1994; Herlocker et al., 1999) and *item-based CF* (Sarwar et al., 2001; Karypis, 2001), among other CF algorithms, have been studied extensively. User-based CF first identifies a set of users (*neighbors*) that are similar to the active user in terms of their rating patterns in the database. It then uses the neighbors' rating patterns to produce recommendations for the active user. On the other hand, item-based CF calculates the similarity between items beforehand and then recommends items that are similar to those preferred by the active user. The performance of item-based CF has been shown to be comparable to or better than that of user-based CF (Sarwar et al., 2001; Karypis, 2001). In contrast to CF, CBF uses the contents (e.g., texts, genres, authors, images, and audio) of items to make recommendations for the active user. Because CF and CBF are complementary, much work has been done to combine them (Basu et al., 1998; Yu et al., 2003; Si and Jin, 2004; Basilico and Hofmann, 2004).

The approach we took in this study is designed to solve top-N recommendation problems with im-

Proceedings of the 2006 Conference on Empirical Methods in Natural Language Processing (EMNLP 2006), pages 449–456, plicit ratings by using an item-based combination of CF and CBF. The methods described in this paper will be applied to recommending English Wikipedia[1] articles based on those articles edited by active users. (This is discussed in Section 3.) We use their editing histories and the contents of their articles to make top-N recommendations. We regard users' editing histories as implicit ratings. That is, if users have edited articles, we consider that they have positive attitudes toward the articles. Those implicit ratings are regarded as positive examples. We do not have negative examples for learning their negative attitudes toward articles. Consequently, handling our application with standard machine learning algorithms that require both positive and negative examples for classification (e.g., support vector machines) is awkward.

Our approach is based on the advancement in language modeling approaches to information retrieval (IR) (Croft and Lafferty, 2003) and extends these to incorporate CF. The motivation behind our approach is the analogy between CF and IR, especially between CF and relevance feedback (RF). Both CF and RF recommend items based on user preference/relevance judgments. Indeed, RF techniques have been applied to CBF, or adaptive filtering, successfully (Allan, 1996; Schapire et al., 1998). Thus, it is likely that RF can also be applied to CF.

To apply RF, we first extend the representation of items to combine CF and CBF under the models developed in Section 2. In Section 3, we report our experiments with the models. Future work and conclusion are in Sections 4 and 5.

2 Relevance feedback models

The analogy between IR and CF that will be exploited in this paper is as follows.[2] First, a document in IR corresponds to an item in CF. Both are represented as vectors. A document is represented as a vector of words (bag-of-words) and an item is represented as a vector of user ratings (bag-of-user ratings). In RF, a user specifies documents that are relevant to his information need. These documents are used by the system to retrieve new relevant documents. In CF, an active user (implicitly) specifies items that he likes. These items are used to search new items that will be preferred by the active user.

We use *relevance models* (Lavrenko and Croft, 2001; Lavrenko, 2004) as the basic framework of our relevance feedback models because (1) they perform relevance feedback well (Lavrenko, 2004) and (2) they can simultaneously handle different kinds of features (e.g., different language texts (Lavrenko et al., 2002), such as texts and images (Leon et al., 2003). These two points are essential in our application.

We first introduce a multinomial model following the work of Lavrenko (2004). This model is a novel one that extends relevance feedback approaches to incorporate CF. It is like a combination of relevance feedback (Lavrenko, 2004) and cross-language information retrieval (Lavrenko et al., 2002). We then generalize that model to an approximated Polya distribution model that is better suited to CF and CBF. This generalized model is the main technical contribution of this work.

2.1 Preparation

Lavrenko (2004) adopts the method of kernels to estimate probabilities: Let $\mathbf{d}$ be an item in the database or training data, the probability of item $\mathbf{x}$ is estimated as $p(\mathbf{x}) = \frac{1}{M}\sum_{\mathbf{d}} p(\mathbf{x}|\theta_{\mathbf{d}})$, where M is the number of items in the training data, $\theta_{\mathbf{d}}$ is the parameter vector estimated from $\mathbf{d}$, and $p(\mathbf{x}|\theta_{\mathbf{d}})$ is the conditional probability of $\mathbf{x}$ given $\theta_{\mathbf{d}}$.[3] This means that once we have defined a probability distribution $p(\mathbf{x}|\theta)$ and the method of estimating $\theta_{\mathbf{d}}$ from $\mathbf{d}$, then we can assign probability $p(\mathbf{x})$ to $\mathbf{x}$ and apply language modeling approaches to CF and CBF.

To begin with, we define the representation of item $\mathbf{x}$ as the concatenation of two vectors $\{\mathbf{w_x}, \mathbf{u_x}\}$, where $\mathbf{w_x} = w_{\mathbf{x}1}w_{\mathbf{x}2}\ldots$ is the sequence of words (contents) contained in $\mathbf{x}$ and $\mathbf{u_x} = u_{\mathbf{x}1}u_{\mathbf{x}2}\ldots$ is the sequence of users who have rated $\mathbf{x}$ implicitly. We use V_w and V_u to denote the set of words and users in the database. The parameter vector θ is also the concatenation of two vectors $\{\omega, \mu\}$, where ω and μ are the parameter vectors for V_w and V_u, respectively. The probability of $\mathbf{x}$ given θ is defined as $p(\mathbf{x}|\theta) = p_\omega(\mathbf{w_x}|\omega)p_\mu(\mathbf{u_x}|\mu)$.

[1] http://en.wikipedia.org/wiki/Main_Page

[2] The analogy between IR and CF has been recognized. For example, Breese et al. (1998) used the vector space model to measure the similarity between users in a user-based CF framework. Wang et al. (2005) used a language modeling approach different from ours. These works, however, treated only CF. In contrast with these, our model extends language modeling approaches to incorporate both CF and CBF.

[3] Item $\mathbf{d}$ in summation $\sum_{\mathbf{d}}$ and word w in $\sum_w$ and $\prod_w$ go over every distinct item d and word w in the training data, unless otherwise stated.

2.2 Multinomial model

Our first model regards that both p_ω and p_μ follow multinomial distributions. In this case, $\omega(w)$ and $\mu(u)$ are the probabilities of word w and user u. Then, $p_\omega(\mathbf{w_x}|\omega)$ is defined as

$$p_\omega(\mathbf{w_x}|\omega) = \prod_{i=1}^{|\mathbf{w_x}|} \omega(w_{\mathbf{x}i}) = \prod_{w \in V_w} \omega(w)^{n(w,\mathbf{w_x})} \quad (1)$$

where $n(w, \mathbf{w_x})$ is the number of occurrences of w in $\mathbf{w_x}$. In this model, we use a linear interpolation method to estimate probability $\omega_\mathbf{d}(w)$.

$$\omega_\mathbf{d}(w) = \lambda_\omega P_l(w|\mathbf{w_d}) + (1 - \lambda_\omega)P_g(w) \quad (2)$$

where $P_l(w|\mathbf{w_d}) = \frac{n(w,\mathbf{w_d})}{\sum_{w'} n(w',\mathbf{w_d})}$, $P_g(w) = \frac{\sum_\mathbf{d} n(w,\mathbf{w_d})}{\sum_\mathbf{d}\sum_{w'} n(w',\mathbf{w_d})}$ and λ_ω $(0 \leq \lambda_\omega \leq 1)$ is a smoothing parameter. The estimation of user probabilities goes similarly: Let $n(u, \mathbf{u_x})$ be the number of times user u implicitly rated item $\mathbf{x}$, we define or estimate p_μ, λ_μ and $\mu_\mathbf{d}$ in the same way. In summary, we have defined a probability distribution $p(\mathbf{x}|\theta)$ and the method of estimating $\theta_\mathbf{d} = \{\omega_\mathbf{d}, \mu_\mathbf{d}\}$ from $\mathbf{d}$.

To recommend top-N items, we have to rank items in the database in response to the implicit ratings of active users. We call those implicit ratings *query* $\mathbf{q}$. It is a set of items and is represented as $\mathbf{q} = \{\mathbf{q}_1 \ldots \mathbf{q}_k\}$, where $\mathbf{q}_i$ is an item implicitly rated by an active user and k is the size of $\mathbf{q}$. We next estimate $\theta_\mathbf{q} = \{\omega_\mathbf{q}, \mu_\mathbf{q}\}$. Then, we compare $\theta_\mathbf{q}$ and $\theta_\mathbf{d}$ to rank items by using Kullback-Leibler divergence $D(\theta_\mathbf{q}||\theta_\mathbf{d})$ (Lafferty and Zhai, 2001; Lavrenko, 2004).

$\omega_\mathbf{q}(w)$ can be approximated as

$$\omega_\mathbf{q}(w) = \frac{1}{k}\sum_{i=1}^{k} \omega_{\mathbf{q}_i}(w) \quad (3)$$

where $\omega_{\mathbf{q}_i}(w)$ is obtained by Eq. 2 (Lavrenko, 2004). However, we found in preliminary experiments that smoothing query probabilities hurt performance in our application. Thus, we use

$$\omega_{\mathbf{q}_i}(w) = P_l(w|\mathbf{w}_{\mathbf{q}_i}) = \frac{n(w, \mathbf{w}_{\mathbf{q}_i})}{\sum_{w'} n(w', \mathbf{w}_{\mathbf{q}_i})} \quad (4)$$

instead of Eq. 2 when $\mathbf{q}_i$ is in a query.

Because KL-divergence is a distance measure, we use a score function derived from $-D(\theta_\mathbf{q}||\theta_\mathbf{d})$ to rank items. We use $S_\mathbf{q}(\mathbf{d})$ to denote the score of $\mathbf{d}$ given $\mathbf{q}$. $S_\mathbf{q}(\mathbf{d})$ is derived as follows. (We ignore terms that are irrelevant to ranking items.)

$$-D(\theta_\mathbf{q}||\theta_\mathbf{d}) = -D(\omega_\mathbf{q}||\omega_\mathbf{d}) - D(\mu_\mathbf{q}||\mu_\mathbf{d})$$

$$-D(\omega_\mathbf{q}||\omega_\mathbf{d}) \overset{rank}{=} \frac{1}{k}\sum_{i=1}^{k} S(\omega_{\mathbf{q}_i}||\omega_\mathbf{d}) \quad (5)$$

where

$$S(\omega_{\mathbf{q}_i}||\omega_\mathbf{d}) = \sum_w P_l(w|\mathbf{w}_{\mathbf{q}_i}) \times \log\left(\frac{\lambda_\omega P_l(w|\mathbf{w_d})}{(1-\lambda_\omega)P_g(w)} + 1\right). \quad (6)$$

The summation goes over every word w that is shared by both $\mathbf{w}_{\mathbf{q}_i}$ and $\mathbf{w_d}$. We define $S(\mu_{\mathbf{q}_i}||\mu_\mathbf{d})$ similarly.[4] Then, the score of $\mathbf{d}$ given $\mathbf{q}_i$, $S_{\mathbf{q}_i}(\mathbf{d})$ is defined as

$$S_{\mathbf{q}_i}(\mathbf{d}) = \lambda_s S(\mu_{\mathbf{q}_i}||\mu_\mathbf{d}) + (1-\lambda_s)S(\omega_{\mathbf{q}_i}||\omega_\mathbf{d}) \quad (7)$$

where λ_s $(0 \leq \lambda_s \leq 1)$ is a free parameter. Finally, the score of $\mathbf{d}$ given $\mathbf{q}$ is

$$S_\mathbf{q}(\mathbf{d}) = \frac{1}{k}\sum_{i=1}^{k} S_{\mathbf{q}_i}(\mathbf{d}). \quad (8)$$

The calculation of $S_\mathbf{q}(\mathbf{d})$ can be very efficient because once we cache $S_{\mathbf{q}_i}(\mathbf{d})$ for each item pair of $\mathbf{q}_i$ and $\mathbf{d}$ in the database, we can reuse it to calculate $S_\mathbf{q}(\mathbf{d})$ for any query $\mathbf{q}$. We further optimize the calculation of top-N recommendations by storing only the top 100 items (*neighbors*) in decreasing order of $S_{\mathbf{q}_i}(\cdot)$ for each item $\mathbf{q}_i$ and setting the scores of lower ranked items as 0. (Note that $S_{\mathbf{q}_i}(\mathbf{d}) >= 0$ holds.) Consequently, we only have to search small part of the search space without affecting the performance very much. These two types of optimization are common in item-based CF (Sarwar et al., 2001; Karypis, 2001).

2.3 Polya model

Our second model is based on the Polya distribution. We first introduce (hyper) parameter $\Theta = \{\alpha^\omega, \alpha^\mu\}$ and denote the probability of $\mathbf{x}$ given Θ as $p(\mathbf{x}|\Theta) = p_\omega(\mathbf{w_x}|\alpha^\omega)p_\mu(\mathbf{u_x}|\alpha^\mu)$. α^ω and α^μ are the parameter vectors for words and users. $p_\omega(\mathbf{w_x}|\alpha^\omega)$ is defined as follows.

$$p_\omega(\mathbf{w_x}|\alpha^\omega) = \frac{\Gamma(\sum_w \alpha_w^\omega)}{\Gamma(\sum_w n_w^\mathbf{x} + \alpha_w^\omega)} \prod_w \frac{\Gamma(n_w^\mathbf{x} + \alpha_w^\omega)}{\Gamma(\alpha_w^\omega)} \quad (9)$$

[4] $S(\mu_{\mathbf{q}_i}||\mu_\mathbf{d}) = \sum_u P_l(u|\mathbf{u}_{\mathbf{q}_i}) \times \log\left(\frac{\lambda_\mu P_l(u|\mathbf{u_d})}{(1-\lambda_\mu)P_g(u)} + 1\right)$, where $P_l(u|\mathbf{u}_{\mathbf{q}_i}) = \frac{n(u,\mu_{\mathbf{q}_i})}{\sum_{u'} n(u',\mu_{\mathbf{q}_i})}$, $P_l(u|\mathbf{u_d}) = \frac{n(u,\mathbf{u_d})}{\sum_{u'} n(u',\mathbf{u_d})}$, and $P_g(u) = \frac{\sum_\mathbf{d} n(u,\mathbf{u_d})}{\sum_\mathbf{d}\sum_{u'} n(u',\mathbf{u_d})}$.

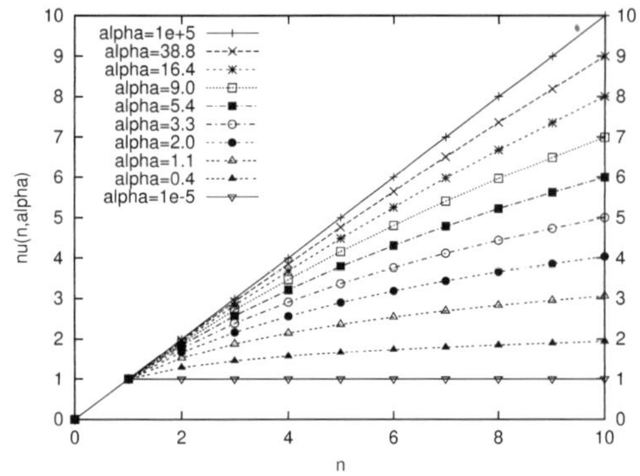

Figure 1: Relationship between original count n and dumped count $\nu(n, \alpha)$

where Γ is known as the gamma function, α_w^ω is a parameter for word w and $n_w^{\mathbf{x}} = n(w, \mathbf{w_x})$. This can be approximated as follows (Minka, 2003).

$$p_\omega(\mathbf{w_x}|\alpha^\omega) \sim \prod_w \omega(w)^{\tilde{n}(w,\mathbf{w_x})} \tag{10}$$

where

$$\begin{aligned} \tilde{n}(w, \mathbf{w_x}) &= \alpha_w^\omega(\Psi(n_w^{\mathbf{x}} + \alpha_w^\omega) - \Psi(\alpha_w^\omega)) \\ &\equiv \nu(n_w^{\mathbf{x}}, \alpha_w^\omega) \end{aligned} \tag{11}$$

Ψ is known as the digamma function and is similar to the natural logarithm. We call Eq. 10 the approximated Polya model or simply the Polya model in this paper.

Eq. 10 indicates that the Polya distribution can be interpreted as a multinomial distribution over a modified set of counts $\tilde{n}(\cdot)$ (Minka, 2003). These modified counts are *dumped* as shown in Fig. 1. When $\alpha_w^\omega \rightarrow \infty$, $\nu(n_w^{\mathbf{x}}, \alpha_w^\omega)$ approaches $n_w^{\mathbf{x}}$. When $\alpha_w^\omega \rightarrow 0$, $\nu(n_w^{\mathbf{x}}, \alpha_w^\omega) = 0$ if $n_w^{\mathbf{x}} = 0$ otherwise it is 1. For intermediate values of α_w^ω, the mapping ν dumps the original counts.

Under the approximation of Eq. 10, the estimation of parameters can be understood as the maximum-likelihood estimate of a multinomial distribution from dumped counts $\tilde{n}(\cdot)$ (Minka, 2003). Indeed, all we have to do to estimate the parameters for ranking items is replace P_l and P_g from Section 2.2 with $P_l(w|\mathbf{w_d}) = \frac{\tilde{n}(w,\mathbf{w_d})}{\sum_{w'} \tilde{n}(w',\mathbf{w_d})}$, $P_g(w) = \frac{\sum_{\mathbf{d}} \tilde{n}(w,\mathbf{w_d})}{\sum_{\mathbf{d}} \sum_{w'} \tilde{n}(w',\mathbf{w_d})}$, and $P_l(w|\mathbf{w_{q_i}}) = \frac{\tilde{n}(w,\mathbf{w_{q_i}})}{\sum_{w'} \tilde{n}(w',\mathbf{w_{q_i}})}$. Then, as in the multinomial model, we can define $S(\omega_{\mathbf{q}_i}||\omega_{\mathbf{d}})$ with these probabilities. This argument also applies to $S(\mu_{\mathbf{q}_i}||\mu_{\mathbf{d}})$.

The approximated Polya model is a generalization of the multinomial model described in Section 2.2. If we set α_w^ω and α_u^μ very large then the Polya model is identical to the multinomial model. By comparing Eqs. 1 and 10, we can see why the Polya model is superior to the multinomial model for modeling the occurrences of words (and users). In the multinomial model, if a word with probability p occurs twice, its probability becomes p^2. In the Polya model, the word's probability becomes $p^{1.5}$, for example, if we set $\alpha_w^\omega = 1$. Clearly, $p^2 < p^{1.5}$; therefore, the Polya model assigns higher probability. In this example, the Polya model assigns probability p to the first occurrence and $p^{0.5} (> p)$ to the second. Since words that occur once are likely to occur again (Church, 2000), the Polya model is better suited to model the occurrences of words and users. See Yamamoto and Sadamitsu (2005) for further discussion on applying the Polya distribution to text modeling.

Zaragoza et al.(2003) applied the Polya distribution to ad hoc IR. They introduced the exact Polya distribution (see Eq. 9) as an extension to the Dirichlet prior method (Zhai and Lafferty, 2001). However, we have introduced a multinomial approximation of the Polya distribution. This approximation allows us to use the linear interpolation method to mix the approximated Polya distributions. Thus, our model is similar to two-stage language models (Zhai and Lafferty, 2002) that combine the Dirichlet prior method and the linear interpolation method. In contrast to our model, Zaragoza et al.(2003) had difficulty in mixing the Polya distributions and did not treat that in their paper.

3 Experiments

We first examined the behavior of the Polya model by varying the parameters. We tied α_w^ω for every w and α_u^μ for every u; for any w and u, $\alpha_w^\omega = \alpha_\omega$ and $\alpha_u^\mu = \alpha_\mu$. We then compared the Polya model to an item-based CF method.

3.1 Behavior of Polya model

3.1.1 Dataset

We made a dataset of articles from English Wikipedia[5] to evaluate the Polya model. English Wikipedia is an online encyclopedia that anyone

[5]We downloaded `20050713_pages_full.xml.gz` and `20050713_pages_current.xml.gz` from `http://download.wikimedia.org/wikipedia/en/`.

can edit, and it has many registered users. Our aim is to recommend a set of articles to each user that is likely to be of interest to that user. If we can successfully recommend interesting articles, this could be very useful to a wide audience because Wikipedia is very popular. In addition, because wikis are popular media for sharing knowledge, developing effective recommender systems for wikis is important.

In our Wikipedia dataset, each item (article) $\mathbf{x}$ consisted of $\mathbf{w_x}$ and $\mathbf{u_x}$. $\mathbf{u_x}$ was the sequence of users who had edited $\mathbf{x}$. If users had edited $\mathbf{x}$ multiple times, then those users occurred in $\mathbf{u_x}$ multiple times. $\mathbf{w_x}$ was the sequence of words that were typical in $\mathbf{x}$. To make $\mathbf{w_x}$, we removed stop words and stemmed the remaining words with a Porter stemmer. Next, we identified 100 typical words in each article and extracted only those words ($|\mathbf{w_x}| \geq 100$ because some of them occurred multiple times). Typicality was measured using the log-likelihood ratio test (Dunning, 1993). We needed to reduce the number of words to speed up our recommender system.

To make our dataset, we first extracted 302,606 articles, which had more than 100 tokens after the stop words were removed. We then selected typical words in each article. The implicit rating data were obtained from the histories of users editing these articles. Each rating consisted of {*user*, *article*, *number of edits*}. The size of this original rating data was 3,325,746. From this data, we extracted a dense subset that consisted of users and articles included in at least 25 units of the original data. We discarded the users who had edited more than 999 articles because they were often software robots or system operators, not casual users. The resulting 430,096 ratings consisted of 4,193 users and 9,726 articles. Each user rated (edited) 103 articles on average (the median was 57). The average number of ratings per item was 44 and the median was 36.

3.1.2 Evaluation of Polya model

We conducted a four-fold cross validation of this rating dataset to evaluate the Polya model. We used three-fourth of the dataset to train the model and one-fourth to test it.[6] All users who existed in both training and test data were used for evaluation. For each user, we regarded the articles in the training data that had been edited by the user as a query and ranked articles in response to it. These ranked top-N articles were then compared to the articles in the test data that were edited by the same user to measure the precisions for the user. We used P@N (precision at rank N = the ratio of the articles edited by the user in the top-N articles), S@N (success at rank $N = 1$ if some top-N articles were edited by the user, else 0), and R-precision (= P@N, where N is the number of articles edited by the user in the test data). These measures for each user were averaged over all users to get the mean precision of each measure. Then, these mean precisions were averaged over the cross validation repeats.

Here, we report the averaged mean precisions with standard deviations. We first report how R-precision varied depending on α (α_ω or α_μ). α was varied over $10^{-5}, 0.4, 1.1, 2, 3.3, 5.4, 9, 16.4, 38.8$, and 10^5. The values of $\nu(10, \alpha)$ were approximately 1, 2, 3, 4, 5, 6, 7, 8, 9, and 10, respectively, as shown in Fig. 1. When $\alpha = 10^5$, the Polya model represents the multinomial model as discussed in Section 2.3. For each value of α, we varied λ (λ_ω or λ_μ) over 0.01, 0.05, 0.1, 0.2, 0.3, 0.4, 0.5, 0.6, 0.7, 0.8, 0.9, 0.95, and 0.99 to obtain the optimum R-precision. These optimum R-precisions are shown in Fig. 2. In this figure, CBF and CF represent the R-precisions for the content-based and collaborative filtering part of the Polya model. The values of CBF and CF were obtained by setting $\lambda_s = 0$ and $\lambda_s = 1$ in Eq. 7 (which is applied to the Polya model instead of the multinomial model), respectively. The error bars represent standard deviations.

At once, we noticed that CBF outperformed CF. This is reasonable because the contents of Wikipedia articles should strongly reflect the users (authors) interest. In addition, each article had about 100 typical words, and this was richer than the average number of users per article (44). This observation contrasts with other work where CBF performed poorly compared with CF, e.g., (Ali and van Stam, 2004).

Another important observation is that both curves in Fig. 2 are concave. The best R-precisions were obtained at intermediate values of α for both CF and CBF as shown in Table 1.

[6] We needed to estimate probabilities of users and words. We used only training data to estimate the probabilities of users. However, we used all 9,726 articles to estimate the probabilities of words because the articles are usually available even when editing histories of users are not.

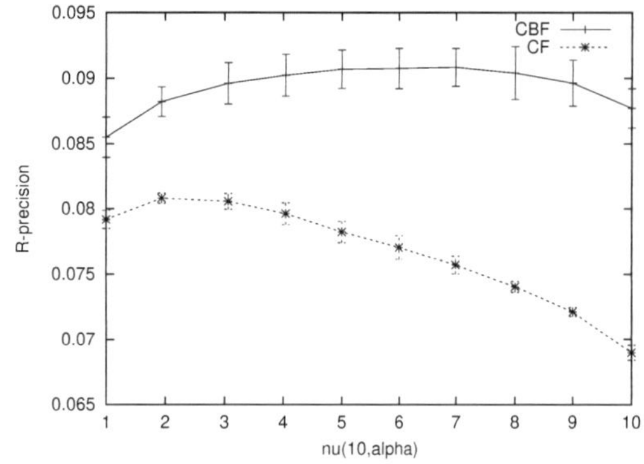

Figure 2: R-precision for Polya model

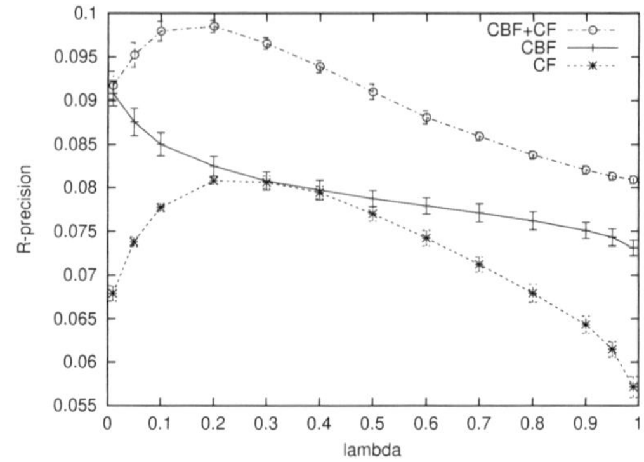

Figure 3: Combination of CBF and CF.

Table 1: Improvement in R-precision (RP)

	best RP ($\nu(\cdot)/\alpha$)	RP ($\nu(\cdot)/\alpha$)	%change
CBF	0.091 (7/9.0)	0.088 ($10/10^5$)	+3.4%
CF	0.081 (2/0.4)	0.069 ($10/10^5$)	+17.4%

When $\alpha = 10^5$ or $\nu(10, \alpha) \sim 10$, the Polya model represents the multinomial model as discussed in Section 2.3. Thus, Fig. 2 and Table 1 show that the best R-precisions achieved by the Polya model were better than those obtained by the multinomial model. The improvement was 3.4% for CBF and 17.4% for CF as shown in Table 1. The improvement of CF was larger than that of CBF. This implies that the occurrences of users are more clustered than those of words. In other words, the degree of repetition in the editing histories of users is greater than that in word sequences. A user who edits an article are likely to edit the article again.

From Fig. 2 and Table 1, we concluded that the generalization of a multinomial model achieved by the Polya model is effective in improving recommendation performance.

3.1.3 Combination of CBF and CF

Next, we show how the combination of CBF and CF improves recommendation performance. We set α (α_ω and α_μ) to the optimum values in Table 1 and varied λ (λ_s, λ_ω and λ_μ) to obtain the R-precisions for CBF+CF, CBF and CF in Fig. 3. The values of CBF were obtained as follows. We first set $\lambda_s = 0$ in Eq. 7 to use only CBF scores and then varied λ_ω, which is the smoothing parameter for word probabilities, in Eq. 2. To get the values of CF, we set $\lambda_s = 1$ in Eq. 7 and then varied λ_μ, which is the smoothing parameter for user probabilities. The values of CBF+CF were obtained by varying λ_s in Eq. 7 while setting λ_ω and λ_μ to the optimum values obtained from CBF and CF (see Table 2). These parameters (λ_s, λ_ω and λ_μ) were defined in the context of the multinomial model in Section 2.2 and used similarly in the Polya model in this experiment.

Table 2: Precision and Success at top-N

	CBF+CF		CBF		CF	
N	P@N	S@N	P@N	S@N	P@N	S@N
5	0.166	0.470	0.149	0.444	0.137	0.408
10	0.135	0.585	0.123	0.562	0.112	0.516
15	0.117	0.650	0.107	0.628	0.098	0.582
20	0.105	0.694	0.096	0.671	0.089	0.627
R-precision	0.099		0.091		0.081	
optimum λ	$\lambda_s = 0.2$		$\lambda_\omega = 0.01$		$\lambda_\mu = 0.2$	

We can see that the combination was quite effective as CBF+CF outperformed both CBF and CF. Table 2 shows R-precision, P@N and S@N for $N = 5, 10, 15, 20$. These values were obtained by using the optimum values of λ in Fig. 3.

Table 2 shows the same tendency as Fig. 3. For all values of N, CBF+CF outperformed both CBF and CF. We attribute this effectiveness of the combination to the feature independence of CBF and CF. CBF used words as features and CF used user ratings as features. They are very different kinds of features and thus can provide complementary information. Consequently, CBF+CF can exploit the benefits of both methods. We need to do further work to confirm this conjecture.

3.2 Comparison with a baseline method

We compared the Polya model to an implementation of a state-of-the-art item-based CF method, *CProb* (Karypis, 2001). CProb has been tested with various datasets and found to be effective in top-N recommendation problems. CProb has also been used in recent work as a baseline method (Ziegler et al., 2005; Wang et al., 2005).

In addition to the Wikipedia dataset, we used two other datasets for comparison. The first was

	R-precision			P@10		
	WP	ML	BX	WP	ML	BX
Polya-CF	0.081	0.272	0.066	0.112	0.384	0.054
CProb	0.082	0.258	0.071	0.113	0.373	0.057
%change	-1.2%	+5.4%	-7.0%	-0.9%	+2.9%	-5.3%

Table 3: Comparison of Polya-CF and CProb

the 1 million MovieLens dataset.[7] This data consists of 1,000,209 ratings of 3,706 movies by 6,040 users. Each user rated an average of 166 movies (the median was 96). The average number of ratings per movie was 270 and the median was 124. The second was the BookCrossing dataset (Ziegler et al., 2005). This data consists of 1,149,780 ratings of 340,532 books by 105,283 users. From this data, we removed books rated by less than 20 users. We also removed users who rated less than 5 books. The resulting 296,471 ratings consisted of 10,345 users and 5,943 books. Each user rated 29 books on average (the median was 10). The average number of ratings per book was 50 and the median was 33. Note that in our experiments, we regarded the ratings of these two datasets as implicit ratings. We regarded the number of occurrence of each rating as one.

We conducted a four-fold cross validation for each dataset to compare CProb and Polya-CF, which is the collaborative filtering part of the Polya model as described in the previous section. For each cross validation repeat, we tuned the parameters of CProb and Polya-CF on the test data to get the optimum R-precisions, in order to compare best results for these models.[8] P@N and S@N were calculated with the same parameters. These measures were averaged as described above. R-precision and P@10 are in Table 3. The maximum standard deviation of these measures was 0.001. We omitted reporting other measures because they had similar tendencies. In Table 3, WP, ML and BX represent the Wikipedia, MovieLens, and BookCrossing datasets.

In Table 3, we can see that the variation of performance among datasets was greater than that between Polya-CF and CProb. Both methods performed best against ML. We think that this is because ML had the densest ratings. The average number of ratings per item was 270 for ML while that for WP was 44 and that for BX was 50.

Table 3 also shows that Polya-CF outperformed CProb when the dataset was ML and CProb was better than Polya-CF in the other cases. However, the differences in precision were small. Overall, we can say that the performance of Polya-CF is comparable to that of CProb.

An important advantage of the Polya model over CProb is that the Polya model can unify CBF and CF in a single language modeling framework while CProb handles only CF. Another advantage of the Polya model is that we can expect to improve its performance by incorporating techniques developed in IR because the Polya model is based on language modeling approaches in IR.

4 Future work

We want to investigate two areas in our future work. One is the parameter estimation and the other is the refinement of the query model.

We tuned the parameters of the Polya model by exhaustively searching the parameter space guided by R-precision. We actually tried to learn α_ω and α_μ from the training data by using an EM method (Minka, 2003; Yamamoto and Sadamitsu, 2005). However, the estimated parameters were about 0.05, too small for better recommendations. We need further study to understand the relation between the probabilistic quality (*perplexity*) of the Polya model and its recommendation quality.

We approximate the query model as Eq. 3. This allows us to optimize score calculation considerably. However, this does not consider the interaction among items, which may deteriorate the quality of probability estimation. We want to investigate more efficient query models in our future work.

5 Conclusion

Recommender systems help users select particular items from a large number of choices by providing recommendations. Much work has been done to combine content-based filtering (CBF) and collaborative filtering (CF) to provide better recommendations. The contributions reported in this paper are twofold: (1) we extended relevance feedback approaches to incorporate CF and (2) we introduced the approximated Polya model as a gen-

[7] `http://www.grouplens.org/`

[8] CProb has two free parameters. Polya-CF also has two free parameters (α_μ and λ_μ). However, for MovieLens and BookCrossing datasets, Polya-CF has only one free parameter λ_μ, because we regarded the number of occurrence of each rating as one, which means $\nu(1, \alpha_\mu) = 1$ for all $\alpha_\mu > 0$ (See Fig. 1). Consequently, we don't have to tune α_μ. Since the number of free parameters is small, the comparison of performance shown in Table 3 is likely to be reproduced when we tune the parameters on separate development data instead of test data.

eralization of the multinomial model and showed that it is better suited to CF and CBF. The performance of the Polya model is comparable to that of a state-of-the-art item-based CF method.

Our work shows that language modeling approaches in information retrieval can be extended to CF. This implies that a large amount of work in the field of IR could be imported into CF. This would be interesting to investigate in future work.

References

Kamal Ali and Wijnand van Stam. 2004. TiVo: Making show recommendations using a distributed collaborative filtering architecture. In *KDD'04*.

James Allan. 1996. Incremental relevance feedback for information filtering. In *SIGIR'96*.

Justin Basilico and Thomas Hofmann. 2004. Unifying collaborative and content-based filtering. In *ICML'04*.

Chumki Basu, Haym Hirsh, and William Cohen. 1998. Recommendation as classification: Using social and content-based information in recommendation. In *AAAI-98*.

John S. Breese, David Heckerman, and Carl Kadie. 1998. Empirical analysis of predictive algorithms for collaborative filtering. Technical report, MSR-TR-98-12.

Kenneth W. Church. 2000. Empirical estimates of adaptation: The chance of two Noriegas is closer to $p/2$ than p^2. In *COLING-2000*, pages 180–186.

W. Bruce Croft and John Lafferty, editors. 2003. *Language Modeling for Information Retrieval*. Kluwer Academic Publishers.

Ted Dunning. 1993. Accurate methods for the statistics of surprise and coincidence. *Computational Linguistics*, 19(1):61–74.

Jonathan L. Herlocker, Joseph A. Konstan, Al Borchers, and John Riedl. 1999. An algorithmic framework for performing collaborative filtering. In *SIGIR'99*, pages 230–237.

George Karypis. 2001. Evaluation of item-based top-N recommendation algorithms. In *CIKM'01*.

John Lafferty and ChengXiang Zhai. 2001. Document language models, query models and risk minimization for information retrieval. In *SIGIR'01*.

Victor Lavrenko and W. Bruce Croft. 2001. Relevance-based language models. In *SIGIR'01*.

Victor Lavrenko, Martin Choquette, and W. Bruce Croft. 2002. Cross-lingual relevance models. In *SIGIR'02*, pages 175–182.

Victor Lavrenko. 2004. *A Generative Theory of Relevance*. Ph.D. thesis, University of Massachusetts.

J. Leon, V. Lavrenko, and R. Manmatha. 2003. Automatic image annotation and retrieval using cross-media relevance models. In *SIGIR'03*.

Thomas P. Minka. 2003. Estimating a Dirichlet distribution. http://research.microsoft.com/~minka/papers/dirichlet/.

Paul Resnick and Hal R. Varian. 1997. Recommender systems. *Communications of the ACM*, 40(3):56–58.

Paul Resnick, Neophytos Iacovou, Mitesh Suchak, Peter Bergstrom, and John Riedl. 1994. GroupLens: An open architecture for collaborative filtering of netnews. In *CSCW'94*, pages 175–186.

Badrul Sarwar, George Karypis, Joseph Konstan, and John Riedl. 2001. Item-based collaborative filtering recommendation algorithms. In *WWW10*.

Robert E. Schapire, Yoram Singer, and Amit Singhal. 1998. Boosting and Rocchio applied to text filtering. In *SIGIR'98*, pages 215–223.

Luo Si and Rong Jin. 2004. Unified filtering by combining collaborative filtering and content-based filtering via mixture model and exponential model. In *CIKM-04*, pages 156–157.

Jun Wang, Marcel J.T. Reinders, Reginald L. Lagendijk, and Johan Pouwelse. 2005. Self-organizing distributed collaborative filtering. In *SIGIR'05*, pages 659–660.

Mikio Yamamoto and Kugatsu Sadamitsu. 2005. Dirichlet mixtures in text modeling. Technical report, University of Tsukuba, CS-TR-05-1.

Kai Yu, Anton Schwaighofer, Volker Tresp, Wei-Ying Ma, and HongJiang Zhang. 2003. Collaborative ensemble learning: Combining collaborative and content-based information filtering via hierarchical Bayes. In *UAI-2003*.

Hugo Zaragoza, Djoerd Hiemstra, and Michael Tipping. 2003. Bayesian extension to the language model for ad hoc information retrieval. In *SIGIR'03*.

ChengXiang Zhai and John Lafferty. 2001. A study of smoothing methods for language models applied to ad hoc information retrieval. In *SIGIR'01*.

ChengXiang Zhai and John Lafferty. 2002. Two-stage language models for information retrieval. In *SIGIR'02*, pages 49–56.

Cai-Nicolas Ziegler, Sean M. McNee, Joseph A. Konstan, and Georg Lausen. 2005. Improving recommendation lists through topic diversification. In *WWW'05*, pages 22–32.

Random Indexing using Statistical Weight Functions

James Gorman and **James R. Curran**
School of Information Technologies
University of Sydney
NSW 2006, Australia
{jgorman2,james}@it.usyd.edu.au

Abstract

Random Indexing is a vector space technique that provides an efficient and scalable approximation to distributional similarity problems. We present experiments showing Random Indexing to be poor at handling large volumes of data and evaluate the use of weighting functions for improving the performance of Random Indexing. We find that Random Index is robust for small data sets, but performance degrades because of the influence high frequency attributes in large data sets. The use of appropriate weight functions improves this significantly.

1 Introduction

Synonymy relations between words have been used to inform many Natural Language Processing (NLP) tasks. While these relations can be extracted from manually created resources such as thesauri (e.g. Roget's Thesaurus) and lexical databases (e.g. WordNet, Fellbaum, 1998), it is often beneficial to extract these relationships from a corpus representative of the task.

Manually created resources are expensive and time-consuming to create, and tend to suffer from problems of bias, inconsistency, and limited coverage. These problems may result in an inappropriate vocabulary, where some terms are not present or an unbalanced set of synonyms. In a medical context it is more likely that administration will refer to the giving of medicine than to paper work, whereas in a business context the converse is more likely.

The most common method for automatically creating these resources uses distributional similarity and is based on the *distributional hypothesis* that *similar words appear in similar contexts*. Terms are described by collating information about their occurrence in a corpus into vectors. These *context vectors* are then compared for similarity. Existing approaches differ primarily in their definition of *context*, e.g. the surrounding words or the entire document, and their choice of distance metric for calculating similarity between the context vectors representing each term.

In this paper, we analyse the use of Random Indexing (Kanerva et al., 2000) for semantic similarity measurement. Random Indexing is an approximation technique proposed as an alternative to Latent Semantic Analysis (LSA, Landauer and Dumais, 1997). Random Indexing is more scalable and allows for the incremental learning of context information.

Curran and Moens (2002) found that dramatically increasing the volume of raw input data for distributional similarity tasks increases the accuracy of synonyms extracted. Random Indexing performs poorly on these volumes of data. Noting that in many NLP tasks, including distributional similarity, statistical weighting is used to improve performance, we modify the Random Indexing algorithm to allow for weighted contexts.

We test the performance of the original and our modified system using existing evaluation metrics. We further evaluate against bilingual lexicon extraction using distributional similarity (Sahlgren and Karlgren, 2005). The paper concludes with a more detailed analysis of Random Indexing in terms of both task and corpus composition. We find that Random Index is robust for small corpora, but larger corpora require that the contexts be weighted to maintain accuracy.

Proceedings of the 2006 Conference on Empirical Methods in Natural Language Processing (EMNLP 2006), pages 457–464,
Sydney, July 2006.

2 Random Indexing

Random Indexing is an approximating technique proposed by Kanerva et al. (2000) as an alternative to Singular Value Decomposition (SVD) for Latent Semantic Analysis (LSA, Landauer and Dumais, 1997). In LSA, it is assumed that there is some underlying dimensionality in the data, so that the attributes of two or more terms that have similar meanings can be *folded* onto a single axis.

Sahlgren (2005) criticise LSA for being both computationally inefficient and requiring the formation of a full co-occurrence matrix and its decomposition before any similarity measurements can be made. Random Indexing avoids both these by creating a short *index vector* for each unique context, and producing the *context vector* for each term by summing index vectors for each context as it is read, allowing an incremental building of the context space.

Hecht-Nielsen (1994) observed that there are many more nearly orthogonal directions in high-dimensional space than there are truly orthogonal directions. The random index vectors are *nearly-orthogonal*, resulting in an approximate description of the context space. The approximation comes from the Johnson-Lindenstrauss lemma (Johnson and Lindenstrauss, 1984), which states that if we project points in a vector space into a randomly selected subspace of sufficiently high dimensionality, the distances between the points are approximately preserved. Random Projection (Papadimitriou et al., 1998) and Random Mapping (Kaski, 1998) are similar techniques that use this lemma. Achlioptas (2001) showed that most zero-mean distributions with unit variance, including very simple ones like that used in Random Indexing, produce a mapping that satisfies the lemma. The following description of Random Indexing is taken from Sahlgren (2005) and Sahlgren and Karlgren (2005).

We allocate a d length index vector to each unique context as is it found. These vectors consist of a large number of 0s and a small number (ϵ) of ± 1s. Each element is allocated one of these values with the following probability:

$$\begin{cases} +1 & \text{with probability } \frac{\epsilon/2}{d} \\ 0 & \text{with probability } \frac{d-\epsilon}{d} \\ -1 & \text{with probability } \frac{\epsilon/2}{d} \end{cases}$$

Context vectors are generated *on-the-fly*. As the corpus is scanned, for each term encountered, its contexts are extracted. For each new context, an index vector is produced for it as above. The context vector is the sum of the index vectors of all the contexts in which the term appears.

The context vector for a term t appearing in one each in the contexts $c_1 = [1, 0, 0, -1]$ and $c_2 = [0, 1, 0, -1]$ would be $[1, 1, 0, -2]$. If the context c_1 encountered again, no new index vector would be generated and the existing index vector for c_1 would be added to the existing context vector to produce a new context vector for t of $[2, 1, 0, -3]$.

The distance between these context vectors can then be measured using any vector space distance measure. Sahlgren and Karlgren (2005) use the cosine measure:

$$\cos(\theta(u, v)) = \frac{\vec{u} \cdot \vec{v}}{|\vec{u}|\ |\vec{v}|} = \frac{\sum_{i=1}^{d} \vec{u}_i \vec{v}_i}{\sqrt{\sum_{i=1}^{d} \vec{u}_i^2}\sqrt{\sum_{i=1}^{d} \vec{v}_i^2}}$$

Random Indexing allows for incremental sampling. This means that the entire data set need not be sampled before similarity between terms can be measured. It also means that additional context information can be added at any time without invalidating the information already produced. This is not feasible with most other word-space models. The approach used by Grefenstette (1994) and Curran (2004) requires the re-computation of all non-linear weights if new data is added, although some of these weights can be approximated when adding new data incrementally. Similarly, new data can be *folded* into a reduced LSA space, but there is no guarantee that the original smoothing will apply correctly to the new data (Sahlgren, 2005).

3 Weights

Our initial experiments using Random Indexing to extract synonymy relations produced worse results than those using full vector measures, such as JACCARD (Curran, 2004), when the full vector is weighted. We experiment using weight functions with Random Indexing.

Only a linear weighting scheme can be applied while maintaining incremental sampling. While incremental sampling is part of the rationale behind its development, it is not required for Random Indexing to work as a dimensionality reduction technique.

To this end, we revise Random Indexing to enable us to use weight functions. For each unique

IDENTITY	1.0	FREQ	$f(w, r, w')$
RELFREQ	$\frac{f(w,r,w')}{f(w,*,*)}$	TF-IDF	$\frac{f(w,r,w')}{n(*,r,w')}$
TF-IDF†	$\frac{\log_2(f(w,r,w')+1)}{\log_2(1+\frac{N_{(r,w')}}{n(*,r,w')})}$	MI	$\log(\frac{p(w,r,w')}{p(w,*,*)p(*,r,w')})$
TTEST	$\frac{p(w,r,w')-p(*,r,w')p(w,*,*)}{\sqrt{p(*,r,w')p(w,*,*)}}$	GREF94	$\frac{\log_2(f(w,r,w')+1)}{\log_2(n(*,r,w')+1)}$
LIN98A	$\log(\frac{f(w,r,w')f(*,r*)}{f(*,r,w')f(w,r,*)})$	LIN98B	$-\log(\frac{n(*,r,w')}{N_w})$
CHI2	*cf.* *Manning and Schütze (1999)*	LR	*cf.* *Manning and Schütze (1999)*
DICE	$\frac{2p(w,r,w')}{p(w,*,*)+p(*,r,w')}$		

Table 1: Weight Functions Evaluated

context attribute, a d length index vector will be generated. The context vector of a term w is then created by the weighted sum of each of its attributes. The results of the original Random Indexing algorithm are reproduced using frequency weighting (FREQ).

Weights are generated using the frequency distribution of each term and its contexts. This increases the overhead, as we must store the context attributes for each term. Rather than the context vector being generated by adding each individual context, it is generated by adding each the index vector for each unique context multiplied by its weight.

The time to calculate the weight of all attributes of all terms is negligible. The original technique scales to $O(dnm)$ in construction, for n terms and m unique attributes. Our new technique scales to $O(d(a + nm))$ for a non-zero context attributes per term, which since $a \ll m$ is also $O(dnm)$.

Following the notation of Curran (2004), a *context relation* is defined as a tuple (w, r, w') where w is a term, which occurs in some grammatical relation r with another word w' in some sentence. We refer to the tuple (r, w') as an *attribute* of w. For example, (dog, direct-obj, walk) indicates that dog was the direct object of walk in a sentence.

An asterisk indicates the set of all existing values of that component in the tuple.

$$(w, *, *) \equiv \{(r, w')|\exists(w, r, w')\}$$

The frequency of a tuple, that is the number of times a word appears in a context is $f(w, r, w')$. $f(w, *, *)$ is the *instance* or *token* frequency of the contexts in which w appears. $n(w, *, *)$ is the *type* frequency. This is the number of attributes of w.

$$\begin{aligned} f(w, *, *) &\equiv \textstyle\sum_{(r,w') \in (w,*,*)} f(w, r, w') \\ p(w, *, *) &\equiv \frac{f(w,*,*)}{f(*,*,*)} \\ n(w, *, *) &\equiv |(w, *, *)| \\ N_w &\equiv |\{w|n(w, *, *) > 0\}| \end{aligned}$$

Most experiments limited weights to the positive range; those evaluated with an unrestricted range are marked with a $^{\pm}$ suffix. Some weights were also evaluated with an extra $\log_2(f(w, r, w') + 1)$ factor to promote the influence of higher frequency attributes, indicated by a LOG suffix. Alternative functions are marked with a dagger.

The context vector of each term w is thus:

$$\bar{w} = \sum_{(r,w') \in (w,*,*)} (r, \vec{w'}) \, \mathrm{wgt}(w, r, w')$$

where $(r, \vec{w'})$ is the index vector of the context (r, w'). The weights functions we evaluate are those from Curran (2004) and are given in Table 1.

4 Semantic Similarity

The first use of Random Indexing was to measure semantic similarity using distributional similarity. Kanerva et al. (2000) used Random Indexing to find the best synonym match in Test of English as a Foreign Language (TOEFL). TOEFL was used by Landauer and Dumais (1997), who reported an accuracy 36% using un-normalised vectors, which was improved to 64% using LSA. Kanerva et al. (2000) produced an accuracy of 48–51% using the same type of document based contexts and Random Indexing, which improved to 62–70% using narrow context windows. Karlgren and Sahlgren (2001) improved this to 72% using lemmatisation and POS tagging.

4.1 Distributional Similarity

Measuring distributional similarity first requires the extraction of context information for each of the vocabulary terms from raw text. The contexts for each term are collected together and counted, producing a vector of context attributes and their frequencies in the corpus. These terms are then compared for similarity using a nearest-neighbour search based on distance calculations between the statistical descriptions of their contexts.

The simplest algorithm for finding synonyms is a k-nearest-neighbour search, which involves pair-wise vector comparison of the context vector of the target term with the context vector of every other term in the vocabulary.

We use two types of context extraction to produce both high and low quality context descriptions. The high quality contexts were extracted from grammatical relations extracted using the SEXTANT relation extractor (Grefenstette, 1994) and are lemmatised. This is the same data used in Curran (2004).

The low quality contexts were extracted taking a window of one word to the left and right of the target term. The context is marked as to whether it preceded or followed the term. Curran (2004) found this extraction technique to provided reasonable results on the non-speech portion of the BNC when the data was lemmatised. We do not lemmatise, which produces noisier data.

4.2 Bilingual Lexicon Acquisition

A variation on the extraction of synonymy relations, is the extraction of bilingual lexicons. This is the task of finding for a word in one language words of a similar meaning in a second language. The results of this can be used to aid manual construction of resources or directly aid translation.

This task was first approached as a distributional similarity-like problem by Brown et al. (1988). Their approach uses aligned corpora in two or more languages: the *source language*, from which we are translating, and the *target language*, to which we are translating. For a each aligned segment, they measure *co-occurrence scores* between each word in the source segment and each word in the target segment. These co-occurrence scores are used to measure the similarity between source and target language terms

Sahlgren and Karlgren's approach models the problem as a distributional similarity problem using the paragraph as context. In Table 2, the source language is limited to the words a, b and c and the target language to the words x, y and z. Three paragraphs in each of these languages are presented as pairs of translations labelled as a context: aaabbc is translated as xxyzzz and labelled context I. The frequency weighted context vector for a is {I:3, III:2} and for x is {I:2, II:1, III:1}.

Source Language	Context	Target Language
aaabbc	I	xxyzzz
bcc	II	wxy
aab	III	xzz

Table 2: Paragraph Aligned Corpora

A translation candidate for a term in the source language is found by measuring the similarity between its context vector and the context vectors of each of the terms in the target language. The most similar target language term is the most likely translation candidate.

Sahlgren and Karlgren (2005) use Random Indexing to produce the context vectors for the source and target languages. We re-implement their system and apply weighting functions in an attempt to achieve improved results.

5 Experiments

For the experiments extracting synonymy relations, high quality contexts were extracted from the non-speech portion of the British National Corpus (BNC) as described above. This represents 90% of the BNC, or 90 million words.

Comparisons between low frequency terms are less accurate than between high frequency terms as there is less evidence describing them (Curran and Moens, 2002). This is compounded in randomised vector techniques because the randomised nature of the representation means that a low frequency term may have a similar context vector to a high frequency term while not sharing many contexts. A frequency cut-off of 100 was found to balance this inaccuracy with the reduction in vocabulary size. This reduces the original 246,046 word vocabulary to 14,862 words. Experiments showed $d = 1000$ and $\epsilon = 10$ to provide a balance between speed and accuracy.

Low quality contexts were extracted from portions of the entire of the BNC. These formed corpora of 100,000, 500,000, 1 million, 5 million, 10 million, 50 million and 100 million words, chosen from random documents. This allowed us test the effect of both corpus size and context quality. This produced vocabularies of between 10,380 and 522,163 words in size. Because of the size of the smallest corpora meant that a high cutoff would remove to many terms for a fair test, a cutoff of 5 was applied. The values $d = 1000$ and $\epsilon = 6$ were used.

For our experiments in bilingual lexicon acquisition we follow Sahlgren and Karlgren (2005). We use the Spanish-Swedish and the English-German portions of the Europarl corpora (Koehn, 2005).[1] These consist of 37,379 aligned paragraphs in Spanish–Swedish and 45,556 in English-German. The text was lemmatised using Connexor Machinese (Tapanainen and Jävinen, 1997)[2] producing vocabularies of 42,671 terms of Spanish, 100,891 terms of Swedish, 40,181 terms of English and 70,384 terms of German. We use $d = 600$ and $\epsilon = 6$ and apply a frequency cutoff of 100.

6 Evaluation Measures

The simplest method for evaluation is the direct comparison of extracted synonyms with a manually created gold standard (Grefenstette, 1994). To reduce the problem of limited coverage, our evaluation of the extraction of synonyms combines three electronic thesauri: the Macquarie, Roget's and Moby thesauri.

We follow Curran (2004) and use two performance measures: direct matches (DIRECT) and inverse rank (INVR). DIRECT is the number of returned synonyms found in the gold standard. INVR is the sum of the inverse rank of each matching synonym, e.g. matches at ranks 3, 5 and 28 give an inverse rank score of $\frac{1}{3} + \frac{1}{5} + \frac{1}{28}$. With at most 100 matching synonyms, the maximum INVR is 5.187. This more fine grained as it incorporates the both the number of matches and their ranking.

The same 300 single word nouns were used for evaluation as used by Curran (2004) for his large scale evaluation. These were chosen randomly from WordNet such that they covered a range over the following properties: *frequency*, *number of senses*, *specificity* and *concreteness*. On average each evaluation term had 301 gold-standard synonyms. For each of these terms, the closest 100 terms and their similarity scores were extracted.

Weight	DIRECT	INVR
FREQ	**2.87**	**0.94**
IDENTITY	3.18	0.95
RELFREQ	2.87	0.94
TF-IDF	0.30	0.07
TF-IDF†	**3.92**	**1.39**
MI	1.52	0.54
MILOG	3.38	1.39
MI$^{\pm}$	1.87	0.65
MILOG$^{\pm}$	**3.49**	**1.41**
TTEST	1.06	0.52
TTESTLOG	1.53	0.62
TTEST$^{\pm}$	1.06	0.52
TTESTLOG$^{\pm}$	1.52	0.61
GREF94	2.82	0.86
LIN98A	1.52	0.50
LIN98B	2.95	0.84
CHI2	0.46	0.25
DICE	3.32	1.11
DICELOG	2.56	0.81
LR	1.96	0.58

Table 3: Evaluation of synonym extraction

For the evaluation of bilingual lexicon acquisition we use two online lexical resources used by Sahlgren and Karlgren (2005) as gold standards: Lexin's online Swedish-Spanish lexicon[3] and TU Chemnitz' online English-German dictionary.[4] Each of the elements in a compound or multi-word expression is treated as a potential translation. The German abblendlicht (low beam light) is treated as a translation candidate for low, beam and light separately.

Low coverage is more of problem than in our thesaurus task as we have not used combined resources. There are an average of 19 translations for each of the 3,403 Spanish terms and 197 translations for each of the 4,468 English terms. The English-German translation count is skewed by the presence of connectives in multi-word expressions, such as of and on, producing mistranslations. Sahlgren and Karlgren (2005) provide good commentary on the evaluation of this task.

Spanish and English are used as the source languages. The 200 closest terms in the target language are found for all terms in both the source vocabulary and the gold-standards.

We measure the DIRECT score and INVR as above. In addition we measure the precision of the closest translation candidate, as used in Sahlgren and Karlgren (2005).

[1] http://www.statmt.org/europarl/

[2] http://www.connexor.com/

[3] http://lexin.nada.kth.se/sve-spa.shtml

[4] http://dict.tu-chemnitz.de/

Weight	English-German			Spanish-Swedish		
	DIRECT	Precision	INVR	DIRECT	Precision	INVR
FREQ	6.1	58%	0.97	0.8	47%	0.53
IDENTITY	6.0	58%	0.91	0.8	47%	0.53
RELFREQ	6.1	58%	0.97	0.8	47%	0.53
TF-IDF	4.9	53%	0.84	0.8	43%	0.50
TF-IDF†	6.3	58%	0.94	0.8	47%	0.53
MI	2.3	58%	0.76	0.8	48%	0.56
MILOG	2.1	58%	0.76	0.8	49%	0.56
MI$^{\pm}$	4.6	57%	0.86	0.8	46%	0.53
MILOG$^{\pm}$	4.6	57%	0.87	0.8	47%	0.54
TTEST	2.1	57%	0.75	0.8	48%	0.56
TTESTLOG	1.9	56%	0.72	0.8	46%	0.54
TTEST$^{\pm}$	4.3	57%	0.85	0.8	45%	0.53
TTESTLOG$^{\pm}$	4.0	56%	0.80	0.8	46%	0.53
GREF94	6.1	58%	0.95	0.8	48%	0.54
LIN98A	4.0	59%	0.82	0.8	48%	0.56
LIN98B	5.9	58%	0.91	0.8	48%	0.54
CHI2	3.1	50%	0.71	0.7	41%	0.48
DICE	5.7	58%	0.95	0.8	47%	0.53
DICELOG	4.7	57%	0.90	0.8	46%	0.52
LR	4.5	57%	0.86	0.8	47%	0.54

Table 4: Evaluation of bilingual lexicon extraction

7 Results

Table 3 shows the results for the experiments extracting synonymy. The basic Random Indexing algorithm (FREQ) produces a DIRECT score of 2.87, and an INVR of 0.94. It is interesting that the only other linear weight, IDENTITY, produces more accurate results. This shows high frequency, low information contexts reduce the accuracy of Random Indexing. IDENTITY removes this effect by ignoring frequency, but does not address the information aspect. A more accurate weight will consider the information provided by a context in its weighting.

There was a large variance in the effectiveness of the other weights and most proved to be detrimental to Random Indexing. TF-IDF was the worst, reducing the DIRECT score to 0.30 and the INVR to 0.07. TF-IDF†, which is a log-weighted alternative to TF-IDF, produced very good results.

With the exception of DICELOG, adding an additional log factor improved performance (TF-IDF†, MILOG and TTESTLOG). Unrestricted ranges improved the MI family, but made no difference to TTEST. Grefenstette's variation on TF-IDF (GREF94) does not perform as well as TF-IDF†, and Lin's variations on MI$^{\pm}$ (LIN98A, LIN98B) do not perform as well as MILOG$^{\pm}$.

MILOG$^{\pm}$ had a higher INVR than TF-IDF†, but a lower DIRECT score, indicating that it forces more correct results to the top of the results list, but also forces some correct results further down so that they no longer appear in the top 100.

Weight	BNC		LARGE	
	DIRECT	INVR	DIRECT	INVR
FREQ	8.9	0.93	7.2	0.85
TF-IDF†	11.8	1.39	12.5	1.50
MILOG$^{\pm}$	10.5	1.41	13.8	1.75

Table 5: Evaluation of Random Indexing using a very large corpus

The effect of high frequency contexts is increased further as we increase the size of the corpus. Table 5 presents results using the 2 billion word corpus used by Curran (2004). This consists of the non-speech portion of the BNC, the Reuter's Corpus Volume 1 and most of the English news holdings of the LDC in 2003. Contexts were extracted as presented in Section 4. A frequency cut-off of 100 was applied and the values $d = 1000$ and $\epsilon = 5$ for FREQ and $\epsilon = 10$ for the improved weights were used.

We see that the very large corpus has reduced the accuracy of frequency weighted Random Indexing. In contrast, our two top performers have both substantially increased in accuracy, presenting a 75–100% improvment in performance over FREQ. MILOG$^{\pm}$ is more accurate than TF-IDF† for both measures of accuracy now, indicating it is a better weight function for very large data sets.

7.1 Bilingual Lexicon Acquisition

When the same function were applied to the bilingual lexicon acquisition task we see substantially different results: neither the improvement nor the extremely poor results are found (Table 4).

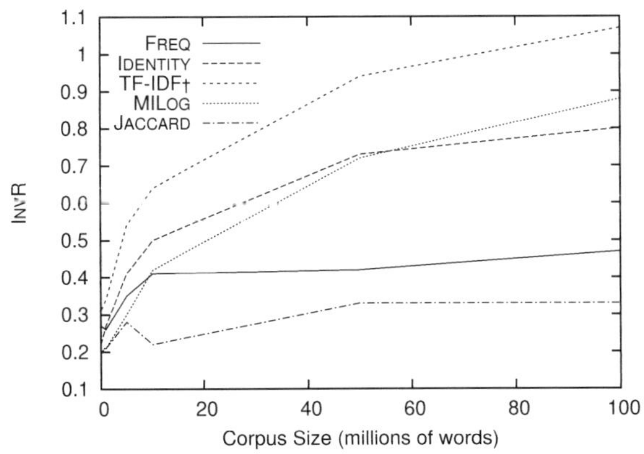

Figure 1: Random Indexing using window-based context

In the English-German corpora we replicate Sahlgren and Karlgren's (2005) results, with a precision of 58%. This has a DIRECT score of 6.1 and an INVR of 0.97. The only weight to make an improvement is TF-IDF†, which has a DIRECT score of 6.3, but a lower INVR and all weights perform worse in at least one measure.

Our results for the Spanish-Swedish corpora show similar results. Our accuracy is down from that in Sahlgren and Karlgren (2005). This is explained by our application of the frequency cut-off to both the source and target languages. There are more weights with higher accuracies, and fewer with significantly lower accuracies.

7.2 Smaller Corpora

The absence of a substantial improvement in bilingual lexicon acquisition requires further investigation. Three main factors differ between our monolingual and bilingual experiments: that we are smoothing a homogeneous data set in our monolingual experiments and a heterogeneous data set in our bilingual experiments; we are using local grammatical contexts in our monolingual experiments and paragraph contexts in our bilingual experiments; and, the volume of raw data used in our monolingual experiments is many times that used in our bilingual experiments.

Figure 1 presents results for corpora extracted from the BNC using the window-based context. Results are shown for the original Random Indexing (FREQ) and using IDENTITY, MILOG$^{\pm}$ and TF-IDF†, as well as for the full vector measurement using JACCARD measure and the TTEST$^{\pm}$ weight (Curran, 2004). Of the Random Indexing results FREQ produces the lowest overall results. It performs better than MILOG$^{\pm}$ for very small corpora, but produces near constant results for greater corpus sizes. Curran and Moens (2002) found that increasing the volume of input data increased the accuracy of results generated using a full vector space model. Without weighting, Random Indexing fails this, but after weighting is applied Curran and Moens' results are confirmed.

The quality of context extracted influences how weights perform individually, but Random Indexing using weights still outperforms not using weights. The relative performance of MILOG$^{\pm}$ has been reduced when compared with TF-IDF†, but is still greater then FREQ.

Gorman and Curran (2006) showed Random Indexing to be much faster than full vector space techniques, but with a 46–56% reduction in accuracy compared to using JACCARD and TTEST$^{\pm}$. Using the MI$^{\pm}$ weight kept the improvement in speed but with only a 10–18% reduction in accuracy. When JACCARD and TTEST$^{\pm}$ are used with our low quality contexts they perform consistently worse that Random Indexing. This indicates Random Indexing is stable in the presence of noisy data. It would be interesting to further compare these results to those produced by LSA.

The results we have presented have shown that applying weights to Random Indexing can improve its performance for thesaurus extraction tasks. This improvement is dependent on the volume of raw data used to generate the context information. It is less dependent on the quality of contexts extracted.

What we have not shown is whether this extends to the extraction of bilingual lexicons. The bilingual corpora have 12-16 million words per language, and for this sized corpora we already see substantial improvement with corpora as small as 5 million words (Figure 1). It may be that extracting paragraph-level contexts is not well suited to weighting, or that the heterogeneous nature of the aligned corpora reduces the meaningfulness of weighting. There is also the question as to whether it can be applied to all languages. There is a lack of freely available large-scale multi-lingual resources that makes this difficult to examine.

8 Conclusion

We have applied weighting functions to the vector space approximation Random Indexing. For large data sets we found a significant improvement when weights were applied. For smaller data sets we found that Random Indexing was sufficiently robust that weighting had at most a minor effect.

Our weighting schemes removed the possibility of incremental learning of the term space. An interesting direction would be the development of algorithms that allowed the incremental application of weights, perhaps by re-weighting vectors when a new context is learned.

Other areas left open for investigation are the interaction between Random Indexing, weights and the type of context extracted, the use of large-scale bilingual corpora, the acquisition of lexicons for non-Indo-European languages and across language family boundaries, and the difference in effect term and paragraph/document contexts for thesaurus extraction.

We have demonstrated that the accuracy of Random Indexing can be improved by applying weight functions, increasing accuracy by up to 50% on the BNC and 100% on a 2 billion word corpus.

Acknowledgements

We would like to thank Magnus Sahlgren for generously supplying his training and evaluation data and our reviewers for their helpful feedback and corrections. This work has been supported by the Australian Research Council under Discovery Project DP0453131.

References

Dimitris Achlioptas. 2001. Database-friendly random projections. In *Symposium on Principles of Database Systems*, pages 274–281, Santa Barbara, CA, USA, 21–23 May.

Peter F. Brown, John Cocke, Stephen A. Della Pietra, Vincent J. Della Pietra, Frederick Jelinek, Robert L. Mercer, and Paul S. Roossin. 1988. A statistical approach to language translation. In *Proceedings of the 12th Conference on Computational linguistics*, pages 71–76, Budapest, Hungry, 22–27 August.

James R. Curran and Marc Moens. 2002. Scaling context space. In *Proceedings of the 40th Annual Meeting of the Association for Computational Linguistics*, pages 231–238, Philadelphia, PA, USA, 7–12 July.

James R. Curran. 2004. *From Distributional to Semantic Similarity*. Ph.D. thesis, University of Edinburgh.

Christiane Fellbaum, editor. 1998. *WordNet: an electronic lexical database*. The MIT Press, Cambridge, MA, USA.

James Gorman and James R. Curran. 2006. Scaling distributional similarity to large corpora. In *Proceedings of the 44th Annual Meeting of the Association for Computational Linguistics*, Sydney, Australia, 17–21 July. To appear.

Gregory Grefenstette. 1994. *Explorations in Automatic Thesaurus Discovery*. Kluwer Academic Publishers, Boston.

Robert Hecht-Nielsen. 1994. Context vectors: general purpose approximate meaning representations self-organized from raw data. *Computational Intelligence: Imitating Life*, pages 43–56.

William B. Johnson and Joram Lindenstrauss. 1984. Extensions to Lipshitz mapping into Hilbert space. *Contemporary mathematics*, 26:189–206.

Pentti Kanerva, Jan Kristoferson, and Anders Holst. 2000. Random indexing of text samples for latent semantic analysis. In *Proceedings of the 22nd Annual Conference of the Cognitive Science Society*, page 1036, Philadelphia, PA, USA, 13–15 August.

Jussi Karlgren and Magnus Sahlgren. 2001. From words to understanding. In Y. Uesaka, P. Kanerva, and H Asoh, editors, *Foundations of Real-World Intelligence*, pages 294–308. CSLI Publications, Stanford, CA, USA.

Samuel Kaski. 1998. Dimensionality reduction by random mapping: Fast similarity computation for clustering. In *Proceedings of the International Joint Conference on Neural Networks*, pages 413–418. Piscataway, NJ, USA, 31 July–4 August.

Philipp Koehn. 2005. Europarl: A parallel corpus for statistical machine translation. In *MT Summit X*, Phuket, Thailand, 12–16 September.

Thomas K. Landauer and Susan T. Dumais. 1997. A solution to plato's problem: The latent semantic analysis theory of acquisition, induction, and representation of knowledge. *Psychological Review*, 104(2):211–240, April.

Christopher D. Manning and Hinrich Schütze. 1999. *Foundations of Statistical Natural Language Processing*. The MIT Press, Cambridge, MA, USA.

Christos H. Papadimitriou, Hisao Tamaki, Prabhakar Raghavan, and Santosh Vempala. 1998. Latent semantic indexing: A probabilistic analysis. In *Proceedings of the 17th ACM Symposium on the Principle of Database Systems*, pages 159–168, Seattle, WA, USA, 2–4 June.

Magnus Sahlgren and Jussi Karlgren. 2005. Automatic bilingual lexicon acquisition using random indexing of parallel corpora. *Journal of Natural Language Engineering, Special Issue on Parallel Texts*, 11(3), June.

Magnus Sahlgren. 2005. An introduction to random indexing. In *Methods and Applications of Semantic Indexing Workshop at the 7th International Conference on Terminology and Knowledge Engineering*, Copenhagen, Denmark, 16 August.

Pasi Tapanainen and Timo Jävinen. 1997. A non-projective dependency parser. In *Proceedings of the 5th Conference on Applied Natural Language Processing*, pages 64–71, 31 March–3 April.

A Hybrid Markov/Semi-Markov Conditional Random Field for Sequence Segmentation

Galen Andrew
Microsoft Research
One Microsoft Way
Redmond, WA 98052
galena@microsoft.com

Abstract

Markov order-1 conditional random fields (CRFs) and semi-Markov CRFs are two popular models for sequence segmentation and labeling. Both models have advantages in terms of the type of features they most naturally represent. We propose a hybrid model that is capable of representing both types of features, and describe efficient algorithms for its training and inference. We demonstrate that our hybrid model achieves error reductions of 18% and 25% over a standard order-1 CRF and a semi-Markov CRF (resp.) on the task of Chinese word segmentation. We also propose the use of a powerful feature for the semi-Markov CRF: the log conditional odds that a given token sequence constitutes a chunk according to a generative model, which reduces error by an additional 13%. Our best system achieves 96.8% F-measure, the highest reported score on this test set.

1 Introduction

The problem of segmenting sequence data into chunks arises in many natural language applications, such as named-entity recognition, shallow parsing, and word segmentation in East Asian languages. Two popular discriminative models that have been proposed for these tasks are the conditional random field (CRFs) (Lafferty et al., 2001) and the semi-Markov conditional random field (semi-CRF) (Sarawagi and Cohen, 2004).

A CRF in its basic form is a model for labeling tokens in a sequence; however it can easily be adapted to perform segmentation via labeling each token as BEGIN or CONTINUATION, or according to some similar scheme. CRFs using this technique have been shown to be very successful at the task of Chinese word segmentation (CWS), starting with the model of Peng et al. (2004). In the Second International Chinese Word Segmentation Bakeoff (Emerson, 2005), two of the highest scoring systems in the closed track competition were based on a CRF model. (Tseng et al., 2005; Asahara et al., 2005)

While the CRF is quite effective compared with other models designed for CWS, one wonders whether it may be limited by its restrictive independence assumptions on non-adjacent labels: an order-M CRF satisfies the order-M Markov assumption that, globally conditioned on the input sequence, each label is independent of all other labels given the M labels to its left and right. Consequently, the model only "sees" word boundaries within a moving window of $M + 1$ characters, which prohibits it from explicitly modeling the tendency of strings longer than that window to form words, or from modeling the lengths of the words. Although the window can in principle be widened by increasing M, this is not a practical solution as the complexity of training and decoding a linear sequence CRF grows exponentially with the Markov order.

The semi-CRF is a sequence model that is designed to address this difficulty via careful relaxation of the Markov assumption. Rather than recasting the segmentation problem as a labeling problem, the semi-CRF directly models the distribution of chunk boundaries.[1] In terms of inde-

[1] As it was originally described, the semi-CRF also assigns labels to each chunk, effectively performing joint segmentation and labeling, but in a pure segmentation problem such as CWS, the use of labels is unnecessary.

Proceedings of the 2006 Conference on Empirical Methods in Natural Language Processing (EMNLP 2006), pages 465–472,
Sydney, July 2006.

pendence, using an order-M semi-CRF entails the assumption that, globally conditioned on the input sequence, the position of each chunk boundary is independent of all other boundaries given the positions of the M boundaries to its left and right *regardless of how far away they are*. Even with an order-1 model, this enables several classes of features that one would expect to be of great utility to the word segmentation task, in particular *word length* and *word identity*.

Despite this, the only work of which we are aware exploring the use of a semi-Markov CRF for Chinese word segmentation did not find significant gains over the standard CRF (Liang, 2005). This is surprising, not only because the additional features a semi-CRF enables are intuitively very useful, but because as we will show, an order-M semi-CRF is strictly more powerful than an order-M CRF, in the sense that any feature that can be used in the latter can also be used in the former, or equivalently, the semi-CRF makes strictly weaker independence assumptions. Given a judicious choice of features (or simply enough training data) the semi-CRF should be superior.

We propose that the reason for this discrepancy may be that despite the greater representational power of the semi-CRF, there are some valuable features that are more naturally expressed in a CRF segmentation model, and so they are not typically included in semi-CRFs (indeed, they have not to date been used in any semi-CRF model for any task, to our knowledge). In this paper, we show that semi-CRFs are strictly more expressive, and also demonstrate how CRF-type features can be used in a semi-CRF model for Chinese word segmentation. Our experiments show that a model incorporating both types of features can outperform models using only one or the other type.

Orthogonally, we explore in this paper the use of a very powerful feature for the semi-CRF derived from a generative model.

It is common in statistical NLP to use as features in a discriminative model the (logarithm of the) estimated probability of some event according to a generative model. For example, Collins (2000) uses a discriminative classifier for choosing among the top N parse trees output by a generative baseline model, and uses the log-probability of a parse according to the baseline model as a feature in the reranker. Similarly, the machine translation system of Och and Ney uses log-probabilities of phrasal translations and other events as features in a log-linear model (Och and Ney, 2002; Och and Ney, 2004). There are many reasons for incorporating these types of features, including the desire to combine the higher accuracy of a discriminative model with the simple parameter estimation and inference of a generative one, and also the fact that generative models are more robust in data sparse scenarios (Ng and Jordan, 2001).

For word segmentation, one might want to use as a local feature the log-probability that a segment is a word, given the character sequence it spans. A curious property of this feature is that it induces a counterintuitive asymmetry between the *is-word* and *is-not-word* cases: the component generative model can effectively dictate that a certain chunk is *not* a word, by assigning it a very low probability (driving the feature value to negative infinity), but it cannot dictate that a chunk *is* a word, because the log-probability is bounded above.[2] If instead the *log conditional odds* $\log \frac{P_i(\mathbf{y}|\mathbf{x})}{P_i(\neg\mathbf{y}|\mathbf{x})}$ is used, the asymmetry disappears. We show that such a log-odds feature provides much greater benefit than the log-probability, and that it is useful to include such a feature even when the model also includes indicator function features for every word in the training corpus.

2 Hybrid Markov/Semi-Markov CRF

The model we describe is formally a type of semi-Markov CRF, distinguished only in that it also involves CRF-style features. So we first describe the semi-Markov model in its general form.

2.1 Semi-Markov CRF

An (unlabeled) semi-Markov conditional random field is a log-linear model defining the conditional probability of a segmentation given an observation sequence. The general form of a log-linear model is as follows: given an input $\mathbf{x} \in X$, an output $\mathbf{y} \in Y$, a feature mapping $\Phi : X \times Y \mapsto \mathbb{R}^n$, and a weight vector $\mathbf{w}$, the conditional probability of $\mathbf{y}$ given $\mathbf{x}$ is estimated as:

$$P(\mathbf{y} \mid \mathbf{x}) = \frac{\exp(\mathbf{w} \cdot \Phi(\mathbf{x}, \mathbf{y}))}{Z(\mathbf{x})}$$

where $Z : \mathbf{x} \mapsto R$ is a normalizing factor. $\mathbf{w}$ is typically chosen to maximize the conditional likelihood of a labeled training set. In the word

[2] We assume the weight assigned to the log-probability feature is positive.

segmentation task, $\mathbf{x}$ is an ordered sequence of characters $(x_1, x_2, \ldots, x_n)$, and $\mathbf{y}$ is a set of indices corresponding to the start of each word: $\{y_1, y_2, \ldots, y_m\}$ such that $y_1 = 1$, $y_m \leq n$, and for all j, $y_j < y_{j+1}$. A log-linear model in this space is an order-1 semi CRF if its feature map Φ decomposes according to

$$\Phi(\mathbf{x}, \mathbf{y}) = \sum_{j=1}^{m} \phi^S(y_j, y_{j+1}, \mathbf{x}) \quad (1)$$

where ϕ^S is a local feature map that only considers one chunk at a time (defining $y_{m+1} = n+1$). This decomposition is responsible for the characteristic independence assumptions of the semi-CRF.

Hand-in-hand with the feature decomposition and independence assumptions comes the capacity for exact decoding using the Viterbi algorithm, and exact computation of the objective gradient using the forward-backward algorithm, both in time quadratic in the lengths of the sentences. Furthermore, if the model is constrained to propose only chunkings with maximum word length k, then the time for inference and training becomes linear in the sentence length (and in k). For Chinese word segmentation, choosing a moderate value of k does not pose any significant risk, since the vast majority of Chinese words are only a few characters long: in our training set, 91% of word tokens were one or two characters, and 99% were five characters or less.

Using a semi-CRF as opposed to a traditional Markov CRF allows us to model some aspects of word segmentation that one would expect to be very informative. In particular, it makes possible the use of local indicator function features of the type "the chunk consists of character sequence $\chi_1, \ldots, \chi_\ell$," or "the chunk is of length ℓ." It also enables "pseudo-bigram language model" features, firing when a given word occurs in the context of a given character unigram or bigram.[3] And crucially, although it is slightly less natural to do so, any feature used in an order-1 Markov CRF can also be represented in a semi-CRF. As Markov CRFs are used in the most competitive Chinese word segmentation models to date, one might expect that incorporating both types of features could yield a superior model.

[3]We did not experiment with this type of feature.

2.2 CRF vs. Semi-CRF

In order to compare the two types of linear CRFs, it is convenient to define a representation of the segmentation problem in terms of character labels as opposed to sets of whole words. Denote by $L(\mathbf{y}) \in \{B, C\}^n$ (for BEGIN vs. CONTINUATION) the sequence $\{L_1, L_2, \ldots L_n\}$ of labels such that $L_i = B$ if and only if $y_i \in \mathbf{y}$. It is clear that if we constrain $L_1 = B$, the two representations $\mathbf{y}$ and $L(\mathbf{y})$ are equivalent. An order-1 Markov CRF is a log-linear model in which the global feature vector Φ decomposes into a sum over local feature vectors that consider bigrams of the label sequence:

$$\Phi(\mathbf{x}, \mathbf{y}) = \sum_{i=1}^{n} \phi^M(L_i, L_{i+1}, i, \mathbf{x}) \quad (2)$$

(where L_{n+1} is defined as B). The local features that are most naturally expressed in this context are indicators of some joint event of the label bigram (L_i, L_{i+1}) and nearby characters in $\mathbf{x}$. For example, one might use the feature "the current character x_i is χ and $L_i = C$", or "the current and next characters are identical and $L_i = L_{i+1} = B$."

Although we have heretofore disparaged the CRF as being incapable of representing such powerful features as word identity, the type of features that it most naturally represents should be helpful in CWS for generalizing to unseen words. For example, the first feature mentioned above could be valuable to rule out certain word boundaries if χ were a character that typically occurs only as a suffix but that combines freely with a variety of root forms to create new words. This type of feature (specifically, a feature indicating the *absence* as opposed to the *presence* of a chunk boundary) is a bit less natural in a semi-CRF, since in that case local features $\phi^S(y_j, y_{j+1}, \mathbf{x})$ are defined on pairs of adjacent boundaries. Information about which tokens are *not* on boundaries is only implicit, making it a bit more difficult to incorporate that information into the features. Indeed, neither Liang (2005) nor Sarawagi and Cohen (2004) nor any other system using a semi-Markov CRF on any task has included this type of feature to our knowledge. We hypothesize (and our experiments confirm) that the lack of this feature explains the failure of the semi-CRF to outperform the CRF for word segmentation in the past.

Before showing how CRF-type features can be used in a semi-CRF, we first demonstrate that the semi-CRF is indeed strictly more expressive than the CRF, meaning that any global feature map Φ that decomposes according to (2) also decomposes according to (1). It is sufficient to show that for any feature map Φ^M of a Markov CRF, there exists a semi-Markov-type feature map Φ^S such that for any $\mathbf{x}, \mathbf{y}$,

$$\Phi^M(\mathbf{x}, \mathbf{y}) = \sum_{i=1}^{n} \phi^M(L_i, L_{i+1}, i, \mathbf{x}) \quad (3)$$
$$= \sum_{j=1}^{m} \phi^S(y_j, y_{j+1}, \mathbf{x}) = \Phi^S(\mathbf{x}, \mathbf{y})$$

To this end, note that there are only four possible label bigrams: BB, BC, CB, and CC. As a direct result of the definition of $L(\mathbf{y})$, we have that $(L_i, L_{i+1}) = (B, B)$ if and only if some word of length one begins at i, or equivalently, there exists a word j such that $y_j = i$ and $y_{j+1} - y_j = 1$. Similarly, $(L_i, L_{i+1}) = (B, C)$ if and only if some word of length > 1 begins at i, etc. Using these conditions, we can define ϕ^S to satisfy equation 3 as follows:

$$\phi^S(y_j, y_{j+1}, \mathbf{x}) = \phi^M(B, B, y_j, \mathbf{x})$$

if $y_{j+1} - y_j = 1$, and

$$\phi^S(y_j, y_{j+1}, \mathbf{x}) = \phi^M(B, C, y_j, \mathbf{x}) + \sum_{k=y_j+1}^{y_{j+1}-2} \phi^M(C, C, k, \mathbf{x}) + \phi^M(C, B, y_{j+1} - 1, \mathbf{x}) \quad (4)$$

otherwise. Defined thus, $\sum_{j=1}^{m} \phi^S$ will contain exactly n ϕ^M terms, corresponding to the n label bigrams.[4]

2.3 Order-1 Markov Features in a Semi-CRF

While it is fairly intuitive that any feature used in a 1-CRF can also be used in a semi-CRF, the above argument reveals an algorithmic difficulty that is likely another reason that such features are not typically used. The problem is essentially an effect of the sum for CC label bigrams in (4): quadratic time training and decoding assumes that the features of each chunk $\phi^S(y_j, y_{j+1}, \mathbf{x})$ can be multiplied with the weight vector $\mathbf{w}$ in a number of operations that is roughly constant over all chunks,

[4]We have discussed the case of Markov order-1, but the argument can be generalized to show that an order-M CRF has an equivalent representation as an order-M semi-CRF, for any M.

procedure $ComputeScores(\mathbf{x}, \mathbf{w})$
for $i = 2 \ldots (n-1)$ **do**
  $\sigma_i^{CC} \leftarrow \phi^M(C, C, i, \mathbf{x}) \cdot \mathbf{w}$
end for
for $a = 1 \ldots n$ **do**
  $CCsum \leftarrow 0$
  for $b = (a+1) \ldots (n+1)$ **do**
    if $b - a = 1$ **then**
      $\sigma_{ab} \leftarrow \phi^M(B, B, a, \mathbf{x}) \cdot \mathbf{w}$
    else
      $\sigma_{ab} \leftarrow \phi^M(B, C, a, \mathbf{x}) \cdot \mathbf{w} + CCsum + \phi^M(C, B, b-1, \mathbf{x}) \cdot \mathbf{w}$
      $CCsum \leftarrow CCsum + \sigma_{b-1}^{CC}$
    end if
  end for
end for

Figure 1: Dynamic program for computing chunk scores σ_{ab} with 1-CRF-type features.

but if one naïvely distributes the product over the sum, longer chunks will take proportionally longer to score, resulting in cubic time algorithms.[5]

In fact, it is possible to use these features without any asymptotic decrease in efficiency by means of a dynamic program. Both Viterbi and forward-backward involve the scores $\sigma_{ab} = \mathbf{w} \cdot \phi^S(a, b, \mathbf{x})$. Suppose that before starting those algorithms, we compute and cache the score σ_{ab} of each chunk, so that remainder the algorithm runs in quadratic time, as usual. This pre-computation can be done quickly if we first compute the values $\sigma_i^{CC} = \mathbf{w} \cdot \phi^M(C, C, i, \mathbf{x})$, and use them to fill in the values of σ_{ab} as shown in Figure 1.

In addition, computing the gradient of the semi-CRF objective requires that we compute the expected value of each feature. For CRF-type features, this is tantamount to being able to compute the probability that each label bigram (L_i, L_{i+1}) takes any value. Assume that we have already run standard forward-backward inference so that we have for any (a, b) the probability that the subsequence $(\mathbf{x}_a, \mathbf{x}_{a+1}, \ldots, \mathbf{x}_{b-1})$ segments as a chunk, $P(chunk(a, b))$. Computing the probability that (L_i, L_{i+1}) takes the values BB, BC or CB is simple to compute:

$$P(L_i, L_{i+1} = BB) = P(chunk(i, i+1))$$

[5]Note that the problem would arise even if only zero-order Markov (label unigram) features were used, only in that case the troublesome features would be those that involved the label unigram C.

and, e.g.,

$$P(L_i, L_{i+1} = BC) = \sum_{j>i+1} P(chunk(i, j)),$$

but the same method of summing over chunks cannot be used for the value CC since for each label bigram there are quadratically many chunks corresponding to that value. In this case, the solution is deceptively simple: using the fact that for any given label bigram, the sum of the probabilities of the four labels must be one, we can deduce that

$$P(L_i, L_{i+1} = CC) = 1.0 - P(L_i, L_{i+1} = BB) \\ - P(L_i, L_{i+1} = BC) - P(L_i, L_{i+1} = CB).$$

One might object that features of the C and CC labels (the ones presenting algorithmic difficulty) are unnecessary, since under certain conditions, their removal would not in fact change the expressivity of the model or the distribution that maximizes training likelihood. This will indeed be the case when the following conditions are fulfilled:

1. All label bigram features are of the form

$$\phi^M(L_i, L_{i+1}, i, \mathbf{x}) = \\ \mathbf{1}\{(L_i, L_{i+1}) = \alpha \ \&\ pred(i, \mathbf{x})\}$$

for some label bigram α and predicate $pred$, and any such feature with a given predicate has variants for all four label bigrams α.

2. No regularization is used during training.

A proof of this claim would require too much space for this paper, but the key is that, given a model satisfying the above conditions, one can obtain an equivalent model via adding, for each feature type over $pred$, some constant to the four weights corresponding to the four label bigrams, such that the CC bigram features all have weight zero.

In practice, however, one or both of these conditions is always broken. It is common knowledge that regularization of log-linear models with a large number of features is necessary to achieve high performance, and typically in NLP one defines feature templates and chooses only those features that occur in some positive example in the training set. In fact, if both of these conditions are fulfilled, it is very likely that the optimal model will have some weights with infinite values. We conclude that it is not a practical alternative to omit the C and CC label features.

2.4 Generative Features in a Discriminative Model

When using the output of a generative model as a feature in a discriminative model, Raina et al. (2004) provide a justification for the use of log conditional odds as opposed to log-probability: they show that using log conditional odds as features in a logistic regression model is equivalent to discriminatively training weights for the features of a Naïve Bayes classifier to maximize conditional likelihood.[6] They demonstrate that the resulting classifier, termed a "hybrid generative/discriminative classifier", achieves lower test error than either pure Naïve Bayes or pure logistic regression on a text classification task, regardless of training set size.

The hybrid generative/discriminative classifier also uses a unique method for using the same data used to estimate the parameters of the component generative models for training the discriminative model parameters $\mathbf{w}$ without introducing bias. A "leave-one-out" strategy is used to choose $\mathbf{w}$, whereby the feature values of the i-th training example are computed using probabilities estimated with the i-th example held out. The beauty of this approach is that since the probabilities are estimated according to (smoothed) relative frequency, it is only necessary during feature computation to maintain sufficient statistics and adjust them as necessary for each example.

In this paper, we experiment with the use of a single "hybrid" local semi-CRF feature, the smoothed log conditional odds that a given subsequence $\mathbf{x}_{ab} = (\mathbf{x}_a, \ldots, \mathbf{x}_{b-1})$ forms a word:

$$\log \frac{wordcount(\mathbf{x}_{ab}) + 1}{nonwordcount(\mathbf{x}_{ab}) + 1},$$

where $wordcount(\mathbf{x}_{ab})$ is the number of times $\mathbf{x}_{ab}$ forms a word in the training set, and $nonwordcount(\mathbf{x}_{ab})$ is the number of times $\mathbf{x}_{ab}$ occurs, not segmented into a single word. The models we test are not strictly speaking hybrid generative/discriminative models, since we also use indicator features not derived from a generative model. We did however use the leave-one-out approach for computing the log conditional odds feature during training.

[6] In fact, one more step beyond what is shown in that paper is required to reach the stated conclusion, since their features are not actually log conditional odds, but $\log \frac{P(\mathbf{x}|\mathbf{y})}{P(\mathbf{x}|\neg\mathbf{y})}$. It is simple to show that in the given context this feature is equivalent to log conditional odds.

3 Experiments

To test the ideas discussed in this paper, we compared the performance of semi-CRFs using various feature sets on a Chinese word segmentation task. The data used was the Microsoft Research Beijing corpus from the Second International Chinese Word Segmentation Bakeoff (Emerson, 2005), and we used the same train/test split used in the competition. The training set consists of 87K sentences of Beijing dialect Chinese, hand segmented into 2.37M words. The test set contains 107K words comprising roughly 4K sentences. We used a maximum word length k of 15 in our experiments, which accounted for 99.99% of the word tokens in our training set. The 249 training sentences that contained words longer than 15 characters were discarded. We did not discard any test sentences.

In order to be directly comparable to the Bakeoff results, we also worked under the very strict "closed test" conditions of the Bakeoff, which require that no information or data outside of the training set be used, not even prior knowledge of which characters represent Arabic numerals, Latin characters or punctuation marks.

3.1 Features Used

We divide our main features into two types according to whether they are most naturally used in a CRF or a semi-CRF.

The CRF-type features are indicator functions that fire when the character label (or label bigram) takes some value and some predicate of the input at a certain position relative to the label is satisfied. For each character label unigram L at position i, we use the same set of predicate templates checking:

- The identity of $\mathbf{x}_{i-1}$ and $\mathbf{x}_i$
- The identity of the character bigram starting at positions $i-2$, $i-1$ and i
- Whether $\mathbf{x}_j$ and $\mathbf{x}_{j+1}$ are identical, for $j = (i-2) \dots i$
- Whether $\mathbf{x}_j$ and $\mathbf{x}_{j+2}$ are identical, for $j = (i-3) \dots i$
- Whether the sequence $\mathbf{x}_j \dots \mathbf{x}_{j+3}$ forms an $AABB$ sequence for $j = (i-4) \dots i$
- Whether the sequence $\mathbf{x}_j \dots \mathbf{x}_{j+3}$ forms an $ABAB$ sequence for $j = (i-4) \dots i$

The latter four feature templates are designed to detect character or word reduplication, a morphological phenomenon that can influence word segmentation in Chinese. The first two of these were also used by Tseng et al. (2005).

For label bigrams (L_i, L_{i+1}), we use the same templates, but extending the range of positions by one to the right.[7] Each label uni- or bigram also has a "prior" feature that always fires for that label configuration. All configurations contain the above features for the label unigram B, since these are easily used in either a CRF or semi-CRF model. To determine the influence of CRF-type features on performance, we also test configurations in which both B and C label features are used, and configurations using all label uni- and bigrams.

In the semi-Markov conditions, we also use as feature templates indicators of the length of a word ℓ, for $\ell = 1 \dots k$, and indicators of the identity of the corresponding character sequence.

All feature templates were instantiated with values that occur in positive training examples. We found that excluding CRF-type features that occur only once in the training set consistently improved performance on the development set, so we use a count threshold of two for the experiments. We do not do any thresholding of the semi-CRF features, however.

Finally, we use the single generative feature, log conditional odds that the given string forms a word. We also present results using the more typical log conditional probability instead of the odds, for comparison. In fact, these are both semi-Markov-type features, but we single them out to determine what they contribute over and above the other semi-Markov features.

3.2 Results

The results of test set runs are summarized in table 3.2. The columns indicate which CRF-type features were used: features of only the label B, features of label unigrams B and C, or features of all label unigrams and bigrams. The rows indicate which semi-Markov-type features were used:

[7] For both label unigram and label bigram features, the indices are chosen so that the feature set exhibits no asymmetry with respect to direction: for each feature considering some boundary and some property of the character(s) at a given offset to the left, there is a corresponding feature considering that boundary and the same property of the character(s) at the same offset to the right, and vice-versa.

Features	B only	uni	uni+bi
none	92.33	94.71	95.69
semi	95.28	96.05	96.46
prob	93.86	95.40	96.04
semi+prob	95.51	96.24	96.55
odds	95.10	96.06	96.40
semi+odds	96.27	96.77	96.84

Table 1: Test F-measure for different model configurations.

"semi" means length and word identity features were used, "prob" means the log-probability feature was used, and "odds" means the log-odds feature was used.

To establish the impact of each type of feature (C label unigrams, label bigrams, semi-CRF-type features, and the log-odds feature), we look at the reduction in error brought about by adding each type of feature. First consider the effect of the CRF-type features. Adding the C label features reduces error by 31% if no semi-CRF features are used, by 16% when semi-CRF indicator features are turned on, and by 13% when all semi-CRF features (including log-odds) are used. Using all label bigrams reduces error by 44%, 25%, and 15% in these three conditions, respectively.

Contrary to previous conclusions, our results show a significant impact due to the use of semi-CRF-type features, when CRF-type features are held constant. Adding semi-CRF indicator features results in a 38% error reduction without CRF-type features, and 18% with them. Adding semi-CRF indicator features plus the log-odds feature gives 52% and 27% in these two conditions, respectively.

Finally, across configurations, the log conditional odds does much better than log conditional probability. When the log-odds feature is added to the complete CRF model (uni+bi) as the only semi-CRF-type feature, errors are reduced by 24%, compared to only 7.6% for the log-probability. Even when the other semi-CRF-type features are present as well, log-odds reduces error by 13% compared to 2.5% for log-probability.

Our best model, combining all features, resulted in an error reduction of 12% over the highest score on this dataset from the 2005 Sighan closed test competition (96.4%), achieved by the pure CRF system of Tseng et al. (2005).

3.3 Discussion

Our results indicate that both Markov-type and semi-Markov-type features are useful for generalization to unseen data. This may be because the two types of features are in a sense complementary: semi-Markov-type features such as word identity are valuable for modeling the tendency of known strings to segment as words, while label based features are valuable for modeling properties of sub-lexical components such as affixes, helping to generalize to words that have not previously been encountered. We did not explicitly test the utility of CRF-type features for improving recall on out-of-vocabulary items, but we note that in the Bakeoff, the model of Tseng et al. (2005), which was very similar to our CRF-only system (only containing a few more feature templates), was consistently among the best performing systems in terms of test OOV recall (Emerson, 2005).

We also found that for this sequence segmentation task, the use of log conditional odds as a feature results in much better performance than the use of the more typical log conditional probability. It would be interesting to see the log-odds applied in more contexts where log-probabilities are typically used as features. We have presented the intuitive argument that the log-odds may be advantageous because it does not exhibit the 0-1 asymmetry of the log-probability, but it would be satisfying to justify the choice on more theoretical grounds.

4 Relation to Previous Work

There is a significant volume of work exploring the use of CRFs for a variety of chunking tasks, including named-entity recognition, gene prediction, shallow parsing and others (Finkel et al., 2005; Culotta et al., 2005; Sha and Pereira, 2003). The current work indicates that these systems might be improved by moving to a semi-CRF model.

There have not been a large number of studies using the semi-CRF, but the few that have been done found only marginal improvements over pure CRF systems (Sarawagi and Cohen, 2004; Liang, 2005; Daumé III and Marcu, 2005). Notably, none of those studies experimented with features of chunk *non*-boundaries, as is achieved by the use of CRF-type features involving the label C, and we take this to be the reason for their not obtaining higher results.

Although it has become fairly common in NLP to use the log conditional probabilities of events as features in a discriminative model, we are not aware of any work using the log conditional odds.

5 Conclusion

We have shown that order-1 semi-Markov conditional random fields are strictly more expressive than order-1 Markov CRFs, and that the added expressivity enables the use of features that lead to improvements on a segmentation task. On the other hand, Markov CRFs can more naturally incorporate certain features that may be useful for modeling sub-chunk phenomena and generalization to unseen chunks. To achieve the best performance for segmentation, we propose that both types of features be used, and we show how this can be done efficiently.

Additionally, we have shown that a log conditional odds feature estimated from a generative model can be superior to the more common log conditional probability.

6 Acknowledgements

Many thanks to Kristina Toutanova for her thoughtful discussion and feedback, and also to the anonymous reviewers for their suggestions.

References

Masayuki Asahara, Kenta Fukuoka, Ai Azuma, Chooi-Ling Goh, Yotaro Watanabe, Yuji Matsumoto, and Takahashi Tsuzuki. 2005. Combination of machine learning methods for optimum chinese word segmentation. In *Proc. Fourth SIGHAN Workshop on Chinese Language Processing*, pages 134–137.

Michael Collins. 2000. Discriminative reranking for natural language parsing. In *Proc. 14th International Conf. on Machine Learning*.

Aron Culotta, David Kulp, and Andrew McCallum. 2005. Gene prediction with conditional random fields. Technical report, University of Massachusetts Dept. of Computer Science, April.

Hal Daumé III and Daniel Marcu. 2005. Learning as search optimization: Approximate large margin methods for structured prediction. In *Proc. 19th International Conf. on Machine Learning*.

Thomas Emerson. 2005. The second international chinese word segmentation bakeoff. In *Proc. Fourth SIGHAN Workshop on Chinese Language Processing*, pages 123–133.

Jenny Finkel, Trond Grenager, and Christopher D. Manning. 2005. Incorporating non-local information into information extraction systems by gibbs sampling. *Proc. 41th Annual Meeting of the Assiciation of Computation Linguistics*.

John Lafferty, Andrew McCallum, and Fernando Pereira. 2001. Conditional random fields: Probabilistic models for segmenting and labeling sequence data. In *Proc. 18th International Conf. on Machine Learning*, pages 282–289. Morgan Kaufmann, San Francisco, CA.

Percy Liang. 2005. Semi-supervised learning for natural language. Master's thesis, Massachusetts Institute of Technology.

Andrew Y. Ng and Michael I. Jordan. 2001. On discriminative vs. generative classifiers: A comparison of logistic regression and Naïve Bayes. In *Proc. Advances in Neural Information Processing 14*.

Franz Josef Och and Hermann Ney. 2002. Discriminative training and maximum entropy models for statistical machine translation. *Proc. 38th Annual Meeting of the Assiciation of Computation Linguistics*.

Franz Josef Och and Hermann Ney. 2004. The alignment template approach to statistical machine translation. *Computational Linguistics*, 30(4):417–449, December.

Fuchun Peng, Fangfang Feng, and Andrew McCallum. 2004. Chinese segmentation and new word detection using conditional random fields. In *Proc. 20th International Conf. on Computational Linguistics*.

Rajat Raina, Yirong Shen, Andrew Y. Ng, and Andrew McCallum. 2004. Classification with hybrid generative/discriminative models. In *Proc. Advances in Neural Information Processing 17*.

Brian Roark and Seeger Fisher. 2005. OGI/OHSU baseline multilingual multi-document sumarization system. In *Proc. Multilingual Summarization Evaluation in ACL Workshop: Intrinsic and Extrinsic Evaluation Measures for MT and/or Summarization*.

Sunita Sarawagi and William Cohen. 2004. Semi-markov conditional random fields for information extraction. In *Proc. 18th International Conf. on Machine Learning*.

Fei Sha and Fernando Pereira. 2003. Shallow parsing with conditional random fields. *Proc. HLT-NAACL*.

Huihsin Tseng, Pichuan Chang, Galen Andrew, Daniel Jurafsky, and Christopher Manning. 2005. A conditional random field word segmenter for sighan bakeoff 2005. In *Proc. Fourth SIGHAN Workshop on Chinese Language Processing*, pages 168–171.

Boosting Unsupervised Relation Extraction by Using NER

Ronen Feldman
Computer Science Department
Bar-Ilan University
Ramat-Gan, ISRAEL
feldman@cs.biu.ac.il

Benjamin Rosenfeld
Computer Science Department
Bar-Ilan University
Ramat-Gan, ISRAEL
grurgrur@gmail.com

Abstract

Web extraction systems attempt to use the immense amount of unlabeled text in the Web in order to create large lists of entities and relations. Unlike traditional IE methods, the Web extraction systems do not label every mention of the target entity or relation, instead focusing on extracting as many different instances as possible while keeping the precision of the resulting list reasonably high. URES is a Web relation extraction system that learns powerful extraction patterns from unlabeled text, using short descriptions of the target relations and their attributes. The performance of URES is further enhanced by classifying its output instances using the properties of the extracted patterns. The features we use for classification and the trained classification model are independent from the target relation, which we demonstrate in a series of experiments. In this paper we show how the introduction of a simple rule based NER can boost the performance of URES on a variety of relations. We also compare the performance of URES to the performance of the state-of-the-art KnowItAll system, and to the performance of its pattern learning component, which uses a simpler and less powerful pattern language than URES.

1 Introduction

Information Extraction (IE) (Riloff 1993; Cowie and Lehnert 1996; Grishman 1996; Grishman 1997; Kushmerick, Weld et al. 1997; Freitag 1998; Freitag and McCallum 1999; Soderland 1999) is the task of extracting factual assertions from text.

Most IE systems rely on knowledge engineering or on machine learning to generate extraction patterns – the mechanism that extracts entities and relation instances from text. In the machine learning approach, a domain expert labels instances of the target relations in a set of documents. The system then learns extraction patterns, which can be applied to new documents automatically.

Both approaches require substantial human effort, particularly when applied to the broad range of documents, entities, and relations on the Web. In order to minimize the manual effort necessary to build Web IE systems, we have designed and implemented URES (Unsupervised Relation Extraction System). URES takes as input the names of the target relations and the types of their arguments. It then uses a large set of unlabeled documents downloaded from the Web in order to learn the extraction patterns.

URES is most closely related to the KnowItAll system developed at University of Washington by Oren Etzioni and colleagues (Etzioni, Cafarella et al. 2005), since both are unsupervised and both leverage relation-independent extraction patterns to automatically generate seeds, which are then fed into a pattern-learning component. KnowItAll is based on the observation that the Web corpus is highly redundant. Thus, its selective, high-precision extraction patterns readily ignore most sentences, and focus on sentences that indicate the presence of relation instances with very high probability.

In contrast, URES is based on the observation that, for many relations, the Web corpus has *limited redundancy*, particularly when one is concerned with less prominent instances of these relations (e.g., the acquisition of Austria Tabak). Thus, URES utilizes a more expressive extraction pattern language, which enables it to extract information from a broader set of sentences. URES relies on a sophisticated mechanism to

Proceedings of the 2006 Conference on Empirical Methods in Natural Language Processing (EMNLP 2006), pages 473–481,
Sydney, July 2006.

assess its confidence in each extraction, enabling it to sort extracted instances, thereby improving its recall without sacrificing precision.

Our main contributions are as follows:

- We introduce the first domain-independent system to extract relation instances from the Web with both high precision and high recall.
- We show how to minimize the human effort necessary to deploy URES for an arbitrary set of relations, including automatically generating and labeling positive and negative examples of the relation.
- We show how we can integrate a simple NER component into the classification scheme of URES in order to boost recall between 5-15% for similar precision levels.
- We report on an experimental comparison between URES, URES-NER and the state-of-the-art KnowItAll system, and show that URES can double or even triple the recall achieved by KnowItAll for relatively rare relation instances.

The rest of the paper is organized as follows: Section 2 describes previous work. Section 3 outlines the general design principles of URES, its architecture, and then describes each URES component in detail. Section 4 presents our experimental evaluation. Section 5 contains conclusions and directions for future work.

2 Related Work

The IE systems most similar to URES are based on bootstrap learning: Mutual Bootstrapping (Riloff and Jones 1999), the DIPRE system (Brin 1998), and the Snowball system (Agichtein and Gravano 2000). (Ravichandran and Hovy 2002) also use bootstrapping, and learn simple surface patterns for extracting binary relations from the Web.

Unlike those unsupervised IE systems, URES patterns allow gaps that can be matched by any sequences of tokens. This makes URES patterns much more general, and allows to recognize instances in sentences inaccessible to the simple surface patterns of systems such as (Brin 1998; Riloff and Jones 1999; Ravichandran and Hovy 2002). The greater power of URES requires different and more complex methods for learning, scoring, and filtering of patterns.

Another direction for unsupervised relation learning was taken in (Hasegawa, Sekine et al. 2004; Chen, Ji et al. 2005). These systems use a NER system to identify pairs of entities and then cluster them based on the types of the entities and the words appearing between the entities. Only pairs that appear at least 30 times were considered. The main benefit of this approach is that all relations between two entity types can be discovered simultaneously and there is no need for the user to supply the relations definitions. Such a system could have been used as a preliminary step to URES, however its relatively low precision makes it unfeasible. Unlike URES, the evaluations performed in these papers ignored errors that were introduced by the underlying NER component. The precision reported by these systems (77% breakeven for the COM-COM domain) is inferior to that of URES.

We compared our results directly to two other unsupervised extraction systems, the Snowball (Agichtein and Gravano 2000) and KnowItAll. Snowball is an unsupervised system for learning relations from document collections. The system takes as input a set of seed examples for each relation, and uses a clustering technique to learn patterns from the seed examples. It does rely on a full fledged Named Entity Recognition system. Snowball achieved fairly low precision figures (30-50%) on relations such as *Merger* and *Acquisition* on the same dataset we used in our experiments.

KnowItAll is a system developed at University of Washington by Oren Etzioni and colleagues (Etzioni, Cafarella et al. 2005). We shall now briefly describe it and its pattern learning component.

Brief description of KnowItAll

KnowItAll uses a set of generic extraction patterns, and automatically instantiates rules by combining those patterns with user supplied relation labels. For example, KnowItAll has patterns for a generic "of" relation:

NP1 <relation> NP2
NP1 's <relation> , NP2
NP2 , <relation> of NP1

where NP1 and NP2 are simple noun phrases that extract values of attribute1 and attribute2 of a relation, and <relation> is a user-supplied string associated with the relation. The rules may also constrain NP1 and NP2 to be proper nouns.

The rules have alternating context strings (exact string match) and extraction slots (typically an NP or head of an NP). Each rule has an associated query used to automatically find candidate sentences from a Web search engine.

KnowItAll also includes mechanisms to control the amount of search, to merge redundant extractions, and to assign a probability to each extraction based on frequency of extraction or on Web statistics (Downey, Etzioni et al. 2004).

KnowItAll-PL. While those generic rules lead to high precision extraction, they tend to have low recall, due to the wide variety of contexts describing a relation. KnowItAll includes a simple pattern learning scheme (KnowItAll-PL) that builds on the generic extraction mechanism (KnowItAll-baseline). Like URES, this is a self-supervised method that bootstraps from seeds that are automatically extracted by the baseline system.

KnowItAll-PL creates a set of positive training sentences by downloading sentences that contain both argument values of a seed tuple and also the relation label. Negative training is created by downloading sentences with only one of the seed argument values, and considering a nearby NP as the other argument value. This does not guarantee that the negative example will actually be false, but works well in practice.

Rule induction tabulates the occurrence of context tokens surrounding the argument values of the positive training sentences. Each candidate extraction pattern has a left context of zero to k tokens immediately to the left of the first argument, a middle context of all tokens between the two arguments, and a right context of zero to k tokens immediately to the right of the second argument. A pattern can be generalized by dropping the furthest terms from the left or right context. KnowItAll-PL retains the most general version of each pattern that has training frequency over a threshold and training precision over a threshold.

3 Description of URES

The goal of URES is extracting instances of relations from the Web without human supervision. Accordingly, the input of the system is limited to (reasonably short) definition of the target relations (composed of the relation's schema and a few keywords that enable gathering relevant sentences). For example, this is the description of the acquisition relation:

Acquisition(ProperNP, ProperNP) ordered
keywords={"acquired" "acquisition"}

The word ordered indicates that Acquisition is not a symmetric relation and the order of its arguments matters. The ProperNP tokens indicate the types of the attributes. In the regular mode, there are only two possible attribute types – ProperNP and CommonNP, meaning proper and common noun phrases, respectively. When using the NER Filter component described in the section 4.1 we allow further subtypes of ProperNP, and the predicate definition becomes:

acquisition(Company, Company) ...

The keywords are used for gathering sentences from the Web and for instantiating the generic patterns for seeds generation. Additional keywords (such as "acquire", "purchased", "hostile takeover", etc), which can be used for gathering more sentences, are added automatically by using WordNet [18].

URES consists of several largely independent components; their layout is shown on the Figure 1. The Sentence Gatherer generates (e.g., downloads from the Web) a large set of sentences that may contain target instances. The Seeds Generator, which is essentially equal to the KnowItAll-baseline system, uses a small set of generic patterns instantiated with the predicate keywords to extract a small set of high-confidence instances of the target relations. The Pattern Learner uses the seeds to learn likely patterns of relation occurrences. Then, the Instance Extractor uses the patterns to extracts the instances from the sentences. Those instances can be filtered by a NER Filter, which is an optional part of the system. Finally, the Classifier assigns the confidence score to each extraction.

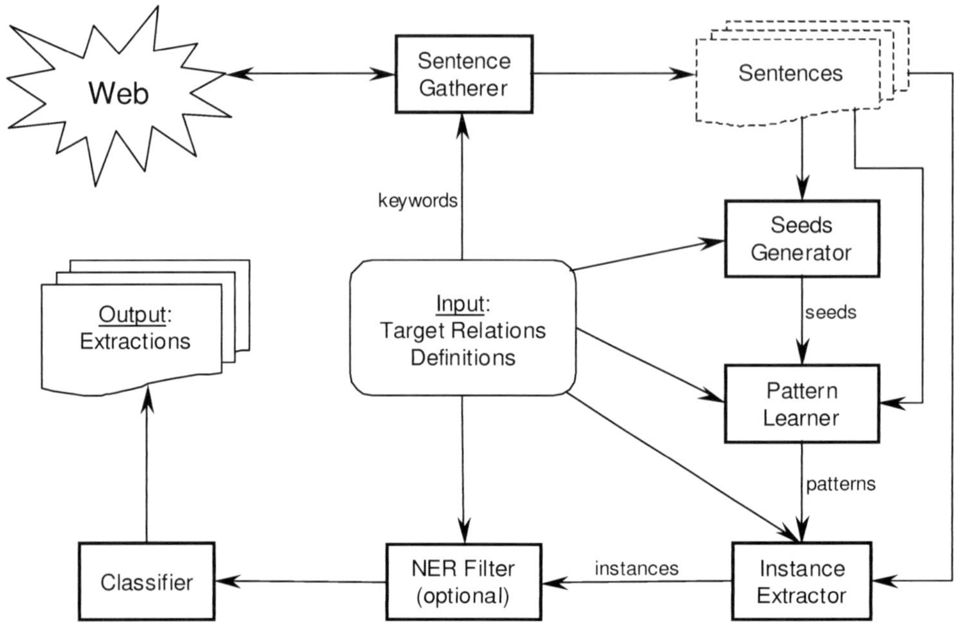

Figure 1. The architecture of URES

3.1 Pattern Learner

The task of the *Pattern Learner* is to learn the patterns of occurrence of relation instances. This is an inherently supervised task, because at least some occurrences must be known in order to be able to find patterns among them. Consequently, the input to the Pattern Learner includes a small set (10 instances in our experiments) of known instances for each target relation. Our system assumes that the seeds are a part of the target relation definition. However, the set of seeds need not be created manually. Instead, the seeds can be taken automatically from the top-scoring results of a high-precision low-recall unsupervised extraction system, such as KnowItAll. The seeds for our experiments were produced in exactly this way: we used two generic patterns instantiated with the relation name and keywords. Those patterns have a relatively high precision (although low recall), and the top-confidence results, which are the ones extracted many times from different sentences, have close to 100% probability of being correct.

The Pattern Learner proceeds as follows: first, the gathered sentences that contain the seed instances are used to generate the positive and negative sets. From those sets the patterns are learned. Finally, the patterns are post-processed and filtered. We shall now describe those steps in detail.

PREPARING THE POSITIVE AND NEGATIVE SETS

The positive set of a predicate (the terms *predicate* and *relation* are interchangeable in our work) consists of sentences that contain a known instance of the predicate, with the instance attributes changed to "<*AttrN*>", where *N* is the attribute index. For example, assuming there is a seed instance *Acquisition*(*Oracle*, *PeopleSoft*), the sentence

The Antitrust Division of the U.S. Department of Justice evaluated the likely competitive effects of Oracle's proposed acquisition of PeopleSoft.

will be changed to

The Antitrust Division... ...of <*Attr1*>*'s proposed acquisition of* <*Attr2*>.

The positive set of a predicate *P* is generated straightforwardly, using substring search. The negative set of a predicate consists of sentences with known false instances of the predicate similarly marked (with <*AttrN*> substituted for attributes). The negative set is used by the pattern learner during the scoring and filtering step, to filter out the patterns that are overly general. We generate the negative set from the sentences in the positive set by changing the assignment of one or both attributes to other suitable entities in the sentence. In the shallow parser based mode of operation, any suitable noun phrase can be assigned to an attribute.

GENERATING THE PATTERNS

The patterns for the predicate *P* are generalizations of pairs of sentences from the positive set of *P*. The function *Generalize*(s_1, s_2) is applied to each pair of sentences s_1 and s_2 from the positive set of the predicate. The function generates a pattern that is the best (according to the objective function defined below) generalization of its two arguments.

The following pseudocode shows the process of generating the patterns for the predicate *P*:

For each pair s_1, s_2 from PositiveSet(P)

Let Pattern = Generalize(s_1, s_2).

Add Pattern to PatternsSet(P).

The patterns are sequences of *tokens*, *skips* (denoted *), *limited skips* (denoted *?) and *slots*. The tokens can match only themselves, the skips match zero or more arbitrary tokens, and slots match instance attributes. The limited skips match zero or more arbitrary tokens, which must not belong to entities of the types equal to the types of the predicate attributes. In the shallow parser based mode, there are only two different entity types – *ProperNP* and *CommonNP*, standing for proper and common noun phrases.

The *Generalize*(s_1, s_2) function takes two sentences and generates the least (most specific) common generalization of both. The function does a dynamical programming search for the best match between the two patterns (Optimal String Alignment algorithm), with the cost of the match defined as the sum of costs of matches for all elements. The exact costs of matching elements are not important as long as their relative order is maintained. We use the following numbers: two identical elements match at cost 0, a token matches a skip or an empty space at cost 10, a skip matches an empty space at cost 2, and different kinds of skip match at cost 3. All other combinations have infinite cost. After the best match is found, it is converted into a pattern by copying matched identical elements and adding skips where non-identical elements are matched. For example, assume the sentences are

Toward this end, <Attr1> in July acquired <Attr2>

Earlier this year, <Attr1> acquired <Attr2> from X

After the dynamic programming-based search, the following match will be found:

Toward		(cost 10)
	Earlier	(cost 10)
this	*this*	(cost 0)
end		(cost 10)
	year	(cost 10)
,	,	(cost 0)
<Attr1>	*<Attr1>*	(cost 0)
in July		(cost 20)
acquired	*acquired*	(cost 0)
<Attr2>	*<Attr2>*	(cost 0)
	from	(cost 10)
	X	(cost 10)

at total cost = 80. Assuming that "X" belongs to the same type as at least one of the attributes while the other tokens are not entities, the match will be converted to the pattern

**? this *? , <Attr1> *? acquired <Attr2> **

3.2 Classifying the Extractions

The goal of the final classification stage is to filter the list of all extracted instances, keeping the correct extractions and removing mistakes that would always occur regardless of the quality of the patterns. It is of course impossible to know which extractions are correct, but there exist properties of patterns and pattern matches that increase or decrease the confidence in the extractions that they produce. Thus, instead of a binary classifier, we seek a real-valued confidence function c, mapping the set of extracted instances into the [0, 1] segment.

Since confidence value depends on the properties of particular sentences and patterns, it is more properly defined over the set of single pattern matches. Then, the overall confidence of an instance is the maximum of the confidence values of the matches that produce the instance.

Assume that an instance E was extracted from a match of a pattern P at a sentence S.

The following set of binary features may influence the confidence c(E, P, S):

f1(E, P, S) = 1, if the number of sentences producing E is greater than one.

f2(E, P, S) = 1, if the number of sentences producing E is greater than two.

f3(E, P, S) = 1, if at least one slot of the pattern P is adjacent to a non-stop-word token.

f4(E, P, S) = 1, if both slots of the pattern P are adjacent to non-stop-word tokens.

f5...f9(E, P, S) = 1, if the number of nonstop words in P is 0 (f5), 1 or greater (f6), 2 or greater (f7), 3 or greater (f8), and 4 or greater (f9).

f10...f15(E, P, S) = 1, if the number of words between the slots of the match M that were matched to skips of the pattern P is 0 (f10), 1 or less (f11), 2 or less (f12) , 3 or less(f13), 5 or less (f14), and 10 or less (f15).

Utilizing the NER

In the URES-NER version the entities of each candidate instance are passed through a simple rule-based NER filter, which attaches a score ("yes", "maybe", or "no") to the argument(s) and optionally fixes the arguments boundaries. The NER is capable of identifying entities of type PERSON and COMPANY (and can be extended to identify additional types).

The scores mean:

"yes" – the argument is of the correct entity type.

"no" – the argument is not of the right entity type, and hence the candidate instance should be removed.

"maybe" – the argument type is uncertain, can be either correct or no.

If "no" is returned for one of the arguments, the instance is removed. Otherwise, an additional binary feature is added to the instance's vector:

f16 = 1 iff the score for both arguments is "yes".

For bound predicates, only the second argument is analyzed, naturally.

As can be seen, the set of features above is small, and is not specific to any particular predicate. This allows us to train a model using a small amount of labeled data for one predicate, and then use the model for all other predicates:

Training: The patterns for a single model predicate are run over a relatively small set of sentences (3,000-10,000 sentences in our experiments), producing a set of extractions (between 150-300 extractions in our experiments).

The extractions are manually labeled according to whether they are correct or not. For each pattern match Mk = (Ek, Pk, Sk), the value of the feature vector fk = (f1(Mk), ..., f15(Mk)) is calculated, and the label Lk = ±1 is set according to whether the extraction Ek is correct or no.

A regression model estimating the function L(f) is built from the training data {(fk, Lk)}. For our classifier we used the BBR (Genkin, Lewis et al. 2004), but other models, such as SVM or NaiveBayes are of course also possible.

Confidence estimation: For each pattern match M, its score L(f(M)) is calculated by the trained regression model. Note that we do not threshold the value of L, instead using the raw probability value between zero and one.

The final confidence estimates c(E) for the extraction E is set to the maximum of L(f(M)) over all matches M that produced E.

4 Experimental Evaluation

Our experiments aim to answer three questions:

1. Can we train URES's classifier once, and then use the results on all other relations?
2. What boost will we get by introducing a simple NER into the classification scheme of URES?
3. How does URES's performance compare with KnowItAll and KnowItAll-PL?

Our experiments utilized five relations:

Acquisition(BuyerCompany,AcquiredCompany),
Merger(Company1, Company2),
CEO_Of(Company, Person),
MayorOf(City, Person),
InventorOf(Person, Invention).

Merger is a symmetric predicate, in the sense that the order of its attributes does not matter. Acquisition is antisymmetric, and the other three are tested as bound in the first attribute. For the bound predicates, we are only interested in the instances with particular prespecified values of the first attribute. The Invention attribute of the InventorOf predicate is of type CommonNP. All other attributes are of type ProperName.

The data for the experiments were collected by the KnowItAll crawler. The data for the Acquisition and Merger predicates consist of about 900,000 sentences for each of the two predicates, where each sentence contains at least one predicate keyword. The data for the bounded predicates consist of sentences that contain a predicate keyword and one of a hundred values of the first (bound) attribute. Half of the hundred are frequent entities (>100,000 search engine hits), and another half are rare (<10,000 hits).

The pattern learning for each of the predicates was performed using the whole corpus of sentences for the predicate. For testing the precision of each of the predicates in each of the systems we manually evaluated sets of 200 instances that were randomly selected out of the full set of instances extracted from the whole corpus.

In the first experiment, we test the performance of the classification component using different predicates for building the model. In the second experiment we evaluate the full system over the whole dataset.

4.1 Cross-Predicate Classification Performance

In this experiment we test whether the choice of the model predicate for training the classifier is significant.

The pattern learning for each of the predicates was performed using the whole corpus of sentences for the predicate. For testing we used a small random selection of sentences, run the Instance Extractor over them, and manually evaluated each extracted instance. The results of the evaluation for Acquisition, CEO_Of, and Merger are summarized in Figure 2. As can be seen, using any of the predicates as the model produces similar results. The graphs for the other two predicates are similar. We have used only the first 15 features, as the NER-based feature (f_{16}) is predicate-dependent.

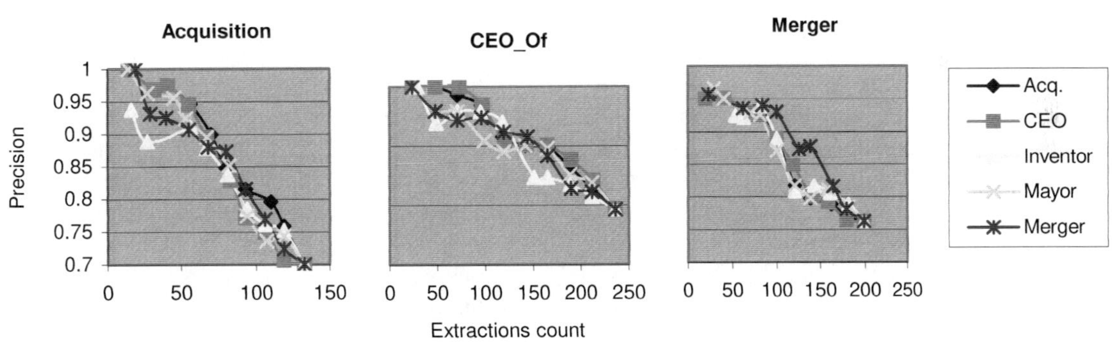

Figure 2. Cross-predicate classification performance results. Each graph shows the five precision-recall curves produced by using the five different model predicates. As can be seen, the curves on each graph are very similar.

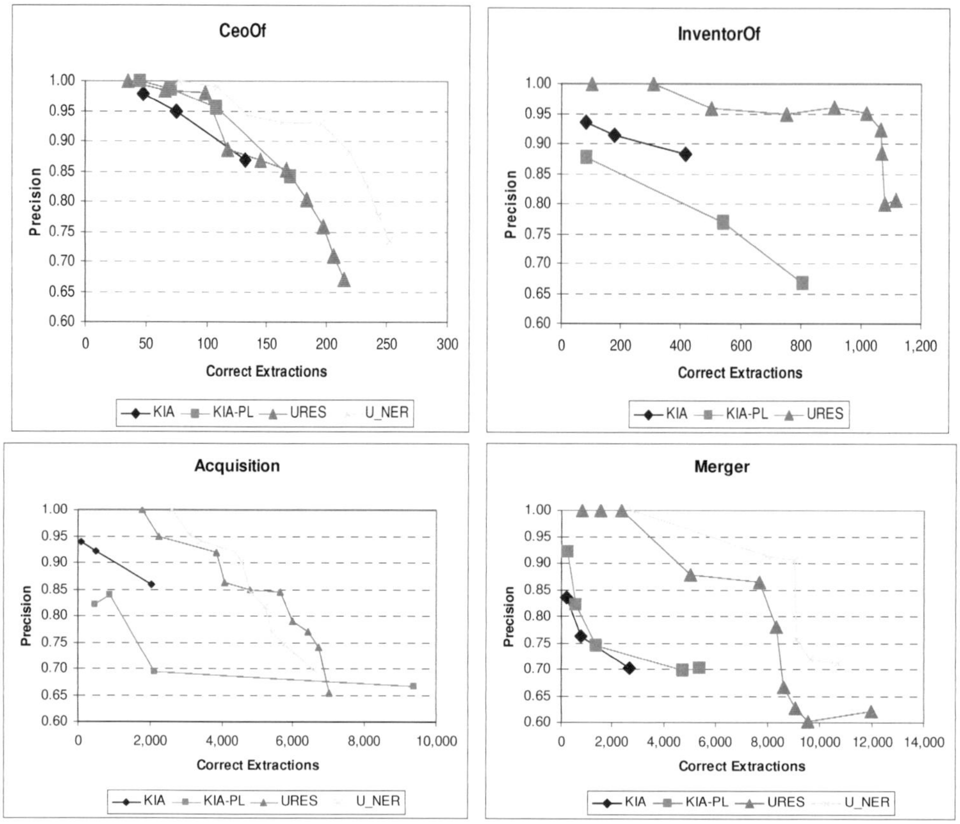

Figure 3. Comparision between URES, URES-NER, KnowItAll-baseline, and KnowItAll-PL.

4.2 Performance of the whole system

In this experiment we compare the performance of URES with classification to the performance of KnowItAll. To carry out the experiments, we used extraction data kindly provided by the KnowItAll group. They provided us with the extractions obtained by the KnowItAll system and by its pattern learning component (KnowItAll-PL). Both are sketched in Section 2.1 and are described in detail in (Etzioni, Cafarella et al. 2005).

In this experiment we used Acquisition as the model predicate for testing all other predicates except itself. For testing Acquisition we used CEO_Of as the model predicate. The results are summarized in the five graphs in the Figure 3.

For three relations (Acquisition, Merger, and InventorOf) URES clearly outperforms KnowItAll. Yet for the other two (CEO_Of and MayorOf), the simpler method of KnowItAll-PL or even the KnowItAll-baseline do as well as URES. Close inspection reveals that the key difference is the amount of redundancy of instances of those relations in the data. Instances of CEO_Of and MayorOf are mentioned frequently in a wide variety of sentences whereas instances of the other relations are relatively infrequent.

KnowItAll extraction works well when redundancy is high and most instances have a good chance of appearing in simple forms that KnowItAll is able to recognize. The additional machinery in URES is necessary when redundancy is low. Specifically, URES is more effective in identifying low-frequency instances, due to its more expressive rule representation, and its classifier that inhibits those rules from overgeneralizing.

In the same graphs we can see that URES-NER outperforms URES by 5-15% in recall for similar precision levels. We can also see that for Person-based predicates the improvement is much more pronounced, because Person is a much simpler entity to recognize. Since in the InventorOf predicate the 2nd attribute is of type CommonNP, the NER component adds no value and URES-NER and URES results are identical for this predicate.

5 Conclusions

We have presented the URES system for autonomously extracting relations from the Web. We showed how to improve the precision of the system by classifying the extracted instances using the properties of the patterns and sentences that generated the instances and how to utilize a simple NER component. The cross-predicate tests showed that classifier that performs well for all relations can be built using a small amount of labeled data for any particular relation. We performed an experimental comparison between URES, URES-NER and the state-of-the-art KnowItAll system, and showed that URES can double or even triple the recall achieved by KnowItAll for relatively rare relation instances, and get an additional 5-15% boost in recall by utilizing a simple NER. In particular we have shown that URES is more effective in identifying low-frequency instances, due to its more expressive rule representation, and its classifier (augmented by NER) that inhibits those rules from overgeneralizing.

References

Agichtein, E. and L. Gravano (2000). Snowball: Extracting Relations from Large Plain-Text Collections. Proceedings of the 5th ACM International Conference on Digital Libraries (DL).

Brin, S. (1998). Extracting Patterns and Relations from the World Wide Web. WebDB Workshop at 6th International Conference on Extending Database Technology, EDBT'98, Valencia, Spain.

Chen, J., D. Ji, et al. (2005). Unsupervised Feature Selection for Relation Extraction IJCNLP-05, Jeju Island, Korea.

Cowie, J. and W. Lehnert (1996). "Information Extraction." Communications of the Association of Computing Machinery **39**(1): 80-91.

Downey, D., O. Etzioni, et al. (2004). Learning Text Patterns for Web Information Extraction and Assessment (Extended Version). Technical Report UW-CSE-04-05-01.

Etzioni, O., M. Cafarella, et al. (2005). "Unsupervised named-entity extraction from the Web: An experimental study." Artificial Intelligence **165**(1): 91-134.

Freitag, D. (1998). Machine Learning for Information Extraction in Informal Domains. Computer Science Department. Pittsburgh, PA, Carnegie Mellon University**:** 188.

Freitag, D. and A. K. McCallum (1999). Information extraction with HMMs and shrinkage. Proceedings of the AAAI-99 Workshop on Machine Learning for Information Extraction.

Genkin, A., D. D. Lewis, et al. (2004). Large-Scale Bayesian Logistic Regression for Text Categorization. New Brunswick, NJ, DIMACS**:** 1-41.

Grishman, R. (1996). The role of syntax in Information Extraction. Advances in Text Processing: Tipster Program Phase II, Morgan Kaufmann.

Grishman, R. (1997). Information Extraction: Techniques and Challenges. SCIE**:** 10-27.

Hasegawa, T., S. Sekine, et al. (2004). Discovering Relations among Named Entities from Large Corpora. ACL 2004.

Kushmerick, N., D. S. Weld, et al. (1997). Wrapper Induction for Information Extraction. IJCAI-97**:** 729-737.

Ravichandran, D. and E. Hovy (2002). Learning Surface Text Patterns for a Question Answering System. 40th ACL Conference.

Riloff, E. (1993). Automatically Constructing a Dictionary for Information Extraction Tasks. AAAI-93.

Riloff, E. and R. Jones (1999). Learning Dictionaries for Information Extraction by Multi-level Boot-strapping. AAAI-99.

Soderland, S. (1999). "Learning Information Extraction Rules for Semi-Structured and Free Text." Machine Learning **34**(1-3): 233-272.

Short Text Authorship Attribution via Sequence Kernels, Markov Chains and Author Unmasking: An Investigation

Conrad Sanderson and Simon Guenter
Australian National University, Canberra, ACT 0200, Australia
National ICT Australia, Locked Bag 8001, ACT 2601, Australia
conrad.sanderson @ anu.edu.au, simon.guenter @ rsise.anu.edu.au

Abstract

We present an investigation of recently proposed character and word sequence kernels for the task of authorship attribution based on relatively short texts. Performance is compared with two corresponding probabilistic approaches based on Markov chains. Several configurations of the sequence kernels are studied on a relatively large dataset (50 authors), where each author covered several topics. Utilising Moffat smoothing, the two probabilistic approaches obtain similar performance, which in turn is comparable to that of character sequence kernels and is better than that of word sequence kernels. The results further suggest that when using a realistic setup that takes into account the case of texts which are not written by any hypothesised authors, the amount of training material has more influence on discrimination performance than the amount of test material. Moreover, we show that the recently proposed author unmasking approach is less useful when dealing with short texts.

1 Introduction

Applications of authorship attribution include plagiarism detection (e.g. college essays), deducing the writer of inappropriate communications that were sent anonymously or under a pseudonym (e.g. threatening or harassing e-mails), as well as resolving historical questions of unclear or disputed authorship. Specific examples are the Federalist papers (Hanus and Hagenauer, 2005; Mosteller, 1984) and the forensic analysis of the Unabomber manifesto (Foster, 2001).

Within the area of automatic author attribution, recently it has been shown that encouraging performance can be achieved via the use of probabilistic models based on n-grams (Clement and Sharp, 2003) and Markov chains of characters and words (Peng et al., 2004). Diederich et al. (2003) showed that Support Vector Machines (SVMs), using the bag-of-words kernel, can obtain promising performance, while in another study, SVMs with kernels based on character collocations obtained mixed performance (Corney, 2003). Gamon (2004) utilised SVMs with syntactic and semantic features to obtain relatively minor accuracy improvements over the use of function word frequencies and part-of-speech trigrams. Koppel & Schler (2004) proposed a word-level heuristic, resembling recursive feature elimination used for cancer classification (Guyon et al., 2002; Huang and Kecman, 2005), to obtain *author unmasking* curves. The curves were processed to obtain feature vectors that were in turn classified in a traditional SVM setting.

The studies listed above have several limitations. In (Clement and Sharp, 2003), a rudimentary probability smoothing technique was used to handle n-grams which were unseen during the training phase. In the dataset used by (Peng et al., 2004) each author tended to stick to one or two topics, raising the possibility that the discrimination was based on topic rather than by author style.

In (Corney, 2003; Gamon, 2004; Peng et al., 2004; Koppel and Schler, 2004) the datasets were rather small in terms of the number of authors, indicating the results may not be generalisable. Specifically, in (Corney, 2003) the largest dataset contains texts from five authors, in (Gamon, 2004) from three, while in (Peng et al., 2004) and (Koppel and Schler, 2004) from ten.

In (Clement and Sharp, 2003; Gamon, 2004; Peng et al., 2004), the attribution of a given document was forced to one of the authors from a set of possible authors (i.e. a closed set identification setup), thus not taking into account the realistic case of having a document which was not

Proceedings of the 2006 Conference on Empirical Methods in Natural Language Processing (EMNLP 2006), pages 482–491,
Sydney, July 2006.

written by any of the authors. In (Koppel and Schler, 2004), the unmasking method was evaluated exclusively on books, raising the question as to whether the method is applicable to considerably shorter texts.

Lastly, all of the studies used different datasets and experiment setups, thus making a quantitative performance comparison of the different approaches infeasible.

Recently, various practical character and word sequence kernels have been proposed (Cancedda et al., 2003; Leslie et al., 2004; Vishwanathan and Smola, 2003) for the purposes of text and biological sequence analysis. This allows kernel based techniques (such as SVMs) to be used in lieu of traditional probabilistic approaches based on Markov chains. In comparison to the latter, SVMs have the advantage of directly optimising the discrimination criterion.

This paper has four main aims: **(i)** to evaluate the usefulness of sequence kernel based approaches for the task of authorship attribution; **(ii)** to compare their performance with two probabilistic approaches based on Markov chains of characters and words; **(iii)** to appraise the applicability of the author unmasking approach for dealing with short texts; and **(iv)** to address some of the limitations of the previous studies.

Several configurations of the sequence kernels are studied. The evaluations are done on a relatively large dataset (50 authors) where each author covers several topics. Rather than using long texts (such as books), in almost all of the experiments the amount of training and test material per author is varied from approx. 300 to 5000 words for both cases. Moreover, rather than using a closed set identification setup, the evaluations are done using a verification setup. Here, a given text material is classified as either having been written by a hypothesised author or as not written by that author (i.e. a two class discrimination task).

The paper is structured as follows. Section 2 describes author attribution systems based on Markov chains of characters and words, followed by a description of the corresponding sequence kernel based approaches in Section 3. Section 4 provides an empirical performance comparison of the abovementioned approaches, while in Section 5 the author unmasking method is appraised. Section 6 concludes the paper by presenting the main findings and suggesting future directions.

2 Markov Chain Based Approaches

The opinion on how likely a given text X was written by author A, rather than any other author, can be found by a log likelihood ratio:

$$\mathcal{O}_{A,G}(X) = |e_z(X)|^{-1} \log \left[p_A(e_z(X)) \, / \, p_G(e_z(X)) \right]$$

where $z \in \{words, chars\}$, $e_z(X)$ extracts an ordered set of items from X (where the items are either words or characters, indicated by z), $|e_z(X)|^{-1}$ is used as a normalisation for varying number of items, while $p_A(e_z(X))$ and $p_G(e_z(X))$ estimate the likelihood of the text having been written by author A and a *generic* author[1], G, respectively.

Given a threshold t, text X is classified as having been written by author A when $\mathcal{O}_{A,G}(X) > t$, or as written by someone else when $\mathcal{O}_{A,G}(X) \leq t$. The $|e_z(X)|^{-1}$ normalisation term allows for the use of a common threshold (i.e. shared by all authors), which facilitates the interpretation of performance (e.g. via the use of the Equal Error Rate (EER) point on a Receiver Operating Characteristic (ROC) curve (Ortega-Garcia et al., 2004)).

Appropriating a technique originally used in language modelling (Chen and Goodman, 1999), the likelihood of author A having written a particular sequence of items, $X = (i_1, i_2, \cdots, i_{|X|})$, can be approximated using the joint probability of all present m-th order Markov chains:

$$p_A(X) \approx \prod\nolimits_{j=(m+1)}^{|X|} p_A\left(i_j | i_{j-m}^{j-1}\right) \qquad (1)$$

where i_{j-m}^{j-1} is a shorthand for $i_{j-m} \cdots i_{j-1}$ and m indicates the length of the history. Given training material for author A, denoted as X_A, the maximum likelihood (ML) probability estimate for a particular m-th order Markov chain is:

$$p_A^{ml}\left(i_j | i_{j-m}^{j-1}\right) = C\left(i_{j-m}^{j} | X_A\right) / \, C\left(i_{j-m}^{j-1} | X_A\right) \qquad (2)$$

where $C\left(i_{j-m}^{j} | X_A\right)$ is the number of times the sequence i_{j-m}^{j} occurs in X_A. For chains that have not been seen during training, elaborate smoothing techniques (Chen and Goodman, 1999) are utilised to avoid zero probabilities in Eqn. (1).

The probabilities for the generic author are estimated from a dataset comprised of texts from many authors.

In this work we utilise interpolated Moffat smoothing[2], where the probability of an m-th or-

[1] A *generic* author is a composite of a number of authors.

[2] Moffat smoothing is often mistakenly referred to as Witten-Bell smoothing. Witten & Bell (1991) referred to this technique as *Method C* and cited Moffat (1988).

der chain is a linear interpolation of its ML estimate and the smoothed probability estimate of the corresponding (m-1)-th order chain:

$$p_A^{mof}\left(i_j|i_{j\text{-}m}^{j\text{-}1}\right) = \alpha_{i_{j\text{-}m}^{j\text{-}1}}\, p_A^{ml}\left(i_j|i_{j\text{-}m}^{j\text{-}1}\right) + \beta_{i_{j\text{-}m}^{j\text{-}1}}\, p_A^{mof}\left(i_j|i_{j\text{-}(m\text{-}1)}^{j\text{-}1}\right)$$

where $\alpha_{i_{j\text{-}m}^{j\text{-}1}} = 1 - \beta_{i_{j\text{-}m}^{j\text{-}1}}$, and

$$\beta_{i_{j-m}^{j-1}} = \frac{\left|i_j : \mathcal{C}\left(i_{j-m}^{j-1} i_j | X_A\right) > 0\right|}{\left|i_j : \mathcal{C}\left(i_{j-m}^{j-1} i_j | X_A\right) > 0\right| + \sum_{i_j} \mathcal{C}\left(i_{j-m}^{j} | X_A\right)}$$

Here, $\left|i_j : \mathcal{C}\left(i_{j-m}^{j-1} i_j | X_A\right) > 0\right|$ is the number of unique (m+1)-grams that have the same i_{j-m}^{j-1} history items. Further elucidation of this method is given in (Chen and Goodman, 1999; Witten and Bell, 1991).

The (m-1)-th order probability will typically correlate with the m-th order probability and has the advantage of being estimated from a larger number of examples (Chen and Goodman, 1999). The 0-th order probability is interpolated with the uniform distribution, given by: $p_A^{unif} = 1/|V_A|$, where $|V_A|$ is the vocabulary size (Chen and Goodman, 1999).

When an m-th order chain has a history (i.e. the items i_{j-m}^{j-1}) which hasn't been observed during training, a back-off to the corresponding reduced order chain is done[3]:

$$\text{if } \mathcal{C}\left(i_{j-m}^{j-1}|X_A\right) = 0,\ \ p_A^{mof}\left(i_j|i_{j-m}^{j-1}\right) = p_A^{mof}\left(i_j|i_{j-(m-1)}^{j-1}\right)$$

Note that if the 0-th order chain also hasn't been observed during training, we are effectively backing off to the uniform distribution.

A caveat: the training dataset for an author can be much smaller (and hence have a smaller vocabulary) than the combined training dataset for the generic author, resulting in $p_A^{unif} > p_G^{unif}$. Thus when a previously unseen chain is encountered there is a dangerous bias towards author A, i.e., $p_A^{mof}\left(i_j|i_{j-m}^{j-1}\right) > p_G^{mof}\left(i_j|i_{j-m}^{j-1}\right)$. To avoid this, p_A^{unif} must be set equal to p_G^{unif}.

3 Sequence Kernel Based Approaches

Kernel based techniques, such as SVMs, allow the comparison of, and discrimination between, vectorial as well as non-vectorial objects. In a binary SVM, the opinion on whether object X belongs to class -1 or +1 is given by:

$$\mathcal{O}_{+1,-1}(X) = \sum_{j=1}^{|S|} \lambda_j\, y_j\, k(s_j, X) + b \quad (3)$$

where $k(X_A, X_B)$ is a symmetric kernel function which reflects the degree of similarity between objects X_A and X_B, while $S = (s_j)_{j=1}^{|S|}$ is a set of support objects with corresponding class labels $(y_j \in \{-1, +1\})_{j=1}^{|S|}$ and weights $\Lambda = (\lambda_j)_{j=1}^{|S|}$. The kernel function, b as well as sets S and Λ define a hyperplane which separates the +1 and -1 classes. Given a training dataset, quadratic programming based optimisation is used to maximise the separation margin[4] (Schölkopf and Smola, 2002; Shawe-Taylor and Cristianini, 2004).

Recently, kernels for measuring the similarity of texts based on sequences of characters and words have been proposed (Cancedda et al., 2003; Leslie et al., 2004; Vishwanathan and Smola, 2003). One kernel belonging to this family is:

$$k(X_A, X_B) = \sum_{q \in Q^\star} w_q\, \mathcal{C}(q|X_A)\, \mathcal{C}(q|X_B) \quad (4)$$

where $Q^\star$ represents all possible sequences, in X_A and X_B, of the symbols in Q. In turn, Q is a set of possible symbols, which can be characters, e.g. $Q = \{$ 'a', 'b', 'c', $\cdots\}$, or words, e.g. $Q = \{$'kangaroo', 'koala', 'platypus', $\cdots\}$. Furthermore, $\mathcal{C}(q|X)$ is the number of occurrences of sequence q in X, and w_q is the weight for sequence q. If the sequences are restricted to have only one item, Eqn. (4) for the case of words is in effect a bag-of-words kernel (Cancedda et al., 2003; Shawe-Taylor and Cristianini, 2004).

In this work we have utilised weights that were dependent only on the length of each sequence, i.e. $w_q = w_{|q|}$. By default $w_{|q|} = 0$, modified by one of the following functions:

specific length: $w_{|q|} = 1$, if $|q| = \tau$
bounded range: $w_{|q|} = 1$, if $|q| \in [1, \tau]$
bounded linear decay: $w_{|q|} = 1 + \frac{1-|q|}{\tau}$, if $|q| \in [1, \tau]$
bounded linear growth: $w_{|q|} = |q| / \tau$, if $|q| \in [1, \tau]$

where τ indicates a user defined maximum sequence length.

To allow comparison of texts with different lengths, a normalised version (Schölkopf and Smola, 2002; Shawe-Taylor and Cristianini, 2004) of the kernel can be used:

$$\hat{k}(X_A, X_B) = k(X_A, X_B) \,/\, \sqrt{k(X_A, X_A)\, k(X_B, X_B)}$$

with constraints $|X_A| \geq 1$ and $|X_B| \geq 1$.

It has been suggested that SVM discrimination based on character sequence kernels in effect utilises a noisy version of stemming (Cancedda et al., 2003). As such, word sequence kernels could be more effective than character sequence

[3]Personal correspondence with the authors of (Chen and Goodman, 1999).

[4]Based on preliminary experiments, the regularisation constant C, used in SVM training, was set to 100.

kernels, since proper word stems, instead of full words, can be explicitly used. However, it must be noted that Eqn. (4) implicitly maps texts to a feature space which has one dimension for each of the possible sequences comprised of the symbols from Q (Cancedda et al., 2003). When using words, the number of unique symbols (i.e. $|Q|$) can be much greater than when using characters (e.g. 10,000 vs 100); furthermore, for a given text the number of words is always smaller than the number of characters. For a given sequence length, these observations indicate that for word sequence kernels the implicit feature space representation can have considerably higher dimensionality and be sparser than for character sequence kernels, which could lead to poorer generalisation of the resulting classifier.

4 Evaluation

4.1 "Columnists" Dataset

We have compiled a dataset that is comprised of texts from 50 newspaper journalists, with a minimum of 10,000 words per journalist. Journalists were selected based on their coverage of several topics; any journalist who covered only one specific area (e.g. sports or economics) was not included in the dataset. Apart from removing all advertising material and standardising the representation by converting any unicode characters to their closest ASCII counterparts, no further editing was performed. The dataset is available for use by other researchers by contacting the authors.

4.2 Setup

The experiments followed a verification setup, where a given text material was classified as either having been written by a hypothesised author or as not written by that author (i.e. a two class discrimination task). This is distinct from a closed set identification setup, where a text is assigned as belonging to one author out of a pool of authors. The presentation of an *impostor text* (a text known not to be written by the hypothesised author) will be referred to as an *impostor claim*, while the presentation of a *true text* (a text known to be written by the hypothesised author) will be referred to as a *true claim*.

For a given text, one of the following two classification errors can occur: **(i)** a false positive, where an impostor text is incorrectly classified as a true text; **(ii)** a false negative, where a true text is incorrectly classified as an impostor text. The errors are measured in terms of the false positive rate (FPR) and the false negative rate (FNR). Following the approach often used within the biometrics field, the decision threshold was then adjusted so that the FPR is equal to the FNR, giving Equal Error Rate (EER) performance (Ortega-Garcia et al., 2004; Sanderson et al., 2006).

The authors in the database were randomly assigned into two disjoint sections: **(i)** 10 background authors; **(ii)** 40 evaluation authors. For the case of Markov chain approaches, texts from the background authors were used to construct the generic author model, while for kernel based approaches they were used to represent the negative class. In both cases, text materials each comprised of approx. 28,000 characters were used, via randomly choosing a sufficient number of sentences from the pooled texts. Table 1 shows a correspondence between the number of characters and words, using the average word length of 5.6 characters including a trailing whitespace (found on the whole dataset).

For each author in the evaluation section, their material was randomly split[5] into two continuous parts: training and testing. The split occurred without breaking sentences. The training material was used to construct the author model, while the test material was used to simulate a true claim as well as impostor claims against all other authors' models. Note that if material from the evaluation section was used for constructing the generic author model, the system would have prior knowledge about the writing style of the authors used for the impostor claims.

For each configuration of an approach (where, for example, the configuration is the order of the Markov chains), the above procedure was repeated ten times, with the randomised assignments and splitting being done each time. The final results

Table 1: Approximate correspondence between the number of characters and number of words. For comparison purposes, this paper has about 5900 words.

No. characters	1750	3500	7000	14000	28000
No. words	312	625	1250	2500	5000

[5]By 'randomly split' we mean that the location of the training and testing parts within the text material is random.

were then obtained in terms of the mean and the corresponding standard deviation of the ten EERs (the standard deviations are shown as error bars in the result figures). Based on preliminary experiments, stemming was used for word based approaches (Manning and Schütze, 1999).

4.3 Experiments and Discussion

In the first experiment we studied the effects of varying the order for character and word Markov chain approaches, while the amount of training material was fixed at approx. 28,000 characters and the test material (for evaluation authors) was decreased from approx. 28,000 to 1,750 characters. Results are presented in Fig. 1.

The results show that 2nd order chains of characters generally obtain the best performance. However, the difference in performance between 1st order and 2nd order chains could be considered as statistically insignificant due to the large overlap of the error bars. The best performing word chain approach had an order of zero, with higher orders (not shown) having virtually the same performance as the 0th order. Its performance is largely similar to the 2nd order character chain approach, with the latter obtaining a somewhat lower error rate at 28,000 characters.

The second experiment was similar to the first, with the difference being that the amount of training material *and* test material was decreased from approx. 28,000 to 1,750 characters. The main change between the results of this experiment (shown in Fig. 2) and the previous experiment's results is the faster degradation in performance as the number of characters is decreased. We comment on this effect later.

In the third experiment we utilised SVMs with character sequence kernels and studied the effects of chunk size. As SVMs employ support objects in the definition of the discriminant function (see Section 3), the training material was split into varying size chunks, ranging from approximately 62 to 4000 characters. Each of the chunks can become a support chunk. Naturally, the smaller the chunk size, the larger the number of chunks. As the split was done without breaking sentences, the effective chunk size tended to be somewhat larger. If there is less words available than a given chunk size, then all of the remaining words are used for forming a chunk. Based on preliminary experiments, the bounded range weight function with

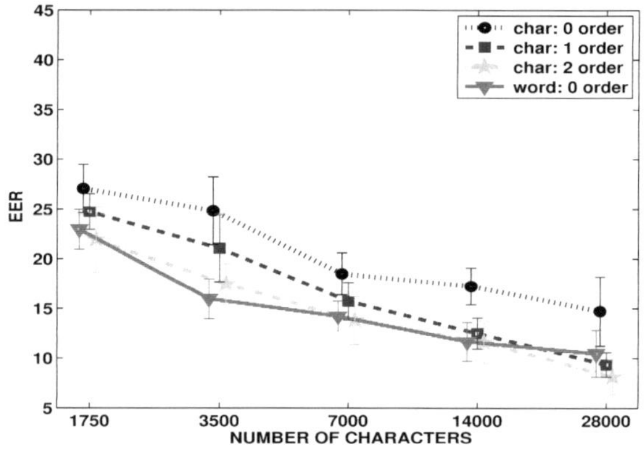

Figure 1: Performance of character and word Markov chain approaches using fixed size training material (approx. 28,000 characters) and varying size test material.

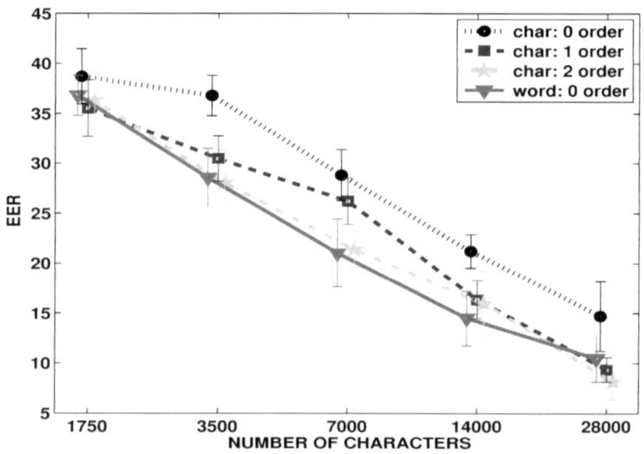

Figure 2: Performance of character and word Markov chain approaches for varying size of training and test material. At each point the size of the training and test materials is equal.

τ=3 was used. The amount of training and test material was equal and three cases were evaluated: 28,000, 14,000 and 7,000 characters. Results, presented in Fig. 3, indicate that the optimum chunk size is approximately 500 characters for the three cases. Furthermore, the optimum chunk size appears to be independent of the number of available chunks for training.

In the fourth experiment we studied the effects of various weight functions and sequence lengths for the character sequence kernel. The amount of training and test material was fixed at approx. 28,000 characters. Based on the results from the previous experiment, chunk size was set at 500. Results for specific length (Fig. 4) suggest that most of the reliable discriminatory information is contained in sequences of length 2. The error rates for the bounded range and bounded lin-

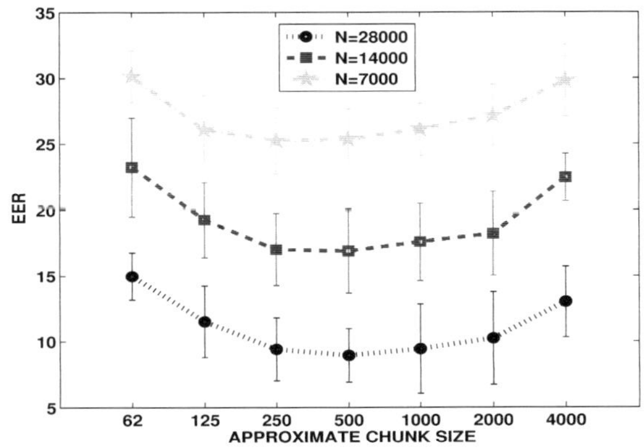

Figure 3: Performance of the character sequence kernel approach for varying chunk sizes. Bounded range weight function with τ=3 was used.

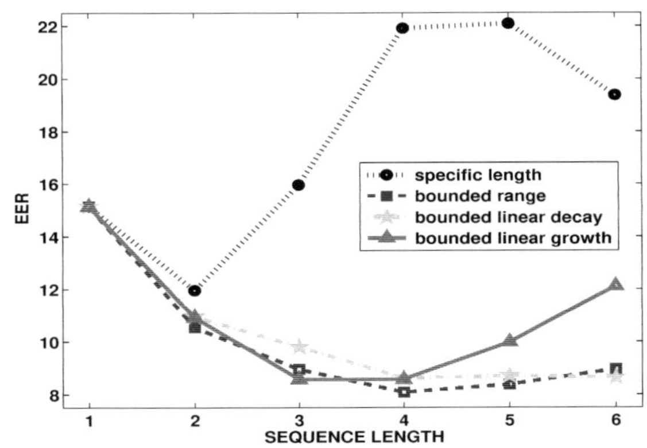

Figure 4: Performance of the character sequence kernel approach for various weight functions. The size of training and test materials was fixed at approx. 28,000 characters. Chunk size of 500 characters was used. Error bars were omitted for clarity.

ear decay functions are quite similar, with both reaching minima for sequences of length 4; most of the improvement occurs when the sequences reach a length of 3. This indicates that while sequences with a specific length of 3 and 4 are less reliable than sequences with a specific length of 2, they contain (partly) complementary information which is useful when combined with information from shorter lengths. Emphasising longer lengths of 5 and 6 (via the bounded linear growth function) achieves a minor, but noticeable, performance degradation. We conjecture that the degradation is caused by the sparsity of relatively long sequences, which affects the generalisation of the classifier.

The fifth experiment was devoted to an evaluation of the effects of chunk size for the word se-

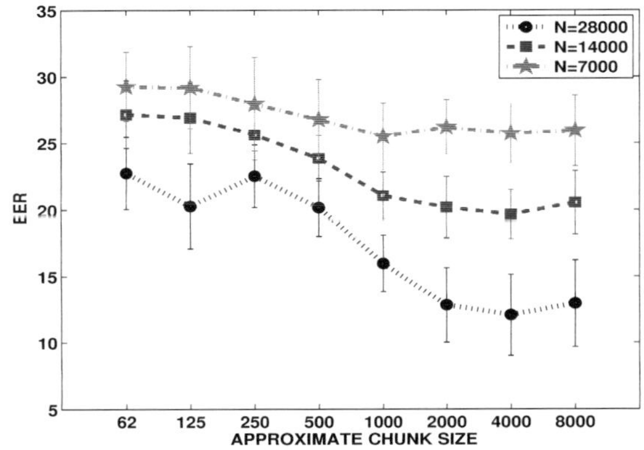

Figure 5: Performance of the word sequence kernel approach for varying chunk sizes. Specific length weight function with τ=1 was used.

quence approach. To keep the results comparable with the character sequence approach (third experiment), the training material was split into varying size chunks, ranging from approximately 62 to 8000 characters. Based on the results from the first experiment, the specific length weight function with τ=1 was used[6] (resulting in a bag-of-words kernel).

The amount of training and test material was equal and three cases were evaluated: 28,000, 14,000 and 7,000 characters. Results, shown in Fig. 5, suggest that the optimum chunk size is approximately 4000 characters for the three cases.

As mentioned in Section 3, for the word based approach the implicit feature space representation can have considerably higher dimensionality and be sparser than for the character based approach. Consequently, longer texts would be required to adequately populate the feature space. This is reflected by the optimum chunk size for the word based approach, which is roughly an order of magnitude larger than the optimum chunk size for the character based approach.

In the sixth experiment we compared the performance of character sequence kernels (using the bounded range function with τ=4) and several configurations of the word sequence kernels. The amount of training material was fixed at approx. 28,000 characters and the test material was decreased from approx. 28,000 to 1,750 characters. Based on the results of previous experiments, chunk size was set to 500 for the character based approach and to 4000 for the word based

[6] Note that for τ=1, all of the weight functions presented in Section 3 are equivalent.

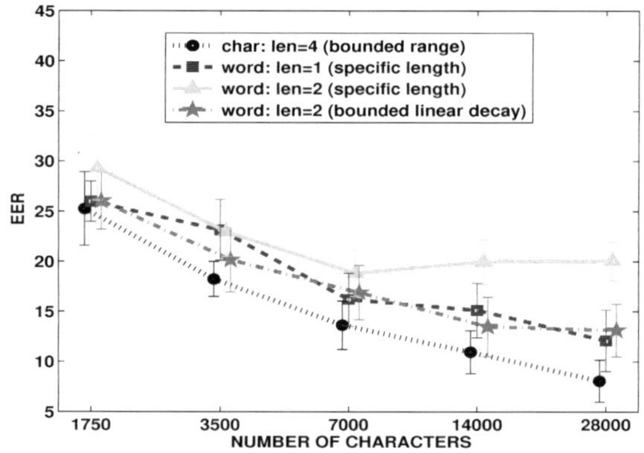

Figure 6: Performance of character and word sequence kernel approaches using fixed size training material (approx. 28,000 characters) and varying size test material.

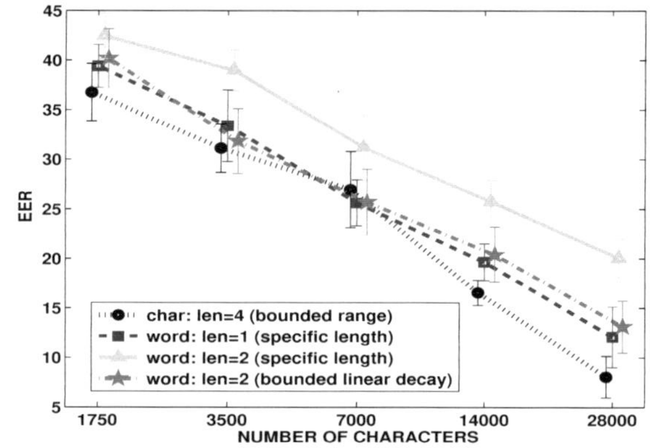

Figure 7: Performance of character and word sequence kernel approaches for varying size of training and test material. At each point the size of the training and test materials is equal.

approach. Fig. 6 shows that word sequences with a specific length of 2 lead to considerably worse performance than sequences of length 1 (i.e. individual words). Furthermore, the best performing combination of lengths (i.e. via the bounded linear decay function[7]) does not provide better performance than using individual words. The character sequence kernels consistently achieve a lower error rate than the best performing word sequence kernel. This suggests that the sparse feature space representation, described in Section 3, is becoming an issue.

The final experiment was similar to the sixth, with the difference being that the amount of training material and test material was decreased from approx. 28,000 to 1,750 characters. As observed for the Markov chain approaches, the main change between the results of this experiment (shown in Fig. 7) and the previous experiment's results is the faster degradation in performance as the number of characters is decreased. Along with the results from experiments 1 and 2, this indicates that the amount of training material has considerably more influence on discrimination performance than the amount of test material.

In Fig. 8 it can be observed that the best performing Markov chain based approach (characters, 2nd order) obtains comparable performance to the character sequence kernel based approach (using the bounded range function with τ=4).

[7]Other combinations of lengths were also evaluated, though the results are not shown here.

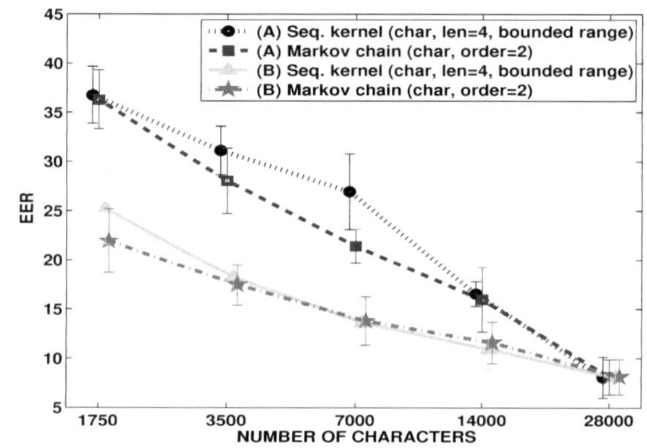

Figure 8: Comparison between the best sequence kernel approach with the best Markov chain approach for two cases: **(A)** varying size of training and test material, **(B)** fixed size training material (approx. 28,000 characters) and varying size test material.

5 Author Unmasking On Short Texts

Koppel & Schler (2004) proposed an alternative method for author verification. Rather than treating the verification problem directly as a two-class discrimination task (as done in Section 4), an "author unmasking" curve is first built. A vector representing the "essential features" of the curve is then classified in a traditional SVM setting. The unmasking procedure is reminiscent of the recursive feature elimination procedure first proposed in the context of gene selection for cancer classification (Guyon et al., 2002).

Instead of having an author specific model (as in the Markov chain approach) or an author specific SVM, a reference text is used. The text to be

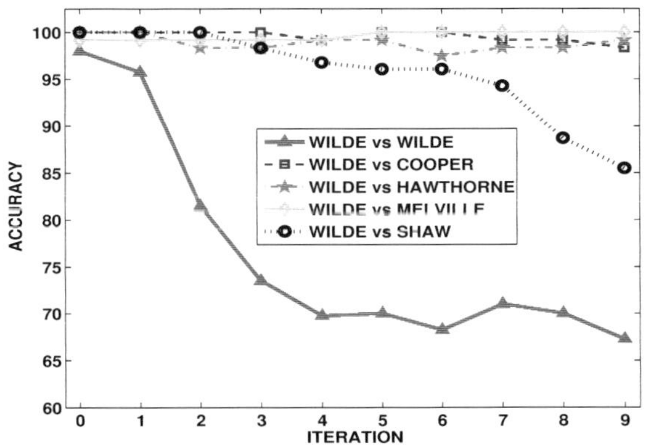

Figure 9: Unmasking of Wilde's *An Ideal Husband* using Wilde's *Woman of No Importance* as well as the works of other authors as reference texts.

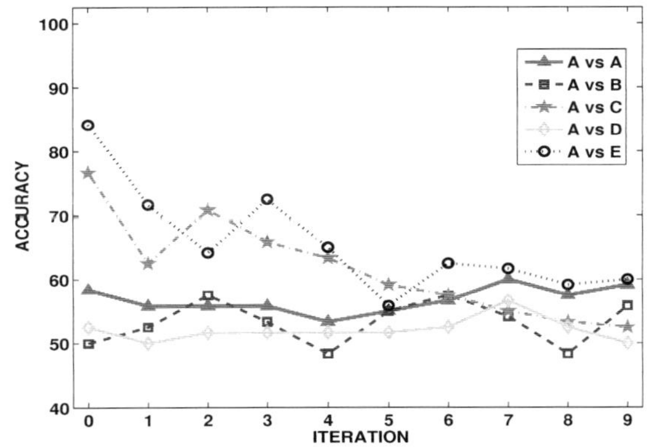

Figure 10: Unmasking of a text from author A from the Columnists dataset, using A's as well as other authors' reference texts.

classified as well as the reference text are divided into chunks; the features representing each chunk are the counts of pre-selected words. Each point in the author unmasking curve is the cross-validation accuracy of discriminating between the two sets of chunks (using a linear SVM). At each iteration, several of the most discriminative features are removed from further consideration.

The underlying hypothesis is that if the two given texts have been written by the same author, the differences between them will be reflected in a relatively small number of features. Koppel & Schler (2004) observed that for texts authored by the same person, the extent of the cross-validation accuracy degradation is much larger than for texts written by different authors. Encouraging classification results were obtained for long texts (books available from Project Gutenberg[8]).

In this section we first confirm the unmasking effect for long texts and then show that for shorter texts (i.e. approx. 5000 words), the effect is considerably less distinctive.

For the first experiment we followed the setup in (Koppel and Schler, 2004), i.e. the same books, chunks with a size of approximately 500 words, 10 fold cross-validation, removing 6 features at each iteration, and using 250 words with the highest average frequency in both texts as the set of pre-selected words. Fig. 9 shows curves for unmasking Oscar Wilde's *An Ideal Husband* using Wilde's *Woman of No Importance* (same-author curve) as well as the works of other authors as reference texts (different-author curves). As can be observed, the unmasking effect is most pronounced for Wilde's text. Furthermore, this figure has a close resemblance to Fig. 2 in (Koppel and Schler, 2004).

[8]http://www.gutenberg.org

Table 2: Performance of author unmasking, character sequence kernel approach ($\tau = 4$, bounded range) and character Markov chain approach (2nd order).

Approach	mean EER	std. dev.
Author unmasking	30.88	4.32
Character sequence kernel	8.08	2.08
Character Markov chain	8.14	1.79

In the second experiment we used text materials from the Columnists dataset. Each author's text material was divided into two sections of approximately 5000 words, with the one of the sections randomly selected to be the reference material, leaving the other as the test material. Based on preliminary experiments, the number of preselected words was set to 100 (with the highest average frequency in both texts) and the size of the chunks was set to 200 words. The remainder of the unmasking procedure setup was the same as for the first experiment. The setup for verification trials was similar to the setup in Section 4.2, with the difference being that the background authors were used to generate same-author and different-author curves for training the secondary SVM. In all cases features from each curve were extracted, as done in (Koppel and Schler, 2004), prior to further processing.

Table 2 provides a comparison between the performance of the unmasking approach with that of the character sequence kernel and character

Markov chain based approaches, as evaluated in Section 4. Fig. 10 shows representative curves resulting from unmasking of the test material from author A, using A's as well as other authors' reference materials. Generally, the unmasking effect for the same-author curves is considerably less pronounced and in some cases it is non-existent. More dangerously, different-author curves often have close similarities to same-author curves. The results and the above observations hence suggest that the unmasking method is less useful when dealing with relatively short texts.

6 Main Findings and Future Directions

In this paper we investigated the use of character and word sequence kernels for the task of authorship attribution and compared their performance with two probabilistic approaches based on Markov chains of characters and words. The evaluations were done on a relatively large dataset (50 authors), where each author covered several topics. Rather than using the restrictive closed set identification setup, a verification setup was used which takes into account the realistic case of texts which are not written by any hypothesised authors. We also appraised the applicability of the recently proposed author unmasking approach for dealing with relatively short texts.

In the framework of Support Vector Machines, several configurations of the sequence kernels were studied, showing that word sequence kernels do not achieve better performance than a bag-of-words kernel. Character sequence kernels (using sequences with a length of 4) generally have better performance than the bag-of-words kernel and also have comparable performance to the two probabilistic approaches.

A possible advantage of character sequence kernels over word-based kernels is their inherent ability to do partial matching of words. Let us consider two examples. **(i)** Given the words "negotiation" and "negotiate", the character sequence kernel can match "negotiat", while a standard word-based kernel requires explicit word stemming beforehand in order to match the two related words (as done in our experiments). **(ii)** Given the words "negotiation" and "desalination", a character sequence kernel can match the common ending "ation". Particular word endings may be indicative of a particular author's style; such information would not be picked up by a standard word-based kernel.

Interestingly, the bag-of-words kernel based approach obtains worse performance than the corresponding word based Markov chain approach. Apart from the issue of sparse feature space representation, factors such as the chunk size and the setting of the C parameter in SVM training can also affect the generalisation performance.

The results also show that the amount of training material has more influence on discrimination performance than the amount of test material; about 5000 training words are required to obtain relatively good performance when using between 1250 and 5000 test words.

Further experiments suggest that the author unmasking approach is less useful when dealing with relatively short texts, due to the unmasking effect being considerably less pronounced than for long texts and also due to different-author unmasking curves having close similarities to the same-author curves.

In future work it would be useful to appraise composite kernels (Joachims et al., 2001) in order to combine character and word sequence kernels. If the two kernel types use (partly) complementary information, better performance could be achieved. Furthermore, more sophisticated character sequence kernels can be evaluated, such as mismatch string kernels used in bioinformatics, where mutations in the sequences are allowed (Leslie et al., 2004).

Acknowledgements

The authors thank the anonymous reviewers as well as Simon Burton, Ari Chanen, Arvin Dehghani, Etienne Grossmann, Adam Kowalczyk and Silvia Richter for useful suggestions and discussions.

National ICT Australia (NICTA) is funded by the Australian Government's *Backing Australia's Ability* initiative, in part through the Australian Research Council.

References

N. Cancedda, E. Gaussier, C. Goutte, and J.-M. Renders. 2003. Word-sequence kernels. *J. Machine Learning Research*, 3:1059–1082.

S.F. Chen and J. Goodman. 1999. An empirical study of smoothing techniques for language modeling. *Computer Speech and Language*, 13:359–394.

R. Clement and D. Sharp. 2003. Ngram and Bayesian classification of documents for topic and authorship. *Literary and Linguistic Computing*, 18(4):423–447.

M. W. Corney. 2003. Analysing e-mail text authorship for forensic purposes. Master's thesis, Queensland University of Technology, Australia.

J. Diederich, J. Kindermann, E. Leopold, and G. Paass. 2003. Authorship attribution with support vector machines. *Applied Intelligence*, 19(1-2):109–123.

D. W. Foster. 2001. *Author Unknown: On the Trail of Anonymous*. Henry Holt & Company, 2nd ed.

M. Gamon. 2004. Linguistic correlates of style: authorship classification with deep linguistic analysis features. In *Proc. 20th Int. Conf. Computational Linguistics (COLING)*, pages 611–617, Geneva.

I. Guyon, J. Weston, S. Barnhill, and V. Vapnik. 2002. Gene selection for cancer classification using support vector machines. *Machine Learning*, 46:389–422.

P. Hanus and J. Hagenauer. 2005. Information theory helps historians. *IEEE Information Theory Society Newsletter*, 55(September):8.

T.-M. Huang and V. Kecman. 2005. Gene extraction for cancer diagnosis by support vector machines – an improvement and comparison with nearest shrunken centroid method. In *Proc. 15th Int. Conf. Artificial Neural Networks (ICANN)*, pages 617–624, Warsaw.

T. Joachims, N. Cristianini, and J. Shawe-Taylor. 2001. Composite kernels for hypertext categorisation. In *Proc. 18th Int. Conf. Machine Learning (ICML)*, pages 250–257, Massachusetts.

M. Koppel and J. Schler. 2004. Authorship verification as a one-class classification problem. In *Proc. 21st Int. Conf. Machine Learning (ICML)*, Banff, Canada.

C. Leslie, E. Eskin, A. Cohen, J. Weston, and W. Noble. 2004. Mismatch string kernels for discriminative protein classification. *Bioinformatics*, 20(4):467–476.

C.D Manning and H. Schütze. 1999. *Foundations of Statistical Natural Language Processing*. MIT Press.

A. Moffat. 1988. A note on the PPM data compression algorithm, Res. Report. 88/7, Dept. Comput. Sci., University of Melbourne, Australia.

F. Mosteller. 1984. *Applied Bayesian and Classical Inference: The Case of the Federalist Papers*. Springer, 2nd edition.

J. Ortega-Garcia, J. Bigun, D. Reynolds, and J. Gonzalez-Rodriguez. 2004. Authentication gets personal with biometrics. *IEEE Signal Processing Magazine*, 21(2):50–62.

F. Peng, D. Schuurmans, and S. Wang. 2004. Augmenting naive Bayes classifiers with statistical language models. *Information Retrieval*, 7:317–345.

C. Sanderson, S. Bengio, and Y. Gao. 2006. On transforming statistical models for non-frontal face verification. *Pattern Recognition*, 39(2):288–302.

B. Schölkopf and A. Smola. 2002. *Learning with Kernels: Support Vector Machines, Regularization, Optimization and Beyond*. The MIT Press, USA.

J. Shawe-Taylor and N. Cristianini. 2004. *Kernel Methods for Pattern Analysis*. Cambridge University Press, UK.

S.V.N. Vishwanathan and A. Smola. 2003. Fast kernels for string and tree matching. In *Advances in Neural Information Processing Systems (NIPS) 15*, pages 569–576, Cambridge. MIT Press.

I.H. Witten and T.C. Bell. 1991. The zero-frequency problem: Estimating the probabilities of novel events in adaptive text compression. *IEEE Trans. Information Theory*, 37(4):1085–1094.

Entity Annotation based on Inverse Index Operations

Ganesh Ramakrishnan, Sreeram Balakrishnan, Sachindra Joshi
IBM India Research Labs
IIT Delhi, Hauz Khas,
New Delhi, India
{ganramkr, sreevb, jsachind}@in.ibm.com

Abstract

Entity annotation involves attaching a label such as 'name' or 'organization' to a sequence of tokens in a document. All the current rule-based and machine learning-based approaches for this task operate at the document level. We present a new and generic approach to entity annotation which uses the inverse index typically created for rapid key-word based searching of a document collection. We define a set of operations on the inverse index that allows us to create annotations defined by cascading regular expressions. The entity annotations for an entire document corpus can be created purely of the index with no need to access the original documents. Experiments on two publicly available data sets show very significant performance improvements over the document-based annotators.

1 Introduction

Entity Annotation associates a well-defined label such as 'person name', 'organization', 'place', *etc.*, with a sequence of tokens in unstructured text. The dominant paradigm for annotating a document collection is to annotate each document separately. The computational complexity of annotating the collection in this paradigm, depends linearly on the number of documents and the cost of annotating each document. More precisely, it depends on the total number of tokens in the document collection. It is not uncommon to have millions of documents in a collection. Using this paradigm, it can take hours or days to annotate such big collections even with highly parallel server farms. Another drawback of this paradigm is that the entire document collection needs to be re-processed whenever new annotations are required.

In this paper, we propose an alternative paradigm for entity annotation. We build an index for the tokens in the document collection first. Using a set of operators on the index, we can generate new index entries for sequences of tokens that match any given regular expression. Since a large class of annotators (*e.g.*, GATE (Cunningham et al., 2002)) can be built using cascading regular expressions, this approach allows us to support annotation of the document collection purely from the index.

We show both theoretically and experimentally that this approach can lead to substantial reductions in computational complexity, since the order of computation is dependent on the size of the indexes and not the number of tokens in the document collection. In most cases, the index sizes used for computing the annotations will be a small fraction of the total number of tokens.

In (Cho and Rajagopalan, 2002) the authors develop a method for speeding up the evaluation of a regular expression 'R' on a large text corpus by use of an optimally constructed multi-gram index to filter documents that will match 'R'. Unfortunately, their method requires access to the document collection for the final match of 'R' to the filtered document set, which can be very time consuming. The other bodies of related prior work concern indexing annotated data (Cooper et al., 2001; Li and Moon, 2001) and methods for document level annotation (Agichtein and Gravano, 2000; McCallum et al., 2000). The work on indexing annotated data is not directly relevant, since our method creates the index to the annotations directly as part of the algorithm for computing the annotation. (Eikvil, 1999) has a good survey of existing document level IE methods. The relevance to our work is that only a certain class of annotators can be implemented using our method: namely anything that can be implemented using cascading weighted regular expressions. Fortu-

Proceedings of the 2006 Conference on Empirical Methods in Natural Language Processing (EMNLP 2006), pages 492–500,
Sydney, July 2006.

nately, this is still powerful enough to enable a large class of highly effective entity annotators.

The rest of the paper is organized as follows. In Section 2, we present an overview of the proposed approach for entity annotation. In Section 3, we construct an algorithm for implementing a deterministic finite automaton (DFA) using an inverse index of a document collection. We also compare the complexity of this approach against the direct approach of running the DFA over the document collection, and show that under typical conditions, the index-based approach will be an order of magnitude faster. In Section 4, we develop an alternative algorithm which is based on translating the original regular expression directly into an ordered AND/OR graph with an associated set of index level operators. This has the advantage of operating directly on the much more compact regular expressions instead of the equivalent DFA (which can become very large as a result of the NFA to DFA conversion and epsilon removal steps). We provide details of our experiments on two publicly available data sets in Section 5. Finally we present our conclusions in Section 6.

2 Overview

Figure 1 shows the process for entity annotation presented in the paper. A given document collection $\mathcal{D}$ is tokenized and segmented into sentences. The tokens are stored in an inverse index I. The inverse index I has an ordered list $\mathcal{U}$ of the unique tokens u_1, u_2, $..u_W$ that occur in the collection, where W is the number of tokens in I. Additionally, for each unique token u_i, I has a postings list $L(u_i) =< l_1, l_2, \ldots l_{cnt(u_i)} >$ of locations in $\mathcal{D}$ at which u_i occurs. $cnt(u_i)$ is the length of $L(u_i)$. Each entry l_k, in the postings list $L(u_i)$, has three fields: (1) a sentence identifier, $l_k.sid$, (2) the begin position of the particular occurrence of u_i, $l_k.first$ and (3) the end position of the same occurrence of u_i, $l_k.last$.

We require the input grammar to be the same as that used for named entity annotations in GATE (Cunningham et al., 2002). The GATE architecture for text engineering uses the Java Annotations Pattern Engine (JAPE) (Cunningham, 1999) for its information extraction task. JAPE is a pattern matching language. We support two classes of properties for tokens that are required by grammars such as JAPE: (1) orthographic properties such as an uppercase character followed by lower case characters, and (2) gazetteer (dictionary) containment properties of tokens and token sequences such as 'location' and 'person name'. The set of tokens along with entity types specified by either of these two properties are referred to as *Basic Entities*. The instances of basic entities specified by orthographic properties must be single tokens. However, instances of basic entities specified using gazetteer containment properties can be token sequences.

The module (1) of our system shown in Figure 1, identifies postings lists for each basic entity type. These postings lists are entered as index entries in I for the corresponding types. For example, if the input rules require tokens/token sequences that satisfy *Capsword* or *Location Dictionary* properties, a postings list is created for each of these basic types. Constructing the postings list for a basic entity type with some orthographic property is a fairly straightforward task; the postings lists of tokens satisfying the orthographic properties are merged (while retaining the sorted order of each postings list). The mechanism for generating the postings list of basic entities with gazetteer properties will be developed in the following sections. A rule for NE annotation may require a token to satisfy multiple properties such as *Location Dictionary* as well as *Capsword*. The posting list for tokens that satisfy multiple properties are determined by performing an operation $parallelint(L, L')$ over the posting lists of the corresponding basic entities. The $parallelint(L, L')$ operation returns a posting list such that each entry in the returned list occurs in both L as well as L'. The module (2) of our system shown in Figure 1 identifies instances of each annotation type, by performing index-based operations on the postings lists of *basic entity* types and other tokens.

3 Annotation using Cascading Regular Expressions

Regular expressions over basic entities have been extensively used for NE annotations. The Common Pattern Specification Language (CSPL)[1] specifies a standard for describing Annotators that can be implemented by a series of cascading regular expression matches.

Consider a regular expression R over an alphabet Σ of basic entities, and a token sequence

[1]http://www.ai.sri.com/~appelt/TextPro

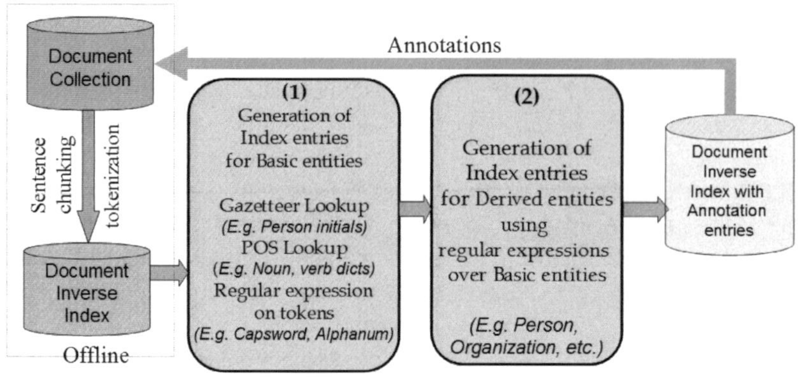

Figure 1: Overview of the entity annotation process described in this paper

$T = \{t_1, \ldots, t_W\}$. The annotation problem aims at determining all matches of regular expression R in the token sequence T. Additionally, NE annotations do not span multiple sentences. We will therefore assume that the length of any annotated token sequence is bounded by Δ, where Δ can be the maximum sentence length in the document collection of interest. In practice, Δ can be even smaller.

3.1 Computing Annotations using a DFA

Given a regular expression R, we can convert it into a deterministic finite automate (DFA) D_R. A DFA is a finite state machine, where for each pair of state and input symbol, there is one and only one transition to a next state. D_R starts processing of an input sequence from a start state s_R, and for each input symbol, it makes a transition to a state given by a transition function Φ_R. Whenever D_R lands in an accept state, the symbol sequence till that point is accepted by D_R. For simplicity of the document and index algorithms, we will ignore document and sentence boundaries in the following analysis.

Let $@t_{i,i+\Delta}, 1 \leq i \leq W - \Delta$ be a subsequence of T of length Δ. On a given input $@t_{i,i+\Delta}$, D_R will determine all token sequences originating at t_i that are accepted by the regular expression grammar specified through D_R. Figure 2 outlines the algorithm *findAnnotations* that locates all token sequences in T that are accepted by D_R.

Let D_R have $\{S_1, \ldots, S_N\}$ states. We assume that the states have been topologically ordered so that S_1 is the start state. Let α be the time taken to consume a single token and advance the DFA to the next state (this is typically implemented as a table or hash look-up). The time taken by the algorithm *findAnnotations* can be obtained by summing up the number of times each state is visited as the input tokens are consumed. Clearly, the state S_1 is visited W times, W being the total number of symbols in the token sequence T. Let $cnt(S_i)$ give the total number of times the state S_i has been visited. The complexity of this method is:

$$C_D = \alpha \sum_{i=1}^{i=N} cnt(S_i) = \alpha \left[W + \sum_{i=2}^{i=N} cnt(S_i) \right] \quad (1)$$

findAnnotations(T, D_R)
Let $T = \{t_1, \ldots, t_W\}$
for i = 1 to $W - \Delta$ **do**
  let $@t_{i,i+\Delta}$ be a subsequence of length Δ starting from t_i in T
  use D_R to annotate $@t_{i,i+\Delta}$
end for

Figure 2: The algorithm for finding all the occurrences of R in a token sequence T.

3.2 Computing Regular Expression Matches using Index

In this section, we present a new approach for finding all matches of a regular expression R in a token sequence T, based on the inverse index I of T. The structure of the inverse index was presented in Section 2. We define two operations on postings lists which find use in our annotation algorithm.

1. $merge(L, L')$: Returns a postings list such that each entry in the returned list occurs either in L or L' or both. This operation takes $O(|L| + |L'|)$ time.

2. $consint(L, L')$: Returns a postings list such that each entry in the returned list points to a token sequence which consists of two consecutive

subsequences @sa and @sb within the same sentence, such that, L has an entry for @sa and L' has an entry for @sb. There are several methods for computing this depending on the relative size of L and L'. If they are roughly equal in size, a simple linear pass through L and L', analogous to a merge, can be performed. If there is a significant difference in sizes, a more efficient modified binary search algorithm can be implemented. The details are shown in Figure 3. The complexity of this algorithm is determined by the size q_i of the interval required to satisfy $l'_j.first \leq l_i.last < l'_{j+q_i}.first$ (assuming $|L| < |L'|$). It will take an average of $\log_2(q_i)$ operations to determine the size of interval and $\log_2(q_i)$ operations to perform the binary search, giving a total of $2\log_2(q_i)$. Let $q_1 \cdots q_M$ be the sequence of intervals. Since the intervals will be at most two times larger than the actual interval between the nearest matches in L' to L, we can see that $|L'| \leq \sum_{i=1}^{M} q_i \leq 2 * |L'|$. Hence the worst case will be reached when $q_i = 2|L'|/|L|$ with a time complexity given by $2|L|(\log_2(|L'|/|L|) + 1)$, assuming $|L| < |L'|$.

```
consint(L, L')
Let M elements of L be l_1 ··· l_M
Let N elements of L' be l'_1 ··· l_N
if M < N then
  set j = 1
  for i = 1 to M do
    set k = 1, keep doubling k until
    l'_j.first ≤ l_i.last < l'_{j+k}.first
    binary search the L' in the interval j ··· k
    to determine the value of p such that
    l'_p.first ≤ l_i.last < l'_{p+1}.first
    if l'_p.first = l_i.last a match exists, copy to output
    set j = p + 1
  end for
else
  Same as above except l and l' are reversed
end if
```

Figure 3: The modified binary search algorithm for consint

To support annotation of a token sequence that matches a regular expression only in the context of some regular expression match on its left and/or right, we implement simple extensions to the $consint(L_1, L_2)$ operator. Details of the extensions are left out from this paper owing to space constraints.

3.3 Implementing a DFA using the Inverse Index

In this section, we present a method that takes a DFA D_R and an inverse index I of a token sequence T, to compute a postings list of subsequences of length at most Δ, that match the regular expression R.

Let the set $S = \{S_1, \ldots, S_N\}$ denote the set of states in D_R, and let the states be topologically ordered with S_1 as the start state. We associate an object $list_{s,k}$ with each state $s \in S$ and $\forall 1 \leq k \leq \Delta$. The object $list_{s,k}$ is a posting list of all token sequences of length exactly k that end in state s. The $list_{s,k}$ is initialized to be empty for all states and lengths. We iteratively compute $list_{s,k}$ for all the states using the algorithm given in Figure 4. The function $dest(S_i)$ returns a set of states, such that for each $s \in dest(S_i)$, there is an arc from state S_i to state s. The function $label(S_i, S_j)$ returns the token associated with the edge (S_i, S_j).

```
for k = 1 to Δ do
  for i = 1 to N do
    for s ∈ dest(S_i) do
      if i == 1 then
        t = L(label(S_i, s))
      else
        t = consint(list_{S_i,k-1}, L(label(S_i, s)))
      end if
      list_{s,k} = merge(list_{s,k}, t)
    end for
  end for
end for
```

Figure 4: The algorithm for building the index to all token sequences in T that match R.

At the end of the algorithm, all token sequences corresponding to postings lists $list_{s,i}, s \in S, 1 \leq i \leq \Delta$ are sequences that are matched by the regular expression R.

3.4 Complexity Analysis for the Index-based Approach

The complexity analysis of the algorithm given in Figure 4 is based on the observation that, $\sum_{k=1}^{k=\Delta} |list_{S_i,k}| = cnt(S_i)$. This holds, since $list_{S_i,k}$ contains an entry for all sequences that visit the state S_i and are of length exactly k. Summing the length of these lists for a particular state S_i across all the values of k will yield the total number of sequences of length at most Δ that visit the state S_i.

For the algorithm in Figure 3, the time taken by

one $consint$ operation is given by $2\beta(|list_{S_i,k}| * (\log(\rho_{ijk}) + 1))$ where β is a constant that varies with the lower level implementation. $\rho_{ijk} = \frac{|L(label(S_i,S_j))|}{|list_{S_i,k}|}$ is the ratio of the postings list size of the label associated with the arc from S_i to S_j to the list size of S_i at step k. Note that $\rho_{ijk} \geq 1$. Let $prev(S_i)$ be the list of predecessor states to S_i. The time taken by all the $merge$ operations for a state S_i at step k is given by $\gamma(\log(|prev(S_i)|)|list_{S_i,k}|)$ Assuming all the merges are performed simultaneously, $\gamma(log(|prev(S_i)|)$ is the time taken to create each entry in the final merged list, where γ is a constant that varies with the lower level implementation. Note this scales as the log of the number of lists that are being merged.

The total time taken by the algorithm given in Figure 4 can be computed using the time spent on $merge$ and $consint$ operations for all states and all lengths. Setting $\bar{\rho_{is}} = \max_k \rho_{isk}$, the total time C_I can be given as:

$$C_I = \sum_{i=2}^{i=N} \left[\gamma \log(|prev(S_i)|) + 2\beta \sum_{s \in dest(S_i)} \log(\bar{\rho_{is}}) \right] cnt(S_i) \quad (2)$$

Note that in deriving Equation 2, we have ignored the cost of merging $list(S_a, k)$ for $k = 1 \cdots \Delta$ for the accept states.

3.5 Comparison of Complexities

To simplify further analysis, we can replace $cnt(S_i)$ with $fcnt(S_i)$ where $fcnt(S_i) = cnt(S_i)/W$. If we assume that the token distribution statistics of the document collection remain constant as the number of documents increases, we can also assume that $fcnt(S_i)$ is invariant to W. Since ρ_{ijk} is given by a ratio of list sizes, we can also consider it to be invariant to W. We now assume $\alpha \approx \beta \approx \gamma$ since these are implementation specific times for similar low level compute operations. With this assumptions from Equations 1 and 2, the ratio C_D/C_I can be approximated by:

$$\frac{1 + \sum_{i=2}^{N} fcnt(S_i)}{\sum_{i=2}^{N} \left[\sum_{s \in dest(S_i)} 2\log(\bar{\rho_{is}}) + \log(|prev(S_i)|) \right] fcnt(S_i)} \quad (3)$$

The overall ratio of C_D to C_I is invariant to W and depends on two key factors $fcnt(S_i)$ and $\sum_{s \in dest(S_i)} \log(\bar{\rho_{is}})$. If $fcnt(S_i) \ll 1$, the ratio will be large and the index-based approach will be much faster. However, if either $fcnt(S_i)$ starts approaching 1 or $\sum_{s \in dest(S_i)} \log(\bar{\rho_{is}})$ starts getting very large (caused by a large fan out from S_i), the direct match using the DFA may be more efficient.

Intuitively, this makes sense since the main benefit of the index is to eliminate unnecessary hash lookups for tokens do not match the arcs of the DFA. As $fcnt(S_i)$ approaches 1, this assumption breaks down and hence the inherent efficiency of the direct DFA approach, where only a single hash lookup is required per state regardless of the number of destination states, becomes the dominant factor.

3.6 Comparison of Complexities for Simple Dictionary DFA

To illustrate the potential gains from the index-based annotation, consider a simple DFA D_R with two states S_1 and S_2. Let the set of unique tokens A be $\{a, b, c \cdots z\}$. Let E be the dictionary $\{a, e, i, o, u\}$. Let D_R have five arcs from S_1 to S_2 one for each element in E. The DFA D_R is a simple acceptor for the dictionary E, and if run over a token sequence T drawn from A, it will match any single token that is in E. For this simple case $fcnt(S_2)$ is just the fraction of tokens that occur in E and hence by definition $fcnt(S_2) \leq 1$. Substituting into 3 we get

$$\frac{C_D}{C_I} = \frac{1 + fcnt(S_2)}{2\log(5) fcnt(S_2)} \quad (4)$$

As long as $fcnt(S_2) < 0.27$, this ratio will always be greater than 1.

4 Inverse Index-based Annotation using Regular Expressions

A DFA corresponding to a given regular expression can be used for annotation, using the inverse index approach as described in Section 3.3. However, the NFA to DFA conversion step may result in a DFA with a very large number of states. We develop an alternative algorithm that translates the original regular expression directly into an ordered AND/OR graph. Associated with each node in the graph is a regular expression and a postings list that points to all the matches for the node's regular expression in the document collection. There are two node types: AND nodes where the output list is computed from the $consint$ of the postings lists of two children nodes and OR nodes where the output list is formed by merging the posting lists of all the children nodes. Additionally, each node has two binary properties: isOpt and selfLoop. The first property is set if the regular expression being matched is of the form 'R?', where '?' denotes that the regular expression R is optional. The second property is set if the regular expression is of the form 'R+', where '+' is the Kleen operator denoting one or more occurrences. For the case of 'R*', both properties are set.

The AND/OR graph is recursively built by scanning the regular expression from left to right and identifying every sub-regular expression for which a sub-graph can be built. We use capital letters R, X to denote regular expressions and small letters a, b, c, *etc.*, to denote terminal symbols in the symbol set Σ. Figure 5 details the algorithm used to build the AND/OR graph. Effectively, the AND/OR graph decomposes the computation of the postings list for R into a ordered set of $merge$ and $consint$ operations, such that the output $L(v)$ for node v become the input to its parents. The graph specifies the ordering, and by evaluating all the nodes in dependency order, the root node will end up with a postings list that corresponds to the desired regular expression.

```
if R is empty then
  Return NULL
else if R is a symbol a ∈ Σ then
  Return createNode(name = a)
else
  Decompose R such that R → R' <regexp>
  if <regexp> is empty then
    if R' == (X) or X+ or X* or X? then
      node = createGraph(X)
      if R' == X+ or X* then
        node.selfLoop = 1
      end if
      if R' == X? or X* then
        node.isOpt = 1
      end if
    else if R' == (X_1|X2|..|X_k) then
      node = createNode(name = R)
      node.nodetype = OR
      for i = 1 to k do
        node.children[i] = createGraph(X_i)
      end for
    end if
  else
    node = createNode(name = R)
    node.nodetype = AND
    node.children[1] = createGraph(R')
    node.children[2] = createGraph(<regexp>)
  end if
  Return node
end if
```

Figure 5: $createGraph(R)$

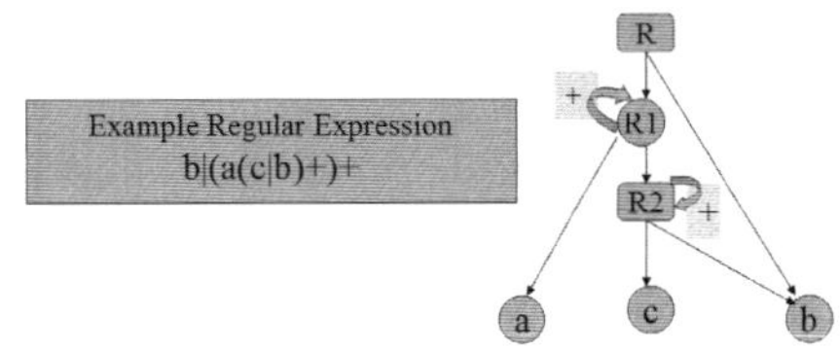

Figure 6: An example regular expression and corresponding AND/OR graph

4.1 Handling '?' and Kleen Operators

The isOpt and selfLoop properties of a node are set if the corresponding regular expression is of the form $R?$, $R+$ or $R*$. To handle the $R?$ case we associate a new property $isOpt$ with the output list $L(v)$ from node v, such that $L(v).isOpt = 1$ if the $v.isOpt = 1$. We also define two operations $consint_\epsilon$ in Figure 7 and $merge_\epsilon$ which account for the $isOpt$ property of their argument lists. For $consint_\epsilon$, the generated list has its $isOpt$ set to 1 if and only if both the argument lists have their $isOpt$ property set to 1. The $merge_\epsilon$ operation remains the same as $merge$, except that the resultant list has $isOpt$ set to 1 if any of its argument lists has $isOpt$ set to 1. The worst case time taken by $consint_\epsilon$ is bounded by 1 $consint$ and 2 $merge$ operations.

To handle the $R+$ case, we define a new operator $consint_\epsilon(L, +)$ which returns a postings list L', such that each entry in the returned list points to a token sequence consisting of all $k \in [1, \Delta]$ consecutive subsequences $@s_1, @s_2 \ldots @s_k$, each $@s_i, 1 \leq i \leq k$ being an entry in L. A simple linear pass through L is sufficient to obtain $consint(L, +)$. The time complexity of this operation is linear in the size of L'. The $isOpt$ property of the result list L' is set to the same value as its argument list L.

Figure 6 shows an example regular expression and its corresponding AND/OR graph; AND nodes are shown as circles whereas OR nodes are shown as square boxes. Nodes having isOpt and selfLoop properties are labeled with $+$, $*$ or $?$. Any AND/OR graph thus constructed is acyclic. The edges in the graph represent dependency between computing nodes. The main regular expression is at the root node of the graph. The leaf nodes correspond to symbols in Σ. Figure 8 outlines the algorithm for computing the postings list of a regular expression by operating bottom-up on the AND/OR graph.

```
consint_ε(L, L')
if ((L.isOpt == 0) and (L'.isOpt == 0)) then
  Return consint(L, L')
end if
if ((L.isOpt == 0) and (L'.isOpt == 1)) then
  Return merge(L, consint(L, L'))
end if
if ((L.isOpt == 1) and (L'.isOpt == 0)) then
  Return merge(consint(L, L'), L')
end if
if ((L.isOpt == 1) and (L'.isOpt == 1)) then
  t = merge(consint(L, L'), L')
  Return merge(t, L)
end if
```

Figure 7: $consint_\epsilon$

```
for Each node v in the reverse topological sorting of G_R
do
  if v.nodetype == AND then
    Let v_1 and v_2 be the children of v
    L(v) = consint_ε(L(v_1), L(v_2))
  else if v.type == OR then
    L(v) = merge_ε(L(v.child1), ···, L(v.childn))
  end if
  if v.selfLoop == 1 then
    L(v) = consint_ε(L(v), +)
  end if
  if v.isOpt == 1 then
    L(v).isOpt = 1
  end if
end for
```

Figure 8: The algorithm for computing postings list of a regular expression R using the inverse index I and the corresponding AND/OR graph G_R

5 Experiments and Results

In this section, we present empirical comparison of performance of the index-based annotation technique (Section 4) against annotation based on the 'document paradigm' using GATE. The experiments were performed on two data sets, *viz.*, (i) the enron email data set[2] and (ii) a combination of Reuters-21578 data set[3] and the 20 Newsgroups data set[4]. After cleaning, the former data set was 2.3 GB while the latter was 93 MB in size. Our code is entirely in Java. The experiments were performed on a dual 3.2GHz Xeon server with 4 GB RAM. The code for creation of the index was custom-built in Java. Prior to indexing, the sentence segmentation and tokenization of each data set was performed using in-house Java versions of standard tools[5].

5.1 Rule Specification using JAPE

JAPE is a version of CPSL[6] (Common Pattern Specification Language). JAPE provides finite state transduction over annotations based on regular expressions. The JAPE grammar requires information from two main resources: (i) a tokenizer and (ii) a gazetteer.

(1) *Tokenizer:* The tokenizer splits the text into very simple tokens such as numbers, punctuation and words of different types. For example, one might distinguish between words in uppercase and lowercase, and between certain types of punctuation. Although the tokenizer is ca pable of much deeper analysis than this, the aim is to limit its work to maximise efficiency, and enable greater flexibility by placing the burden on the grammar rules, which are more adaptable. A rule has a left hand side (LHS) and a right hand side (RHS). The LHS is a regular expression which has to be matched on the input; the RHS describes the annotations to be added to the Annotation Set. The LHS is separated from the RHS by '>'. The following four operators can be used on the LHS: '|', '?', '*' and '+'. The RHS uses ';' as a separator between statements that set the values of the different attributes. The following tokenizer rule identifies each character sequence that begins with a letter in upper case and is followed by 0 or more letters in lower case:

```
"UPPERCASELETTER" "LOWERCASELETTER"*
>>> Token; orth=upperInitial; kind=word;
```

Each such character sequence will be annotated as type "Token". The attribute "orth" (orthography) has the value "upperInitial"; the attribute "kind" has the value "word".

(2) *Gazetteer:* The gazetteer lists used are plain text files, with one entry per line. Each list represents a set of names, such as names of cities, organizations, days of the week, *etc.* An index file is used to access these lists; for each list, a major type is specified and, optionally, a minor type. These lists are compiled into finite state machines. Any text tokens that are matched by these machines will be annotated with features specifying the major and minor types. JAPE grammar rules

[2] http://www.cs.cmu.edu/~enron/

[3] http://www.daviddlewis.com/resources/testcollections/reuters21578/

[4] http://people.csail.mit.edu/jrennie/20Newsgroups/

[5] http://l2r.cs.uiuc.edu/~cogcomp/tools.php

[6] A good description of the original version of this language is in Doug Appelt's TextPro manual: http://www.ai.sri.com/~appelt/TextPro.

then specify the types to be identified in particular circumstances.

The JAPE Rule: Each JAPE rule has two parts, separated by "–>". The LHS consists of an annotation pattern to be matched; the RHS describes the annotation to be assigned. A basic rule is given as:

```
Rule::=
<rule> <ident> ( <priority> <integer> )?
LeftHandSide ">>>" RightHandSide
```

(1) *Left hand side:* On the LHS, the pattern is described in terms of the annotations already assigned by the tokenizer and gazetteer. The annotation pattern may contain regular expression operators (*e.g.* $*$, ?, $+$). There are 3 main ways in which the pattern can be specified:

1. *value:* specify a string of text, *e.g.* {Token.string == "of"}
2. *attribute:* specify the attributes (and values) of a token (or any other annotation), *e.g.* {Token.kind == number}
3. *annotation:* specify an annotation type from the gazetteer, *e.g.* {Lookup.minorType == month}

(2) *Right hand side:* The RHS consists of details of the annotations and optional features to be created. Annotations matched on the LHS of a rule may be referred to on the RHS by means of labels that are attached to pattern elements. Finally, attributes and their corresponding values are added to the annotation. An example of a complete rule is:

```
Rule: NumbersAndUnit
(({Token.kind=="number"})+:numbers
{Token.kind=="unit"})
>>>
:numbers.Name={rule="NumbersAndUnit"}
```

This says 'match sequences of numbers followed by a unit; create a *Name* annotation across the span of the numbers, and attribute rule with value *NumbersAndUnit*'.

Use of context: Context can be dealt with in the grammar rules in the following way. The pattern to be annotated is always enclosed by a set of round brackets. If preceding context is to be included in the rule, this is placed before this set of brackets. This context is described in exactly the same way as the pattern to be matched. If context following the pattern needs to be included, it is placed after the label given to the annotation. Context is used where a pattern should only be recognised if it occurs in a certain situation, but the context itself does not form part of the pattern to be annotated.

```
Macro: CWORDGROUP
(
({Token.orth == upperInitial})
({Token.orth == upperInitial})?
({Token.orth == upperInitial})?
({Token.orth == upperInitial})?
({Token.orth == upperInitial})?
({Token.orth == upperInitial})?
)

Rule:Person1
Priority: 1
{Token.kind == word,
            Lookup.majorType == INITIAL}
({Token.string == "."})?
(
(CWORDGROUP)
):person1
-->
:person1.Person={rule=Person1}
```

Figure 9: An example JAPE rule used in the experiments

For example, the following rule for 'email-id's (assuming an appropriate regular expression for "EMAIL-ADD") would mean that an email address would only be recognized if it occurred inside angled brackets (which would not themselves form part of the entity):

```
Rule: Emailaddress1
({Token.string=="<"})
(
{Token.kind==EMAIL-ADD}
)
:email
({Token.string==">"})
>>>
:email.Address={kind="email",
rule="Emailaddress1"}
```

5.2 Results

In our first experiment, we performed annotation of the two corpora for 4 annotation types using 2 JAPE rules for each type. The 4 annotation types were 'Person name', 'Organization', 'Location' and 'Date'. A sample JAPE rule for identifying person names is shown in Figure 9. This rule identifies a sequence of words as a person name when each word in the sequence starts with an alphabet in upper-case and when the sequence is immediately preceded by a word from a dictionary of 'INITIAL's. Example words in the 'INITIAL' dictionary are: 'Mr.', 'Dr.', 'Lt.', *etc.*

Table 1 compares the time taken by the index-based annotator against that taken by GATE for the 8 JAPE rules. The index-based annotator performs 8-13 times faster than GATE. Table 2 splits the time mentioned for the index-based annotator in Table 1 into the time taken for the task of computing postings lists for basic entities and derived entities (*c.f.* Section 2) for each of the data sets. We can also observe that a greater speedup is achieved for the larger corpus.

Data set	GATE	Index-based
Enron	4974343	374926
Reuters	752287	92238

Table 1: Time (in milliseconds) for computing annotations using the two techniques

Data set	Orthographic entity types	Gazetteer entity types	Derived entity types
Enron	38285	105870	230771
Reuters	28493	21531	42214

Table 2: Time (in milliseconds) for computing postings lists of entity types

An important advantage of performing annotations over the inverse index is that index entries for basic entity types can be preserved and reused for annotation types as additional rules for annotation are specified by users. For instance, the index entry for 'Capsword' might find reuse in several annotation rules. As against this, a document-based annotator has to process each document from scratch for every newly introduced annotation rule. To verify this, we introduced 1 additional rule for each of the 4 named entity types. In Table 3, we compare the time required by the index-based annotator against that required by GATE for annotating the two corpora using the 4 additional rules. We achieve a greater speedup factor of 23-37 for incremental annotation.

Data set	GATE	Index-based
Enron	1479954	62227
Reuters	661157	17929

Table 3: Time (in milliseconds) for computing annotations using the two techniques for the additional 4 rules

6 Conclusions

In this paper we demonstrated that a suitably constructed inverse index contains all the necessary information to implement entity annotators that use cascading regular expressions. The approach has the key advantage of not requiring access to the original unstructured data to compute the annotations. The method uses a basic set of operators on the inverse index to construct indexes to all matches for a regular expression in the tokenized data set. We showed theoretically, that for a DFA implementation, the index approach can be much faster if the index sizes corresponding to the labels on the DFA are a small fraction of the total number of tokens in the data set. We also provided a more efficient index-based implementation that is directly computed from the regular expressions without the need of a DFA conversion and experimentally demonstrated the gains.

References

Eugene Agichtein and Luis Gravano. 2000. Snowball: Extracting relations from large plain-text collections. In *Proceedings of the Fifth ACM International Conference on Digital Libraries*.

Junghoo Cho and Sridhar Rajagopalan. 2002. A fast regular expression indexing engine. In *Proceedings of the* 18th *International Conference on Data Engineering*.

Brian Cooper, Neal Sample, Michael J. Franklin, Gísli R. Hjaltason, and Moshe Shadmon. 2001. A fast index for semistructured data. In *The VLDB Conference*, pages 341–350.

H. Cunningham, D. Maynard, K. Bontcheva, and V. Tablan. 2002. GATE: A framework and graphical development environment for robust NLP tools and applications.

H. Cunningham. 1999. Jape – a java annotation patterns engine.

Line Eikvil. 1999. Information extraction from world wide web - a survey. Technical Report 945, Norweigan Computing Center.

Quanzhong Li and Bongki Moon. 2001. Indexing and querying XML data for regular path expressions. In *The VLDB Journal*, pages 361–370.

Andrew McCallum, Dayne Freitag, and Fernando Pereira. 2000. Maximum entropy Markov models for information extraction and segmentation. In *Proc. 17th International Conf. on Machine Learning*, pages 591–598. Morgan Kaufmann, San Francisco, CA.

Unsupervised Information Extraction Approach Using Graph Mutual Reinforcement

Hany Hassan **Ahmed Hassan** **Ossama Emam**

IBM Cairo Technology Development Center
Giza, Egypt
P.O. Box 166 Al-Ahram

hanyh@eg.ibm.com hasanah@eg.ibm.com emam@eg.ibm.com

Abstract

Information Extraction (IE) is the task of extracting knowledge from unstructured text. We present a novel unsupervised approach for information extraction based on graph mutual reinforcement. The proposed approach does not require any seed patterns or examples. Instead, it depends on redundancy in large data sets and graph based mutual reinforcement to induce generalized "extraction patterns". The proposed approach has been used to acquire extraction patterns for the ACE (Automatic Content Extraction) Relation Detection and Characterization (RDC) task. ACE RDC is considered a hard task in information extraction due to the absence of large amounts of training data and inconsistencies in the available data. The proposed approach achieves superior performance which could be compared to supervised techniques with reasonable training data.

1 Introduction

In this paper we propose a novel, and completely unsupervised approach for information extraction. We present a general technique; however we focus on relation extraction as an important task of Information Extraction. The approach depends on constructing generalized extraction patterns, which could match many instances, and deploys graph based mutual reinforcement to weight the importance of these patterns. The mutual reinforcement is used to automatically identify the most informative patterns, where patterns that match many instances tend to be correct. Similarly, instances matched by many patterns tend to be correct. The intuition is that large unsupervised data is redundant, i.e. different instances of information could be found many times in different contexts and by different representation. The problem can therefore be seen as hubs (instances) and authorities (patterns) problem which can be solved using the Hypertext Induced Topic Selection (HITS) algorithm (Kleinberg, 1998).

HITS is an algorithmic formulation of the notion of authority in web pages link analysis, based on a relationship between a set of relevant "authoritative pages" and a set of "hub pages". The HITS algorithm benefits from the following observation: when a page (hub) links to another page (authority), the former confers authority over the latter.

By analogy to the authoritative web pages problem, we could represent the patterns as authorities and instances as hubs, and use mutual reinforcement between patterns and instances to weight the most authoritative patterns. Highly weighted patterns are then used in extracting information.

The proposed approach does not need any seeds or examples. Human involvement is only needed in determining the entities of interest; the entities among which we are seeking relations.

The paper proceeds as follows: in Section 2 we discuss previous work followed by a brief definition of our general notation in Section 3. A detailed description of the proposed approach then follows in Section 4. Section 5 discusses the application of the proposed approach to the prob-

Proceedings of the 2006 Conference on Empirical Methods in Natural Language Processing (EMNLP 2006), pages 501–508,
Sydney, July 2006.

lem of detecting semantic relations from text. Section 6 discusses experimental results while the conclusion is presented in Section 7.

2 Previous Work

Most of the previous work on Information Extraction (IE) focused on supervised learning. Relation Detection and Characterization (RDC) was introduced in the Automatic Content Extraction Program (ACE) (ACE, 2004). The approaches proposed to the ACE RDC task such as kernel methods (Zelenko et al., 2002) and Maximum Entropy methods (Kambhatla, 2004) required the availability of large set of human annotated corpora which are tagged with relation instances. However human annotated instances are limited, expensive, and time consuming to obtain, due to the lack of experienced human annotators and the low inter-annotator agreements.

Some previous work adopted weakly supervised or unsupervised learning approaches. These approaches have the advantage of not needing large tagged corpora but need seed examples or seed extraction patterns. The major drawback of these approaches is their dependency on seed examples or seed patterns which may lead to limited generalization due to dependency on handcrafted examples. Some of these approaches are briefed here:

(Brin,98) presented an approach for extracting the authorship information as found in books description on the World Wide Web. This technique is based on dual iterative pattern relation extraction wherein a relation and pattern set is iteratively constructed. This approach has two major drawbacks: the use of handcrafted seed examples to extract more examples similar to these handcrafted seed examples and the use of a lexicon as the main source for extracting information.

(Blum and Mitchell, 1998) proposed an approach based on co-training that uses unlabeled data in a particular setting. They exploit the fact that, for some problems, each example can be described by multiple representations.

(Riloff & Jones, 1999) presented the Meta-Bootstrapping algorithm that uses an un-annotated training data set and a set of seeds to learn a dictionary of extraction patterns and a domain specific semantic lexicon. Other works tried to exploit the duality of patterns and their extractions for the purpose of inferring the semantic class of words like (Thelen & Riloff, 2002) and (Lin et al, 2003).

(Muslea et al., 1999) introduced an inductive algorithm to generate extraction rules based on user labeled training examples. This approach suffers from the labeled data bottleneck.

(Agichtein et. al, 2000) presented an approach using seed examples to generate initial patterns and to iteratively obtain further patterns. Then ad-hoc measures were deployed to estimate the relevancy of the patterns that have been newly obtained. The major drawbacks of this approach are: its dependency on seed examples leads to limited capability of generalization, and the estimation of patterns relevancy requires the deployment of ad-hoc measures.

(Hasegawa et. al. 2004) introduced unsupervised approach for relation extraction depending on clustering context words between named entities; this approach depends on ad-hoc context similarity between phrases in the context and focused on certain types of relations.

(Etzioni et al, 2005) proposed a system for building lists of named entities found on the web. Their system uses a set of eight domain-independent extraction patterns to generate candidate facts.

All approaches, proposed so far, suffer from either requiring large amount of labeled data or the dependency on seed patterns (or examples) that result in limited generalization.

3 General Notation

In graph theory, a graph is a set of objects called vertices joined by links called edges. A bipartite graph, also called a bigraph, is a special graph where the set of vertices can be divided into two disjoint sets with no two vertices of the same set sharing an edge.

The Hypertext Induced Topic Selection (HITS) algorithm is an algorithm for rating, and therefore ranking, web pages. The HITS algorithm makes use of the following observation: when a page (hub) links to another page (authority), the former confers authority over the latter. HITS uses two values for each page, the "authority value" and the "hub value". "Authority value" and "hub value" are defined in terms of one another in a mutual recursion. An authority value is computed as the sum of the scaled hub values that point to that authority. A hub value is the sum of the scaled authority values of the authorities it points to.

A template, as we define for this work, is a sequence of generic forms that could generalize over the given instances. An example template is:

```
GPE POS   (PERSON)+

GPE: Geographical Political En-
tity
POS: possessive ending
PERSON: PERSON Entity
```

This template could match the sentence: "France's President Jacque Chirac...". This template is derived from the representation of the Named Entity tags, Part-of-Speech (POS) tags and semantic tags. The choice of the template representation here is for illustration purpose only; any combination of tags, representations and tagging styles might be used.

A pattern is more specific than a template. A pattern specifies the role played by the tags (first entity, second entity, or relation). An example of a pattern is:

```
GPE(E2)  POS    (PERSON)+(E1)
```

This pattern indicates that the word(s) with the tag GPE in the sentence represents the second en-tity (Entity 2) in the relation, while the word(s) tagged PERSON represents the first entity (Entity 1) in this relation, the "+" symbol means that the (PERSON) entity is repetitive (i.e. may consist of several tokens).

A tuple, in our notation during this paper, is the result of the application of a pattern to unstructured text. In the above example, one result of applying the pattern to some raw text is the following tuple:

```
Entity 1:       Jacque Chirac
Entity 2:       France
Relation:       EMP-Executive
```

4 The Approach

The unsupervised graph-based mutual reinforcement approach, we propose, depends on the construction of generalized "extraction patterns" that could match many instances. The patterns are then weighted according to their importance by deploying graph based mutual reinforcement techniques. This duality in patterns and extracted information (tuples) could be stated that patterns could match different tuples, and tuples in turn could be matched by different patterns. The proposed approach is composed of two main steps namely, initial patterns construction and pattern weighting or induction. Both steps are detailed in the next sub-sections.

4.1 Initial Patterns Construction

As shown in Figure 1, several syntactic, lexical, and semantic analyzers could be applied to the unstructured text. The resulting analyses could be employed in the construction of extraction patterns. It is worth mentioning that the proposed approach is general enough to accommodate any pattern design; the introduced pattern design is for illustration purposes only.

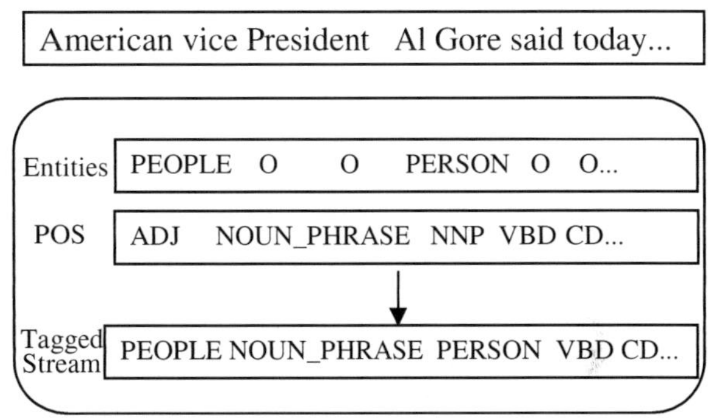

Figure 1: An example of the output of analysers applied to the unstructured text

Initially, we need to start with some templates and patterns to proceed with the induction process. Relatively large amount of text data is tagged with different taggers to produce the previously mentioned patterns styles. An n-gram language model is built on this data and used to construct weighted finite state machines.

Paths with low cost (high language model probabilities) are chosen to construct the initial set of templates; the intuition is that paths with low cost (high probability) are frequent and could represent potential candidate patterns.

The resulting initial set of templates is applied to a very large text data to produce all possible patterns. The number of candidate initial patterns could be reduced significantly by specifying the candidate types of entities; for example we might specify that the first entity could be PEROSN or PEOPLE while the second entity could be ORGANIZATION, LOCATION, COUNTRY and etc...

The candidate patterns are then applied to the tagged stream and the unstructured text to collect a set of patterns and matched tuples pairs.

The following procedure briefs the Initial Pattern Construction Step:

- Select a random set of text data.

- Apply various taggers on text data and construct templates style.
- Build n-gram language model on template style data.
- Construct weighted finite state machines from the n-gram language model.
- Choose n-best paths in the finite state machines.
- Use best paths as initial templates.
- Apply initial templates on large text data.
- Construct initial patterns and associated tuples sets.

4.2 Pattern Induction

The inherent duality in the patterns and tuples relation suggests that the problem could be interpreted as a hub authority problem. This problem could be solved by applying the HITS algorithm to iteratively assign authority and hub scores to patterns and tuples respectively.

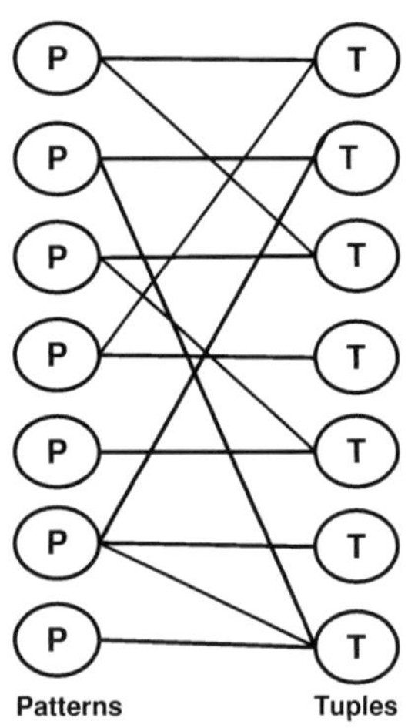

Figure 2: A bipartite graph representing patterns and tuples

Patterns and tuples are represented by a bipartite graph as illustrated in figure 2. Each pattern or tuple is represented by a node in the graph. Edges represent matching between patterns and tuples. The pattern induction problem can be formulated as follows: Given a very large set of data *D* containing a large set of patterns *P* which match a large set of tuples T, the problem is to identify $\tilde{P}$, the set of patterns that match the set of the most correct tuples $\tilde{T}$. The intuition is that the tuples matched by many different patterns tend to be correct and the patterns matching many different tuples tend to be good patterns. In other words; we want to choose, among the large space of patterns in the data, the most informative, highest confidence patterns that could identify correct tuples; i.e. choosing the most *"authoritative"* patterns in analogy with the hub authority problem. However, both $\tilde{P}$ and $\tilde{T}$ are unknown. The induction process proceeds as follows: each pattern *p* in *P* is associated with a numerical authority weight a_v which expresses how many tuples match that pattern. Similarly, each tuple *t* in *T* has a numerical hub weight h_t which expresses how many patterns were matched by this tuple. The weights are calculated iteratively as follows:

$$a^{(i+1)}(p) = \sum_{u=1}^{T(p)} \frac{h^{(i)}(u)}{H^{(i)}} \qquad (1)$$

$$h^{(i+1)}(t) = \sum_{u=1}^{P(t)} \frac{a^{(i)}(u)}{A^{(i)}} \qquad (2)$$

where *T(p)* is the set of tuples matched by *p*, *P(t)* is the set of patterns matching *t*, $a^{(i+1)}(p)$ is the authoritative weight of pattern p at iteration $(i+1)$, and $h^{(i+1)}(t)$ is the hub weight of tuple *t* at iteration $(i+1)$. *H(i)* and *A(i)* are normalization factors defined as:

$$H^{(i)} = \sum_{p=1}^{|P|} \sum_{u=1}^{T(p)} h^{(i)}(u) \qquad (3)$$

$$A^{(i)} = \sum_{v=1}^{|T|} \sum_{u=1}^{P(t)} a^{(i)}(u) \qquad (4)$$

Highly weighted patterns are identified and used for extracting relations.

4.3 Tuple Clustering

The tuple space should be reduced to allow more matching between pattern-tuple pairs. This space reduction could be accomplished by seeking a tuple similarity measure, and constructing a weighted undirected graph of tuples. Two tuples are linked with an edge if their similarity measure exceeds a certain threshold. Graph clustering algorithms could be deployed to partition the graph into a set of homogeneous communities or clusters. To reduce the space of tuples, we seek a matching criterion that group similar tuples together. Using WordNet, we can measure the semantic similarity or relatedness between a pair of concepts (or word senses), and by extension, between a pair of sentences. We use the similarity measure described in (Wu and Palmer, 1994) which finds the path length to the root node from the least common subsumer (LCS) of the two word senses which is the most specific word sense they share as an ancestor. The similarity score of two tuples, S_T, is calculated as follows:

$$S_T = \sqrt{S_{E1}^2 + S_{E2}^2} \qquad (5)$$

where S_{E1}, and S_{E2} are the similarity scores of the first entities in the two tuples, and their second entitles respectively.

The tuple matching procedure assigns a similarity measure to each pair of tuples in the dataset. Using this measure we can construct an undirected graph G. The vertices of G are the tuples. Two vertices are connected with an edge if the similarity measure between their underlying tuples exceeds a certain threshold. It was noticed that the constructed graph consists of a set of semi isolated groups as shown in figure 3. Those groups have a very large number of inter-group edges and meanwhile a rather small number of intra-group edges. This implies that using a graph clustering algorithm would eliminate those weak intra-group edges and produce separate groups or clusters representing similar tuples. We used Markov Cluster Algorithm (MCL) for graph clustering (Dongen, 2000). MCL is a fast and scalable unsupervised clustering algorithm for graphs based on simulation of stochastic flow.

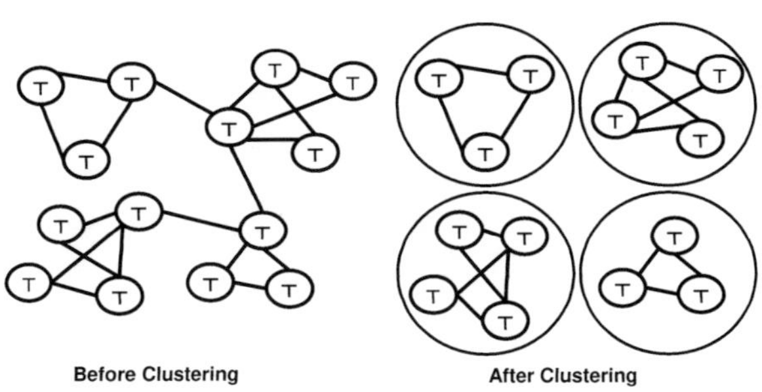

Figure 3: Applying Clustering Algorithms to Tuple graph

An example of a couple of tuples that could be matched by this technique is:

```
United Stated(E2) presi-
dent(E1)
 US(E2) leader(E1)
```

A bipartite graph of patterns and tuple clusters is constructed. Weights are assigned to patterns and tuple clusters by iteratively applying the HITS algorithm and the highly ranked patterns are then used for relation extraction.

5 Experimental Setup

5.1 ACE Relation Detection and Characterization

In this section, we describe Automatic Content Extraction (ACE). ACE is an evaluation conducted by NIST to measure Entity Detection and Tracking (EDT) and Relation Detection and Characterization (RDC). The EDT task is concerned with the detection of mentions of entities, and grouping them together by identifying their coreference. The RDC task detects relations between entities identified by the EDT task. We choose the RDC task to show the performance of the graph based unsupervised approach we propose. To this end we need to introduce the notion of mentions and entities. Mentions are any instances of textual references to objects like people, organizations, geopolitical entities (countries, cities ...etc), locations, or facilities. On the other hand, entities are objects containing all mentions to the same object. Here, we present some examples of ACE entities and relations:

```
Spain's Interior Minister
announced this evening the
arrest of separatist organi-
zation Eta's presumed leader
Ignacio Garcia Arregui. Ar-
regui, who is considered to
be the Eta organization's
top man, was arrested at
17h45 Greenwich. The Spanish
judiciary suspects Arregui
of ordering a failed attack
on King Juan Carlos in 1995.
```

In this fragment, all the underlined phrases are mentions to "Eta" organization, or to "Garcia Arregui". There is a management relation between "leader" which references to "Garcia Arregui" and "Eta".

5.2 Patterns Construction and Induction

We used the LDC English Gigaword Corpus, AFE source from January to August 1996 as a source for unstructured text. This provides a total of 99475 documents containing 36 M words. In the performed experiments, we focus on two types of relations EMP-ORG relations and GPE-AFF relations which represent almost 50% of all relations in RDC – ACE task.

POS (part of speech) tagger and mention tagger were applied to the data, the used pattern design consists of a mix between the part of speech (POS) tags and the mention tags for the words in the unsupervised data. We use the mention tag, if it exists; otherwise we use the part of speech tag. An example of the analyzed text and the presumed associated pattern is shown:

```
Text: Eta's presumed leader
Arregui …
Pos: NNP POS JJ NN NNP
Mention: ORG 0 0 0 PERSON
Pattern: ORG(E2) POS JJ
NN(R) PERSON(E1)
```

An n-gram language model, 5-gram model and back off to lower order n-grams, was built on the data tagged with the described patterns' style. Weighted finite states machines were constructed with the language model probabilities. The n-best paths, 20 k paths, were identified and deployed as the initial template set. Sequences that do not contain the entities of interest, and hence cannot represent relations, were automatically filtered out. This resulted in an initial templates set of around 3000 element. This initial templates set was applied on the text data to establish initial patterns and tuples pairs. Graph based mutual reinforcement technique was deployed with 10 iterations on the patterns and tuples pairs to weight the patterns.

We conducted two groups of experiments, the first with simple syntactic tuple matching, and the second with semantic tuple clustering as described in section 4.3

6 Results and Discussion

We compare our results to a state-of-the-art supervised system similar to the system described in (Kambhatla, 2004). Although it is unfair to make a comparison between a supervised system and a completely unsupervised system, we chose to make this comparison to test the performance of the proposed unsupervised approach on a real task with defined test set and state-of-the-art performance. The supervised system was trained on 145 K words which contain 2368 instances of the two relation types we are considering.

The system performance is measured using precision, recall and F-Measure with various amounts of induced patterns. Table 1 presents the precision, recall and F-measure for the two relations using the presented approach with the utilization of different amount of highly weighted patterns. Table 2 presents the same results using semantic tuple matching and clustering, as described in section 4.3.

No. of Patterns	Precision	Recall	F-Measure
1500	35.9	66.3	46.58
1000	41.2	59.7	48.75
700	43.1	58.1	49.49
500	**46**	**56.5**	**50.71**
400	46.9	52.9	49.72
200	50.1	44.9	47.36

Table 1: The effect of varying the number of induced patterns on the system performance (syntactic tuple matching)

No. of Patterns	Precision	Recall	F-Measure
1500	36.1	67.2	46.97
1000	43.7	59.6	50.43
700	44.1	59.3	50.58
500	46.3	57.2	51.18
400	**47.3**	**57.6**	**51.94**
200	48.1	45.9	46.97

Table 2: The effect of varying the number of induced patterns on the system performance (semantic tuple matching)

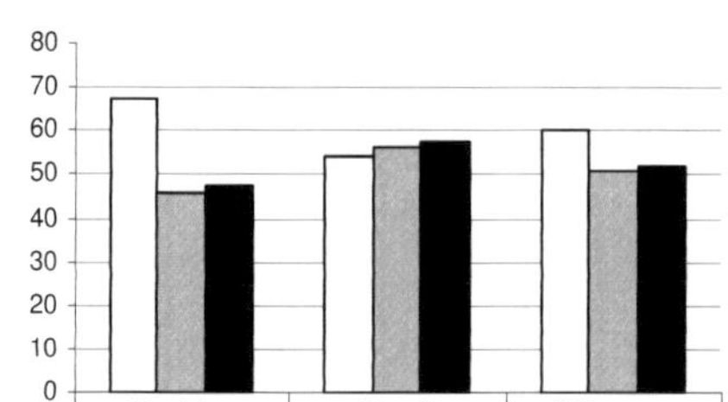

	Precision	Recall	F Measure
Sup	67.1	54.2	59.96
Unsup-Syn	46	56.5	50.71
Unsup-Sem	47.3	57.6	51.94

Figure 4: A comparison between the supervised system (Sup), the unsupervised system with syntactic tuple matching (Unsup-Syn), and with semantic tuple matching (Unsup-Sem)

Best F-Measure is achieved using relatively small number of induced patterns (400 and 500 patterns) while using more patterns increases the recall but degrades the precision.

Table 2 indicates that the semantic clustering of tuples did not provide significant improvement; although better performance was achieved with less number of patterns (400 patterns). We think that the deployed similarity measure and it needs further investigation to figure out the reason for that.

Figure 4 presents the comparison between the proposed unsupervised systems and the reference supervised system. The unsupervised systems achieves good results even in comparison to a state-of-the-art supervised system.

Sample patterns and corresponding matching text are introduced in Table 3 and Table 4. Table 3 shows some highly ranked patterns while Table 4 shows examples of low ranked patterns.

Pattern	Matches
GPE (PERSON)+	Peruvian President Alberto Fujimori
GPE (PERSON)+	Zimbabwean President Robert Mugabe
GPE (PERSON)+	PLO leader Yasser Arafat
GPE POS (PERSON)+	Zimbabwe 's President Robert Mugabe
GPE JJ PERSON	American clinical neuropsychologist
GPE JJ PERSON	American diplomatic personnel
PERSON IN JJ GPE	candidates for local government
ORGANIZATION PERSON	Airways spokesman
ORGANIZATION PERSON	Ajax players
PERSON IN DT (ORGANIZATION)+	chairman of the opposition parties
(ORGANIZATION)+ PERSON	opposition parties chairmans

Table3: Examples of patterns with high weights

Pattern	Matches
GPE CC (PERSON)+	Barcelona and Johan Cruyff
GPE , CC PERSON	Paris , but Riccardi
GPE VBZ VBN PERSON	Pyongyang has accepted Gallucci
GPE VBZ VBN PERSON	Russia has abandoned us
GPE VBZ VBN P PERSON	Rwanda 's defeated Hutu
GPE VBZ VBN PERSON	state has pressed Arafat
GPE VBZ VBN TO VB PERSON	Taiwan has tried to keep Lee
(PERSON)+ VBD GPE ORGANIZATION	Alfred Streim told German radio
(PERSON)+ VBD GPE ORGANIZATION	Dennis Ross met Syrian army
(PERSON)+ VBD GPE ORGANIZATION	Van Miert told EU industry

Table4: Examples of patterns with low weights

7 Conclusion and Future Work

In this work, a general framework for unsupervised information extraction based on mutual reinforcement in graphs has been introduced. We construct generalized extraction patterns and deploy graph based mutual reinforcement to automatically identify the most informative patterns. We provide motivation for our approach from a graph theory and graph link analysis perspective. Experimental results have been presented supporting the applicability of the proposed approach to ACE Relation Detection and Characterization (RDC) task, demonstrating its applicability to hard information extraction problems. The proposed approach achieves remarkable results comparable to a state-of-the-art supervised system, achieving 51.94 F-measure compared to 59.96 F-measure of the state-of-the-art supervised system which requires huge amount of human annotated data. The proposed approach represents a powerful unsupervised technique for information extraction in general and particularly for relations extraction that requires no seed patterns or examples and achieves significant performance.

In our future work, we plan to focus on generalizing the approach for targeting more NLP problems.

8 Acknowledgements

We would like to thank Salim Roukos for his invaluable suggestions and support. We would also like to thank Hala Mostafa for helping with the early investigation of this work. Finally we would like to thank the anonymous reviewers for their constructive criticism and helpful comments.

References

ACE. 2004. The NIST ACE evaluation website. http://www.nist.gov/speech/tests/ace/

Eugene Agichtein and Luis Gravano. 2000. *Snowball: Extracting Relations from Large Plain-Text Collections.* Proceedings of the 5th ACM Conference on Digital Libraries (DL 2000).

Sergy Brin. 1998. *Extracting Patterns and Relations from the World Wide Web.* Proceedings of the 1998 International Workshop on the Web and Databases"

Stijn van Dongen. 2000. *A Cluster Algorithm for Graphs.* Technical Report INS-R0010, National Research Institute for Mathematics and Computer Science in the Netherlands.

Stijn van Dongen. 2000. *Graph Clustering by Flow Simulation*. PhD thesis, University of Utrecht

Oren Etzioni, Michael Cafarella, Doug Downey, Ana-Maria Popescu, Tal Shaked, Stephen Soderland, Daniel S. Weld, and Alexander Yates. 2004. *Web-scale information extraction in KnowItAll (preliminary results)*. In Proceedings of the 13th World Wide Web Conference, pages 100-109.

Oren Etzioni, Michael Cafarella, Doug Downey, Ana-Maria Popescu, Tal Shaked, Stephen Soderland, Daniel S. Weld, and Alexander Yates. 2005. *Unsupervised Named-Entity Extraction from the Web: An Experimental Study*. Artificial Intelligence, 2005.

Radu Florian, Hany Hassan, Hongyan Jing, Nanda Kambhatla, Xiaqiang Luo, Nicolas Nicolov, and Salim Roukos. 2004. *A Statistical Model for multilingual entity detection and tracking*. Proceedings of the Human Language Technologies Conference (HLT-NAACL 2004).

Dayne Freitag, and Nicholas Kushmerick. 2000. *Boosted wrapper induction*. The 14th European Conference on Artificial Intelligence Workshop on Machine Learning for Information Extraction

Rayid Ghani and Rosie Jones. 2002. *A Comparison of Efficacy and Assumptions of Bootstrapping Algorithms for Training Information Extraction Systems*. Workshop on Linguistic Knowledge Acquisition and Representation: Bootstrapping Annotated Data at the Linguistic Resources and Evaluation Conference (LREC 2002).

Takaaki Hasegawa, Satoshi Sekine, Ralph Grishman. 2004. *Discovering Relations among Named Entities from Large Corpora*. Proceedings of The 42nd Annual Meeting of the Association for Computational Linguistics (ACL 2004).

Taher Haveliwala. 2002. *Topic-sensitive PageRank*. Proceedings of the 11th International World Wide Web Conference

Thorsten Joachims. 2003. *Transductive Learning via Spectral Graph Partitioning*. Proceedings of the International Conference on Machine Learning (ICML 2003).

Nanda Kambhatla. 2004. *Combining Lexical, Syntactic, and Semantic Features with Maximum Entropy Models for Information Extraction*. Proceedings of The 42nd Annual Meeting of the Association for Computational Linguistics (ACL 2004).

John Kleinberg. 1998. *Authoritative Sources in a Hyperlinked Environment*. Proceedings of the 9th ACM-SIAM Symposium on Discrete Algorithms.

N. Kushmerick, D.S. Weld, R.B. Doorenbos. 1997. *Wrapper Induction for Information Extraction*. Proceedings of the International Joint Conference on Artificial Intelligence.

Winston Lin, Roman Yangarber, Ralph Grishman. *2003. Bootstrapped Learning of Semantic Classes from Positive and Negative Examples*. Proceedings of the 20th International Conference on Machine Learning (ICML 2003) Workshop on The Continuum from Labeled to Unlabeled Data in Machine Learning and Data Mining.

Ion Muslea, Steven Minton, and Craig Knoblock.1999. *A hierarchical approach to wrapper induction*. Proceedings of the Third International Conference on Autonomous Agents.

Ted Pedersen, Siddharth Patwardhan, and Jason Michelizzi. 2004, *WordNet::Similarity - Measuring the Relatedness of Concepts*. Proceedings of Fifth Annual Meeting of the North American Chapter of the Association for Computational Linguistics (NAACL 2004)

Ellen Riloff and Rosie Jones. 2003. *Learning dictionaries for information extraction by multilevel bootstrapping*. Proceedings of the Sixteenth national Conference on Artificial Intelligence (AAAI 1999).

Michael Thelen and Ellen Riloff. 2002. *A Bootstrapping Method for Learning Semantic Lexicons using Extraction Pattern Contexts*. Proceedings of the 2002 Conference on Empirical Methods in Natural Language Processing (EMNLP 2002).

Scott White, and Padhraic Smyth. 2003. *Algorithms for Discoveing Relative Importance in Graphs*. Proceedings of Ninth ACM SIGKDD International Conference on Knowledge Discovery and Data Mining.

Zhibiao Wu, and Martha Palmer. 1994. *Verb semantics and lexical selection*. Proceedings of the 32nd Annual Meeting of the Association for Computational Linguistics (ACL 1994).

Xiaojin Zhu, Zoubin Ghahramani, and John Lafferty. 2003. *Semi-supervised Learning using Gaussian Fields and Harmonic Functions*. Proceedings of the 20th International Conference on Machine Learning (ICML 2003).

Empirical Study on the Performance Stability of Named Entity Recognition Model across Domains

Hong Lei Guo   Li Zhang   and   Zhong Su
IBM China Research Laboratory
Building 19, Zhongguancun Software Park
8 Dongbeiwang WestRoad, Haidian District, Beijing, 100094, P.R.C.
{guohl, lizhang , suzhong }@cn.ibm.com

Abstract

When a machine learning-based named entity recognition system is employed in a new domain, its performance usually degrades. In this paper, we provide an empirical study on the impact of training data size and domain information on the performance stability of named entity recognition models. We present an informative sample selection method for building high quality and stable named entity recognition models across domains. Experimental results show that the performance of the named entity recognition model is enhanced significantly after being trained with these informative samples.

1 Introduction

Named entities (NE) are phrases that contain names of persons, organizations, locations, etc. Named entity recognition (NER) is an important task in many natural language processing applications, such as information extraction and machine translation. There have been a number of conferences aimed at evaluating NER systems, for example, MUC6, MUC7, CoNLL2002 and CoNLL2003, and ACE (automatic content extraction) evaluations.

Machine learning approaches are becoming more attractive for NER in recent years since they are trainable and adaptable. Recent research on English NER has focused on the machine learning approach (Sang and Meulder, 2003). The relevant algorithms include Maximum Entropy (Borthwick, 1999; Klein et al., 2003), Hidden Markov Model (HMM) (Bikel et al., 1999; Klein et al., 2003), AdaBoost (Carreras et al., 2003), Memory-based learning (Meulder and Daelemans, 2003), Support Vector Machine (Isozaki and Kazawa, 2002), Robust Risk Minimization (RRM) Classification method (Florian et al., 2003), etc.

For Chinese NER, most of the existing approaches use hand-crafted rules with word (or character) frequency statistics. Some machine learning algorithms also have been investigated in Chinese NER, including HMM (Yu et al., 1998; Jing et al., 2003), class-based language model (Gao et al., 2005; Wu et al., 2005), RRM (Guo et al., 2005; Jing et al., 2003), etc.

However, when a machine learning-based NER system is directly employed in a new domain, its performance usually degrades. In order to avoid the performance degrading, the NER model is often retrained with domain-specific annotated corpus. This retraining process usually needs more efforts and costs. In order to enhance the performance stability of NER models with less efforts, some issues have to be considered in practice. For example, how much training data is enough for building a stable and applicable NER model? How does the domain information and training data size impact the NER performance?

This paper provides an empirical study on the impact of training data size and domain information on NER performance. Some useful observations are obtained from the experimental results on a large-scale annotated corpus. Experimental results show that it is difficult to significantly enhance the performance when the training data size is above a certain threshold. The threshold of the training data size varies with domains. The performance stability of each NE type recognition also varies with domains. Corpus statistical data show that NE types have different distribution across domains. Based on the empirical investigations, we present an informative sample selection method

Proceedings of the 2006 Conference on Empirical Methods in Natural Language Processing (EMNLP 2006), pages 509–516,
Sydney, July 2006.

for building high quality and stable NER models. Experimental results show that the performance of the NER model is enhanced significantly across domains after being trained with these informative samples. In spite of our focus on Chinese, we believe that some of our observations can be potentially useful to other languages including English.

This paper is organized as follows. Section 2 describes a Chinese NER system using multi-level linguistic features. Section 3 discusses the impact of domain information and training data size on the NER performance. Section 4 presents an informative sample selection method to enhance the performance of the NER model across domains. Finally the conclusion is given in Section 5.

2 Chinese NER Based on Multilevel Linguistic Features

In this paper, we focus on recognizing four types of NEs: Persons (PER), Locations (LOC), Organizations (ORG) and miscellaneous named entities (MISC) which do not belong to the previous three groups (e.g. products, conferences, events, brands, etc.). All the NER models in the following experiments are trained with a Chinese NER system. In this section, we simply describe this Chinese NER system. The Robust Risk Minimization (RRM) Classification method and multi-level linguistic features are used in this system (Guo et al., 2005).

2.1 Robust Risk Minimization Classifier

We can view the NER task as a sequential classification problem. If tok_i $(i = 0, 1, ..., n)$ denotes the sequence of tokenized text which is the input to the system, then every token tok_i should be assigned a class-label t_i.

The class label value t_i associated with each token tok_i is predicted by estimating the conditional probability $P(t_i = c|x_i)$ for every possible class-label value c, where x_i is a feature vector associated with token tok_i.

We assume that $P(t_i = c|x_i) = P(t_i = c|tok_i, \{t_j\}_{j \leq i})$. The feature vector x_i can depend on previously predicted class labels $\{t_j\}_{j \leq i}$, but the dependency is typically assumed to be local. In the RRM method, the above conditional probability model has the following parametric form:

$$P(t_i = c|x_i, t_{i-l}, ..., t_{i-1}) = T(w_c^T x_i + b_c),$$

where $T(y) = \min(1, \max(0, y))$ is the truncation of y into the interval [0, 1]. w_c is a linear weight vector and b_c is a constant. Parameters w_c and b_c can be estimated from the training data. Given training data (x_i, t_i) for $i = 1, ..., n$, the model is estimated by solving the following optimization problem for each c (Zhang et al., 2002):

$$\inf_{w,b} \frac{1}{n} \sum_{i=1}^{n} f(w_c^T x_i + b_c, y_c^i),$$

where $y_c^i = 1$ when $t_i = c$, and $y_c^i = -1$ otherwise. The function f is defined as:

$$f(p, y) = \begin{cases} -2py & py < 1 \\ \frac{1}{2}(py - 1)^2 & py \in [-1, 1] \\ 0 & py > 1 \end{cases}$$

Given the above conditional probability model, the best possible sequence of t_i's can be estimated by dynamic programming in the decoding stage (Zhang et al., 2002).

2.2 Multilevel Linguistic Features

This Chinese NER system uses Chinese characters (not Chinese words) as the basic token units, and then maps word-based features that are associated with each word into corresponding features of those characters that are contained in the word. This approach can effectively incorporate both character-based features and word-based features. In general, we may regard this approach as information integration from linguistic views at different abstraction levels.

We integrate a diverse set of local linguistic features, including word segmentation information, Chinese word patterns, complex lexical linguistic features (e.g. part of speech and semantic features), aligned at the character level. In additional, we also use external NE hints and gazetteers, including surnames, location suffixes, organization suffixes, titles, high-frequency Chinese characters in Chinese names and translation names, and lists of locations and organizations. In this system, local linguistic features of a token unit are derived from the sentence containing this token unit. All special linguistic patterns (i.e. date, time, numeral expression) are encoded into pattern-specific class labels aligned with the tokens.

3 Impact of Training Data Size And Domain Information on the NER Performance

It is very important to keep the performance stability of NER models across domains in practice.

However, the performance usually becomes unstable when NER models are applied in different domains. We focus on the impact of the training data size and domain information on the NER performance in this section.

3.1 Data

We built a large-scale high-quality Chinese NE annotated corpus. The corpus size is 114.25M Chinese characters. All the data are news articles selected from several Chinese newspapers in 2001 and 2002. All the NEs in the corpus are manually tagged. Documents in the corpus are also manually classified into eight domain categories, including politics, sports, science, economics, entertainment, life, society and others. Cross-validation is employed to ensure the tagging quality.

All the training data and test data in the experiments are selected from this Chinese annotated corpus. The general training data are randomly selected from the corpus without distinguishing their domain categories. All the domain-specific training data are selected from the corpus according to their domain categories. One general test data set and seven domain-specific test data sets are used in our experiments (see Table 1). The size of the general test data set is 1.34M Chinese characters. Seven domain-specific test sets are extracted from the general test data set according to the document domain categories.

Domain	NE distribution in the domain-oriented test data set					Test set Size
	PER	ORG	LOC	MISC	Total	
General	11,991	9,820	12,353	1,820	35,984	1.34M
Politics	2,470	1,528	2,540	480	7,018	0.2M
Economics	1,098	2,971	2,362	493	6,924	0.26M
Sports	1,802	1,323	1,246	478	4,849	0.10M
Entertainment	2,458	526	738	542	4,264	0.10M
Society	916	418	823	349	2,506	0.08M
Life	2,331	1,690	3,634	763	8,418	0.39M
Science	1,802	1,323	1,246	478	4,849	0.10M

Table 1: NE distribution in the general and domain-specific test data sets

In our evaluation, only NEs with correct boundaries and correct class labels are considered as the correct recognition. We use the standard P (i.e. Precision), R (i.e. Recall), and F-measure (defined as 2PR/(P+R)) to measure the performance of NER models.

3.2 Impact of Training Data Size on the NER Performance across Domains

The amount of annotated data is always a bottleneck for supervised learning methods in practice.

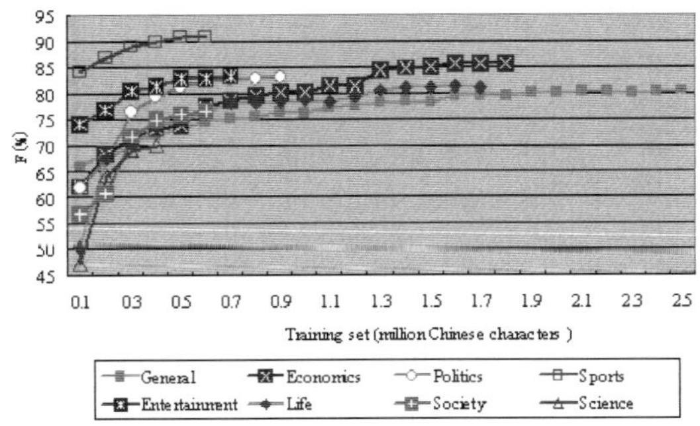

Figure 1: Performance curves of the general and specific domain NER models

Thus, we evaluate the impact of training data size on the NER performance across domains.

In this baseline experiment, an initial general NER model is trained with 0.1M general data at first. Then the NER model is incrementally retrained by adding 0.1M new general training data each time till the performance isn't enhanced significantly. The NER performance curve (labelled with the tag "General") in the whole retraining process is shown in Figure 1. Experimental results show that the performance of the general NER model is significantly enhanced in the first several retraining cycles since more training data are used. However, when the general training data set size is more than 2.4M, the performance enhancement is very slight.

In order to analyze how the training data size impacting the performance of NER models in specific domains, seven domain-specific NER models are built using the similar retraining process. Each domain-specific NER model is also trained with 0.1M domain-specific data at first. Then, each initial domain-specific NER model is incrementally retrained by adding 0.1M new domain-specific data each time.

NER Model	F(%)	Size threshold (M)	NE distribution in the training set				
			PER	ORG	LOC	MISC	Total
General	80.38	2.4	24,960	27,231	21,098	7,439	80,728
Politics	83.09	0.9	11,388	6,618	14,350	1,974	34,330
Economics	85.46	1.7	7,197	21,113	15,582	3,466	47,358
Sports	90.78	0.6	11,647	8,105	7,468	3,070	30,290
Entertainment	83.31	0.6	12,954	2,823	4,665	3,518	32,860
Society	76.55	0.6	7,099	3,279	6,946	1,909	19,233
Life	81.06	1.7	10,502	5,675	18,980	2,420	37,577
Science	70.02	0.4	1,625	3,010	2,083	902	7,620

Table 2: Performance of NER models, size threshold and NE distribution in the corresponding training data sets

The performance curves of these domain-specific NER models are also shown in Figure 1 (see the curves labelled with the domain tags). Although the initial performance of each domain-specific NER model varies with domains, the performance is also significantly enhanced in the first several retraining cycles. When the size of the domain-specific training data set is above a certain threshold, the performance enhancement is very slight as well.

The final performance of the trained NER models, and the corresponding training data sets are shown in Table 2.

From these NER performance curves, we obtain the following observations.

1. More training data are used, higher NER performance can be achieved. However, it is difficult to significantly enhance the performance when the training data size is above a certain threshold.

2. The threshold of the training data size and the final achieved performance vary with domains (see Table 2). For example, in entertainment domain, the threshold is 0.6M and the final F-measure achieves 83.31%. In economic domain, the threshold is 1.7M, and the corresponding F-measure is 85.46%.

3.3 The Performance Stability of Each NE Type Recognition across Domains

Statistic data on our large-scale annotated corpus (shown in Table 3) show that the distribution of NE types varies with domains. We define " NE density " to quantitatively measure the NE distribution in an annotated data set. NE density is defined as "the count of NE instances in one thousand Chinese characters". Higher NE density usually indicates that more NEs are contained in the data set. We may easily measure the distribution of each NE type across domains using NE density. In this annotated corpus, PER, LOC, and ORG have similar NE density while MISC has the smallest NE density. All the NE types also have different NE density in each domain. For example, the NE density of ORG and LOC is much higher than that of PER in economic domain. PER and LOC have higher NE density than ORG in politics domain. PER has the highest NE density among these NE types in both sports and entertainment domains. The unbalanced NE distribution across domains shows that news articles on different domains usually focus on different specific NE types. These NE distribution features imply that each NE type has different domain dependency feature. The performance stability of domain-focused NE type recognition becomes more important in domain-specific applications. For example, since economic news articles usually focus on ORG and LOC NEs, the high-quality LOC and ORG recognition models will be more valuable in economic domain. In addition, these distribution features also can be used to guide training and test data selection.

Domain	NE distribution in the specific domain					
	PER	LOC	ORG	MISC	ALL	Ratio (%)
Politics	167,989	180,193	105,936	30,830	484,948	16.43
Economics	117,459	200,261	352,323	76,320	746,363	25.29
Sports	129,137	73,435	98,618	33,304	334,494	11.33
Entertainment	154,193	50,408	40,444	52,460	297,505	10.08
Life	200,222	234,150	145,138	65,733	645,243	21.86
Society	63,793	53,724	43,657	21,162	182,336	6.18
Science	27,878	30,737	72,413	16,824	147,852	5.00
Others	31,723	40,730	26,666	13,926	113,045	3.83
All	892,394	863,638	885,195	310,559	2,951,786	–
Domain	NE density in the Chinese annotated corpus					Size (M)
	PER	LOC	ORG	MISC	ALL	
Politics	10.70	11.48	6.75	1.96	31.21	15.70
Economics	4.18	7.13	12.55	2.72	26.58	28.08
Sports	16.43	9.34	12.55	4.24	42.57	7.86
Entertainment	16.81	5.05	4.14	5.72	32.44	9.17
Life	5.64	6.59	4.09	1.85	18.17	35.52
Society	8.57	7.22	5.87	2.84	24.51	7.44
Science	4.30	4.74	11.17	2.60	22.82	6.48
Others	7.9	10.18	6.67	3.48	28.26	4.00
All	7.81	7.56	7.75	2.72	25.89	114.25

Table 3: NE distribution in the Chinese annotated corpus

In this experiment, the performance stability of NER models across domains is evaluated, especially the performance stability of each NE type recognition. The general NER model is trained with 2.4M general data. Seven domain-specific models are trained with the corresponding domain-specific training sets (see Table 2 in Section 3.2).

The performance stability of the general NER model is firstly evaluated on the general and domain-specific test data sets (see Table 1 in Section 3.1). The experimental results are shown in Table 4. The performance curves of the general model are shown in Figure 2, including the total F-measure curve of the NER model (labelled with the tag "All") and F-measure curves of each NE type recognition in the specific domains (labelled with the NE tags respectively).

The performance stability of the seven domain-specific NER models are also evaluated. Each domain-specific NER model is tested on the gen-

Domain	F(%) of general NER model				
	PER	LOC	ORG	MISC	ALL
General	86.69	85.55	73.59	56.00	80.38
Economic	85.11	88.22	75.91	49.53	80.50
Politics	86.26	87.00	71.31	61.50	81.90
Sports	91.87	89.03	81.67	67.41	86.10
Entertainment	84.24	85.85	68.65	60.96	79.31
Life	86.62	83.54	70.30	58.49	79.73
Society	84.53	76.16	68.89	41.14	74.50
Science	87.74	86.42	65.85	24.10	69.55

Table 4: Performance of the general NER model in specific domains

NER Model	F(%) in specific domain							
	General	Economic	Politics	Sports	Entertainment	Life	Society	Science
General	80.38	80.50	81.90	86.10	79.31	79.73	74.50	69.55
Economic	75.30	85.46	74.32	72.89	68.46	76.23	65.75	68.97
Politics	73.37	66.39	83.09	76.37	71.51	74.83	67.31	53.76
Sports	71.23	62.56	68.99	90.78	73.48	71.18	64.82	53.85
Entertainment	70.82	61.52	72.04	75.34	83.31	71.80	69.10	52.50
Life	73.53	66.92	75.07	73.86	72.68	81.06	69.61	57.36
Society	70.29	62.55	72.70	70.69	72.24	74.10	76.55	53.42
Science	67.26	67.57	69.00	64.32	63.84	69.05	64.85	70.02

Table 5: Performance of NER models in specific domains

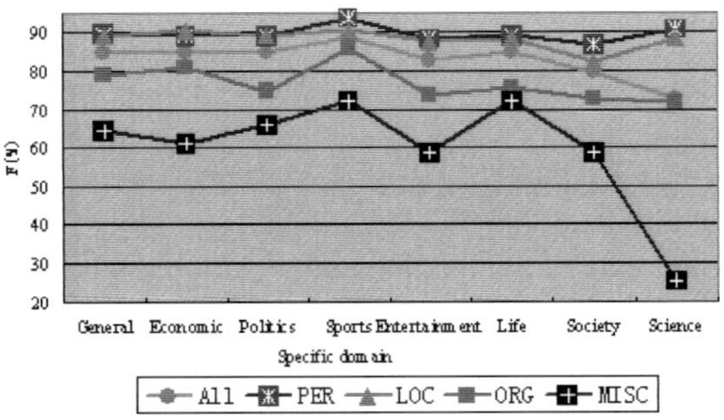

Figure 2: Performance curves of the general NER model in specific domains

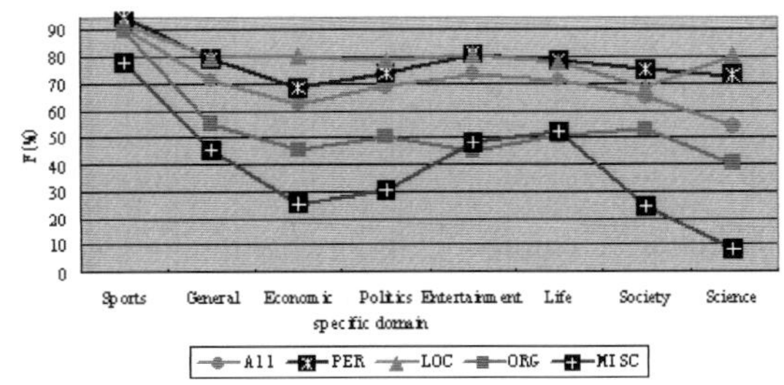

Figure 4: Performance curves of sports domain NER model in the other specific domains

eral test data and the other six different domain-specific test data sets. The experimental results are shown in Table 5. The performance curves of three domain-specific NER models are shown in Figure 3, Figure 4 and Figure 5 respectively.

From these experimental results, we have the following conclusions.

1. The performance stability of all the NER models is limited across domains. When a NER model is employed in a new domain, its performance usually decreases. Moreover, its performance is usually much lower than the performance of the corresponding domain-specific model.

2. The general NER model has better performance stability than the domain-specific NER model when they are applied in new domains (see Table 5). Domain-specific models usually could achieve a higher performance in its corresponding domain after being trained with a smaller amount of domain-specific annotated data (see Table 2 in Section 3.2). However, the performance stability of domain-specific NER model is poor across different domains. Thus, it is very popular to build a general NER model for the general applications in practice.

3. The performance of PER, LOC and ORG recognition is better than that of MISC recog-

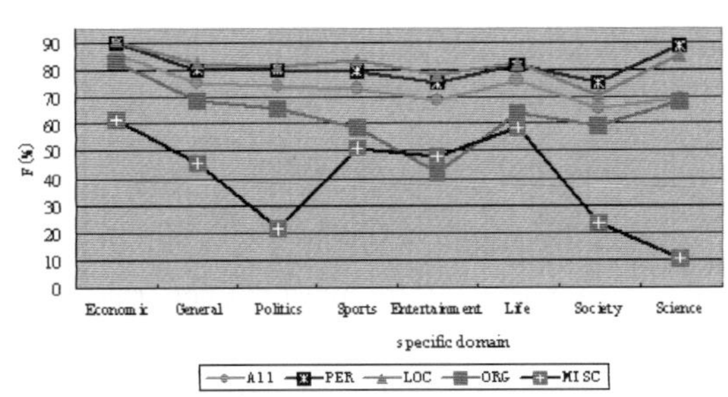

Figure 3: Performance curves of economic domain NER model in the other specific domains

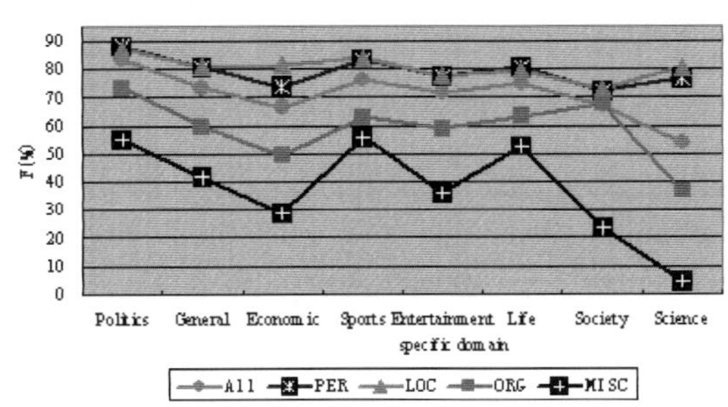

Figure 5: Performance curves of politics domain NER model in the other specific domains

nition in NER (see Figure 2 ~ Figure 5). The main reason for the poor performance of MISC recognition is that there are less common indicative features among various MISC NEs which we do not distinguish. In addition, NE density of MISC is much less than that of PER, LOC, and ORG. There are a relatively small number of positive training samples for MISC recognition.

4. NE types have different domain dependency attribute. The performance stability of each NE type recognition varies with domains (see Figure 2 ~ Figure 5). The performance of PER and LOC recognition are more stable across domains. Thus, few efforts are needed to adapt the existing high-quality general PER and LOC recognition models in domain-specific applications. Since ORG and MISC NEs usually contain more domain-specific semantic information, ORG and MISC are more domain-dependent than PER and LOC. Thus, more domain-specific features should be mined for ORG and MISC recognition.

4 Use Informative Training Samples to Enhance the Performance of NER Models across Domains

A higher performance system usually requires more features and a larger number of training data. This requires larger system memory and more efficient training method, which may not be available. Within the limitation of available training data and computational resources, it is necessary for us to either limit the number of features or select more informative data which can be efficiently handled by the training algorithm. Active learning method is usually employed in text classification (McCallum and Nigam et al., 1998). It is only recently employed in NER (Shen et al., 2004).

In order to enhance the performance and overcome the limitation of available training data and computational resources, we present an informative sample selection method using a variant of uncertainty-sampling (Lewis and Catlett, 1994). The main steps are described as follows.

1. Build an initial NER model (F-measure=76.24%) using an initial data set. The initial data set (about 1M Chinese characters) is randomly selected from the large-scale candidate data set (about 9M).

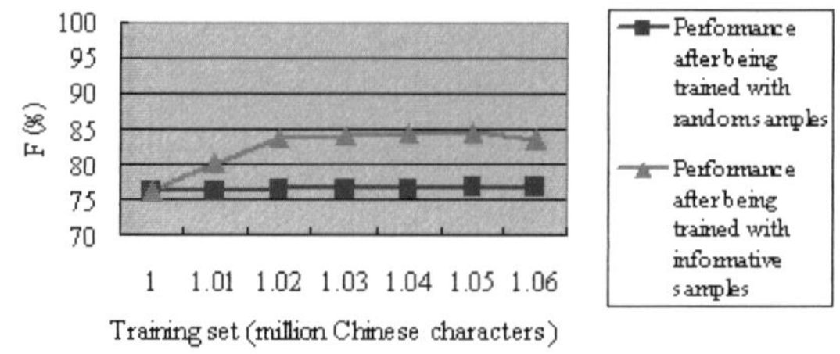

Figure 6: Performance curves of general NER models after being trained with informative samples and random samples respectively

2. Refine the training set by adding more informative samples and removing those redundant samples. In this refinement phase, all of the data are annotated by the current recognition model (e.g. the initial model built in Step 1). Each annotation has a confidence score associated with the prediction. In general, an annotation with lower confidence score usually indicates a wrong prediction. The confidence score of the whole sample sentence is defined as the average of the confidence scores of all the annotations contained in the sentence. Thus, we add those sample sentences with lower confidence scores into the training set. Meanwhile, in order to keep a reasonable size of the training set, those old training sample sentences with higher confidence scores are removed from the current training set. In each retraining phase, all of the sample sentences are sorted by the confidence score. The top 1000 new sample sentences with lowest confidence scores are added into the current training set. The top 500 old training sample sentences with highest confidence scores are removed from the current training set.

3. Retrain a new Chinese NER model with the newly refined training set

4. Repeat Step 2 and Step 3, until the performance doesn't improve any more.

We apply this informative sample selection method to incrementally build the general domain NER model. The size of the final informative training sample set is 1.05M Chinese characters. This informative training sample set has higher NE density than the random training data set (see Table 6).

We denote this general NER model trained with the informative sample set as "general informative model", and denote the general-domain model which is trained with 2.4M random general training data as "general random model". The performance curves of the general NER models after being trained with informative samples and random data respectively are shown in Figure 6. Experiment results (see Table 6) show that there is a significant enhancement in F-measure if using informative training samples. Compared with the random model, the informative model can increase F-measure by 4.21 percent points.

Type	Using informative sample set (1.05M)			Using random training set (2.4M)		
	F(%)	NEs	NE density	F(%)	NEs	NE density
PER	89.87	18,898	18.00	86.69	24,960	10.38
LOC	89.68	24,862	23.68	85.55	21,089	11.33
ORG	79.22	22,173	21.12	73.59	27,231	8.78
MISC	64.27	8,067	7.68	56.00	7,439	3.10
Total	84.59	74,000	70.48	80.38	80,728	33.58

Table 6: Performance of informative model and random model in the general domain

Domain	F(%) of general informative model				
	PER	LOC	ORG	MISC	ALL
Economic	89.26	90.66	81.24	61.14	84.63
Politics	89.36	89.37	74.76	65.95	84.70
Sports	93.65	90.66	86.00	72.05	88.71
Entertainment	88.38	87.54	73.88	58.32	82.74
Life	89.15	88.35	75.68	72.01	84.66
Society	86.61	82.15	72.99	58.55	79.49
Science	90.91	88.35	71.69	25.16	72.71

Table 7: Performance of the general informative model in specific domains

This informative model is also evaluated on the domain-specific test sets. Experimental results are shown in Table 7. We view the performance of the domain-specific NER model as the baseline performance in its corresponding domain (see Table 8), denoted as $F_{baseline}$. The performance of informative model in specific domains is very close to the corresponding $F_{baseline}$ (see Figure 7). We define the domain-specific average F-measure as the average of all the F-measure of the NER model in seven specific domains, denote as $\overline{F}$. The average of all the $F_{baseline}$ in specific domains is denoted as $\overline{F}_{baseline}$. The average F-measure of the informative model and the random model in specific domains is denoted as $\overline{F}_{informative}$ and $\overline{F}_{random}$ respectively. Compared with $\overline{F}_{baseline}$ ($\overline{F}$ =81.47%), the informative model increases $\overline{F}$ by 1.05 percent points. However, $\overline{F}$ decreases by 2.67 percent points if using the random model. Especially, the performance of the informative model is better than the corresponding baseline performance in politics, life, society and science domains. Moreover, the size of the informative sample set is much less than the life domain training set (1.7M).

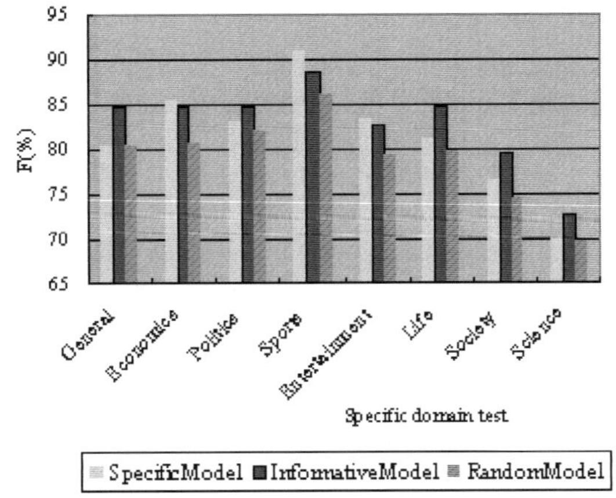

Figure 7: Performance comparison of informative model, random model, and the corresponding domain-specific models

NER model	F(%) in specific domains							$\overline{F}$
	Economic	Politics	Sports	Entertainment	Life	Society	Science	
domain-specific (baseline)	85.46	83.09	90.78	83.31	81.06	76.55	70.02	81.47
Informative	84.63	84.70	88.71	82.74	84.66	79.49	72.71	82.52
Random	80.50	81.90	86.10	79.31	79.73	74.50	69.55	78.80
NER model	$\delta(F)$ in specific domain $\delta(F) = (F - \overline{F})$							σ
	Economic	Politics	Sports	Entertainment	Life	Society	Science	
Informative	2.11	2.18	6.19	0.22	2.14	-3.03	-9.81	4.74
Random	1.7	3.1	7.3	0.51	0.93	-4.3	-9.25	4.94

Table 8: Performance comparison of informative model, random model and the corresponding domain-specific model in each specific domain

The informative model has much better performance than the random model in specific domains (see Table 8 and Figure 7). $\overline{F}_{informative}$ is 82.52% while $\overline{F}_{random}$ is 78.80%. The informative model can increase $\overline{F}$ by 3.72 percent points. The informative model is also more stable than the random model in specific domains (see Table 8). Standard deviation of F-measure for the informative model is 4.74 while that for the random model is 4.94.

Our experience with the incremental sample selection provides the following hints.

1. The performance of the NER model across domains can be significantly enhanced after being trained with informative samples. In

order to obtain a high-quality and stable NER model, it is only necessary to keep the informative samples. Informative sample selection can alleviate the problem of obtaining a large amount of annotated data. It is also an effective method for overcoming the potential limitation of computational resources.

2. In learning NER models, annotated results with lower confidence scores are more useful than those samples with higher confidence scores. This is consistent with other studies on active learning.

5 Conclusion

Efficient and robust NER model is very important in practice. This paper provides an empirical study on the impact of training data size and domain information on the performance stability of NER. Experimental results show that it is difficult to significantly enhance the performance when the training data size is above a certain threshold. The threshold of the training data size varies with domains. The performance stability of each NE type recognition also varies with domains. The large-scale corpus statistic data also show that NE types have different distribution across domains. These empirical investigations provide useful hints for enhancing the performance stability of NER models across domains with less efforts. In order to enhance the NER performance across domains, we present an informative training sample selection method. Experimental results show that the performance is significantly enhanced by using informative training samples.

In the future, we'd like to focus on further exploring more effective methods to adapt NER model to a new domain with much less efforts, time and performance degrading.

References

Daniel M. Bikel, Richard L. Schwartz, and Ralph M. Weischedel. 1999. An algorithm that learns what's in a name. *Machine Learning*, 34(1-3):211–231.

Andrew Borthwick. 1999. *A Maximum Entropy Approach to Named Entity Recognition*. Ph.D. thesis, New York University.

Xavier Carreras, Lluís Màrquez, and Lluís Padró. 2003. A simple named entity extractor using adaboost. In *Proceedings of CoNLL-2003*, pages 152–155.

Radu Florian, Abe Ittycheriah, Hongyan Jing, and Tong Zhang. 2003. Named entity recogintion through classifier combination. In *Proceedings CoNLL-2003*, pages 168–171.

Jian F. Gao, Mu Li, Anndy Wu, and Chang N., Huang. 2005. Chinese Word Segmentation and Named Entity Recognition: A Pragmatic Approach. *Computational Linguisitc*,31(4):531-574.

Hong L. Guo, Jian M. Jiang, Gang Hu, and Tong Zhang. 2005. Chinese Named Entity Recognition Based on Multilevel Linguistic Features. *Lecture Notes in Artificial Intelligence*,3248:90-99,Springer.

Hideki Isozaki and Hideto Kazawa. 2002. Efficient support vector classifiers for named entity recognition. In *Proceedings of Coling-2002*, pages 1-7.

Hongyan Jing, Radu Florian, Xiaoqiang Luo, Tong Zhang, and Abraham Ittycheriah. 2003. Howtogetachinesename (entity) : Segmentation and combination issues. In *EMNLP 2003*, pages 200-207.

Dan Klein, Joseph Smarr, Huy Nguyen, and Christopher D. Manning. 2003. Named entity recognition with character-level models. In *Proceedings of CoNLL-2003*, pages 180–183.

David D. Lewis and Jason Catlett. 1994. Heterogeneous uncertainty sampling for supervised learning. In *Proceedings of the Eleventh International Conference on Machine Learning*, pages 148–156.

Andrew Kamal McCallum and K. Nigam. 1998. Employing EM in pool-based active learning for text classification. *Proceedings of 15th International Conference on Machine Learning*, pages 350-358.

Fien De Meulder and Walter Daelemans. 2003. Memory-based named entity recognition using unannotated data. In *Proceedings of CoNLL-2003*, pages 208–211.

Erik F. Tjong Kim Sang and Fien De Meulder. 2003. Introduction to the conll-2003 shared task: Language independent named entity recognition. In Walter Daelemans and Miles Osborne, editors, *Proceedings of CoNLL-2003*, pages 142–147.

Dan Shen, Jie Zhang, Jian Su, Gou D. Zhou, and Chew L.Tan, 2004. Multi-Criteria-based Active Learning for Named Entity Recognition. *Proceedings of ACL04*, pages 589-596.

Yu Z. Wu, Jun Zhao, Bo Xu, and Hao Yu. 2005. Chinese Named Entity Recognition Based on Multiple Features. *Proceedings of EMNLP05*, pages 427-434

Shi H. Yu, Shuan H. Bai, and Paul Wu. 1998. Description of the kent ridge digital labs system used for muc-7. In *Proceedings of the Seventh Message Understanding Conference (MUC-7)*.

Tong Zhang, Fred Damerau, and David E. Johnson. 2002. Text chunking based on a generalization of Winnow. *Journal of Machine Learning Research*, 2:615–637.

Statistical Ranking in Tactical Generation

Erik Velldal
University of Oslo (Norway)
erik.velldal@ifi.uio.no

Stephan Oepen
University of Oslo (Norway)
and CSLI Stanford (CA)
oe@csli.stanford.edu

Abstract

In this paper we describe and evaluate several statistical models for the task of *realization ranking*, i.e. the problem of discriminating between competing surface realizations generated for a given input semantics. Three models (and several variants) are trained and tested: an n-gram language model, a discriminative maximum entropy model using structural information (and incorporating the language model as a separate feature), and finally an SVM ranker trained on the same feature set. The resulting hybrid tactical generator is part of a larger, semantic transfer MT system.

1 Introduction

This paper describes the application of several different statistical models for the task of *realization ranking* in tactical generation, i.e. the problem of choosing among multiple paraphrases that are generated for a given meaning representation. The specific realization component we use is the open-source chart generator of the Linguistic Knowledge Builder (LKB; Carroll, Copestake, Flickinger, & Poznanski, 1999; Carroll & Oepen, 2005). Given a meaning representation in the form of Minimal Recursion Semantics (MRS; Copestake, Flickinger, Malouf, Riehemann, & Sag, 1995), the generator outputs English realizations in accordance with the HPSG LinGO English Resource Grammar (ERG; Flickinger, 2002).

As an example of generator output, a sub-set of alternate realizations that are produced for a single input MRS is shown in Figure 1. For the two data sets considered in this paper, the average number of realizations produced by the generator is 85.7 and 102.2 (the maximum numbers are 4176 and 3408, respectively). Thus, there is immediate demand for a principled way of choosing a single output among the generated candidates. For this task we train and test three different statistical models: an n-gram language model, a maximum entropy model (MaxEnt) and a (linear) support vector machine (SVM). These are all models that have proved popular within the NLP community, but it is usually only the first of these three that has been applied to the task of ranking in sentence generation. The latter two models that we present here go beyond the surface information used by the n-gram model, and are trained on a *symmetric treebank* with features defined over the full HPSG analyses of competing realizations. Furthermore, such discriminative models are suitable for 'on-line' use within our generator—adopting the technique of *selective unpacking* from a packed forest (Carroll & Oepen, 2005)—which means our hybrid realizer obviates the need for exhaustive enumeration of candidate outputs. The present results extend our earlier work (Velldal, Oepen, & Flickinger, 2004)—and the related work of Nakanishi, Miyao, & Tsujii (2005)—to an enlarged data set, more feature types, and additional learners.

The rest of this paper is structured as follows. Section 2 first gives a general summary of the various statistical models we will be considering, as well as the measures used for evaluating them. We then go on to define the task we are aiming to solve in terms of treebank data and feature types in Section 3. By looking at different variants of the MaxEnt model we review some results for the relative contribution of individual features and the impact of frequency cutoffs for feature selection. Keeping these parameters constant then, Section 4 provides an array of empirical results on the relative performance of the various approaches.

2 Models

In this section we briefly review the different types of statistical models that we use for ranking the output of the generator. We start by describing the language model, and then go on to review the framework for discriminative MaxEnt models and SVM rankers. In the following we will use s and r to denote semantic inputs and generated realizations respectively.

Proceedings of the 2006 Conference on Empirical Methods in Natural Language Processing (EMNLP 2006), pages 517–525,
Sydney, July 2006.

Remember that dogs must be on a leash.
Remember dogs must be on a leash.
On a leash, remember that dogs must be.
On a leash, remember dogs must be.
A leash, remember that dogs must be on.
A leash, remember dogs must be on.
Dogs, remember must be on a leash.

Table 1: A small example set of generator outputs using the ERG. Where the input semantics is no specified for aspects of information structure (e.g. requesting foregrounding of a specific entity), paraphrases include all grammatically legitimate topicalizations. Other choices involve, for example, the optionality of complementizers and relative pronouns, permutation of (intersective) modifiers, and lexical and orthographic alternations.

2.1 Language Models

The use of n-gram language models is the most common approach to statistical selection in generation (Langkilde & Knight, 1998; and White (2004); inter alios). In order to better assert the relative performance of the discriminative models and the structural features we present below, we also apply a trigram model to the ranking problem. Using the freely available CMU SLM Toolkit (Clarkson & Rosenfeld, 1997), we trained a trigram model on an unannotated version of the British National Corpus (BNC), containing roughly 100 million words (using Witten-Bell discounting and back-off). Given such a model p_n, the score of a realization r_i with surface form $w_{i1}^k = (w_{i1}, \ldots, w_{ik})$ is then computed as

(1) $$F(s, r_i) = \sum_{j=1}^{k} p_n(w_{i,j} | w_{i,j-n}, \ldots, w_{i,j-1})$$

Given the scoring function F, the best realization is selected according to the following decision function:

(2) $$\hat{r} = \arg\max_{r' \in \mathcal{Y}(s)} F(s, r')$$

Although in this case scoring is not conditioned on the input semantics at all, we still include it to make the function formulation more general as we will be reusing it later.

Note that, as the realizations in our symmetric treebank also include punctuation marks, these are also treated as separate tokens by the language model (in addition to pseudo-tokens marking sentence boundaries).

2.2 Maximum Entropy Models

Maximum entropy modeling provides a very flexible framework that has been widely used for a range of tasks in NLP, including parse selection (e.g. Johnson, Geman, Canon, Chi, & Riezler, 1999; Malouf & Noord, 2004) and reranking for machine translation (e.g. Och et al., 2004). A model is specified by a set of real-valued *feature functions* that describe properties of the data, and an associated set of *learned weights* that determine the contribution of each feature.

Let us first introduce some notation before we go on. Let $\mathcal{Y}(s_i) = \{r_1, \ldots, r_m\}$ be the set of realizations licensed by the grammar for a semantic representation s_i. Now, let our (positive) training data be given as $X_p = \{x_1, \ldots, x_N\}$ where each x_i is a pair (s_i, r_j) for which $r_j \in \mathcal{Y}(s_i)$ and r_j is annotated in the treebank as being a correct realization of s_i. Note that we might have several different members of $\mathcal{Y}(s_i)$ that pair up with s_i in X_p. In our set-up, this is the case where multiple HPSG derivations for the same input semantics project identical surface strings.

Given a set of d features (as further described in Section 3.2), each pair of semantic input s and hypothesized realization r is mapped to a feature vector $\Phi(s, r) \in \Re^d$. The goal is then to find a vector of weights $w \in \Re^d$ that optimize the likelihood of the training data. A conditional MaxEnt model of the probability of a realization r given the semantics s, is defined as

(3) $$p_w(r|s) = \frac{e^{F_w(s,r)}}{Z_w(s)}$$

where the function F_w is simply the sum of the products of all feature values and feature weights, given by

(4) $$F_w(s, r) = \sum_{i=1}^{d} w_i \Phi_i(s, r) = w \cdot \Phi(s, r)$$

The normalization term Z_w is defined as

(5) $$Z_w(s) = \sum_{r' \in \mathcal{Y}(s)} e^{F_w(s,r)}$$

When we want to find the best realization for a given input semantics according to a model p_w, it is sufficient to compute the score function as in Equation (4) and then use the decision function previously given in Equation (2) above. When it comes to estimating[1] the parameters w, the procedure seeks to maximize the (log of) a penalized likelihood function as in

$$(6) \quad \hat{w} = \arg\max_{w} \log L(w) - \frac{\sum_{i=1}^{d} w_i^2}{2\sigma^2}$$

where $L(w)$ is the 'conditionalized' likelihood of the training data X_p (Johnson et al., 1999), computed as $L(w) = \prod_{i=1}^{N} p_w(r_i|s_i)$. The second term of the likelihood function in Equation (6) is a penalty term that is commonly used for reducing the tendency of log-linear models to over-fit, especially when training on sparse data using many features (Chen & Rosenfeld, 1999; Johnson et al., 1999; Malouf & Noord, 2004). More specifically it defines a zero-mean Gaussian prior on the feature weights which effectively leads to less extreme values. After empirically tuning the prior on our 'Jotunheimen' treebank (training and testing by 10-fold cross-validation), we ended up using $\sigma^2 = 0.003$ for the MaxEnt models applied in this paper.

2.3 SVM Rankers

In this section we briefly formulate the optimization problem in terms of support vector machines. Our starting point is the SVM approach introduced in Joachims (2002) for learning ranking functions for information retrieval. In our case the aim is to learn a ranking function from a set of preference relations on sentences generated for a given input semantics.

In contrast to the MaxEnt approach, the SVM approach has a geometric rather than probabilistic view on the problem. Similarly to the the MaxEnt set-up, the SVM learner will try to learn a linear scoring function as defined in Equation (4) above. However, instead of maximizing the probability of the preferred or positive realizations, we try to maximize their value for F_w directly.

Recall our definition of the set of positive training examples in Section 2.2. Let us here analogously define $X_n = \{x_1, \ldots, x_Q\}$ to be the negative counterpart, so that for a given pair $x = (s_i, r_j) \in X_n$, we have that $r_j \in \mathcal{Y}(s_i)$ but r_j is not annotated as a preferred realization of s_i. Following Joachims (2002), the goal is to minimize

$$(7) \quad V(w, \xi) = \frac{1}{2} w \cdot w + C \sum \xi_{i,j,k}$$

subject to the following constraints,

$$(8) \quad \forall ijk \text{ s.t. } (s_k, r_i) \in X_p \wedge (s_k, r_j) \in X_n : \\ w \cdot \Phi(s_k, r_i) \geq w \cdot \Phi(s_k, r_j) + 1 - \xi_{i,j,k}$$

$$(9) \quad \forall ijk : \ \xi_{i,j,k} \geq 0$$

Joachims (2002) shows that the preference constraints in Equation (8) can be rewritten as

$$(10) \quad w \cdot (\Phi(s_k, r_i) - \Phi(s_k, r_j)) \geq 1 - \xi_{i,j,k}$$

so that the optimization problem is equivalent to training a classifier on the pairwise difference vectors $\Phi(s_k, r_i) - \Phi(s_k, r_j)$. The (non-negative) slack variables $\xi_{i,j,k}$ are commonly used in SVMs to make it possible to approximate a solution by allowing some error in cases where a separating hyperplane can not be found. The trade-off between maximizing the margin size and minimizing the training error is governed by the constant C. Using the SVM^{light} package by Joachims (1999), we empirically specified $C = 0.005$ for the model described in this paper. Note that, for the experiments reported here, we will only be making binary distinctions of preferred/non-preferred realizations, although the approach presented in (Joachims, 2002) is formulated for the more general case of learning ordinal ranking functions.

Finally, given a linear SVM, we score and select realizations in the same way as we did with the MaxEnt model, according to Equations (4) and (2). Note, however, that it is also possible to use non-linear kernel functions with this set-up, since the ranking function can be represented as a linear combination of the feature vectors as in

$$(11) \quad w \cdot \Phi(s, r_i) = \sum \alpha_{j,k} \Phi(s_j, r_k) \Phi(s, r_i)$$

2.4 Evaluation Measures

The models presented in this paper are evaluated with respect to two simple metrics: exact match accuracy and word accuracy. The exact match measure simply counts the number of times that the model assigns the highest score to a string that exactly matches a corresponding 'gold' or reference sentence (i.e. a sentence that is marked as preferred in the treebank). This score is discounted appropriately in the case of ties between preferred and non-preferred candidates.

[1]We use the TADM open-source package (Malouf, 2002) for training the models, using its *limited-memory variable metric* as the optimization method and experimentally determine the optimal convergence threshold and variance of the prior.

if several realizations are given the top rank by the model. We also include the exact match accuracy for the five best candidates according to the models (see the n-best columns of Table 6).

The simple measure of exact match accuracy offers a very intuitive and transparent view on model performance. However, it is also in some respects too harsh as an evaluation measure in our setting since there will often be more than just one of the candidate realizations that provides a reasonable rendering of the input semantics. We therefore also include WA as similarity-based evaluation metric. This measure is based on the *Levensthein distance* between a candidate string and a reference, also known as *edit distance*. This is given by the minimum number of deletions, substitutions and insertions of words that are required to transform one string into another. If we let d, s and i represent the number of necessary deletions, substitutions and insertions respectively, and let l be the length of the reference, then WA is defined as

$$\text{WA} = 1 - \frac{d+s+i}{l} \qquad (12)$$

The scores produced by similarity measures such as WA are often difficult to interpret, but at least they provide an alternative view on the relative performance of the different models that we want to compare. We could also have used several other similarity measures here, such as the BLEU score which is a well-established evaluation metric within MT, but in our experience the various string similarity measures usually agree on the relative ranking of the different models.

3 Data Sets and Features

The following sections summarize the data sets and the feature types used in the experiments.

3.1 Symmetric Treebanks

Conditional parse selection models are standardly trained on a treebank consisting of strings paired with their optimal analyses. For our discriminative realization ranking experiments we require training corpora that provide the inverse relation. By assuming that the preferences captured in a standard treebank can constitute a *bidirectional* relation, Velldal et al. (2004) propose a notion of symmetric treebanks as the combination of (a) a set of pairings of surface forms and associated semantics; combined with (b) the sets of alternative analyses for each surface form, and (c) sets of alternate realizations of each semantic form. Using the semantics of the preferred analyses in an existing treebank as input to the generator, we can produce all equivalent paraphrases of the original string. Furthermore, assuming that the original surface form is an optimal verbalization of the corresponding semantics, we can automatically label the preferred realization(s) by matching the *yields* of the generated trees against the original strings in the 'source' treebank. The result is what we call a *generation treebank*, which taken together with the original parse-oriented pairings constitute a full symmetrical treebank.

We have successfully applied this technique to the tourism segments of the LinGO Redwoods treebank, which in turn is built atop the ERG.[2]

Jotunheimen

Bin	Items	Words	Trees	Gold	Chance
$100 \leq n$	396	21.7	367.4	20.7	0.083
$50 \leq n < 100$	246	18.5	73.7	11.5	0.160
$10 \leq n < 50$	831	14.8	24.2	6.3	0.277
$5 \leq n < 10$	426	10.1	7.0	3.0	0.436
$1 < n < 5$	291	11.2	3.3	1.6	0.486
Total	**2190**	**15.1**	**85.7**	**8.2**	**0.287**

Rondane

Bin	Items	Words	Trees	Gold	Chance
$100 \leq n$	107	21.8	498.4	17.8	0.060
$50 \leq n < 100$	63	19.1	72.9	12.0	0.162
$10 \leq n < 50$	244	15.2	23.4	4.9	0.234
$5 \leq n < 10$	119	11.9	7.2	2.7	0.377
$1 < n < 5$	101	9.3	3.21	1.5	0.476
Total	**634**	**15.1**	**102.2**	**6.8**	**0.263**

Table 2: Some core metrics for the symmetric treebanks *'Jotunheimen'* (top) and *'Rondane'* (bottom). The former data set was used for development and cross-validation testing, the latter for cross-genre held-out testing. The data items are aggregated relative to their number of realizations. The columns are, from left to right, the subdivision of the data according to the number of realizations, total number of items scored (excluding items with only one realization and ones where all realizations are marked as preferred), average string length, average number of realizations, and average number of references. The rightmost column shows a random choice baseline, i.e. the probability of selecting the preferred realization by chance.

[2] See '`http://www.delph-in.net/erg/`' for fur-

Table 2 summarizes the two resulting data sets, which are both comprised of instructional texts on tourist activities, the application domain of the background MT system.

3.2 Feature Templates

For the purpose of parse selection, Toutanova, Manning, Shieber, Flickinger, & Oepen (2002) and Toutanova & Manning (2002) train a discriminative log-linear model on the Redwoods parse treebank, using features defined over *derivation trees* with non-terminals representing the *construction types* and *lexical types* of the HPSG grammar (see Figure 1). The basic feature set of our MaxEnt realization ranker is defined in the same way (corresponding to the PCFG-S model of Toutanova & Manning, 2002), each feature capturing a sub-tree from the derivation limited to depth one. Table 3 shows example features in our MaxEnt and SVM models, where the feature template # 1 corresponds to local derivation sub-trees. To reduce the effects of data sparseness, feature type # 2 in Table 3 provides a back-off to derivation sub-trees, where the sequence of daughters is reduced, in turn, to just one of the daughters. Conversely, to facilitate sampling of larger contexts than just sub-trees of depth one, feature template # 1 allows optional grandparenting, including the upward chain of dominating nodes in some features. In our experiments, we found that grandparenting of up to three dominating nodes gave the best balance of enlarged context vs. data sparseness.

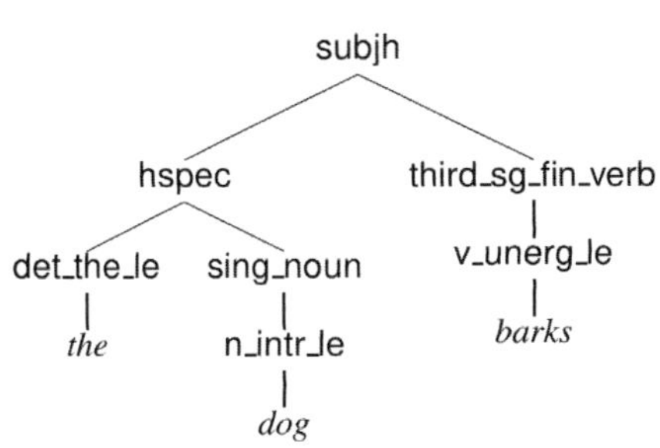

Figure 1: Sample HPSG derivation tree for the sentence *the dog barks*. Phrasal nodes are labeled with identifiers of grammar rules, and (preterminal) lexical nodes with class names for types of lexical entries.

In addition to these dominance-oriented features taken from the derivation trees of each realization, our models also include more surface-oriented features, viz. n-grams of lexical types with or without lexicalization. Feature type # 3 in Table 3 defines n-grams of variable size, where (in a loose analogy to part of speech tagging) sequences of lexical types capture syntactic category assignments. Feature templates # 3 and # 4 only differ with regard to lexicalization, as the former includes the surface token associated with the rightmost element of each n-gram. Unless otherwise noted, we used a maximum n-gram size of three in the experiments reported here, again due to its empirically determined best overall performance.

Id	Sample Features
1	⟨0 subjh hspec third_sg_fin_verb⟩
1	⟨1 $\triangle$ subjh hspec third_sg_fin_verb⟩
1	⟨0 hspec det_the_le sing_noun⟩
1	⟨1 subjh hspec det_the_le sing_noun⟩
1	⟨2 $\triangle$ subjh hspec det_the_le sing_noun⟩
2	⟨0 subjh third_sg_fin_verb⟩
2	⟨0 subjh hspce⟩
2	⟨1 subjh hspec det_the_le⟩
2	⟨1 subjh hspec sing_noun⟩
3	⟨1 n_intr_le *dog*⟩
3	⟨2 det_the_le n_intr_le *dog*⟩
3	⟨3 $\lhd$ det_the_le n_intr_le *dog*⟩
4	⟨1 n_intr_le⟩
4	⟨2 det_the_le n_intr_le⟩
4	⟨3 $\lhd$ det_the_le n_intr_le⟩

Table 3: Examples of structural features extracted from the derivation tree in Figure 1. The first column identifies the feature template corresponding to each example; in the examples, the first integer value is a parameter to feature templates, i.e. the depth of grandparenting (types 1 and 2) or n-gram size (types 3 and 4). The special symbols $\triangle$ and $\lhd$ denote the root of the tree and left periphery of the yield, respectively.

The number of instantiated features produced by the feature templates easily grows quite large. For the 'Jotunheimen' data the total number of distinct feature instantiations is 312,650. For the experiments in this paper we implemented a simple frequency based cutoff by removing features that are observed as *relevant* less than c times. We here follow the approach of Malouf & Noord (2004) where *relevance* of a feature is simply defined as taking on a different value for any two competing candidates for the same input. A feature is only included in training if it is relevant for more than c items in the training data. Table 4 shows the effect on the accuracy of the MaxEnt model when varying the cutoff. We see that a model can be

ther information and download pointers.

Cutoff	Features	Accuracy
–	312,650	71.18
1	264,455	71.18
2	112,051	70.03
3	66,069	70.28
4	46,139	69.30
5	35,295	67.93
10	16,036	65.36
20	7,563	63.05
50	2,605	59.10
100	889	54.21
200	261	50.11
500	34	34.70

Table 4: The effects of frequency-based feature selection with respect to model size and accuracy.

model configuration	match	WA
basic model of (Velldal et al., 2004)	63.09	0.904
basic plus partial daughter sequence	64.64	0.910
basic plus grandparenting	67.54	0.923
basic plus lexical type trigrams	68.61	0.921
basic plus all of the above	70.28	0.927
basic plus language model	67.96	0.912
basic plus all of the above	72.28	0.928

Table 5: Performance summaries of best-performing realization rankers using various feature configurations, when compared to the set-up of Velldal et al. (2004). These scores where computed using a relevance cutoff of 3 and optimizing the variance of the prior for individual configurations.

compacted quite aggressively without sacrificing much in performance. For all models presented below we use a cutoff of $c = 3$.

4 Results

In this section we present contrastive results for the models defined in Section 2 above, evaluated against the exact match accuracy and word accuracy as described in Section 2.4.

As can be seen in Table 6, both the MaxEnt and SVM learner does a much better job than the n-gram model at identifying the correct reference strings. The two discriminative models perform very similarly, however, although the MaxEnt model often seems to do slightly better.

When working with a cross-validation set-up the difference between the learners can conveniently be tested using an approach such as the cross-validated paired t-test described by Dietterich (1998). We also tried this approach using the Wilcoxon Matched-Pairs Signed-Ranks test as a non-parametric alternative without the assumption of normality of differences made in the t-test. However, none of the two tests found that the differences between the MaxEnt model and the SVM model were significant for $\alpha = 0.05$ (using two-sided tests).

Note that, due to memory constraints, we only included a random sample of maximum 50 non-preferred realizations per item in the training data used for the SVM ranker. Even so, the SVM trained on the full 'Jotunheimen' data had a total of 66,621 example vectors in its training data, which spawned a total of 639,301 preference constraints with respect to the optimization problem of Equations 8 and 10. We did not try to maximize performance on the development data by repeatedly training with different random samples, but this might be one way to improve the results.

Although we were only able to present results using linear kernels for the SVM ranker in this paper, preliminary experiments using a *polynomial* kernel seem to give promising results. Due to memory constraints and long convergence times, we were only able to train such a model on half of the 'Jotunheimen' data. However, when testing on the remaining half, it achieved an exact match accuracy of 71.03%. This is comparable to the performance achieved by the linear SVM through full 10-fold training and testing. Moreover, there is reason to believe that these results will improve once we manage to train on the full data set.

In order to assess the effect of increasing the size of the training set, Figure 3 presents learning curves for two MaxEnt configurations, viz. the basic configurational model and the one including all features but the language model. Each data point

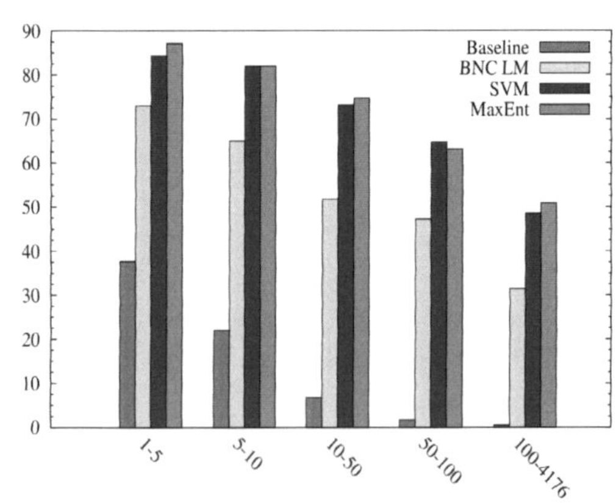

Figure 2: Exact match accuracy scores for the different models. Data items are binned with respect to the number of distinct realizations.

Model	Jotunheimen accuracy	Jotunheimen n-best	Jotunheimen WA	Rondane accuracy	Rondane n-best	Rondane WA
BNC LM	53.24	78.81	0.882	54.19	77.19	0.891
SVM	71.11	84.69	0.922	63.64	83.12	0.906
MaxEnt	72.28	84.59	0.927	64.28	83.60	0.903

Table 6: Performance of the different learners. The results on the 'Jotunheimen' treebank for the discriminative models are averages from 10-fold cross-validation. A model trained on the entire 'Jotunheimen' data was used when testing on 'Rondane'. Note that the training accuracy of the SVM learner on the 'Jotunheimen' training set is 91.69%, while it's 92.99% for the MaxEnt model.

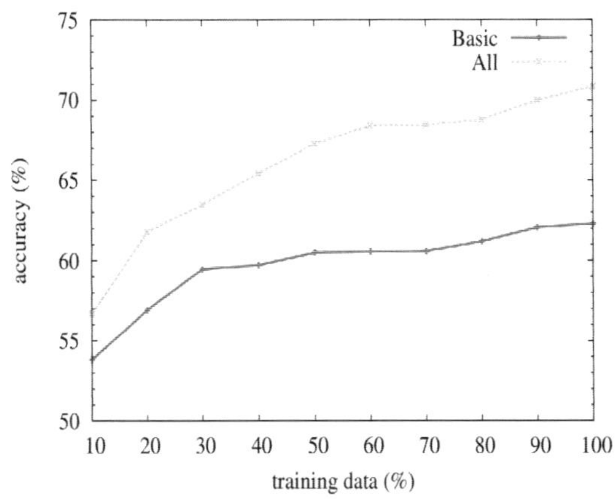

Figure 3: Learning curves for two MaxEnt model configurations (trained without cutoffs). Although there appears to be a saturation effect in model performance with increasing amounts of 'Jotunheimen' training data, for the richer configuration (using all features but the language model) further enlarging the training data still seems attractive.

corresponds to average exact match performance for 10-fold cross-validation on 'Jotunheimen', but restricting the amount of training data presented to the learner to between 10 and 100 per cent of the total. At 60 per cent training data, the two models already perform at 60.6% and 68.4% accuracy, and the learning curves are starting to flatten out. Somewhat remarkably, the richer model including partial daughter back-off, grandparenting, and lexical type trigrams already outperforms the baseline model by a clear margin with just a small fraction of the training data, so the MaxEnt learner appears to make effective use of the greatly enlarged feature space.

When testing against the 'Rondane' held-out set and comparing to performance on the 'Jotunheimen' cross-validation set, we see that the performance of both the MaxEnt model and the SVM degrades quite a bit. Of course, some drop in performance is to be expected as the estimation parameters had been tuned to this development set. Furthermore, as can be seen from Table 2, the baseline is also slightly lower for the 'Rondane' test set as the average number of realizations is higher. Also, while basically from the same domain, the two text collections differ noticeably in style: 'Jotunheimen' is based on edited, high-quality guide books; 'Rondane' has been gathered from a variety of web sites. Note, however, that the performance of the BNC n-gram model seems to be more stable across the different data sets.

In any case we see that, for our realization ranking task, the use of discriminative models in combination with structural features extracted from treebanks, clearly outperforms the surface oriented, generative n-gram model. This is in spite of the relatively modest size of the treebanked training data available to the discriminative models. On the 'Rondane' test set the reduction in error rate for the combined MaxEnt model relative to the n-gram LM, is 22.03%. The error reduction for the SVM over the LM on 'Rondane' is 20.63%.

Another factor that is likely to be important for the differences in performance is the fact that the treebank data is better tuned to the domain of application or the test data. The n-gram language model, on the other hand, was only trained on the general-domain BNC data. Note, however, that when testing on 'Rondane', we also tried to combine this general-domain model with an additional in-domain model trained only on the text that formed the basis of the 'Jotunheimen' treebank, a total of 5024 sentences. The optimal weights for linearly combining these two models were calculated using the interpolation tool in the CMU toolkit (using the expectation maximization (EM) algorithm, minimizing the perplexity on a held out data set of 330 sentences). However, when applied to the 'Rondane' test set, this in-

model	error	ties	correct
BNC LM	253	68	313
MaxEnt (sans LM)	222	63	349
MaxEnt (combined)	225	3	404

Table 7: Exact match error counts for three models, viz. the BNC LM only, the MaxEnt model by itself (using all feature types except the LM probability), and the combined MaxEnt model. The intermediate column corresponds to *ties* or *partial* errors, i.e. the number of items for which multiple candidates were ranked at the top, of which some were actually preferred and some not. Primarily this latter error type is reduced by including the LM feature in the MaxEnt universe.

terpolated model failed to improve on the results achieved by just using the larger general-domain model alone. This is probably due to the small amount of domain specific data that we presently have available for training.

Another observation about our n-gram experiments that is worth a mention is that we found that ranking realizations according to non-normalized log probabilities directly resulted in much better accuracy than using a length normalized score such as the geometric mean.

Finally, Table 7 breaks down per-item exact match errors for three distinct ranking configurations, viz. the BNC LM only, the structural MaxEnt model only, and the combined MaxEnt model, which includes the LM probability as an additional feature; all numbers are for application to the held-out 'Rondane' test set. Further contrasting the first two of these, the BNC LM yields 129 unique errors, in the sense that the structural MaxEnt makes the correct predictions on these items, contrasted to 98 unique errors in the structural MaxEnt model. When compared to the only 124 errors made equally by both rankers, we conclude that the different approaches have partially complementary strengths and weaknesses. This observation is confirmed in the relatively substantial improvement in ranking performance of the combined model on the 'Rondane' test: The exact match accuracies of the n-gram model, the basic MaxEnt model and the combined model are 54.19%, 59.43% and 64.28%, respectively.

5 Summary and Outlook

Applying three alternate statistical models to the realization ranking task, we found that discriminative models with access to structural information substantially outperform the traditional language model approach. Using comparatively small amounts of annotated training data, we were able to boost ranking performance from around 54% to more than 72%, albeit for a limited, reasonably coherent domain and genre. The incremental addition of feature templates into the MaxEnt model suggests a trend of diminishing return, most likely due to increasing overlap in the portion of the problem space captured across templates, and possibly reflecting limitations in the amount of training data. The comparison of the MaxEnt and SVM rankers suggest comparable performance on our task, not showing statistically significant differences. Nevertheless, in terms of scalability when using large data sets, it seems clear that the MaxEnt framework is a more practical and manageable alternative, both in terms of training time and memory requirements.

As further work we would like to try to train an SVM that takes full advantage of the ranking potential of the set-up described in (Joachims, 2002). Instead of just making binary (right/wrong) distinctions, we could grade the realizations in the training data according to their WA scores toward the references and try to learn a similar ranking. So far we have only been able to do preliminary experiments with this set-up on a small sub-set of the data. When evaluated with the accuracy measures used in this paper the results were not as good as those obtained when training with only two ranks, however this might very well look different if we evaluate the full rankings (e.g. number of swapped pairs) instead of just focusing on the top ranked candidates. Note that it is also possible to use such graded training data with the MaxEnt models, by letting the probabilities of the empirical distribution be based on similarity scores such as WA instead of frequencies.

Acknowledgments

The work reported here is part of the Norwegian LOGON project on precision MT, and we are grateful to numerous colleagues; please see '`http://www.emmtee.net`' for background. Furthermore, we warmly acknowledge the support and productive criticism provided by Dan Flickinger (the ERG developer), Francis Bond, John Carrol, and three anonymous reviewers.

References

Carroll, J., Copestake, A., Flickinger, D., & Poznanski, V. (1999). An efficient chart generator for (semi-)lexicalist grammars. In *Proceedings of the 7th European Workshop on Natural Language Generation*. Toulouse.

Carroll, J., & Oepen, S. (2005). High-efficiency realization for a wide-coverage unification grammar. In R. Dale & K. fai Wong (Eds.), *Proceedings of the 2nd International Joint Conference on Natural Language Processing* (Vol. 3651, pp. 165 – 176). Jeju, Korea: Springer.

Chen, S. F., & Rosenfeld, R. (1999). *A Gaussian prior for smoothing maximum entropy models* (Tech. Rep.). Carnegie Mellon University. (Technical Report CMUCS-CS-99-108)

Clarkson, P., & Rosenfeld, R. (1997). Statistical language modeling using the CMU-Cambridge Toolkit. In *Proceedings of ESCA Eurospeech*.

Copestake, A., Flickinger, D., Malouf, R., Riehemann, S., & Sag, I. (1995). Translation using minimal recursion semantics. In *Proceedings of the Sixth International Conference on Theoretical and Methodological Issues in Machine Translation*. Leuven, Belgium.

Dietterich, T. G. (1998). Approximate statistical test for comparing supervised classification learning algorithms. *Neural Computation, 10*(7), 1895–1923.

Flickinger, D. (2002). On building a more efficient grammar by exploiting types. In S. Oepen, D. Flickinger, J. Tsujii, , & H. Uszkoreit (Eds.), *Collaborative language engineering: A case study in efficient grammar-based processing* (pp. 1–17). CSLI Press.

Joachims, T. (1999). Making large-scale svm learning practical. In B. Schölkopf, C. Burges, & A. Smola (Eds.), *Advances in kernel methods - support vector learning*. MIT-Press.

Joachims, T. (2002). Optimizing search engines using clickthrough data. In *Proceedings of the ACM conference on knowledge discovery and data mining (KDD)*. ACM.

Johnson, M., Geman, S., Canon, S., Chi, Z., & Riezler, S. (1999). Estimators for stochastic 'unification-based' grammars. In *Proceedings of the 37th Meeting of the Association for Computational Linguistics* (pp. 535 – 541). College Park, MD.

Langkilde, I., & Knight, K. (1998). The practical value of n-grams in generation. In *International natural language generation workshop*.

Malouf, R. (2002). A comparison of algorithms for maximum entropy parameter estimation. In *Proceedings of the 6th Conference on Natural Language Learning* (pp. 49–55). Taipei, Taiwan.

Malouf, R., & Noord, G. van. (2004). Wide coverage parsing with stochastic attribute value grammars. In *Proceedings of the IJCNLP workshop Beyond Shallow Analysis*. Hainan, China.

Nakanishi, H., Miyao, Y., & Tsujii, J. (2005). Probabilistic models for disambiguation of an HPSG-based chart generator. In *Proceedings of the 9th International Workshop on Parsing Technologies* (pp. 93 – 102). Vancouver, Canada: Association for Computational Linguistics.

Och, F. J., Gildea, D., Khudanpur, S., Sarkar, A., Yamada, K., Fraser, A., Kumar, S., Shen, L., Smith, D., Eng, K., Jain, V., Jin, Z., & Radev, D. (2004). A smorgasbord of features for statistical machine translation. In *Proceedings of the 5th Conference of the North American Chapter of the ACL*. Boston.

Toutanova, K., & Manning, C. D. (2002). Feature selection for a rich HPSG grammar using decision trees. In *Proceedings of the 6th Conference on Natural Language Learning*. Taipei, Taiwan.

Toutanova, K., Manning, C. D., Shieber, S. M., Flickinger, D., & Oepen, S. (2002). Parse disambiguation for a rich hpsg grammar. In *First workshop on treebanks and linguistic theories*. Sozopol, Bulgaria.

Velldal, E., Oepen, S., & Flickinger, D. (2004). Paraphrasing treebanks for stochastic realization ranking. In *Proceedings of the 3rd workshop on Treebanks and Linguistic Theories*. Tübingen, Germany.

White, M. (2004). Reining in CCG chart realization. In *Proceedings of the 3rd International Conference on Natural Language Generation*. Hampshire, UK.

Sentence Ordering with Manifold-based Classification in Multi-Document Summarization

Paul D Ji
Centre for Linguistics and Philology
University of Oxford
paul_dji@yahoo.co.uk

Stephen Pulman
Centre for Linguistics and Philology
University of Oxford
sgp@clg.ox.ac.uk

Abstract

In this paper, we propose a sentence ordering algorithm using a semi-supervised sentence classification and historical ordering strategy. The classification is based on the manifold structure underlying sentences, addressing the problem of limited labeled data. The historical ordering helps to ensure topic continuity and avoid topic bias. Experiments demonstrate that the method is effective.

1. Introduction

Sentence ordering has been a concern in text planning and concept-to-text generation (Reiter et al., 2000). Recently, it has also drawn attention in multi-document summarization (Barzilay et al., 2002; Lapata, 2003; Bollegala et al., 2005). Since summary sentences generally come from different sources in multi-document summarization, an optimal ordering is crucial to make summaries coherent and readable.

In general, the strategies for sentence ordering in multi-document summarization fall in two categories. One is chronological ordering (Barzilay et al., 2002; Bollegala et al., 2005), which is based on time-related features of the documents. However, such temporal features may be not available in all cases. Furthermore, temporal inference in texts is still a problem, in spite of some progress in automatic disambiguation of temporal information (Filatova et al., 2001).

Another strategy is majority ordering (MO) (McKeown et al., 2001; Barzilay et al., 2002), in which each summary sentence is mapped to a theme, i.e., a set of similar sentences in the documents, and the order of these sentences determines that for summary sentences. To do that, a directed theme graph is built, in which if a theme A occurs behind another theme B in a document, B is linked to A no matter how far away they are located. However, this may lead to wrong theme correlations, since B's occurrence may rely on a third theme C and have nothing to do with A. In addition, when outputting theme orders, MO uses a kind of heuristic that chooses a theme based on its in-out edge difference in the directed theme graph. This may cause topic disruption, since the next choice may have no link with previous choices.

Lapata (2003) proposed a probabilistic ordering (PO) method for text structuring, which can be adapted to majority ordering if the training texts are those documents to be summarized. The primary evidence for the ordering are informative features of sentences, including words and their grammatical dependence relations, which needs reliable parsing of the text. Unlike in MO, selection of the next sentence here is based on the most recent one. However, this may lead to topic bias: i.e. too many sentences on the same topic.

In this paper, we propose a historical ordering (HO) strategy, in which the selection of the next sentence is based on the whole history of selection, not just the most recent choice. This

Proceedings of the 2006 Conference on Empirical Methods in Natural Language Processing (EMNLP 2006), pages 526–533,
Sydney, July 2006.

strategy helps to ensure continuity of topics but to avoid topic bias at the same time.

To do that, we need to map summary sentences to those in documents. We formalize this as a kind of classification problem, with summary sentences as class labels. Since there are very few (only one) labeled examples for each class, we adopt a kind of semi-supervised classification method, which makes use of the manifold structure underlying the sentences to do the classification. A common assumption behind this learning paradigm is that the manifold structure among the data, revealed by higher density, provides a global comparison between data points (Szummer et al., 2001; Zhu et al., 2003; Zhou et al., 2003). Under such an assumption, even one labeled example is enough for classification, if only the structure is determined.

The remainder of the paper is organized as follows. In section 2, we give an overview of the proposed method. In section 3~5, we talk about the method including sentence networks, classification and ordering. In section 6, we present experiments and evaluations. Finally in section 7, we give some conclusions and future work.

2. Overview

Fig. 1 gives the overall structure of the proposed method, which includes three modules: construction of sentence networks, sentence classification and sentence ordering.

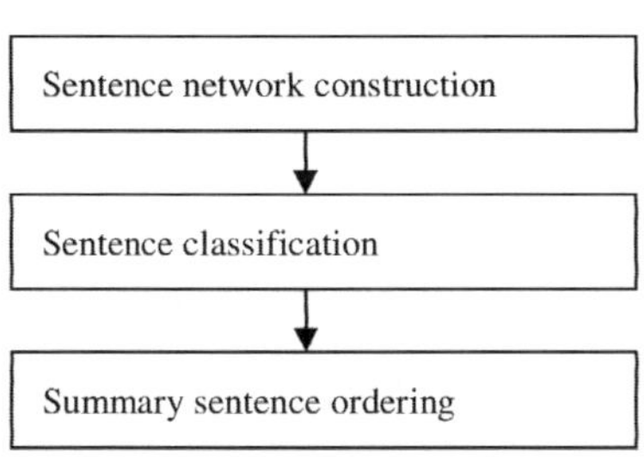

Fig. 1. Algorithm Overview

The first step is to build a sentence neighborhood network with weights on edges, which can serve as the basis for a Markov random walk (Tishby et al., 2000). The neighborhood is based on similarity between sentences, and weights on edges can be seen as transition probabilities for the random walk. From this network, we can derive new representations for sentences.

The second step is to make a classification of sentences, with each summary sentence as a class label. Since only one labeled example exists for each class, we use a semi-supervised method based on a Markov random walk to reveal the manifold structure for the classification.

The third step is to order summary sentences according to the original positions of their partners in the same class. During this process, the next selection of a sentence is based on the whole history of selection, i.e., the association of the sentence with all those already selected.

3. Sentence Network Construction

Suppose S is the set of all sentences in the documents and a summary (a summary sentence may be not a document sentence), let $S=\{s_1, s_2, \ldots, s_N\}$ with a distance metric $d(s_i,s_j)$, the distance between two sentences s_i and s_j, which is based on the Jensen-Shannon divergence (Lin, 1991). We construct a graph with sentences as points by sorting the distances among the points in an ascending order and repeatedly connecting two points according to the order until a connected graph is obtained. Then, we assign a weight $w_{i,j}$, as in (1), to each edge based on the distance.

1) $w_{i,j} = \exp(-d(s_i, s_j)/\delta)$

The weights are symmetric, $w_{i,i}=1$ and $w_{i,j}=0$ for all non-neighbors (δ is set as 0.6 in this work). 2) is the one-step transition probability $p(s_i, s_j)$ from s_i to s_j based on weights of neighbors.

2) $p(s_i, s_j) = \dfrac{w_{i,j}}{\sum_k w_{i,k}}$

Let M be the $N \times N$ matrix and $M_{i,j} = p(s_i, s_j)$, then M^t is the tth Markov random walk matrix, whose i, j-th entry is the probability $p_t(s_i, s_j)$ of the transition from s_i to s_j after t steps. In this way, each sentence s_j is associated with a vector of conditional probabilities $p_t(s_i, s_j)$, $i=1, \ldots, N$, which form a new manifold-based representation for s_j. With such representations, sentences are close whenever they have a similar distribution over the starting points. Notice that the representations depend on the step parameter t (Tishby et al., 2000). With smaller values of t, unlabeled points may be not connected with labeled ones; with bigger values of t, the points may be indistinguishable. So, an appropriate t should be estimated.

4. Sentence Classification

Suppose $s_1, s_2, \ldots, s_L$ are summary sentences and their labels are $c_1, c_2, \ldots, c_L$ respectively. In our case, each summary sentence is assigned with a unique class label c_i, $1 \le i \le L$. This also means that for each class c_i, there is only one labeled example, i.e., the summary sentence, s_i.

Let $S=\{(s_1, c_1), (s_2, c_2), \ldots, (s_L, c_L), s_{L+1}, \ldots, s_N\}$, then the task of sentence classification is to infer the labels for unlabeled sentences, $s_{L+1}, \ldots, s_N$. Through the classification, we can get similar sentences for each summary sentence. To do that, we assume that each sentence has a distribution $p(c_k|s_i)$, $1 \le k \le L$, $1 \le i \le N$, and these probabilities are to be estimated from the data.

Seeing a sentence as a sample from the t step Markov random walk in the sentence graph, we have the following interpretation of $p(c_k|s_i)$.

3) $$p(c_k \mid s_i) = \sum_j p(c_k \mid s_j) p_t(j,i)$$

This means that the probability of s_i belonging to c_k is dependent on the probabilities of those sentences belonging to c_k which will transit to s_i after t steps and their transition probabilities.

With the conditional log-likelihood of labeled sentences 4) as the estimation criterion, we can use the EM algorithm to estimate $p(c_k|s_i)$, in which the E-step and M-step are 5) and 6) respectively.

4) $$\sum_{k=1}^{L} \log p(c_k \mid s_k) = \sum_{k=1}^{L} \log \sum_{j=1}^{N} p(c_k \mid s_j) p_t(j,k)$$

5) $$p(s_i \mid s_k, c_k) = p(c_k \mid s_i) p_t(i,k) / \sum_{k=1}^{L} p(c_k \mid s_i) p_t(i,k)$$

6) $$p(c_k \mid s_i) = p(s_i \mid s_k, c_k) / \sum_{1 \le k \le L} p(s_i \mid s_k, c_k)$$

The final class c_i for s_i is given in 7).

7) $$c_i = \arg\max_{c_k} p(c_k \mid s_i)$$

$p(c_i|s_i)$ is called the membership probability of s_i. After classification, each sentence is assigned a label according to 7).

One key problem in this setting is to estimate the parameter t. A possible strategy for that is by cross validation, but it needs a large amount of labeled data. Here, following Szummer et al., 2001, we use marginal difference of probabilities of sentences falling in different classes as the estimation criterion, which is given in 8).

8) $$m(S) = \sum_{s \in S} (L \max_{1 \le k \le L} p(c_k \mid s) - \sum_{1 \le k \le L} p(c_k \mid s))$$

To maximize 8), we can get an appropriate value for the parameter t, which means that a better t should make sentences belong to some classes more prominently. Notice that the classes represented by summary sentences may be incomplete for all the sentences occurring in the documents, so some sentences will belong to the classes without obviously different probabilities. To avoid such sentences in the estimation of t, we only choose the top (40%) sentences in a class based on their membership probabilities.

5. Sentence Ordering

After sentence classification, we get a class of similar sentences for each summary sentence, which is also a member of the class. With these sentence classes, we create a directed class graph based on the order of their member sentences in documents. In the graph, each sentence class is a node, and there exists a directed edge $e_{i,j}$ from one node c_i to another c_j if and only if there is s_i in c_i immediately appearing before s_j in c_j in the documents (the sentences not in classes are neglected). The weight of $e_{i,j}$, $F_{i,j}$, captures the frequency of such occurrence. We add one additional node denoting an initial class c_0, and it links to each class with a directed edge $e_{0,j}$, the weight $F_{0,j}$ of which is the frequency of the member sentences of the class appearing at the beginning of the documents.

Suppose the input is the class graph $G=<C, E>$, where $C = \{c_1, c_2, \ldots, c_L\}$ is the set of the classes, $E=\{e_{i,j}|1\leq i, j\leq L\}$ is the set of the directed edges, and o is the ordering of the classes. Fig. 2 gives the ordering algorithm.

---

i) $c_k \leftarrow \max_{c_i \in C} F_{0,i}$

ii) $o \leftarrow o\, c_k$

iii) For all c_i in C, $F_{0,i} \leftarrow F_{0,i} + F_{k,i}$

iv) Remove c_k from C and $e_{k,j}$ and $e_{i,k}$ from E;

v) Repeat i)-iv) while $C \neq \{c_0\}$

vi) Return the order o.

Fig. 2 Ordering algorithm

In the algorithm, there are two main steps. Step i) selects the class whose member sentences occur most frequently immediately after those in c_0. Step iii) updates the weights of the edges $e_{0,i}$. In fact, it can be seen as merge of the original c_0 and c_k, and in this sense the updated c_0 represents the history of selections.

In contrast to the MO algorithm, the ordering algorithm here (HO) uses immediate back-front co-occurrence, while the MO algorithm uses relative back-front locations. On the other hand, the selection of a class is dependent on previous selections in HO, while in MO, the selection of a class is mainly dependent on its in-out edge difference.

In contrast to the PO algorithm, the selection of a class in HO is dependent on all previous selections, while in PO, the selection is only related to the most recent one.

As an example, Fig. 3 gives an initial class graph. The output orderings by PO and HO are $[c_1, c_3, c_4, c_2]$ and $[c_1, c_3, c_2, c_4]$ respectively. The difference lies in whether to select c_4 or c_2 after selection of c_3. PO selects c_4 since it only considers the most recent selection, while HO selects c_2 because it considers all previous selections including c_1.

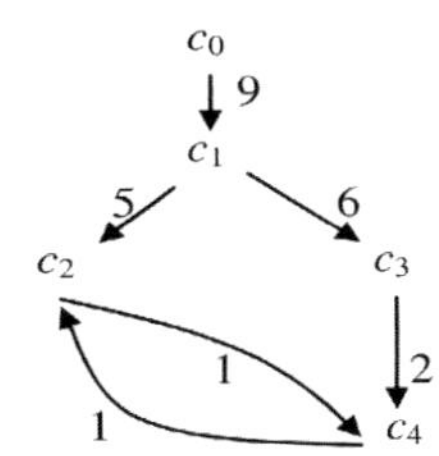

Fig. 3 Initial graph for PO and HO

As another example, Fig. 4 gives the order of the classes in individual documents.

1) c_2 c_3 c_1
2) c_2 c_3 c_1
3) c_3 c_2 c_1
4) c_3 c_2 c_1
5) c_3 c_2
6) c_2 c_3
7) c_1 c_2 c_3 c_2 c_3 c_2 c_3 c_2

Fig. 4. Class orders in documents

From 1)-6), we can see some regularity among the order of the classes: c_2 and c_3 are interchangeable, while c_1 always appears behind c_2 or c_3. From 7), we can see that c_2 and c_3 still co-occur, while c_1 happens to occur at the beginning of the document. Thus, the appropriate ordering should be $[c_2, c_3, c_1]$ or $[c_3, c_2, c_1]$. Fig. 5 is the graph built by MO.

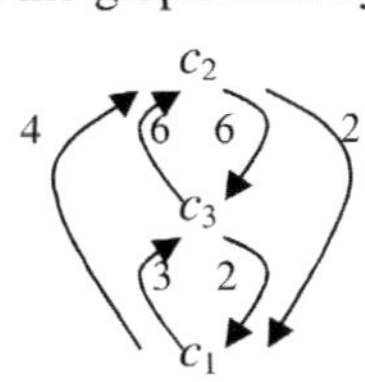

Fig. 5 Graph by MO

According to MO, the first node to be selected will be c_1, since the difference of its in-out edges (+3) is bigger than that (-2, -1) of other two nodes. Then the in-out edge differences for c_2 or c_3 are both 0 after removing edges associated with c_1, and either c_2 or c_3 will be selected. Thus, the output ordering should be $[c_1, c_2, c_3]$ or $[c_1, c_3, c_2]$.

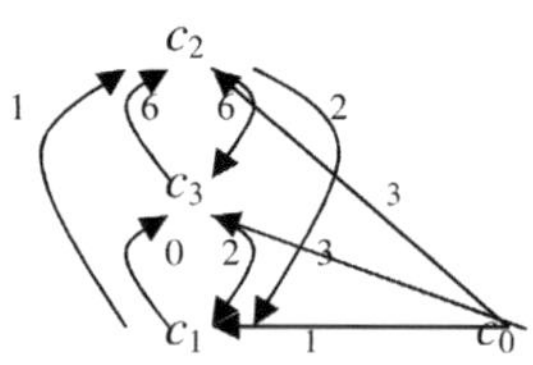

Fig. 6 Graph by HO

Fig. 6 is the class graph built by HO. According to HO, the first node to be selected will be c_2 or c_3, since $e_{0,1}=e_{0,2}=3>e_{0,1}=1$. Suppose c_2 is firstly selected, then $e_{0,3} \Leftarrow e_{0,3}+e_{2,3}=3+6=9$, while $e_{0,1} \Leftarrow e_{0,1}+e_{2,1}=1+2=3$, so c_3 will be selected then. Finally the output ordering will be $[c_2, c_3, c_1]$. Similarly, if c_3 is firstly selected, the output ordering will be $[c_3, c_2, c_1]$.

6 Experiments and Evaluation

6.1 Data

We used the DUC04 document dataset. The dataset contains 50 document clusters and each cluster includes 20 content-related documents. For each cluster, 4 manual summaries are provided.

6.2 Evaluation Measure

The proposed method in this paper consists of two main steps: sentence classification and sentence ordering. For classification, we used pointwise entropy (Dash et al., 2000) to measure the quality of the classification result due to lack of enough labeled data. For a $n\times m$ matrix M, whose row vectors are normalized as 1, its pointwise entropy is defined in 9).

$$9) \; E(M) = -\sum_{1\le i\le n}\sum_{1\le j\le m}(M_{i,j}\log M_{i,j} + (1-M_{i,j})\log(1-M_{i,j}))$$

Intuitively, if $M_{i,j}$ is close to 0 or 1, $E(M)$ tends towards 0, which corresponds to clearer distinctions between classes; otherwise $E(M)$ tends towards 1, which means there are no clear boundaries between classes. For comparison between different matrices, $E(M)$ needs to be averaged over $n\times m$.

For sentence ordering, we used Kendall's τ coefficient (Lapata, 2003), as defined in 10),

$$10) \quad \tau = 1 - \frac{2(N_I)}{N(N-1)/2}$$

where, N_I is number of inversions of consecutive sentences needed to transform output of the algorithm to manual summaries. The measure ranges from -1 for inverse ranks to +1 for identical ranks, and can also be seen as a kind of edit similarity between two ranks: smaller values for lower similarity, and bigger values for higher similarity.

6.3 Evaluation of Classification

For sentence classification, we need to estimate the parameter t. We randomly chose 5 document clusters and one manual summary from the four. Fig. 7 shows the change of the average margin over all the top 40% sentences in a cluster with t varying from 3 to 25.

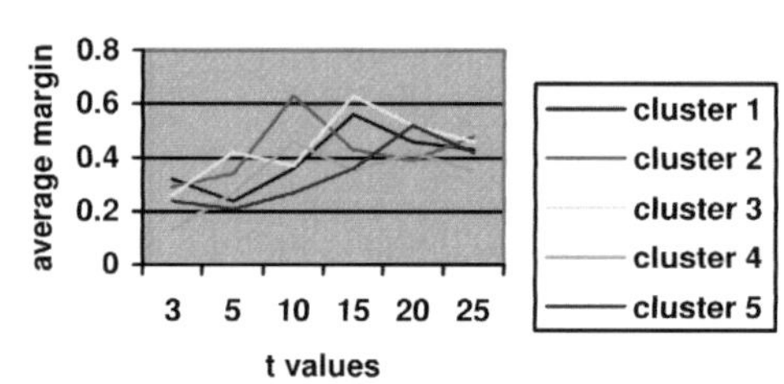

Fig. 7. Average margin and t

Fig. 7 indicates that the average margin changes with t for each cluster and the values of t maximizing the margin are different for different clusters. For the 5 clusters, the estimated t is 16, 8, 14, 12 and 21 respectively. So we need to estimate the best t for each cluster.

After estimation of t, EM was used to estimate the membership probabilities. Table 1 gives the average pointwise entropy for top 10% to top 100% sentences in each cluster, where sentences were ordered by their membership probabilities. The values were averaged over 20 runs, and for each run, 10 document clusters and one summary were randomly selected, and the entropy was averaged over the summaries.

Sentences	E_Semi	E_SVM	Significance
10%	0.23	0.22	~
20%	0.26	0.27	~
30%	0.32	0.43	*
40%	0.35	0.49	**
50%	0.42	0.51	*
60%	0.46	0.55	*
70%	0.48	0.57	*
80%	0.59	0.62	~
90%	0.65	0.69	~
100%	0.70	0.73	~

Table 1. Entropy of classification result

In Table 1, the column E_Semi shows entropies of the semi-supervised classification. It indicates that the entropy increases as more sentences are considered. This is not surprising since the sentences are ordered by their membership probabilities in a cluster, which can be seen as a kind of measure for closeness between sentences and cluster centroids, and the boundaries between clusters become dim with more sentences considered.

To compare the performance between this semi-supervised classification and a standard supervised method like Support Vector Machines (SVM), Table 1 also lists the average entropy of a SVM (E_SVM) over the runs. Similarly, we found that the entropy also increases as sentences increase. Table 2 also gives the significance sign over the runs, where *, ** and ~ represent p-values <=0.01, (0.01, 0.05] and >0.05, and indicate that the entropy of the semi-supervised classification is lower, significantly lower, or almost the same as that of SVM respectively.

Table 1 demonstrates that when the top 10% or 20% sentences are considered, the performance between the two algorithms shows no difference. The reason may be that these top sentences are closer to cluster centroids in both cases, and the cluster boundaries in both algorithms are clear in terms of these sentences.

For the top 30% sentences, the entropy for semi-supervised classification is lower than that for a SVM, and for the top 40%, the difference becomes significantly lower. The reason may go to the substantial assumptions behind the two algorithms. SVM, based on local comparison, is successful only when more labeled data is available. With only one sentence labeled as in our case, the semi-supervised method, based on global distribution, makes use of a large amount of unlabeled data to reveal the underlying manifold structure. Thus, the performance is much better than that of a SVM when more sentences are considered.

For the top 50% to 70% sentences, E_Semi is still lower, but not by much. The reason may be that some noisy documents are starting to be included. For the top 80% to 100% sentences, the performance shows no difference again. The reason may be that the lower ranking sentences may belong to other classes than those represented by summary sentences, and with these sentences included, the cluster boundaries become unclear in both cases.

6.4 Evaluation of Ordering

We used the same classification results to test the performance of our ordering algorithm HO as well as MO and PO. Table 2 lists the Kendall's τ coefficient values for the three algorithms (τ_1). The value was averaged over 20 runs, and for each run, 10 summaries were randomly selected and the τ score was averaged over summaries. Since a summary sentence tends to generalize some sentences in the documents, we also tried to combine two or three consecutive sentences into one, and tested their ordering performance (τ_2 and τ_3) respectively.

τ	HO	MO	PO
τ_1	0.42	0.31	0.33
τ_2	0.33	0.26	0.29
τ_3	0.27	0.21	0.25

Table 2. τ scores for HO, MO and PO

Table 2 indicates that the combination of sentences harms the performance. To see why, we checked the classification results, and found that the pointwise entropies for two and three sentence combinations (for the top 40% sentence in each cluster) increase 12.4% and 18.2% respectively. This means that the cluster structure becomes less clear with two or three sentence combinations, which would lead to less similar sentences being clustered with summary sentences. This result also suggests that if the summary sentence subsumes multiple sentences in the documents, they tend to be not consecutive.

Fig. 8 shows change of τ scores with different number of sentences used for ordering, where x axis denotes top (1-x)*100% sentences in each cluster. The score was averaged over 20 runs, and for each run, 10 summaries were randomly selected and evaluated.

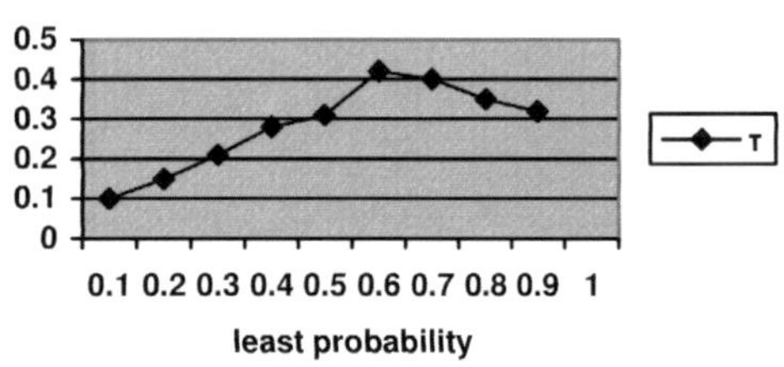

Fig. 8. τ scores and number of sentences

Fig. 8 indicates that with fewer sentences (x >=0.7) used for ordering, the performance decreases. The reason may be that with fewer and fewer sentences used, the result is deficient training data for the ordering. On the other hand, with more sentences used (x <0.6), the performance also decreases. The reason may be that as more sentences are used, the noisy sentences could dominate the ordering. That's why we considered only the top 40% sentences in each cluster as training data for sentence reordering here.

As an example, the following is a summary for a cluster of documents about Central American storms, in which the ordering is given manually.

1) A category 5 storm, Hurricane Mitch roared across the northwest Caribbean with 180 mph winds across a 350-mile front that devastated the mainland and islands of Central America.

2) Although the force of the storm diminished, at least 8,000 people died from wind, waves and flood damage.

3) The greatest losses were in Honduras where some 6,076 people perished.

4) Around 2,000 people were killed in Nicaragua, 239 in El Salvador, 194 in Guatemala, seven in Costa Rica and six in Mexico.

5) At least 569,000 people were homeless across Central America.

6) Aid was sent from many sources (European Union, the UN, US and Mexico).

7) Relief efforts are hampered by extensive damage.

Compared with the manual ordering, our algorithm HO outputs the ordering [1, 3, 4, 2, 5, 6, 7]. In contrast, PO and MO created the orderings [1, 3, 4, 5, 6, 7, 2] and [1, 3, 2, 6, 4, 5, 7] respectively. In HO's output, sentence 2 was put in the wrong position. To check why this was so, we found that sentences in cluster 2 and cluster 3 (clusters containing sentence 2 or sentence 3) were very similar, and the size of cluster 3 was bigger than that of cluster 2. Also we found that sentences in cluster 4 mostly followed those in cluster 3. This may explain why the ordering [1, 3, 4] occurred. Due to the link between cluster 2 and cluster 1 or 3, sentence 2 followed sentence 4 in the ordering. In PO, sentence 2 was put at the end of the ordering, since it only considered the most recent selection when determining next, so cluster 1 would not be considered when determining the

4th position. This suggests that consideration of selection history does in fact help to group those related sentences more closely, although sentence 2 was ranked lower than expected in the example.

In MO, we found sentence 2 was put immediately behind sentence 3. The reason was that, after sentence 1 and 3 were selected, the in-edges of the node representing cluster 2 became 0 in the cluster directed graph, and its in-out edge difference became the biggest among all nodes in the graph, so it was chosen. For similar reasons, sentence 6 was put behind sentence 2. This suggests that it may be difficult to consider the selection history in MO, since its selection is mainly based on the current status of clusters.

6. Conclusion and Future Work

In this paper, we propose a sentence ordering method for multi-document summarization based on semi-supervised classification and historical ordering. For sentence classification, the semi-supervised classification groups sentences based on their global distribution, rather than on local comparisons. Thus, even with a small amount of labeled data (just 1 labeled example in our case) we nevertheless ensure good performance for sentence classification.

For sentence ordering, we propose a kind of history-based ordering strategy, which determines the next selection based on the whole selection history, rather than the most recent single selection in probabilistic ordering, which could result in topic bias, or in-out difference in MO, which could result in topic disruption.

In this work, we mainly use sentence-level information, including sentence similarity and sentence order, etc. In future, we may explore the role of term-level or word-level features, e.g., proper nouns, in the ordering of summary sentences. To make summaries more coherent and readable, we may also need to discover how to detect and control topic movement automatic summaries. One specific task is how to generate co-reference among sentences in summaries. In addition, we will also try other semi-supervised classification methods, and other evaluation metrics, etc.

Reference

Barzilay, R N. Elhadad, and K. McKeown. 2002. *Inferring strategies for sentence ordering in multidocument news summarization.* Journal of Artificial Intelligence Research, 17:35–55.

Bollegala D. Okazaki, N. Ishizuka, M. 2005. *A Machine Learning Approach to Sentence Ordering for Multidocument Summarization*, in Proceedings of IJCNLP.

Dash M. and H. Liu, (2000) *Unsupervised feature selection*, proceedings of PAKDD.

Filatova, E. & Hovy, E. (2001) *Assigning time-stamps to event-clauses.* In Proceedings of AACL/EACL workshop on Temporal and Spatial Information Processing.

Lapata, M. 2003. *Probabilistic text structuring: Experiments with sentence ordering.* In Proceedings of the annual meeting of ACL 545–552.

Lin, J. 1991. *Divergence Measures Based on the Shannon Entropy.* IEEE Transactions on Information Theory, 37:1, 145–150.

McKeown K., Barzilay R. Evans D., Hatzivassiloglou V., Kan M., Schiffman B., &Teufel, S. (2001). *Columbia multi-document summarization: Approach and evaluation.* In Proceedings of DUC.

Reiter, Ehud and Robert Dale. 2000. *Building Natural Language Generation Systems.* Cambridge University Press, Cambridge.

Szummer M. and T. Jaakkola. (2001) *Partially labeled classification with markov random walks.* NIPS14.

Tishby, N, Slonim, N. (2000) *Data clustering by Markovian relaxation and the Information Bottleneck Method.* NIPS 13.

Zhu, X., Ghahramani, Z., & Lafferty, J. (2003) *Semi-Supervised Learning Using Gaussian Fields and Harmonic Functions.* ICML-2003.

Zhou D., Bousquet, O., Lal, T.N., Weston J. & Schokopf B. (2003). *Learning with local and Global Consistency.* NIPS 16. pp: 321-328.

Quality Assessment of Large Scale Knowledge Resources

Montse Cuadros
IXA NLP Group
EHU/UPV
Donostia, Basque Country
mcuadros001@ikasle.ehu.es

German Rigau
IXA NLP Group
EHU/UPV
Donostia, Basque Country
german.rigau@ehu.es

Abstract

This paper presents an empirical evaluation of the quality of publicly available large-scale knowledge resources. The study includes a wide range of manually and automatically derived large-scale knowledge resources. In order to establish a fair and neutral comparison, the quality of each knowledge resource is indirectly evaluated using the same method on a Word Sense Disambiguation task. The evaluation framework selected has been the Senseval-3 English Lexical Sample Task. The study empirically demonstrates that automatically acquired knowledge resources surpass both in terms of precision and recall the knowledge resources derived manually, and that the combination of the knowledge contained in these resources is very close to the most frequent sense classifier. As far as we know, this is the first time that such a quality assessment has been performed showing a clear picture of the current state-of-the-art of publicly available wide coverage semantic resources.

1 Introduction

Using large-scale semantic knowledge bases, such as WordNet (Fellbaum, 1998), has become a usual, often necessary, practice for most current Natural Language Processing systems. Even now, building large and rich enough knowledge bases for broad–coverage semantic processing takes a great deal of expensive manual effort involving large research groups during long periods of development. This fact has severely hampered the state-of-the-art of current Natural Language Processing (NLP) applications. For example, dozens of person-years have been invested in the development of wordnets for various languages (Vossen, 1998), but the data in these resources seems not to be rich enough to support advanced concept-based NLP applications directly. It seems that applications will not scale up to working in open domains without more detailed and rich general-purpose (and also domain-specific) linguistic knowledge built by automatic means.

For instance, in more than eight years of manual construction (from version 1.5 to 2.0), WordNet passed from 103,445 semantic relations to 204,074 semantic relations[1]. That is, around twelve thousand semantic relations per year. However, during the last years the research community has devised a large set of innovative processes and tools for large-scale automatic acquisition of lexical knowledge from structured or unstructured corpora. Among others we can mention eXtended WordNet (Mihalcea and Moldovan, 2001), large collections of semantic preferences acquired from SemCor (Agirre and Martinez, 2001; Agirre and Martinez, 2002) or acquired from British National Corpus (BNC) (McCarthy, 2001), large-scale Topic Signatures for each synset acquired from the web (Agirre and de la Calle, 2004) or acquired from the BNC (Cuadros et al., 2005).

Obviously, all these semantic resources have been acquired using a very different set of methods, tools and corpora, resulting on a different set of new semantic relations between synsets. In fact, each resource has different volume and accuracy figures. Although isolated evaluations have been performed by their developers in different experi-

[1] Symmetric relations are counted only once.

Proceedings of the 2006 Conference on Empirical Methods in Natural Language Processing (EMNLP 2006), pages 534–541,
Sydney, July 2006.

mental settings, to date no comparable evaluation has been carried out in a common and controlled framework.

This work tries to establish the relative quality of these semantic resources in a neutral environment. The quality of each large-scale knowledge resource is indirectly evaluated on a Word Sense Disambiguation (WSD) task. In particular, we use a well defined WSD evaluation benchmark (Senseval-3 English Lexical Sample task) to evaluate the quality of each resource.

Furthermore, this work studies how these resources complement each other. That is, to which extent each knowledge base provides new knowledge not provided by the others.

This paper is organized as follows: after this introduction, section 2 describes the large-scale knowledge resources studied in this work. Section 3 describes the evaluation framework. Section 4 presents the evaluation results of the different semantic resources considered. Section 5 provides a qualitative assessment of this empirical study and finally, the conclusions and future work are presented in section 6.

2 Large Scale Knowledge Resources

This study covers a wide range of large-scale knowledge resources: WordNet (WN) (Fellbaum, 1998), eXtended WordNet (Mihalcea and Moldovan, 2001), large collections of semantic preferences acquired from SemCor (Agirre and Martinez, 2001; Agirre and Martinez, 2002) or acquired from the BNC (McCarthy, 2001), large-scale Topic Signatures for each synset acquired from the web (Agirre and de la Calle, 2004) or acquired from the BNC (Cuadros et al., 2005).

However, although these resources have been derived using different WN versions, the research community has the technology for the automatic alignment of wordnets (Daudé et al., 2003). This technology provides a mapping among synsets of different WN versions, maintaining the compatibility to all the knowledge resources which use a particular WN version as a sense repository. Furthermore, this technology allows to port the knowledge associated to a particular WN version to the rest of WN versions already connected.

Using this technology, most of these resources are integrated into a common resource called Multilingual Central Repository (MCR) (Atserias et al., 2004). In particular, all WordNet versions, eXtended WordNet, and the semantic preferences acquired from SemCor and BNC.

2.1 Multilingual Central Repository

The Multilingual Central Repository (MCR)[2] follows the model proposed by the EuroWordNet project. EuroWordNet (Vossen, 1998) is a multilingual lexical database with wordnets for several European languages, which are structured as the Princeton WordNet. The Princeton WordNet contains information about nouns, verbs, adjectives and adverbs in English and is organized around the notion of a *synset*. A synset is a set of words with the same part-of-speech that can be interchanged in a certain context. For example, *<party, political_party>* form a synset because they can be used to refer to the same concept. A synset is often further described by a gloss, in this case: "an organization to gain political power". Finally, synsets can be related to each other by semantic relations, such as hyponymy (between specific and more general concepts), meronymy (between parts and wholes), cause, etc.

The current version of the MCR (Atserias et al., 2004) is a result of the 5th Framework MEANING project. The MCR integrates into the same EuroWordNet framework wordnets from five different languages (together with four English WordNet versions). The MCR also integrates WordNet Domains (Magnini and Cavaglià, 2000) and new versions of the Base Concepts and Top Concept Ontology. The final version of the MCR contains 1,642,389 semantic relations between synsets, most of them acquired by automatic means. This represents almost one order of magnitude larger than the Princeton WordNet (204,074 unique semantic relations in WordNet 2.0). Table 1 summarizes the main sources for semantic relations integrated into the MCR.

Table 2 shows the number of semantic relations between synsets pairs in the MCR and its overlappings. Note that, most of the relations in the MCR between synsets-pairs are unique.

Hereinafter we will refer to each semantic resource as follows:

- **WN** (Fellbaum, 1998): This knowledge resource uses the direct relations encoded in WordNet 1.6 or 2.0. We also tested WN-2 (using relations at distance 1 and 2) and WN-3 (using relations at distance 1, 2 and 3).

[2] http://nipadio.lsi.upc.es/˜nlp/meaning

Source	#relations
Princeton WN1.6	138,091
Selectional Preferences from SemCor	203,546
Selectional Preferences from the BNC	707,618
New relations from Princeton WN2.0	42,212
Gold relations from eXtended WN	17,185
Silver relations from eXtended WN	239,249
Normal relations from eXtended WN	294,488
Total	1,642,389

Table 1: Main sources of semantic relations

Type of Relations	#relations
Total Relations	1,642,389
Different Relations	1,531,380
Unique Relations	1,390,181
Non-unique relations (>1)	70,425
Non-unique relations (>2)	341
Non-unique relations (>3)	8

Table 2: Overlapping relations in the MCR

- **XWN** (Mihalcea and Moldovan, 2001): This knowledge resource uses the direct relations encoded in eXtended WordNet.

- **XWN+WN**: This knowledge resource uses the direct relations included in WN and XWN.

- **spBNC** (McCarthy, 2001): This knowledge resource contains the selectional preferences acquired from the BNC.

- **spSemCor** (Agirre and Martinez, 2001; Agirre and Martinez, 2002): This knowledge resource contains the selectional preferences acquired from SemCor.

- **spBNC+spSemCor**: This knowledge resource uses the selectional preferences acquired from the BNC and SemCor.

- **MCR** (Atserias et al., 2004): This knowledge resource uses the direct relations included in MCR.

2.2 Automatically retrieved Topic Signatures

Topic Signatures (TS) are word vectors related to a particular topic (Lin and Hovy, 2000). Topic Signatures are built by retrieving context words of a target topic from large volumes of text. In our case, we consider word senses as topics. Basically, the acquisition of TS consists of A) acquiring the best possible corpus examples for a particular word sense (usually characterizing each word sense as a query and performing a search on the corpus for those examples that best match the queries), and then, B) building the TS by deriving the context words that best represent the word sense from the selected corpora.

For this study, we use the large-scale Topic Signatures acquired from the web (Agirre and de la Calle, 2004) and those acquired from the BNC (Cuadros et al., 2005).

- **TSWEB**[3]: Inspired by the work of (Leacock et al., 1998), these Topic Signatures were constructed using monosemous relatives from WordNet (synonyms, hypernyms, direct and indirect hyponyms, and siblings), querying Google and retrieving up to one thousand snippets per query (that is, a word sense). In particular, the method was as follows:

  - Organizing the retrieved examples from the web in collections, one collection per word sense.
  - Extracting the words and their frequencies for each collection.
  - Comparing these frequencies with those pertaining to other word senses using TFIDF (see formula 1).
  - Gathering in an ordered list, the words with distinctive frequency for one of the collections, which constitutes the Topic Signature for the respective word sense.

  This constitutes the largest available semantic resource with around 100 million relations (between synsets and words).

- **TSBNC**: These Topic Signatures have been constructed using ExRetriever[4], a flexible tool to perform sense queries on large corpora.

  - This tool characterizes each sense of a word as a specific query using a declarative language.
  - This is automatically done by using a particular query construction strategy, defined *a priori*, and using information from a knowledge base.

  In this study, ExRetriever has been evaluated using the BNC, WN as a knowledge base and

[3] http://ixa.si.ehu.es/Ixa/resources/sensecorpus
[4] http://www.lsi.upc.es/~nlp/meaning/downloads.html

TFIDF (as shown in formula 1) (Agirre and de la Calle, 2004)[5].

$$TFIDF(w, C) = \frac{wf_w}{max_w wf_w} \times log\frac{N}{Cf_w} \quad (1)$$

Where w stands for word context, wf for the word frecuency, C for Collection (all the corpus gathered for a particular word sense), and Cf stands for the Collection frecuency.

In this study we consider two different query strategies:

- Monosemous A (**queryA**): (OR monosemous-words). That is, the union set of all synonym, hyponym and hyperonym words of a WordNet synset which are monosemous nouns (these words can have other senses as verbs, adjectives or adverbs).
- Monosemous W (**queryW**): (OR monosemous-words). That is, the union set of all words appearing as synonyms, direct hyponyms, hypernyms indirect hyponyms (distance 2 and 3) and siblings. In this case, the nouns collected are monosemous having no other senses as verbs, adjectives or adverbs.

While TSWEB use the query construction queryW, ExRetriever use both.

3 Indirect Evaluation on Word Sense Disambiguation

In order to measure the quality of the knowledge resources described in the previous section, we performed an indirect evaluation by using all these resources as Topic Signatures (TS). That is, word vectors with weights associated to a particular synset which are obtained by collecting those word senses appearing in the synsets directly related to them [6]. This simple representation tries to be as neutral as possible with respect to the evaluation framework.

All knowledge resources are indirectly evaluated on a WSD task. In particular, the noun-set of Senseval-3 English Lexical Sample task which consists of 20 nouns. All performances are evaluated on the test data using the fine-grained scoring system provided by the organizers.

Furthermore, trying to be as neutral as possible with respect to the semantic resources studied, we applied systematically the same disambiguation method to all of them. Recall that our main goal is to establish a fair comparison of the knowledge resources rather than providing the best disambiguation technique for a particular semantic knowledge base.

A common WSD method has been applied to all knowledge resources. A simple word overlapping counting (or weighting) is performed between the Topic Signature and the test example[7]. Thus, the **occurrence** evaluation measure counts the amount of overlapped words and the **weight** evaluation measure adds up the weights of the overlapped words. The synset having higher overlapping word counts (or weights) is selected for a particular test example. However, for TSWEB and TSBNC the better results have been obtained using occurrences (the weights are only used to order the words of the vector). Finally, we should remark that the results are not skewed (for instance, for resolving ties) by the most frequent sense in WN or any other statistically predicted knowledge.

Figure 3 presents an example of Topic Signature from TSWEB using queryW and the web and from TSBNC using queryA and the BNC for the first sense of the noun party. Although both automatically acquired TS seem to be closely related to the first sense of the noun party, they do not have words in common.

As an example, table 4 shows a test example of Senseval-3 corresponding to the first sense of the noun party. In bold there are the words that appear in TSBNC-queryA. There are several important words that appear in the text that also appear in the TS.

4 Evaluating the quality of knowledge resources

In order to establish a clear picture of the current state-of-the-art of publicly available wide coverage knowledge resources we also consider a number of basic baselines.

[5] Although other measures have been tested, such as Mutual Information or Association Ratio, the best results have been obtained using TFIDF formula.

[6] A weight of 1 is given when the resource do not has associated weight.

[7] We also consider multiword terms.

democratic	0.0126	socialist	0.0062
tammany	0.0124	organization	0.0060
alinement	0.0122	conservative	0.0059
federalist	0.0115	populist	0.0053
missionary	0.0103	dixiecrats	0.0051
whig	0.0099	know-nothing	0.0049
greenback	0.0089	constitutional	0.0045
anti-masonic	0.0083	pecking	0.0043
nazi	0.0081	democratic-republican	0.0040
republican	0.0074	republicans	0.0039
alcoholics	0.0073	labor	0.0039
bull	0.0070	salvation	0.0038

party	4.9350	trade	1.5295
political	3.7722	parties	1.4083
government	2.4129	politics	1.2703
election	2.2265	campaign	1.2551
policy	2.0795	leadership	1.2277
support	1.8537	movement	1.2156
leader	1.8280	general	1.2034
years	1.7128	public	1.1874
people	1.7044	member	1.1855
local	1.6899	opposition	1.1751
conference	1.6702	unions	1.1563
power	1.6105	national	1.1474

Table 3: Topic Signatures for party#n#1 using TSWEB (24 out of 15881 total words) and TS-BNC(queryA) with TFIDF (24 out of 9069 total words)

<instance id="party.n.bnc.00008131" docsrc="BNC"> <context> Up to the **late** 1960s , catholic nationalists were **split** between two **main political** groupings . There was the Nationalist Party , a weak **organization** for which **local** priests had to **provide** some **kind** of legitimation . As a <head>party</head> , it really only exercised a modicum of **power** in relation to the Stormont administration . Then there were the republican **parties** who focused their attention on Westminster **elections** . The disorganized **nature** of catholic nationalist **politics** was only turned round with the emergence of the **civil rights movement** of 1968 and the subsequent forming of the SDLP in 1970 . </context> </instance>

Table 4: Example of test num. 00008131 for party#n which its correct sense is 1

4.1 Baselines

We have designed several baselines in order to establish a relative comparison of the performance of each semantic resource:

- **RANDOM**: For each target word, this method selects a random sense. This baseline can be considered as a lower-bound.
- **WordNet MFS (WN-MFS)**: This method selects the most frequent sense (the first sense in WordNet) of the target word.
- **TRAIN-MFS**: This method selects the most frequent sense in the training corpus of the target word.
- **Train Topic Signatures (TRAIN)**: This baseline uses the training corpus to directly build a Topic Signature using TFIDF measure for each word sense. Note that in this case, this baseline can be considered as an upper-bound of our evaluation framework.

Table 5 presents the F1 measure (harmonic mean of recall and precision) of the different baselines. In this table, TRAIN has been calculated with a fixed vector size of 450 words. As expected, RANDOM baseline obtains the poorest result while the most frequent sense of WordNet (WN-MFS) is very close to the most frequent sense of the training corpus (TRAIN-MFS), but both are far below to the Topic Signatures acquired using the training corpus (TRAIN).

Baselines	**F1**
TRAIN	65.1
TRAIN-MFS	54.5
WN-MFS	53.0
RANDOM	19.1

Table 5: Baselines

4.2 Performance of the knowledge resources

Table 6 presents the performance of each knowledge resource uploaded into the MCR and the average size of its vectors. In bold appear the best results for precision, recall and F1 measures. The lowest result is obtained by the knowledge directly gathered from WN mainly because of its poor coverage (Recall of 17.6 and F1 of 25.6). Its performance is improved using words at distance 1 and 2 (F1 of 33.3), but it decreases using words at distance 1, 2 and 3 (F1 of 30.4). The best precision is obtained by WN (46.7), but the best performance is achieved by the combined knowledge of MCR-spBNC[8] (Recall of 42.9 and F1 of 44.1). This represents a recall 18.5 points higher than WN. That is, the knowledge integrated into the MCR (WordNet, eXtended WordNet and the selectional preferences acquired from SemCor) although partly derived by automatic means performs much better

[8]MCR without Selectional Preferences from BNC

KB	P	R	F1	Av. Size
MCR-spBNC	45.4	**42.9**	**44.1**	115
MCR	41.8	40.4	41.1	235
spSemCor	43.1	38.7	40.8	56
spBNC+spSemCor	41.4	30.1	40.7	184
WN+XWN	45.5	28.1	34.7	68
WN-2	38.0	29.7	33.3	72
XWN	45.0	25.6	32.6	55
WN-3	31.6	29.3	30.4	297
spBNC	36.3	25.4	29.9	128
WN	**46.7**	17.6	25.6	13

Table 6: P, R and F1 fine-grained results for the resources integrated into the MCR.

in terms of recall and F1 measures than using the knowledge currently present in WN alone (with a small decrease in precision). It also seems that the knowledge from spBNC always degrades the performance of their combinations[9].

Regarding the baselines, all knowledge resources integrated into the MCR surpass RANDOM, but none achieves neither WN-MFS, TRAIN-MFS nor TRAIN.

Figure 1 plots F1 results of the fine-grained evaluation on the nominal part of the English lexical sample of Senseval-3 of the baselines (including upper and lower-bounds), the knowledge bases integrated into the MCR, the best performing Topic Signatures acquired from the web and the BNC evaluated individually and in combination with others. The figure presents F1 (Y-axis) in terms of the size of the word vectors (X-axis)[10].

In order to evaluate more deeply the quality of each knowledge resource, we also provide some evaluations of the combined outcomes of several knowledge resources. The combinations are performed following a very simple voting method: first, for each knowledge resource, the scoring results obtained for each word sense are normalized, and then, for each word sense, the normalized scores are added up selecting the word sense with higher score.

Regarding Topic Signatures, as expected, in general the knowledge gathered from the web (TSWEB) is superior to the one acquired from the BNC either using queryA or queryW (TSBNC-queryA and TSBNC-queryW). Interestingly, the performance of TSBNC-queryA when using the first two hundred words of the TS is slightly better than using queryW (both using the web or the BNC).

Although TSBNC-queryA and TSBNC-queryW perform very similar, both knowledge resources contain different knowledge. This is shown when combining the outcomes of these two different knowledge resources with TSWEB. While no improvement is obtained when combining the knowledge acquired from the web and the BNC when using the same acquisition method (queryW), the combination of TSWEB and TSBNC-queryA (TSWEB+ExRetA) obtains better F1 results than TSWEB (TSBNC-queryA have some knowledge not included into TSWEB).

Surprisingly, the knowledge integrated into the MCR (MCR-spBNC) surpass the knowledge from Topic Signatures acquired from the web or the BNC, using queryA, queryW or their combinations.

Furthermore, the combination of TSWEB and MCR-spBNC (TSWEB+MCR-spBNC) outperforms both resources individually indicating that both knowledge bases contain complementary information. The maximum is achieved with TS vectors of at most 700 words (with 49.3% precision, 49.2% recall and 49.2% F1). In fact, the resulting combination is very close to the most frequent sense baselines. This fact indicates that the resulting large-scale knowledge base almost encodes the knowledge necessary to behave as a most frequent sense tagger.

4.3 Senseval-3 system performances

For sake of comparison, tables 7 and 8 present the F1 measure of the fine-grained results for nouns of the Senseval-3 lexical sample task for the best and worst unsupervised and supervised systems, respectively. We also include in these tables some of the baselines and the best performing combination of knowledge resources (including TSWEB and MCR-spBNC)[11]. Regarding the knowledge resources evaluated in this study, the best combination (including TSWEB and MCR-spBNC) achieves an F1 measure much better than some supervised and unsupervised systems and it is close to the most frequent sense of WordNet (WN-MFS) and to the most frequent sense of the training corpora (TRAIN-MFS).

[9]All selectional preferences acquired from SemCor or the BNC have been considered including those with very low confidence score.

[10]Only varying the size of TS for TSWEB and TSBNC.

[11]Although we maintain the classification of the organizers, system s3_wsdiit used the train data.

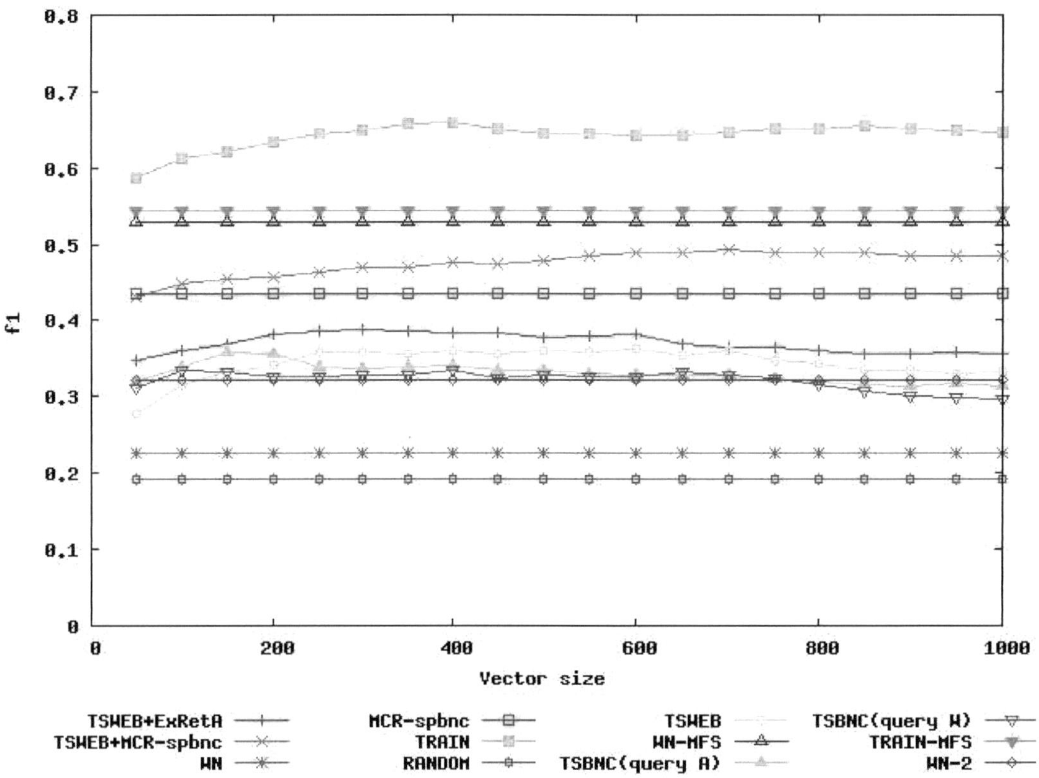

Figure 1: Fine-grained evaluation results for the knowledge resources

s3 systems	F1
s3_wsdiit	68.0
WN-MFS	53.0
Comb TSWEB MCR-spBNC	49.2
s3_DLSI	17.8

Table 7: Senseval-3 Unsupervised Systems

s3 systems	F1
htsa3 U.Bucharest (Grozea)	74.2
TRAIN	65.1
TRAIN-MFS	54.5
DLSI-UA-LS-SU U.Alicante (Vazquez)	41.0

Table 8: Senseval-3 Supervised Systems

We must recall that the main goal of this research is to establish a clear and neutral view of the relative quality of available knowledge resources, not to provide the best WSD algorithm using these resources. Obviously, much more sophisticated WSD systems using these resources could be devised.

5 Quality Assessment

Summarizing, this study provides empirical evidence for the relative quality of publicly available large-scale knowledge resources. The relative quality has been measured indirectly in terms of precision and recall on a WSD task.

The study empirically demonstrates that automatically acquired knowledge bases clearly surpass both in terms of precision and recall the knowledge manually encoded from WordNet (using relations expanded to one, two or three levels).

Surprisingly, the knowledge contained into the MCR (WordNet, eXtended WordNet, Selectional Preferences acquired automatically from SemCor) is of a better quality than the automatically acquired Topic Signatures. In fact, the knowledge resulting from the combination of all these large-scale resources outperforms each resource individually indicating that these knowledge bases contain complementary information. Finally, we should remark that the resulting combination is very close to the most frequent sense classifiers.

Regarding the automatic acquisition of large-scale Topic Signatures it seems that those acquired from the web are slightly better than those acquired from smaller corpora (for instance, the BNC). It also seems that queryW performs better than queryA but that both methods (queryA and queryW) also produce complementary knowledge. Finally, it seems that the weights are not useful for measuring the strength of a vote (they are only useful for ordering the words in the Topic Signature).

6 Conclusions and future work

During the last years the research community has derived a large set of semantic resources using a very different set of methods, tools and corpus, resulting on a different set of new semantic relations between synsets. In fact, each resource has different volume and accuracy figures. Although isolated evaluations have been performed by their developers in different experimental settings, to date no complete evaluation has been carried out in a common framework.

In order to establish a fair comparison, the quality of each resource has been indirectly evaluated in the same way on a WSD task. The evaluation framework selected has been the Senseval-3 English Lexical Sample Task. The study empirically demonstrates that automatically acquired knowledge bases surpass both in terms of precision and recall to the knowledge bases derived manually, and that the combination of the knowledge contained in these resources is very close to the most frequent sense classifier.

Once empirically demonstrated that the knowledge resulting from MCR and Topic Signatures acquired from the web is complementary and close to the most frequent sense classifier, we plan to integrate the Topic Signatures acquired from the web (of about 100 million relations) into the MCR. This process will be performed by disambiguating the Topic Signatures. That is, trying to obtain word sense vectors instead of word vectors. This will allow to enlarge the existing knowledge bases in several orders of magnitude by fully automatic methods. Other evaluation frameworks such as PP attachment will be also considered.

7 Acknowledgements

This work is being funded by the IXA NLP group from the Basque Country University, EHU/UPV-CLASS project and Basque Government-ADIMEN project. We would like to thank also the three anonymous reviewers for their valuable comments.

References

E. Agirre and O. Lopez de la Calle. 2004. Publicly available topic signatures for all wordnet nominal senses. In *Proceedings of LREC*, Lisbon, Portugal.

E. Agirre and D. Martinez. 2001. Learning class-to-class selectional preferences. In *Proceedings of CoNLL*, Toulouse, France.

E. Agirre and D. Martinez. 2002. Integrating selectional preferences in wordnet. In *Proceedings of GWC*, Mysore, India.

J. Atserias, L. Villarejo, G. Rigau, E. Agirre, J. Carroll, B. Magnini, and Piek Vossen. 2004. The meaning multilingual central repository. In *Proceedings of GWC*, Brno, Czech Republic.

M. Cuadros, L. Padró, and G. Rigau. 2005. Comparing methods for automatic acquisition of topic signatures. In *Proceedings of RANLP*, Borovets, Bulgaria.

J. Daudé, L. Padró, and G. Rigau. 2003. Validation and Tuning of Wordnet Mapping Techniques. In *Proceedings of RANLP*, Borovets, Bulgaria.

C. Fellbaum, editor. 1998. *WordNet. An Electronic Lexical Database*. The MIT Press.

C. Leacock, M. Chodorow, and G. Miller. 1998. Using Corpus Statistics and WordNet Relations for Sense Identification. *Computational Linguistics*, 24(1):147–166.

C. Lin and E. Hovy. 2000. The automated acquisition of topic signatures for text summarization. In *Proceedings of COLING*. Strasbourg, France.

B. Magnini and G. Cavaglià. 2000. Integrating subject field codes into wordnet. In *Proceedings of LREC*, Athens. Greece.

D. McCarthy. 2001. *Lexical Acquisition at the Syntax-Semantics Interface: Diathesis Aternations, Subcategorization Frames and Selectional Preferences*. Ph.D. thesis, University of Sussex.

R. Mihalcea and D. Moldovan. 2001. extended wordnet: Progress report. In *Proceedings of NAACL Workshop on WordNet and Other Lexical Resources*, Pittsburgh, PA.

P. Vossen, editor. 1998. *EuroWordNet: A Multilingual Database with Lexical Semantic Networks* . Kluwer Academic Publishers .

Graph-based Word Clustering using a Web Search Engine

Yutaka Matsuo
National Institute of Advanced
Industrial Science and Technology
1-18-13 Sotokanda, Tokyo 101-0021
y.matsuo@aist.go.jp

Takeshi Sakaki
University of Tokyo
7-3-1 Hongo
Tokyo 113-8656

Kôki Uchiyama
Hottolink Inc.
2-11-17 Nishi-gotanda
Tokyo 141-0031
uchi@hottolink.co.jp

Mitsuru Ishizuka
University of Tokyo
7-3-1 Hongo
Tokyo 113-8656
ishizuka@i.u-tokyo.ac.jp

Abstract

Word clustering is important for automatic thesaurus construction, text classification, and word sense disambiguation. Recently, several studies have reported using the web as a corpus. This paper proposes an unsupervised algorithm for word clustering based on a word similarity measure by web counts. Each pair of words is queried to a search engine, which produces a co-occurrence matrix. By calculating the similarity of words, a word co-occurrence graph is obtained. A new kind of graph clustering algorithm called *Newman clustering* is applied for efficiently identifying word clusters. Evaluations are made on two sets of word groups derived from a web directory and WordNet.

1 Introduction

The web is a good source of linguistic information for several natural language techniques such as question answering, language modeling, and multilingual lexicon acquisition. Numerous studies have examined the use of the web as a corpus (Kilgarriff, 2003).

Web-based models perform especially well against the *sparse data problem*: Statistical techniques perform poorly when the words are rarely used. For example, F. Keller et al. (2002) use the web to obtain frequencies for unseen bigrams in a given corpus. They count for adjective-noun, noun-noun, and verb-object bigrams by querying a search engine, and demonstrate that web frequencies (web counts) correlate with frequencies from a carefully edited corpus such as the British National Corpus (BNC). Aside from counting bigrams, various tasks are attainable using web-based models: spelling correction, adjective ordering, compound noun bracketing, countability detection, and so on (Lapata and Keller, 2004). For some tasks, simple unsupervised models perform better when n-gram frequencies are obtained from the web rather than from a standard large corpus; the web yields better counts than the BNC.

The web is an excellent source of information on new words. Therefore, automatic thesaurus construction (Curran, 2002) offers great potential for various useful NLP applications. Several studies have addressed the extraction of hypernyms and hyponyms from the web (Miura et al., 2004; Cimiano et al., 2004). P. Turney (2001) presents a method to recognize synonyms by obtaining word counts and calculating pointwise mutual information (PMI). For further development of automatic thesaurus construction, word clustering is beneficial, e.g. for obtaining synsets. It also contributes to word sense disambiguation (Li and Abe, 1998) and text classification (Dhillon et al., 2002) because the dimensionality is reduced efficiently.

This paper presents an unsupervised algorithm for word clustering based on a word similarity measure by web counts. Given a set of words, the algorithm clusters the words into groups so that the similar words are in the same cluster. Each pair of words is queried to a search engine, which results in a co-occurrence matrix. By calculating the similarity of words, a word co-occurrence graph is created. Then, a new kind of graph clustering algorithm, called *Newman clustering*, is applied. Newman clustering emphasizes betweenness of an edge and identifies densely connected subgraphs.

To the best of our knowledge, this is the first attempt to obtain word groups using web counts. Our contributions are summarized as follows:

Proceedings of the 2006 Conference on Empirical Methods in Natural Language Processing (EMNLP 2006), pages 542–550, Sydney, July 2006.

- A new algorithm for word clustering is described. It has few parameters and thus is easy to implement as a baseline method.
- We evaluate the algorithm on two sets of word groups derived from a web directory and WordNet. The chi-square measure and Newman clustering are both used in our algorithm, they are revealed to outperform PMI and hierarchical clustering.

We target Japanese words in this paper. The remainder of this paper is organized as follows: We overview the related studies in the next section. Our proposed algorithm is described in Section 3. Sections 4 and 5 explain evaluations and advance discussion. Finally, we conclude the paper.

2 Related Works

A number of studies have explained the use of the web for NLP tasks e.g., creating multilingual translation lexicons (Cheng et al., 2004), text classification (Huang et al., 2004), and word sense disambiguation (Turney, 2004). M. Baroni and M. Ueyama summarize three approaches to use the web as a corpus (Baroni and Ueyama, 2005): using web counts as frequency estimates, building corpora through search engine queries, and crawling the web for linguistic purposes. Commercial search engines are optimized for ordinary users. Therefore, it is desirable to crawl the web and to develop specific search engines for NLP applications (Cafarella and Etzioni, 2005). However, considering that great efforts are taken in commercial search engines to maintain quality of crawling and indexing, especially against spammers, it is still important to pursue the possibility of using the current search engines for NLP applications.

P. Turney (Turney, 2001) presents an unsupervised learning algorithm for recognizing synonyms by querying a web search engine. The task of recognizing synonyms is, given a target word and a set of alternative words, to choose the word that is most similar in meaning to the target word. The algorithm uses pointwise mutual information (PMI-IR) to measure the similarity of pairs of words. It is evaluated using 80 synonym test questions from the Test of English as a Foreign Language (TOEFL) and 50 from the English as a Second Language test (ESL). The algorithm obtains a score of 74%, contrasted to that of 64% by Latent Semantic Analysis (LSA). Terra and Clarke (Terra and Clarke, 2003) provide a comparative investigation of co-occurrence frequency estimation on the performance of synonym tests. They report that PMI (with a certain window size) performs best on average. Also, PMI-IR is useful for calculating semantic orientation and rating reviews (Turney, 2002).

As described, PMI is one of many measures to calculate the strength of word similarity or word association (Manning and Schütze, 2002). An important assumption is that similarity between words is a consequence of word co-occurrence, or that the proximity of words in text is indicative of relationship between them, such as synonymy or antonymy. A commonly used technique to obtain word groups is distributional clustering (Baker and McCallum, 1998). Distributional clustering of words was first proposed by Pereira Tishby & Lee in (Pereira et al., 1993): They cluster nouns according to their conditional verb distributions.

Graphic representations for word similarity have also been advanced by several researchers. Kageura et al. (2000) propose automatic thesaurus generation based on a graphic representation. By applying a minimum edge cut, the corresponding English terms and Japanese terms are identified as a cluster. Widdows and Dorow (2002) use a graph model for unsupervised lexical acquisition. A graph is produced by linking pairs of words which participate in particular syntactic relationships. An incremental cluster-building algorithm achieves 82% accuracy at a lexical acquisition task, evaluated against WordNet classes. Another study builds a co-occurrence graph of terms and decomposes it to identify relevant terms by duplicating nodes and edges (Tanaka-Ishii and Iwasaki, 1996). It focuses on transitivity: if transitivity does not hold between three nodes (e.g., if edge *a*-*b* and *b*-*c* exist but edge *a*-*c* does not), the nodes should be in separate clusters.

A network of words (or named entities) on the web is investigated also in the context of the Semantic Web (Cimiano et al., 2004; Bekkerman and McCallum, 2005). Especially, a social network of persons is mined from the web using a search engine (Kautz et al., 1997; Mika, 2005; Matsuo et al., 2006). In these studies, the Jaccard coefficient is often used to measure the co-occurrence of entities. We compare Jaccard coefficients in our evaluations.

In the research field on complex networks,

Table 1: Web counts for each word.

printer	*print*	*InterLaser*	*ink*	*TV*	*Aquos*	*Sharp*	
17000000	103000000	215	18900000	69100000	1760000000	2410000	186000000

Table 2: Co-occurrence matrix by web counts.

	printer	*print*	*InterLaser*	*ink*	*TV*	*Aquos*	*Sharp*
printer	—	4780000	179	4720000	4530000	201000	990000
print	4780000	—	183	4800000	8390000	86400	1390000
InterLaser	179	183	—	116	65	0	0
ink	4720000	4800000	116	—	10600000	144000	656000
TV	4530000	8390000	65	10600000	—	1660000	42300000
Aquos	201000	86400	0	144000	1660000	—	1790000
Sharp	990000	1390000	0	656000	42300000	1790000	—

structures of various networks are investigated in detail. For example, Motter (2002) targeted a conceptual network from a thesaurus and demonstrated its small-world structure. Recently, numerous works have identified communities (or densely-connected subgraphs) from large networks (Newman, 2004; Girvan and Newman, 2002; Palla et al., 2005) as explained in the next section.

3 Word Clustering using Web Counts

3.1 Co-occurrence by a Search Engine

A typical word clustering task is described as follows: given a set of words (nouns), cluster words into groups so that the similar words are in the same cluster [1]. Let us take an example. Assume a set of words is given: プリンタ (*printer*), 印刷 (*print*), インターレーザー (*InterLaser*), インク (*ink*), TV (*TV*), Aquos (*Aquos*), and Sharp (*Sharp*). Apparently, the first four words are related to a printer, and the last three words are related to a TV [2]. In this case, we would like to have two word groups: the first four and the last three.

We query a search engine[3] to obtain word counts. Table 1 shows web counts for each word. Table 2 shows the web counts for pairs of words. For example, we submit a query *printer AND InterLaser* to a search engine, and are directed to 179 documents. Thereby, ${}_nC_2$ queries are necessary to obtain the matrix if we have n words. We call Table 2 a *co-occurrence matrix*.

We can calculate the pointwise mutual information between word w_1 and w_2 as

$$PMI(w_1, w_2) = \log_2 \frac{p(w_1, w_2)}{p(w_1)p(w_2)}.$$

Probability $p(w_1)$ is estimated by f_{w_1}/N, where f_{w_1} represents the web count of w_1 and N represents the number of documents on the web. Probability of co-occurrence $p(w_1, w_2)$ is estimated by $f_{w_1,w_2}/N$ where f_{w_1,w_2} represents the web count of w_1 *AND* w_2.

The PMI values are shown in Table 3. We set $N = 10^{10}$ according to the number of indexed pages on Google. Some values are inconsistent with our intuition: *Aquos* is inferred to have high PMI to *TV* and *Sharp*, but also to *printer*. None of the words has high PMI with *TV*. These are because the range of the word count is broad. Generally, mutual information tends to provide a large value if either word is much rarer than the other.

Various statistical measures based on co-occurrence analysis have been proposed for estimating term association: the DICE coefficient, Jaccard coefficient, chi-square test, and the log-likelihood ratio (Manning and Schütze, 2002). In our algorithm, we use the chi-square (χ^2) value instead of PMI. The chi-square value is calculated as follows: We denote the number of pages containing both w_1 and w_2 as a. We also denote b, c, d as follows[4].

	w_2	$\neg w_2$
w_1	a	b
$\neg w_1$	c	d

Thereby, the expected frequency of (w_1, w_2) is $(a+c)(a+b)/N$. Eventually, chi-square is calculated as follows (Manning and Schütze, 2002).

[1] In this paper, we limit our scope to clustering nouns. We discuss the extension in Section 4.

[2] InterLaser is a laser printer made by Epson Corp. Aquos is a liquid crystal TV made by Sharp Corp.

[3] Google (www.google.co.jp) is used in our study.

[4] Note that $N = a + b + c + d$.

Table 3: A matrix of pointwise mutual information.

	printer	*print*	*InterLaser*	*ink*	*TV*	*Aquos*	*Sharp*
printer	—	4.771	8.936	7.199	0.598	5.616	1.647
print	4.771	—	6.369	4.624	-1.111	1.799	-0.463
InterLaser	8.936	6.369	—	8.157	0.781	$-\infty$*	$-\infty$*
ink	7.199	4.624	8.157	—	1.672	4.983	0.900
TV	0.598	-1.111	0.781	1.672	—	1.969	0.370
Aquos	5.616	1.799	$-\infty$*.	4.983	1.969	—	5.319
Sharp	1.647	-0.463	$-\infty$*	0.900	0.370	5.319	—

* represents that the PMI is not available because the co-occurrence web count is zero, in which case we set $-\infty$.

Table 4: A matrix of chi-square values.

	printer	*print*	*InterLaser*	*ink*	*TV*	*Aquos*	*Sharp*
printer	—	6880482.6	399.2	5689710.7	0.0*	0.0*	0.0*
print	6880482.6	—	277.8	3321184.6	176855.5	0.0*	0.0*
InterLaser	399.2	277.8	—	44.8	0.0*	0.0	0.0
ink	5689710.7	3321184.6	44.8	—	1419485.5	0.0*	0.0*
TV	0.0*	176855.5	0.0*	1419485.5	—	26803.2	70790877.6
Aquos	0.0*	0.0*	0.0	0.0*	26803.2	—	729357.7
Sharp	0.0*	0.0*	0.0	0.0*	70790877.6	729357.7	—

* represents that the observed co-occurrence frequency is below the expected value, in which case we set 0.0.

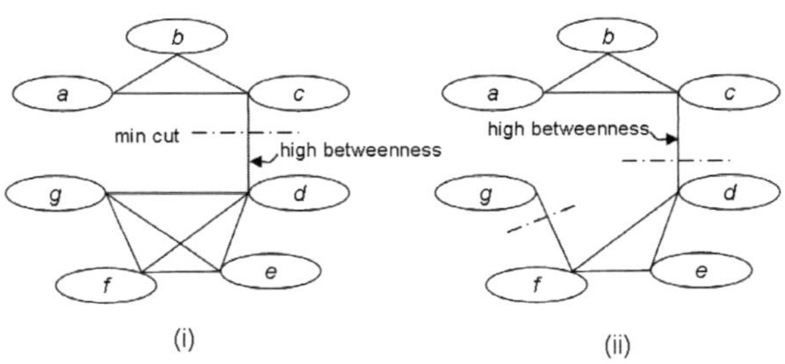

Figure 1: Examples of Newman clustering.

$$\chi^2(w_1, w_2) = \frac{N \times (a \times d - b \times c)^2}{(a+b) \times (a+c) \times (b+d) \times (c+d)}$$

However, N is a huge number on the web and sometimes it is difficult to know exactly. Therefore we regard the co-occurrence matrix as a contingency table:

$$b' = \sum_{w \in W; w \neq w_2} f_{w_1, w}, \quad c' = \sum_{w \in W; w \neq w_1} f_{w_2, w};$$

$$d' = \sum_{w, w' \in W; w \text{ and } w' \neq w_1 \text{ nor } w2} f_{w, w'}, \quad N' = \sum_{w, w' \in W} f_{w, w'},$$

where W represents a given set of words. Then chi-square (within the word list W) is defined as

$$\chi^2_W(w_1, w_2) = \frac{N' \times (a \times d' - b' \times c')^2}{(a+b') \times (a+c') \times (b'+d') \times (c'+d')}.$$

We should note that χ^2_W depends on a word set W. It calculates the relative strength of co-occurrences. Table 4 shows the χ^2_W values. *Aquos* has high values only with *TV* and *Sharp* as expected.

3.2 Clustering on Co-occurrence Graph

Recently, a series of effective graph clustering methods has been advanced. Pioneering work that specifically emphasizes edge betweenness was done by Girvan and Newman (2002): we call the method as GN algorithm. Betweenness of an edge is the number of shortest paths between pairs of nodes that run along it. Figure 1 (i) shows that two "communities" (in Girvan's term), i.e. $\{a,b,c\}$ and $\{d,e,f,g\}$, which are connected by edge *c-d*. Edge *c-d* has high betweenness because numerous shortest paths (e.g., from *a* to *d*, from *b* to *e*, ...) traverse the edge. The graph is likely to be separated into densely connected subgraphs if we cut the high betweenness edge.

The GN algorithm is different from the minimum edge cut. For (i), the results are identical: By cutting edge *c-d*, which is a minimum edge cut, we can obtain two clusters. However in case of (ii), there are two candidates for the minimum edge cut, whereas the highest betweenness edge is still only edge *c-d*. Girvan et al. (2002) shows that this clustering works well to various networks from biological to social networks. Numerous studies have been inspired by that work. One prominent effort is a faster variant of GN algorithm (Newman, 2004), which we call *Newman clustering* in

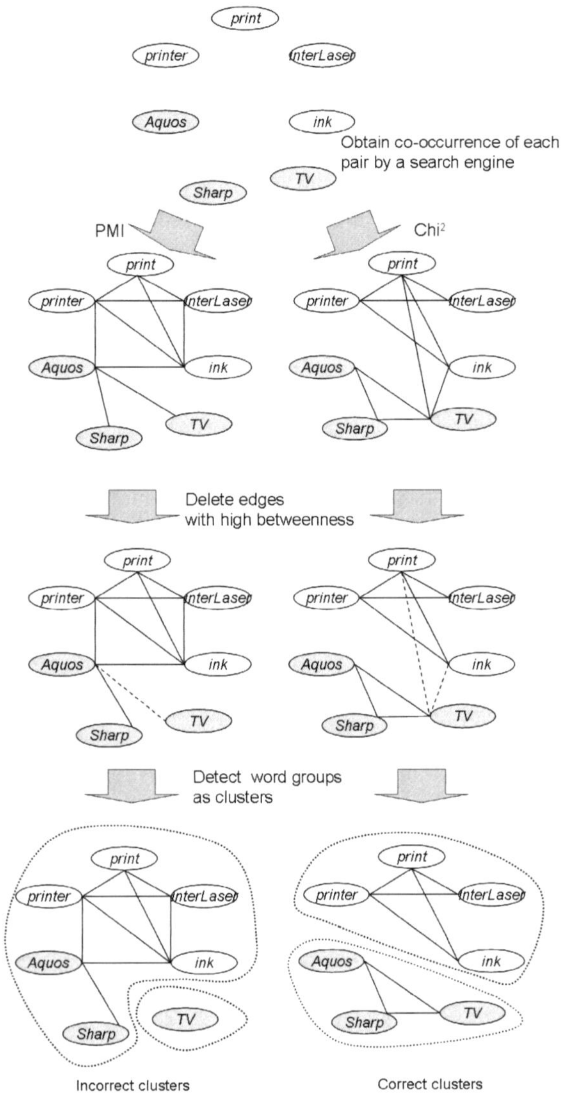

Figure 2: An illustration of graph-based word clustering.

this paper.

In Newman clustering, instead of explicitly calculating high-betweenness edges (which is computationally demanding), an objective function is defined as follows:

$$Q = \sum_i \left(e_{ii} - \left(\sum_j e_{ij} \right)^2 \right) \quad (1)$$

We assume that we have separate clusters, and that e_{ij} is the fraction[5] of edges in the network that connect nodes in cluster i to those in cluster j. The term e_{ii} denotes the fraction of edges within the clusters. The term $\sum_j e_{ij}$ represents the expected fraction of edges within the cluster. If a particular division gives no more within-community edges than would be expected by random chance, then we would obtain $Q = 0$. In practice, values greater than about 0.3 appear to indicate significant group structure (Newman, 2004).

Newman clustering is agglomerative (although we can intuitively understand that a graph without high betweenness edges is ultimately obtained). We repeatedly join clusters together in pairs, choosing at each step the joint that provides the greatest increase in Q. Currently, Newman clustering is one of the most efficient methods for graph-based clustering.

The illustration of our algorithm is shown in Fig. 2. First, we obtain web counts among a given set of words using a search engine. Then PMI or the chi-square values are calculated. If the value is above a certain threshold[6], we invent an edge between the two nodes. Then, we apply graph clustering and finally identify groups of words. This illustration shows that the chi-square measure yields the correct clusters.

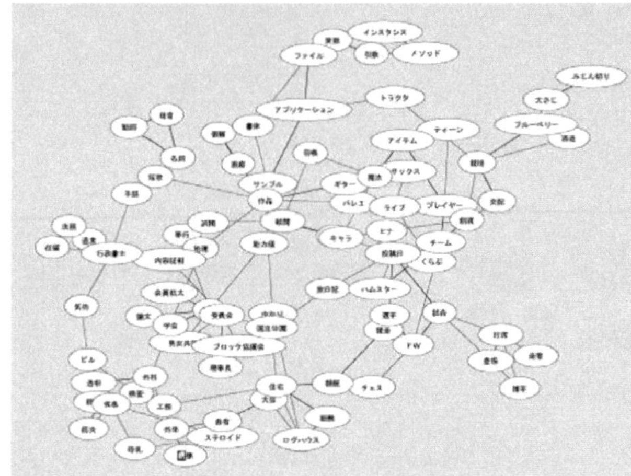

Figure 3: A word graph for 88 Japanese words.

The algorithm is described in Fig. 4. The parameters are few: a threshold d_{thre} for a graph and, optionally, the number of clusters n_c. This enables easy implementation of the algorithm. Figure 3 is a small network of 88 Japanese words obtained through 3828 search queries. We can see that some parts in the graph are densely connected.

4 Experimental Results

This section addresses evaluation. Two sets of word groups are used for the evaluation: one is derived from documents on a web directory; another is from WordNet. We first evaluate the co-

[5]We can calculate e_{ij} using the number of edges between cluster i and j divided by the number of all edges.

[6]In this example, 4.0 for PMI and 200 for χ^2.

1. **Input** A set of words is given. The number of words is denoted as n.

2. **Obtain frequencies** Put a query for each pair of words to a search engine, and obtain a co-occurrence matrix. Then calculate the chi-square matrix (alternatively a PMI matrix, or a Jaccard matrix.)

3. **Make a graph** Set a node for each word, and an edge to a pair of nodes whose χ^2 value is above a threshold. The threshold is determined so that the network density (the number of edges divided by ${}_nC_2$) is d_{thre}.

4. **Apply Newman clustering** Initially set each node as a cluster. Then merge two clusters repeatedly so that Q is maximized. Terminate if Q does not increase anymore, or when a given number of clusters n_c is obtained. (Alternatively, apply average-link hierarchical clustering.)

5. **Output** Output groups of words.

Figure 4: Our algorithm for word clustering.

occurrence measures, then we evaluate the clustering methods.

4.1 Word Groups from an Open Directory

We collected documents from the Japanese Open Directory (dmoz.org/World/Japanese). The dmoz japanese category contains about 130,000 documents and more than 10,000 classes. We chose 9 categories out of the top 12 categories: *art*, *sports*, *computer*, *game*, *society*, *family*, *science*, and *health*. We crawled 1000 documents for each category, i.e., 9000 documents in all.

For each category, a word group is obtained through the procedure in Fig. 5. We consider that the specific words to a category are relevant to some extent, and that they can therefore be regarded as a word group. Examples are shown in Table 5. In all, 90 word sets are obtained and merged. We call the word set DMOZ-J data.

Our task is, given 90 words, to cluster the words into the correct nine groups. Here we investigate whether the correct nine words are selected for each word using the co-occurrence measure. We compare pointwise mutual information (PMI), the Jaccard coefficient (Jaccard), and chi-square (χ^2). We chose these methods for comparison because PMI performs best in (Terra and Clarke, 2003). The Jaccard coefficient is often used in social network mining from the web. Table 7 shows the precision of each method. Experiments are repeated five times. We keep each method that outputs the

1. For each category, crawl 1000 documents randomly[a]

2. Apply the Japanese morphological analysis system ChaSen (Matsumoto et al., 2000) to the documents. Calculate the score of each word w in category c similarly to *TF-IDF*:

$$score(w, c) = f_c(w) \times \log(N_{all}/f_{all}(w))$$

where f_c denotes the document frequency of word w in category c, N_{all} denotes the number of all documents, and $f_{all}(w)$ denotes the frequency of word w in all documents.

3. For each category, the top 10 words are selected as the word group.

[a]We first get all urls, sort them, and select a sample randomly.

Figure 5: Procedure for obtaining word groups for a category.

Table 7: Precision for DMOZ-J set.

	PMI	Jaccard	χ^2
Mean	0.415	0.402	0.537
Min	0.396	0.376	0.493
Max	0.447	0.424	0.569
SD	0.020	0.020	0.032

highest nine words for each word, groups of ten words. Therefore, recall is the same as the precision. From the table, the chi-square performs best. PMI is slightly better than the Jaccard coefficient.

4.2 Word Groups from WordNet

Next, we make a comparison using WordNet [7]. By extracting 10 words that have the same hypernym (i.e. coordinates), we produce a word group. Examples are shown in Table 6. Nine word groups are merged into one, as with DMOZ-J. The experiments are repeated 10 times. Table 8 shows the result. Again, the chi-square performs best among the methods that were compared.

Detailed analyses of the results revealed that word groups such as bacteria and diseases are clustered correctly. However, word groups such as *computers* (in which *homepage*, *server* and *client* are included) are not well clustered: these words tend to be polysemic, which causes difficulty.

4.3 Evaluation of Clustering

We compare two clustering methods: Newman clustering and average-link agglomerative cluster-

[7]We use a partly-translated version of WordNet.

Table 5: Examples of word groups from DMOZ-J.

category	specific words to a category as a word group
アート (*art*)	画廊 (*gallery*), 作品 (*artwork*), 劇場 (*theater*), サックス (*saxophone*), 短歌 (*verse*), ライブ (*live concert*), ギター (*guitar*), 披露 (*performance*), バレエ (*ballet*), 個展 (*personal exhibition*)
レクリエーション (*recreation*)	飼育 (*raising*), ヒナ (*poult*), ハムスター (*hamster*), 旅日記 (*travel diary*), 国立公園 (*national park*), 酒造 (*brewing*), 競艇 (*boat race*), 競争 (*competition*), 釣り堀 (*fishing pond*)
健康 (*health*)	疾患 (*illness*), 患者 (*patient*), 筋炎 (*myositis*), 外科 (*surgery*), 透析 (*dialysis*), ステロイド (*steroid*), 検査 (*test*), 病棟 (*medical ward*), 膠原病 (*collagen disease*), 外来 (*clinic*)

Table 6: Examples of word groups from WordNet.

hypernym	hyponyms as a word group
宝石 (*gem*)	アメジスト (*amethyst*), アクアマリン (*aquamarine*), ダイアモンド (*diamond*), エメラルド (*emerald*), ムーンストーン (*moonstone*), ペリドット (*peridot*), ルビー (*ruby*), サファイア (*sapphire*), トパーズ (*topaz*), トルマリン (*tourmaline*)
学問 (*academic field*)	自然科学 (*natural science*), 数学 (*mathematics*), 農学 (*agronomics*), 建築学 (*architectonics*), 地質学 (*geology*), 心理学 (*psychology*), 情報工学 (*computer science*), 認知科学 (*cognitive science*), 社会学 (*sociology*), 言語学 (*linguistics*)
飲み物 (*drink*)	牛乳 (*milk*), アルコール (*alcohol*), 清涼飲料 (*cooling beverage*), 炭酸飲料 (*carbonated beverage*), サイダー (*soda*), ココア (*cocoa*), フルーツジュース (*fruit juice*), コーヒー (*coffee*), お茶 (*tea*), ミネラルウォーター (*mineral water*)

Table 8: Precision of WordNet set.

	PMI	Jaccard	χ^2
Mean	0.549	0.484	0.584
Min	0.473	0.415	0.498
Max	0.593	0.503	0.656
SD	0.037	0.027	0.048

Table 9: Precision, recall and the F-measure for each clustering.

		PMI	Jaccard	χ^2
Average -link	precision	0.633	0.603	0.486
	recall	0.102	0.101	0.100
	F-measure	0.179	0.173	0.164
Newman	precision	0.751	0.739	0.546
	recall	0.103	0.103	0.431
	F-measure	0.182	0.181	0.480

ing, which is often used in word clustering.

A word co-occurrence graph is created using PMI, Jaccard, and chi-square measures. The threshold is determined so that the network density d_{thre} is 0.3. Then, we apply clustering to obtain nine clusters; $n_c = 9$. Finally, we compare the resultant clusters with the correct categories.

Clustering results for DMOZ-J sets are shown in Table 9. Newman clustering produces higher precision and recall. Especially, the combination of chi-square and Newman is the best in our experiments.

5 Discussion

In this paper, the scope of co-occurrence is document-wide. One reason is that major commercial search engines do not support a type of query w_1 *NEAR* w_2. Another reason is in (Terra and Clarke, 2003) document-wide co-occurrences perform comparable to other Windows-based co-occurrences.

Many types of co-occurrence exist other than noun-noun. We limit our scope to noun-noun co-occurrences in this paper. Other types of co-occurrence such as verb-noun can be investigated in future studies. Also, co-occurrence for the second-order similarity can be sought. Because web documents are sometimes difficult to analyze, we keep our algorithm as simple as possible. Analyzing semantic relations and applying distributional clustering is another goal for future work.

A salient weak point of our algorithm is the number of necessary queries allowed to a search engine. For obtaining a graph of n words, $O(n^2)$ queries are required, which discourages us from undertaking large experiments. However some devices are possible: if we analyze the texts of the top retrieved pages by query w, we can guess what words are likely to co-occur with w. This preprocessing seems promising at least in social network extraction: we can eliminate 85% of queries in the 500 nodes case while retaining more than 90% precision (Asada et al., 2005).

In our evaluation, the chi-square measure performed well. One reason is that the PMI performs worse when a word group contains rare or frequent words, as is generally known for mutual information measure (Manning and Schütze, 2002). Another reason is that if we put one word and two words to a search engine, the result might be inconsistent. In an extreme case, the web count of w_1 is below the web count of $w_1 AND w_2$. This phenomenon depends on how a search engine processes *AND* operator, and results in unstable values for the PMI. On the other hand, our method by the chi-square uses a co-occurrence matrix as a contingency table. For that reason, it suffers less from the problem. Other statistical measures such as the likelihood ratio are also applicable.

6 Conclusion

This paper describes a new approach for word clustering using a search engine. The chi-square measure is used to overcome the broad range of word counts for a given set of words. We also apply recently-developed Newman clustering, which yields promising results through our evaluations.

Our algorithm has few parameters. Therefore, it can be used easily as a baseline, as suggested by (Lapata and Keller, 2004). New words are generated day by day on the web. We believe that to automatically identify new words and obtain word groups potentially enhances many NLP applications.

References

Yohei Asada, Yutaka Matsuo, and Mitsuru Ishizuka. 2005. Increasing scalability of researcher network extraction from the web. *Journal of Japanese Society for Artificial Intelligence*, 20(6).

D. Baker and A. McCallum. 1998. Distributional clustering of words for text classification. In *Proc. SIGIR-98*.

M. Baroni and M. Ueyama. 2005. Building general- and special-purpose corpora by web crawling. In *Proc. NIJL International Workshop on Language Corpora*.

R. Bekkerman and A. McCallum. 2005. Disambiguating web appearances of people in a social network. In *Proc. WWW 2005*.

M. Cafarella and O. Etzioni. 2005. A search engine for natural language applications. In *Proc. WWW2005*.

P. Cheng, W. Lu, J. Teng, and L. Chien. 2004. Creating multilingual translation lexicons with regional variations using web corpora. In *Proc. ACL 2004*, pages 534–541.

P. Cimiano, S. Handschuh, and S. Staab. 2004. Towards the self-annotating web. In *Proc. WWW2004*, pages 462–471.

J. Curran. 2002. Ensemble methods for automatic thesaurus extraction. In *Proc. EMNLP 2002*.

I. Dhillon, S. Mallela, and R. Kumar. 2002. Enhanced word clustering for hierarchical text classification. In *Proc. KDD-2002*, pages 191–200.

Michelle Girvan and M. E. J. Newman. 2002. Community structure in social and biological networks. *Proceedings of National Academy of Sciences USA*, 99:8271–8276.

C. Huang, S. Chuang, and L. Chien. 2004. Categorizing unknown text segments for information extraction using a search result mining approach. In *Proc. IJCNLP 2004*, pages 576–586.

K. Kageura, K. Tsuji, and A. Aizawa. 2000. Automatic thesaurus generation through multiple filtering. In *Proc. COLING 2000*.

H. Kautz, B. Selman, and M. Shah. 1997. The hidden Web. *AI magazine*, 18(2):27–35.

F. Keller, M. Lapata, and O. Ourioupina. 2002. Using the web to overcome data sparseness. In *EMNLP-02*, pages 230–237.

A. Kilgarriff. 2003. Introduction to the special issue on the web as corpus. *Computer Linguistics*, 29(3).

M. Lapata and F. Keller. 2004. The web as a baseline: Evaluating the performance of unsupervised web-based models for a range of nlp tasks. In *Proc. HLT-NAACL 2004*, pages 121–128.

H. Li and N. Abe. 1998. Word clustering and disambiguation based on co-occurrence data. In *Proc. COLING-ACL98*.

C. D. Manning and H. Schütze. 2002. *Foundations of statistical natural language processing*. The MIT Press, London.

Y. Matsumoto, A. Kitauchi, T. Yamashita, Y. Hirano, H. Matsuda, K. Takaoka, and M. Asahara. 2000. Morphological analysis system ChaSen version 2.2.1 manual. Technical report, NIST.

Y. Matsuo, J. Mori, M. Hamasaki, H. Takeda, T. Nishimura, K. Hasida, and M. Ishizuka. 2006. POLYPHONET: An advanced social network extraction system. In *Proc. WWW 2006*.

P. Mika. 2005. Flink: Semantic web technology for the extraction and analysis of social networks. *Journal of Web Semantics*, 3(2).

K. Miura, Y. Tsuruoka, and J. Tsujii. 2004. Automatic acquisition of concept relations from web documents with sense clustering. In *Proc. IJCNLP04*.

A. Motter, A. de Moura, Y. Lai, and P. Dasgupta. 2002. Topology of the conceptual network of language. *Physical Review E*, 65.

M. Newman. 2004. Fast algorithm for detecting community structure in networks. *Phys. Rev. E*, 69.

G. Palla, I. Derenyi, I. Farkas, and T. Vicsek. 2005. Uncovering the overlapping community structure of complex networks in nature and society. *Nature*, 435:814.

F. Pereira, N. Tishby, and L. Lee. 1993. Distributional clustering of English words. In *Proc. ACL93*, pages 183–190.

K. Tanaka-Ishii and H. Iwasaki. 1996. Clustering co-occurrence graph using transitivity. In *Proc. 16th International Conference on Computational Linguistics*, pages 680–585.

E. Terra and C. Clarke. 2003. Frequency estimates for statistical word similarity measures. In *Proc. HLT/NAACL 2003*.

P. Turney. 2001. Mining the web for synonyms: PMI-IR versus LSA on TOEFL. In *Proc. ECML-2001*, pages 491–502.

P. Turney. 2002. Thumbs up or thumbs down? semantic orientation applied to unsupervised classification of reviews. In *Proc. ACL'02*, pages 417–424.

P. Turney. 2004. Word sense disambiguation by web mining for word co-occurrence probabilities. In *Proc. SENSEVAL-3*.

D. Widdows and B. Dorow. 2002. A graph model for unsupervised lexical acquisition. In *Proc. COLING 2002*.

Context-Dependent Term Relations for Information Retrieval

Jing Bai **Jian-Yun Nie** **Guihong Cao**
DIRO, University of Montreal
CP. 6128, succ. Centre-ville, Montreal,
Quebec H3C 3J7, Canada
{baijing,nie,caogui}@iro.umontreal.ca

Abstract

Co-occurrence analysis has been used to determine related words or terms in many NLP-related applications such as query expansion in Information Retrieval (IR). However, related words are usually determined with respect to a single word, without relevant information for its application context. For example, the word "*programming*" may be considered to be strongly related to "*Java*", and applied inappropriately to expand a query on "*Java travel*". To solve this problem, we propose to add another context word in the relation to specify the appropriate context of the relation, leading to term relations of the form "(*Java*, *travel*) → *Indonesia*". The extracted relations are used for query expansion in IR. Our experiments on several TREC collections show that this new type of context-dependent relations performs much better than the traditional co-occurrence relations.

1. Introduction

A query usually is a poor expression of an information need. This is not only due to its short length (usually a few words), but also due to the inability of users to provide the best terms to describe their information need. At best, one can expect that some, but not all, relevant terms are used in the query. Query expansion thus aims to improve query expression by adding related terms to the query. However, the effect of query expansion is strongly determined by the term relations used (Peat and Willett, 1991). For example, even if "*programming*" is strongly related to "*Java*", if this relation is used to expand a query on "*Java travel*", the retrieval result will likely deteriorate because the irrelevant term "*programming*" is introduced, leading to the retrieval of irrelevant documents about "*programming*".

A number of attempts have been made to deal with the problem of selecting appropriate expansion terms. For example, Wordnet has been used in (Voorhees, 1994) to determine the expansion terms. However, the experiments did not show improvement on retrieval effectiveness. Many experiments have been carried out using associative relations extracted from term co-occurrences; but they showed variable results (Peat and Willett, 1991). In (Qiu and Frei, 1993), it is observed that one of the reasons is that one tried to determine expansion terms according to each original query term separately, which may introduce much noise. Therefore, they proposed to determine the expansion terms by summing up the relations of a candidate expansion term to each of the query terms. In so doing, a candidate expansion term is preferred if it has a strong relationship with many of the query terms. However, it is still difficult to prevent the expansion process from adding "*programming*" to a query on "*Java travel*" because of its very strong relation with "*Java*".

The approach used in (Qiu and Frei, 1993) indeed tries to correct a handicap inherent in the relations: as term relations are created between two single words such as "*Java* → *programming*", no information is available to help determine the appropriate context to apply it. The approach used in (Qiu and Frei, 1993) can simply alleviate the problem without solving it radically.

In this paper, we argue that the solution lies in the relations themselves. They have to contain more information to help determine the appropriate context to apply them. We thus propose a way to add some context information into the relations: we introduce an additional word into the condition part of the relation, such as "(*Java*, *computer*) → *programming*", which

Proceedings of the 2006 Conference on Empirical Methods in Natural Language Processing (EMNLP 2006), pages 551–559,
Sydney, July 2006.

means "*programming*" is related to "(*Java*, *computer*)" together. In so doing, we would be able to prevent from extracting and applying a relation such as "(*Java*, *travel*) → *programming*".

In this paper, we will test the extracted relations in query expansion for IR. We choose to implement query expansion within the language modeling (LM) framework because of its flexibility and high performance. The experiments on several TREC collections will show that our query expansion approach can bring large improvements in retrieval effectiveness.

In the following sections, we will first review some of the relevant approaches on query expansion and term relation extraction. Then we will describe our general IR models and the extraction of term relations. The experimental results will be reported and finally some conclusions will be drawn.

2. Query Expansion and Term Relations

It has been found that a key factor that determines the effect of query expansion is the selection of appropriate expansion terms (Peat and Willett, 1991). To determine expansion terms, one possible resource is thesauri constructed manually, such as Wordnet. Thesauri contain manually validated relations between terms, which can be used to suggest related terms. (Voorhees, 1994) carried out a series of experiments on selecting related terms (e.g. synonyms, hyonyms, etc.) from Wordnet. However, the experiments did not show that this can improve retrieval effectiveness. Some of the reasons are as follows: Although Wordnet contains many relations validated by human experts, the coverage is far from complete for the purposes of IR: not only linguistically motivated relations, but also association relations, are useful in IR. Another problem is the lack of information about the appropriate context to apply relations. For example, Wordnet contains two synsets for "*computer*", one for the sense of "*machine*" and another for "*human expert*". It is difficult to automatically select the correct synset to expand the word "*computer*" even if we know that the query's area is computer science.

Another often used resource is associative relations extracted from co-occurrences: two terms that co-occur frequently are thought to be associated to each other (Jing and Croft, 1994). However, co-occurrence relations are noisy: Frequently co-occurring terms are not necessarily related. On the other hand, they can also miss true relations. The most important problem is still that of ambiguity: when one term is associated with another, it may be related for one sense and not for other possible senses. It is then difficult to determine when the relation applies.

In most of the previous studies, relations extracted are restricted between one word and another. This limitation makes the relations ambiguous, and their utilization in query expansion often introduces undesired terms. We believe that the key to make a relation less ambiguous is to add some contextual information.

In an attempt to select better expansion terms, (Qiu and Frei, 1993) proposed the following approach to select expansion terms: terms are selected according to their relation to the whole query, which is calculated as the sum of their relations to each of the query terms. Therefore, a term that is related to several query terms will be favored. In a similar vein, (Bai et al. 2005) also try to determine the relationship of a word to a group of words by combining its relationships to each of the words in the group. This can indeed select better expansion terms. The consideration of other query terms produces a weak contextual effect. However, this effect is limited due to the nature of the relations extracted, in which a term depends on only one other term. Much of the noise in the sets will remain after selection.

For a query composed of several words, what we would really like to have is a set of terms that are related to all the words taken together (and not separately). By combining words in the condition part such as "(*Java, travel*)" or "(*base, bat*)", each word will serve as a context to the other in order to constrain the related terms. In these cases, we would expect that "*hotel*", "*island*" or "*Indonesia*" would co-occur much more often with "(*Java, travel*)" than "*programming*", and "*ball*", "*catcher*" etc. co-occur much more often with "(*base, bat*)" than "*animal*" or "*foundation*".

One naturally would suggest that compound terms can be used for this purpose. However, for many queries, it is difficult to form a legitimate compound term. Even if we can detect one occurrence of a compound, we may miss others that use its variants. For example, if "*Java travel*" is used as a query, we will likely be able to consider it as a compound term. The same compound (or its variant) would be difficult to detect in a document talking about traveling to Java: the two words may appear at some distance or not in some specific syntactic structure as required in (Lin, 1997). This will lead to the problem of mismatching between document and query.

In fact, compound terms are not the only way to add contextual information to a word. By putting two words together (without forming a compound term), we usually obtain a more precise sense for each word. For example, from "*Java travel*", we can guess that the intended meaning is likely related to "*traveling to Java Island*". People will not interpret this combination in the sense of "*Java programming*". In the same way, people would not consider "*animal*" to be a related term to "*base, bat*". These examples show that in a combination of words, each word indeed serves to specify a context to interpret another word. It then suggests the following approach: we can adjunct some additional word(s) in the condition part of a relation, such as "*(Java, travel)* → *Indonesia*", which means "*Indonesia*" is related to "*(Java, travel)*" together. It is expected that one would not obtain "*(Java, travel)* → *programming*".

Owing to the context effect explained above, we will call the relations with multiple words in the condition part *context-dependent* relations. In order to limit the computation complexity, we will only consider adding one additional word into relations.

The proposed approach follows the same principle as (Yarowsky, 1995), which tried to determine the appropriate word sense according to one relevant context word. However, the requirement for query expansion is less than word sense disambiguation: we do not need to know the exact word sense to make expansion. We only need to determine the relevant expansion terms. Therefore, there is no need to determine manually a set of seeds before the learning process takes place.

To some extent, the proposed approach is also related to (Schütze and Pedersen, 1997), which calculate term similarity according to the words appearing in the same context, or to second-order co-occurrences. However, a key difference is that (Schütze and Pedersen, 1997) consider only separate context words, while we consider multiple context words together.

Once term relations are determined, they will be used in query expansion. The basic IR process will be implemented in a language modeling framework. This framework is chosen for its flexibility to integrate term relations. Indeed, the LM framework has proven to be capable of integrating term relations and query expansion (Bai et al., 2005; Berger and Lafferty, 1999; Zhai and Lafferty, 2001). However, none of the above studies has investigated the extraction of strong context-dependent relations from text collections.

In the next section, we will describe the general LM framework and our query expansion models. Then the extraction of term relation will be explained.

3. Context-Dependent Query Expansion in Language Models

The basic IR approach based on LM (Ponte and Croft, 1998) determines the score of relevance of a document D by its probability to generate the query Q. By assuming independence between query terms, we have:

$$P(Q \mid D) = \prod_{w_i \in Q} P(w_i \mid D) \propto \sum_{w_i \in Q} \log P(w_i \mid D)$$

where $P(w_i \mid D)$ denotes the probability of a word in the language model of the document D. As no ambiguity will arise, we will use D to mean both the language model of the document and the document itself (similarly for a query model and a query Q).

Another score function is based on KL-divergence or cross entropy between the document model and the query model:

$$score(D,Q) = \sum_{w_i \in V} P(w_i \mid Q) \log P(w_i \mid D)$$

where V is the vocabulary. Although we have both document and query models in the above formulation, usually only the document model is smoothed, while the query model uses Maximum Likelihood Estimation (MLE) $P_{ML}(w_i \mid Q)$. Then we have:

$$score(D,Q) = \sum_{w_i \in Q} P_{ML}(w_i \mid Q) \log P(w_i \mid D)$$

However, it is obvious that a distance (KL-divergence) measured between a short query of a few words and a document cannot be precise. A better expression would contain all the related terms. The construction of a better query expression is the very motivation for query expansion in traditional IR systems. It is the same in LM for IR: to create a better query expression (model) to be able to measure the distance to a document in a more precise way. The key to creating the new model is the integration of term relations.

3.1 LM for Query Expansion

Term relations have been used in several recent language models in IR. (Berger and Lafferty, 1999) proposed a translation model that expands the document model. The same approach can also be used to expand the query model. Following (Berger and Lafferty, 1999), we arrive at the first expansion model as follows, which has also been used in (Bai et al., 2005):

Model 1: Context-independent query expansion model (CIQE)

$$P_R(w_i \mid Q) = \sum_{q_j \in V} P_R(w_i, q_j \mid Q) = \sum_{q_j \in Q} P_R(w_i \mid q_j) P_{ML}(q_j \mid Q)$$

In this model, each original query term q_j is expanded by related terms w_i. The relations between them are determined by $P_R(w_i \mid q_j)$. We will explain how this probability is defined in Section 3.2. However, we can already see here that w_i is determined solely by one of the query term q_j. So, we call this model "context-independent query expansion model" (CIQE).

The above expanded query model enables us to obtain new related expansion terms, to which we also have to add the original query. This can be obtained through the following smoothing:

$$P(w_i \mid Q) = \lambda_1 P_{ML}(w_i \mid Q) + (1-\lambda_1) \sum_{q_j \in Q} P_R(w_i \mid q_j) P_{ML}(q_j \mid Q) \quad (1)$$

where λ_1 is a smoothing parameter.

However, if the query model is expanded on all the vocabulary (V), the query evaluation will be very time consuming because the query and the document have to be compared on every word (dimension). In practice, we observe that only a small number of terms have strong relations with a given term, and the terms having weak relations usually are not truly related. So we can limit the expansion terms only to the strongly related ones. By doing this, we can also expect to filter out some noise and considerably reduce the retrieval time.

Suppose that we have selected a set E of strong expansion terms. Then we have:

$$score(D,Q) = \sum_{w_i \in V} P(w_i \mid Q) \log P(w_i \mid D) \approx \sum_{w_i \in E \cup Q} P(w_i \mid Q) \log P(w_i \mid D)$$

This query expansion method uses the same principle as (Qiu and Frei, 1993), but in a LM setting: the selected expansion terms are those that are strongly related to all the query terms (this is what the summation means). The approach used in (Bai et al., 2005) is slightly different: A context vector is first built for each word; then a context vector for a group of words (e.g. a multi-word query) is composed from the context vectors of the words of the group; finally related terms to the group of words are determined according to the similarity of their context vectors to that of the group. This last step uses second-order co-occurrences similarly to (Schütze and Pedersen, 1997). In both (Qiu and Frei, 1993) and (Bai et al., 2005), the terms related to a group of words are determined from their relations to each of the words in the group, while the latter relations are extracted separately. Irrelevant expansion terms can be retained.

As we showed earlier, in many cases, when one additional word is used with another word, the sense of each of them can usually be better determined. This additional word may be sufficient to interpret correctly many multi-word user queries. Therefore, our goal is to extract stronger context-dependent relations of the form (q_j q_k) → w_i, or to build a probability function $P_R(w_i \mid q_j q_k)$. Once this function is determined, it can be integrated into a new language model as follows.

Model 2: Context-dependent query expansion model (CDQE)

$$P_R(w_i \mid Q) = \sum_{q_j, q_k \in V} P_R(w_i \mid q_j q_k) P(q_j q_k \mid Q) \approx \sum_{q_j, q_k \in Q} P_R(w_i \mid q_j q_k) P(q_j q_k \mid Q)$$

As $P_R(w_i \mid q_j q_k)$ is a relation with two terms as condition, we will also call it a *biterm* relation. The name "biterm" is due to (Srikanth and Srihari, 2002), which means two terms co-occurring within some distance. Similarly, $P_R(w_i \mid q_j)$ will be called *unigram* relation. The corresponding query models will be called biterm relation model and unigram relation model.

As in general LM, the biterm relation model can be smoothed with a unigram model. Then we have the following score function:

$$P_R(w_i \mid Q) = \lambda_2 P_{ML}(w_i \mid Q) + (1-\lambda_2) \sum_{q_j, q_k \in Q} P_R(w_i \mid q_j q_k) P(q_j q_k \mid Q) \quad (2)$$

where λ_2 is another smoothing parameter.

3.2 Extraction of Term Relations

The key problem now is to obtain the relations we need: $P_R(w_i \mid w_j)$ and $P_R(w_i \mid w_j w_k)$. For the first probability, as in many previous studies, we exploit term co-occurrences. $P_R(w_i \mid w_j)$ could be built as a traditional bigram model. However, this is not a good approach for IR because two related terms do not necessarily co-occur side by side. They often appear at some distance. Therefore, this model is indeed a *biterm* model (Srikanth and Srihari, 2002), i.e., we allow two terms be separated within some distance. We use the following formula to determine this probability:

$$P_R(w_i \mid w_j) = \frac{c(w_i, w_j)}{\sum_{w_l} c(w_l, w_j)}$$

where $c(w_i, w_j)$ is the frequency of co-occurrence of the biterm (w_i, w_j), i.e. two terms in the same window of fixed size across the collection. In our case, we set the window size at 10 (because this size turned out to be reasonable in our pilot experiments).

For $P(w_i \mid w_j w_k)$, we further extend the biterm to triterm, and we use the frequency of co-occurrences of three terms $c(w_i, w_j, w_k)$ within the same windows in the document collection:

$$P_R(w_i \mid w_j w_k) = \frac{c(w_i, w_j, w_k)}{\sum_{w_l} c(w_l, w_j, w_k)}$$

The number of relations determined in this way can be very large. The upper bound for $P(w_i \mid w_j)$ and $P(w_i \mid w_j w_k)$ are respectively $O(|V|^2)$ and $O(|V|^3)$. However, many relations have very low probabilities and are often noise. As we only consider a subset of strong expansion terms, the relations with low probability are almost never used. Therefore, we set two filtering criteria:

- The biterm in the condition of a relation should be higher than a threshold (10 in our case);
- The probability of a relation should be higher than another threshold (0.0001 in our case).
- One more filtering criterion is mutual information (*MI*), which reflects the relatedness of two terms in their combination (w_j, w_k). To keep a relation $P(w_i \mid w_j w_k)$, we require (w_j, w_k) be a meaningful combination. We use the following pointwise *MI* (Church and Hanks 1989):

$$MI(w_j, w_k) = \log \frac{P(w_j, w_k)}{P(w_j)P(w_k)}$$

We only keep meaningful combinations such that $MI(w_j, w_k) > 0$.

By these filtering criteria, we are able to reduce considerably the number of biterms and triterms. For example, on a collection of about 200MB, with a vocabulary size of about 148K, we selected only about 2.7M useful biterms and about 137M triterms, which remain tractable.

3.3 Probability of Biterms

In LM used in IR, each query term is attributed the same weight. This is equivalent to a uniform probability distribution, i.e.:

$$P(q_i \mid Q) = \frac{1}{|Q|_U}$$

where $|Q|_U$ is the number of unigrams in the query. In CIQE model, we use the same method.

In CDQE, we also need to attribute a probability $P(q_j q_k \mid Q)$, to the biterm (q_j, q_k). Several options are possible.

Uniform probability

This simple approach distributes the probability uniformly among all biterms in the query, i.e.:

$$P(q_j q_k \mid Q) = \frac{1}{|Q|_B}$$

where $|Q|_B$ is the number of biterms in Q.

According to mutual information

In a query, if two words are strongly associated, this also means that their association is more meaningful to the query, thus should be weighted higher. Therefore, a natural way to assign a probability to a biterm in the query is to use mutual information, which denotes the strength of association between two words. We use again the pointwise mutual information $MI(q_j, q_k)$. If it is negative, we consider that the biterm is not meaningful, and is ignored. Therefore, we arrive at the following probability function:

$$P(q_j q_k \mid Q) = \frac{MI(q_j, q_k)}{\sum_{(q_l q_m) \in Q} MI(q_l, q_m)}$$

where $(q_l q_m) \in Q$ means all the meaningful biterms in the query.

Statistical parsing

In (Gao et al., 2002), a statistical parsing approach is used to determine the best combination of translation words for a query. The approach is similar to building a minimal spanning tree, which is also used in (Smeaton and Van Rijsbergen, 1983), to select the strongest term relations that cover the whole query. This approach can also be used in our model to determine the minimal set of the strongest biterms that cover the query.

In our experiments, we tested all the three weighting schemas. It turns out that the best weighting is the one with *MI*. Therefore, in the next section, we will only report the results with the second option.

4. Experimental Evaluation

We evaluate query expansion with different relations on four TREC collections, which are described in Table 1. All documents have been processed in a standard manner: terms are stemmed using Porter stemmer and stopwords are removed. We only use titles of topics as queries, which contain 3.58 words per query on average.

Table 1. TREC collection statistics

Coll.	Description	Size (Mb)	Vocab.	# Doc.	Query
AP	*Associated Press* (1988-89)	491	196,933	164,597	51-100
SJM	*San Jose Mercury News* (1991)	286	146,514	90,257	101-150
WSJ	*Wall Street Journal* (1990-92)	242	121,946	74,520	51-100

In our experiments, the document model remains the same while the query model changes. The document model uses the following Dirichlet smoothing:

$$P(w_i \mid D) = \frac{tf(w_i, D) + \mu P_{ML}(w_i \mid C)}{\mid D \mid_U + \mu}$$

where $tf(w_i, D)$ is the term frequency of w_i in *D*, $P_{ML}(w_i \mid C)$ is the collection model and μ is the Dirichlet prior, which is set at 1000 following (Zhai and Lafferty, 2001).

There are two other smoothing parameters λ_1, and λ_2 to be determined. In our experiments, we use a simple method to set them: the parameters are tuned empirically using a training collection containing AP1989 documents and queries 101-150. These preliminary tests suggest that the best value of λ_1 and λ_2 (in Equations 1-2) are relatively stable (we will show this later). In the experiments reported below, we will use $\lambda_1 = 0.4$, and $\lambda_2 = 0.3$.

4.1 Experimental Results

The main experimental results are described in Table 2, which reports average precision with different methods as well as the number of relevant documents retrieved. **UM** is the basic unigram model without query expansion (i.e. we use MLE for the query model, while the document model is smoothed with Dirichlet method). **CIQE** is the context-independent query expansion model using unigram relations (Model 1). **CDQE** is the context-dependent query expansion model using biterm relations (Model 2). In the table, we also indicate whether the improvement in average precision obtained is statistically significant (t-test).

Table 2. Avg. precision and Recall

Coll. #Rel.	UM	CIQE	CDQE
AP	0.2767	0.2902 (+5%*)	0.3383 (+22%**) [+17%**]
6101	3677	3897	4029
SJM	0.2017	0.2225 (+10%**)	0.2448 (+21%**) [+10%*]
2559	1641	1761	1873
WSJ	0.2373	0.2393 (+1%)	0.2710 (+14%**) [+13%*]
2172	1588	1626	1737

* and ** indicate that the difference is statistically significant according to t-test: * indicates $p<0.05$, ** indicates $p<0.01$; (.) is compared to UM and [.] is compared to CIQE.

CIQE and CDQE vs. UM

It is interesting to observe that query expansion, either by CIQE or CDQE, consistently outperforms the basic unigram model on all the collections. In all the cases except CIQE for WSJ, the improvements in average precision are statistically significant. At the same time, the increases in the number of relevant documents retrieved are also consistent with those in average precision.

The improvement scales obtained with CIQE are relatively small: from 1% to 10%. These correspond to the typical figure using this method.

Comparing **CIQE** and **CDQE**, we can see that context-dependent query expansion (**CDQE**) always produces better effectiveness than context-independent expansion (**CIQE**). The improvements range between 10% and 17%. All the improvements obtained by CDQE are statistically significant. This result strongly suggests that in general, the context-dependent term relations identify better expansion terms than context-independent unigram relations. This confirms our earlier hypothesis.

Indeed, when we look at the expansion results, we see that the expansion terms suggested by biterm relations are usually better. For example, the (stemmed) expansion terms for the query *"insider trading"* suggested respectively by **CIQE** and **CDQE** are as follows:

CIQE: stock:0.0141 market:0.0113 US:0.0112 year:0.0102 exchang:0.0101 trade:0.0092 report:0.0082 price:0.0076 dollar:0.0071 1:0.0069 govern:0.0066 state:0.0065 futur:0.0061 million:0.0061 dai:0.0060 offici:0.0059 peopl:0.0059 york:0.0057 issu:0.0057 …

CDQE: **secur**:0.0161 charg:0.0158 stock:0.0137 **scandal**:0.0128 **boeski**:0.0125 inform:0.0119 street:0.0113 wall:0.0112 case:0.0106 year:0.0090 million:0.0086 **investig**:0.0082 exchang:0.0080 govern:0.0077 **sec**:0.0077 **drexel**:0.0075 **fraud**:0.0071 law:0.0063 ivan:0.0060 …

We can see that in general, the terms suggested by **CDQE** are much more relevant. In particular, it has been able to suggest "**boeski**" (Boesky) who is involved in an insider trading scandal. Several other terms are also highly relevant, such as **scandal, investing, sec, drexel, fraud**, etc.

The addition of these new terms does not only improve recall. Precision of top-ranked documents is also improved. This can be seen in Figure 1 where we compare the full precision-recall curve for the AP collection for the three models. We can see that at all the recall levels, the precision values always follow the following order: CDQE > UM. The same observation is also made on the other collections. This shows that the CDQE method does not increase recall to the detriment of precision, but both of them. In contrast, CIQE increases precision at all but 0.0 recall points: the precision at the 0.0 recall point is 0.6565 for CIQE and 0.6699 for UM. This shows that CIQE can slightly deteriorate the top-ranked few documents.

Figure 1. Comparison of three models on AP

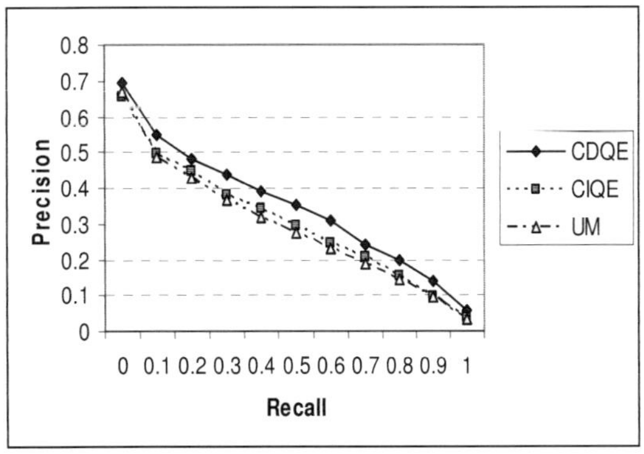

CDQE vs. Pseudo-relevance feedback

Pseudo-relevance feedback is widely considered to be an effective query expansion method. In many previous experiments, it produced very good results. The mixture model (Zhai and Lafferty, 2001) is a representative and effective method to implement pseudo-relevance feedback: It uses a set of feedback documents to smooth the original query model. Compared to the mixture model, our CDQE method is also more effective: By manually tuning the parameters of the mixture model to their best, we obtained the average precisions of 0.3171, 0.2393 and 0.2565 respectively for AP, SJM and WSJ collections. These values are lower than those obtained with CDQE, which has not been heavily tuned.

For the same query *"insider trading"*, the mixture model determines the following expansion terms:

Mixture: stock:0.0259256 secur:0.0229553 market:0.0157057 sec:0.013992 inform:0.011658 firm:0.0110419 exchang:0.0100346 law:0.00827076 bill:0.007996 case:0.00764544 profit:0.00672575 investor:0.00662856 japan:0.00625859 compani:0.00609675 commiss:0.0059618 foreign:0.00582441 bank:0.00572947 investig:0.00572276

We can see that some of these terms overlap with those suggested by biterm relations. However, interesting words such as *boeski*, *drexel* and *scandal* are not suggested.

The above comparison shows that our method outperforms the state-of-the-art methods of query expansion developed so far.

4.2 Effect of the Smoothing Parameter

In the previous experiments, we have fixed the smoothing parameters. In this series of tests, we analyze the effect of this smoothing parameter on retrieval effectiveness. The following figure shows the change of average precision (AvgP) using **CDQE** (Model 2) along with the change of the parameter λ_2 (UM is equivalent to $\lambda_2 = 1$).

Figure 2. Effectiveness w.r.t. λ_2

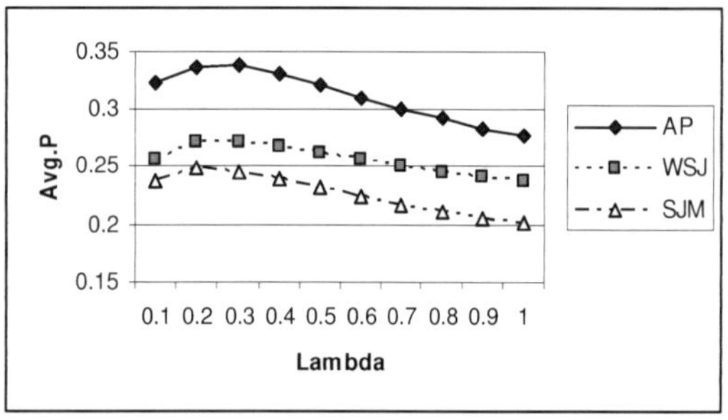

We can see that for all the three collections, the effectiveness is good when the parameter is set in the range of 0.1-0.5. The best value for different collections remains stable: 0.2-0.3.

The effect of λ_1 on Model 1 is slightly different, but we observe the same trend.

4.3 Number of Expansion Terms

In the previous tests, we limit the number of expansion terms to 80. When different numbers of expansion terms are used, we obtain different effectiveness measures. The following figure shows the variation of average precision (AvgP) with different numbers of expansion terms, using **CDQE** method.

Figure 3. Effectiveness w.r.t. #expansion terms

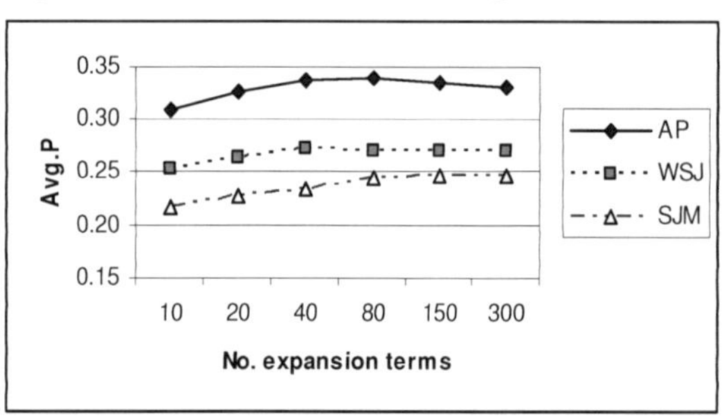

We can see that when more expansion terms are added, the effectiveness does not always increase. In general, a number around 80 will produce good results. In some cases, even if better effectiveness can be obtained with more expansion terms, the retrieval time is also longer. The number 80 seems to produce a good compromise between effectiveness and retrieval speed: the retrieval time remains less than 1 sec. per query.

4.4 Suitability of Relations Across Collections

In many real applications (e.g. Web search), we do not have a static document collection from which relations can be extracted. The question is whether it is possible and beneficial to extract relations from one text collection and use them to retrieve documents in another text collection. Our intuition is that this is possible because the relations (especially context-dependent relations) encode general knowledge, which can be applied to a different collection. In order to show this, we extracted term relations from each collection, and applied them on other collections. The following tables show the effectiveness produced using respectively unigram and bi-term relations.

Table 3. Cross-utilization of relations

Rel. / Coll.	Unigram relation			Biterm relation		
	AP	**SJM**	**WSJ**	**AP**	**SJM**	**WSJ**
AP	**0.2902**	0.2803	0.2793	**0.3383**	0.3057	0.2987
SJM	**0.2271**	0.2225	0.2267	0.2424	0.2448	**0.2453**
WSJ	**0.2541**	0.2445	0.2393	**0.2816**	0.2636	0.2710

From this table, we can observe that relations extracted from any collection are useful to some degree: they all outperform **UM** (see Table 2). In particular, the relations extracted from AP are the best for almost all the collections. This can be explained by the larger size and wider coverage of the AP collection. This suggests that we do not necessarily need to extract term relations from the same text collection on which retrieval is performed. It is possible to extract relations from a large text collection, and apply them to other collections. This opens the door to the possibility of constructing a general relation base for various document collections.

5. Related Work

Co-occurrence analysis is a common method to determine term relations. The previous studies have been limited to relations between two words, which we called unigram relations. This expansion approach has been integrated both in traditional retrieval models (Jing and Croft, 1994) and in LM (Berger and Lafferty 1999). As we observed, this type of relation will introduce much noise into the query, leading to unstable effectiveness.

Several other studies tried to filter out noise expansion (or translation) terms by considering the relations between them (Gao et al., 2002;

Jang et al. 1999; Qiu and Frei, 1993; Bai et al. 2005). However, this is insufficient to detect all the noise. The key issue is the ambiguity of relations due to the lack of context information in the relations. In this paper, we proposed a method to add some context information into relations.

(Lin, 1997) also tries to solve word ambiguity by adding syntactic dependency as context. However, our approach does not require determining syntactic dependency. The principle of our approach is more similar to (Yarowsky, 1995). Compared to this latter, our approach is less demanding: we do not need to identify manually the exact word senses and seed context words. The process is fully automatic. This simplification is made possible due to the requirement for IR: only in-context related words are required, but not the exact senses.

Our work is also related to (Smadja and McKeown, 1996), which tries to determine the translation of collocations. Term combinations or biterms we used can be viewed as collocations. Again, there is much less constraint for our related terms than translations in (Smadja and McKeown, 1996).

6. Conclusions

In many NLP applications such as IR, we need to determine relations between terms. In most previous studies, one tries to determine the related terms to one single term (word). This makes the resulting relations ambiguous. Although several approaches have been proposed to remove afterwards some of the inappropriate terms, this only affects part of the noise, and much still remains. In this paper, we argue that the solution to this problem lies in the addition of context information in the relations between terms. We proposed to add another word in the condition of the relations so as to help constrain the context of application. Our experiments confirm that this addition of limited context information can indeed improve the quality of term relations and query expansion in IR.

In this paper, we only compared biterm relations and unigram relations, the general method can be extended to triterm relations or more complex relations, provided that they can be extracted efficiently.

This paper only investigated the utilization of context-dependent relations in IR. These relations can be applied in many other tasks, such as machine translation, word sense disambiguation / discrimination, and so on. These are some interesting research work in the future.

References

Bai, J., Song, D., Bruza, P., Nie, J. Y. and Cao, G. 2005. Query expansion using term relationships in language models for information retrieval, *ACM CIKM*, pp. 688-695.

Berger, A. and Lafferty, J. 1999. Information retrieval as statistical translation. *ACM SIGIR*, pp. 222-229.

Church, K. W. and Hanks, P. 1989. Word association norms, mutual information, and lexicography. *ACL*, Vol. 16, pp. 22-29.

Gao, J., Nie, J.Y., He, H, Chen, W., Zhou, M. 2002. Resolving query translation ambiguity using a decaying co-occurrence model and syntactic dependency relations. *ACM SIGIR*, pp. 11-15.

Jang, M. G., Myaeng, S. H., and Park, S. Y. 1999. Using mutual information to resolve query translation ambiguities and query term weighting. *ACL*, pp. 223-229.

Jing, Y. and Croft, W.B. 1994. An association thesaurus for information retrieval. *RIAO*, pp. 146-160.

Lin, D. 1997. Using syntactic dependency as local context to resolve word sense ambiguity, *ACL*, pp. 64-71.

Peat, H.J. and Willett, P. 1991. The limitations of term co-occurrence data for query expansion in document retrieval systems. *JASIS*, 42(5): 378-383.

Ponte, J. and Croft, W.B. 1998. A language modeling approach to information retrieval. *ACM SIGIR*, pp. 275-281.

Qiu, Y. and Frei, H.P. 1993. Concept based query expansion. *ACM SIGIR*, pp.160-169.

Schütze, H. and Pedersen J.O. 1997. A cooccurrence-based thesaurus and two applications to information retrieval, *Information Processing and Management*, 33(3): 307-318.

Smeaton, A. F. and Van Rijsbergen, C. J. 1983. The retrieval effects of query expansion on a feedback document retrieval system. *Computer Journal*, 26(3): 239-246.

Smadja, F., McKeown, K.R., 1996. Translating collocations for bilingual lexicons: A statistical approach, *Computational Linguistics*, 22(1): 1-38.

Srikanth, M. and Srihari, R. 2002. Biterm language models for document retrieval. *ACM SIGIR*, pp. 425-426

Voorhees, E. 1994. Query expansion using lexical-semantic relations. *ACM SIGIR*, pp. 61-69.

Yarowsky, D. 1995. Unsupervised word sense disambiguation rivaling supervised methods. *ACL*, pp. 189-196.

Zhai, C. and Lafferty, J. 2001. Model-based feedback in the language modeling approach to information retrieval. *ACM SIGIR*, pp. 403-410.

Loss Minimization in Parse Reranking

Ivan Titov
Department of Computer Science
University of Geneva
24, rue Général Dufour
CH-1211 Genève 4, Switzerland
ivan.titov@cui.unige.ch

James Henderson
School of Informatics
University of Edinburgh
2 Buccleuch Place
Edinburgh EH8 9LW, United Kingdom
james.henderson@ed.ac.uk

Abstract

We propose a general method for reranker construction which targets choosing the candidate with the least expected loss, rather than the most probable candidate. Different approaches to expected loss approximation are considered, including estimating from the probabilistic model used to generate the candidates, estimating from a discriminative model trained to rerank the candidates, and learning to approximate the expected loss. The proposed methods are applied to the parse reranking task, with various baseline models, achieving significant improvement both over the probabilistic models and the discriminative rerankers. When a neural network parser is used as the probabilistic model and the Voted Perceptron algorithm with data-defined kernels as the learning algorithm, the loss minimization model achieves 90.0% labeled constituents F_1 score on the standard WSJ parsing task.

1 Introduction

The reranking approach is widely used in parsing (Collins and Koo, 2005; Koo and Collins, 2005; Henderson and Titov, 2005; Shen and Joshi, 2003) as well as in other structured classification problems. For structured classification tasks, where labels are complex and have an internal structure of interdependency, the 0-1 loss considered in classical formulation of classification algorithms is not a natural choice and different loss functions are normally employed. To tackle this problem, several approaches have been proposed to accommodate loss functions in learning algorithms (Tsochantaridis et al., 2004; Taskar et al., 2004; Henderson and Titov, 2005). A very different use of loss functions was considered in the areas of signal processing and machine translation, where direct minimization of expected loss (Minimum Bayes Risk decoding) on word sequences was considered (Kumar and Byrne, 2004; Stolcke et al., 1997). The only attempt to use Minimum Bayes Risk (MBR) decoding in parsing was made in (Goodman, 1996), where a parsing algorithm for constituent recall minimization was constructed. However, their approach is limited to binarized PCFG models and, consequently, is not applicable to state-of-the-art parsing methods (Charniak and Johnson, 2005; Henderson, 2004; Collins, 2000). In this paper we consider several approaches to loss approximation on the basis of a candidate list provided by a baseline probabilistic model.

The intuitive motivation for expected loss minimization can be seen from the following example. Consider the situation where there are a group of several very similar candidates and one very different candidate whose probability is just slightly larger than the probability of any individual candidate in the group, but much smaller than their total probability. A method which chooses the maximum probability candidate will choose this outlier candidate, which is correct if you are only interested in getting the label exactly correct (i.e. 0-1 loss), and you think the estimates are accurate. But if you are interested in a loss function where the loss is small when you choose a candidate which is similar to the correct candidate, then it is better to choose one of the candidates in the group. With this choice the loss will only be large if the outlier turns out to be correct, while if the outlier is chosen then the loss will be large if any of the group are correct. In other words, the expected loss of

Proceedings of the 2006 Conference on Empirical Methods in Natural Language Processing (EMNLP 2006), pages 560–567,
Sydney, July 2006.

choosing a member of the group will be smaller than that for the outlier.

More formally, the Bayes risk of a model $y = h(x)$ is defined as

$$R(h) = E_{x,y}\Delta(y, h(x)), \tag{1}$$

where the expectation is taken over all the possible inputs x and labels y and $\Delta(y, y')$ denotes a loss incurred by assigning x to y' when the correct label is y. We assume that the loss function possesses values within the range from 0 to 1, which is equivalent to the requirement that the loss function is bounded in (Tsochantaridis et al., 2004). It follows that an optimal reranker $h^\star$ is one which chooses the label y that minimizes the expected loss:

$$h^\star(x) = \arg\min_{y' \in G(x)} \sum_y P(y|x)\Delta(y, y'), \tag{2}$$

where $G(x)$ denotes a candidate list provided by a baseline probabilistic model for the input x. In this paper we propose different approaches to loss approximation. We apply them to the parse reranking problem where the baseline probabilistic model is a neural network parser (Henderson, 2003), and to parse reranking of candidates provided by the (Collins, 1999) model. The resulting reranking method achieves very significant improvement in the considered loss function and improvement in most other standard measures of accuracy.

In the following three sections we will discuss three approaches to learning such a classifier. The first two derive a classification criteria for use with a predefined probability model (the first generative, the second discriminative). The third defines a kernel for use with a classification method for minimizing loss. All use previously proposed learning algorithms and optimization criteria.

2 Loss Approximation with a Probabilistic Model

In this section we discuss approximating the expected loss using probability estimates given by a baseline probabilistic model. Use of probability estimates is not a serious limitation of this approach because in practice candidates are normally provided by some probabilistic model and its probability estimates are used as additional features in the reranker (Collins and Koo, 2005; Shen and Joshi, 2003; Henderson and Titov, 2005).

In order to estimate the expected loss on the basis of a candidate list, we make the assumption that the total probability of the labels not in the candidate list is sufficiently small that the difference $\delta(x, y')$ of expected loss between the labels in the candidate list and the labels not in the candidate list does not have an impact on the loss defined in (1):

$$\delta(x, y') = \frac{\sum_{y \notin G(x)} P(y|x)\Delta(y, y')}{\sum_{y \notin G(x)} P(y|x)} - \frac{\sum_{y \in G(x)} P(y|x)\Delta(y, y')}{\sum_{y \in G(x)} P(y|x)} \tag{3}$$

This gives us the following approximation to the expected loss for the label:

$$l(x, y') = \frac{\sum_{y \in G(x)} P(y|x)\Delta(y, y')}{\sum_{y \in G(x)} P(y|x)}. \tag{4}$$

For the reranking case, often the probabilistic model only estimates the joint probability $P(x, y)$. However, neither this difference nor the denominator in (4) affects the classification. Thus, replacing the true probabilities with their estimates, we can define the classifier

$$\hat{h}(x) = \arg\min_{y' \in G(x)} \sum_{y \in G(x)} P(x, y|\hat{\theta})\Delta(y, y'), \tag{5}$$

where $\hat{\theta}$ denotes the parameters of the probabilistic model learned from the training data. This approach for expected loss approximation was considered in the context of word error rate minimization in speech recognition, see for example (Stolcke et al., 1997).

3 Estimating Expected Loss with Discriminative Classifiers

In this section we propose a method to improve on the loss approximation used in (5) by constructing the probability estimates using a trained discriminative classifier. Special emphasis is placed on linear classifiers with data-defined kernels for reranking (Henderson and Titov, 2005), because they do not require any additional domain knowledge not already encoded in the probabilistic model, and they have demonstrated significant improvement over the baseline probabilistic model for the parse reranking task. This kernel construction can be motivated by the existence of a function which maps a linear function in the feature space of the kernel to probability estimates which are superior to the estimates of the original probabilistic model.

3.1 Estimation with Fisher Kernels

The Fisher kernel for structured classification is a trivial generalization of one of the best known data-defined kernels for binary classification (Jaakkola and Haussler, 1998). The Fisher score of an example input-label pair (x, y) is a vector of partial derivatives of the log-likelihood of the example with respect to the model parameters[1]:

$$\phi_{\hat{\theta}}^{FK}(x, y) = \tag{6}$$

$$(\log P(x, y|\hat{\theta}), \frac{\partial \log P(x,y|\hat{\theta})}{\partial \theta_1}, \ldots, \frac{\partial \log P(x,y|\hat{\theta})}{\partial \theta_l}).$$

This kernel defines a feature space which is appropriate for estimating the discriminative probability in the candidate list in the form of a normalized exponential

$$\frac{P(x, y)}{\sum_{y' \in G(x)} P(x, y')} \approx \tag{7}$$

$$\frac{\exp(w^{\star T} \phi_{\hat{\theta}}^{FK}(x, y))}{\sum_{y' \in G(x)} \exp(w^{\star T} \phi_{\hat{\theta}}^{FK}(x, y'))}$$

for some choice of the decision vector $w = w^{\star}$ with the first component equal to one.

It follows that it is natural to use an estimator of the discriminative probability $P(y|x)$ in exponential form and, therefore, the appropriate form of the loss minimizing classifier is the following:

$$\hat{h}_{FK}(x) = \tag{8}$$

$$\arg\min_{y' \in G(x)} \sum_{y \in G(x)} exp(A \hat{w}^T \phi_{\hat{\theta}}^{FK}(x, y')) \Delta(y, y'),$$

where $\hat{w}$ is learned during classifier training and the scalar parameter A can be tuned on the development set. From the construction of the Fisher kernel, it follows that the optimal value A is expected to be close to inverse of the first component of $\hat{w}$, $1/\hat{w}_1$.

If an SVM is used to learn the classifier, then the form (7) is the same as that proposed by (Platt, 1999), where it is proposed to use the logistic sigmoid of the SVM output as the probability estimator for binary classification problems.

[1]The fi rst component $logP(x, y|\hat{\theta})$ is not in the strict sense part of the Fisher score, but usually added to kernel features in practice (Henderson and Titov, 2005).

3.2 Estimation with TOP Kernels for Reranking

The TOP Reranking kernel was defined in (Henderson and Titov, 2005), as a generalization of the TOP kernel (Tsuda et al., 2002) proposed for binary classification tasks. The feature extractor for the TOP reranking kernel is given by:

$$\phi_{\hat{\theta}}^{TK}(x, y) = \tag{9}$$

$$(v(x, y, \hat{\theta}), \frac{\partial v(x, y, \hat{\theta})}{\partial \theta_1}, \ldots, \frac{\partial v(x, y, \hat{\theta})}{\partial \theta_l}),$$

where

$$v(x, y, \hat{\theta}) = \log P(x, y|\hat{\theta}) - \log \sum_{y' \in G(x) - \{y\}} P(x, y'|\hat{\theta}).$$

The TOP reranking kernel has been demonstrated to perform better than the Fisher kernel for the parse reranking task (Henderson and Titov, 2005). The construction of this kernel is motivated by the minimization of the classification error of a linear classifier $w^T \phi_{\hat{\theta}}(x, y)$. This linear classifier has been shown to converge, assuming estimation of the discriminative probability in the candidate list can be in the form of the logistic sigmoid (Titov and Henderson, 2005):

$$\frac{P(x, y)}{\sum_{y' \in G(x)} P(x, y')} \approx \tag{10}$$

$$\frac{1}{1 + \exp(-w^{\star T} \phi_{\hat{\theta}}^{TK}(x, y))}$$

for some choice of the decision vector $w = w^{\star}$ with the first component equal to one. From this fact, the form of the loss minimizing classifier follows:

$$\hat{h}_{TK}(x) = \tag{11}$$

$$\arg\min_{y' \in G(x)} \sum_{y \in G(x)} g(A \hat{w}^T \phi_{\hat{\theta}}^{TK}(x, y')) \Delta(y, y'),$$

where g is the logistic sigmoid and the scalar parameter A should be selected on the development set. As for the Fisher kernel, the optimal value of A should be close to $1/\hat{w}_1$.

3.3 Estimates from Arbitrary Classifiers

Although in this paper we focus on approaches which do not require additional domain knowledge, the output of most classifiers can be used to estimate the discriminative probability in equation (7). As mentioned above, the form of (7) is appropriate for the SVM learning task with arbitrary kernels, as follows from (Platt, 1999). Also, for models which combine classifiers using votes (e.g. the Voted Perceptron), the number of votes cast for each candidate can be used to define this discriminative probability. The discriminative probability of a candidate is simply the number of votes cast for that candidate normalized across candidates. Intuitively, we can think of this method as treating the votes as a sample from the discriminative distribution.

4 Expected Loss Learning

In this section, another approach to loss approximation is proposed. We consider learning a linear classifier to choose the least loss candidate, and propose two constructions of data-defined loss kernels which define different feature spaces for the classification. In addition to the kernel, this approach differs from the previous one in that the classifier is assumed to be linear, rather than the nonlinear functions in equations (8) and (11).

4.1 Loss Kernel

The Loss Kernel feature extractor is composed of the logarithm of the loss estimated by the probabilistic model and its first derivatives with respect to each model parameter:

$$\phi_{\hat{\theta}}^{LK}(x,y) = \tag{12}$$
$$(v(x,y,\hat{\theta}), \frac{\partial v(x,y,\hat{\theta})}{\partial \theta_1}, \ldots, \frac{\partial v(x,y,\hat{\theta})}{\partial \theta_l}),$$

where

$$v(x,y,\hat{\theta}) = \log(\sum_{y' \in G(x)} P(y',x|\hat{\theta})\Delta(y',y)).$$

The motivation for this kernel is very similar to that for the Fisher kernel for structured classification. The feature space of the kernel guarantees convergence of an estimator for the expected loss if the estimator is in normalized exponential form. The standard Fisher kernel for structured classification is a special case of this Loss Kernel when $\Delta(y,y')$ is 0-1 loss.

4.2 Loss Logit Kernel

As the Loss kernel was a generalization of the Fisher kernel to arbitrary loss function, so the Loss Logit Kernel is a generalization of the TOP kernel for reranking. The construction of the Loss Logit Kernel, like the TOP kernel for reranking, can be motivated by the minimization of the classification error of a linear classifier $w^T \phi_{\hat{\theta}}^{LLK}(x,y)$, where $\phi_{\hat{\theta}}^{LLK}(x,y)$ is the feature extractor of the kernel given by:

$$\phi_{\hat{\theta}}^{LLK}(x,y) = \tag{13}$$
$$(v(x,y,\hat{\theta}), \frac{\partial v(x,y,\hat{\theta})}{\partial \theta_1}, \ldots, \frac{\partial v(x,y,\hat{\theta})}{\partial \theta_l}),$$

where

$$v(x,y,\hat{\theta}) = \log(\sum_{y' \in G(x)} P(y'|x,\hat{\theta})(1-\Delta(y',y))) - \log(\sum_{y' \in G(x)} P(y'|x,\hat{\theta})\Delta(y',y)).$$

5 Experimental Evaluation

To perform empirical evaluations of the proposed methods, we considered the task of parsing the Penn Treebank Wall Street Journal corpus (Marcus et al., 1993). First, we perform experiments with SVM Struct (Tsochantaridis et al., 2004) as the learner. Since SVM Struct already uses the loss function during training to rescale the margin or slack variables, this learner allows us to test the hypothesis that loss functions are useful in parsing not only to define the optimization criteria but also to define the classifier and to define the feature space. However, SVM Struct training for large scale parsing experiments is computationally expensive[2], so here we use only a small portion of the available training data to perform evaluations of the different approaches. In the other two sets of experiments, described below, we test our best model on the standard Wall Street Journal parsing benchmark (Collins, 1999) with the Voted Perceptron algorithm as the learner.

5.1 The Probabilistic Models of Parsing

To perform the experiments with data-defined kernels, we need to select a probabilistic model of parsing. Data-defined kernels can be applied to any kind of parameterized probabilistic model.

For our first set of experiments, we choose to use a publicly available neural network based probabilistic model of parsing (Henderson, 2003).

[2]In (Shen and Joshi, 2003) it was proposed to use an ensemble of SVMs trained the Wall Street Journal corpus, but the generalization performance of the resulting classifi er might be compromised in this approach.

This parsing model is a good candidate for our experiments because it achieves state-of-the-art results on the standard Wall Street Journal (WSJ) parsing problem (Henderson, 2003), and data-defined kernels derived from this parsing model have recently been used with the Voted Perceptron algorithm on the WSJ parsing task, achieving a significant improvement in accuracy over the neural network parser alone (Henderson and Titov, 2005). This gives us a baseline which is hard to beat, and allows us to compare results of our new approaches with the results of the original data-defined kernels for reranking.

The probabilistic model of parsing in (Henderson, 2003) has two levels of parameterization. The first level of parameterization is in terms of a history-based generative probability model. These parameters are estimated using a neural network, the weights of which form the second level of parameterization. This approach allows the probability model to have an infinite number of parameters; the neural network only estimates the bounded number of parameters which are relevant to a given partial parse. We define data-defined kernels in terms of the second level of parameterization (the network weights).

For the last set of experiments, we used the probabilistic model described in (Collins, 1999) (model 2), and the Tree Kernel (Collins and Duffy, 2002). However, in these experiments we only used the estimates from the discriminative classifier, so the details of the probabilistic model are not relevant.

5.2 Experiments with SVM Struct

Both the neural network probabilistic model and the kernel based classifiers were trained on section 0 (1,921 sentences, 40,930 words). Section 24 (1,346 sentences, 29,125 words) was used as the validation set during the neural network learning and for choosing parameters of the models. Section 23 (2,416 sentences, 54,268 words) was used for the final testing of the models.

We used a publicly available tagger (Ratnaparkhi, 1996) to provide the part-of-speech tags for each word in the sentence. For each tag, there is an unknown-word vocabulary item which is used for all those words which are not sufficiently frequent with that tag to be included individually in the vocabulary. For these experiments, we only included a specific tag-word pair in the vocabulary if it occurred at least 20 time in the training set, which (with tag-unknown-word pairs) led to the very small vocabulary of 271 tag-word pairs. The same model was used both for choosing the list of candidate parses and for the probabilistic model used for loss estimation and kernel feature extraction. For training and testing of the kernel models, we provided a candidate list consisting of the top 20 parses found by the probabilistic model. For the testing set, selecting the candidate with an oracle results in an F_1 score of 89.1%.

	R	P	F_1	CM
SSN	80.9	81.7	81.3	18.3
TRK	81.1	82.4	81.7	18.2
SSN-Estim	81.4	82.3	81.8	18.3
LLK-Learn	81.2	82.4	81.8	17.6
LK-Learn	81.5	82.2	81.8	17.8
FK-Estim	81.4	82.6	82.0	18.3
TRK-Estim	81.5	82.8	82.1	18.6

Table 1: Percentage labeled constituent recall (R), precision (P), combination of both (F_1) and percentage complete match (CM) on the testing set.

We used the SVM Struct software package (Tsochantaridis et al., 2004) to train the SVM for all the approaches based on discriminative classifier learning, with slack rescaling and linear slack penalty. The loss function is defined as $\Delta(y, y') = 1 - F_1(y, y')$, where F_1 denotes F_1 measure on bracketed constituents. This loss was used both for rescaling the slacks in the SVM and for defining our classification models and kernels.

We performed initial testing of the models on the validation set and preselected the best model for each of the approaches before testing it on the final testing set. Standard measures of parsing accuracy, plus complete match accuracy, are shown in table 1.[3] As the baselines, the table includes the results of the standard TOP reranking kernel (TRK) (Henderson and Titov, 2005) and the baseline probabilistic model (SSN) (Henderson, 2003). SSN-Estim is the model using loss estimation on the basic probabilistic model, as explained in section 2. LLK-Learn and LK-Learn are the models which define the kernel based on loss, using the Loss Logit Kernel (equation (13)) and the Loss Kernel (equation (12)), respectively. FK-Estim and TRK-Estim are the models which esti-

[3] All our results are computed with the evalb program (Collins, 1999).

mate the loss with data-defined kernels, using the Fisher Kernel (equation (8)) and the TOP Reranking kernel (equation (11)), respectively.

All our proposed models show better F_1 accuracy than the baseline probabilistic model SSN, and all these differences are statistically significant.[4] The difference in F_1 between TRK-Estim and FK-Estim is not statistically significant, but otherwise TRK-Estim demonstrates a statistically significant improvement over all other models. It should also be noted that exact match measures for TRK-Estim and SSN-Estim are not negatively affected, even though the F_1 loss function was optimized. It is important to point out that SSN-Estim, which improves significantly over SSN, does not require the learning of a discriminative classifier, and differs from the SSN only by use of the different classification model (equation (5)), which means that it is extremely easy to apply in practice.

One surprising aspect of these results is the failure of LLK-Learn and LK-Learn to achieve improvement over SSN-Estim. This might be explained by the difficulty of learning a linear approximation to (4). Under this explanation, the performance of LLK-Learn and LK-Learn could be explained by the fact that the first component of their kernels is a monotonic function of the SSN-Estim estimation. To test this hypothesis, we did an additional experiment where we removed the first component of Loss Logit Kernel (13) from the feature vector and performed learning. Surprisingly, the model achieved virtually the same results, rather than the predicted worse performance. This result might indicate that the LLK-Learn model still can be useful for different problems where discriminative learning gives more advantage over generative approaches.

These experimental results demonstrate that the loss approximation reranking approaches proposed in this paper demonstrate significant improvement over the baseline models, achieving about the same relative error reduction as previously achieved with data-defined kernels (Henderson and Titov, 2005). This improvement is despite the fact that the loss function is already used in the definition of the training criteria for all the models except SSN. It is also interesting to note that the best result on the validation set for estimation of the loss with data-defined kernels (12) and (13) was achieved when the parameter A is close to the inverse of the first component of the learned decision vector, which confirms the motivation for these kernels.

[4]We measured significance of all the experiments in this paper with the randomized significance test (Yeh, 2000).

5.3 Experiments with Voted Perceptron and Data-Defined Kernels

The above experiments with the SVM Struct demonstrate empirically the viability of our approaches. The aim of experiments on the entire WSJ is to test whether our approaches still achieve significant improvement when more accurate generative models are used, and also to show that they generalize well to learning methods different from SVMs. We perform experiments on the standard WSJ parsing data using the standard split into training, validation and testing sets. We replicate completely the setup of experiments in (Henderson and Titov, 2005). For a detailed description of the experiment setup, we refer the reader to (Henderson and Titov, 2005). We only note here that the candidate list has 20 candidates, and, for the testing set, selecting the candidate with an oracle results in an F_1 score of 95.4%.

We selected the TRK-Estim approach for these experiments because it demonstrated the best results in the previous set of experiments (5.2). We trained the Voted Perceptron (VP) modification described in (Henderson and Titov, 2005) with the TOP Reranking kernel. VP is not a linear classifier, so we were not able to use a classifier in the form (11). Instead the normalized counts of votes given to the candidate parses were used as probability estimates, as discussed in section 3.3.

The resulting accuracies of this model are presented in table 2, together with results of the TOP Reranking kernel VP (Henderson and Titov, 2005) and the SSN probabilistic model (Henderson, 2003). Model TRK-Estim achieves significantly better results than the previously proposed models, which were evaluated in the same experimental setup. Again, the relative error reduction is about the same as that of TRK. The resulting system, consisting of the generative model and the reranker, achieves results at the state-of-the-art level. We believe that this method can be applied to most parsing models to achieve a significant improvement.

	R	P	F_1
Henderson, 2003	88.8	89.5	89.1
Henderson&Titov, 2005	89.1	90.1	89.6
TRK-Estim	89.5	90.5	90.0

Table 2: Percentage labeled constituent recall (R), precision (P), combination of both (F_1) on the testing set.

5.4 Experiments with Voted Perceptron and Tree Kernel

In this series of experiments we validate the statement in section 3.3, where we suggested that loss approximation from a discriminative classifier is not limited only to models with data-defined kernels. We apply the same method as used in the TRK-Estim model above to the Tree Kernel (Collins and Duffy, 2002), which we call the TK-Estim model.

We replicated the parse reranking experimental setup used for the evaluation of the Tree Kernel in (Collins and Duffy, 2002), where the candidate list was provided by the generative probabilistic model (Collins, 1999) (model 2). A list of on average 29 candidates was used, with an oracle F_1 score on the testing set of 95.0%. We trained VP using the same parameters for the Tree Kernel and probability feature weighting as described in (Collins and Duffy, 2002). A publicly available efficient implementation of the Tree Kernel was utilized to speed up computations (Moschitti, 2004). As in the previous section, votes of the perceptron were used to define the probability estimate used in the classifier.

The results for the MBR decoding method (TK-Estim), defined in section 3.3, along with the standard Tree Kernel VP results (Collins and Duffy, 2002) (TK) and the probabilistic baseline (Collins, 1999) (CO99) are presented in table 3. The proposed model improves in F_1 score over the standard VP results. Differences between all the models are statistically significant. The error reduction of TK-Estim is again about the same as the error reduction of TK. This improvement is achieved without adding any additional linguistic features. It is important to note that the model improves in other accuracy measures as well. We would expect even better results with MBR-decoding if larger n-best lists are used. The n-best parsing algorithm (Huang and Chiang, 2005) can be used to efficiently produce candidate lists as large as 10^6 parse trees with the model of (Collins, 1999).

	R	P	F_1*	CB	0C	2C
CO99	88.1	88.3	88.2	1.06	64.0	85.1
TK	88.6	88.9	88.7	0.99	66.5	86.3
TK-Estim	89.0	89.5	89.2	0.91	66.6	87.4

* F_1 for previous models may have rounding errors.

Table 3: Result on the testing set. Percentage labeled constituent recall (R), precision (P), combination of both (F_1), an average number of crossing brackets per sentence (CB), percentage of sentences with 0 and ≤ 2 crossing brackets (0C and 2C, respectively).

6 Conclusions

This paper considers methods for the estimation of expected loss for parse reranking tasks. The proposed methods include estimation of the loss from a probabilistic model, estimation from a discriminative classifier, and learning of the loss using a specialized kernel. An empirical comparison of these approaches on parse reranking tasks is presented. Special emphasis is given to data-defined kernels for reranking, as they do not require the introduction of any additional domain knowledge not already encoded in the probabilistic model. The best approach, estimation of the loss on the basis of a discriminative classifier, achieves very significant improvements over the baseline generative probabilistic models and the discriminative classifier itself. Though the largest improvement is demonstrated in the measure which corresponds to the considered loss functional, other measures of accuracy are also improved. The proposed method achieves 90.0% F_1 score on the standard Wall Street Journal parsing task when the SSN neural network is used as the probabilistic model and VP with a TOP Reranking kernel as the discriminative classifier.

Acknowledgments

We would like to thank Michael Collins and Terry Koo for providing us their data and useful comments on experimental setup, and Alessandro Moschitti for providing us the source code for his Tree Kernel implementation. We also thank anonymous reviewers for their constructive comments.

References

Eugene Charniak and Mark Johnson. 2005. Coarse-to-fine n-best parsing and MaxEnt discriminative reranking. In *Proc. 43rd Meeting of Association for Computational Linguistics*, pages 173–180, Ann Arbor, MI.

Michael Collins and Nigel Duffy. 2002. New ranking algorithms for parsing and tagging: Kernels over discrete structures and the voted perceptron. In *Proc. 40th Meeting of Association for Computational Linguistics*, pages 263–270, Philadelphia, PA.

Michael Collins and Terry Koo. 2005. Discriminative reranking for natural language parsing. *Computational Linguistics*, 31(1):25–69.

Michael Collins. 1999. *Head-Driven Statistical Models for Natural Language Parsing*. Ph.D. thesis, University of Pennsylvania, Philadelphia, PA.

Michael Collins. 2000. Discriminative reranking for natural language parsing. In *Proc. 17th Int. Conf. on Machine Learning*, pages 175–182, Stanford, CA.

Joshua Goodman. 1996. Parsing algorithms and methods. In *Proc. 34th Meeting of the Association for Computational Linguistics*, pages 177–183, Santa Cruz, CA.

James Henderson and Ivan Titov. 2005. Data-defined kernels for parse reranking derived from probabilistic models. In *Proc. 43rd Meeting of Association for Computational Linguistics*, Ann Arbor, MI.

James Henderson. 2003. Inducing history representations for broad coverage statistical parsing. In *Proc. joint meeting of North American Chapter of the Association for Computational Linguistics and the Human Language Technology Conf.*, pages 103–110, Edmonton, Canada.

James Henderson. 2004. Discriminative training of a neural network statistical parser. In *Proc. 42nd Meeting of Association for Computational Linguistics*, Barcelona, Spain.

Liang Huang and David Chiang. 2005. Better k-best parsing. In *Proc. 9th Int. Workshop on Parsing Technologies*, Vancouver, Canada.

Tommi S. Jaakkola and David Haussler. 1998. Exploiting generative models in discriminative classifiers. *Advances in Neural Information Processes Systems 11*.

Terry Koo and Michael Collins. 2005. Hidden-variable models for discriminative reranking. In *Proc. Conf. on Empirical Methods in Natural Language Processing*, Vancouver, B.C., Canada.

Shankar Kumar and William Byrne. 2004. Minimum bayes-risk decoding for statistical machine translation. In *Proceedings of the Human Language Technology Conference and Meeting of the North American Chapter of the Association for Computational Linguistics*, Boston, MA.

Mitchell P. Marcus, Beatrice Santorini, and Mary Ann Marcinkiewicz. 1993. Building a large annotated corpus of English: The Penn Treebank. *Computational Linguistics*, 19(2):313–330.

Alessandro Moschitti. 2004. A study on convolutional kernels for shallow semantic parsing. In *Proc. 42nd Meeting of the Association for Computational Linguistics*, Barcelona, Spain.

John C. Platt. 1999. Probabilistic outputs for support vector machines and comparision to regularized likelihood methods. In A. Smola, P. Bartlett, B. Scholkopf, and D. Schuurmans, editors, *Advances in Large Margin Classifiers*, pages 61–74. MIT Press.

Adwait Ratnaparkhi. 1996. A maximum entropy model for part-of-speech tagging. In *Proc. Conf. on Empirical Methods in Natural Language Processing*, pages 133–142, Univ. of Pennsylvania, PA.

Libin Shen and Aravind K. Joshi. 2003. An SVM based voting algorithm with application to parse reranking. In *Proc. of the 7th Conf. on Computational Natural Language Learning*, pages 9–16, Edmonton, Canada.

Andreas Stolcke, Yochai Konig, and Mitchel Weintraub. 1997. Explicit word error minimization in n-best list rescoring. In *Proc. of 5th European Conference on Speech Communication and Technology*, pages 163–165, Rhodes, Greece.

Ben Taskar, Dan Klein, Michael Collins, Daphne Koller, and Christopher Manning. 2004. Max-margin parsing. In *Proc. Conf. on Empirical Methods in Natural Language Processing*, Barcelona, Spain.

Ivan Titov and James Henderson. 2005. Deriving kernels from MLP probability estimators for large categorization problems. In *International Joint Conference on Neural Networks*, Montreal, Canada.

Ioannis Tsochantaridis, Thomas Hofmann, Thorsten Joachims, and Yasemin Altun. 2004. Support vector machine learning for interdependent and structured output spaces. In *Proc. 21st Int. Conf. on Machine Learning*, pages 823–830, Banff, Alberta, Canada.

K. Tsuda, M. Kawanabe, G. Ratsch, S. Sonnenburg, and K. Muller. 2002. A new discriminative kernel from probabilistic models. *Neural Computation*, 14(10):2397–2414.

Alexander Yeh. 2000. More accurate tests for the statistical significance of the result differences. In *Proc. 17th International Conf. on Computational Linguistics*, pages 947–953, Saarbruken, Germany.

Unsupervised Relation Disambiguation with Order Identification Capabilities

Jinxiu Chen[1] **Donghong Ji**[1] **Chew Lim Tan**[2] **Zhengyu Niu**[1]
[1]Institute for Infocomm Research
21 Heng Mui Keng Terrace
119613 Singapore
{jinxiu,dhji,zniu}@i2r.a-star.edu.sg
[2]Department of Computer Science
National University of Singapore
117543 Singapore
tancl@comp.nus.edu.sg

Abstract

We present an unsupervised learning approach to disambiguate various relations between name entities by use of various lexical and syntactic features from the contexts. It works by calculating eigenvectors of an adjacency graph's Laplacian to recover a submanifold of data from a high dimensionality space and then performing cluster number estimation on the eigenvectors. This method can address two difficulties encoutered in Hasegawa et al. (2004)'s hierarchical clustering: no consideration of manifold structure in data, and requirement to provide cluster number by users. Experiment results on ACE corpora show that this spectral clustering based approach outperforms Hasegawa et al. (2004)'s hierarchical clustering method and a plain k-means clustering method.

1 Introduction

The task of relation extraction is to identify various semantic relations between name entities from text. Prior work on automatic relation extraction come in three kinds: supervised learning algorithms (Miller et al., 2000; Zelenko et al., 2002; Culotta and Soresen, 2004; Kambhatla, 2004; Zhou et al., 2005), semi-supervised learning algorithms (Brin, 1998; Agichtein and Gravano, 2000; Zhang, 2004), and unsupervised learning algorithm (Hasegawa et al., 2004).

Among these methods, supervised learning is usually more preferred when a large amount of labeled training data is available. However, it is time-consuming and labor-intensive to manually tag a large amount of training data. Semi-supervised learning methods have been put forward to minimize the corpus annotation requirement. Most of semi-supervised methods employ the bootstrapping framework, which only need to pre-define some initial seeds for any particular relation, and then bootstrap from the seeds to acquire the relation. However, it is often quite difficult to enumerate all class labels in the initial seeds and decide an "optimal" number of them.

Compared with supervised and semi-supervised methods, Hasegawa et al. (2004)'s unsupervised approach for relation extraction can overcome the difficulties on requirement of a large amount of labeled data and enumeration of all class labels. Hasegawa et al. (2004)'s method is to use a hierarchical clustering method to cluster pairs of named entities according to the similarity of context words intervening between the named entities. However, the drawback of hierarchical clustering is that it required providing cluster number by users. Furthermore, clustering is performed in original high dimensional space, which may induce non-convex clusters hard to identified.

This paper presents a novel application of spectral clustering technique to unsupervised relation extraction problem. It works by calculating eigenvectors of an adjacency graph's Laplacian to recover a submanifold of data from a high dimensional space, and then performing cluster number estimation on a transformed space defined by the first few eigenvectors. This method may help us find non-convex clusters. It also does not need to pre-define the number of the context clusters or pre-specify the similarity threshold for the clusters as Hasegawa et al.

Proceedings of the 2006 Conference on Empirical Methods in Natural Language Processing (EMNLP 2006), pages 568–575,
Sydney, July 2006.

(2004)'s method.

The rest of this paper is organized as follows. Section 2 formulates unsupervised relation extraction and presents how to apply the spectral clustering technique to resolve the task. Then section 3 reports experiments and results. Finally we will give a conclusion about our work in section 4.

2 Unsupervised Relation Extraction Problem

Assume that two occurrences of entity pairs with similar contexts, are tend to hold the same relation type. Thus unsupervised relation extraction problem can be formulated as partitioning collections of entity pairs into clusters according to the similarity of contexts, with each cluster containing only entity pairs labeled by the same relation type. And then, in each cluster, the most representative words are identified from the contexts of entity pairs to induce the label of relation type. Here, we only focus on the clustering subtask and do not address the relation type labeling subtask.

In the next subsections we will describe our proposed method for unsupervised relation extraction, which includes: 1) Collect the context vectors in which the entity mention pairs co-occur; 2) Cluster these Context vectors.

2.1 Context Vector and Feature Design

Let $X = \{x_i\}_{i=1}^n$ be the set of context vectors of occurrences of all entity mention pairs, where x_i represents the context vector of the i-th occurrence, and n is the total number of occurrences of all entity pairs.

Each occurrence of entity mention pairs can be denoted as follows:

$$R \rightarrow (C_{pre}, e_1, C_{mid}, e_2, C_{post}) \qquad (1)$$

where e_1 and e_2 represents the entity mentions, and C_{pre},C_{mid},and C_{post} are the contexts before, between and after the entity pairs respectively.

We extracted features from e_1, e_2, C_{pre}, C_{mid}, C_{post} to construct context vectors, which are computed from the parse trees derived from Charniak Parser (Charniak, 1999) and the Chunklink script [1] written by Sabine Buchholz from Tilburg University.

[1] Software available at http://ilk.uvt.nl/ sabine/chunklink/

Words: Words in the two entities and three context windows.

Entity Type: the entity type of both entity mentions, which can be PERSON, ORGANIZATION, FACILITY, LOCATION and GPE.

POS features: Part-Of-Speech tags corresponding to all words in the two entities and three context windows.

Chunking features: This category of features are extracted from the chunklink representation, which includes:

- **Chunk tag information** of the two entities and three context windows. The "0" tag means that the word is outside of any chunk. The "I-XP" tag means that this word is inside an XP chunk. The "B-XP" by default means that the word is at the beginning of an XP chunk.
- **Grammatical function** of the two entities and three context windows. The last word in each chunk is its head, and the function of the head is the function of the whole chunk. "NP-SBJ" means a NP chunk as the subject of the sentence. The other words in a chunk that are not the head have "NO-FUNC" as their function.
- **IOB-chains** of the heads of the two entities. So-called IOB-chain, noting the syntactic categories of all the constituents on the path from the root node to this leaf node of tree.

We combine the above lexical and syntactic features with their position information in the context to form the context vector. Before that, we filter out low frequency features which appeared only once in the entire set.

2.2 Context Clustering

Once the context vectors of entity pairs are prepared, we come to the second stage of our method: cluster these context vectors automatically.

In recent years, spectral clustering technique has received more and more attention as a powerful approach to a range of clustering problems. Among the efforts on spectral clustering techniques (Weiss, 1999; Kannan et al., 2000; Shi et al., 2000; Ng et al., 2001; Zha et al., 2001), we adopt a modified version (Sanguinetti et al., 2005) of the algorithm by Ng et al. (2001) because it can provide us model order selection capability.

Since we do not know how many relation types in advance and do not have any labeled relation

Table 1: Context Clustering with Spectral-based Clustering technique.

	Input: A set of context vectors $X = \{x_1, x_2, ..., x_n\}$, $X \in \Re^{n \times d}$;
	Output: Clustered data and number of clusters;
1.	Construct an affinity matrix by $A_{ij} = \exp(-\frac{s_{ij}^2}{\sigma^2})$ if $i \neq j$, 0 if $i = j$. Here, s_{ij} is the similarity between x_i and x_j calculated by Cosine similarity measure. and the free distance parameter σ^2 is used to scale the weights;
2.	Normalize the affinity matrix A to create the matrix $L = D^{-1/2}AD^{-1/2}$, where D is a diagonal matrix whose (i,i) element is the sum of A's ith row;
3.	Set $q = 2$;
4.	Compute q eigenvectors of L with greatest eigenvalues. Arrange them in a matrix Y.
5.	Perform elongated K-means with $q + 1$ centers on Y, initializing the $(q + 1)$-th mean in the origin;
6.	If the $q + 1$-th cluster contains any data points, then there must be at least an extra cluster; set $q = q + 1$ and go back to step 4. Otherwise, algorithm stops and outputs clustered data and number of clusters.

training examples at hand, the problem of model order selection arises, i.e. estimating the "optimal" number of clusters. Formally, let k be the model order, we need to find k in Equation: $k = argmax_k\{criterion(k)\}$. Here, the criterion is defined on the result of spectral clustering.

Table 1 shows the details of the whole algorithm for context clustering, which contains two main stages: 1) Transformation of Clustering Space (Step 1-4); 2) Clustering in the transformed space using Elongated K-means algorithm (Step 5-6).

2.3 Transformation of Clustering Space

We represent each context vector of entity pair as a node in an undirected graph. Each edge (i,j) in the graph is assigned a weight that reflects the similarity between two context vectors i and j. Hence, the relation extraction task for entity pairs can be defined as a partition of the graph so that entity pairs that are more similar to each other, e.g. labeled by the same relation type, belong to the same cluster. As a relaxation of such NP-hard discrete graph partitioning problem, spectral clustering technique computes eigenvalues and eigenvectors of a Laplacian matrix related to the given graph, and construct data clusters based on such spectral information.

Thus the starting point of context clustering is to construct an *affinity matrix* A from the data, which is an $n \times n$ matrix encoding the distances between the various points. The affinity matrix is then normalized to form a matrix L by conjugating with the the diagonal matrix $D^{-1/2}$ which has as entries the square roots of the sum of the rows of A. This is to take into account the different spread of the various clusters (points belonging to more rarified clusters will have lower sums of the corresponding row of A). It is straightforward to prove that L is positive definite and has eigenvalues smaller or equal to 1, with equality holding in at least one case.

Let K be the true number of clusters present in the dataset. If K is known beforehand, the first K eigenvectors of L will be computed and arranged as columns in a matrix Y. Each row of Y corresponds to a context vector of entity pair, and the above process can be considered as transforming the original context vectors in a d-dimensional space to new context vectors in the K-dimensional space. Therefore, the rows of Y will cluster upon mutually orthogonal points on the K dimensional sphere,rather than on the coordinate axes.

2.4 The Elongated K-means algorithm

As the step 5 of Table 1 shows, the result of elongated K-means algorithm is used to detect whether the number of clusters selected q is less than the true number K, and allows one to iteratively obtain the number of clusters.

Consider the case when the number of clusters q is less than the true cluster number K present in the dataset. In such situation, taking the first $q < K$ eigenvectors, we will be selecting a q-dimensional subspace in the clustering space. As the rows of the K eigenvectors clustered along mutually orthogonal vectors, their projections in a lower dimensional space will cluster along radial directions. Therefore, the general picture will be of q clusters elongated in the radial direction, with possibly some clusters very near the origin (when the subspace is orthogonal to some of the discarded eigenvectors).

Hence, the K-means algorithm is modified as the elongated K-means algorithm to downweight distances along radial directions and penalize distances along transversal directions. The elongated K-means algorithm computes the distance of point x from the center c_i as follows:

- If the center is not very near the origin, $c_i^T c_i > \epsilon$ (ϵ is a parameter to be fixed by the user), the distances are cal-

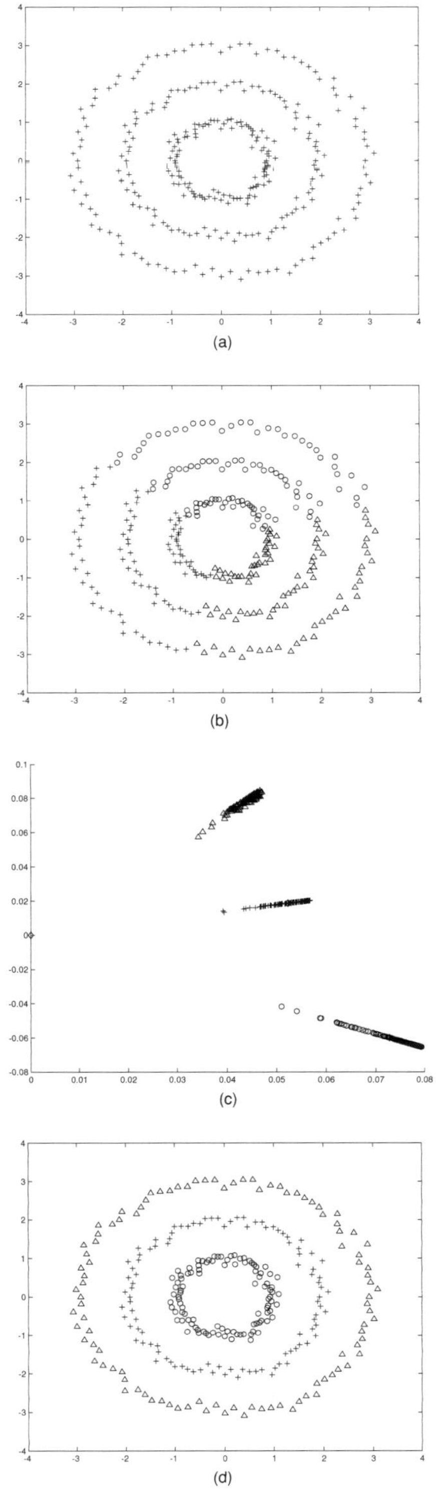

Figure 1: An Example:(a) The Three Circle Dataset. (b) The clustering result using K-means; (c) Three elongated clusters in the 2D clustering space using Spectral clustering: two dominant eigenvectors; (d) The clustering result using Spectral-based clustering (σ^2=0.05). ($\triangle$,$\circ$ and $+$ denote examples in different clusters)

culated as: $edist(x, c_i) = (x - c_i)^T M(x - c_i)$, where $M = \frac{1}{\lambda}(I_q - \frac{c_i c_i^T}{c_i^T c_i}) + \lambda \frac{c_i c_i^T}{c_i^T c_i}$, λ is the *sharpness* parameter that controls the elongation (the smaller, the more elongated the clusters) [2].

- If the center is very near the origin,$c_i^T c_i < \epsilon$, the distanccs are measured using the Euclidean distance.

In each iteration of procedure in Table 1, elongated K-means is initialized with q centers corresponding to data points in different clusters and one center in the origin. The algorithm then will drag the center in the origin towards one of the clusters not accounted for. Compute another eigenvector (thus increasing the dimension of the clustering space to $q + 1$) and repeat the procedure. Eventually, when one reach as many eigenvectors as the number of clusters present in the data, no points will be assigned to the center at the origin, leaving the cluster empty. This is the signal to terminate the algorithm.

2.5 An example

Figure 1 visualized the clustering result of three circle dataset using K-means and Spectral-based clustering. From Figure 1(b), we can see that K-means can not separate the non-convex clusters in three circle dataset successfully since it is prone to local minimal. For spectral-based clustering, as the algorithm described, initially, we took the two eigenvectors of L with largest eigenvalues, which gave us a two-dimensional clustering space. Then to ensure that the two centers are initialized in different clusters, one center is set as the point that is the farthest from the origin, while the other is set as the point that simultaneously farthest the first center and the origin. Figure 1(c) shows the three elongated clusters in the 2D clustering space and the corresponding clustering result of dataset is visualized in Figure 1(d), which exploits manifold structure (cluster structure) in data.

3 Experiments and Results

3.1 Data Setting

Our proposed unsupervised relation extraction is evaluated on ACE corpus, which contains 519 files from sources including broadcast, newswire, and newspaper. We only deal with intra-sentence explicit relations and assumed that all entities have

[2] In this paper, the *sharpness* parameter λ is set to 0.2

Table 2: Frequency of Major Relation SubTypes in the ACE training and devtest corpus.

Type	SubType	Training	Devtest
ROLE	General-Staff	550	149
	Management	677	122
	Citizen-Of	127	24
	Founder	11	5
	Owner	146	15
	Affiliate-Partner	111	15
	Member	460	145
	Client	67	13
	Other	15	7
PART	Part-Of	490	103
	Subsidiary	85	19
	Other	2	1
AT	Located	975	192
	Based-In	187	64
	Residence	154	54
SOC	Other-Professional	195	25
	Other-Personal	60	10
	Parent	68	24
	Spouse	21	4
	Associate	49	7
	Other-Relative	23	10
	Sibling	7	4
	GrandParent	6	1
NEAR	Relative-Location	88	32

been detected beforehand in the EDT sub-task of ACE. To verify our proposed method, we only collect those pairs of entity mentions which have been tagged relation types in the given corpus. Then the relation type tags were removed to test the unsupervised relation disambiguation. During the evaluation procedure, the relation type tags were used as ground truth classes. A break-down of the data by 24 relation subtypes is given in Table 2.

3.2 Evaluation method for clustering result

When assessing the agreement between clustering result and manually annotated relation types (ground truth classes), we would encounter the problem that there was no relation type tags for each cluster in our clustering results.

To resolve the problem, we construct a contingency table T, where each entry $t_{i,j}$ gives the number of the instances that belong to both the i-th estimated cluster and j-th ground truth class. Moreover, to ensure that any two clusters do not share the same labels of relation types, we adopt a permutation procedure to find an one-to-one mapping function Ω from the ground truth classes (relation types) TC to the estimated clustering result EC. There are at most $|TC|$ clusters which are assigned relation type tags. And if the number of the estimated clusters is less than the number of the ground truth clusters, empty clusters should be added so that $|EC| = |TC|$ and the one-to-one mapping can be performed, which can be formulated as the function: $\hat{\Omega} = \arg\max_{\Omega} \sum_{j=1}^{|TC|} t_{\Omega(j),j}$, where $\Omega(j)$ is the index of the estimated cluster associated with the j-th class.

Given the result of one-to-one mapping, we adopt *Precision*, *Recall* and *F-measure* to evaluate the clustering result.

3.3 Experimental Design

We perform our unsupervised relation extraction on the devtest set of ACE corpus and evaluate the algorithm on relation subtype level. Firstly, we observe the influence of various variables, including Distance Parameter σ^2, Different Features, Context Window Size. Secondly, to verify the effectiveness of our method, we further compare it with supervised method based on SVM and other two unsupervised methods.

3.3.1 Choice of Distance Parameter σ^2

We simply search over σ^2 and pick the value that finds the best aligned set of clusters on the transformed space. Here, the scattering criterion $trace(P_W^{-1} P_B)$ is used to compare the cluster quality for different value of σ^2 [3], which measures the ratio of between-cluster to within-cluster scatter. The higher the $trace(P_W^{-1} P_B)$, the higher the cluster quality.

In Table 3 and Table 4, with different settings of feature set and context window size, we find out the corresponding value of σ^2 and cluster number which maximize the $trace$ value in searching for a range of value σ^2.

3.3.2 Contribution of Different Features

As the previous section presented, we incorporate various lexical and syntactic features to extract rela-

[3] $trace(P_W^{-1} P_B)$ is $trace$ of a matrix which is the sum of its diagonal elements. P_W is the within-cluster scatter matrix as: $P_W = \sum_{j=1}^{c} \sum_{X_i \in X_j} (X_i - m_j)(X_i - m_j)^t$ and P_B is the between-cluster scatter matrix as: $P_B = \sum_{j=1}^{c} (m_j - m)(m_j - m)^t$, where m is the total mean vector and m_j is the mean vector for j^{th} cluster and $(X_j - m_j)^t$ is the matrix transpose of the column vector $(X_j - m_j)$.

Table 3: Contribution of Different Features

Features	σ^2	cluster number	$trace$ value	Precison	Recall	F-measure
Words	0.021	15	2.369	41.6%	30.2%	34.9%
+Entity Type	0.016	18	3.198	40.3%	42.5%	41.5%
+POS	0.017	18	3.206	37.8%	46.9%	41.8%
+Chunking Infomation	0.015	19	3.900	43.5%	49.4%	46.3%

Table 4: Different Context Window Size Setting

Context Window Size	σ^2	cluster number	$trace$ value	Precision	Recall	F-measure
0	0.016	18	3.576	37.6%	48.1%	42.2%
2	0.015	19	3.900	43.5%	49.4%	46.3%
5	0.020	21	2.225	29.3%	34.7%	31.7%

tion. To measure the contribution of different features, we report the performance by gradually increasing the feature set, as Table 3 shows.

Table 3 shows that all of the four categories of features contribute to the improvement of performance more or less. Firstly,the addition of entity type feature is very useful, which improves *F-measure* by 6.6%. Secondly, adding POS features can increase *F-measure* score but do not improve very much. Thirdly, chunking features also show their great usefulness with increasing *Precision/Recall/F-measure* by 5.7%/2.5%/4.5%.

We combine all these features to do all other evaluations in our experiments.

3.3.3 Setting of Context Window Size

We have mentioned in Section 2 that the context vectors of entity pairs are derived from the contexts before, between and after the entity mention pairs. Hence, we have to specify the three context window size first. In this paper, we set the mid-context window as everything between the two entity mentions. For the pre- and post- context windows, we could have different choices. For example, if we specify the outer context window size as 2, then it means that the pre-context (post-context)) includes two words before (after) the first (second) entity.

For comparison of the effect of the outer context of entity mention pairs, we conducted three different settings of context window size (0, 2, 5) as Table 4 shows. From this table we can find that with the context window size setting, 2, the algorithm achieves the best performance of 43.5%/49.4%/46.3% in *Precision/Recall/F-measure*. With the context window size setting, 5, the performance becomes worse because extending the context too much may include more features, but at the same time, the noise also increases.

Table 5: Performance of our proposed method (Spectral-based clustering) compared with supervised method (SVM) and unsupervised methods((Hasegawa et al., 2004))'s method and K-means clustering.

	Precision	Recall	F-measure
SVM	61.2%	49.6%	54.8%
Hasegawa's Method1	38.7%	29.8%	33.7%
Hasegawa's Method2	37.9%	36.0%	36.9%
Kmeans	34.3%	40.2%	36.8%
Our Proposed Method	43.5%	49.4%	46.3%

3.3.4 Comparison with Supervised methods and other Unsupervised methods

To explore the effectiveness of our unsupervised method compared to supervised method, we perform SVM technique with the same feature set defined in our proposed method. The *LIBSVM* tool is used in this test [4]. The kernel function we used is linear and SVM models are trained using the training set of ACE corpus.

In (Hasegawa et al., 2004), they preformed unsupervised relation extraction based on hierarchical clustering and they only used word features between entity mention pairs to construct context vectors. We reported the clustering results using the same clustering strategy as Hasegawa et al. (2004) proposed. In Table 5, Hasegawa's Method1 means the test used the word feature as Hasegawa et al. (2004) while Hasegawa's Method2 means the test used the same feature set as our method. In both tests, we specified

[4] *LIBSVM*: a library for support vector machines. Software available at http://www.csie.ntu.edu.tw/ cjlin/libsvm. It supports multi-class classification.

Table 6: Comparison of the existing efforts on ACE RDC task.

		Relation Dectection			Relation Classification on Types			on Subtypes		
	Method	P	R	F	P	R	F	P	R	F
Culotta and Soresen (2004)	Tree kernel based	81.2	51.8	63.2	67.1	35.0	45.8	-	-	-
Kambhatla (2004)	Feature based, Maximum Entropy	-	-	-	-	-	-	63.5	45.2	52.8
Zhou et al. (2005)	Feature based,SVM	84.8	66.7	74.7	77.2	60.7	68.0	63.1	49.5	55.5

the cluster number as the number of ground truth classes.

We also approached the relation extraction problem using the standard clustering technique, K-means, where we adopted the same feature set defined in our proposed method to cluster the context vectors of entity mention pairs and pre-specified the cluster number as the number of ground truth classes.

Table 5 reports the performance of our proposed method comparing with SVM-based supervised method and the other two unsupervised methods. As the result shows, SVM-based method by using the same feature set in our proposed method can achieve 61.2%/49.6%/54.8% in *Precision/Recall/F-measure*. Table 5 also shows our proposed spectral based method clearly outperforms the other two unsupervised methods by 12.5% and 9.5% in *F-measure* respectively. Moreover, the incorporation of various lexical and syntactic features into Hasegawa et al. (2004)'s method2 makes it outperform Hasegawa et al. (2004)'s method1 which only uses word feature.

3.4 Discussion

In this paper, we have shown that the modified spectral clustering technique, with various lexical and syntactic features derived from the context of entity pairs, performed well on the unsupervised relation disambiguation problem. Our experiments show that by the choice of the distance parameter σ^2, we can estimate the cluster number which provides the tightest clusters. We notice that the estimated cluster number is less than the number of ground truth classes in most cases. The reason for this phenomenon may be that some relation types can not be easily distinguished using the context information only. For example, the relation subtypes "Located", "Based-In" and "Residence" are difficult to disambiguate even for human experts to differentiate.

The results also show that various lexical and syntactic features contain useful information for the task. Especially, although we did not concern the dependency tree and full parse tree information as other supervised methods (Miller et al., 2000; Culotta and Soresen, 2004; Kambhatla, 2004; Zhou et al., 2005), the incorporation of simple features, such as words and chunking information, still can provide complement information for capturing the characteristics of entity pairs. Another observation from the result is that extending the outer context window of entity mention pairs too much may not improve the performance since the process may incorporate more noise information and affect the clustering result.

As regards the clustering technique, the spectral-based clustering performs better than direct clustering, K-means. Since the spectral-based algorithm works in a transformed space of low dimensionality, data can be easily clustered so that the algorithm can be implemented with better efficiency and speed. And the performance using spectral-based clustering can be improved due to the reason that spectral-based clustering overcomes the drawback of K-means (prone to local minima) and may find non-convex clusters consistent with human intuition.

Currently most of works on the RDC task of ACE focused on supervised learning methods. Table 6 lists a comparison of these methods on relation detection and relation classification. Zhou et al. (2005) reported the best result as 63.1%/49.5%/55.5% in *Precision/Recall/F-measure* on the extraction of ACE relation subtypes using feature based method, which outperforms tree kernel based method by Culotta and Soresen (2004). Although our unsupervised method still can not outperform these supervised methods, from the point of view of unsupervised resolution for relation extraction, our approach already achieves best performance of 43.5%/49.4%/46.3% in *Precision/Recall/F-measure* compared with other clustering methods.

4 Conclusion and Future work

In this paper, we approach unsupervised relation disambiguation problem by using spectral-based clustering technique with diverse lexical and syntactic features derived from context. The advantage of our method is that it doesn't need any manually labeled relation instances, and pre-definition the number of the context clusters. Experiment results on the ACE corpus show that our method achieves better performance than other unsupervised methods.

Currently we combine various lexical and syntactic features to construct context vectors for clustering. In the future we will further explore other semantic information to assist the relation extraction problem. Moreover, instead of cosine similarity measure to calculate the distance between context vectors, we will try other distributional similarity measures to see whether the performance of relation extraction can be improved. In addition, if we can find an effective unsupervised way to filter out unrelated entity pairs in advance, it would make our proposed method more practical.

References

Agichtein E. and Gravano L.. 2000. *Snowball: Extracting Relations from large Plain-Text Collections, In Proc. of the* 5th *ACM International Conference on Digital Libraries (ACMDL'00).*

Brin Sergey. 1998. *Extracting patterns and relations from world wide web. In Proc. of WebDB Workshop at 6th International Conference on Extending Database Technology (WebDB'98).* pages 172-183.

Charniak E.. 1999. *A Maximum-entropy-inspired parser. Technical Report CS-99-12..* Computer Science Department, Brown University.

Culotta A. and Soresen J. 2004. *Dependency tree kernels for relation extraction, In proceedings of 42th Annual Meeting of the Association for Computational Linguistics.* 21-26 July 2004. Barcelona, Spain.

Defense Advanced Research Projects Agency. 1995. *Proceedings of the Sixth Message Understanding Conference (MUC-6)* Morgan Kaufmann Publishers, Inc.

Hasegawa Takaaki, Sekine Satoshi and Grishman Ralph. 2004. *Discovering Relations among Named Entities from Large Corpora, Proceeding of Conference ACL2004.* Barcelona, Spain.

Kambhatla N. 2004. *Combining lexical, syntactic and semantic features with Maximum Entropy Models for extracting relations, In proceedings of 42th Annual Meeting of the Association for Computational Linguistics.* 21-26 July 2004. Barcelona, Spain.

Kannan R., Vempala S., and Vetta A.. 2000. *On clustering: Good,bad and spectral. In Proceedings of the 41st Foundations of Computer Science.* pages 367-380.

Miller S.,Fox H.,Ramshaw L. and Weischedel R. 2000. *A novel use of statistical parsing to extract information from text. In proceedings of 6th Applied Natural Language Processing Conference.* 29 April-4 may 2000, Seattle USA.

Ng Andrew.Y, Jordan M., and Weiss Y.. 2001. *On spectral clustering: Analysis and an algorithm. In Proceedings of Advances in Neural Information Processing Systems.* pages 849-856.

Sanguinetti G., Laidler J. and Lawrence N.. 2005. *Automatic determination of the number of clusters using spectral algorithms.In: IEEE Machine Learning for Signal Processing.* 28-30 Sept 2005, Mystic, Connecticut, USA.

Shi J. and Malik.J. 2000. *Normalized cuts and image segmentation. IEEE Transactions on Pattern Analysis and Machine Intelligence.* 22(8):888-905.

Weiss Yair. 1999. *Segmentation using eigenvectors: A unifying view. ICCV(2).* pp.975-982.

Zelenko D., Aone C. and Richardella A.. 2002. *Kernel Methods for Relation Extraction, Proceedings of the Conference on Empirical Methods in Natural Language Processing (EMNLP).* Philadelphia.

Zha H.,Ding C.,Gu.M,He X.,and Simon H.. 2001. *Spectral Relaxation for k-means clustering. In Neural Information Processing Systems (NIPS2001).* pages 1057-1064, 2001.

Zhang Zhu. 2004. *Weakly-supervised relation classification for Information Extraction, In proceedings of ACM 13th conference on Information and Knowledge Management (CIKM'2004).* 8-13 Nov 2004. Washington D.C.,USA.

Zhou GuoDong, Su Jian, Zhang Jie and Zhang min. 2005. *Exploring Various Knowledge in Relation Extraction, In proceedings of 43th Annual Meeting of the Association for Computational Linguistics.* USA.

Competitive generative models with structure learning for NLP classification tasks

Kristina Toutanova
Microsoft Research
Redmond, WA
kristout@microsoft.com

Abstract

In this paper we show that generative models are competitive with and sometimes superior to discriminative models, when both kinds of models are allowed to learn structures that are optimal for discrimination. In particular, we compare Bayesian Networks and Conditional log-linear models on two NLP tasks. We observe that when the structure of the generative model encodes very strong independence assumptions (*a la* Naive Bayes), a discriminative model is superior, but when the generative model is allowed to weaken these independence assumptions via learning a more complex structure, it can achieve very similar or better performance than a corresponding discriminative model. In addition, as structure learning for generative models is far more efficient, they may be preferable for some tasks.

1 Introduction

Discriminative models have become the models of choice for NLP tasks, because of their ability to easily incorporate non-independent features and to more directly optimize classification accuracy. State of the art models for many NLP tasks are either fully discriminative or trained using discriminative reranking (Collins, 2000). These include models for part-of-speech tagging (Toutanova et al., 2003), semantic-role labeling (Punyakanok et al., 2005; Pradhan et al., 2005b) and Penn Treebank parsing (Charniak and Johnson, 2005).

The superiority of discriminative models has been shown on many tasks when the discriminative and generative models use exactly the same model structure (Klein and Manning, 2002). However, the advantage of the discriminative models can be very slight (Johnson, 2001) and for small training set sizes generative models can be better because they need fewer training samples to converge to the optimal parameter setting (Ng and Jordan, 2002). Additionally, many discriminative models use a generative model as a base model and add discriminative features with reranking (Collins, 2000; Charniak and Johnson, 2005; Roark et al., 2004), or train discriminatively a small set of weights for features which are generatively estimated probabilities (Raina et al., 2004; Och and Ney, 2002). Therefore it is important to study generative models and to find ways of making them better even when they are used only as components of discriminative models.

Generative models may often perform poorly due to making strong independence assumptions about the joint distribution of features and classes. To avoid this problem, generative models for NLP tasks have often been manually designed to achieve an appropriate representation of the joint distribution, such as in the parsing models of (Collins, 1997; Charniak, 2000). This shows that when the generative models have a good model structure, they can perform quite well.

In this paper, we look differently at comparing generative and discriminative models. We ask the question: given the same set of input features, what is the best a generative model can do if it is allowed to learn an optimal *structure* for the joint distribution, and what is the best a discriminative model can do if it is also allowed to learn an optimal structure. That is, we do not impose any independence assumptions on the generative or discriminative models and let them learn the best representation of the data they can.

Structure learning is very efficient for generative models in the form of directed graphical models (Bayesian Networks (Pearl, 1988)), since the optimal parameters for such models can be estimated in closed form. We compare Bayesian Net-

Proceedings of the 2006 Conference on Empirical Methods in Natural Language Processing (EMNLP 2006), pages 576–584,
Sydney, July 2006. ©2006 Association for Computational Linguistics

works with structure learning to their closely related discriminative counterpart – conditional log-linear models with structure learning. Our conditional log-linear models can also be seen as Conditional Random Fields (Lafferty et al., 2001), except we do not have a structure on the labels, but want to learn a structure on the features.

We compare the two kinds of models on two NLP classification tasks – prepositional phrase attachment and semantic role labelling. Our results show that the generative models are competitive with or better than the discriminative models. When a small set of interpolation parameters for the conditional probability tables are fit discriminatively, the resulting hybrid generative-discriminative models perform better than the generative only models and sometimes better than the discriminative models.

In Section 2, we describe in detail the form of the generative and discriminative models we study and our structure search methodology. In Section 3 we present the results of our empirical study.

2 Model Classes and Methodology

2.1 Generative Models

In classification tasks, given a training set of instances $D = \{[x_i, y_i]\}$, where x_i are the input features for the i-th instance, and y_i is its label, the task is to learn a classifier that predicts the labels of new examples. If $\mathcal{X}$ is the space of inputs and $\mathcal{Y}$ is the space of labels, a classifier is a function $f : \mathcal{X} \to \mathcal{Y}$. A generative model is one that models the joint probability of inputs and labels $P_D(x, y)$ through a distribution $P_\theta(x, y)$, dependent on some parameter vector θ. The classifier based on this generative model chooses the most likely label given an input according to the conditionalized estimated joint distribution. The parameters θ of the fitted distribution are usually estimated using the maximum joint likelihood estimate, possibly with a prior.

We study generative models represented as Bayesian Networks (Pearl, 1988), because their parameters can be estimated extremely fast as the maximizer of the joint likelihood is the closed form relative frequency estimate. A Bayesian Network is an acyclic directed graph over a set of nodes. For every variable Z, let $Pa(Z)$ denote the set of parents of Z. The structure of the Bayesian Network encodes the following set of independence assumptions: every variable is conditionally independent of its non-descendants given its parents. For example, the structure of the Bayesian Network model in Figure 1 encodes the independence assumption that the input features are conditionally independent given the class label.

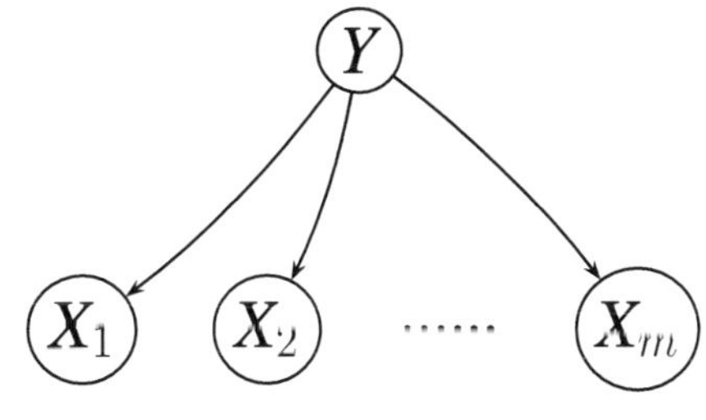

Figure 1: Naive Bayes Bayesian Network

Let the input be represented as a vector of m nominal features. We define Bayesian Networks over the m input variables $X_1, X_2, \ldots, X_m$ and the class variable Y. In all networks, we add links from the class variable Y to all input features. In this way we have generative models which estimate class-specific distributions over features $P(X|Y)$ and a prior over labels $P(Y)$. Figure 1 shows a simple Bayesian Network of this form, which is the well-known Naive Bayes model.

A specific joint distribution for a given Bayesian Network (BN) is given by a set of conditional probability tables (CPTs) which specify the distribution over each variable given its parents $P(Z|Pa(Z))$. The joint distribution $P(Z_1, Z_2, \ldots, Z_m)$ is given by:

$$P(Z_1, Z_2, \ldots, Z_m) = \prod_{i=1\ldots m} P(Z_i|Pa(Z_i))$$

The parameters of a Bayesian Network model given its graph structure are the values of the conditional probabilities $P(Z_i|Pa(Z_i))$. If the model is trained through maximizing the joint likelihood of the data, the optimal parameters are the relative frequency estimates: $\hat{P}(Z_i = v|Pa(Z_i) = \vec{u}) = \frac{count(Z_i=v,Pa(Z_i)=\vec{u})}{count(Pa(Z_i)=\vec{u})}$ Here v denotes a value of Z_i and $\vec{u}$ denotes a vector of values for the parents of Z_i.

Most often smoothing is applied to avoid zero probability estimates. A simple form of smoothing is add-α smoothing which is equivalent to a Dirichlet prior. For NLP tasks it has been shown that other smoothing methods are far superior to add-α smoothing – see, for example, Goodman

(2001). In particular, it is important to incorporate lower-order information based on subsets of the conditioning information. Therefore we assume a structural form of the conditional probability tables which implements a more sophisticated type of smoothing – interpolated Witten-Bell (Witten and Bell, 1991). This kind of smoothing has also been used in the generative parser of (Collins, 1997) and has been shown to have a relatively good performance for language modeling (Goodman, 2001).

To describe the form of the conditional probability tables, we introduce some notation. Let Z denote a variable in the BN and $Z_1, Z_2, \ldots, Z_k$ denote the set of its parents. The probability $P(Z = z | Z_1 = z_1, Z_2 = z_2, \ldots, Z_k = z_k)$ is estimated using Witten-Bell smoothing as follows: (below the tuple of values $z_1, z_2, \ldots, z_k$ is denoted by z_{1k}).

$$P_{WB}(z|z_{1k}) = \lambda(z_{1k}) \times \hat{P}(z|z_{1k}) + (1 - \lambda(z_{1k})) \times P_{WB}(z|z_{1k-1})$$

In the above equation, $\hat{P}$ is the relative frequency estimator. The recursion is ended by interpolating with a uniform distribution $\frac{1}{V_z}$, where V_z is the vocabulary of values for the prediction variable Z. We determine the interpolation back-off order by looking at the number of values of each variable. We apply the following rule: the variable with the highest number of values observed in the training set is backed off first, then the variable with the next highest number of values, and so on. Typically, the class variable will be backed-off last according to this rule.

In Witten-Bell smoothing, the values of the interpolation coefficients are as follows: $\lambda(z_{1k}) = \frac{count(z_{1k})}{count(z_{1k}) + d \times |z : count(z, z_{1k}) > 0|}$. The weight of the relative frequency estimate based on a given context increases if the context has been seen more often in the training data and decreases if the context has been seen with more different values for the predicted variable z.

Looking at the form of our conditional probability tables, we can see that the major parameters are estimated directly based on the counts of the events in the training data. In addition, there are interpolation parameters (denoted by d above), which participate in computing the interpolation weights λ. The d parameters are hyper-parameters and we learn them on a development set of samples. We experimented with learning a single d parameter which is shared by all CPTs and learning multiple d parameters – one for every type of conditioning context in every CPT – i.e., each CPT has as many d parameters as there are back-off levels.

We place some restrictions on the Bayesian Networks learned, for closer correspondence with the discriminative models and for tractability: Every input variable node has the label node as a parent, and at most three parents per variable are allowed.

2.1.1 Structure Search Methodology

Our structure search method differs slightly from previously proposed methods in the literature (Heckerman, 1999; Pernkopf and Bilmes, 2005). The search space is defined as follows. We start with a Bayesian Network containing only the class variable. We denote by CHOSEN the set of variables already in the network and by REMAINING the set of unplaced variables. Initially, only the class variable Y is in CHOSEN and all other variables are in REMAINING. Starting from the current BN, the set of next candidate structures is defined as follows: For every unplaced variable R in REMAINING, and for every subset Sub of size at most two from the already placed variables in CHOSEN, consider adding R with parents $Sub \cup Y$ to the current BN. Thus the number of candidate structures for extending a current BN is on the order of m^3, where m is the number of variables.

We perform a greedy search. At each step, if the best variable B with the best set of parents $Pa(B)$ improves the evaluation criterion, move B from REMAINING to CHOSEN, and continue the search until there are no variables in REMAINING or the evaluation criterion can not be improved.

The evaluation criterion for BNs we use is classification accuracy on a development set of samples. Thus our structure search method is discriminative, in the terminology of (Grossman and Domingos, 2004; Pernkopf and Bilmes, 2005). It is very easy to evaluate candidate BN structures. The main parameters in the CPTs are estimated via the relative frequency estimator on the training set, as discussed in the previous section. We do not fit the hyper-parameters d during structure search. We fit these parameters only after we have selected a final BN structure. Throughout the structure search, we use a fixed value of 1 for d for all CPTs and levels of back-off. Therefore we are using generative parameter estimation and discriminative structure search. See Section 4 for discussion on how this method relates to previous work.

Notice that the optimal parameters of the conditional probability tables of variables already in the current BN do not change at all when a new variable is added, thus making update very efficient. After the stopping criterion is met, the hyper-parameters of the resulting BN are fit on the development set. As discussed in the previous subsection, we fit either a single or multiple hyper-parameters d. The fitting criterion for the generative Bayesian Networks is joint likelihood of the development set of samples with a Gaussian prior on the values $log(d)$. [1]

Additionally, we explore fitting the hyper-parameters of the Bayesian Networks by optimizing the conditional likelihood of the development set of samples. In this case we call the resulting models *Hybrid Bayesian Network* models, since they incorporate a number of discriminatively trained parameters. Hybrid models have been proposed before and shown to perform very competitively (Raina et al., 2004; Och and Ney, 2002). In Section 3.2 we compare generative and hybrid Bayesian Networks.

2.2 Discriminative Models

Discriminative models learn a conditional distribution $P_\theta(Y|\vec{X})$ or discriminant functions that discriminate between classes. Here we concentrate on conditional log-linear models. A simple example of such model is logistic regression, which directly corresponds to Naive Bayes but is trained to maximize the conditional likelihood. [2]

To describe the form of models we study, let us introduce some notation. We represent a tuple of nominal variables (X_1,X_2,...,X_m) as a vector of 0s and 1s in the following standard way: We map the tuple of values of nominal variables to a vector space with dimensionality the sum of possible values of all variables. There is a single dimension in the vector space for every value of each input variable X_i. The tuple (X_1,X_2,...,X_m) is mapped to a vector which has 1s in m places, which are the corresponding dimensions for the values of each variable X_i. We denote this mapping by Φ.

In logistic regression, the probability of a label $Y = y$ given input features $\Phi(X_1, X_2, \ldots, X_k) = \vec{x}$ is estimated as:

$$P(y|\vec{x}) = \frac{\exp\langle \vec{w_y}, \vec{x}\rangle}{\sum_{y'} \exp\langle \vec{w_{y'}}, \vec{x}\rangle}$$

There is a parameter vector of feature weights $\vec{w_y}$ for each label y. We fit the parameters of the log-linear model by maximizing the conditional likelihood of the training set including a gaussian prior on the parameters. The prior has mean 0 and variance σ^2. The variance is a hyper-parameter, which we optimize on a development set.

In addition to this simple logistic regression model, as for the generative models, we consider models with much richer structure. We consider more complex mappings Φ, which incorporate conjunctions of combinations of input variables. We restrict the number of variables in the combinations to three, which directly corresponds to our limit on number of parents in the Bayesian Network structures. This is similar to considering polynomial kernels of up to degree three, but is more general, because, for example, we can add only some and not all bigram conjunctions of variables. Structure search (or feature selection) for log-linear models has been done before e.g. (Della Pietra et al., 1997; McCallum, 2003). We devise our structure search methodology in a way that corresponds as closely as possible to our structure search for Bayesian Networks. The exact hypothesis space considered is defined by the search procedure for an optimal structure we apply, which we describe next.

2.2.1 Structure Search Methodology

We start with an initial empty feature set and a candidate feature set consisting of all input features: CANDIDATES=$\{X_1,X_2,\ldots,X_m\}$. In the course of the search, the set CANDIDATES may contain feature conjunctions in addition to the initial input features. After a feature is selected from the candidates set and added to the model, the feature is removed from CANDIDATES and all conjunctions of that feature with all input features are added to CANDIDATES. For example, if a feature conjunction $\langle X_{i_1},X_{i_2},\ldots,X_{i_n}\rangle$ is selected, all of its expansions of the form $\langle X_{i_1},X_{i_2},\ldots,X_{i_n},X_i\rangle$, where X_i is not in the conjunction already, are added to CANDIDATES.

We perform a greedy search and at each step select the feature which maximizes the evaluation criterion, add it to the model and extend the set

[1] Since the d parameters are positive we convert the problem to unconstrained optimization over parameters γ such that $d = e^\gamma$.

[2] Logistic regression additionally does not have the sum to one constraint on weights but it can be shown that this does not increase the representational power of the model.

CANDIDATES as described above. The evaluation criterion for selecting features is classification accuracy on a development set of samples, as for the Bayesian Network structure search.

At each step, we evaluate all candidate features. This is computationally expensive, because it requires iterative re-estimation. In addition to estimating weights for the new features, we re-estimate the old parameters, since their optimal values change. We did not preform search for the hyper-parameter σ when evaluating models. We fit σ by optimizing the development set accuracy after a model was selected. Note that our feature selection algorithm adds an input variable or a variable conjunction with all of its possible values in a single step of the search. Therefore we are adding hundreds or thousands of binary features at each step, as opposed to only one as in (Della Pietra et al., 1997). This is why we can afford to perform complete re-estimation of the parameters of the model at each step.

3 Experiments

3.1 Problems and Datasets

We study two classification problems – prepositional phrase (PP) attachment, and semantic role labeling.

Following most of the literature on prepositional phrase attachment (e.g., (Hindle and Rooth, 1993; Collins and Brooks, 1995; Vanschoenwinkel and Manderick, 2003)), we focus on the most common configuration that leads to ambiguities: V NP PP. Here, we are given a verb phrase with a following noun phrase and a prepositional phrase. The goal is to determine if the PP should be attached to the verb or to the object noun phrase. For example, in the sentence: *Never* $[hang]_V$ $[a\ painting]_{NP}$ $[with\ a\ peg]_{PP}$, the prepositional phrase *with a peg* can either modify the verb *hang* or the object noun phrase *a painting*. Here, clearly, *with a peg* modifies the verb *hang*.

We follow the common practice in representing the problem using only the head words of these constituents and of the NP inside the PP. Thus the example sentence is represented as the following quadruple: [v:hang n_1:painting p:with n_2:peg]. Thus for the PP attachment task we have binary labels Att, and four input variables – v, n_1, p, n_2.

We work with the standard dataset previously used for this task by other researchers (Ratnaparkhi et al., 1994; Collins and Brooks, 1995). It is extracted from the the Penn Treebank Wall Street Journal data (Ratnaparkhi et al., 1994). Table 1 shows summary statistics for the dataset.

Task	Training	Devset	Test
PP	20,801	4,039	3,097
SRL	173,514	5,115	9,272

Table 1: Data sizes for the PP attachment and SRL tasks.

The second task we concentrate on is semantic role labeling in the context of PropBank (Palmer et al., 2005). The PropBank corpus annotates phrases which fill semantic roles for verbs on top of Penn Treebank parse trees. The annotated roles specify agent, patient, direction, etc. The labels for semantic roles are grouped into two groups, *core* argument labels and *modifier* argument labels, which correspond approximately to the traditional distinction between arguments and adjuncts.

There has been plenty of work on machine learning models for semantic role labeling, starting with the work of Gildea and Jurafsky (2002), and including CoNLL shared tasks (Carreras and Màrquez, 2005). The most successful formulation has been as learning to classify nodes in a syntactic parse tree. The possible labels are NONE, meaning that the corresponding phrase has no semantic role and the set of core and modifier labels. We concentrate on the subproblem of *classification* for core argument nodes. The problem is, given that a node has a core argument label, decide what the correct label is. Other researchers have also looked at this subproblem (Gildea and Jurafsky, 2002; Toutanova et al., 2005; Pradhan et al., 2005a; Xue and Palmer, 2004).

Many features have been proposed for building models for semantic role labeling. Initially, 7 features were proposed by (Gildea and Jurafsky, 2002), and all following research has used these features and some additional ones. These are the features we use as well. Table 2 lists the features. State-of-the-art models for the subproblem of classification of core arguments additionally use other features of individual nodes (Xue and Palmer, 2004; Pradhan et al., 2005a), as well as global features including the labels of other nodes in parse tree. Nevertheless it is interesting to see how well we can do with these 7 features only.

We use the standard training, development, and

Feature Types (Gildea and Jurafsky, 2002)
PHRASE TYPE: Syntactic Category of node
PREDICATE LEMMA: Stemmed Verb
PATH: Path from node to predicate
POSITION: Before or after predicate?
VOICE: Active or passive relative to predicate
HEAD WORD OF PHRASE
SUB-CAT: CFG expansion of predicate's parent

Table 2: Features for Semantic Role Labeling.

test sets from the February 2004 version of Propbank. The training set consists of sections 2 to 21, the development set is from section 24, and the test set is from section 23. The number of samples is listed in Table 1. As we can see, the training set size is much larger compared to the PP attachment training set.

3.2 Results

In line with previous work (Ng and Jordan, 2002; Klein and Manning, 2002), we first compare Naive Bayes and Logistic regression on the two NLP tasks. This lets us see how they compare when the generative model is making strong independence assumptions and when the two kinds of models have the same structure. Then we compare the generative and discriminative models with learned richer structures.

Table 3 shows the Naive Bayes/Logistic regression results for PP attachment. We list results for several conditions of training the Naive Bayes classifier, depending on whether it is trained as strictly generative or as a hybrid model, and whether a single or multiple hyper-parameters d are trained. In the table, we see results for generative Naive Bayes, where the d parameters are trained to maximize the joint likelihood of the development set, and for Hybrid Naive Bayes, where the hyper-parameters are trained to optimize the conditional likelihood. The column H-Params (for hyper-parameters) indicates whether a single or multiple d parameters are learned.

Logistic regression is more fairly comparable to Naive Bayes trained using a single hyper-parameter, because it also uses a single hyper-parameter σ trained on a development set. However, for the generative model it is very easy to train multiple weights d since the likelihood of a development set is differentiable with respect to the parameters. For logistic regression, we may want to choose different variances for the different types of features but the search would be prohibitively expensive. Thus we think it is also fair to fit multiple interpolation weights for the generative model and we show these results as well.

Model	H-params	Test set acc
Naive Bayes	1	81.2
Naive Bayes	9	81.2
Logistic regression	1	**82.6**
Hybrid Naive Bayes	1	81.2
Hybrid Naive Bayes	9	81.5

Table 3: Naive Bayes and Logistic regression PP attachment results.

As we can see from the table, logistic regression outperforms both Naive Bayes and Hybrid Naive Bayes. The performance of Hybrid Naive Bayes with multiple interpolation weights improves the accuracy, but performance is still better for logistic regression. This suggests that the strong independence assumptions are hurting the classifier. According to McNemar's test, logistic regression is statistically significantly better than the Naive Bayes models and than Hybrid Naive Bayes with a single interpolation weight ($p < 0.025$), but is not significantly better than Hybrid Naive Bayes with multiple interpolation parameters at level 0.05.

However, when both the generative and discriminative models are allowed to learn optimal structures, the generative model outperforms the discriminative model. As seen from Table 4, the Bayesian Network with a single interpolation weight achieves an accuracy of 84.6%, whereas the discriminative model performs at 83.8%. The hybrid model with a single interpolation weight does even better, achieving 85.0% accuracy. For comparison, the model of Collins & Brooks has accuracy of 84.15% on this test set, and the highest result obtained through a discriminative model with this feature set is 84.8%, using SVMs and a polynomial kernel with multiple hyper-parameters (Vanschoenwinkel and Manderick, 2003). The Hybrid Bayes Nets are statistically significantly better than the Log-linear model ($p < 0.05$), and the Bayes Nets are not significantly better than the Log-linear model. All models from Table 4 are significantly better than all models in Table 3.

For semantic role labelling classification of core arguments, the results are listed in Tables 5 and 6. We can see that the difference in performance between Naive Bayes with a single interpolation parameter d – 83.3% and the performance of Logistic regression – 91.1%, is very large. This shows that the independence assumptions are quite

Model	H-params	Test set acc
Bayes Net	1	84.6
Bayes Net	13	84.6
Log-linear model	1	83.8
Hybrid Bayes Net	1	**85.0**
Hybrid Bayes Net	13	84.8

Table 4: Bayesian Network and Conditional log-linear model PP attachment results.

Model	H-params	Test set acc
Naive Bayes	1	83.3
Naive Bayes	15	85.2
Logistic regression	1	**91.1**
Hybrid Naive Bayes	1	84.1
Hybrid Naive Bayes	15	86.5

Table 5: Naive Bayes and Logistic regression SRL classificaion results.

strong, and since many of the features are not sparse lexical features and training data for them is sufficient, the Naive Bayes model has no advantage over the discriminative logistic regression model. The Hybrid Naive Bayes model with multiple interpolation weights does better than Naive Bayes, performing at 86.5%. All differences between the classifiers in Table 5 are statistically significant at level 0.01. Compared to the PP attachment task, here we are getting more benefit from multiple hyper-parameters, perhaps due to the diversity of the features for SRL: In SRL, we use both sparse lexical features and non-sparse syntactic ones, whereas all features for PP attachment are lexical.

From Table 6 we can see that when we compare general Bayesian Network structures to general log-linear models, the performance gap between the generative and discriminative models is much smaller. The Bayesian Network with a single interpolation weight d has 93.5% accuracy and the log-linear model has 93.9% accuracy. The hybrid model with multiple interpolation weights performs at 93.7%. All models in Table 6 are in a statistical tie according to McNemar's test, and thus the log-linear model is not significantly better than the Bayes Net models. We can see that the generative model was able to learn a structure with a set of independence assumptions which are not as strong as the ones the Naive Bayes model makes, thus resulting in a model with performance competitive with the discriminative model.

Figures 2(a) and 2(b) show the Bayesian Networks learned for PP Attachment and Semantic Role Labeling. Table 7 shows the conjunctions

Model	H-params	Test set acc
Bayes Net	1	93.5
Bayes Net	20	93.6
Log-linear model	1	**93.9**
Hybrid Bayes Net	1	93.5
Hybrid Bayes Net	20	93.7

Table 6: Bayesian Network and Conditional log-linear model SRL classification results.

PP Attachment Model
⟨P⟩, ⟨P,V⟩, ⟨P,N_1⟩, ⟨P,N_2⟩
⟨N_1⟩,⟨V⟩, ⟨P,N_1,N_2⟩
SRL Model
⟨PATH⟩, ⟨PATH,PLEMMA⟩,⟨SUB-CAT⟩,⟨PLEMMA⟩
⟨HW,PLEMMA⟩,⟨PATH,PLEMMA,VOICE⟩
,⟨HW,PLEMMA,PTYPE⟩,⟨SUB-CAT,PLEMMA⟩
⟨SUB-CAT,PLEMMA,POS⟩,⟨HW⟩

Table 7: Log-linear models learned for PP attachment and SRL.

learned by the Log-linear models for PP attachment and SRL.

We should note that it is much faster to do structure search for the generative Bayesian Network model, as compared to structure search for the log-linear model. In our implementation, we did not do any computation reuse between successive steps of structure search for the Bayesian Network or log-linear models. Structure search took 2 hours for the Bayesian Network and 24 hours for the log-linear model.

To put our results in the context of previous work, other results on core arguments using the same input features have been reported, the best being 91.4% for an SVM with a degree 2 polynomial kernel (Pradhan et al., 2005a).[3] The highest reported result for independent classification of core arguments is 96.0% for a log-linear model using more than 20 additional basic features (Toutanova et al., 2005). Therefore our resulting models with 93.5% and 93.9% accuracy compare favorably to the SVM model with polynomial kernel and show the importance of structure learning.

4 Comparison to Related Work

Previous work has compared generative and discriminative models having the same structure, such as the Naive Bayes and Logistic regression models (Ng and Jordan, 2002; Klein and Manning, 2002) and other models (Klein and Manning, 2002; Johnson, 2001).

[3]This result is on an older version of Propbank from July 2002.

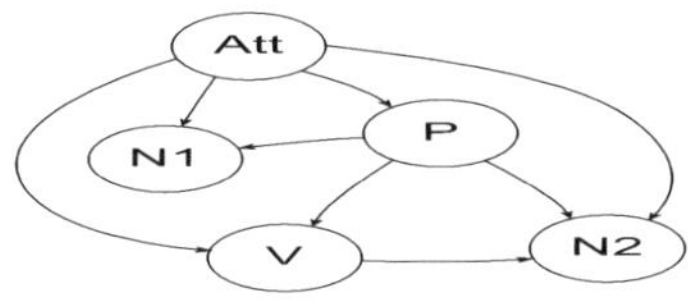

(a) Learned Bayesian Network for PP attachment.

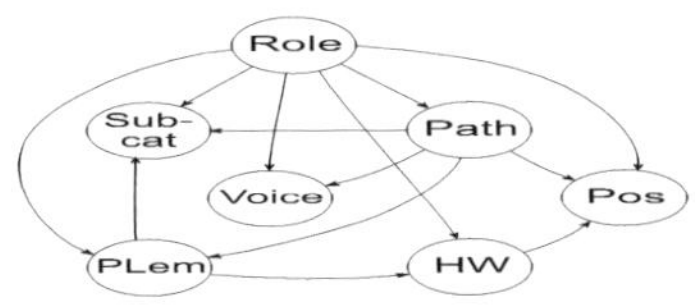

(b) Learned Bayesian Network for SRL.

Figure 2: Learned Bayesian Network structures for PP attachment and SRL.

Bayesian Networks with special structure of the CPTs – e.g. decision trees, have been previously studied in e.g. (Friedman and Goldszmidt, 1996), but not for NLP tasks and not in comparison to discriminative models. Studies comparing generative and discriminative models with structure learning have been previously performed ((Pernkopf and Bilmes, 2005) and (Grossman and Domingos, 2004)) for other, non-NLP domains. There are several important algorithmic differences between our work and that of (Pernkopf and Bilmes, 2005; Grossman and Domingos, 2004). We detail the differences here and perform an empirical evaluation of the impact of some of these differences.

Form of the generative models. The generative models studied in that previous work do not employ any special form of the conditional probability tables. Pernkopf and Bilmes (2005) use a simple smoothing method: fixing the probability of every event that has a zero relative frequency estimate to a small fixed ϵ. Thus the model does not take into account information from lower order distributions and has no hyper-parameters that are being fit. Grossman and Domingos (2004) do not employ a special form of the CPTs either and do not mention any kind of smoothing used in the generative model learning.

Form of the discriminative models. The works (Pernkopf and Bilmes, 2005; Grossman and Domingos, 2004) study Bayesian Networks whose parameters are trained discriminatively (by maximizing conditional likelihood), as representatives of discriminative models. We study more general log-linear models, equivalent to Markov Random Fields. Our models are more general in that their parameters do not need to be interpretable as probabilities (sum to 1 and between 0 and 1), and the structures do not need to correspond to Bayes Net structures. For discriminative classifiers, it is not important that their component parameters be interpretable as probabilities; thus this restriction is probably unnecessary. Like for the generative models, another major difference is in the smoothing algorithms. We smooth the models both by fitting a gaussian prior hyper-parameter and by incorporating features of subsets of cliques. Smoothing in (Pernkopf and Bilmes, 2005) is done by substituting zero-valued parameters with a small fixed ϵ. Grossman and Domingos (2004) employ early stopping using held-out data which can achieve similar effects to smoothing with a gaussian prior.

To evaluate the importance of the differences between our algorithm and the ones presented in these works, and to evaluate the importance of fitting hyper-parameters for smoothing, we implemented a modified version of our structure search. The modifications were as follows. For Bayes Net structure learning: (*i*) no Witten-Bell smoothing is employed in the CPTs, and (*ii*) no backoffs to lower-order distributions are considered. The only smoothing remaining in the CPTs is an interpolation with a uniform distribution with a fixed weight of $\alpha = .1$. For discriminative log-linear model structure learning: (*i*) the gaussian prior was fixed to be very weak, serving only to keep the weights away from infinity ($\sigma = 100$) and (*ii*) the conjunction selection was restricted to correspond to a Bayes Net structure with no features for subsets of feature conjunctions. Thus the only difference between the class of our modified discriminative log-linear models and the class of models considered in (Pernkopf and Bilmes, 2005; Grossman and Domingos, 2004) is that we do not restrict the parameters to be interpretable as probabilities.

The results shown in Table 8 summarize the results obtained by the modified algorithm on the two tasks. Both the generative and discriminative learners suffered a statistically significant (at level .01) loss in performance. Notably, the log-linear model for PP attachment performs worse than logistic regression with better smoothing.

PP Attachment Results		
Model	**H-params**	**Test set acc**
Bayes Net	0	82.8
Log-linear model	0	81.2
SRL Classification Results		
Model	**H-params**	**Test set acc**
Bayes Net	0	92.5
Log-linear model	0	92.7

Table 8: Bayesian Network and Conditional log-linear model: PP & SRL classification results using minimal smoothing and no backoff to lower order distributions.

In summary, our results showed that by learning the structure for generative models, we can obtain models which are competitive with or better than corresponding discriminative models. We also showed the importance of employing sophisticated smoothing techniques in structure search algorithms for natural language classification tasks.

References

Xavier Carreras and Luís Màrquez. 2005. Introduction to the CoNLL-2005 shared task: Semantic role labeling. In *Proceedings of CoNLL*.

Eugene Charniak and Mark Johnson. 2005. Coarse-to-fi ne n-best parsing and MaxEnt discriminative reranking. In *Proceedings of ACL*.

Eugene Charniak. 2000. A maximum-entropy-inspired parser. In *Proceedings of NAACL*, pages 132–139.

Michael Collins and James Brooks. 1995. Prepositional attachment through a backed-off model. In *Proceedings of the Third Workshop on Very Large Corpora*, pages 27–38.

Michael Collins. 1997. Three generative, lexicalised models for statistical parsing. In *Proceedings of ACL*, pages 16–23.

Michael Collins. 2000. Discriminative reranking for natural language parsing. In *Proceedings of ICML*, pages 175–182.

Stephen Della Pietra, Vincent J. Della Pietra, and John D. Lafferty. 1997. Inducing features of random fi elds. *IEEE Transactions on Pattern Analysis and Machine Intelligence*, 19(4):380–393.

Nir Friedman and Moises Goldszmidt. 1996. Learning Bayesian networks with local structure. In *Proceeding of UAI*, pages 252–262.

Daniel Gildea and Daniel Jurafsky. 2002. Automatic labeling of semantic roles. *Computational Linguistics*, 28(3):245–288.

Joshua T. Goodman. 2001. A bit of progress in language modeling. In *MSR Technical Report MSR-TR-2001-72*.

Daniel Grossman and Pedro Domingos. 2004. Learning bayesian network classifi ers by maximizing conditional likelihood. In *Proceedings of ICML*, pages 361—368.

David Heckerman. 1999. A tutorial on learning with bayesian networks. In *Learning in Graphical Models*. MIT Press.

Donald Hindle and Mats Rooth. 1993. Structural ambiguity and lexical relations. *Computational Linguistics*, 19(1):103–120.

Mark Johnson. 2001. Joint and conditional estimation of tagging and parsing models. In *Proceedings of ACL*.

Dan Klein and Christopher Manning. 2002. Conditional structure versus conditional estimation in NLP models. In *Proceedings of EMNLP*.

John Lafferty, Andrew McCallum, and Fernando Pereira. 2001. Conditional random fi elds: Probabilistic models for segmenting and labeling sequence data. In *Proc. 18th International Conf. on Machine Learning*, pages 282–289. Morgan Kaufmann, San Francisco, CA.

Andrew McCallum. 2003. Effi ciently inducing features of conditional random fi elds. In *Proceedings of UAI*.

Andrew Ng and Michael Jordan. 2002. On discriminative vs. generative classifi ers: A comparison of logistic regression and Naive Bayes. In *NIPS 14*.

Franz Josef Och and Hermann Ney. 2002. Discriminative training and maximum entropy models for statistical machine translation. In *Proceedings of ACL*, pages 295–302.

Martha Palmer, Dan Gildea, and Paul Kingsbury. 2005. The proposition bank: An annotated corpus of semantic roles. *Computational Linguistics*.

Judea Pearl. 1988. *Probabilistic reasoning in intelligent systems: Networks of plausible inference*. Morgan Kaufmann.

Franz Pernkopf and Jeff Bilmes. 2005. Discriminative versus generative parameter and structure learning of bayesian network classifi ers. In *Proceedings of ICML*.

Sameer Pradhan, Kadri Hacioglu, Valerie Krugler, Wayne Ward, James Martin, and Dan Jurafsky. 2005a. Support vector learning for semantic argument classifi cation. *Machine Learning Journal*.

Sameer Pradhan, Wayne Ward, Kadri Hacioglu, James Martin, and Daniel Jurafsky. 2005b. Semantic role labeling using different syntactic views. In *Proceedings of ACL*.

Vasin Punyakanok, Dan Roth, and Wen tau Yih. 2005. The necessity of syntactic parsing for semantic role labeling. In *Proceedings of IJCAI*.

Rajat Raina, Yirong Shen, Andrew Y. Ng, and Andrew McCallum. 2004. Classifi cation with hybrid generative/discriminative models. In Sebastian Thrun, Lawrence Saul, and Bernhard Schölkopf, editors, *Advances in Neural Information Processing Systems 16*. MIT Press, Cambridge, MA.

Adwait Ratnaparkhi, Jeff Reynar, and Salim Roukos. 1994. A maximum entropy model for prepositional phrase attachment. In *Workshop on Human Language Technology*.

Brian Roark, Murat Saraclar, Michael Collins, and Mark Johnson. 2004. Discriminative language modeling with conditional random fi elds and the perceptron algorithm. In *Proceedings of ACL*.

Kristina Toutanova, Dan Klein, and Christopher D. Manning. 2003. Feature-rich part-of-speech tagging with a cyclic dependency network. In *Proceedings of HLT-NAACL*.

Kristina Toutanova, Aria Haghighi, and Christopher D. Manning. 2005. Joint learning improves semantic role labeling. In *Proceedings of ACL*.

Bram Vanschoenwinkel and Bernard Manderick. 2003. A weighted polynomial information gain kernel for resolving prepositional phrase attachment ambiguities with support vector machines. In *IJCAI*.

Ian H. Witten and Timothy C. Bell. 1991. The zero-frequency problem: Estimating the probabilities of novel events in adaptive text compression. *IEEE Transactions on Information Theory*, 37,4:1085–1094.

Nianwen Xue and Martha Palmer. 2004. Calibrating features for semantic role labeling. In *Proceedings of EMNLP*.

Two graph-based algorithms for state-of-the-art WSD

Eneko Agirre, David Martínez, Oier López de Lacalle and Aitor Soroa
IXA NLP Group
University of the Basque Country
Donostia, Basque Contry
a.soroa@si.ehu.es

Abstract

This paper explores the use of two graph algorithms for unsupervised induction and tagging of nominal word senses based on corpora. Our main contribution is the optimization of the free parameters of those algorithms and its evaluation against publicly available gold standards. We present a thorough evaluation comprising supervised and unsupervised modes, and both lexical-sample and all-words tasks. The results show that, in spite of the information loss inherent to mapping the induced senses to the gold-standard, the optimization of parameters based on a small sample of nouns carries over to all nouns, performing close to supervised systems in the lexical sample task and yielding the second-best WSD systems for the Senseval-3 all-words task.

1 Introduction

Word sense disambiguation (WSD) is a key enabling-technology. Supervised WSD techniques are the best performing in public evaluations, but need large amounts of hand-tagged data. Existing hand-annotated corpora like SemCor (Miller et al., 1993), which is annotated with WordNet senses (Fellbaum, 1998) allow for a small improvement over the simple most frequent sense heuristic, as attested in the all-words track of the last Senseval competition (Snyder and Palmer, 2004). In theory, larger amounts of training data (SemCor has approx. 700K words) would improve the performance of supervised WSD, but no current project exists to provide such an expensive resource.

Supervised WSD is based on the "fixed-list of senses" paradigm, where the senses for a target word are a closed list coming from a dictionary or lexicon. Lexicographers and semanticists have long warned about the problems of such an approach, where senses are listed separately as discrete entities, and have argued in favor of more complex representations, where, for instance, senses are dense regions in a continuum (Cruse, 2000).

Unsupervised WSD has followed this line of thinking, and tries to induce word senses directly from the corpus. Typical unsupervised WSD systems involve clustering techniques, which group together similar examples. Given a set of induced clusters (which represent word *uses* or senses[1]), each new occurrence of the target word will be compared to the clusters and the most similar cluster will be selected as its sense.

Most of the unsupervised WSD work has been based on the vector space model, where each example is represented by a vector of features (e.g. the words occurring in the context), and the induced senses are either clusters of examples (Schütze, 1998; Purandare and Pedersen, 2004) or clusters of words (Pantel and Lin, 2002). Recently, Véronis (Véronis, 2004) has proposed HyperLex, an application of graph models to WSD based on the small-world properties of cooccurrence graphs. Graph-based methods have gained attention in several areas of NLP, including knowledge-based WSD (Mihalcea, 2005; Navigli and Velardi, 2005) and summarization (Erkan and Radev, 2004; Mihalcea and Tarau, 2004).

The HyperLex algorithm presented in (Véronis, 2004) is entirely corpus-based. It builds a cooccurrence graph for all pairs of words cooccurring in the context of the target word. Véronis shows that this kind of graph fulfills the properties of small world graphs, and thus possesses highly connected

[1] Unsupervised WSD approaches prefer the term 'word uses' to 'word senses'. In this paper we use them interchangeably to refer to both the induced clusters, and to the word senses from some reference lexicon.

Proceedings of the 2006 Conference on Empirical Methods in Natural Language Processing (EMNLP 2006), pages 585–593,
Sydney, July 2006. ©2006 Association for Computational Linguistics

components (hubs) in the graph. These hubs eventually identify the main word uses (senses) of the target word, and can be used to perform word sense disambiguation. These hubs are used as a representation of the senses induced by the system, the same way that clusters of examples are used to represent senses in clustering approaches to WSD (Purandare and Pedersen, 2004).

One of the problems of unsupervised systems is that of managing to do a fair evaluation. Most of current unsupervised systems are evaluated in-house, with a brief comparison to a re-implementation of a former system, leading to a proliferation of unsupervised systems with little ground to compare among them.

In preliminary work (Agirre et al., 2006), we have shown that HyperLex compares favorably to other unsupervised systems. We defined a semi-supervised setting for optimizing the free-parameters of HyperLex on the Senseval-2 English Lexical Sample task (S2LS), which consisted on mapping the induced senses onto the official sense inventory using the training part of S2LS. The best parameters were then used on the Senseval-3 English Lexical Sample task (S3LS), where a similar semi-supervised method was used to output the official sense inventory.

This paper extends the previous work in several aspects. First of all, we adapted the PageRank graph-based method (Brin and Page, 1998) for WSD and compared it with HyperLex.

We also extend the previous evaluation scheme, using measures in the clustering community which only require a gold standard clustering and no mapping step. This allows for having a purely unsupervised WSD system, and at the same time comparing supervised and unsupervised systems according to clustering criteria.

We also include the Senseval-3 English All-words testbed (S3AW), where, in principle, unsupervised and semi-supervised systems have an advantage over purely supervised systems due to the scarcity of training data. We show that our system is competitive with supervised systems, ranking second.

This paper is structured as follows. We first present two graph-based algorithms, HyperLex and PageRank. Section 3 presents the two evaluation frameworks. Section 4 introduces parameter optimization. Section 5 shows the experimental setting and results. Section 6 analyzes the results and presents related work. Finally, we draw the conclusions and advance future work.

2 A graph algorithm for corpus-based WSD

The basic steps for our implementation of HyperLex and its variant using PageRank are common. We first build the cooccurrence graph, then we select the hubs that are going to represent the senses using two different strategies inspired by HyperLex and PageRank. We are then ready to use the induced senses to do word sense disambiguation.

2.1 Building cooccurrence graphs

For each word to be disambiguated, a text corpus is collected, consisting of the paragraphs where the word occurs. From this corpus, a cooccurrence graph for the target word is built. Vertices in the graph correspond to words[2] in the text (except the target word itself). Two words appearing in the same paragraph are said to cooccur, and are connected with edges. Each edge is assigned a weight which measures the relative frequency of the two words cooccurring. Specifically, let w_{ij} be the weight of the edge[3] connecting nodes i and j, then $w_{ij} = 1 - \max[P(i \mid j), P(j \mid i)]$, where $P(i \mid j) = \frac{\text{freq}_{ij}}{\text{freq}_j}$ and $P(j \mid i) = \frac{\text{freq}_{ij}}{\text{freq}_i}$.

The weight of an edge measures how tightly connected the two words are. Words which always occur together receive a weight of 0. Words rarely cooccurring receive weights close to 1.

2.2 Selecting hubs: HyperLex vs. PageRank

Once the cooccurrence graph is built, Véronis proposes a simple iterative algorithm to obtain its hubs. At each step, the algorithm finds the vertex with highest relative frequency[4] in the graph, and, if it meets some criteria, it is selected as a hub. These criteria are determined by a set of heuristic parameters, that will be explained later in Section 4. After a vertex is selected to be a hub, its neighbors are no longer eligible as hub candidates. At any time, if the next vertex candidate has a relative frequency below a certain threshold, the algorithm stops.

Another alternative is to use the PageRank algorithm (Brin and Page, 1998) for finding hubs in the

[2]Following Véronis, we only work on nouns.

[3]The cooccurrence graph is undirected, i.e. $w_{ij} = w_{ji}$

[4]In cooccurrence graphs, the relative frequency of a vertex and its degree are linearly related, and it is therefore possible to avoid the costly computation of the degree.

coocurrence graph. PageRank is an iterative algorithm that ranks all the vertices according to their relative importance within the graph following a random-walk model. In this model, a link between vertices v_1 and v_2 means that v_1 *recommends* v_2. The more vertices recommend v_2, the higher the rank of v_2 will be. Furthermore, the rank of a vertex depends not only on how many vertices point to it, but on the rank of these vertices as well.

Although PageRank was initially designed to work with directed graphs, and with no weights in links, the algorithm can be easily extended to model undirected graphs whose edges are weighted. Specifically, let $G = (V, E)$ be an undirected graph with the set of vertices V and set of edges E. For a given vertex v_i, let $\mathrm{In}(v_i)$ be the set of vertices pointing to it[5]. The rank of v_i is defined as:

$$P(v_i) = (1 - d) + d \sum_{j \in \mathrm{In}(v_i)} \frac{w_{ji}}{\sum_{k \in \mathrm{In}(v_j)} w_{jk}} P(v_j)$$

where w_{ij} is the weight of the link between vertices v_i and v_j, and $0 \leq d \leq 1$. d is called the *damping factor* and models the probability of a web surfer standing at a vertex to follow a link from this vertex (probability d) or to jump to a random vertex in the graph (probability $1 - d$). The factor is usually set at 0.85.

The algorithm initializes the ranks of the vertices with a fixed value (usually $\frac{1}{N}$ for a graph with N vertices) and iterates until convergence below a given threshold is achieved, or, more typically, until a fixed number of iterations are executed. Note that the convergence of the algorithms doesn't depend on the initial value of the ranks.

After running the algorithm, the vertices of the graph are ordered in decreasing order according to its rank, and a number of them are chosen as the main hubs of the word. The hubs finally selected depend again of some heuristics and will be described in section 4.

2.3 Using hubs for WSD

Once the hubs that represent the senses of the word are selected (following any of the methods presented in the last section), each of them is linked to the target word with edges weighting 0, and the *Minimum Spanning Tree* (MST) of the whole graph is calculated and stored.

[5] As G is undirected, the in-degree of a vertex v is equal to its out-degree.

The MST is then used to perform word sense disambiguation, in the following way. For every instance of the target word, the words surrounding it are examined and looked up in the MST. By construction of the MST, words in it are placed under exactly one hub. Each word in the context receives a set of scores s, with one score per hub, where all scores are 0 except the one corresponding to the hub where it is placed. If the scores are organized in a score vector, all values are 0, except, say, the i-th component, which receives a score $d(h_i, v)$, which is the distance between the hub h_i and the node representing the word v. Thus, $d(h_i, v)$ assigns a score of 1 to hubs and the score decreases as the nodes move away from the hub in the tree.

For a given occurrence of the target word, the score vectors of all the words in the context are added, and the hub that receives the maximum score is chosen.

3 Evaluating unsupervised WSD systems

All unsupervised WSD algorithms need some addition in order to be evaluated. One alternative, as in (Véronis, 2004), is to manually decide the correctness of the hubs assigned to each occurrence of the words. This approach has two main disadvantages. First, it is expensive to manually verify each occurrence of the word, and different runs of the algorithm need to be evaluated in turn. Second, it is not an easy task to manually decide if an occurrence of a word effectively corresponds with the use of the word the assigned hub refers to, specially considering that the person is given a short list of words linked to the hub. Besides, it is widely acknowledged that people are leaned not to contradict the proposed answer.

A second alternative is to evaluate the system according to some performance in an application, e.g. information retrieval (Schütze, 1998). This is a very attractive idea, but requires expensive system development and it is sometimes difficult to separate the reasons for the good (or bad) performance.

A third alternative would be to devise a method to map the hubs (clusters) returned by the system to the senses in a lexicon. Pantel and Lin (2002) automatically mapped the senses to WordNet, and then measured the quality of the mapping. More recently, tagged corpora have been used to map the induced senses, and then compare the systems over publicly available benchmarks (Purandare and Pedersen, 2004; Niu et al., 2005; Agirre et al., 2006), which offers the advantage of comparing to other systems, but converts the whole system into semi-supervised. See Section 5 for more details on these systems. Note that the mapping introduces noise and information loss, which is a disadvantage when comparing to other systems that rely on the gold-standard senses.

Yet another possibility is to evaluate the induced senses against a gold standard as a clustering task. Induced senses are clusters, gold standard senses are classes, and measures from the clustering literature like entropy or purity can be used. In this case the manually tagged corpus is taken to be the gold standard, where a class is the set of examples tagged with a sense.

We decided to adopt the last two alternatives, since they allow for comparison over publicly available systems of any kind.

3.1 Evaluation of clustering: hubs as clusters

In this setting the selected hubs are treated as clusters of examples and gold standard senses are classes. In order to compare the clusters with the classes, hand annotated corpora are needed (for instance Senseval). The test set is first tagged with the induced senses. A perfect clustering solution will be the one where each cluster has exactly the same examples as one of the classes, and vice versa. The evaluation is completely unsupervised.

Following standard cluster evaluation practice (Zhao and Karypis, 2005), we consider three measures: entropy, purity and Fscore. The entropy measure considers how the various classes of objects are distributed within each cluster. In general, the smaller the entropy value, the better the clustering algorithm performs. The purity measure considers the extent to which each cluster contained objects from primarily one class. The larger the values of purity, the better the clustering algorithm performs. The Fscore is used in a similar fashion to Information Retrieval exercises, with precision and recall defined as the percentage of correctly "retrieved" examples for a cluster (divided by total cluster size), and recall as the percentage of correctly "retrieved" examples for a cluster (divided by total class size). For a formal definition refer to (Zhao and Karypis, 2005). If the clustering is identical to the original classes in the datasets, FScore will be equal to one which means that the higher the FScore, the better the clustering is.

3.2 Evaluation as supervised WSD: mapping hubs to senses

(Agirre et al., 2006) presents a straightforward framework that uses hand-tagged material in order to map the induced senses into the senses used in a gold standard . The WSD system first tags the training part of some hand-annotated corpus with the induced hubs. The hand labels are then used to construct a matrix relating assigned hubs to existing senses, simply counting the times an occurrence with sense s_j has been assigned hub h_i. In the testing step we apply the WSD algorithm over the test corpus, using the hubs-to-senses matrix to select the sense with highest weights. See (Agirre et al., 2006) for further details.

4 Tuning the parameters

The behavior of the original HyperLex algorithm was influenced by a set of heuristic parameters, which were set by Véronis following his intuition. In (Agirre et al., 2006) we tuned the parameters using the mapping strategy for evaluation. We set a range for each of the parameters, and evaluated the algorithm for each combination of the parameters on a fixed set of words (S2LS), which was different from the final test sets (S3LS and S3AW). This ensures that the chosen parameter set can be used for any noun, and is not overfitted to a small set of nouns.

In this paper, we perform the parameter tuning according to four different criteria, i.e., best supervised performance and best unsupervised entropy/purity/FScore performance. At the end, we have four sets of parameters (those that obtained the best results in S2LS for each criterion), and each set is then selected to be run against the S3LS and S3AW datasets.

The parameters of the graph-based algorithm can be divided in two sets: those that affect how the cooccurrence graph is built (p1–p4 below), and those that control the way the hubs are extracted from it (p5–p8 below).

- p1 Minimum frequency of edges (occurrences)
- p2 Minimum frequency of vertices (words)
- p3 Edges with weights above this value are removed
- p4 Context containing fewer words are not processed
- p5 Minimum number of adjacent vertices in a hub
- p6 Max. mean weight of the adjacent vertices of a hub
- p7 Minimum frequency of hubs
- p8 Number of selected hubs

	Vr	Vr_opt Range	Best	Pr_fr (p7) and Pr_fx (p8) Range	Best
p1	5	1-3	1	1-3	2
p2	10	2-4	3	2-4	3
p3	.9	.3-.7	.4	.4-.5	.5
p4	4	4	4	4	4
p5	6	1-7	1	–	–
p6	.8	.6-.95	.95	–	–
p7	.001	.0009-.003	.001	.0015-.0025	.0016
p8	–	–	–	50-65	55

Table 1: Parameters of the HyperLex algorithm

Both strategies to select hubs from the coocurrence graph (cf. Sect. 2.2) share parameters p1–p4. The algorithm proposed by Véronis uses p5–p6 as requirements for hubs, and p7 as the threshold to stop looking for more hubs: candidates with frequency below p7 are not eligible to be hubs.

Regarding PageRank the original formulation does not have any provision for determining which are hubs and which not, it just returns a weighted list of vertices. We have experimented with two methods: a threshold for the frequency of the hubs (as before, p7), and a fixed number of hubs for every target word (p8). For a shorthand we use Vr for Veronis' original formulation with default parameters, Vr_opt for optimized parameters, and Pr_fr and Pr_fx respectively for the two ways of using PageRank.

Table 1 lists the parameters of the HyperLex algorithm, with the default values proposed for them in the original work (second column), the ranges that we explored, and the optimal values according to the supervised recall evaluation (cf. Sect. 3.1). For Vr_opt we tried 6700 combinations. PageRank has less parameters, and we also used the previous optimization of Vr_opt to limit the range of p4, so Pr_fr and Pr_fx get respectively 180 and 288 combinations.

5 Experiment setting and results

To evaluate the HyperLex algorithm in a standard benchmark, we will first focus on a more extensive evaluation of S3LS and then see the results in S3AW (cf. Sec. 5.4). Following the design for evaluation explained in Section 3, we use the standard train-test split for the supervised evaluation, while the unsupervised evaluation only uses the test part.

Table 2 shows the results of the 4 variants of our algorithm. Vr stands for the original Veronis algorithm with default parameters, Vr_opt to our optimized version, and Pr_fr and Pr_fx to the two variants of PageRank. In the columns we find the evaluation results according to our 4 criteria. For supervised evaluation we indicate only recall, which in our case equals precision, as the coverage is 100% in all cases (values returned by the official Senseval scorer). We also include 2 baselines, a system returning a single cluster (that of the most frequent sense, MFS), and another returning one cluster for each example (1ex-1hub). The last rows list the results for 3 supervised and 5 unsupervised systems (see Sect. 5.1). We will comment on the result of this table from different perspectives.

	Sup. Rec.	Unsupervised Entr.	Pur.	FS
Vr	59.9	50.3	58.2	**44.1**
Vr_opt	**64.6**	**18.3**	**78.5**	35.0
Pr_fr	64.5	18.7	77.2	34.3
Pr_fx	62.2	25.4	72.2	33.3
1ex-1hub	40.1	0.0	100.0	14.5
MFS	54.5	53.2	52.8	28.3
S3LS-best	**72.9**	**19.9**	**67.3**	**63.8**
kNN-all	70.6	21.2	64.0	60.6
kNN-BoW	63.5	22.6	61.1	57.1
Cymfony (10%-S3LS)	**57.9**	**25.0**	**55.7**	**52.0**
Prob0 (MFS-S3)	54.2	28.8	49.3	46.0
clr04 (MFS-Sc)	48.8	25.8	52.5	46.2
Ciaosenso (MFS-Sc)	48.7	28.0	50.3	48.8
duluth-senserelate	47.5	27.2	51.1	44.9

Table 2: Results for the nouns in S3LS using the 4 methods (Vr, Vr_opt, Pr_fr and Pr_fx). Each of the methods was optimized in S2LS using the 4 evaluation criteria (Supervised recall, Entropy, Purity and Fscore) and evaluated on S3LS according to the respective evaluation criteria (in the columns). Two baselines, plus 3 supervised and 5 unsupervised systems are also shown. Bold is used for best results in each category.

5.1 Supervised evaluation

In this subsection we will focus in the first four evaluation rows in Table 2. All variants of the algorithm outperform by an ample margin the MFS and the 1ex-1hub baselines when evaluated on S3LS recall. This means that the method is able to learn useful hubs. Note that we perform this supervised evaluation just for comparison with other systems, and to prove that we are able to provide high performance WSD.

The default parameter setting (Vr) gets the worst results, followed by the fixed-hub implementation of PageRank (Pr_fx). Pagerank with frequency threshold (Pr_fr) and the optimized Veronis (Vr_opt) obtain a 10 point improvement over the MFS baseline with very similar results (the difference is not statistically significant according to McNemar's test at 95% confidence level).

Table 2 also shows the results of three supervised systems. These results (and those of the other unsupervised systems in the table) where obtained from the Senseval website, and the only processing we did was to filter nouns. S3LS-best stands for the the winner of S3LS (Mihalcea et al., 2004), which is 8.3 points over our method. We also include the results of two of our in-house systems. kNN-all is a state-of-the-art system (Agirre et al., 2005) using wide range of local and topical features, and only 2.3 points below the best S3LS system. kNN-BoW which is the same supervised system, but restricted to bag-of-words features only, which are the ones used by our graph-based systems. The table shows that Vr_opt and Pr_fr are one single point from kNN-BoW, which is an impressive result if we take into account the information loss of the mapping step and that we tuned our parameters on a different set of words.

The last 5 rows of Table 2 show several unsupervised systems, all of which except Cymfony (Niu et al., 2005) and (Purandare and Pedersen, 2004) participated in S3LS (check (Mihalcea et al., 2004) for further details on the systems). We classify them according to the amount of "supervision" they have: some have access to most-frequent information (MFS-S3 if counted over S3LS, MFS-Sc if counted over SemCor), some use 10% of the S3LS training part for mapping (10%-S3LS). Only one system (Duluth) did not use in any way hand-tagged corpora.

The table shows that Vr_opt and Pr_fr are more than 6 points above the other unsupervised systems, but given the different typology of unsupervised systems, it's unfair to draw definitive conclusions from a raw comparison of results. The system coming closer to ours is that described in (Niu et al., 2005). They use hand tagged corpora which does not need to include the target word to tune the parameters of a rather complex clustering method which does use local features. They do use the S3LS training corpus for mapping. For every sense of the target word, three of its contexts in the train corpus are gathered (around 10% of the training data) and tagged. Each cluster is then related with its most frequent sense. The mapping method is similar to ours, but we use all the available training data and allow for different hubs to be assigned to the same sense.

Another system similar to ours is (Purandare and Pedersen, 2004), which unfortunately was evaluated on Senseval 2 data and is not included in the table. The authors use first and second order bag-of-word context features to represent each instance of the corpus. They apply several clustering algorithms based on the vector space model, limiting the number of clusters to 7. They also use all available training data for mapping, but given their small number of clusters they opt for a one-to-one mapping which maximizes the assignment and discards the less frequent clusters. They also discard some difficult cases, like senses and words with low frequencies (10% of total occurrences and 90, respectively). The different test set and mapping system make the comparison difficult, but the fact that the best of their combinations beats MFS by 1 point on average (47.6% vs. 46.4%) for the selected nouns and senses make us think that our results are more robust (nearly 10% over MFS).

5.2 Clustering evaluation

The three columns corresponding to fully unsupervised evaluation in Table 2 show that all our 3 optimized variants easily outperform the MFS baseline. The best results are in this case for the optimized Veronis, followed closely by Pagerank with frequency threshold.

The comparison with the supervised and unsupervised systems shows that our system gets better entropy and purity values, but worse FScore. This can be explained by the bias of entropy and purity towards smaller and more numerous clusters. In fact the 1ex-1hub baseline obtains the best entropy and purity scores. Our graph-based system tends to induce a large number of senses (with averages of 60 to 70 senses). On the other hand FScore penalizes the systems inducing a different number of clusters. As the supervised and unsupervised systems were designed to return the same (or similar) number of senses as in the gold standard, they attain higher FScores. This motivated us to compare the results of the best parameters across evaluation methods.

5.3 Comparison across evaluation methods

Table 3 shows all 16 evaluation possibilities for each variant of the algorithm, depending of the evaluation criteria used in S2LS (in the rows) and the evaluation criteria used in S3LS (in the columns). This table shows that the best results (in bold for each variant) tend to be in the diagonal, that is, when the same evaluation criterion is used for optimization and test, but it is not decisive. If we take the first row (supervised evaluation) as the most credible criterion, we can see that optimizing according to entropy and purity get similar and sometimes better result (Pr_fr and Pr_fx). On the contrary the Fscore yields worse results by far.

This indicates that a purely unsupervised system evaluated according to the gold standard (based on entropy or purity) yields optimal parameters similar to the supervised (mapped) version. This is an important result, as it shows that the quality in performance does not come from the mapping step, but from the algorithm and optimal parameter setting. The table shows that optimization on purity and entropy criteria do correlate with good performance in the supervised evaluation.

The failure of FScore based optimization, in our opinion, indicates that our clustering algorithm prefers smaller and more numerous clusters, compared to the gold standard. FScore prefers clustering solutions that have a similar number of clusters to that of the gold standard, but it is unable to drive the optimization or our algorithm towards good results in the supervised evaluation.

All in all, the best results are attained with smaller and more numerous hubs, a kind of micro-senses. This effect is the same for all three variants tried and all evaluation criteria, with Fscore yielding less clusters. At first we were uncomfortable with this behavior, so we checked whether HyperLex was degenerating into a trivial solution. This was the main reason to include the 1ex-1hub baseline, which simulates a clustering algorithm returning one hub per example, and its precision was 40.1, well below the MFS baseline. We also realized that our results are in accordance with some theories of word meaning, e.g. the "indefinitely large set of prototypes-within-prototypes" envisioned in (Cruse, 2000). Ted Pedersen has also observed a similar behaviour in his vector-space model clustering experiments (PC). We now think that the idea of having many micro-senses is attractive for further exploration, specially if we are able to organize them into coarser hubs in future work.

		Sup.	Unsupervised		
Alg.	Opt.	Rec.	Entr.	Pur.	FS
Vr	Sup	**64.6**	18.4	77.9	30.0
	Ent	**64.6**	**18.3**	78.3	29.1
	Pur	63.7	19.0	**78.5**	30.8
	Fsc	60.4	38.2	63.5	**35.0**
Pr_fr	Sup	64.5	20.8	76.1	28.6
	Ent	64.6	**18.7**	**77.7**	27.2
	Pur	**64.7**	19.3	77.2	27.6
	Fsc	61.2	36.0	65.2	**34.3**
Pr_fx	Sup	62.2	28.2	69.3	29.5
	Ent	**63.1**	**25.4**	**72.2**	28.4
	Pur	**63.1**	**25.4**	**72.2**	28.4
	Fsc	54.5	32.9	66.5	**33.3**

Table 3: Cross-evaluation comparison. In the rows the evaluation method for optmizing over S2LS is shown, and in the columns the result over S3LS according to the different evaluation methods.

	recall
kuaw	70.9
Pr_fr	70.7
Vr_opt	70.1
GAMBL	70.1
MFS	69.9
LCCaw	68.6

Table 4: Results for the nouns in S3AW, compared to the most frequent baseline and the top three supervised systems

5.4 S3AW task

In the Senseval-3 all-words task (Snyder and Palmer, 2004) all words in three document excerpts need to be disambiguated. Given the scarce amount of training data available in Semcor (Miller et al., 1993), supervised systems barely improve upon the simple most frequent heuristic. In this setting the unsupervised evaluation schemes are not feasible, as many of the target words occur only once, so we used the mapping strategy with Semcor to produce the required WordNet senses in the output.

Table 4 shows the results for our systems with the best parameters according to the supervised criterion on S2LS, plus the top three S3AW supervised systems and the most frequent sense heuristic. In order to focus the comparison, we only kept noun occurrences of all systems and filtered out multiwords, target words with two different lemmas and unknown tags, leaving a total of 857 occurrences of nouns. We can see that Pr_fr is only 0.2 from the S3AW winning system, demonstrating that our unsupervised graph-based systems that use Semcor for mapping are nearly equivalent to the most powerful supervised systems to date. In fact, the differences in performance for the systems are not statistically significant (McNemar's test at 95% significance level).

6 Conclusions and further work

This paper has explored the use of two graph algorithms for corpus-based disambiguation of nominal senses. We have shown that the parameter optimization learnt over a small set of nouns significantly improves the performance for all nouns, and produces a system which (1) in a lexical-sample setting (Senseval 3 dataset) is 10 points over the Most-Frequent-Sense baseline, 1 point over a supervised system using the same kind of information (i.e. bag-of-words features), and 8 points below the best supervised system, and (2) in the all-words setting is à la par the best supervised system. The performance of PageRank is statistically the same as that of HyperLex, with the advantage of PageRank of using less parameters.

In order to compete on the same test set as supervised systems, we do use hand-tagged data, but only to do the mapping from the induced senses into the gold standard senses. In fact, we believe that using our WSD system as a purely unsupervised system (i.e. returning just hubs), the perfomance would be higher, as we would avoid the information loss in the mapping. We would like to test this on Information Retrieval, perhaps on a setting similar to that of (Schütze, 1998), which would allow for an indirect evaluation of the quality and a comparison with supervised WSD system on the same grounds.

We have also shown that the optimization according to purity and entropy values (which does not need the supervised mapping step) yields very good parameters, comparable to those obtained in the supervised optimization strategy. This indicates that we are able to optimize the algorithm in a completely unsupervised fashion for a small number of words, and then carry over to tag new text with the induced senses.

Regarding efficiency, our implementation of HyperLex is extremely fast. Trying the 6700 combinations of parameters takes 5 hours in a 2 AMD Opteron processors at 2GHz and 3Gb RAM. A single run (building the MST, mapping and tagging the test sentences) takes only 16 sec. For this reason, even if an on-line version would be in principle desirable, we think that this batch version is readily usable as a standalone word sense disambiguation system.

Both graph-based methods and vector-based clustering methods rely on local information, typically obtained by the occurrences of neighbor words in context. The advantage of graph-based techniques over over vector-based clustering might come from the fact that the former are able to measure the relative importance of a vertex in the whole graph, and thus combine both local and global cooccurrence information.

For the future, we would like to look more closely the micro-senses induced by HyperLex, and see if we can group them into coarser clusters. We would also like to integrate different kinds of information, specially the local or syntactic features so successfully used by supervised systems, but also more heterogeneous information from knowledge bases.

Graph models have been very successful in some settings (e.g. the PageRank algorithm of Google), and have been rediscovered recently for natural language tasks like knowledge-based WSD, textual entailment, summarization and dependency parsing. Now that we have set a robust optimization and evaluation framework we would like to test other such algorithms (e.g. HITS (Kleinberg, 1999)) in the same conditions.

Acknowledgements

Oier Lopez de Lacalle enjoys a PhD grant from the Basque Government. We thank the comments of the three anonymous reviewers.

References

E. Agirre, O. Lopez de Lacalle, and D. Martinez. 2005. Exploring feature spaces with svd and unlabeled data for word sense disambiguation. In *Proc. of RANLP*.

E. Agirre, O. Lopez de Lacalle, D. Martinez, and A. Soroa. 2006. Evaluating and optimizing the parameters of an unsupervised graph-based wsd algorithm. In *Proc. of the NAACL Texgraphs workshop*.

S. Brin and L. Page. 1998. The anatomy of a large-scale hypertextual web search engine. *Computer Networks and ISDN Systems*, 30(1-7).

D. A. Cruse, 2000. *Polysemy: Theoretical and Computational Approaches*, chapter Aspects of the Micro-structure of Word Meanings, pages 31–51. OUP.

G Erkan and D. R. Radev. 2004. Lexrank: Graph-based centrality as salience in text summarization. *Journal of Artificial Intelligence Research (JAIR)*.

C. Fellbaum. 1998. *WordNet: An Electronic Lexical Database*. MIT Press.

Jon M. Kleinberg. 1999. Authoritative sources in a hyperlinked environment. *Journal of the ACM*, 46(5):604–632.

R. Mihalcea and P Tarau. 2004. Textrank: Bringing order into texts. In *Proc. of EMNLP2004*.

R. Mihalcea, T. Chklovski, and A. Kilgarriff. 2004. The senseval-3 english lexical sample task. In R. Mihalcea and P. Edmonds, editors, *Senseval-3 proccedings*, pages 25–28. ACL, July.

R. Mihalcea. 2005. Unsupervised large-vocabulary word sense disambiguation with graph-based algorithms for sequence data labeling. In *Proc. of EMNLP2005*.

G.A. Miller, C. Leacock, R. Tengi, and R.Bunker. 1993. A semantic concordance. In *Proc. of the ARPA HLT workshop*.

R. Navigli and P. Velardi. 2005. Structural semantic interconnections: a knowledge-based approach to word sense disambiguation. *IEEE Transactions on Pattern Analysis and Machine Intelligence*, 7(27):1063–1074, June.

C. Niu, W. Li, R. K. Srihari, and H. Li. 2005. Word independent context pair classification model for word sense disambiguation. In *Proc. of CoNLL-2005*.

P. Pantel and D. Lin. 2002. Discovering word senses from text. In *Proc. of KDD02*.

A. Purandare and T. Pedersen. 2004. Word sense discrimination by clustering contexts in vector and similarity spaces. In *Proc. of CoNLL-2004*, pages 41–48.

H. Schütze. 1998. Automatic word sense discrimination. *Computational Linguistics*, 24(1):97–123.

B. Snyder and M. Palmer. 2004. The english all-words task. In *Proc. of SENSEVAL*.

J. Véronis. 2004. Hyperlex: lexical cartography for information retrieval. *Computer Speech & Language*, 18(3):223–252.

Y Zhao and G Karypis. 2005. Hierarchical clustering algorithms for document datasets. *Data Mining and Knowledge Discovery*, 10(2):141–168.

Broad-Coverage Sense Disambiguation and Information Extraction with a Supersense Sequence Tagger*

Massimiliano Ciaramita
Inst. of Cognitive Science and Technology
Italian National Research Council
m.ciaramita@istc.cnr.it

Yasemin Altun
Toyota Technological Institute
at Chicago
altun@tti-c.org

Abstract

In this paper we approach word sense disambiguation and information extraction as a unified tagging problem. The task consists of annotating text with the tagset defined by the 41 Wordnet supersense classes for nouns and verbs. Since the tagset is directly related to Wordnet synsets, the tagger returns partial word sense disambiguation. Furthermore, since the noun tags include the standard named entity detection classes – person, location, organization, time, etc. – the tagger, as a by-product, returns extended named entity information. We cast the problem of supersense tagging as a sequential labeling task and investigate it empirically with a discriminatively-trained Hidden Markov Model. Experimental evaluation on the main sense-annotated datasets available, i.e., Semcor and Senseval, shows considerable improvements over the best known "first-sense" baseline.

1 Introduction

Named entity recognition (NER) is the most studied *information extraction* (IE) task. NER typically focuses on detecting instances of "person", "location", "organization" names and optionally instances of "miscellaneous" or "time" categories. The scalability of statistical NER allowed researchers to apply it successfully on large collections of newswire text, in several languages, and biomedical literature. Newswire NER performance, in terms of F-score, is in the upper 80s (Carreras et al., 2002; Florian et al., 2003), while Bio-NER accuracy ranges between the low 70s and 80s, depending on the data-set used for training/evaluation (Dingare et al., 2005). One shortcoming of NER is its over-simplified ontological model, leaving instances of other potentially informative categories unidentified. Hence, the utility of named entity information is limited. In addition, instances to be detected are mainly restricted to (sequences of) proper nouns.

Word sense disambiguation (WSD) is the task of deciding the intended sense for ambiguous words in context. With respect to NER, WSD lies at the other end of the semantic tagging spectrum, since the dictionary defines tens of thousand of very specific word senses, including NER categories. Wordnet (Fellbaum, 1998)[1], possibly the most used resource for WSD, defines word senses for verbs, common and proper nouns. Word sense disambiguation, at this level of granularity, is a complex task which resisted all attempts of robust broad-coverage solutions. Many distinctions are too subtle to be captured automatically, and the magnitude of the class space – several orders larger than NER's – makes it hard to approach the problem with sophisticated, but scalable, machine learning methods. Lastly, even if the methods would scale up, there are not enough manually tagged data, at the word sense level, for training a model. The performance of state of the art WSD systems on realistic evaluations is only comparable to the "first sense" baseline (cf. Section 5.3). Notwithstanding much research, the benefits of disambiguated lexical information for language processing are still mostly speculative.

This paper presents a novel approach to broad-

*The first author is now at Yahoo! Research. The tagger described in this paper is free software and can be downloaded from http://www.loa-cnr.it/ciaramita.html.

[1]When referring to Wordnet, throughout the paper, we mean Wordnet version 2.0.

Proceedings of the 2006 Conference on Empirical Methods in Natural Language Processing (EMNLP 2006), pages 594–602, Sydney, July 2006.

NOUNS			
SUPERSENSE	NOUNS DENOTING	SUPERSENSE	NOUNS DENOTING
act	acts or actions	object	natural objects (not man-made)
animal	animals	quantity	quantities and units of measure
artifact	man-made objects	phenomenon	natural phenomena
attribute	attributes of people and objects	plant	plants
body	body parts	possession	possession and transfer of possession
cognition	cognitive processes and contents	process	natural processes
communication	communicative processes and contents	person	people
event	natural events	relation	relations between people or things or ideas
feeling	feelings and emotions	shape	two and three dimensional shapes
food	foods and drinks	state	stable states of affairs
group	groupings of people or objects	substance	substances
location	spatial position	time	time and temporal relations
motive	goals	Tops	abstract terms for unique beginners
VERBS			
SUPERSENSE	VERBS OF	SUPERSENSE	VERBS OF
body	grooming, dressing and bodily care	emotion	feeling
change	size, temperature change, intensifying	motion	walking, flying, swimming
cognition	thinking, judging, analyzing, doubting	perception	seeing, hearing, feeling
communication	telling, asking, ordering, singing	possession	buying, selling, owning
competition	fighting, athletic activities	social	political and social activities and events
consumption	eating and drinking	stative	being, having, spatial relations
contact	touching, hitting, tying, digging	weather	raining, snowing, thawing, thundering
creation	sewing, baking, painting, performing		

Table 1. Nouns and verbs supersense labels, and short description (from the Wordnet documentation).

coverage information extraction and word sense disambiguation. Our goal is to simplify the disambiguation task, for both nouns and verbs, to a level at which it can be approached as any other tagging problem, and can be solved with state of the art methods. As a by-product, this task includes and extends NER. We define a tagset based on Wordnet's lexicographers classes, or *supersenses* (Ciaramita and Johnson, 2003), cf. Table 1. The size of the supersense tagset allows us to adopt a structured learning approach, which takes local dependencies between labels into account. To this extent, we cast the supersense tagging problem as a sequence labeling task and train a discriminative Hidden Markov Model (HMM), based on that of Collins (2002), on the manually annotated Semcor corpus (Miller et al., 1993). In two experiments we evaluate the accuracy of the tagger on the Semcor corpus itself, and on the English "all words" Senseval 3 shared task data (Snyder and Palmer, 2004). The model outperforms remarkably the best known baseline, the first sense heuristic – to the best of our knowledge, for the first time on the most realistic "all words" evaluation setting.

The paper is organized as follows. Section 2 introduces the tagset, Section 3 discusses related work and Section 4 the learning model. Section 5 reports on experimental settings and results. In Section 6 we summarize our contribution and consider directions for further research.

2 Supersense tagset

Wordnet (Fellbaum, 1998) is a broad-coverage machine-readable dictionary which includes 11,306 verbs mapped to 13,508 word senses, called *synsets*, and 114,648 common and proper nouns mapped to 79,689 synsets. Each noun or verb synset is associated with one of 41 broad semantic categories, in order to organize the lexicographer's work of updating and managing the lexicon (see Table 1). Since each lexicographer category groups together many synsets they have been also called *supersenses* (Ciaramita and Johnson, 2003). There are 26 supersenses for nouns, 15 for verbs. This coarse-grained ontology has a number of attractive features, for the purpose of natural language processing. First, the small size of the set makes it possible to build a single tagger which has positive consequences on robustness. Second, classes, although fairly general, are easily recognizable and not too abstract or vague. More importantly, similar word senses tend to be merged together.

As an example, Table 2 summarizes all senses of the noun "box". The 10 synsets are mapped to 6 supersenses: "artifact", "quantity", "shape", "state", "plant", and "act". Three similar senses (2), (7) and (9), and the probably related (8), are merged in the "artifact" supersense. This process can help disambiguation because it removes sub-

1. {box} (container) "he rummaged through a box of spare parts" - n.artifact
2. {box, loge} (private area in a theater or grandstand where a small group can watch the performance) "the royal box was empty" - n.artifact
3. {box, boxful} (the quantity contained in a box) "he gave her a box of chocolates" - n.quantity
4. {corner, box} (a predicament from which a skillful or graceful escape is impossible) "his lying got him into a tight corner" - n.state
5. {box} (a rectangular drawing) "the flowchart contained many boxes" - n.shape
6. {box, boxwood} (evergreen shrubs or small trees) - n.plant
7. {box} (any one of several designated areas on a ball field where the batter or catcher or coaches are positioned) "the umpire warned the batter to stay in the batter's box" - n.artifact
8. {box, box seat} (the driver's seat on a coach) "an armed guard sat in the box with the driver" - n.artifact
9. {box} (separate partitioned area in a public place for a few people) "the sentry stayed in his box to avoid the cold" - n.artifact
10. {box} (a blow with the hand (usually on the ear)) "I gave him a good box on the ear" - n.act

Table 2. The noun "box" in Wordnet: each line lists one synset, the set of synonyms, a definition, an optional example sentence, and the supersense label.

tle distinctions, which are hard to discriminate and increase the size of the class space. One possible drawback is that senses which one might want to keep separate, e.g., the most common sense box/container (1), can be collapsed with others. One might argue that all "artifact" senses share semantic properties which differentiate them from the other senses and can support useful semantic inferences. Unfortunately, there are no general solutions to the problem of sense granularity. However, major senses identified by Wordnet are maintained at the supersense level. Hence, supersense-disambiguated words are also, at least partially, synset-disambiguated.

Since Wordnet includes both proper and common nouns, the new tagset suggests an extended notion of named entity. As well as the usual NER categories, "person", "group", "location", and "time"[2], supersenses include categories such as artifacts, which can be fairly frequent, but usually neglected. To a greater extent than in standard NER, research in Bio-NER has focused on the adoption of richer ontologies for information extraction. Genia (Ohta et al., 2002), for example, is an ontology of 46 classes – with annotated corpus – designed for supporting information extraction in the molecular biology domain. In addition, there is growing interest for extracting *relations* between entities, as a more useful type of IE (cf. (Rosario and Hearst, 2004)).

Supersense tagging is inspired by similar considerations, but in a domain-independent setting; e.g., verb supersenses can label semantic interactions between nominal concepts. The following sentence (Example 1), extracted from the data – further described in Section 5.1 – shows the information captured by the supersense tagset:

(1) *Clara Harris*$_{n.person}$, one of the *guests*$_{n.person}$ in the *box*$_{n.artifact}$, *stood up*$_{v.motion}$ and *demanded*$_{v.communication}$ *water*$_{n.substance}$.

As Example 1 shows there is more information that can be extracted from a sentence than just the names; e.g. the fact that "Clara Harris" and the following "guests" are both tagged as "person" might suggest some sort of co-referentiality, while the coordination of verbs of motion and communication, as in "stood up and demanded", might be useful for language modeling purposes. In such a setting, structured learning methods, e.g., sequential, can help tagging by taking the senses of the neighboring words into account.

3 Related Work

Sequential models are common in NER, POS tagging, shallow parsing, etc.. Most of the work in WSD, instead, has focused on labeling each word individually, possibly revising the assignments of senses at the document level; e.g., following the "one sense per discourse" hypothesis (Gale et al., 1992). Although it seems reasonable to assume that occurrences of word senses in a sentence can be correlated, hence that structured learning methods could be successful, there has not been much work on sequential WSD. Segond et al. (1997) are possibly the first to have applied an HMM tagger to semantic disambiguation. Interestingly, to make the method more tractable, they also used the supersense tagset and estimated the model on Semcor. By cross-validation they show a marked improvement over the first sense baseline. However, in (Segond et al., 1997) the tagset is used differently, by defining equivalence classes of words with the same set of senses. From a similar perspective, de Loupy et al. (de Loupy et al., 1998)

[2]The supersense category "group" is rather a superordinate of "organization" and has wider scope.

also investigated the potential advantages of using HMMs for disambiguation. More recently, variants of the generative HMM have been applied to WSD (Molina et al., 2002; Molina et al., 2004) and evaluated also on Senseval data, showing performance comparable to the first sense baseline.

Previous work on prediction at the supersense level (Ciaramita and Johnson, 2003; Curran, 2005) has focused on lexical acquisition (nouns exclusively), thus aiming at word type classification rather than tagging. As far as applications are concerned, it has been shown that supersense information can support supervised WSD, by providing a partial disambiguation step (Ciaramita et al., 2003). In syntactic parse re-ranking supersenses have been used to build useful latent semantic features (Koo and Collins, 2005). We believe that supersense tagging has the potential to be useful, in combination with other sources of information such as part of speech, domain-specific NER models, chunking or shallow parsing, in tasks such as question answering and information extraction and retrieval, where large amounts of text need to be processed. It is also possible that this kind of shallow semantic information can help building more sophisticated linguistic analysis as in full syntactic parsing and semantic role labeling.

4 Sequence Tagging

We take a sequence labeling approach to learning a model for supersense tagging. Our goal is to learn a function from input vectors, the observations from labeled data, to response variables, the supersense labels. POS tagging, shallow parsing, NP-chunking and NER are all examples of sequence labeling tasks in which performance can be significantly improved by optimizing the choice of labeling over whole sequences of words, rather than individual words. The limitations of the generative approach to sequence tagging, i. e. Hidden Markov Models, have been overcome by discriminative approaches proposed in recent years (McCallum et al., 2000; Lafferty et al., 2001; Collins, 2002; Altun et al., 2003). In this paper we apply perceptron trained HMMs originally proposed in (Collins, 2002).

4.1 Perceptron-trained HMM

HMMs define a probabilistic model for observation/label sequences. The joint model of an observation/label sequence $(\mathbf{x}, \mathbf{y})$, is defined as:

$$P(\mathbf{y}, \mathbf{x}) = \prod_i P(y_i|y_{i-1})P(x_i|y_i)), \qquad (2)$$

where y_i is the ith label in the sequence and x_i is the ith word. In the NLP literature, a common approach is to model the conditional distribution of label sequences given the label sequences. These models have several advantages over generative models, such as not requiring questionable independence assumptions, optimizing the conditional likelihood directly and employing richer feature representations. This task can be represented as learning a discriminant function $F : \mathcal{X} \times \mathcal{Y} \to \mathbb{R}$, on a training data of observation/label sequences, where F is linear in a feature representation Φ defined over the joint input/output space

$$F(\mathbf{x}, \mathbf{y}; \mathbf{w}) = \langle \mathbf{w}, \Phi(\mathbf{x}, \mathbf{y}) \rangle. \qquad (3)$$

Φ is a global feature representation, mapping each $(\mathbf{x}, \mathbf{y})$ pair to a vector of feature counts $\Phi(\mathbf{x}, \mathbf{y}) \in \mathbb{R}^d$, where d is the total number of features. This vector is given by

$$\Phi(\mathbf{x}, \mathbf{y}) = \sum_{i=1}^{d} \sum_{j=1}^{|\mathbf{y}|} \phi_i(y_{j-1}, y_j, \mathbf{x}). \qquad (4)$$

Each individual feature ϕ_i typically represents a morphological, contextual, or syntactic property, or also the inter-dependence of consecutive labels. These features are described in detail in Section 4.2. Given an observation sequence $\mathbf{x}$, we make a prediction by maximizing F over the response variables:

$$f_{\mathbf{w}}(\mathbf{x}) = \arg\max_{\mathbf{y} \in \mathcal{Y}} F(\mathbf{x}, \mathbf{y}; \mathbf{w}). \qquad (5)$$

This involves computing the Viterbi decoding with respect to the parameter vector $\mathbf{w} \in \mathbb{R}^d$. The complexity of the Viterbi algorithm scales linearly with the length of the sequence.

There are different ways of estimating $\mathbf{w}$ for the described model. We use the perceptron algorithm for sequence tagging (Collins, 2002). The perceptron algorithm focuses on minimizing the error rate, without involving any normalization factors. This property makes it very efficient which is a desirable feature in a task dealing with a large tagset such as ours. Additionally, the performance of perceptron-trained HMMs is very competitive on a number of tasks; e.g., in shallow parsing, where

Algorithm 1 Hidden Markov average perceptron algorithm.

```
Initialize w_0 = 0⃗
for t = 1...., T do
    Choose x^i
    Compute ŷ = arg max_{y∈Y} F(x^i, y; w)
    if y^i ≠ ŷ then
        w_{t+1} ← w_t + Φ(x^i, y^i) − Φ(x^i, ŷ)
    end if
    w = (1/T) Σ_t w_t
end for
return w
```

the perceptron performance is comparable to that of Conditional Random Field models (Sha and Pereira, 2003), The tendency to overfit of the perceptron can be mitigated in a number of ways including regularization and voting. Here we apply averaging and straightforwardly extended Collins algorithm, summarized in Algorithm 1.

4.2 Features

We used the following combination of spelling/morphological and contextual features. For each observed word x_i in the data ϕ extracts the following features:

1. **Words:** x_i, x_{i-1}, x_{i-2}, x_{i+1}, x_{i+2};

2. **First sense:** supersense baseline prediction for x_i, $\mathsf{fs}(x_i)$, cf. Section 5.3;

3. **Combined (1) and (2):** $x_i + \mathsf{fs}(x_i)$;

4. **Pos:** $\mathsf{pos_i}$ (the POS of x_i), $\mathsf{pos_{i-1}}$, $\mathsf{pos_{i-2}}$, $\mathsf{pos_{i+1}}$, $\mathsf{pos_{i+2}}$, $\mathsf{pos_i}[0]$, $\mathsf{pos_{i-1}}[0]$, $\mathsf{pos_{i-2}}[0]$, $\mathsf{pos_{i+1}}[0]$, $\mathsf{pos_{i+2}}[0]$, $\mathsf{pos\_comm_i}$ if x_i's POS tags is "NN" or "NNS" (common nouns), and $\mathsf{pos\_prop_i}$ if x_i's POS is "NNP" or "NNPS" (proper nouns);

5. **Word shape:** $\mathsf{sh}(x_i)$, $\mathsf{sh}(x_{i-1})$, $\mathsf{sh}(x_{i-2})$, $\mathsf{sh}(x_{i+1})$, $\mathsf{sh}(x_{i+2})$, where $\mathsf{sh}(x_i)$ is as described below. In addition $\mathsf{sh_i} = \mathsf{low}$ if the first character of x_i is lowercase, $\mathsf{sh_i} = \mathsf{cap\_brk}$ if the first character of x_i is uppercase and x_{i-1} is a full stop, question or exclamation mark, or x_i is the first word of the sentence, $\mathsf{sh_i} = \mathsf{cap\_nobrk}$ otherwise;

6. **Previous label:** supersense label y_{i-1}.

Word features (1) are morphologically simplified using the morphological functions of the Wordnet library. The first sense feature (2) is the label predicted for x_i by the baseline model, cf. Section 5.3. POS labels (4) were generated using Brants' TnT tagger (Brants, 2002). POS features of the form $\mathsf{pos_i}[0]$ extract the first character from the POS label, thus providing a simplified representation of the POS tag. Finally, word shape features (5) are regular expression-like transformation in which each character c of a string s is substituted with X if c is uppercase, if lowercase, c is substituted with x, if c is a digit it is substituted with d and left as it is otherwise. In addition each sequence of two or more identical characters c is substituted with $c*$. For example, for s = "Merrill Lynch& Co.", $\mathsf{sh}(s) = \mathsf{Xx} * \mathsf{Xx} * \&\mathsf{Xx}.$.

Exploratory experiments with richer feature sets, including syntactic information, affixes, and topic labels associated with words, did not result in improvements in terms of performance. While more experiments are needed to investigate the usefulness of other sources of information, the feature set described above, while basic, offers good generalization properties.

5 Experiments

5.1 Data

We experimented with the following data-sets[3]. The Semcor corpus (Miller et al., 1993), a fraction of the Brown corpus (Kučera and Francis, 1967) which has been manually annotated with Wordnet synset labels. Named entities of the categories "person", "location" and "group" are also annotated. The original annotation with Wordnet 1.6 synset IDs has been converted to the most recent version 2.0 of Wordnet. Semcor is divided in three parts: "brown1" and "brown2", here referred to as "SEM", in which nouns, verbs, adjectives and adverbs are annotated. In addition, the section "brownv", "SEMv" here, contains annotations only for verbs. We also experimented with the Senseval-3 English all-words tasks data (Snyder and Palmer, 2004), here called "SE3". The Senseval all-words task evaluates the performance of WSD systems on all open class words in complete documents. The Senseval-3 data consists of two Wall Street Journal Articles, "wsj_1778" and

[3] These datasets are available in a consistent format and can be downloaded from http://www.cs.unt.edu/ rada/downloads.html

	Dataset		
Counts	SE3	SEM	SEMv
Sentences	300	20,138	17,038
Tokens	5,630	434,774	385,546
Supersenses	1,617	135,135	40,911
Verbs	725	47,710	40,911
Nouns	892	87,425	0
Avg-poly-N-WS	4.66	4.41	4.33
Avg-poly-N-SS	2.86	2.75	2.66
Avg-poly-V-WS	11.17	10.87	11.05
Avg-poly-V-SS	4.20	4.11	4.16

Table 3. Statistics of the datasets. The row "Supersenses" lists the number of instances of supersense labels, partitioned, in the following two rows, between verb and noun supersense labels. The lowest four rows summarize average polysemy figures at the synset and supersense level for both nouns and verbs.

"wsj_1695", and a fiction excerpt, "cl_23", from the unannotated portion of the Brown corpus. Table 3 summarizes a few statistics about the composition of the datasets. The four lower rows report the average polysemy of nouns ("N") and verbs ("V"), in each dataset, both at the synset level ("WS") and supersense ("SS") level. The average number of senses decreases significantly when the more general sense inventory is considered.

We substituted the corresponding supersense to each noun and verb synset in all three data-sets: SEM, SEMv and SE3. All other tokens were labeled "0". The supersense label "noun.Tops" refers to 45 synsets which lie at the very top of the Wordnet noun hierarchy. Some of these synsets are expressed by very general nouns such as "biont", "benthos", "whole", and "nothing". However, others undoubtedly refer to other supersenses, for which they provide the label, such as "food", "person", "plant" or "animal". Since these nouns tend to be fairly frequent, it is confusing and inconsistent to label them "noun.Tops"; e.g., nouns such as "chowder" and "Swedish meatball" would be tagged as "noun.food", but the noun "food" would be tagged as "noun.Tops". For this reason, in all obvious cases, we substituted the "noun.Tops" label with the more specific supersense label for the noun[4].

The SEMv dataset only includes supersense labels for verbs. In order to avoid unwanted false negatives, that is, thousands of nouns labeled "0", we applied the following procedure. Rather than using the full sentences from the SEMv dataset, from each sentence we generated the fragments including a verb but no common or proper nouns; e.g., from a sentence such as "Karns' ruling *pertained*$_{verb.stative}$ to eight of the 10 cases." only the fragment "*pertained*$_{verb.stative}$ to eight of the 10" is extracted and used for training.

Sometimes more than one label is assigned to a word, in all data-sets. In these cases we adopted the heuristic of only using the first label in the data as the correct synset/supersense. We leave the extension of the tagger to the multilabel case for future research. As for now, we can expect that this solution will simply lower, somewhat, both the baseline and the tagger performance. Finally, we adopted a beginning (B) and continuation of entity (I) plus no label (0), encoding; i.e., the actual class space defines 83 labels.

5.2 Setup

The supersense tagger was trained on the Semcor datasets SEM and SEMv. The only free parameter to set in evaluation is the number of iterations to perform T (cf. Algorithm 1). We evaluated the model's accuracy on Semcor by splitting the SEM data randomly in training, development and evaluation. In a 5-fold cross-validation setup the tagger was trained on 4/5 of the SEM data, the remaining data was split in two halves, one used to fix T the other for evaluating performance on test. The full SEMv data was always added to the training portion of SEM. We also evaluated the model on the Senseval-3 data, using the same value for T set by cross-validation on the SEM data[5]. The ordering of the training instances is randomized across different runs, therefore the algorithm outputs different results after each run, even if the evaluation set is fixed, as is the case for the Senseval evaluation. The variance in the results on the SE3 data was measured in this way.

5.3 Baseline tagger

The first sense baseline is the supersense of the most frequent synset for a word, according to Wordnet's sense ranking. This baseline is very competitive in WSD tasks, and it is extremely hard to improve upon even slightly. In fact, the baseline has been proposed as a good alternative to WSD

[4]The nouns which are left with the "noun.Top" label are: entity, thing, anything, something, nothing, object, living thing, organism, benthos, heterotroph, life, and biont.

[5]On average T is equal to 12 times the size of the training data.

	Semcor			Senseval-3		
Method	Recall	Precision	F-score [σ]	Recall	Precision	F-score [σ]
Rand	42.99	38.17	40.44	42.09	35.84	38.70
Baseline	69.25	63.90	66.47	68.65	60.10	64.09
Supersense-Tagger	77.71	76.65	77.18 0.45	73.74	67.60	70.54 0.21

Table 4. Summary of results for random and first sense baselines and supersense tagger, σ is the standard error computed on the five trials results.

altogether (cf. (McCarthy et al., 2004)). For this reason we include the first sense prediction as one of the features of our tagging model.

We apply the heuristic as follows. First, in each sentence, we identify the longest sequence which has an entry in Wordnet as either noun or verb. We carry out this step using the Wordnet's library functions, which perform also morphological simplification. Hence, in Example 1 the entry "stand up" is detected, although also "stand" has an entry in Wordnet. Then, each word identified in this way is assigned its most frequent sense – the only one available if the word is unambiguous. To reduce the number of candidate supersenses we distinguish between common and proper nouns; e.g. "Savannah" (city/river) is distinguished from "savannah" (grassland). This method improves slightly the accuracy of the baseline which does not distinguish between different types of nouns.

5.4 Results

Table 4 summarizes overall performance[6]. The first line shows the accuracy of a baseline which assigns possible supersenses of identified words at random. The second line shows the performance of the first sense baseline (cf. Section 5.3), the marked difference between the two is a measure of the robustness of the first sense heuristic. On the Semcor data the tagger improves over the baseline by 10.71%, 31.19% error reduction, while on Senseval-3 the tagger improves over the baseline by 6.45%, 17.96% error reduction. We can put these results in context, although indirectly, by comparison with the results of the Senseval-3 all words task systems. There, with a baseline of 62.40%, only 4 out of 26 systems performed above the baseline, with the two best systems (Mihalcea and Faruque, 2004; Decadt et al., 2004) achieving an F-score of 65.2% (2.8% improvement, 7.45% error reduction). The system based on the HMM tagger (Molina et al., 2004), achieved an F-score of 60.9%. The supersense tagger improves mostly on precision, while also improving on recall. Overall the tagger achieves F-scores between 70.5 and 77.2%. If we compare these figures with the accuracy of NER taggers the results are very encouraging. Given the considerably larger – one order of magnitude – class space some loss has to be expected. Experiments with augmented tagsets in the biomedical domain also show performance loss with respect to smaller tagsets; e.g., Kazama et al. (2002) report an F-score of 56.2% on a tagset of 25 Genia classes, compared to the 75.9% achieved on the simplest binary case. The sequence fragments from SEMv contribute about 1% F-score improvement.

Table 5 focuses on subsets of the evaluation. The upper part summarizes the results on Semcor for the classes comparable to standard NER's: "person", "group", "location" and "time". However, these categories here are composed of common nouns as well as proper names/named entities. On this four tags the tagger achieves an average 82.46% F-score, not too far from NER results. The lower portion of Table 5 summarizes the results on the five most frequent noun and verb supersense labels on the Senseval-3 data, providing more specific evidence for the supersense tagger's disambiguation accuracy. The tagger outperforms the first sense baseline on all categories, with the exception of "verb.cognition" and "noun.person". The latter case has a straightforward explanation, named entities (e.g., "Phil Haney", "Chevron" or "Marina District") are not annotated in the Senseval data, while they are in Semcor. Hence the tagger learns a different model for nouns than the one used to annotate the Senseval data. Because of this discrepancy the tagger tends to return false positives for some categories. In fact, the other noun categories on which the tagger performs poorly in SE3 are "group" and "location" (baseline 52.10 tagger 44.72 and baseline 47.62% tagger 47.54% F-score). Naturally, the lower performance on Senseval is also explained by the fact that the eval-

[6] Scoring was performed with a re-implementation of the "conlleval" script .

NER supersenses in Semcor							
		Supersense-Tagger			Baseline		
Supersense	# Supersenses	R	P	F	R	P	F
n.person	1526	92.04	87.94	**89.94**	56.29	77.35	65.16
n.group	665	75.38	79.56	**77.40**	62.42	66.81	64.54
n.location	459	77.21	75.37	**76.25**	67.88	63.33	65.53
n.time	412	88.36	84.30	**86.27**	78.26	83.88	80.98
5 most frequent verb supersenses in Senseval-3							
Supersense	# Supersenses	R	P	F	R	P	F
v.stative	184	80.33	81.30	**80.81**	72,83	63.81	68.02
v.communication	88	77.53	83.36	**80.33**	71.91	74.42	73.14
v.motion	81	69.63	64.54	**66.98**	58.02	60.26	59.12
v.cognition	61	73.44	67.91	70.56	75.41	71.87	**73.60**
v.change	60	68.33	67.47	**67.89**	56.67	57.63	57.14
5 most frequent noun supersenses in Senseval-3							
Supersense	# Supersenses	R	P	F	R	P	F
n.person	148	92.24	60.49	73.06	89.12	79.39	**83.97**
n.artifact	131	80.91	77.73	**79.29**	74.24	75.97	75.10
n.act	96	61.46	72.37	**66.45**	58.33	65.12	61.54
n.cognition	67	45.80	52.87	**49.06**	49.28	46.58	47.89
n.event	60	70.33	89.83	**78.87**	71.67	75.44	73.50

Table 5. Summary of results of baseline and tagger on selected subsets of labels: NER categories evaluated on Semcor (upper section), and 5 most frequent verb (middle) and noun (bottom) categories evaluated on Senseval.

uation comes from different sources than training.

6 Conclusions

In this paper we presented a novel approach to broad-coverage word sense disambiguation and information extraction. We defined a tagset based on Wordnet supersenses, a much simpler and general semantic model than Wordnet which, however, preserves significant polysemy information and includes standard named entity recognition categories. We showed that in this framework it is possible to perform accurate broad-coverage tagging with state of the art sequence learning methods. The tagger considerably outperformed the most competitive baseline on both Semcor and Senseval data. To the best of our knowledge the results on Senseval data provide the first convincing evidence of the possibility of improving by considerable amounts over the first sense baseline.

We believe both the tagset and the structured learning approach contribute to these results. The simplified representation obviously helps by reducing the number of possible senses for each word (cf. Table 3). Interestingly, the relative improvement in performance is not as large as the relative reduction in polysemy. This indicates that sense granularity is only one of the problems in WSD. More needs to be understood concerning sources of information, and processes, that affect word sense selection in context. As far as the tagger is concerned, we applied the simplest feature representation, more sophisticated features can be used, e.g., based on kernels, which might contribute significantly by allowing complex feature combinations. These results also suggest new directions of research within this model. In particular, the labels occurring in each sequence tend to coincide with predicates (verbs) and arguments (nouns and named entities). A sequential dependency model might not be the most accurate at capturing the grammatical dependencies between these elements. Other conditional models, e.g., designed on head to head, or similar, dependencies could prove more appropriate.

Another interesting issue is the granularity of the tagset. Supersenses seem more practical then synsets for investigating the impact of broad-coverage semantic tagging, but they define a very simplistic ontological model. A natural evolution of this kind of approach might be one which starts by defining a semantic model at an intermediate level of abstraction (cf. (Ciaramita et al., 2005)).

References

Y. Altun, T. Hofmann, and M. Johnson. 2003. Discriminative Learning for Label Sequences via Boosting. In *Proceedings of NIPS 2003*.

T. Brants. 2002. TnT - A Statistical Part-of-Speech Tagger. In *Proceedings of ANLP 2000*.

X. Carreras, L. Marquez, and L. Padro. 2002. Named Entity Extraction Using AdaBoost. In *Proceedings of CONLL 2002*.

M. Ciaramita and M. Johnson. 2003. Supersense Tagging of Unknown Nouns in WordNet. In *Proceedings of EMNLP 2003*.

M. Ciaramita, T. Hofmann, and M. Johnson. 2003. Hierarchical Semantic Classification: Word Sense Disambiguation with World Knowledge. In *Proceedings of IJCAI 2003*.

M. Ciaramita, S. Sloman, M. Johnson, and E. Upfal. 2005. Hierarchical Preferences in a Broad-Coverage Lexical Taxonomy. In *Proceedings of CogSci 2005*.

M. Collins. 2002. Discriminative Training Methods for Hidden Markov Models: Theory and Experiments with Perceptron Algorithms. In *Proceedings of EMNLP 2002*, pages 1–8.

J. Curran. 2005. Supersense Tagging of Unknown Nouns Using Semantic Similarity. In *Proceedings of ACL 2005*, pages 26–33.

C. de Loupy, M. El-Beze, and P.F. Marteau. 1998. Word Sense Disambiguation Using HMM Tagger. In *Proceedings of LREC 1998*, pages 1255–1258.

B. Decadt, V. Hoste, W. Daelemans, and A. van der Bosch. 2004. GAMBL, Genetic Algorithm Optimization of Memory-Based WSD. In *Proceedings of SENSEVAL-3/ACL 2004*.

S. Dingare, M. Nissim, J. Finkel, C. Manning, and C. Grover. 2005. A System for Identifying Named Entities in Biomedical Text: How Results from Two Evaluations Reflect on Both the System and the Evaluations. *Comparative and Functional Genomics*, 6:77–85.

C. Fellbaum, editor. 1998. *WordNet: An Electronic Lexical Database*. MIT Press, Cambridge.

R. Florian, A. Ittycheriah, H. Jing, and T. Zhang. 2003. Named Entity Extraction through Classifier Combination. In *Proceedings of CONLL 2003*.

W. Gale, K. Church, and D. Yarowsky. 1992. One Sense per Discourse. In *Proceedings of the DARPA Workshop on Speech and Natural Language*.

J. Kazama, T. Makino, Y. Ohta, and J. Tsujii. 2002. Tuning Support Vector Machines for Biomedical Named Entity Recognition. In *Proceedings of the Workshop on Natural Language Processing in the Biomedical Domain (ACL 2002)*.

T. Koo and M. Collins. 2005. Hidden-Variable Models for Discriminative Reranking. In *Proceedings of EMNLP 2005*.

H. Kučera and W. Francis. 1967. *Computational Analysis of Present-Day American English*. Brown University Press, Providence, RI.

J. Lafferty, A. McCallum, and F. Pereira. 2001. Conditional Random Fields: Probabilistic Models for Segmenting and Labeling Sequence Data. In *Proceedings of ICML 2001*, pages 282–289.

A. McCallum, D. Freitag, and F. Pereira. 2000. Maximum Entropy Markov Models for Information Extraction and Segmentation. In *Proceedings of ICML 2000*, pages 591–598.

D. McCarthy, R. Koeling, and J. Carroll. 2004. Finding Predominant Senses in Untagged Text. In *Proceedings of ACL 2004*.

R. Mihalcea and E. Faruque. 2004. SenseLearner: Minimally Supervised Word Sense Disambiguation for All Words in Open Text. In *Proceedings of SENSEVAL-3/ACL 2004*.

G.A. Miller, C. Leacock, T. Randee, and R. Bunker. 1993. A Semantic Concordance. In *Proceedings of the 3 DARPA Workshop on Human Language Technology*, pages 303–308.

A. Molina, F. Pla, and E. Segarra. 2002. A Hidden Markov Model Approach to Word Sense Dsiambiguation. In *Proceedings of IBERAMIA 2002*.

A. Molina, F. Pla, and E. Segarra. 2004. WSD System Based on Specialized Hidden Markov Model (upv-shmm-eaw). In *Proceedings of SENSEVAL-3/ACL 2004*.

Y. Ohta, Y. Tateisi, J. Kim, H. Mima, and J. Tsujii. 2002. The GENIA Corpus: An Annotated Research Abstract Corpus in the Molecular Biology Domain. In *Proceedings of HLT 2002*.

B. Rosario and M. Hearst. 2004. Classifying Semantic Relations in Bioscience Text. In *Proceedings of ACL 2004)*.

F. Segond, A. Schiller, G. Grefenstette, and J.P. Chanod. 1997. An Experiment in Semantic Tagging Using Hidden Markov Model. In *Proceedings of the Workshop on Automatic Information Extraction and Building of Lexical Semantic Resources (ACL/EACL 1997)*, pages 78–81.

F. Sha and F. Pereira. 2003. Shallow Parsing with Conditional Random Fields. In *Proceedings of HLT-NAACL 2003*, pages 213–220.

B. Snyder and M. Palmer. 2004. The english All-Words Tasks. In *Proceedings of SENSEVAL-3/ACL 2004*.

Learning Field Compatibilities to Extract Database Records from Unstructured Text

Michael Wick, Aron Culotta and **Andrew McCallum**
Department of Computer Science
University of Massachusetts
Amherst, MA 01003
{mwick, culotta, mccallum}@cs.umass.edu

Abstract

Named-entity recognition systems extract entities such as people, organizations, and locations from unstructured text. Rather than extract these mentions in isolation, this paper presents a *record extraction* system that assembles mentions into records (i.e. database tuples). We construct a probabilistic model of the compatibility between field values, then employ graph partitioning algorithms to cluster fields into cohesive records. We also investigate compatibility functions over *sets* of fields, rather than simply pairs of fields, to examine how higher representational power can impact performance. We apply our techniques to the task of extracting contact records from faculty and student homepages, demonstrating a 53% error reduction over baseline approaches.

1 Introduction

Information extraction (IE) algorithms populate a database with facts discovered from unstructured text. This database is often used by higher-level tasks such as question answering or knowledge discovery. The richer the structure of the database, the more useful it is to higher-level tasks.

A common IE task is named-entity recognition (NER), the problem of locating mentions of entities in text, such as people, places, and organizations. NER techniques range from regular expressions to finite-state sequence models (Bikel et al., 1999; Grishman, 1997; Sutton and McCallum, 2006). NER can be viewed as method of populating a database with single-tuple records, e.g. PERSON=*Cecil Conner* or ORGANIZATION= *IBM*.

We can add richer structure to these single-tuple records by extracting the associations among entities. For example, we can populate multi-field records such as a contact record [PERSON=*Steve Jobs*, JOBTITLE = *CEO*, COMPANY = *Apple*, CITY = *Cupertino*, STATE = *CA*]. The relational information in these types of records presents a greater opportunity for text analysis.

The task of associating together entities is often framed as a binary *relation extraction* task: Given a pair of entities, label the relation between them (e.g. *Steve Jobs* LOCATED-IN *Cupertino*). Common approaches to relation extraction include pattern matching (Brin, 1998; Agichtein and Gravano, 2000) and classification (Zelenko et al., 2003; Kambhatla, 2004).

However, binary relation extraction alone is not well-suited for the contact record example above, which requires associating together many fields into one record. We refer to this task of piecing together many fields into a single record as *record extraction*.

Consider the task of extracting contact records from personal homepages. An NER system may label all mentions of cities, people, organizations, phone numbers, job titles, etc. on a page, from both semi-structured an unstructured text. Even with a highly accurate NER system, it is not obvious which fields belong to the same record. For example, a single document could contain five names, three phone numbers and only one email. Additionally, the layout of certain fields may be convoluted or vary across documents.

Intuitively, we would like to learn the *compatibility* among fields, for example the likelihood that the organization *University of North Dakota* is located in the state *North Dakota*, or that phone numbers with area code *212* co-occur with the

Proceedings of the 2006 Conference on Empirical Methods in Natural Language Processing (EMNLP 2006), pages 603–611, Sydney, July 2006.

city *New York*. Additionally, the system should take into account page layout information, so that nearby fields are more likely to be grouped into the same record.

In this paper, we describe a method to induce a probabilistic compatibility function between sets of fields. Embedding this compatibility function within a graph partitioning method, we describe how to cluster highly compatible fields into records.

We evaluate our approach on personal homepages that have been manually annotated with contact record information, and demonstrate a 53% error reduction over baseline methods.

2 Related Work

McDonald et al. (2005) present clustering techniques to extract *complex relations*, i.e. relations with more than two arguments. Record extraction can be viewed as an instance of complex relation extraction. We build upon this work in three ways: (1) Our system learns the compatibility between *sets* of fields, rather than just pairs of field; (2) our system is not restricted to relations between entities in the same sentence; and (3) our problem domain has a varying number of fields per record, as opposed to the fixed schema in McDonald et al. (2005).

Bansal et al. (2004) present algorithms for the related task of *correlational clustering*: finding an optimal clustering from a matrix of pairwise compatibility scores. The correlational clustering approach does not handle compatibility scores calculated over sets of nodes, which we address in this paper.

McCallum and Wellner (2005) discriminatively train a model to learn binary coreference decisions, then perform joint inference using graph partitioning. This is analogous to our work, with two distinctions. First, instead of binary coreference decisions, our model makes binary *compatibility* decisions, reflecting whether a set of fields belong together in the same record. Second, whereas McCallum and Wellner (2005) factor the coreference decisions into pairs of vertices, our compatibility decisions are made between sets of vertices. As we show in our experiments, factoring decisions into sets of vertices enables more powerful features that can improve performance. These higher-order features have also recently been investigated in other models of coreference, both discriminative (Culotta and McCallum, 2006) and generative (Milch et al., 2005).

Viola and Narasimhan (2005) present a probabilistic grammar to parse contact information blocks. While this model is capable of learning long-distance compatibilities (such as *City* and *State* relations), features to enable this are not explored. Additionally, their work focuses on labeling fields in documents that have been presegmented into records. This record segmentation is precisely what we address in this paper.

Borkar et al. (2001) and Kristjannson et al. (2004) also label contact address blocks, but ignore the problem of clustering fields into records. Also, Culotta et al. (2004) automatically extract contact records from web pages, but use heuristics to cluster fields into records.

Embley et al. (1999) provide heuristics to detect record boundaries in highly structured web documents, such as classified ads, and Embley and Xu (2000) improve upon these heuristics for slightly more ambiguous domains using a vector space model. Both of these techniques apply to data for which the records are highly contiguous and have a distinctive separator between records. These heuristic approaches are unlikely to be successful in the unstructured text domain we address in this paper.

Most other work on relation extraction focuses only on binary relations (Zelenko et al., 2003; Miller et al., 2000; Agichtein and Gravano, 2000; Culotta and Sorensen, 2004). A serious difficulty in applying binary relation extractors to the record extraction task is that rather than enumerating over all *pairs* of entities, the system must enumerate over all *subsets* of entities, up to subsets of size k, the maximum number of fields per record. We address this difficulty by employing two sampling methods: one that samples uniformly, and another that samples on a focused subset of the combinatorial space.

3 From Fields to Records

3.1 Problem Definition

Let a field F be a pair $\langle a, v \rangle$, where a is an attribute (column label) and v is a value, e.g. $F_i = \langle$CITY, *San Francisco*$\rangle$. Let record R be a set of fields, $R = \{F_1 \ldots F_n\}$. Note that R may contain multiple fields with the same attribute but different values (e.g. a person may have multiple job titles). Assume we are given the output of a named-entity recognizer, which labels tokens in a document with their attribute type (e.g. NAME or CITY). Thus, a document initially contains a set of fields, $\{F_1 \dots F_m\}$.

The task is to partition the fields in each annotated document into a set of records $\{R_1 \dots R_k\}$ such that each record R_i contains exactly the set of fields pertinent to that record. In this paper, we assume each field belongs to exactly one record.

3.2 Solution Overview

For each document, we construct a fully-connected weighted graph $G = (V, E)$, with vertices V and weighted edges E. Each field in the document is represented by a vertex in V, and the edges are weighted by the compatibility of adjacent fields, i.e. a measure of how likely it is that F_i and F_j belong to the same record.

Partitioning V into k disjoint clusters uniquely maps the set of fields to a set of k records. Below, we provide more detail on the two principal steps in our solution: (1) estimating the compatibility function and (2) partitioning V into disjoint clusters.

3.3 Learning field compatibility

Let $\mathcal{F}$ be a candidate cluster of fields forming a partial record. We construct a compatibility function C that maps two sets of fields to a real value, i.e. $C : \mathcal{F}_i \times \mathcal{F}_j \rightarrow \mathcal{R}$. We abbreviate the value $C(\mathcal{F}_i, \mathcal{F}_j)$ as C_{ij}. The higher the value of C_{ij} the more likely it is that $\mathcal{F}_i$ and $\mathcal{F}_j$ belong to the same record.

For example, in the contact record domain, C_{ij} can reflect whether a city and state should co-occur, or how likely a company is to have a certain job title.

We represent C_{ij} by a maximum-entropy classifier over the binary variable S_{ij}, which is *true* if and only if field set $\mathcal{F}_i$ belongs to the same record as field set $\mathcal{F}_j$. Thus, we model the conditional distribution

$$P_\Lambda(S_{ij}|\mathcal{F}_i, \mathcal{F}_j) \propto \exp\left(\sum_k \lambda_k f_k(S_{ij}, \mathcal{F}_i, \mathcal{F}_j)\right)$$

where f_k is a binary feature function that computes attributes over the field sets, and $\Lambda = \{\lambda_k\}$ is the set of real-valued weights that are the parameters of the maximum-entropy model. We set $C_{ij} = P_\Lambda(S_{ij} = \textit{true}|\mathcal{F}_i, \mathcal{F}_j)$. This approach can be viewed as a logistic regression model for field compatibility.

Examples of feature functions include formatting evidence ($\mathcal{F}_i$ appears at the top of the document, $\mathcal{F}_j$ at the bottom), conflicting value information ($\mathcal{F}_i$ and $\mathcal{F}_j$ contain conflicting values for the *state* field), or other measures of compatibility (a *city* value in $\mathcal{F}_i$ is known to exist in a state in $\mathcal{F}_j$). A feature may involve more than one field, for example, if a name, title and university occurs consecutively in some order. We give a more detailed description of the feature functions in Section 4.3.

We propose learning the Λ weights for each of these features using supervised machine learning. Given a set of documents $\mathcal{D}$ for which the true mapping from fields to set of records is known, we wish to estimate $P(S_{ij}|\mathcal{F}_i, \mathcal{F}_j)$ for all pairs of field sets $\mathcal{F}_i, \mathcal{F}_j$.

Enumerating all positive and negative pairs of field sets is computationally infeasible for large datasets, so we instead propose two sampling methods to generate training examples. The first simply samples pairs of field sets uniformly from the training data. For example, given a document D containing true records $\{R_1 \dots R_k\}$, we sample positive and negative examples of field sets of varying sizes from $\{R_i \dots R_j\}$. The second sampling method first trains the model using the examples generated by uniform sampling. This model is then used to cluster the training data. Additional training examples are created during the clustering process and are used to retrain the model parameters. This second sampling method is an attempt to more closely align the characteristics of the training and testing examples.

Given a sample of labeled training data, we set the parameters of the maximum-entropy classifier in standard maximum-likelihood fashion, performing gradient ascent on the log-likelihood of the training data. The resulting weights indicate how important each feature is in determining whether two sets of fields belong to the same record.

3.4 Partitioning Fields into Records

One could employ the estimated classifier to convert fields into records as follows: Classify each pair of fields as *positive* or *negative*, and perform transitive closure to enforce transitivity of decisions. That is, if the classifier determines that A and B belong to the same record and that B and C belong to the same record, then by transitivity

A and C must belong to the same record. The drawback of this approach is that the compatibility between A and C is ignored. In cases where the classifier determines that A and C are highly *incompatible*, transitive closure can lead to poor precision. McCallum and Wellner (2005) explore this issue in depth for the related task of noun coreference resolution.

With this in mind, we choose to avoid transitive closure, and instead employ a graph partitioning method to make record merging decisions jointly.

Given a document D with fields $\{F_1 \ldots F_n\}$, we construct a fully connected graph $G = (V, E)$, with edge weights determined by the learned compatibility function C. We wish to partition vertices V into clusters with high intra-cluster compatibility.

One approach is to simply use greedy agglomerative clustering: initialize each vertex to its own cluster, then iteratively merge clusters with the highest inter-cluster edge weights. The compatibility between two clusters can be measured using single-link or average-link clustering. The clustering algorithm converges when the inter-cluster edge weight between any pair of clusters is below a specified threshold.

We propose a modification to this approach. Since the compatibility function we have described maps two *sets* of vertices to a real value, we can use this directly to calculate the compatibility between two clusters, rather than performing average or single link clustering.

We now describe the algorithm more concretely.

- **Input:** (1) Graph $G = (V, E)$, where each vertex v_i represents a field F_i. (2) A threshold value τ.

- **Initialization:** Place each vertex v_i in its own cluster $\hat{R}_i$. (The hat notation indicates that this cluster represents a possible record.)

- **Iterate:** Re-calculate the compatibility function C_{ij} between each pair of clusters. Merge the two most compatible clusters, $\hat{R}_i^*, \hat{R}_j^*$.

- **Termination:** If there does not exist a pair of clusters $\hat{R}_i, \hat{R}_j$ such that $C_{ij} > \tau$, the algorithm terminates and returns the current set of clusters.

A natural threshold value is $\tau = 0.5$, since this is the point at which the binary compatibility classifier predicts that the fields belong to different records. In Section 4.4, we examine how performance varies with τ.

3.5 Representational power of cluster compatibility functions

Most previous work on inducing compatibility functions learns the compatibility between *pairs* of vertices, not *clusters* of vertices. In this section, we provide intuition to explain why directly modeling the compatibility of clusters of vertices may be advantageous. We refer to the cluster compatibility function as C_{ij}, and the pairwise (binary) compatibility function as B_{ij}.

First, we note that C_{ij} is a generalization of single-link and average-link clustering methods that use B_{ij}, since the output of these methods can simply be included as features in C_{ij}. For example, given two clusters $\hat{R}_i = \{v_1, v_2, v_3\}$ and $\hat{R}_j = \{v_4, v_5, v_6\}$, average-link clustering calculates the inter-cluster score between $\hat{R}_i$ and $\hat{R}_j$ as

$$S_{AL}(\hat{R}_i, \hat{R}_j) = \frac{1}{|\hat{R}_i||\hat{R}_j|} \sum_{a \in \hat{R}_i, b \in \hat{R}_j} B_{ab}$$

$S_{AL}(\hat{R}_i, \hat{R}_j)$ can be included as a feature for the compatibility function C_{ij}, with an associated weight estimated from training data.

Second, there may exist phenomena of the data that can only be captured by a classifier that considers "higher-order" features. Below we describe two such cases.

In the first example, consider three vertices of mild compatibility, as in Figure 1(a). (For these examples, let $B_{ij}, C_{ij} \in [0, 1]$.) Suppose that these three phone numbers occur nearby in a document. Since it is not uncommon for a person to have two phone numbers with different area codes, the pairwise compatibility function may score any pair of nearby phone numbers as relatively compatible. However, since it is fairly uncommon for a person to have three phone numbers with *three* different area codes, we would not like all three numbers to be merged into the same record.

Assume an average-link clustering algorithm. After merging together the *333* and *444* numbers, B_{ij} will recompute the new inter-cluster compatibility as 0.51, the average of the inter-cluster edges. In contrast, the cluster compatibility function C_{ij} can represent the fact that three numbers with different area codes are to be merged, and can penalize their compatibility accordingly. Thus, in

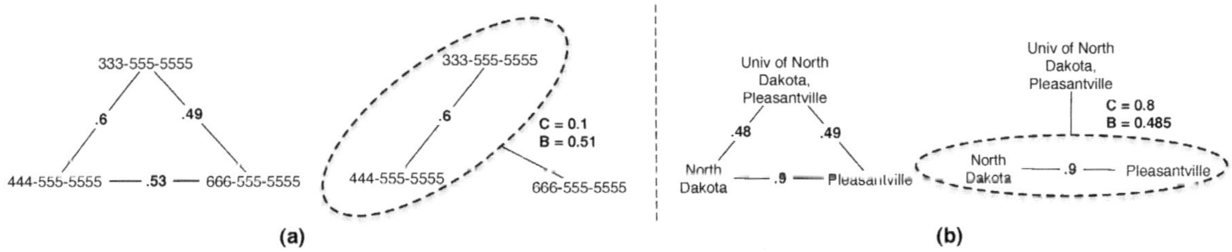

Figure 1: Two motivating examples illustrating why the cluster compatibility measure (**C**) may have higher representational power than the pairwise compatibility measure (**B**). In (a), the pairwise measure *over*-estimates the inter-cluster compatibility when there exist higher-order features such as *A person is unlikely to have phone numbers with three different area codes.* In (b), the pairwise measure *under*-estimates inter-cluster compatibility when weak features like string comparisons can be combined into a more powerful feature by examining multiple field values.

this example, the pairwise compatibility function over-estimates the true compatibility.

In the second example (Figure 1(b)), we consider the opposite case. Consider three edges, two of which have weak compatibility, and one of which has high compatibility. For example, perhaps the system has access to a list of city-state pairs, and can reliably conclude that *Pleasantville* is a city in the state *North Dakota.*

Deciding that *Univ of North Dakota, Pleasantville* belongs in the same record as *North Dakota* and *Pleasantville* is a bit more difficult. Suppose a feature function measures the string similarity between the city field *Pleasantville* and the company field *Univ of North Dakota, Pleasantville.* Alone, this string similarity might not be very strong, and so the pairwise compatibility is low. However, after *Pleasantville* and *North Dakota* are merged together, the cluster compatibility function can compute the string similarity of the *concatenation* of the city and state fields, resulting in a higher compatibility. In this example, the pairwise compatibility function underestimates the true compatibility.

These two examples show that the cluster compatibility score can have more representational power than the average of pairwise compatibility scores.

FirstName	MiddleName
LastName	NickName
Suffix	Title
JobTitle	CompanyName
Department	AddressLine
City1	City2
State	Country
PostalCode	HomePhone
Fax	CompanyPhone
DirectCompanyPhone	Mobile
Pager	VoiceMail
URL	Email
InstantMessage	

Table 1: The 25 fields annotated in the contact record dataset.

4 Experiments

4.1 Data

We hand-labeled a subset of faculty and student homepages from the WebKB dataset[1]. Each page was labeled with the 25 fields listed in Table 1. In addition, we labeled the records to which each field belonged. For example, in Figure 2, we labeled the contact information for Professor Smith into a separate record from that of her administrative assistant. There are 252 labeled pages in total, containing 8996 fields and 16679 word tokens. We perform ten random samples of 70-30 splits of the data for all experiments.

4.2 Systems

We evaluate five different record extraction systems. With the exception of **Transitive Closure**, all methods employ the agglomerative clustering

[1]http://www.cs.cmu.edu/afs/cs.cmu.edu/project/theo-20/www/data/

Figure 2: A synthetic example representative of the labeled data. Note that Record 1 contains information both from an address block and from free text, and that Record 2 must be separated from Record 1 even though fields from each may be nearby in the text.

algorithm described previously. The difference is in how the inter-cluster compatibility is calculated.

- **Transitive Closure:** The method described in the beginning of Section 3.4, where hard classification decisions are made, and transitivity is enforced.

- **Pairwise Compatibility:** In this approach, the compatibility function only estimates the compatibility between *pairs* of fields, not *sets* of fields. To compute inter-cluster compatibility, the mean of the edges between the clusters is calculated.

- **McDonald:** This method uses the pairwise compatibility function, but instead of calculating the mean of inter-cluster edges, it calculates the geometric mean of all pairs of edges in the potential new cluster. That is, to calculate the compatibility of records R_i and R_j, we construct a new record R_{ij} that contains all fields of R_i and R_j, then calculate the geometric mean of all pairs of fields in R_{ij}. This is analogous to the method used in McDonald et al. (2005) for relation extraction.

- **Cluster Compatibility (uniform):** Inter-cluster compatibility is calculated directly by the cluster compatibility function. This is the method we advocate in Section 3. Training examples are sampled uniformly as described in Section 3.3.

- **Cluster Compatibility (iterative):** Same as above, but training examples are sampled using the iterative method described in Section 3.3.

4.3 Features

For the pairwise compatibility classifier, we exploit various formatting as well as knowledge-based features. Formatting features include the number of hard returns between fields, whether the fields occur on the same line, and whether the fields occur consecutively. Knowledge-based features include a mapping we compiled of cities and states in the United States and Canada. Additionally, we used compatibility features, such as which fields are of the same type but have different values.

In building the cluster compatibility classifier, we use many of the same features as in the binary classifier, but cast them as first-order existential features that are generated if the feature exists between any pair of fields in the two clusters. Additionally, we are able to exploit more powerful compatibility and knowledge-base features. For example, we examine if a title, a first name and a last name occur consecutively (i.e., no other fields occur in-between them). Also, we examine multiple telephone numbers to ensure that they have the same area codes. Additionally, we employ count features that indicate if a certain field occurs more than a given threshold.

4.4 Results

For these experiments, we compare performance on the *true* record for each page. That is, we calculate how often each system returns a complete and accurate extraction of the contact record pertaining to the owner of the webpage. We refer to this record as the *canonical record* and measure performance in terms of precision, recall and F1 for each field in the canonical record.

Table 2 compares precision, recall and F1 across the various systems. The cluster compatibility method with iterative sampling has the highest F1, demonstrating a 14% error reduction over the next best method and a 53% error reduction over the transitive closure baseline.

Transitive closure has the highest recall, but it comes at the expense of precision, and hence obtains lower F1 scores than more conservative compatibility methods. The McDonald method also has high recall, but drastically improves precision over the transitivity method by taking into consideration all edge weights.

The pairwise measure yields a slightly higher F1 score than McDonald mostly due to precision improvements. Because the McDonald method calculates the mean of *all* edge weights rather than just the inter-cluster edge weights, inter-cluster weights are often outweighed by intra-cluster weights. This can cause two densely-connected clusters to be merged despite low inter-cluster edge weights.

To further investigate performance differences, we perform three additional experiments. The first measures how sensitive the algorithms are to the threshold value τ. Figure 3 plots the precision-recall curve obtained by varying τ from 1.0 to 0.1. As expected, high values of τ result in low recall but high precision, since the algorithms halt with a large number of small clusters. The highlighted points correspond to $\tau = 0.5$. These results indicate that setting τ to 0.5 is near optimal, and that the cluster compatibility method outperforms the pairwise across a wide range of values for τ.

In the second experiment, we plot F1 versus the size of the canonical record. Figure 4 indicates that most of the performance gain occurs in smaller canonical records (containing between 6 and 12 fields). Small canonical records are most susceptible to precision errors simply because there are more extraneous fields that may be incorrectly assigned to them. These precision errors are often addressed by the cluster compatibility method, as shown in Table 2.

In the final experiment, we plot F1 versus the total number of fields on the page. Figure 5 indicates that the cluster compatibility method is best at handling documents with large number of fields.

	F1	Precision	Recall
Cluster (I)	**91.81** (.013)	92.87 (.005)	90.78 (.007)
Cluster (U)	90.02 (.012)	**93.56 (.007)**	86.74 (.011)
Pairwise	90.51 (.013)	91.07 (.004)	89.95 (.006)
McDonald	88.36 (.012)	83.55 (.004)	93.75 (.005)
Trans Clos	82.37 (.002)	70.75 (.009)	**98.56** (.020)

Table 2: Precision, recall, and F1 performance for the record extraction task. The standard error is calculated over 10 cross-validation trials.

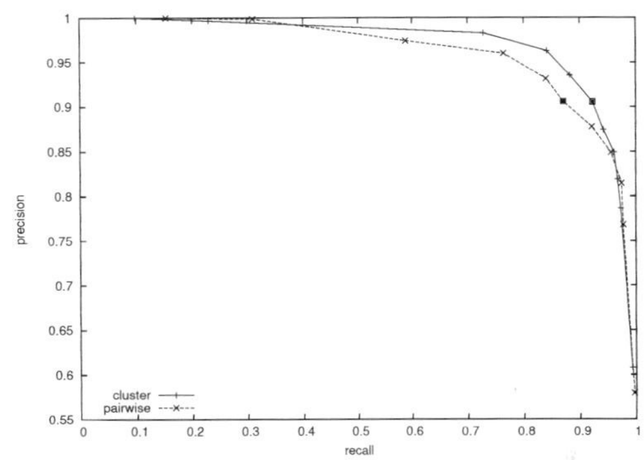

Figure 3: Precision-recall curve for cluster, pairwise, and mcdonald. The graph is obtained by varying the stopping threshold τ from 1.0 to 0.1. The highlighted points correspond to $\tau = 0.5$.

When there are over 80 fields in the document, the performance of the pairwise method drops dramatically, while cluster compatibility only declines slightly. We believe the improved precision of the cluster compatibility method explains this trend as well.

We also examine documents where cluster compatibility outperforms the pairwise methods. Typically, these documents contain interleaving contact records. Often, it is the case that a single pair of fields is sufficient to determine whether a cluster should *not* be merged. For example, the cluster classifier can directly model the fact that a contact record should not have multiple first or last names. It can also associate a weight with the fact that several fields overlap (e.g., the chances that a cluster has two first names, two last names and two cities). In contrast, the binary classifier only examines pairs of fields in isolation and averages these probabilities with other edges. This averaging can dilute the evidence from a single pair of fields. Embarrassing errors may result, such as a contact record with two first names or two last

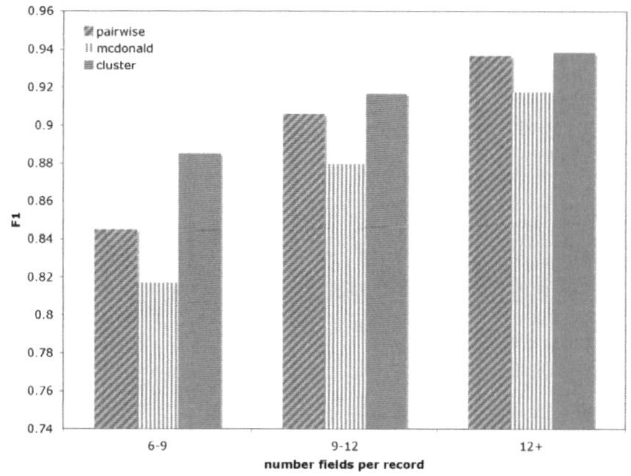

Figure 4: Field F1 as the size of the canonical record increases. This figure suggests that cluster compatibility is most helpful for small records.

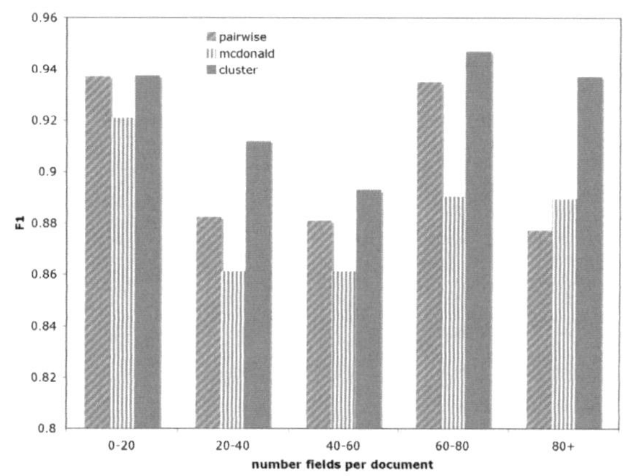

Figure 5: Field F1 as the number of fields in the document increases. This figure suggests that cluster compatibility is most helpful when the document has more than 80 fields.

names. These errors are particularly prevalent in interleaving contact records since adjacent fields often belong to the same record.

5 Conclusions and Future Work

We have investigated graph partitioning methods for discovering database records from fields annotated in text. We have proposed a cluster compatibility function that measures how likely it is that two *sets* of fields belong to the same cluster. We argue that this enhancement to existing techniques provides more representational power.

We have evaluated these methods on a set of hand-annotated data and concluded that (1) graph partitioning techniques are more accurate than performing transitive closure, and (2) cluster compatibility methods can avoid common mistakes made by pairwise compatibility methods.

As information extraction systems become more reliable, it will become increasingly important to develop accurate ways of associating disparate fields into cohesive records. This will enable more complex reasoning over text.

One shortcoming of this approach is that fields are not allowed to belong to multiple records, because the partitioning algorithm returns non-overlapping clusters. Exploring overlapping clustering techniques is an area of future work.

Another avenue of future research is to consider syntactic information in the compatibility function. While performance on contact record extraction is highly influenced by formatting features, many fields occur within sentences, and syntactic information (such as dependency trees or phrase-structure trees) may improve performance.

Overall performance can also be improved by increasing the sophistication of the partitioning method. For example, we can examine "block moves" to swap multiple fields between clusters in unison, possibly avoiding local minima of the greedy method (Kanani et al., 2006). This can be especially helpful because many mistakes may be made at the start of clustering, before clusters are large enough to reflect true records.

Additionally, many personal web pages contain a time-line of information that describe a person's educational and professional history. Learning to associate time information with each contact record enables *career path modeling*, which presents interesting opportunities for knowledge discovery techniques, a subject of ongoing work.

Acknowledgments

We thank the anonymous reviewers for helpful suggestions. This work was supported in part by the Center for Intelligent Information Retrieval, in part by U.S. Government contract #NBCH040171 through a subcontract with BBNT Solutions LLC, in part by The Central Intelligence Agency, the National Security Agency and National Science Foundation under NSF grant #IIS-0326249, and in part by the Defense Advanced Research Projects Agency (DARPA), through the Department of the Interior, NBC, Acquisition Services Division, under contract number NBCHD030010. Any opinions, findings and conclusions or recommendations expressed in this material are the author(s) and do not necessarily reflect those of the sponsor.

References

Eugene Agichtein and Luis Gravano. 2000. Snowball: Extracting relations from large plain-text collections. In *Proceedings of the Fifth ACM International Conference on Digital Libraries*.

Nikhil Bansal, Avrim Blum, and Shuchi Chawla. 2004. Correlation clustering. *Machine Learining*, 56:89–113.

Daniel M. Bikel, Richard Schwartz, and Ralph M. Weischedel. 1999. An algorithm that learns what's in a name. *Machine Learning*, 34:211–231.

Vinayak R. Borkar, Kaustubh Deshmukh, and Sunita Sarawagi. 2001. Automatic segmentation of text into structured records. In *SIGMOD Conference*.

Sergey Brin. 1998. Extracting patterns and relations from the world wide web. In *WebDB Workshop at 6th International Conference on Extending Database Technology*.

Aron Culotta and Andrew McCallum. 2006. Practical Markov logic containing first-order quantifiers with application to identity uncertainty. In *HLT Workshop on Computationally Hard Problems and Joint Inference in Speech and Language Processing*, June.

Aron Culotta and Jeffrey Sorensen. 2004. Dependency tree kernels for relation extraction. In *ACL*.

Aron Culotta, Ron Bekkerman, and Andrew McCallum. 2004. Extracting social networks and contact information from email and the web. In *First Conference on Email and Anti-Spam (CEAS)*, Mountain View, CA.

David W. Embley and Lin Xu. 2000. Record location and reconfiguration in unstructured multiple-record web documents. In *WebDB*, pages 123–128.

David W. Embley, Xiaoyi Jiang, and Yiu-Kai Ng. 1999. Record-boundary discovery in web documents. In *SIGMOD Conference*, pages 467–478.

Ralph Grishman. 1997. Information extraction: Techniques and challenges. In *SCIE*, pages 10–27.

Nanda Kambhatla. 2004. Combining lexical, syntactic, and semantic features with maximum entropy models for extracting relations. In *ACL*.

Pallika Kanani, Andrew McCallum, and Chris Pal. 2006. Improving author coreference by resource-bounded information gathering from the web. Technical note.

Trausti Kristjannson, Aron Culotta, Paul Viola, and Andrew McCallum. 2004. Interactive information extraction with conditional random fields. *Nineteenth National Conference on Artificial Intelligence (AAAI 2004)*.

Andrew McCallum and Ben Wellner. 2005. Conditional models of identity uncertainty with application to noun coreference. In Lawrence K. Saul, Yair Weiss, and Léon Bottou, editors, *Advances in Neural Information Processing Systems 17*. MIT Press, Cambridge, MA.

Ryan McDonald, Fernando Pereira, Seth Kulick, Scott Winters, Yang Jin, and Pete White. 2005. Simple algorithms for complex relation extraction with applications to biomedical ie. In *43rd Annual Meeting of the Association for Computational Linguistics*.

Brian Milch, Bhaskara Marthi, and Stuart Russell. 2005. BLOG: Probabilistic models with unknown objects. In *IJCAI*.

Scott Miller, Heidi Fox, Lance A. Ramshaw, and Ralph Weischedel. 2000. A novel use of statistical parsing to extract information from text. In *ANLP*.

Charles Sutton and Andrew McCallum. 2006. An introduction to conditional random fields for relational learning. In Lise Getoor and Ben Taskar, editors, *Introduction to Statistical Relational Learning*. MIT Press. To appear.

Paul Viola and Mukund Narasimhan. 2005. Learning to extract information from semi-structured text using a discriminative context free grammar. In *SIGIR '05: Proceedings of the 28th annual international ACM SIGIR conference on Research and development in information retrieval*, pages 330–337, New York, NY, USA. ACM Press.

Dmitry Zelenko, Chinatsu Aone, and Anthony Richardella. 2003. Kernel methods for relation extraction. *Journal of Machine Learning Research*, 3:1083–1106.

Discriminative Methods for Transliteration

Dmitry Zelenko
SRA International
4300 Fair Lakes Ct.
Fairfax VA 22033
dmitry_zelenko@sra.com

Chinatsu Aone
SRA International
4300 Fair Lakes Ct.
Fairfax VA 22033
chinatsu_aone@sra.com

Abstract

We present two discriminative methods for name transliteration. The methods correspond to local and global modeling approaches in modeling structured output spaces. Both methods do not require alignment of names in different languages – their features are computed directly from the names themselves. We perform an experimental evaluation of the methods for name transliteration from three languages (Arabic, Korean, and Russian) into English, and compare the methods experimentally to a state-of-the-art joint probabilistic modeling approach. We find that the discriminative methods outperform probabilistic modeling, with the global discriminative modeling approach achieving the best performance in all languages.

1 Introduction

Name transliteration is an important task of transcribing a name from alphabet to another. For example, an Arabic "وليام", Korean "윌리엄", and Russian "Вильям" all correspond to English "William". We address the problem of transliteration in the general setting: it involves trying to recover original English names from their transcription in a foreign language, as well as finding an acceptable spelling of a foreign name in English.

We apply name transliteration in the context of cross-lingual information extraction. Name extractors are currently available in multiple languages. Our goal is to make the extracted names understandable to monolingual English speakers by transliterating the names into English.

The extraction context of the transliteration application imposes additional complexity constraints on the task. In particular, we aim for the transliteration speed to be comparable to that of extraction speed. Since most current extraction systems are fairly fast (>1 Gb of text per hour), the complexity requirement reduces the range of techniques applicable to the transliteration. More precisely, we cannot use WWW and the web count information to hone in on the right transliteration candidate. Instead, all relevant transliteration information has to be represented within a compact and self-contained transliteration model.

We present two methods for creating and applying transliteration models. In contrast to most previous transliteration approaches, our models are discriminative. Using an existing transliteration dictionary D (a set of name pairs $\{(\boldsymbol{f},\boldsymbol{e})\}$), we learn a function that directly maps a name $\boldsymbol{f}$ from one language into a name $\boldsymbol{e}$ in another language. We do not estimate either direct conditional $p(\boldsymbol{e}|\boldsymbol{f})$ or reverse conditional $p(\boldsymbol{f}|\boldsymbol{e})$ or joint $p(\boldsymbol{e},\boldsymbol{f})$ probability models. Furthermore, we do away with the notion of alignment: our transliteration model does not require and is not defined of in terms of aligned $\boldsymbol{e}$ and $\boldsymbol{f}$. Instead, all features used by the model are computed directly from the names $\boldsymbol{f}$ and $\boldsymbol{e}$ without any need for their alignment.

The two discriminative methods that we present correspond to local and global modeling paradigms for solving complex learning problems with structured output spaces. In the local setting, we learn linear classifiers that predict a letter e_i from the previously predicted letters $e_1 \dots e_{i-1}$ and the original name $\boldsymbol{f}$. In the global setting, we learn a function W mapping a pair $(\boldsymbol{f},\boldsymbol{e})$ into a score $W(\boldsymbol{f},\boldsymbol{e}) \in R$. The function W is linear in features computed from the pair $(\boldsymbol{f},\boldsymbol{e})$. We describe the pertinent feature spaces as well as pre-

Proceedings of the 2006 Conference on Empirical Methods in Natural Language Processing (EMNLP 2006), pages 612–617,
Sydney, July 2006.

sent both training and decoding algorithms for the local and global settings.

We perform an experimental evaluation for three language pairs (transliteration from Arabic, Korean, and Russian into English) comparing our methods to a joint probabilistic modeling approach to transliteration, which was shown to deliver superior performance. We show experimentally that both discriminative methods outperform the probabilistic approach, with global discriminative modeling achieving the best performance in all languages.

2 Preliminaries

Let E and F be two finite alphabets. We will use lowercase latin letters e, f to denote letters $e \in E$, $f \in F$, and we use bold letters $\mathbf{e} \in E^*$, $\mathbf{f} \in F^*$ to denote strings in the corresponding alphabets. The subscripted e_i, f_j denote ith and jth symbols of the strings $\mathbf{e}$ and $\mathbf{f}$, respectively. We use $\mathbf{e}[i,j]$ to represent a substring $e_i \ldots e_j$ of $\mathbf{e}$. If $j<i$, then $\mathbf{e}[i,j]$ is an empty string Λ.

A transliteration model is a function mapping a string $\mathbf{f}$ to a string $\mathbf{e}$. We seek to learn a transliteration model from a transliteration dictionary $D=\{(\mathbf{f},\mathbf{e})\}$. We apply the model in conjunction with a *decoding algorithm* that produces a string $\mathbf{e}$ from a string $\mathbf{f}$.

3 Local Transliteration Modeling

In local transliteration modeling, we represent a transliteration model as a sequence of local prediction problems. For each local prediction, we use the *history* h representing the context of making a single transliteration prediction. That is, we predict each letter e_i based on the pair $h=(\mathbf{e}[1,i-1], \mathbf{f}) \in H$.

Formally, we map $H \times E$ into a d-dimensional feature space φ: $H \times E \rightarrow R^d$, where each $\varphi_k(h,e)(k \in \{1,..,d\})$ corresponds to a condition defined in terms of the history h and the currently predicted letter e.

In order to model string termination, we augment E with a sentinel symbol $\$$, and we append $\$$ to each $\mathbf{e}$ from D.

Given a transliteration dictionary D, we transform the dictionary in a set of $|E|$ binary learning problems. Each learning problem L_e corresponds to predicting a letter $e \in E$. More precisely, for a pair $(\mathbf{f}[1,m], \mathbf{e}[1,n]) \in D$ and $i \in \{1,\ldots,n\}$, we generate a positive example $\varphi((\mathbf{e}[1,i-1], \mathbf{f}), e_i)$ for the learning problem L_e, where $e=e_i$, and a negative example $\varphi((\mathbf{e}[1,i-1], \mathbf{f}), e)$ for each L_e, where $e \neq e_i$.

Each of the learning problems is a binary classification problem and we can use our favorite binary classifier learning algorithm to induce a collection of binary classifiers $\{c_e : e \in E\}$. From most classifiers we can also obtain an estimate of conditional probability $p(e|h)$ of a letter e given a history h.

For decoding, in our experiments we use the beam search to find the sequence of letters (approximately) maximizing p(e|h).

3.1 Local Features

The features used in local transliteration modeling correspond to pairs of substrings of $\mathbf{e}$ and $\mathbf{f}$. We limit the length of substrings as well as their relative location with respect to each other.

- For $\varphi((\mathbf{e}[1,i-1], \mathbf{f}), e)$, generate a feature for every pair of substrings $(\mathbf{e}[i-w,i-1], \mathbf{f}[j-v,j])$, where $1 \leq w < W(E)$ and $0 \leq v < W(F)$ and $|i-j| \leq d(E,F)$. Here, $W(\cdot)$ is the upper bound on the length of strings in the corresponding alphabet, and $d(E,F)$ is the upper bound on the relative distance between substrings.
- For $\varphi((\mathbf{e}[1,i-1], \mathbf{f}[1,m]), e)$, generate the length difference feature $\varphi_{len}=i-m$. In experiments, we discretize φ_{len} to obtain 9 binary features: $\varphi_{len}=l$ $(l \in [-3,3])$, $\varphi_{len} \leq -4$, $4 \leq \varphi_{len}$.
- For $\varphi((\mathbf{e}[1,i-1], \mathbf{f}[1,m]), e)$, generate a language modeling feature $p(e| e_{[1,i-1]})$.
- For $\varphi((\mathbf{e}[1,i-1], \mathbf{f}), e)$ and $i=1$, generate "start" features: $(\hat{}f_1, \hat{}e)$, $(\hat{}f_1 f_2, \hat{}e)$.
- For $\varphi((\mathbf{e}[1,i-1], \mathbf{f}), e)$ and $i=2$, generate "start" features: $(\hat{}f_1, \hat{}e_1 e_2)$, $(\hat{}f_1 f_2, \hat{}e_1 e_2)$.
- For $\varphi((\mathbf{e}[1,i-1], \mathbf{f}), e)$ and $e=\$$, generate "end" features: $(f_m\$, e\$)$, $(f_{m-1} f_m\$, e\$)$.

The parameters $W(E)$, $W(F)$, and $d(E,F)$ are, in general, language-specific, and we will show, in the experiments, that different values of the parameters are appropriate for different languages.

4 Global Transliteration Modeling

In global transliteration modeling, we directly model the agreement function between **f** and **e**. We follow (Collins 2002) and consider the global feature representation Φ: $F^* \times E^* \rightarrow R^d$.

Each global feature corresponds to a condition on the pair of strings. The value of a feature is the number of times the condition holds true for a given pair of strings. In particular, for every local feature $\varphi_k((\boldsymbol{e}[1,i-1], \boldsymbol{f}), e_i)$ we can define the corresponding global feature:

$$\Phi_k(\boldsymbol{f}, \boldsymbol{e}) = \sum_i \varphi_k((\boldsymbol{e}[1,i-1], \boldsymbol{f}), e_i) \qquad (1)$$

We seek a transliteration model that is linear in the global features. Such a transliteration model is represented by d-dimensional weight vector $W \in R^d$. Given a string $\boldsymbol{f}$, model application corresponds to finding a string $\boldsymbol{e}$ such that

$$\boldsymbol{e} = \arg\max_{e'} \sum_k W_k \Phi_k(\boldsymbol{f}, \boldsymbol{e'}) \qquad (2)$$

As with the case of local modeling, due to computational constraints, we use beam search for decoding in global transliteration modeling.

(Collins 2002) showed how to use the Voted Perceptron algorithm for learning W, and we use it for learning the global transliteration model. We use beam search for decoding within the Voted Perceptron training as well.

4.1 Global Features

The global features used in local transliteration modeling directly correspond to local features described in Section 3.1.

- For $\boldsymbol{e}[1,n]$ and $\boldsymbol{f}[1,m]$, generate a feature for every pair of substrings $(\boldsymbol{e}[i\text{-}w,i], \boldsymbol{f}[j\text{-}v,j])$, where $1 \leq w < W(E)$ and $0 \leq v < W(F)$ and $|i\text{-}j| \leq d(E,F)$.
- For $\boldsymbol{e}[1,n]$ and $\boldsymbol{f}[1,m]$, generate the length difference feature $\Phi_{len}=n\text{-}m$. In experiments, we discretize Φ_{len} to obtain 9 binary features: $\Phi_{len}=l$ $(l\in[-3,3])$, $\varphi_{len} \leq -4$, $4 \leq \varphi_{len}$.
- For $\boldsymbol{e}[1,n]$, generate a language modeling feature $(p(\boldsymbol{e}))^{1/n}$.
- For $\boldsymbol{e}[1,n]$ and $\boldsymbol{f}[1,m]$,, generate "start" features: $(\hat{\ }f_1,\hat{\ }e_1)$, $(\hat{\ }f_1f_2,\hat{\ }e_1)$, $(\hat{\ }f_1,\hat{\ }e_1e_2)$, $(\hat{\ }f_1f_2,\hat{\ }e_1e_2)$.
- For $\boldsymbol{e}[1,n]$ and $\boldsymbol{f}[1,m]$, generate "end" features: $(f_m\$,e_n\$)$, $(f_{m-1}f_m\$,e_n)$.

5 Joint Probabilistic Modeling

We compare the discriminative approaches to a joint probabilistic approach to transliteration introduced in recent years.

In the joint probabilistic modeling approach, we estimate a probability distribution $p(\boldsymbol{e},\boldsymbol{f})$. We also postulate hidden random variables $\boldsymbol{a}$ representing the alignment of $\boldsymbol{e}$ and $\boldsymbol{f}$. An alignment $\boldsymbol{a}$ of $\boldsymbol{e}$ and $\boldsymbol{f}$ is a sequence $a_1,a_2,\ldots a_L$, where $a_l = (\boldsymbol{e}[i_l\text{-}w_l,i_l],\boldsymbol{f}[j_l\text{-}v_l,j_l])$, $i_{l-1}+1=i_l\text{-}w_l$, and $j_{l-1}+1=j_l\text{-}v_l$. Note that we allow for at most one member of a pair a_l to be an empty string.

Given an alignment $\boldsymbol{a}$, we define the joint probability $p(\boldsymbol{e},\boldsymbol{f}|\boldsymbol{a})$:

$$p(\boldsymbol{e},\boldsymbol{f} \mid \boldsymbol{a}) = \prod_l p(\boldsymbol{e}[i_l - w_l, i_l], \boldsymbol{f}[j_l - v_l, j_l])$$

We learn the probabilities $p(\mathbf{e}[i_l\text{-}w_l,i_l],\mathbf{f}[j_l\text{-}v_l,j_l])$ using a version of EM algorithm. In our experiments, we use the Viterbi version of the EM algorithm: starting from random alignments of all string pairs in D, we use maximum likelihood estimates of the above probabilities, which are then employed to induce the most probable alignments in terms of the probability estimates. The process is repeated until the probability estimates converge.

During the decoding process, given a string $\boldsymbol{f}$, we seek both a string $\boldsymbol{e}$ and an alignment $\boldsymbol{a}$ such that $p(\boldsymbol{e},\boldsymbol{f}|\boldsymbol{a})$ is maximized. In our experiments, we used beam search for decoding.

Note that with joint probabilistic modeling use of a language model $p(\boldsymbol{e})$ is not strictly necessary. Yet we found out experimentally that an adaptive combination of the language model with the joint probabilistic model improves the transliteration performance. We thus combine the joint log-likelihood $log(p(\boldsymbol{e},\boldsymbol{f}|\boldsymbol{a}))$ with $log(p(\boldsymbol{e}))$:

$$score(e|f) = log(p(\boldsymbol{e},\boldsymbol{f}|\boldsymbol{a})) + \alpha log(p(\boldsymbol{e})) \qquad (3)$$

We estimate the parameter α on a held-out set by generating, for each $\boldsymbol{f}$, the set of top $K=10$ candidates with respect to $log(p(\boldsymbol{e},\boldsymbol{f}|\boldsymbol{a}))$, then using (3) for re-ranking the candidates, and picking α to minimize the number of transliteration errors among re-ranked candidates.

6 Experiments

We present transliteration experiments for three language pairs. We consider transliteration from Arabic, Korean, and Russian into English. For all language pairs, we apply the same training and decoding algorithms.

6.1 Data

The training and testing transliteration dataset sizes are shown in Table 1. For Arabic and Russian, we created the dataset manually by keying in and translating Arabic, Russian, and English names. For Korean, we obtained a dataset of transliterated names from a Korean government website. The dataset contained mostly foreign names transliterated into Korean. All datasets were randomly split into training and (blind) testing parts.

	Training	Testing
Arabic	935	233
Korean	11973	1363
Russian	545	121

Table 1. Transliteration Data.

Prior to transliteration, the Korean words of the Korean transliteration data were converted from their Hangul (syllabic) representation to Jamo (letter-based) representation to effectively reduce the alphabet size for Korean. The conversion process is completely automatic (see Unicode Standard 3.0 for details).

6.2 Algorithm Details

For language modeling, we used the list of 100,000 most frequent names downloaded from the US Census website. Our language model is a 5-gram model with interpolated Good-Turing smoothing (Gale and Sampson 1995).

We used the learning-to-classify version of Voted Perceptron for training local models (Freund and Schapire 1999). We used Platt's method for converting scores produced by learned linear classifiers into probabilities (Platt 1999). We ran both local and global Voted Perceptrons for 10 iterations during training.

6.3 Transliteration Results

Our discriminative transliteration models have a number of parameters reflecting the length of strings chosen in either language as well as the relative distance between strings. While we found that choice of $W(E)=W(F)=2$ always produces the best results for all of our languages, the distance $d(E,F)$ may have different optimal values for different languages.

Table 2 presents the transliteration results for all languages for different values of *d*. Note that the joint probabilistic model does not depend on *d*. The results reflect the accuracy of transliteration, that is, the proportion of times when the top English candidate produced by a transliteration model agreed with the correct English transliteration. We note that such an exact comparison may be too inflexible, for many foreign names may have more than one legitimate English spelling. In future experiments, we plan to relax the requirement and consider alternative variants of transliteration scoring (e.g., edit distance, top-N candidate scoring).

	Local	Global	Prob
Arabic (d=1)	31.33	**32.61**	
Arabic (d=2)	30.04	30.04	25.75
Arabic (d=3)	26.61	27.03	
Korean (d=1)	26.93	30.44	
Korean (d=2)	28.84	34.26	26.93
Korean (d=3)	30.96	**35.28**	
Russian (d=1)	44.62	**46.28**	
Russian (d=2)	38.84	41.32	39.67
Russian (d=3)	38.01	38.01	

Table 2. Transliteration Results for Different Values of Relative Distance (*d*).

Table 2 shows that, for all three languages, the discriminative methods convincingly outperform the joint probabilistic approach. The global discriminative approach achieves the best performance in all languages. It is interesting that different values of relative distance are optimal for different languages. For example, in Korean, the Hangul-Jamo decomposition leads to fairly redundant strings of Korean characters thereby making transliterated characters to be relatively far from each other. Therefore, Korean requires a larger relative distance bound. In Arabic and Russian, on the other hand, transliterated characters are relatively close to each other, so the distance *d* of 1 suffices. While for Russian such a small distance is to be expected, we are surprised by such a small relative distance for Arabic. Our intuition was that omitting short vowels in spelling names in Arabic will increase *d*.

We have the following explanation of the low value of *d* for Arabic from the machine learning perspective: incrementing *d* implies adding a lot of extraneous features to examples, that is, increasing attribute noise. Increased attribute noise requires a corresponding increase in the number of training examples to achieve adequate performance. While for Korean the number of training examples is sufficient to cope with the attribute noise, the relatively small Arabic training sample is not. We hypothesize that with increasing the number of training examples for Arabic, the optimal value of *d* will also increase.

7 Related Work

Most work on name transliteration adopted a source-channel approach (Knight and Grael 1998; Al-Onaizan and Knight 2002a; Virga and Khudanpur 2003; Oh and Choi 2000) incorporating phonetics as an intermediate representation. (Al-Onaizan and Knight 2002) showed that use of outside linguistic resources such as WWW counts of transliteration candidates can greatly boost transliteration accuracy. (Li *et al.* 2004) introduced the joint transliteration model whose variant augmented with adaptive re-ranking we used in our experiments.

Among direct (non-source-channel) models, we note the work of (Gao et al. 2004) on applying Maximum Entropy to English-Chinese transliteration, and the English-Korean transliteration model of (Kang and Choi 2000) based on decision trees.

All of the above models require alignment between names. We follow the recent work of (Klementiev and Roth 2006) who addressed the problem of discovery of transliterated named entities from comparable corpora and suggested that alignment may not be necessary for transliteration.

Finally, our modeling approaches follow the recent work on both local classifier-based modeling of complex learning problems (McCallum et al. 2000; Punyakanok and Roth 2001), as well as global discriminative approaches based on CRFs (Lafferty et al. 2001), SVM (Taskar et al. 2005), and the Perceptron algorithm (Collins 2002) that we used in our experiments.

8 Conclusions

We presented two novel discriminative approaches to name transliteration that do not employ the notion of alignment. We showed experimentally that the approaches lead to superior experimental results in all languages, with the global discriminative modeling approach achieving the best performance.

The results are somewhat surprising, for the notion of alignment seems very intuitive and useful for transliteration. We will investigate whether similar alignment-free methodology can be extended to full-text translation. It will also be interesting to study the relationship between our discriminative alignment-free methods and recently proposed discriminative alignment-based methods for transliteration and translation (Taskar et al. 2005a; Moore 2005).

We also showed that for name transliteration, global discriminative modeling is superior to local classifier-based discriminative modeling. This may have resulted from poor calibration of scores and probabilities produced by individual classifiers. We plan to further investigate the relationship between the local and global approaches to complex learning problems in natural language.

References

Y. Al-Onaizan and K. Knight. 2002. Translating Named Entities Using Monolingual and Bilingual Resources. *Proceedings of ACL.*

Y. Al-Onaizan and K. Knight. 2002a. Machine Transliteration of Names in Arabic Text. *Proceedings of ACL Workshop on Computational Approaches to Semitic Languages.*

M. Collins. 2002. Discriminative Training for Hidden Markov Models: Theory and Experiments with Perceptron Algorithms. In *Proceedings of EMNLP.*

Y. Freund and R. Shapire. 1999. Large margin classification using the perceptron algorithm. *Machine Learning*, 37, 277–296.

W. Gale and G. Sampson. 1995. Good-Turing frequency estimation without tears. *Journal of Quantitative Linguistics* 2:217-235.

Gao Wei, Kam-Fai Wong, and Wai Lam. 2004. Phoneme-based transliteration of foreign names for OOV problem. *Proceedings of the First International Joint Conference on Natural Language Processing.*

B.J. Kang and Key-Sun Choi, 2000. Automatic Transliteration and Back-transliteration by Decision Tree Learning, *Proceedings of the 2nd International Conference on Language Resources and Evaluation.*

A. Klementiev and D. Roth. 2006. Named Entity Transliteration and Discovery from Multilingual Comparable Corpora. *Proceedings of ACL.*

K. Knight and J. Graehl. 1998. Machine Transliteration, *Computational Linguistics*, 24(4).

J. Lafferty, A. McCallum, and F. Pereira. 2001. Conditional Random Fields: Probabilistic Models for Segmenting and Labeling Sequence Data. *Proceedings of the Eighteenth International Conference on Machine Learning.*

Li Haizhou, Zhang Min, and Su Jian. 2004. A Joint Source-channel Model for Machine Transliteration. *Proceedings of ACL 2004.*

A. McCallum, D. Freitag, and F. Pereira. 2000. Maximum entropy Markov models for information extraction and segmentation. *Proceedings of ICML.*

R. Moore. 2005. A Discriminative Framework for Bilingual Word Alignment. *Proceedings of the Conference on Empirical Methods in Natural Language Processing.*

Jong-Hoon Oh and Key-Sun Choi. 2000. An English-Korean Transliteration Model Using Pronunciation and Contextual Rules. *Proceedings of COLING.*

J. Platt. 1999. Probabilistic outputs for support vector machines and comparison to regularized likelihood methods. In *Advances in Large Margin Classifers.*

V. Punyakanok and D. Roth. 2001. The Use of Classifiers in Sequential Inference. *Proceedings of the Conference on Advances in Neural Information Processing Systems.*

B. Taskar, V. Chatalbashev, D. Koller and C. Guestrin. 2005. Learning Structured Prediction Models: A Large Margin Approach. *Proceedings of Twenty Second International Conference on Machine Learning.*

B. Taskar, S. Lacoste-Julien, and D. Klein. 2005a. A Discriminative Matching Approach to Word Alignment. *Proceedings of the Conference on Empirical Methods in Natural Language Processing.*

P. Virga and S. Khudanpur. 2003. Transliteration of Proper Names in Cross-lingual Information Retrieval. *Proceedings of ACL 2003 workshop MLNER.*

Solving the Problem of Cascading Errors: Approximate Bayesian Inference for Linguistic Annotation Pipelines

Jenny Rose Finkel, Christopher D. Manning and Andrew Y. Ng
Computer Science Department
Stanford University
Stanford, CA 94305
{jrfinkel, manning, ang}@cs.stanford.edu

Abstract

The end-to-end performance of natural language processing systems for compound tasks, such as question answering and textual entailment, is often hampered by use of a greedy 1-best pipeline architecture, which causes errors to propagate and compound at each stage. We present a novel architecture, which models these pipelines as Bayesian networks, with each low level task corresponding to a variable in the network, and then we perform approximate inference to find the best labeling. Our approach is extremely simple to apply but gains the benefits of sampling the entire distribution over labels at each stage in the pipeline. We apply our method to two tasks – semantic role labeling and recognizing textual entailment – and achieve useful performance gains from the superior pipeline architecture.

1 Introduction

Almost any system for natural language understanding must recover hidden linguistic structure at many different levels: parts of speech, syntactic dependencies, named entities, etc. For example, modern semantic role labeling (SRL) systems use the parse of the sentence, and question answering requires question type classification, parsing, named entity tagging, semantic role labeling, and often other tasks, many of which are dependent on one another and must be pipelined together. Pipelined systems are ubiquitous in NLP: in addition to the above examples, commonly parsers and named entity recognizers use part of speech tags and chunking information, and also word segmentation for languages such as Chinese. Almost no NLP task is truly standalone.

Most current systems for higher-level, aggregate NLP tasks employ a simple 1-best feed forward architecture: they greedily take the best output at each stage in the pipeline and pass it on to the next stage. This is the simplest architecture to build (particularly if reusing existing component systems), but errors are frequently made during this pipeline of annotations, and when a system is given incorrectly labeled input it is much harder for that system to do its task correctly. For example, when doing semantic role labeling, if no syntactic constituent of the parse actually corresponds to a given semantic role, then that semantic role will almost certainly be misidentified. It is therefore disappointing, but not surprising, that F-measures on SRL drop more than 10% when switching from gold parses to automatic parses (for instance, from 91.2 to 80.0 for the joint model of Toutanova (2005)).

A common improvement on this architecture is to pass k-best lists between processing stages, for example (Sutton and McCallum, 2005; Wellner et al., 2004). Passing on a k-best list gives useful improvements (e.g., in Koomen et al. (2005)), but efficiently enumerating k-best lists often requires very substantial cognitive and engineering effort, e.g., in (Huang and Chiang, 2005; Toutanova et al., 2005).

At the other extreme, one can maintain the entire space of representations (and their probabilities) at each level, and use this full distribution to calculate the full distribution at the next level. If restricting oneself to weighted finite state transducers (WFSTs), a framework applicable to a number of NLP applications (as outlined in Karttunen (2000)), a pipeline can be compressed down

Proceedings of the 2006 Conference on Empirical Methods in Natural Language Processing (EMNLP 2006), pages 618–626,
Sydney, July 2006.

into a single WFST, giving outputs equivalent to propagating the entire distribution through the pipeline. In the worst case there is an exponential space cost, but in many relevant cases composition is in practice quite practical. Outside of WFSTs, maintaining entire probability distributions is usually infeasible in NLP, because for most intermediate tasks, such as parsing and named entity recognition, there is an exponential number of possible labelings. Nevertheless, for some models, such as most parsing models, these exponential labelings can be compactly represented in a packed form, e.g., (Maxwell and Kaplan, 1995; Crouch, 2005), and subsequent stages can be reengineered to work over these packed representations, e.g., (Geman and Johnson, 2002). However, doing this normally also involves a very high cognitive and engineering effort, and in practice this solution is infrequently adopted. Moreover, in some cases, a subsequent module is incompatible with the packed representation of a previous module and an exponential amount of work is nevertheless required within this architecture.

Here we present an attractive middle ground in dealing with linguistic pipelines. Rather than only using the 1 or k most likely labelings at each stage, we would indeed like to take into account all possible labelings and their probabilities, but we would like to be able to do so without a lot of thinking or engineering. We propose that this can be achieved by use of approximate inference. The form of approximate inference we use is very simple: at each stage in the pipeline, we draw a sample from the distribution of labels, conditioned on the samples drawn at previous stages. We repeat this many times, and then use the samples from the last stage, which corresponds to the ultimate, higher-level task, to form a majority vote classifier. As the number of samples increases, this method will approximate the complete distribution. Use of the method is normally a simple modification to an existing piece of code, and the method is general. It can be applied not only to all pipelines, but to multi-stage algorithms which are not pipelines as well.

We apply our method to two problems: semantic role labeling and recognizing textual entailment. For semantic role labeling we use a two stage pipeline which parses the input sentence, and for recognizing textual entailment we use a three stage pipeline which tags the sentence with named entities and then parses it before passing it to the entailment decider.

2 Approach

2.1 Overview

In order to do approximate inference, we model the entire pipeline as a Bayesian network. Each stage in the pipeline corresponds to a variable in the network. For example, the parser stage corresponds to a variable whose possible values are all possible parses of the sentence. The probabilities of the parses are conditioned on the parent variables, which may just be the words of the sentence, or may be the part of speech tags output by a part of speech tagger.

The simple linear structure of a typical linguistic annotation network permits exact inference that is quadratic in the number of possible labels at each stage, but unfortunately our annotation variables have a very large domain. Additionally, some networks may not even be linear; frequently one stage may require the output from multiple previous stages, or multiple earlier stages may be completely independent of one another. For example, a typical QA system will do question type classification on the question, and from that extract keywords which are passed to the information retreival part of the system. Meanwhile, the retreived documents are parsed and tagged with named entities; the network rejoins those outputs with the question type classification to decide on the correct answer. We address these issues by using approximate inference instead of exact inference. The structure of the nodes in the network permits direct sampling based on a topological sort of the nodes. Samples are drawn from the conditional distributions of each node, conditioned on the samples drawn at earlier nodes in the topological sort.

2.2 Probability of a Complete Labeling

Before we can discuss how to sample from these Bayes nets, we will formalize how to move from an annotation pipeline to a Bayes net. Let $\mathbf{A}$ be the set of n annotators A_1, A_2, ..., A_n (e.g., part of speech tagger, named entity recognizer, parser). These are the variables in the network. For annotator a_i, we denote the set of other annotators whose input is directly needed as $Parents(A_i) \subset \mathbf{A}$ and a particular assignment to those variables is $parents(A_i)$. The possible values for a particular annotator A_i are a_i (e.g., a particular parse tree or named entity tagging). We can now formulate the probability of a complete annotation (over all annotators) in the standard way for Bayes nets:

$$\mathrm{P_{BN}}(a_1, a_2, ..., a_n) = \prod_{i=1}^{N} P(a_i|parents(A_i)) \quad (1)$$

2.3 Approximate Inference in Bayesian Networks

This factorization of the joint probability distribution facilitates inference. However, exact inference is intractable because of the number of possible values for our variables. Parsing, part of speech tagging, and named entity tagging (to name a few) all have a number of possible labels that is exponential in the length of the sentence, so we use approximate inference. We chose Monte Carlo inference, in which samples drawn from the joint distribution are used to approximate a marginal distribution for a subset of variables in the distribution. First, the nodes are sorted in topological order. Then, samples are drawn for each variable, conditioned on the samples which have already been drawn. Many samples are drawn, and are used to estimate the joint distribution.

Importantly, for many language processing tasks our application only needs to provide the most likely value for a high-level linguistic annotation (e.g., the guessed semantic roles, or answer to a question), and other annotations such as parse trees are only present to assist in performing that task. The probability of the final annotation is given by:

$$\mathrm{P_{BN}}(a_n) = \sum_{a_1, a_2, ..., a_{n-1}} \mathrm{P_{BN}}(a_1, a_2, ..., a_n) \quad (2)$$

Because we are summing out all variables other than the final one, we effectively use only the samples drawn from the final stage, ignoring the labels of the variables, to estimate the marginal distribution over that variable. We then return the label which had the highest number of samples. For example, when trying to recognize textual entailment, we count how many times we sampled "yes, it is entailed" and how many times we sampled "no, it is not entailed" and return the answer with more samples.

When the outcome you are trying to predict is binary (as is the case with RTE) or n-ary for small n, the number of samples needed to obtain a good estimate of the posterior probability is very small. This is true even if the spaces being sampled from during intermediate stages are exponentially large (such as the space of all parse trees). Ng and Jordan (2001) show that under mild assumptions, with only N samples the relative classification error will be at most $O(\frac{1}{N})$ higher than the error of the Bayes optimal classifier (in our case, the classifier which does exact inference). Even if the outcome space is not small, the sampling technique we present can still be very useful, as we will see later for the case of SRL.

3 Generating Samples

The method we have outlined requires the ability to sample from the conditional distributions in the factored distribution of (1): in our case, the probability of a particular linguistic annotation, conditioned on other linguistic annotations. Note that this differs from the usual annotation task: taking the argmax. But for most algorithms the change is a small and easy change. We discuss how to obtain samples efficiently from a few different annotation models: probabilistic context free grammars (PCFGs), and conditional random fields (CRFs).

3.1 Sampling Parses

Bod (1995) discusses parsing with probabilistic tree substitution grammars, which, unlike simple PCFGs, do not have a one-to-one mapping between output parse trees and a derivation (a bag of rules) that produced it, and hence the most-likely derivation may not correspond to the most likely parse tree. He therefore presents a bottom-up approach to sampling derivations from a derivation forest, which does correspond to a sample from the space of parse trees. Goodman (1998) presents a top-down version of this algorithm. Although we use a PCFG for parsing, it is the grammar of (Klein and Manning, 2003), which uses extensive state-splitting, and so there is again a many-to-one correspondence between derivations and parses, and we use an algorithm similar to Goodman's in our work.

PCFGs put probabilities on each rule, such as *S* → *NP VP* and *NN* → *'dog'*. The probability of a parse is the product of the probabilities of the rules used to construct the parse tree. A dynamic programing algorithm, the *inside algorithm*, can be used to find the probability of a sentence. The *inside probability* $\beta_k(p,q)$ is the probability that words p through q, inclusive, were produced by the non-terminal k. So the probability of the sentence *The boy pet the dog.* is equal to the inside probability $\beta_S(1,6)$, where the first word, w_1 is *The* and the sixth word, w_6, is *[period]*. It is also useful for our purposes to view this quantity as the sum of the probabilities of all parses of the sentence which have *S* as the start symbol. The probability can be defined recursively (Manning and Schütze, 1999) as follows:

$$\beta_k(p,q) = \begin{cases} P(N^k \rightarrow w_p) \quad \text{if} \quad p = q \\ \sum_{r,s} \sum_{d=p}^{q-1} P(N^k \rightarrow N^r N^s) \beta_r(p,d) \beta_s(d+1,q) \\ \qquad \text{otherwise} \end{cases} \tag{3}$$

where N^k, N^r and N^s are non-terminal symbols and w_p is the word at position p. We have omitted the case of unary rules for simplicity since it requires a closure operation.

These probabilities can be efficiently computed using a dynamic program. or memoization of each value as it is calculated. Once we have computed all of the inside probabilities, they can be used to generate parses from the distribution of all parses of the sentence, using the algorithm in Figure 1.

This algorithm is called after all of the inside probabilities have been calculated and stored, and take as parameters S, 1, and $length(sentence)$. It works by building the tree, starting from the root, and recursively generating children based on the posterior probabilities of applying each rule and each possible position on which to split the sentences. Intuitively, the algorithm is given a non-terminal symbol, such as *S* or *NP*, and a span of words, and has to decide (a) what rule to apply to expand the non-terminal, and (b) where to split the span of words, so that each non-terminal resulting from applying the rule has an associated word span, and the process can repeat. The inside probabilities are calculated just once, and we can then generate many samples very quickly; *DrawSamples* is linear in the number of words, and rules.

3.2 Sampling Named Entity Taggings

To do named entity recognition, we chose to use a conditional random field (CRF) model, based on Lafferty et al. (2001). CRFs represent the state of

```
function DRAWSAMPLE(N^k, r, s)
 if r = s
    tree.label = N^k
    tree.child = word(r)
    return (tree)
 for each rule m ∈ {m' : head(m') = N^k}
    N^i ← lChild(m)
    N^j ← rChild(m)
    for q ← r to s − 1
       scores(m, q) ← P(m)β_i(r, q)β_j(q + 1, s)
 (m, q) ← SAMPLEFROM(scores)
 tree.label = head(m)
 tree.lChild = DRAWSAMPLE(lChild(m), r, q)
 tree.rChild = DRAWSAMPLE(rChild(m), q + 1, s)
 return (tree)
```

Figure 1: Pseudo-code for sampling parse trees from a PCFG. This is a recursive algorithm which starts at the root of the tree and expands each node by sampling from the distribution of possible rules and ways to split the span of words. Its arguments are a non-terminal and two integers corresponding to word indices, and it is initially called with arguments *S*, 1, and the length of the sentence. There is a call to *sampleFrom*, which takes an (unnormalized) probability distribution, normalizes it, draws a sample and then returns the sample.

the art in sequence modeling – they are discriminatively trained, and maximize the joint likelihood of the entire label sequence in a manner which allows for bi-directional flow of information. In order to describe how samples are generated, we generalize CRFs in a way that is consistent with the Markov random field literature. We create a linear chain of *cliques*, each of which represents the probabilistic relationship between an adjacent set of n states using a *factor table* containing $|S|^n$ values. These factor tables on their own should *not* be viewed as probabilities, unnormalized or otherwise. They are, however, defined in terms of exponential models conditioned on features of the observation sequence, and must be instantiated for each new observation sequence. The probability of a state sequence is then defined by the sequence of factor tables in the clique chain, given the observation sequence:

$$\mathrm{P}_{\mathrm{CRF}}(\mathbf{s}|\mathbf{o}) = \frac{1}{Z(\mathbf{o})} \prod_{i=1}^{N} F_i(s_{i-n} \ldots s_i) \tag{4}$$

where $F_i(s_{i-n} \ldots s_i)$ is the element of the factor table at position i corresponding to states s_{i-n} through s_i, and $Z(o)$ is the partition function which serves to normalize the distribution.[1] To in-

[1] To handle the start condition properly, imagine also that we define a set of distinguished start states $s_{-(n-1)} \ldots s_0$.

fer the most likely state sequence in a CRF it is customary to use the Viterbi algorithm.

We then apply a process called *clique tree calibration*, which involves passing *messages* between the cliques (see Cowell et al. (2003) for a full treatment of this topic). After this process has completed, the factor tables can be viewed as unnormalized probabilities, which can be used to compute conditional probabilities, $P_{CRF}(s_i|s_{i-n} \dots s_{i-1}, o)$. Once these probabilities have been calculated, generating samples is very simple. First, we draw a sample for the label at the first position,[2] and then, for each subsequent position, we draw a sample from the distribution for that position, conditioned on the label sampled at the previous position. This process results in a sample of a complete labeling of the sequence, drawn from the posterior distribution of complete named entity taggings.

Similarly to generating sample parses, the expensive part is calculating the probabilities; once we have them we can generate new samples very quickly.

3.3 k-Best Lists

At first glance, k-best lists may seem like they should outperform sampling, because in effect they are the k best samples. However, there are several important reasons why one might prefer sampling. One reason is that the k best paths through a word lattice, or the k best derivations in parse forest do not necessarily correspond to the k best sentences or parse trees. In fact, there are no known sub-exponential algorithms for the best outputs in these models, when there are multiple ways to derive the same output.[3] This is not just a theoretical concern – the Stanford parser uses such a grammar, and we found that when generating a 50-best derivation list that on average these derivations corresponded to about half as many unique parse trees. Our approach circumvents this issue entirely, because the samples are generated from the actual output distribution.

Intuition also suggests that sampling should give more diversity at each stage, reducing the likelihood of not even considering the correct output. Using the Brown portion of the SRL test set (discussed in sections 4 and 6.1), and 50-samples/50-best, we found that on average the 50-samples system considered approximately 25% more potential SRL labelings than the 50-best system.

When pipelines have more than two stages, it is customary to do a beam search, with a beam size of k. This means that at each stage in the pipeline, more and more of the probability mass gets "thrown away." Practically, this means that as pipeline length increases, there will be increasingly less diversity of labels from the earlier stages. In a degenerate 10-stage, k-best pipeline, where the last stage depends mainly on the first stage, it is probable that all but a few labelings from the first stage will have been pruned away, leaving something much smaller than a k-best sample, possibly even a 1-best sample, as input to the final stage. Using approximate inference to estimate the marginal distribution over the last stage in the pipeline, such as our sampling approach, the pipeline length does not have this negative impact or affect the number of samples needed. And unlike k-best beam searches, there is an entire research community, along with a large body of literature, which studies how to do approximate inference in Bayesian networks and can provide performance bounds based on the method and the number of samples generated.

One final issue with the k-best method arises when instead of a linear chain pipeline, one is using a general directed acyclic graph where a node can have multiple parents. In this situation, doing the k-best calculation actually becomes exponential in the size of the largest in-degree of a node – for a node with n parents, you must try all k^n combinations of the values for the parent nodes. With sampling this is not an issue; each sample can be generated based on a topological sort of the graph.

4 Semantic Role Labeling

4.1 Task Description

Given a sentence and a target verb (the *predicate*) the goal of semantic role labeling is to identify and label syntactic constituents of the parse tree with semantic roles of the predicate. Common roles are *agent*, which is the thing performing the action, *patient*, which is the thing on which the action is being performed, and *instrument*, which is the thing with which the action is being done. Additionally, there are *modifier arguments* which can specify the location, time, manner, etc. The following sentence provides an example of a predi-

[2] Conditioned on the distinguished start states.

[3] Many thanks to an anonymous reviewer for pointing out this argument.

cate and its arguments:

> [The luxury auto maker]$_{agent}$ [last year]$_{temp}$ [sold]$_{pred}$ [1,214 cars]$_{patient}$ in [the U.S]$_{location}$.

Semantic role labeling is a key component for systems that do question answering, summarization, and any other task which directly uses a semantic interpretation.

4.2 System Description

We modified the system described in Haghighi et al. (2005) and Toutanova et al. (2005) to test our method. The system uses both local models, which score subtrees of the entire parse tree independently of the labels of other nodes not in that subtree, and joint models, which score the entire labeling of a tree with semantic roles (for a particular predicate).

First, the task is separated into two stages, and local models are learned for each. At the first stage, the *identification stage*, a classifier labels each node in the tree as either *ARG*, meaning that it is an argument (either core or modifier) to the predicate, or *NONE*, meaning that it is not an argument. At the second stage, the *classification stage*, the classifier is given a set of arguments for a predicate and must label each with its semantic role.

Next, a Viterbi-like dynamic algorithm is used to generate a list of the k-best joint (identification and classification) labelings according to the local models. The algorithm enforces the constraint that the roles should be non-overlapping. Finally, a joint model is constructed which scores a completely labeled tree, and it is used to re-rank the k-best list. The separation into local and joint models is necessary because there are an exponential number of ways to label the entire tree, so using the joint model alone would be intractable. Ideally, we would want to use approximate inference instead of a k-best list here as well. Particle filtering would be particularly well suited - particles could be sampled from the local model and then reweighted using the joint model. Unfortunately, we did not have enough time modify the code of (Haghighi et al., 2005) accordingly, so the k-best structure remained.

To generate samples from the SRL system, we take the scores given to the k-best list, normalize them to sum to 1, and sample from them. One consequence of this, is that any labeling not on the k-best list has a probability of 0.

5 Recognizing Textual Entailment

5.1 Task Description

In the task of recognizing textual entailment (RTE), also commonly referred to as robust textual inference, you are provided with two passages, a *text* and a *hypothesis*, and must decide whether the hypothesis can be inferred from the text. The term *robust* is used because the task is not meant to be domain specific. The term *inference* is used because this is not meant to be logical entailment, but rather what an intelligent, informed human would infer. Many NLP applications would benefit from the ability to do robust textual entailment, including question answering, information retrieval and multi-document summarization. There have been two PASCAL workshops (Dagan et al., 2005) with shared tasks in the past two years devoted to RTE. We used the data from the 2006 workshop, which contains 800 text-hypothesis pairs in each of the test and development sets[4] (there is no training set). Here is an example from the development set from the first RTE challenge:

Text: *Researchers at the Harvard School of Public Health say that people who drink coffee may be doing a lot more than keeping themselves awake – this kind of consumption apparently also can help reduce the risk of diseases.*

Hypothesis: *Coffee drinking has health benefits.*

The positive and negative examples are balanced, so the baseline of guessing either all *yes* or all *no* would score 50%. This is a hard task – at the first challenge no system scored over 60%.

5.2 System Description

MacCartney et al. (2006) describe a system for doing robust textual inference. They divide the task into three stages – linguistic analysis, graph alignment, and entailment determination. The first of these stages, *linguistic analysis* is itself a pipeline of parsing and named entity recognition. They use the syntactic parse to (deterministically) produce a typed dependency graph for each sentence. This pipeline is the one we replace. The second stage, *graph alignment* consists of trying to find good alignments between the typed dependency graphs

[4]The dataset and further information from both challenges can be downloaded from *http://www.pascal-network.org/Challenges/RTE2/Datasets/*

Figure 2: The pipeline for recognizing textual entailment.

for the text and hypothesis. Each possible alignment has a score, and the alignment with the best score is propagated forward. The final stage, *entailment determination*, is where the decision is actually made. Using the score from the alignment, as well as other features, a logistic model is created to predict entailment. The parameters for this model are learned from development data.[5] While it would be preferable to sample possible alignments, their system for generating alignment scores is not probabilistic, and it is unclear how one could convert between alignment scores and probabilities in a meaningful way.

Our modified linguistic analysis pipeline does NER tagging and parsing (in their system, the parse is dependent on the NER tagging because some types of entities are pre-chunked before parsing) and treats the remaining two sections of their pipeline, the alignment and determination stages, as one final stage. Because the entailment determination stage is based on a logistic model, a probability of entailment is given and sampling is straightforward.

6 Experimental Results

In our experiments we compare the greedy pipelined approach with our sampling pipeline approach.

6.1 Semantic Role Labeling

For the past two years CoNLL has had shared tasks on SRL (Carreras and Màrquez (2004) and Carreras and Màrquez (2005)). We used the CoNLL 2005 data and evaluation script. When evaluating semantic role labeling results, it is common to present numbers on both the core arguments (i.e., excluding the modifying arguments) and all arguments. We follow this convention and present both sets of numbers. We give precision,

[5]They report their results on the first PASCAL dataset, and use only the development set from the first challenge for learning weights. When we test on the data from the second challenge, we use all data from the first challenge and the development data from the second challenge to learn these weights.

SRL Results – Penn Treebank Portion			
Core Args	Precision	Recall	F-measure
Greedy	79.31%	77.7%	78.50%
K-Best	80.05%	78.45%	79.24%
Sampling	80.13%	78.25%	79.18%
All Args	Precision	Recall	F-measure
Greedy	78.49%	74.77%	76.58%
K-Best	79.58%	74.90%	77.16%
Sampling	79.81%	74.85%	77.31%
SRL Results – Brown Portion			
Core Args	Precision	Recall	F-measure
Greedy	68.28%	67.72%	68.0%
K-Best	69.25%	69.02%	69.13%
Sampling	69.35%	68.93%	69.16%
All Args	Precision	Recall	F-measure
Greedy	66.6%	60.45%	63.38%
K-Best	68.82%	61.03%	64.69%
Sampling	68.6%	61.11%	64.64%

Table 1: Results for semantic role labeling task. The sampled numbers are averaged over several runs, as discussed.

recall and F-measure, which are based on the number of arguments correctly identified. For an argument to be correct both the span and the classification must be correct; there is no partial credit.

To generate sampled parses, we used the Stanford parser (Klein and Manning, 2003). The CoNLL data comes with parses from Charniak's parser (Charniak, 2000), so we had to re-parse the data and retrain the SRL system on these new parses, resulting in a lower baseline than previously presented work. We choose to use Stanford's parser because of the ease with which we could modify it to generate samples. Unfortunately, its performance is slightly below that of the other parsers.

The CoNLL data has two separate test sets; the first is section 23 of the Penn Treebank (PTB), and the second is "fresh sentences" taken from the Brown corpus. For full results, please see Table 1. On the Penn Treebank portion we saw an absolute F-score improvement of 0.7% on both core and all arguments. On the Brown portion of the test set we saw an improvement of 1.25% on core and 1.16% on all arguments. In this context, a gain of over 1% is quite large: for instance, the scores for the top 4 systems on the Brown data at CoNLL 2005 were within 1% of each other. For both portions, we generated 50 samples, and did this 4 times, averaging the results. We most likely saw better performance on the Brown portion than the PTB portion because the parser was trained on the Penn Treebank training data, so the most likely parses will be of higher quality for the PTB portion of the test data than for the Brown portion. We also

RTE Results		
	Accuracy	Average Precision
Greedy	59.13%	59.91%
Sampling	60.88%	61.99%

Table 2: Results for recognizing textual entailment. The sampled numbers are averaged over several runs, as discussed.

ran the pipeline using a 50-best list, and found the two results to be comparable.

6.2 Textual Entailment

For the second PASCAL RTE challenge, two different types of performance measures were used to evaluate labels and confidence of the labels for the text-hypothesis pairs. The first measure is accuracy – the percentage of correct judgments. The second measure is *average precision*. Responses are sorted based on entailment confidence and then average precision is calculated by the following equation:

$$\frac{1}{R}\sum_{i=1}^{n} E(i)\frac{\text{\# correct up to pair } i}{i} \quad (5)$$

where n is the size of the test set, R is the number of positive (entailed) examples, $E(i)$ is an indicator function whose value is 1 if the ith pair is entailed, and the is are sorted based on the entailment confidence. The intention of this measure is to evaluate how well calibrated a system is. Systems which are more confident in their correct answers and less confident in their incorrect answers will perform better on this measure.

Our results are presented in Table 2. We generated 25 samples for each run, and repeated the process 7 times, averaging over runs. Accuracy was improved by 1.5% and average precision by 2%. It does not come as a surprise that the average precision improvement was larger than the accuracy improvement, because our model explicitly estimates its own degree of confidence by estimating the posterior probability of the class label.

7 Conclusions and Future Work

We have presented a method for handling language processing pipelines in which later stages of processing are conditioned on the results of earlier stages. Currently, common practice is to take the best labeling at each point in a linguistic analysis pipeline, but this method ignores information about alternate labelings and their likelihoods. Our approach uses all of the information available, and has the added advantage of being extremely simple to implement. By modifying your subtasks to generate samples instead of the most likely labeling, our method can be used with very little additional overhead. And, as we have shown, such modifications are usually simple to make; further, with only a "small" (polynomial) number of samples k, under mild assumptions the classification error obtained by the sampling approximation approaches that of exact inference. (Ng and Jordan, 2001) In contrast, an algorithm that keeps track only of the k-best list enjoys no such theoretical guarantee, and can require an exponentially large value for k to approach comparable error. We also note that in practice, k-best lists are often more complicated to implement and more computationally expensive (e.g. the complexity of generating k sample parses or CRF outputs is substantially lower than that of generating the k best parse derivations or CRF outputs).

The major contribution of this work is not specific to semantic role labeling or recognizing textual entailment. We are proposing a general method to deal with all multi-stage algorithms. It is common to build systems using many different software packages, often from other groups, and to string together the 1-best outputs. If, instead, all NLP researchers wrote packages which can generate samples from the posterior, then the entire NLP community could use this method as easily as they can use the greedy methods that are common today, and which do not perform as well.

One possible direction for improvement of this work would be to move from a Bayesian network to an undirected Markov network. This is desirable because influence should be able to flow in both directions in this pipeline. For example, the semantic role labeler should be able to tell the parser that it did not like a particular parse, and this should influence the probability assigned to that parse. The main difficulty here lies in how to model this reversal of influence. The problem of using parse trees to help decide good semantic role labelings is well studied, but the problem of using semantic role labelings to influence parses is not. Furthermore, this requires building joint models over adjacent nodes, which is usually a non-trivial task. However, we feel that this approach would improve performance even more on these pipelined tasks and should be pursued.

8 Acknowledgements

We would like to thank our anonymous reviewers for their comments and suggestions. We would also like to thank Kristina Toutanova, Aria Haghighi and the Stanford RTE group for their assistance in understanding and using their code.

This paper is based on work funded in part by a Stanford School of Engineering fellowship and in part by the Defense Advanced Research Projects Agency through IBM. The content does not necessarily reflect the views of the U.S. Government, and no official endorsement should be inferred.

References

Rens Bod. 1995. The problem of computing the most probable tree in data-oriented parsing and stochastic tree grammars. In *Proceedings of EACL 1995*.

Xavier Carreras and Lluís Màrquez. 2004. Introduction to the CoNLL-2004 shared task: Semantic role labeling. In *Proceedings of CoNLL 2004*.

Xavier Carreras and Lluís Màrquez. 2005. Introduction to the CoNLL-2005 shared task: Semantic role labeling. In *Proceedings of CoNLL 2005*.

Eugene Charniak. 2000. A maximum-entropy-inspired parser. In *Proceedings of the 14th National Conference on Artificial Intelligence*.

Robert G. Cowell, A. Philip Dawid, Steffen L. Lauritzen, and David J. Spiegelhalter. 2003. *Probabilistic Networks and Expert Systems*. Springer.

Richard Crouch. 2005. Packed rewriting for mapping semantics to KR. In *Proceedings of the 6th International Workshop on Computational Semantics*.

Ido Dagan, Oren Glickman, and Bernardo Magnini. 2005. The PASCAL recognizing textual entailment challenge. In *Proceedings of the PASCAL Challenges Workshop on Recognizing Textual Entailment*.

Stuart Geman and Mark Johnson. 2002. Dynamic programming for parsing and estimation of stochastic unification-based grammars. In *Proceedings of ACL 2002*.

Joshua Goodman. 1998. *Parsing Inside-Out*. Ph.D. thesis, Harvard University.

Aria Haghighi, Kristina Toutanova, and Christopher D. Manning. 2005. A joint model for semantic role labeling. In *Proceedings of CoNLL 2005*.

Liang Huang and David Chiang. 2005. Better k-best parsing. In *Proceedings of the 9th International Workshop on Parsing Technologies*.

Lauri Karttunen. 2000. Applications of finite-state transducers in natural-language processing. In *Proceesings of the Fifth International Conference on Implementation and Application of Automata*.

Dan Klein and Christopher D. Manning. 2003. Accurate unlexicalized parsing. In *Proceedings of ACL 2003*.

Peter Koomen, Vasin Punyakanok, Dan Roth, and Wen tau Yih. 2005. Generalized inference with multiple semantic role labeling systems. In *Proceedings of CoNLL 2005*, pages 181–184.

John Lafferty, Andrew McCallum, and Fernando Pereira. 2001. Conditional Random Fields: Probabilistic models for segmenting and labeling sequence data. In *Proceedings of the Eighteenth International Conference on Machine Learning*, pages 282–289.

Bill MacCartney, Trond Grenager, Marie de Marneffe, Daniel Cer, and Christopher D. Manning. 2006. Learning to recognize features of valid textual entailments. In *Proceedings of NAACL-HTL 2006*.

Christopher D. Manning and Hinrich Schütze. 1999. *Foundations of Statistical Natural Language Processing*. The MIT Press, Cambridge, Massachusetts.

John T. Maxwell, III and Ronald M. Kaplan. 1995. A method for disjunctive constraint satisfaction. In Mary Dalrymple, Ronald M. Kaplan, John T. Maxwell III, and Annie Zaenen, editors, *Formal Issues in Lexical-Functional Grammar*, number 47 in CSLI Lecture Notes Series, chapter 14, pages 381–481. CSLI Publications.

Andrew Ng and Michael Jordan. 2001. Convergence rates of the voting Gibbs classifier, with application to Bayesian feature selection. In *Proceedings of the Eighteenth International Conference on Machine Learning*.

Charles Sutton and Andrew McCallum. 2005. Joint parsing and semantic role labeling. In *Proceedings of CoNLL 2005*, pages 225–228.

Kristina Toutanova, Aria Haghighi, and Christopher D. Manning. 2005. Joint learning improves semantic role labeling. In *Proceedings of ACL 2005*.

Kristina Toutanova. 2005. *Effective statistical models for syntactic and semantic disambiguation*. Ph.D. thesis, Stanford University.

Ben Wellner, Andrew McCallum, Fuchun Peng, and Michael Hay. 2004. An integrated, conditional model of information extraction and coreference with application to citation matching. In *Proceedings of the 20th Annual Conference on Uncertainty in Artificial Intelligence*.

AUTHOR INDEX

AUTHOR INDEX

Association for Computational Linguistics
209 N. Eighth Street
Stroudsburg, Pennsylvania 18360

CURRAN ASSOCIATES INC
proceedings.com